International Conference on Recent Advances in Natural Language Processing 2009 (RANLP 2009)

Borovets, Bulgaria
14 - 16 September 2009

Editors:

Galia Angelova
Kalina Bontcheva
Ruslan Mitkov
Nicolas Nicolov
Nikolai Nikolov

ISBN: 978-1-5108-1327-4

Printed from e-media with permission by:

Curran Associates, Inc.
57 Morehouse Lane
Red Hook, NY 12571

CURRAN ASSOCIATES INC. proceedings.com

Some format issues inherent in the e-media version may also appear in this print version.

Printed by Curran Associates, Inc. (2016)

Association for Computational Linguistics
209 N. Eighth Street
Stroudsburg, Pennsylvania 18360

Phone: 1-570-476-8006
Fax: 1-570-476-0860

acl@aclweb.org

Additional copies of this publication are available from:

Curran Associates, Inc.
57 Morehouse Lane
Red Hook, NY 12571 USA
Phone: 845-758-0400
Fax: 845-758-2634
Email: curran@proceedings.com
Web: www.proceedings.com

INTERNATIONAL CONFERENCE

RECENT ADVANCES IN

NATURAL LANGUAGE PROCESSING

PROCEEDINGS

Edited by

Galia Angelova, Kalina Bontcheva, Ruslan Mitkov, Nicolas Nicolov, Nikolai Nikolov

Borovets, Bulgaria

14-16 September 2009

ORGANISERS AND SPONSORS

The International Conference RANLP–2009 is organised by:

Linguistic Modelling Department, Institute for Parallel Processing (IPP), Bulgarian Academy of Sciences (BAS)

Association for Computational Linguistics, Bulgaria

and

Research Group in Computational Linguistics, University of Wolverhampton, U.K.

RANLP–2009 is partially supported by:

Ontotext Semantic Technology Lab, Bulgaria

Research Institute of Information and Language Processing, University of Wolverhampton, UK

IPP-BAS (BIS-21 Centre of Excellence)

Association for Computational Linguistics, Bulgaria

The team behind RANLP–2009:

Galia Angelova	Bulgarian Academy of Sciences, Bulgaria, OC Chair
Kalina Bontcheva	University of Sheffield, U.K.
Ruslan Mitkov	University of Wolverhampton, U.K., PC Chair
Nicolas Nicolov	Umbria, Inc., Boulder, U.S.A.
Nikolai Nikolov	INCOMA Ltd., Shoumen, Bulgaria
Kiril Simov	Bulgarian Academy of Sciences, Bulgaria, Workshop Coordinator

PROGRAMME COMMITTEE CHAIR

Ruslan Mitkov (*University of Wolverhampton, UK*)

PROGRAMME COMMITTEE

Roberto Basili (*Univ. of Roma "Tor Vergata", Italy*)
Marco De Boni (*Unilever, UK*)
Kalina Bontcheva (*University of Sheffield, UK*)
António Branco (*University of Lisbon, Portugal*)
Michael Carl (*Copenhagen Business School, Denmark*)
Eugene Charniak (*Brown University, USA*)
Kevin Cohen (*University of Colorado School of Medicine, USA*)
Gloria Corpas (*University of Malaga, Spain*)
Dan Cristea (*"Al. I. Cuza" University of Iasi, Romania*)
Gael Dias (*Univ. of Beira Interior, Portugal*)
Arantza Diaz de Ilarraza (*Un. of Basque Country, Spain*)
Atefeh Farzindar (*NLP Technologies, Canada*)
Robert Gaizauskas (*University of Sheffield, UK*)
Alexander Gelbukh (*Nat. Polytechnic Inst., Mexico*)
Ralph Grishman (*New York University, USA*)
Le An Ha (*University of Wolverhampton, UK*)
Johann Haller (*IAI Saarbrücken, Germany*)
Patrick Hanks (*Charles University, Czech Republic*)
Erhard Hinrichs (*University of Tübingen, Germany*)
Veronique Hoste (*University College Ghent, Belgium*)
Diana Inkpen (*University of Ottawa, Canada*)
Richard J. Evans (*University of Wolverhampton, UK*)
Dimitar Kazakov (*University of York, UK*)
Alma Kharrat (*Microsoft, USA*)
Udo Kruschwitz (*University of Essex, UK*)
Hristo Krushkov (*Plovdiv University, Bulgaria*)
Sandra Kuebler (*Indiana University, USA*)
Shalom Lappin (*King's College London, UK*)
Montse Maritxalar (*Univ. of the Basque Country, Spain*)
M. Antonia Marti (*University of Barcelona, Spain*)
Patricio Martinez-Barco (*Univ. of Alicante, Spain*)
Yuji Matsumoto (*NAIST, Japan*)
Diana Maynard (*University of Sheffield, UK*)
Wolfgang Menzel (*University of Hamburg, Germany*)
Rada Mihalcea (*University of North Texas, USA*)
Andrei Mikheev (*Infogistics Ltd & Daxtra Tech. Ltd, UK*)
Paola Monachesi (*Utrecht University, The Netherlands*)
Andres Montonyo (*University of Alicante, Spain*)
Rafael Munoz Guillena (*University of Alicante, Spain*)
Preslav Nakov (*National Univ. of Singapore, Singapore*)
Roberto Navigli (*Univ. di Roma La Sapienza, Italy*)
John Nerbonne (*Univ. of Groningen, The Netherlands*)
Michael Oakes (*University of Sunderland, UK*)
Kemal Oflazer (*Carnegie Mellon University, Qatar*)
Constantin Orasan (*University of Wolverhampton, UK*)
Petya Osenova (*Bulgarian Academy of Sciences, Bulgaria*)
Manuel Palomar (*University of Alicante, Spain*)
Viktor Pekar (*Oxford University Press, UK*)
Stelios Piperidis (*ILSP, Greece*)
Massimo Poesio (*Univ. of Trento, Italy & Univ. of Essex, UK*)
John Prager (*IBM, USA*)
Gabor Proszeky (*MorphoLogic, Hungary*)
Paul Rayson (*Lancaster University, UK*)
Horacio Rodriguez (*Technical Univ. of Catalonia, Spain*)
Satoshi Sekine (*New York University, USA*)
Khalil Sima'an (*University of Amsterdam, The Netherlands*)
Kiril Simov (*Bulgarian Academy of Sciences, Bulgaria*)
Thamar Solorio (*Univ. of Alabama at Birmingham, USA*)
Lucia Specia (*University of Wolverhampton, UK*)
Ralf Steinberger (*European Commission - Joint Research Centre, Italy*)
Joel Tetreault (*University of Pittsburgh, UK*)
L. Alfonso Urena Lopez (*University of Jaen, Spain*)
Karin Verspoor (*University of Colorado School of Medicine, USA*)
Yorick Wilks (*University of Sheffield, UK*)
Michael Zock (*LIF, CNRS, France*)

REVIEWERS

In addition to the members of the Programme Committee, the following colleagues were involved in the reviewing process:

Naveed Afzal (*University of Wolverhampton, UK*)
Itziar Aldabe (*Univ. of the Basque Country, Spain*)
Afra Alishahi (*University of Saarland, Gemany*)
Alexandra Balahur-Dobrescu (*Univ. Alicante, Spain and European Commission – Joint Research Centre, Italy*)
Verginica Barbu Mititelu (*Rom. Academy, Romania*)
Leonor Becerra-Bonache (*Univ. Rovira i Virgili, Spain*)
Lamia Hadrich Belguith (*University of Sfax, Tunisia*)
Svetla Boytcheva (*State Univ. LS and IT, Bulgaria*)
Guadalupe Aguado de Cea (*Polytechn. Univ. Madrid*)
Rosita Chan (*Ins. Comercial and Univ. of Panama*)
Atanas Chanev (*Bulgaria*)
Andras Csomai (*University of North Texas, USA*)
Iustin Dornescu (*University of Wolverhampton, UK*)
Robert M. Foster (*University of Wolverhampton, UK*)
Kuzman Ganchev (*University of Pennsylvania, USA*)
Lisette Garcia Moya (*University Jaume I, Spain*)
Kallirroi Georgila (*Univ. of Southern California, USA*)
Jose M. Gomez (*University of Alicante, Spain*)
Laura Hasler (*University of Wolverhampton, UK*)
Jesus M. Hermida (*Univ. of Alicante, Spain*)
Adrian Iftene (*"Al. I. Cuza" University of Iasi, Romania*)
Iustina Ilisei (*University of Wolverhampton, UK*)
Radu Ion (*Romanian Academy, Romania*)
Heng Ji (*City University of New York, USA*)
Jason Kessler (*Indiana University, USA*)
Kiril Kolev (*University of Wolverhampton, UK*)
Natalia Konstantinova (*Univ. of Wolverhampton, UK*)
Zornitsa Kozareva (*USC ISI, California, USA*)
Elina Lagoudaki (*Imperial College London, UK*)
Els Lefever (*University College Ghent, Belgium*)
Fang Li (*University of Wolverhampton, UK*)
Elena Lloret (*University of Alicante, Spain*)
Annie Louis (*University of Pennsylvania, USA*)
Oier Lopez de Lacalle (*Univ. of the Basque Country, Spain*)
Lieve Macken (*University College Ghent, Belgium*)
Ruslana Margova (*Journal 'Geomedia', Bulgaria*)
Dalila Mekhaldi (*University of Wolverhampton, UK*)
Neil Millar (*Lancaster University, UK*)
Arturo Montejo Raez (*University of Jaen, Spain*)
Rumen Moraliyski (*Univ. of Beira Interior, Portugal*)
Andrea Mulloni (*University of Wolverhampton, UK*)
Shiyan Ou (*Nanjing University, China*)
Slav Petrov (*Google Research New York, USA*)
Ionut Pistol (*"Al. I. Cuza" University of Iasi, Romania*)
Emily Pitler (*University of Pennsylvania, USA*)
Natalia Ponomareva (*Univ. of Wolverhampton, UK*)
Jelena Prokic (*Univ. of Groningen, The Netherlands*)
Prokopis Prokopidis (*ILSP / R.C. "Athena", Greece*)
Georgiana Puscasu (*Univ. of Wolverhampton, UK*)
Marta Recasens (*University of Barcelona, Spain*)
Luz Rello (*University of Wolverhampton, UK*)
Julie Renahy (*Université de Franche-Comté, France*)
Estela Saquete Boro (*University of Alicante, Spain*)
Armando Suarez Cueto (*University of Alicante, Spain*)
Horacio Saggion (*University of Sheffield, UK*)
Doaa Samy (*Cairo University, Egypt*)
Smriti Singh (*Indian Inst. of Technology, Bombay, India*)
Yvonne Skalban (*University of Wolverhampton, UK*)
Veselin Stoyanov (*Cornell University, USA*)
Ang Sun (*New York University, USA*)
Irina Temnikova (*University of Wolverhampton, UK*)
Rafael M. Terol (*Univ. of Alicante, Spain*)
Diana Trandabat (*"Al. I. Cuza" Univ. of Iasi, Romania*)
Andrea Varga (*University of Wolverhampton, UK*)
Sonia Vazquez Perez (*University of Alicante, Spain*)
Cristina Vertan (*University of Hamburg, Germany*)
Roman Yangarber (*University of Helsinki, Finland*)
Nick Webb (*University at Albany, SUNY, USA*)
Jakub Zavrel (*Textkernel, The Netherlands*)
Kalliopi Zervanou (*ILK, Tilburg Univ., The Netherlands*)

PROGRAMME COMMITTEE COORDINATOR

Ivelina Nikolova (*Bulgarian Academy of Sciences, Bulgaria*)

PROGRAMME COMMITTEE SUPPORT

Natalia Konstantinova (*University of Wolverhampton, UK*)
Irina Temnikova (*University of Wolverhampton, UK*)

Table of Contents

RANLP-09 Programme, 14 September 2009

8^{45}- 9^{00} Opening

9^{00}-10^{00} **Ricardo Baeza-Yates:** *Towards Semantic Search* (*invited talk*)

Morning session 1a

Semantics

10^{00}-10^{30} **Unsupervised Extraction of False Friends from Parallel Bi-Texts Using the Web as a Corpus**
Svetlin Nakov, Preslav Nakov and Elena Paskaleva

10^{30}-11^{00} **Identifying Semantic Relations in Context: Near-misses and Overlaps**
Alla Rozovskaya and Roxana Girju

Morning session 1b

Parsing

10^{00}-10^{30} **Lexicalized Semi-Incremental Dependency Parsing**
Hany Hassan, Khalil Sima'an and Andy Way

10^{30}-11^{00} **Co-Parsing with Competitive Models**
Lidia Khmylko, Kilian Foth and Wolfgang Menzel

11^{00}-11^{30} Coffee break

Morning session 2a

Sentiment analysis

11^{30}-12^{00} **Classification of Opinions with Non-affective Adverbs and Adjectives**
Marina Sokolova and Guy Lapalme

12^{00}-12^{25} **Multi-entity Sentiment Scoring**
Karo Moilanen and Stephen Pulman

12^{25}-12^{50} **Sentiment Analysis of Figurative Language using a Word Sense Disambiguation Approach**
Vassiliki Rentoumi, George Giannakopoulos, Vangelis Karkaletsis and George Vouros

Morning session 2b

Lexicon, dictionary

11^{35}-12^{00} **A morphological and syntactic wide-coverage lexicon for Spanish: The Leffe**
Miguel Angel Molinero, Benoît Sagot and Lionel Nicolas

12^{00}-12^{25} **Exploring the Vector Space Model for Finding Verb Synonyms in Portuguese**
Luís Sarmento, Paula Carvalho and Eugénio Oliveira

12^{25}-12^{50} **Grouping synonyms by definitions**
Ingrid Falk, Claire Gardent, Evelyne Jacquey and Fabienne Venant

12^{50}-14^{30} Lunch

14^{30}-15^{30} **Kevin Bretonnel Cohen:** *Paradigms for Evaluation in Natural Language Processing (invited talk)*

Afternoon session 1a	Afternoon session 1b
Summarisation	*Grammars, POS tagging*
15^{30}-15^{55} **A Semi-supervised Approach for Generating a Table-of-Contents** *Viet Cuong Nguyen, Le Minh Nguyen and Akira Shimazu*	15^{30}-15^{55} **An Interaction Grammar of Interrogative & Relative Clauses in French** *Guy Perrier*
15^{55}-16^{20} **Summary Generation for Toponym-referenced Images using Object Type Language Models** *Ahmet Aker and Robert Gaizauskas*	15^{55}-16^{20} **Evaluating the Impact of Morphosyntactic Ambiguity in Grammatical Error Detection** *Arantza Díaz de Ilarraza, Koldo Gojenola and Maite Oronoz*
16^{20}-16^{45} **Contextual Salience in Query-based Summarization** *Wauter Bosma*	16^{20}-16^{45} **Amharic Part-of-Speech Tagger for Factored Language Modeling** *Martha Yifiru Tachbelie and Wolfgang Menzel*

16^{45}-17^{15} Coffee break

17^{15}-18^{30} ***Poster presentations: session 1***

RANLP-09 CONFERENCE POSTERS

Global Evaluation of Random Indexing through Swedish Word Clustering Compared to the People's Dictionary of Synonyms, *Magnus Rosell, Martin Hassel and Viggo Kann*

Exploiting Latent Semantic Relations in Highly Linked Hypertext for Information Retrieval in Wikis, *Tristan Miller, Bertin Klein and Elisabeth Wolf*

From Partial toward Full Parsing, *Heshaam Faili*

Unsupervised Word Sense Induction from Multiple Semantic Spaces with Locality Sensitive Hashing, *Claire Mouton, Guillaume Pitel, Gaël de Chalendar and Anne Vilnat*

A Model for the Cross-Modal Influence of Visual Context upon Language Processing, *Patrick McCrae*

Detection of Opinions and Facts. A Cognitive Approach
Yann Vigile Hoareau, Adil El-Ghali and Charles Tijus

STUDENT RESEARCH WORKSHOP POSTERS

Normalized Accessor Variety in Chinese Word Segmentation Based on Conditional Random Fields, *Saike He, Tao Zheng Zxhang, Xue Bai, Xiaojie Wang and Yuan Dong*

LOGICON: A System for Extracting Semantic Structure using Partial Parsing, *Kais Dukes*

An Evaluation of Output Quality of Machine Translation Program, *Mitra Shahabi*

Pronunciation Modeling for Dialectal Arabic Speech Recognition, *Hassan Al-Haj and Roger Hsiao*

Hierarchical Discourse Parsing based on Similarity Metrics, *Ravikiran Vadlapudi, Poornima Malepati and Suman Yelati*

Does Language Shape Thought? Time Estimation in Speakers of English and Persian, *Omid Tabatabaei, Ali Reza Ahmadi and Bahar Assarzadegan*

A Study of Machine Learning Algorithms for Recognizing Textual Entailment, *Julio Javier Castillo*

Exploring Context Variation and Lexicon Coverage in Projection-based Approach for Term Translation, *Raphaël Rubino*

ZAC.PB: An Annotated Corpus for Zero Anaphora Resolution in Portuguese, *Simone Pereira*

A Rule Based Approach to the Identification of Spanish Zero Pronouns, *Luz Rello and Iustina Ilisei*

Context Driven XML Retrieval, *Aneliya Tincheva*

Framework for Using a Natural Language Approach to Object Identification, *Mosa Elbendak*

Improving the Output from Software that Generates Multiple Choice Question (MCQ) Test Items Automatically using Controlled Rhetorical Structure Theory, *Robert Foster*

18^{30}-19^{15} Demonstration of Ontotext software products

Integrating Language Technologies in Modern Semantic Processing
Atanas Kiryakov and Georgi Georgiev, Ontotext AD, SIRMA group

RANLP-09 Programme, 15 September 2009

9^{00}-10^{00} **Mirella Lapata:** *Vector-based Models of Semantic Composition (invited talk)*

Morning session 1a	Morning session 1b
Applications: MT and QA	*Semantics*
10^{00}-10^{30} **Interactive Machine Translation Based on Partial Statistical Phrase-based Alignments** *Daniel Ortiz-Martínez, Ismael García-Varea and Francisco Casacuberta*	10^{00}-10^{30} **Extracting Synonyms from Dictionary Definitions** *Tong Wang and Graeme Hirst*
10^{30}-11^{00} **Question Answering over Structured Data: an Entailment-Based Approach to Question Analysis** *Matteo Negri and Milen Kouylekov*	10^{30}-11^{00} **Combining Lexical Resources for Contextual Synonym Expansion** *Ravi Sinha and Rada Mihalcea*

11^{00}-11^{30} Coffee break

Morning session 2a	Morning session 2b
Parsing	*Term extraction*
11^{30}-11^{55} **Prepositional Phrase Attachment in Shallow Parsing** ***Vincent Van Asch and Walter Daelemans***	11^{30}-11^{55} **Evaluating Term Extraction** *Adeline Nazarenko and Haïfa Zargayouna*
11^{55}-12^{20} **Exploring Treebank Transformations in Dependency Parsing** *Kepa Bengoetxea and Koldo Gojenola*	11^{55}-12^{20} **Too Many Mammals: Improving the Diversity of Automatically Recognized Terms** *Ziqi Zhang, Lei Xia, Mark A. Greenwood and José Iria*
12^{20}-12^{45} **Dependency Parsing and Semantic Role Labeling as a Single Task** *Roser Morante, Vincent Van Asch and Antal van den Bosch*	

12^{45}-14^{30} Lunch

14^{30}-15^{30} **Shalom Lappin:** *Restricting Probability Distributions to Expand the Class of Learnable Languages (invited talk)*

Afternoon session 1a	Afternoon session 1b
Word-sense disambiguation, temporal processing	*Language learning*
15^{30}-15^{55} **Integrating WordNet and FrameNet using a Knowledge-based Word Sense Disambiguation Algorithm** *Egoitz Laparra and German Rigau*	15^{30}-15^{55} **Singular Value Decomposition for Feature Selection in Taxonomy Learning** *Francesca Fallucchi and Fabio Massimo Zanzotto*
15^{55}-16^{20} **Semi-Supervised Learning for Word Sense Disambiguation: Quality vs. Quantity** *Sandra Kübler and Desislava Zhekova*	15^{55}-16^{20} **Prototype-based Active Learning for Lemmatization** *Walter Daelemans, Hendrik J. Groenewald and Gerhard B. van Huyssteen*
16^{20}-16^{45} **Using Semantic Networks to Identify Temporal Expressions from Semantic Roles** *Hector Llorens, Borja Navarro and Estela Saquete*	16^{20}-16^{45} **Sources of Performance in CRF Transfer Training: a Business Name-tagging Case Study** *Marc Vilain, Jonathan Huggins and Ben Wellner*

16^{45}-17^{15} Coffee break

17^{00} - 18^{30}	*Student Research Workshop Oral Presentations*
Poster presentations: session 2 **RANLP-09 CONFERENCE POSTERS**	17^{15}-17^{45} **A Two-stage Bootstrapping Algorithm for Relation Extraction** *Ang Sun* 17^{45}-18^{15} **Mink: An Incremental Data-Driven Dependency Parser with Integrated Conversion to Semantics** *Rachael Cantrell* 18^{15}-18^{45} **Event Ordering. Temporal Annotation on Top of the BulTreeBank** *Laska Laskova*

Poster session 2: **RANLP-09 CONFERENCE POSTERS**

String Distance-based Stemming of the Highly Inflected Croatian Language, *Jan Šnajder and Bojana Dalbelo Bašić*

All Words Unsupervised Semantic Category Labeling for Hindi, *Siva Reddy, Abhilash Inumella, Rajeev Sangal and Soma Paul*

The Influence of Text Pre-processing on Plagiarism Detection, *Zdenek Ceska and Chris Fox*

Combining Finite State and Corpus-based Techniques for Unknown Word Prediction, *Kostadin Cholakov and Gertjan van Noord*

Identification of Parallel Text Pairs Using Fingerprints, *Martin Hassel and Hercules Dalianis*

Unsupervised Relation Extraction for Automatic Generation of Multiple-Choice Questions, *Naveed Afzal and Viktor Pekar*

Bimodal Corpora Terminology Extraction: Another Brick in the Wall, *Claudiu Mihăilă and Dalila Mekhaldi*

Integrating Document Structure into a Multi-Document Summarizer, *Aurélien Bossard and Thierry Poibeau*

Classification of Emotion Words in Russian and Romanian Languages, *Marina Sokolova and Victoria Bobicev*

Cross-Linguistic Sentiment Analysis: From English to Spanish
Julian Brooke, Milan Tofiloski and Maite Taboada

A Comparative Study of Open Domain and Opinion Question Answering Systems for Factual and Opinionated Queries, *Alexandra Balahur, Ester Boldrini, Andrés Montoyo and Patricio Martínez-Barco*

Sampling-based Multilingual Alignment, *Adrien Lardilleux and Yves Lepage*

Language-Independent Sentiment Analysis Using Subjectivity and Positional Information, *Veselin Raychev and Preslav Nakov*

Ontology Engineering and Knowledge Extraction for Crosslingual Retrieval, *Jantine Trapman and Paola Monachesi*

User's Choice of Precision and Recall in Named Entity Recognition, *Roman Klinger and Christoph M. Friedrich*

Learning to Identify Educational Materials, *Samer Hassan and Rada Mihalcea*

RANLP-09 Programme, 16 September 2009

9^{00}-10^{00} **Walter Daelemans:** *Robust Features for Computational Stylometry (invited talk)*

Morning session 1a

Dialogue, lexical resources

10^{00}-10^{30} **Improving Unsegmented Statistical Dialogue Act Labelling**
Vicent Tamarit, Carlos-D. Martínez-Hinarejos and José-Miguel Benedí Ruíz

10^{30}-11^{00} **Three Issues in Cross-language Frame Information Transfer**
Sara Tonelli and Emanuele Pianta

Morning session 1b

Named Entity Recognition, Diacritization

10^{00}-10^{30} **Feature Subset Selection in Conditional Random Fields for Named Entity Recognition**
Roman Klinger and Christoph M. Friedrich

10^{30}-11^{00} **Diacritization for Real-World Arabic Texts**
Emad Mohamed and Sandra Kübler

11^{00}-11^{30} Coffee break

Morning session 2a

Topic segmentation and modelling

11^{30}-11^{55} **Improving Text Segmentation by Combining Endogenous and Exogenous Methods**
Olivier Ferret

11^{55}-12^{20} **Topic Modeling of Research Fields: An Interdisciplinary Perspective**
Michael Paul and Roxana Girju

12^{20}-12^{45} **Topic-based Multi-Document Summarization with Probabilistic Latent Semantic Analysis**
Leonhard Hennig

Morning session 2b

Natural Language Generation, keyphrase extraction

11^{30}-11^{55} **Text Content and Task Performance in the Evaluation of a Natural Language Generation System**
Albert Gatt and François Portet

11^{55}-12^{20} **A Classification-driven Approach to Document Planning**
Rafael Oliveira, Eder Novais, Roberto Araujo and Ivandré Paraboni

12^{20}-12^{45} **Approximate Matching for Evaluating Keyphrase Extraction**
Torsten Zesch and Iryna Gurevych

12^{45}-14^{30} Lunch

Afternoon session 1a	Afternoon session 1b
Similarity, Information Extraction	*Language resources, language models, anaphora resolution*
14^{30}-14^{55} **A Study on Linking Wikipedia Categories to Wordnet Synsets using Text Similarity** *Antonio Toral, Óscar Ferrández, Eneko Agirre and Rafael Muñoz*	14^{30}-14^{55} **Towards Efficient Production of Linguistic Resources: the Victoria Project** *Lionel Nicolas, Miguel Molinero, Benoît Sagot, Elena S. Trigo, Éric de la Clergerie, Miguel Al. Pardo, Jacques Farré and Joan Miquel Vergés*
14^{55}-15^{20} **Comparing Statistical Similarity Measures for Stylistic Multivariate Analysis** *Marius Popescu and Liviu Dinu*	14^{55}-15^{20} **Structured Output Learning with Polynomial Kernel** *Hajime Morita, Hiroya Takamura and Manabu Okumura*
15^{20}-15^{45} **Cross-document Event Extraction and Tracking: Task, Evaluation, Techniques and Challenges** *Heng Ji, Ralph Grishman, Zheng Chen and Prashant Gupta*	15^{20}-15^{45} **Instance Sampling Methods for Pronoun Resolution** *Holger Wunsch, Sandra Kübler and Rachael Cantrell*

15^{45} - Coffee Break

16^{00} - 17^{30} *Poster presentations: session 3*

RANLP-09 CONFERENCE POSTERS

17^{30}-18^{30} **Massimo Poesio:** *Conceptual Knowledge: Evidence from Corpora and the Brain (invited talk)*

18^{30} **Closure**

Poster session 3: **RANLP-09 CONFERENCE POSTERS**

Statistical Confidence Measures for Probabilistic Parsing, *Ricardo Sánchez-Sáez, Joan Andreu Sánchez and José-Miguel Benedí*

Robust Compositional Polarity Classification, *Manfred Klenner, Stefanos Petrakis and Angela Fahrni*

Fast Boosting-based Part-of-Speech Tagging and Text Chunking with Efficient Rule Representation for Sequential Labeling, *Tomoya Iwakura*

Unsupervised Knowledge Extraction for Taxonomies of Concepts from Wikipedia, *Eduard Barbu and Massimo Poesio*

A Unified Method for Extracting Simple and Multiword Verbs with Valence Information and Application for Hungarian, *Bálint Sass*

The Design of an Experiment in Anaphora Resolution for Referring Expressions Generation, *Diego Jesus de Lucena and Ivandré Paraboni*

How Limited is the Limit? *Prakash Mondal*

Acquisition of Common Sense Knowledge for Basic Level Concepts, *Eduard Barbu*

Uncertainty Detection for Information Extraction, *Bénédicte Goujon*

Stochastic Definite Clause Grammars, *Christian Theil Have*

A Method to Restrict the Blow-up of Hypotheses of a Non-disambiguated Shallow Machine Translation System, *Jernej Vičič, Petr Homola and Vladislav Kuboň*

From Bag of Languages to Family Trees from Noisy Corpus, *Taraka Rama and Anil Kumar Singh*

Treelex Meets Adjectival Tables, *Anna Kupść*

Feature-Rich Named Entity Recognition for Bulgarian Using Conditional Random Fields, *Georgi Georgiev, Preslav Nakov, Kuzman Ganchev, Petya Osenova and Kiril Simov*

Exploiting the Use of Prior Probabilities for Passage Retrieval in Question Answering, *Surya Ganesh and Vasudeva Varma*

Exploiting Structure and Content of Wikipedia for Query Expansion in the Context of Question Answering, *Surya Ganesh and Vasudeva Varma*

Edlin: an Easy to Read Linear Learning Framework, *Kuzman Ganchev and Georgi Georgiev*

Large Vocabulary Continuous Speech Recognition for Bulgarian, *Petar Mitankin, Stoyan Mihov and Tinko Tinchev*

Unsupervised Relation Extraction for Automatic Generation of Multiple-Choice Questions

Naveed Afzal
Research Institute for Information and Language Processing
University of Wolverhampton
Wolverhampton, UK
n.afzal@wlv.ac.uk

Viktor Pekar
Oxford University Press
Great Clarendon St.
Oxford, OX2 6DP, UK
viktor.pekar@oup.com

Abstract

In this paper, we investigate an unsupervised approach to Relation Extraction to be applied in the context of automatic generation of multiple-choice questions (MCQs). The approach aims to identify the most important semantic relations in a document without assigning explicit labels to them in order to ensure broad coverage, unrestricted to predefined types of relations. The paper examines three different surface pattern types, each implementing different assumptions about linguistic expression of semantic relations between named entities. Our main findings indicate that the approach is capable of achieving high precision rates and its enhancement with linguistic knowledge helps to produce significantly better patterns. The intended application for the method is an e-learning system for automatic assessment of students' comprehension of training texts; however it can also be applied to other NLP scenarios, where it is necessary to recognise important semantic relations without any prior knowledge as to their types.

Keywords
Information Extraction, Relation Extraction, Biomedical domain, MCQ generation.

1. Introduction

Information Extraction (IE) is an important problem in many information access applications. The goal is to identify instances of specific semantic relations between named entities of interest in the text. As is known from the literature, Relation Extraction in the biomedical domain is quite difficult compared to other domains, such as news domain, due to the inherently complex nature of its texts: biomedical Named Entities (NEs) are expressed in various linguistic forms such as abbreviations, plurals, compounds, coordination, cascades, acronyms and apposition. Sentences in such texts are syntactically complex as the subsequent Relation Extraction phase depends upon the correct identification of the named entities and correct analysis of linguistic constructions expressing relations between them (e.g., [3, 21]).

The main advantage of the approach presented in this paper is that it can cover a potentially unrestricted range of semantic relations while most supervised and semi-supervised approaches can learn to extract only those relations that have been exemplified in annotated text, seed patterns or seed named entities. Moreover, our approach is suitable in situations where a lot of unannotated text is available as it does not require manually annotated text or seeds. These properties of the method can be useful, specifically, in such applications as Multiple-Choice Question generation [12] or a pre-emptive approach in which viable IE patterns are created in advance without human intervention [20,15].

In the future, we plan to employ the Relation Extraction method for automatic MCQ generation, where it will be used to find relations and named entities in educational texts that are important for testing students' familiarity with key facts contained in the texts. In order to achieve this, we need an IE method that has a high precision and at the same time works with unrestricted semantic types of relations (i.e. without reliance on seeds), while recall is of secondary importance to precision.

2. Related Work

There is a large body of research dedicated to the problem of extracting relations from general-domain texts, and from biomedical texts in particular. Most previous work focused on supervised methods and tried to both extract relations and assign labels describing their semantic types [16 and 5, among many others]. As a rule, these approaches required a manually annotated corpus, which is very laborious and time-consuming to produce.

Semi-supervised and unsupervised approaches relied on seeds patterns and/or examples of specific types of relations [1, 17, 20, and 15]. They often employ bootstrapping techniques which use a small set of seeds in order to start the learning process. An unsupervised approach based on clustering of candidate patterns for the discovery of the most important relation types among NEs from a newspaper domain was presented by [6]. In the biomedical domain, most approaches were supervised and relied on regular expressions to learn patterns [4], while semi-supervised approaches exploited pre-defined seed patterns and cue words [2, 7, 11].

Supervised approaches or those based on manually-written extraction rules that have been previously used for Relation Extraction in the biomedical domain are inadequate in scenarios where relation types of interest are not known in advance. In the following section, we describe our method for finding such relations in an unsupervised manner.

3. Extraction of candidate patterns

Our general approach to the discovery of interesting extraction patterns consists of two main stages: (i) the construction of potential patterns from an unannotated domain corpus and (ii) their relevance ranking.

3.1 Pre-processing steps

The first step in constructing candidate patterns is to perform part-of-speech tagging and NE recognition in an unannotated domain corpus. To do that, we employed the Genia[1] tagger. The Genia tagger tags the following five types of biomedical named entities: Protein, DNA, RNA, Cell Type, and Cell Line. The Genia PoS tagger has been reported to achieve over 96% accuracy on a general corpus (Wall Street Journal) and over 98% on the biomedical Genia corpus [18, 19].

3.2 Linguistic types of patterns

Once the training corpus has been tagged with the Genia tagger, the process of pattern building takes place. Its goal is to identify which NEs are likely to be semantically related to each other. The procedure for constructing candidate patterns is based on the idea that important semantic relations are expressed with the help of recurrent linguistic constructions, and these constructions can be recognised by examining sequences of content words (nouns, verbs, adjectives and adverbs) appearing between NEs. To find such constructions, we impose a limit on the number of content words intervening between two NEs. We experimented with different thresholds and finally settled on minimum one content word and maximum three content words to be extracted between two NEs. The reason for introducing this condition is that if there are no content words between two NEs then, although some relation might exist between them, it is likely to be a very abstract grammatical relation. For example, in "X of Y" there is a relation between X and Y, but the phrase does not explicitly express any domain-specific knowledge. On the other hand, if there are too many content words intervening between two NEs, then it is likely they are not related at all. We build patterns using this approach and store each pattern along with its frequency in a database. In this paper we describe experiments with three different pattern types:

1. Untagged word patterns
2. PoS-tagged word patterns
3. Verb-centred patterns

Untagged word patterns consist of named entities and the content words intervening between them. The reason for choosing these different types of surface patterns is that verbs typically express semantic relations between nouns that are used as their arguments. Some examples of untagged word patterns along with their frequencies are shown in Table 1. Table 2 (*PoS-tagged word patterns)* contains the PoS of each content word, while Table 3 (*verb-centred patterns*) contains patterns where the presence of a verb is compulsory in each pattern. We require the presence of a verb in the verb-based patterns as verbs are the main predicative class of words, expressing specific semantic relations between two named entities.

Table 1: Examples of untagged word patterns

Patterns	Frequency
PROTEIN activation PROTEIN	53
DNA contain DNA	46
PROTEIN bind DNA	39
CELL_TYPE express PROTEIN	31

Table 2: Examples of PoS-tagged patterns

Patterns	Frequency
PROTEIN activation_n PROTEIN	53
PROTEIN include_v PROTEIN	43
PROTEIN activate_v PROTEIN	32
DNA encode_v PROTEIN	27

Table 3: Examples of verb-centred patterns

Patterns	Frequency
PROTEIN bind_v DNA	39
PROTEIN induce_v PROTEIN	29
PROTEIN express_v CELL_TYPE	19
PROTEIN stimulate_v CELL_LINE	11

Moreover, in the pattern building phase, patterns containing passive forms of the verb like:

PROTEIN be_v express_v CELL_TYPE

are converted into the active voice form of the verb:

CELL_LINE express_v PROTEIN

Because such patterns were taken to express a similar semantic relation between NEs, passive to active conversion was carried out in order to relieve the problem of data sparseness: it helped to increase the frequency of unique patterns and reduce the total number of patterns. For the same reason, negation expressions (not, does not, etc) were also removed from the patterns as they express a semantic relation between NEs equivalent to one expressed in patterns where a negation particle is absent.

4. Pattern Ranking

After candidate patterns have been constructed, the next step is to rank the patterns based on their significance in the domain corpus. The ranking method we use requires

[1] http://www-tsujii.is.s.u tokyo.ac.jp/GENIA/tagger/

a general corpus that serves as a source of examples of pattern use in domain-independent texts. To extract candidates from the general corpus, we treated every noun as a potential named-entity holder and the candidate construction procedure described above was applied to find potential patterns of the three different types in the general corpus. In order to score candidate patterns for domain-relevance, we measure the strength of association of a pattern with the domain corpus as opposed to the general corpus. The patterns are scored using the following methods for measuring the association between a pattern and the domain corpus: Information Gain (IG), Information Gain Ratio (IGR), Mutual Information (MI), Normalised Mutual Information (NMI)[2], Log-likelihood (LL) and Chi-Square (CHI). These association measures were included in the study as they have different theoretical principles behind them: IG, IGR, MI and NMI are information-theoretic concepts while LL and CHI are statistical tests of association.

Information Gain measures the amount of information obtained about domain specialisation of corpus *c*, given that pattern *p* is found in it.

$$IG(p,c) = \sum_{d \in \{c,c'\}} \sum_{g \in \{p,p'\}} P(g,d) \log \frac{P(g,d)}{P(g)P(d)}$$

where *p* is a candidate pattern, *c* – the domain corpus, *p'* – a pattern other than *p*, *c'* – the general corpus, *P*(*c*) – the probability of *c* in "overall" corpus {*c*,*c'*}, and *P*(*p*) – the probability of *p* in the overall corpus.

Information Gain Ratio aims to overcome one disadvantage of IG consisting of the fact that IG grows not only with the increase of dependence between *p* and *c*, but also with the increase of the entropy of *p*. IGR removes this factor by normalizing IG by the entropy of the patterns in the corpora:

$$IGR(p,c) = \frac{IG(g,c)}{-\sum_{g \in \{p,p'\}} P(g) \log P(g)}$$

Pointwise Mutual Information between corpus *c* and pattern *p* measures how much information the presence of *p* contains about *c*, and vice versa:

$$MI(p,c) = \log \frac{P(p,c)}{P(p)P(c)}$$

Chi-Square and Log-likelihood are statistical tests which work with frequencies and rank-order scales, both calculated from a contingency table with observed and expected frequency of occurrence of a pattern in the domain corpus. **Chi-Square** is calculated as follows.

$$x^2(p,c) = \sum_{d \in \{c,c'\}} \frac{(O_d - E_d)^2}{E_d}$$

where *O* is the observed frequency of *p* in domain and general corpus respectively and *E* is the expected frequency of *p* in two corpora.

Log-likelihood is calculated according to the following formula:

$$LL(p,c) = 2\left(O_1 \log\left(\frac{O_1}{E_1}\right) + O_2 \log\left(\frac{O_2}{E_2}\right)\right)$$

where O_1 and O_2 are observed frequencies of *p* in the domain and general corpus respectively, while E_1 and E_2 are its expected frequency values in the two corpora.

In addition to these six measures, we introduce a **meta-ranking** method that combines the scores produced by several individual association measures, in order to leverage agreement between different association measures and downplay idiosyncrasies of individual ones. Because the association functions range over different values (for example, IGR ranges between 0 and 1, and MI between +∞ and -∞), we first normalise the scores assigned by each method[3]:

$$s_{norm}(p) = \frac{s(p)}{\max_{q \in P}(s(q))}$$

where *s*(*p*) is the non-normalised score for pattern *p*, from the candidate pattern set *P*. The normalised scores are then averaged across different methods and used to produce a meta-ranking of the candidate patterns.

Given the ranking of candidate patterns produced by a scoring method, a certain number of highest-ranking patterns can be selected for evaluation. We studied two different ways of selecting these patterns: (i) one based on setting a threshold on the association score below which the candidate patterns are discarded (henceforth, *score-thresholding method*) and (ii) one that selects a fixed number of top-ranking patterns (henceforth, *rank-thresholding method*). During the evaluation, we experimented with different rank- and score-thresholding values.

5. Evaluation

5.1 Experimental data

We used the Genia Corpus as the domain corpus while British National Corpus (BNC) was used as a general corpus. Genia corpus consists of 2,000 abstracts extracted from the MEDLINE containing 18,477 sentences. In the evaluation phase, Genia Event

[2] Mutual Information has a well-known problem of being biased towards infrequent events. To tackle this problem, we normalised the MI score by a discounting factor, following the formula proposed in [9].

[3] Patterns with negative MI scores are discarded.

Annotation corpus[4] is used [8]. It consists of 9,372 sentences.

5.2 Evaluation method

In order to evaluate the quality of the extracted patterns, we examined their ability to capture pairs of related named entities in the manually annotated evaluation corpus, without recognising the type of semantic relation. Selecting a certain number of best-ranking patterns, we measure precision, recall and F-score. To test the statistical significance of differences in the results of different methods and configurations, we used a paired t-test, having randomly divided the evaluation corpus into 20 subsets of equal size; each subset containing 461 sentences on average.

6. Results

Table 4 shows the results of top-ranked patterns for each approach respectively while Table 5 shows the results of the score-thresholding method for each approach respectively (for space considerations, the tables show only precision scores; "Untagged" stands for "untagged word patterns", "PoS" – for "PoS-tagged word patterns", "VC" – for "verb-centred patterns").

Table 4: Precision results of rank-thresholding method

	IG	IGR	MI	NMI	LL	CHI	Meta
Top 100 Ranked Patterns							
Untagged	.56	.62	.33	.68	.62	.74	.69
PoS	.79	.80	.43	.84	.80	.90	.86
VC	.65	.65	.38	.79	.65	.83	.83
Top 200 Ranked Patterns							
Untagged	.55	.55	.30	.54	.55	.63	.56
PoS	.74	.74	.42	.71	.74	.75	.76
VC	.70	.69	.36	.72	.69	.74	.76
Top 300 Ranked Patterns							
Untagged	.53	.52	.34	.53	.52	.56	.55
PoS	.72	.73	.46	.72	.72	.74	.73
VC	.71	.70	.41	.60	.70	.62	.67
Top 400 Ranked Patterns							
Untagged	.51	.53	.33	.49	.53	.52	.50
PoS	.70	.70	.45	.64	.70	.69	.69
VC	.65	.66	.42	.55	.66	.55	.59
Top 500 Ranked Patterns							
Untagged	.51	.51	.32	.47	.51	.49	.48
PoS	.68	.68	.42	.61	.68	.62	.63
VC	.59	.59	.45	.51	.59	.51	.54

Table 5: Precision results of score-thresholding method

	IG	IGR	MI	NMI	LL	CHI	Meta
Threshold score > .06							
Untagged	.68	.68	.34	.34	.68	.72	.33
PoS	.72	.73	.43	.43	.73	.88	.44
VC	.68	.68	.44	.44	.68	.76	.44
Threshold score > .07							
Untagged	.65	.65	.34	.34	.65	.73	.55
PoS	.74	.74	.43	.43	.74	.87	.44
VC	.70	.71	.44	.44	.71	.89	.44
Threshold score > .08							
Untagged	.62	.62	.34	.34	.62	.78	.55
PoS	.71	.71	.43	.43	.71	.92	.72
VC	.66	.69	.44	.44	.69	.88	.76
Threshold score > .09							
Untagged	.57	.57	.34	.34	.57	.82	.56
PoS	.70	.72	.43	.43	.72	.96	.72
VC	.67	.67	.44	.44	.67	.88	.75
Threshold score > .1							
Untagged	.50	.50	.34	.34	.50	.81	.55
PoS	.70	.70	.43	.43	.70	.95	.74
VC	.65	.66	.44	.44	.65	.95	.75
Threshold score > .2							
Untagged	0	0	.34	.34	0	.86	.82
PoS	.86	.86	.43	.44	.86	1.00	.90
VC	.85	.85	.43	.44	.85	1.00	.87

6.1 Ranking methods

In both tables, the results of the best performing ranking method are shown in bold font.

The CHI-score method performs best for the selected 100 top ranked patterns while the meta-ranking method comes out second best in all three patterns types. The difference between CHI-score and the second-best method (meta-ranking) is significant at $p < 0.05$ level. In Table 5, the CHI-score ranking method outperforms all the other ranking methods for all three patterns types while IG, IGR and LL come out second best for most of the thresholding score values. Here also the difference from the second-best ranking method is significant ($p < 0.05$). IG, IGR and LL ranking methods perform quite similarly to each other and in general, there is no statistically significant difference between them. While literature on the topic suggests that IGR performs better than the IG [14, 10], we found that in general there is no statistically significant difference between IG and IGR, IGR and LL in all three pattern types. In both sets of experiments, obviously due to the aforementioned problem, MI performs quite poorly; the normalised version of MI helps to alleviate this problem. Moreover, there exists a statistically significant difference ($p < 0.01$) between NMI and the other ranking methods in all three pattern types.

The meta-ranking method did not improve on the best individual ranking method as expected. In Table 4, the meta- ranking method comes out second best for 100, 200 and 300 top ranked patterns but then its performance decreases. Similarly for thresholding score values it comes out second best for all thresholds greater than 0.09. Moreover, we found that there is a statistically significant difference ($p < 0.05$) between the meta-ranking method and all the other ranking methods for all three patterns types.

6.2 Score vs. rank thresholding

We also find out that score-thresholding method produces better results than rank-thresholding as we are

[4]http://www-tsujii.is.s.u-tokyo.ac.jp/GENIA/home/wiki.cgi?page=Event+Annotation

able to achieve up to 100% precision with the former technique.

6.3 Types of patterns

PoS-tagged word patterns and verb-centred patterns perform better than untagged word patterns. Verb-centred patterns work well, because verbs are known to express semantic relations between named entities using syntactic arguments to the verb; PoS-tagged word patterns add important semantic information into the pattern and possibly disambiguate words appearing in the pattern. In order to find out that whether the differences between the three patterns types are statistically significant, we carried out a paired t-test again. We found that there is no statistically significant difference between PoS-tagged word patterns and verb-centred patterns. Apart from IG, IGR and LL there is a statistically significant difference between all the ranking methods of untagged word patterns and PoS-tagged word patterns, untagged word patterns and verb-centred patterns respectively.

6.4 Precision vs. F-measure optimisation

The score-thresholding method achieves higher precision than the rank-thresholding method. High precision is quite important in applications such as MCQ generation. In thresholding scores, it is possible to optimise for high precision (up to 100%), though F-measure is generally quite low. MCQ applications rely on the production of good questions rather than the production of all possible questions, so high precision plays a vital role in such applications.

7. Conclusion

In this paper, we have presented an unsupervised approach for Relation Extraction from surface-based patterns intended to be deployed in an e-Learning system for automatic generation of multiple choice questions. We experimented with three different surface-based approaches and showed that PoS-based and verb-centred patterns achieve higher precision compared to untagged word patterns. We explored different ranking methods and found that the Chi-Square ranking method obtained higher precision than the other ranking methods. We employed two techniques: the rank-thresholding method and score-thresholding method and found that thresholding scores perform better.

For future work, we are going to investigate other meta-ranking methods and carry out a task-embedded evaluation, in the context of the multiple-choice question generation problem.

8. References

[1] Agichtein E. and Gravano L. Snowball: Extracting Relations from Large Plaintext Collections. In Proc. of the 5th ACM International Conference on Digital Libraries (DL-00), 2000.

[2] Blaschke A., Andrade M. A., Ouzounis C., and Valencia A. Automatic Extraction of Biological Information from Scientific Text: Protein-Protein interactions, in Proc. of ISMB99, pp. 60-67, 1999.

[3] Cohen A. M., and Hersh W. R. A Survey of Current Work in Biomedical Text Mining. Briefings in Bioinformatics, pp. 57-71, 2005.

[4] Corney D. P., Jones D., Buxton B., and Langdon W. BioRAT: Extracting Biological Information from Full-length Papers. Bioinformatics, pp. 3206-3213, 2004.

[5] Cunningham H., Maynard D., Bontcheva K., and Tablan V. GATE: A framework and graphical development environment for robust NLP tools and applications. In Proc. of ACL'02, Philadelphia, 2002.

[6] Hasegawa T., Sekine S., and Grishman R. Discovering relations among named entities from large corpora. In Proc. of ACL'04, 2004.

[7] Huang M., Zhu X., Payan G. D., Qu K., and Li M. Discovering patterns to extract protein-protein interactions from full biomedical texts. Bioinformatics, pp. 3604-3612, 2004.

[8] Kim J-D., Ohta T., and Tsujii J. Corpus Annotation for Mining Biomedical Events from Literature, BMC Bioinformatics, 2008.

[9] Lin D. and Pantel P. Concept Discovery from Text. In Proc. of Conference on CL 2002. pp. 577-583. Taipei, Taiwan, 2002.

[10] Manning C. and Schütze H. Foundations of Statistical Natural Language Processing. The MIT Press, Cambridge, US, 1999.

[11] Martin E. P., Bremer E., Guerin G., DeSesa M-C., Jouve O. Analysis of Protein/Protein Interactions through Biomedical Literature: Text Mining of Abstracts vs. Text Mining of Full Text Articles. Berlin: Springer-Verlag, pp. 96-108, 2004.

[12] Mitkov, R., Ha, L. A. and Karamanis, N. A computer-aided environment for generating multiple-choice test items. Natural Language Engineering 12(2). Cambridge University Press, pp. 177-194, 2006.

[13] Ono T., Hishigaki H., Tanigami A. and Takagi T. Automated Extraction of Information on Protein–Protein Interactions from the Biological Literature. Bioinformatics, pp. 155-161, 2001.

[14] Quinlan J.R. Induction of decision trees. Machine Learning, 1(1), pp. 81-106, 1986.

[15] Satoshi Sekine. On-Demand Information Extraction. Proc. of the COLING/ACL. Sydney, pp. 731-738, 2006.

[16] Soderland S. Learning Information Extraction Rules for Semi-Structured and Free Text. Machine Learning, 34(1-3):233–272, 1999.

[17] Stevenson M. and Greenwood. A Semantic Approach to IE Pattern Induction. In Proc. of ACL'05, pages 379-386, 2005.

[18] Tsuruoka Y., Tateishi Y., Kim J-D., Ohta T., McNaught J., Ananiadou S., and Tsujii J. Developing a Robust PoS Tagger for Biomedical Text. Advances in Informatics - 10th Panhellenic Conference on Informatics, LNCS 3746, pp. 382-392, 2005.

[19] Tsuruoka Y. and Tsujii J. Bidirectional Inference with the Easiest-First Strategy for Tagging Sequence Data. Proc. of HLT/EMNLP, pp. 467-474, 2005.

[20] Yusuke Shinyama and Satoshi Sekine. Preemptive Information Extraction using Unrestricted Relation Discovery. Proc. of the HLT Conference of the North American Chapter of the ACL. New York, pp. 304-311, 2006.

[21] Zhou G., Su J., Shen D. and Tan C. Recognizing Name in Biomedical Texts: A Machine Learning Approach. Bioinformatics, pp. 1178-1190, 2004.

Summary Generation for Toponym-Referenced Images using Object Type Language Models

Ahmet Aker & Robert Gaizauskas
Department of Computer Science
University of Sheffield
Sheffield, S1 4DP, UK
A.Aker, R.Gaizauskas@dcs.shef.ac.uk

Abstract

This paper presents a novel approach to automatic captioning of toponym-referenced images. The automatic captioning procedure works by summarizing multiple web-documents that contain information related to an image's location. Our summarizer can generate both query-based and language model-biased multi-document summaries. The models are created from large numbers of existing articles pertaining to places of the same "object type". Evaluation relative to human written captions shows that when language models are used to bias the summarizer the summaries score more highly than the non-biased ones.

Keywords

Multi-Document Summarization, Image Captioning, Language Models, Statistical Methods, NLP

1 Introduction

In recent years the number of images on the web has grown immensely, facilitated by the development of cheap digital hardware and the availability of online image sharing social sites. Many of these images are tagged only with place names or contain minimal captions that include locational information. This small amount of textual information associated with the image is of limited usefulness for image indexing, organization and search. What would be useful is a means to generate or augment captions automatically based on existing data.

Attempts towards automatic generation of image captions have been previously reported. Deschacht & Moens [6] and Mori et al. [14] generate image captions automatically by analyzing image-related text from the immediate context of the image, e.g. the surrounding text in HTML documents. The authors identify named entities and other noun phrases in the image-related text and assign these to the image as captions. Other approaches create image captions by taking into consideration image features (colour, shape and texture) as well as image-related text [22, 14, 4, 7, 3, 15, 8]. These approaches analyze only the immediate textual context of the image. However, generating image captions based on the immediate context of the image can result in an image description which does not describe the image at all. Marsch & White [13] argue that the content of an image and its immediate text have little semantic agreement and this can, according to Purves et al. [16], be misleading to image retrieval. Furthermore, these approaches assume that the image has been obtained from a document. In cases where there is no document associated with the image, which is the scenario we are principally concerned with, these techniques are not applicable.

In this paper, we propose a technique for automatic image captioning or caption enhancement starting with only a set of place names pertaining to an image. The technique applies just to images of static features of the built or natural landscape (e.g. buildings, mountains, etc.) and not to images of objects which move about in such landscapes (e.g. people, cars, clouds, etc.).

Our approach is based on extractive multi-document summarization techniques, where the documents to be summarized are web-documents retrieved using the place names associated with an image. In earlier work [1] we have shown that in this scenario query-based summaries outperform generic summaries, i.e. extractive summaries of multiple web pages retrieved using the place names which bias the summarizer to include sentences mentioning these place names tend to be better than generic summaries of the same pages. However, the resulting summaries were still far from ideal. We examined information selected by humans for inclusion in a caption from the same place-name-retrieved web-documents made available to the summarizer and observed high levels of agreement between humans on which information to include. This led us to hypothesize that humans have a conceptual model of what is salient regarding a certain scene or object type (e.g. church, bridge, etc.) and that they use this in providing a description of the scene or object. Our qualitative analysis of Wikipedia articles (section 2) confirmed this hypothesis.

Given the observation that humans appear to have a conceptual model of what is salient regarding a specific object type, the question arises as to whether we can represent or approximate such a conceptual model in a way that allows us to improve content selection for our caption summaries. While there are many ways this could be done, one simple way is to view a corpus of descriptions of objects of a given type as containing an implicit model of that type and use language models derived from the corpus to bias sentence selection by an extractive summarizer.

In this paper we explore the use of signature words [12] and language models [21] to represent such conceptual models and investigate their impact on the quality of automatically generated image captions. Our results show that using these conceptual models does indeed improve the results over those of a standard query-based summarizer. In the following we first describe how the object type corpora were collected (section 2) and how language models are generated from these corpora (section 3). Next, we describe the set of our images, their categorization by object type and the retrieval of related web-documents (section 4). In section 5 we present the multi-document summarizer used to caption images. We discuss the results of evaluating automatic summaries against the human created captions in section 6, and conclude the paper in section 7.

2 Object Type Corpora

An object type corpus for our purposes is a collection of texts about a specific static object type such as *church, bridge, etc.* Objects can be named places or locations such as *Parc Guell, etc.* To refer to such object names we use the term *toponym*.

To build object type corpora we categorized Wikipedia articles about places by object types. For this categorization a Wikipedia dump[1] was used. The object types were identified automatically using *Is-A* patterns in the fashion of [10] and as described in [9]. The Is-A patterns were applied to the first ten sentences of each article. They match sentences which contain the type description of an object such as ... *is a ... <object type>*. For *Westminster Abbey*, for instance, our Is-A patterns found the sentence which contains ... *is a ... church*, extracted *church* as an object type from this sentence and assigned the article about the abbey to the *church* category. In this way we collected 107 categories containing articles about places around the world (cf. Table 1).

To assess the accuracy of the categorization we randomly selected 35 object type corpora and 50 articles from each corpus. Then we checked for each of these articles whether it is correctly assigned to its object type. Finally, we calculate an accuracy value for each object type by dividing the number of correctly assigned articles by 50 (cf. Table 2). We observed an average accuracy of 80% for all 35 object types.

We examined articles about different objects of the same type to investigate whether they contained recurring information. For this analysis we randomly selected 15 different object types from our entire set of 107. From each object type corpus we selected 20 articles about different objects. For each of the 15 object types we read all 20 associated articles and manually identified information that was repeated in at least two of the 20 articles. For illustration Table 3 shows the results of the analysis for three object types. From Table 3 we can observe that for each object type there is a common case of information used to describe instances of that type. This supports our hypothesis that humans have a shared idea about what is important information for an object type. Capturing this shared idea in conceptual models about object types could be used to bias a summarizer towards sentences that contain the information contained in the models.

[1] English Wikipedia dump from 24/07/2008

Table 1: *Object types and the number of articles. Object types which are bold are covered by our image set.*

village 39970, school 15794, city 14233, organization 9393, **university** 7101, **area** 6934, **district** 6565, airport 6493, **island** 6400, **railway station** 5905, **river** 5851, company 5734, **mountain** 5290, **park** 3754, **college** 3749, **stadium** 3665, **lake** 3649, **road** 3421, country 3186, **church** 3005, way 2508, **museum** 2320, **railway** 2093, **house** 2018, arena 1829, field 1731, club 1708, shopping centre 1509, highway 1464, **bridge** 1383, **street** 1352, **theatre** 1330, bank 1310, property 1261, **hill** 1072, **castle** 1022, forest 995, court 949, hospital 937, peak 906, bay 899, **skyscraper** 843, **valley** 763, **hotel** 741, **garden** 739, **building** 722, market 712, **monument** 679, port 651, sea 645, **temple** 625, **beach** 614, **square** 605, store 547, campus 525, **palace** 516, **tower** 496, cemetery 457, **volcano** 426, **cathedral** 402, **glacier** 392, **residence** 371, dam 363, **waterfall** 355, **gallery** 349, **prison** 348, **cave** 341, **canal** 332, restaurant 329, path 312, observatory 303, **zoo** 302, coast 298, **statue** 283, **venue** 269, **parliament** 258, shrine 256, desert 248, synagogue 236, bar 229, **ski resort** 227, arch 223, landscape 220, **avenue** 202, casino 179, farm 179, seaside 173, waterway 167, tunnel 167, ruin 166, **chapel** 165, **observation wheel** 158, **basilica** 157, woodland 154, wetland 151, cinema 144, **gate** 142, **aquarium** 136, entrance 136, opera **house** 134, **spa** 125, shop 124, **abbey** 108, **boulevard** 108, **pub** 92, bookstore 76, **mosque** 56

Table 2: *Object types and the categorization accuracy.*

Object Type	Accuracy	Object Type	Accuracy
shopping center	0.9	**ski resort**	1.0
mountain	0.92	highway	0.82
railway station	1.0	mosque	0.66
waterfall	0.88	street	0.58
landscape	0.5	restaurant	0.86
island	0.92	**airport**	1.0
area	0.64	volcano	0.92
village	0.96	zoo	0.96
arena	0.96	wetland	0.79
bank	0.74	monument	0.62
university	0.98	building	0.52
park	0.96	gallery	0.725
museum	0.7	canal	0.82
temple	0.74	tower	0.52
prison	0.83	residence	0.8
aquarium	0.62	castle	0.86
bridge	0.72	waterway	0.83
river	0.94	**average accuracy**	**0.80**

3 Constructing Models

For constructing primitive conceptual models of shared information about object types we use two approaches: signature words [12] and generative language models as commonly used in information retrieval [21]. Using these two approaches we build unigram and bi-gram models for each object type using the corpus for that type constructed from Wikipedia articles as described above.

3.1 Signature Words

Signature words are a family of related terms [12]. Lin and Hovy use these terms to bias the sentence selection during the summarization process when creating topic-oriented summaries. They classify documents from the TREC collection as relevant or non-relevant for each given topic. Then, based on the relevant and non-relevant documents they generate for each topic a set of topic related terms or signature words. For each term in the set a weight is generated which expresses the importance of the term to the topic. The non-relevant documents are used to filter non-specific words from the topic-related documents. In the summarization process each sentence from the documents to be summarized is checked for whether it contains any word from the set of signature words. The score of the sentence is the sum of the weights of signature words it contains. Lin and Hovy showed that signature words lead to better summaries. There-

Table 3: *Information commonly provided among the 20 Wikipedia articles for each object type.*

river:	where it originates; where it flows and ends/empties; length; other water bodies it joins; size of the area it drains; how fast it flows; tributaries it has;amount of water it discharges annually on average; location
church:	architecture; size (height, width); type of church (catholic, etc.); foundation year; architect; location;
mountain:	location; height(above see level); range; structure/shape; comparison to other mountains; when it was first climbed

fore we investigated the usefulness of this idea for the automatic image captioning task.

Similarly to Lin and Hovy we use our object type corpus to generate signature words. For each object type corpus we generate a uni-gram and a bi-gram signature word model:

$$ngram = \{corpus, [(ngram_1, score_1), .., (ngram_n, score_n)]\} \quad (1)$$

where *ngram* is either a single word (uni-gram) or two words (bi-gram). Lemmas of the words are used for both uni-gram and bi-gram models[2]. The score we use is the count of the n-gram lemma over the entire corpus divided by the most frequently occurring n-gram (to ensure that the n-gram score ranges between 0 and 1).

3.2 Language Models

Language models are used in different fields with different purposes. In information retrieval (IR), for instance, language models are used to retrieve documents relevant to a query. For each document a distinct n-gram language model is derived and used to estimate the probabilities of producing each term in the query [21]. The query is treated as a generation process, i.e. based on each language model the probability of generating each term in the query is computed. The probability of generating the query is the product of terms occurring in the query. Finally, the documents are ranked in descending order based on the probability assigned to the query. Therefore, if terms of a document lead to higher generation probabilities, the more relevant this document is to the query.

As an alternative to the signature word method we also generated language models from the object type corpora. Similar to [21] our language models are used in a generative way, i.e. we calculate the probability that a sentence is generated based on an n-gram language model. As for the signature word models we generate a uni-gram and a bi-gram model from each object type corpus:

$$ngram = \{corpus, [(ngram_1, prob_1), .., (ngram_n, prob_n)]\} \quad (2)$$

where again *ngram* is either the lemma of an uni-gram or bi-gram. $prob_i$ is the probability of an n-gram calculated using Good-Turing estimation:

$$prob(ngram) = \frac{(r+1)\frac{E(N_{r+1})}{E(N_r)}}{N} \quad (3)$$

where r is the number of times an n-gram is seen, N_r is the number of different n-grams seen exactly r times in the entire corpus, $E(N_r)$ is the expected value of N_r and N is the number of words in the entire corpus. However, in case $r=0$ (an n-gram is not seen) the probability is calculated as $E(N_1)/E(N_0 N)$. N_0 is the number of n-grams which have not been seen. It is calculated by taking the square of the number of all seen n-gram types minus their sum.

[2] Lemmatizing was performed using OpenNLP tools, http://opennlp.sourceforge.net/.

4 Images & related Documents

Our image collection has 203 different images which are toponym-referenced, i.e. are assigned toponyms. The subjects of our images are locations around the world such as *Parc Guell, Edinburgh Castle*, etc. We manually categorized these images by object type. For each image we used its toponyms to search for a Wikipedia article using the Yahoo! search engine. We then selected the object type of the image from the Wikipedia article. For the image showing *Westminster Abbey*, for instance, we used the toponym *Westminster Abbey* to retrieve the Wikipedia article about the abbey, selected from this article the object type *church* and assigned the image showing the abbey to the object type category *church*. This process was repeated for our entire image set. Our images cover 60 of the 107 object types (cf. Table 1).

To generate automatic captions for these images we automatically retrieved the top ten related web-documents for each image from the Yahoo! search engine using the toponym associated with the image as a query. The text from these documents was extracted using an HTML parser and passed to the summarizer.

5 Summary Generation

The image captions are generated using *the-MDS* (the-multi-document summarizer), an extractive, language independent, multi-document, query-based summarization system implemented in Java. It uses a single cluster approach to summarize n related documents which are given as input. The summarizer creates image captions in a three step process. First, it applies shallow text analysis to the given documents. Then extracts features from the document sentences. Finally, it performs sentence selection to create the summary. The latter two tasks are language independent and can be performed for any UTF-8 encoded language. This means that *the-MDS* needs only a shallow text analyzer for any specific language in order to perform summarization. The three steps are described in more detail in the following subsections.

5.1 Shallow Text Analysis

The-MDS first applies shallow text analysis including sentence detection, tokenization, lemmatization and POS-tagging to the given documents using the OpenNLP tools.

5.2 Feature Extraction

After text analysis, *the-MDS* represents each sentence in the documents as a vector, where each vector position contains a term (word) and a value which is a product of the *term frequency* in the document and the *inverse document frequency (IDF)*, a measurement of the term's distribution over the set of documents [18]. The IDF table is generated from the n related documents. Furthermore, *the-MDS* enhances the sentence vector representation with four further features:

1. ***querySimilarity***: Sentence similarity to the query.
2. ***sentencePosition***: Position of the sentence within its document. The first sentence in the document gets the score 1 and

the last one gets $\frac{1}{n}$ where n is the number of sentences in the document.
3. ***centroidSimilarity***: Similarity to the centroid.
4. ***starterSimilarity***: A sentence gets a binary score if it starts with the query term (e.g. *Westminster Abbey, The Westminster Abbey, The Westminster* or *The Abbey*) or with the object type, e.g. *The church*.

For calculating vector similarities (*querySimilarity* and *centroidSimilarity*), the cosine similarity measure is used [19]. If there is an object type model, then for each sentence in the documents an additional fifth feature, the similarity to the given model (*modelSimilarity*), is added. In case of signature words this *modelSimilarity* is the sum of scores (*score*) of n-grams from a sentence S found also in the signature word model M (cf. Formula 4).

$$modelScore(S, M) = \sum_{ngram \in M \cap S} score_{ngram} \quad (4)$$

The *modelSimilarity* score with language models is calculated according to Formula 5.

$$modelScore(S, M) = \prod_{ngram \in s} (prob_{ngram} + 1) \quad (5)$$

In this case the *modelSimilarity* score of a sentence S is the product of scores (*prob*) of its n-grams where the *prob* values are obtained from the language model M. Finally, the feature vector representation of each sentence is passed to the sentence scoring process.

5.2.1 Sentence Scoring

We have two different approaches (signature word and language models) to determine the value for the *modelSimilarity* score. Both models, however, produce different value ranges for the same feature. To unify this score we apply a technique similar to the one described by Alfonseca et al. [2]. The authors produce a final ranked list for sentences from three different ranked lists for the same sentence by positioning the sentence which occurs in the top position in all three lists also in the top position of the final ranked list.

Following this idea *The-MDS* calculate the final sentence score. First, the first four features are used in a weighted linear combination to rank the sentences based on Formula 6.

$$S_{firstScore} = \sum_{i=1}^{n} feature_i * weight_i \quad (6)$$

The values for the weights are set to *.3* for the *querySimilarity*, *.1* for the *sentencePosition*, *.8* for the *centroidSimilarity* and *.9* for the *starterSimilarity*. We obtained these values empirically based on a set of 20 images selected randomly from our larger corpus of images. None of these 20 images is contained in the image set that we use for our evaluation. For this set of 20 images we generate summaries with different weight-value combinations, compare these summaries with human written captions and keep the weight-value combination which produces a summary with the highest ROUGE score.

The first ranking produces a ranked list of sentences in descending order by the $S_{firstScore}$. Then *the-MDS* uses the *modelSimilarity* feature to produce a second ranked list. Like the first ranked list the second list contains in its first position the sentence with the highest score. Finally, *the-MDS* combines these two lists to a final ranked list which is used to generate the summary. To produce the final list *the-MDS* takes for each sentence its position from the first and second ranked list and adds this sentence to the final list with a final score which is calculated using Formula 7.

$$S_{finalScore} = pos_{firstList} + 0.1 * pos_{secondList} \quad (7)$$

5.3 Sentence Selection

After the scoring process, *the-MDS* selects sentences for summary generation by selecting the sentence from the first position from the final list, followed by the next sentence in the list until the compression rate is reached. As in [17], before a sentence is selected a similarity metric for redundancy detection is applied to each sentence to decide whether a sentence is distinct enough from already selected sentences to be included in the summary or not. *The-MDS* measures lemma overlap between the words of the current sentence with the lemmas of previous selected sentences and includes the current sentence to the summary if the similarity measure is less than 30% which is obtained experimentally based on our training set images.

Using *the-MDS*, query-based (using first four features) and model-biased (using all five features) summaries are generated for the image-related documents obtained from the web. Each summary contains a maximum of 200 words. The queries used are the toponyms.

6 Evaluation

To evaluate our approach we compared the automatically generated summaries against model captions written by humans. Model captions were generated based on image captions taken from *Virtualtourist*[3]. Virtualtourist is one of the largest online travel communities in the world containing 3 million photos with captions (in English) of more than 58,000 destinations worldwide.

As with all information found in online knowledge sharing systems, there is no quality check for Virtualtourist captions. Members can describe places in anyway they want, resulting in image captions of different length, coherence, focus, grammaticality etc. To ensure a good standard for our model captions we asked 11 human subjects to generate up to four model captions per object by modifying Virtualtourist captions. The modifications included deleting personal information, ensuring consistency and coherence of the text and generating a summary of 190-210 words in length (because our automatic summaries have similar word counts). An example model summary about *Parc Guell* is shown in Table 6. For comparison between summaries the ROUGE metric [11] is used. ROUGE compares automatically generated summaries against human-created reference summaries and can be used to estimate content coverage in an automatically generated summary. Following the Document Understanding Conference (DUC) [5] evaluation standards we use ROUGE 2 and ROUGE SU4 as evaluation metrics. ROUGE 2 gives recall scores for bi-gram overlap between the automatically generated summaries and the reference ones. ROUGE SU4 allows bi-grams to be composed of non-contiguous words, with a maximum of four words between the bi-grams.

[3] www.virtualtourist.com

Table 4: *ROUGE scores for the first document (F), Wikipedia (W) and the query-based (qB) baselines. The last 3 columns show z scores and the significance of the Wilcoxon signed ranked test.*

Recall	F	W	qB	F<W	F<qB	W>qB
R2	.045	**.095**	.066	-10.4***	-7***	-8.9***
RSU4	.081	**.14**	.114	-10.8***	-8.6***	-8.6***

Table 5: *ROUGE results for uni-gram and bi-gram biased models (signature words (WS) and language models (WL)). The first 2 rows show the results for uni-gram and the last 2 rows for the bi-gram models. The last 4 columns show z scores and the significance of the Wilcoxon signed ranked test.*

Recall	WS	WL	WS<WL	WL>qB	WS>qB	WL<W
R2	.068	**.07**	-1.9	-4***	-1.5	-8.3***
RSU4	.115	**.118**	-2.6**	-4.8***	-1.5	-7.3***
R2	.068	**.071**	-2.4*	-5.2***	-1.9	-8***
RSU4	.115	**.119**	-4***	-5.9***	-.67	-7.3***

As baselines for evaluation we use three summary types. Firstly, we generate summaries for each image using the top-ranked non Wikipedia document retrieved in the Yahoo! search results for the given toponyms. From this document we create a baseline summary by selecting sentences from the beginning until the summary reaches a length of 200 words. As a second baseline we use the Wikipedia article for a given toponym list from which we again select sentences from the beginning until the summary length limit is reached. Thirdly, we include query-based summaries generated without language models. Table 4 shows the ROUGE scores when baseline summaries are compared to the Virtualtourist model summaries. To assess the statistical significance of ROUGE score differences between multiple summarization results we performed a pairwise Wilcoxon signed-rank test with Bonferroni correction[4] for multiple testing.

Both Wikipedia baseline and query-based summaries score significantly higher than the first document baseline. The Wikipedia baseline scores are also significantly higher than the query-based ones. It follows from these results that the Wikipedia baseline summaries have the best coverage of the content in our model captions. Table 6 shows the Wikipedia baseline summary about *Parc Guell.*

Using the same Virtualtourist model captions we also evaluated the uni-gram and bi-gram model-biased summaries. It should be noted that the set of documents we used to generate our summaries do not contain any Virtualtourist related sites, as these are used to generate our model summaries. The results are given in Table 5 and show that the highest scoring summaries are the ones biased with language models. Table 6 shows the language model-biased summary about *Parc Guell.* In both uni-gram and bi-gram models the language models score significantly higher than signature word models as well as query-based summaries. The signature words summaries perform moderately higher than query-based summaries. However, both signature words and language model summaries are significantly lower than the Wikipedia baseline summaries (Due to limited space Table 5 shows only the comparison between the language model and Wikipedia baseline summaries). These results show that language model biased summaries lead to significant improvement in ROUGE results compared to the query-based summaries. One reason for this might be that the query-based summarizer takes relevant sentences according to the query given to it and does not take into more general consideration the information typically provided for the, albeit simple, object type. Our language models are one way of capturing shared interests about some particular object type. To assess whether and to what extent language model biased summaries contain more shared information than query-based ones, we also qualitatively analyze the sentences in query-based and language model-biased summaries. First, we delete all sentences that occur in both summary types to focus only on differences between the two methods. Then, for each remaining sentence, we check whether it carries one of the facets of information about an object type commonly presented in Wikipedia articles (cf. section 2). If this is the case, the sentence is selected. Finally, we count the number of selected sentences in query-based and language model-biased summaries. Language model-biased summaries covered 76 sentences containing shared information whereas query-based summaries covered only 34 such sentences. While this is not the total number of sentences containing shared information, it highlights the differences between the two summarization methods with respect to capturing shared information about object types. Language model-biased summaries contain 51% more of the information commonly provided in the Wikipedia articles than the query-based summaries. This implies that the model-biased summaries do indeed help to bias the summarizer towards information commonly used for certain object types, which in turn improves the quality of summaries or image captions.

6.1 Discussion

There are several application areas for our automatically generated image captions. They could provide useful information about objects to interested users, e.g. a tourist who is looking for some basic information about a place to visit. Also they could be used as a way to automatically index images. The automatic summary shown in Table 6 could serve both these purposes. It contains only sentences relevant to *Parc Guell* without any unrelated information. Furthermore, the summary contains terms such as *park*, *Barcelona centre*, *Gaudi's creations*, etc. These terms could be used to index an image showing *Parc Guell*, which would potentially provide better indexing than using the park's name only. Sanderson & Kohler [20], for example, analyzed search engine queries containing place names and other geographic terms such as object types (street, island, lake, etc.), address and direction information, etc. They showed that more than 40% of the queries contained other geographic terms beside the place name. Thus indexing images with the place name and the terms from the automatically

[4] After Bonferroni correction all effects are reported at a *p=.0167* level of significance. We use the following conventions for indicating significance level in the tables: *** = p < .0001, ** = p < .001, * = p < .0167 and no star indicates non-significance. We also use Wilcoxon test for all pairwise comparisons reported in the text, in which case no correction is applied, and the results are reported relative to significance level *p<.05*.

Table 6: *Model, Wikipedia baseline and language model-biased summary for Parc Guell.*

Model Summary	Wikipedia baseline summary	Language model-biased summary
One of the star attractions of Barcelona is the Parc Guell, the second most visited park after the Ciutadella probably only because of its location in the north of the city. The park owes its magnetic attraction to the fact that it was designed by Gaudi. In creating the park, Gaudi used shapes which harmonized with the landscape. Always aware of the struggle betwen man and nature, he built a complex garden of staircases, animal like sculptures, curvy ramps, and viaducts. Today, the park is declared a monument of world interest by UNESCO and has had this status since 1984. The most interesting part of the park consists of the large snake bench. Each part of the bench has a different looking pattern and color. Then down below this part is the famous lizard. Above this more popular area are pathways to walk on and even these are decorated with palm trees and unique benches made of rock. The best way to get there is with the bus. The bus number 24 bus stops close to the park. The bus stop is located near placa catalunya, The Metro is a much longer walk away from the park. Admission to the park is free!	The park was originally part of a commercially unsuccessful housing site, the idea of Count Eusebi Guell, whom the park was named after. It was inspired by the English garden city movement; hence the original English name Park (in the Catalan language spoken in Catalonia where Barcelona is located, the word for "Park" is "Parc", and the name of the place is "Parc Guell" in its origin language). The site was a rocky hill with little vegetation and few trees, called Montana Pelada (Bare Mountain). It already included a large country house called Larrard House or Muntaner de Dalt House, and was next to a neighborhood of upper class houses called La Salud. The intention was to exploit the fresh air (well away from smoky factories) and beautiful views from the site, with sixty triangular lots being provided for luxury houses. Count Eusebi Guell added to the prestige of the development by moving in 1906 to live in Larrard House. Ultimately, only two houses were built, neither designed by Gaudi.	The park is huge with many different sights to enjoy. The park is full of narrow twisting pathways which meander through thepark. The park contains amazing stone structures (see below), stunning tiling and fascinating buildings. In every sense, Barcelona has become one of the hottest destinations in Spain. The park was built between 1900-1914, originally planned to be a garden city on the estate of Eusebi Guell. More: everything looks like it wasn't created by man, but by nature. Great park, quite a lot so see as you walk around, some mad buildings! The walk from the metro will take you about 20 mins. Park Gueell is another of Gaudi's creations and lies north of Barcelona centre, 20 mins walk from Lesseps Metro (Green Line, L3). The extraordinary craftsmanship and unusual use of materials and plants throughout the park catch and delight the eye, making Parc Guell one of the great parks of the world. Ultimately, only two houses were built, neither designed by Gaudi.

generated caption or summary could indeed lead to better retrieval. This would be the case for all search engine queries which do not contain a specific place name but rather are more general query such as *parks in Barcelona*. However, one could argue that the same benefits would be achieved by simply taking Wikipedia articles as image captions, rendering multi-document summarization unnecessary for captioning. Our results showed that initial sentences from Wikipedia articles are indeed a tough baseline for evaluation of image captions. One problem with this, however, is that Wikipedia does not contain an article for every location that may be described on the web. In our larger image set, for instance, no Wikipedia article exits for 30 images. This gives us the motivation to further develop multi-document summarization techniques for image captioning.

7 Conclusion

In this work we have proposed an approach to automatic captioning of toponym-referenced images using query-based multi-document summarization techniques. We showed that query-based summarizers biased with a language model for a specific object type perform significantly better than standard query-based summarizers without such models. The language models are generated from object/scene type corpora built from Wikipedia articles which have been automatically categorized by object type. In future work we plan to investigate alternative ways of modelling conceptual knowledge about object types and also ways of producing more coherent summaries. We also plan to investigate the application of the same technique to other languages.

8 Acknowlegment

The research reported was funded by the TRIPOD project supported by the European Commission under the contract No. 045335. We would like to thank Mark Greenwood for discussions and comments.

References

[1] A. Aker and R. Gaizauskas. Evaluating automatically generated user-focused multi-document summaries for geo-referenced images. *Proc. of COLING08, Workshop on Multi-source, Multilingual Information Extraction and Summarization (MMIES2)*, 2008.

[2] E. Alfonseca, M. Okumura, J. Guirao, and A. Moreno-Sandoval. Googling answers models in question-focused summarisation. *Document Understanding Conference*, 2006.

[3] K. Barnard, P. Duygulu, D. Forsyth, N. de Freitas, D. Blei, and M. Jordan. Matching words and pictures. *The Journal of Machine Learning Research*, 3:1107–1135, 2003.

[4] K. Barnard and D. Forsyth. Learning the semantics of words and pictures. In *International Conference on Computer Vision*, volume 2, pages 408–415. Vancouver: IEEE, 2001.

[5] H. Dang. Overview of DUC 2006. *National Institute of Standards and Technology*, 2006.

[6] K. Deschacht and M. Moens. Text Analysis for Automatic Image Annotation. *Proc. of the 45th Annual Meeting of the Association for Computational Linguistics*, 2007.

[7] P. Duygulu, K. Barnard, J. de Freitas, and D. Forsyth. Object Recognition as Machine Translation: Learning a Lexicon for a Fixed Image Vocabulary. *In 7th European Conference on Computer Vision (ECCV)*, 4:97–112, 2002.

[8] Y. Feng and M. Lapata. Automatic Image Annotation Using Auxiliary Text Information. *Proc. of Association for Computational Linguistics*, 2008.

[9] T. Gornostay and A. Aker. Development and Implementation of Multilingual Object Type Toponym-Referenced Text Corpora for Optimizing Automatic Image Description. *Proc. of the 15th International Conference on Computational Linguistics*, 2009.

[10] M. Hearst. Automatic acquisition of hyponyms from large text corpora. *Proc. of the 14th conference on Computational linguistics*, 1992.

[11] C. Lin. ROUGE: A Package for Automatic Evaluation of Summaries. *Proc. of the Workshop on Text Summarization Branches Out*, 2004.

[12] C. Lin and E. Hovy. The automated acquisition of topic signatures for text summarization. In *Proc. of the COLING Conference*, 2000.

[13] E. Marsh and M. White. A taxonomy of relationships between images and text. *Journal of Documentation*, 2003.

[14] Y. Mori, H. Takahashi, and R. Oka. Automatic word assignment to images based on image division and vector quantization. *Proc. of RIAO 2000: Content-Based Multimedia Information Access*, 2000.

[15] J. Pan, H. Yang, P. Duygulu, and C. Faloutsos. Automatic image captioning. *Multimedia and Expo. ICME'04. IEEE International Conference on Multimedia and Expo*, 2004.

[16] R. Purves, A. Edwardes, and M. Sanderson. Describing the where–improving image annotation and search through geography. *1st Intl. Workshop on Metadata Mining for Image Understanding, Funchal, Madeira-Portugal*, 2008.

[17] H. Saggion. Topic-based Summarization at DUC 2005. *Document Understanding Conference*, 2005.

[18] G. Salton and C. Buckley. Term-weighting approaches in automatic text retrieval. *Information Processing and Management: an International Journal*, 1988.

[19] G. Salton and M. Lesk, E. Computer evaluation of indexing and text processing. *Journal of the ACM*, 1968.

[20] M. Sanderson and J. Kohler. Analyzing geographic queries. In *SIGIR Workshop on Geographic Information Retrieval*, 2004.

[21] F. Song and W. Croft. A general language model for information retrieval. *Proc. of the eighth international conference on Information and knowledge management*, 1999.

[22] T. Westerveld. Image retrieval: Content versus context. *Content-Based Multimedia Information Access, RIAO 2000 Conference*, 2000.

Prepositional Phrase Attachment in Shallow Parsing

Vincent Van Asch
CLiPS - Computational Linguistics
University of Antwerp
Prinsstraat 13
B-2000 Antwerpen, Belgium
Vincent.VanAsch@ua.ac.be

Walter Daelemans
CLiPS - Computational Linguistics
University of Antwerp
Prinsstraat 13
B-2000 Antwerpen, Belgium
Walter.Daelemans@ua.ac.be

Abstract

In this paper we extend a shallow parser [6] with prepositional phrase attachment. Although the PP attachment task is a well-studied task in a discriminative learning context, it is mostly addressed in the context of artificial situations like the quadruple classification task [18] in which only two possible attachment sites, each time a noun or a verb, are possible. In this paper we provide a method to evaluate the task in a more natural situation, making it possible to compare the approach to full statistical parsing approaches. First, we show how to extract anchor-pp pairs from parse trees in the GENIA and WSJ treebanks. Next, we discuss the extension of the shallow parser with a PP-attacher. We compare the PP attachment module with a statistical full parsing approach [4] and analyze the results. More specifically, we investigate the domain adaptation properties of both approaches (in this case domain shifts between journalistic and medical language).

Keywords

prepositional phrase attachment, shallow parsing, machine learning of language

1 Introduction

Shallow parsing (also called partial parsing) is an approach to language processing that computes a basic analysis of sentence structure rather than attempting full syntactic analysis.

Originally defined by Abney [1] as a task to be solved with handcrafted regular expressions (finite state methods) and limited to finding basic (non-recursive) phrases in text, the label shallow parsing has meanwhile broadened its scope to machine learning methods and to a set of related tasks including part of speech tagging, finding phrases (chunking), clause identification, grammatical role labeling, etc. Especially the machine learning approach to shallow parsing, pioneered by Ramshaw and Marcus [17] has been investigated intensively, in part because of the availability of benchmark datasets and competitions (CoNLL shared tasks 1999 to 2001)[1].

[1] See `http://ifarm.nl/signll/conll/`

It has been argued in [10] and by others that full parsing often provides too much (or not enough) information for some frequent natural language processing tasks. For example, for information retrieval, finding basic NPs and VPs is arguably sufficient, and for information extraction and other text mining tasks, finding syntactic-semantic relations between verbs and base NPs (who did what when and where) is more important than having an elaborate configurational syntactic analysis, provided this shallow analysis can be computed in a deterministic, efficient, robust, and accurate way. Another advantage is that the modules in a machine learning based shallow parser can be trained independently, and allow the inclusion of more information sources (input features) than is possible in statistical parsing (because of sparse data problems). This flexibility in feature engineering, inherent in discriminative, supervised learning approaches to shallow parsing should make the approach more flexible, e.g. when engineering features robust for domain shifts.

However, a shallow approach also has its shortcomings, an important one being that prepositional phrases, which contain important semantic information for interpreting events, are left unattached. Furthermore, while statistical full parsing used to be more noise-sensitive and less efficient than shallow parsing, that is no longer necessarily the case with recent developments in parse ranking.

In this paper, we extend an existing memory based shallow parser, MBSP [5, 6], with a machine learning based prepositional phrase attachment module, and compare it to PP attachment in a state of the art statistical parser. The machine learning method chosen is memory-based learning. We also investigate the ability of this Memory-based PP attachment (MBPA) to cope with the problem of domain adaptation, i.e. the often dramatic decrease in accuracy when testing a trained system on data from a domain different from the domain of the data on which it was trained.

The remainder of this paper starts with an explanation of how the corpus is prepared in order to use it for PP attachment, Section 2. In Section 3 we explain the architecture of the memory-based PP-attacher. Section 4 discusses the experiments and shows the results. In this section we also compare our system to a statistical parser, the Collins parser [3, 4]. An overview of related work can be found in Section 5. Finally, Section 6 concludes this paper and discusses options for further research.

International Conference RANLP 2009 - Borovets, Bulgaria, pages 12–17

2 Data preparation

In this section, we explain the extraction of the training and test data and the algorithm used to create instances from treebanks.

2.1 Training and test data

The memory-based PP-attacher is trained on sections 2 through 21 of the Penn Treebank 2 Wall Street Journal corpus (WSJ) [14]. The development of the system is done using the first 2000 PPs of sections 0-1 of WSJ. Evaluation of the system is done on the next set of 2000 PPs and additional evaluation is done using the first 2000 PPs of the GENIA corpus [20].

The corpora used for training and testing consist of tree structures representing the syntactic structure of sentences, as shown in Figures 1a and 1b. We transform the trees into a flat representation in order to be able to define one unique attachment site (anchor) for every prepositional phrase (PP). A flat representation of an anchor-PP pair consists of a pair of indices. The first element of the pair is the index in the sentence of the anchor; the second element is the index of the preposition. Word count starts at zero. For the sentence in Figure 1a the representation is (3, 4). For the sentence in Figure 1b the representation is (1, 4).

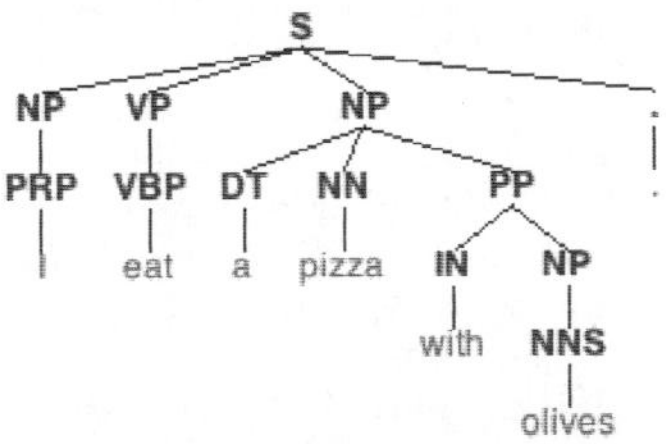

(a) I eat a pizza with olives.

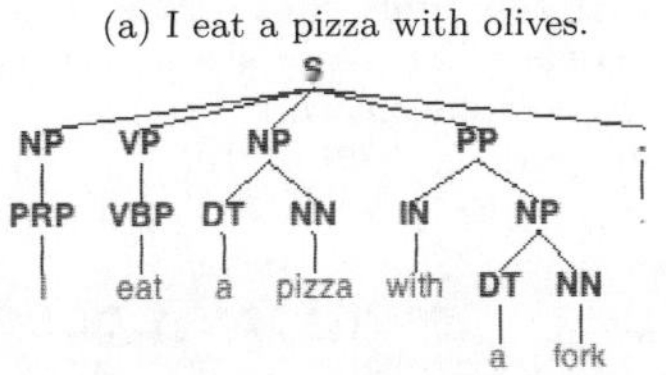

(b) I eat a pizza with a fork.

Fig. 1: Example tree structures

The example tree structures in Figure 1 are relatively straightforward to rewrite into a flat representation.

The basic setup had to be extended by rules for specific cases. A good example is conjunction. In the sentence:

I see cats on the roof and behind the windows.

the parent node of the PP-nodes is a node that also holds the conjunction. Therefore, in this case the algorithm does not take the sibling of the PP-node but it takes a sibling of the parent node of the PP-node.

The extraction algorithm yields 8933 prepositions from sections 0-1 of the WSJ corpus. For 1.95% of the PP-nodes in those two sections no anchor is found. For sections 2-21 1.99% of the 95,955 PP-nodes remain without an anchor. Some anchor-PP pairs are removed in a post-processing step because we limit the task to preposition-NP PPs and disregard preposition-ADJP sequences.

Table 1 shows the chunk type distribution of the anchors. A fairly equal amount of the anchors are nouns and verbs. A minor part has an adjective, comparative adjective or something else as the anchor point.

NP	50.5%
VP	45.8%
Other	3.7%

Table 1: The distribution of the anchors among the chunk types

2.2 Extracting chunks and prepositional phrases

The memory-based PP-attacher (MBPA) is defined as a module within a shallow parser [6]. The MBPA is trained on the WSJ, and it needs chunk and pos tag information from other modules in that shallow parser. In order to prevent indirect contamination of the training data with test data, we retrained the modules of the shallow parser delivering input to the PP attachment module on Wall Street Journal sections 2-21, using the script of the 2000 CoNLL shared task to extract IOB-style chunks from WSJ trees.

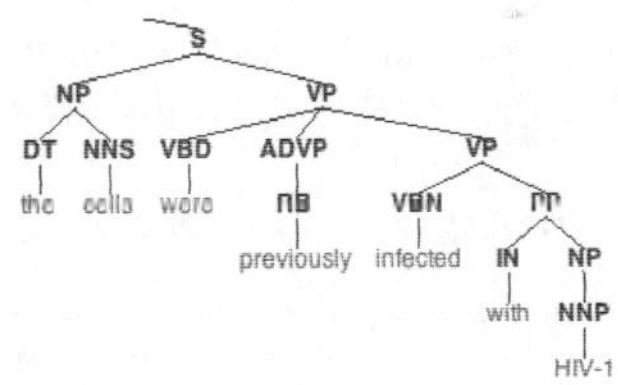

Fig. 2: A tree structure with undetermined cut-off

Converting syntactic trees into a flat representation introduces approximation errors. Figure 2 is an illustration of the problems encountered when looking for syntactic phrases. It is unclear which node should be used as the break point. Since the evaluation is based on chunks, the decisions made in the flattening step may have an influence on the final results. To minimize the bias we use the algorithm that was used to prepare the training data for the memory-based chunker to extract chunks from the syntactic trees output by Collins.

Table 2 shows the results of the comparison between the shallow parser and the Collins parser. The table shows the scores at chunk level. A chunk is correctly identified if it has the same label and it spans the same words as the gold standard chunk. When either the label or the span is not correct, the chunk is a false

	Our system prec	recall	f-score	Collins prec	recall	f-score	share
-	0.97	0.97	0.97	0.96	0.88	0.92	20.76%
ADJP	0.79	0.74	0.76	0.76	0.77	0.76	1.41%
ADVP	0.84	0.83	0.83	0.86	0.81	0.83	2.75%
CONJP	0.56	0.80	0.66	0.60	0.60	0.60	0.04%
INTJ	0.67	0.20	0.31	0.40	0.20	0.27	0.02%
LST	1.00	0.53	0.70	0.88	0.47	0.61	0.03%
NP	0.94	0.95	0.94	0.93	0.92	0.93	41.21%
PreP	0.97	0.98	0.97	0.97	0.97	0.97	15.57%
PRT	0.77	0.79	0.78	0.79	0.87	0.83	0.37%
SBAR	0.88	0.88	0.88	0.89	0.91	0.90	1.83%
UCP	0.00	0.00	0.00	0.00	0.00	0.00	0.00%
VP	0.94	0.93	0.93	0.83	0.88	0.85	16.01%
weighted mean	0.94	0.95	0.94	0.92	0.91	0.91	100%

Table 2: Results of chunking with our system and Collins

positive, when a chunk in the gold standard is not present in the system's output it is considered a false negative. The shallow parser chunking module and Collins perform comparably well although the former has slightly better results. This implies that there is no reason not to use the memory-based chunker as the basis for the PP-attacher. The PreP chunk in Table 2 is not equal to a PP. In this paper, the label PP is used for the combination of a preposition and a noun phrase, the PreP chunk is a chunk that consists of one or more prepositions only.

The logical first step in finding anchors for prepositional noun phrases is finding the PPs. When extracting the anchor-PP pairs (see Section 2.1) PPs are recognized by the label of the nodes. Since there are no nodes in the input of the MBPA a different strategy is used. PPs are retrieved by a regular expression-like algorithm. All *preposition NP* sequences are considered to be PPs. There are two exceptions to this regular expression rule. Sequences like *preposition " NP* ('in "very modest amounts"') and *preposition VBG NP* ('in making paper') are also considered PPs.

2.3 Creating the instances

The core of the PP-attacher is a memory-based machine learner (supervised, classification-based learning). Every PP found by the algorithm discussed in the previous subsection is a trigger for creating several instances. One instance is created for every combination of the PP in focus and a candidate-anchor. Candidate-anchors are the NPs and VPs of the sentence that are not part of the PP itself. For example,

I eat a pizza with olives.

will induce the creation of 3 instances. One instance for the combination *I–with*, one for the combination *eat–with* and one for the combination *pizza–with*. In the classification task, the machine learner will have to decide whether an instance suggests a true anchor or not. The advantage of this approach is that the machine learner can investigate every possible anchor for its validity and not only the VP and NP in front of the PP. The drawback of this approach is that we have skewed data. There will be many more negative instances in the instance base as can be seen in Table 3.

The features of the instances were chosen on the basis of previous work in machine learning based PP

	count	percentage
NP	43,049	6.0%
VP	42,285	5.9%
NONE	630,720	88.1%
TOTAL	716,054	100%

Table 3: Distribution of classes in sections 2-21 of WSJ

attachment and related tasks: the number of commas between the PP and the candidate anchor, the number of other punctuation marks between the PP and the candidate anchor, the token-distance between the PP and the candidate anchor, the preposition if the candidate anchor is an NP that is part of a PP, the lemma and POS-tag of the last token of the candidate anchor, the lemma and POS tag of the token just in front of the preposition of the PP, the lemma of the preposition, the lemma and POS-tag of the last token of the NP of the PP, the number of NPs between the candidate anchor and the PP, the number of PPs between the candidate anchor and the PP, and NP anchor tendency. If a preposition is for 10% of the cases in the training corpus attached to an NP, the NP anchor tendency will be 10.

3 The memory-based PP-attacher

The input of the MBPA module consists of sentences tagged with Part-of-Speech tags, IOB-chunk tags and the lemmata for every word by other modules of the shallow parser. The output of the system is a set of pairs, where each pair represents a PP with its corresponding attachment point.

3.1 Machine Learning Approaches

The machine learning approach we chose is memory-based learning, as implemented in the open source software package TiMBL[2]. We used version 6.1 [7]. Memory-based learning (MBL) is a supervised inductive algorithm for learning classification tasks based on the k-nearest neighbor classification rule.

[2] Available from `http://ilk.uvt.nl`.

However, the machine learner used to train the PP attachment module can be any algorithm that assigns classes to instances. For comparison, we also implemented a system using maxent, an eager learning method, as the machine learner. Maxent[3] is an implementation of maximum entropy modeling. It is a general purpose machine learning framework that constructs a model that captures the distribution of outcomes for a given context in the training data [13].

3.2 Heuristic decision making

If the classifier would be able to predict the anchors with 100% accuracy, no post-processing would be necessary. Only one instance, the one with the correct anchor, would carry a positive class label and all other instances would have a negative classlabel. But due to misclassifications, multiple or no anchors may be identified by the machine learner. An extra step ensures that the system presents one unique anchor for every PP. In case the PP in focus is classified positively with exactly one anchor, that anchor-PP pair is returned as the solution. The other possible outcomes of the classification step are:

1. No instance for the PP in focus got a positive class ⇒ There is no anchor identified yet.
2. More than one instance for the PP in focus got a positive class ⇒ We have a decrease of possible anchors but still no unique anchor.

To resolve these cases, we need an extra step. A baseline algorithm is used if no anchor has been found (case 1). If there are still several candidate anchors to choose from, the entropy is used to reduce the set of candidates to just one unique anchor (case 2).

Baseline

The baseline is computed using a simple rule-based PP-attacher. If a rule fails, the next rule in the hierarchy is checked. The hierarchy of the rules of the baseline algorithm is:

1. Take the nearest NP or VP in front of the PP. We take an NP if in the training corpus the preposition of the PP is associated more frequently with NP anchors. Otherwise we take the VP anchor.
2. Take the nearest anchor in front of the PP.
3. Take the nearest VP anchor behind the PP.
4. Take the nearest anchor behind the PP.

Entropy

When the classification step results in a draw, the candidate with the lowest entropy will be the anchor. The entropy is calculated using the distribution of the classes of the nearest neighbors. When processing an instance with TiMBL we can obtain the (weighted) distribution of the classes of instances in memory that are in the neighborhood of the test instance. The entropy of an instance is computed using this distribution. The formula is:

$$-\sum_{i=1}^{n} P(c_i)log_2(P(c_i)) \qquad (1)$$

with
- n: the total number of different classes in the distribution
- $P(c_i)$: $\frac{\text{the number of instances in the neighborhood with class i}}{\text{the total number of instances in the neighborhood}}$

The memory-based learner has an optional weighing parameter. If weighing is applied, $P(c_i)$ is calculated using the weighted counts instead of the plain counts.

The candidate anchor with the lowest entropy is regarded as the correct and unique anchor for a given PP. The rationale behind this decision is that choosing the candidate anchor with the lowest entropy means choosing the anchor for which the classifier was the most certain of its class.

Post-processing rules

For completeness, we also mention two post-processing rules that are applied because of some idiosyncrasies in the treebank data and common errors of the attacher-system. These rules are:

- If there are 2 consecutive prepositions the second preposition will always be attached to the first.
- If a PP is attached to a noun phrase anchor between parentheses, and the PP is not inside the parentheses, then the noun phrase before the parentheses becomes the anchor. This is done because the NP between the parentheses is most of the time an elaboration/abbreviation of the noun phrase in front.

4 Experiments and results

We train 4 systems (baseline, MBL, maxent and a statistical parser) on sections 2-21 of WSJ. In the first set of experiments, Section 4.1, we used the trained systems to attach the second set of 2000 PPs of WSJ sections 0-1 to their anchors. In the second set of experiments, Section 4.2, we reuse the trained systems to attach 2000 PPs extracted from the GENIA corpus to their anchors.

For comparison, we parse every sentence fed to the MBPA with a state-of-the-art statistical parser, viz. Bikel's implementation of the Collins parser. Applying the PP extraction algorithm from Section 2.1 on the syntactic trees output by Collins will yield all anchor-PP pairs needed for evaluation.

4.1 Training and testing on WSJ corpus

Table 4 shows the accuracies of systems trained and tested on the WSJ corpus. We performed a χ^2 statistical test and found that maxent, MBL and Collins all significantly ($p < 5\%$) differ from the baseline system. The variation between the accuracies of the machine learning systems is not found to be significant. The 'not retrieved' column is due to POS, chunking and/or syntactic tree errors in the pre-processing step. Looking at the first 200 errors MBPA and Collins made,

[3] Available from `http://homepages.inf.ed.ac.uk/s0450736/maxent_toolkit.html`.

shows that MBPA tends to misattach PPs at the start of the sentence. E.g. 'At the meeting, etc.' Collins has a higher number of 'not retrieved' PPs because it often inserts adverbs and quotes into the PP. E.g. 'by commenting [PP publicly on the case]'.

Table 5 shows the accuracies of the steps involved in the PP-attacher system. The 91.21% accuracy for TiMBL means that for 79.05% of the PPs TiMBL identified a unique anchor and that 91.21% of these anchors were correct. For 11.7% of the PPs, TiMBL could not find an anchor so baseline had to take over. 44.4% of the PPs baseline handled, were correctly assigned to their head. For 6.35% of the PPs, TiMBL found multiple anchors. Entropy handled these cases and found the correct anchor for 67% of them. After finding a unique anchor for every PP, the system made sure that for a sequence of PPs the last PP got attached to the previous. This happened for 1.2% of the PPs.

	Correct	Incorrect	Not retrieved
Baseline	69.85%	25.45%	1.70%
Collins	83.85%	13.30%	2.85%
MBL	82.65%	15.65%	1.70%
Maxent	81.40%	16.90%	1.70%

Table 4: The accuracies on 2000 anchor-PP pairs from WSJ

	Accuracy (%)	proportion (%)
TiMBL	91.21	79.05
Baseline	44.44	11.70
Entropy	66.93	6.35
consecutive preps	91.67	1.20

Table 5: The accuracies split into the different steps of MBPA

These results show that it is possible to develop a PP attachment module using supervised machine learning techniques, integrated as a module within a shallow parser, and reach state of the art accuracy when comparing to one of the best statistical parsers available today. This way the semantically important information carried by relations between PPs and their anchors becomes available to shallow analysis approaches with their advantages in terms of efficiency and flexibility. We were not able to find significant differences between lazy (TiMBL) and eager (Maxent) learning approaches for this problem.

4.2 Domain Adaptation

Adaptation of NLP systems to domains different from the one on which they were developed, is a crucial functionality to make the technology useful. Accuracy of systems deteriorates enormously when moving between different domains. Accuracy drops of 20 to 40 percent are not uncommon for tasks such as parsing, named-entity recognition, word sense disambiguation, and machine translation when moving from the source domain to the new target domain. Usually, no or limited labeled data exists for the target domain. We evaluated the PP attachment systems trained on the WSJ using 2000 anchor-PP pairs from the GENIA corpus. The WSJ corpus consists of news articles on mainly financial issues in contrast to the medical abstracts of the GENIA corpus. Although one cannot always clearly say where the boundaries between domains are, we assume that medical and financial texts are sufficiently different. Table 6 shows the accuracies for the different systems. We performed these experiments to gain more insight into the relative robustness of different approaches to PP attachment to domain shifts. The χ^2 test gave the same results as in the previous section: all systems perform significantly better than baseline but do not differ significantly from each other. As expected, the accuracy significantly decreases compared to the same-domain experiments.

	Correct	Incorrect	Not retrieved
Baseline	69.20%	27.00%	3.80%
Collins	78.80%	19.35%	1.85%
MB-attacher	77.70%	19.10%	3.20%
Maxent-attacher	77.15%	19.65%	3.20%

Table 6: The accuracies on 2000 anchor-PP pairs from GENIA

Table 7 shows the robustness of the systems to a domain shift from mainly financial to medical language. The higher the ratio, the lower the drop of accuracy. As can be seen, if no learning is involved (baseline) the system is most robust. A shallow approach is at an advantage here compared to full parsing because it allows more flexible feature engineering to alleviate the domain adaptation problem (e.g. by adding or removing specific lexical, syntactic, and semantic features to the classifiers. This is in general more difficult in a statistical parsing approach because of data sparseness.

5 Related work

As Atterer and Schütze [2] state, the classic formulation of the task of PP attachment, as defined in [19] and [11], is a simplification. The classic formulation uses quadruples (v, n_1, p, n_2) that were manually selected from a corpus. This helps performance of PP attachment systems but for a natural language application these quadruples are not available. In their experiments, the PP attachment systems they evaluated did not significantly improve on a state-of-the-art parser, Collins parser [3, 4]. The PP-attacher system in this paper does not make use of this simplified representation and therefore can be regarded as more fit for the task of natural language PP attachment.

Foth and Menzel [9] implemented a PP attachment predictor for German and incorporated it in a rule-based dependency parser [8]. The PP attachment pre-

	Ratio
Baseline	0.991
Collins	0.940
MB-attacher	0.940
Maxent-attacher	0.948

Table 7: The ratio of the accuracies GENIA/WSJ

dictor was based on a collocation measure and significantly increased the accuracy on the PP attachment subtask. Basically, the collocation measure is a number indicating whether a word and a preposition co-occur more often than chance. In this paper, we did not compute a collocation measure but for the NP anchor tendency feature we draw upon the same underlying idea.

As noticed in [21], the algorithm used to extract the pairs from the corpus has an influence on the accuracies reported, and makes comparing of results among systems for different corpora and languages difficult. The noun attachment rate and the extraction procedure are two important features when comparing results obtained using different corpora. As we tested our system and Collins' using the same training and test data, the comparison is reliable.

Other memory-based approaches to the problem of PP attachment can be found in [12] and [22]. [12] uses a memory-based PP-attacher combined with the MALTParser [16]. They showed that the dependency parser could not fully benefit from the separate PP-attacher although the PP-attacher module assigns PPs to their heads with a reasonable accuracy. The features they use for their PP-attacher system are lemmata, POS-tags and distances between words.

In their paper, [15] mainly focus on how to disambiguate between argument and adjunct PPs, but they provide an alternative way of extracting PPs from the WSJ treebank. Their final data contains quadruples and sets of multiple PP sequences.

6 Conclusion

In this paper we compared a shallow parsing approach to PP-attachment with a state of the art full parser. We used a flat representation of prepositional phrases and their associated attachment sites to train a machine learner for the PP attachment task. We showed that a memory-based approach can obtain results for the PP attachment task comparable to a state-of-the-art full parser. The PP attachment system proposed in this article is not limited to the classical quadruple approximation of the PP attachment task and therefore the system can be combined with any (shallow) parser that assigns part-of-speech tags, lemmata and chunk tags to natural language sentences. Such a PP attachment module can also be easily added to a full parser as a reattacher.

The shallow memory-based PP attachment module is fairly robust to a domain shift of the testing corpus but further research should focus on how to improve the robustness. Building a more robust PP attachment system would legitimate the use of the PP-attacher system as a reattachment module in any full parser.

Acknowledgements

This research was made possible through financial support from the University of Antwerp (BIOGRAPH GOA-project).

References

[1] S. Abney. Parsing by chunks. In *Principle-Based Parsing*, pages 257–278. Kluwer Academic Publishers, 1991.

[2] M. Atterer and H. Schütze. Prepositional phrase attachment without oracles. *Computational Linguistics*, 33(4):469–476, 2007.

[3] D. Bikel. Intricacies of Collins' parsing model. *Computational Linguistics*, 30(4):479–512, 2004.

[4] M. Collins. Head-driven statistical models for natural language parsing. *Computational Linguistics*, 29(4):589–637, 2003.

[5] W. Daelemans, S. Buchholz, and J. Veenstra. Memory-based shallow parsing. In *Proceedings of CoNLL-99*, pages 53–60, Bergen, Norway, 1999.

[6] W. Daelemans and A. van den Bosch. *Memory-Based Language Processing*. Studies in Natural Language Processing. Cambridge University Press, Cambridge, 2005.

[7] W. Daelemans, J. Zavrel, K. van der Sloot, and A. van den Bosch. Timbl: Tilburg memory-based learner, version 6.1. Technical Report ILK 07-07, Tilburg University, 2007.

[8] K. Foth, M. Daum, and W. Menzel. Parsing unrestricted german text with defeasible constraints. In *Constraint Solving and Language Processing*, volume 3438 of *Lecture Notes in Computer Science*, pages 140–157. Springer, Berlin/Heidelberg, 2005.

[9] K. Foth and W. Menzel. The benefit of stochastic PP attachment to a rule-based parser. In *Proceedings of the COLING/ACL 2006 Main Conference Poster Sessions*, pages 223–230, 2006.

[10] J. Hammerton, M. Osborne, S. Armstrong, and W. Daelemans. Introduction to special issue on machine learning approaches to shallow parsing. *Journal of Machine Learning Research*, 2(Mar):551–558, 2002.

[11] D. Hindle and M. Rooth. Structural ambiguity and lexical relations. *Computational Linguistics*, 19(1):103–120, 1993.

[12] S. Kübler, S. Ivanova, and E. Klett. Combining dependency parsing with PP attachment. In *Fourth Midwest Computational Linguistics Colloquium*, 2007.

[13] Z. Le. Maximum Entropy Modeling Toolkit for Python and C++, 2004. Version 20061005.

[14] M. Marcus, G. Kim, M. A. Marcinkiewicz, R. MacIntyre, A. Bies, M. Ferguson, K. Katz, and B. Schasberger. The Penn treebank: annotating predicate argument structure. In *HLT '94: Proceedings of the workshop on Human Language Technology*, pages 114–119, Morristown, NJ, USA, 1994. Association for Computational Linguistics.

[15] P. Merlo and E. E. Ferrer. The notion of argument in prepositional phrase attachment. *Computational Linguistics*, 32(3):341–377, 2006.

[16] J. Nivre. *Inductive Dependency Parsing*, volume 34 of *Text, Speech and Language Technology*. Springer, 2006.

[17] L. Ramshaw and M. Marcus. Text chunking using transformation-based learning. In D. Yarovsky and K. Church, editors, *Proceedings of the Third Workshop on Very Large Corpora*, pages 82–94. Association for Computational Linguistics, 1995.

[18] A. Ratnaparkhi. *Maximum Entropy Models for Natural Language Ambiguity Resolution*. PhD thesis, Computer and Information Science, University of Pennsylvania, 1998.

[19] A. Ratnaparkhi, J. Reynar, and S. Roukos. A maximum entropy for prepositional phrase attachment. In *Workshop on Human Language Technology*, pages 250–255, 1994.

[20] Y. Tateisi, A. Yakushiji, T. Ohta, and J. Tsujii. Syntax annotation for the genia corpus. In *Proceedings of the IJCNLP 2005, Companion volume*, pages 222–227, October 2005.

[21] M. Volk. How bad is the problem of PP-attachment? A comparison of English, German and Swedish. In *Proceedings of the Third ACL-SIGSEM Workshop on Prepositions*, pages 81–88, 2006.

[22] J. Zavrel, W. Daelemans, and J. Veenstra. Resolving PP attachment ambiguities with memory-based learning. In *Proceedings CoNLL 1997*, pages 136–144, 1997.

A Comparative Study of Open Domain and Opinion Question Answering Systems for Factual and Opinionated Queries

Alexandra Balahur, Ester Boldrini, Andrés Montoyo, Patricio Martínez-Barco
Natural Language Processing and Information Systems Group, Department of Software and Computing Systems.
Apartado de Correos 99, 03080, Alicante

{abalahur, eboldrini, montoyo, patricio}@dlsi.ua.es

Abstract

The development of the Web 2.0 led to the birth of new textual genres such as blogs, reviews or forum entries. The increasing number of such texts and the highly diverse topics they discuss make blogs a rich source for analysis. This paper presents a comparative study on open domain and opinion QA systems. A collection of opinion and mixed fact-opinion questions in English is defined and two Question Answering systems are employed to retrieve the answers to these queries. The first one is generic, while the second is specific for emotions. We comparatively evaluate and analyze the systems' results, concluding that opinion Question Answering requires the use of specific resources and methods.

Keywords Question Answering, Multi-perspective Question Answering, Opinion Annotation, Opinion Mining, Non-Traditional Textual Genres.

1. Introduction

Recent years' statistics show that the number of blogs has been increasing at an exponential rate. A research of the Pew Institute [1] shows that 2-7% of Internet users created a blog and that 11% usually read them. Moreover, researches in different fields proved that this new textual genre is a valuable resource for large community behavior analysis, since blogs address a great variety of topics from a high diversity of social spheres. A common belief is that they are written in a colloquial style, but [2] shows that the language of these texts is not restricted to the more informal levels of expression and a large number of different genres are involved. As a consequence, free expressions, literary prose and newspaper writing coexist without a clear predominance. When using this textual genre, people tend to express themselves freely, using colloquial expressions employed only in day-by-day conversations. Moreover, they can introduce quotes from newspaper articles, news or other sources of information to support their arguments, make references to previous posts or the opinion expressed by others in the discussion thread. Users intervening in debates over one specific topic are from different geographical regions and belong to diverse cultures. All the abovementioned features make blogs a valuable source of information that can be exploited for different purposes. However, due to their language being heterogeneous, it is complex to understand and formalize in order to create effective Natural Language Processing (NLP) tools. At the same time, due to the high volume of data contained in blogs, automatic NLP systems are needed to manage the language understanding and generation. Analyzing emotions and/ or opinions expressed in blog posts could also be useful to predict people's opinion or preferences about a product or an event. One of the other possible applications is an effective Question Answering (QA) system, able to recognize different queries and give the correct answer to both factoid and opinion questions.

2. Related work

QA is the task in which, given a set of questions and a collection of documents where the answers can be found, an automatic NLP system is employed to retrieve the answer to these queries in Natural Language. The main difference between QA and Information Retrieval (IR) is that in the first one, the system is supposed to output the exact answer snippet, whereas in the second task whole paragraphs or even documents are retrieved. Research in building factoid QA systems has a long tradition; however, it is only recently that studies have started to focus on the creation and development of opinion QA systems. Recent years have seen the growth of interest in this field, both by the research and publishing of studies on the requirements and peculiarities of opinion QA systems [4] as well as the organization of international conferences that promote the creation of effective QA systems both for general and subjective texts, such as the Text Analysis Conference (TAC)[1]. Last year's TAC 2008 Opinion QA track proposed a mixed setting of factoid and opinion questions (so called "rigid list" and "squishy list"), to which the traditional systems had to be adapted. Participating systems employed different resources, techniques and methods to overcome the newly introduced difficulties related to opinion mining and polarity classification. The Alyssa system [5], which performed better in the "squishy list" questions than in the

[1] http://www.nist.gov/tac/

International Conference RANLP 2009 - Borovets, Bulgaria, pages 18–22

"rigid list" questions, had additional components implemented for classifying the polarity of the question and of the extracted answer snippet, using a Support Vector Machines (SVM) classifier trained on the MPQA corpus [6], English NTCIR[2] data and rules based on the subjectivity lexicon [7]. Another system introducing new modules to tackle opinion is [8]. They perform query analysis to detect the polarity of the question using defined rules. They filter opinion from fact retrieved snippets using a classifier based on Naïve Bayes with unigram features, assigning for each sentence a score that is a linear combination between the opinion and the polarity scores. The PolyU [9] system determines the sentiment orientation of the sentence and it uses the Kullback-Leibler divergence measure with the two estimated language models for the positive versus negative categories. The UOFL system [10] generates a non-redundant summary of the query for the opinion questions, to take into consideration all the information present in the question, and not only the separated words.

3. Motivation and contribution

Opinion Mining is the task of extracting, given a collection of texts, the opinion expressed on a given target within the documents. It has been proven that performing this task, several other subtasks of NLP can be improved: *Information Extraction* (where opinion mining techniques can be used as a preprocessing step to separate among factual and subjective information), *Authorship Determination* (as subjective language can be considered as a personality mark), *Word Sense Disambiguation, multi-source (multi-perspective) summarization* and more informative Answer Retrieval for definition questions [16] (as it can constitute a measure for *credibility, sentiment* and *contradictions).* Related work presented research in determining the differences in the characteristics of the fact versus opinion queries and their corresponding answers [11]. However, certain types of questions, which are factual in nature, require the use of Opinion Mining resources and techniques in order to retrieve the correct answers. Our first contribution relies in the analysis and definition of the criteria for the discrimination among different types of factual versus opinionated questions. Furthermore, we created and annotated a set of questions and answers over a multilingual blog collection for English and Spanish. Thus, we also analyze the effect of the textual genre characteristics on the properties of the opinion answers retrieved/missed. A further contribution lies in the evaluation of two different approaches to QA; one is fact oriented (based on Named Entities –NEs–) and the other is specifically designed for opinion QA scenarios. We analyze their different elements, specifications, behavior, evaluated performance and present conclusions on the needs and requirements of systems designed for the presented categories of questions. Last, but not least, using the annotated answers and their corresponding corpus, we analyze possible methods for keyword expansion in an opinion versus fact setting. We present some possible solutions to the shortcomings of direct keyword expansion for opinion QA, employing "polarity-based" expansion using our corpus annotations.

[2] http://research.nii.ac.jp/ntcir/

4. Corpus collection and analysis

The corpus we employed for our evaluation is composed of blog posts extracted form the Web. It has been collected taking into account the requirements of coherence, authenticity, equilibrium and quality. Our main purpose was to collect a corpus in which the blog posts were about a topic, forming a coherent discussion. Moreover, our collection had to provide a real example of this textual genre, it had to be of the same length for each topic and language, and originated from reliable Web sites. We selected three topics: the Kyoto Protocol, the 2008 Zimbabwe and the USA elections. After having collected the three corpora, we analyzed the characteristic of this textual genre also looking for the subjective expressions and for the way they are formulated in NL. The following step of our research consisted in building up the initial version of *EmotiBlog* [18], an annotation scheme focused on emotions detection in non-traditional textual genres. The annotation scheme is briefly presented in the following section.

5. Annotation scheme

As we mentioned in the previous section, *EmotiBlog* [12] is an annotation scheme for detecting opinion in non-traditional textual genres. It is the first version of a fine-grained and multilingual annotation model that could be useful for an exhaustive comprehension of NL. The first version has been created for English, Italian and Spanish; however, it could be easily adapted for the annotation of other languages. Firstly, we detect the overall sentiment of the blogs and subsequently a distinction between objective and subjective sentences is done. Moreover, for each element, we annotate the source, the target and also a wide range of attributes for the elements (sentiment type, its intensity and polarity, for example). Sentiments are grouped according to [13], who created an alternative dimensional structure of the semantic space for emotions grouping emotions between obstructive and conductive, and finally, between high power and low power control. The annotation task has been carried out by two non-native speakers with extensive knowledge of Spanish and English. The labeling of the 100 texts took approximately one month and a half, working in a part-time schedule. Finally, the last step consisted in labeling the answers to our list of questions to create a *gold standard* for detecting the mistakes of the QA systems presented in the next section. The list of questions is composed by 20 factual and opinionated queries. Table 1 shows the list of questions.

Table 1: Example of questions

NUM	TYPE	QUESTION
1	F	What international organization do people criticize for its policy on carbon emissions?
2	O	What motivates people's negative opinions on the Kyoto Protocol?
3	F	What country do people praise for not signing the Kyoto Protocol?
4	F	What is the nation that brings most criticism to the Kyoto Protocol?
5	O	What are the reasons for the success of the Kyoto Protocol?
6	O	What arguments do people bring for their criticism of media as far as the Kyoto Protocol is concerned?
7	O	Why do people criticize Richard Branson?
8	F	What president is criticized worldwide for his reaction to the Kyoto Protocol?

As we can see in Table 1, we have a list of opinionated and factoid queries. Factual need a name, date, time, etc as answer, while opinionated ones something more complex. The system should be able firstly to recognize the subjective expressions and after that, discriminate them in order to retrieve the correct answer. In this case the answer can be expressed by an idiom, a saying, or by a sentence and as a consequence it is not a simple name or a date. It is complex because it could be everything; there are no fixed categories of answer types for opinionated questions. As a consequence, we formulated the opinion questions explicitly in order not to increase the difficulty level of the analysis.

6. Evaluation

6.1 Open QA system

With the purpose of evaluating the performance of a general QA system in a mixed fact and opinion setting, we used the QA system of the University of Alicante [14] [15]. It is an open domain QA system employed to deal with factual questions both for English and Spanish. The queries this system can support are *location*, *person*, *organization*, *date-time* and *number*. Furthermore, its architecture is divided into three modules. The first one is the Question Analysis in which the language object of the study is determined using dictionaries with the criterion of selecting the language for which more words are found. Therefore, the question type is selected using a set of regular expressions and the keywords of each question are obtained with morphological and dependencies analysis. For that purpose, MINIPAR[3] for Spanish and Freeling[4] for English are used. The second module is the IR in which the system, originally, relied on the Internet search engines. However, in order to look for information among the Web Log collection, an alternative approach has been developed. A simple keyword-based document retrieval method has been implemented in order to get relevant documents given the question keywords. The last module is called Answer Extraction (AE). The potential answers are selected using a NE recognizer for each retrieved document. LingPipe[5] and Freeling have been used for English and Spanish respectively. Furthermore, NE of the obtained question type and question keywords are marked up in the text. Once selected they are scored and ranked using answer-keywords distances approach. Finally, when all relevant documents have been explored, the system carries out an answer clustering process which groups all answers that are equal or contained by others to the most scored.

6.2 Specific QA system

For the opinion specific QA system, our approach was similar to [16]. Given an opinion question, we try to determine its *polarity*, the *focus*, its *keywords* (by eliminating stopwords) and the *expected answer type* (EAT) (while also marking the NE appearing in it); once this information is extracted from the question, blog texts are split into sentences and NE are marked. Finally, sentences in the blogs are sought which have the highest similarity score with the question keywords, whose polarity is the same as the determined question polarity and which contains a NE of the EAT. As the traditional QA system outputs 50 answers, we also take the 50 most similar sentences and extract the NEs they contain. In the future, when training examples will be available, we plan to set a threshold for similarity, thus not limiting the number of output answers, but setting a border to the similarity score (this is related to the observation in [4] that opinion questions have a highly variable number of answers. In order to extract the topic and determine the question polarity, we define question patterns. These patterns take into consideration the interrogation formula and extract the opinion words (nouns, verbs, adverbs, adjectives and their determiners). They are then classified to determine the polarity of the question, using the WordNet Affect emotion lists, the emotion triggers resource [17], a list of four attitudes containing the verbs, nouns, adjectives and adverbs for the categories of **criticism**, **support**, **admiration** and **rejection** and a list of positive and negative opinion words taken from the system in [18]. On the other hand, we preprocessed the blog texts in order to prepare the answer retrieval. Starting from the focus, keywords and topic of the question, we sought sentences in

[3] http://www.cs.ualberta.ca/~lindek/minipar.htm

[4] http://garraf.epsevg.upc.es/freeling/

[5] http://alias-i.com/lingpipe/

the blog collection (which was split into sentences and where Named Entity Recognition was performed using LingPipe) that could constitute possible answers to the questions, according to their similarity to the latter. The similarity score was computed with Pedersen's Text Similarity Package[6]. The condition we subsequently set was that the polarity of the retrieved snipped be the same as the one of the question and, in the case of questions with EAT PERSON, ORGANIZATION or LOCATION, that a Named Entity of the appropriate type was present in the retrieved snippets. In case retrieved snippets containing Named Entities in the question were found, their score was boosted to the score of the most similar snippet retrieved. In case more than 50 snippets were retrieved, we only considered for evaluation the first 50 in the order of their polarity score (which proved to be a good indicator of the snippet's importance [22].

6.3 Evaluation process

We evaluate the performance of the two QA systems in terms of the number of found answers within the top 1, 5, 10 and 50 output answers (TQA is the indicator for the traditional QA system and OQA is the indicator for the opinion QA system). In Table 2 we present the results of the evaluations in the case of each of the 20 questions (the table also contains the type of each questions – F (factual) and O (opinion)). The first observation we can make is the fact that the traditional QA system was able to answer only 8 of the 20 questions we formulated. We will thus compare the performance of the systems at the level of these 8 questions they both answered and separately analyze the faults and strong points, as well as the difficulties of each individual question separately).

Table 2: The QA systems' performance

Question	Type	Number of answers	Number of found answers							
			@1		@5		@10		@ 50	
			TQA	OQA	TQA	OQA	TQA	OQA	TQA	OQA
1	F	5	0	0	0	2	0	3	4	4
2	O	5	0	0	0	1	0	1	0	3
3	F	2	1	1	2	1	2	1	2	1
4	F	10	1	1	2	1	6	2	10	4
5	O	11	0	0	0	0	0	0	0	0
6	O	2	0	0	0	0	0	1	0	2
7	O	5	0	0	0	0	0	1	0	3
8	F	5	1	0	3	1	3	1	5	1
9	F	5	0	1	0	2	0	2	1	3
10	F	2	1	0	1	0	1	1	2	1
11	O	2	0	1	0	1	0	1	0	1
12	O	3	0	0	0	1	0	1	0	1
13	F	1	0	0	0	0	0	0	0	1
14	F	7	1	0	1	1	1	2	1	2
15	F(O)	1	0	0	0	0	0	1	0	1
16	F(O)	6	0	1	0	4	0	4	0	4
17	F	10	0	1	0	1	4	1	0	2
18	F(O)	1	0	0	0	0	0	0	0	0
19	F(O)	27	0	1	0	5	0	6	0	18
20	F(O)	4	0	0	0	0	0	0	0	0

[6] http://www.d.umn.edu/~tpederse/text-similarity.html

As we can observe in Table 2, as expected, the questions for which the traditional QA system performed better were the pure factual ones (1, 3, 4, 8, 10 and 14), although in some cases (like the one of question number 14) the OQA system retrieved more correct answers. At the same time, purely opinion questions, although revolving around NEs, were not answered by the traditional QA system, but were satisfactorily answered by the opinion QA system (2, 5, 6, 7, 11, 12), taking into consideration that a purely word-overlap approach was taken. Questions 18 and 20 were not correctly answered by any of the two systems. We believe this is due to the fact that question 18 was ambiguous as far as polarity of the opinions expressed in the answer snippets ("improvement" does not translate to either "positive" or "negative") and question 20 referred to the title of a project proposal that was not annotated by any of the tools used. Thus, as part of the future work in our OQA system, we must add a component for the identification of quotes and titles, as well as explore a wider range of polarity/opinion scales. Questions 15, 16, 18, 19 and 20 contain both factual as well as opinion aspects and the OQA system performed better than the TQA, although in some cases, answers were lost due to the artificial boosting of the queries containing NEs of the EAT. Therefore, it is obvious that an extra method for answer ranking should be used, as Answer Validation techniques using Textual Entailment.

7. Issues and discussion

There are many problems involved when trying to perform opinion QA. Explanations for this fact include ambiguity of the questions (*What is the nation that brings most criticism to the Kyoto Protocol?* – the answer can be explicitly stated in one of the blog sentences, or a system might have to infer them; therefore, the answer is highly contextual and depends on the texts one is analyzing, the need for extra knowledge on the NEs (i.e. *Al Gore is an American politician – should we first look for people that are in favor of environmental measures and test which one is an American politician?)* and the fact that, as opposed to purely factoid questions, most of the opinion questions have answers longer than a single sentence. In many of the cases, the opinion mining system missed on the answers due to erroneous sentence splitting. Another source of problems was the fact that we gave a high weight to the presence of the NE of the sought type within the retrieved snippet and in some cases the NER performed by LingPipe either attributed the wrong category to an entity, failed to annotate it or wrongfully annotated words as being NEs when that was not the case. As we could notice, problems of temporal expressions and the coreference need to be taken into account in order to retrieve the correct answer. In most of the time, the QA system need to understand the temporal context of the questions and also of the sentences that compose the corpus, because the present President the USA is different from two years ago, for example. At the other hand, an effective coreference resolution system is indispensable to understand some retrieved answers.

8. Conclusions and future work

In this article, we first presented *EmotiBlog*, an annotation scheme for opinion annotation in blogs and the blog posts collection we gathered to label with our scheme. Subsequently, we presented the collection of mixed opinion and fact questions we created, whose answers we annotated in our corpus. We finally evaluated and discussed on the results of two different QA systems, one that is fact oriented and one that is designed for opinion question answering. Some conclusions that we draw from this analysis are that, even when using specialized resources, the task of opinion QA is still difficult and extra techniques and methods have to be investigated in order to solve the problems we found, parallel to a deeper analysis of the issues involved in this type of QA. In many cases, opinion QA can benefit from a snippet retrieval at a paragraph level, since usually the answers were not mere parts of sentences, but consisted in two or more consecutive sentences. On the other hand, however, we have seen cases in which each of three different consecutive sentences was a separate answer to a question. Future work includes the study of the impact anaphora resolution has on the task of opinion QA, as well as the possibility to use Answer Validation techniques in order to increase the system's performance by answer re-ranking.

9. Acknowledgments

The authors would like to thank Paloma Moreda, Hector Llorens, Estela Saquete and Manuel Palomar for evaluating the questions on their QA system. This research has been partially funded by the Spanish Government under the project TEXT-MESS (TIN 2006-15265-C06-01), by the European project QALL-ME (FP6 IST 033860) and by the University of Alicante, through its doctoral scholarship.

10. References

[1] A. Lenhart, J. Horrigan, D. Fallow, *Content Creation Online, Pew Internet & American Life Project.* Available at www.pewinternet.org/pdfs/PIP_Content_Creation_Report.pdf

[2] B. Pang, and L. Lee, *Opinion mining and sentiment analysis. Foundations and Trends R* In Information Retrieval Vol. 2, Nos. 1–2 (2008) 1–135, 2008.

[3] M.,Tavosanis. *Linguistic features of Italian blogs: literary language.* New Text. Wikis and blogs and other dynamic text sources, pp 11-15, Trento,vol. 1, 2006.

[4] V., Stoyanov, C., Cardie, J., Wiebe. *Multi-Perspective Question Answering Using the OpQA Corpus*. HLT/EMNLP. 2005.

[5] D. Shen,. M. Wiegand, A. Merkel, S. Kazalski, S. Hunsicker, J.L. Leidner, and D. Klakow. *The Alyssa system at TREC QA 2007: Do we need Blog06?* In Proceedings of The Sixteenth Text Retrieval Conference (TREC 2007), Gaithersburg, MD, USA, 2007.

[6] J. Wiebe, T. Wilson, and C. Cardie *Annotating expressions of opinions and emotions in language.* Language Resources and Evaluation, volume 39, issue 2-3, pp. 165-210, 2005.

[7] T. Wilson, J.Wiebe, and P. Hoffmann. *Recognising Contextual Polarity in Phrase-level sentiment Analysis.* In Proceedings of Human language Technologies Conference/Conference on Empirical methods in Natural Language Processing (HLT/EMNLP), Vancouver, BC, Canada, 2005.

[8] V. Varma, P. Pingali, R. Katragadda, S. Krishna, S. Ganesh, K. Sarvabhotla, H. Garapati, H. Gopisetty, K. Reddy and R. Bharadwaj. In Proceedings of Text Analysis Conference, at the joint annual meeting of TAC and TREC, Gaithersburg, Maryland, USA, 2008.

[9] L. Wenjie, Y. Ouyang, Y. Hu, F. Wei. *PolyU at TAC 2008.* In Proceedings of Human Language Technologies Conference/Conference on Empirical methods in Natural Language Processing (HLT/EMNLP), Vancouver, BC, Canada, 2008.

[10] Y. Chali, S.A. Hasan, S.R. Joty. *(University of Lethbridge) UofL: QA, Summarization (Update Task).* In Proceedings of Human Language Technologies Conference/Conference on Empirical methods in Natural Language Processing (HLT/EMNLP), Vancouver, BC, Canada, 2008.

[11] V. Stoyanov, C. Cardie, J. Wiebe. *Multi-Perspective Question Answering using the OpQA corpus.* In Proceedings of EMNLP 2005.

[12] A. Balahur, E. Boldrini, A. Montoyo and P. Martínez- Barco. *Cross-topic Opinion Mining for Real-time Human-Computer Interaction.* To appear in Proceedings of ICEIS 2009 Conference, Milan, Italy, 2009.

[13] Scherer, K. R. *What are emotions? And how can they be measured?* Social Science Information. 44(4), 693–727. 2005.

[14] P. Moreda, H. Llorens, E. Saquete, M. Palomar. *The influence of semantic roles in QA: a comparative analysis.* In Proceedings of the SEPLN. MAdris, Spain, pages 55-62, 2008.

[15] P. Moreda, H. Llorens, E. Saquete, M. Palomar. *Automatic Generalization of a QA Answer Extraction Module Based on Semantic Roles.* In: AAI - IBERAMIA, Lisbon, Portugal, pages 233-242, Springer, 2008.

[16] Balahur, A., Lloret, E., Ferrandez, O., Montoyo, A., Palomar, M., Munoz, R. *The DLSIUAES Team's Participation in the TAC 2008 Tracks.* Proceedings of the Text Analysis Conference 2008.

[17] A., Balahur and A., Montoyo. *Applying a culture dependent emotion triggers database for text valence and emotion classification.* In Procesamiento del Lenguaje Natural, Revista nº 40, marzo de 2008, pp. 107-114. 2008a.

[18] A., Balahur, A., Montoyo. Multilingual Feature-Driven Opinion Extraction and Summarization from Customer Reviews. In Proceedings of NLDB 2008 – LNCS 5039, pp. 345-346. 2008b.

Acquisition of common sense knowledge for basic level concepts

Eduard Barbu
Center for Mind/Brain Sciences
Rovereto
Trento, Italy
eduard.barbu@unitn.it

Abstract

Feature norms can be regarded as repositories of common sense knowledge for basic level concepts. We acquire from very large corpora feature-norm-like concept descriptions using a combination of a weakly supervised method and an unsupervised method. The success in identifying the specific properties listed in the feature norms as well as the success in acquiring the classes of properties present in the norms are reported.

Keywords

basic level categories, common-sense knowledge, feature norms

1 Introduction

The acquisition of common sense knowledge is the focus of a series of projects originated in AI like CYC [5] or Open Mind [10]. The aim of this paper is the acquisition of every day knowledge for a restricted category of concepts: basic level concepts denoting concrete objects.

One of the main criteria for concept organization in initial studies carried both in psychology and AI [2] was thought to be the taxonomic criteria. Early work in psychology [9] showed that not all levels of taxonomy are equal with respect to object categorization. There is a privileged level at which people consistently classify the objects in common speech called the basic level. For example, encountering an object (e.g. 19th century dinning table) in ordinary discussion we do not categorize it at its specific level (19th century dinning table) nor to its more general level (e.g. entity) but to its basic level (table). The basic level concept is the most inclusive level at which concepts share common features, it carves the world at its joints. Examples of basic level concepts are bird, dog, cat or car.

To acquire common-sense knowledge for basic level concepts we rely on an ongoing effort in cognitive psychology: the feature norms.

In a task called feature-generation subjects list what they believe the most important properties for a set of test concepts are. The experimenter processes the resulting conceptual descriptions and registers the final representation in the norm. Thus, a feature norm is a database containing a set of concepts and their most salient features (properties). The recorded properties are pieces of common sense knowledge. For example, in a norm one finds statements like:

- An **apple** (concept) *is a fruit* (property)[1].
- An **airplane** (concept) *is used for people transportation* (property).

In this paper we explore the possibility to acquire common-sense knowledge from very large corpora. The type of properties one finds in the norms guides the knowledge-extraction task. A double classification of the properties in the norms is used. At the morphological level the properties are grouped according to the part of speech of the words used to express them (noun properties, adjective properties, verb properties). At the semantic level we group the properties in semantic classes (taxonomic properties, part properties, etc.).

The properties in certain semantic classes are learnt using a pattern-based approach, while other classes of properties are learnt using a novel method based on co-occurrence associations.

The rest of the paper has the following organization. The second section discusses the structure of feature norms and presents the procedure for property learning. The third section reports and discusses the results. The fourth section puts our work in context briefly surveying the related work. The paper ends with the conclusions.

2 Feature Norm like Knowledge Acquisition

2.1 Property Classification

For our experiments we choose the feature norm obtained by McRae and colleagues [6]. The norm lists conceptual descriptions for 541 basic level concepts representing living and non-living things and was produced interviewing 725 participants.

We classify each property in the norm at two levels: morphological and semantic.

The morphological level contains the part of speech of the word representing the property. The semantic classification is inspired by a perceptually based taxonomy discussed later in this section. Table 1 shows a

[1] In this paper the concepts will be typed in **bold** and the properties in *italics*

International Conference RANLP 2009 - Borovets, Bulgaria, pages 23–27

part of the conceptual description for the focal concept **axe** (in this paper the focal concepts are the concept for which the subjects list properties in the feature generation task) and the double classification of the concept properties.

Property	Morphological Classification	Semantic Classification
Tool	Noun	Superordinate
Blade	Noun	Part
Chop	Noun	Action

Table 1: *The double classification of the properties of the concept axe*

The semantic classification is based on Wu and Barsalou (WB) taxonomy [12]. This taxonomy gives a perceptually oriented categorization of properties in the norms. WB taxonomy classifies the properties in 27 distinct classes. Some of these classes contain very few properties and therefore are of marginal interest. For example, the Affect Emotion class classifies only 11 properties. Therefore, we consider only the classes of properties with more than 100 members.

Unfortunately, we cannot directly use the WB taxonomy in the learning process because some of the distinctions it makes are too fine-grained. For example, the taxonomy distinguishes between external components of an object and its internal components. On this account the heart of an animal is an internal component whereas its legs are external components. Keeping these distinctions otherwise relevant from a psychological point of view will hinder the learning of feature norm concept descriptions . Therefore we remap the WB initial property classes on a new set of property classes more adequate for our task. Table 2 presents the new set of property classes together with the morphological classification of the properties in each class.

Morphological Classification	Semantic Classification
Superordinate	Noun
Part	Noun
Stuff	Noun
Location	Noun
Action	Verb
Quality	Adjective

Table 2: *The semantic and morphological classification of properties in McRae feature norm*

The meaning of each semantic class of properties is the following:

- Superordinate. The superordinate properties are those properties that classify a concept from a taxonomic point of view. For example, the **dog** (focal concept) *is an animal* (taxonomic property).

- Part. The category part includes the properties denoting external and internal components of an object. For example *blade* (part property) is a part of an **axe** (focal concept).

- Stuff. The properties in this semantic class denote the stuff an object is made of. For example, **bottle** (focal concept) *is made of glass* (stuff property).

- Location. The properties in this semantic class denote typical places where instances of the focal concepts are found. For example, **airplanes** (focal concept) *are found in airports* (location property).

- Action. This class of properties represents the characteristic actions defining the behavior of an entity (the **cat** (focal concept) *meow* (action property)) or the function, instances of the focal concepts typically fulfill (the **heart** (focal concept) *pumps blood* (function property)).

- Quality. This class of properties denotes the qualities (color, taste, etc.) of the objects instances of the focal concepts. For example, the **apple** (focal concept) *is red* (quality property) or *is sweet* (quality property).

The most relevant properties produced by the subjects in the feature production experiments are in the categories presented above. Thus, asked to list the defining properties of the concepts representing concrete objects subjects will typically: classify the objects (Superordinate), list their parts and the stuff they are made from (Parts and Stuff), specify the location the objects are typically found in (Location), their intended functions, and their typical behavior (Action), or name their perceptual qualities (Quality).

3 Property Learning

To learn the property classes discussed in the preceding section we employ two different strategies. Superordinate, Part, Stuff and Location properties are learnt using a pattern-based approach. Quality and Action properties are learnt using a novel method that quantifies the strength of association between the nouns representing the focal concepts and the adjective and verbs co-occurring with them in a corpus. The learning decision is motivated by the following experiment. We took a set of concepts and their properties from McRae feature norm and extracted sentences from a corpus where a pair concept - property appears in the same sentence.

We noticed that, in general, the quality properties are expressed by the adjectives modifying the noun representing the focal concept. For example, for the concept property pair (**apple**, *red*) we find contexts like:

"She took the red apple" .

The action properties are expressed by verbs. The pair (**dog**, *bark*) is conveyed by contexts like:

"The ugly dog is barking".

where the verb expresses an action to which the dog (i.e. the noun representing the concept) is a participant.

The experiment suggests that to learn Quality and Action properties we should filter the adjectives and verbs co-occurring with the focal concepts.

For the rest of the property classes the extracted contexts suggest that the best learning strategy should be a pattern-based approach. Moreover with the exception of the Location relation, that, to our knowledge, has not been studied yet, for the relations Superordinate, Part and Stuff some patterns are already known. The properties we try to find lexico-syntactic patterns for are classified at the morphological level as nouns (see Table 2). The rest of the properties are classified as either adjectives (Qualities) or verbs (Action). To generate candidate patterns for Superordinate, Part, Stuff and Location relation we follow the procedure discussed in [1]. Basically the hypothesis we pursue is that the best lexico syntactic patterns are those highly associated with the instances representing the relation of interest. The idea is not new and was used in the past by other researchers.However, they used only frequency [8] or pointwise mutual information [7] to calculate the strength of association between patterns and instances. We improve previous work and employ two statistical association measures (Chi Squared and Log Likelihood) for the same task.

The precision of each candidate pattern is evaluated in the following way. A set of 50 concept-feature pairs is selected from a corpus using the devised pattern. For example, to evaluate the precision of the pattern: "Noun made of Noun " for the Stuff relation we extract concept feature pairs like **hammer** - *wood*, **bottle** - *glass*, **car** - *cheese*, etc. Then we label a pair as a hit if the semantic relation holds between the concept and the feature in the pair and a miss otherwise. The pattern precision is defined as the percent of hits. In the case of the three pairs in the example above we have two hits: **hammer** - *wood* and **bottle** - *glass* and one miss: **car** - *cheese*. Thus we have a pattern precision of 66 %.

The Quality and Action properties are learnt using an unsupervised approach. First the association strength between the nouns representing the focal concepts and the adjectives or verbs co-occurring with them in a corpus is computed. The co-occurring adjectives are those adjectives found one word at the left of the nouns representing the focal concepts. A co-occurring verb is a verb found one word at the right of the nouns representing the focal concepts or a verb separated from an auxiliary verb by the nouns representing the focal concepts.

The strongest 30 associated adjectives are selected as Quality properties and the strongest 30 associated verbs are selected as Action properties.

To quantify the attraction strength between the concept and the potential properties of type adjective or verb we use the log-likelihood measure.

4 Results and discussion

4.1 Experimental setup

The corpus used for learning feature-norm-like concept descriptions is ukWaC [3]. UkWaC is a very large corpus of British English, containing more than 2 billion words, constructed by crawling the web. For evaluating the success of our method we have chosen a test set of 44 concepts from McRae feature norm. In the next two subsections we report and discuss the results obtained for Superordinate, Stuff, Location and Part properties and Quality and Action properties respectively. All our experiments were performed using the CWB and UCS toolkits (`http://www.collocations.de/software.html`).

4.2 Results for Superordinate, Stuff, Location and Part properties

For the concepts in the test set we extract properties using the manually selected patterns reported in table 3.

Relation	Pattern
Superordinate	Noun [JJ]-such [IN]-as Noun Noun [CC]-and [JJ]-other Noun Noun [CC]-or [JJ]-other Noun
Stuff	Noun [VVN]-make [IN]-of Noun
Location	Noun [IN]-from [DT]-the Noun
Part	Noun [VVP]-comprise Noun Noun [VVP]-consists [IN]-of Noun

Table 3: *The selected patterns*

The results of property extraction phase are reported in Table 4. The columns of the table represent in order: the name of the class of semantic properties to be extracted, the recall of our procedure and the pattern precision. The recall tells how many properties in the test set are found using the patterns in Table 3. The pattern precision states how precise the selected pattern is in finding the properties in a certain semantic class and it is computed as shown at the end of the section 2.2. In case more than one pattern have been selected, the pattern precision is the average precision for all selected patterns.

Property Class	Recall	Pattern Precission
Superordinate	87%	85%
Stuff	21%	70%
Location	33%	40%
Part	0%	51%

Table 4: *The results for each property class*

As one can see from Table 4, the recall for the superordinate relation is very good and the precision of the patterns is not bad either (average precision 85%). However, many of the extracted superordinate properties are roles and not types. For example, **banana**, one of the concepts in the test set, has the superordinate property: *is a fruit* (type). Using the patterns for superordinate relation we find that **banana** *is a fruit* (a type) but also *is an ingredient* and *is a product* (roles). The lexico-syntactic patterns for the superordinate relation blur the type-role distinction. Other extracted pairs for the superordinates relation include (the left side of the pair contains a concept from the test set, while the right side lists its extracted superordinates): **cat**- (*pet*, *animal*), **potato**-(*vegetable*, *food*),

chicken-(*bird*, *product*). In general, as we see from the pattern precision, the extracted taxonomic knowledge is accurate.

The pattern used to represent the Stuff relation has a bad recall (21 %) and an estimated precision of 70 %. To be fair, the pattern expresses better than the estimated precision the substance an object is made of. The problem is that in many cases constructions of type "Noun made of Noun" are used in a metaphoric way as in: "car made of cheese". In the actual context the car was not made of cheese but the construction is used to show that the respective car was not resistant to impact. Other examples of extracted relations are: **bottle**-(*glass*, *aluminum*), **ship** -(*oak*, *metal*), **cup**-(*stone*, *paper*). The extracted information should be carefully assessed because many times the properties extracted are highly contextual and do not qualify as common-sense knowledge.

The pattern for Location relation has bad precision and bad recall. The properties of type Location listed in the norm represent typical places where objects can be found. For example, in the norm it is stated that **bananas** *are found in tropical climates* (the tropical climate being the typical place where banana-trees grow). However what one can hope from a pattern-based approach is to find patterns representing with good precision the concept of Location in general. We found a more precise Location pattern than the selected one: "N is found in N". Unfortunately, this pattern has 0% recall for our test set. The extracted properties are in general imprecise: **duck**- (*exploit*), **hammer**-(*north*).

The patterns for Part relation have 0% recall for the concepts in the test set and their precision for the general domain is not very good either. As others have shown [4] a pattern based approach is not enough to learn the part relation and one needs to use a supervised approach to achieve a relevant degree of success.

4.3 Results for Quality and Action properties

We computed the association strength between the concepts in the test set and the co-occurring verbs and adjectives using the log-likelihood measure. Some of the extracted properties for the concepts in the test set are shown in Table 5.

The results for Quality and Action properties are presented in Table 6. The columns of the table represent in order: the name of the class of semantic properties, the Recall and the Property Precision. The Recall represents the percent of properties in the test set our procedure found. The Property Precision computes the precision with which our procedure finds properties in a semantic class. The property precision is the percent of quality and action properties found among the strongest 30 adjectives and verbs associated with the focal concepts.Because the number of potential properties is reasonable for hand checking, the validation for this procedure was performed manually.

The manual comparison between the corpus extracted properties and the norm properties confirm the hypothesis regarding the relation between the association strength of features of type adjective and verbs and their degree of relevance as properties of concepts.

Concept	Quality	Action
Duck	*wild, tufted* *lame, ruddy*	*waddle, fly* *swim, quack*
Eagle	*golden, bald* *white-tailed, spotted*	*soar, fly* *perch, swoop*
Turtle	*marine, green* *giant, engendered*	*dive, nest* *hatch, crawl*

Table 5: *Some quality and action properties for the concepts in the test set*

Property Class	Recall	Property Precission
Quality	60%	60%
Action	70%	83%

Table 6: *The results for Quality and Action property classes*

For each concept in the test set roughly 18 adjectives and 25 verbs in the extracted set of potential properties represent qualities and action respectively (see Property Precision column in Table 6). This can be explained by the fact that all concepts in the test set denote concrete objects. Many of the adjectives modifying nouns denoting concrete objects express the objects qualities, whereas the verbs usually denote actions different actors perform or to which various objects are subject.

Many of the properties found using this method encode pieces of common sense knowledge not present in the norms. For example, the semantic representation of the concept **turtle** has the following Quality properties listed in the norm: *green, hard, small.* The strongest adjectives associated in the UkWaC corpus with the noun turtle ordered by the loglikelihood score are: *marine, green, giant.* The property *marine* carries a greater distinctiveness than any of similar feature listed in the norms.

Likewise, the actions typically associated with the concept **turtle** in the McRae feature norm are: *lays eggs, swims, walks slowly.* The strongest verbs associated in the UkWaC corpus with the noun turtle are: *dive, nest, hatch.* The *dive* action is more specific and therefore more distinct than the *swim* action registered in the feature norm. The *hatch* property is characteristic to reptiles and birds and thus a good candidate for the representation of the concept turtle.

5 Related Work

The need of acquiring common-sense knowledge to enable computers understand and reason with natural language was recognized long time ago. The first large-scale effort for acquisition of common sense knowledge is the project CYC. Human users codify by hand millions of rules representing every-day knowledge (in CYC one finds concepts like cat and mammal and assertions like the cat is a mammal).

A more up to date effort to acquire knowledge about

daily life is the project OpenMind. It attempts at building a huge database of common sense knowledge exploiting the wisdom of crowds. Thousands of non-expert contributors introduce knowledge inside a set of predefined scenarios like: Story telling, Typical arguments of verbs or the Listing of objects appearing usually together.

An interesting method to gather the common-sense knowledge is von Ahns work, who draws on the data collected with the help of online games [11].

The work reported here uses an alternative basis for common-sense property acquisition, it builds on the effort in cognitive psychology to extract kinds of properties people are likely to know about the concepts. Of course, as the experience of CYC shows, there is much more to common sense knowledge than the acquisition of concept properties. However we think that our work, having a sound empirical basis, is a step in the right direction.

6 Conclusions

The presented method for acquiring common-sense knowledge based on feature-norm concept description has been successful at learning semantic property classes Superordinate, Quality and Action. For learning the superordinates of the focal concepts one needs to use a high precision pattern. For Quality and Action properties one needs to apply the method based on co-occurrence association presented in section 2.2.

To learn all other property classes other methods (probably a supervised approach) must be devised.

Acknowledgments

The author would like to thank Verginica Barbu Mititelu and three anonymous reviewers for their suggestions and corrections.

References

[1] E. Barbu. Combining methods to learn feature-norm-like concept descriptions. In *Proceedings of the ESSLLI Workshop on Distributional Lexical Semantics*, pages 9–17, August 2008.

[2] A. M. Collins and M. R. Quillian. Retrieval time from semantic memory. *Journal of Verbal Learning and Verbal Behavior*, 8:241–248, 1969.

[3] A. Ferraresi, E. Zanchetta, M. Baroni, and S. Bernardini. Introducing and evaluating ukwac, a very large web-derived corpus of english. In *WAC4 Workshop Conference Proceedings*, pages 84–89, 2008.

[4] R. Girju, A. Badulescu, and D. Moldovan. Automatic discovery of part-whole relations. *Computational Linguistics*, 32(1):83–135, March 2006.

[5] D. B. Lenat. Cyc: A large-scale investment in knowledge infrastructure. *Communications of the ACM*, 38(11):33–38, 1995.

[6] K. McRae, G. S. Cree, M. S. Seidenberg, and C. McNorgan. Semantic feature production norms for a large set of living and nonliving things. *Behavior Research Methods*, 37(4):547–559, Nov. 2005.

[7] P. Pantel and M. Pennacchiotti. Espresso: A bootstrapping algorithm for automatically harvesting semantic relations. In *Proceedings of Conference on Computational Linguistics / Association for Computational Linguistics (COLING/ACL-06)*, 2006.

[8] D. Ravichandran and E. Hovy. Learning learning surface text patterns for a question answering system. In *Proceedings of ACL*, 2002.

[9] E. Rosch and C. Mervis. Family resemblance: Studies in the internal structure of categories. *Cognitive Psychology*, 7:573–605, 1975.

[10] P. Singh. The public acquisition of commonsense knowledge. In *AAAI Spring Symposium on Acquiring (and Using) Linguistic (and World) Knowledge for Information Access*, 2002.

[11] L. von Ahn. Games with a purpose. *IEEE Computer Magazine*, 39(6):96–98, June 2006.

[12] L. Wu and L. Barsalou. Perceptual simulation in conceptual combination. *Acta Psychologica*, page In press, 2009.

Unsupervised Knowledge Extraction for Taxonomies of Concepts from Wikipedia

Eduard Barbu
Center for Mind/Brain Sciences
Rovereto
Trento, Italy
eduard.barbu@unitn.it

Massimo Poesio
Center for Mind/Brain Sciences
Rovereto
Trento, Italy
massimo.poesio@unitn.it

Abstract

A novel method for unsupervised acquisition of knowledge for taxonomies of concepts from raw Wikipedia text is presented. We assume that the concepts classified under the same node in a taxonomy are described in a comparable way in Wikipedia. The concepts in 6 taxonomies extracted from WordNet are mapped onto Wikipedia pages and the lexico-syntactic patterns describing semantic structures expressing relevant knowledge for the concepts are automatically learnt.

Keywords

wikipedia, unsupervised knowledge acquisition, taxonomy

1 Introduction

A crucial phase in ontology acquisition from text is the extraction of relevant knowledge for ontology concepts, the focus of the current work. Our framework extracts in an unsupervised way knowledge for a set of concepts hierarchically ordered. For example, for the concept **bewick's swan**, one of the concepts in bird taxonomy, some extracted properties are: *have few natural predator*[1], *live in water*, *is a small Holarctic swan*. From a logical/ontological point of view the extracted knowledge can be classified as: quantifier restrictions (e. g. *most birds build nests*), parts of the instances of the concepts in the taxonomy (e.g. *small head* and *long thick mane* for the concept **shetland pony**), alternative classification of the concepts in the taxonomy (*herd animal* and *social creature* for the concept **horse**), etc.

The knowledge relevant for concepts can be automatically extracted from a variety of sources: dictionaries, databases, corpora, web directories and others. Recently, Wikipedia drew the attention of various research groups as a goldmine resource for information retrieval [3], information extraction [9] and ontology building [8].

There are some characteristics that make Wikipedia an appropriate resource for information extraction. Firstly, its coverage is impressive: the English Wikipedia has almost three million articles currently maintained and updated by thousands of voluntary contributors, thus surpassing any other encyclopedia in history. Secondly, the style of writing Wikipedia articles is more homogeneous than the mixed bag of styles one encounters in general corpora or in unrestricted text found on the web. Thirdly, Wikipedia has a large network of links, categories and info-boxes allowing a combination of techniques for information extraction.

This paper introduces a novel method for acquisition of knowledge for taxonomies of concepts from the raw Wikipedia text. We assume that similar concepts (i.e. those classified under the same node in a taxonomy) are described in a comparable way in Wikipedia. More precisely, we suppose that the relevant knowledge of these similar concepts is expressed using equivalent surface patterns. The learning process starts with the generation of concept hierarchies from WordNet. The concepts in each hierarchy are mapped onto Wikipedia pages and the knowledge appropriate to the concepts is automatically extracted at a precision ranging from 55 to 66 percents depending on the taxonomy.

The remaining of the paper is organized as follows. In section 2 we present the mapping of concept taxonomy onto Wikipedia pages and discuss the algorithm for knowledge extraction. Section 3 presents, evaluates and discusses the results. Section 4 compares our work with related approaches and the last section summarizes the results and concludes the paper.

2 Knowledge Extraction for Taxonomies of Concepts

The knowledge extraction precision depends on the accuracy of the classification of Wikipedia pages. Each concept from the taxonomy should be precisely mapped on the corresponding Wikipedia article. Therefore, to generate the taxonomy of concepts and map the generated taxonomy onto Wikipedia articles we follow the next steps:

- First, we pick a concept of interest representing the higher level node of the taxonomy to be extracted and map it onto a WordNet synset. For example, if you have chosen the concept **dog** and you want to get the sense corresponding to the animal, you map the concept to the sense number 1 in WordNet.

[1] In this paper the concepts will be typed in **bold** and the properties in *italics*

International Conference RANLP 2009 - Borovets, Bulgaria, pages 28–32

- Second, the hyponymy (sub)tree having as root the concept chosen in the previous step is produced and the concepts in the tree are mapped onto Wikipedia pages. As others have shown [5] the best mapping heuristic is to choose that member of a synset which has the sense number 1 . Even so, the ambiguity problem is not completely solved. For it is possible that concepts having low or no ambiguity in WordNet to be highly ambiguous in Wikipedia. Fortunately, in this case the Wikipedia server returns a page having a standard structure and allows us to reject the ambiguous concept or to guess the right mapping. The disambiguation is performed concatenating the ambiguous concept with each of its WordNet hyperonyms and searching again in Wikipedia until an unambiguos entry is found. For example, the concept **buckskin** appears in two synsets in WordNet and in 8 possible entries in Wikipedia. Because we are interested in the sense of **buckskin** having the hyperonym horse we concatenate the two words (buckskin_(horse)) and send the new entry to Wikipedia server. Fortunately, in this case no ambiguity results and the correct mapping is automatically performed.

The generated taxonomy is used as input by the system in Figure 1. The Extracted taxonomy is mapped onto the Wikipedia pages (the first part of Figure 1) and the pipeline of the system is made by a set of modules, each of them working on the output produced by the preceding module in the pipeline.

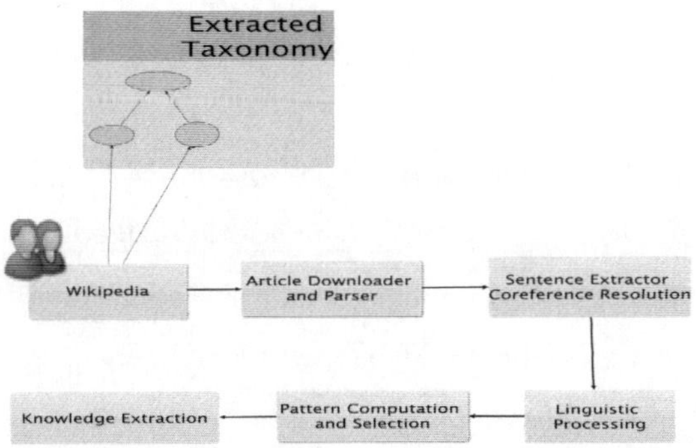

Fig. 1: *The pipeline of the system for knowledge extraction*

The module **Article Downloader and Parser** downloads the Wikipedia articles corresponding to the categories in the taxonomy. From the rough downloaded content of Wikipedia articles we eliminate the useless html tags and the head structure of the article is recovered (e.g. to each higher order head in the article its corresponding text is assigned). In addition, the module eliminates the content of some heads not used by the system, like: Links, Miscellaneous, See also.

The next module, **Sentence Extractor and Co-Reference Resolution**, extracts from the Wikipedia text of an article all sentences containing references to the title concept. The idea behind extracting all sentences containing the title concept is that these sentences express in a direct way relevant information about the categories in the taxonomy. To extend the range of the sentences extracted, the module performs a basic co-reference resolution. It assumes that pronouns like their, it, he, they found within the first three words of a sentence refer back to the title concept. Further, all references at the beginning of a sentence (within the first five words) to any concept in the taxonomic chain of the title concept are also extracted.

Then the module **Linguistic Processing** performs part-of-speech tagging, lemmatization and term identification for the extracted sentences. In order to harvest multi-word expressions and to achieve a better generalization across multiple similar sentences we use the following regular expression of a term definition:

$$(NPrep)?((Adv)?Adj)*(Noun)+$$

The abbreviation NPrep denotes a noun preposition and the straightforward abreviations Adv and Adj denote a adverb an an adjective respectively. The output of this module is a list of sentences in simplified term form (where the terms containing the title concepts are replaced with the generic label TitleConcept and the rest of the terms are replaced with the label T).

The task of the module **Pattern Computation and Selection** is to identify the patterns expressing relevant knowledge for the title concepts. This module has two sub-modules: the first one is called **Pattern Generation** and computes candidate patterns. The second one is named **Pattern Ranking and Selection** and it implements heuristics for ranking and selecting the relevant patterns. The idea behind pattern generation is that the patterns originated should express knowledge characteristic to similar concepts. We judge concepts as similar if they are classified under the same node in the taxonomy and we assume that the relevant knowledge of similar concepts is stated in using the same lexico-syntactic patterns. Therefore, one expects the patterns expressing knowledge of these concepts to appear in the extracted Wikipedia sentences for more than one concept. To produce candidate patterns the Cartesian Product between all sentences in simplified term form (as outputted by the **Linguistic Processing** module) belonging to each pair of similar concepts is performed. For each pair of sentences in the Cartesian product we consider as candidate patterns the longest common substring including the title concept between the sentences. The submodule **Pattern Ranking and Selection** filters the patterns produced by the sub-module **Pattern Generation**. We assume that the best patterns have the shape given by the following regular expression form:

$$(TitleConcept|T)(.+)(T|TitleConcept).$$

Thus we accept the following patterns: "T of TitleConcept be T", "TitleConcept be T", "TitleConcept be design by T" and reject the next patterns: "in

T , TitleConcept be", "of TitleConcept, T". While the former patterns have both topic (what is being talked about; it always contains the TitleConcept) and focus (what is being said about the topic), the latter are incomplete, missing either topic or focus, thus being useless for information extraction. We also reject all patterns having a frequency lower than an experimentally determined threshold.

The module **Knowledge extraction** extracts knowledge for the concepts in taxonomy using the patterns voted in the previous step. For example, applying the voted pattern "TitleConcept consists_of T" to one of the sentences in the entry of the concept **knife** we get part relations:

- **knife** *consist_of a blade*

Moreover, applying the pattern "TitleConcept be_use_in T" to the entries corresponding to the concepts **razor** and **sickle** we extract the function relations:

- **razor** *be_use_in carpentry*
- **sickle** *be_use_in druidic ritual*

3 Results and discussions

3.1 Experimental setup

The input to the knowledge generation experiment is a set of six taxonomies extracted from WordNet as explained in the previous section. The root nodes of taxonomies are three animals (**Horse**, **Dog**, **Bird**), two vehicles (**Aircraft** and **Boat**) and one tool (**Cutlery**). The distribution of concepts for each taxonomy together with examples of concepts is given in Table 1. The number of concepts in the six taxonomies varies from a minimum of 34 concepts to a maximum 128 concepts with an average number of 64 concepts per category. The encyclopedia entries corresponding to the taxonomies categories are downloaded with the software module WWW::Wikipedia. The Wikipedia text is part-of-speech tagged and lemmatized with TreeTagger, a language independent POS tagger.

3.2 Pattern Voting

Table 2 shows examples of patterns voted for each of the six taxonomies. Inspecting the table we observe that a pattern voted in all taxonomies is "TitleConcept be T". This pattern is present in almost all articles in Wikipedia and it is usually found in the first three sentences of the abstract. Included in the term connected with the title concept by the verb to be there is a noun phrase giving the taxonomic classification of the title concept together with other interesting information. However, the taxonomic classification extracted with the help of this pattern is not always found among the superordinate terms in the taxonomy we started with. For example, the extracted superordinate for the concept **red_eyed_vireo** is **songbird**. In WordNet the relevant superordinates of the concept **red_eyed_vireo** are: **oscine**, **passerine** and **bird**, none of which is **songbird**.

Taxonomic Root	Number of Concepts	Examples
Aircraft	34	**monoplane, seaplane airliner, stealth_fighter**
Boat	30	**wherry, fireboat motorboat, steamboat**
Horse	34	**tarpan, shetland_pony percheron, palomino**
Dog	128	**belgian_sheepdog, collie rottweiler, dalmatian**
Bird	121	**crossbill, oscine nightingale, tailorbird**
Cutlery	34	**knife, chisel sickle, razor**

Table 1: *The roots of the extracted taxonomies and concept examples*

As we expected, some of the voted patterns express knowledge specific to the concepts in certain taxonomies. For example, the pattern "T build TitleConcept" is related to concepts in the taxonomy **Aircraft** and the pattern "TitleConcept eat T" is specific to the concepts in the taxonomy **Bird**[2] . In the first case, the knowledge extracted are constructors of aircraft models like: *Pan Am One* or *Edison*. In the second case, the properties obtained are kinds of food (*insects*, *snail*) consumed by different types of birds.

Taxonomic Root	Examples of voted Patterns
Aircraft	TitleConcept be T T use TitleConcept T build TitleConcept
Boat	TitleConcept be T TitleConcept use T TitleConcept have T
Horse	TitleConcept be T TitleConcept be use in T TitleConcept require T
Dog	TitleConcept be T TitleConcept need T TitleConcept also know as T
Bird	TitleConcept be T TitleConcept forage on T TitleConcept eat T
Cutlery	TitleConcept be T TitleConcept consist of T TitleConcept be T with T

Table 2: *Examples of extracted patterns for taxonomy classes*

3.3 Knowledge Evaluation

In the Table 3 we give examples of the generated knowledge for three concepts: **andean_condor**, **air-**

[2] Although we expected that the second pattern "TitleConcept eat T" to appear also in the concepts of the taxonomies **Dog** and **Horse** it turned out that it did not appear or it was not voted as relevant.

ship and knife belonging to the taxonomies **Bird**, **Aircraft** and **Cutlery** respectively.

Concept	Examples of Properties
andean_condor	*be_find_in South_America* *be_call the Argentinean_Condor* *Vultur gryphus*
airship	*use dynamic helium volume* *have a natural buoyancy* *be_know_as dirigible*
knife	*consists_of a blade* *come_in many forms* *make_of copper*

Table 3: *Examples of extracted properties for three concepts*

Two raters evaluate the quality of the generated knowledge using a 3-point scale:

- Ideal Knowledge - (2 points). The extracted properties are necessary for the concepts in the taxonomy. They should be part of an ideal list of properties for the taxonomy concepts (e.g. *is omnivorous* for the concept **australian magpie** or *consists of a blade* for the concept **knife**)
- Partially Correct - (1 point) if the extracted properties correctly describe the taxonomy concepts but are not among their ideal list of properties (e.g. *is related to butcher birds* or *described by English Ornithologist John Latham* for the concept **australian magpie**)
- Incorrect Knowledge - (0 points) if the extracted properties do not apply in any way to the category (e.g. the property *number* for the concept **knife** or the property *be on average* for the concept **andean condor**).

The precision of the extracted knowledge is computed using the following formula.

$$Precission = \frac{2N_{IK} + 1N_{PC}}{2N_{Properties}}$$

where

- N_{IK} counts the number of ideal knowledge labels
- N_{PC} represents the number of partially correct labels
- $N_{Properties}$ counts all properties evaluated

Approximately 10 concepts per category are chosen for evaluation. When the two raters disagreed about a label the judge solves the disagreement adding the final label. The inter-rater agreement is computed using the Kappa score [7] and the precision is computed for the judge scores (see table 4).

Each property generated in the rater file was annotated with a type (e.g. classification property, part property, behaviour property, etc.). For the concepts in all taxonomies the algorithm generates part properties (e.g. *leg* for the concept **king vulture**, *blade* for the concept **knife**) and classification properties

Taxonomic Root	Kappa Score	Precission
Aircraft	0.62	0.55
Boat	0.65	0.57
Horse	0.62	0.63
Dog	0.65	0.66
Bird	0.68	0.60
Cutlery	0.79	0.61

Table 4: *The inter-rater agreement and the precision for the extracted knowledge*

(e.g. *medium-large grebe* for the concept **red_necked grebe** or *scent hound* for the concept **beagle**). Then, depending on the taxonomy, the algorithm generates different types of properties. For example, for all animals (the concepts in the taxonomies dominated by **Horse**, **Dog** and **Bird**) a common property type generated is Behaviour (e.g. *sensitive to insecticide* for the concept **greyhound** or *builds a large nest* for the concept **bald eagle**). For tools a common generated property type is the function (e.g. *used by barbers* for **razor** or *used in druidic ritual* for **golden sickle**). Interestingly enough, some extracted knowledge are rules, like: *most birds build nests* or *most helicopters have a single main rotor.*

4 Related Work

With the advent of new information sources many teams are developing methods for large-scale information extraction taking advantage of the huge amounts of unstructured text currently available. In this framework relevant is the work of Pasca ([4]) who exploits both query logs and Web documents to acquire instances and knowledge for open domain classes.

Recently the potential of Wikipedia for information extraction in general and knowledge extraction in particular was acknowledged by many research groups. The methods that use Wikipedia for knowledge extraction can be grouped in two major classes. The first class of methods takes profit of the internal link structure and the structured information in Wikipedia (e.g. infoboxes or templates), while the second class of methods use Wikipedias raw text.

Representative for the second class of methods is the work of [6]. They acquire from Simple English Wikipedia (an Wikipedia variant intended for people whose first language is not English) patterns expressing the semantic relations linking nouns in Princeton WordNet 1.7 (hyperonymy, hyponymy, holonymy and meronymy). Then they gather new instances for these relations improving in this way the WordNet coverage. The reported precision for the newly extracted relationships is between 60 and 70 depending on the relation. A direct comparison between their system and our system is not possible because, in the first place, the framework they use is weakly supervised, while our framework is completely unsupervised. Secondly, their system is tuned to acquire certain kinds of relations (hyperonyms, parts), while our framework does not make any assumption about the relations that should be extracted. However, there is an important overlap between the patterns for hyperonyms and part relation generated by both methods.

Much sophisticated frameworks for relation acquisition from Wikipedia include the work of [2] who uses a dependency parser to extract hyponymy relations from Wikipedia sentences containing the verb to be. Our approach is different from the other methods mentioned in the way we make use of the Wikipedia text to generate concept knowledge. We do not identify patterns by defining a certain relation using seeds, as it is the standard procedure in CL after the seminal work of Hearst [1]. We assume instead that similar concepts are described in similar ways in encyclopedia-like resources. If the main assumption behind the work of Hearst is that semantic relations can be mapped with a certain precision on lexico-syntactic patterns, we go a step forward and assume that semantic structures describing concept knowledge can be mapped on sets of lexico-syntactic patterns.

5 Conclusions

In this paper we presented a novel method for unsupervised knowledge extraction for taxonomies of concepts using Wikipedia as information source. Departing from previous methods for knowledge acquisition we seek to extract semantic structures from wikipedia descriptions of similar concepts. These structures are formalized as surface patterns linking the title concepts with their properties. Future work includes:

1. usage of more formalized taxonomies.
2. the extension of the set of taxonomies to include abstract concepts like **cognition**.
3. a better evaluation framework for the results.

Acknowledgments

The authors would like to thank to Verginica Barbu Mititelu and Gianluca Lebani for support in the data collection and data rating. We also want to thank three anonymous reviewers for suggestions and criticism.

References

[1] M. A. Hearst. Automated discovery of wordnet relations. In C. Fellbaum, editor, *WordNet: An Electronic Lexical Database*. MIT Press, 1998.

[2] A. Herbelot and A. Copestake. Acquiring ontological relationships from wikipedia using rmrs. In *ISWC Workshop On Web Content*, 2006.

[3] D. N. Milne, I. H. Witten, and D. M.Nichols. A knowledge-based search engine powered by wikipedia. In *CIKM '07: Proceedings of the sixteenth ACM conference on Conference on information and knowledge management*, pages 445–454, New York, NY, USA, 2007. ACM.

[4] M.Pasca and B. Durme. Weakly-supervised acquisition of open-domain classes and class knowledge from web documents and query logs. In *Proceedings of the 46th Annual Meeting of the Association for Computational Linguistics: Human Language Technologies*, 2008.

[5] S. Pradhan, E. Loper, D. Dligach, and M. Palmer. Semeval-2007 task-17: English lexical sample, srl and all words. In *Proceedings of the Fourth International Workshop on Semantic Evaluations (SemEval-2007)*, pages 87–92, Prague, Czech Republic, June 2007. Association for Computational Linguistics.

[6] M. Ruiz-Casado, E. Alfonseca, and P. Castells. Automatising the learning of lexical patterns: An application to the enrichment of wordnet by extracting semantic relationships from wikipedia. *Data and Knowledge Engineering*, 61(3):484–499, 2007. Advances on Natural Language Processing - NLDB 05.

[7] S. Siegel and N. J. Castellan. *Nonparametric statistics for the Behavioral Sciences*. McGraw-Hill, 2nd edition, 1988.

[8] F. M. Suchanek, G. Kasneci, and G. Weikum. Yago: a core of semantic knowledge. In *WWW '07: Proceedings of the 16th international conference on World Wide Web*, pages 697–706, New York, NY, USA, 2007. ACM.

[9] G. Wang, Y. Yu, and H. Zhu. Positive-only relation extraction from wikipedia text. In *Proceedings of the 6th International Semantic Web Conference and 2nd Asian Semantic Web Conference, ISWC/ASWC'07*, 2007.

Exploring Treebank Transformations in Dependency Parsing

Kepa Bengoetxea
IXA NLP Group
Technical School of Engineering, Bilbao
University of the Basque Country
Plaza La Casilla 3, 48012, Bilbao
kepa.bengoetxea@ehu.es

Koldo Gojenola
IXA NLP Group
Technical School of Engineering, Bilbao
University of the Basque Country
Plaza La Casilla 3, 48012, Bilbao
koldo.gojenola@ehu.es

Abstract

This paper presents a set of experiments performed on parsing the Basque Dependency Treebank. We have concentrated on treebank transformations, maintaining the same basic parsing algorithm across the experiments. The experiments can be classified in two groups: 1) feature optimization, which is important mainly due to the fact that Basque is an agglutinative language, with a rich set of morphosyntactic features attached to each word, 2) graph transformations, ranging from language independent methods, such as projectivization, to language specific approaches, as coordination and subordinated sentences, where syntactic properties of Basque have been used to reshape the dependency trees used for training the system. The transformations have been tested independently and also in combination, showing that their order of application is relevant. The experiments were performed using a freely available state of the art data-driven dependency parser [11].

Keywords

Dependency parsing, treebank parsing, agglutinative language.

1 Introduction

This work presents several experiments performed on dependency parsing of the Basque Dependency Treebank (BDT) [1]. Several syntactic analyzers based on dependencies have been developed, with proposals ranging from systems that directly construct dependency structures [9] to other systems based on the more traditional constituency structures that allow the extraction of dependencies [2]. The present work has been developed in the context of dependency parsing exemplified by the CoNLL[1] shared task on dependency parsing in years 2006 and 2007 [12], where several systems had to compete analyzing data from a typologically varied range of 11 languages. The treebanks for all languages were standardized using a previously agreed CONLL-X format (see Figure 1). BDT was one of the evaluated treebanks, which will allow us to make a direct comparison of results.

Many works on treebank parsing have dedicated an effort to the task of pre-processing training trees [4, 13]. This paper extends these works, applying treebank transformations [7, 10] to a morphologically rich, agglutinative language.

The rest of the paper is organized as follows. Section 2 presents the main resources used in this work, including the BDT and a data-driven open source parser. Section 3 presents the different proposals for Treebank transformation that have been devised in order to improve the parser's accuracy. Next, section 4 will evaluate the results of each transformation. Section 5 examines related work, and the last section outlines the main conclusions.

2 Resources

This section will describe the main elements that have been used in the experiments. First, subsection 2.1 will present the Basque Treebank data, while subsection 2.2 will describe the main characteristics of Maltparser, a state of the art and data-driven dependency parser.

2.1 The Basque Dependency Treebank

BDT [2] can be considered a pure dependency treebank, as its initial design considered that all the dependency arcs would connect sentence tokens. Although this decision had consequences on the annotation process, its simplicity is also an advantage when applying several of the most efficient parsing algorithms. The treebank consists of 55,469 tokens forming 3,700 sentences, 334 of which were used as test data[2].

```
(1) Etorri de-la eta joan de-la  esan  zien.
come has-that and go has-that tell he-to-them
```
He told them that he has come and he has gone.

Figure 1 contains an example of a sentence (1), annotated in the CONLL-X format. The text is organized in eight tab-separated columns: word-number, form, lemma, category (coarse POS), fine-grained POS, morphosyntactic features, and the dependency relation (headword + dependency). Basque is an agglutinative language, and it presents a high power to generate inflected word-forms.. Verbs offer a lot of grammatical information, as each verb form conveys information about the subject, the two objects, as well as the tense and aspect. As a result of this wealth of information contained within word-forms,

[1] *CoNLL: Computational Natural Language Learning.*

[2] The corpus is freely available. The treebank converted to the *CONLL-X* format can also be obtained from the authors.

International Conference RANLP 2009 - Borovets, Bulgaria, pages 33–38

W	Form	Lemma	CPOS	POS	Features	Head	Dependency
1	Etorri	etorri	V	V	_	3	coord
2	dela	izan	AUXV	AUXV	COMPL|3S	1	auxmod
3	eta	eta	CONJ	CONJ	_	6	ccomp_obj
4	joan	joan	V	V	_	3	coord
5	dela	izan	AUXV	AUXV	COMPL|3S	4	auxmod
6	esan	esan	V	V	_	0	ROOT
7	zien	*edun	AUXV	AUXV	SUBJ3S|OBJ3P	6	auxmod
8	.	.	PUNT	PUNT_PUNT	_	7	PUNC

Figure 1: Example of BDT sentence in the CONLL-X format

(V = main verb, AUXV = auxiliary verb, COMPL = completive subordinate marker, ccomp_obj = clausal complement object, 3S: third person sing., SUBJ3S: subject in 3rd person sing., OBJ3P: object in 3rd person pl.).

complex structures have to be built to represent complete morphological information at word level. The information in Figure 1 has been simplified due to space reasons, as typically the Features column will contain lots of morphosyntactic features, which are relevant for parsing.

2.2 Maltparser

Maltparser [11] is a state of the art dependency parser that has been successfully applied to typologically different languages and treebanks. While several variants of the base parser have been implemented, we will use one of its standard versions (Maltparser version 0.4).

The parser is based on two basic data-structures. A stack stores the dependency-graph that is formed by linking the input sentence's words, while an input sequence contains the elements that have not yet been examined. The basic algorithm applies a set of four parsing actions (shift into the stack, reduce, left-arc, or right-arc) and obtains deterministically a dependency tree in linear-time in a single pass over the input. To determine which is the best action at each step, the parser uses history-based feature models and discriminative machine learning. In all the following experiments, we made use of a SVM[3] classifier. The specification of the features used by the classifier, allows to select the number of elements of both stack and input to be considered during learning, and also indicates the kind of information for each element, which can in principle be any kind of data described in Figure 1 (such as word-form, lemma, category or morphosyntactic features).

3 Experiments

We have performed two classes of experiments. First, we have tested the effect of simplifying morphosyntactic features. Second, we have applied three different tree transformations to the treebank.

3.1 Feature optimization

Basque is an agglutinative and morphologically rich language, and this opens the way to experiment with many combinations of morphological features. The original annotation of the BDT contained 359 different morphosyntactic feature values. This led us to experiment with several modifications:

- Grouping complex features into a set of simpler ones. For example, complex case suffixes were simplified, as in DAT_INS (a complex case suffix that is internally formed by the dative case followed by the instrumental case), which was changed to INS(trumental), as the last case suffix is syntactically more relevant.
- Deletion of several features that were interesting in the description of the internal morphology of a word but were not relevant for syntactic analysis.
- The original annotation of 359 values marked them as totally unrelated values, without indicating which feature (say, case) each value was an instance of. We added a label prefix to each value, which allowed us to experiment the inclusion of a feature. For example, ABS(olutive) was transformed to CASE:ABS.

After these steps, there were 127 values of morphosyntactic features, grouped in 14 features (case, number, tense, aspect, countable, …).

3.2 Graph transformations

Algorithms for dependency-tree transformations are applied in a black box manner in four steps: 1) apply the transformation to the training data, 2) train a parser on the transformed data, 3) parse the test set, and 4) apply the inverse transformation to the parse output, so that the final evaluation is carried over the original tree representations.

We will experiment with three different tree transformations, ranging from a language independent method in one extreme, like projectivization, to a pure language specific approach on the other, going through a transformation on coordinated structures, which lies in the middle, as coordination is present in all languages but needs an adaptation depending on each language and parser.

3.2.1 *Projectivization (T_P)*

Several parsing algorithms are unable to deal with non-projective arcs, that is, arcs that cross each other. The solution can be either to design a modified algorithm (e.g., Covington's, see [11]) or transform the tree into a projective one. This option is more attractive if the original

[3] We used SVM with a polinomial kernel of degree 2 (LIVSM parameters: -s 0 –t 1 –d 2 –g 0.2 –c 0.4 –r 0 –e 0.1 –S 0)

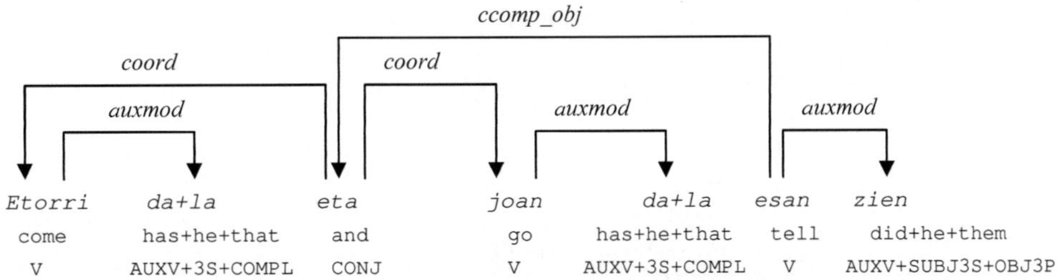

Figure 2: Dependency tree for the sentence in Figure 1,

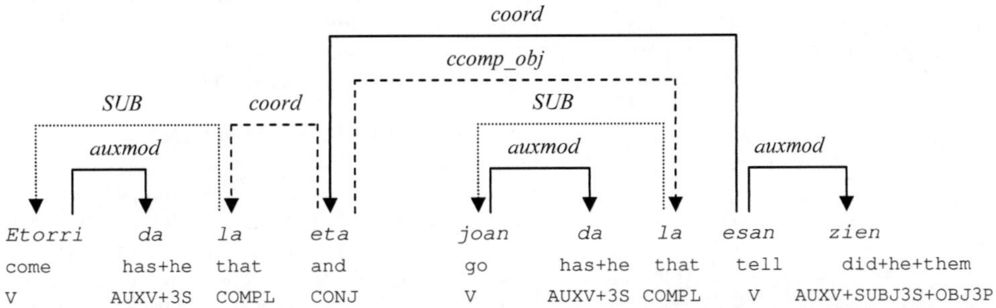

Figure 3: Transformed tree (T_S) (new arcs: dotted lines; modified arcs: discontinuous lines).

algorithm is simple, efficient and accurate, as is the case with Nivre's transition-based algorithm [11]. This transformation is totally language independent, and can be considered a standard transformation. We include it because:

- We want to test the effect of consecutive transformations against the base treebank.
- Its performance on BDT has been already tested [13]. This is in accordance with BDT having a 2.9% of non-projective arcs.

[10] proposes three types of projective transformations: path, head, and head+path. After testing them we found that the head transformation gave the best results, so this will be the one used in the following work.

3.2.2 Subordinated sentences (T_S)

Subordinated sentences are formed in Basque by attaching the corresponding morphemes to verbs, either the main verb (non-finite verbs) or the auxiliary verb (finite verbs). However, in BDT the verbal elements are organized around the main verb (semantic head) while the syntactic head corresponds to the subordination morpheme, which appears usually attached to the auxiliary. Its main consequence for parsing is that the elements bearing the relevant information for parsing are situated far in the tree with respect to their head. In Figure 2, we can see that the morpheme *–la*, indicating the presence of a subordinated completive sentence, appears down in the tree, and this could affect their correct attachment of the two coordinated verbs to the conjunction (*eta*), as conjunctions should link elements showing similar grammatical features (*-la* in this example). Similarly, it could affect the decision about the dependency type of *eta* with respect to the main verb *esan* (to say), as the dependency relation ccomp_obj is defined by means of the *–la* (completive) morpheme, far down in the tree.

Figure 3 shows the effect of transforming the original tree given in Figure 2. The subordination morpheme (*-la*) is separated from the auxiliary verb (*da*), and is "promoted" as the syntactic head of the subordinated sentence. New arcs are created from the main verbs (*etorri* and *joan*) to the morpheme (which is now the head), also adding a new dependency relation (SUB). Figure 3 shows that the tree suffers important transformations. However, as the order of sentence elements is maintained, the transformation does not so greatly affect the annotated treebank (see Figure 1), and the transformations can be described by changes in dependency links and splitting of words together with each morpheme's morphological features.

A similar solution was proposed by [6] when parsing the Prague Dependency Treebank, where relative clauses are annotated introducing an additional level with a new

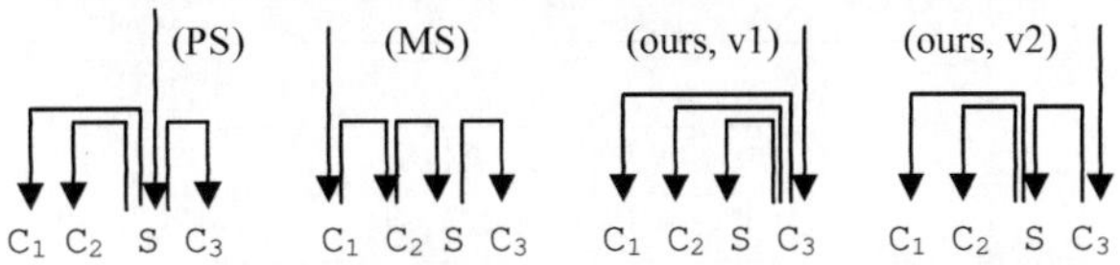

Figure 4: Dependency structures for coordination.

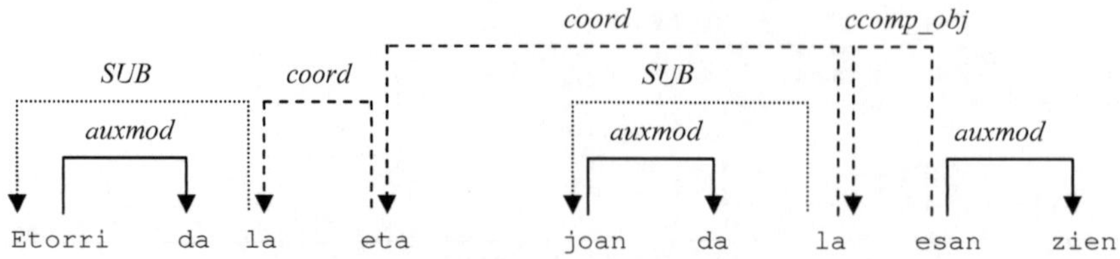

Figure 5: Transformed tree ($T_S + T_{C(v1)}$).

category (SBAR), that helps distinguish simple VPs from relative subordinated sentences. We have extended this idea to most types of subordinated sentences, as relative clauses, temporal clauses and completive, indirect interrogative, causal, adversative and modal clauses. An important difference with respect to this work is that in [4] the change is performed on the shape of the (constituency) trees, not affecting the input sequence of words, while in our case the morphemes are detached from the root words.

Transformations on finite verbs are similar to those in Figure 3 (e.g., *dela* is transformed to *da*(AUXV) + *-la*(COMPletive)). Non-finite verbs are transformed separating the suffix from the main verb (so, *etortzea* is transformed to *etorri*(V) + *-tzea*(COMPletive)).

3.2.3 Coordination (T_C)

This transformation can be considered general but it is also language dependent, as it depends on the specific configurations present in each different language, mainly the set of coordination conjunctions and also the types of elements that can be coordinated, together with their morphosyntactic properties (such as head initial or head final). Basque is considered a head final language, where many important syntactic features, like case or subordinating conjunction are located at the end of constituents. Coordination in BDT has been annotated in the so called Prague Style (PS, see Figure 4), where the conjunction (represented as S in Fig. 4) is taken as the head, and the conjuncts depend on it. [10] advocates the Mel´cuk style (MS) for parsing Czech, taking the first conjunct as the head, and creating a chain where each element depends on the preceding one (they also test its effectiveness with Arabic and Slovene). Being Basque head-final, we propose two symmetric variations of MS. In the first one (v(ersion)1 in Figure 4) the coordinated elements will all be dependents of the last conjunct (which will be the head), going from left to right. In the second version (v2), the final conjunct is again the head, and the coordination conjunction dependent on it, while the rest of the dependents attach to the conjunction. Figure 5 shows the effect of applying the v1 transformation to the tree in Figure 3.

Table 1. Top scores for Basque dependency parsing.

	System	LAS
CoNLL 2007	Nivre et al. [12]	76.94%
	Carreras [3]	75.75%
	Titov and Henderson [14]	75.49%
	Hall et al. (singlemalt) [8]	74.99%

3.3 Impact of transformations

Figure 5 shows that an important number of arcs can be modified. A negative consequence could be that the original tree structure could be lost. This would have the effect that the expected improvement could be compensated by the noise introduced by the algorithms. In this regard, we have evaluated that the transformations can be recovered with more than 97% precision.

4 Evaluation

Training and testing of the system have been performed on the same datasets presented at the CoNLL 2007 shared task, which will allow for direct comparison of the results (see Table 1). The best system obtained a score of 76.94% on Labeled Attachment Score (LAS). This system combined six different variants of a base parser (Maltparser), being the first system in 5 (out of 11) languages, competing with 19 systems in the case of Basque.

Our work will consist in applying different treebank transformations using the same treebank and the same base parser, so we can consider the last system in Table 1 as our baseline. The singlemalt parser described in [8] obtained the fifth position at CoNLL 2007. This system tried to optimize Maltparser's results on BDT by tuning parameters and selecting different training configurations. This system applied the projectivization transformation (T_P).

Evaluation was performed dividing the treebank in two sets: training set (50,000 tokens, using 10-fold cross validation) and test set (5,000 tokens). Table 2[4] presents the LAS scores of the different tests. First, we calculated the result for the system trained in the absence of morphosyntactic features (except POS and CPOS), which

[4] Statistical significance was assessed using Dan Bikel's randomized parsing evaluation comparator with the default setting of 10,000 iterations (*: Statistically significant, with $p < 0.05$; (**: Statistically significant, with $p < 0.01$)

Table 2. Evaluation results
(F+: feature optimization, T_P, T_C, T_S: transformations for projectivization, coordination and subordinated sentences).

		LAS			
	System	**10-fold cross validation**		**Test**	
1	Without morphological features	69.93% 68.35%		66.89%	
2	**Full morphology (baseline)**	76.15%		74.52%	
3	Hall et al., 2007 (full morphology + T_P) [8]	-		74.99%	(+0.47)
4	T_P	76.59%	(+0.44)	**75.54%	(+1.02)
5	$T_{C(MS)}$	72.05%	(-4.10)	69.99%	(-4.53)
6	$T_{C(v1)}$	76.43%	(+0.28)	**75.25%	(+0.73)
7	$T_{C(v2)}$	76.35%	(+0.20)	**74.93%	(+0.41)
8	T_S	76.06%	(-0.09)	73.94%	(-0.58)
9	F_+	75.98%	(-0.17)	75.01%	(+0.49)
10	$T_S + T_P + T_C$	77.32%	(+1.17)	*75.84%	(+1.32)
11	$T_S + T_P$	77.03%	(+0.88)	*75.44%	(+0.92)
12	$F_+ + T_P + T_{C(v1)}$	76.55%	(+0.40)	**75.89%	(+1.37)
13	$F_+ + T_{C(v1)} + T_S + T_P$	77.52%	(+1.37)	**76.51%	(+2.03)
14	$F_+ + T_S + T_P + T_{C(v1)}$	77.52%	(+1.37)	****76.80%**	(+2.28)

gives 66.89% LAS. The second row shows the results using the full set of morphological features, which we take as the baseline, as it presents a system optimized on the basic BDT version (regarding coordination, this version contained the original Prague Style annotation). The second and third rows in Table 2 can be considered a strong baseline, as the CoNLL systems tested many variants of training and parse configurations, mainly taking into account morphological features, that are crucial when dealing with morphologically rich languages.

The table shows the LAS scores calculated on several of the multiple combinations that were experimented. Rows 5, 6, and 7 show the effect of transforming coordinate structures, compared to the baseline (PS, row 2). MS presents the worst results (-4.53 lower than PS on the test set). They also shows that v1 and v2 transformations are more suitable than PS as the target representation. A partial explanation can be found in the effect of "short-dependency preference", as MS presents the longest average dependency-length, followed by PS, v2 and v1. The rest of the tests were performed using the best transformation (v1).

The results show how the application of all kinds of transformations improves significantly the results, giving a best score of 76.80% (14th row) on the test set, which is near the best CoNLL 2007 (combined) system.

The table also shows how the order of application of the tree transformation affects the overall results in both cross validation and test set. For example, T_S is dependent on T_P, as the results vary changing their relative order of application. We corroborated this result when examining the transformed treebanks, and found that T_S leads to loss of projectivity, adding a new set of non-projective arcs. This implies that the results are better if T_S precedes T_P. We made a study of the relations involved between subordinated sentences and their heads, such as cmod (clausal modifier) or xcomp_subj (clausal complement acting as subject), and found that T_S maintained recall on the set of subordinating dependency relations and also augmented precision significantly (for dependencies that link subordinate and main sentences, recall and precision increase 3.05% and 4.13%, respectively).

5 Related work

Collins [4] applied his parser to Czech, a highly-inflected language, which shares several characteristics with Basque. [6] applies Collin's parser to Spanish, concluding that morphological information improves the analyzer.

[7] experiments the use of several types of morphosyntactic information in the analysis of Turkish, showing how the richest the information improves precision. In a related work, Eryiğit and Oflazer (2006) also show that using morphemes as the unit of analysis (instead of words) gets better results, in line with T_S results

[6] conclude that an integrated model of morphological disambiguation and syntactic parsing in Hebrew Treebank parsing, improves the results of a pipelined approach. Dividing words into morphemes fits into this idea, as we postpone the treatment of subordination morphemes from morphology to syntax.

[9, 10] present the application of pseudoprojective and coordination transformations to several languages using maltparser, showing that they improves the results. As for coordination, they only test the PS and MS variants.

6 Conclusions

We have tested a number of transformations in the Basque Dependency Treebank, such as:

- Feature optimization. Basque is a morphologically rich language and presents many opportunities to tune the set of morphosyntactic features, adding, deleting, generalizing or specializing features.

- Projectivization. This is a language independent transformation already tested in several languages.
- We also tested two language specific transformations, such as coordination and modification of subordinated sentences. They cause important changes in the trees, but also help to improve results. In the case of coordination, we have shown that it is dependent on the specific features of each language.
- We also have found that the order of transformations can be relevant. This effect opens the study of which factors affect the order of transformations, as the creation of non projective arcs or the average length of dependency arcs.

Overall, one of the applied transformations is totally language-independent (projectivization, T_P). T_C (coordination) can be considered in the middle, as it depends on the general characteristics of the language. Finally, feature optimization, and the transformation of subordinated sentences (T_S) are specific to the treebank and intrinsecally linked to the agglutinative nature of Basque. The transformations affect a considerable number of dependencies (between 5.94% and 11.97% of all arcs). The best system, after applying all the transformations, obtains a 76.80% LAS (2.24% improvement over the baseline) on the test set, which is the best reported result for Basque dependency parsing using a single parser, and close to the better published result for a combined parser (76.94%).

The results on feature optimization do not allow us to extract a definite conclusion, as it does not help on development data but gives an improvement on test data. [7] argues that "adding inflectional features as atomic values was better than taking certain subsets with linguistic intuition …" due to the ability of SVMs to do this successfully. However, Table 2 shows that feature optimization slightly increases LAS when transformations are combined (see the improvement in $T_S + T_P + T_C$ with and without F+).

$T_S + T_P$ shows how the use of morphological information gives a substantial improvement in accuracy, even when the number of modified dependency links is modest in relation with the full size of the treebank (this transformation affects 5.94% of all arcs). Another interesting result is that when applying several types of transformations, the order of application is significant, as earlier transformations can condition the following ones. This has been demonstrated in the case of T_S, which introduces a new set of non-projective arcs, and does not give an improvement unless it is combined with T_P. The relations among the rest of the transformations deserve future examination, as the actual results do not allow us to extract a precise conclusion. For example, T_C seems to be independent of the rest of transformations.

7 Acknowledgements

This research was supported in part by the Basque Government (EPEC-RS: Basque corpus annnotated with argumental structures and semantic roles, S-PE08UN48) and the University of the Basque Country (EHU-EJIE: a semantically annotated corpus for Basque, EJIE07/05).

8 References

[1] Itziar Aduriz, Maria J. Aranzabe, Jose M. Arriola, Aitziber Atutxa, Arantza Diaz de Ilarraza, Aitzpea Garmendia and Maite Oronoz. 2003. Construction of a Basque dependency treebank. Workshop on Treebanks and Linguistic Theories.

[2] Dan Bikel. 2004. On the Parameter Space of Generative Lexicalized Statistical Parsing Models. PhD Thesis, University of Pennsylvania.

[3] Xavier Carreras. 2007. Experiments with a high-order projective dependency parser. In Proceedings of the CoNLL 2007 Shared Task (EMNLP-CoNLL).

[4] Michael Collins. 1999. Head-Driven Statistical Models for Natural Language Parsing. Ph.D. thesis, Univ. of Pennsylvania.

[5] Shay B. Cohen and Noah A. Smith. 2007. Joint Morphological and Syntactic Disambiguation. In Proceedings of the CoNLL 2007 Shared Task.

[6] Brooke Cowan and Michael Collins. 2005. Morphology and Reranking for the Statistical Parsing of Spanish. In Proceedings of EMNLP 2005.

[7] Gülsen Eryiğit, Joakim Nivre and Kemal Oflazer. 2008. Dependency Parsing of Turkish. Computational Linguistics, Vol. 34 (3).

[8] Johan Hall, Jens Nilsson, Joakim Nivre J., Eryigit G., Megyesi B., Nilsson M. and Saers M. 2007. Single Malt or Blended? A Study in Multilingual Parser Optimization. Proceedings of the CoNLL Shared Task EMNLP-CoNLL.

[9] Timo Järvinen, Pasi Tapanainen. 1998. Towards an Implementable Dependency Grammar. Workshop on Processing of Dependency-Based Grammars, COLING-ACL.

[10] Jens Nilsson, Joakim Nivre and Johan Hall. 2007. Tree Transformations for Inductive Dependency Parsing. In Proceedings of the 45th Annual Meeting of the ACL.

[11] Joakim Nivre, Johan Hall, Jens Nilsson, Chanev A., Gülsen Eryiğit, Sandra Kübler, Marinov S., and Marsi, E. 2007a. MaltParser: A language-independent system for data-driven dependency parsing. Natural Language Engineering,.

[12] Joakim Nivre, Johan Hall, Sandra Kübler, Ryan McDonald, Jens Nilsson, Sebastian Riedel and Deniz Yuret. 2007b. The CoNLL 2007 Shared Task on Dependency Parsing. In Proceedings of EMNLP-CoNLL 2007, Prague.

[13] Nivre, J. and Nilsson, J. (2005) Pseudo-Projective Dependency Parsing. In Proceedings of the 43rd ACL.

[14] Ivan Titov and James Henderson. 2007. Fast and robust multilingual dependency parsing with a generative latent variable model. Proceedings of EMNLP-CoNLL.

Contextual salience in query-based summarization

Wauter Bosma
CLTL, VU University Amsterdam
Boelelaan 1105, 1081HV Amsterdam
w.bosma@let.vu.nl

Abstract

Discourse theories claim that text gets meaning in context. Most summarization systems do not take advantage of this. They assess the relevance of each passage individually rather than modeling the way context affects the relevance of passages. This paper presents a framework for graph-based summarization in order to model relations in text, so that the passages can be viewed in a broader context. The result is a summarization system which is more in line with discourse theory but still fully automatic. I evaluated the content selection performance of an implementation of the framework in different configurations. The system significantly outperforms a competitive baseline (and participant systems) on the DUC 2005 evaluation set.

Keywords

Query-based summarization, content selection, semantic networks, discourse structure, graph theory.

1 Introduction

One of the challenges in automatic summarization is content selection – deciding what should be in a summary, and what shouldn't. Summarization systems typically do this by determining the relevance of each passage independently, and then composing a summary of the top passages. Classical features for scoring sentences include the presence of cue phrases, term frequency, stop word lists, etc. [4, 7].

Systems which assess the relevance of each sentence individually violate insights in discourse organization (e.g., [9]), which claim that meaning is tightly related to discourse organization. The meaning in a text is not merely the sum of the meaning in its passages, but a passage should be interpreted in the context shaped by other passages. For example, given the two passages in Fig. 1, the second passage had little meaning if the context provided by the first would be omitted. Hence, a generic summarization system should include the second sentence in a summary only if the first (or similar) is also included. Recently, summarization systems have broadened their scope from generic single document summarization to multi-document summarization, query-based summarization and update summarization [11]. These summarization tasks have made the need for dealing with issues like redundancy and coherence even more critical. For instance, in case of query-based summarization, the query is part of the summary's context. Update summarization extends the context to prior knowledge, represented by a number of documents which are assumed to be read by the user.

A number of ad-hoc solutions to redundancy and coherence emerged in response to the increasingly complex summarization tasks. For instance, [3] introduced the concept of *marginal relevance*: i.e., that the salience of a content unit is reduced by its redundancy with respect to the summary thus far. [1] divided the source into topics by identifying *lexical chains*. They composed summaries of one sentence from each of the strongest topics, as to maximize coverage. The summarization system of [2] prefers to include sentences in the summary which have a coherence relation to another summary sentence. Each of these answers to the problem of coherence represent a small change to an existing summarization system, rather than a new methodology based on the notion of coherence. Some summarization systems (e.g., [10, 13]) do assign a prominent and explicit role to coherence relations, but they require high level knowledge which can only be annotated manually. A fully automatic graph-based summarization system was built by [5], but their aim was to select sentences which represent a particular (sub)topic in the text, rather than to model coherence or contextual salience.

This paper presents a graph-based framework for content selection in automatic summarization which is based on *contextual salience* – all evidence of salience of a particular passage is based on the salience of related passages (its context). In the evaluation setting, the features used to calculate salience include a graph to express relations between sentences of the same document based on cosine similarity, and a graph to express redundancy, also based on cosine similarity. Section 2 describes the evaluated task and the data set used for evaluation. Section 3 describes the summarization framework. Section 4 describes the experiments to evaluate the framework, and section 5 describes the results.

1A	A commercial airliner crashed in northwestern Iran on Wednesday.
1B	All 168 people on board were killed.

Fig. 1: *Related passages.*

2 Evaluation procedure

The DUC 2006 data set is used in this paper for training, and the DUC 2005 data set is used for testing.[1] This is possible because the data sets for DUC 2005 and DUC 2006 are similar. The task posed by the evaluation set is to automatically generate a summary of a maximum of 250 words, given a *topic*. A topic consists of a title, a query, and a set of source documents. The summary should answer the query, using the source documents. An example of a topic is given in Fig. 2. The DUC 2006 document set consists of 50 topics with 25 source documents each. The DUC 2005 document set consists of 50 topics with 25–50 source documents each (approx. 32 on average).

The summarization task is given to professional human summarizers as well as automatic summarization systems. The human summaries are used as *reference summaries* for evaluating *candidate summaries* (i.e., generated summaries). Each DUC 2005 topic has six corresponding reference summaries; each DUC 2006 topic has four. I use Rouge-2 (i.e. bigram recall with respect to reference summaries) and Rouge-SU4 (skip bigram recall) as performance metrics for evaluation [6], because these metrics are also used (with the same configuration) at DUC 2005 and DUC 2006. Although Rouge metrics provide only a partial evaluation of a summarization system, they are very suitable for these experiments since they require no manual intervention. Other evaluation methods (including extrinsic methods) may be applied at a later stage.

To measure if one summarization algorithm performs better (or worse) than another with a particular metric, I count the number of topics for which it outperformed the other, and vice versa. Then, an approximate randomization test is run to measure statistical significance.

Title:	former President Carter's international activities
Query:	Describe former President Carter's international efforts including activities of the Carter Center.

Fig. 2: *A DUC 2006 topic (D0650E).*

3 A framework for summarization

The aim of this paper is to investigate the content selection sub task of summarization. Nonetheless, the evaluation methods used are designed to measure the quality of abstracts, and require a full summarization system. I briefly describe the summarization system, and then focus on the content selection components. The summarization system consists of the following components.

Segmentation. The source documents as well as the query are segmented into sentences. In addition to the textual content, the document name, the paragraph number and sentence number are associated with each sentence. The document name can be used to detect whether sentences are from the same document, or whether they are query sentences. Paragraph boundaries are derived from annotations provided with the source documents. The segmenter also attempts to remove meta data from the text, such as the date and location of publication. These meta data are not part of the running text and may introduce noise in the summary.

Feature extraction. The source text and the query are processed and converted to a feature graph to prepare for content selection. Multiple modules may be used in parallel so that multiple graphs are generated. This may include coherence analysis, measuring redundancy, etc. The generated graphs are integrated into a combined graph, as described later.

Salience estimation. A salience value is derived for each sentence from the (possibly combined) feature graph.

Presentation. A summary is created using the most salient content units, up to the word limit of 250 words. If adding the next-salient sentence would cause the word limit to be exceeded, no more sentences are added. Where possible, the linear ordering of the sentences in the source text is retained. If the summary contains sentences from multiple source documents, sentences from the document containing the largest number of sentences are presented first. Although the ordering of the sentences may be important for readability, it has little effect on Rouge scores.

The components of *segmentation* and *presentation* remain constant. The experiments described in the next section are used to compare different methods for *feature extraction* and *salience estimation.*

4 Experiments in query-based summarization

This section describes a number of experiments, starting with a rudimentary summarization system, and adding features to build increasingly sophisticated systems. The modular summarization framework allows for the flexibility to add feature graphs or replace the salience estimation algorithm.

The first summarization system, called *query-relevance*, just measures the similarity of candidate sentences with query sentences. The only feature graph – the *query-relevance graph* – relates candidate sentences to query sentences by cosine similarity. The most similar candidate sentences are included in the summary.

Next, a feature graph is added which relates candidate sentences to other sentences of the same document, by means of cosine similarity. This is the *cohesion graph.* Two salience estimation algorithms are used: an adapted version of the *normalized centrality* algorithm, first published in [5], and the *probabilistic relevance* algorithm.

Finally, another feature graph is added – the *redundancy graph* – which relates candidate sentences to sentences of another document, by means of cosine

[1] These data are available from `http://duc.nist.gov`

Table 1: *Performance on DUC 2006 data: Rouge scores, and the system rank among 36 systems (bracketed) if it had participated in DUC 2006.*

System	Rouge-2		Rouge-SU4	
Query-relevance	0.0818	(11)	0.138	(11)
Normalized c.	0.0820	(11)	0.136	(11)
Probabilistic r.	0.0888	(3)	0.143	(7)
Redundancy-aware n.c.	0.0929	(2)	0.150	(2)
Redundancy-aware p.r.	0.0930	(2)	0.150	(2)

Table 2: *Percentage of DUC 2006 topics (Rouge-2/Rouge-SU4) for which one system (rows) beat another (columns). Note that percentages do not add up to 100 if both systems receive the same score for at least one topic. The compared systems are (a) query-relevance (Δ_q); (b) normalized centrality ($\Delta_{q,c}$); (c) probabilistic relevance ($\Delta_{q,c}$); (d) normalized centrality ($\Delta_{q,c,r}$); (e) probabilistic relevance ($\Delta_{q,c,r}$; P_r).*

%	(a)	(b)	(c)	(d)	(e)
(a)	–	50/52	34[a]/28[a]	30[a]/28[a]	26[a]/26[a]
(b)	46/48	–	34[a]/36[b]	38[b]/34[a]	30[a]/24[a]
(c)	64[a]/70[a]	66[a]/62[b]	–	56/58	44/50
(d)	66[a]/66[a]	60[b]/62[a]	42/42	–	30[a]/30[a]
(e)	70[a]/72[a]	68[a]/72[a]	48/46	64[a]/68[a]	–

[a] Significant at $p < 0.01$.
[b] Significant at $p < 0.05$.
[c] Significant at $p < 0.1$.

similarity. This graph can be used in combination with the previously used graphs as well as both salience estimation algorithms.

The remainder of this section describes the summarization systems in greater detail, and gives preliminary comparative performance statistics on DUC 2006 data. Table 1 gives an overview of the Rouge scores of each system. A pair-wise comparison of the systems is shown in Table 2.

4.1 Query-relevance

A simple form of query-based summarization is to determine sentence salience by measuring its cosine similarity with the query. The sentences most similar to the query are presented as a summary. This constitutes a competitive baseline system for query-based summarization. The graph used for salience estimation is the graph where each candidate sentence is related to each query sentence, and the strength of this relation is the cosine similarity of the two sentences. The sentences closest to a query sentence are then included in the summary. The cosine similarity graph is generated in three steps:

1. words of all sentences are stemmed using Porter's stemmer [12];
2. the inverse document frequency (IDF) is calculated for each word;
3. the cosine similarity of each candidate sentence and each query sentence is calculated using the *tf · idf* weighting scheme.

Stemming is a way to normalize syntactic variation. The inverse document frequency is used to weight words higher than other words if they occur in fewer sentences. Rare words typically characterize the sentence they appear in to a greater extent than frequent words.

Using this method for calculating IDF values for query terms as well appeared not appropriate because there is a mismatch between the language use in the query and in the source documents. For instance, queries frequently used phrases such as 'Discuss ...' or 'Describe ...'. These words have a low frequency in the source documents, and are thus assigned a high IDF value, but they are hardly descriptive if they appear in the query. Therefore, the IDF values for query terms are calculated from the set of sentences from all DUC 2006 queries instead of the source document sentences specific for the topic.

The query-relevance graph (δ_q) is defined by a function determining the strength of the relation between two sentences:

$$\begin{aligned} \delta_q(i,j) &= cosim(i,j) \qquad &, \text{if } i \in Q;\ j \in S \\ \delta_q(i,j) &= 0 \qquad &, \text{otherwise} \end{aligned} \tag{1}$$

where $\delta_q(i,j)$ is the strength of the relation between sentences i and j; Q is the set of query sentences; S is the set of candidate sentences; $cosim(i,j)$ is the cosine similarity of sentences i and j. The strength of a relation is a value in the range of 0 (no relation) to 1 (a strong relation).

The query-relevance $R_{query\_relevance}(j)$ of a sentence j is then calculated as follows.

$$R_{query\_relevance}(j) = \min_{q \in Q} \delta_q(q,j) \tag{2}$$

where $R_{query\_relevance}(j)$ is the salience of sentence j; Q is the set of query sentences.

A summary is then generated from the most salient sentences. The results are shown in Table 1 and Table 2.

4.2 Contextual relevance

The *cohesion graph* (δ_c) is added as a feature graph for calculating contextual relevance. This graph is constructed indentically to the way the query-relevance graph is constructed, except that it relates candidate sentences of the same document, rather than query sentences and candidate sentences.

The graphs δ_q and δ_c are integrated into a single multi-graph $\Delta_{q,c}$. A multi-graph is a graph that can have two edges between the same two vertices, expressing simultaneous relations. As a result, not a single relation but a set of relations hold between two sentences, and each relation may have a different strength between 0 and 1. The integrated graph is expressed as follows.

$$\Delta_{q,c}(i,j) = \{w_q\delta_q(i,j), w_c\delta_c(i,j)\} \tag{3}$$

where $\Delta_{q,i}(i,j)$ is a set of values, each representing the strength of an edge from i to j in the multi-graph $\Delta_{q,c}$. The values of $w_q, w_c \in [0..1]$ are weighting factors. The smaller w_q and the greater w_c, the greater the relative importance of indirect evidence of relevance, and the more sentences are selected which are not directly query-relevant.

The salience estimation algorithms calculate the salience of each sentence, given a graph of relations between sentences. A relation from sentence X to sentence Y increases the relevance of Y if X is relevant. This immediately poses a problem if X is a candidate sentence, because initially, its relevance is unknown, and the relevance of Y depends on the relevance of X. Literature provides two solutions [8, 5], both of which iteratively recalculate the salience of a sentence from a similarity graph and the salience of neighboring sentences. Following this process, relevance is calculated as follows.

1. Initiate the salience of all candidate sentences (source document sentences) at 0. The salience of query sentences is initiated at 1.
2. Recalculate the salience of each candidate sentence, using the feature graphs and the salience of neighboring (i.e. related) sentences. Salient sentences increase the salience of their neighbors.
3. Repeat step 2 unless the change in salience in the last iteration falls below a certain (pre-defined) threshold.

I used two salience estimation algorithms, *normalized centrality* and *probabilistic relevance*. They differ in how they recalculate relevance (step 2).

The first, based on [5], recalculates the salience by dividing the salience of each sentence among its neighboring sentences. Because no salience is created or lost (the total 'amount of salience' of all sentences remains approximately constant), I call this *normalized centrality*.

The *probabilistic relevance* algorithm regards the feature graph as a probabilistic semantic network. The salience of a sentence represents the probability that the sentence is relevant, and a relation from sentence X to Y is the probability that Y is relevant, given X is relevant.

Normalized centrality

At each iteration, the normalized centrality is calculated as follows:

$$\begin{aligned} \mu_j(t) &= 1 && \text{, if } j \in Q \\ \mu_j(0) &= 0 && \text{, if } j \in S \\ \mu_j(t+1) &= \frac{d}{\|D\|} + (1-d)\sum_{i \in D} x(i,j) && \text{, if } j \in S \\ x(i,j) &= \sum_{r \in \Delta_{q,c} ij} r \cdot \mu_i(t) \cdot degree(i)^{-1} \end{aligned} \quad (4)$$

where $D = Q \cup S$; and $\mu_j(t)$ is the normalized centrality of sentence j at iteration $t \geq 0$; and $\Delta_{q,c} ij$ is the set of edges between i and j in the relevance graph. The constant d is a small value which is required in generic summarization in order to guarantee a salience ranking under all circumstances by giving each sentence a small prior non-zero salience.[2] The degree of a sentence i in the graph ($degree(i)$) is measured as the number of outgoing edges:

$$degree(i) = \sum_{k \in D} \sum_{(r \in \Delta_{q,c}(i,k))} r \quad (5)$$

The result is a salience value μ between 0 and 1 associated with each passage. The content units with the highest salience values are selected for inclusion in the summary. In this configuration, normalization cancels out the effect of graph weighting: changing the graph weights w_q and w_c (eq. 3) does not affect the summaries in any way because the relevance distribution is normalized and the sets of sentences with outgoing edges in δ_q and δ_c are disjunct.

As shown in Table 2, the average quality of normalized centrality summaries does not significantly differ (at $p < 0.05$) from the quality of query-relevance summarization.

Probabilistic relevance

In the probabilistic approach, contrary to the normalized approach, the relevance of Y given X is unaffected by any other sentence whose relevance may depend on X. Viewing edges as relevance probabilities also has implications on how evidence of relevance is combined. Rather than accumulating weighted relevance of neighbors, the relevance of a sentence is calculated as the product of inverse conditional probabilities. This is based on the idea that, if we have several pieces of evidence that a sentence is salient, it suffices if one of them is true. The probabilistic relevance algorithm calculates salience as follows.

$$\begin{aligned} \nu_j(t) &= 1 && \text{, if } j \in Q \\ \nu_j(0) &= 0 && \text{, if } j \in S \quad (6) \\ \nu_j(t+1) &= 1 - \prod_{(i \in Q \cup S)} z(i,j) && \text{, if } j \in S \\ z(i,j) &= \prod_{r \in \Delta_{q,c}(i,j)} (1 - r \cdot \nu_i(t) \cdot y) \end{aligned}$$

where $\nu_j(t)$ is the probabilistic relevance value of sentence j at iteration t. The value of y is the *decay* value, a global constant in the range $\langle 0..1 \rangle$. The constant y has a function similar to the constant d in normalized centrality: it is necessary to ensure that the salience value keeps increasing at each iteration.

The graph weights w_q and w_c are determined by measuring Rouge-2 performance for different weight values. First, w_q is incremented in steps of 0.1 from 0 to 1 with $w_c = 1$, and then w_c is incremented in steps of 0.1 from 0 to 1 with $w_q = 1$. The optimal weight settings are $w_q = 1$; $w_c = 0.1$ (see Table 1 for Rouge scores). As shown in Table 2, the system significantly outperforms the query-relevance system ($p < 0.01$ for Rouge-2 and Rouge-SU4) and the normalized centrality system ($p < 0.05$ for Rouge-2 and Rouge-SU4).

[2] Throughout this section, the value of 0.15 is used, as suggested in [5], but the actual value of d has no effect on the final salience ranking as long as it is non-zero.

4.3 Redundancy-aware summarization

One of the assumptions usually made implicitly in the design of single-document summarization systems, is that the source document does not contain redundancy. Consequently, there is no risk of including a sentence in the summary which does not contain any information not already present. This changes when a summary is generated from multiple source documents, where non-redundancy of sentences from different documents cannot be taken for granted. The content selection procedures outlined previously concentrate entirely on relevancy, not redundancy. However, in multi-document summarization, presented content should be relevant to the query and novel with respect to what is already mentioned in the summary. In other words, salience comprises both relevance and novelty.

To accommodate representing novelty, the model is extended with a redundancy feature graph P which is used in addition to the previously mentioned relevancy feature graph Δ. Similarly to relevance, redundancy relations have a strength in the range [0..1]. The strength of a redundancy relation between two sentences expresses the likelihood that a sentence is redundant, given the fact that another sentence is redundant. The redundancy of sentence j, given sentence i, is defined by $\delta_r(i,j)$. The form of the redundancy graph is identical to that of the relevance graph. The strengths of relations in the redundancy feature graph δ_r are defined as follows:

$$\begin{aligned}\delta_r(i,j) &= cosim(i,j) \quad &, \text{if } i,j \in S;\ doc(i) \neq doc(j) \\ \delta_r(i,j) &= 0 \quad &, \text{otherwise}\end{aligned} \tag{7}$$

The redundancy-aware summarization system uses a set of redundancy feature graphs P for determining salience of sentences, in addition to the relevancy feature graphs Δ:

$$\begin{aligned}\Delta_{q,o,r}(i,j) &= \{w_q \cdot \delta_q(i,j), w_c \cdot \delta_c(i,j), w_{r\Delta} \cdot \delta_r(i,j)\} \\ P_r(i,j) &= \{w_{rP} \cdot \delta_r(i,j)\}\end{aligned} \tag{8}$$

where $\delta_q(i,j)$, $\delta_c(i,j)$ and $\delta_r(i,j)$ are the query-relevance graph, the cohesion graph, and the redundancy graph respectively. The set of relations between sentences i and j are represented by $\Delta_{q,c,r}(i,j)$ (relevancy) and $P_r(i,j)$ (redundancy). Since redundancy implies 'relatedness', I regard a redundancy graph a special case of a relevance graph. Therefore, δ_r is not only included in P_r but also in $\Delta_{q,c,r}$.

The calculation of redundancy-adjusted salience was inspired by [3]. First, the relevance of each sentence is calculated using $\Delta_{q,c,r}$. Then, the novelty is calculated – novelty is the reciprocal of redundancy. If two sentences are redundant, this affects only the novelty of the less-relevant of the two. The stronger the redundancy relation, the greater the reduction of novelty. Novelty is calculated as follows:

$$\begin{aligned}N(j) &= \prod_{i \in F_j} \prod_{r \in P_r(i,j)} (1 - r \cdot R(i)) \\ F_j &= \{k : S \mid R(k) > R(j)\}\end{aligned} \tag{9}$$

where $N(j)$ is a value in the range [0..1], representing the novelty of sentence j; $P_r(i,j)$ is a set of redundancy relations, expressing the redundancy of j given i; F_j is the set of content units more relevant than j. The function $R(i)$ denotes the relevance of sentence i, as previously calculated.

Now, the redundancy-adjusted salience can be calculated as the product of relevancy and novelty:

$$\sigma_j = R(j) \cdot N(j) \tag{10}$$

where σ_j is the redundancy-adjusted salience of sentence j. The calculation of σ_j ensures that:

- if one content unit is selected, all content units redundant to that unit are less likely to be selected: if two content units are redundant with respect to each other, the salience of the less-relevant content unit is reduced;
- redundancy of a content unit does not prevent relevancy to propagate: a redundant content unit may still be relevant.

The graph weights are determined by starting from the optimal values for w_q and w_c in section 4.2. The remaining weights are determined by means of a similar procedure as in section 4.2: first, $w_{r\Delta}$ is incremented in steps of 0.1 from 0 to 1 with $w_{rP} = 0$, and then w_{rP} is incremented in steps of 0.1 from 0 to 1 without changing the other weights.

For the normalized centrality algorithm, the resulting optimal weight settings are $w_q = 1$; $w_c = 1$ and $w_{rP} = 0$; $w_{r\Delta} = 1$. Increasing the value of $w_{rP} = 0$ has no effect on the quality of the summaries. Table 1 shows the system's performance with these settings on DUC 2006 data. As shown in Table 2, the redundancy-aware normalized centrality system significantly outperforms the normalized centrality system ($p < 0.05$ for Rouge-2 and Rouge-SU4).

For the probabilistic relevance algorithm, the resulting optimal weight settings are $w_q = 1$; $w_c = 0.1$; $w_{r\Delta} = 0.2$, $w_{rP} = 1$. This configuration shows a significant performance gain compared to all previously mentioned systems ($p < 0.01$ for Rouge-2 and Rouge-SU4) except the (non-redundancy aware) probabilistic relevance system. Compared to the latter, the performance was increased but no significant differences were found.

5 Validating the results

The previous section outlined a comparison of different configurations of the summarization framework. However, the way the graph weight configurations are determined implies that the weights are tailored to the DUC 2006 data set. As a result, there is a risk that the weights are overfitted to this particular set. In order to validate the results, I ran the experiments on the DUC 2005 data set with the graph weight configurations determined in section 4.

Fig. 3 shows the average Rouge-2 and Rouge-SU4 scores achieved with the DUC 2005 corpus. Table 3 shows an overview of the pair-wise significance tests. The redundancy-aware probabilistic relevance system significantly outperformed all other systems when Rouge-2 is used ($p < 0.1$), and all except the

Table 3: *Percentage of DUC 2005 topics (Rouge-2/Rouge-SU4) for which one system (rows) beat another (columns). Note that percentages do not add up to 100 if both systems receive the same score for at least one topic. The compared systems are (a) query-relevance (Δ_q); (b) normalized centrality ($\Delta_{q,c}$); (c) probabilistic relevance ($\Delta_{q,c}$); (d) normalized centrality ($\Delta_{q,c,r}$); (e) probabilistic relevance ($\Delta_{q,c,r}$; P_r).*

%	(a)	(b)	(c)	(d)	(e)
(a)	–	46/44	42/42	50/50	40[c]/40[c]
(b)	52/54	–	50/34[a]	50/54	38[b]/34[a]
(c)	54/58	50/66[a]	–	58[b]/64[a]	36[c]/42
(d)	44/44	46/44	38[b]/36[a]	–	30[a]/30[a]
(e)	58[c]/60[c]	60[b]/66[a]	54[c]/54	60[a]/70[a]	–

[a] Significant at $p < 0.01$.
[b] Significant at $p < 0.05$.
[c] Significant at $p < 0.1$.

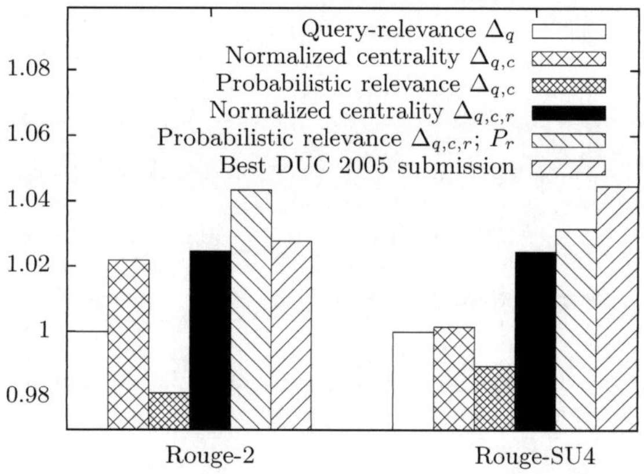

Fig. 3: *Indexed performance on DUC 2005 data:* 1 *indicates the performance of the query-relevance system.*

redundancy-aware normalized centrality system according to Rouge-SU4. This system would have ranked first (Rouge-2) or second (Rouge-SU4) if it had participated in DUC 2005.

Note that it is not guaranteed that the combination of graph weights that leads to the best performance has been found. Apart from the risk of overfitting, the number of possible graph weight combinations is infinite and a greater number of graphs makes it more difficult to find the best combination of weights. A future extension would use machine learning methods such as genetic algorithms to be better suited to find the optimal solution. As mentioned before, Rouge measured only one aspect of a summarization system. That said, the results may teach us the following:

1. The graph-based approach to summarization represents a promising direction, given the good results in spite of the superficial linguistic analysis performed by the evaluated systems. Even better results are to be expected when more sophisticated features are used.
2. The probabilistic interpretation of semantic networks (i.e., *probabilistic relevance*) seems to be more suitable for content selection than the social network interpretation (i.e., *normalized centrality*).

6 Conclusion

The aim of this paper is to bring automatic summarization practice in line with insights from discourse theory. To this end, it provides a framework for automatic summarization which is founded on graph theory. The content selection algorithm is entirely based on relations between text passages. The evaluated system is just one implementation of this framework; it can be extended to exploit more textual features, and discourse oriented features in particular. The framework represents a step toward context aware summarization. Previous work on query-based summarization has mainly focused on extracting the set of sentences which best match the query, ignoring their broader context.

The features used for relating sentences are computationally cheap and easy to port to other languages, but knowledge-intensive methods may detect relations between sentences more accurately. Despite this, the graph-based approach showed good results compared to DUC participant systems (the redundancy-aware probabilistic relevance system would have ranked first for Rouge-2 and second for Rouge-SU4 if it had participated in DUC 2005), which indicates that we are on the right track. Further performance gains may be achieved by using more different sources of information for detecting relations, including knowledge-intensive methods such as rhetorical relation detection or anaphora resolution.

References

[1] R. Barzilay and M. Elhadad. Using lexical chains for text summarization. In *Proceedings of the ACL Workshop on Intelligent Scalable Text Summarization*, pages 10–17, Aug. 1997.

[2] S. Blair-Goldensohn and K. McKeown. Integrating rhetorical-semantic relation models for query-focused summarization. In *Proceedings of DUC*, 2006.

[3] J. Carbonell and J. Goldstein. The use of MMR, diversity-based reranking for reordering documents and producing summaries. In *Proceedings of the 21st annual international ACM SIGIR conference on Research and development in information retrieval*, pages 335–336, New York, NY, USA, 1998.

[4] H. Edmundson. New methods in automatic extracting. *Journal of the ACM*, 16(2):264–285, Apr. 1969.

[5] G. Erkan and D. Radev. Lexrank: Graph-based centrality as salience in text summarization. *Journal of Artificial Intelligence Research (JAIR)*, 2004.

[6] C.-Y. Lin. Rouge: a package for automatic evaluation of summaries. In *Proceedings of the ACL workshop: Text Summarization Branches Out*, Barcelona, Spain, 2004.

[7] H. Luhn. The automatic creation of literature abstracts. *IBM Journal of Research and Development*, 2(2):159–165, 1958.

[8] I. Mani and E. Bloedorn. Multi-document summarization by graph search and matching. In *Proceedings of the Fourteenth National Conference on Artificial Intelligence (AAAI'97)*, pages 622–628, 1997.

[9] W. Mann and S. Thompson. Rhetorical Structure Theory: Toward a functional theory of text organization. *Text*, 8:243–281, 1988.

[10] D. Marcu. Discourse trees are good indicators of importance in text. In I. Mani and M. Maybury, ed., *Advances in Automatic Text Summarization*, pages 123–136. MIT Press, 1999.

[11] P. Over, H. Dang, and D. Harman. DUC in context. *Information processing and management*, 43(6):1506–1520, 2007.

[12] M. Porter. Snowball: A language for stemming algorithms, 2001. `http://snowball.tartarus.org/texts/introduction.html`.

[13] F. Wolf and E. Gibson. Representing discourse coherence: A corpus-based study. *Computational Linguistics*, 31(2):249–288, 2005.

Integrating Document Structure into a Multi-Document Summarizer

Aurélien Bossard and Thierry Poibeau
Laboratoire d'Informatique de Paris-Nord
CNRS and Université Paris 13
99, avenue Jean-Baptiste Clément — F-93430 Villetaneuse
{firstname.lastname}@lipn.univ-paris13.fr

Abstract

In this paper, we present a novel approach for automatic summarization. CBSEAS, the system implementing this approach, integrates a method to detect redundancy at its very core, in order to produce more expressive summaries than previous approaches. The evaluation of our system during TAC 2008 —the Text Analysis Conference— revealed that, even if our system performed well on blogs, it had some failings on news stories. A *post-mortem* analysis of the weaknesses of our original system showed the importance of text structure for automatic summarization, even in the case of short texts like news stories. We describe some ongoing work dealing with these issues and show that first experiments provide a significant improvement of the results.

Keywords

Multi-document Summarization; Text structure; Evaluation; Text Analysis Conference.

1 Introduction

During the past decade, automatic summarization, supported by evaluation campaigns and a large research community, has shown fast and deep improvements. Indeed, the research in this domain is guided by strong industrial needs: fast processing despite ever increasing amount of data.

We have developed a system called CBSEAS that integrates a new method to detect redundancy at its very core, in order to produce more expressive summaries than previous approaches. We have evaluated our system by participating in two tasks of TAC 2008 (the Text Analysis Conference):

- Opinion Task (Summarizing opinions found in blogs);
- Update Task (News stories summarization and detecting updates).

We obtained very competitive results during TAC 2008 on the "Opinion Task". However, our system did not rank as well on the "Update Task". A *post-mortem* analysis of the weaknesses of our original system revealed the importance of text structure for automatic summarization, even in the case of short texts like news stories.

Therefore, we will only focus on the "Update task" in this paper. We present our approach for automatic summarization and the first results of our current work dealing with the detection of document structure along with its integration for the production of summaries. The reader who wants to get information on the system we have developed for the Opinion task —for which we obtained among the best results— may refer to the system description in the TAC 2008 proceedings, see [1].

The rest of this paper is structured as follows: we first give a quick overview of the state of the art. We then describe our system, focusing on the most important novel features implemented and on the results obtained for the TAC 2008 "Update" task. Lastly, we show that news stories structure is meaningful and we detail some preliminary techniques that improve the results.

2 Related Works

Interest in creating automatic summaries began as soon as in the 1950s with the work by Luhn at IBM [8]. Following this line of research, Edmundson [3] proposed a set of features in order to assign a score to each sentence of a corpus and rank them accordingly: the sentences which get the highest scores are the ones to be extracted. The features that Edmundson used were the sentence position (in a news stories for example, the first sentences are the most important ones), the presence of proper names and keywords in the document title, the presence of indicative phrases and the sentence length.

More recently, research has mainly focused on multi-document summarization. In this context, a central issue consists in eliminating redundancy since the risks of extracting two sentences conveying the same information is more important than in the single-document paradigm. Moreover, identifying redundancy is a critical task, as information appearing several times in different documents is supposed to be important.

The "centroid-based summarization" method developed by Radev and his colleagues [9] is probably the most popular one in the field. It consists in identifying the centroid of a cluster of documents, that is to say the terms which best describe the documents to summarize. Then, the sentences to be extracted are the ones that are closest to the centroid. Radev implemented this method in an online multi-document summarizer called MEAD.

Radev further improved MEAD using a method inspired by the concept of *prestige* in social networks. This method called "graph-based centrality" [4] consists in computing similarity between sentences, and then selecting sentences which are considered as "central" in a graph where nodes are sentences and edges are similarities. Sentence selection is then performed by picking the sentences which have been visited most after a random walk on the graph. The main limitation of this method is that it only selects central sentences, which means that most of them can be redundant. It is thus necessary to add a module to detect redundancy before producing the final summary.

In order to avoid dealing with redundancy as a post-processing task, various methods have been proposed to integrate redundancy detection during the summarization process itself. For example, Goldberg [10] uses a "Markov absorbing chain random walk" on a graph representing the different sentences of the corpus to summarize.

MMR-MD, introduced by Carbonnel in [2], is a measure that needs a "passage" (snippet) clustering: all passages considered as paraphrases are grouped into the same clusters. MMR-MD takes into account the similarity to a query, the coverage of a passage (clusters that it belongs to), the content of the passage, the similarity to passages already selected for the summary, the fact that it belongs to a cluster or to a document that has already contributed a passage to the summary. The problem of this measure lies in the clustering method: in the literature, clustering is generally fulfilled using a threshold. If a passage has a similarity to a cluster centroid higher than a threshold, then it is added to this cluster. This threshold has to be specifically defined for each new corpus, which is the main weakness of this approach.

Our method is inspired from these last series of work: we think that it is crucial to integrate redundancy identification as soon as possible, and not as a last processing step. The main novelty of our approach is that we try to better characterize the content of news stories depending on their type. Most summarizers keep using standard features introduced in [3] to rank the sentences and do not take into account the document structure itself. Our goal is to determine the impact of the type and structure of news stories in automatic summarization, since these features have rarely been used.

3 CBSEAS: A Clustering-Based Sentence Extractor for Automatic Summarization

We give in this section a brief overview of our TAC-2008 summarization system. Since we are most interested in the improvements we have added to the system since then, we will not give the full details but the reader may have a look at our TAC-2008 paper to get a more thorough description [1].

for all $e_j inE$
    $C_1 \leftarrow e_j$
for i from 1 to k do
    for j from 1 to i
        center$(C_j) \leftarrow e_m | e_m maximizes \sum_{e_n in C_j} sim(e_m, e_n)$
    for all e_j in E
        $e_j \rightarrow C_l | C_l maximizessim(center(C_l, e_j)$
    add a new cluster: C_i. It initially contains only its center, the worst represented element in its cluster.
done

Fig. 1: *Fast global k-means algorithm*

We assume that, for multi-document summarization, redundant pieces of information are the most important elements to produce a good summary. Therefore, the sentences which carry those pieces of information have to be extracted. Detecting groups of sentences conveying the same information is the first step of our approach. The developed algorithm first establishes the similarities between all sentences of the documents to summarize, and then apply a clustering algorithm — fast global k-means [6] — to the similarity matrix in order to create clusters in which sentences convey the same information.

First, our system ranks all the sentences according to their similarity to the documents centroid, or to the user query if there is one. We have chosen to build up the documents centroid with the m most important terms, importance being reflected by the tf/idf of each terms. We then select, to create a n sentences long summary, the n^2 best ranked sentences. We do so because the clustering algorithm we use to detect sentences conveying the same information, fast global k-means, behaves better when it has to group n^2 elements into n clusters. The similarity with the centroid is a weighted sum of terms appearing in both centroid and sentence, normalized by sentence length.

Once the similarities are computed, we cluster the sentences using fast-global kmeans (description of the algorithm is in figure 1) using the similarity matrix. It works well on a small data set with a small number of dimensions, although it has not yet scaled up as well as we would have expected.

This clustering step completed, we select one sentence per cluster in order to produce a summary that contains most of the relevant information/ideas from the original documents. We do so by choosing the central sentence in each cluster. The central sentence is the one which maximizes the sum of similarities with the other sentences of its cluster. It should be the one that characterizes best the cluster in terms of conveyed information.

The overall process of our summarization system is shown in fig. 2.

4 CBSEAS at TAC 2008

In this section, we briefly describe the TAC 2008 "Update" task and the adaptation we had to implement in order to make our system compliant with the task requirements. Here again, the interested reader can

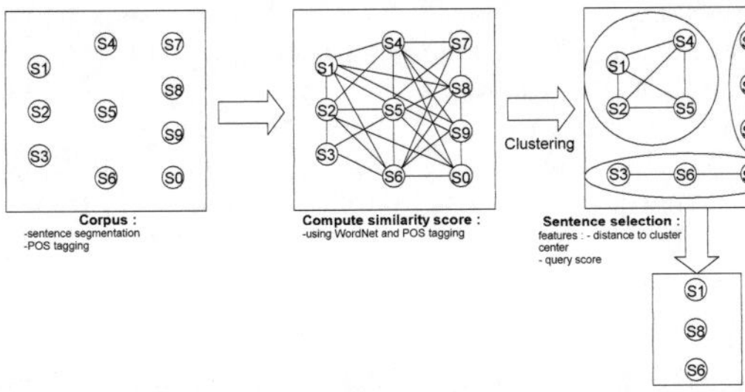

Fig. 2: *Summarization system*

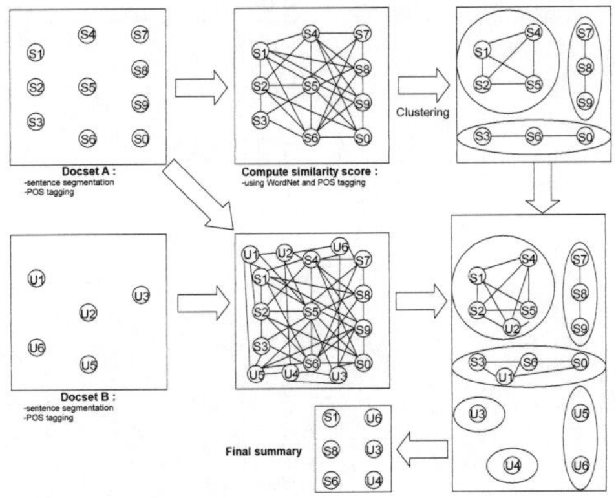

Fig. 3: *CBASES Update system*

refer to [1] for more details.

4.1 Description of the Update Task

The "Update task" consists in generating two types of summaries for each evaluation topic. Each topic is composed of a user query and of two groups of documents. Documents are extracted from the AQUAINT-2 corpus (a collection of news stories issued by several press agencies). The first type of summary is the "standard" one, a simple summary of the first document set. The second type of summary is more complex: it has to summarize the information found in the second document set that was not already present in the first document set. Summaries are to be 100 words long at most.

For the *Update task*, two evaluations were given to participants: the first one using PYRAMID, the second one using ROUGE scores [5]. The PYRAMID score depends on the number of basic semantic units the summary contains which are considered as important by human annotators (the importance of a semantic unit depends on the number of times it appears in the summaries generated by human annotators). Summaries have also been scored using five different scores attributed manually for grammaticality, non-redundancy, structure, fluency and overall responsiveness (responsiveness is a subjective score corresponding to the question "How much would you pay for that summary?"). ROUGE metrics are based on n-gram comparison between the automatic summary and a reference summary which has been written by TAC annotators.

4.2 Adaptation of CBSEAS for the "Update Task"

Our system, CBSEAS, is a "standard" summarization system. We had to adapt it in order to deal with the specific requirements of TAC 2008.

The adaptation for the "Update Task" mainly consisted in managing update. The first step, summarizing the first document set, is done using CBSEAS as it stands. After the selection of sentences for the first document set, we re-compute all sentence similarities including the new sentences (i.e. sentences from the second document set).

We cluster the first document set and mark all the concerned sentences as immobile. Using fast global kmeans, we continue the clustering process by adding new clusters, with the following constraints:

- sentences from the first document set cannot be moved to another cluster;
- the cluster centres from the first clustering must not be recalculated.

Doing so, sentences from the second document set which are supposed to be (semantically) close to sentences from the first document set are added to old clusters, whereas sentences which appear to bring novelty are added to new clusters. These new clusters include the sentences from which the second summary will be produced. Fig. 3 gives an overview of the "Update" system.

The way *update* is managed is very specific to our system, and taking into account its results should distort the pure summarizing results obtained by CBSEAS. For this reason, we will only present in 4.3 the results obtained by the summaries of the first documents sets.

4.3 TAC 2008 Results for the "Update task"

Contrary to our system for the Opinion Task that behaved quite well, the system used for the "Update Task" did not obtain good results. Results presented in fig. 4 are results computed with ROUGE [5], an automatic scoring measure that compares automatic summaries to a gold standard. Manual evaluation has been provided to participants, but the results presented here are those of TAC for CBSEAS 0.2 and results obtained after TAC on the same evaluation dataset for CBSEAS 0.5. We only provide ROUGE results since those can be calculated automatically and, therefore, provide a good basis for comparison (even if we are conscious that a manual evaluation would give a more thorough insight on our results).

CBSEAS 0.2 obtained poor results. Our system tried to always create summaries under the 100 words

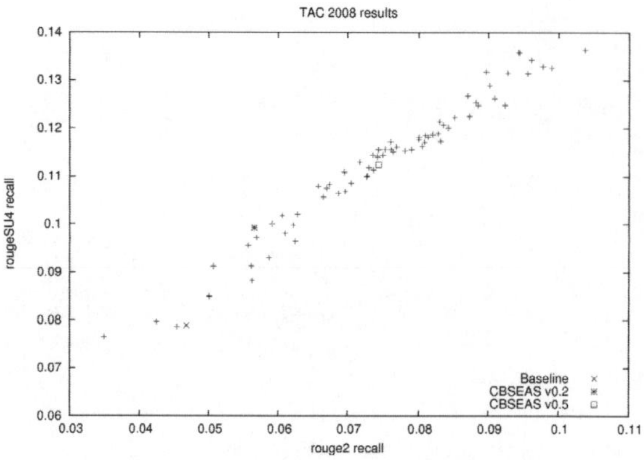

Fig. 4: *Results of our system on the "Update" task*

limit given by TAC organizers, eliminating one by one all the sentences, starting from the worst ranked. Our summaries were 67 words long on average. We corrected that point in CBSEAS 0.5, cutting every summary exactly at 100 words, even if this means removing abruptly the end of a sentence. One can see that CBSEAS 0.5, just by using this trick, obtained significantly better results than CBSEAS 0.2. However, CBSEAS 0.5 is still not among the ten best systems. One hypothesis is that most of the evaluated systems used features that were specifically tuned for this task and this type of texts. For example, favouring the first sentence of an article is a strategy often used. Our system does not use such information.

However, the studies on which those features are based neither take into account the document type nor its structure. That is why we propose to study news stories structure and integrate it to our summarizing system (see section 5).

4.4 Studying the Impact of the Clustering Step

As most of the actual summarization systems do not use any clustering techniques to group related sentences together, we wanted to check whether this clustering phase does improve the summaries quality or not. For this purpose, we made two different tests: one running the system and attributing random classes to the sentences, and the other selecting the n best ranked sentences using the same scoring function, as shown above.

These two tests allow us to see if we get more benefit by eliminating redundant sentences and eventually false positive redundant sentences that could be essential to the creation of a summary than selecting the best ranked sentences, and if our clustering algorithm behaves well for this task in combination to our sentence similarity measure.

We can see in fig. 5 the results of these two experiments, marked as "Random" and "No-Clust". These results prove that the clustering step has an impact on the quality of our summaries. If the redundancy is well managed, the overall results obtained by CBSEAS v0.5 on the two tests tend to show that our system does not necessarily integrate the best suited sentences into the final summary, and does not optimize the number of information that can be found in a text (using for example sentence compression techniques).

In what follows, we propose a method to improve sentence selection, not simply based on statistical measures, but taking into account the document structure in order to weight sentence centrality.

5 Analysing News Story Structure

In this section, we present the work done on the analysis of news story structure.

5.1 Categorizing news stories

A recent study on news stories has been held by N. Lucas [7]. In this study, Lucas proposes the following news story categorization:

- "Commented" news stories (made of two different parts; first part: factual explanation; second part: projection in the future of the expected evolution of the current situation)
- "Elaborated" news stories (concerning more than one event)
- "Action" news stories (reporting a line of events directly linked together; according to N. Lucas, market newswires also belong to this type of news).

She also stated that "commented" news always follow the same temporal presentation. First, the author presents the current event. Then, he gives an explanation of this event based on past events. In the end, the author tells the reader what could or will be the consequences of this event in the future. Identifying these three parts can be very useful, as they follow the classic rule of news writing: the first sentence is the most important one.

Studying the AQUAINT-2 corpus, we identified more types of news:

- Opinion reviews,
- Speech reports,
- Chronologies,
- Comparative news,
- Enumerative news.

The last three categories are very interesting for an automatic summarization task. In fact, they make up at most 5% of the total number of news stories in AQUAINT-2 but, in the training corpus of the "Update Task", they contain 80% of the relevant information. Moreover, they are written in a concise style, and the sentences these news contain have specific characteristics that make them easier to categorize than the other ones:

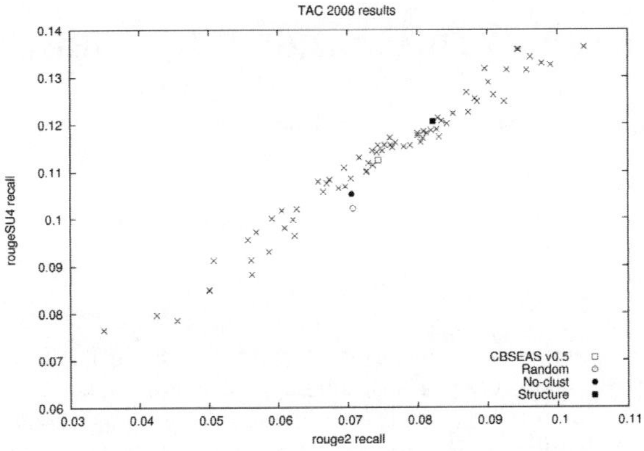

Fig. 5: *Post-Campaigns Experiments*

- Chronologies have almost all their paragraphs beginning with a time reference;
- Chronologies often start with a key phrase such as "*Here is a timeline of events surrounding the election:*";
- Comparative news and enumerative news contain lists which are well structured;
- The elements of a list in a comparative news begin with terms that belong to the same category (for example, country names).

We have implemented a simple categorizer which classifies the news in four groups: chronologies, comparative news, enumerative news and classic news. We plan to develop a more complete system that classifies all the news into the different categories we have identified.

We have evaluated our categorizer on a part of AQUAINT-2 (300 documents) that has been manually annotated. We obtained 100% precision and 81% recall for chronologies, 73% precision and 65% recall for comparative newswire, and 65% precision and 67% recall for enumerative newswire.

We have integrated the categorization to CBSEAS, and forced the system to favor sentences extracted from non-classic news, giving them a 15% bonus on the scoring function. This method is too discriminating, but this is only a preliminary study. We compared the ROUGE-SU4 scores of summaries of groups of documents which contain at least one non classic news and noted a 10% improvement. This ranks our system 21st instead of 39th.

These results encourage us to keep on studying the news structure and integrating it to CBSEAS.

5.2 Future work

Our news categorizer still needs to be worked on: the method to categorize news only recognizes the three categories which are the simplest ones to identify. The other categories have their own properties and ranking sentences by importance using document structure is different from one category to another. News structure and temporality are bound together. Using machine learning techniques on temporaly annotated documents can be a solution to categorize news.

6 Conclusion

We have presented a new approach for multi-document summarization. It uses an unsupervised clustering method to group semantic related sentences together. It can be compared to approaches using sentence neighbourhood [4], because the sentences which are highly related to the highest number of sentences are those which will be extracted first. However, our approach is different since sentence selection is directly dependent on redundancy analysis. This is the reason why redundancy elimination, which is crucial in multi-document summarization, takes place at the same time as sentence selection. We also proposed a way to improve the quality of news summaries using the news story structure. We showed, by integrating some basic structure traits in the summarization process, that it really boosts the quality of the summaries.

References

[1] A. Bossard, M. Généreux, and T. Poibeau. Description of the LIPN Systems at TAC2008: Summarizing Information and Opinions. In *Text Analysis Conference 2008, Workshop on Summarization Tracks*, National Institute of Standards and Technology, Gaithersburg, Maryland USA, 2004.

[2] J. Carbonell and J. Goldstein. The use of MMR, diversity-based reranking for reordering documents and producing summaries. In *SIGIR '98: Proceedings of the 21st annual international ACM SIGIR conference on Research and development in information retrieval*, pages 335–336, New York, NY, USA, 1998. ACM.

[3] H. P. Edmundson and R. E. Wyllys. Automatic Abstracting and Indexing—Survey and Recommendations. *Commun. ACM*, 4(5):226–234, 1961.

[4] G. Erkan and D. R. Radev. LexRank: Graph-based Centrality as Salience in Text Summarization. *Journal of Artificial Intelligence Research (JAIR)*, 2004.

[5] C.-Y. Lin. ROUGE: a Package for Automatic Evaluation of Summaries. In *Proceedings of the Workshop on Text Summarization Branches Out (WAS 2004)*, Barcelona, Spain, 2004.

[6] S. López-Escobar, J. A. Carrasco-Ochoa, and J. F. M. Trinidad. Fast Global k-Means with Similarity Functions Algorithm. In E. Corchado, H. Yin, V. J. Botti, and C. Fyfe, editors, *IDEAL*, volume 4224 of *Lecture Notes in Computer Science*, pages 512–521. Springer, 2006.

[7] N. Lucas. The Enunciative Structure of News Dispatches, a Contrastive Rhetorical Approach. In *Proceedings of the ASLA Conference*, pages 154–164, 2005.

[8] H. Luhn. The Automatic Creation of Literature Abstracts. *IBM Journal*, 2(2):159–165, 1958.

[9] D. Radev, T. Allison, S. Blair-Goldensohn, J. Blitzer, A. Çelebi, S. Dimitrov, E. Drabek, A. Hakim, W. Lam, D. Liu, J. Otterbacher, H. Qi, H. Saggion, S. Teufel, M. Topper, A. Winkel, and Z. Zhu. MEAD — a Platform for Multi-document Multilingual Text Summarization. In *Proceedings of LREC 2004*, Lisbon, Portugal, May 2004.

[10] X. Zhu, A. Goldberg, J. Van Gael, and D. Andrzejewski. Improving Diversity in Ranking using Absorbing Random Walks. *Proceedings of HLT-NAACL*, pages 97–104, 2007.

Cross-Linguistic Sentiment Analysis: From English to Spanish

Julian Brooke
Department of Linguistics
Simon Fraser University
Burnaby, BC, Canada
jab18@sfu.ca

Milan Tofiloski
School of Computing Science
Simon Fraser University
Burnaby, BC, Canada
mta45@sfu.ca

Maite Taboada
Department of Linguistics
Simon Fraser University
Burnaby, BC, Canada
mtaboada@sfu.ca

Abstract

We explore the adaptation of English resources and techniques for text sentiment analysis to a new language, Spanish. Our main focus is the modification of an existing English semantic orientation calculator and the building of dictionaries; however we also compare alternate approaches, including machine translation and Support Vector Machine classification. The results indicate that, although language-independent methods provide a decent baseline performance, there is also a significant cost to automation, and thus the best path to long-term improvement is through the inclusion of language-specific knowledge and resources.

1. Introduction

Sentiment analysis refers to the automatic determination of subjectivity (whether a text is objective or subjective), polarity (positive or negative) and strength (strongly or weakly positive/negative). It is a growing field of research, especially given the gains to be obtained from mining opinions available online. Approaches to sentiment analysis have tackled the problem from two different angles: a word-based or semantic approach, or a machine learning (ML) approach. The word-based approach uses dictionaries of words tagged with their *semantic orientation* (SO), and calculates sentiment by aggregating the values of those present in a text or sentence [17]. The ML approach uses collections of texts that are known to express a favorable or unfavorable opinion as training data, and learns to recognize sentiment based on those examples [13].

Our approach is semantic, and makes use of a series of dictionaries, additionally taking into account the role of negation, intensification and irrealis expressions. We believe that a semantic approach offers the advantage of taking many different aspects of a text into account.

One of the disadvantages of a semantic approach is that the resources necessary for a new domain or a new language need to be built from scratch, whereas a machine-learning approach only needs enough data to train. In this paper we show that porting to a new language, Spanish, requires only a small initial investment, while providing the opportunities for further improvement available only to semantic methods.

For comparison, we have taken three approaches to performing sentiment analysis in a new language. Our main approach involves deploying Spanish-specific resources, which we build both manually and automatically. The second approach, used in Bautin et al. [4] and Wan [18], consists of translating the texts into English, and using an existing English calculator. Finally, the third approach builds unigram Support Vector Machine classifiers from our Spanish corpora.

Our evaluation on multi-domain corpora indicates that, although translation and machine learning classification both perform reasonably well, there is a significant cost to automated translation. A language-specific SO Calculator with dictionaries built using words that actually appear in relevant texts gives the best performance, with significant potential for improvement.

2. The English SO Calculator

Our semantic orientation calculator (SO-CAL) uses five main dictionaries: four lexical dictionaries with 2,257 adjectives, 1,142 nouns, 903 verbs, and 745 adverbs, and a fifth dictionary containing 177 intensifying words and expressions. Although the vast majority of the entries are single words, our calculator also allows for multiword entries written in regular expression-like language.

The SO-carrying words in these dictionaries were taken from a variety of sources, the three largest a corpus of 400 mixed reviews from Epinions.com, a 100 text subset of the 2,000 movie reviews in the Polarity Dataset [12], and positive and negative words from the General Inquirer dictionary [15]. Each of the open-class words were given a hand-ranked SO value between 5 and -5 by a native English speaker. The numerical values were chosen to reflect both the prior polarity and strength of the word, averaged across likely interpretations. For example, the word *phenomenal* is a 5, *nicely* a 2, *disgust* a -3, and *monstrosity* a -5. The dictionary was later reviewed by a committee of three other researchers in order to minimize the subjectivity of ranking SO by hand.

SO-CAL also implements a modified version of contextual valence shifting as originally proposed by Polanyi and Zaenen [14], including negation and intensification. We have also added irrealis blocking.

Our approach to negation differs from Polanyi and Zaenen's in that negation involves a polarity shift instead of a switch: A negated adjective is shifted by a fixed amount (4) toward the origin. This means that the negation of a strongly negative word (like *terrible*) will be neutral or weakly negative (*not terrible* -5 + 4 = -1 instead of 5), while the negation of a weakly positive word like *nice* is equally negative (*not nice* 2 – 4 = -2).

International Conference RANLP 2009 - Borovets, Bulgaria, pages 50–54

The calculation of intensification is somewhat more sophisticated than simple addition and subtraction. Each expression in our intensifier dictionary is associated with a multiplier value. For instance, *very* has a value of .25, which means the SO value of any adjective modified by *very* is increased by 25%. We also included three other kinds of intensification that are common within our genre: the use of all capital letters, the use of exclamation points, and the use of discourse *but* to indicate more salient information (e.g., *...but the movie was GREAT!*).

Some markers indicate that the words appearing in a sentence might not be reliable for the purposes of sentiment analysis. We refer to these using the linguistic term *irrealis*. Irrealis markers in English include modals (*would, could*), some verbs (*expect, doubt*), and certain kinds of punctuation (questions, quotations). When SO-carrying words appear within the scope of these markers, our calculator ignores them.

Lexicon-based sentiment classifiers generally show a positive bias [10], likely the result of a human tendency to favor positive language [6]. In order to overcome this bias, we increase the final SO of any negative expression (after other modifiers have applied) by a fixed amount (currently 50%).

For initial testing, we use the 400 text Epinions corpus (50 texts in each of eight different product types), the other 1,900 texts in the Polarity Dataset (Movie), and a 2,400 text corpus of camera, printer, and stroller reviews (Camera) taken from a larger set of Epinions reviews also used by Bloom et al. [5], for a total of 4,700 texts split equally between positive and negative. Table 1 shows the performance of the English calculator with all features, and disabling the three types of valence shifters (negation, intensification and irrealis) and the extra weight on negative words. An asterisk (*) indicates that a chi square test yielded significance at the $p<0.05$ level, as compared to the result with all features enabled. Whereas not all the differences are statistically significant, it does seem that the set of features that we have chosen has a positive effect on performance.

Table 1. Effects of disabling various features

	Percent Correct by Corpus			
Features	**Epinions**	**Movie**	**Camera**	**Total**
All	80.3	76.4	80.3	78.7
No Neg	75.8*	74.6	76.1*	75.4*
No Int	79.0	74.7	77.5*	76.5*
No Irreal	78.8	74.8	79.6	77.6
No Neg W	71.8*	75.6	71.5*	73.2*

3. The Spanish SO Calculator

Compared to English, Spanish is a highly inflected language, with gender and plural markers on nouns, as well as a rich system of verbal inflection (45 possible verb forms). In the English version of SO-CAL, the only external software we made use of was the Brill tagger [7]; lemmatization of noun and verbs was simple enough to be carried out during the calculation. For Spanish, we used a high-accuracy statistical tagger, the SVMTool [9], and we adapted a 500,000+ word lemma dictionary included in the FreeLing software package[1], which we used to both lemmatize the words and to add more detail to the basic verb tags assigned by SVMTool (each verb is lemmatized, but tagged with information about its tense and mood). We found that some sentiment-relevant words were not being lemmatized properly, so we also implemented a second layer of lemmatization within the calculator.

Most of the Python code written for the English version of SO-CAL could be reused. With regards to detecting negation, intensification, and modifier blocking, it was necessary to take into account the fact that in Spanish adjectives appear both before and (more commonly) after the noun. The most interesting difference was the fact that verb forms in Spanish provide irrealis information. In particular, the conditional tense and the imperative and subjunctive moods often serve to indicate that the situation being referred to is not in fact the case. Thus, in Spanish we used a mixture of word and inflection-based irrealis blocking, using the same words as the English version whenever possible.

We built new Spanish dictionaries, including dictionaries for adjectives, nouns, verbs, adverbs and intensifiers. For intensifiers, given the fact that they are closed-class and highly idiosyncratic, we simply created a new list of 157 expressions, based on the English list. For the open-class dictionaries, we tested three different methods of dictionary-building; we compare their performance on the Spanish corpus in Section 5.

The first set of dictionaries started with the English dictionaries for each part of speech, which we translated automatically into Spanish, preserving the semantic orientation value for each word. For the automatic translation we used, in turn, two different methods. The first was an online bilingual dictionary, from the site www.spanishdict.com. We extracted the first definition under the appropriate syntactic category, ignoring any cases where either the English or the Spanish were multi-word expressions. The second automatic translation method involved simply plugging our English dictionaries into the Google translator and parsing the results.

For the second method of dictionary creation, we took the lists from Spanishdict.com and manually fixed entries that were obviously wrong. This involved mostly removing words in the wrong dictionary for their part of speech, but also changing some of the values (less than 10% for each dictionary). This hand-correction took a native speaker of Spanish about two hours to complete.

Finally, the third method consisted in creating all dictionaries from scratch. Our source corpora created for this project consists of reviews extracted from the Ciao.es review website. Following the basic format of the Epinions corpus, we collected 400 reviews from the domains of hotels, movies, music, phones, washing machines, books, cars, and computers. Each category

[1] http://garraf.epsevg.upc.es/freeling/

contained 50 reviews: 25 positive and 25 negative. Whenever possible, exactly two reviews, one positive and one negative, were taken for any particular product, so that the machine learning classifier described in Section 4.2 could not use names as sentiment clues.

We tagged the Spanish corpus collected from Ciao.es, and extracted all adjectives, nouns, adverbs and verbs. This resulted in large lists for each category (e.g., over 10,000 nouns). We manually pruned the lists, removing words that did not convey sentiment, misspelled and inflected words, and words with the wrong part of speech tag. Finally, semantic orientation values were assigned for each. This process took a native speaker of Spanish about 12 hours. We decided against a committee review of the Spanish dictionaries for the time being.

Another type of dictionary tested was a merging of the dictionaries created using the second and third methods, i.e., the automatically-created (but hand-fixed) dictionaries and the ones created from scratch (Ciao manual). We created two versions of these dictionaries, depending on whether we used the value from the Fixed Spanishdict.com or Ciao dictionary.

The dictionaries range from smallest (Spanishdict.com) to largest (Ciao+Fixed). The first one contains 1,160 adjectives, 979 nouns, 500 verbs and 422 adverbs. The combined dictionary has 2,049 adjectives, 1,324 nouns, 739 verbs, and 548 adverbs.

We performed a comparison of fully automated and fully manual methods, comparing the unedited Spanishdict.com dictionaries and the ones created by hand. We calculated the percentage of words in common, as a percentage of the size for the larger of the two sets (the Spanishdict.com dictionaries). The commonalities ranged from roughly 20% of the words for nouns to 41% for adjectives (i.e., 41%, or 480 of the hand-ranked adjectives were also found in the automatic dictionary). We also compared the values assigned to each word: The variance of the error ranged from 1.001 (verbs) to 1.518 (adjectives). Automatically translated dictionaries tend to include more formal words, whereas the ones created by hand include many more informal and slang words

4. Alternative approaches

4.1 Corpus translation

For translation, we used Google's web-based translation system. Google Translate (translate.google.com) uses phrase-based statistical machine translation. We used only one translator, but Bautin et al. [4] discuss the use of different Spanish translating systems, and Wan [18] compare Chinese machine translators; the latter found that Google gave the best performance, which is consistent with our preliminary testing of other systems.

4.2 Machine Learning

A popular approach to sentiment analysis has been the automatic training of a text classifier. Cross-linguistic sentiment detection seems particularly amenable to machine learning, since classifiers can be easily trained in any language. Following Pang et al. [13], we used Support Vector Machine (SVM) classifiers, built with the sequential minimal optimization algorithm included in the WEKA software suite [20], with a linear kernel and testing done with 10-fold cross-validation. We trained using unigram features that appeared at least four times in the dataset (the same cut-off was used by Pang and Lee [12]). To test the efficacy of the WEKA classifiers, we first trained a classifier on the full 2,000 text Polarity Dataset, a collection of balanced positive and negative movie reviews [12], comparing the cross-validated results with the baseline for SVM unigram classifiers on this dataset (before other improvements) given in Pang and Lee [12]. The difference (about 1%) was not statistically significant. It is worth noting that more recent work in SVM-based sentiment analysis has shown significant improvement on this baseline [19], however relevant resources are not available for Spanish.

In order to compare the classifier across languages, we trained separately on each of our two 400-text development corpora. In each case we used the output after pre-processing, with lemmatizing in the case of Spanish. In addition to basic unigrams we also tested unigrams with full POS tags and, for Spanish, partial tags (retaining word class but disregarding inflection such as number and person). The results were identical or in some cases worse than a simple unigram model.

5. Evaluation

We built two additional 400 text corpora, in English and Spanish, with the same basic constituency as the Epinions and Ciao Corpus discussed earlier. The English corpus (Epinions 2) is also from the Epinions site, while the Spanish corpus came from Dooyoo.es. This second set of texts for each language has never been used for training or development of any of our resources

All four corpora were translated using the appropriate Google translator, and for each version the accuracy identifying the polarity of reviews for all possible dictionaries and methods was tested. Note that when the corpus and the dictionary are the same language, the original version of the corpus is used, and when the corpus and the dictionary are in different languages, we use the translated version. The results are given in Table 2.

There are a number of clear patterns in Table 2. First, for the original Spanish versions, the translated Spanish dictionaries, taken together, do poorly compared to the versions of the dictionaries derived from actual Spanish texts; this is significant at the $p<0.05$ level for all possible dictionary combinations (all significance results are derived from chi-square tests). For Spanish, including words from translated dictionaries has little or no benefit. The opposite is true for Spanish translations of English texts, where the Ciao (manual) dictionary performance is low, and performance improves dramatically with the addition of translated (although manually fixed) resources; in the case of the Epinions 2 corpus, this improvement is significant ($p<0.05$). We attribute this to the fact that translated texts and translated dictionaries "speak the same language"; translated English corpora

Table 2. Accuracy of polarity detection for various corpora and methods

Method		Corpus				
		English		Spanish		Overall
SO Calculator	Dictionary	Epinions	Epinions2	Ciao	Dooyoo	
English	English SO-CAL	**80.25**	**79.75**	72.50	**73.50**	**76.50**
Spanish	Google-translated	66.00	68.50	66.75	66.50	66.50
Spanish	Spanishdict.com	68.75	68.00	67.25	67.25	67.94
Spanish	Fixed Spanishdict.com	69.25	69.75	68.25	68.00	68.81
Spanish	Ciao (manual)	66.00	67.50	**74.50**	72.00	70.00
Spanish	Ciao + Fixed Combined, Ciao value preferred	68.75	**72.50**	74.25	72.25	**71.93**
Spanish	Ciao + Fixed Combined, Fixed value preferred	69.50	68.75	73.50	70.75	70.87
Support Vector Machine, English versions		76.50	71.50	72.00	64.75	71.25
Support Vector Machine, Spanish versions		71.50	68.75	72.25	69.75	70.56

are unlikely to contain the colloquial Spanish found in the Ciao dictionary, and are more likely to contain the kind of formal language we saw in our translated dictionaries.

Turning now to machine learning methods, the SVM classifiers show the worse performance overall, however only the difference seen in the Epinions 2 corpus is significant (at the $p<0.01$ level). The relatively poor performance of the SVM classifier in this case can be attributed to the small size of the training set and the heterogeneity of the corpora; SVM classifiers have been shown to have poor cross-domain performance in text sentiment tasks [2], a problem that can be remedied somewhat by integrating a lexicon-based system [1].

The numbers in Table 2 do not indicate a clear winner with respect to the performance of Spanish SO-CAL as compared to English SO-CAL with translated texts, although it is clear that translating English texts into Spanish is, at present, a bad approach ($p<0.01$). The totals for all corpora for each method suggest that Spanish SO-CAL is performing well below English SO-CAL ($p<0.01$).

Table 3 summarizes the effects of translation. Original refers to all the 1,600 original versions and Translated to all 1,600 translated versions. For SO calculation, we use the best performing dictionary in the relevant language.

Table 3. Accuracy for translated/original corpora

Method	Texts	Accuracy
SO Calculation	Original	76.62
	Translated	71.81
SVM	Original	72.56
	Translated	69.25

Table 3 shows a general deficit for translated texts; for SO calculation, this is significant at the $p<0.01$ level. The fact that it is also visible in SVMs (which are not subject to dictionary biases) suggests that it is a general phenomenon. One potential criticism here is our use of corpora whose words were the basis for our dictionary, unfairly providing two of the four original corpora with high coverage which would not pass to the translations. Indeed, there is some evidence in Table 3 to suggest that these high coverage corpora do outperform their low coverage counterparts to some degree in relevant dictionaries (compared with the Subjective dictionary, for instance); in general, though, there were no significant differences among same-language corpora tested using the same dictionary. Note also that using high-coverage corpora is not analogous to testing and training on the same corpora, since words are rated for SO independently of the texts in which they appear.

6. Related Work

Wan [18] created a hybrid classifier which combined the scores from a Chinese lexicon-based system and an English lexicon-based system (with translated texts). In contrast to our results, his Chinese lexicon-based system performed quite poorly compared to the English system. Similar to our results, Chinese lexicons created by translating English lexicons did not help performance.

Although they are concerned with sentence level subjectivity instead of text-level polarity, the work of Mihalcea et al. [11] is quite relevant, since their focus, like ours, is on exploring ways to deriving new resources from existing resources for English. In adapting subjectivity cues to Romanian, they also saw limited benefits to straight translation of dictionaries, but obtained promising results from the projection of English annotations into Romanian.

Bautin et al. [4] used online resources from multiple languages, including Spanish, into English, using the output from an existing sentiment analyzer to track attitudes in different language communities. Yao et al. [21] made use of a bilingual lexicon to build a Chinese sentiment dictionary using English glosses. Lexicon-based sentiment analysis has also been pursued independently in a number of East Asian languages, including Japanese [16], Chinese [22], and Korean [8]. As far as we know, ours is the first Spanish SO calculator. Banea et al. [3] report on work in Spanish, but theirs is a subjectivity classification task.

In terms of approaches to calculation of text level sentiment in English, the work of Kennedy and Inkpen [10] is the most directly comparable. Their main focus was the comparison of lexicon-based versus machine learning approaches; in contrast to our results, they found that performance of their semantic model was significantly below that of an SVM classifier.

To facilitate comparisons with other approaches, the corpora and some of the resources described in the paper are available[2].

7. Conclusion

The surge in attention paid to automated analysis of text sentiment has largely been focused on English. In this paper, we have discussed how to adapt an existing English semantic orientation system to Spanish while at the same time comparing several alternative approaches.

Our results indicate that SVMs, at least the fairly simple SVMs we have tested here, do not do very well in our Spanish corpora. There are a number of obvious reasons for this, and our rejection of SVMs is far from decisive; on the contrary, machine learning might be useful, for instance, in identifying parts of the text that should be disregarded during the SO calculation [12].

For calculation of semantic orientation using lexicons, translation of any kind seems to come with a price, even between closely related languages such as English and Spanish. Our Spanish SO calculator (SO-CAL) is clearly inferior to our English SO-CAL, probably the result of a number of factors, including a small, preliminary dictionary, and a need for additional adaptation to a new language. Translating our English dictionary also seems to result in significant semantic loss, at least for original Spanish texts. Although performance of Spanish texts translated into English is comparable to native SO-CAL performance, the overall accuracy of translated texts in both English and Spanish suggests that there is 3-5% performance cost for any (automated) translation. This, together with the fact that translation seems to have a disruptive effect on previous reliable improvements, as well as the relatively small time investment required to develop Spanish SO-CAL, lead us to conclude that there is value in pursuing the development of language-specific resources, notwithstanding new breakthroughs in machine translation.

8. Acknowledgments

This work was supported by a NSERC Discovery Grant (261104-2008) to Maite Taboada.

9. References

[1] A. Andreevskaia and S. Bergler. When specialists and generalists work together: Domain dependence in sentiment tagging. Proc. of 46th ACL. Columbus, OH, 2008.

[2] A. Aue and M. Gamon. Customizing sentiment classifiers to new domains: A case study. Proc. of RANLP. Borovets, Bulgaria, 2005.

[3] C. Banea, R. Mihalcea, J. Wiebe and S. Hassan. Multilingual subjectivity analysis using machine translation. Proc. of EMNLP. Honolulu, 2008.

[4] M. Bautin, L. Vijayarenu and S. Skiena. International sentiment analysis for news and blogs. Proc. of 3rd AAAI International Conference on Weblogs and Social Media. San Jose, CA, 2008.

[5] K. Bloom, G. Navendu and S. Argamon. Extracting appraisal expressions. Proc. of HLT/NAACL. Rochester, NY, 2007.

[6] J.D. Boucher and C.E. Osgood. The Pollyanna hypothesis. Journal of Verbal Learning and Verbal Behaviour 8: 1-8, 1969.

[7] E. Brill. A simple rule-based part of speech tagger. Proc. of 3rd Conference on Applied Natural Language Processing. Trento, Italy, 1992.

[8] Y.H. Cho and K.J. Lee. Automatic affect recognition using natural language processing techniques and manually built affect lexicon. IEICE Transactions on Information and Systems 89(12): 2964-2971, 2006.

[9] J. Giménez and L. Màrquez. SVMTool: A general POS tagger generator based on support vector machines. Proc. of Conference on Language Resources and Evaluation (LREC). Lisbon, Portugal, 2004.

[10] A. Kennedy and D. Inkpen. Sentiment classification of movie and product reviews using contextual valence shifters. Computational Intelligence 22(2): 110-125, 2006.

[11] R. Mihalcea, C. Banea and J. Wiebe. Learning multilingual subjective language via cross-lingual projections. Proc. of ACL. Prague, Czech Republic, 2007.

[12] B. Pang and L. Lee. A sentimental education: Sentiment analysis using subjectivity summarization based on minimum cuts. Proc. of ACL. Barcelona, Spain, 2004.

[13] B. Pang, L. Lee and S. Vaithyanathan. Thumbs up? Sentiment classification using Machine Learning techniques. Proc. of EMNLP, 2002.

[14] L. Polanyi and A. Zaenen. Contextual valence shifters. In Computing Attitude and Affect in Text: Theory and Applications, J.G. Shanahan, Y. Qu, and J. Wiebe, Eds. Springer: Dordrecht, pp. 1-10, 2006.

[15] P.J. Stone. Thematic text analysis: New agendas for analyzing text content. In Text Analysis for the Social Sciences, C. Roberts, Ed. Lawrence Erlbaum: Mahwah, NJ, 1997.

[16] H. Takamura, T. Inui and M. Okumura. Extracting semantic orientations of words using spin model. Proc. of ACL. Ann Arbor, 2005.

[17] P. Turney. Thumbs up or thumbs down? Semantic orientation applied to unsupervised classification of reviews. Proc. of ACL, 2002.

[18] X. Wan. Using bilingual knowledge and ensemble techniques for unsupervised Chinese sentiment analysis. Proc of EMNLP. Honolulu, 2008.

[19] C. Whitelaw, N. Garg and S. Argamon. Using Appraisal groups for sentiment analysis. Proc. of ACM SIGIR Conference on Information and Knowledge Management (CIKM 2005). Bremen, Germany, 2005.

[20] I.H. Witten and E. Frank. Data Mining: Practical Machine Learning Tools and Techniques. 2nd ed. San Francisco: Morgan Kaufmann, 2005.

[21] J. Yao, G. Wu, J. Liu and Y. Zheng. Using bilingual lexicon to judge sentiment orientation of Chinese words. Proc. of 6th International Conference on Computer and Information Technology (CIT'06). Seoul, Korea, 2006.

[22] Q. Ye, B. Lin and Y.-J. Li. Sentiment classification for Chinese reviews: A comparison between SVM and semantic approaches. Fourth Int. Conference on Machine Learning and Cybernetics. Guangzhou, China, 2005.

[2] http://www.sfu.ca/~mtaboada/research/nserc-project.html

The Influence of Text Pre-processing on Plagiarism Detection

Zdenek Ceska
Computer Science and Engineering
Faculty of Applied Sciences
University of West Bohemia
Pilsen, 306 14, Czech Republic
zceska@kiv.zcu.cz

Chris Fox
School of Computer Science
and Electronic Engineering
University of Essex
Colchester, CO4 3SQ, United Kingdom
foxcj@essex.ac.uk

Abstract

This paper explores the influence of text pre-processing techniques on plagiarism detection. We examine stop-word removal, lemmatization, number replacement, synonymy recognition, and word generalization. We also look into the influence of punctuation and word-order within N-grams. All these techniques are evaluated according to their impact on F_1-measure and speed of execution. Our experiments were performed on a Czech corpus of plagiarized documents about politics. At the end of this paper, we propose what we consider to be the best combination of text pre-processing techniques.

Keywords

Plagiarism, Copy Detection, Natural Language Processing, Stop-words, Lemmatization, Synonymy, WordNet, Thesaurus.

1 Introduction

Recently, there has been much interest in automatic plagiarism. Written-text plagiarism is a wide-spread problem which many organizations have to deal with. Various methods are used in this field, such as SCAM [9] and Kopi [5]. SVDPLAG [1] is another technique whose performance outperforms all these other methods.

Text pre-processing can have a significant influence on the performance of many Natural Language Processing (NLP) tasks, including plagiarism detection. Although many studies on pre-processing techniques have been performed for applications such as text categorization [10], it is appropriate to look at such pre-processing techniques again when when considering a new application. Plagiarism detection is a distinct field that should be given particular attention, as it may be appropriate to apply a wide range of pre-processing techniques. Various pre-processing have different effects, some improve the accuracy, some just decrease the time requirements, and some do both. This paper aims to clarify the influence of text pre-processing on this task when using the SVDPLAG method.

2 Pre-processing Techniques

Plagiarism detection can employ various pre-processing techniques in order to improve the accuracy or decrease the number of features that need to be processed.

Figure 1 shows the text pre-processing step-by-step. The most essential block is Tokenization, which extracts single words from the structured text. Punctuation marks can be extracted if they are required by other processes. The other blocks represent optional techniques that can be applied if the user wishes.

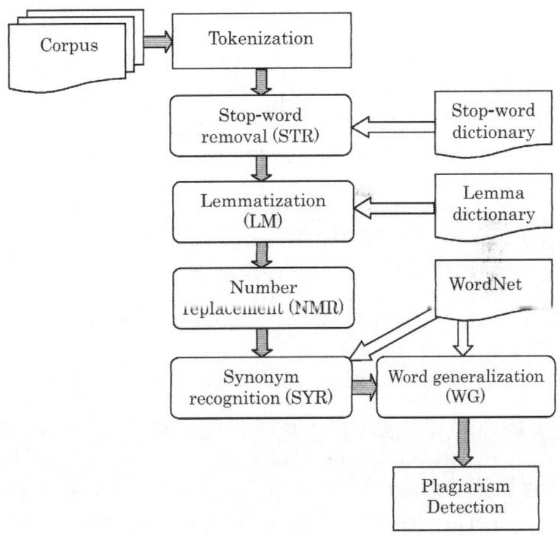

Fig. 1: *Text pre-processing scheme*

Below we describe each technique in detail. The impact of these techniques on accuracy and processing time is given in Section 4, where we also explore the impact of maintaining word-order, and the boundaries between sentences and phrases, as marked by punctuation.

2.1 Stop-word Removal (STR)

Stop-word removal is a fundamental pre-processing approach that removes common words. Its primary use is to prevent the following processing being over-influenced by very frequent words.

For plagiarism detection, there may be a complication to remove such words that could break up an

International Conference RANLP 2009 - Borovets, Bulgaria, pages 55–59

author's writing style. For this reason, the effect of stop-word removal is rather unpredictable. The usual way of determining what counts as a stop-word is just to use a dictionary that lists them. We used a pre-existing list for Czech [8].

2.2 Lemmatization (LM)

Lemmatization is the process of determining the base form of a given word [4]. During this process, the context of the word is used to determine the word sense.

Sometimes lemmatization is mistaken for stemming; however, there is an essential difference. Stemming operates only with single words without any knowledge of the context, and therefore cannot distinguish among words having several different meanings. As an example of stemming, the words "does" and "done" may be transformed into the stem "do". The resulting word does not need to be a real English word.

Lemmatization, on the other hand, makes use of the context to disambiguate word meaning. This is particularly important for languages that have rich systems of inflexion, such as Czech. We employed a method by Toman [10].

2.3 Number Replacement (NMR)

Number replacement is a particular approach that transforms all numbers into a dummy symbol. We suggest this approach may be highly appropriate in some cases. Let us imagine the situation when a student submits a plagiarized essay that focuses on an economic analysis of a company. It is very simple to use someone else's work just by replacing any numeric values, in combination with any necessary rewording. On the other hand, the number replacement could lead to lower accuracy in the case of factual dates.

2.4 Synonymy Recognition (SYR)

The motivation for using synonymy recognition comes from considering human behaviour, whereby people may seek to hide plagiarism by replacing words with appropriate synonyms.

If a sufficient number of words are replaced by synonyms, then most of the common copy detection methods fail. Regardless of the features the methods use, the best solution is to transform words having the same meaning onto a unique identifier. A consideration has to be given to words that have more than one meaning; if a significant impact on the accuracy is expected, a disambiguation process is required to determine the appropriate meaning.

We consider three possible solutions for synonymy recognition. These all exploit the WordNet thesaurus [12]. In WordNet, all words that have the same meaning are grouped together into a so-called *synset*. Moreover, each WordNet synset is mapping onto an *inter-lingual index* (ILI) that is used as a unique identifier.

2.4.1 First Meaning Selection (FMS)

To implement *first meaning selection* we search for an equivalent word in WordNet. If a match is found, then the algorithm returns the corresponding ILI. This approach does not care about ambiguity; even if there is more than one meaning for the word, it still just returns the first ILI.

2.4.2 Disambiguation and Proper Meaning Selection (DPMS)

A more advanced approach is to use a disambiguation process based on a Naïve Bayes classifier [6]. This aims to select the best word meaning depending on the adjacent words. For more information about the disambiguation process see [4]. Because the adjacent words do not always provide sufficient information for full disambiguation, this process sometimes fails.

2.4.3 Every Meaning Selection (EMS)

The last approach is a generalized variant of FMS. This selects all corresponding meanings contained in WordNet and returns their ILIs. For two words to be matched, at least one of their possible meanings has to correspond. There is a potential risk that this it too permissive.

2.5 Word Generalization (WG)

The last technique is word generalization. The main idea of this process rests in replacing various specific words by a more general word. For example, the words "dog" and "cat" could both be replaced by the word "animal", or some other hypernym, such as "mammal". This has two aims. First, it reduces the number of distinct words that have to be processed. Second, it may reveal evidence of plagiarism where some paraphrasing and generalization, or specialization, has been used in an attempt to hide the offence.

The WordNet thesaurus interconnects synsets by many *inter-lingual references* (ILR), where a synset consists of one or more synonyms. The hypernym relation defines a synset hierarchy.

The idea of replacing specific words by more general words is simple. The issue we have to address is how to decide which words to use. If we are insufficiently general, then there may be little benefit. If too general, then all nominals would be replaced by "entity", thus eliminating the information content.

The best solution might be to define an individual generalization level for every sub-hierarchy. However, this is rather impractical. We adopt the more practical alternative of specifying a fixed, global generalization level. All words from deeper, more specific levels of the hierarchy are replaced by the word occurring at that level. Words that are associated with shallower, more general levels are left unchanged.

Although we have been talking about replacing words with more general ones, in practice all that is required is to record the appropriate ILI of the relevant synset to which a given word belongs. All words have to be mapped onto their ILIs before the word generalization process. It turns out that this notion of word generalization is closely connected with the synonym recognition (SYR).

3 Plagiarism Detection Method

All the following experiments were performed using a variant of the SVDPLAG method published in [1]. We modified this method in order to improve the evaluation when the documents are of differing length. The modification rests in an asymmetric document similarity normalization (Formula (1)). The modified method is called SVDPLAG$_{\mathrm{ASYM}}$. The original method (which we shall call SVDPLAG$_{\mathrm{SYM}}$) used symmetric normalization.

$$\mathrm{sim}_{\mathrm{ASYM}}(R,S) = \mathrm{sim}_{\mathrm{SVD}}(R,S) \cdot \frac{\sqrt{|G_{red}(R)| \cdot |G_{red}(S)|}}{\min(|G_{orig}(R)|,\ |G_{orig}(S)|)} \quad (1)$$

In this formula, $\mathrm{sim}_{\mathrm{ASYM}}(R,S)$ represents the resulting similarity between documents R and S. The term $\mathrm{sim}_{\mathrm{SVD}}(R,S)$ is a similarity measure given by the SVD process [1], $G_{orig}(D)$ denotes a set of N-grams contained in document D before reduction, and $G_{red}(D)$ is a set of N-grams after reduction.

4 Experiments

For our experiments we used a corpus of plagiarized documents, written in Czech. In total, the corpus contains 1,500 text documents about politics. The corpus was created as follows. Initially, 350 documents were selected from the Czech News Agency (CTK) source [3], volume 1999. A group of students was then set the task of manually plagiarizing these documents to create 550 plagiarized texts. A further 600 documents from CTK on the same topic were then added to the corpus. These documents effectively act as an unplagiarized control.

In order to produce the 550 plagiarized documents, students were asked to combine two or more randomly selected documents from the initial corpus of 350 CTK documents. During this task the following rules had to be taken into account: (i) copy several paragraphs from the selected documents; (ii) remove about 20% of sentences from the new created document; (iii) remove about 10% of words with consideration of the sentence meaning; (iv) exchange about 20% of sentences from different paragraphs; (v) modify some words or reword at most 10% of sentences to add new ideas; (vi) insert new words to fix any "broken" meanings.

To evaluate various pre-processing techniques the standard measures from Information Retrieval (IR) are used. We define precision p and recall r according to Rijsbergen [11]. Further we define F_1-measure to be a harmonic mean of precision and recall, see the following formula.

$$F_1 = \frac{2 \cdot p \cdot r}{p + r} \quad (2)$$

To make a comparison of time requirements, all the following experiments were performed on Intel Core 2 Duo E6600, 4GB RAM, and Windows Server 2003 R2 operating system in 64-bit mode.

Through all the experiments, the Student's t-test of significance at the confidence level of 99.5% was employed.

4.1 Punctuation and Word-Order

In the first experiment we look at the influence of considering punctuation and word-order on the accuracy, see Table 1. At the same time, we determine which features (N-grams) achieve the best results. We performed all the experiments on the asymmetric variant of SVDPLAG.

We use the term "punctuation" to refer to the case where N-grams are ignored if they cross sentential and phrase boundaries, as marked by punctuation such as full-stops, question marks, commas, etc.

Table 1: *The influence of punctuation and word-order on the plagiarism detection accuracy*

Punctuation	–	+	–	+
Word-order	–	–	+	+
Features	F_1 [%]	F_1 [%]	F_1 [%]	F_1 [%]
Words	86.29	86.29	86.29	86.29
Bigrams	91.93	91.74	92.03	91.85
Trigrams	94.59	93.16	94.50	93.21
4-grams	95.68	93.23	95.56	93.33
5-grams	94.64	92.18	94.48	92.15
6-grams	93.16	90.29	93.07	90.33
7-grams	92.05	88.16	92.00	88.21
8-grams	90.54	85.69	90.41	85.58

¿From our experiments it is evident that people usually copy segments of text that include more than one sentence, or phrase. The F_1-measure decreases when N-grams that link sentences and phrases that may have been copied together are ignored. Moreover, the longer N-gram the larger the decrease in F_1-measure. Short sentences that have fewer words than the specified N-gram length are left out of computation process. Overall, this has the effect of reducing the number of features extracted from the text, which has the advantage of speeding-up the subsequent computation. Although the computation time for the SVD method decreases, the pre-processing takes more time due to the need to examine and process the sentential structure of the documents. Overall, just a few seconds are saved by applying this approach (Table 2).

Table 2: *The number of 4-gram features and the time requirements when punctuation and/or word order is taking into account*

Punctuation	Word-order	Num. of features	Preproc. time [s]	Comp. time [s]	Total time [s]
–	–	240159	23.65	60.73	84.38
+	–	155871	32.92	44.63	77.54
–	+	238903	23.48	60.33	83.81
+	+	155092	32.84	44.61	77.45

Next, we examine the impact of word-order by comparing the case where the order of the words within each N-gram is preserved with one where the words are sorted into ascending alphabetic order, effectively ignoring the original word order. This can be thought of as using an N-bag of words, where word-order is unimportant. It turns out that ignoring word-order gives slightly worse results (Table 2).

The number of features, and the time taken to process them, are reduced. Despite that, we do not recommend these techniques, especially with languages that do not support free word-order. All of the subsequent experiments were performed without considering punctuation, and with the word-order being maintained within the N-grams.

4.2 Pre-processing Techniques

Now we observe the influence of the individual pre-processing techniques, described in Section 2. Figure 2 presents the F_1-measure (the line) and the total computation time (the bars) for different pre-processing techniques, using 4-grams. The first case is where no pre-processing technique is applied. In this case, the F_1-measure is 95.68% and the total computation takes 84.38 seconds.

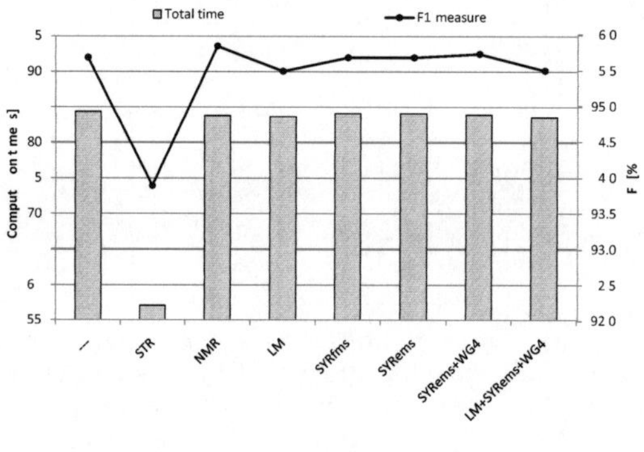

Fig. 2: *The influence of individual pre-processing techniques on F_1-measure and computation time, when* SVDPLAG$_{ASYM}$ *and 4-gram features are used*

Stop word removal (STR) significantly reduces the number of 4-grams and decreases time requirements to 57.08 seconds. Unfortunately, the F_1-measure falls down on 93.89%. This suggests that very frequent stop-words make a measurable contribution in determining the identity of fragments of text.

Number replacement (NMR) gives very promising result. A higher F_1-measure of 95.84% is obtained, together with a slightly lower execution time.

Lemmatization (LM) looses some relevant information; our experiments indicate a decrease in F_1-measure to 95.49%.

In the case of synonym replacement (SYR), we initially examine only the SYR$_{FMS}$ and SYR$_{EMS}$ approaches. This is because there is no training data for Czech word-meaning disambiguation. We discuss SYR$_{DPMS}$ later in Section 4.2.3. Both SYR$_{FMS}$ and SYR$_{EMS}$ have no influence F_1-measure. We just notice a small decrease in the time required. In the case of single words (Figure 3), there is a tiny improvement of just several hundredths of a percent, which is not significant. Generally, SYR$_{EMS}$ performs better than SYR$_{FMS}$.

These results suggest that in our data-set people often copy longer sentences without any modification. Nevertheless, sometimes a word is replaced by its synonym, which is reflected in the better results for single words. It seems the extra performance obtained by using N-grams (rather than single words) is not further improved by considering synonyms.

For word generalization (WG), we use the 4th generalization level (WG$_4$). As already mentioned in Section 2.5, WG cannot be applied by itself; it always has to be combined with a synonym replacement (SYR) technique. Word generalization has more impact on the computation time for shorter N-grams, and in particular for single words (see Section 4.2.1). However, we do also notice some improvement for 4-grams. It also gives a very slightly better results in F_1-measure (+0.05%) for both single words and 4-grams than single SYR techniques, although this may not be significant.

We explored the use of different generalization levels for WG. If the generalization level is too abstract, e.g. effectively replacing all words by "entity", then this has a negative impact on the F_1-measure. According to our experiments, the 4th generalization level achieves the best results, with the benefits gradually disappearing as greater levels of generalization are used.

4.2.1 Single Words

It is worth looking at the performance for single-word features, see Figure 3. Perhaps the most interesting result is the much smaller reduction in the F_1-measure and time requirements when STR is applied.

The Czech language has a rich system of word inflections, resulting in large reduction in the number of features, and overall computation time, when using LM with single words. Intuitively at least, it would seem that longer word sequence, e.g. 4-grams, contain implicit constraints on the occurrence of inflected forms of individual words, which reduces the impact of the LM technique.

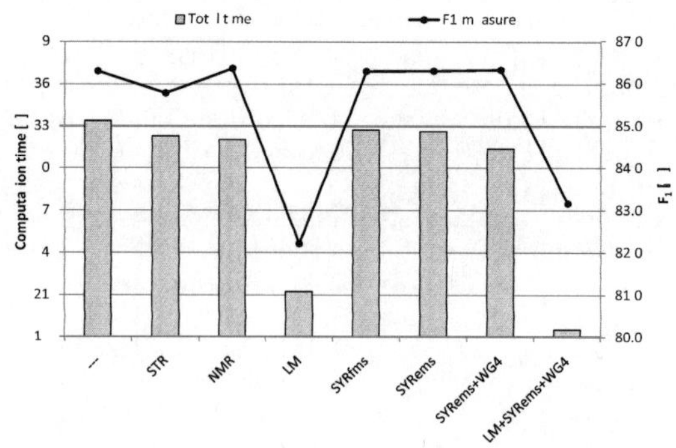

Fig. 3: *The influence of individual techniques on F_1-measure and the computation time, when* SVDPLAG$_{ASYM}$ *and single-word features are used*

The results for SYR and WG with single words were described above.

The last case for single words is the combination of LM, SYR$_{EMS}$ and WG$_4$. This combination resulted in an even greater reduction in time taken, and better results for F_1-measure.

4.2.2 Combinations of Techniques

It is possible to consider various combinations of text pre-processing techniques. Here there is only space to outline the results for a couple of combinations. The combination of NMR, SYR_{EMS} and WG_4 gives promising result; the F_1-measure is 95.92% in comparison with 95.68% when no pre-processing is used.

Using all the techniques together, i.e. STR, LM, NMR, SYR_{EMS}, and WG_4, yields a lower F_1-measure of 94.52% but is the best choice for obtaining a lower total execution time. In this case, using the combination of all the various techniques seems to gain the benefit of each one.

4.2.3 Sense Disambiguation (DPMS)

Finally, we examine SYR_{DPMS}, including the disambiguation process. Since there are no training data available for Czech language, we performed our experiments on the METER corpus [2]. This consists of news stories published in nine British newspapers, some of which are based on common news-wire sources.

For our experiments we used the $\text{SVDPLAG}_{\text{ASYM}}$ method with single-word features. Every piece of news is written in a novel style, which may explain why longer N-grams yield worse results. As a training corpus for English word disambiguation, we employed the Semantic Concordance Corpus [7].

According to our experiments, we achieve 87.07% F_1-measure without the use of pre-processing. Applying the SYR techniques slightly improves the results: 87.07% for FMS; 87.09% for DPMS, using a six word context centered on the word being disambiguated (DPMS-6); and 87.10% for EMS. According to the statistical significance testing, the measured differences are not significant. Using anything other than a six word context for DPMS gave F_1-measures that were worse than those without pre-processing.

The results suggest that DPMS has a worse performance than EMS. The reason for this appears to be that if a word is not recognized among the training data, a random meaning is selected. We would argue that EMS is good choice not only for this corpus, but also for the plagiarism detection problem in general.

5 Conclusion

On the basis of our experiments, text pre-processing cannot significantly improve the accuracy of plagiarism detection. Only number replacement (NMR), synonymy recognition (SYR), and word generalization (WG) improve the accuracy slightly. Their combination yields the highest score 95.92% F_1-measure in comparison with the situation when no pre-processing is employed, i.e. 95.68%.

If speed of execution is the main priority, then stop-word removal (STR) and lemmatization (LM) should be considered. Stop-word removal gives a greater reduction in execution time as longer N-grams are used. However, we should be aware that this throws away information that is useful for plagiarism detection, with the F_1-measure decreasing to 93.89%. Lemmatization (LM), on the other hand, has a greater impact on execution time with shorter N-grams. In case of single words, F_1-measure declines from 86.29% to 82.21%. We hypothesis that lemmatization has less impact because the word collocation contains implicit information about the legitimate inflexions.

Taking punctuation into account has a significant, but negative impact. Although it reduces the number of features that have to be analyzed, the overall execution time does not decrease. This is because of the additional time required to perform the pre-processing. The longer the N-grams, the greater is the reduction in the F_1-measure. An explanation for this is that short sentences do not fill the longer N-grams, and are simply discarded. Maintainingm or ignoring word-order has no influence on the results.

Synonymy recognition itself (SYR) does not improve the performance with longer N-grams. Out of all synonymy techniques, the approach that considers all of the word meanings, i.e. EMS, appears to have the best performance. Word generalization (WG) works in combination with the synonymy recognition and makes additional use of the WordNet thesaurus. According to our experiments, the 4th generalization level achieves the best results for this technique.

Acknowledgments

This research was supported in part by National Research Programme II, project 2C06009 (COT-SEWing). Special thanks go to Michal Toman who helped us to employ the disambiguation process.

References

[1] Z. Ceska. Plagiarism Detection Based on Singular Value Decomposition. *Advances in Natural Language Processing*, 5221: 108–119, August 2008.

[2] P. Clough and S. Piao. The METER Corpus. Last update 12/2/2000. Available at http://www.dcs.shef.ac.uk/nlp/meter/Metercorpus/metercorpus.htm.

[3] CTK. Czech News Agency: Political and General News Service. Available at http://www.ctk.eu/services/news/political_and_general/.

[4] K. Jezek and M. Toman. Documents Categorization in Multilingual Environment. In *Proceedings of ElPub 2005*, pages 97–104, Leuven, Belgium, 2005. ISBN 90-429-1645-1.

[5] L. Kovacs and M. Pataki. KOPI Protection instead of Copy Protection. In *Proceedings of AXMEDIS 2006*, pages 38–41, Washington, DC, USA, 2006. ISBN 88-8453-526-3.

[6] C. Manning and H. Schutze. *Foundation of Statistical Natural Language Processing*. The MIT Press, Massachusetts Institute of Technology, Cambridge, USA, 1999. ISBN 0-262-13360-1.

[7] G. A. Miller, C. Leacock, R. Tengi, and R. T. Bunker. A Semantic Concordance. In *Proceedings of Human Language Technology Conference*, pages 303–308, Princeton, USA, 1993.

[8] RANKS.NL. Czech stopwords. Available at http://www.ranks.nl/.

[9] N. Shivakumar and H. Garcia-Molina. SCAM: A copy detection mechanism for digital documents. In *Proceedings of Digital Libraries '95*, pages 303–308, Austin, USA, 1995.

[10] M. Toman, R. Tesar, and K. Jezek. Influence of Word Normalization on Text Classification. In *Proceedings of InSciT 2006*, pages 354–358, Merida, Spain, 2006. ISBN 84-611-3105-3.

[11] C. van Rijsbergen. *Information Retrieval*. Butterworth-Heinemann, 2 edition, 1979. ISBN 0-408-70929-4.

[12] P. Vossen. Global WordNet Association: EuroWordNet. Last update 9/1/2001. Available at http://www.illc.uva.nl/EuroWordNet/.

Combining Finite State and Corpus-based Techniques for Unknown Word Prediction

Kostadin Cholakov and Gertjan van Noord
University of Groningen
PO Box 716
9700 AS Groningen, The Netherlands
k.cholakov@rug.nl, *g.j.m.van.noord@rug.nl*

Abstract

Many NLP systems make use of various lexicons and dictionaries. However, unknown words are a major problem for such resources when applied to real-life data. We propose a method that combines finite state techniques and web queries to deliver possible analyses for a given unknown word and to generate its paradigm. We ensure the general applicability of our approach by applying it to a test set of Dutch words.

1 Introduction

Unknown words are a major hindrance for the performance of NLP tools that make use of lexicons and dictionaries. To overcome this problem, most applications try to extract (partially) the necessary morphological knowledge by implementing various heuristics and unknown word guessers.

In this paper, we present a two-phase method which delivers an accurate morphological analysis for a given unknown word and generates its paradigm. It deals with *open-class* words– nouns, adjectives and verbs based on the assumption that the other word classes are already covered by most lexicons. We test its efficiency and accuracy by applying it to real-life Dutch data. Dutch is a language with a productive inflectional morphology that exhibits quite a few interesting phenomena and thus poses a challenge for morphological processing.

In the first phase we use finite state techniques which are one of the most common approaches for morphological processing (Beesley and Karttunen, 2003; Petitpierre and Russel, 1995) since they can conveniently be used for both analysis and generation. We employ a small set of *non-deterministic* 'unweighted' finite state transducers (FSTs) whose manually encoded rules cover *regular* morphological phenomena.

Since our method deals with unknown words, it does not have access to any additional information apart from the limited knowledge provided by the word structure. Restricted only by that limited knowledge the FSTs, in *analysis mode*, identify all *possible* forms and roots allowed by the word structure. For example, the word *schnabbel* (a gig) is analysed as a singular noun, a base adjective and a first person singular present verb. As a consequence, three possible roots are produced. Since there is no way to know which of them is the correct one, in *generation mode*, all possible paradigms for each of these roots are generated.

The problem of *disambiguating* the output of the FSTs is dealt with in the second phase. We use Yahoo to search the web for each root and generated paradigm form and, based on the number of occurrences found, we try to identify the correct root and paradigm of the unknown word. Commercial search engines have already been successfully used for various NLP tasks (Keller and Lapata, 2003) and it is our claim that they are sufficient for ours as well. Since the *whole paradigm* of the unknown word is generated, it would be very difficult to find a large number of occurrences for each form in a wrong paradigm. For example, the generated adjective and verb forms for *schnabbel* have no or very few occurrences on the web and they can be safely rejected.

A similar approach, described in (Adolphs, 2008), applies finite state techniques to generate possible inflectional classes for unknown German words. However, disambiguation is done by using metrics based on frequency counts obtained from a corpus. Thus disambiguation depends heavily on the size and the gender of the corpus which is a drawback in comparison with the virtually unlimited data in the web our method has access to. If a word is, for instance, both a noun and a verb, it is possible that it would occur only as a noun in a given corpus and the method would fail to deal with the morphological ambiguity. (Nakov et al., 2003) use a rule-based approach to guess the morphological classes of unknown German nouns where each induced rule is ranked in the manner of (Mikheev, 1997). However, it is not clear if the method can scale to other word classes. (van den Bosch and Daelemans, 1999) apply memory-based learning to provide a detailed morphological analysis of Dutch. The method is tested on frequent dictionary words and only an *estimate* is provided about its expected performance on real-world data.

We should mention that the work described here is part of an algorithm for the automated acquisition of lexical types for words unknown to the Alpino grammar and parser (van Noord, 2006). The information provided by the generated paradigms is used as features in a statistical classifier which predicts lexical types for each unknown word. We also take into account occurrences of the unknown word in different contexts to extract additional features, including the type(s) assigned by the Alpino POS tagger (Prins and

International Conference RANLP 2009 - Borovets, Bulgaria, pages 60–64

van Noord, 2001) and types which Alpino allows as plausible in the particular context. Therefore, *both* the morphology of the unknown word and its context are considered in the prediction process. For more details, see (Cholakov, 2009).

The remainder of the paper is organised as follows. Section 2 presents the morphological phenomena which are relevant for our experiments. Section 3 describes the FSTs and investigates their coverage and degree of non-determinism. Section 4 describes the web heuristics used to disambiguate the output of the FSTs and presents the experiments with the test data. Section 5 concludes the paper.

2 Morphological Phenomena

In this section we present the morphological phenomena which the FSTs account for. We begin by presenting some rules that have effect on all the three POS classes we consider.

In Dutch, the vowels **a, e, o, u** and **i** are either long or short. A vowel is long if it is doubled (e.g., *m**aa**n*– moon), if it is in a vowel combination (***lief***– sweet, dear) or when it is at the end of a syllable (***ma**-ken*– to make). The general rule is that the type of a vowel, short or long, is preserved in all word forms. In particular contexts, a vowel is kept long by doubling it:

(1) *ma-ken–m**aa**k*
(to make, INF–1st PER.SG.PRES)

After removing the *-en* suffix from the infinitive, we get the form **mak* and the vowel turns into a short one. To prevent this, *a* is doubled. When *en* is added to form plural in (2), *u* would become a long vowel– ****stu**-ken*. To prevent this, the following consonant is doubled– *stuk-ken*.

(2) *stuk–stu**kk**en* (piece–pieces)

However, there are some exceptions to these rules. Depending on whether the syllable containing the vowel in question is stressed or not, the type of the vowel can change for words with stems ending in *-el*, *-er* and *-ig*. If the syllable is stressed, then the vowel preserves its type in all word forms as shown in (3-a). If the respective syllable is not stressed, then the vowel is not doubled and it turns into a short one as in (3-b).

(3) a. *de-len–deel* (parts–part)
b. *re-ge-len–re-gel* (rules–rule)

The same also applies to the doubling of consonants. In (4-a) *r* is doubled to keep the vowel short. However, this is not the case in (4-b) because the stress falls on another syllable and thus, *e* turns into a long vowel.

(4) a. *sper–sper-ren*
(to bar, 1st PER.SG.PRES–INF)
b. *coun-ter–coun-te-ren* (to strike back, 1st PER.SG.PRES–INF)

One last important rule is that a morpheme cannot end in *-v* or *-z* and they are replace by *f* and *s*, respectively: *rei-zen–reis* (to travel, INF–1st PER.SG.PRES) and *le-ven–leef* (to live, INF–1st PER.SG.PRES).

Noun Inflection. Most Dutch nouns form plural by adding *-en* to the singular form, as shown in (2). However, some nouns take *-s* to form their plural: *jongen-jongens* (boy-boys), *tram-trams*.

Adjective Inflection. Most adjectives in Dutch have base, comparative and superlative forms. Comparative is normally formed by adding *-er* to the base form: *snel-sneller* (fast-faster). Superlative is formed by adding the suffix *-st* to the base form: *snel-snelst.* However, base forms that end in *-s* take only *-t* to form superlative:

(5) *geeps-geepst* (pale–the most pale)

Additionally, when adjectives are used attributively, they get an *-e* suffix. The only exception is when they precede a neutral noun which is not used with a definite article or a pronoun. Some adjectives, for example the ones ending in *-en* which are mostly adjectives denoting material, do not exhibit that kind of inflection: *de gouden ring* (the gold ring).

Verb Inflection. The starting point for verb inflection is the verb stem. The only thing which needs to be explained in connection with the results of our experiments is the formation of the past participle (psp). It is formed by adding the prefix *ge-* to the stem and, depending on the final consonant of the stem, either a *t* or *d* suffix is attached. However, if the stem already ends in *-t* or *-d*, no suffix is added.

An exception to these rules are verbs with *separable* particles which form psp by inserting *ge* between the separable particle and the verb stem–*op**ge**ruimd* (to clean). Verbs starting with *be-, er-, ge-, her-, mis-, ont-* and *ver-* form psp without *ge-*: *vertel-verteld* (to tell). These particles are also known as *inseparable.* For a detailed discussion of Dutch morphology, see (de Haas and Trommelen, 1993).

3 Finite State Morphology

We employ a set of FSTs to cover the morphological phenomena presented in the previous section. For example, if the input word is *stukken* from (2), the transducer for plural nouns should produce *stuk* as a possible root form in analysis mode, and then, given this root form, it should output *stukken* in generation mode. In our experiments, the root of a given noun is its singular form, the root of an adjective– its base form, and the one of a verb is its stem.

We have used the Stuttgart Finite State Transducer (SFST) tools to implement and run a number of separate transducers which are shown in Table 1.

POS	transducers
nouns	singular, plural
adj	base, comparative, superlative
verbs	sg1, sg2/3, pl/inf, past-sg, past-pl, psp

Table 1: *Transducers used*

We use words from the CELEX morphological database (CELEX, 1995) as a development set in order to: **i)** investigate if all target phenomena are covered by the FSTs and **ii)** to have some notion of their degree of non-determinism. CELEX contains about

380K word forms corresponding to nearly 125K headwords. It is a very suitable resource for our purposes since it covers a large number of different morphological phenomena.

Three word sets are randomly selected: 2000 plural nouns, 2000 superlative adjectives and 2000 first person singular verbs and they are processed with the FSTs. We take superlative adjective forms and plural nouns in order to ensure that we deal with comparable adjectives and countable nouns. The paradigms of the selected words are extracted from CELEX, so we can check the paradigms generated by the FSTs against them.

The results for the analysis of the three extracted word sets are given in Table 2. First, the words of each set are analysed with the respective transducer and the output is a set of possible root forms for each word. The number of analyses is divided by the number of analysed words to get the *analyses per word* ratio. This indicates how deterministic the applied transducer is in analysis mode.

Next, we use the candidate roots to generate paradigms for each word and we check them against the paradigm we extracted from CELEX for the respective word. If the correct paradigm was found, the root which it was generated from is saved and thus, a list of correct roots for each of the three word sets is produced.

	nouns	adj	verbs
analysed	1995	1999	1963
analyses/word	1.18	2.93	1.11
correct roots	1946	1998	1567

Table 2: *Analysis mode results*

The words which failed to be analysed are very irregular forms which makes it impossible for an analysis to be produced, e.g. *vaklui-vakman* (experts-expert), since our method deals only with regular inflection.

The FSTs do not have access to information about the word stress and therefore, cases like (3-a) and (3-b) are ambiguous because it is not clear whether the vowel should be doubled or not. For example, the possible roots for *regelen* would be **regeel* and *regel*.

The number of analyses for adjectives is so high because it is not clear whether the word is an adjective that ends in *s* and takes only *-t* to form superlative as shown in (5). If so, there is also no way to know if the root form ends in *-s* or if *s* is a replacement for a *-z*. Thus, for almost each adjective three analyses will be delivered– *boost* (angry): **boo*, **boos* and *booz*. This is also the reason for the non-determinism of the first person singular verb transducer– the output of the analysis for *leef* is *leev* and **leef*.

There are also words for which no correct paradigms are generated. This is due to the fact that those words have at least one irregular form in their paradigms–*schip-schepen* (ship-ships). However, we do not see these irregularities as an obstacle for the performance of our method since they form a closed class and are supposed to be already included in most lexicons and dictionaries.

Next, each of the three lists with correct roots is processed by the transducers for the respective POS in generation mode to investigate the non-determinism of the generation. Table 3 shows the average number of *generated forms per root* for the transducers with non-deterministic generation.

transducer	forms/root
plural	1.21
base	1.21
comparative	1.38
pl/inf	1.36
psp	1.11

Table 3: *Generation: non-deterministic transducers*

Except for the psp transducer, the non-determinism is caused by cases like (4-a) and (4-b) where, depending on which syllable is stressed, the final *l*, *r* and *g* can be doubled or not. The non-determinism of the psp generator is due to the fact that some of the verb particles can be both separable and inseparable. For example, we have *omklemd* (to clasp) but there is also *omgekanteld* (to tip over). Therefore, both **omkanteld* and *omgekanteld* are generated.

4 Disambiguation Phase

4.1 Web Search Heuristics

Since we showed that the FSTs cover all target morphological phenomena, the only remaining issue is to disambiguate their non-deterministic output. We resolve this problem by using Yahoo to obtain the search hits for a given root and the word forms it generates. If a given form is found more times than a certain threshold (500 in our experiments), it is very likely that the form is a valid member of the paradigm. A paradigm is considered valid if all its forms have passed the threshold. Further, we limit the search only to pages considered by Yahoo to be in Dutch and which are from the Netherlands.

In order to evaluate the performance of our method, a test set that consists of nouns, adjectives and verbs which have between 40 and 100 occurrences in large Dutch newspaper corpora (~530M words) has been created. This selection is based on the assumption that unknown words are typically *less frequent*. The corpora have already been parsed with the Alpino parser and many words have been added to the lexicon of the Alpino grammar. The lexical entries of the chosen words provide our gold standard.

Verbs are the easiest POS for processing with our method because in most cases, all 6 forms– *sg1, sg2/3, pl/inf, past-sg, past-pl* and *psp*– are different and the chance of finding enough counts for all forms in a wrong paradigm is minimal. We start by checking if there are enough search hits for the root, i.e. the sg1 form in this case. In order to be sure that the occurrences found are actually the ones of the root, the query sent to Yahoo consists of the first person singular personal pronoun and the root– *ik* + root.

However, it is very difficult to capture cases like *opruimen* with that query since the separable particle occurs at the end of the sentence. To deal with this, we automatically check whether the given candidate root starts with a separable particle and if so, we ignore that particle and search only for the verb stem– *ik ruim*.

Since the combination of *ik* and the root form can be very rare for some verbs, we set a threshold of only 50 occurrences. Even if a wrong root is able to get through, it would be always discarded, if there are not enough search hits for one of the forms it generates. The same threshold is also used for the past singular and the past plural forms since those are not that frequently used in Dutch.

For adjectives, we want to find the base, comparative and superlative forms and their inflected counterparts. However, not every adjective has all six forms. Non-comparable adjectives like *amorf* (amorphous) have only the base and the base inflected form. There are also some adjectives like *romantisch* (romantic) which form superlative by using the word *meest* (most) in front of the base form.

We start again by looking if there are enough search hits for the proposed root which is the base adjective form in this case. If all six forms are found, then the generated paradigm is taken to be the final result. However, in order to be able to deal with cases like *romantisch*, we also allow for paradigms where only the two base and the two comparative forms are found.

The adjectives for which no paradigm has been generated are processed again but this time we assume that these adjectives are non-comparable and thus, we search only for the two base forms. If their counts are above the threshold, the paradigm is considered to be valid. We do this in a separate round in order to avoid situations where a wrong root is able to produce two valid base forms due to chance.

Nouns are the most complicated POS to process because there are only 2 forms, singular and plural, which makes it more difficult to obtain reliable results. One example is *schel-schellen* (bell-bells). If the input word is *schellen*, there are two possible roots for it– *schel* and **schellen*. In the latter case, there are enough hits for the generated plural form **schellens* because *schellen* happens to be a family name and *schellens* is its genitive form– *Schellens methode* (Schellen's method). Thus a wrong paradigm will be generated.

To prevent this, we search for the combination of the indefinite article *een* and the root. However, not all nouns combine with *een* (e.g. mass nouns) and that is why, if there are not enough search hits, we also search for the combination of the root and *is* (to be, 3rd PER.SG.PRES). The queries for *een schellen* and *schellen is* return less than 100 hits and this root is correctly discarded.

Once a root form has passed the threshold, we can also determine the definite article of the noun. Depending on their gender and number, Dutch nouns are used either with the *de* definite article (for masculine and feminine, and also plural) or the *het* article (for neuter). We search for occurrences of *de* + root and *het* + root and return the article with the higher number of search hits.

The query for the generated noun plural form is *de+plural*. Since the generation is not deterministic, there might be more than one plural form which passes the threshold. In this case, the most frequent one is taken to be the final output. If there is more than one root that was able to generate a paradigm, the paradigm of the one with the most search hits is taken to be the final outcome.

However, there are many compounds whose root forms, combined with the indefinite article have very low number of occurrences: *Marshall-plan* (the Marshall plan), *zaak-Bouterse* (the Bouterse case), *zendingswerk* (missionary work). Normally, the compound head is a common word and the paradigm could be generated by processing the head instead of the whole compound. In most of the cases, the head is the rightmost part of the compound– *plan* in *Marshall-plan* and *werk* (work) in *zendingswerk*.

For words which are joined by a hyphen, splitting the compound is straightforward– the word on the right side is considered to be the head of the compound. However, if this word starts with a capital letter, like in *zaak-Bouterse*, we assume that the head of the compound is on the left side since the right part is most probably a name. For compounds without a hyphen, we take the chunk from the third letter to the end of the word. If there are at least 10,000 search hits for this chunk, it is considered to be the head of the compound. Otherwise, the chunk from the fourth letter is taken and so on, until we find a chunk with enough occurrences.

Let us put it all together. The query for the root is sent but the threshold set for it is 100 because nouns tend to occur less frequently together with the indefinite article. After a valid root is found, the definite article is determined and then the search hits for the generated plural form(s) are obtained. If no paradigm was generated for a given word, we assume that it might be a low-frequent compound and we try to split it. If there is a valid head, the same procedure is applied to it in an attempt to generate its paradigm which is also the paradigm of the whole compound.

4.2 Results and Error Analysis

The test set, described in Section 4.1, consists of 2593 unique words but the gold standard contains a total of 2781 entries– 1368 nouns, 729 adjectives and 684 verbs. This is due to the fact that some morphologically ambiguous words have more than one valid paradigm. For instance, many psp can also act as adjectives: *gebruind* is the psp of the verb *bruinen* (to turn/make brown) but it is also an adjective– 'tanned, sunburnt'. That is why this word is listed both as an adjective and a verb. There are 188 cases of morphological ambiguity.

However, our method is able do deal with them. When an input word comes in, the FSTs for each POS try to process it and if some of them manage to generate a paradigm, the web heuristics for the respective POS are applied. After the disambiguation phase, only the verb and the adjective paradigms for *gebruind* 'survived' and they are correctly taken to be the final outcome. However, in very rare cases there is morphological ambiguity within the same POS. For instance, the word *kussen* is the plural form of *kus* (a kiss) but it also means 'a cushion' whose plural form is *kussens*. In that case, only the paradigm whose root form has more search hits is returned.

Table 4 presents the overall results and the results for each POS. *Coverage* indicates the number of words with a paradigm generated and *accuracy* is the number of the generated correct paradigms.

	overall	nouns	adjectives	verbs
total	2781	1368	729	684
coverage	96.55%	98%	98.91%	90.94%
accuracy	99.63%	99.33%	100%	99.84%

Table 4: *Web experiment results*

No paradigm has been generated for the uncountable noun *smelt* (smelt). All other nouns without paradigms are compounds which form plural in an irregular way. The same is also valid for the verbs which have not been covered– all of them have irregular past or psp forms which are not handled by our technique. Most of the adjectives not covered are non-comparable adjectives ending in *-en* and designating material, e.g. *satijnen* (satin). Such adjectives have only a base form and thus, no valid paradigm is found for them.

Next, we see in Table 4 that some of the generated noun and verb paradigms are wrong. Most of the wrong noun ones are compounds whose head is the word *kind* (child). For example, the compound *pleegkind* (foster child) is correctly split and we try to generate a paradigm for its head *kind*. However, it has an irregular plural form– *kinderen*. Nevertheless, the 'regular' plural form **kinden* has more than 1000 occurrences in the web and it is taken to be a valid one. A manual examination of the results of the web search showed that all the occurrences were actually a typo– the actual meaning was *kind en* (child and) but in many web forums, blogs, etc. they were written as one word.

Another source of error for the noun paradigms are words from French origin, e.g. *secretaris-generaal* (secretary-general). In this case the head of the compound is on the left of the hyphen and thus it is the part that is inflected. The right plural form is *secretarissen-generaal*. However, our compound splitting heuristics takes the right part to be the head which, in this case, happens to be the noun *generaal* (general). Its paradigm is generated but this is not the correct paradigm of the compound.

The only verb with a wrong paradigm generated is the irregular verb *schijten* (to shit). The incorrect psp generated by the psp FST, *geschijt*, has enough search hits because it happens to be a less frequent case of nominalisation– namely, *ge* + *root*. This error, however, can be tolerated, since it is potentially possible in the rare case of irregular verbs which allow for such nominalisation and have roots that end in *-t* or *-d*.

The achieved results show clearly that simple but carefully designed web queries can be successfully used to disambiguate the output of a non-deterministic finite state morphology for Dutch. Our method is able to deal with all major and common morphological phenomena except for few cases that include irregular forms or very rare combinations of factors.

5 Conclusion

We proposed a combination of finite state techniques and specially designed web queries and heuristics to deliver morphological analyses for a given unknown word and to generate its paradigm. Our approach does not require access to sophisticated linguistic information but instead employs the web as a linguistic resource. The successful application of the method to real-life Dutch data proved its efficiency and high accuracy.

Naturally, languages with a large number of inflectional variants would be more problematic for our approach due to the much larger morphological ambiguity they exhibit. However, we also expect that the high number of forms in the paradigms would facilitate the disambiguation of the FSTs output. As we showed, it is much easier to validate a paradigm that consists of 6 forms since the web results are more reliable for it. We will investigate the scalability of our method in future research.

References

Adolphs, P. (2008). Acquiring a poor man's inflectional lexicon for German. In *Proceedings of the 6th International Conference on Language Resources and Evaluation (LREC)*, Marrakech, Morocco.

Beesley, K. R. and Karttunen, L. (2003). *Finite State Morphology*. CSLI Publications, Palo Alto, CA, USA.

CELEX (1995). The CELEX lexical database-Dutch, English, German. CD-ROM.

Cholakov, K. (2009). Towards morphologically enhanced automated lexical acquisition. In *Proceedings of the 14th ESSLLI Student Session*, Bordeaux, France.

de Haas, W. and Trommelen, M. (1993). *Morfologisch Handboek van het Nederlands: Een overzicht van de woordvorming*. SDU, 's Gravenhage, The Netherlands.

Keller, F. and Lapata, M. (2003). Using the web the obtain frequencies for unseen bigrams. *Computational Linguistics*, 29(3):459–484.

Mikheev, A. (1997). Automatic rule induction for unknown-word guessing. *Computational Linguistics*, 23.

Nakov, P., Bonev, Y., Angelova, G., Gius, E., and von Hahn, W. (2003). Guessing morphological classes of unknown German nouns. In *Proceedings of RANLP 2003*, Borovets, Bulgaria.

Petitpierre, D. and Russel, G. (1995). Mmorph– the multext morphology program. Technical report, Carouge, Switzerland.

Prins, R. and van Noord, G. (2001). Unsupervised POS-tagging improves parcing accuracy and parsing efficiency. In *Proceedings of IWPT*, Beijing, China.

van den Bosch, A. and Daelemans, W. (1999). Memory-based morphological analysis. In *Proceedings of the 37th Annual Meeting of the ACL*, pages 285–292, San Francisco, CA.

van Noord, G. (2006). At last parsing is now operational. In *Proceedings of TALN*, Leuven, Belgium.

Prototype-based Active Learning for Lemmatization

Walter Daelemans
Centre for Dutch Language and Speech (CNTS)
University of Antwerp
Antwerp, Belgium
walter.daelemans@ua.ac.be

Hendrik J. Groenewald
Centre for Text Technology (CTexT)
North-West University
Potchefstroom, South Africa
handre.groenewald@nwu.ac.za

Gerhard B. van Huyssteen
Centre for Text Technology (CTexT)
North-West University
Potchefstroom, South Africa
gvhuyssteen@csir.co.za

Abstract

Annotation of training data for machine learning is often a laborious and costly process. In Active Learning (AL), criteria are investigated that allow ordering the unannotated data in such a way that those instances potentially contributing most to the speed of learning can be annotated first. Within this context we explore a new approach that focuses on prototypicality as a criterion for the selection of instances to act as training data in order to optimize prediction accuracy. In parallel with the prototype-based active classification (PBAC) approach of Cebron & Berthold (2009), we investigate whether the basic PBAC assumption rings true for linguistic data. The NLP task we address is lemmatization, the reduction of inflected word forms to their base-form. We operationalize prototypicality as features (i.e. word frequency and word length) of the already available training data items, and combine this with a measure of uncertainty (entropy). We show that the selection of less prototypical instances first, provides performance that is better than when data is randomly selected or when state of the art AL methods are used. We argue that this improvement is possible due to the fact that language processing tasks have highly disjunctive instance spaces, as there are often few regularities and many irregularities.

Keywords

Active Learning; Prototype Theory; Lemmatization; Afrikaans.

1. Introduction

Supervised machine learning techniques are still superior to unsupervised machine learning techniques for many NLP tasks. However, annotation of training data is often a laborious and costly process. In Active Learning (AL) [1,2] criteria are investigated that allow ordering the unannotated data in such a way that those instances potentially contributing most to the speed of learning can be annotated first. Rather than relying on random samples to act as instances in training data, AL entails the selection of instances to act as training data in order to optimize prediction accuracy. Ideally, AL leads to the creation of a supervised learning classifier at a fraction of the annotation effort needed when selecting new training items to be annotated randomly, and without loss in accuracy. Also in domain adaptation, AL has been proposed [3] as a feasible approach. Research on AL centers around the development and comparison of different approaches that could be used to order the available unannotated examples in such a way that those selected first are the ones most informative for learning. Another research area is the design of suitable stopping criteria.

In this paper, we explore a new approach that focuses on prototypicality (i.e. the degree to which some examples are better, more representative examples of a category than others) as a criterion for ordering the data. In parallel with the prototype-based active classification (PBAC) approach of Cebron & Berthold [4], we investigate whether the basic PBAC assumption rings true for linguistic data. We operationalize prototypicality on the basis of different features of the already available training data items and show that the selection of less prototypical instances first provides performance that is better than when data is randomly selected or when state of the art AL methods are used (i.e. a committee-based entropy method). The NLP task we address is lemmatization, the reduction of inflected word forms to their base-form.

In Section 2 work related to Prototype Theory, Active Learning, and lemmatization is discussed. Section 3 outlines our approach, Section 4 describes our experiments on Afrikaans lemmatization and the remainder of the paper discusses these results.

2. Related work

2.1 Prototype Theory

In studies on human cognition, prototypes have been studied for many years [5]. Prototype effects are especially prevalent in language structure and language usage, and have been a central topic in the Cognitive Linguistics paradigm [6,7]. It is widely accepted that language structures (including lexical items) show prototype effects: some instances are better examples than others. For example, with regard to plural formation the {s} morpheme (like in *tables*) could be considered more prototypical than the {en} morpheme (as in *oxen*); likewise, the lexical item *chair* would probably be considered to be a more proto-

International Conference RANLP 2009 - Borovets, Bulgaria, pages 65–70

typical English lexical item than, say, *cache*. In both these cases frequency plays a central role in determining which example is more prototypical than the other (e.g. *chair* is more frequently used than *cache*). When working with linguistic data for natural language processing (NLP) purposes, we can therefore safely assume that some examples in a data set (of unknown examples) are better examples, or more representative, than others.

Various interdependent physiological, referential, statistical and/or psychological factors determine prototypicality [7]; in our current research we focus on frequency (i.e. most commonly or productively used; cf. the statistical hypothesis in Prototype Theory), and size/length (i.e. prototypical concepts are often represented by shorter words; cf. insights on basic-level effects in Prototype Theory [6]). Other factors include membership function (i.e. centrality and salience within a family resemblance model), activation time (i.e. time to process/classify/identify), association/chaining (i.e. the link between form, function, and meaning), conventionalization (i.e. how well-known a word is), acquisition (i.e. more prototypical items are learned first), etc. [6]). These factors are not considered in our current research, but could also be operationalized in future work.

2.2 Active Learning

Predominant approaches to AL include uncertainty-based sampling [8], Support Vector Machine methods [9], and query-by-committee [2]. The latter is a popular method in Active Learning, where entropy computed on the basis of a committee of classifiers is used as a criterion for sample selection.

Recently, Cebron & Berthold [4] presented a novel approach to AL, which they call prototype-based active classification (PBAC). In their algorithm a new, labeled prototype is added in each learning iteration to fine-tune the classification of the datasets; prototypical (i.e. representative) examples are selected first, and examples at the classification boundary (i.e. less prototypical examples) are only selected/focused on automatically when it becomes necessary. In all their experiments, they only use non-linguistic data.

In the PBAC algorithm the relative importance of each data point is calculated as a combination of (a) its representativeness of the data set as a whole (i.e. based on density estimates on the unannotated data), and (b) the uncertainty of a classifier to assign a class to it (i.e. measured as entropy – based on the annotated data – that is inversely related to the voting confidence of the classifier). These two measures are then combined as a new data selection criterion (i.e. the uncertainty distribution), which is calculated as the weighted sum of the representativeness (called potentials) and the classification uncertainty, to the extent that "the remaining potential on the data point still prevents unrepresentative samples from being chosen", which "helps to prevent selection of rare or borderline cases"; see Mazzoni et al. [10] for the detrimental effects of choosing irrelevant data points in AL). Thus, the uncertainty distribution is being used to choose prototypical examples for classification, an approach which promises, with regard to non-linguistic data, to outperform AL with random initialization and closest-to-boundary selection; the algorithm also proved to be stable, and reaches levels of accuracy close to the final one after only a few iterations.

One central aspect of Prototype Theory that is important for the PBAC algorithm is the radial model of categorization. Lakoff [6] makes it clear that "the center, or prototype, of the category is predictable. And while the non-central members are not predictable from the central members, they are 'motivated' by it, in the sense that they bear family resemblances to it." Hence, in the PBAC algorithm, the value of the radius of the neighborhood (i.e. a positive constant defining a neighborhood) is one of the parameters that determine the performance of the algorithm. Cebron & Berthold [4] found that a "...larger radius seems to be beneficial in the first iterations, whereas a small radius leads to more regions with high potential. This causes more exploration and leads to a more detailed (but slower) exploration of the datasets, which proves beneficial in later iterations".

In their conclusion, Cebron & Berthold [4] indicate that future work could include tuning the parameters of the PBAC algorithm to a specific problem; in this research, we look at a specific linguistic problem, viz. lemmatization.

2.3 Lemmatization

AL has been applied to a large range of natural language processing (NLP) tasks, including document classification ([9], Part-of-Speech tagging [11], and parse selection [12]. To our knowledge, no literature has been published on using AL in the development of lemmatizers.

Lemmatization is a common NLP task for most languages, and can simply be defined as "a normalisation step on textual data, where all inflected forms of a lexical word are reduced to its common headword-form, i.e. lemma" [13]. For example, the grouping of the inflected forms *swim*, *swimming* and *swam* under the base-form *swim* is seen as an instance of lemmatization. The last part of this definition applies to this project, as the emphasis is on recovering the base-form from the inflected form of the word. The base-form or lemma is the simplest form of a word as it would appear as headword in a dictionary.

Our experiments in this paper deal specifically with lemmatization for Afrikaans. Inflection is a productive, but rather simple (in comparison to languages like Spanish or Finnish) morphological process in Afrikaans, with nine basic categories of inflection, viz. plural, diminutive, comparative, superlative, partitive genitive, infinitive, past tense, participle, and attributive. The *-e* suffix is by far the most frequent affix, occurring across many of these inflectional categories [14]. We could therefore predict that words ending on *-e* would be prototypical examples of inflected words in Afrikaans.

3. Using prototypes in AL

3.1 Assumptions

The broad aim of our research is to investigate whether the basic PBAC assumption rings true for linguistic data. Note that we don't implement the PBAC algorithm directly; our implementation was developed in parallel with the research of Cebron & Berthold [4], and is merely related to and compatible with the broad approach taken in the PBAC algorithm. As such, our research can be seen as a contribution towards a better understanding of the representativeness parameter in the PBAC approach.

A central assumption of the PBAC approach is that less prototypical cases (i.e. peripheral cases or exceptions) are not important for machine classification, since they do not contribute much information to the construction of a global model. This contrasts directly with our view that, with regard to linguistic data, less prototypical instances are in actual fact important for learning. Our view is based on two grounds: firstly, it is generally accepted in Cognitive Linguistics [6] that outliers contribute as much to the construction of cognitive models as central members (see Section 2.2); hence the interest that Cognitive Linguistics takes in studying not only prototypical instances, but also those peripheral, less prototypical instances of language usage [15]. Secondly, in memory-based language processing [16] it has been argued, on the basis of comparative machine learning experiments on natural language processing data, that exceptions are crucial for obtaining high generalization accuracy. It therefore seems as if the assumption of the PBAC approach is at odds with what is widely believed about natural language data.

For purposes of this paper, our assumption is that long words (e.g. *manifestations*) are less prototypical than short words (e.g. *chair*); likewise, we assume that low frequency words (e.g. *cache*) are less prototypical than high frequency words (e.g. *chair*). (See 2.1 above for a motivation of these assumptions.)

3.2 Hypothesis

Based on our above stated point of view, we hypothesize that less prototypical linguistic examples should provide better results quicker in AL; this is in contrast with the PBAC approach that would predict that more prototypical instances should provide better results quicker.

Our basic hypothesis is that, contrary to what is expected from the PBAC approach, adding less prototypical instances to a baseline classifier (seeded with randomly selected data) at the start of the learning process has a bigger impact than adding prototypical instances (specifically with regard to linguistic data). The reason for this is that less prototypical instances (in our case long, low frequency words, such as *manifestations*) contribute new information to the classifier, and are therefore more informative for learning than prototypical instances (i.e. short, high frequency words, such as *chair*).

Similarly, words with high entropy should provide more information to the construction of a classification model than words with low entropy. Hence, using long, low frequency words with high entropy should provide better results in AL.

3.3 Approach

Recall that in the PBAC approach the criterion for data selection is calculated as the weighted sum of (1) the representativeness, and (2) the classification uncertainty.

With regard to (1), we must determine for a certain dataset and/or a certain task what factors determine the representativeness (i.e. prototypicality) of category members. These factors must then be operationalized as density estimates on the unannotated data so that it could be used to select the data point with the highest estimate as prototype. Such operationalizations could be implemented as features of the training instances, or otherwise as organizational principles of the data set. In our current research, our experiments are geared towards the exploration of word frequency and word length as density estimates in the task of lemmatization (see Section 3).

With regard to (2), we follow the PBAC approach by using entropy as an indicator of the degree of uncertainty or disagreement among different classifiers to assign a class to it, where entropy is inversely related to the voting confidence of the classifier. High entropy therefore indicates higher levels of uncertainty. Words with high entropy are believed to be less prototypical and should therefore be beneficial at the start of the learning process. Entropy correlates with exploitation in the PBAC approach.

Our criterion for data selection, called the combination distribution (CD), is calculated as a weighted combination of word frequency, word length and entropy. The formula for the combination distribution is as follows:

$$CD = w_1(Entropy) + w_2(WL) + w_3(WF) \qquad (1)$$

where w_1, w_2 *and* w_3 indicate the different weights.

4. Experiments

4.1 Setup

For purposes of our experiments, we want to construct a model of the data where we can (a) distinguish between more or less prototypical instances; and (b) select different subsets of the data for AL purposes. In this way, we want to explore, for the task of lemmatization, word frequency and word length as parameters of representativeness, and entropy as an indication of classifier uncertainty. In our experiments, we operationalize these three factors in the following way.

Concerning word frequency, the data set (see 4.2) is ordered based on frequency counts for the words in the data set, which were calculated on the basis of frequency counts (on types) obtained from an Afrikaans corpus containing more than 160 million tokens [17]. It should be noted that, if frequency is viewed as a density estimate of the distribution of instances in memory, it means that such a distribution will have a high density with regard to low frequency words, which could be viewed as a large group of similar training instances (i.e. in the core of a radial representation). High frequency words (which are less frequent in the data set) will appear, on the other hand, outside the boundaries of this core. Since words appearing inside the boundaries are deemed to be more prototypical than words that fall outside of the boundaries, this representation of the word frequency is so to speak the inverse of a commonsense representation; if viewed as a density estimate, low frequency words are therefore actually more prototypical than high frequency words.

The same argument is also valid when considering word length as a feature. Longer words are less prototypical than shorter words, since the data set contains larger numbers of short words grouped together, than longer words. Short words will appear inside the boundaries and are therefore viewed as more prototypical than longer words. Word length was calculated by counting the number of characters comprising each word in the data set.

Entropy is calculated on the basis of a class distribution obtained from a committee of three different classifiers, each using a different machine learning algorithm. The algorithms that were used are the default TiMBL implementations of IB1, IGTree and IB2 [18], where k=1. k refers to the k-nearest distances, rather than the k-nearest neighbors. This means the class distribution may contain several instances, despite k having a value of 1. The class distribution therefore consists of all the classes of the instances contained within a distance of 1 from the classified instance, as indicated by the committee of classifiers. The formula used for the calculation of the entropy of a word is shown in Equation 1:

$$Entropy(w) = -\sum_{i=1}^{n} p(w_i)\log p(w_i) \qquad (2)$$

where n is the number of classes in the distribution and $p(w_i)$ is the proportional number of a particular class relative to the total number of classes in the class distribution output by the committee.

4.2 Data

Data for the Afrikaans lemmatiser was constructed by extracting word-forms that contain substrings that correspond to inflectional affixes (at the surface level) from an Afrikaans lexicon, together with an equal number of instances where lemma and word-form are equal. The extraction yielded 72,226 instances, which were manually lemmatized as training data. Each instance consisted of 20 features (letters of the word-form as separate features).

271 classes were automatically derived by means of a comparison based on the longest common substring of the extracted word-forms and their manually provided lemmas. The classes indicate the transformation that a word-form must undergo in order to obtain its linguistically correct lemma, specifying the character string to be removed, the relative position of the operation (i.e. L (left), R (right) and M (middle)), and the replacement string. If a word-form and its lemma are identical, the class awarded will be "0", denoting the word should be left in the same form. This annotation scheme yields classes like those in the third column of Table 1. The classifiers are not prohibited from predicting impossible classes (e.g. “Lge>” is not a valid class for the word bote, since the word does not containing the string “ge”).

Table 1. Inflected words with their lemmas and classes as found in the Afrikaans training data

Word-form	Lemma	Class
"geel" 'yellow'	"geel" 'yellow'	0
"geslaap" 'slept'	"slaap" 'sleep"	Lge>
"hondjie" 'puppy'	"hond" 'dog'	Rjie>
"bote" 'ships'	"boot" 'ship'	Rte>ot

4.3 Implementation

In all our experiments, we use a k-Nearest Neighbor (k-NN) approach as learner (i.e. memory-based learning). In this approach, classification of a new instance is based on local extrapolation from memorized similar instances. We employed the standard k-NN algorithm, IB1, with default algorithmic parameter settings as implemented in the TiMBL software package [18].This package also contains implementations of IGTree (a decision tree based approximation of k-NN, and IB2 (a variation of IB1 in which only instances misclassified with the current contents of memory are added to that memory). These variations were used in computing the entropy measure (see 4.1 above).

Experiments were performed by using the entire data set, consisting of 72,226 words, where every word is a single instance in the training data. 10-fold cross validation was used throughout the evaluation process.

We started by training the system with a seed memory (10% of the data set) containing randomly-selected instances. We then arranged the remaining instances in the training data set according to the parameters to be evaluated (i.e. word frequency (WF), word length (WL), and entropy, as well as using the combination distribution (CD) described in 3.3 above). In each case the instances were added both in a high-to-low and in a low-to-high order to the learner in sets of 6,500 instances.

We are interested in obtaining a learning curve with a steeper gradient than that of the baseline experiment (indicated as “Random” in Figure 1) in order to show that our

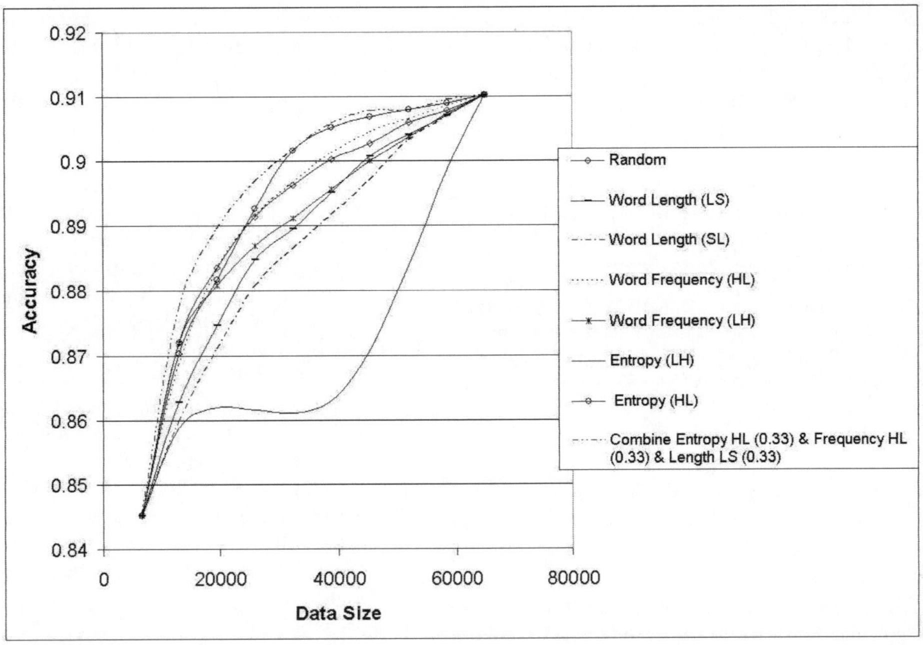

Figure 1. Learning curves

data selection method performs better than a random selection. We also want to compare our method with a standard state of the art approach in AL, which we consider to be the committee-based entropy method (indicated as "Entropy (HL)" in Figure 1).

5. Results

The learning curves for the various parameters, the combination distribution, as well as a random distribution (the base-line experiment) are indicated in Figure 1. Using the same set of randomly selected instances for computing the accuracy obtained in the first fold of every 10-fold cross-validation experiment results in the learning curves of all experiments starting at the same point on the graph. For the calculation of the combination distribution (see Equation 1), we also experimented with different weight values, but found that the best combination distribution curve was obtained with equal weight values.

Figure 1 shows that adding unprototypical words to the seed memory at the start of the learning process clearly outperforms the experiments where prototypical words were added first. This is true for both the evaluated parameters and can be observed by comparing the unprototypical learning curves (e.g. Word Frequency [Low to High] and Word Length [Long to Short] with the prototypical curves (e.g. Word Frequency [High to Low] and [Word Length Short to Long]). (With regard to the learning curves representing word frequency, refer to 4.1 for an explanation of why [High to Low] is indicated as better than [Low to High] in Figure 1.) Another finding from Figure 1 is that the combination distribution (CD) with equal weights yields a steeper learning curve than any of the other individual parameters, including that of the committee-based entropy method.

Even though the gains of this approach seem small at first, the significance of our results is appreciated when considering the difference in the number of training instances required by each of the distributions to reach a certain accuracy figure. The combination distribution, for example, requires 19,864 instances to achieve an accuracy of 0.89, compared to the 24,656 instances required by the random distribution to achieve the same accuracy. In this case it means that 4,792 less instances are needed when using the combination distribution, representing a significant saving in terms of the annotation effort.

6. Discussion

Entropy computed on the basis of a committee of classifiers is a popular method for selecting instances in AL (see 2.2 above). Our results indicate that the performance of this method can be improved by combining entropy with other parameters of representativeness, selected on the basis of Prototype Theory. This approach also improves notably upon the random baseline. However, contrary to intuition and to results for AL in other areas than language processing, it is the selection of less prototypical instances first that provides the best improvement, both for word frequency and word length. A possible explanation for this is that language processing tasks have highly disjunctive instance spaces, as there are often few regularities and many irregularities, and pockets of exceptions [16]. Starting from a random seeding may already provide sufficient structure (as there is little structure of the instance space), and in such a case, finding the boundary cases is as least as important as finding the central cases of classes. A meta-learning analysis in which the prototype-based selection approach is investigated for a larger range of language processing tasks with class systems of different complexities could shed more light on this issue.

Our research shows in any case that a prototype-based selection approach indeed improves upon a committee-based and random baseline approach, but not necessarily the way expected in the PBAC approach.

7. Conclusion

In this paper we have shown that a prototype-based selection strategy for AL improves upon both random baseline and entropy-based committee approaches. Interestingly, for our language processing problem, prototypicality works not in the way expected and documented in other research (more prototypical instances first is better than less prototypical first), but exactly the other way round. A possible explanation for this is the lack of structure found in instance spaces of language processing problems, which typically show large disjunctivity.

Future work includes the investigation of more natural language processing tasks with more operationalizations of prototypicality to investigate whether our findings indeed point to a different superior selection strategy for language processing tasks than for other types of problems. Another aspect to be investigated is the interaction of this approach with possible stopping criteria for AL.

8. Acknowledgments

Van Huyssteen is jointly affiliated with the Human Language Technologies Research Group, Meraka Institute, CSIR, Pretoria, South Africa. Support by the CSIR is hereby acknowledged.

We would like to extend our gratitude to JA Pienaar, who was involved in the initial conceptualization of this project.

Part of this research was made possible through a research grant by the South African National Research Foundation (GUN: 65462).

9. References

[1] Cohn, D.A., Ghahramani, Z. & Jordan, M.I. 1996. Active Learning with Statistical Models. *Journal of Artificial Intelligence Research*. 4: 129-145.

[2] Freund, Y., Seung, H.S., Shamir, E. & Tishby, N. 1997. Selective sampling using the query by committee algorithm. *Machine Learning*. 28: 133-168.

[3] Chan, Y. & Ng, H. 2007. Domain adaptation with active learning for word sense disambiguation. In *Proceedings of the 45th Conference of the Association for Computational Linguistics*. pp. 49-56.

[4] Cebron, N. & Berthold, M.R. 2009. Active learning for object classification: from exploration to exploitation. *Data Mining and Knowledge Discovery*. 18: 283-299.

[5] Rosch, E. & Lloyd, B.B. (eds.). 1978. *Cognition and categorization*. Hillsdale: Lawrence Erlbaum.

[6] Lakoff, G. 1987. *Women, Fire, and Dangerous Things*. Chicago: University of Chicago Press.

[7] Geeraerts, D. 2006. *Words and other wonders: papers on lexical and semantic topics*. Berlin: Walter de Gruyter.

[8] Hwa, R. 2000. Sample selection for statistical grammar induction. In *Proceedings of the Joint SIGDAT Conference on Empirical Methods in NLP and Very Large Corpora*. pp. 45–52.

[9] Schohn, G. & Cohn, D. 2000. Less is more: Active learning with support vector machines. In *Proceedings of the 17th International Conference on Machine Learning*. San Francisco: Morgan Kaufmann. pp. 839-846.

[10] Mazzoni, D., Wagstaff, K.L. & Burl, M. 2006. Active learning with irrelevant examples. In *Proceedings of the 17th European Conference on Machine Learning*. pp. 695-702.

[11] Engelson, S. & Dagan, I. 1996. Minimizing manual annotation cost in supervised training from corpora. In *Proceedings of the 34th Meeting of the Association for Computational Natural Language Learning*. San Fransico: Morgan Kaufmann. pp. 319-326.

[12] Baldridge, J. & Osborne, M. 2004. Active learning and the total cost of annotation. In *Proceedings of the 2004 Conference on Empirical Methods in Natural Language Processing*. Barcelona, Spain. pp. 9-16.

[13] Erjavec, T. & Džeroski, S. 2004. Machine Learning of Morphosyntactic Structure: Lemmatising Unknown Slovene Words. *Applied Artificial Intelligence*. 18(1): 17-40.

[14] Groenewald, H.J. & Van Huyssteen, G.B. 2008. Outomatiese Lemma-identifisering vir Afrikaans [Automatic Lemmatisation for Afrikaans]. *Literator*. 29(1): 65-91.

[15] Langacker, R.W. 2008. *Cognitive Grammar: A Basic Introduction*. Oxford: Oxford University Press.

[16] Daelemans, W. & Van den Bosch, A. 2005. *Memory-based language processing*. Cambridge: Cambridge University Press.

[17] Pharos Dictionaries. 2007. *Media24 Corpus*. Media24: Cape Town.

[18] Daelemans, W., Zavrel, J., Van der Sloot, K. & Van den Bosch, A. 2004. *TiMBL: Tilburg Memory Based Learner, version 5.1, Reference Guide*. ILK Technical Report 04-02. Tilburg: University of Tilburg.

From Partial toward Full Parsing

Heshaam Faili
Department of Electrical and Computer Engineering
University of Tehran
Tehran, Iran
hfaili@ut.ac.ir

Abstract

Full-Parsing systems able to analyze sentences robustly and completely at an appropriate accuracy can be useful in many computer applications like information retrieval and machine translation systems. Increasing the domain of locality by using tree-adjoining-grammars (TAG) caused some researchers to use it as a modeling formalism in their language application. But parsing with a rich grammar like TAG faces two main obstacles: low parsing speed and a lot of ambiguous syntactical parses. In order to decrease the parse time and these ambiguities, we use an idea of combining statistical chunker based on TAG formalism, with a heuristically rule-based search method to achieve the full parses. The partial parses induced from statistical chunker are basically resulted from a system named supertagger, and are followed by two different phases: error detection and error correction, which in each phase, different completion heuristics apply on the partial parses. The experiments on Penn Treebank show that by using a trained probability model considerable improvement in full-parsing rate is achieved.

Keywords

Full Parsing, Partial Parsing, Tree Adjoining Grammar, SuperTagging

1. Introduction

In many applications like information retrieval and Rule-based machine translation systems, accurate deep parse structure of a sentence is required; hence a lot of research is being done on introducing methods to produce deep hierarchical syntactical structure of a given natural language sentence [6]. Over the last decade, there has been a great increase in the performance of parsers. Current parsers achieve to a score of about 90% when measuring just the accuracy of choosing these dependencies [4, 5 and 7]. The choice of formalism does not change the parsers' accuracy significantly, because in all approaches word-word dependencies are used as the only underlying information. But because of the inherent ambiguity in the natural languages, achieving to a full parses of a sentence is a big challenges.

Tree-adjoining-grammars (TAG) have some specific features, which are interested by researchers to be used as modeling formalisms in their language application. The parsing methods based on this formalism involve different problems such as a lot of ambiguities and low parsing speed. One of the main parsing algorithms based on TAG formalism is presented by Van Noord [10] which runs in $O(n^6)$ time complexity. This complexity in a real-size grammar (like XTAG [9]) is not acceptable, especially for a more complicated system like information retrieval and machine translation systems. Also, because of the ambiguities in the resulted parses, the output of this algorithm must be disambiguated by another approach.

To overcome the mentioned problems, we use an alternative approach which is based on statistical partial parsers. One of the partial parser systems which alleviate the TAG formalism problems in time complexity and ambiguity is named supertagging, proposed by (Bangalore and Joshi [2]). The idea behind supertagging is to extend the notion of "tag" from a part of speech to a tag that represents rich syntactic information. Each supertag can be thought as an element in TAG formalism.

They also introduced "lightweight" parsing which follows the supertagging. If words in a string can be tagged with this rich syntactic information, then Bangalore and Joshi claim, the remaining step of determining the actual syntactic structure is trivial [2]. They propose a "lightweight dependency parser" (LDA) which is a heuristically-driven, very simple program that creates a dependency structure from the supertags of the words. While the supertagging only requires a notion of syntactically relevant features, the stage of determining a syntactic structure requires a grammar that uses these syntactically relevant features. Given the correct supertags, LDA performs with an unlabeled accuracy of about 95%.

Although supertagging is a worthwhile notion pursuing the full-parsing, but approaching to a full-parse by the proposed lightweight parser has a major obstacle. Bangalore announced the accuracy of supertagging to be about 92% based on the experiments done on Penn Treebank [1]. This accuracy is not satisfiable to generate a complete deep structure of the sentence by using lightweight dependency analyzer. In a sentence with 15-words length, LDA parser determines the correct full-parse of the sentence with the probability about $95\% * (0.92)^{15} = 27.5\%$. For longer sentences, lower accuracy has been achieved. Nasr and Rambow try to improve the accuracy by changing the heuristic dependency linker with a non-lexical chart parser [8]. Like the original supertagger, their

International Conference RANLP 2009 - Borovets, Bulgaria, pages 71–75

method still has no access to lexical information and only information about the supertags is combined with a chart parser. They cut the error rate of the heuristic LDA by more than half.

In this paper, we present a full-parsing method by combining different heuristics with lightweight shallow parser. Our approach is still in the spirit of Bangalore's work in the sense that lexical information is only used during supertagging. The idea of this paper is based on finding the erroneous supertags which are most probable to be wrongly assigned, and then replacing them with proper candidates.

2. Full Parsing

Although full parsing based on fully correct supertags is very time-efficient [8], but acquiring the fully correct supertagging itself is the main obstacle. The probability of assigning correct supertag set $S=\{s_1,s_2,\ldots,s_n\}$ to all words of a sentence $W=\{w_1,w_2,\ldots,w_n\}$ is equal to product of the probability of correct assigning a single supertag s_i to i-th word w_i (i.e. $p(s_i \mid w_i)$). Based on the experiments done by Bangalore, the probability $p(s_i \mid w_i)$ is equal to 92.2%. So full parsing probability by linking all supertags resulted from supertagging process for a sentence with 15 words length is equal almost be 29.5% and with 25 words near to 13.1%. To overcome this problem, n-best supertagging that assign n-best supertags to each word was proposed by [1]. Based on this approach, by setting n = 3, supertagging correctness increased to 97.1% and accordingly the rate of fully-parsing for whole words in a sentence improved efficiently. (e.g. 74.5% for sentences with 15 words length and 64.3% for sentences with 25 words length). But using n-best supertags followed by lightweight analyzer is equal to find a combination of these supertags which satisfies all available syntactical constraints on TAG. For 3-best supertagger in 15 words length sentence, there are 3^{15} = 14,348,907 combinations which should be checked in order to choose the correct combination. In [8] a dynamic programming method to resolve this complexity is used.

This problem can be seen as a search problem in the state space of all supertags assigned to the words of the sentence. The initial state is a combination of those tags which are assigned by supertagger and the goal states are those which LDA succeed to make a fully dependency linkage between the supertags and hence in those states full-syntactic structure of the sentence is generated. Hill-climbing approach is chosen for search method and the accuracy of LDA is calculated as a heuristic performance measure of problem.

3. Search in the Supertag State Space

Same as other local search problems, the search can be divided into two distinct phases: error detection and correction. In fact, instead of associating n-best supertag to every word of the sentence, the most probable erroneous supertags resulted from n-best supertagging are detected and substituted with proper alternatives which are proposed by an error correction algorithm.

In each non-goal state (i.e. partial parse), error nodes are supertags that are wrongly assigned and therefore they are the cause of preventing LDA to produce exactly one dependency diagram as the correct full parse tree of the sentence. The result of LDA is a dependency diagram which links all supertags based on its syntactical behavior [1]. Four our experiments, we gathered 341 sentences, which are failed to be parsed by LDA, and analyzed the failing reasons. In the case of failing LDA to generate the full connected structure, one of the three cases may happen. These cases are shown in Table 1. As it's shown in the table, different heuristics for detecting the faulty nodes are demonstrated too. These heuristics show the supertags which are most probable to be wrong and should to be replaced with proper candidates.

Table 1. The cases in which supertagger fails to generate the full syntactic structure

Case 1	The LDA output diagram is not fully connected graph and it contains multiple partial graphs. In this case, substitution slots of some supertags are not filled by other tags. From the total 341 faulty test sentences, this case appears in 172 sentences, that is about 50% of all corpus fails to be parsed because of this problem.
Proposed faulty nodes in case 1	The partial trees' root is mostly an erroneous node, which its supertag should be substituted to better one (i.e. should to replace with another supertag which contains more substitution slots in order to make a link with other partial trees). Changing this node with proper one could correct 150 sentences from the total 172 faulty sentences of this case.
Case 2	Supertags of some words do not participate in the dependency diagram and so some child nodes are not included in its parent diagram. Either footnode or substitution slots are required to make a link between the orphan child and parent node. This case appears in more than 30% of test sentences.
Proposed faulty nodes in case 2	The root node of trees that some of their children are missed has a large potential to be wrongly assigned supertag. These missed children can be seen as slots that are not filled. In our experiments, the total faulty sentences of this case have been corrected by changing this node.

Case 3	In the 15% of mentioned faulty test sentences, the LDA output diagram has cycles in its dependencies and therefore is not a valid dependency structure diagram.
Proposed faulty nodes in case 3	In the case of existence any loop in the diagram, the verb nodes are usually ambiguous and have a large potential to be erroneous. By using this heuristic, the full parse structure of 70% of all unparsed sentences of case 3 is correctly acquired.

In each of the mentioned cases, the noisy nodes are detected and then replaced with some other supertags which will be proposed by other heuristics. So, the whole search for finding the full-parse can be summarized as the follows:

```
1- Use supertagger to achieve partial parse
2- Detect the full linkage by using LDA
3- In the case of using full linkage, stop
4- In the case of failure the full parses,
   check if one of the three mentioned cases
   happened
5- In the case of happening one of the
   mentioned cases, replace the faulty node
   proposed by error detection heuristic
   with a better candidate
6- Go to step 2
```

4. Error Correction Heuristics

After detecting the erroneous nodes, a list of proper candidates required to be substituted with the erroneous supertags. Three heuristics are presented here to propose the candidates to be replaced with the erroneous nodes, where each of which improves the full parsing rate and speed. These heuristics are as follows:

4.1 N-Best Heuristic

In this heuristic, the outputs of n-best supertagger are used as successor candidates. The n-best supertagger is a modified version of simple supertagger which proposes n supertags for each word of the sentence. Suppose that *m* is the number of faulty nodes which are detected by the previously mentioned heuristics and *n* is the number of n-best candidates which are predicted by supertagger, so finding the best combination in this space involves $O(m^n)$ cases. Breath first search (BFS) strategy is used to find the best match in this state space. That is for each node; all its successor nodes are generated first and then are evaluated by LDA as an evaluation function. The search terminated when the full parse structure of the input sentence is acquired.

4.2 XTAG-Based Heuristic

In this heuristic, a human-crafted grammar based on tree-adjoining formalism, named XTAG, is used. XTAG is an on-going project to develop a wide-coverage grammar for English using TAG formalism [9]. XTAG uses Lexicalized TAG, where each lexical item is associated to many elementary trees which can satisfy its structural constraints. In this heuristic, these associations between each lexical item and elementary trees are used as candidates to be replaced with the detected faulty nodes.

When an error node is detected, other TAGs, which are associated to those nodes' lexical in the XTAG grammar bank, are chosen as a substitution list. XTAG grammar contains 1226 elementary trees which are categorized into 26 different family trees, and each lexical item especially verb, associated to more than 10 elementary trees. Thus, the candidate list to be substituted with erroneous nodes in this method is much larger than previous one. Therefore, both the time and performance are much higher than n-best correction heuristic.

4.3 Trained Probability Model Heuristic

Although n-best is faster than XTAG heuristic, but the performance of full-parsing is much lower. In the first method the candidate list for correcting the error nodes is so shorter than the later one, and thus it needs less time to search among the combinations. Here a method using a trained probability model is proposed. In fact, for any supertags s_i, s_j, the probability of changing a faulty supertag s_j to supertag s_i (i.e. $P(s_i \mid s_j)$) which concludes a full-parse tree is calculated.

These probabilities are estimated by using maximum likelihood estimation method with counting the number of successful changes of faulty supertag (s_j) to correct supertag (s_i). By using from an annotated corpus of 40,000 sentences and their syntactic parses, these changes are computed in an iterative fashion. At each iteration, the sentences are tagged by the supertagger and the correctness of LDA algorithms is checked by the previously mentioned error detection heuristics and the erroneous nodes are detected. The faulty nodes then substituted with other supertags proposed by a combination of XTAG-based and 10-best heuristics. Each time an error supertag s_j is replaced with supertag s_i, the resulting parse structure is evaluated by PARSEVAL metrics [3]. If the result is a satisfiable full deep structure, the frequency of successful changing s_i to s_j increases one unit. The whole process of calculating the probability model $P(s_i \mid s_j)$ is shown in figure 1.

The training algorithm is terminated when the changes of the probabilities after running the experiment on the whole 40,000 sentences become ignorable. That is the total number of changes in whole probabilities becomes less that a predefined threshold. In our method, we set this threshold to be less than 0.05% of all entry values. At the end of process, all frequencies of changes in any faulty node should be normalized by using equation (1) in order to get the probability $P(s_j \mid s_i)$. Having these probabilities, an ordered list of candidate nodes for any error supertag si is achieved, which can be used in the error correction method:

$$P(s_i \mid s_j) = count(s_i, s_j) / \Sigma_k\, count(s_k, s_j) \qquad (1)$$

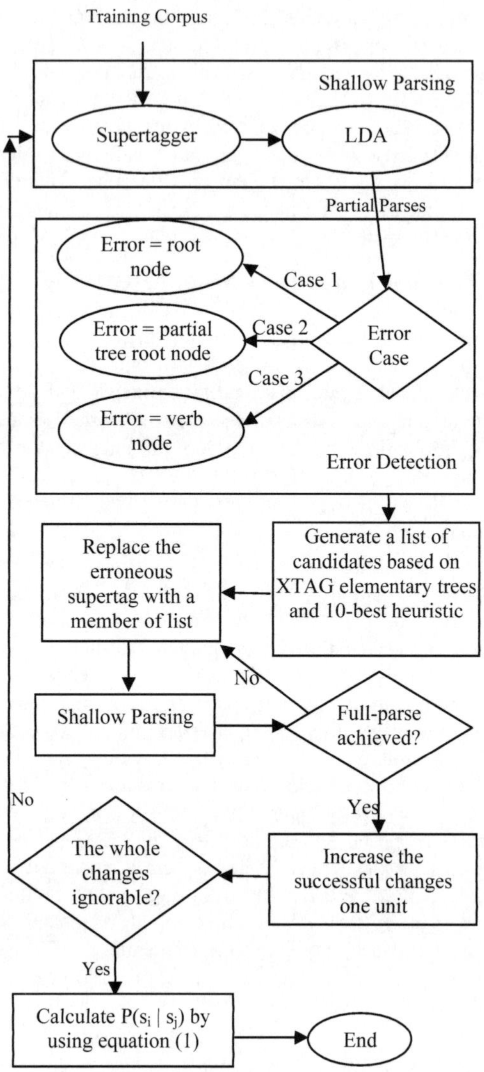

Figure 1. The whole process of calculating the probability model $P(s_i \mid s_j)$

5. Evaluation

In order to evaluate the proposed methods, 3000 sentences with their syntactic structure from Penn Treebank are selected as test corpus. These sentences are completely different from those that are used in the process of calculating the changing probabilities.

We divided the test corpus into three different categories based on the sentence length: the sentences shorter than 16 words, sentences with length between 16 and 25 words and sentences longer than 25 words[1].

The experiments include the evaluation of mentioned heuristics such as 1-best, 10-best, 25-best, XTAG based and trained probability model heuristics. In each experiment, the percentage of full-parsed sentences and parsing time are computed. Also, in order to evaluate the resulting full-parse quality, PARSEVAL metrics, introduced by [3], are calculated. We measure PARSEVAL metric only for those sentences which have been fully-parsed successfully.

Figure 2, 3 and 4 show the results of these experiments on each of the mentioned category. The evaluations show that considerable improvements both in time and percentage of full-parsed sentences are achieved by using the trained probability model heuristic. This method increases the full-parse rate from the native supertagger (1-best heuristic) by a factor of 3 in the first category, by a factor of 11 in the second category and by the factor of 21 in the third category. That is, the effects of the trained probability model in long sentences are more than short sentences.

Comparing the mentioned figures, shows that by increasing the sentence length, the percentage of full-parsing rate and parsing speed decreases dramatically. Also, in the trained probability model heuristic, the parsing speed increases about twice than XTAG-based heuristic, while the full-parsing rate also increases about 20%.

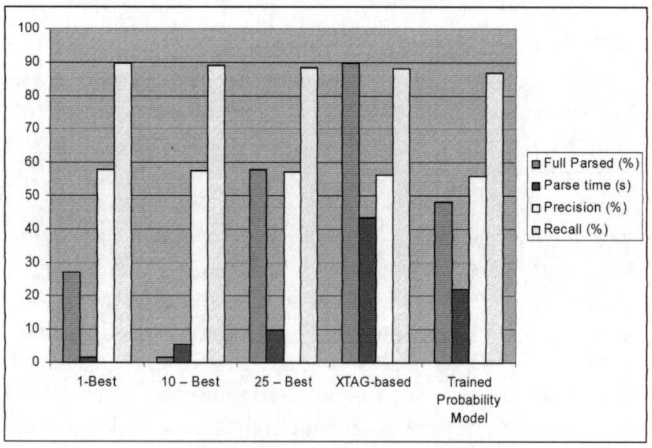

Figure 2: Experimental results on sentences shorter than 16 words

[1] Maximum length of selected sentences is bounded on 45 words.

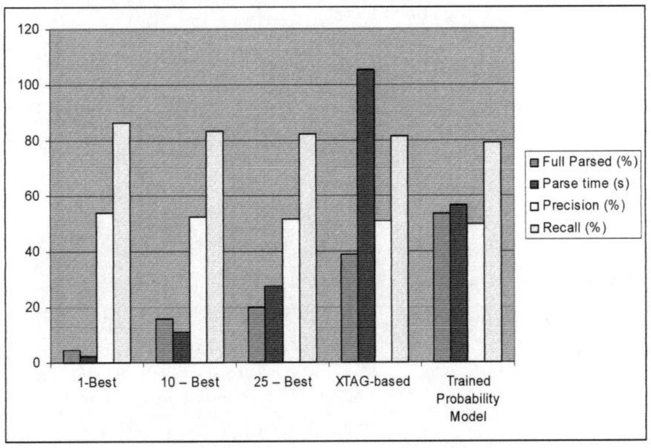

Figure 3: Experimental results on sentences between 16 and 25 words

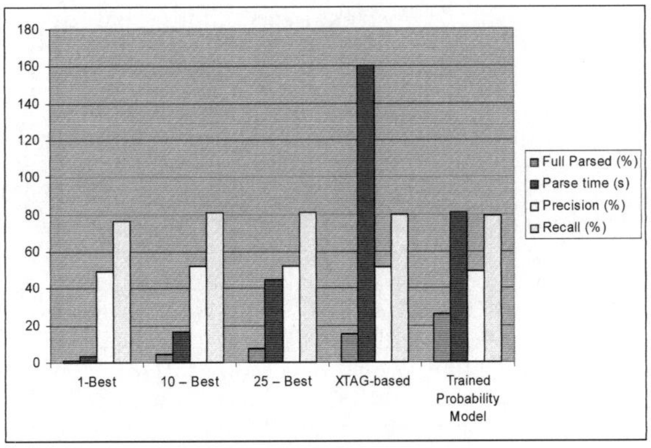

Figure 4: Experimental results on sentences longer than 25 words

6. Conclusion

Parsing is the one of the most important phases in many natural language applications, like information retrieval and rule-based machine translation systems, where it needs full-syntactic analysis for the input sentence. Although using more enriched grammar model, like TAG, is preferred because of its power in the descriptive model, but this kind of formalism lacks both in parsing speed and accuracy.

To overcome these problems, we've taken the benefits of speed and accuracy of a shallow parsing algorithm named supertagger. We introduced several heuristics which get the partial parses as the input and generate the full-parse structure of the sentence.

Several experiments on different data set selected from Penn Treebank show that by using error detection heuristics with a trained probability model to propose correcting candidates, the full-parsing rate as well as parsing speed have been improved significantly.

7. References

[1] Bangalore S., Complexity of Lexical Descriptions and its Relevance to Partial Parsing, PhD thesis, Department of Computer and Information Sciences, University of Pennsylvania, 1997.

[2] Bangalore S. and Joshi A., Supertagging: An approach to almost parsing, Computational Linguistics, 25(2), pp. 237–266, 1999.

[3] Black, E., Abnery, S., Flickinger, D. and et al., A procedure for quantitatively comparing the syntactic coverage of English grammars, DARPA Speech and Natural Language Workshop, pp. 306-311, 1991.

[4] Clark S., Hockenmaier J., and Steedman M., Building deep dependency structures with a wide coverage CCG parser. In Proceedings of the 40th Annual Meeting on Association for Computational Linguistics, Philadelphia, Pennsylvania, pp. 327–334, July 2002.

[5] Collins, M., Three generative, lexicalized models for statistical parsing, In Proceedings of the 35th Annual Meeting of the Association for Computational Linguistics, Madrid, Spain, July 1997.

[6] Faili, H. and Ghassem-Sani, G., An Application of Lexicalized Grammars in English-Persian Translation, Proceedings of the 16th European Conference on Artificial Intelligence (ECAI 2004), Universidad Politecnica de Valencia, Spain, pp. 596-600, 2004.

[7] Hockenmaier J. and Steedman M., Generative models for statistical parsing with combinatory categorial grammar, In Proceedings of the 40th Annual Meeting on Association for Computational Linguistics, Philadelphia, Pennsylvania, pp. 335–342, July 2002.

[8] Nasr A., and Rambow O., supertagging and full parsing, In Proceedings of the Workshop on Tree Adjoining Grammar and Related Formalisms (TAG+7), Vancouver, BC, Canada, 2004.

[9] XTAG research group, A Lexicalized Tree Adjoining Grammar for English, Technical Report IRCS 98-18, Institute for Research in Cognitive Science, University of Pennsylvania, pp. 5-10, 1998.

[10] Van Noord G., Head-corner parsing for TAG, In Computational Intelligence, 10(4), pp. 525–534, 1994.

Grouping synonyms by definitions

Ingrid Falk*
INRIA / Université Nancy 2
ingrid.falk@loria.fr

Claire Gardent
CNRS / LORIA, Nancy
claire.gardent@loria.fr

Evelyne Jacquey
CNRS / ATILF, Nancy
evelyne.jacquey@atilf.fr

Fabienne Venant
Université Nancy 2 / LORIA, Nancy
fabienne.venant@loria.fr

Abstract

We present a method for grouping the synonyms of a lemma according to its dictionary senses. The senses are defined by a large machine readable dictionary for French, the TLFI (Trésor de la langue française informatisé) and the synonyms are given by 5 synonym dictionaries (also for French). To evaluate the proposed method, we manually constructed a gold standard where for each (word, definition) pair and given the set of synonyms defined for that word by the 5 synonym dictionaries, 4 lexicographers specified the set of synonyms they judge adequate. While inter-annotator agreement ranges on that task from 67% to at best 88% depending on the annotator pair and on the synonym dictionary being considered, the automatic procedure we propose scores a precision of 67% and a recall of 71%. The proposed method is compared with related work namely, word sense disambiguation, synonym lexicon acquisition and WordNet construction.

Keywords

Similarity measures, Synonyms, Lexical Acquisition

1 Introduction

Synonymic resources for French are still limited in scope, quality and/or availability. Thus the French WordNet (FREWN) created within the EuroWordNet project [16] has limited scope (3 777 verbs and 14 618 nouns vs. 7 384 verbs and 42 849 nouns in the morphological lexicon for French Morphalou) and has not been widely used mainly due to licensing issues. The alternative open-source WordNet for French called WOLF (WordNet Libre du Francais, [24]) remedies the first shortcoming (restrictive licensing) and aims to achieve a wider coverage by automating the WordNet construction process using an *extend* approach which in essence, translates the synsets from Princeton WordNet (PWN) into French. However, compared to Morphalou, WOLF is still incomplete (979 verbs and 34 827 nouns). Finally, the synonym lexicon DicoSyn [19] is restricted to assigning sets of synonyms to lemmas thereby lacking both categorial information and definitions.

In this paper, we present a method for grouping synonyms by senses and evaluate it on the synonyms given by 5 synonym dictionaries included in the ATILF synonym database. The long term aim is to apply this method to these synonym dictionaries so as to build a uniform synonymic resource for French in which each lemma is assigned a part of speech, a set of (TLFI) definitions and for each given definition, a set of synonyms. The resulting resource should complement DicoSyn and WOLF. Contrary to DicoSyn, it will include categorial information and associate groups of synonyms with definitions. It will furthermore complement WOLF by providing an alternative synonymic resource which, being built on handbuilt high quality resources, should differ from WOLF both in coverage and in granularity.

The paper is structured as follows. Section 2 presents the data we are working from, namely a set of synonym dictionaries for French and the TLFI, the largest machine readable dictionary available for French. Section 3 describes the basic algorithm used to assign a verb synonym to a given definition. Section 4 presents the experiments we did to assess the impact of the similarity measures used and of a linguistic preprocessing on the definitions. Section 5 discusses related work. Section 6 concludes and gives pointers for further research.

2 The source data

We have at our disposal a general purpose machine readable dictionary for French, the Trésor de la Langue Française informatisé (TLFI, [11, 8]) and 5 synonym dictionaries namely, *Dictionnaire des synonymes de la langue française* [2], *Dictionnaire des synonymes* [5], *Nouveau dictionnaire des synonymes* [12], *Dictionnaire alphabétique et analogique de la langue française* [23], *Grand Larousse de la Langue Française* [17].

One driving motivation behind our method is the question of how to merge these 5 synonym lexicons in a meaningful way. Indeed although one of them (namely, [23]) covers most of the verbs present in the five synonym lexicons (5 027 verbs out of 5 736), a merge of the lexicons would permit an increased "synonymic coverage" (11 synonyms in average per verb with the 5 lexicons against 6 per verb using only [23]). To merge the

*The research presented in this paper was partially supported by the TALC theme of the CPER "Modélisation, Information et Systèmes Numériques" funded by the Région Lorraine. We also gratefully acknowledge the ATILF for letting us access their synonym database and the TLFi.

International Conference RANLP 2009 - Borovets, Bulgaria, pages 76–81

five lexicons, we plan to apply the method presented here to each of the synonyms assigned to a word by the 5 synonym lexicons. In this way, we aim to obtain a merged lexicon in which each word is associated with a part of speech, a set of TLFi definitions and for each definition, the set of synonyms associated to this definition.

For our experiment, we worked on a restricted dataset. First, we handled only verbs. Since they are in average more polysemous[1] than other categories, they nevertheless provide an interesting benchmark. Second, we based our evaluation on a single synonym dictionary, namely [23]. As mentioned above, this is the largest of the five lexicons (cf. Fig. 2). Moreover, it is unlikely that the quality of the results obtained vary greatly when considering more synonyms since, as we shall see in Section 3, the synonym-to-definition mapping performed by our method is independent of the number of synonyms assigned to a given word.

The TLFi is the largest machine readable dictionary available for French (54 280 entries, 92 997 lemmas, 271 166 definitions, 430 000 examples). It has a rich XML markup which supports a selective treatment of entry subfields. Moreover, the definitions have been part-of-speech tagged and lemmatised.

For our experiment, we extracted from the TLFi all the verb entries and their associated definitions. Definitions were extracted by selecting the XML elements identifying an entry definition and checking their content. If a selected definitional element contained either some text (i.e., a definition), a synonym or a domain specification, the XML element was taken to indeed identify a definition. Else, no definition was stored. In this way, XML elements that did not contain any definitional information such as subdefinitions containing only examples, were not taken into account.

For each selected definitional element, a definition index was then constructed by taking the open class lemmas associated with the definition and, if any, the synonyms and/or the domain information contained in the definitional element. For instance, given the TLFi definitions for *projeter* (*to project*) listed in Fig. 1, the indexes extracted will be as indicated below each definition. In (a), the index contains the open class lemmas of the definition; in (b) the domain information is also included and in (c), synonymic information is added.

The synonym dictionaries. The table in Fig. 2 gives a quantitative summary of the data contained in the five available synonym dictionaries. Each entry in the synonym dictionaries is associated with one or more sets of synonyms, each set corresponding to a different meaning of the entry. The synonym dictionaries however contain neither part of speech information nor definitions. An example entry of [23] is given in Figure 3. For the experiment, we extracted the verb entries (using a morphological lexicon) of these dictionaries that were also present in the TLFi. Synonyms or entries that were present in the synonym dictionaries but not in the TLFi were discarded.

[1] The average polysemy recorded by the Princeton WordNet for the various parts of speech is: 2.17 for verbs, 1.4 for adjectives, 1.25 for adverbs and 1.24 for nouns.

a. Jeter loin en avant avec force.
To throw far ahead and with strength
⟨ *jeter, loin, avant, force* ⟩

b. CIN. AUDIOVISUEL. Passer dans un projecteur.
CIN. AUDIOVISUAL. To show on a projector.
⟨ *cinéma, audiovisuel, passer, projecteur* ⟩

c. Eclaircir. Synon. jeter quelque lumière
To lighten. Synonym. To throw some light.
⟨ *lighten. throw, light* ⟩

Fig. 1: *Some definitions and extracted indexes for* projeter *(*to project*).*

Syn. Dic.	Verbs	-Refl	+Refl	Syn/verb
Bailly	2600	2370	230	1.
Benac	2656	2298	358	1.5
Chazaud	3808	3267	541	5.25
Larousse	3835	3194	641	4.7
Rey	5027	4071	956	6.
ALL	5736	4554	1182	11.

Fig. 2: *Verbs from* TLFi*, also present in the synonym dictionaries. -Refl indicates the number of non reflexive verb entries (laver), +Refl the number of reflexive verb entries (se laver).*

Reference. To evaluate our results, we built a reference sample as follows. First, we selected a sample of French verbs using the combination of three features: genericity, polysemy and frequency. Each feature could have one of the three values "high", "medium" and "low" thus yielding a sample of 27 verbs. Genericity was assessed using the position of the verb in the French EuroWordNet (the higher the more generic). Polysemy was defined by the number of definitions assigned to the verb by the TLFi. Frequency was extracted from a frequency list built from 10 years of Le Monde newspaper parsed with the Syntex parser [7].

For these 27 verbs, we extracted the corresponding definitions and synonyms from the TLFi and the synonym dictionaries respectively. To facilitate the assignment by the annotators of synonyms to definitions, we manually reconstructed some of the definitions from the information contained in the TLFi entries. Indeed a dictionary entry has a hierarchical structure (a definition can be the child of another definition) which is often used by the lexicographer to omit information in definitions occurring lower down in the hierarchy. The assumption is that the missing information is inherited from the higher levels. To facilitate the assignment by the annotator of a given synonym to a given definition, we manually reconstructed the information that had been omitted on an inheritance assumption. Note though that this manual reconstruction is only intended to facilitate the annotation task.

It does not affect the evaluation since the numbering of the definitions within a given dictionary entry remains the same and what is being compared is solely the assignment of synonyms to definition identifiers made by the system and that made by the annotators.

Third, we asked four professional lexicographers to manually assign synonyms to definitions. The lexicographers were given for each verb v in the sample, the set of (possibly reconstructed) definitions assigned by the TLFI to v and the set of synonyms associated to v by the synonym base. They then had to decide which definition(s) the synonym should be associated with.

We computed the agreement rate between pairs of annotators and all four annotators. No pair achieved a perfect agreement. The proportions of triples for which two annotators agree range from 87.07% (highest) to 74.06% (lowest) and the agreement rate for four annotators was even lower, 63.37%. This indicates that matching synonyms with definitions is a difficult task even for humans. On the other hand, the reasonably high agreement rate suggests that the sample provides a reasonable basis for evaluation. Accordingly we used the rating produced by the first annotator of the pair with the highest agreement as a baseline for our system.

3 The basic procedure

Given a verb V, a synonym Syn_V of that verb and a set of definitions $D_V = \{d_1 \dots d_n\}$ given for V by the TLFI, the task is to identify the definitions $d_i \in D_V$ of V for which Syn_V is a synonym of V.

Mapping synonyms to definitions. To assign a synonym Syn_V to a definition d_i of V, we proceed as follows: First we compare the index of the merged definitions of Syn_V with the index of each definition $d_i \in D_V$ using a gloss-based similarity measure. Note that since the intended meaning of the synonym is not given, we do not attempt to identify it and use as the basis for comparison the union of the definitions given by the TLFI for each synonym. Next, the synonym Syn_V is mapped onto the definition that gets the highest (non null) similarity score.

Evaluation. We evaluated the results obtained with respect to the reference sample presented in the previous section as follows.

From the reference, we extracted the set of tuples $\langle$ V, Syn$_V$, Def$_i\rangle$ such that Syn$_V$, is a synonym of V which is associated with the definition Def$_i$ of V.

Recall is then the number of correct tuples produced by the system divided by the total number of tuples contained in the reference. Precision is the number of correct tuples produced by the system divided by the total number of tuples produced by the system.

The baseline gives the results obtained when randomly assigning the synonyms of a verb to its definitions.

4 Experiments

4.1 Comparing similarity measures

To assess the impact of the similarity method used, we applied the 6 similarity measures listed in Table 1 namely, simple word overlap, extended word overlap, extended word overlap normalised, 1st order vectors and 2nd order vectors with and without a tfidf threshold. These methods were implemented using Ted Pedersen's Perl library `search.cpan.org/dist/WordNet-Similarity/` and adapting it to fit our data[2].

Simple word overlap. Simple word overlap between glosses were introduced by [18] to perform word sense disambiguation. The Lesk Algorithm which is used there, assigns a sense to a target word in a given context by comparing the glosses of its various senses with those of the other words in the context. That sense of the target word whose gloss has the most words in common with the glosses of the neighbouring words is chosen as its most appropriate sense.

Similarly, here we use word overlap to assess the similarity between a verb definition and the merged definitions of a synonym. Given a set of verb definitions and a synonym, the synonym will be matched to the definition(s) with which its definitions has the most words in common (and at least one).

Extended word overlap. The scoring mechanism of the original Lesk Algorithm does not differentiate between single word and phrasal overlaps. [3] modifies the Lesk method of comparison in two ways. First, the glosses used for comparison are extended by those of related WordNet concepts and second, the scoring mechanism is modified to favour glosses containing phrasal overlaps. An n word overlap is assigned an n^2 score. Because the French EuroWordNet is relatively under-developed[3] we did not modify the comparison to take into account WordNet related glosses[4]. We did however modify it to take into account phrase overlaps using the same scoring mechanism as Banerjee and Pedersen in [3][5].

Extended word overlap normalised. The extended word overlap is normalised by the number of words occurring in the definitions being compared.

First order vectors. A first order word vector for a given word indicates all the first order co-occurrences

[2] In particular, calls to the Princeton WordNet were removed.

[3] The French EuroWordNet (FREWN) contains 3 777 verbs. Since [23] alone lists 5 027 verbs, it is clear that a FREWN based extended gloss overlap measure would only partially be applicable.

[4] As mentioned in the introduction 1, an alternative WordNet for French is being developed by [24]. It cannot be used to integrate in the comparison glosses of WordNet related words however because the glosses associated with synsets are the Princeton WordNet English glosses.

[5] Recall (cf. Section 2) that the index of a definition is the *list* of lemmas for the open class words occurring in that definition. The order in the list reflects the linear order of the corresponding words in the definition.

of that word found in a given context (e.g., a TLFi definition). Similarity between words can then be computed using some vector similarity measure. For each verb V, we build weighted word vectors for each of its definitions d_V^i and for each of its synonyms. The dimensions of these vectors are the lemmatised words occurring in the definitions of V whose tf.idf is different from 0. [6] The similarity score between a verb definition d_V^i and a synonym Syn_V is the product of the two corresponding vectors.

Second order word vectors with and without tf.idf cutoff. Second order vectors are derived from first order vectors as follows. For each verb/synonym definition, the corresponding second order vector is the sum of the first order vectors[7] defined over the words occurring in this definition. The second order vectors "average" the direction of a set of vectors. If many of the words occurring in the definition have a strong component in one of the dimensions, then this dimension will be strong in the second order vector. In other words, the second order vector helps pinning down the strength of the different dimensions in a given definition.

The similarity score between a verb definition and a synonym is the product of the two corresponding second order vectors. We compare two versions of the second order word vectors approach, one where a tf.idf cut-off is used to trim down the word space and another where it isn't.

The results obtained by the various measures are given in Table 1 (left side).

A first observation is that our synonym-to-definition mapping procedure systematically outperforms the random assignment baseline. Thus, despite the brevity of dictionary definitions, gloss based similarity measures appear to be reasonably effective in associating a synonym with a definition on the basis of its own definitions.

A second observation is that no similarity measure clearly yields better results than the others. This suggests that word overlap between TLFi definitions is a richer source of information for synonym sense disambiguation (SSD) than other more indirect contextual cues such as the distributional similarity of the words occurring in the definitions (first order word vector approach) or of the words defined by the words occurring in the definitions (second order word vector approach).

[6] The weights are computed as follows: For a definition d_V^i, the weight of each word w_j is the number of occurrences of w_j in d_V^i divided by the number of occurrences of w_j in all definitions of V. For a synonym Syn_V, the weight of w_j is the number of occurrences of w_j in the definitions of Syn_V divided by the number of occurrences of w_j in all definitions of V.

[7] In contrast to the vectors used in the first order approach, the dimensions of the first-order vectors used to compute the 2nd order vectors are the lemmatised open class words of all definitions in the TLFi (not just the words occurring in the definitions of a given verb).

[9] Please note that the values shown here have been computed with higher precision and then rounded, therefore some differences in scores may no longer be visible.

	No refl. dist.			With refl. dist.		
Meas.	**R**	**P**	**F**	**R**	**P**	**F**
baseline	0.45	0.32	0.38	0.44	0.43	0.44
Over 1	0.72	0.51	0.60	0.70	0.68	0.69
Over 2	0.72	0.51	0.60	0.70	0.68	0.69
Over 3	**0.73**	**0.51**	**0.60**	**0.71**	0.67	**0.71**
WV 1	0.73	0.51	0.60	0.70	0.69	0.70
WV 2	0.71	0.50	0.59	0.70	0.69	0.69
WV 3	0.72	0.50	0.59	0.70	**0.70**	0.69

Table 1: ***Precision, recall and F-measure for various similarity measures, with (right side) and without (left side) reflexive/non reflexive distinction.*** *The similarity measures are the following:* Over 1*: Simple word overlap,* Over 2*: Extended word overlap,* Over 3*: Extended word overlap normalised,* WV 1*: First order vectors,* WV 2*: Second order vectors, without tf.idf cut-off,* WV 3*: Second order vectors, with tf.idf cut-off. Best scores are set in bold face*[9]*.*

ABANDONNER: (1) se dessaisir, renoncer à, se déposséder, se dépouiller, abdiquer, se démettre, démissionner, se désister, résigner, renoncer à, sacrifier, céder, confier, donner, léguer (2) concéder, accorder (3) exposer (ancient), délaisser, lâcher, tomber, larguer (fam.), plaquer (fam.) ...
S'ABANDONNER: se livrer, succomber, céder, se donner, s'épancher, se fier, se reposer sur

Fig. 3: *Sample (reflexive and non-reflexive) synonym dictionary entry of* (s') abandonner*, (*to abandon*).*

4.2 Linguistic preprocessing

A single TLFi verb entry might encompass several very different uses/meanings of this verb. Typically, it might include definitions that relate to the reflexive use of that verb, to a non reflexive use and/or to collocational use.

The approach presented in the previous section does not take such distinctions into account and is therefore prone to compare apples and oranges. It will for instance select the synonyms of a verb V and match these into all its definitions independent of whether these definitions reflect a reflexive or a non reflexive usage. This is clearly incorrect because the synonyms of a verb V are not necessarily synonyms of its reflexive form. For example, the synonyms of the non reflexive form *abandonner* (to abandon) listed in Fig. 3 are clearly distinct from those of the reflexive form *s'abandonner* (to give way).

Hence matching e.g., the synonyms of *abandonner* onto definitions corresponding to a reflexive use of the verb will result in incorrect synonym/definition associations.

To account for these observations, we developed an approach that aims to take into account the reflexive/non reflexive distinction. The approach differs from the procedure described in the previous section as follows: First, we automatically differentiated both in the handbuilt reference and in the automatically extracted verb entries between the reflexive and the non reflexive usage of a verb. For each verb with the two types of usage, we constructed two entries each with the appropriate definitions. The synonym selection is then done with respect to a verb entry i.e., with respect to either a reflexive or a non reflexive usage.

As a result, similarity measures were applied between the definitions of verbs corresponding to the same type of usage. In other words, the definitions of a synonym associated with a given verb usage (reflexive *vs.* non-reflexive) were compared only with the definitions of this particular usage.

The results obtained on the basis of this modified procedure are given in Table 1, right side.

Unsurprisingly while precision increases, recall decreases. The increase in precision indicates that this linguistically more constrained approach does indeed support a better matching between synonyms and definitions. The decrease in recall can be explained by several factors. First, the information contained in the TLFi concerning reflexive and non reflexive usage is irregular so that it is sometimes difficult to automatically distinguish between the definition of a reflexive usage and that of a non reflexive usage. Second, the synonym dictionary might fail to provide synonyms for a reflexive usage listed by the TLFi. Third, a reflexive verb listed in the synonym dictionary might fail to have a corresponding entry (and hence definition) in the TLFi. All of these cases introduce discrepancies between the reference and the system results thereby negatively impacting recall.

In short, while a finer linguistic processing of the data contained in the TLFi might help improve precision, a better recall would involve enriching both the synonym and the TLFi dictionaries.

5 Related work

Our work has connections to several research areas namely, word sense disambiguation (we aim to identify the meaning of a synonym and more specifically, to map a synonym to one or more dictionary definitions associated by a dictionary with the verb of which it is a synonym), synonym lexicon acquisition (we plan to use the method presented here to merge the five synonym lexicons into one) and WordNet construction (by identifying sense based synonym sets i.e., synsets).

Word sense disambiguation (WSD) uses four main types of approaches namely, lexical knowledge-based methods which rely primarily on dictionaries, thesauri, and lexical knowledge bases [18, 21], without using any corpus evidence; supervised and semi-supervised approaches [20] which make use of sense annotated data to train or start from and unsupervised methods [22] .

The approach presented here squarely fits within the lexical knowledge-based methods in that it exclusively uses dictionary definitions to disambiguate words. Supervised and semi-supervised approaches were not considered because of the absence of sense annotated data for French. Moreover, as shown by the construction of the reference sample and the agreement rate obtained (cf. Section 2), the fact that we are working on disambiguating synonyms (as opposed to a set of arbitrary words) out of context makes sense annotation a lot more difficult than for the standard WSD task.

It would in principle be possible to use an unsupervised approach and attempt to disambiguate synonyms on the basis of raw corpora. Such approaches however are not based on a fixed list of senses where the senses for a target word are a closed list coming from a dictionary. Instead they induce word senses directly from the corpus by using clustering techniques, which group together similar examples. To associate synonyms with definitions, it would therefore be necessary to define an additional mapping between corpus induced word senses and dictionary definitions. As noted in [1], such a mapping usually introduces noise and information loss however.

Synonym lexicon construction. As noted above and further discussed in Section 6, the method described in this paper can be used to merge the five synonym dictionaries mentioned in section 2 into a single one. In this sense, it is related to work on synonym lexicon construction. Much work has recently focused on extracting synonyms from dictionaries and/or from corpora to build synonym lexicons or thesauri. Thus, [15, 9, 14] extract synonyms from large monolingual corpora based on the idea that similar words occur in similar context; [4] used a bilingual corpus; [6] use the structure of monolingual dictionaries; and [25] combine both monolingual and bilingual resources. Such approaches are fundamentally different from the work presented here in two main ways. First, they aim to extract synonyms from linguistic data and thereby often yield "associative" lexicons rather than synonymic ones. In other words, these approaches yield lexicons which often associate with a word, synonyms but also antonyms, hypernyms or simply words that belong to the same semantic field. In contrast, we work on a predefined base of synonyms and the lexicon we produce is therefore a purely synonymic lexicon. Second, whereas we associate synonyms with a predefined list of senses, existing work on synonym lexicon construction usually doesn't and is restricted to identifying sets of synonyms (or semantically related words).

WordNet and thesaurus construction. Grouping synonyms in sets reflecting their possible senses effectively boils down to identifying synsets i.e., sets of words having a common meaning. In this sense, our work has some connections with work on WordNet development and more precisely, with a *merge* approach to WordNet development that is, with an approach that aims to first create a WordNet for a given language and then map it to existing WordNets. Recently, [24, 13] have presented an *extend* approach to WordNet construction for French based on a parallel corpus for 5 languages (French, English, Romanian, Czech, Bulgarian). Briefly the approach consists in first extracting a multilingual lexicon from the aligned parallel corpora and second, in using the Balkanet WordNets to disambiguate polysemous words. The approach relies on the fact that the WordNets for English, Romanian, Czech and Bulgarian all use the same synset identifiers. First, the synset identifiers of the translations of the French words are gathered. Second, the synset identifier shared by all translations is assigned the French word. In this way, and using various other techniques and resources to assign a synset identifier to monosemous words, [24, 13] produces a WordNet for French called WOLF (freely available WordNet for French) that replicates the Princeton WordNet structure.

Like work on synonym extraction, the WOLF approach differs from ours in that synonyms are automatically extracted from linguistic data (i.e., a parallel corpus and the Balkanet WordNets) rather than taken from a set of existing synonym dictionaries thereby introducing errors in the synsets. [24, 13] report a precision of 63.2% for verbs with respect to the French EuroWordNet. A second difference is that our approach associates synsets with a French definition (from the TLFI) rather than an English one (from the Princeton WordNet via the synset identifier). A third difference is that we do not map definitions to a Princeton WordNet synset identifier and therefore cannot reconstruct a network of lexical relations between synsets. More generally, the two approaches are complementary in that ours provides the seeds for a *merge* construction of a French WordNet whilst [24, 13] pursue an extend approach.

6 Conclusion and future work

We have presented an automatic method for assigning synonyms to definitions with a reasonably high F-score of at best, 0.70 (P=0.67,R=0.71). Future work will focus on two main points.

First, we will explore ways of improving these results. In particular, we will investigate in how much the structure of a dictionary entry can be used to enrich a definition. As mentioned in Section 2, a dictionary entry has a hierarchical structure which is often used by the lexicographer to omit information in definitions occurring lower down in the hierarchy. Automatically enriching the TLFI definitions by inheriting information from higher up in the dictionary entry might result in definitions which, because they contain more information, provide a better basis for similarity measures. Similarly to the distinguishing treatment of reflexive/non reflexive usages discussed in section 4.2, we will also develop a separate treatment of definitions involving verbal collocations (as opposed to isolated verbs).

Second, we will use this method to merge the synonym dictionaries into one where each word is associated with a set of (TLFI) definitions and each definition with a set of synonyms. We will then investigate, on the basis of the resulting merged synonym dictionary, how to reconstruct the lexical relation links used in WordNet. To this end, we intend to explore in how far translation and ontology enrichment techniques [10] can be applied to enrich our synonym lexicon and align it with the Princeton WordNet. In this way, we can build on the WordNet structure given by the Princeton WordNet and enrich the synsets derived from the five synonym dictionaries with translations of the related English synonyms.

References

[1] E. Agirre, O. L. de Lacalle, D. Martinez, and A. Soroa. Evaluating and optimizing the parameters of an unsupervised graph-based wsd algorithm. In *Proc. of the NAACL Texgraphs workshop*, 2006.

[2] R. Bailly, editor. *Dictionnaire des synonymes de la langue franaise*. Larousse, 1947.

[3] S. Banerjee and T. Pedersen. Extended gloss overlaps as a measure of semantic relatedness. In *Proceedings of the Eighteenth International Conference on Artificial Intelligence (IJCAI-03)*, 2003.

[4] R. Barzilay and K. McKeown. Extracting paraphrases from a parallel corpus. In *Proc. of ACL/EACL*, 2001.

[5] H. Bénac, editor. *Dictionnaire des synonymes*. Hachette, 1974.

[6] V. D. Blondel and P. Sennelart. Automatic extraction of synonyms in a dictionary. In *Proc. of the SIAM Workshop on Text Mining*, 2002.

[7] D. Bourigault and C. Fabre. Approche linguistique pour l'analyse syntaxique de corpus. Technical report, Université Toulouse - Le Mirail, 2000. Cahiers de Grammaires, no. 25.

[8] CNRS. *Trésor de la langue franaise, dictionnaire de la langue du 19e et du 20e siècle*. Gallimard, 1976-1993.

[9] C. Crouch and B. Yang. Experiments in automatic statistical thesaurs construction. In *Proc. of the 15th Annual International ACL SIGIR conference on Research and Development in Information Retrieval*, pages 77–88, 1992.

[10] J. de Bruijn, F. Martin-Recuerda, D. Manov, and M. Ehrig. State of the art survey on ontology merging and aligning. Technical report, EU-IST Project SEKT, 2004.

[11] J. Dendien and J. Pierrel. Le trésor de la langue franaise informatisé : un exemple dinformatisation dun dictionnaire de langue de référence. *Traitement Automtique des langues*, 44(2):11–37, 2003.

[12] H. B. du Chazaud, editor. *Nouveau dictionnaire des synonymes*. Hachette, 1979.

[13] D. Fišer and B. Sagôt. Combining multiple resources to build reliable wordnets. In *Proc. of TSD*, Brno, Tchéquie, 2008.

[14] G. Grefenstette. *Explorations in Automatic Thesaurus Discovery*. Kluwer Academic Press, 1994.

[15] D. Hindle. Noun classification from predicate-argument structure. In *Proc. of ACL*, 1990.

[16] C. Jacquin, E. Desmontils, and L. Monceaux. French euroword-net lexical database improvements. In *Proceedings of CICLing 2007*, pages 12–22, 2007.

[17] Larousse, editor. *Grand Larousse de la langue française*. Larousse, 1971-1978.

[18] M. Lesk. Word sense disambiguation: Algorithms and applications. In *Proceedings of SIGDOC*, 1986.

[19] J.-L. Manguin, J. François, R. Eufe, L. Fesenmeier, C. Ozouf, and M. Sénéchal. Le dictionnaire électronique des synonymes du crisco : un mode d'emploi à trois niveaux. *Les Cahiers du CRISCO*, 17, 2004.

[20] L. Màrquez, G. Escudero, D. Martínez, and G. Rigau. *Word Sense Disambiguation: Algorithms and Applications*, chapter Supervised Corpus-Based Methods for WSD. Springer, 2007.

[21] R. Mihalcea. *Word Sense Disambiguation: Algorithms and Applications*, volume 33 of *Text, Speech and Language Technology*, chapter Knowledge-Based Methods for WSD. Springer, 2007.

[22] T. Pedersen. *Word Sense Disambiguation: Algorithms and Applications*, chapter Unsupervised Corpus-Based Methods for WSD. Springer, 2007.

[23] A. Rey and al, editors. *Dictionnaire alphabétique et analogique de la langue française*. Editions Le Robert, 2e ed. edition, 1985. (9 vol.).

[24] B. Sagôt and D. Fišer. Building a free french wordnet from multilingual resources. In *Proc. of Ontolex*, Marrakech, Maroc, 2008.

[25] H. Wu and M. Zhou. Optimizing synonym extraction using monolingual and bilingual resources. In *Proceedings of the second international workshop on Paraphrasing*, pages 72–79, Morristown, NJ, USA, 2003. Association for Computational Linguistics.

Singular Value Decomposition for Feature Selection in Taxonomy Learning

Francesca Fallucchi and Fabio Massimo Zanzotto *
Via del Politecnico 00133 Rome, Italy
{*fallucchi,zanzotto*}@*info.uniroma2.it*

Abstract

In this paper, we propose a novel way to include unsupervised feature selection methods in probabilistic taxonomy learning models. We leverage on the computation of logistic regression to exploit unsupervised feature selection of singular value decomposition (SVD). Experiments show that this way of using SVD for feature selection positively affects performances.

1 Introduction

Taxonomies and, in general, networks of words connected with transitive relations are extremely important knowledge repositories for a variety of applications in natural language processing (NLP) and knowledge representation (KR). In NLP, taxonomies such as WordNet [17] are widely used in intermediate tasks such as word sense disambiguation (e.g. [1]) and selectional preference induction (e.g., [25]) as well as in final applications such as question answering (e.g., [4]) and textual entailment recognition (e.g. [5]). In KR, taxonomies as well as other word networks are the bulk of domain ontologies.

To be effectively used in NLP and KR applications, taxonomies and knowledge repositories have to be large or, at least, adapted to specific domains. Yet, even huge knowledge repositories such as WordNet [17] are extremely poor when used in specific domains such as the medical domain (see [29]). Automatically creating, adapting, or extending existing knowledge repositories using domain texts is, then, a very important and active area. A large variety of methods have been proposed: ontology learning methods [16, 3, 19] in KR as well as knowledge harvesting methods in NLP such as [13, 21]. These learning methods use variants of the distributional hypothesis [12] or exploit some induced lexical-syntactic patterns (originally used in [26]). The task is generally seen as a classification (e.g., [22, 27]) or a clustering (e.g., [3]) problem. This allows the use of machine learning models.

Yet, as any other machine learning problem, knowledge harvesting and ontology learning models exploit the above hypothesis to build feature spaces where instances, i.e., words as in [22] or word pairs as in [27], are represented. These feature spaces are used to determine whether or not new word pairs coming from the text collection have to be included in existing knowledge repositories. Decision models are learnt using existing knowledge repositories and then applied to new words or word pairs. Generally, these models use as features all the possible and relevant generalized contexts where words or word pairs can appear. For example, possible features in the word pair classification problem are *"is a"* and *"as well as"*. Given the nature of the problem, these feature spaces can then be huge as they include all potential relevant features for a particular relation among words. Relevant features are not known in advance. Yet, large feature spaces can have negative effects on machine learning models such as increasing the computational load and introducing redundant or noisy features. Feature selection is the solution (see [11]).

In this paper, we want to study how to improve performances of taxonomy learning methods by using feature selection. We focus on the probabilistic taxonomy learning model introduced by [27] as it uses existing taxonomies exploiting the transitivity of the *isa* relation. Leveraging on the particular model, we propose a novel way of using singular value decomposition (SVD) as unsupervised model for feature selection. In a nutshell, given the probabilistic model for taxonomy learning, we use SVD as a way to compute the pseudo-inverse matrix needed in logistic regression. We will analyze if our method for using unsupervised feature selection positively affect performances.

Before staring, in Sec. 2 we will shortly review methods for taxonomy learning and for feature selection. We motivate our choice of working within the probabilistic setting. In Sec. 3, as SVD is the core of our method, we will then introduce SVD as unsupervised feature selection model. In Sec. 4 we then describe how we introduced SVD as natural feature selector in the probabilistic taxonomy learning model introduced by [27]. To describe how we use SVD as natural feature selector, we will shortly review the logistic regression used to compute the taxonomy learning model. We will describe our experiments in Sec. 5. Finally, in Sec. 6, we will draw some conclusions and describe our future work.

2 Related work

Extracting knowledge bases from texts is one of the major goal of NLP and KR. These methods can give an important boost to knowledge-based systems. In this section we want to shortly analyze some of these methods in order to motivate our choice to work within an existing probabilistic model for learning taxonomies. We also review the more traditional models for super-

*DISP University Rome "Tor Vergata"

International Conference RANLP 2009 - Borovets, Bulgaria, pages 82–87

vised and unsupervised feature selection.

The models for automatically extracting structured knowledge, such as taxonomies, from texts use variants of the distributional hypothesis [12] exploit some induced lexical-syntactic patterns (originally used in [26]).

The distributional hypothesis is widely used in many approaches for taxonomy induction from texts. For example, it is used in [3] for populating lattices, i.e. graphs of a particular class, of formal concepts.

Lexical syntactic patterns are also a source of relevant information for deciding whether or not a particular relation holds between two words. This approach has been widely used for detecting hypernymy relations such as in [13, 18], for other ontological relations such as in [21], or for more generic relations such as in [24, 28]. These learning models generally use the hypothesis that two words are related according to a particular relation if these often appear in specific text fragments.

Despite the wide range of models for taxonomy learning, only very few exploit the structure of existing taxonomies. The task is seen as building taxonomies from scratch. In [3], for example, lattices and the related taxonomies are the target. Yet, existing taxonomies may be used to drive the process of building new taxonomies. In [19], WordNet [17] and WordNet glosses are used to drive the construction of domain specific ontologies. In [22], taxonomies are augmented exploiting their structure. Inserting a new word in the network is seen as a classification problem. The target classes are the nodes of the existing hierarchy. The distributional description of the word as well as the existing taxonomy structure is used to make the decision. This model is purely distributional. In [27], a probabilistic model exploiting existing taxonomies is introduced. This model is purely based on lexical-syntactical patterns. Also in this case, the insertion of a new word in the hierarchy is seen as a binary classification problem. Yet, the classification decision is taken over a pair of words, i.e., a word and its possible generalization. The probabilistic classifier should decide if this pair belongs or not to the taxonomy.

The probabilistic taxonomy learning models has at least two advantages with respect to the other models. The first advantage is that it coherently uses existing taxonomies in the expansion phase. Both existing and new information is modeled in the same probabilistic way. The second advantage is that classification problem is binary, i.e., a word pair belongs or not to the taxonomy. This allows to build a unique binary classifier. This is not the case for models such as the one of [22], where we need a multi-class classifier or a set of binary classifiers. For these two reasons, we are using the probabilistic taxonomy learning setting for our study.

Yet, in applications involving texts such as taxonomy learning, machine learning models are exposed to huge feature spaces. This has not always positive effects. A first important problem is that huge feature spaces require large computational and storage resources for applying machine learning models. A second problem is that more features not always result in better accuracies of learnt classification models. Many features can be noise. Feature selection, i.e., the reduction of the feature space offered to machine learners, is seen as a solution (see [11]).

There is a wide range of feature selection models that can be classified in two main families: *supervised* and *unsupervised*. Supervised models directly exploit the class of the instances for determining if a feature is relevant or not. The idea is to select features that are highly correlated with final target classes. Information theoretic ranking criteria such as mutual information and information gain are often used (see [8]). Unsupervised models are instead used when the information on classes of instances is not available at the training time or it is inapplicable such as in information retrieval. Straightforward and simple models for unsupervised feature selection can be derived from information retrieval weighting schemes, e.g., term frequency times inverse document frequency ($tf * idf$). In this case, relevant features are respectively those appearing more often or those more selective, i.e., appearing in fewer instances.

Feature selection models are also widely used in taxonomy learning. For example, attribute selection for building lattices of concepts in [3] is done applying specific thresholds on specific information measures on the attributes extracted from corpora. This models uses conditional probabilities, point-wise mutual information, and a selectional-preference-like measure as the one introduced in [25].

3 Unsupervised Feature Selection with SVD

A very important way of unsupervised feature selection is the application of the SVD. As this is the bulk of our methodology we will review how SVD can be used for this purpose. SVD has been largely used in information retrieval for reducing the dimension of the document vector space [7].

SVD, originally, is a decomposition of a rectangular matrix. Given a generic rectangular $n \times m$ matrix A, its singular value decomposition is $A = U \Sigma V^T$ where U is a matrix $n \times r$, V^T is a $r \times m$ and Σ is a diagonal matrix $r \times r$. The diagonal elements of the Σ are the *singular values* such as $\delta_1 \geq \delta_2 \geq ... \geq \delta_r > 0$ where r is the rank of the matrix A. For the decomposition, SVD exploits the linear combination of rows and columns of A.

There are different ways of using SVD as unsupervised feature reduction. An interesting way is to exploit its approximated computations, i.e. :

$$A \approx A_k = U_{m \times k} \Sigma_{k \times k} V_{k \times n}^T \quad (1)$$

where k is smaller than the rank r. The computation algorithm [10] allows to stop at a given k different from the real rank r. The property of the singular values, i.e., $\delta_1 \geq \delta_2 \geq ... \geq \delta_r > 0$, guarantees that the first k are bigger than the discarded ones. There is a direct relation between the informativeness of the i-th new dimension and the singular value δ_i. High singular values correspond to dimensions of the new space where examples have more variability whereas low singular values determine dimensions where examples have a smaller variability (see [15]). These latter dimensions can be then hardly used as efficient features in learning. The possibility of computing approximated versions of matrices gives a powerful method for feature selection and filtering as we can decide in advance how many features or, better, linear combination of original features we want to use.

4 Probabilistic Taxonomy Learning and SVD

In this section we will firstly introduce the probabilistic model (Sec. 4.1) and, then, we will describe how SVD is used as feature selector in the logistic regression that estimates the probabilities of the model (Sec. 4.2). To describe this part we need to go in depth into the definition of the logistic regression and some ways of computing it.

4.1 Probabilistic model

In the probabilistic formulation [27], the task of learning taxonomies from a corpus is seen as a maximum likelihood problem. The taxonomy is seen as a set T of assertions R over pairs $R_{i,j}$. If $R_{i,j}$ is in T, i is a concept and j is one of its generalization (i.e., the direct or the indirect generalization). For example, $R_{dog,animal} \in T$ describes that *dog* is an *animal* according to the taxonomy T.

The main probabilities are then: (1) the prior probability $P(R_{i,j} \in T)$ of an assertion $R_{i,j}$ to belong to the taxonomy T and (2) the posterior probability $P(R_{i,j} \in T|\overrightarrow{e}_{i,j})$ of an assertion $R_{i,j}$ to belong to the taxonomy T given a set of evidences $\overrightarrow{e}_{i,j}$ derived from the corpus. These evidences are derived from the contexts where the pair (i,j) is found in the corpus. The vector $\overrightarrow{e}_{i,j}$ is a feature vector associated with a pair (i,j). For example, a feature may describe how many times i and j are seen in patterns like *"i as j"* or *"i is a j"*. These among many other features are indicators of an is-a relation between i and j (see [13]).

Given a set of evidences E over all the relevant word pairs, the probabilistic taxonomy learning task is defined as the problem of finding a taxonomy $\widehat{T}$ that maximizes the probability of having the evidences E, i.e.:

$$\widehat{T} = \arg\max_{T} P(E|T)$$

In [27], this maximization problem is solved with a local search. What is maximized at each step is the ratio between the likelihood $P(E|T')$ and the likelihood $P(E|T)$ where $T' = T \cup N$ and N are the relations added at each step. This ratio is called multiplicative change $\Delta(N)$ and is defined as follows $\Delta(N) = P(E|T')/P(E|T)$.
The main innovation of the model in [27] is the possibility of adding at each step the best relation $N = \{R_{i,j}\}$ as well as $R_{i,j}$ with all the relations induced from $R_{i,j}$, i.e., $N = \{R_{i,j}\} \cup I(R_{i,j})$ where $I(R_{i,j})$ are the relations induced using the existing taxonomy and $R_{i,j}$. Given the taxonomy T and the relation $R_{i,j}$, the set $I(R_{i,j})$ contains $R_{i,k}$ if $R_{j,k}$ is in T and contains $R_{k,j}$ if $R_{k,i}$ is in T. [1]

We will experiment with our feature selection methodology in two different models:

flat: at each iteration step, a single relation is added, i.e. $\widehat{R}_{i,j} = \arg\max_{R_{i,j}} \Delta(R_{i,j})$

inductive: at each iteration step, a set of relations is added, i.e. $I(\widehat{R}_{i,j})$ where $\widehat{R}_{i,j} = \arg\max_{R_{i,j}} \Delta(I(R_{i,j}))$.

The last important fact is that it is possible to demonstrate that

$$\begin{aligned}\Delta(R_{i,j}) &= k \cdot \frac{P(R_{i,j} \in T|\overrightarrow{e}_{i,j})}{1 - P(R_{i,j} \in T|\overrightarrow{e}_{i,j})} = \\ &= k \cdot odds(R_{i,j}) \qquad (2)\end{aligned}$$

where k is a constant (see [27]) that will be neglected in the maximization process. This last equation gives the possibility of using the logistic regression as it is. In the next sections we will see how SVD and the related feature selection can be used to compute the odds.

4.2 Exploiting SVD in Logistic Regression

We here show that the $odds(R_{i,j})$ in eq. 2 can be computed with logistic regression (Sec. 4.2.1). We then describe how we can compute logistic regression using a particular pseudo-inverse matrix (Sec. 4.2.2). Finally, we show that approximated pseudo-inverse matrices can be computed using SVD (Sec. 4.2.3).

4.2.1 Logistic Regression

Logistic Regression [6] is a particular type of statistical model for relating responses Y to linear combinations of predictor variables X. It is a specific kind of Generalized Linear Model (see [20]) where its function is the *logit function* and the dependent variable Y is a *binary* or *dichotomic* variable which has a Bernoulli distribution. The dependent variable Y takes value 0 or 1. The probability that Y has value 1 is function of the regressors $x = (1, x_1, ..., x_k)$.

The probabilistic taxonomy learner model introduced in the previous section falls in the category of probabilistic models where the logistic regression can be applied as $R_{i,j} \in T$ is the binary dependent variable and $\overrightarrow{e}_{i,j}$ is the vector of its regressors. In the rest of the section we will see how the *odds*, i.e., the multiplicative change, can be computed.

We start from formally describing the Logistic Regression Model. Given the two stochastic variables Y and X, we can define as p the probability of Y to be 1 given that X=x, i.e.$p = P(Y = 1|X = x)$ The distribution of the variable Y is a Bernoulli distribution. Given the definition of the $logit(p)$ as $logit(p) = \ln\left(\frac{p}{1-p}\right)$ and given the fact that Y is a Bernoulli distribution,

[1] For example: given T and $R_{dog,animal}$ if $R_{animal,organism} \in T$ then $I(R_{dog,animal})$ contains $R_{dog,organism}$.
Moreover given T and $R_{bird,beast}$ if $R_{turkey,beast} \in T$ then $I(R_{bird,beast})$ contains $R_{turkey,bird}$.

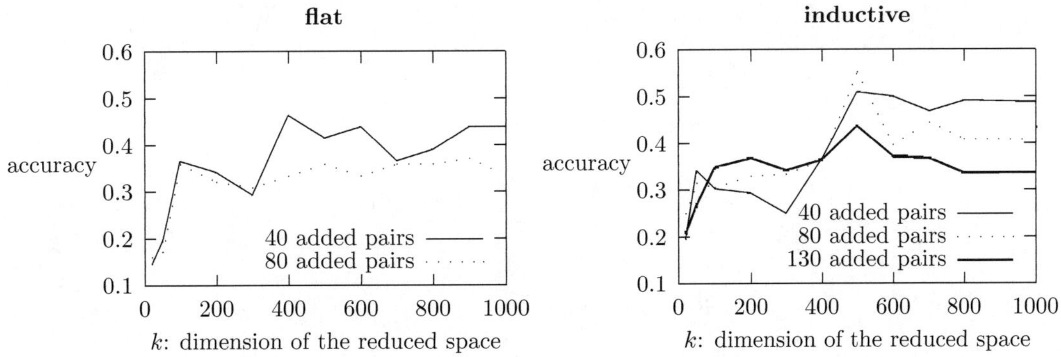

Fig. 1: *Accuracy over different cuts with SVD of the feature space*

the logistic regression foresees that the logit is a linear combination of the values of the regressors, i.e.,

$$logit(p) = \beta_0 + \beta_1 x_1 + ... + \beta_k x_k \quad (3)$$

where $\beta_0, \beta_1, ..., \beta_k$ are called *regression coefficients* of the variables $x_1, ..., x_k$ respectively.

It is obviously trivial to determine the $odds(R_{i,j})$ related to the multiplicative change of the probabilistic taxonomy model. The *odds*, the ratio between the positive and the negative event, can be determined as follows:

$$odds(R_{i,j}) = \frac{P(R_{i,j} \in T | \vec{e}_{i,j})}{1 - P(R_{i,j} \in T | \vec{e}_{i,j})} = \exp(\beta_0 + \vec{e}^{\,T}_{i,j} \beta) \quad (4)$$

4.2.2 Estimating Coefficients with Pseudoinverse

The remaining problem is how to estimate the regression coefficients. This estimation is done using the maximal likelihood estimation to prepare a set of linear equations using the above *logit* definition and, then, solving a linear problem. This will give us the possibility of introducing the necessity of determining a pseudo-inverse matrix where we will use the singular value decomposition and its natural possibility of performing feature selection. Once we have the regression coefficients, we have the possibility of estimating a probability $P(R_{i,j} \in T | \vec{e}_{i,j})$ given any configuration of the values of the regressors $\vec{e}_{i,j}$, i.e., the observed values of the features. Let assume we have a multiset O of observations extracted from $Y \times E$ where $Y \in \{0, 1\}$ and we know that some of them are positive observations (i.e., $Y = 1$) and some of them are negative observations (i.e., $Y = 0$). For each pair, the relative configuration $\vec{e}_l \in E$ appears at least once in O and can be determined using the maximal likelihood estimation $P(Y = 1 | \vec{e}_l)$. Then, from the equation of the logit (Eq. 3), we have a linear equation system, i.e.:

$$\overrightarrow{logit(p)} = Q\beta \quad (5)$$

where Q is a matrix that includes a constant column of 1, necessary for the β_0 of the linear combination of the values of the regression. Moreover it includes the set of evidences, i.e. $Q = (1, \vec{e}_1 ... \vec{e}_m)$.

The set of equations in Eq. 5 are a particular case multiple linear regression [2]. As Q is a rectangular and singular matrix, the system (Eq.5) has no solution. This problem can be solved by the **Moore-Penrose pseudoinverse** Q^+ [23]. Then, we determine the regressors as $\widehat{\beta} = Q^+ \overrightarrow{logit(p)}$.

4.2.3 Computing Pseudoinverse with SVD

We finally reached the point where it is possible to explain our idea that is naturally using singular value decomposition (SVD) as feature selection in a probabilistic taxonomy learner. In previous sections we described how the probabilities of the taxonomy learner can be estimated using logistic regressions and we concluded that a way to determine the regression coefficients β is computing the **Moore-Penrose pseudoinverse** Q^+. It is possible to compute the **Moore-Penrose pseudoinverse** using the SVD in the following way [23]. Given an SVD decomposition of the matrix $Q = U \Sigma V^T$ the pseudo-inverse matrix is:

$$Q^+ = V \Sigma^+ U^T \quad (6)$$

The diagonal matrix Σ^+ is a matrix $r \times r$ obtained calculating the reciprocals of the singular value of Σ.

We have now our opportunity of using SVD as natural feature selector as we can compute different approximations of the pseudo-inverse matrix. The algorithm for computing SVD is iterative (Sec. 3). The firstly derived dimensions are those with higher singular value. We can then decide how many dimensions we want to use. The first k dimensions are more informative than the $k + 1$. We can consider different k in order to obtain different SVD as approximations of the original matrix (Eq. 1). We can define different approximations of the inverse matrix Q^+ as Q^+_k, i.e.:

$$Q^+_k = V_{n \times k} \Sigma^+_{k \times k} U^T_{k \times m}$$

5 Experimental Evaluation

In this section, we want to empirically explore whether our use of SVD feature selection positively affects performances of the probabilistic taxonomy learner. The

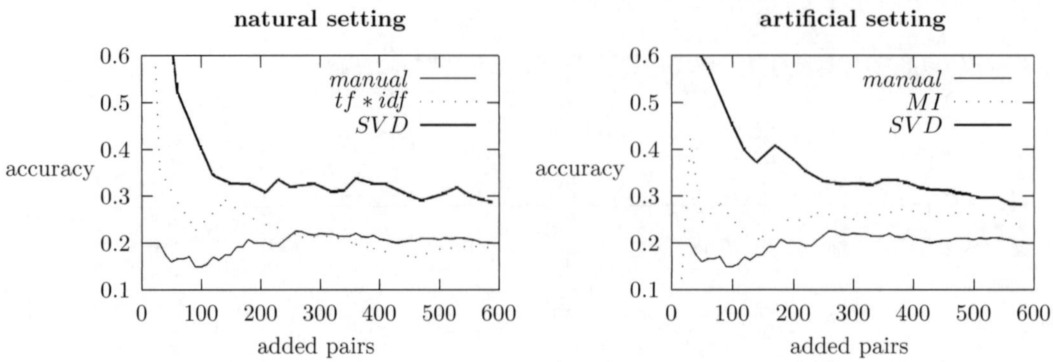

Fig. 2: *Comparison of different feature selection models*

best way of determining how a taxonomy learner is performing is to see if it can replicate an existing "taxonomy". We will experiment with the attempt of replicating a portion of WordNet [17]. In the experiments, we will address two issues: determining to what extent SVD feature selection affect performances of the taxonomy learner and determining if, for the probabilistic taxonomy learner, SVD is better than other simpler models for supervised and unsupervised feature selection. We will explore the effects on both the **flat** and the **inductive** probabilistic taxonomy learner.

In the rest of the section we will describe: the experimental set-up (Sec. 5.1) and the results of the experiments in term of performance (Sec. 5.2).

5.1 Experimental Set-up

To completely define the experiments we need to describe some issues: how we defined the taxonomy to replicate, which corpus we have used to extract evidences for pairs of words, which feature space we used, and, finally, the feature selection models we compared against. As target taxonomy we selected a portion of WordNet[2] [17]. Namely, we started from the 44 concrete nouns divided in 3 classes: animal, artifact, and vegetable. For each word w, we selected the synset s_w that is compliant with the class it belongs to. We then obtained a set S of synsets. We then expanded the set to S' adding the siblings (i.e., the coordinate terms) for each synset in S. The set S' contains 265 coordinate terms plus the 44 original concrete nouns. For each element in S we collected its hypernyms, obtaining the set H. We then removed from the set H the 4 topmosts: *entity*, *unit*, *object*, and *whole*. The set H contains 77 hypernyms. For the purpose of the experiments we both derived from the previous sets a taxonomy T and produced a set of negative examples $\overline{T}$. The two sets have been obtained as follows. The taxonomy T is the portion of WordNet implied by $O = H \cup S'$, i.e. T contains all the $(s,h) \in O \times O$ that are in WordNet and $\overline{T}$ contains all the $(s,h) \in O \times O$ that are not in WordNet. We have 5108 positive pairs in T and 52892 negative pairs in $\overline{T}$.

[2] We used the version 3.0

We then produced two experimental settings: a *natural* and an *artificial* one. In the *natural setting* we used only positive pairs in the training set. This is the natural situation when augmenting existing taxonomies. Only positive word pairs can be derived from existing taxonomies. Yet, negative pairs cannot. In the *artificial setting* we used both positive and negative examples.

To obtain the training and the testing sets, we randomly divided the set $T \cup \overline{T}$ in two parts T_{tr} and T_{ts}, respectively, of 70% and 30% of the original $T \cup \overline{T}$.

As corpus we used ukWaC [9]. This is a web extracted corpus of about 2700000 web pages containing more than 2 billion words. The corpus contains documents of different topics such as web, computers, education, public sphere, etc.. It has been largely demonstrated that the web documents are good models for natural language [14].

As the focus of the paper is the analysis of the effect of the SVD feature selection, we used as feature spaces both n-grams and bag-of-words. Out of the $T \cup \overline{T}$, we selected only those pairs that appeared at a distance of at most 3 tokens. Using this 3 tokens, we generated two spaces: (1) *bag-of-word* and (2) the bigram space that contains bigrams and monograms. For the purpose of this experiment, we used a reduced stop list as classical stop words as punctuation, parenthesis, the verb *to be* are very relevant in the context of features for learning a taxonomy.

Finally, we want define the feature selection models we compared against. As *unsupervised feature selection models* we used the term frequency times the inverse document frequency (*tf*idf*). Instances $\overrightarrow{e}$ have the role of the documents. As *supervised feature selection models* we used the mutual information (mi). For all the feature selection models, we selected the first k features. Finally, we used a manual feature selection model based on the Heart's patterns [13]. In this model that we call *manual*, we used as features only the classical Hearst's patterns.

5.2 Results

In the first set of experiments we want to focus on the issue whether or not performances of the probabilistic taxonomy learner is positively affected by the proposed feature selection model based on the singular value decomposition. We then determined the performance with respect to different values of k. This latter represents the number of surviving dimensions where the pseudo-inverse is computed. The features of this experiment are unigrams derived from a 3-sized-window. Punctuation has been considered. Figures 1 plots the accuracy of the probabilistic learner with respect to the size of the feature set, i.e. the number k of single values considered for computing the pseudo-inverse matrix. To determine if the effect of the feature selection is preserved during the iteration of the local search algorithm, we report curves at different sizes of the set of added pairs. Curves are reported for both the *flat* model and the *inductive* model. The *flat* algorithm adds one pair at each iteration. Then, we reported curves for 40 and 80 added pairs. The curves show that accuracy doesn't increase after a dimension of k=400. For the *inductive* model we report the accuracies for around 40, 80, 130 added pairs. The optimal dimension of the feature space seems to be around 500 as after that value performances decrease or stay stable. SVD feature selection has then a positive effect for both the *flat* and the *inductive* probabilistic taxonomy learners. This has beneficial effects both on the performances and on the computation time.

In the second set of experiments we want to determine whether or not SVD feature selection for the probabilistic taxonomy learner behaves better than other feature selection models. We then fixed k to 600 both for the SVD selection model and for the other feature selection models. In this experiments, the original feature space is the bigram space. Figure 2 shows results. Curves report accuracies of the different models after n added pairs. In the *natural setting*, we compared our model against the $tf * idf$ and the *manual feature selection*. Our SVD model outperforms both models of feature selection. The same happened against mutual information (*MI*) in the *artificial setting*. Our SVD way of selecting features seems to be very effective.

6 Conclusions and Future Work

We presented a model to naturally introduce SVD feature selection in a probabilistic taxonomy learner. The method is effective as allows the designing of better probabilistic taxonomy learners. We still need to explore whether or not the positive effect of SVD feature selection is preserved in more complex feature spaces such as syntactic feature spaces as those used in [27].

References

[1] E. Agirre and G. Rigau. Word sense disambiguation using conceptual density. In *Proc. of the 16th COLING*, pages 16–22, Morristown, NJ, USA, 1996. ACL.

[2] D. Caron, W. Hospital, and P. N. Corey. Variance estimation of linear regression coefficients in complex sampling situation. *Sampling Error: Methodology, Software and Application*, pages 688–694, 1988.

[3] P. Cimiano, A. Hotho, and S. Staab. Learning concept hierarchies from text corpora using formal concept analysis. *JAIR*, 24:305–339, 2005.

[4] P. Clark, C. Fellbaum, and J. Hobbs. Using and extending wordnet to support question-answering. In *Proc. 4th GWC*, 2008.

[5] C. Corley and R. Mihalcea. Measuring the semantic similarity of texts. In *Proc. of the ACL Workshop on Empirical Modeling of Semantic Equivalence and Entailment*, pages 13–18, Ann Arbor, Michigan, June 2005. ACL.

[6] D. R. Cox. The regression analysis of binary sequences. *JRSS,B*, 20(2):215–242, 1958.

[7] S. Deerwester, S. T. Dumais, G. W. Furnas, T. K. L, and R. Harshman. Indexing by latent semantic analysis. *Journal of the American Society for Information Science*, 41:391–407, 1990.

[8] I. S. Dhillon, S. Mallela, I. Guyon, and A. Elisseeff. A divisive information-theoretic feature clustering algorithm for text classification. *Journal of Machine Learning Research*, 3:2003, 2003.

[9] A. Ferraresi, E. Zanchetta, M. Baroni, and S. Bernardini. Introducing and evaluating ukwac, a very large web-derived corpus of english. In *Proc. of the WAC4 Workshop at LREC 2008*, Marrakesh, Morocco, 2008.

[10] G. Golub and W. Kahan. Calculating the singular values and pseudo-inverse of a matrix. *J Soc Ind Appl Math B Num Anal*, 2(2):205–224, 1965.

[11] I. Guyon and A. Elisseeff. An introduction to variable and feature selection. *JMLR*, 3:1157–1182, March 2003.

[12] Z. Harris. Distributional structure. In J. J. Katz and J. A. Fodor, editors, *The Philosophy of Linguistics*, New York, 1964. Oxford University Press.

[13] M. A. Hearst. Automatic acquisition of hyponyms from large text corpora. In *Proc. of the 15th CoLing*, Nantes, France, 1992.

[14] M. Lapata and F. Keller. The web as a baseline: Evaluating the performance of unsupervised web-based models for a range of nlp tasks. In *Proc. of the HLT-NAACL*, Boston, MA, 2004.

[15] B. Liu. *Web Data Mining: Exploring Hyperlinks, Contents, and Usage Data.* Data-Centric Systems and Applications. Springer, 2007.

[16] A. Medche. *Ontology Learning for the Semantic Web*, volume 665 of *Engineering and Computer Science.* Kluwer International, 2002.

[17] G. A. Miller. WordNet: A lexical database for English. *Communications of the ACM*, 38(11):39–41, Nov. 1995.

[18] E. Morin. *Extraction de liens sémantiques entre termes à partir de corpus de textes techniques.* PhD thesis, Univesité de Nantes, Faculté des Sciences et de Techniques, 1999.

[19] R. Navigli and P. Velardi. Learning domain ontologies from document warehouses and dedicated web sites. *Comput. Linguist.*, 30(2):151–179, 2004.

[20] J. A. Nelder and R. W. M. Wedderburn. Generalized linear models. *JRSS,A*, 135(3):370–384, 1972.

[21] P. Pantel and M. Pennacchiotti. Espresso: Leveraging generic patterns for automatically harvesting semantic relations. In *Proc. of the 21st COLING and 44th Annual Meeting of the ACL*, pages 113–120, Sydney, Australia, July 2006. ACL.

[22] V. Pekar and S. Staab. Taxonomy learning: factoring the structure of a taxonomy into a semantic classification decision. *Proc. of the 19th COLING*, 2:786–792, 2002.

[23] R. Penrose. A generalized inverse for matrices. In *Proc. Cambridge Philosophical Society*, 1955.

[24] D. Ravichandran and E. Hovy. Learning surface text patterns for a question answering system. In *Proceedings of the 40th ACL Meeting*, Philadelphia, Pennsilvania, 2002.

[25] P. Resnik. *Selection and Information: A Class-Based Approach to Lexical Relationships.* PhD thesis, Dept. of Computer and Information Science, Univ. of Pennsylvania, 1993.

[26] H. R. Robison. Computer-detectable semantic structures. *Information Storage and Retrieval*, 6(3):273–288, 1970.

[27] R. Snow, D. Jurafsky, and A. Y. Ng. Semantic taxonomy induction from heterogenous evidence. In *ACL*, pages 801–808, 2006.

[28] I. Szpektor, H. Tanev, I. Dagan, and B. Coppola. Scaling web-based acquisition of entailment relations. In *Proc. of the EMNLP*, Barcellona, Spain, 2004.

[29] A. Toumouth, A. Lehireche, D. Widdows, and M. Malki. Adapting wordnet to the medical domain using lexicosyntactic patterns in the ohsumed corpus. In *Proc. of the AICCSA*, pages 1029–1036, Washington, DC, USA, 2006. IEEE Computer Society.

Improving text segmentation by combining endogenous and exogenous methods

Olivier Ferret
CEA, LIST
18 route du Panorama, BP6, Fontenay-aux-Roses, F-92265 France
olivier.ferret@cea.fr

Abstract

Topic segmentation was addressed by a large amount of work from which it is not easy to draw conclusions, especially about the need for knowledge. In this article, we propose to combine in the same framework two methods for improving the results of a topic segmenter based on lexical reiteration. The first one is endogenous and exploits the distributional similarity of words in a document for discovering its topics. These topics are then used to facilitate the detection of topical similarity between discourse units. The second approach achieves the same goal by relying on external resources. Two resources are tested: a network of lexical co-occurrences built from a large corpus and a set of word senses induced from this network. An evaluation of the two approaches and their combination is performed in a reference framework and shows the interest of this combination both for French and English.

1 Introduction

In this article, we address the problem of linear topic segmentation, which consists in segmenting documents into topically homogeneous non-overlapping segments. This Discourse Analysis problem has received a constant interest since works such as [11]. One criterion for classifying topic segmentation systems is the kind of knowledge they depend on. Most of them only rely on surface features of documents: word reiteration in [11, 4, 20, 10], and more recently [14, 7], or discourse cues in [16, 10]. As they don't exploit external knowledge, such systems are not domain-dependent but they can be successfully applied only to some types of documents: word reiteration is reliable only if concepts are not expressed by too different means (synonyms, etc.); discourse cues are often rare and corpus-specific.

To overcome these difficulties, some systems make use of domain-independent knowledge about lexical cohesion: a lexical network built from a dictionary in [13]; a thesaurus in [15]; a large set of lexical co-occurrences collected from a corpus in [5] or [6]. To some extent, these lexical networks enable segmenters to rely on a sort of concept reiteration. However, their lack of any topical structure makes this kind of knowledge difficult to use when lexical ambiguity is high.

The most simple solution to this problem is to exploit knowledge about the topics that may occur in documents. Such topic models are generally built from a large set of example documents as in [21], [2] or in one component of [1]. These statistical topic models enable segmenters to improve their precision but they also restrict their scope.

Hybrid systems that combine the approaches we have presented were also developed and illustrated the interest of such a combination: [12] combined word recurrence, co-occurrences and a thesaurus; [1] relied on both lexical modeling and discourse cues; [10] made use of word reiteration through lexical chains and discourse cues.

The work we report in this article takes place in the last category we have presented. More precisely, it first confirms the interest of combining lexical recurrence with an external resource about lexical cohesion of texts. Second, it shows that the improvement brought by the use of a resource about lexical cohesion and the improvement brought by an endogenous method such as the one presented in [9] are complementary and can be fruitfully combined.

2 Overview

In most of the algorithms in the text segmentation field, documents are represented as sequences of basic discourse units. When they are written texts, these units are generally sentences, which is also the case in our work. Each unit is turned into a vector of words, following the principles of the *Vector Space* model. Then, the similarity between the basic units of a text is evaluated by computing a similarity measure between the vectors that represent them. Such a similarity is considered as representative of the topical closeness of the corresponding units. This principle is also applied to groups of basic units, such as text segments, because of the properties of the *Vector Space* model. Segments are finally delimited by locating the areas where the similarity between units or groups of units is weak.

This quick overview highlights the important role of the evaluation of the similarity between discourse units in the segmentation process. When no external knowledge is used, this similarity is only based on the reiteration of words. But it can be enhanced by taking into account semantic relations between words. Such relations can be found in manually-built semantic resources such as WordNet or Roget's Thesaurus. Although their coverage is large, these resources can't obviously cover all domains in depth. As a consequence, it can also be interesting to rely on resources whose relations are less well defined but that can be easily extended to a new domain in an unsupervised way

International Conference RANLP 2009 - Borovets, Bulgaria, pages 88–93

from a representative corpus. The cohesion relations that are captured through the lexical co-occurrences extracted from a set of texts fulfill these constraints and were already exploited with success together with word reiteration in [12].

In [9], another way to improve the evaluation of the similarity between two sentences of a text is proposed: the idea is to define each topic of the text as a subset of its vocabulary and to use the implicit relation between each couple of words that are part of the same topic for detecting the topical similarity of sentences. A large repository of topics doesn't exist and similarly to semantic resources, it couldn't cover all domains. As a consequence, [9] performs the discovering of the topics of a text in an unsupervised way and its method can be qualified as endogenous as it doesn't rely on any external resource. This method is used in conjunction with a method based on word reiteration that is implemented in the same framework.

The first objective of the work we report here is to generalize this framework for evaluating the use of different types of lexical relations to improve the detection of similarity between text units in the context of topic segmentation. Its second objective is to test an exogenous approach in this framework in conjunction with word reiteration. More precisely, two sources of knowledge have been used to support the exogenous approach: a network of lexical co-occurrences and a set of word senses induced from this network. The first one aims at confirming the results of [12] while the second one aims at testing the interest of selecting the most significant co-occurrences from a semantic viewpoint. The last main objective of this work is to determine if the association in the same framework of two different kinds of methods for improving the detection of similarity between text units, endogenous and exogenous methods, can lead to better results.

3 The F06 framework for text segmentation

3.1 Overall principles

The F06 framework is globally based on the same principles as *TextTiling* [11]. Its first stage, the linguistic pre-processing of texts, splits each text into sentences and represents each of them as the sequence of its normalized plain words, that is, nouns (proper and common nouns), verbs and adjectives. It is performed by the *TreeTagger* tool both for French and English, our two target languages. Finally, each sentence is turned into a vector of normalized plain words.

The evaluation of the lexical cohesion of a text, the second stage, relies as for *TextTiling* on a fixed-size focus window that is moved over the text to segment and stops at each sentence break. A cohesion value is computed at each position of this window and is associated to the sentence break at the transition between the two sides of the window. The final result is a cohesion graph of the text.

The last stage of F06 is mainly taken from the *LCseg* system [10]. It starts by evaluating the likelihood of each minimum m of the cohesion graph to be a topic shift. First, the pair of maxima l and r around m is found. Then, its score as a topic shift is computed as:

$$score(m) = \frac{LC(l) + LC(r) - 2 \cdot LC(m)}{2} \quad (1)$$

This score favors as possible topic shifts minima that correspond to sharp falls of lexical cohesion.

The next step is done by removing as a possible topic shift each minimum that is not farther than 2 sentences from its preceding neighbor. Finally, the selection of topic shifts is performed by applying a threshold computed from the distribution of minimum scores. Thus, a minimum m is kept as a topic shift if $score(m) > \mu - \alpha \cdot \sigma$, where μ is the average of minimum scores, σ their standard deviation and α is a modulator ($\alpha = 0.6$ in all our experiments).

3.2 Evaluation of lexical cohesion

As pointed out in Section 2, the evaluation of the cohesion in the sliding window of the text segmenter is the most important stage of the segmentation process and is the focus of the improvements we explore in this article. Globally, this evaluation is performed following [12]: each side of the window is represented by a vector and the cohesion in the window is evaluated by applying the *Dice coefficient* between its two sides. When the evaluation of the cohesion is only based on word reiteration, this principle is applied literally: if W_l refers to the vocabulary of the left side of the focus window and W_r to the vocabulary of its right side, the cohesion in the window at a text position is given by:

$$LC_{rec} = \frac{2 \cdot card(W_l \cap W_r)}{card(W_l) + card(W_r)} \quad (2)$$

More generally, this definition is suitable for relations of equivalence between words, which are limited in the present case to the equality between lemmas. For the other types of lexical cohesion relations, the *Dice coefficient* is extended in the following way: instead of focusing on words that are shared by the two sides of the window, the measure takes into account the words of one side of the window that are linked to words of the other side of the window according to the considered type of relations. More precisely, the cohesion in the window for a relation type rel_i takes the form:

$$LC_{rel_i} = \frac{card(W_{rel_i}(l) - W_{rec} - \bigcup_{j \neq i} W_{rel_j}(l))}{card(W_l) + card(W_r)} + \frac{card(W_{rel_i}(r) - W_{rec} - \bigcup_{j \neq i} W_{rel_j}(r))}{card(W_l) + card(W_r)} \quad (3)$$

where

$W_{rel_i}(x)$ is the set of words from the (x=l)eft or the (x=r)ight side of the window that are selected according to lexical relations of type rel_i,

$W_{rec} = card(W_l \cap W_r)$, words in a recurrence relation,

$\bigcup_{j \neq i} W_{rel_j}(x)$ gathers the set of words from the x side of the window that are selected according to lexical relations that are different from rel_i.

By removing from $W_{rel_i}(x)$ words that also appear in W_{rec} or $\bigcup_{j \neq i} W_{rel_j}(x)$, we make LC_{rel_i} measure the specific contribution of rel_i relations to the detection of the cohesion between the two sides of the window.

Finally, the global cohesion inside the window is the result of the sum of the cohesion values computed for each kind of lexical relations:

$$LC = LC_{rec} + \sum_i LC_{rel_i} \quad (4)$$

4 Improving text segmentation by an endogenous method

In this section, we will not present F06T in detail, the method described in [9] for improving text segmentation in an endogenous way. We will only remind its main principles and show how it can be defined in the F06 framework.

The specificity of the F06T segmenter in relation to the F06 framework is the use of the topics of the text to segment in the evaluation of the cohesion of the focus window. These topics are identified in an unsupervised way by clustering the words of the text according to their co-occurrents in this text. Thus, each of its topic is represented by a subset of its vocabulary.

In this context, the evaluation of the cohesion of the focus windows starts by the determination of the topics of the window that are actually representative of its content. Several topics may be associated to the focus window as a theme of a text may be scattered over several identified topics due to the absence of external reference topics. A topic is considered as representative of the content of the focus window only if it matches each side of this window. In practice, this matching is evaluated by applying the *Cosine* measure between the vector that represents one side of the window and the vector that represents the topic.

The computation of the cohesion of the focus windows from these selected text topics first consists in determining for each side of this window the number of its words that belong to one of these topics. The topical cohesion of the window, LC_{top}, is then given by Equation 5, derived from Equation 3:

$$\frac{card(W_{top}(l) - W_{rec})}{card(W_l) + card(W_r)} + \frac{card(W_{top}(r) - W_{rec})}{card(W_l) + card(W_r)} \quad (5)$$

where $W_{top}(i)_{i \in \{l,r\}} = W_i \cap T_w$ and T_w is the union of all the representations of the topics associated to the window. $W_{top}(i)$ corresponds to the words of the i side of the window that belong to the topics of the window.

Finally, the global cohesion in the focus window for F06T is computed as the sum of the cohesion computed from word reiteration, LC_{rec}, and the one computed from text topics LC_{top}, in accordance with Equation 4.

5 Improving text segmentation by exogenous methods

We present now the use in the F06 framework of external resources about relations between words. We first consider lexical co-occurrences, a resource that can be extracted from large corpora in an easy way.

5.1 Using lexical co-occurrences

5.1.1 Co-occurrence networks

For the experiments of Section 6, two networks of lexical co-occurrences were built: one for French, from the *Le Monde* newspaper, and one for English, from the *L.A. Times* newspaper. The size of each corpus was around 40 million words.

The building process was the same for the two networks. First, the initial corpus was pre-processed similarly to the texts to segment (see Section 3.1). Co-occurrences were classically extracted by moving a fixed-size window on texts with parameters for catching topical relations: the window was rather large, 20-word wide, took into account the boundaries of texts and co-occurrences were indifferent to word order. We adopted the Pointwise Mutual Information as the cohesion measure of each co-occurrence. This measure was normalized according to the maximal mutual information relative to the considered corpus. After filtering the less frequent and cohesive co-occurrences, we got a network with approximately 23,000 words and 5.2 million co-occurrences for French, 30,000 words and 4.8 million co-occurrences for English.

5.1.2 Using co-occurrence networks for segmentation

Similarly to F06T, F06C, the topic segmenter based on lexical co-occurrences, evaluates the cohesion inside the focus window in two steps. First, it uses its resource for selecting the words of one side of the focus window ($W_{coo}(x)$) that are the most strongly linked to words of the other side of this window. As lexical co-occurrences are not as reliable as semantic relations coming from a resource such as WordNet, this selection is only based on the most cohesive co-occurrences and must rely on several co-occurrence relations. More precisely, a word of one side of the focus window is selected if:

- it has direct co-occurrence relations with at least N words of the other side of the window ($N = 2$ in the experiments of Section 6);
- the frequency and the cohesion of these support co-occurrence relations are higher than a fixed threshold (14 for frequency and 0.14 for cohesion).

The second step is the computation of the cohesion in F06C's focus window following Equations 3 and 4. $LC_{F06C} = LC_{rec} + LC_{coo}$, where LC_{coo}, the cohesion from co-occurrence relations, is equal to:

$$\frac{card(W_{coo}(l) - W_{rec})}{card(W_l) + card(W_r)} + \frac{card(W_{coo}(r) - W_{rec})}{card(W_l) + card(W_r)} \quad (6)$$

5.2 Using word senses

Lexical co-occurrences represent a rather crude resource and it is interesting to test if more elaborated resources can lead to better results. In this section, we consider word senses that were discriminated from a corpus, a resource that can be seen halfway between co-occurrences and semantic knowledge.

mouse-device	computer#n, disk#n, pc#n, software#n, user#n, machine#n, screen#n, compatible#a ...
mouse-animal	hormone#n, tumour#n, immune#a, researcher#n, animal#n, disease#n, gene#n ...

Table 1: *Two senses of the word "mouse"*

5.2.1 Word senses discriminated from texts

The word senses we use in this work were built according to the method described in [8]. More precisely, the building process starts from a network of lexical co-occurrences as the ones described in Section 5.1.1. First, the subgraph of the co-occurrents of the target word is delimited and turned into a similarity graph where the similarity between two co-occurrents is equal to their cohesion in the network. Then, a clustering algorithm is applied for detecting high-density areas in this graph. Finally, a word sense is defined from each resulting cluster. An example of such word senses is given by Table 1 with the two senses found for the noun *mouse*.

A set of word senses were built from the two co-occurrence networks of Section 5.1.1. Due to the sparsity of these networks, senses are not discriminated for all their words. For French, the word sense base is made of 7,373 lemmas with an average number of senses by word equal to 2.8 whereas for English, the base is made of 9,838 lemmas with 2.0 senses by word.

5.2.2 Using word senses for segmentation

The discrimination of the senses of a word evoked in the previous section can also be seen as a way of filtering and structuring its co-occurrents. As a consequence, the use of lexical co-occurrences for topic segmentation described in Section 5.1.2 can be extended rather straightforwardly to the use of such word senses. The resulting segmenter is called F06WS.

This extension mainly consists in adding a preliminary step: before selecting the words of each side of the focus window that are the most strongly linked to words of the other side of this window, a word sense disambiguation process is applied to them to determine which of their senses are actually present. The selection is then performed as in Section 5.1.2 except that it is only based on the co-occurrents that are part of the definition of the senses kept by the word sense disambiguation process. More precisely, this process follows the principles defined by Lesk: it selects a sense for a word according to the overlap between its definition and the side of the window this word is part of. This overlap is evaluated here by computing the *Cosine* measure between the definition of the sense and the side of the window, both turned into vectors of lemmas. The sense with the highest similarity is kept.

6 Evaluation

6.1 Evaluation methodology

Choi proposed in [4] an evaluation methodology for topic segmentation systems that has became a kind of standard. This methodology is based on the building of artificial texts made of segments extracted from different documents. Because it is not well adapted to the evaluation of endogenous approaches, [9] proposed to adapt this methodology concerning the way the document segments are selected.

Instead of taking each segment from a different document, [9] uses two source documents referring to two different topics. This ensures that the boundary between two adjacent segments of an evaluation document actually corresponds to a topic shift. Each of the two source documents is split into a set of segments whose size is between 3 and 11 sentences, as for Choi, and an evaluation document is built by concatenating these segments in an alternate way from the beginning of the source documents until 10 segments are extracted. The topics of the source documents are controlled by taking them from the corpus of the CLEF 2003 evaluation for crosslingual information retrieval: each evaluation document is built from two source documents that were judged as relevant for two different CLEF 2003 topics. We used for our evaluations the two corpora of [9], one for French, one for English, as the results of F06R and F06T on these corpora were already known.

6.2 Using external resources

First, we evaluated the interest of using external resources in F06 by applying F06C and F06WS to the two evaluation corpora. We classically used the error metric P_k proposed in [1] and its variant *WindowDiff* (*WD*) [17] to measure segmentation accuracy. P_k and *WD* are given as percentages in the next tables (smallest values are best results).

Systems	P_k	WD
U00	25.91	27.42
C99	27.57	35.42
TextTiling*	21.08	27.43
LCseg	20.55	28.31
F06R	21.58	27.83
F06C	16.48	20.94
F06WS	18.17	23.14

Table 2: *Evaluation of F06 with external resources for the French corpus*

Tables 2 and 3 show both the results of our evaluations for F06C and F06WS and the results reported in [9] for F06R (F06 with only word recurrence) and several reference topic segmenters: U00 [20], C99 [4] and *LCseg* [10]; *TextTiling** is a variant of *TextTiling* in which the final identification of topic shifts from the cohesion graph is taken from [10]. All these systems were used without fixing the number of topic shifts to find. As pointed out in [9], the results of these reference systems show that the corpora we used are more difficult than Choi's corpus.

In the F06 framework, the results are globally similar for the two corpora: the use of external resources in

Systems	P_k	WD
U00	19.42	21.22
C99	21.63	30.64
TextTiling*	15.81	19.80
LCseg	14.78	19.73
F06R	16.90	20.93
F06C	14.85	21.00
F06WS	15.89	19.30

Table 3: *Evaluation of F06 with external resources for the English corpus*

addition to word recurrence improves topic segmentation but the use of word senses instead of co-occurrence relations is not as interesting as we could expected.

Nevertheless, the detailed situation is a little bit different for French and English. For French, the results of F06C and F06WS are higher than those of F06R in a significant way[1] and the difference between F06C and F06WS is not significant. For English, the difference between F06C and F06R or between F06WS and F06R are not statistically significant. There is no obvious explanation of this fact but we can notice that the average level of P_k and WD values of methods based on word recurrence is clearly higher for English than for French, which means that word recurrence is a more reliable way to detect topic similarity in English than in French. As a consequence, the use of external resources is less necessary for English than for French. Moreover, the high level of results based on word recurrence make them difficult to increase.

The lack of interest of word senses is also difficult to interpret. Their use was supposed to restrict the number of words that are wrongly detected as topically linked in the focus window of the segmenter. The results show that in practice, such restriction is too strict and certainly leads to discard relevant links. This loss is at least partially due to two characteristics of the clustering algorithm used for discriminating senses: it removes some of the co-occurrents of the word and it performs hard clustering, which means that some co-occurrents that should be shared by several senses are assigned to only one of them.

6.3 Combining endogenous and exogenous approaches

The general definition of the cohesion in the focus window of a F06 segmenter given by Equation 3 offers a direct means of integrating the endogenous approach of F06T and the exogenous approaches of F06C and F06WS. More precisely, as the evaluation of the previous section has shown that F06WS tends to have worst results than F06C, even if the difference is not significant, we will only consider F06C for this integration. Hence, the cohesion in the focus window of this integrating segmenter, called F06CT, is given by this instance of Equation 7:

$$LC = LC_{rec} + LC_{top-coo} + LC_{coo-top} \quad (7)$$

[1] The significance level of differences is evaluated by a one-side t-test with a null hypothesis of equal means. Levels lower than 0.05 are considered as statistically significant.

where $LC_{top-coo}$, the contribution of the endogenous approach, is equal to LC_{top} without taking into account words of $W_{coo}(x)$ and $LC_{coo-top}$, the contribution of the exogenous approach, is equal to $LC_{F06C} - LC_{rec}$ without taking into account words of $W_{top}(x)$.

Systems	P_k	WD
F06R	21.58	27.83
F06T	18.46	24.05
F06C	16.48	20.94
F06CT	14.59	18.41

Table 4: *Evaluation of the combination of approaches in F06 for the French corpus*

Tables 4 and 5 show the results of F06CT on the two evaluation corpora together with the results of the other F06 segmenters. The first point to note is that F06CT have the highest results among all the F06 segmenters. Both for French and English, F06CT significantly outperforms F06. Moreover, [9] reports that F06T also outperforms F06 in both cases. But as for F06C, there are also some differences for the two languages: the difference between F06CT and F06C is not significant for French while it is significant for English and the difference between F06CT and F06T is significant for French but not for English. This globally confirms our findings from the first evaluation. For English, the use of lexical co-occurrences is less effective than for French. As a consequence, a significant part of F06CT's results for English can certainly be explained by its endogenous approach while for French, the dominant part in F06CT's results seems rather come from its exogenous approach.

Systems	P_k	WD
F06R	16.90	20.93
F06T	14.06	18.31
F06C	14.85	21.00
F06CT	12.30	14.88

Table 5: *Evaluation of the combination of approaches in F06 for the English corpus*

Nevertheless, the results of this evaluation also show that the two kinds of approaches, exogenous and endogenous, are complementary: for French, F06CT significantly outperforms F06 and F06T while F06T significantly outperforms F06. This means that the cohesion relations brought by lexical co-occurrences are different from the endogenous relations extracted from the unsupervised topic identification and can be fruitfully associated.

7 Related work

Our work has two main characteristics. First, it focuses on the detection of the topical similarity of text units. Second, it tests and integrates several approaches for performing this detection. These two aspects are not tackled by many works as most of the work in this field concentrates on the application of statistical models to topic segmentation and relies on a basic similarity measure between text units. This can be partly explained by the differences we have observed in our evaluations between French and English: almost all works are dedicated to English, a language in which word recurrence seems to be particularly effective for topic segmentation. As a consequence, the use of external resources is not considered as a priority. But we have seen that the situation can be different for other languages, such as French.

Some works were done following this trend nevertheless. One way that was commonly adopted for improving the evaluation of this similarity without being dependent of a particular domain was to exploit a semantic space built from a large corpus. In CWM [5], a variant of C99, each word of a sentence is replaced by its representation in a *Latent Semantic Analysis* (LSA) space. In the work of Ponte and Croft [18], the representations of sentences are expanded by adding to them words selected from an external corpus by the means of the *Local Context Analysis* (LCA) method. Finally in [3], a set of concepts are learnt from a corpus in an unsupervised way by using the X-means clustering algorithm and the paragraphs of documents are represented in the space defined by these concepts. Co-occurrence relations were more directly used by [6] for supporting a similarity measure between sentences. Works that exploit manually-built resources such as [13], [15] or [19] also exist but they generally don't use these resources for evaluating directly the similarity of text units: in [15] and [19] for instance, they help in identifying lexical chains.

More globally, these works explore one way to detect the similarity of text units but they don't try to integrate several approaches. Hybrid systems are rare for topic segmentation and as [10] or [1], they aims at integrating content-based approaches with discourse cues. The only work that can be compared to ours from this viewpoint is [12], which combines word recurrence, co-occurrence relations and relations from a thesaurus. Although their evaluation framework is different from ours, their results also confirm the interest of combining word recurrence with external resources.

8 Conclusion and future work

In this article, we have first proposed to generalize the framework of [9] for topic segmentation to integrate external resources about lexical cohesion. Then, we have presented how to exploit in this new framework, F06, two such resources: a network of lexical co-occurrences and a repository of word senses induced from this network. The evaluation of the segmenters integrating word recurrence with these resources have shown that both of them improve segmentation results but that word senses don't outperform co-occurrences. Finally, we have combined the endogenous approach of [9] and the best exogenous approach we have tested and shown the interest of such a combination.

As future work, we plan to extend this work in three ways. First, we want to add to the tested external resources a manually-built resource about synonymy relations between words. This will be comparable to the use of a thesaurus in [12]. The second extension will test further the use of word senses by considering senses defined by similar words instead of co-occurrents. The last extension concerns the unsupervised topic identification process that underlies the endogenous approach. In [9], this identification only relies on the distributional similarity of words in documents. Using external resources such as lexical co-occurrences or synonyms could also improve this process, with finally a positive impact on topic segmentation.

References

[1] D. Beeferman, A. Berger, and J. Lafferty. Statistical models for text segmentation. *Machine Learning*, 34(1):177–210, 1999.

[2] D. M. Blei and P. J. Moreno. Topic segmentation with an aspect hidden markov model. In *24th ACM SIGIR*, pages 343–348, 2001.

[3] M. Caillet, J.-F. Pessiot, M. Amini, and P. Gallinari. Unsupervised learning with term clustering for thematic segmentation of texts. In *RIAO'04*, pages 1–11, 2004.

[4] F. Y. Y. Choi. Advances in domain independent linear text segmentation. In *NAACL'00*, pages 26–33, 2000.

[5] F. Y. Y. Choi, P. Wiemer-Hastings, and J. Moore. Latent semantic analysis for text segmentation. In *EMNLP'01*, pages 109–117, 2001.

[6] G. Dias, E. Alves, and J. G. P. Lopes. Topic segmentation algorithms for text summarization and passage retrieval: An exhaustive evaluation. In *22th AAAI*, pages 1334–1340, 2007.

[7] J. Eisenstein and R. Barzilay. Bayesian unsupervised topic segmentation. In *EMNLP 2008*, pages 334–343, 2008.

[8] O. Ferret. Discovering word senses from a network of lexical cooccurrences. In *20th COLING*, pages 1326–1332, 2004.

[9] O. Ferret. Finding document topics for improving topic segmentation. In *45th ACL*, pages 480–487, 2007.

[10] M. Galley, K. McKeown, E. Fosler-Lussier, and H. Jing. Discourse segmentation of multi-party conversation. In *ACL'03*, pages 562–569, 2003.

[11] M. A. Hearst. Multi-paragraph segmentation of expository text. In *ACL'94*, pages 9–16, 1994.

[12] A. C. Jobbins and L. J. Evett. Text segmentation using reiteration and collocation. In *ACL-COLING'98*, pages 614–618, 1998.

[13] H. Kozima. Text segmentation based on similarity between words. In *ACL'93 (Student Session)*, pages 286–288, 1993.

[14] I. Malioutov and R. Barzilay. Minimum cut model for spoken lecture segmentation. In *COLING-ACL 2006*, pages 25–32, 2006.

[15] J. Morris and G. Hirst. Lexical cohesion computed by thesaural relations as an indicator of the structure of text. *Computational Linguistics*, 17(1):21–48, 1991.

[16] R. J. Passonneau and D. J. Litman. Discourse segmentation by human and automated means. *Computational Linguistics*, 23(1):103–139, 1997.

[17] L. Pevzner and M. A. Hearst. A critique and improvement of an evaluation metric for text segmentation. *Computational Linguistics*, 28(1):19–36, 2002.

[18] J. M. Ponte and B. W. Croft. Text segmentation by topic. In *First European Conference on research and advanced technology for digital libraries*, 1997.

[19] N. Stokes, J. Carthy, and A. Smeaton. Segmenting broadcast news streams using lexical chains. In *STAIRS'02*, pages 145–154, 2002.

[20] M. Utiyama and H. Isahara. A statistical model for domain-independent text segmentation. In *ACL'01*, pages 491–498, 2001.

[21] J. Yamron, I. Carp, L. Gillick, S. Lowe, and P. van Mulbregt. A hidden markov model approach to text segmentation and event tracking. In *23th ICASSP*, pages 333–336, 1998.

Edlin: an easy to read linear learning framework

Kuzman Ganchev *
University of Pennsylvania
3330 Walnut St, Philaldelphia PA
kuzman@seas.upenn.edu

Georgi Georgiev
Ontotext AD
135 Tsarigradsko Ch., Sofia , Bulgaria
georgi.georgiev@ontotext.com

Abstract

The Edlin toolkit provides a machine learning framework for linear models, designed to be easy to read and understand. The main goal is to provide easy to edit working examples of implementations for popular learning algorithms. The toolkit consists of 27 Java classes with a total of about 1400 lines of code, of which about 25% are I/O and driver classes for examples. A version of Edlin has been integrated as a processing resource for the GATE architecture, and has been used for gene tagging, gene name normalization, named entity recognition in Bulgarian and biomedical relation extraction.

Keywords

Information Extraction, Classification, Software Tools

1 Introduction

The Edlin toolkit provides a machine learning framework for linear models, designed to be easy to read and understand. The main goal is to provide easy to edit working examples of implementations for popular learning algorithms. To minimize programmer overhead, Edlin depends only on GNU Trove[1] for fast data structures and JUnit[2] for unit tests. A version of Edlin has been integrated as a processing resource for the GATE [7] architecture, and has been used in-house for gene tagging, gene name normalization, named entity recognition in Bulgarian and biomedical relation extraction. For researchers we expect the main advantage of Edlin is that its code is easy to read, understand and modify, meaning that variations are easy to experiment with. For industrial users, the simplicity of the code as well as relatively few dependencies means that it is easier to integrate into existing codebases.

Edlin implements learning algorithms for linear models. Currently implemented are: Naive Bayes, maximum entropy models, the Perceptron and one-best MIRA (optionally with averaging), AdaBoost, structured Perceptron and structured one-best MIRA (optionally with averaging) and conditional random fields. Because of the focus on clarity and conciseness, some optimizations that would make the code harder to read have not been made. This makes the framework slightly slower than it could be, but implementations are asymptotically fast and suitable for use on medium to large datasets.

The rest of this paper is organized as follows: §2 describes the code organization; §3-§4 describes an integration with the GATE framework and an example application; §5 describes related software; and §6 discusses future work and concludes the paper.

2 Overview of the code

The goal of machine learning is to choose from a (possibly infinite) set of functions mapping from some input space to some output space. Let $x \in X$ be a variable denoting an input example and $y \in Y$ range over possible labels for x. A linear model will choose a label according to

$$h(x) = \arg\max_y f(x, y) \cdot w \qquad (1)$$

where $f(x, y)$ is a feature function and w is a parameter vector. We take the inner product of the feature vector with the model parameters w and select the output y that has high-

*Supported by ARO MURI SUBTLE W911NF-07-1-0216 and by the European projects AsIsKnown (FP6-028044) and LTfLL (FP7-212578)

[1] http://trove4j.sourceforge.net/

[2] http://www.junit.org

est such score. The feature function $f(x, y)$ is specified by the user, while the parameter vector w is learned using training data.

Even though the learning and inference algorithms are generic, and can be used for different applications, Edlin is implemented with an natural language tasks in mind. The classes related to classification, are implemented in the `classification` package, while those related to sequence tasks are implemented in the `sequence` package. The code to perform gradient ascent and conjugate gradient is in an `algo` package. There are three helper packages. Two (`experiments` and `io`) are code for reading input and for driver classes for the examples. The final package, called `types` contains infrastructure code such as an implementation of sparse vectors, elementary arithmetic operations such as the inner product, and other widely used operations whose implementation is not interesting from the point of view of understanding the learning algorithms. This code organization, as well as the data structures we employ are similar to other learning packages such as StructLearn [12] and MALLET [11]. One attribute that distinguishes Edlin from both of these packages is the decomposition of the feature function into

$$f(x, y) = f_2(f_1(x), y) \quad (2)$$

where f_1 maps the input into a sparse vector and f_2 combines it with a possible output in order to generate the final sparse vector used to assess the compatibility of the label for this input. By contrast, many other learning frameworks only allow the user to specify f_1 and hard-code an implementation of f_2 as conjoining the input predicates (f_1 in the notation above) with the label. By allowing the user to specify f_2, we allow them to tie parameters and add domain information about how different outputs are related. See the illustration below for an example.

2.1 Example Application

Perhaps the best way to describe the minimal amount to make reading the code easy is to trace how information is propagated and transformed in an example application. Take a POS tagging task as an example. Suppose we are given a collection of sentences that have been manually annotated and these have been split for us into a training set and a testing set. The sentences are read from disk and converted to a sparse vector representing $f_1(x)$ by a class in the `io` package. For example we might extract suffixes of length 2 to 5 from each word in a sentence. We look these up in an alphabet that maps them to a unique dimension, and store the counts of the words in a sparse vector for each word. The alphabet and sparse vector are implemented in `Alphabet` and `SparseVector` respectively. The array of sparse vectors for a sentence (recall there is one for each word) and alphabet are bundled together in an `SequenceInstance` object along with the true label. Next we want to train a linear sequence model using the perceptron algorithm on the training portion of our data. We construct a `sequence.Perceptron` object and call its `batchTrain` method. Figure 1 reproduces the implementation. The method takes the training data as a Java `ArrayList` of `SequenceInstance` objects, and the `Perceptron` class has parameters for whether averaging is turned on and the number of passes to make over the data. It also contains a `SequenceFeatureFunction` object (`fxy` in Figure 1) that implements f_2 from above. For part of speech tagging, it is typical to let $f_t(x, y^{(t-1)}, y^{(t)})$ conjoin $f_1(x)$ with $y^{(t)}$ and also conjoin $y^{(t)}$ with $y^{(t-1)}$, but not to have any features that look at x, $y^{(t)}$ and $y^{(t-1)}$ all at the same time. By contrast for named entities it is typical to have features that look at all three. The linear sequence model is created in the first line of the `batchTrain` method as a `LinearTagger` object, which has access to the alphabet used in the initial construction of the sparse vectors, the label alphabet (`yAlphabet` in Figure 1) and f_2 (`fxy` in Figure 1). It computes the prediction which is represented as an `int` array, with the interpretation `yhat[t]=j` as word t has the label at position j in the label alphabet (accessible via `yAlphabet.lookupIndex(j)`). The `batchTrain` method returns the linear sequence model.

3 GATE integration

GATE [8, 7] is a framework for engineering NLP applications along with a graphical development environment for developing components. GATE divides language processing resources into language resources, processing re-

```
public LinearTagger batchTrain(
        ArrayList<SequenceInstance> trainingData) {
  LinearTagger w = new LinearTagger(xAlphabet,
                                   yAlphabet, fxy);
  LinearTagger theta = null;
  if (performAveraging)
    theta = new LinearTagger(xAlphabet, yAlphabet,
                                               fxy);
  for (int iter = 0; iter < numIterations; iter++) {
    for (SequenceInstance inst : trainingData) {
      int[] yhat = w.label(inst.x);
      // if y = yhat then this update won't change w.
      StaticUtils.plusEquals(w.w, fxy.apply(inst.x,
                                            inst.y));
      StaticUtils.plusEquals(w.w, fxy.apply(inst.x,
                                          yhat), -1);
      if (performAveraging)
        StaticUtils.plusEquals(theta.w, w.w, 1);
    }
  }
  if (performAveraging) return theta;
  return w;
}
```

Fig. 1: *Edlin's perceptron implementation, reproduced verbatim to show code organization.*

sources, and graphical interfaces. We have integrated a version of Edlin into the GATE framework as a set of processing resources, by defining interfaces in Edlin for training, classification, and sequence tagging. These interfaces are used to communicate between Edlin's machine learning implementations and the concrete implementations of tagger and classifier processors in GATE. The integration allows Edlin to be used for robust, complex text processing applications, relying on GATE processors such as tokenizers, sentence splitters and parsers, to preprocess the data. The integration also makes it easy to pipeline Edlin-trained linear models using the GATE infrastructure for processing pipelines. Since Edlin has very readable code, this makes it easy for a researcher or engineer to try a modified learning algorithm if they already use the GATE framework.

4 Biomedical Relation Extraction

In this section we show an example text processing application within the Edlin and GATE architectures, focusing on the text processing components organization. Our problem domain is the BioNLP 2009 shared task [17], a biomedical relation extraction task. The goal is to identify relations between genes/gene products. We chose this task as an example because it is relatively complex and uses both Edlin and several GATE processing components. The results are described in [9].

Following BioNLP terminology, we use the term proteins to refer to both genes and gene products. Both trigger chunks and proteins are called *participants*. For example, the text "... phosphorylation of TRAF2 ..." would be a relation of type Phosphorylation with a theme of TRAF2. The relation is called an *event*, while the string "phosphorylation" is called a trigger. Gene boundary annotations are provided by the task organizers. In general, there are events with multiple participants in addition to the trigger. The event instances are organized into the structure of the Gene Ontology [5].

We separated the task in two main sub-tasks (i) recognition of trigger chunks using an Edlin sequence tagger and, (ii) classification of triggers and proteins as either forming an event from one of 9 predefined types or not participating in an event together. At the end of the section we discuss the final pipeline of processors used in this relation extraction task.

4.1 Gene and Trigger Tagging

The trigger chunks are simply words and phrases that describe the events linking proteins. For instance *binds* is such a trigger word that would link two or more genes in a *Binding* event. We used the Edlin GATE integration described in Section 3 to create one GATE processing resource that trains an Edlin linear sequence model and another that uses that Edlin sequence model to tag trigger chunks.

Both processors work in a pipeline with GATE preprocessors including a tokenizer, sentence splitter, POS tagger and chunker. Because Edlin represents linear models trained using different algorithms in the same way it was easy for us to compare different learning algorithms for the task. For this application tagger recall is an upper bound on system performance, and used MIRA with a loss function designed to achieve high recall since that performed best.

4.2 Relation Extraction

We separate the process of relation extraction into two stages: in the first stage, we generate events corresponding to relations between a trigger word and one or more proteins (*simple* events), while in the second stage, we generate events that correspond to relations between trigger words, proteins and simple events (we call the new events *complex* events).

For the purpose of this task we designed and implemented four GATE processing resources for two for training and two for classification of genes and trigger chunks into the 9 predefined types of events. The training of an Edlin linear model and classification using that model are again done using the Edlin-GATE integration, and are integrated in a GATE pipeline that now also includes dependency and phrase-structure parsers.

As with finding trigger words in the previous section, the uniform representation of linear models allowed us to compare different learning methods. We compared max entropy, perceptron and one-best MIRA, and again chose MIRA with a loss function designed to increase recall, since getting high recall was the most challenging part of the task. Finally, this tunable loss function was appealing for us because it allows application-specific tuning. For example, a search might require high recall, but high precision might be more important for adding relations to a knowledge base.

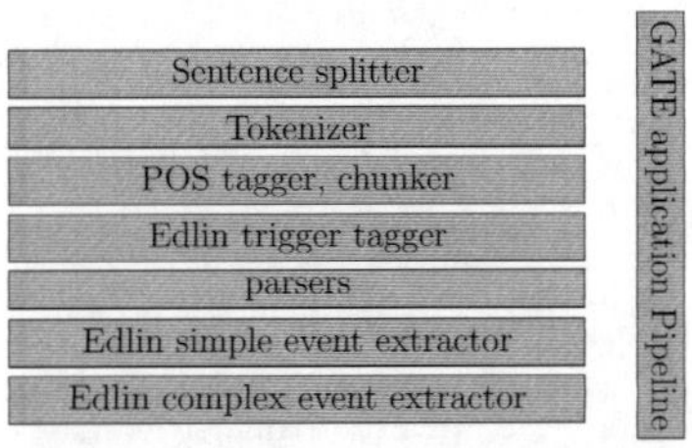

Fig. 2: *Graphical view of our relation extraction system pipeline.*

Figure 2 shows our event extraction pipeline, stringing together different GATE text processors. The first stages of the pipeline as well as the parsers are included in order to create features useful for later stages.

As described above, the trigger tagging stage uses an Edlin GATE processor trained using one-best MIRA. Furthermore, we employ a maximum entropy constituency parser [1] and a dependency parser [13]. These components are also represented as GATE processors. In the last stage of the pipeline we use two components, one for *simple* and one for *complex* events, based on the classification version of one-best MIRA algorithm implemented in Edlin and used as GATE processors.

5 Related Work

There are a number of machine learning tools available either as open source packages, or with source code for research purposes. To our knowledge Edlin is the only framework that represents linear models in a uniform fashion, and is also the only learning framework that prioritizes code readability. The NLTK [3, 4] (natural language toolkit) emphasizes code readability but focuses on natural language processing rather than learning.

MALLET [11] is a Java toolkit for machine learning. MALLET implements most of the learning algorithms available in Edlin in addition to many others. The exceptions are perceptron and MIRA, which are available as a separate MALLET-compatible package called StructLearn [12, 6]. For sequence data, one of MALLET's main strengths is a way to easily create predicate functions (f_1 in the notation of Section 2). Edlin does not have sophisticated code for feature engineering, and in our experiments we used GATE to generate features. MALLET also contains a very general implementation of CRFs that allows linear-chain models with varying order n Markov properties. These enhancements lead to a larger and hence harder to read code-base. For example the CRF model implementation in MALLET comprises 1513 lines of code compared to 56 for Edlin's simplistic implementation.[3] Note that the authors actively recommend MALLET in particular for CRFs, however it serves a different need than Edlin. While MALLET is very general and easy to use, Edlin is very simple and easy to understand.

LingPipe[2] is a Java toolkit for linguistic analysis of free text. The framework provides tools for classification, sequence tagging, clustering and a variety of problem-specific tasks such as spelling correction, word segmentation named entity normalization and parsing for biomedical text among others. Some trained models are provided, but it is possible to train a new models for new tasks and data. The software is available along with source code. We did not investigate source code complexity due to time constraints, but the full featured nature of the software and its marketing to enterprise customers suggests that its focus is on stability, and scalability rather than code simplicity and readability.

[3] Counted with *cloc* `http://cloc.sourceforge.net/`

Weka [18] is a widely used framework developed at the University of Waikato in New Zealand and comprises a collection of learning algorithms for classification, clustering, feature selection, and visualizations. Weka includes a very friendly graphical user interface, and is targeted largely at researchers in the sciences or social sciences who would like to experiment with different algorithms to analyze their data. Weka does not contain code for structured learning and is more suitable for use as a versatile black box than for reading and modifying source code. For example Weka's perceptron algorithm is implemented in 600 lines of code compared to 38 for Edlin. By contrast Weka has a very good graphical user interface and allows visualization not implemented in Edlin. GATE integration allows some visualizations and evaluation for Edlin, but specialized only for text.

ABNER [16] is a tool for processing natural language text aimed at the biomedical domain. ABNER is widely used for annotation of biomedical named entities such as genes and gene products. It contains a CRF implementation and a graphical user interface for visualization and modification of annotations, in addition to domain specific tokenizers and sentence segmenters. BioTagger [14] is a different tool for named entity recognition in biomedical text also using linear-chain CRFs. It has been applied to genes/gene products [14], malignancy mentions [10] and genomic variations in the oncology domain [15].

6 Conclusions and Future Work

We have presented a linear modeling toolkit of implementations written specifically for readability. We described the toolkit's layout, learning algorithms and an application we have found it useful for. The main goal of Edlin is to be easy to read and modify and we have used the toolkit in teaching a Master's level class. While we have not performed a scientific evaluation, initial feedback from students has been positive and at least one fellow researcher commented that he liked the organization and simplicity of the code.

Future work includes the implementation of maximal margin learning (i.e. support vector machines) and further improvements to the integration between Edlin and GATE. Finally, we intend to improve the implementation of the optimization algorithms to improve training run-time for maximum entropy models and CRFs.

References

[1] OpenNLP. `http://opennlp.sourceforge.net`, 2009.

[2] Alias-i. LingPipe. `http://alias-i.com/lingpipe`, 2008. (accessed 2008-04-20).

[3] S. Bird and E. Loper. Nltk: The natural language toolkit. In *Proceedings ACL*. ACL, 2004.

[4] S. Bird and E. Loper. Natural language toolkit. `http://www.nltk.org/`, 2008.

[5] T. G. O. Consortium. Gene ontology: tool for the unification of biology. *Nature Genetics*, 25(1):25–29, 2000.

[6] K. Crammer, R. McDonald, and F. Pereira. Scalable large-margin online learning for structured classification. Department of Computer and Information Science, University of Pennsylvania, 2005.

[7] H. Cunningham. GATE – general architecture for text engineering. `http://gate.ac.uk/`.

[8] H. Cunningham, D. Maynard, K. Bontcheva, and V. Tablan. GATE: A framework and graphical development environment for robust NLP tools and applications. In *Proceedings of the 40th Anniversary Meeting of the Association for Computational Linguistics*, 2002.

[9] G. Georgiev, K. Ganchev, V. Momchev, D. Peychev, P. Nakov, and A. Roberts. Tunable domain-independent event extraction in the mira framework. In *Proceedings of BioNLP*. ACL, June 2009.

[10] Y. Jin, R. McDonald, K. Lerman, M. Mandel, M. Liberman, F. Pereira, R. Winters, and P. White. Identifying and extracting malignancy types in cancer literature. In *BioLink*, 2005.

[11] A. McCallum. Mallet: A machine learning for language toolkit. http://mallet.cs.umass.edu, 2002.

[12] R. McDonald, K. Crammer, K. Ganchev, S. P. Bachoti, and M. Dredze. Penn StructLearn. `http://www.seas.upenn.edu/~strctlrn/StructLearn/StructLearn.html`.

[13] R. McDonald, K. Crammer, and F. Pereira. Online large-margin training of dependency parsers. In *Proceedings of ACL*. ACL, 2005.

[14] R. McDonald and F. Pereira. Identifying gene and protein mentions in text using conditional random fields. *BMC Bioinformatics*, (Suppl 1):S6(6), 2005.

[15] R. McDonald, R. Winters, M. Mandel, Y. Jin, P. White, and F. Pereira. An entity tagger for recognizing acquired genomic variations in cancer literature. *Journal of Bioinformatics*, 2004.

[16] B. Settles. ABNER: An open source tool for automatically tagging genes, proteins, and other entity names in text. *Bioinformatics*, 21(14):3191–3192, 2005.

[17] J. Tsujii. BioNLP'09 Shared Task on Event Extraction. `http://www-tsujii.is.s.u-tokyo.ac.jp/GENIA/SharedTask/index.html`, 2009.

[18] I. H. Witten and E. Frank. *Data Mining: Practical machine learning tools and techniques*. Morgan Kaufmann, San Francisco, 2nd edition, 2005.

Exploiting the use of Prior Probabilities for Passage Retrieval in Question Answering

Surya Ganesh, Vasudeva Varma
Language Technologies Research Centre,
IIIT-Hyderabad, India
suryag@research.iiit.ac.in, vv@iiit.ac.in

Abstract

Document Retrieval assumes that a document is independent of its relevance, and non-relevance. Previous works showed that the same assumption is being considered for passage retrieval in the context of Question Answering. In this paper, we relax this assumption and describe a method for estimating the prior of a passage being relevant, and non-relevant to a question. These prior probabilities are used in the process of ranking passages. We also describe a trivial method for identifying relevant and non-relevant text to a question using the Web and AQUAINT corpus as information sources. An empirical evaluation on TREC 2006 Question Answering test set showed that in the context of Question Answering prior probabilities are necessary in ranking the passages.

1 Introduction

Passage Retrieval is an intermediate step between document retrieval and answer extraction in a typical Question Answering (QA) system. It reduces the search space for finding an answer from a massive collection of documents to a fixed number of passages (say top 100). Unless the answer is present in one of the retrieved passages, QA systems will not find the answer to a given question. So, passage retrieval is considered as one of the most important components of a QA system.

The Probability Ranking Principle [13] states that a retrieval system should rank the documents in decreasing order of their probability of relevance to the query. According to the Language Modeling [11] decomposition [8] of this ranking principle, the documents should be ranked using the following equation:

$$\log rank(D) = \log p(Q|D, R) + \log \frac{p(D|R)}{p(D|N)} \qquad (1)$$

Here the first term $p(Q|D, R)$ measures the likelihood of the query given a document that is relevant and Language Modeling is being used to estimate this value. The second term measures the prior probabilities of document being relevant, and non relevant. But, document retrieval assumes that a document is independent of its relevance, and non-relevance. So, documents are just ranked based on Language Modeling i.e., the probability of a query being generated by a document. Previous works [9] [10] showed that the same approach is being used even for passage retrieval in the context of QA.

Previously Jagadeesh et al. [5] used prior probabilities in Query-Based Multi-Document Summarization task. They defined an entropy based measure called Information Measure to capture the prior of a sentence. This information measure was computed using external information sources like the Web and Wikipedia. Their experimental results showed that prior probabilities are necessary for ranking sentences in the summarization task. We use a similar approach to exploit the use of prior probabilities for passage retrieval in QA.

In this paper we describe a mutual information measure called KullbackLeibler divergence (KL divergence) [3] to compute the prior of a passage. We also describe a trivial method for identifying relevant and non-relevant text to a question using the Web and AQUAINT corpus (used in TREC[1] QA evaluations) as information sources. The rest of this paper is organized as follows: Section 2 describes the estimation of prior probabilities of passages; Section 3 describes the identification of relevant and non-relevant text to a question; Section 4 describes the experiments conducted and their results and Section 5 concludes the paper.

2 Estimation of prior probability

In this section we assume that relevant (R) and non-relevant (N) text is identified for a given question. In Information Retrieval, KullbackLeibler divergence is often used to measure the distance between two language models [2] [14]. We use this mutual information measure to estimate prior probabilities of passages. Let U_A denotes the unigram language model of passage A and U_R, U_N denote the unigram language models of relevant and non-relevant text respectively. KL divergence between U_A, U_R and U_A, U_N are computed as follows:

$$D(U_A||U_R) = \sum_{v \in V} U_A(v) \log \frac{U_A(v)}{U_R(v)}$$

$$D(U_A||U_N) = \sum_{v \in V} U_A(v) \log \frac{U_A(v)}{U_N(v)}$$

[1] Text REtrieval Conference, http://trec.nist.gov

International Conference RANLP 2009 - Borovets, Bulgaria, pages 99–102

Where v is a term in the vocabulary V and $U_A(v)$, $U_R(v)$, $U_N(v)$ are the unigram probabilities of v in the passage, relevant and non-relevant text respectively. With the increase in the divergence between passage and relevant text, the probability of passage being relevant decreases. So, the prior probabilities are estimated as follows:

$$p(A|R) = \frac{1}{1 + D(U_A||U_R)}$$

$$p(A|N) = \frac{1}{1 + D(U_A||U_N)}$$

As KL divergence is always non-negative, both $p(A|R)$ and $p(A|N)$ always lie in the range $[0, 1]$. This satisfies the basic law of probability i.e., the probability of an event should always lie in the range $[0, 1]$. $p(A|R) = 1$ when $U_A = U_R$, as the divergence of two equivalent distributions is zero. Similarly, $p(A|N) = 1$ when $U_A = U_N$. Substituting the above estimates for prior probabilities in equation 1 gives the final ranking ranking function for passage retrieval.

$$\log rank(A) = \log p(Q|A, R) - \log \frac{1 + D(U_A||U_R)}{1 + D(U_A||U_N)}$$

3 Identifying relevant and non-relevant text

In the previous section we have assumed that the relevant and non-relevant text for a given question is known. Here we will discuss a method to extract the required information based on different query formulation strategies.

3.1 Relevant text

Breck et al. [1] noticed a correlation between the number of times an answer appeared in the TREC corpus and the average performance of TREC systems on that particular question. This shows that, the more times an answer appears in the text collection, the easier it is to find it. As a text collection, the Web is larger in size than any research corpus by several orders of magnitude. An important implication of this size is the amount of data redundancy inherent in the Web i.e., each item of information has been stated in a variety of ways in different documents in the Web.

Data redundancy in the Web indicates that the answer for a given natural language question exists in many different forms in different documents. So, our methodology for extracting relevant text relies on Web search engines. Currently, the Yahoo search engine is used to retrieve this text from the Web. Assuming that an answer is likely to be found within the vicinity of set of keywords in the question, a query composed of keywords in it is given to the search engine. For example, given the question *"Which position did Warren Moon play in professional football?"*, the following query *"position warren moon play professional football"* is given to the search engine. The top N snippets/summaries provided by the search engine are extracted to form relevant text.

Most of the snippets provided by the search engine consist of broken sentences. These broken sentences may miss a part of answer pattern or entire answer pattern which is originally present in them. In either case, an automatic evaluation using a set of questions and their corresponding answer patterns will fail to show the actual quality of snippets. So, we manually examined the snippets for a set of 50 randomly selected questions from TREC 2006 test set [4]. We observed that on an average about 6 snippets out of top 10 snippets provided by the search engine are relevant to the question. As the quality of snippets is considerably high, we use them as relevant text to a given question.

3.2 Non-relevant text

The methodology for extracting non-relevant text is independent of the size of a text collection unlike the methodology for relevant text. Here the structure of a question is used to extract the required information. An input question is parsed to get POS tags corresponding to all the terms in it. We have used the stanford parser [6] [7] to get POS tag sequence corresponding to a question. Based on POS tags, all keywords in a question are splitted into two sets: Topic and Keyword.

Topic: Typically, questions ask for a specific information within a broad topic. For example, the question *"Which position did Warren Moon play in professional football?"*, asks for a specific information regarding *"Warren Moon"*. A topic can be a person, location, organization, event or any other entity, which are proper nouns. So, a topic set consists of all the proper nouns within a question. And, in questions where there are no proper nouns like *"Which country is the leading producer of rice?"*, nouns *"rice"* and *"country"* are considered as individual topics and these terms form topic set.

Keywords: This set contains all the keywords in a question which are not members of topic set. So, for the question *"Which position did Warren Moon play in professional football?"*, the constituents of this set are "*position*", "*play*", "*professional*" and "*football*".

Using the above two sets, two distinct queries are formulated which represent their non-relevance to a question.

QUERY I: It is formulated using topic set terms alone, which is based on the idea that text which covers general information regarding a topic in the question can be considered as non-relevant to it. So, for the above example question "*warren moon*" is expected to retrieve non-relevant text.

QUERY II: It is formulated using terms from both topic and keyword sets. The idea behind this query formulation is that text which covers information about a topic in the question but does not contain any of the keywords in it, can be considered as non-relevant to it. So, for the above example question, "*warren moon -position -play -professional -football*" is expected to retrieve non-relevant text. The negative operator (-) in the above query restricts the Information Retrieval system to retrieve only information without terms in the query that succeed '-' operator.

As the methodology is independent of the size of a corpus, two text collections which include Web and AQUAINT corpus, are used to extract the required information. An empirical evaluation using TREC 2006 QA test set was performed to test the quality of text extracted by using the two queries described previously. Redundancy, a passage retrieval performance evaluation metric, is used to measure the average number of answer bearing passages found within the top N passages retrieved for each query formulation. So, here the quality of text is inversely proportional to redundancy i.e., lower the redundancy value better is the quality of text extracted. All the FACTOID questions from the test set were used to measure redundancy. Table 1 shows the average redundancy scores for the top N passages retrieved from AQUAINT corpus in the test set. QUERY I and QUERY II are the query formulations from a question as described previously and QUERY is a keyword query formulated for retrieving relevant snippets from the Web. These results show that QUERY II produces better quality of non-relevant text than QUERY I. And, compared to QUERY both QUERY I and QUERY II have significantly lower redundancy scores. A similar evaluation could not be performed on snippets retrieved from Web because of broken sentences as described in the previous section.

Query	Top 1	Top 10	Top 20	Top 100
QUERY	0.222	0.844	1.202	2.227
QUERY I	0.020	0.116	0.236	0.597
QUERY II	0.006	0.057	0.122	0.270

Table 1: *Redundancy scores for the passages retrieved from AQUAINT corpus using different queries*

As the extracted relevant and non-relevant text is not truly relevant and non-relevant to a question, a linear interpolation of Language Modeling score and prior probabilities are used to rank passages as shown in the equation below.

$$\log rank(A) = (1-\alpha)\log p(Q|A,R) - \alpha \log \frac{1 + D(U_A||U_R)}{1 + D(U_A||U_N)}$$

Where α is a weighting parameter which lies between 0 and 1.

4 Experiments

In the context of QA, coverage and redundancy [12] are the two principal measures used to measure the performance of passage retrieval. The coverage gives the proportion of questions for which a correct answer can be found within the top N passages retrieved for each question. The redundancy gives the average number of answer bearing passages found within the top N passages retrieved for each question. In our experiments we have set N as 20 i.e., the top 20 passages are used for evaluation.

The data used to test the effectiveness of prior probabilities of passages includes: AQUAINT corpus, factoid questions from TREC 2006 QA task, and answer judgments provided by NIST for these questions. The AQUAINT corpus consists of 1,033,461 documents taken from AP newswire, the New York Times newswire and the English portion of the Xinhua News Agency newswire. The documents in this corpus contain paragraph markers which are used as passage level boundaries for our experiments. The answer judgments consist of answer patterns and document ids in which they occur. This allows the evaluation to be performed under two criteria: strict and lenient. For strict scoring, the answer pattern must occur in the passage, and the passage must be from one of the documents listed as relevant in the answer judgments. For lenient scoring, the answer pattern must occur in the passage.

We used two open source retrieval engines, Lucene and Indri, to test the effect of prior probabilities on passage retrieval. Lucene supports Boolean query language and ranked retrieval using BM25. Indri is a state-of-the-art retrieval engine that combines the merits of language model and inference network. We incorporated our approach for passage retrieval as a re-ranking step into these retrieval engines. After Lucene or Indri retrieves a ranked set of passages for a given question, top 200 passages are re-ranked, of which top 20 passages are considered for evaluation. The scores for top 20 passages returned by respective engines act as baseline to compare the re-ranked results using our approach.

We performed two experiments in which QUERY and QUERY II were used to extract relevant and non-relevant text respectively. In the first experiment, we compared the re-ranked and baseline results from the two retrieval engines, and they are shown in tables 2 and 3. Only Web was used to extract relevant text but for extracting non-relevant text both AQUAINT and Web were used. So, to analyze the effect of two text collections on computing the prior of a passage, we showed results for both of them. The results listed under AQUAINT and Web show considerable improvements over the baseline and in between the two, scores are marginally higher when Web was used.

Criteria	Metric	Lucene	AQUAINT	Web
Strict	Coverage	0.597	0.639	0.662
	Redundancy	1.202	1.313	1.341
Lenient	Coverage	0.719	0.770	0.781
	Redundancy	3.514	3.790	3.957

Table 2: *Lucene evaluation results under strict and lenient criteria*

In the second experiment we tested our methodology for different values of weighting parameter (α) between 0.0 and 1.0 in the ranking function. Figure 1 shows the performance of passage retrieval for differ-

Criteria	Metric	Indri	AQUAINT	Web
Strict	Coverage	0.548	0.554	0.582
	Redundancy	1.043	1.074	1.114
Lenient	Coverage	0.685	0.707	0.719
	Redundancy	3.349	3.514	3.730

Table 3: *Indri evaluation results under strict and lenient criteria*

ent α values under strict and lenient criteria. In all the cases, the performance of passage retrieval improves over the baseline ($\alpha = 0.0$) for α values between 0.0 and 0.8, and from then it is below the baseline. And, the performance reaches maximum for α values between 0.3 and 0.5 which shows that performance is biased towards query likelihood scores.

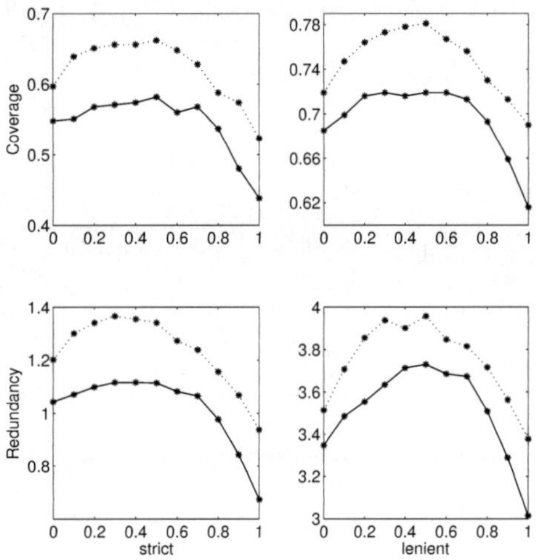

Fig. 1: *Performance of passage retrieval for different* α *values from* 0.0 *to* 1.0 *under strict and lenient criteria. In all the cases '(—*—)' and '(··· *···)' denotes re-ranked scores from Indri and Lucene.*

5 Conclusion

Question Answering aims at finding exact answers to natural language questions from a large collection of documents. Within a QA system, passage retrieval reduces the search space for finding an answer from such large collection of documents to a fixed number of passages. In this paper, we have explored the use of prior probabilities of a passage being relevant, and non-relevant to a question in the process of ranking passages. We described a method for estimating these prior probabilities using KullbackLeibler divergence, and a method for extracting relevant and non-relevant text to a question.

Our experiments on factoid questions from TREC 2006 test set showed that in the context of QA, use of prior probabilities improves the performance of passage retrieval. The experimental results also showed that performance is biased towards query likelihood scores. This could be because the information used for computing prior of a passage is not strictly relevant or non-relevant. In the future, we aim to further enhance the performance of our passage retrieval methodology by exploring different text classification algorithms to derive better prior probability estimates, and different techniques to extract relevant and non-relevant information to a question.

References

[1] E. Breck, M. Light, G. S. Mann, E. Riloff, B. Brown, P. Anand, M. Rooth, and M. Thelen. Looking under the hood : Tools for diagnosing your question answering engine. *CoRR*, cs.CL/0107006, 2001.

[2] C. Carpineto, R. de Mori, G. Romano, and B. Bigi. An information-theoretic approach to automatic query expansion. *ACM Trans. Inf. Syst.*, 19(1):1–27, 2001.

[3] T. M. Cover and J. A. Thomas. *Elements of information theory.* Wiley-Interscience, New York, NY, USA, 1991.

[4] H. T. Dang, J. J. Lin, and D. Kelly. Overview of the trec 2006 question answering track 99. In *TREC*, 2006.

[5] J. Jagarlamudi, P. Pingali, and V. Varma. Capturing sentence prior for query-based multi-document summarization. In D. Evans, S. Furui, and C. Soulupuy, editors, *RIAO*. CID, 2007.

[6] D. Klein and C. D. Manning. Accurate unlexicalized parsing. In *ACL '03: Proceedings of the 41st Annual Meeting on Association for Computational Linguistics*, pages 423–430, Morristown, NJ, USA, 2003. Association for Computational Linguistics.

[7] D. Klein and C. D. Manning. Fast exact inference with a factored model for natural language parsing. In *In Advances in Neural Information Processing Systems 15 (NIPS)*, pages 3–10. MIT Press, 2003.

[8] J. Lafferty and C. Zhai. *Probabilistic Relevance Models Based on Document and Query Generation*, volume 13. Kluwer International Series on Information Retrieval, 2003.

[9] X. Liu and W. B. Croft. Passage retrieval based on language models. In *CIKM '02: Proceedings of the eleventh international conference on Information and knowledge management*, pages 375–382, New York, NY, USA, 2002. ACM.

[10] V. Murdock and W. B. Croft. A translation model for sentence retrieval. In *HLT '05: Proceedings of the conference on Human Language Technology and Empirical Methods in Natural Language Processing*, pages 684–691, Morristown, NJ, USA, 2005. Association for Computational Linguistics.

[11] J. M. Ponte. A language modeling approach to information retrieval. Master's thesis, Amherst, MA, USA, 1998.

[12] I. Roberts and R. Gaizauskas. Evaluating passage retrieval approaches for question answering. In *In Proceedings of 26th European Conference on Information Retrieval*, pages 72–84, 2003.

[13] S. E. Robertson. The probability ranking principle in ir. pages 281–286, 1997.

[14] C. Zhai and J. Lafferty. Model-based feedback in the language modeling approach to information retrieval. In *CIKM '01: Proceedings of the tenth international conference on Information and knowledge management*, pages 403–410, New York, NY, USA, 2001. ACM.

Exploiting structure and content of Wikipedia for Query Expansion in the context of Question Answering

Surya Ganesh, Vasudeva Varma
Language Technologies Research Centre,
IIIT-Hyderabad, India
suryag@research.iiit.ac.in, vv@iiit.ac.in

Abstract

Retrieving answer containing passages is a challenging task in Question Answering. In this paper we describe a novel query expansion method which aims to rank the answer containing passages better. It uses content and structured information (link structure and category information) of Wikipedia to generate a set of terms semantically related to the question. As Boolean model allows a fine-grained control over query expansion, these semantically related terms are added to the original query to form an expanded Boolean query. We conducted experiments on TREC 2006 QA data. The experimental results show significant improvements of about 24.6%, 11.1% and 12.4% in precision at 1, MRR at 20 and TDRR scores respectively using our query expansion method.

1 Introduction

Question Answering (QA) aims at finding exact answers to natural language questions in a large collection of documents (such as World Wide Web). Within a QA system, passage retrieval reduces the search space for finding the answer from such large collection of documents to a fixed number of passages (say top 20). But this could lead to the case where the set of passages considered may not contain the answer. In such cases any QA system would not answer the question. One of the reasons for not retrieving answer containing passages is attributed to the problem of vocabulary mismatch i.e., passages holding the answer to a question have semantic alterations of original terms in the question. Moldovan [5] showed that their system failed to answer 25.7% of questions solely because of vocabulary mismatch. In Information Retrieval (IR) such a problem is addressed using the technique of Query Expansion. It is the process of expanding the search query to match additional relevant documents. Query expansion techniques like adding synonyms of the query terms and relevance feedback have performed well in many IR applications. But most of these techniques as described by Derczynski [4] were not successful in the context of QA.

In this paper we describe a novel query expansion method using Wikipedia. Wikipedia is the leading open encyclopedia with a wide coverage on diverse topics, events, entities, etc. It is a reliable data-source and has found its use in many applications [1]. Another factor which motivated us to use it, is based on the simple experiment we conducted using TREC 2006 QA test set [3]. The test set consists of question series where each series asks for information regarding a particular target. The targets in the test set include people, organizations, events and other entities. Because of low data redundancy in Wikipedia, the coverage of its articles is directly proportional to the size of the text content in them. So in this experiment, we search for size of the text content present in Wikipedia for each target and the results are shown in table 1.

Target	Count
Rich Content	64
Partial Content	8
Zero Content	3

Table 1: *Targets from TREC 2006 QA test set*

As most of the targets as seen in Table 1, have rich content in Wikipedia, we used it as a knowledge source for our Query expansion method. Apart from the content of Wikipedia, we also used its structured information in our method. The structured data we used includes category information and link structure. Each article in Wikipedia belongs to one or more categories and the links between articles signify a semantic relationship between source and target articles.

2 Related Work

Different query expansion methods have been studied to enhance the performance of passage retrieval in the context of QA. Monz [6] tested a blind relevance feedback technique which selects terms based on standard Rocchio term weighting from top N documents. His experiments in the context of QA, showed a reduction in the performance compared to original query's performance. On the other hand, the same technique was found effective for the ad-hoc retrieval task. Pizzato [7] employed a blind relevance feedback technique which uses the named entities of the relevant answer type from the top ranked documents to form an expanded query. His experiments on PERSON type factoid questions have not shown a considerable improvement.

Yang et al. [10] used WordNet and Web to expand queries for QA. Only marginal improvements were attained when Web was used to extract expansion terms and when WordNet was used to rank these extracted terms the improvement was reduced. On semantic

International Conference RANLP 2009 - Borovets, Bulgaria, pages 103–106

grouping the candidate expansion terms based on the relations between them, best results were obtained. Bilotti et al. [2] studied the effect of stemming and explicit query expansion using inflectional variants on document retrieval in the context of QA. The experimental results showed high recall for explicit query expansion and comparably low recall when stemming was used. Sun et al. [8] studied two query expansion techniques which make use of dependency relation analysis to extract contextual terms and relations from external corpuses. These techniques were used to enhance the performance of density based and relation based passage retrieval frameworks. The experimental results showed that relation based term expansion method with density based passage retrieval system outperformed the local content analysis method for query expansion. And, relation expansion method outperformed relation based passage retrieval system.

Arguello [1] described a technique for mining the links and anchor text in Wikipedia for query expansion terms and phrases. The technique yielded consistent and significant improvements in both recall and precision for blog recommendation. Our query expansion method is intended to rank the answer containing passages higher, by using the content and structure of Wikipedia.

3 Methodology

Our query expansion method first defines a query expansion term space ($QETS$) and then selects terms in this space based on proximity between terms and category information of outlink pages in Wikipedia. The query expansion term space consists of terms which could enhance the performance of passage retrieval for a given question. So, defining $QETS$ plays a major role in query expansion methods and it depends on different factors. In the case of Document Retrieval, query expansion methods are intended to bridge the gap between a high level general topic (expressed by the query) and the more nuanced facets of that topic likely to be written about in the documents. So, they use terms from top ranked documents or user selected documents to form $QETS$ for a given query. But, in the case of QA, query expansion methods are intended to rank the answer containing passages higher, as only fixed number of top ranked passages are considered to find the answer. So, constructing $QETS$ with the terms that are semantically related to the question could help in ranking the answer containing passages higher.

We use the content of Wikipedia to define $QETS$ for a given question in the following way. First, the Wikipedia article (A) corresponding to the question target is found and then a set of sentences (S) from this article which consist of question keywords is found. The above process of retrieving relevant sentences to a question is similar to that of passage retrieval. The terms in these sentences excluding stopwords and question keywords, constitute to form $QETS$ for a given question. It also includes terms in the anchor text of outlinks from the relevant sentences. Each term in this $QETS$ is weighted based on its semantic relatedness to the question. And, the strength of this semantic relation is captured using a linear combination of proximity score and outlink score as shown in the equation below.

$$score(t \in QETS) = ps(t, Q) + ls(t, C) \qquad (1)$$

Where t is a term in $QETS$, Q is a string of keywords in the question, C is the category information of outlink page, $ps(t, Q)$ and $ls(t, C)$ are proximity and outlink scores of term t. The significance and computation of proximity and outlink scores are described below.

3.1 Proximity score

The assumption behind selection of terms based on proximity scores is that semantically related terms are usually located in proximity, and the distance between two terms could indicate the strength of their association. The proximity score of a term is computed using its frequency and its minimum distance to a keyword in the question over a fixed window size of single sentence. Normally, within a sentence most of the terms occur only once. So, effectively our proximity score of a term is the summation of its minimum distances to a keyword in the question over all the relevant sentences (S) found in Wikipedia. Finally, each term in $QETS$ is weighted using the equation below.

$$ps(t \in QETS, Q) = \sum_{i=1}^{|S|} tf_{s_i}(t) * \frac{1}{dt_{s_i}(t, Q)}$$

Where $tf_{s_i}(t)$ is the term frequency of t in the sentence s_i and $dt_{s_i}(t, Q)$ is the minimum distance between term t and a keyword from Q.

3.2 Outlink score

This scoring method exploits the structured information (link structure and category information) of Wikipedia to rank the terms in $QETS$. All the outlinks present in the relevant sentence set (S) may not be semantically related to the question. So to find only the semantically related outlinks to the question, the category information of these outlink pages is used. Only those outlinks with their category information matching the question are considered semantically relevant. For example, given the question "*Which position did Warren Moon play in professional football?*", only the outlinks that fall into any one of these categories "*position/play/football/professional*" are considered semantically relevant to the question. Finally, all the terms from anchor texts of these relevant outlinks are weighted based on their frequencies in the relevant sentences (S) as shown in the equation below. And, for the rest of the terms in $QETS$, the outlink score is zero.

$$ls(t \in QETS, C) = tf_S(t)$$

The final scores of all the terms in $QETS$ is computed using equation 1, and they are sorted based on these scores. After sorting, the top N terms are picked for query expansion. The top 10 query expansion terms for the sample question "*Which position did Warren Moon play in professional football?*" from TREC 2006 QA dataset are shown in Table 2. One of the query expansion terms "*quarterback*" is the name of a position in football and even all other terms are semantically related to the keywords in the question. We use the term expansion length (el) which defines the number of terms considered for query expansion, in the rest of this paper. To trade off the balance between length of original query and expansion length, the latter must be proportional to the number of terms in the former.

$$el = k * |Q| \quad (2)$$

Where, k is a constant and $|Q|$ is number of terms in the query. So, for short queries the expansion length will be small and for long queries the expansion length will be large.

quarterback	surpassed
league	canadian
american	record
completions	attempts
touchdowns	unmatched

Table 2: *Top 10 expansion terms for the question "Which position did Warren Moon play in professional football?".*

Boolean model allows a fine-grained control over query expansion. Tellex [9], in his study of different passage retrieval algorithms found that Boolean querying schemes perform well in the QA task. So, we use Boolean model to form the expanded query from the original query with appropriate weights. The expanded Boolean query is a combination of question target, keywords in the question and expansion terms from Wikipedia. Finally, the expanded Boolean query is given to the passage retrieval which searches for relevant paragraphs that are likely to contain the answer.

4 Experiments

The three principal measures used to measure the performance of passage retrieval in the context of QA are: Precision at 1, Mean Reciprocal Rank (MRR) at N, and Total Document Reciprocal Rank (TDRR). Precision at 1 is the proportion of questions for which a correct answer appears in the first retrieved passage. The MRR at N is the mean of the inverse of highest ranked correct answer if that answer appears in the top N. TDRR extends MRR with a notion of recall. It is the sum of all reciprocal ranks of all answer bearing passages per question (averaged over all questions) and attains maximum if all retrieved passages are relevant. In the experiments described below we considered top 20 passages for evaluation i.e. both MRR at N and TDRR are measured for top 20 passages.

We tested our query expansion method on TREC 2006 QA test set. The test set consists of AQUAINT corpus: contains 1,033,461 documents taken from the New York Times, the Associated Press, and the Xinhua News Agency newswires; question set: contains a series of 75 targets and each target contains a minimum of five factoid questions; answer judgments: contains answer patterns and document IDs in which they occur. TREC also provides the top 1000 documents for every target in the question set. These documents are retrieved from the AQUAINT collection using Prise[1] search engine. In our experiments we use Wikipedia dump as of October 13, 2008. The dump consists of about 4.0 million articles in XML format. We use Lucene[2] (a freely available open-source IR engine) for indexing and searching the Wikipedia articles. Lucene supports a Boolean query language, although it performs ranked retrieval using BM25. So, we used Lucene for retrieving relevant passages from top 1000 documents set in our experiments.

We conducted three experiments to test our query expansion method and in each experiment we did two separate evaluations, with strict and lenient criteria. For a passage to be judged correct within the strict criteria, the answer pattern must occur in the passage, and the passage must be from a document listed as relevant in the answer judgments. Under the lenient criteria, the answer pattern must occur in the passage. Strict scoring suffers from false negatives i.e., valid answer containing passages are scored as incorrect, since the list of document IDs supplemented in answer judgments is not exhaustive, and lenient scoring suffers from false positives i.e., wrong answer containing passages are scored as correct, since some of the answer patterns are not discriminating enough. So, strict and lenient scoring measure lower and upper bound performance of passage retrieval.

In the first experiment, we compared the performance of passage retrieval using expanded queries with the expansion length of $k = 8$ (in equation 2), against the one which is using seed/original queries. The results for this experiment over all the factoid questions in the test set are shown in Table 3. These results show improvements of about 24.6%, 11.1% and 12.4% in precision at 1, MRR at 20 and TDRR scores respectively under strict criteria and improvements of about 18.4%, 10.5% and 13.8% under lenient criteria.

Criteria	Metric	SQ	EQ
Strict	Prec@1	0.158	0.197
	MRR@20	0.252	0.280
	TDRR	0.330	0.371
Lenient	Prec@1	0.282	0.334
	MRR@20	0.387	0.428
	TDRR	0.742	0.845

Table 3: *Strict and lenient evaluation results for seed queries (SQ) and expanded queries (EQ)*

In the second experiment, we analyzed the two scoring methods to show how much does each of the two scores contribute to the overall performance of passage retrieval. For each question in the test set, two expanded queries with the expansion length of $k = 8$ (in equation 2) were constructed, where expansion terms for first and second queries were selected from $QETS$

[1] http://www-nlpir.nist.gov/works/papers/zp2/psearch_design.html
[2] http://lucene.apache.org/

by using proximity and outlink scores respectively. The performance of passage retrieval using the above two queries are shown in Table 4. Comparing these results with seed and expanded queries performance from Table 3 shows an increase in the performance over the former but not as much as latter. So, the linear combination of proximity and outlink score results in better ranking of terms in *QETS*. And, in between the two scoring methods, outlink scoring performs better under strict criteria and proximity scoring performs better under lenient criteria.

Criteria	Metric	PS	OS
Strict	Prec@1	0.174	0.192
	MRR@20	0.262	0.279
	TDRR	0.351	0.373
Lenient	Prec@1	0.313	0.298
	MRR@20	0.413	0.396
	TDRR	0.825	0.786

Table 4: *Statistical analysis of proximity scoring (PS) and outlink scoring (OS) methods*

Finally, we tested our methodology for different expansion lengths by varying k value in the equation 2. Figure 1 shows the performance of passage retrieval for different expansion lengths under strict and lenient criteria. For both the criteria, the performance of our methodology has improved for all expansion lengths corresponding to k (in equation 2) values from 1 to 10 over the baseline ($k = 0$), and it attains maximum for the expansion length with $k = 8$.

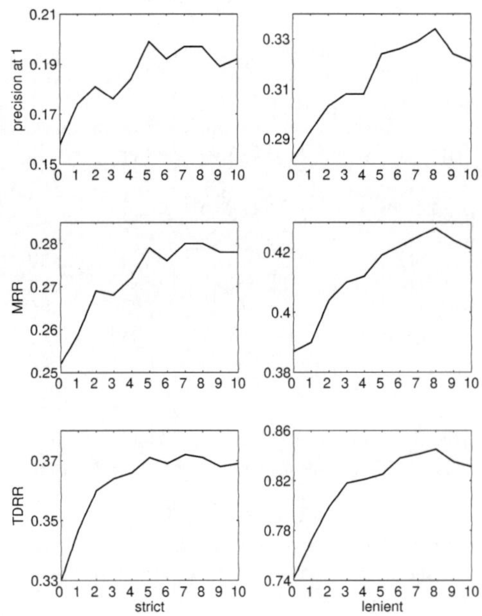

Fig. 1: *Performance of passage retrieval for different expansion lengths corresponding to k values from 1 to 10 under strict and lenient criteria.*

5 Conclusion

In a Question Answering system, an answer to a question cannot be retrieved unless it is present in one of the retrieved passages. So, passage retrieval is considered as one of the most important components of a QA system. Techniques like query expansion are often used to improve the performance of information retrieval systems. In this paper, we have described a new query expansion method which aims to rank the answer containing passages better. It used content and structured information (link structure and category information) of Wikipedia to generate a set of semantically related terms to the question. An empirical evaluation using TREC 2006 QA data set showed significant improvements using our query expansion method.

References

[1] J. Arguello, J. Elsas, J. Callan, and J. Carbonell. Document representation and query expansion models for blog recommendation. In *Int. Conf. on Weblogs and Social Media (ICWSM)*, 2008.

[2] K. B. Bilotti, M.W. and J. Lin. What works better for question answering: Stemming or morphological query expansion? In *ACM SIGIR'04 Workshop Information Retrieval for QA*, 2004.

[3] H. T. Dang, J. J. Lin, and D. Kelly. Overview of the trec 2006 question answering track 99. In *TREC*, 2006.

[4] L. Derczynski, J. Wang, R. Gaizauskas, and M. A. Greenwood. A data driven approach to query expansion in question answering. In *Proceedings of the 22nd International Conference on Computational Linguistics (COLING 2008) Workshop on Information Retrieval for Question Answering (IR4QA08)*, 2008.

[5] D. Moldovan, M. Paca, S. Harabagiu, A. Harabagiu, and M. Surdeanu. Performance issues and error analysis in an open-domain question answering system. In *ACM Trans. Inf. Syst*, page 2003, 2002.

[6] C. Monz. From document retrieval to question answering. In *ILLC Dissertation Series*, 2003.

[7] L. Pizzato, D. Mollá, and C. Paris. Pseudo relevance feedback using named entities for question answering. In *Proceedings ALTW*, volume 4, pages 83–90, 2006.

[8] R. Sun, C.-H. Ong, and T.-S. Chua. Mining dependency relations for query expansion in passage retrieval. In *SIGIR '06: Proceedings of the 29th annual international ACM SIGIR conference on Research and development in information retrieval*, pages 382–389, New York, NY, USA, 2006. ACM.

[9] S. Tellex, B. Katz, J. Lin, A. Fernandes, and G. Marton. Quantitative evaluation of passage retrieval algorithms for question answering. In *SIGIR '03: Proceedings of the 26th annual international ACM SIGIR conference on Research and development in informaion retrieval*, pages 41–47, New York, NY, USA, 2003. ACM.

[10] H. Yang, T.-S. Chua, S. Wang, and C.-K. Koh. Structured use of external knowledge for event-based open domain question answering. In *SIGIR '03: Proceedings of the 26th annual international ACM SIGIR conference on Research and development in informaion retrieval*, pages 33–40, New York, NY, USA, 2003. ACM.

Text content and task performance in the evaluation of a Natural Language Generation system

Albert Gatt
Department of Computing Science
University of Aberdeen
a.gatt@abdn.ac.uk

François Portet
Laboratoire d'Informatique de Grenoble
Grenoble Institute of Technology
francois.portet@imag.fr

Abstract

An important question in the evaluation of Natural Language Generation systems concerns the relationship between textual characteristics and task performance. If the results of task-based evaluation can be correlated to properties of the text, there are better prospects for improving the system. The present paper investigates this relationship by focusing on the outcomes of a task-based evaluation of a system that generates summaries of patient data, attempting to correlate these with the results of an analysis of the system's texts, compared to a set of gold standard human-authored summaries.

Keywords

Natural Language Generation, evaluation, decision support, domain ontology

1 Introduction

In the evaluation of NLP systems, an important distinction is that between *intrinsic* criteria, which typically measure aspects of output quality, and *extrinsic* ones, which assess a system in terms of its adequacy in its target setting [9]. The relationship between the two is important. A systematic relationship between the outcomes of extrinsic evaluation and properties of a system's output can indicate directions for improvement in output, leading to improvements in the system's utility in its target setting.

This paper focusses on the evaluation of a a Natural Language Generation (NLG) system, BT-45 [13], which generates summaries of clinical patient data in a Neonatal Intensive Care Unit (NICU). It was been evaluated in an experiment comparing decision making by clinicians based on the system output and other ways of presenting the same information, including human-authored summaries [17]. The aims of this paper are twofold. First, we investigate the relationship between intrinsic properties of generated text – particularly its informativeness and relevance – and its utility for decision-making. Second, we propose a novel intrinsic evaluation method. Rather than comparing BT-45 texts to a gold standard based on surface characteristics, such as matching $n-$grams, we make explicit use of domain knowledge in the form of an ontology and attempt to quantify the differences in the content selection strategies underlying the BT-45 and the gold standard texts.

2 Background

Intrinsic evaluation in NLG has often relied on human input, typically in the form of ratings of or responses to questionnaires [12, 4, 7]. Automatic intrinsic methods exploiting corpora have mostly been used in evaluations of morphosyntactic realisers [11, 3]. Extrinsic, task-based methods are also widespread [14, 10, 15]. While such studies tend to be more expensive and labour-intensive, extrinsic evaluation criteria give a reliable assessment of the system's utility in doing what it was designed to do.

The relationship between these different classes of evaluation methods is not straightforward. Recent work has shown that corpus-based intrinsic methods do not correlate with the results of intrinsic evaluation based on human judgements, suggesting that they are measuring different aspects of output quality [2]. Cautionary notes have also been sounded in Machine Translation [5] and summarisation [6], with some recent work in NLG showing that intrinsic measures also correlate poorly with task-based measures NLG [1]. On the other hand, the relationship between task-based measures and textual characteristics bears on several important questions. Task-based evaluations tend to yield global scores from which it is often hard to extract specific indicators of a system's weaknesses. While judgement elicitation studies may be better suited to this purpose, these do not necessarily reflect a system's utility in a task, while corpus-based studies necessarily depend on a finite number of reference outputs against which to compare a system, which do not exhaust the space of possibilities.

3 The BT-45 system and evaluation

In this section, we briefly summarise the main aspects of the BT-45 architecture and the task-based evaluation (see [13] and [17] for a complete description). BT-45 produces a textual summary of 45 minutes of NICU data, in the form of physiological signals measured from a patient using sensors, and data relating to discrete events, which are logged by clinicians in a database in the course of a shift. A snapshot of the input data is displayed in Figure 1(a). Figure 1(b) shows a summary of this data written by two expert neonatologists, while Figure 1(c) presents the BT-45 output for the same period. As the summary shows, BT-45 texts kept interpretation and diagnosis to a minimum, generating a descriptive summary of the salient events related to a patient. This involved a four-stage process, each making use of a domain-specific ontology. First, the main features of the signal data are identified, and the discrete data are extracted. Both form the input to a *data interpretation* stage,

International Conference RANLP 2009 - Borovets, Bulgaria, pages 107–112

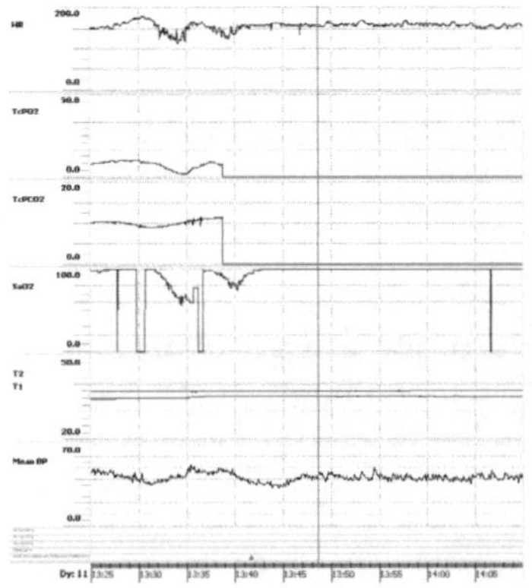

(a) Graphical presentation

You saw the baby between 13:25 and 14:10.

At the start of the monitoring period: HR baseline is 145-155, oxygen saturation is 99%, pO2 = 4.9 and CO2 = 10.3 Mean BP is 37-47; T1 and T2 are 37.3degC and 34.6degC respectively.

At 13:33 there is a desaturation to 59%, which is accompanied by a drop in pO2 to 1.3 and a decrease in HR to 122. The blood pressure rises toward the end of this episode to 49. These parameters return to their baselines by 13:37.

At 13:38 the transcutaneous probe is taken off the baby to be re-sited. With this there is a desaturation to 80% and a decrease in HR to 129. The FiO2 is changed to 27%. The BP decreases to 33, then rises over the next 2 minutes to a baseline of 42 until the end of the trace.

By 13:43 the HR = 155 and oxygen saturation = 100%. The baby's observations remain steady around these values until the end of the monitoring period.

(b) Human-authored summary

You saw the baby between 13:25 and 14:10. Heart Rate (HR) = 149. Core Temperature (T1) = 37.4. Peripheral Temperature (T2) = 34.6. Transcutaneous Oxygen (TcPO2) = 4.8. Transcutaneous CO2 (TcPCO2) = 10.2. Mean Blood Pressure (mean BP) = 45. Oxygen Saturation (SaO2) = 96.

Over the next 38 minutes T1 stayed at around 37.4.

By 13:33 TcPO2 had rapidly decreased to 2.7. Previously HR had increased to 173.

By 13:35 there had been 2 successive desaturations down to 56. Previously T2 had increased to 35.5.

By 13:40 SaO2 had rapidly decreased to 79.

Over the next 30 minutes HR gradually increased to 157.

At 13:41 Fraction of Inspired Oxygen (FIO2) was set to 27%. Previously mean BP had decreased to 35.

(c) BT-45 summary

Fig. 1: NICU *data presented in different formats*

which creates abstractions from the raw data and relates events to eachother via causal and other links. *Document planning* selects important events and structures them into a document plan, while *microplanning* fleshes out their semantic content and realises the text.

The system was evaluated during an off-ward experiment during which 35 clinicians in 4 groups (junior and senior doctors and junior and senior nurses) were asked to select the most appropriate clinical actions to take in relation to a patient, based on around 45 minutes of data. 24 scenarios were presented to each participant in one of the three conditions shown in Figure 1: **(G)** Graphically; **(H)** textual summary written by human experts; and **(C)** textual summary generated by BT-45. Participants were asked to select the appropriate clinical actions to take at the end of the period from a predefined set of 18 actions. Prior to the experiment, a senior neonatal nurse and consultant neonatologist identified, for each scenario, the subsets of appropriate, inappropriate (potentially harmful) and neutral actions from this set. Moreover, for each scenario there was one *target action* which was deemed to be the most important out of all the appropriate ones. For each participant p and scenario s, a performance score S_s^p was computed based on the proportion P_{AP_s} of actions selected out of the set of appropriate actions for the scenario, AP_s, and the proportion P_{INAP_s} selected out of the set of inappropriate actions INAP_s:

$$S_s^p = P_{\text{AP}_s} - P_{\text{INAP}_s} \in [-1, 1] \quad (1)$$

Overall, the human expert texts (H) led to the best decision making ($.45^{SD=.10}$) followed by the Computer texts (C) ($.41^{SD=.13}$) and the Graphical (G) condition ($.40^{SD=.15}$). A 3 (Condition) x 4 (Group) by-subjects ANOVA showed no main effect of participant Group, but an effect of Condition that approached significance ($F(2,31) = 2.939, p = 0.06$). There was no interaction. Separate ANOVAs showed a difference between the G and H conditions ($F(1,31) = 4.975, p < 0.05$) and the C and H conditions ($F(1,31) = 5.266, p < 0.05$), but none between G and C. Thus, human texts proved most useful to decision-making, but generated texts were found to be no worse than presentation in the graphical condition, which is the modality used in current clinical practice. A follow-up analysis comparing the scenarios based on their main target action showed a significant difference in performance between H and C texts ($F(1,7) = 8.002; p < 001$).

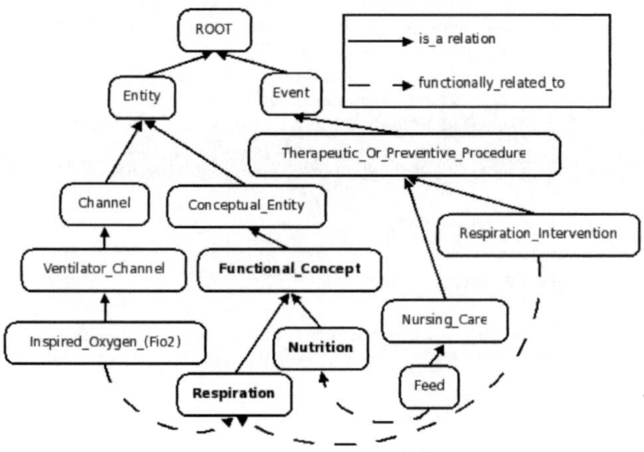

Fig. 2: *Excerpt from the ontology showing relations to functional concepts (in bold)*

Although this evaluation tells us that textual presentation can be very effective, it does not give direct information about which aspects of the experimental texts played a role in decision-making. On the other hand, the significant effect of main target action does suggest that some of the burden is carried by the content selection strategies in the H and C texts, with the human-authored summaries incorporating more information that was relevant to the appropriate actions. This was the focus of our follow-up evaluation.

4 The role of the ontology

Much of the processing in BT-45 relied on an ontology, an excerpt of which is shown in Figure 2. The complete ontology represented more than 550 concepts, though only a subset was used to a significant extent in BT-45. The principal top-level nodes are EVENT and ENTITY. The latter subsumes domain objects, such as VENTILATOR, which are not subject to significant change over time, whereas

EVENTs are inherently temporal and subsume INTERVENTION (e.g. drug administration), OBSERVATION (e.g. the observation that a baby has poor capillary refill), DATA COLLECTION (e.g. adjusting sensors), etc. While the ontology was a relatively static repository of declarative knowledge, procedural knowledge used for inference (e.g. causal associations between concepts, abstractions, etc), was encoded in production rules in the data interpretation module.

Following the BT-45 evaluation, a senior consultant was asked to udpate the ontology by linking entities and events to functional concepts (FC) corresponding to physiological systems, such as BLOOD PRODUCTION and RESPIRATION. These `functionally_related_to` links, shown in Figure 2, reflect the tendency of clinicians to link concepts in terms of their clinical significance (rather than, say, their structure). The underlying principle is that each event is related to an FC that clinicians monitor, and each clinical action has a purpose that is itself related to one or several FCs (e.g. VENTILATION to support RESPIRATION). A reasoning module can thus relate different events via their common relations to FCs. For example, if an alteration of the FiO2 (Fraction of inspired oxygen) on the ventilator is recorded, then this event can be linked to all other events that are related to RESPIRATION. In what follows, we shall use $\text{FC}(x)$ to abbreviate the set of functional concepts that a concept x is functionally related to.

5 Quantitative evaluation methods

To identify the characteristics of the texts which contributed to the decision-making performance, two kinds of quantitative methods were used. The first compared the computer (C) and human-authored (H) texts in terms of *informativeness*. This was based on the expectation that differences in informativeness between texts would covary with differences in decision-making, since more information should increase the likelihood of making the correct decisions. However, the extent to which information impacts decision-making also depends on the *relevance* of the information. Hence, the second evaluation measure quantified the extent to which a text was relevant to the appropriate actions on a given scenario. Presumably, higher relevance would give rise to a greater probability of a reader making the right decisions. Both methods relied on a prior annotation of the H and C texts, using the ontology as the central repository of domain knowledge.

Corpus annotation The corpus consists of 48 texts representing the 24 scenarios generated by BT-45 and the 24 scenarios written by the clinical experts. Annotation was consensus-based and was carried out manually by the authors, with a scheme to mark up text segments representing an event or an aggregation of events, as shown in the excerpt below.

```
<EVENT CARDINALITY="3" TYPE="TREND"
       SOURCE="TcPO2,HR,mean BP">
   These parameters return to their baselines
</EVENT>
[...]
<EVENT CARDINALITY="1" TYPE="RE-SITE_PROBES"
       DONE_TO="TCM_SENSOR">
   the transcutaneous probe is [...] re-sited
</EVENT>
```

An EVENT tag has a TYPE whose value is an ontology concept; CARDINALITY is used to account for reference to multiple events (e.g. *These parameters* in line 1, which refers to several physiological parameters mentioned earlier in the example text); optionally, the SOURCE attribute indicates the location of an event (usually a physiological parameter, such as heart rate in the case of trends like *a decrease in HR*), while the DONE_TO attribute is used when the event involves the use or modification of an entity (e.g. an instrument or a drug). Once the texts were marked up, the relation of an event to its FC was found by instantiating the event in the ontology based either on its TYPE attribute or the value of its DONE_TO or SOURCE attributes, to retrieve the value of its `functionally_related_to` property.

Informativeness Informativeness of a text was computed as a global estimate of the amount of information conveyed, irrespective of what the appropriate decisions to be taken were. This measure indicates whether the C and H texts convey a different amount of descriptive information, which could explain some differences in decision-making performance. In this work, we used two definitions of informativeness: (i) the number of (clinical) events NE that a text references; (ii) the length of the text in tokens (words) NW. Differentiating them allows us to distinguish between informativeness based solely on events (NE), and informativeness which also includes expressions which are not annotated (including adverbials and discourse connectives).

Relevance The relevance of a text for a given experimental scenario s was defined in terms of whether the events it mentioned have some relationship to the clinical actions which are appropriate for that scenario (AP_s). Let $\text{E}_{s,t}$ be the set of events mentioned in text t for scenario s. The relevance of an event is defined as follows:

Definition 1 (relevance) *An event* $e \in \text{E}_{s,t}$ *is relevant iff* $\exists a \in \text{AP}_s \,.\, \text{FC}(e) \cap \text{FC}(a) \neq \emptyset$

Of course an event can be relevant to more than one action. Likewise, we define the *ir*relevance of an event e if it is functionally associated to an element of the set of inappropriate actions for a scenario (INAP_s).

Though this definition gives a fair handle on the notion of relevance, it only approximates the information clinicians bring to bear on their decisions. Our hypothesis is that an appropriate action which is related to some FCs is more likely to be taken if these FCs are referenced in the text by mentioning events which are functionally related to them. For instance, if a text gives no information related to RESPIRATION, a clinician cannot make a decision related to managing a patient's artificial ventilation. Another noteworthy aspect of this method is its reliance on the knowledge (i.e. the ontology) that is already available in the system, rather than on human expert judgements, which could be subject to expert bias. For both human and computer texts, two scores were computed: $\text{REL}_{s,t}$, the number of relevant events in text t for scenario s; and $\text{IRREL}_{s,t}$, the number of irrelevant events in the text.

As defined above, relevance does not take into account the prior probability of the actions. In a clinical environment, some actions, such as taking a blood gas from an arterial line, are performed routinely, while others, such as

Table 1: *Examples of prior probability of actions*

Action	P(Action)
blood gas	0.0034
monitor equipment	0.0077
CPR	2.28E-5
manage temperature	0.0071
manage ventilation	0.0326
CPAP	0.0015

	Human (H)		BT-45 (C)		Overall
	Mean (SD)	r	*Mean (SD)*	r	r_{diff}
NW	146.75 (86.8)	-.24	122.33 (41.4)	-.47*	.434*
NE	19.75 (12.5)	-.25	17.35 (6.4)	-.47*	.458*
REL	0.326 (.37)	-.09	0.217 (.17)	-.10	.16
IRREL	0.324 (.31)	-.15	0.242 (.16)	-.32	.25

Table 2: *Mean scores across groups on informativeness and relevance, with correlations. r = Pearson's correlation between intrinsic and extrinsic performance score. r_{diff} = correlation between difference in performance and difference in score between H and C. Asterisk (∗) indicates significance at $p \leq .05$*

resuscitating a patient, are only taken in exceptional circumstances. To account for the potential effects of this on decision making, we computed the prior probability of each clinical action used in the experiment, as a maximum likelihood estimate based on a large database of 43,889 clinical actions recorded by an on-site research nurse over a period of 4 months in a NICU [8]. Some example probabilities for each action are displayed in Table 1. These were used to weight the relevance scores, which are now defined as follows:

$$\text{REL}_{s,t} = \sum_{a \in \text{AP}_s} P(a).N(a)_t \quad (2)$$

$$\text{IRREL}_{s,t} = \sum_{a \in \text{INAP}_s} P(a).N(a)_t \quad (3)$$

where a is any action and $N(a)_t$ stands for the number of times action a was referenced by the events in text t.

6 Evaluation results

In this section, we present the results of our comparison of the 24 pairs of human and computer-generated texts. All results are reported using scenarios ($N = 24$) as source of variance. For each measure, we report (a) the correlation (r) between the performance score and the measure in a given condition (H or C); (b) differences between H and C on the measure; (c) the correlation between the *absolute* differences in the scores obtained by H and C texts and those in decision-making performance (r_{diff}). Table 2 displays all descriptives and correlation coefficients. In what follows, we summarise the main observations, discussing their implications in Section 7.

6.1 Effect of informativeness

The means for NE and NW in Table 2 indicates that human texts tend to mention more events and are slightly longer than the BT-45 texts, but with much higher variability (higher SD) between scenarios. No significant correlations (r) were observed between NE or NW and performance in the H condition; in the C condition, both correlations are significant. However, in all cases, the r scores are negative, suggesting that more information tended to be linked to *lower* decision-making performance. Paired t-tests showed that there was no significant difference between the two sets of texts on NE ($t(23) = 1.24, p > .2$), though the difference on the NW score approached significance ($t(23) = 1.90, p = .07$).

There was a significant positive correlation between the absolute differences in informativeness scores and decision-making (r_{diff}). We also investigated the correlation within user groups, finding a significant correlation only in the case of Senior Doctors for both measures (NW: $r = 45$; NE: $r = .53$; $p \leq .05$). The differences in scores are plotted against differences in performance in Figures 3(a) and 3(b). In both cases, a linear relationship accounts for approximately 20% of the variance, as reflected by the R^2 value associated with the regression line. Omitting the 'outliers' where the differences between H and C in NW and NE seems highest (4 points in Figure 3(a), 5 in Figure 3(a)) does not improve the models.

In summary, human expert texts shown more variability than BT-45 texts on our informativeness measures. Separate correlations for H and C show a surprising negative covariation between the measures and decision-making, while a weak positive relationship can be observed between the difference in the scores and decision-making differences in the two conditions.

6.2 Effect of relevance

Table 2 shows that the H texts achieved higher scores on both REL and IRREL, that is, the events mentioned by human experts referenced more appropriate actions, but also more 'inappropriate' ones. Once again, the variation is higher in the H texts. There were significant differences on both measures between H and C texts (REL: $t(23) = 2.23, p < .05$; IRREL: $t(23) = 2.11, p < .05$). As for the correlations within each condition (r), they are once again negative, and never reach significance.

On the other hand, we do observe a significant positive correlation between difference in performance and both REL and IRREL. Once again, this seems to be primarily due to the Senior Doctor group, where differences in REL and difference in performance were significantly correlated ($r = .54; p < .05$). The correlations were not significant for any other user group, and never significant for differences in IRREL.

These trends are further reflected in Figures 3(c) and 3(d), which again plot the difference in performance between H and C against difference in the REL and IRREL. Once again, both figures show that the linear relationship accounts for a very low proportion of the variance ($< 2\%$); removing the outliers in either case again results in no improvement.

7 Discussion

The results reported above do not offer very strong support for our initial hypotheses that differences in informativeness or relevance would account for differences in performance. Despite some significant differences in content, as shown by the difference between H and C on REL and IRREL, the relationship between content and task performance is weak at best. Although this is consistent with previous results comparing intrinsic and extrinsic evaluation

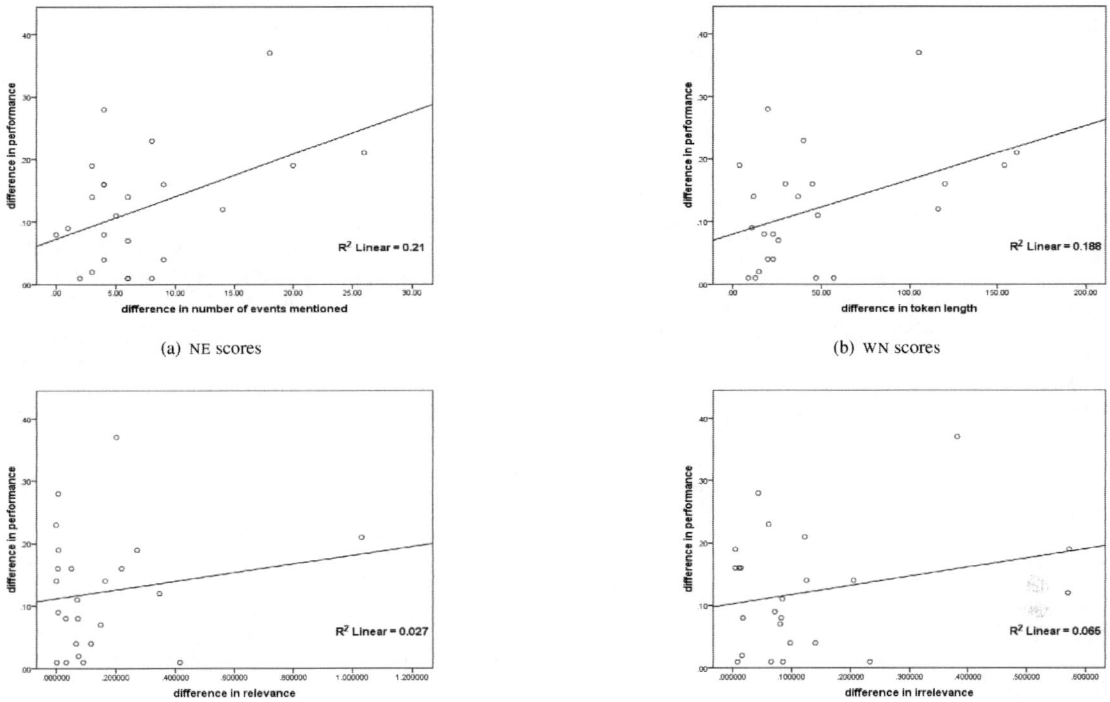

(a) NE scores

(b) WN scores

(c) REL scores

(d) IRREL scores

Fig. 3: *Difference in task performance against differences in* NW, NE, REL *and* IRREL *scores*

measures, taking the present conclusions as final would seem to be premature, for a number of reasons which we outline in this section.

Content vs. structure In focussing exclusively on a definition of content based on the events referenced by a text, our evaluation scores ignore aspects of discourse and information structure, such as the extent to which the texts link the events mentioned via discourse or temporal connectives, as in the human-authored excerpt below:

Example 1 (Human text) *The pCO2 continues to rise to 10.1. The baby is pale and unresponsive. ET suction is given, baby is turned and at 17:02 the ETT is removed; the baby is again given Neopuff ventilation.*

BT-45 texts often lacked the kind of linking exemplified above. Hence, the relationship between intrinsic and extrinsic evaluation measures may need to account for both content and discourse structure.

Differences among users It is likely that some of the statistically weak results reported in the previous section are due to differences between participants in our evaluation. These differences are in part individual, as reflected by the comparatively high variance in performance scores (cf. Section 3). Perhaps more importantly, differences are also likely to arise between user groups. Although no main effect of Group was found on performance, it seems likely that different users will focus on different aspects of a text when reading summaries. For instance, whether a user is a doctor or a nurse will have an impact on how likely they are to consider taking a particular action, given their different aims, and the fact that some actions fall within their remit and others tend not to. Some support for this conclusion comes from the observation that the correlation between differences in performance and differences in informativeness and relevance were primarily due to one group of users, namely, Senior Doctors. If this interpretation is correct, then it reflects the necessity of tailoring the NLG system output to different users, particularly in a medical context, where roles tend to be fixed and a single 'one size fits all' solution is unlikely to be adequate [16].

Granularity Another limitation is related to the information captured by our annotations, which do not make sufficiently fine-grained distinctions and do not use the full expressivity available in the ontology. For example, *SaO2 decreases to 60%* and *SaO2 stays stable* are both represented by the same event, with TYPE = TREND and SOURCE = OXYGEN SATURATION; however, their relative importance is clearly different, since only the former suggests that something must be done. We are seeking to make finer-grained distinctions of this kind in our current work.

The role of context An issue which is related to granularity is the degree to which context must be taken into account. As shown in Table 2, human-authored texts displayed considerably higher variance in their informativeness and relevance scores compared to the BT-45 texts. BT-45's document planner had a relatively deterministic content selection strategy which selected events based on their clinical importance, computed using rules obtained from clinicians. By contrast, our expert authors may have been selecting content using much more sophisticated heuristics, in part based on the salient patterns in the data and possibly also their knowledge of the most important observations given a patient's current and previous state. As an example, BT-45 seldom mentioned noise or artifacts in the input signals, deeming these to be unimportant; in contrast, these were mentioned in some cases by the human texts because they drew a clinician's attention to the need for managing the sensors which were sampling the physiological parameters. In short, humans probably do a better job at taking context into account. Modulo differences in the probability of actions, our measures of informativeness and relevance gave equal weight to the different events mentioned, without reference to context, whereby an event can become relevant not through its association with a potential target action, but because it can shed light on the nature and provenance of the rest of the events described in the text. Thus, when we focus on those events which are indirectly linked to possible actions, BT-45 does not seem to differ very much from the H texts, but this should be interpreted in light of the fact that the two texts did differ on overall informativeness, as reflected by the NE measure.

8 Conclusions

This paper began by arguing that extrinsic evaluation methodologies, though useful and necessary, often leave open the question of which aspects of a system are contributing to the results, and why. The present paper attempted to identify some of these aspects, focusing primarily on the content selection strategy of a system to generate patient summaries in a Neonatal Intensive Care context. Our results showed that the relationship between our measures of textual content, and performance on a task is somewhat weak. Our interpretation of these results is that content-based intrinsic measures need to be more granular, and take into account other textual characteristics, such as discourse structure, as well as the role of different user groups. We have also proposed an intrinsic evaluation methodology which relies on domain knowledge to quantify informativeness and relevance. In our ongoing work, we are extending this methodology to address the shortcomings identified in our results.

Acknowledgments

Thanks to Professor Neil McIntosh, senior consultant at the Royal Infirmary of Edinburgh, who helped with the development of the ontology. Thanks also to Jim Hunter and Ehud Reiter. The BabyTalk project is supported by UK Engineering and Physical Sciences Research Council (EPSRC), under grants EP/D049520/1 and EP/D05057X/1.

References

[1] A. Belz and A. Gatt. Intrinsic vs. extrinsic evaluation measures for referring expression generation. In *Proc. ACL-08*, 2008.

[2] A. Belz and E. Reiter. Comparing automatic and human evaluation of NLG systems. In *Proc. EACL-06*, 2006.

[3] C. B. Callaway. Evaluating coverage for large symbolic NLG grammars. In *Proc. IJCAI-03*, 2003.

[4] C. B. Callaway and J. C. Lester. Narrative prose generation. *Artificial Intelligence*, 139(2):213–252, 2002.

[5] C. Calliston-Burch, M. Osborne, and P. Koehn. Reevaluating the role of BLEU in machine translation research. In *Proc. EACL-06*, 2006.

[6] B. J. Dorr, C. Monz, S. President, R. Schwartz, and D. Zajic. A methodology for extrinsic evaluation of text summarization: Does ROUGE correlate? In *Proc. Workshop on Intrinsic and Extrinsic Evaluation Measures*, 2005.

[7] M. Foster. Automated metrics that agree with human judgements on generated output for an embodied conversational agent. In *Proc. INLG-08*, 2008.

[8] J. Hunter, G. Ewing, L. Ferguson, Y. Freer, R. Logie, P. McCue, and N. McIntosh. The NEONATE database. In *Proc. IDAMAP-03*, 2003.

[9] K. S. Jones and J. Galliers. *Evaluating natural language processing systems: An analysis and review*. Springer, Berlin, 1996.

[10] A. Karasimos and A. Isard. Multilingual evaluation of a natural language generation system. In *Proc. LREC-04*, 2004.

[11] I. Langkilde-Geary. An empirical verification of coverage and correctness for a general-purpose sentence generator. In *Proc. INLG-02*, 2002.

[12] J. Lester and B. Porter. Developing and empirically evaluating robust explanation generators: The KNIGHT experiments. *Computational Linguistics*, 23(1):65–101, 1997.

[13] F. Portet, E. Reiter, A. Gatt, J. Hunter, S. Sripada, Y. Freer, and C. Sykes. Automatic generation of textual summaries from neonatal intensive care data. *Artificial Intelligence*, 173(7–8):789–816, 2009.

[14] E. Reiter, R. Robertson, and L. Osman. Lessons from a failure: Generating tailored smoking cessation letters. *Artificial Intelligence*, 144:41–58, 2003.

[15] O. Stock, M. Zancanaro, P. Busetta, C. Callaway, A. Krueger, M. Kruppa, T. Kuflik, E. Not, and C. Rocchi. Adaptive, intelligent presentation of information for the museum visitor in PEACH. *User Modeling and User-Adapted Interaction*, 17(3):257–304, 2007.

[16] B. Strople and P. Ottani. Can technology improve intershift report? what the research reveals. *Journal of Professional Nursing*, 22(3):197–204, 2006.

[17] M. van der Meulen, R. H. Logie, Y. Freer, C. Sykes, N. McIntosh, and J. Hunter. When a graph is poorer than 100 words: A comparison of computerised Natural Language Generation, human generated descriptions and graphical displays in neonatal intensive care. *Applied Cognitive Psychology*, to appear.

Feature-Rich Named Entity Recognition for Bulgarian Using Conditional Random Fields

Georgi Georgiev*
georgi.georgiev@ontotext.com

Preslav Nakov†§
nakov@comp.nus.edu.sg

Kuzman Ganchev‡
kuzman@cis.upenn.ed

Petya Osenova§
petya@bultreebank.org

Kiril Simov§
kivs@bultreebank.org

Abstract

The paper presents a feature-rich approach to the automatic recognition and categorization of named entities (persons, organizations, locations, and miscellaneous) in news text for Bulgarian. We combine well-established features used for other languages with language-specific lexical, syntactic and morphological information. In particular, we make use of the rich tagset annotation of the BulTreeBank (680 morpho-syntactic tags), from which we derive suitable task-specific tagsets (local and nonlocal). We further add domain-specific gazetteers and additional unlabeled data, achieving F_1=89.4%, which is comparable to the state-of-the-art results for English.

Keywords

Named entity recognition, information extraction, conditional random fields, linear models, machine learning, morphology.

1 Introduction

The earliest work on named entity recognition (NER) was based on hand-crafted rules using pattern matching [1]. For instance, a rule could encode the knowledge that a sequence of capitalized words ending in '*Inc.*' is typically the name of an organization. An example of such a system is ANNIE in the GATE architecture [9]. Such systems could achieve very high precision, but typically suffered from low recall. They also required significant manual tuning, which was time-consuming and could be quite complicated when thousands of rules interact in complex manners.

Since the nineties, statistical models have offered a viable alternative while requiring little or no manual tuning at all. Such models typically treat NER as a sequence tagging problem, where each word is tagged with its entity type if it is part of an entity. Generative models such as Hidden Markov Models (HMM) [3, 26] have demonstrated excellent performance on the *Message Understanding Conference* (MUC) datasets [6].

*Ontotext AD, 135 Tsarigradsko Ch., Sofia 1784, Bulgaria

†Department of Computer Science, National University of Singapore, 13 Computing Drive, Singapore 117417

‡Department of Computer and Information Science, University of Pennsylvania, Philadelphia, PA, USA

§Linguistic Modelling Laboratory, Institute for Parallel Processing, Bulgarian Academy of Sciences, 25A Acad. G. Bonchev St., 1113 Sofia, Bulgaria

Discriminative models such as locally-normalized maximum-entropy [4] and conditional random fields (CRF) [15] have also been explored for NER. Collins [7] used an HMM tagger to generate n-best outputs, which he reranked discriminatively. By using a semi-Markov CRF, [22] recast NER as a segmentation rather than a tagging problem, thus allowing for richer feature sets.

Recent research also includes semi-supervised methods, e.g., [16] use word clusters derived from large sets of unlabeled data in order to enrich their feature set.

NER can also be viewed as a two-stage process: (1) find the named entities in a sentence, and (2) classify each entity into its type, e.g, person, organization, location, etc. [7] mentions that first identifying named entities without classifying them alleviates some data sparsity issues. [8] focus on the second stage, named entity classification, assuming that the boundaries of the named entities have been found already; they use a bootstrapping approach based on co-training in order to leverage unlabeled examples. [21] use a similar bootstrapping approach for information extraction.

Using CRFs has become the dominant approach to NER [15], allowing for effective feature construction, handling very large feature sets, and modeling complex interactions across multiple levels of granularity; Thus, in the present paper, CRFs will be our learning method of choice. We will employ a rich set of features that (*i*) have been found useful for other languages, (*ii*) can handle expert knowledge in the form of gazetteers and domain-specific predicates, (*iii*) can model rich morpho-syntactic characteristics of Bulgarian, (*iv*) can represent complex predicates, (*v*) can be extracted from raw text automatically.

In the remainder of the paper, we will describe feature generation, and we will discuss the results.

2 Sequence tagging model

The identification of named entity mentions in text can be implemented using a sequence tagger, where each token is labeled with a BIO tag indicating whether it begins (B), is inside (I), or is outside (O) of a named entity mention [20]. Following CoNLL-2002 [24], we further indicate whether it is a person (PER), an organization (ORG), a location (LOC), or miscellaneous (MISC), which yields the following nine tags: B-PER, I-PER, B-ORG, I-ORG, B-LOC, I-LOC, B-MISC, I-MISC, and O. See Figure 1 for an example.

International Conference RANLP 2009 - Borovets, Bulgaria, pages 113–117

Георги	Първанов	е	президент	на	България	.
Georgi	*Parvanov*	*is*	*President*	*of*	*Bulgaria*	.
B-PER	I-PER	O	O	O	B-ORG	O

Fig. 1: *Sample tagging using the BIO tagset. The sentence contains two named entity mentions: one person, and one organization.*

3 Feature sets

3.1 Basic features

Feature-based models like CRFs are attractive since they reduce the problem to finding a feature set that adequately represents the target task. We used features based on individual words as well as orthographic predicates, as shown in Table 1, and character-level n-gram predicates, $2 \leq n \leq 4$. Bulgarian is morphologically rich and thus such predicates can help the system recognize informative substrings in words that were not seen in training, e.g., Slavic family name endings like *-ов* ('*-ov*') or *-ова* ('*-ova*'), and the possessive *-во* ('*-vo*') that is often used at the end of Bulgarian location names. We also included word prefix and word suffix predicates, also of lengths $2 \leq n \leq 4$. This may seem redundant, but prefix and suffix predicates also take into account the position of the n-gram in the word, which can often be informative. For example *во* ('*vo*') occurring at the end of a word is much more informative than its presence anywhere in the word, e.g., compare *вода* ('*voda*', i.e., 'water') vs. *Димитрово* ('*Dimitrovo*', a village name). We further included predicates that indicate whether the current token occurs in parentheses or inside a quotation. Finally, in addition to the current token, we also used features on the previous and on the following one.

Table 1 lists the orthographic predicates we used.

Predicate name	Regular expression
Initial capital	[А-Я].*
Capital, followed by any	[А-Я].
Initial capitals, alpha	[А-Я][а-я]*
All capitals	[А-Я]+
All lowercase	[а-я]+
Capitals mix	[А-Яа-я]+
Contains a digit	.*[0-9].*
Single digit	[0-9]
Double digit	[0-9][0-9]
Natural number	[0-9]+
Real number	[-0-9]+[\.,]?[0-9]+
Alpha-numeric	[А-Яа-я0-9]+
Roman	[ivxdlcm]+|[IVXDLCM]+
Contains dash	.*-.*
Initial dash	-.*
Ends with dash	.*-
Punctuation	[,\.;:\?!-+"]
Multidots	\.\.+
Ends with dot	.*\.
Acronym	[А-Я]+
Lonely initial	[А-Я]\.
Single character	[А-Яа-я]
Quote	["']

Table 1: ***The orthographic predicates used in our system.*** *The observation list for each token will include a predicate for each regular expression that matches it.*

Even though simple, the above feature set yielded a very good performance on the development data: see Table 2, row A. In order to add expert knowledge to the model, we used some regular expressions that generate predicates on the word by checking whether it ends with some character sequences that are common for Bulgarian names of persons, e.g., *-ска* ('*-ska*'), *-ски* ('*-ski*'), *-ов* ('*-ov*'), *-ва* ('*-va*') or locations, e.g., *-во* ('*-vo*'); see Table 2, row B for details. Another useful approach for adding domain knowledge to the model, used in previous work for named entity recognition and gene mentions tagging, is predicate generation on the basis of membership in a gazetteer.

In our case, gazetteers are lists of words, multi-token units, and acronyms. A straightforward method of integrating these knowledge sources is to create predicates indicating whether a token occurs in one of these gazetteers. For multi-token entries, we required that all entry tokens be matched. We further created similar predicates for the previous and the next tokens. Table 2, row C summarizes the effect of adding these gazetteers.

The following sections will further explore the morpho-syntactic tagset, the feature induction and using additional raw unannotated text.

3.2 Morpho-syntactic features

We made use of the rich tagset annotation of the BulTreeBank [23], from which we derived suitable task-specific tagsets (local and nonlocal).

Initially, we started with the full morpho-syntactic set of the BulTreeBank (680 morpho-syntactic tags), and we were able to achieve some improvements. However, working with so many distinct tags caused data sparsity issues, and missed opportunities for successful generation. We found the tagset was tightly coupled, thus reducing the possibility to model complex context relationships in the text sequence. Some of the tags were quite rare and apparently not very helpful. Since our NER experiments aim to be practical, we divided the tag characteristics (morpho-syntactic and part of speech) into *local* and *nonlocal.* The *local* predicates (111 tags in this set) are linguistically related to other predicates that hold on the same word, e.g., character n-grams, prefixes and suffixes, the word itself, etc. For nouns, they could be gender (e.g., masculine, feminine, neuter), number (e.g., singular, plural, count form), article (e.g., indefinite, definite). The *nonlocal* predicates (230 tags in this set) are related to predicates that hold on words in a particular context, i.e., window around the target word, e.g., the type of noun: common vs. proper.

This treatment of the BulTreeBank tagset stimulates simple and adequate treatment of the feature functions design for the NER task. The *local* characteristics are used alone and in combination with predicates holding on the current word, while the *nonlocal* ones are combined with predicates and words appearing in the local context at positions $\{-3, -2, -1, 0, +1, +2, +3\}$, where 0 is the current word, -1 is the previous one, $+1$ is the next one, etc. This approach induces many useful predicates, which is shown by the overall increase in the system performance: see Table 2, rows D and E.

	Types of predicates	NE type	Precision	Recall	F_1-Measure
A	Orthographic	Organization	85.50	82.73	84.10
		Person	86.05	79.86	82.84
		Location	88.34	82.97	85.57
		Miscellaneous	44.83	22.41	29.89
		OVERALL	85.67	78.89	**82.14**
B	+Domain-specific	Organization	85.35	83.81	84.57
		Person	86.46	80.40	83.32
		Location	88.51	82.48	85.39
		Miscellaneous	44.83	22.41	29.89
		OVERALL	85.86	79.20	**82.40**
C	+Gazetteers	Organization	87.89	80.94	84.27
		Person	90.70	84.17	87.31
		Location	88.45	87.59	88.02
		Miscellaneous	48.39	25.86	33.71
		OVERALL	88.26	81.96	**85.00**
D	+Local morphology	Organization	88.93	86.69	87.80
		Person	92.96	90.13	91.52
		Location	89.64	90.29	89.96
		Miscellaneous	57.14	27.12	36.78
		OVERALL	90.19	86.60	**88.36**
E	+Nonlocal morphology	Organization	87.23	88.49	87.86
		Person	90.99	92.46	91.72
		Location	90.34	90.78	90.56
		Miscellaneous	60.00	25.42	35.71
		OVERALL	89.36	88.06	**88.70**
F	+Feature induction	Organization	89.45	88.49	88.97
		Person	93.13	92.46	92.79
		Location	88.11	91.75	89.89
		Miscellaneous	60.00	25.42	35.71
		OVERALL	90.02	88.36	**89.18**
G	+Mutual information	Organization	89.89	89.57	89.73
		Person	93.13	92.46	92.79
		Location	88.89	91.26	90.06
		Miscellaneous	60.00	25.42	35.71
		OVERALL	90.38	88.44	**89.40**

Table 2: *Precision, recall and F_1-measure (in %s) for different feature sets on the test dataset.* *(A) Uses orthographic predicates and some simple features like token length. We define this system as our baseline. (B) Adds some simple regular expressions that match common patterns in Bulgarian personal and location names. (C) Adds predicates for gazetteer membership. (D) Adds predicates using local morpho-syntactic characteristics of the current word. (E) Adds nonlocal morpho-syntactic characteristics. (F) Adds feature induction to generate suitable combinations two of or more simple predicates. (G) Further uses unlabeled text.*

For instance, the following feature could be useful:

$$f_i(s,o) = \begin{cases} \mathbf{1} & \textbf{if } \text{'WORD} = \textit{Джина}\text{'} \in o, \\ & \text{'local\_tag} = \text{N} - \text{msi'} \in o, \\ & \textbf{tag}_\mathbf{0}(s) = \text{B} - \text{PER}; \\ \mathbf{0} & \textbf{otherwise}. \end{cases} \quad (1)$$

In the above example, the feature function will have the value of 1 if the the word is *Джина* ('*Dzhina*') and its local tag characteristics are feminine, singular, indefinite, and the named entity tag at this position is 'B-PER'; otherwise, the function value will be 0.

In contrast, we show that *nonlocal* tags would be beneficial in modeling complex context dependencies, for example:

$$f_i(s,o) = \begin{cases} \mathbf{1} & \textbf{if } \text{'WORD}_{+2} = \textit{влезе}\text{'} \in o, \\ & \text{'nonlocal\_tag} = \text{p'} \in o, \\ & \textbf{tag}_\mathbf{0}(s) = \text{B} - \text{PER}; \\ \mathbf{0} & \textbf{otherwise}. \end{cases}$$

In the above example, the function value will be 1 if the nonlocal tag describes a proper noun, the word *влезе* ('*entered*') appears at position +2, and the current tag is 'B-PER'. In all other cases, it will be 0.

The BulTreeBank tagset was further reduced by dropping information about the types of pronouns, the article was limited to indefinite and definite only, and the number and the count forms were merged into a single class. Rows D and E in Table 2 show the results when using these morpho-syntactic features.

3.3 Inducing complex features

So far, we have described features over a single predicate only, except in the design of morpho-syntactic features. However, it is often useful to create features based on the conjunction of several simple predicates:

$$f_i(s,o) = \begin{cases} \mathbf{1} & \textbf{if } \text{'WORD} = \textit{Батенберг}\text{'} \in o, \\ & \text{'WORD}_{+1} = \textit{управлява}\text{'} \in o, \\ & \textbf{tag}_\mathbf{0}(s) = \text{B} - \text{PER}; \\ \mathbf{0} & \textbf{otherwise}. \end{cases}$$

The above feature could be useful for disambiguating the token *Батенберг*[1] ('*Batenberg*'), which can be a person's name (e.g., when followed by *управлява*, '*ruled*'). However, it could be also part of a location (e.g., when preceded by *площад*, '*a square*'), and thus we might want to have a special feature for this case:

$$f_i(s,o) = \begin{cases} \mathbf{1} & \textbf{if } \text{'WORD} = \textit{Батенберг}' \in o, \\ & \text{'WORD}_{-1} = \textit{площад}' \in o, \\ & \mathbf{tag_0}(s) = \text{B} - \text{LOC}; \\ \mathbf{0} & \textbf{otherwise}. \end{cases}$$

The system already uses tens of thousands of features, which makes it infeasible to create predicates for the conjunction of all pairs of simple predicates. Even if it were computationally possible, it would still be hard to gather sufficient statistics for most of them. Thus, we use the method described in [14] to limit the search space. Row F in Table 2 shows the results.

3.4 Using unlabeled text

In this section, we try using additional unlabeled text, from which we extract two kinds of additional features.

The first type is pointwise *mutual information* (MI). It is a standard measure of the strength of association between co-occurring items and has been used successfully in extracting collocations from English text [12] and for performing Chinese word segmentation [21, 13, 25], among other tasks.

The MI for two words x_1 and x_2 is defined as follows:

$$\text{MI}(x_1, x_2) = \log \frac{\Pr(x_1, x_2)}{\Pr(x_1)\Pr(x_2)}$$

where $\Pr(x)$ is the probability of observing x, and $\Pr(x_1, x_2)$ is the probability of x_2 following x_1.

Estimates of the MI are simple and cheap to compute from unlabeled data alone; this can be done in linear time on the text length.

We used 7.4M words of unlabeled newswire text, from which we extracted the top 1M word pairs, ranked according to the MI score. We then distributed these pairs into separate bins based on their MI values, where bins contained approximately equal numbers of pairs, and we created binary features of the following kind to be integrated in the CRF model:

$$f_i(s,o) = \begin{cases} \mathbf{1} & \textbf{if } \text{'WORD} = \textit{Батенберг}' \in o, \\ & \text{'WORD}_{-1} = \textit{площад}' \in o, \\ & \text{MI}(\text{WORD}, \text{WORD}_{+1}) \in \text{bin}_\text{x}, \\ & \mathbf{tag_0}(s) = \text{B} - \text{LOC}; \\ \mathbf{0} & \textbf{otherwise}. \end{cases}$$

Initially, we tried using a high number of bins (50K, 100K, 200K and 500K), but did not observe improvements on the development set, probably because of the limited amount of unlabeled text and the sparsity issues resulting thereof. We thus tried smaller numbers of bins, eventually ending up with just two bins, which yielded the highest improvement on the development set. Table 2, row G shows this also yielded a tiny improvement on the test set: from 89.18% to 89.40%.

We also tried a second kind of features based on the clustering algorithm described in [5], using (1) bottom-up agglomerative word clustering, and (2) the clustering method of [11], but were unable to achieve any performance gains on the development dataset.

[1] Alexander Joseph of Battenberg (April 5, 1857 – October 23, 1893) was the first prince (knyaz) of modern Bulgaria.

4 Experiments and evaluation

In our experiments, we used the Mallet implementation of CRF. We further used manually annotated sentences from the BulTreeBank for training, development and testing:

- *training*: 8,896 sentences (147,339 tokens), including 1,563 organizations, 4,282 persons, 2,300 locations, and 353 miscellaneous named entities;
- *development*: 1,779 sentences (29,467 tokens), including 312 organizations, 856 persons, 383 locations, and 70 miscellaneous named entities;
- *testing*: 2,000 sentences (34,649 tokens), including 315 organizations, 841 persons, 438 locations, and 69 miscellaneous named entities.

In the process of system development, we did many iterations of training and evaluation on the development data, followed by predicate enhancement and new feature construction. For the final evaluation, we trained on a concatenation of the training and the development data and we tested on the unseen test data.

We were very strict in the evaluation and gave no credit for partially discovered named entities: we considered that a named entity was correctly recognized if all tokens it covers were labeled correctly, and no extra tokens were included as part of the entity.

5 Results and discussion

The evaluation results are shown in Table 2. We started with simple orthographic features in our baseline system (row A: F_1=82.14%), and we repeatedly added additional types to improve the performance.

As we can see in rows B and C, using domain-specific features in the form of simple regular expressions and gazetteers yielded about 3% absolute improvement on F_1 to 85%. Adding morpho-syntactic features resulted in additional 3% increase to 88.70% (rows D and E), and using feature induction and mutual information (rows F and G) added 1% more to F_1, which reached 89.40% for our final system (row G).

An examination of system's output on the development dataset shows that the primary source of errors were properly labeled mentions whose boundaries were off by one or more tokens. If the score was relaxed so that tagged entities were considered as true positives if and only if one or more tokens overlap with a correct entry, the performance on the development data would increase a lot. As an extreme example, consider the string *Вашку да Гама* ('*Vashku da Gama*', i.e., '*Vasco da Gama*'), which was incorrectly recognized as covering two entities of type person ('*Вашку*' and '*Гама*').

We should note that our results are not directly comparable to previous publications; we are the first to try a statistical approach for Bulgarian NER, which has attracted very little research interest so far and was dominated by rule-based systems. For example, [17] describe adding manual rules for Bulgarian NER to ANNIE, but provide no formal evaluation.

It is still informative to compare our results to those achieved for other Slavic languages even if we use different kinds/amounts of training data and different sets of named entities types. For example, the best P/R/F_1 results for Russian are 79.9/63.7/70.9 (in %), which was calculated for six types of named entities [19]: persons (70.5/53.9/61.1), organizations (72.5/59.8/65.5), locations (91.2/68.7/78.4), dates (77.0/71.7/74.3), percents (87.5/87.5/87.5), and money (80.8/40.4/60.6). For Polish, the best results are the following [18]: persons (90.6/85.3/87.9), organizations (87.9/56.6/68.9), locations (88.4/43.4/58.2), time (81.3/85.9/83.5), percents (100.0/100.0/100.0), and money (97.8/93.8/95.8); overall this makes 91.0/77.5/82.4. For Czech, the best results are the following [10]: 84.0/70.0/76.0. We can see that our results are superior, especially on F_1 and recall.

The state-of-the-art F_1 scores for English at specialized competitions like the Message Understanding Conference and CoNLL-2003 has been 93.39% and 88.76%, respectively. Similarly, at CoNLL-2002[2] and CoNLL-2003[3], the best F_1 for German, Spanish and Dutch were 72.41%, 81.39% and 77.05%, respectively. The highest reported F_1 score for Arabic, which is morphologically richer than Bulgarian, is 83.5% [2]. All these systems were trained on about 200K tokens as is ours, and thus we can conclude that our F_1=89.4% is comparable to the state-of-the-art.

6 Conclusions and future work

Our experiments show that CRF models with carefully-designed features can identify mentions of named entities (organizations, persons, locations and miscellaneous) in Bulgarian text with fairly high accuracy, even without features containing domain-specific knowledge. However, such features, which in our framework take the form of membership in a gazetteer, simple common endings for personal names and location entities, and rich morpho-syntactic tagsets, can lead to improved system performance. Even on the limited training data we had available, we have shown that using external raw text could potentially help on the system performance. However, broader experiments are needed to measure the scope of influence.

We also demonstrate that proper handling of morpho-syntactic tags for morphologically rich languages like Bulgarian could lead to intelligent feature generation and huge performance gains for the named entity tagger. Still, we consider the construction of morpho-syntactic taggers that can handle the rich tagset of the BulTreeBank as a challenging but demanding task. Finally, using raw text is another promising direction we plan to pursue in future work.

[2] http://www.cnts.ua.ac.be/conll2002/ner/

[3] http://www.cnts.ua.ac.be/conll2003/ner/

References

[1] D. E. Appelt, J. R. Hobbs, J. Bear, D. Israel, M. Kameyama, A. Kehler, D. Martin, K. Myers, and M. Tyson. SRI International FASTUS system: MUC-6 test results and analysis. In *Proceedings of MUC-6*, 1995.

[2] Y. Benajiba, M. Diab, and P. Rosso. Arabic named entity recognition using optimal feature sets. In *EMNLP*, 2008.

[3] D. M. Bikel, R. Schwartz, and R. M. Weischedel. An algorithm that learns what's in a name. *Machine Learning*, 34(1):211–231, February 1999.

[4] A. Borthwick. *Maximum Entropy Approach to Named Entity Recognition*. PhD thesis, New York University, 1999.

[5] P. Brown, V. Pietra, P. deSouza, J. Lai, and R. Mercer. Class-based n-gram models of natural language. computational linguistics. *Proceedings of the IEEE*, 18(4):467479, 1992.

[6] N. A. Chinchor. Overview of MUC-7/MET-2. In *Proceedings of MUC-7*, 1998.

[7] M. Collins. Ranking algorithms for named-entity extraction: Boosting and the voted perceptron, 2002.

[8] M. Collins and Y. Singer. Unsupervised models for named entity classification. In *Proceedings of EMNLP-VLC*, 1999.

[9] H. Cunningham, D. Maynard, K. Bontcheva, and V. Tablan. GATE: A framework and graphical development environment for robust NLP tools and applications. In *Proc. of ACL*, 2002.

[10] J. Kravalova and Z. Zabokrtsky. Czech named entity corpus and SVM-based recognizer. In *Proceedings of the Named Entities Workshop*, 2009.

[11] P. Liang. Semi-supervised learning for natural language. Master's thesis, Massachusetts Institute of Technology. Dept. of Electrical Engineering and Computer Science., 2005.

[12] D. Lin. Extracting collocations from text corpora. In *First Workshop on Computational Terminology*, 1998.

[13] S. Maosong, S. Dayang, and B. Tsou. Chinese word segmentation without using lexicon and hand-crafted training data. In *Proceedings of ACL*, 1998.

[14] A. McCallum. Efficiently inducing features of conditional random fields. In *Proceedings of UAI*, 2003.

[15] A. McCallum and W. Li. Early results for named entity recognition with conditional random fields, feature induction and web-enhanced lexicons. In *Seventh Conference on Natural Language Learning (CoNLL)*, 2003.

[16] S. Miller, J. Guinness, and A. Zamanian. Name tagging with word clusters and discriminative training. In *Proceedings of HLT-NAACL*, pages 277–296, 2004.

[17] E. Paskaleva, G. Angelova, M.Yankova, K. Bontcheva, H. Cunningham, and Y. Wilks. Slavonic named entities in GATE. Technical Report 03, University of Sheffield, 2002.

[18] J. Piskorski, P. Homola, M. Marciniak, A. Mykowiecka, A. Przepirkowski, and M. Wolinski. Information extraction for Polish using the SProUT platform. In *Intelligent Information Systems*, Advances in Soft Computing. Springer, 2004.

[19] B. Popov, A. Kirilov, D. Maynard, and D. Manov. Creation of reusable components and language resources for named entity recognition in Russian. In *Proceedings of LREC*, 2004.

[20] L. Ramshaw and M. Marcus. Text chunking using transformation-based learning. In *Proceedings of the Third Workshop on Very Large Corpora*. ACL, 1995.

[21] E. Riloff and R. Jones. Learning dictionaries for information extraction by multi-level bootstrapping. In *AAAI/IAAI*, pages 474–479, 1999.

[22] S. Sarawagi and W. Cohen. Semi-Markov conditional random fields for information extraction. In *Proceedings of NIPS*, 2004.

[23] K. Simov, P. Osenova, and M. Slavcheva. BTB-TR03: BulTreeBank morphosyntactic tagset. Technical Report CS-02-01, 2004.

[24] E. F. Tjong Kim Sang. Introduction to the CoNLL-2002 shared task: Language-independent named entity recognition. In *Proceedings of CoNLL-2002*, 2002.

[25] J. Zhang, J. Gao, and M. Zhou. Extraction of Chinese compound words: An experimental study on a very large corpus. In *Proceedings of the ACL Chinese Processing Workshop*, 2000.

[26] G. Zhou and J. Su. Named entity recognition using an HMM-based chunk tagger. In *Proceedings of ACL-2001*, 2001.

Uncertainty Detection For Information Extraction

Bénédicte Goujon
Thales Research & Technology
Campus de Polytechnique
1, avenue Augustin Fresnel
91 767 Palaiseau - FRANCE
benedicte.goujon@thalesgroup.com

Abstract

The detection of factual information from texts, like relations or events, is an important task in natural language processing. However most of the tools dealing with information extraction do not take into account the nuances expressed by the author, such as uncertainty. In those applications, the sentence "According to a witness, Y has met X" is reduced to its second part. The lost of the uncertainty expressed by the use of the secondary source "a witness" transforms the understanding of the whole information. The method presented in this paper aims at detecting the uncertainty and the reality of the information described in texts, and captures whether an information is presented as past, with a moderate uncertainty or in a negative way. The method is implemented in a web service for event annotation from texts, which is used in strategic watch applications.

Keywords

Semantic Annotation, Information Extraction, Event Extraction, Uncertainty, Linguistic patterns.

1. Introduction

The automatic extraction of events from texts has to take into account the discursive context in which the events are presented. For example, in the following sentences : "According to a witness, Y has met X", "Y may have met X", "X has met Y", several different levels of certainty are expressed by the author. In the first case, the author presents a reported discourse and the certainty of the event is relative to the reliability of the secondary source ("a witness" in this example). In the second case, the author expresses an uncertainty with "may". In the third case, the author expresses no uncertainty. Our aim is to capture those expressions of uncertainty, coupled with the expressions of reality of the information (for example, future tense is used when events have not occurred yet).

First, we present our context of information extraction. Then, we detail existing approaches in information extraction, modality and uncertainty detection and their limits. Afterwards, we present our model and the associated linguistic knowledge. We end with the implementation as web service and its evaluation.

2. Information Extraction

Our aim is to extract structured information from texts, in order to help the end-user like a strategic watch expert to identify a maximum of information for his or her task. Several difficulties are occurring. First, we want to extract all the information characteristics. For example if the end-user is interested in a Purchase event, we want to identify the agent, the patient, and according to the given details we want to identify all others parameters (date, location...). To do so, we need to build very precise linguistic patterns, if possible easy to build by the end-user. Another difficulty is the identification of all the nuances that are associated to the extracted information. For example, in the following sentence "Laurent Gbagbo might go to Italy.", the Move event relies Laurent Gbagbo and Italy, and is expressed with uncertainty. If this event is extracted and added into a knowledge base without this nuance, the result may not have the same sense as the original information in the text. Those slight differences, obvious when reading a text, must be taken into account by the automatic event extraction tools. The first needs in event extraction, expressed by the NIST MUC 3 (1991) and MUC 4 (1992) campaigns, were aiming at the identification of location, date and victim of past events [8]. They were not concerned by expression of uncertainty. More recently, the ACE (Automatic Content Extraction) campaigns integrated the event extraction, with the identification of attributes such as modality or polarity. However, in 2007, only one candidate (BBN Technologies) performed this test [1], which was suppressed in 2008. We may thus conclude that systems are not yet ready to such evaluations. The importance to manage the uncertainty expressed by the author of the text is now well identified. For example, Auger and Roy of the Defense R&D Canada [2] show the necessity to take into account the ambiguities and characterize automatically certainty/uncertainty expressed into texts in order to fuse information afterwards. Our aim is to identify the uncertainty related to events that are extracted.

3. State of the art and limitations

3.1 Information Extraction from Texts

Here is the presentation of two existing tools aiming at extracting events from texts.

Zenon [6] aims at extracting actions from HUMINT documents of the KFOR, in English. It uses FrameNet [4] to define the actions (KILL, REPORT, KNOW, COMMAND, PROPOSE, EXPLODE) and entities (Company, Person, Number, Date, City, Region, River, ...)

International Conference RANLP 2009 - Borovets, Bulgaria, pages 118–122

to extract. Zenon is based on GATE [3], which is a free open source framework for Natural Language Engineering. This tool extracts actions and their corresponding entities but does not take into account nuances such as uncertainty that can modify the sense of the extracted actions.

The University College Dublin [7] has also developed a tool for the event extraction from heterogeneous sources. Their tool identifies sentences expressing events. Their aim is to cluster the sentences that express a same event, in order to ease the understanding of an event by a user. In this work, the objective is to extract complete sentences, but not to extract structured information from texts. So their approach keeps all the nuances of the author as it keeps the sentences, but it doesn't capture automatically events and their participants.

3.2 Modality and Event Detection

Saurí et al. [10] have worked on the identification of modality values associated to events described in texts. Their aim is to improve for example question-answering systems. Modalities taken into account in their approach are the following: degree of possibility, belief, evidentiality (*Subcomandante Marcos said that the Mexican government is not interested in putting an end to the conflict.*), expectation (*Hans Blix wants the US to allow UN inspectors back into Iraq to verify any weapons found by coalition forces.*), attempting and command. This work is based on the TimeML language. EvITA, a system using this approach, aims at recognize the events, and identifies among other things the modal characteristics. In this work, the certainty modality is not studied, whereas this modality is the most important for us.

3.3 Uncertainty Model for Natural Language

Several linguistic works aim at modeling the use of modality, but very few concentrate on uncertainty, for instance, the Certainty Categorization Model proposed by Rubin et al. in [9]. This model is based on four dimensions, called "level", "perspective", "focus" and "time", to characterize the uncertainty. Each of those dimensions are detailed in Figures 1 and 2 below, and may be illustrated with a few examples as follows.

Let us first consider the Level dimension: sentences (1) and (2) below give examples of an Absolute Level and a Low Level, respectively. (1) *Eventually, however, auditors* ***will almost certainly have to*** *form a tough self-regulatory body that can oversee its members' actions…*

(2) *So far the presidential candidates are more interested in talking about what a surplus* ***might buy*** *than in the painful choices that lie ahead.*

For the Perspective dimension, the example (3) illustrates a reported point of view.

(3) *The historian Ira Berlin, author of "Many Thousands Gone,"* ***estimates*** *that one slave perished for everyone who survived capture in the African interior…*

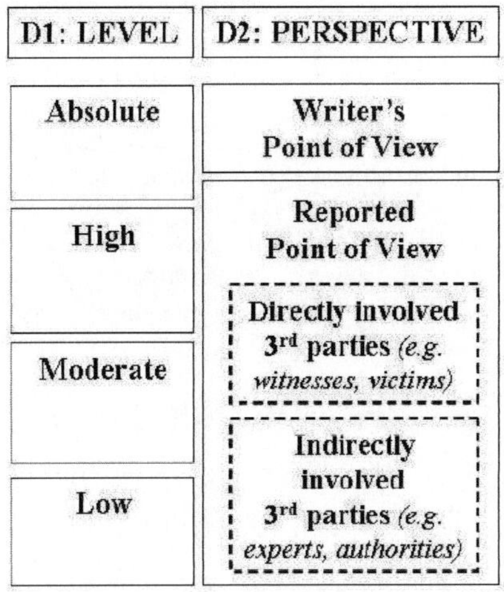

Figure 1: Dimensions 1 and 2, Certainty Categorization Model.

The Focus dimension is illustrated with sentences (4) and (5): sentence (4) is an example of an abstract information and sentence (5) is a factual information.

(4) *In Iraq, the first steps* ***must be taken*** *to put a hard-won new security council resolution on arms inspections into effect.*

(5) *The settlement* ***may not fully compensate*** *survivors for the delay in justice, ...*

At last, the Time dimension is understandable without examples.

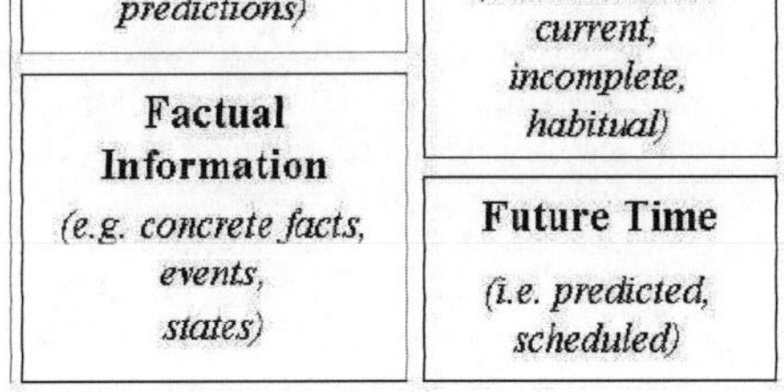

Figure 2: Dimensions 3 and 4, Certainty Categorization Model.

This model was developed for manual annotation. For our objective, the identification of the reported point of view is necessary. For example, if an event is reported by the government spokesperson or by the leader of the rebels, the user may associate quickly the uncertainty of the reported event, according to the reliability of the source. Also, we think that the reality of an event is lacking. For example, if we have "Laurent Gbagbo didn't go to Italy.", the sentence deals with the Move event between Laurent Gbagbo and Italy, but in a negative way. This negative expression has to be captured in order to keep this nuance for further treatment (expansion of a knowledge base). At last, we want to automatically extract those uncertainty and reality information.

4. Event Extraction with Uncertainty and Reality Detection

4.1 Enrichment of the Rubin et al. uncertainty model

We present here our model, which is an enrichment of the Rubin et al. uncertainty model. It includes the identification of the local source, which is necessary for an end-user to evaluate the reliability of the reported discourse. It also takes into account the reality or unreality of an information which is specified in the source text, rather than the Focus dimension. For example, if we have "Laurent Gbagbo didn't go to Italy.", the sentence deals with the Move event between Laurent Gbagbo and Italy, but in a negative way. But it's not an opinion, or an abstract information as in the Focus dimension. Here is the model of uncertainty and reality that we have defined in a context of textual information extraction.

D1 LEVEL: High, Moderate, Low.

D2 PERSPECTIVE: Writer's point of View, Reported Point of View.

D4 TIME: Past Time, Present Time, Future Time.

D5 REALITY: Assertion, Negative.

D6 SOURCE NAME. (only when D2= Reported Point of View)

Figure 3: Our Uncertainty and Reality Model.

In our model, we did not keep the Absolute value of the Level dimension, because in our current implementation we only define three levels of uncertainty. We will have to analyze whether this Absolute value is necessary or not. Also, we did not keep the distinction between the Directly involved 3rd parties and the Indirectly involved 3rd parties for the Perspective dimension, as it seems to be too hard to identify it automatically from text. Finally, we did not keep the Focus dimension, as it was not useful according to our needs.

4.2 Linguistic patterns for uncertainty and reality detection

We have developed linguistic patterns to identify the values of uncertainty in texts according to our five dimensions. This work was done for French, but could be realized for English also. Here is a subset of the linguistic knowledge used to identify uncertainty and reality.

Categories	Linguistic Forms	Dimensions and associated values
Adjectives	*douteux, incertain, peu probable*	Level: Low
	présumé, supposé,	Level: Moderate
	vraisemblable, probable, possible, envisageable, envisagé,	Level: High
Verbs	*dire, déclarer, annoncer* *penser, croire, douter, hésiter, ...*	Level: Moderate
Expressions	*selon toute vraisemblance, sans doute, à ce qu'on dit,* *il se peut que, il paraît*	Level: Moderate
Structures	*selon, d'après , de source(s)* « ... »	Perspective: Reported Point of View
	si (except when followed by an adverb)	Level: Moderate
	aller + infinitive	Time: Future Time
	ne, n' (except « *n'importe* »)	Reality: Negative

Table 1. Linguistic Knowledge used in patterns.

Those words or expressions are used in linguistic patterns in order to identify the sentence part concerned by the uncertainty. Our patterns are finite state automaton, defined with Intex, a linguistic development tool [11]. Here is an example of pattern, which annotates the moderate level of uncertainty.

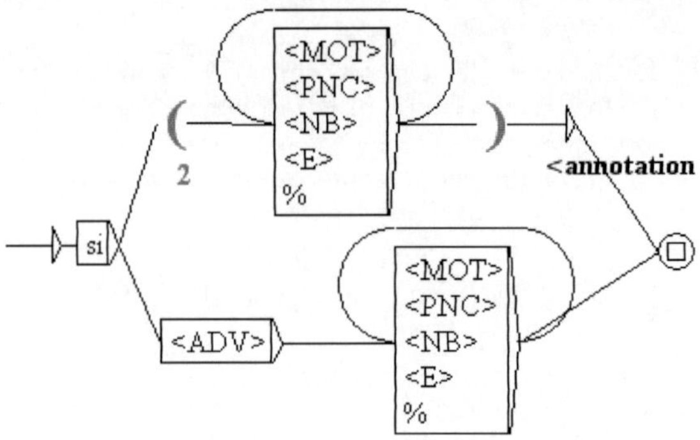

Figure 4. Linguistic Pattern Example.

In the first line of this pattern, "*si*" ("if" in French) introduces a part of sentence annotated with a Moderate level of uncertainty (we can see the beginning of the annotation expression at the right). In the second line no annotation is added when "*si*" is followed with an adverb (<ADV>). In this pattern, a sequence of any word is represented by the loop on boxes with <MOT>+<PNC>+<NB>+<E>+%.

4.3 Combination of Uncertainty and Event Extraction

Usually, uncertainty or other non-factual information are modeled by linguists but not used for automatic detection. On the other hands, some tools are dealing with the information extraction, such as relation or event extraction, but without capturing the nuances of the discourse. In our approach we have combined the automatic detection of events from text with the detection of the uncertainty and reality associated to the events, in order to keep all the contextual information. Our aim is to identify not only the uncertainty, but also the reality or unreality of the event, as sometimes discourses are dealing with events that never occur.

In practical terms, we first associate certainty characteristics to a part of sentence or a whole sentence of a text. Then, we apply event extraction linguistic patterns to extract events from text. When we identify an event, we add it all the certainty characteristics that have been associated to the sentence where the event was found.

5. Implementation

5.1 The WebContent Project Context

This work is done in the French ANR WebContent project context. The objective of WebContent is to provide a platform with services for text analysis for strategic watch applications. It is based on semantic web paradigm, so WebContent uses web services and Ontologies. Several web services (language identification, named entity identification, crawling, classification…) are developed by partners (CEA, EADS, Exalead, INRA, INRIA…) and are used in the strategic watch applications of the project (economic watch in aeronautics, strategic intelligence, microbiological and chemical food risk, watch on seismic events).

5.2 The Event Extraction Web Service

We have developed a web service for the event extraction, which implements also the detection of uncertainty. It is developed in Java. The web service analyses texts by applying linguistic patterns thanks to Intex. Some linguistic patterns are associated to uncertainty, some are associated to events. Linguistic patterns associated to events are built previously with the SemPlusEvent tool. This tool, which is the last version of the SemPlus tool, aims at easing the capture of event linguistic patterns from examples thanks to a learning algorithm [5]. At runtime, to configure the web service, we need an ontology of the domain with instances, which is transformed into dictionaries compatible with SemPlus. Then, for each input text, the web service takes in input a MediaUnit structure, which is a WebContent format containing texts, and adds semantic annotations in RDF to this MediaUnit which is provided as input. Here is an example to illustrate this implementation. We have analyzed the following sentence:

> *Selon des témoins, Laurent Gbagbo aurait rencontré Alassane Ouattara.*

The analysis of this short text produces the following RDF annotations (figure 4, in thick, important information).

The first part of this RDF annotation contains all the characteristics of the Uncertainty#1, which is associated to the Event#0 described in the last RDF annotation. In this event, Personne56 is "*Laurent Gbagbo*", and Personne4 is "*Alassane Ouattara*". Those annotations are related to the corresponding textual segments via others RDF descriptions.

```
...
<rdf:RDF ...> <rdf:Description
rdf:about="weblab://InstanceCandidate//
Uncertainty#0">
<onto:Level>Moderate</onto:Level>
<onto:Time>Past time</onto:Time>
<onto:Reality>Assertion</onto:Reality>
<onto:Source>des témoins</onto:Source>
<onto:Perspective>Reported point of
View</onto:Perspective>
</rdf:Description> </rdf:RDF>
...
<rdf:Description
rdf:about="weblab://InstanceCandidate/Event#0">
<rdf:type rdf:resource="RENCONTRE"/>
<onto:Agent>http://www.owl-
ontologies.com/RCI.owl#Personne56</onto:Agent>
<onto:Patient>http://www.owl-
ontologies.com/RCI.owl#Personne4</onto:Patient>
<onto:related_uncertainty>weblab://InstanceCandidate/U
ncertainty#0</onto:related_uncertainty>
</rdf:Description>
...
```

Figure 5. RDF Annotations produced by the web service.

This web service is used in the economic watch in aeronautics and strategic intelligence applications developed in the WebContent project.

5.3 Evaluation

We have carried out a first evaluation of this work. It was done on a small corpus of 5 French articles dealing with news. This corpus contains 40 reported discourses, 25 uncertainty, 8 negation and 4 future. Here are two sentences from the corpus:

Selon lemonde.fr, les enregistreurs de vol de l'Airbus A330 qui s'est abîmé le 1er juin dans l'Atlantique avec 228 personnes à bord auraient été localisées par les navires de la marine française.[1]

Mir Hossein Moussavi et Mehdi Karoubi estiment que le vote a fait l'objet de vastes fraudes.[2]

Here are the results of the evaluation:

	Recall	*Precision*	*F-measure*
Perspective	0.73	0.95	0.83
Source	0.48	0.98	0.64
Level	0.84	0.58	0.69
Reality	0.88	1	0.94
Time	1	1	1

Table 2. Evaluation results.

Some reported discourses were not identified as the verbs used to introduce them were not taken into account (*commenter, voir,…*). Also, we work at the sentence level. Some sentences were not associated to reported discourses because when several sentences are in a reported discourse, only the first one, introduced with ", is identified. A similar situation occurs at sources identification: sometimes sources appear out of the sentence containing the reported discourse. In this case, they are not identified by our approach. Previously, we considered that a source could not contain ".", but we have to take into account sources such as web sites (lemonde.fr).

We considered at last that all reported discourses were associated to a "Moderate" certainty, according to the writer's point of view. But, we have observed that sometimes the quotation marks are also used to introduce a sentence pronounced by another person, without certainty or uncertainty.

6. Conclusion

We have presented a model that allows the precise characterization of uncertainty in a context of information extraction from texts. We have described our approach based on linguistic patterns and detailed a part of the linguistic knowledge for French analysis. This approach is used in a web service that produces RDF annotations containing the level of uncertainty, the time, the reality, the perspective and the source characteristics. Currently those annotations are used in strategic watch applications.

To improve our approach, we will need to take into account the results of the evaluation. We also will need to compare our annotations to the inputs and needs of fusion tools that may fused events according to their uncertainty characteristics.

7. Acknowledgements

This work was done in the WebContent ANR French Project context (http://www.webcontent.fr).

8. References

[1] ACE 2007, http://www.itl.nist.gov/iad/894.01/tests/ace/2007/.

[2] A. Auger, J. Roy. Expression of Uncertainty in Linguistic Data, in *Fusion 2008*, Cologne, Allemagne.

[3] H. Cunningham, D. Maynard, K. Bontcheva, V. Tablan. GATE: A Framework and Graphical Development Environment for Robust NLP Tools and Applications. *Proceedings of the 40th Anniversary Meeting of the Association for Computational Linguistics (ACL'02)*. Philadelphia, July 2002.

[4] FrameNet, http://framenet.icsi.berkeley.edu/.

[5] B. Goujon. Relation Extraction in an Intelligence Context, in *LangTech 2008*, Roma, Italy.

[6] M. Hecking. System ZENON – Semantic Analysis of Intelligence Reports, in *LangTech 2008*, Roma, Italy.

[7] M. Naughton, N. Kushmerick, and J.Carthy. Event Extraction from Heterogeneous News Sources, in *AAAI 2006 Workshop on Event Extraction and Synthesis*, Boston.

[8] T. Poibeau. Extraction d'information à base de connaissances hybrides, PhD, 2002.

[9] V. L. Rubin, E. D. Liddy, N. Kando. Certainty Identification in Texts: Categorization Model and Manual Tagging Results Computing Attitude and Affect in Text: Theory and Applications, The Information Retrieval Series, Springer Netherlands, vol. 20. pp. 61-76.

[10] R. Saurí, M. Verhagen, J. Pustejovsky. Annotating and Recognizing Event Modality in Text, *FLAIRS 2006*, Floride.

[11] M. Silberztein, 1999. INTEX: a Finite State Transducer toolbox, in *Theoretical Computer Science #231:1*, Elsevier Science.

[1] According to lemonde.fr, the recorders of the flight of the Airbus A330 which … should have been located by the ship of the French navy.

[2] Mir Hossein Moussavi and Mehdi Karoubi consider that the vote was the object of massive frauds.

Learning to Identify Educational Materials

Samer Hassan and Rada Mihalcea
University of North Texas
samer@unt.edu, *rada@cs.unt.edu*

Abstract

In this paper, we explore the task of automatically identifying educational materials, by classifying documents with respect to their educative value. Through experiments carried out on a data set of manually annotated documents, we show that the generally accepted notion of a learning object's "educativeness" is indeed a property that can be reliably assigned through automatic classification.

Keywords

learning objects, educational applications, text classification

1 Introduction

With the rapid growth of the amount of information available online and elsewhere, it becomes increasingly difficult to identify documents that satisfy the user needs. Current search engines target broad coverage of information, at the cost of providing limited support for well defined verticals.

In particular, an increasingly large number of users, consisting primarily of students, instructors and self-taught learners, are often seeking educational materials online, to use as standalone instructional materials or to supplement existing class resources. The typical solution is to either refer to existing collections of learning materials, which often lack breadth of coverage, or to search the Web using one of the current search engines, which frequently lead to many irrelevant results. For example, as shown later in Section 3, from the top 50 documents returned by a search performed on a major search engine[1] for the query "tree data structure," only four were found to be strongly educative, while as many as 29 documents were found to be non-educative.

In this paper, we address the task of automatically identifying educational materials. We formulate the task as a text categorization problem, and try to automatically classify the "educativeness" of a document (defined as a property that reflects the educative value of a document). Through annotation experiments carried out on a data set of materials from the domain of computer science, we show that the educativeness of a document is a property that can be reliably assigned by human judges. We also identify several features characteristic to educational resources, which can be used to identify the educativeness of a document. We perform a number of classification experiments, and show that the document educativeness can be learned and automatically assigned.

2 Background

A learning object is formally defined as "any entity, digital or non-digital, that may be used for learning, education or training" [2], or "any digital resource that can be reused to support learning" [12].

The idea that a document can have an educative property is widely accepted in the growing body of work dedicated to learning objects. Learning object repositories (e.g., [6, 8]) target improved access to learning materials through "sharing and reuse," by providing a common interface to entire collections of learning materials that can be shared among students and instructors and can be reused across courses and disciplines. These definitions are representative for the notion of "educativeness" as used in this paper.

While there has been a large body of work focused toward Learning Object Metadata harnessing [7, 4, 1], we are not aware of any work that has tried to harness the power of the Web as an educational resource through the automatic identification of learning assets on the Web. The work closest to ours is perhaps [9], where the authors addressed the problem of finding educational resources on the Web. However, the focus of their work was limited to metadata extraction for a limited set of fine grained properties. Instead, in this paper, we introduce a method to automatically annotate the educativeness property of a document, which can be used to assist learners in their search for educational materials.

It is important to note that the classification of the educativeness of a document cannot be modeled as a genre classification task. While recognizing the educativeness of a document is relatively easy to do with accomplished readers, different educational materials can have major stylistic inconsistencies, which invalidate their membership to a unified genre [3]. For example, a diagram, textbook, and a blog could all serve as useful and educative resources despite their obvious stylistic differences.

3 Building A Data Set for the Classification of Educational Materials

What is an educational material? The purpose of educational materials is primarily decided by the author

[1] Throughout our experiments, we conduct our searches using the Google search engine.

International Conference RANLP 2009 - Borovets, Bulgaria, pages 123–127

or the presenter of the resource, who furthermore decides the target audience and the delivery style (e.g., textbooks, presentation, diagram). While the purpose of the resource is a property that is mainly determined by its author, the strength of the educative resource ("educativeness") is a property evaluated cumulatively by the target audience of the resource (e.g., students or educational experts) . Hence, in the construction of our data set and in the evaluations we run, we focus on the educativeness property of a learning resource as determined by the agreement of their potential users (students).

Educational materials can be located in a variety of sources and formats, including lectures, tutorials, online books, blog articles, publications, even technical forums or expert networks. Most of these learning objects typically include several of the following components: definitions, examples, questions and answers, diagrams, and illustrations.

In order to build a data set for the classification of educational materials, we mimic a hypothetical learner who tries to locate and identify learning assets using current online resources. We use a typical search scenario, which involves the use of a search engine with a disambiguated query to identify candidate materials, followed by a filtering step that selects only those materials that have educational relevance.

We collect a data set covering the domain of computer science. We select fourteen topics frequently addressed in data structures and algorithms courses, as shown in Table 2. Starting with each of the fourteen topics, a query is constructed and run against the Google search engine, and the top 60 ranked search results are collected.[2] Note that the meaning of some terms can be ambiguous, e.g., "tree" or "list," and thus we explicitly disambiguate the query by adding the phrase "data structure." By performing this explicit disambiguation, we can focus on the educativeness property of the documents returned by the search, rather than on the differences that could arise from ambiguities of meaning.

3.1 Properties of Educational Materials

We define a set of features largely based on the properties associated with learning objects, as defined in standards such as IEEE LOM [2]. Some of the features are also motivated by previous work on educational metadata [11]. The following features are associated with each document in the data set.

Educativeness
To be able to capture the educativeness of a resource, the annotators had to score each page on its overall educative value. This feature serves as the major class of the documents in the data set. The annotators were instructed to evaluate the resource as a necessary asset for a student to understand the topic, and score each document on a four point scale ranging from "non-educative" to "strongly-educative."

[2] From the top 60 documents, some had to be removed prior to any further processing, because they were either unreachable or they contained non-English characters.

Relevance
We want to measure how human-assigned relevance can contribute to our task, and see if an accurate (manual) measure of relevance can result in a better identification of learning objects, as compared to the search engine ranking. We measure relevance on a four point scale ranging from "non-relevant" to "very relevant."

Content Categories
The content category is a feature that classifies the type of content found on the target page. We assume that the typical content of a learning object can be categorized into one or more of the following types:

Definition: The content presents a textual definition of a concept or any of its associated properties.

Example/Use: The content presents examples that help clarify a concept, demonstrative use of a concept, or the use of operations in that concept. (e.g., the queue data structure push and pop operations)

Questions & Answers: The content presents a question and answer dialogue, as usually found in technical forums and sometime in blog articles.

Illustration: The content presents an illustration of a concept or a process, either through the use of images, or through diagrams.

Other: This group contains all the other types that do not fit in the previous categories.

Resource Type
One of the interesting properties of the learning asset is its source. Under the assumption that the type of the resource can contribute to the document educativeness, the annotators were instructed to choose all the possible types that apply from a pre-compiled list. The list was generated by observing and inspecting the collection of retrieved documents. These types are not mutually exclusive.

Class webpage: A typical class home page where the teacher would provide lecture notes, tips, quizzes and answers for the class homework.

Encyclopedia: A resource for educative materials, representing semi-structured or fully structured knowledge contributed by experts in the field.

Blog: Web log or blog represents an online personal journal. It varies in format and purpose and it is an increasing popular online form of self-expression.

Mailing list/forums: It is a typical example of expert network where users pose their questions to an expert (or group of experts) in the field and receive one or more answers. Usually such content is very technical but not always useful.

Online book: This category represents electronic books in an online format (e.g., HTML, PDF).

Presentation: A demonstrative material that consists of a set of slides or pages, representing the main points to be addressed with respect to a topic.

Publication: This group includes scientific publications, such as journal articles, conference proceedings, article abstracts, and patent descriptions.

How-To article: This source type addresses the use of a specific concept on a step by step basis.

Reference manual: A technical reference or manual, which explains the use and the inner workings of a concept (e.g., Java language documentations).

Other: This category includes all other content (e.g. product catalogs, company homepages)

Expertise
Learning objects are very diverse and are subject to the judgment of the learner. An expert in the field needs little introduction to the topic, and may require a high level of technical insight. Instead, the same information might seem non-educative and irrelevant from the perspective of a novice user, who seeks basic fundamentals. To address this problem, we asked the annotators to indicate their expertise in each of the selected topics on a four point scale.

3.2 Final Set of Features

Taken together, all the features defined above are referred to as "user features," and are listed in Table 1. In addition to these features, for each document in the data set we also collect its search engine ranking and its document type (ppt, pdf, html, doc, etc.). We also calculate the hubness of each page as a ratio of its hyper-linked contents to its original content.

HasDefinition	IsForum	HasExamples
HasQA	IsManual	HasIllustrations
HasOther	IsBook	IsOther
IsHowTo	IsClassWebpage	IsPublication
Rank	Relevance	Hubness
IsBlog	IsPresentation	IsEncyclopedia
DocType	Expertise	Educativeness

Table 1: *User features*

3.3 Agreement Study

Two judges individually annotated the collected documents based on a set of annotation guidelines. The annotators were required to identify the value associated with all the document features described above, along with the educativeness property of a document. The annotators were instructed to evaluate the resource from a college student perspective, therefore discarding highly technical and specific resources as non-educative or marginally-educative.

We measure the inter-annotator agreement by calculating the kappa statistic for the annotations made by the two human annotators. The inter-annotator agreement and the kappa statistic for all the features are shown in Figure 1.

The final data set is created by asking a third annotator to arbitrate the disagreements among the first two annotators. The final distribution across the educativeness class labels is shown in Table 2. As seen in the table, the distribution across educative and non-educative classes is relatively balanced with a few exceptions. Topics such as "queue" and "tree" tend to have more non-educative pages, unlike topics such as "binary search," which tend to have more educative pages.

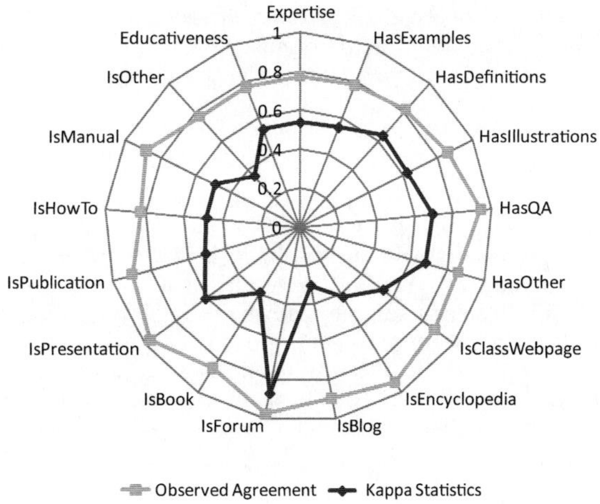

Fig. 1: *Kappa statistic and inter-annotator agreement*

Topic	NE	ME	E	SE	Total
Array	22	13	17	6	48
Queue	23	15	18	4	50
Stack	20	13	20	7	60
Tree	29	11	11	4	55
Linked list	22	10	19	9	60
Skip list	18	3	18	10	49
Heap	21	10	15	6	52
Priority queue	18	7	21	5	51
Hash table	22	9	17	7	55
Dictionary	28	6	17	3	54
Graph	25	9	14	6	54
Sorting algorithms	20	8	22	10	60
Binary search	12	6	28	14	60

Table 2: *Distribution of classes across the topics. Number of non-educational (NE), marginally educational (ME), educational (E) and strongly educational (SE) materials.*

4 Experiments

Using the data set described in the previous section, we experiment with automatic classifiers to annotate the educativeness of a given document. Through these evaluations, we measure the ability of a system to automatically detect and classify documents according to their educative value.

The four-point scale used for the educativeness annotation allows us to perform both a fine grained and a coarse grained evaluation. In the fine grained evaluation, all four dimensions are considered, and thus we run a four-way classification. In the coarse grained evaluation, we combine the non-educative and marginally educative documents into one class (non-educative), and the educative and strongly educative pages into another class (educative), and run a two-way classification. All the evaluations are conducted using a ten-fold cross validation.

Through our experiments, we seek answers to the following questions:

1. Can the content of a document be used to classify its educativeness? We evaluate the use of the document content to learn and detect its educativeness. The content is used to construct a feature representation of each document. The terms appearing in the learning objects serve as features in the learning algorithm, with a weight indicating their frequency in the learning object.

2. Are the user-features useful for the classification of a document educativeness? We evaluate the selected user features as possible dimensions to learn and detect the educativeness of target examples. We use all the user features summarized in Table 1 to construct a feature vector representation for each learning asset. Since these features were manually assigned by the annotators, these annotations serve as an upper bound on the accuracy that can be achieved by using such features.

3. Can the content of a document be used to automatically predict the user-features? We run an evaluation where each of the selected user-features serves as its own class. The learning assets in which this feature has been selected by the annotators serve as positive examples, while the documents in which the feature was not encountered serve as negative examples. The content of the documents is used to build the feature vectors. The examples are then used to train a classifier to classify each of the features automatically.

4. Can the automatically predicted user-features be used to learn and detect the educativeness of a document? Finally, given the set of classifiers generated in the previous experiment, we use their output to construct a machine weighted user-feature representation of the given document. This evaluation is similar to the one relying on manually assigned user-features. However, instead of using the user annotations, we use the output automatically predicted by the classifiers.

For the experiments, we used two classifiers: Naïve Bayes[5] and SVM [10], selected based on their performance and diversity of learning methodologies.

5 Results

We run a first experiment where we use the content of the documents, with minimal pre-processing (tokenization, stopword removal), and classify them with respect to the fine-grained and coarse-grained educativeness class. We use a 10-fold cross validation on the entire data set. The rows labeled with "document content" in Tables 3 show the results of this experiment. To answer the first question, these experiments show that the use of raw content is useful and can be effectively used to classify the educativeness of a document. In fact, compared to the baseline of selecting the most common class across all the documents, the content-based classification results in a 22-23% absolute increase in F-measure.

Next, we use the manual annotations for the user-features to classify the educativeness of a document. The results obtained in this experiment are shown in Table 3 in the rows labeled with "user-features (manual)." The results are clearly superior, which answers the second question and suggests the usefulness of these features for the classification of educativeness. Note that these results represent an upper bound for our evaluations, since they rely on manually annotated features.

Features	NB	SVM
Fine-grained		
Document content	53.88	61.25
User-features (manual)	74.33	76.24
User-features (predicted)	58.70	62.38
Baseline	38.63	38.63
Coarse-grained		
Document content	77.00	78.65
User-features (manual)	87.80	88.56
User-features (predicted)	78.78	77.38
Baseline	55.02	55.02

Table 3: *Classification results*

Since the user-features seem to exhibit the best performance, next we evaluate the ability of automatically labeling these features using the content of the documents. The accuracy of the automatic classification of the user-features is shown in Figure 2. Both SVM and Naive Bayes seem to be able to label these features with relatively high accuracy. The lowest performance is achieved for Relevance (50-56% F-measure) and the highest for IsEncyclopedia (86-95% F-measure). This experiment provides an answer to the third question: all the user-features that proved useful for the classification of educativeness can be predicted based on the document content.

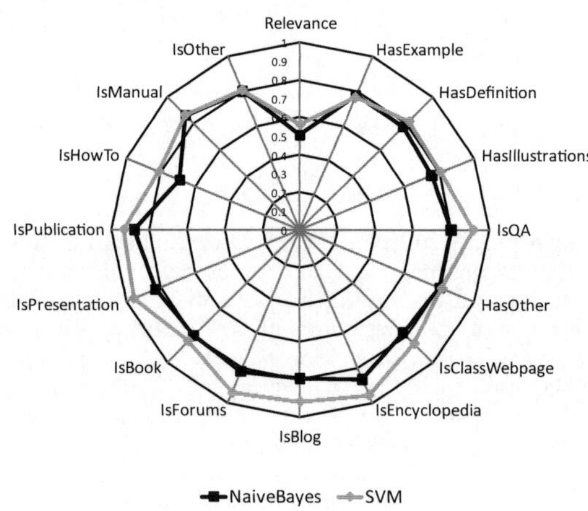

Fig. 2: *Classification results for user-features*

Finally, we answer the fourth question by running an experiment where the automatically predicted user-features are used as input to a classifier to annotate the educativeness of a document. The results obtained in this experiment are shown in Table 3, under the rows labeled "user-features (predicted)." The performance obtained by this classifier shows slight advantage (1-5% absolute increase in F-measure) over the one obtained by using the raw content alone. This indicates that a prediction of high accuracy might help in closing the gap with the upper-bound obtained with the manually annotated user-features. This result can be the basis for future improvements, by seeking improvements in the classification of the individual features prediction (e.g., by using syntactic or semantic features in addition to lexical features).

6 Discussion

Based on our experiments, we found that the educativeness of a document is a property that can be automatically identified. Not surprisingly, the classification with respect to a set of coarse-grained classes is significantly higher than the fine-grained classification. In terms of features, the raw content of a document was found useful, as were other properties associated with a document (referred to as "user-features").

To evaluate how each of the user-features contribute to the accuracy of the classification, we measured the information gain associated with each feature based on the manual annotations. Figure 3 shows the feature weights. Not surprisingly, the content categories (e.g., HasDefinition, HasExample, HasIllustration) score the highest, indicating their significant discriminative power. Interestingly, the Relevance feature has a higher discriminative power than the Rank feature, which indicates that the relevance of a document might be a good feature to consider when modeling its educativeness. Other intuitive features such as resource types (e.g., IsHowTo, IsPresentation) seem to also contribute to the classification. Note however that the degree of their contribution might be affected by the implicit dependency on content categories (e.g., pages classified as IsEncyclopedia often include definitions, which also activate the HasDefinition feature).

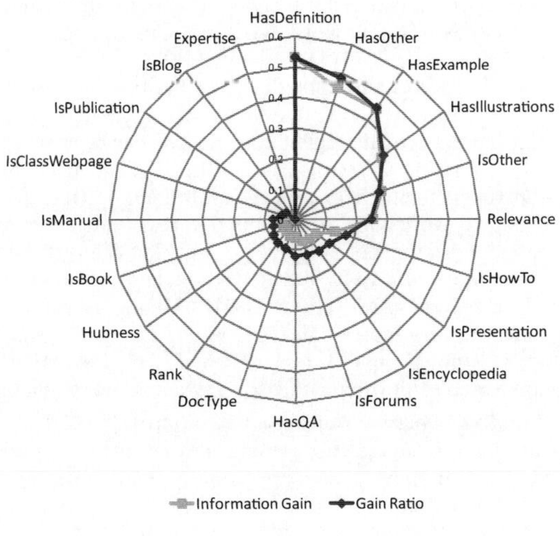

Fig. 3: *Information gain for user-features*

7 Conclusion

In this paper, we addressed the task of automatically identifying learning materials. We constructed a data set by manually annotating the educativeness of the documents retrieved for fourteen topics in computer science. An annotation experiment carried out on this data set showed that the educativeness of a document is a property that can be reliably assigned by human judges. Moreover, through a number of classification experiments, we showed that the educativeness property can also be automatically assigned, with up to 23% absolute increase in F-measure as compared to the most common class baseline.

Through our experiments, we identified several promising lines for future research. First, we plan to explore ways of improving the classification accuracy for the individual user-features, as well as ways of combining them with the features extracted from the content of a document, in order to improve the overall accuracy of the classification of educativeness. Second, we plan to carry out larger-scale experiments to explore the portability across different domains.

The data set introduced in the paper can be downloaded from http://lit.csci.unt.edu/index.php/Downloads

Acknowledgments

The authors are grateful to Carmen Banea and Ravi Sinha for their help with the data annotations.

References

[1] J. Greenberg. Metadata extraction and harvesting. *Journal of Library Metadata*, 6(4):59–82, 2004.

[2] W. Hodgins and E. Duval. Draft standard for learning technology - learning object metadata - iso/iec 11404. Technical report, 2002.

[3] J. Karlgren. The wheres and whyfores for studying textual genre computationally. In *In Proceedings of the AAAI Fall Symposium of Style and Meaning in Language, Art and Music.*, Washington D.C., 2004.

[4] Marek. Categorizing learning objects based on wikipedia as substitute corpus.

[5] A. McCallum and K. Nigam. A comparison of event models for Naive Bayes text classification. In *Proceedings of AAAI Workshop on Learning for Text Categorization*, 1998.

[6] F. Neven and E. Duval. Reusable learning objects: a survey of LOM-based repositories. In *Proceedings of the ACM International Conference on Multimedia*, France, 2002.

[7] L. T. E. Pansanato and R. P. M. Fortes. Strategies for automatic lom metadata generating in a web-based cscl tool. In *WebMedia '05: Proceedings of the 11th Brazilian Symposium on Multimedia and the web*, pages 1–8, New York, NY, USA, 2005. ACM.

[8] S. Smith Nash. Learning objects, learning object repositories and learning theory: Preliminary best practices for online courses. *Interdisciplinary Journal of Knowledge and Learning Objects*, 1, 2005.

[9] C. Thompson, J. Smarr, H. Nguyen, and C. Manning. Finding educational resources on the web: Exploiting automatic extraction of metadata. In *ECML Workshop on Adaptive Text Extraction and Mining*, 2003.

[10] V. Vapnik. *The Nature of Statistical Learning Theory.* Springer, New York, 1995.

[11] E. Westerhout and P. Monachesi. Creating glossaries using pattern-based and machine learning techniques. In *Proceedings of the Sixth International Language Resources and Evaluation*, Marrakech, Morocco, 2008.

[12] D. Wiley. *Learning Object Design and Sequencing Theory.* PhD thesis, Department of Instructional Psychology and Technology Brigham Young University., 2000.

Lexicalized Semi-Incremental Dependency Parsing

Hany Hassan
Cairo TDC
IBM
Cairo, Egypt
hanyh@eg.ibm.com

Khalil Sima'an
Language and Computation
University of Amsterdam
Amsterdam, The Netherlands
k.simaan@uva.nl

Andy Way
School of Computing
Dublin City University
Dublin, Ireland
away@computing.dcu.ie

Abstract

Even leaving aside concerns of cognitive plausibility, incremental parsing is appealing for applications such as speech recognition and machine translation because it could allow the incorporation of syntactic features into the decoding process without blowing up the search space. Nevertheless, incremental parsing is often associated with greedy parsing decisions and intolerable loss of accuracy. Would the use of lexicalized grammars provide a new perspective on incremental parsing?

In this paper we explore incremental left-to-right dependency parsing using a lexicalized grammatical formalism that works with lexical categories (supertags) and a small set of combinatory operators. A strictly incremental parser would conduct only a single pass over the input, use no lookahead and make only local decisions at every word. We show that such a parser suffers heavy loss of accuracy. Instead, we explore the utility of a two-pass approach that incrementally builds a dependency structure by first assigning a supertag to every input word and then selecting an incremental operator that allows assembling every supertag with the dependency structure built thus far to its left. We instantiate this idea in different models that allow a trade-off between aspects of full incrementality and performance, and explore the differences between these models empirically. Our exploration shows that a semi-incremental (two-pass), linear-time parser that employs fixed and limited look-ahead exhibits an appealing balance between the efficiency advantages of incrementality and the achieved accuracy. Surprisingly, taking local or global decisions matters very little for the accuracy of this linear-time parser. Such a parser fits seamlessly with the currently dominant finite-state decoders for machine translation.

1 Introduction

As it processes an input sentence word-by-word in some order (e.g., left-to-right for a language like English), an *incremental* parser builds for each prefix of the input sentence a partial parse that is a subgraph of the partial parse that it builds for a longer prefix. An incremental parser may have access only to a fixed, limited window of lookahead words. The lookahead is equivalent to buffering a number of words before processing them; as stated by [Marcus et. al., 1983], a deterministic parser can buffer and examine a small number of words before adding them to the existing structure. A parser might also make multiple incremental passes over the input sentence where decisions made in an earlier pass are refined in a subsequent pass. In this paper we refer to an incremental, left-to-right parser without lookahead information taking a single pass over the input as a *fully incremental parser*. We refer to an incremental left-to-right parser with limited lookahead capability as a *weakly* incremental parser. And when the incremental parser makes two passes over the input, we refer to it by the term *semi-incremental*.

Besides being cognitively plausible, an incremental parser is more appealing for applications if its time and space (worst-case) complexities are close to linear in input length. For example, an incremental, linear-time parser should constitute a natural match for the word-by-word decoding and pruning schemes used within phrase-based statistical machine translation (PB-SMT) and speech recognition. It is worth noting that fully incremental parsers are cognitively plausible [Marslen-Wilson, 1973, Sturt & Lombardo, 2004], while weakly incremental parsers can serve well for syntax-based language modeling where a local context of the word is usually provided for scoring.

The degree of possible incrementality in parsing depends largely on the syntactic formalism underpinning the parsing process. In this work, we adopt Combinatory Categorial Grammar (CCG) [Steedman, 2000], which would appear to represent an appealing grammatical representation for incremental parsing due to two main reasons. Firstly, as highlighted in [Steedman, 2000], CCG can represent every leftmost string as a constituent even if it is not a syntactic constituent. This enables any left branching (left-to-right) parser to work fully incrementally. Secondly, a fully incremental dependency parser is only possible if the leftmost graph is fully connected at each parse state, which was highlighted in [Nivre, 2004]. This is especially possible with grammars like CCG where the type raising and compositional capabilities can be utilized to keep the graph connected even when not resolving a dependency relation.

In this paper we present a new approach to linear-time, semi-incremental CCG parsing and explore the trade-off between the degree of incrementality and parse accuracy. On the one hand, it turns out to be not so easy to obtain a fully incremental parser that maintains the same level of accuracy as a parser that explores the full parse-forest without worries about incrementality or linear-time processing. On the other hand, we show that reasonable levels of accuracy can be achieved when the requirements of incrementality are somewhat relaxed: allowing a two-pass classification approach (a supertagger followed by an operator tagger) and a limited use of look-ahead. Furthermore, when allowing for global search (as opposed to local classification) during both supertagging and operator-

International Conference RANLP 2009 - Borovets, Bulgaria, pages 128–134

tagging (thereby sacrificing a major aspect of incrementality), small improvements in accuracy can be obtained. The best performing models would fit seamlessly with linear-time, finite state decoders used in MT and speech recognition because they predict a single partial parse at every word position in the input.

The structure of this paper is as follows. In section 2, we discuss related work on incremental parsing, and introduce our model of incremental CCG parsing in section 3. We then detail our method for transforming the canonical derivations in the CCGbank into left-to-right, incremental derivations (section 4). Given this incremental version of the CCGbank, we study in section 5 a range of linear-time parsing models, with varying degrees of incrementality, and provide the results of a number of experiments in section 6. We discuss our findings, and offer some conclusions and avenues for further research in section 7.

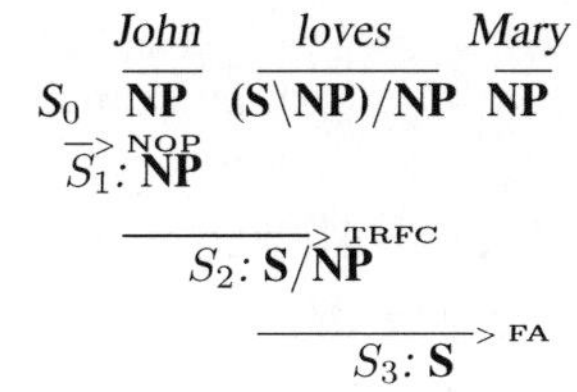

Fig. 1: *A sentence and possible supertag-, operator- and state-sequences. NOP: No Operation; TRFC: Type Raising follwed by Forward Composition.*

2 Related Work

While there exist numerous recent efforts at (deterministic) incremental (shallow) dependency parsing (e.g. [Nivre, 2004, Shen & Joshi, 2005]), most current constituency parsers are hard to classify as incremental. State-of-the-art parsers (e.g. [Collins, 1999, Charniak, 2000]) select the Viterbi parse only when the parse-space has been spanned for the whole sentence; the Viterbi parse may change as the prefix grows, violating incrementality. In contrast, partial parsers such as [Abney, 1991] by default do not output a full sequence of connected phrases, which causes the constraint of incrementality to fail for a quite different reason.

Among the many attempts at efficient (often deterministic) and incremental (dependency) parsing, we concentrate on the quite small number of research papers which are most similar to our work [Yamada & Matsumoto, 2003, Nivre, 2004, Shen & Joshi, 2005, Sagae & Lavie, 2006]. [Nivre, 2004] suggests that deterministic dependency parsing (e.g. [Yamada & Matsumoto, 2003]) is a halfway house between full and partial parsing, in that the building of a full parse of the input string is the aim, whilst at the same time remaining robust, efficient and deterministic. [Nivre, 2004] then describes his own approach to incremental deterministic dependency parsing. While strict incrementality was not possible using his framework, as far as well-formed utterances are concerned, the degree of incrementality achievable approaches 90%. In a similar manner, [Sagae & Lavie, 2006] introduce a statistical shift-reduce parser that uses a probabilistic framework to determine the shift/reduce actions. Multiple possible parse decisions are handled by a beam strategy.

[Shen & Joshi, 2005] use the term 'semi-incremental' to refer to parsers (both left-corner [Collins & Roark, 2004] and head-corner [Yamada & Matsumoto, 2003]) which permit multiple iterations of left-to-right scans, rather than just one. In contrast to these models, [Shen & Joshi, 2005] introduce an approach for incremental parsing of spinal Lexicalized Tree Adjoining Grammar, which supports full adjunction, a dynamic treatment of coordination, as well as non-projective dependencies. This can be seen as an incremental version of Supertagging [Bangalore & Joshi, 1999].

Incremental dependency parsing of Categorial Grammar was attempted in [Milward, 1995] using a state-transition (or dynamic) processing model, where each state consists of a syntactic type together with an associated semantic value. The model of incremental parsing for CCG that we propose here is largely inspired by ideas presented in the latter two papers.

3 Semi-Incremental CCG Parsing

As it processes the sentence left-to-right, word-by-word, our parser specifies for every word a supertag and a combinatory operator, and maintains a parse-state (henceforth 'state'). Each state is represented by a composite CCG category. Apart from the first word in the sentence, this composite CCG category is the result of applying the combinatory operator to the preceding state and current supertag; at the first word in the sentence, the state consists solely of the supertag of that word. In terms of CCG representations, a CCG composite category specifies a functor and the arguments that are expected to the right of the current word. Crucially, given a sentence and its state sequence, the dependency structure can be retrieved unambiguously. At each state the partial dependency structure can be represented as a directed graph with nodes representing words and arcs representing dependency relations. Figure 1 illustrates the workings of this incremental parser, where the sequence of supertags is shown, then the operators that apply from left-to-right in order to build the state sequence incrementaly.

From the description above it is conceptually appealing to describe our parser in two parts: (i) a Supertag-Operator Tagger which proposes a supertag–operator pair for the current word, and (ii) a State-Realizer, which realizes the current state by applying the current operator to the previous state and the current supertag. In this work, the State-Realizer is a deterministic function, whereas the supertag-operator tagger is a statistical one trained on our own incremental version of the CCGbank. While this conceptual view describes a baseline, fully incremental version, in what follows we will consider refinements that trade off some aspects of incrementality for accuracy (i) by employing lookahead in predicting supertag–operator pairs, (ii) by predicting the supertag and using that for predicting the operator (a cascade of per-word classifiers possibly with lookahead), and (iii) by using a two-pass, semi-incremental approach where supertags and operators are chosen globally using Viterbi decoding (rather than per-word by means of classifiers). All these versions remain linear-time and space (worst-case complexity).

To train the statistical components, we transform the CCGbank normal form derivations into strictly left-to-right derivations, with operators specifically chosen to allow incrementality while satisfying the dependencies in the CCGbank. In the next section we present our transformation technique developed to obtain the appropriate training data.

4 Transforming the CCGbank into left-to-right derivations

The goal of the transformation is to obtain training data for our incremental parsing approach. The result of the transform is an incremental CCGbank where sentences are annotated with supertags as well as combinatory operators that allow left-to-right, incremental building of a parse while satisfying the dependencies specified in the CCGbank.

For each sentence in the CCGbank, we apply the following procedure:

- Initialize empty operator sequence and empty unsatisfied dependencies;
- For each word:
    1. Add current dependencies to unsatisfied dependencies.
    2. Check unsatisfied dependencies:
        (a) If adjacent dependency with simple categories, assign *application* operators;
        (b) If adjacent dependency with complex categories, assign *composition* operators;
        (c) If long-range dependency, apply *Type Raising* followed by *Forward Composition*.
    3. Handle special cases if any:
        (a) Coordination (section 4.1),
        (b) Apposition & Interruptions (section 4.2),
        (c) WH-movement (section 4.3),
    4. Update Current state;
    5. Assign selected operator to the operator sequence;
    6. Update the dependencies by removing satisfied dependencies.

This procedure deploys the dependencies available in the CCGbank in order to assign the simplest possible operator sequence that is able to satisfy, and reproduce, the dependency structure of the sentence under investigation.

Figure 2 illustrates the transformation process, step-by-step, on a sentence of the CCGbank. At the beginning of the process, we start with the words, the associated supertags and the dependency relations, indicated by curved dotted arrows in the figure. The purpose of the transformation process is to induce the state sequence and the operator sequence. These sequences should be able to reproduce the given dependency relations.

The transformation process proceeds word-by-word, and at each word position we check all previous and current unsatisfied dependencies. The transformation proceeds as follows:

1. State *S1* being an initial state, it is associated with operator *NOP*.
2. Moving to State *S2*, there is a dependency between the previous word *Mr.* and the current word *Warren*. As this dependency relation is adjacent and in the forward direction, the *FA* operator is associated and so the state is transferred to *S2* with category *NP*.
3. Moving to State *S3* is triggered by the word *will*, which has both backward and forward dependencies. Thus the operator *TRFC* is applied.
4. Moving to State *S4* is triggered by the word *remain*, which being linked with the word *will* by a forward dependency relation, causes the *FC* operator to be assigned. The state becomes *(S/PP)*, indicating that a prepositional phrase is required to the right.
5. Moving to State *S5* is triggered by the word *on* which is linked to the previous verb *remain*, and so the *FC* operator is assigned.
6. Moving to State *S6* is triggered by the word *the*, which has neither backward nor forward dependencies; however, it is linked through a chain of dependencies with a future word *board*. Thus we apply the composite *TRFC* operator to type raise the current word to the required dependency category and then perform forward composition.
7. Moving to State *S7* is triggered by the word *company*, which has a forward dependency with the previous position, and so the *FA* operator is applied.
8. Moving to State *S8* is triggered by the word *'s* which has adjacent forward and backward dependencies, so the *FC* operator is applied. This changes the state to *(S/NP)*.
9. Finally, state *S9* is triggered by the word *board*. The *FA* operator is finally applied to construct the complete category *S*.

This detailed illustration shows how the CCGbank is transformed. We started with a supertag sequence and a dependency graph, and ended with the corresponding operator and state sequences. However, the same procedure applies during parsing, i.e. if we have the supertag and the operator sequences, then we are able to construct both the incremental states and the dependency graph. As an indication of the performance of our transformation process, on section 00 of the WSJ—our dev data (see section 6)—we managed to successfully extract 97% of the CCGbank dependencies, with the incremental approach failing to restore just 3% of the dependencies. This defines the upper bound of the accuracy expected from this incremental representation.

In the next three sections we describe the special operators we added for cases of coordination, apposition and interruptions, and WH-movement.

4.1 Coordination

Cognitive studies [Sturt & Lombardo, 2004] view coordination as an incremental operation. Unfortunately, the CCGbank uses a simple category *conj* for coordination instead of the more elaborate category $(X\backslash X)/X$, which was originally defined for coordination in CCG [Steedman, 2000]. The atomic *conj* operator is not efficient for incremental parsing, because it does not provide information on the coordinated elements. Therefore, we use the dependency information to assign more elaborate coordination categories. For example, if coordination is performed between two noun phrases, the appropriate category is $(NP\backslash NP)/NP$. Furthermore, we added a new coordination operator (*COORD*) to handle coordination in the state-realizer. When such a conjunction is encountered, the

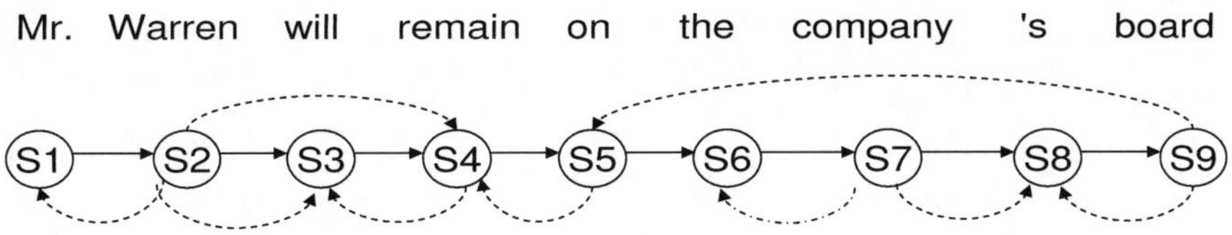

Supertag	NP/NP	NP	(S\NP)/(S\NP)	(S\NP)/PP	PP/NP	NP/NP	NP	(NP/NP)\NP	NP
Operator	NOP	FA	TRFC	FC	FC	TRFC	FA	FC	FA
State Cat.	NP/NP	NP	S/(S\NP)	(S/PP)	(S/NP)	(S/(NP\NP))/NP	(S/(NP\NP))	(S/NP)	S

Fig. 2: *Illustration of the CCGbank transformation process into incremental derivations.*

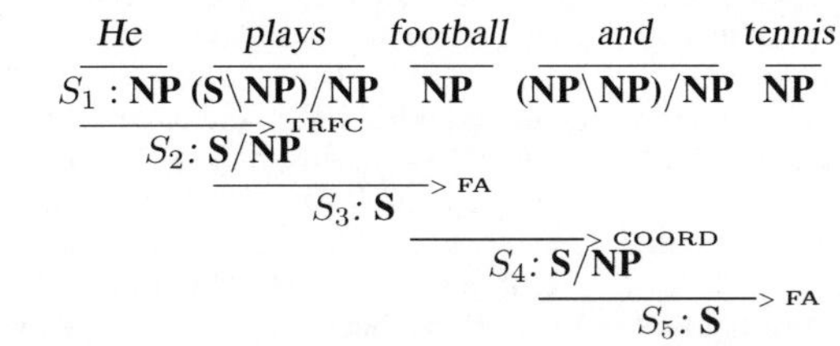

Fig. 3: *Coordination Handling.*

nearest previous state that is able to satisfy the coordination is retrieved from the state stack to become the current state.[1]

The example shown in Figure 3 illustrates the handling of coordination. At the transition from *S3* to *S4* a coordination operator *COORD* is encountered, which causes the current state *S4* to 'go back' to state *S2* with structure *S/NP*, i.e. expecting an *NP* to the right.

4.2 Apposition and Interruptions

Neither the CCGbank nor the WSJ treebank distinguish between the appositive and coordination commas [Hockenmaier & Steedman, 2007]. The comma mostly has a single supertag in the CCGbank that does not indicate its actual role in the syntactic structure of the sentence at hand. We adopted the syntactic patterns in [Bayraktar et al., 1998] as a means of identifying the comma's different possible syntactic categories. Based on these syntactic patterns, we enriched the supertags associated with the comma to indicate the correct syntactic role. Furthermore, we added a new operator INTR for handling cases of both apposition and interruptions.

4.3 WH-movement

A new operator is added to handle cases of WH-movement where a syntactic category is required on the right but, having moved, is available only on the left. Consider the sentence *He believes in what he plays.* Here *plays* is of category (S\NP)/NP, i.e. it is a transitive verb, where if it finds an object NP to its right, and a subject NP to its left, a sentence will have been formed. The NP *what* is expected as the object somewhere to the right of *plays*, but has already moved to an appropriate position somewhere to its left. Accordingly, we added a new operator WHMV to handle such cases in our framework.

[1] This retrieval action of a previous state remains incremental because the previous state sequence is not altered, and the retrieved state is always an extension of the last state (it always adds arguments to a given category rather than changing it to a different one).

5 Implementation Detail

After POS tagging, the parser works its way through the sentence, left-to-right, assigning for every word a supertag–operator pair, and deciding on a state using the deterministic state-realizer. We describe the state-realizer before delving into the implementation of different versions of the supertag-operator tagger.

Parse-State Realizer After assigning supertag–operator pairs for the words of the input sentence (described in the next section), the *state-realizer* deterministically realizes the parse-states as well as the intermediate dependency graphs between words using the CCG incremental operators (as defined in our incremental version of the CCGbank). Starting at the first word with (obviously) a null previous state, the realizer performs the following steps for each word in turn: (i) set the current supertag and operator to those of the current word; (ii) at the current state apply the current operator to the previous state and current supertag; (iii) add edges to the dependency graphs between words that are linked as CCG arguments; and (iv) if not at the end of the sentence, set the previous state to the current one, then set the current word to the next one, and iterate from (i).

Figure 4 illustrates the realizer operation along with the incrementally constructed partial dependency graphs at each state. At the initial state S_0, the *NOP* Operator is applied to the previous state, a Null state, and the current supertag *NP*; the resulting state is S_1 with category *NP* and the resulting dependency graph is simply the node representing the first word *John*. The transition to the next state S_2 is triggered by the verb *likes*, where the *TRFC* operator is applied to the previous state and the current supertag, resulting in a new state *S/NP*. The dependency graph associated with state S_2 shows the realized dependency between *likes* and *John* which has resulted from the previous operation. Finally the last word triggers the final state, and the realizer is able to construct the full dependency graph which is associated with the last state S_3.

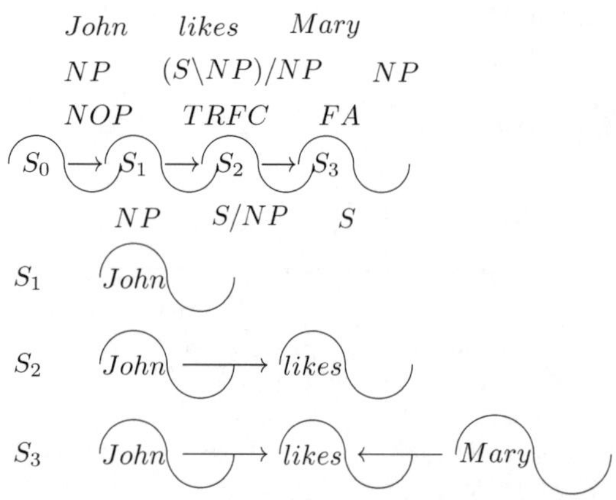

Fig. 4: *Illustration of the operation of the incremental parse-state realizer and the associated intermediate dependency graphs at each state.*

Maximum Entropy Taggers We build different linear-time models for assigning supertag–operator pairs to words in order to explore the effect of the different gradations of incrementality on parsing accuracy. All models present in this paper are based on MaxEnt classifiers [Berger et al., 1996]. A MaxEnt classifier selects the class that gives the highest conditional probability of any class given a set of features of the input, where the probability is expressed as a log-linear interpolation of weights of features. The weights are trained in order to maximize the likelihood of the given training data. In this work we use sequential conditional generalized iterative scaling [Goodman, 2002].

In building classifiers for sequence-tagging, as in the present case, choices arise regarding the search strategy as well as regarding the use of lookahead features:

- *Search (GLOBAL/LOCAL):* A MaxEnt model can be used for sequence classification, either as a classifier (LOCAL) or by converting the classification scores into probabilities and then using standard dynamic programming (Viterbi search, GLOBAL). Naturally, per-word (left-to-right) LOCAL classifiers facilitate a more incremental parser than GLOBAL classifiers; in the latter case, the state-realizer has to wait till the end of the sentence before it can realize the states.
- *Lookahead: (Y-LH/N-LH):* For training the classifiers, lookahead features could either be included (Y-LH) or not (N-LH). When lookahead is used, it refers to the lexical and POS features from a window of two words two words to the right of the focus word. Note that those features to the left are always included in all models as history.

Crucially, the choice for a global search procedure is orthogonal to using a lookahead. This is because in a global search the disambiguation weights are the accumulation (assuming independence given the overlapping features) of the weights of local classification decisions (per word) for the whole input sentence, whereas the lookahead affects the features used to estimate the local weights themselves. Hence, when assuming independence (multiplying) between the local decisions, global search cannot substitute for the use of lookahead.

Furthermore, given any choice of search strategy and lookahead, there are two different architectures for assigning supertag–operator pairs to words:

- *Joint:* We train a MaxEnt module to assign supertag–operator pairs (as a single class) to words.
- *Cascaded:* We train two MaxEnt modules, one for supertags, and one for operators, and use them in a cascade. We limit the options here such that both classifiers (supertag and operator) either use lookahead or not, i.e. we do not explore a mixed situation where one does and the other does not. For the version that does use lookahead, while the supertagger is trained using the standard feature set, the operator tagger is trained with the same window but with POS and supertag features coming from the supertagger (no lexical features).

As a baseline we start out from the Joint classifier, without lookahead (N-LH) and with LOCAL search. We choose this as a baseline as it is the most straightforward implementation of an incremental, linear-time CCG parser without making any extra assumptions. The Cascaded architecture with LOCAL search and without lookahead (N-LH) might be seen as incremental but it embodies an extra set of independence assumptions (i.e. different choices of features for supertag and operator classifiers). Similarly, any model using look-ahead and LOCAL search is slightly less incremental since it employs still more resources than the preceding models. If we move one further step away from full to semi-incremental parsing, we arrive at models which employ GLOBAL search (since the supertag–operator sequences are assigned only after the whole sentence has been processed).

6 Experiments and Results

This section details a number of experiments carried out to test the effectiveness of the supertagger, the operator tagger, and our ability to capture the necessary dependencies using a range of incremental parsers. We used the same data split of the WSJ as in [Clark & Curran, 2007]. Sections 02–21 were used for training, section 00 for devtesting of intermediate taggers, and section 23 for testing dependencies.

6.1 Supertagging Results

Given our introduction of new supertags for coordination, apposition, interruption, and WH-movement, we used section 00 to evaluate our supertagger's accuracy compared to the standard CCGbank set. Although our supertags are more complex, we obtain an F-score of 91.7 (cf. Table 1, last row, 'Supertagging' column), which compares favourably with the supertagger of [Clark & Curran, 2007], which scores 92.39 on the same dataset. While we have not carried out significance testing at this stage, it is clear that there is little difference between the two sets of scores, indicating that our supertagger is robust as well as accurate. As will be seen for all experiments in this section, this is only true when lookahead is utilised; note that our best score of 91.7 dips to 68.62—an absolute drop of 23.08 points, or a 33.6% relative decrease in performance—when lookahead is turned off.

6.2 Operator Tagging Results

In Table 1 we also present the results for our Operator tagger. This displays a very high accuracy (90.9%, cf. last

Architecture	Lookahead	Search	Dependency Accuracy	Supertagging Accuracy	Operator Tagging Accuracy	Incremental
Joint	NO	LOCAL	56.02	67.47		Incr.
	NO	GLOBAL	56.13	68.31		Semi
	YES	LOCAL	82.17	84.34		Incr.+LH
	YES	GLOBAL	83.20	85.02		Semi+LH
Cascaded	NO	LOCAL	59.01	68.11	76.19	Incr.
	NO	GLOBAL	59.30	68.62	76.53	Semi
	YES	LOCAL	86.31	91.62	90.76	Incr.+LH
	YES	GLOBAL	86.70	91.70	90.90	Semi+LH

Table 1: *All results (F-Score) of systems applied to input with POS tags output by POS tagger trained using Maxent with feature window (+/-2) on the CCGbank POS data. The results with no lookahead use only left window features.*

row, 'Operator Tagging' column) even when no lexical features are used. We also contemplated a hypothetical situation in which we feed the correct (gold standard) previous syntactic state as a feature to the system. In this scenario an operator tagging score of 99.22% (8.32% absolute improvement, or 9.15% relative) was obtained, indicating that a high gain is to be expected if this state were to be made available to the operators classifier.

6.3 Dependency Results

In Table 1 we also present the results for unlabeled dependency accuracy using our method. We use the same evaluation criteria as [Clark & Curran, 2007] by comparing the dependency output of the incremental parser with the predicate-argument dependencies in the CCGbank. Testing on section 23 of the WSJ, we obtain an F-score of 86.7 (last row, 'Dependency' column). The score with the gold standard POS and supertags in the input is 87.5, 0.8% absolute (or 0.92% relative) higher than the result when using the POS, supertags and operators hypothesized by the system, but not by much. While this result is considerably below the best known result for a non-incremental, bottom-up chart parser [Clark & Curran, 2007]), we think that our result is reasonably good for an extremely efficient, semi-incremental parser. To put the efficiency gains in perspective, the parsers of [Collins, 1999], [Charniak, 2000] and [Clark & Curran, 2007] take respectively 45, 28 and 1.9 mins to parse section 23 of the WSJ. By contrast, our parser takes only 11 seconds, a speed-up of around ten times relative to the fastest among these parsers [Clark & Curran, 2007] (parsing times are measured on a machine with the same specifications).

6.4 Cascaded vs. Joint Approach

The results reported above demonstrate the accuracy of the cascaded approach using two cascaded taggers: the first for supertags, and the second the operator tagger followed by the deterministic state- realizer. In this section we compare the cascaded model with a joint model, where we train a single classifier that produces the supertags and operators simultaneously in the same step. In Table 1 we give the unlabeled dependency results for section 23 for the cascaded and joint models side-by-side for comparative purposes. The cascaded model significantly outperforms the joint model (by 3.5% absolute, or 4.2% relative; this rises to 4.3% absolute, or 5.17% relative, if we compare the joint model with the dependency score using the gold standard POS and supertags, as described in the previous section). Besides data sparseness, the joint model makes the choice of an operator at a certain position in the sentence based on supertag information only to the left of the current position because the joint model must guess supertag–operator pairs at once.

Note that our Cascaded version with lookahead and GLOBAL search is the semi-incremental model of [Shen & Joshi, 2005]. They report an F-score of 89.3 on section 23 using a semi-incremental approach. While not directly comparable, we consider our performance to be on a par with theirs, with a considerable improvement in parsing time (they report a speed of 0.37 sent./sec.).

6.5 Effect of Lookahead

The present parser is just two words of lookahead away from being fully incremental. Here, we examine the effect of lookahead features on the supertagger, operator tagger and dependency results. We examine two versions of a supertag- and operator-classifier, namely a weakly incremental and a fully incremental version. The weakly incremental version deploys features in a window of two words to the left and two words to the right of the focus word. The fully incremental parser deploys features in a window of two words to the left only.

Looking at all the results in Table 1, the scores for the weakly (semi-)incremental versions of the parser barely differ from their fully incremental counterparts, whether we are concerned with dependency, supertagging or operator accuracy; the scores are higher, on the whole, but not by much.

By contrast, what is *extremely* significant is the extent to which lookahead is utilised. For all accuracy measures—dependency, supertagging or operator—huge improvements are to be seen when the parser avails of lookahead. Clearly, full incrementality at this stage comes at a high cost in accuracy, relative to the weakly incremental version, without any benefit in efficiency.

7 Conclusions and Future work

In this paper we introduced a novel, simple approach for wide-coverage CCG analysis using a weakly incremental parser. In addition to the standard CCG operators, we added extensions to efficiently handle coordination, apposition and interruptions, and WH-movement. Our supertagger achieves results comparable with the state-of-the-art for CCG [Clark & Curran, 2004]. Moreover, the operator tagger, even without lexical features, performs well on our extended operator set.

Our empirical results show three main findings. Firstly, despite being just two words of lookahead away from being fully incremental, our proposed cascaded weakly incremental parser outperforms both the joint and fully incremental approaches. Nevertheless, there is perhaps less of a performance difference between the joint and cascaded architectures on the one hand, and between global search or local classification on the other. The fact that the local search performs almost as well as global search for this model implies that at least the local search could be easily integrated within speech-recognition or machine translation decoders.

Secondly, with respect to dependency parsing, while our overall result is below the result reported in [Clark & Curran, 2007] using a non-incremental bottom-up parser, it is far more efficient being (weakly) incremental. This speedup is, we feel, particularly attractive for applications that incorporate in the decoder a word-prediction (or language) model, since this semi-incremental parser works in a fashion similar to such language models, i.e. the possible states are built on-the-fly from the training data, just like any other non-parametric method.

Thirdly, our results, using a state-of-the-art classifier, highlight the fact that incremental parsing using CCG is attainable at some tolerable cost in accuracy. Perhaps most importantly, incremental parsing for CCG as suggested here gives acceptable levels of accuracy only when lookahead is used. Nevertheless, since our approach to parsing is left-to-right and makes decisions at every word in the input, one might actually question the effectiveness of taking decisions at every word. It might turn out, for example, that when the decision points are selected carefully, the need for lookahead can be less crucial. This conjecture is left for the future.

As for other avenues of future research, work on an improved, fully incremental version is ongoing as well as an investigation of the effect of incremental parsing in machine translation.

References

[Abney, 1991] Abney, S. 1991. Parsing By Chunks. In R. Berwick, S. Abney and C. Tenny (eds.) *Principle-Based Parsing*. Kluwer, Dordrecht, pp.257–278.

[Bangalore & Joshi, 1999] Bangalore, S. and A. Joshi. 1999. Supertagging: An Approach to Almost Parsing. *Computational Linguistics* **25**(2):237–265.

[Bayraktar et al., 1998] Bayraktar, M., B. Say and V. Akman. 1998. An Analysis of English punctuation: The Special Case of Comma. *International Journal of Corpus Linguistics* **3**(1):33–58, .

[Berger et al., 1996] Berger, A., V. Della Pietra, and S. Della Pietra. 1996. A maximum entropy approach to natural language processing. *Computational Linguistics* **22**(1):39–71.

[Charniak, 2000] Charniak, E. 2000. A Maximum-Entropy-Inspired Parser. In *1st Annual Meeting of the North American Association for Computational Linguistics, Proceedings (NAACL 2000)*, Seattle, WA., pp.132–139.

[Clark & Curran, 2004] Clark, S. and J. Curran. 2004. The Importance of Supertagging for Wide-Coverage CCG Parsing. In *Proceedings of the 20th International Conference on Computational Linguistics (COLING'04)*, Geneva, Switzerland, pp.282–288.

[Clark & Curran, 2007] Clark, S. and J. Curran. 2007. Wide-Coverage Efficient Statistical Parsing with CCG and Log-Linear Models. *Computational Linguistics* **33**(4):493–552.

[Collins, 1999] Collins, M. 1999. *Head-Driven Statistical Models for Natural Language Parsing*. PhD Thesis, University of Pennsylvania, Philadelphia, PA.

[Collins & Roark, 2004] Collins, M. and B. Roark. 2004. Incremental Parsing with the Perceptron Algorithm. In *42nd Annual Meeting of the Association for Computational Linguistics (ACL-04)*, Barcelona, Spain, pp.111-118.

[Doran and Bangalore, 1994] Doran, C. and S. Bangalore. 1994. Bootstrapping a Wide-coverage CCG from FB-LTAG. In *Proceedings of Third International Workshop on Tree-Adjoining Grammars (TAG+3)*, Paris, France [no page numbers].

[Goodman, 2002] Goodman, J. 2002. Sequential Conditional Generalized Iterative Scaling. In *40th Annual Meeting of the Association for Computational Linguistics*, Philadelphia, PA., pp.9–16.

[Hockenmaier & Steedman, 2007] Hockenmaier, J. and M. Steedman. 2007. CCGbank: a corpus of CCG derivations and dependency structures extracted from the Penn Treebank. *Computational Linguistics* **33**(3):355–396.

[Marslen-Wilson, 1973] Marslen-Wilson, W. 1973. Linguistic structure and speech shadowing at very short latencies. *Nature* **244**:522–533.

[Milward, 1995] Milward, D. 1995. Incremental Interpretation of Categorial Grammar. In *Proceedings of 7th Conference of the European Chapter of the Association for Computational Linguistics (EACL-95)*, Dublin, Ireland, pp.119–126.

[Nivre, 2004] Nivre, J. 2004. Incrementality in Deterministic Dependency Parsing. In *Proceedings of the ACL Workshop on Incremental Parsing: Bringing Engineering and Cognition Together*, Barcelona, Spain, pp.50–57.

[Sturt & Lombardo, 2004] Sturt, P. and V. Lombardo. 2004. Processing coordinated structures: Incrementality and connectedness. *Cognitive Science* **29**(2):291–305.

[Sagae & Lavie, 2006] Sagae, K. and A. Lavie. 2006. A best-first probabilistic shift-reduce parser. In *Proceedings of the 21st International Conference on Computational Linguistics and 44th Annual Meeting of the Association for Computational Linguistics–Posters*, Sydney, Australia, pp.691–698.

[Shen & Joshi, 2005] Shen, L. and A. Joshi. 2005. Incremental LTAG Parsing. In *Proceedings of the Conference on Human Language Technology and Empirical Methods in Natural Language Processing (HLT/EMNLP 2005)*, Vancouver, Canada, pp.811–818.

[Steedman, 2000] Steedman, M. 2000. *The Syntactic Process*. MIT Press, Cambridge, MA.

[Yamada & Matsumoto, 2003] Yamada, H. and Y. Matsumoto. 2003. Statistical dependency Analysis with Support Vector Machines. In *Proceedings of 8th International Workshop on Parsing Technologies (IWPT-2003)*, Nancy, France, pp.195–206.

[Marcus et. al., 1983] Mitchell Marcus and Donald Hindle and Margaret Fleck. 1983. D-theory: talking about talking about trees. In *Proceedings of the 21st Annual Meeting on Association for Computational Linguistics (1983)*, Cambridge, Massachusetts, pp.129–136.

Identification of Parallel Text Pairs Using Fingerprints

Martin Hassel †
† DSV, KTH - Stockholm University
Forum 100
164 40 Kista, Sweden
xmartin@dsv.su.se

Hercules Dalianis †‡
‡ Euroling AB, SiteSeeker
Igeldammsgatan 22c
112 49 Stockholm, Sweden
hercules@dsv.su.se

Abstract

When creating dictionaries for use in for example cross-language search engines, one often uses a word alignment system that takes parallel or comparable text pairs as input and produces a word list.

Multilingual web sites may contain parallel texts but these can be difficult to detect. In this article we describe an experiment on automatic identification of parallel text pairs.

We utilize the frequency distribution of word initial letters in order to map a text in one language to a corresponding text in another in the JRC-Acquis corpus (European Council legal texts). Using English and Swedish as language pair, and running a ten-fold random pairing, the algorithm made 87 percent correct matches (baseline-random 50 percent). Attempting to map the correct text among nine randomly chosen false matches and one true yielded a success rate of 68 percent (baseline-random 10 percent).

Keywords

Cross Language Information Retrieval, Identification of Parallel Text, Prefix Frequency Distribution, A-priori Probability.

1. Introduction

Dictionaries are an important part of natural language processing tasks and linguistic work. Domain-specific dictionaries can for example be used in cross-language web and intranet search engines.

Word alignment tools are often used for the creation of bilingual word lists. These tools need parallel corpora to work properly. One source is Internet and the multilingual web sites there. Unfortunately these web sites are often only parallel with regard to web pages.

In [6] and in [2] are described different heuristics to download and identify parallel text. However, these methods are not enough since the downloaded parallel text still can be very noisy.

For example [13] found only 45 percent parallel text pairs on the multilingual parallel web site Hallå Norden (Hello Scandinavia) that was intended to be completely parallel and the parallel pages contained 5 percent non-parallel elements.

Therefore, we found a need to develop and evaluate a new method for identifying parallel and non-parallel texts in corpora covering different language pairs.

2. Related Work

The distinction between a parallel and a comparable corpus is very important and has been discussed in for example [10] and also in [3].

Freely available multilingual resources are often noisy and non-parallel sections need to be removed. Many methods for identifying such sections automatically have been proposed. Maximum entropy (ME) classification is used in [7] in order to improve machine translation performance. From large Chinese, Arabic and English non-parallel newspaper corpora, parallel data was extracted. For this method, a bilingual dictionary and a small amount of parallel data for the ME classifier is needed. By selecting pairs of similar documents from two monolingual corpora, all possible sentence pairs are passed through a word-overlap based filter and then sent to the ME classifier. The authors reported significant improvements over the baseline for Arabic-English and for Chinese-English

In [3] a method for extracting parallel sentences through bootstrapping and Expectation Maximization (EM) learning methods is presented. An iterative bootstrapping framework is presented, based on the idea that documents, even those with a low similarity score, containing one pair of parallel sentences must contain others. In particular, the proposed method works well for corpora with very disparate contents. The approach achieves 65.7 percent accuracy and a 50 percent relative improvement over their baseline.

Latent Semantic Indexing (LSI) has been experimented with in [5] in order to identify parallel sequences in corpora. In this work, the hypothesis that LSI reveals similarities between parallel texts not apparent in non-parallel texts is presented and evaluated. Corpora from digital libraries were used with the language combinations English-French, English-Russian, French-Russian and English-Russian-Italian. Applying correlation coefficient analysis, a threshold of 0.75 was reported to successfully hold as a lower bound for identifying parallel text pairs. Non-parallel text pairs did not, in these experiments, exceed a correlation coefficient value of 0.70.

Unfortunately, most work has been performed on different types of corpora and on different language pairs. Moreover, they have been evaluated differently depending

International Conference RANLP 2009 - Borovets, Bulgaria, pages 135–138

on available resources and the nature of the experiments, which makes them difficult to compare. However, the different approaches show the need for these types of methods.

3. Identifying Parallel Texts in Bilingual Corpora using Fingerprints

When comparing documents for content similarity it is common practice to produce some form of document signatures, or "fingerprints". These fingerprints represent the content in some way, often as a vector of features, which are used as the basis for such comparison. One common method when comparing the likeness of two documents is to utilize the so-called Vector Space model [9]. In this model the documents' fingerprints are represented as feature vectors consisting of the words that occur within the documents, with weights attached to each word denoting its importance for the document. We can, for example, for each feature (in this example, a word) record the number of times it occurs within each document. This gives us what is commonly called a document-by-term matrix where the rows represent the documents in the document collection and the columns each represent a specific term existing in any of the documents (a weight can thus be zero). We can now, somewhat simplified, compare the documents' fingerprints by looking at how many times each feature occurs in each document, taking the cosine angle between the vectors, and pair the two most similar together. One obvious drawback of the basic use of this model is that when comparing texts written in different languages we do not necessarily know which feature in one language corresponds to which feature in another.

Another drawback when building a word vector space representing more than one language is that the vocabulary, i.e. the number of features in the feature vectors, grows alarmingly (this is in many cases already a problem representing just one language [8]). Ways of limiting the vocabulary include using stop-word lists to remove "information poor" features, frequency thresholding and conflation into feature classes (for example lemmatization). In word vector spaces the latter is often accomplished by bringing semantically related words to a common lemma or stem. In the experiments described below conflation was attempted by moving from term frequency classes towards prefix frequency classes, i.e. the leading characters of each token. This way a document's fingerprint effectively is represented by a feature vector containing the frequency of each prefix of a set length *n* occurring in the corpus.

Fingerprinting using prefix frequencies has for example been used in information retrieval for filtering of similar documents written in the same language [11]. We here attempt to utilize this notion in cross-language text alignment.

4. Data sets and experimental setup

In this set of experiments we have used the JRC-Acquis corpus [12]. This corpus consists of European Union law texts, which are domain specific and also very specific in their structure. Many texts are listings of regulations with numerical references to other law texts[1] and named entities (such as countries). We have investigated the language pair Swedish-English, i.e. we used Swedish as a source language attempting to find the corresponding parallel text in English. We have also used only those documents that have a counterpart in both languages, resulting in a total of 20.145 document pairs.

In order to delimit the search space for the practicality of this experiment we have not compared each Swedish source text with each and every English text. Instead we, in one experiment, compare the similarity between a true positive (the corresponding, parallel, English text) and one true negative (a randomly chosen non-parallel English text), letting the algorithm choose the closest match (as defined by the cosine angle between the feature vectors for each text). In another experiment we repeated the setup, but instead of only using one true negative we used nine.

This setup gave us a random chance of picking the true positive of 50 percent in the case of one true positive and one true negative, and 10 percent in the case of one true positive and nine true negatives. In order to rule out any random fluke in the choice of true negative(s) for each true positive both experiments were carried out 10 times, making new random pairings each time. An average was then taken, calculated over these ten runs.

As in [11] we have extracted a-priori probabilities of prefix classes from reference corpora. Since we are dealing with the language pair Swedish-English we have used a Swedish reference corpus, the Swedish Parole corpus [4], and an English ditto, the British National Corpus [1]. The Swedish reference corpus is comprised of roughly 20 million words. In order to have a comparable English reference corpus we have only used the first 20 million words of BNC.

These two corpora can be seen as the expected distribution of the prefix classes for each language, while each text's feature vector then is the deviation to the expected distribution. We would like to find if a deviation from the expected frequency distribution pattern in one language in the pair could possibly reflect a similar deviation in the other. In this set of experiments the feature vector for each text was preprocessed in two ways:

---

[1] Referencing systems do however differ between languages. For example, while some use Hindu-Arabic numerals others use Roman.

Table 1: Swedish source, one true positive and one true negative English target (k=2); one true positive and nine true negatives (k=10). Lower case is abbreviated lc. The precision is calculated over 10 random selections of the non-parallel text(s). Also given is the lowest and the highest result of the ten runs. At k=2 baseline-random is 50 percent and our results indicate up to 87 percent precision; at k=10 baseline-random is 10 percent and our results indicate up to 68 percent precision.

model:	1. Parole / BNC normalization using reference corpora		2. no normalization using reference corpora	
prefix size	mean precision	lowest – highest	mean precision	lowest – highest
k=2, n=1	50 %	0.496 - 0.503	**87 %**	0.865 - 0.872
k=2, n=1, lc	50 %	0.497 - 0.502	86 %	0.852 - 0.858
k=2, n=2	50 %	0.497 - 0.502	80 %	0.794 - 0.799
k=2, n=2, lc	50 %	0.498 - 0.502	76 %	0.756 - 0.762
k=2, n=3	50 %	0.496 - 0.502	76 %	0.759 - 0.769
k=2, n=3, lc	50 %	0.495 - 0.505	75 %	0.747 - 0.753
k=10, n=*1*	10 %	0.097 - 0.102	**68 %**	0.674 - 0.678
k=10, n=*1, lc*	10 %	0.098 - 0.102	65 %	0.646 - 0.655
k=10, n=*2*	10 %	0.099 - 0.104	54 %	0.534 - 0.543
k=10, n=*2, lc*	10 %	0.098 - 0.103	45 %	0.450 - 0.455
k=10, n=*3*	10 %	0.100 - 0.102	50 %	0.497 - 0.504
k=10, n=*3, lc*	10 %	0.097 - 0.102	44 %	0.438 - 0.442

1) Using Parole as reference corpus for the Swedish texts and BNC as reference corpus for the English, by calculating the difference in frequency between the occurrences of a prefix in the reference corpus and in each text. The prefixes in these vectors were then sorted by the frequency in each respective reference corpus. The feature with the highest frequency in the source language thus corresponds to the most frequent feature in the target language, and so on. The comparison of the text's feature vectors is then based on the deviation from the expected and normalized distribution for each language.
2) No normalization using reference corpora. Instead the raw frequencies are compared directly. However, matching of features is still based on the frequency in each language's respective reference corpus, i.e. we still sort the features based on respective feature's frequency in the reference corpus. As stated above, feature vectors were created using the leading n characters of each word occurring in each reference corpus, as well as in any of the 20.145 documents used in the tests.

A fingerprint was constructed for each reference corpus and each document, in both languages, for n=1..3, both using all lower case, (lc), prefixes as well as prefixes maintaining their original capitalization. To be noted here is the fact that the vocabulary size grows at an explosive rate as n grows, especially when the original capitalization is preserved.

5. Results

As can be seen in Table 1 it is far more favorable to compare the raw frequencies of the features in the source and target vectors, rather than comparing the deviation based on the frequency distribution in the reference corpus of the respective languages. This is further supported by the fact that model two stands even stronger, relatively speaking, when pin-pointing the right match out of ten possible target texts.

We can also see that the results are very stable – there is only a slight difference in the precision between the best and the least good run – even though there is little overlap between the 10 randomly generated lists of pairs. The highest number of pairs that one of the lists has in common with any of the other lists is 12 (out of 20.145). When it comes to the lists containing 10 target words this number is nearly non-existent.

One possible answer for the success of the second model could of course be that the source and target texts always are lexically very alike. This could be the case if they to a high degree share the same vocabulary, for instance named entities. This does, however, not seem to be the case if we take a look at Table 2.

The degree of precision and the stability of the results are encouraging. However, for the sake of a fairer comparison one might want to reconsider the baselines used in this experiment as being too naïve.

Table 2: Baselines using only basic features, each tracking the number of occurrences of; baseline1={bytes, tokens, dot, comma, percent, digit, 0, 1, 2, 3, 4, 5, 6, 7, 8, 9}, baseline2={bytes, tokens, dot, comma, percent} and baseline3={tokens, dot, comma}

	k=1		*k*=10	
baseline	mean precision	lowest – highest	mean precision	lowest - highest
1	50 %	0.496 - 0.503	10 %	0.097 - 0.102
2	50 %	0.497 - 0.503	10 %	0.099 - 0.102

6. Conclusions and Future Work

In the experiments described above we have shown that our method for identifying and deleting non-parallel texts from corpora covering different language pairs show great potential. In future experiments we plan to use other language pairs from languages that are not closely related as for examples Swedish and Finnish.

Moreover, further experiments on the identification of parallel text pairs should be carried out on more language pairs, preferably such that contain languages belonging to different language groups. An obvious observation here is that the language pairs should also be tested reversely; that is, if one is to investigate the performance on for instance the language pair Swedish-English, it should also be evaluated on the corresponding pair English-Swedish. Also, the experiments should be re-run on other corpora than the JRC-Acquis corpus in order to discern that we are not just investigating peculiarities of this specific corpus. Yet another point to be taken is that when taking care so that reference corpora are of equal size one should perhaps not simply use the first n words in the larger corpus, but instead do a random sampling of the desired amount of words.

We believe methods such as ours will improve, for instance, automatic bilingual dictionary construction from unstructured corpora and our experiments will be further developed and evaluated along these lines.

7. References

[1] Aston, G. and L. Burnard. (1998). The BNC Handbook: Exploring the British National Corpus with SARA. Edinburgh: Edinburgh University Press.

[2] Chen, J and J-Y Nie. 2000. Parallel Web Text Mining for Cross-Language IR. Proceedings of RIAO-2000: Content-Based Multimedia Information Access, pp 62-77.

[3] Fung, P. and B. Cheung (2004) Mining Very-Non-Parallel Corpora: Parallel Sentence and Lexicon Extraction via Bootstrapping and EM. In Proceedings of Conference on Empirical Methods in Natural Language Processing (EMNLP 2004). Barcelona, Spain 25 – 26 July 2004.

[4] Gellerstam, M., Y. Cederholm and T. Rasmark. (2000) The bank of Swedish. In Proceedings of Second International Conference on Language Resources and Evaluation. LREC-2000, pp. 329–333, Athens, Greece, 2000.

[5] Katsnelson, Y. and C. Nicholas (2001). Identifying Parallel Corpora Using Latent Semantic Indexing. In Proceedings of the Corpus Linguistics 2001 Conference. Lancaster, UK 30 March – 2 April 2001.

[6] Ma, Xiaoyi and M. Y. Liberman. 1999. BITS: A Method for Bilingual Text Search over the Web. In Proceedings of MT Summit VII, September, pp. 538-542.

[7] Munteanu, D. S and D. Marcu, (2005). Improving Machine Translation Performance by Exploiting Non-Parallel Corpora. Computational Linguistics, 31(4), pp. 477-504.

[8] Sahlgren, M. (2005). An Introduction to Random Indexing. In Proceedings of the Methods and Applications of Semantic Indexing Workshop at the 7th International Conference on Terminology and Knowledge Engineering, TKE 2005. Copenhagen, Denmark August 16, 2005.

[9] Salton, G. and M. McGill (1983). Introduction to Modern Information Retrieval. New York, NY: McGraw-Hill.

[10] Somers, H. (2001). Bilingual Parallel Corpora and Language Engineering. In Anglo-Indian Workshop "Language Engineering for South-Asian Languages" (LESAL). Mumbai, India April 2001.

[11] Stein, B. (2005). Fuzzy-Fingerprints for Text-Based Information Retrieval. In Tochtermann, K and Maurer, H., eds. Proceedings of the I-KNOW '05, Graz 5th International Conference on Knowledge Management Journal of Universal Computer Science. Graz, Austria: Know-Center, pp. 572-579.

[12] Steinberger, R., B. Pouliquen, A. Widiger, C. Ignat, T. Erjavec, D. Tufiş, and D. Varga, (2006). The JRC-Acquis: A multilingual aligned parallel corpus with 20+ languages. In Proceedings of the Fifth International Conference on Language Resources and Evaluation, LREC'06. Genoa, Italy 24 – 26 May 2006.

[13] Velupillai, S. and H. Dalianis (2008). Automatic Construction of Domain-specific Dictionaries on Sparse Parallel Corpora in the Nordic Languages. In The proceedings of the 2nd MMIES Workshop: Multi-source, Multilingual Information Extraction and Summarization. Manchester, UK, 23 August 2008.

Stochastic Definite Clause Grammars

Christian Theil Have
Research group PLIS: Programming, Logic and Intelligent Systems
Department of Communication, Business and Information Technologies
Roskilde University, P.O.Box 260, DK-4000 Roskilde, Denmark
cth@ruc.dk

Abstract

This paper introduces Stochastic Definite Clause Grammars, a stochastic variant of the well-known Definite Clause Grammars. The grammar formalism supports parameter learning from annotated or unannotated corpora and provides a mechanism for parse selection by means of statistical inference. Unlike probabilistic context-free grammars, it is a context-sensitive grammar formalism and it has the ability to model cross-serial dependencies in natural language. SDCG also provides some syntax extensions which makes it possible to write more compact grammars and makes it straight-forward to add lexicalization schemes to a grammar.

1 Introduction and background

We describe a stochastic variant of the well-known Definite Clause Grammars [12], which we call *Stochastic Definite Clause Grammars* (SDCG).

Definite Clause Grammars (DCG) is a grammar formalism built on top of Prolog, which was developed by Pereira and Warren [12] and was based the principles from Colmerauers metamorphis grammars [6]. The grammars are expressed as rewrite rules which may include logic variables, like normal Prolog rules. DCG exploit Prologs unification semantics, which assures equality between different instances of the same logic-variable. DCG also allows modeling of cross-serial of dependencies, which is known to be beyond the capability of context-free grammars [4].

In stochastic grammar formalisms such as probabilistic context-free grammars (PCFG), every rewrite rule has an associated probability.

For a particular sentence, a grammar can produce an exponential number of derivations. In parsing, we are usually only interested in *one* derivation which best reflects the intended sentence structure. In stochastic grammars, a statistical inference algorithm can be used to find the most probable derivation, and this is a very successful method for parse disambiguation. This is especially true variants of PCFGs which condition rule expansions on lexical features. Charniak [3] reports that "a vanilla PCFG will get around 75% precision/recall whereas lexicalized models achieve 87-88% precision recall". The reason for the impressive precision/recall of stochastic grammars is that the probabilities governing the likelihood of rule expansions are normally derived from corpora using parameter estimation algorithms. Estimation with complete data, where corpus annotations dictate the derivations, can be done by counting expansions used in the annotations. Estimation with incomplete data can be accomplished using the Expectation-Maximization (EM) algorithm [8].

In stochastic unification grammars, the choice of rules to expand is stochastic and the values assigned to unification variables are determined implicitly by rule selection. This means that in some derivations, instances of the same logic variable may get different values and unification will *fail* as result.

Some of the first attempts to define stochastic unification grammars did not address the issue of how they should be trained. Brew [2] and Eisele [9] tries to address this problem using EM, but their methods have problems handling cases where variables fails to unify. The resulting probability distributions are missing some probability mass and normalization results in non-optimal distributions.

Abney [1] defines a sound theory of unification grammars based on Markov fields and shows how to estimate the parameters of these models using Improved Iterative Scaling (IIS). Abney's proposed solution to the parameter estimation problem depends on sampling and only considers complete data. Riezler[13] describes the Iterative Maximization algorithm which also work for incomplete data. Finally, Cussens [7] provide an EM algorithm for stochastic logic programs which handles incomplete data and is not dependent on sampling.

SDCG is implemented as a compiler that translates a grammar into a program in the PRISM language. PRISM [16, 19, 15] is an extension of Prolog that allows expression of complex statistical models as logic programs. A PRISM program is a usual Prolog program augmented with random variables. PRISM defines a probability distribution over the possible Herbrand models of a program. It includes efficient implementations of algorithms for parameter learning and probabilistic inference. The execution, or sampling, of a PRISM program is a simulation where values for the random variables is selected stochastically, according to the underlying probability distribution. PRISM programs can have constraints, usually in the form of equality between unified logic variables. Stochastic selection of values for such variables may lead to unification failure and resulting failed derivations must be taken into account in parameter estimation. PRISM achieves this using the fgEM algorithm [17, 20, 18], which is an adaptation of Cussen's Failure-Adjusted Maximization algorithm [7]. A central part

International Conference RANLP 2009 - Borovets, Bulgaria, pages 139–143

of Cussens algorithm is the estimation of the number of times rules are used in failed derivations. PRISM estimates failed derivations using a failure program, derived through a program transformation called First Order Compilation (FOC) [14].

2 Stochastic Definite Clause Grammars

Stochastic Definite Clause Grammars is a stochastic unification based grammar formalism. The grammar syntax is modeled after, and is compatible with, Definite Clause Grammars. To facilitate writing stochastic grammars in DCG notation, a custom DCG compiler has been implemented. The compiler converts a DCG to a PRISM program, which is a stochastic model of the grammar.

Utilizing the functionality of PRISM, the grammar formalism supports parameter learning from annotated or unannotated corpora and provides and mechanism for parse selection through statistical inference. Parameter learning and inference is performed using PRISMs builtin functionality.

SDCG include some extensions to the DCG syntax. It includes a compact way of expressing recursion, inspired by regular expressions. It has expansion macros used for writing template rules which allow compact expression of multiple similar rules. The grammar syntax also adds a new conditioning operator which makes possible to condition rule expansions on previous expansions.

2.1 Grammar syntax

A grammar consist *grammar rules* and possibly some helper Prolog rules and facts. A grammar rule takes the form,

```
H ==> C1,C2,..,Cn.
```

H is called the *head* or left-hand side of the rule and `C1,C2,...,Cn` is called the *body* or right-hand side of the rule. The head is composed of a `name`, followed by an optional parameter list and an optional conditioning clause. It has the form,

```
name(F1,F2,...,Fn) | V1,V2,...,Vn
```

The `name` of the rule is a Prolog atom. The parameter list is a non-empty parenthesized, comma-separated list of features which may be Prolog variables or atoms. The number of features in rules is referred to as its arity. The optional conditioning clause starts with the pipe (included) and is a non-empty, comma-separated list of Prolog variables or atoms, or a combination of the two. The conditioning clause may also contain expansion macros in the case of unexpanded rules.

The *body* of a rule is a comma-separated list of constituents, of which there are four basic types: Rule constituents, embedded Prolog code, symbol lists and expansion macros.

Rule constituents are references to other SDCG grammar rules. They have the same format of Prolog goals, but may not be variables. A rule constituent consists of a `name` which is a Prolog atom, followed by an optional parenthesized, comma-separated list of *features*; `(F1..Fn)`. Features are either Prolog atoms or variables. Rule constituents may additionally have prefix regular expression modifiers. The allowed modifiers are `*` (kleene star) meaning *zero or more* occurrences, `+` meaning *one or more* occurrences and `?` meaning *zero or one* occurrence.

Embedded code takes the form, `{ P }`, where `P` is a block of Prolog goals and control structures. The allowed subset of Prolog corresponds to what is allowed in the body of a Prolog rule, but with the restriction that every goal must return a ground answer and may not be a variable. Also, while admitted by the syntax, meta-programming goals like `call` are not allowed. The goals unify with facts and rules defined outside the embedded Prolog code, but not in other embedded code blocks.

Symbol lists are Prolog lists of either atoms or variables or a combination of the two. The list usually take the form, `[ S1,S2,..,SN ]`, but the list operator `|` may also be used. However, it is required that every variable in the list is ground. A symbol list may not be empty.

Expansion macros have the form,

```
@name(V1,V2,...,Vn)
```

where `name` is an atom and is followed by a non-empty parenthesized, comma-separated list, `V1...Vn`, consisting of atoms or variables or a combination. A macro corresponds have a corresponding goal, `name/n`, which must be defined.

2.2 Procedural semantics

The grammar rules govern the rewriting the head of a rule into the constituents in the body of a rule. A rule is rewritten when all its constituents have been expanded. The order of the constituents in the body are significant and they are expanded in a left-to-right manner. The rewriting process always begins with the start rule and progress in a depth-first manner. A rule constituent in the body of a rule is thus a reference to one or more other rules of the grammar. A grammar rule is said to be matched by a constituent rule if the `name` and arity of are the same and their features unify. A *constituent rule* is expanded by replacing it with the body of some matching rule. Symbol lists are terminals and are not expanded. Embedded Prolog code is expanded to nothing and executed as a side-effect. The expansion terminates when the body only contains symbols or some constituent cannot be expanded (derivation fails).

When a constituent matches more than one rule there might be more than one derivation. The choice of the rule to expand given such a constituent, should be seen in the light of the probabilistic inference being performed. In general, we can assume that only the derivations relevant to the probabilistic query being used are expanded.

2.3 Statistical semantics

A rule $r \in R^{n,a}$ with the distinct name n and arity a has a probability $P(r) \in [0, 1]$ of being expanded in place of a matching rule constituent.

A rule r_i may have a condition (conditioning clause), in which case the probability of its expansion depend on the probability of the condition $c_i \in C^{n,a}$ being true, $C^{n,a}$ being the set of possible values for condition clauses for rules in $R^{n,a}$. Each distinct condition (clause value) has a separate probability, such that

$$\sum_{i=1}^{|C^{n,a}|} P(c_i) = 1$$

We denote number of rules in $R^{n,a}$ satisfying a particular condition c, $|n, a, c|$.

It holds for the sum of probabilities of such rules $r_i^{n,a} \in R^{n,a}$ that,

$$\sum_{i=1}^{|n,a,c|} P(r_i^{n,a}|c) = 1$$

where the probability of a rule r given a combination of conditions c is their product, $P(r|c) = P(r)P(c)$. If rules with the same head ($R^{n,a}$) occur without conditioning ($C^{n,a} = \emptyset$) then the condition *true* is assumed and $P(true) = 1$.

The probability of a derivation is the product of the probabilities of all rules used in that derivation. The probability of given sentence is the sum of the probabilities for each possible derivation of the sentence. A derivation may be unsuccessful due to failure of variable unification. The probability of all possible derivations, successful and unsuccessful sums to unity, given by the relation, $P_{success} = 1 - P_{failure}$.

2.4 The translated SDCG

The compiler behaves similar to a usual DCG compiler, by transforming rules in a DCG syntax to Prolog rules with difference lists. In addition to these normal Prolog rules, which we call *implementation rules*, special *selection rules* are used to control the stochastic derivation process. Each rule head with the same number and arity in the original DCG grammar are grouped together and managed by one *selection* rule. The selection rule has the same name and number of features as the of the original rule, but any ground atoms in the original rule are replaced by variables in the selection rule. Consider the two rules in the example below,

```
np(Number) ==> det(Number), noun(Number).
np(Number) ==> noun(Number).
```

The generated selection rule for the two rules is shown below:

```
np(Number, In, Out) :-
    msw(np(1), RuleIdentifier),
    np_impl(RuleIdentifer, Number, In, Out).
```

The `msw` goal is a special PRISM primitive which implements simulation of a random variable, which here stochastically unifies `RuleIndentifier` to a value given the name of the random variable. The name of the random variable is assigned according to the name of the nonterminal and its arity. For instance, since `np` has an arity of 1, the corresponding random variable is named `np(1)`. The possible outcomes of this particular random variable are `np_1_1` and `np_1_2`.

The first parameter of the implementation rules uniquely identifies them and this name corresponds to an outcome of the random variable used by the selection rule. The implementation rules for the above grammar is shown below:

```
np_impl(np_1_1, Number, In, Out) :-
    det(Number, In, InOut1),
    noun(Number, InOut1, Out).
np_impl(np_1_2, Number, In, Out) :-
    noun(Number, In, Out).
```

2.5 Grammar extensions

Regular expression operators, expansion macros and conditioning clauses, which are extensions of the usual DCG syntax, makes it possible to express aspects of the grammar more compactly. These operators are implemented in a preprocessing step which expands the compacted grammar.

2.5.1 Regular expression modifiers

Regular expression operators is a way of expressing recursion in a more convenient manner. An example grammar rule containing all the allowed regular expression operators is shown below:

```
name ==> ?(title), *(firstname), +(lastname).
```

The regular expression operators are implemented by generating some additional rules and replacing the original constituent (`orig_const`), which the operator is applied to, with another constituent (`new_const`). All regular expression operators can be implemented generating a subset of the following rules:

```
1) new_const ==> []
2) new_const ==> orig_const
3) new_const ==> new_const, new_const
```

The `?` operator is implemented by adding rules 1-2. The `+` operator is implemented adding rules 2-3 and the `*` operator is implemented adding all the rules. The name `new_const` is symbolic. The compiler use a naming scheme, which avoids conflicting names: The name of the regular expression modifier is prefixed to the constituent name. For instance `*(firstname)` becomes `sdcg_regex_star_firstname/0`. The compiler only adds the implementation rules for the same regular expression once, even if it is used in multiple rules.

2.5.2 Expansion macros

Macros are special Prolog goals embedded in grammar rules. They may occur in both the head and the body of rules. Grammar rules with macros are *meta grammar rules*; they act as templates for the generation similar rules. The result of macro expansion of a rule is a set of rules, equal in structure to the original rule, but where each macro is replaced with selected parameters from an answer for the goal. The ground input to the goal is omitted by default. It is possible to explicitly configure which parameters of a goal should be inserted using an `expand_mode` directive. If the goal contains more than one non-ground/answer parameter, the answer parameters are inserted comma-separated. If a rule contains more than one macro, then the set of expanded rules correspond to a cartesian product of the answers for all the macros. When several macros in the same rule use the same name for a variable, this works as a constraint on the answers for the macros. This is exactly as if the goals of the macros were constituents in the body of a Prolog rule.

The original motivation for expansion macros was integration of lexical resources. Suppose that we wish to integrate the lexicon defined by the following simple Prolog program,

```
word(he,sg,masc). word(she,sg,fem).
number(Word,Number) :- word(Word,Number,_).
gender(Word,Gender) :- word(Word,_,Gender).

expand_mode(number(-,+)).
expand_mode(gender(-,+)).

term(@number(Word,N),@gender(Word,G)) ==>
     [ Word ].
```

We select the variables which should be inserted in the resulting rules. A minus (-) indicates that the parameter is an *input* parameter and will not appear in place of the substituted macro and a plus (+) indicates an output parameter which will appear in place of the macro.

Since the macros in the example share the `Word` variable, it must unify to the same value for all macros. The result of performing macro substitutions on the grammar above is another, macro free, grammar:

```
term(sg,fem)==>[she]. term(sg,masc)==>[he].
```

2.5.3 Conditioning

Conditioning makes it possible to condition an expansion on previous expansions, which is useful for adding lexicalization schemes to the grammar. An example of a rule with a conditioning clause is shown below:

```
n1(A,B,C) | a,b ==> n2, n3.
```

The values of the conditioning clause, (`a,b`), corresponds to values for parameters in the head of the rule. This relation is defined by adding a fact, `conditioning_mode(n1(+,+,-))`, to the grammar. The parameter is a compound term with the same functor as a corresponding nonterminal. The parameters of this term indicate which parameters to grammar rules named by the functor are subject to conditioning. For instance, the conditioning mode in the above example states that the two first parameters of `n1` should be conditioned on (indicated with +), but the last one should not (indicated with -).

In the simple grammar fragment below, we illustrate a simple conditioning scheme, inspired from [5], where we condition on a single headword:

```
sentence ==>
   np(nohead,NPHead),vp(NPHead,VPHead).
np(ParentHead,Head) | @headword(W) ==>
   det(ParentHead,DetHead),noun(DetHead,Head).
vp(ParentHead,Head) | @headword(W) ==>
   verb(ParentHead,Head).
```

We have not specified conditioning modes for the rules, but in each case the condition corresponds to the first parameter in the head. Assume that the macro `@headword` expands to each of the words (terminals) in the grammar. The headword is propagated from the terminals, so for instance in the sentence rule, the choice of which `vp` rule to expand depends on headword propagated from the preceding `np`. Conditioning a rule on every word implicates that the rule *given that word* will have a *distinct* probability distribution.

More advanced lexicalization schemes can easily be created using the conditioning mechanism. The limitation lies in the order in which variables conditioned on are unified (and thus derivation order). It is not possible to condition on a variable which is not yet ground.

2.5.4 Syntax extensions example

As an illustrative example which applies all the syntax extensions, we demonstrate a part of speech tagger expressed with SDCG. A part of speech tagger is can be implemented as a stochastic regular grammar/Hidden Markov Model (HMM). A HMM based POS tagger can be created in SDCG with a single rule,

```
tag_word(Prev, @tag(Cur),  [CurRest])
        | @tag(_) ==>
     @consume_word(W),
     ?(tag_word(Cur,_,Rest)).
```

This assumes definition of words, tags, a conditioning mode declaration. The grammar rule consumes one word for each time it is expanded. Note that there will be separate rules for each word, because of the `@consume_word` macro, which expands the rule for all the words in the lexicon (enclosing them in square brackets). The next constituent in the body is a recursive reference to the rule itself. It is governed by the regular expression operator `?`, which indicates that the constituent may or may not be matched. If it is not matched, we have termination of the recursion. The model defined by the rule is a fully connected second order HMM model, where the expanded grammar has a rule for each possible transition.

To illustrate the use of the tagger we consider an example from [3], defined here as a simple Prolog lexicon,

```
tag(none). tag(det). tag(noun).
tag(verb). tag(modalverb).
word(the). word(can). word(will). word(rust).
```

We introduce a helper rule to interact with the lexicon and also a start rule,

```
consume_word([Word]) :-  word(Word).
start(TagList) ==> tag_word(none,_,TagList).
```

To train the grammar we feed it with tagged sentences,

```
learn([ start([det,noun,modalverb,verb],
    [the,can,will,rust],[]),
  start([det,noun,modalverb,verb],
    [the,can,can,rust],[]),
  start([det,noun,noun], [the,can,rust],[]),
  start([det,noun],[the,rust],[]),
  start([modalverb,noun,verb],
    [will,rust,rust],[]),
  start([noun,modalverb,verb],
    [will,can,rust],[]),
  start([noun,noun],[the,the],[])  ]).
```

When the grammar/tagger has been trained we can pose a viterbi query to find the most likely tag sequence for a sentence,

```
| ?- viterbig(start(T,[the,can,will,rust],[])).
T = [det,noun,modalverb,verb|_4794] ?
yes
```

3 Evaluation

To test the grammar formalism with regard to more realistic grammars, a grammar for a subset of the English language was developed. The grammar consists of about 90 rules, not counting pre-terminal rules, and models various different sentences types. It was originally modeled after the descriptions of context-free grammars for English in [11] and extended with some common agreement features, chosen with the tagset of the Brown corpus in mind.

In a small scale experiment, the grammar was used to parse 4000 select sentences from the Brown corpus [10], between 2 and 60 words in length. Parsing was relatively fast - usually less than 100 milliseconds per sentence excluding the time used to load the grammar and sentences. Training the grammar on the same sentences takes quite a while longer, approximately 4 minutes.

Introducing a lexicalization scheme similar to [5] increases the resulting number of random variables and affects both training time and inference time drastically. Some optimizations are needed to work with such lexicalized grammars in more realistic settings.

A limitation seems to be the first order compilation process in PRISM which takes a lot of time and consumes a lot of memory as the grammar grows larger. With recursion, the process may not complete, which has motivated the addition of an option to limit the depth of the derivation tree.

Precision/Recall was not measured, as the intention was only to measure the performance of the formalism, not the usefulness of the grammar.

4 Conclusion and future work

We introduced Stochastic Definite Clause Grammars, a new stochastic unification-based grammar formalism syntacticly compatible with Definite Clause Grammars. The grammar formalism borrows the expressivity and ability to model natural language phenomena from DCG, but also enjoys the benefits from of statistical models. SDCG extends DCG syntax which allow expression of probabilistic grammars very compactly. This naturally includes probabilistic regular grammars (such as the demonstrated POS tagger) and probabilistic context-free grammars, but also includes context sensitive grammars. It was demonstrated that lexicalization schemes can be compactly expressed in the formalism through conditioning and macros.

Some optimizations are needed in order to utilize large grammars (and training sets) for natural languages. Alternative methods for parameter learning may be explored.

Finally, the success of the grammar formalism depends on the applications that using it. SDCG will evolve with the development of applications using it.

References

[1] S. P. Abney. Stochastic attribute-value grammars. *Computational Linguistics*, 23(4):597–618, 1997.

[2] C. Brew. Stochastic HPSG. In *Proceedings of EACL-95*, February 1995.

[3] E. Charniak. Statistical techniques for natural language parsing. *AI Magazine*, 18(4):33–44, 1997.

[4] N. Chomsky. *Syntactic Structures*. Mouton, The Hague, 1957.

[5] M. J. Collins. *Head-driven statistical models for natural language parsing*. PhD thesis, Penn university, Jan. 01 1999.

[6] A. Colmerauer. Metamorphosis grammars. In L. Bolc, editor, *Natural Language Communication with Computers*. Springer-Verlag, 1978.

[7] J. Cussens. Parameter estimation in stochastic logic programs. *Machine Learning*, 44(3):245, 2001.

[8] A. P. Dempster, N. M. Laird, and D. B. Rubin. Maximum likelihood from incomplete data via the EM algorithm. *Journal of the Royal Statistical Society*, 39:1–38, 1977.

[9] A. Eisele. Towards probabilistic extensions of constraint-based grammars. *DYANA-2 deliverable R 1.2 B*, 1994.

[10] W. N. Francis and H. Kuçera. Brown corpus manual. 1979.

[11] D. Jurafsky and J. H. Martin. *Speech and language processing*. Prentice Hall, 2000.

[12] F. C. N. Pereira and D. H. D. Warren. Definite clause grammars for language analysis – a survey of the formalism and a comparison with augmented transition networks. *Artificial Intelligence*, 13, 1980.

[13] S. Riezler. Probabilistic constraint logic programming. *CoRR*, cmp-lg/9711001, 1997. informal publication.

[14] T. Sato. First order compiler: A deterministic logic program synthesis algorithm. *Journal of Symbolic Computation*, pages 605–627, 1989.

[15] T. Sato. A glimpse of symbolic-statistical modeling by prism. *Journal of Intelligent Information Systems*, 2008.

[16] T. Sato and Y. Kameya. Parameter learning of logic programs for symbolic-statistical modeling. *Journal of Artificial Intelligence Research (JAIR)*, 15:391454, 2001.

[17] T. Sato and Y. Kameya. A dynamic programming approach to parameter learning of generative models with failure. In *Proceedings of ICML Workshop on Statistical Relational Learning and its Connection to the Other Fields (SRL2004)*, 2004.

[18] T. Sato and Y. Kameya. Learning through failure. In L. D. Raedt, T. Dietterich, L. Getoor, and S. H. Muggleton, editors, *Probabilistic, Logical and Relational Learning - Towards a Synthesis*, number 05051 in Dagstuhl Seminar Proceedings, Dagstuhl, Germany, 2006. Internationales Begegnungs- und Forschungszentrum für Informatik (IBFI), Schloss Dagstuhl, Germany.

[19] T. Sato and Y. Kameya. New advances in logic-based probabilistic modeling by prism. *Probabilistic Inductive Logic Programming LNCS 4911, Springer*, page 118155, 2008.

[20] T. Sato, Y. Kameya, and N.-F. Zhou. Generative modeling with failure in prism. In *Proceedings of the 19th International Joint Conference on Artificial Intelligence (IJCAI2005)*, pages 847–852, 2005.

Topic-based Multi-Document Summarization with Probabilistic Latent Semantic Analysis

Leonhard Hennig
DAI Labor, TU Berlin
Berlin, Germany
leonhard.hennig@dai-labor.de

Abstract

We consider the problem of query-focused multi-document summarization, where a summary containing the information most relevant to a user's information need is produced from a set of topic-related documents. We propose a new method based on probabilistic latent semantic analysis, which allows us to represent sentences and queries as probability distributions over latent topics. Our approach combines query-focused and thematic features computed in the latent topic space to estimate the summary-relevance of sentences. In addition, we evaluate several different similarity measures for computing sentence-level feature scores. Experimental results show that our approach outperforms the best reported results on DUC 2006 data, and also compares well on DUC 2007 data.

Keywords

text summarization, probabilistic latent semantic analysis, plsa

1 Introduction

Automatically producing summaries from large textual sources is an extensively studied problem in IR and NLP [17, 12]. In this paper, we investigate the problem of multi-document summarization, where a summary is created from a set of related documents and optionally fulfills a specific information need of a user. In particular, we focus on generating an extractive summary by selecting sentences from a document cluster [8]. Multi-document summarization is an increasingly important task: With the rapid growth of online information, and many documents covering the same topic, the condensation of information from different sources into an informative summary helps to reduce information overload. Automatically created summaries can either consist of the most important information overall (generic summarization) or of the information most relevant with respect to a user's information need (query-focused summarization).

A major aspect of identifying relevant information is to find out what a text is about. A document will generally contain a variety of information centered around a main theme, and covering different aspects of the main topic. Similarly, human summaries tend to cover different topics of the original source text to increase the informative content of the summary. Various approaches have exploited features based on the identification of topics (or thematic foci) to construct generic or query-focused summaries. Often, thematic features rely on identifying and weighting important keywords [21], or creating topic signatures [14, 10]. Sentences are scored by combinations of keyword scores, or by computing similarities between sentences and queries. Yet it is well known that term matching has severe drawbacks due to the ambivalence of words and to differences in word usage and personal style across authors. This is especially important for automatic summarization, as summaries produced by humans may differ significantly, potentially not sharing very many terms [16].

Latent Semantic Indexing (LSI) is an approach to overcome these problems by mapping documents to a latent semantic space, and has been shown to work well for text summarization [9, 23]. However, LSI has a number of drawbacks, namely its unsatisfactory statistical foundations. The technique of probabilistic latent semantic analysis (PLSA) assumes a latent lower dimensional topic model as the origin of observed term co-occurrence distributions, and can be seen as a probabilistic analogue to LSI [11]. It has a solid statistical foundation, is based on the likelihood principle and defines a proper generative model for data. PLSA models documents as a list of mixing proportions for mixture components that can be viewed as representations of "topics" [4].

In this paper, we are primarily interested the capability of the PLSA approach to model documents as mixtures of topics. Unlike previous approaches in PLSA-based extractive summarization, we represent sentences, queries, and documents as probability distributions over topics. We train the probabilistic model on the term-sentence matrix of all sentences in a document cluster, and proceed by folding queries, document titles and cluster centroid vectors into the trained model. This allows us to compute various thematic and query-focused similarity measures, as well as redundancy measures, in the space of latent topics, in order to estimate the summary-worthiness of sentences.

Our system improves on previous approaches in three ways: First, we investigate PLSA in the context of multi-document summarization, modeling topic distributions across documents and taking into account information redundancy. Second, we do not only pick sentences from topics with the highest likelihood in the training data as in [3], but compute a sentence's score based on a linear function of query-focused and

International Conference RANLP 2009 - Borovets, Bulgaria, pages 144–149

thematic features. Third, we examine how a PLSA model can be used to represent documents, sentences and queries in the context of multi-document summarization, and investigate which measures are most useful for computing similarities in the latent topic space. We evaluate our approach on the data sets of the DUC 2006 and DUC 2007 text summarization challenges, and show that the resulting summaries compare favorably on ROUGE metrics with those produced by existing state-of-the-art summarization systems.

The rest of this paper is organized as follows: In Section 2 we describe the probabilistic latent semantic analysis algorithm. Next, in Section 3, we give details of our summarization system, the sentence-level features we use, as well as of the similarity measures we evaluate. In Section 4, we give experimental results showing that our approach leads to improvements over a LSI baseline, and that overall scores compare well with those of existing systems on ROUGE metrics. We then compare our system to related work in Section 5, and finally Section 6 concludes the paper.

2 Probabilistic Latent Semantic Analysis

Probabilistic latent semantic analysis is a latent variable model for co-occurrence data which has been found to provide better results than LSI for term matching in retrieval applications [11]. It associates an unobserved class variable $z \in \mathcal{Z} = \{z_1, \ldots, z_k\}$ with each observation (d, w), where word $w \in \mathcal{W} = \{w_1, \ldots, w_i\}$ occurs in document $d \in \mathcal{D} = \{d_1, \ldots, d_j\}$. Each word in a document is considered as a sample from a mixture model, where the mixture components are multinomial random variables that can be viewed as representations of latent topics. A document is represented as a list of mixing proportions for the mixing components, i.e. it is reduced to a probability distribution over a fixed set of latent classes.

In terms of a generative model, PLSA can be defined as follows:

- select a document d with probability $P(d)$,
- pick a latent class z with probability $P(z|d)$,
- generate a word w with probability $P(w|z)$.

For each observation pair (d, w) the resulting likelihood expression is:

$$P(d,w) = P(d)P(w|d), \text{ where} \quad (1)$$

$$P(w|d) = \sum_{z \in \mathcal{Z}} P(w|z)P(z|d). \quad (2)$$

A document d and a word w are assumed to be conditionally independent given the unobserved topic z. Following the maximum likelihood principle, the mixing components and the mixing proportions are determined by the maximization of the likelihood function

$$\mathcal{L} = \sum_{d \in \mathcal{D}} \sum_{w \in \mathcal{W}} n(d,w) log P(d,w), \quad (3)$$

where $n(d, w)$ denotes the term frequency, i.e. the number of times w occurred in d.

The standard procedure for maximizing the likelihood function in the presence of latent variables is the Expectation Maximization (EM) algorithm. EM is an iterative algorithm where each iteration consists of two steps, an expectation step where the posterior probabilities for the latent classes z are computed, and a maximization step where the conditional probabilities of the parameters given the posterior probabilities of the latent classes are updated. Alternating the expectation and maximization steps, one arrives at a converging point which describes a local maximum of the log likelihood. The output of the algorithm are the mixture components, as well as the mixing proportions over the components for each training document, i.e. the conditional probabilities $P(w|z)$ and $P(z|d)$. For details of the EM algorithm and its application to PLSA, see [11].

3 Topic-based summarization

Our approach for producing a summary consists of three steps: First, we associate sentences and queries with a representation in the latent topic space of a PLSA model by estimating their mixing proportions $P(z|d)$[1]. We then compute several sentence-level features based on the similarity of sentence and query distributions over latent topics. Finally, we combine individual feature scores linearly into an overall sentence score to create a ranking, which we use to select sentences for the summary. We follow a greedy approach for selecting sentences, and penalize candidate sentences based on their similarity to the partial summary.

3.1 Sentence representation in the latent topic space

Given a corpus $\mathcal{D}$ of topic-related documents, we perform sentence splitting on each document using the NLTK toolkit[2]. Each sentence is represented as a bag-of-words $\mathbf{w} = (w_1, \ldots, w_m)$. During preprocessing, we remove stop words, and apply stemming using Porter's stemmer [22]. We discard all sentences which contain less than $l_{min} = 5$ or more than $l_{max} = 20$ content words, as these sentences are unlikely to be useful for a summary [24]. We create a term-sentence matrix TS containing all sentences of the corpus, where each entry $TS(i, j)$ is given by the frequency of term i in sentence j. We then train the PLSA model on the term-sentence matrix TS.

After the model has been trained, it provides a representation of the sentences as probability distributions $P(z|s)$ over the latent topics z. This representation can be interpreted as follows: Since the source documents cover multiple topics related to a central theme, each sentence can be viewed as representing one or more of these topics. By applying PLSA, we arrive at a representation of sentences as a vector in

[1] From hereon, we will use $P(z|s)$ and $P(z|q)$ to denote topic distributions over sentences and queries respectively, but for all purposes these can be considered identical to the notation $P(z|d)$ of the original PLSA model.

[2] http://nltk.org

the "topic-space" of the document cluster $\mathcal{D}$:

$$P(z|s) = (p(z_1|s), p(z_2|s), \ldots, p(z_K|s)), \quad (4)$$

where $p(z_k|s)$ is the conditional probability of topic k given the sentence s. The probability distribution $P(z|s)$ hence tells us how many and which topics this sentence covers[3], and how likely the different topics are for this sentence.

In order to produce a query-focused summary, we also need to represent the query in the latent topic space. This is achieved by folding the query into the trained model. The folding is performed by EM iterations, where the factors $P(w|z)$ are kept fixed, and only the mixing proportions $P(z|q)$ are adapted in each M-step [11]. The representation of sentences and queries in the latent topic space allows us to apply similarity measures in this space. Furthermore, the topic space is much smaller than the original term vector space.

3.2 Computing query-focused and thematic sentence features

Since we are interested in creating a summary that covers the main topics of a document set and is also focused on satisfying a user's information need, specified by a query, we create sentence-level features that attempt to capture these different aspects in the form of per-sentence scores. We then combine the feature scores to arrive at an overall sentence score.

Each of our evaluation data sets contains a title and a narrative for each cluster of topic-related documents. The narrative consists of one or more sentences describing a user's information need. This allows us to compute the following sentence features, where each feature measures the similarity of the sentence's topic distribution S with a "query" topic distribution:

- $r(S, CT)$ - cluster title
- $r(S, N)$ - cluster narrative
- $r(S, T)$ - document title
- $r(S, D)$ - document term vector
- $r(S, C)$ - cluster centroid vector

To compute the features, we fold the title and the narrative of the document clusters, the document titles, and document and cluster term vectors into the trained PLSA model. Query term vectors are preprocessed in the same way as training sentences, except that no sentence splitting is performed. Document and document cluster term vectors are computed by aggregating sentence term vectors.

We evaluate three similarity measures r in our approach: The symmetric Kullback-Leibler (KL) divergence, the Jensen-Shannon (JS) divergence and the cosine similarity, but a variety of other similarity measures can be utilized towards this end.

[3] In terms of topics whose probability is not negligible, i.e. larger than some small quantity ϵ.

The symmetric KL-divergence is defined as follows:

$$\begin{aligned} KL(S,Q) &= D_{KL}(S||Q) + D_{KL}(Q||S) \\ &= \sum_I S(i) \log \frac{S(i)}{Q(i)} \\ &\quad + \sum_I Q(i) \log \frac{Q(i)}{S(i)}. \end{aligned} \quad (5)$$

To use the KL-divergence as a similarity measure, we scale divergence values to $[0, 1]$ and invert by subtracting from 1, hence

$$r_{KL} = 1 - KL(S,Q)_{scaled}. \quad (6)$$

The Jensen-Shannon divergence is a symmetrized and smoothed version of the KL-divergence, computing the KL-divergence of S, Q with respect to the average of the two input distributions. The JS-divergence based similarity r_{JS} is then defined as:

$$\begin{aligned} r_{JS}(S,Q) &= 1 - [D_{JS}(S||Q)] \quad (7) \\ &= 1 - \left[\frac{1}{2} D_{KL}(S||M) + \frac{1}{2} D_{KL}(Q||M)\right], \end{aligned}$$

where $M = 1/2(S+Q)$. Finally, the cosine similarity is defined as $r_{COS}(S,Q) = S^T Q$.

As the training of a PLSA model using the EM algorithm with random initialization converges on a local maximum of the likelihood of the observed data, different initializations will result in different locally optimal models. As the authors of [5] have shown, the effect of random initialization can be reduced by generating several PLSA models, then computing features according to the different models, and finally averaging the feature values. We have implemented this model averaging in our approach using 5 iterations of training the PLSA model.

3.3 Sentence scoring

The system described so far assigns a vector of similarity feature values to each sentence s. The overall score of a sentence s based on the feature vector $(r_1^s, \ldots, r_P^s)$ is:

$$score(s) = \sum_P w_p r_p^s, \quad (8)$$

where w_p is a feature-specific weight. Sentences are ranked by this score, and the highest-scoring sentences are selected for the summary.

For our system, we trained the feature weights by initializing all weights to a default value of 1. We then optimized one feature weight at a time while keeping the others fixed. The training was performed on the DUC 2006 data set. The most dominant features in our experiments are the sentence-narrative similarity $r(S, N)$ and the sentence-document similarity $r(S, D)$, which confirms previous research. On the other hand, the sentence-title similarity $r(S, T)$ did not have a significant influence on the resulting summaries.

When generating a summary, we also need to deal with the problem of repetition of information. This problem is especially important for multi-document summarization, where multiple documents will discuss

System	k	Rouge-1	Rouge-2	Rouge-SU4
PLSA-JS	192	**0.43283**	**0.09698**	**0.15568**
PYTHY	-	-	0.096	0.147
PLSA-COS	256	0.42444	0.09588	0.15409
peer 24	-	0.40980	0.09505	0.15464
PLSA-KL	256	0.42956	0.09465	0.15474
LSI	128	0.42155	0.08880	0.14938
Lead	-	0.30217	0.04947	0.09788

Table 1: *DUC-06: ROUGE recall scores for best number of latent topics k. PLSA-JS, -KL and -COS are system variants using the Jensen-Shannon-divergence, symmetric KL-divergence, and Cosine similarity respectively. Best LSI model based on a rank-k approximation with* $k = 128$.

the same topic. We model redundancy similar to the maximum marginal relevance framework [6]. MMR is a greedy approach that iteratively selects the best-scoring sentence for the summary, and then updates sentence scores by computing a penalty based on the similarity of each sentence with the current summary:

$$score(s) = \lambda(score(s)) - (1 - \lambda)r(S, SUM), \quad (9)$$

where the score of sentence s is scaled to $[0, 1]$ and $r(S, SUM)$ is the cosine similarity of the sentence and the summary centroid vector, which is based on the averaged topic distribution of sentences selected for the summary. λ is set experimentally to 0.5, weighting relevance and redundancy scores equally.

4 Experiments

For the evaluation of our summarization system, we use two data sets from recent summarization tasks: Multi-document summarization in DUC 2006 and in DUC 2007. For all our evaluations, we use ROUGE metrics[4]. ROUGE metrics are recall-oriented and based on n-gram overlap. ROUGE-1 has been shown to correlate well with human judgements [15]. In addition, we also report the performance on ROUGE-2 (bigram overlap) and ROUGE-SU4 (skip bigram) metrics.

We implemented two baseline systems, *Lead* and a system using LSI [9]. The *Lead* system selects the lead sentences from the most recent news article in the document cluster as the summary. The LSI baseline computes the rank-k singular value decomposition of the term-sentence matrix. The resulting right-singular vectors, scaled by the singular values, represent the sentences in the latent semantic space. We compute the same sentence-level features as for the PLSA-based system, using the cosine similarity measure, and apply our greedy ranking and redundancy removal strategy to create a summary.

4.1 DUC 2006

In the multi-document summarization task in DUC-2006, participants are given 50 document clusters, where each cluster contains 25 news articles related to the same topic. Participants are asked to generate summaries of at most 250 words for each cluster. For each cluster, a title and a narrative describing a user's information need are provided. The narrative is usually composed of a set of questions or a multi-sentence task description.

We present the results of our system in Table 1. We compare the results to the best peer (*peer24*) and to the best reported results on this data set by the PYTHY system [25]. In addition, we also give the results for the LSI and the *Lead* baselines.

In the table, system *PLSA-JS* uses the Jensen-Shannon divergence as the similarity measure $r(S, Q)$, *PLSA-KL* the symmetric KL-divergence and *PLSA-COS* the cosine similarity. The results are given for the empirically best value of the parameter k (number of latent topics) for each system variant. The system using the JS-divergence outperforms the best existing systems at $k = 192$ with a ROUGE-2 score of 0.9698, although the improvements for ROUGE-2 and ROUGE-SU4 are not significant at $p < 0.05$. ROUGE-1 scores are significantly better than the results reported by *peer24*. A comparison to the PYTHY system on ROUGE-1 scores was not possible as the authors do not specify this score for their system. All variants of our system outperform the LSI baseline on ROUGE-2.

4.2 DUC 2007

The multi-document summarization task in DUC-2007 is the same as in DUC-2006, with participants asked to produce 250 word multi-document summaries for a total of 45 document clusters. The results of our system are presented in Table 2.

ROUGE-2 and ROUGE-SU4 scores of our system are lower than those of the best system (*peer15*), but still very competitive, with the PLSA-JS variant ranking 5th for ROUGE-2 and 2nd for ROUGE-SU4 when compared to other participating systems. Again we see that all three system variants outperform the LSI baseline. We observe that both the PLSA-JS and the PLSA-COS variant require a much smaller number of latent classes than the LSI model for comparable ROUGE-2 results.

We can also see that the PLSA-JS variant outperforms *peer15* on ROUGE-1, and achieves almost the same score as the top-performing system for ROUGE-SU4, with the differences in both cases not being significant. This suggests that the PLSA model can adequately capture the importance of individual words for ROUGE-1 recall, and word co-occurrences for ROUGE-SU4 skip-bigram recall. The ROUGE-2 score, on the other hand, is significantly lower than that of *peer15*. This indicates that the PLSA model, which was trained on the co-occurrence counts of invididual words, could benefit from the inclusion of bigram co-occurrence counts.

4.3 Effect of system variations

Next, we look at the effect of varying the number of latent topics: For all systems we find that using less than $k = 32$ latent classes, the model cannot cope with

[4] ROUGE version 1.5.5, with arguments -n 4 -w 1.2 -m -2 4 -u -c 95 -r 1000 -f A -p 0.5 -t 0

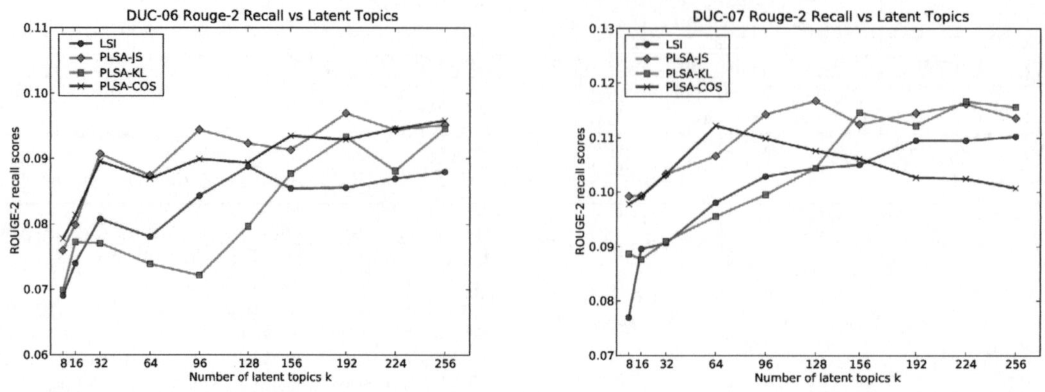

(a) DUC 2006

(b) DUC 2007

Fig. 1: *Summarization performance on DUC 2006 (a) and DUC 2007 data (b) in terms of ROUGE-2 recall for different numbers of latent topics. Also shown are the performance of system variants using different similarity measures and the LSI baseline. The system using Jensen-Shannon divergence with* $k = 192$ *latent classes outperforms existing approaches on DUC 2006 data.*

System	k	Rouge-1	Rouge-2	Rouge-SU4
peer 15	-	0.44508	0.12448	0.17711
PLSA-JS	128	**0.45843**	**0.11675**	**0.17680**
PLSA-KL	224	0.45208	0.11662	0.17306
PLSA-COS	64	0.44329	0.11222	0.16679
LSI	256	0.44891	0.11022	0.16864
Lead	-	0.31250	0.06039	0.10507

Table 2: *DUC-07: ROUGE recall scores for best number of latent topics k. The PLSA-JS variant outperforms the best participating system on ROUGE-1, and ranks 5th for ROUGE-2.*

the complexity of the data. As can be seen in Figure 1(a), ROUGE-2 scores of the PLSA-JS and -COS variants on DUC 2006 data improve when increasing the number of latent topics k, but level out quickly. From there on, the system seems relatively robust to changes of the number of latent topics, with observed performance variations most likely due to the EM algorithm's convergence on local maxima. The scores of the KL-divergence based variant are significantly lower than those of the PLSA-JS variant when using less than $k = 156$ latent classes, but are almost as good as those of PLSA-JS when using more classes.

Similar observations hold for the DUC 2007 data set, as can be seen in Figure 1(b). One notable difference is that the PLSA-COS variant exhibits overfitting for the DUC 2007 data set much earlier than the other systems, with performance dropping for $k > 64$. This can be explained by the fact that the PLSA model assigns near-zero probabilities to most of the latent classes of a sentence, which in turn affects the cosine similarity more strongly than for the distribution divergence measures which smooth near-zero probabilities.

The most interesting observation for both data sets is that the PLSA-JS variant achieves very good performance with only very few latent classes, signifying that a drastic reduction of the original vector space is possible before computing similarity features. Even with $k = 192$ latent classes, the dimensionality of the space in which we compute similarity features is much lower than for the original term vector space.

Both figures also show that the PLSA approach consistently outperforms the LSI approach. Although performance improvements are not significant at $p < 0.05$, they do indicate that the PLSA model can better capture the sparse information contained in sentences than the LSI model. We find that the LSI baseline system's performance improves significantly when increasing the number of latent classes from 32 to 96, while using more latent classes results in only marginal improvements of ROUGE-2 scores.

5 Related work

Most existing approaches to summarization are sentenced-based and extractive. Proposed approaches explore a variety of features, including document structure and term prominence [18], rhethorical structure [19], as well as graph-theoretic [7, 20] and semantic features [13]. Redundancy is often accounted for by implementing some form of MMR [6], or encoded in feature weighting schemes [25].

Topic information is usually encoded with term-based weighting strategies. Topic signatures [14, 10] are a well-known method of representing topic themes in multi-document summarization. Lexical chains, as proposed by [2], model topic progression through a text using WordNet and other linguistic resources. Different chains can be viewed as modeling different topics within the source documents.

Our system focuses on scoring sentences based on a representation of each sentence in the latent topic space provided by a trained PLSA model. Previous work on applying PLSA to the task of text summarization includes [3], who evaluate single document summarization on DUC 2002 data. The system computes a PLSA model on the term-sentence matrix of a single document, then picks the topics with the highest posterior probabilities $p(z)$, and selects sentences with the highest likelihood $p(s|z)$ within these topics for the summary. The approach produces generic summaries based on the most likely topics of the PLSA model. In contrast, our system focuses on query-oriented multi-document summarization, and models redundancy when creating the summary.

More closely related to our approach is recent work by [1], who employ Latent Dirichlet Allocation [4] to create multi-document summaries on DUC 2002 data. The authors report an improvement of ROUGE-1 recall scores over the best known DUC 2002 system. However, their approach is similar to the approach of [3] in being restricted to selecting sentences from the topics with the largest likelihoods. As compared to our approach, their system does not seem to perform any redundancy checking except for relying on the discriminative quality of the latent classes. Furthermore, our approach utilizes narrative and other meta-information of the document cluster to create not only generic, but also query-focused summaries.

6 Conclusion

We introduced an approach to query-focused multi-document summarization based on probabilistic latent semantic analysis. After training a PLSA model on the term-sentence matrix of document clusters from recent summarization tasks, we represent each sentence as a distribution over latent topics. Using this representation, we combine query-focused and thematic sentence features into an overall sentence score. Sentences are ranked and selected for the summary according to this score, choosing a greedy approach for sentence selection and penalizing redundancy with a maximum marginal relevance method.

Our results are among the best reported on the DUC-2006 and DUC-2007 multi-document summarization tasks for ROUGE-1, ROUGE-2 and ROUGE-SU4 scores. Our approach outperforms the previous best performing system on DUC 2006 data, although the improvements are not statistically significant. We have achieved these very competitive results using a simple unsupervised approach. The comparison with a system using latent semantic indexing shows that the PLSA model can better capture the sparse information contained in a sentence than a comparable LSI model. We also studied the effect of different measures to compute sentence-level similarity features in the latent topic space. We found that using the Jensen-Shannon divergence resulted in the best ROUGE scores, as well as being very robust to changes of the number of latent classes.

In future research, we would like to extend our method with additional linguistic knowledge. Given that the unigram, bag-of-words approach ignores syntactic structure information, we would like to study the effect of including such information — by means of bi- or trigram co-occurrence counts — in a PLSA model. The performance differences of our system in terms of ROUGE-2 as compared to ROUGE-1 and ROUGE-SU4 suggests that the model could benefit from including n-gram co-occurrences.

References

[1] R. Arora and B. Ravindran. Latent dirichlet allocation based multi-document summarization. In *Proc. of AND '08*, pages 91–97, 2008.

[2] R. Barzilay and M. Elhadad. *Using Lexical Chains for Text Summarization*, pages 111–121. MIT Press, 1999.

[3] H. Bhandari, M. Shimbo, T. Ito, and Y. Matsumoto. Generic text summarization using probabilistic latent semantic indexing. In *Proc. of IJCNLP 2008*, 2008.

[4] D. M. Blei, A. Y. Ng, M. I. Jordan, and J. Lafferty. Latent dirichlet allocation. *JMLR*, 3:2003, 2003.

[5] T. Brants, F. Chen, and I. Tsochantaridis. Topic-based document segmentation with probabilistic latent semantic analysis. In *Proc. of CIKM '02*, pages 211–218, 2002.

[6] J. Carbonell and J. Goldstein. The use of mmr, diversity-based reranking for reordering documents and producing summaries. In *Proc. of SIGIR '98*, pages 335–336, 1998.

[7] G. Erkan and D. Radev. Lexrank: graph-based centrality as salience in text summarisation. *JAIR*, 2004.

[8] J. Goldstein, V. Mittal, J. Carbonell, and M. Kantrowitz. Multi-document summarization by sentence extraction. In *NAACL-ANLP 2000 Workshop on Automatic summarization*, pages 40–48, 2000.

[9] Y. Gong and X. Liu. Generic text summarization using relevance measure and latent semantic analysis. In *Proc. of SIGIR '01*, pages 19–25, 2001.

[10] S. Harabagiu and F. Lacatusu. Topic themes for multi-document summarization. In *Proc. of SIGIR '05*, pages 202–209, 2005.

[11] T. Hofmann. Probabilistic latent semantic indexing. In *Proc. of SIGIR '99*, pages 50–57, 1999.

[12] K. S. Jones. Automatic summarising: The state of the art. *Inf. Process. Manage.*, 43(6):1449–1481, 2007.

[13] J. Leskovec, N. Milic-Frayling, and M. Grobelnik. Impact of linguistic analysis on the semantic graph coverage and learning of document extracts. In *Proc. of AAAI'05*, 2005.

[14] C.-Y. Lin and E. Hovy. The automated acquisition of topic signatures for text summarization. In *Proc. of Coling '00*, pages 495–501, 2000.

[15] C.-Y. Lin and E. Hovy. Automatic evaluation of summaries using n-gram co-occurrence statistics. In *Proc. of NAACL-HLT 2003*, pages 71–78, 2003.

[16] C.-Y. Lin and E. Hovy. The potential and limitations of automatic sentence extraction for summarization. In *Proc. of the HLT-NAACL 2003 Workshop on Text Summarization*, pages 73–80, 2003.

[17] H. Luhn. The automatic creation of literature abstracts. *IBM J. of Research & Development*, 1958.

[18] I. Mani and E. Bloedorn. Machine learning of generic and user-focused summarization. In *Proc. of AAAI '98/IAAI '98*, pages 820–826, 1998.

[19] D. Marcu. The rhetorical parsing of natural language texts. In *Proc. of the 35th Annual Meeting of the ACL*, pages 96–103, 1997.

[20] R. Mihalcea. Graph-based ranking algorithms for sentence extraction, applied to text summarization. In *Proc. of ACL 2004*, page 20, 2004.

[21] A. Nenkova, L. Vanderwende, and K. McKeown. A compositional context sensitive multi-document summarizer: exploring the factors that influence summarization. In *Proc. of SIGIR '06*, pages 573–580, 2006.

[22] M. F. Porter. An algorithm for suffix stripping. *Program*, 14(3):130–137, 1980.

[23] J. Steinberger, M. A. Kabadjov, M. Poesio, and O. Sanchez-Graillet. Improving LSA-based summarization with anaphora resolution. In *Proc. of HLT-EMNLP '05*, pages 1–8, 2005.

[24] S. Teufel and M. Moens. Sentence extraction as a classification task. In *ACL/EACL-97 Workshop on Intelligent and Scalable Text Summarization*, pages 58–65, 1997.

[25] K. Toutanova, C. Brockett, M. Gamon, J. Jagarlamudi, H. Suzuki, and L. Vanderwende. The PYTHY summarization system: Microsoft research at duc 2007. In *Proc. of DUC 2007*, 2007.

Detection of opinions and facts. A cognitive approach

Yann Vigile Hoareau†
Human and Artificial Cognition Lab.
University of Paris 8 – 2 rue de la Liberté.
93526 St Denis Cedex 02 -FRANCE
hoareau@lutin-userlab.fr

Adil El-Ghali
Human and Artificial Cognition Lab.
University of Paris 8 – 2 rue de la Liberté.
93526 St Denis Cedex 02 -FRANCE
elghali@lutin-userlab.fr

Charles Tijus
Human and Artificial Cognition Lab.
University of Paris 8 – 2 rue de la Liberté.
93526 St Denis Cedex 02 -FRANCE
tijus@lutin-userlab.fr

Abstract

A model of episodic memory is derived to propose algorithms of text categorization with semantic space models. Performances of two algorithms named *Target vector* and *Sub-target vector* are contrasted using textual material of the text-mining context 'DEFT09'. The experience reported here have been realized on the english corpus which is composed of articles of the economic newspaper "*The Financial Times*". The aim of the task was to categorize texts in function of the factuality or subjectivity they expressed. Results confirm (i) that the episodic memory metaphor provides a convenient framework to propose efficient algorithm for text categorization, and (ii) that *Sub-target vector algorithm* outperforms the *Target vector algorithm.*

Keywords

Random Indexing, episodic memory, text-mining, categorization.

1. Introduction

Since its early introduction, the model that is now named Latent Semantic Analysis [14] has been proposed as a method of matrix reduction and vectorial representation of information for indexing textual documents. The model was known as Latent Semantic Indexing [3] at that time.

Originally only concerned by indexing tasks, LSA has been extended to the area of human memory simulation. Researchers in cognitive psychology got interested in it and then proposed it as a plausible model of human behavior in different tasks such as synonymy test [14] and problem solving [17]. The most famous application in cognitive psychology is the coupled CI-LSA model of text comprehension [12], which combines the previous "Construction-Integration" model of reading [11] with LSA as model of semantic memory. Whereas research involving LSA has been split in two main fields with the text-mining on the one hand and cognitive psychology on the other hand, our paper deals with both of those fields. Discussions of MINERVA 2 model of human episodic memory [6][7] allow proposing an operative algorithm for texts categorization.

LSA has been known to perform in synonymy test and other equivalent thematic classification tasks [14]. The model has been recently successfully applied on opinion judgment task [1]. There are very important differences between thematic classification, and opinion judgment classification. Firstly, thematic classification is directly connected to the distributional hypothesis, which states that "words that appear in similar contexts have similar meanings". Here is the reason why LSA is able to find words that *share the same thematic, ie "appear in equivalent contexts".* Secondly, in opinion judgment classification, different thematics could possibly belong to the same category of opinion. For example, I have a good opinion of different movies, which do not deal with the same topic. If I write texts in which I give my opinion of each movie, those texts will be influenced by the topic of the movie for a part, as well as by my motivation to exhibit how and why I loved them for another part. In consequence, the basic application of the distributional hypothesis cannot account for judgment opinion task.

In this paper, we will explore two lines of investigation. In the first line, we will propose the paradigmatic breakthrough that has been realized to find a solution to the limitation of the basic application of the distributional hypothesis. This breakthrough consists in switching from the semantic memory research field to the episodic memory metaphor to drive the similarity comparison stage. The episodic memory metaphor has been tested with LSA [8]. The second line that will be developed in this paper will consist in testing the episodic memory metaphor with an alternative method of Words Vectors construction, named Random Indexing.

2. Abstractive versus non-abstractive models of memory

In the debate within cognitive psychology about the distinction between "abstractive" versus "non-abstractive" models of memory [18][21], LSA has been proposed as belonging to the abstractive family [2]. This proposition is congruent with the affirmation by Landauer, Foltz and Laham that "the representations of passages that LSA forms can be interpreted as abstractions of "episodes", sometimes of episodes of purely verbal content such as philosophical arguments, and sometimes episodes from real or imagined life coded into verbal descriptions" [15: 15]. Tiberghien considers that "it would be more precise and theoretically more adequate, to consider that all the models are 'abstractive' but, for some of them this abstractive process

International Conference RANLP 2009 - Borovets, Bulgaria, pages 150–154

happens during encoding and for some others it happens during retrieval" [21: 145]. Because the abstractive process occurs during encoding, LSA and other Word Vector models are categorized as belonging to the abstractive model family.

A model like MINERVA 2 or other Multiple-Trace models are considered as "non-abstractive" because the abstractive process occurs during retrieval. According to MINERVA 2, memory consists of events or episodes that are represented and stored as vectors. The activation value of each coordinate stores features of episodes. Each vector corresponds to an episode in the system's life. Retrieval consists of a two stage calculation. First, a similarity calculation is carried out between the probe-vector and all the episode-vectors in memory (see ***Eq 1***). Episodes that are most similar will be affected by a higher level of activation than episodes that are least similar. Second, a calculation is made to compare the level of activation of each feature and this corresponds to the "echo" phenomena of memory. The "echo" calculation produces a new vector that inherits the features of the most activated vectors, even those parts that did not actually exist in the probes. The "echo" has two components: intensity which is denoted *I* (see ***Eq 2***), and content which corresponds to the sum of the content of all traces in memory, weighted by their activation level (see ***Eq 3***). "Echo" constitutes the process of abstraction that Rousset (2000) qualified as "re-creation.

$$S_i = \sum_{j=1}^{N} \frac{P_j T_{i,j}}{N_i}$$

Eq 1 Similarity of a trace i, where P_j is the value of feature j in the probe, and $T_{i,j}$ the value of feature j in trace I

$$\mathbf{I} = \sum_{i=1}^{M} A_i, \text{ whoro } A_i = S_i^3$$

Eq 2 Intensity of the « echo »

$$C_j = \sum_{i=1}^{M} A_i T_{i,j}$$

Eq 3 The content of the « echo »

3. The episodic memory metaphor in opinion judgment classification task

LSA has been successfully applied in tasks of text classification with texts expressing subjective opinion in the DEFT07 contest [1]. The Multiple-Trace approach has been proposed to account for semantic space performance when modifying factors like generality/specificity of episodes that compose the space [8]. Two predictions of MINERVA 2 model has been tested and confirmed. First, two methods of semantic space construction are compared.

In one method, different categories of episodes are blended in the same *global* semantic space. In the other method, each semantic space is built from a single category of episodes. These spaces are named *specific*. For each method of semantic space construction (*global vs specific*), two experimental conditions are compared. In the first condition, the number of episodes corresponding to each category is equalized. In the other condition, the number of episodes corresponding to each category is not controlled.

For the global space condition, correlation analysis showed that the relationship between relative amount of episodes and F-score was more important than the relationship between absolute amount of episode and F-score (r = .96, $\alpha > .001$ *versus* r = .74, $\alpha > .05$). For the specific space condition, the relationship between F-score and relative amount of data was almost the same as the relationship between F-score and absolute amount of data (r = .84, $\alpha > .01$ *versus* r = .87, $\alpha > .01$).

As predicted by MINERVA 2, modifying the relative amount of episodes or the absolute amount of episodes has an almost equivalent effect on performance for specialized spaces, whereas modifying relative amount of episodes has a more important effect on performance than modifying absolute amount of episode for general spaces.

4. The episodic memory metaphor for similarity judgment algorithm

The algorithm used in Deft07 to identify opinion judgment expressed by unknown texts, consisted in creating a target vector for each type of opinion that should be identified. These target vectors are created by the sum of vectors of all documents that belong to a given category of opinion[1]. For example, the target vector that was used to identify "good critics of movies" was a summed vector of all documents known to be a "good critic of movie". In-comings "text-to-be-indexed" were compared to the target vectors of each category of opinion. Then, the text was categorized with the opinion of the target vector to which it was the more similar. The comparison of similarity used the calculation of the cosine of the angle between the vector of the "text-to-be-indexed" and the target vector. The use of cosine calculation makes it possible to compare the very large target-vectors (hundreds of documents) to the very small text-to-be-indexed vector (one document).

The intuition that was underlying the construction of these very large target-vectors was that the classical distributional hypothesis approach has to be derived to perform in opinion judgment task. The idea was to sum vectors of all documents corresponding to a given opinion

[1]In data-mining contests, a classified corpus is given in what is called a *learning stage* to make it possible to implement algorithms that will be used to categorize un-classified documents in the *test stage*.

category to take advantage of the great number of documents to draw a vector that (i) would not correspond to any topic in particular, and in contrast, (ii) would hold information that would correspond to the linguistic way a given opinion is statistically expressed in numbers of texts. Applying the Multiple-Trace approach specifically to the stage of similarity comparison makes it possible to consider a target vector as an episodic memory that should behave like MINERVA 2 model predicts. Indeed, in considering each document as a specific episode, target-vectors become episodic memories, which are constituted of different episodes of the same category of opinion. As described above, the calculus of "echo" of MINERVA 2 predicts that the more a probe is similar to great numbers of episodes, the more the memory system would react by a strong value of "echo". It is neither mathematically nor psychologically wrong to consider that the value of "echo" in MINERVA 2 and the value of the cosine in LSA behave and can be interpreted in the same way. In consequence, MINERVA 2 gives a theoretical basement to our first intuitive method of vector target construction. The large size target vector method functioned pretty well and contributed to rank second in the Deft07.

5. Target-vectors as homogeneous episodic memory

The use of the episodic memory metaphor accounts for the limitation of the basic application of the distributional hypothesis for opinion judgment task. In creating these large target vectors, we are creating episodic memories, which behaviors became understandable with the MINERVA 2 model. Predictions concerning "echo" involve that the episodic memories will be more sensitive to probe episodes that are well represented in the memory and less sensible to probe episodes that are less represented. In other words, target vectors will be more sensible to typical documents and less sensible to non-typical documents. Theories of categorization showed that some items are typical of the category they belong, others are not. The typicality of an item is generally defined as (i) a high similarity with items of a given category and (ii) a low similarity with items of other categories.

Target vectors have been produced with the aim of creating episodic memories, which would hold the statistical linguistic signature of a given category of opinion. "Echo" predicts that target vectors will not identify non-typical documents as well as typical documents. We assume that a homogeneous episodic memory, which holds non-typical documents of a given category will be more sensitive to non-typical documents than a heterogeneous episodic memory, which holds typical and non-typical documents, all blended.

Our hypothesis has been implemented for the DEFT09. The aim of the task 1 was to classify texts that express facts or opinions, respectively corresponding "objective" *versus* "subjective" categories. First, we created a target vector in summing all vectors of all documents for each category. These target vectors had the same properties than those of the Deft07. Second, to be able to identify and regroup typical *versus* non-typical documents, a calculation of similarity is realized between (i) each document that composes the target vector, and (ii) the target vector. Documents that compose the target vector are ordered in function of their similarity with the target vector. Third, documents are regrouped in n sub-target vectors in a way that (i) each sub-target vector has the same amount of documents, and (ii) documents of the same degree of similarity with the target vector are regrouped in the same sub-target vector. The number of sub-target vectors for each category is a parameter of the algorithm we developed. Whereas the target vector algorithm has been tested with LSA, we propose to compare the *target-vector algorithm* with the *sub-target vector algorithm* using an alternative method of Word vector named Random Indexing.

6. Random Indexing

Word vectors correspond to a family of models in which LSA is the most known. Several principles are common to all of these models (see [18]):

- They are based on the distributional hypothesis
- They involve a method of counting words in a given unit of context
- They have a statistical method, which abstracts the meaning of concepts from large distributions of words in context
- They use a vectorial representation of word meaning.

As we will see, Random Indexing is not a typical item of its category. In the other models, the list of principles enounced above is also the stages of a semantic space construction. Particularities of the Random Indexing (RI) model are that (i) it does not create co-occurrence matrix (but it is possible if needed) and (ii) it does not need heavy statistical treatments like SVD for LSA. Contrary to the other Word Vector models, RI is not based on statistics but on random projections. The construction of a semantic space with RI is as follows:

- Create a matrix A (d x N), containing *Index vectors*, where d is the number of documents or contexts and N, the number of dimensions ($N >$ 1000) decided by the experimenter. *Index vectors* are sparse and randomly generated. They consist in small numbers +1 and -1 and thousands of 0.
- Create a matrix B (t x N), containing *term vectors*, where t is the number of different terms in the

corpus. Set all vectors with null values to start the semantic space construction.

- Scan each document of the corpus. Each time a term *t* appears in a document *d*, accumulate the randomly generated *d-index vector* to the *t-term vector*.

At the end of the process, *term vectors* that appeared in similar contexts have accumulated similar *index vectors*. There is a training cycle option in the model. When the scan has been computed for all documents, the matrix B is charged for all *term vectors*. Then a matrix A' (d' x N), with $d' = d$ can be computed with the output of *term vectors*. The number of training cycle is a parameter in the model. The training process output is consistent with what has been described for neural network learning. The RI model has performed in TOEFL synonymy test [9][10] as well as in text categorization [18].

7. Experiment

7.1 Method and material

The experiment reported here has been realized the task 1 of the DEFT09 using the english corpus. The purpose of the task 1 was the detection of the subjectivity or objectivity character of a text. As described by the committee, "the reference is established by projecting each section on both the subjective and the objective dimension. For instance, the Letter from the editor, which usually states an opinion, has the type subjective, while the News, describing actual facts, have the type objective"[2]. The english corpus was composed of articles of the economic newspaper "*The Financial Time*". In the learning stage, 60% of the total corpus is given to each team engaged to allow them to implement algorithms that will then be applied on the 40% of uncategorized documents during the test stage. We realized our learning session using the "ten cross-folder" method. Table 1 give a description of the corpus.

Table 1. Description of the corpus of learning and test

	Learning		Test	
	Number of documents	Size (Kb)	Number of documents	Size (Kb)
Objective	3440	15840	5245	27996
Subjective	4426	26016		

7.2 Results

Precision and recall performances are reported for the *Target vector algorithm* and the *Sub-target vector algorithm.* Taking account that the value of 1 for recall means that all documents have been categorized in the same category. Hence those scores should be considered as aberrant.

This is the case for two reported results: the *Target vector algorithm*, which have 1 target and the *Sub-target vector algorithm* using 11 targets (indicated by the double slash in Table 2) both have 0.432 for Precision and 1 in Recall. Those results demonstrate that the *Target vector algorithm* was not able to perform in the considered task.

Concerning the *Sub-target vector algorithm,* the systems performs better using 9 sub-targets (Precision of 0.740 and Recall of 0.708 using 1000 dimensions and respectively 0.746 and 0.718 using 2000 dimensions). This result involves that there is an optimum threshold for the number of sub-target vectors. Considering Multiple-Trace approach, this threshold corresponds to the moment where episodic memories or sub-targets are the most homogeneous.

Runs realized changing the specific parameters of Random Indexing as the number of dimensions and the number of training cycles show that the optimum partition realized with the *Sub-target vector algorithm* using 9 sub-targets doest not change significantly (between 0.740 and 0.746 for the Precision and between 0.708 and 0.718 for Recall). Those results show that performance of the *Sub-target vector algorithm* is more dependent of the number of sub-target used and less dependent of the parameters of Random Indexing.

Table 2. Parameters and scores

Parameters			Score	
Dimensions	Cycles	Sub-target	Precision	Recall
Target-vector algorithm				
1500	10	1	0.432	1//
Sub-target vector algorithm				
1500	10	3	0.648	0.508
1500	10	5	0.688	0.530
1500	10	7	0.652	0.503
1000	10	9	0.740	0.708
1500	10	9	0.738	0.704
2000	10	9	0.746	0.718
1500	10	11	0.432	1//

8. Conclusions

Target vector algorithm consisted in creating a very large vector composed of each and every documents of a given category as target vector used to identify the category a document belongs to. The proposed theoretical switching from abstractive to non-abstractive model of memory has

[2] DEFT09 website: http://deft09.limsi.fr/index.php?id=1&lang=en

been described and tested to account for the *Target-vector algorithm*. Those large target vectors have been considered as episodic memories and MINERVA 2 has been used as a metaphor to predict and interpret behaviors of such episodic memories. The *Target-vector algorithm,* which has been developped for the DEFT07, has been applied on the DEFT09 corpus. Results reported demonstrate very bad performance.

Computing the *Sub-target algorithm* with different numbers of homogeneous sub-targets was congruent with predictions derived from the "echo" calculation of Minerva 2. Indeed, performance reported for the *Sub-target algorithm* using 9 sub-targets demonstrated that there is an optimal partition of similar episodes in sub-target that upgrades the system's performance.

The work presented here is in the line of researches that study the effect of typicality or the effect of frequency of episodes on the capability of the memory system to recognize or to recall a particular event or item. Future developments of our research should highlight, in a more reliable way, how mathematical description of the human cognitive system could upgrade artificial computing systems, particularly in Natural Language Processing applications.

9. References

[1] M. Ahat, W. Lenhart, H. Baier, Y. V. Hoareau, S. Jhean-Larose, & G. Denhière,(2007) "Le concours DEFT'07 envisagé du point de vue de l'Analyse de la Sémantique Latente (LSA)". In Proceedings of the conference DEFT'07, Grenoble, 2007.

[2] C. Bellissens, P. Thérouane, & G. Denhière, Les modèles vectoriels de la mémoire sémantique : description, validation et perspectives, Le Langage et L'Homme, 34 (2004), 101-122.

[3] S. Deerwester, S. T. Dumais, G. W. Furnas, T. K. Landauer, & R. Harshman, Indexing By Latent Semantic Analysis, Journal of the American Society For Information Science, 41(1990), 391-407.

[4] G. Denhière, B. Lemaire, C. Bellissens, & S. Jhean-Larose, A semantic space for modeling children's semantic memory, In T. K. Landauer, D. McNamara, S. Dennis, W. Kintsch (Eds) The Handbook of Latent Semantic Analysis, Lawrence Erlbaum Associates, Mahwah, 2007.

[5] S. T. Dumais, Improving the retrieval of information from external resources, Behavior Research Methods, Instruments, & Computers, 23 (1991), 229-236.

[6] D. L. Hintzman, MINERVA 2: A simulation of human memory, Behavior Research Methods, Intruments, & Computers, 16 (1984), 96-101.

[7] D. L. Hintzman, Judgments of frequency and recognition memory in a Multiple-Trace Model, Psychological Review, 95 (1988), 528-551.

[8] Y. V. Hoareau, M. Ahat, G. Denhière, S. Jean-Lharose, W. Lenhard & H. Baier & L. Legros, Indexing with LSA : the Multiple Trace approach, (submitted).

[9] P. Kanerva, J. Kristoferson, & A. Holst, Random Indexing of Text Samples for Latent Semantic Analysis, In L.R. Gleitman, and A.K. Josh (Eds.), Proceedings of the 22nd Annual Conference of the Cognitive Science Society, Lawrence Erlbaum Associates, Mahwah, 2000.

[10] J. Karlgren, & M. Sahlgren, From Words to Understanding, In Y. Uesaka, P. Kanerva, & H. Asoh (Eds.) Foundations of Real-World Intelligence, CSLI Publications, Stanford, 2001.

[11] W. Kintsch, The role of knowledge in discourse comprehension : a construction-integration model, Psychological Review, 95 (1988), 163-182

[12] W. Kintsch, Comprehension: a paradigm for cognition, Cambridge University Press, Cambridge, 1998.

[13] T. K. Landauer, LSA as a Theory of Meaning. In T. K. Landauer, D. McNamara, S. Dennis, W. Kintsch (Eds). The Handbook of Latent Semantic Analysis, Lawrence Erlbaum Associates, Mahwah, 2007.

[14] T. K. Landauer, & S. T.Dumais, A solution to Plato's problem: The Latent Semantic Analysis theory of the acquisition, induction, and representation of knowledge, Psychological Review, 104 (1997), 211-240.

[15] T. K. Landauer, P. W. Foltz, & D. Laham, Introduction to Latent Semantic Analysis, Discourse Processes, 25 (1998), 259-284.

[16] K. Lund, C. Burgess. Producing high-dimensional semantic spaces from lexical co-occurrence, Behavior Research Methods, Instrumentation, and Computers, 28 (1996), 203-208.

[17] J.F. Quesada, W. Kintsch, & E. Gomez, A theory of Complex Problem Solving using Latent Semantic Analysis, In W. D. Gray & C. D. Schunn (Eds.) Proceedings of the 24th Annual Conference of the Cognitive Science Society, Lawrence Erlbaum Associates, Mahwah, NJ, 2002.

[18] S. Rousset, Les conceptions "système unique" de la mémoire : aspect théorique, Revue de neuropsychologie, 10 (2000), 30-56.

[19] M. Sahlgren, The Word-Space Model: Using distributional analysis to represent syntagmatic and paradigmatic relations between words in high-dimensional vector spaces. Ph.D. dissertation, Department of Linguistics, Stockholm University, (2006).

[20] M. Sahlgren, & R. Cöster, Using Bag-of-Concepts to Improve the Performance of Support Vector Machines in Text Categorization, Proceedings of the 20th International Conference on Computational Linguistics, Geneva, 2004.

[21] G. Tiberghien, La mémoire oubliée, Mardaga, Liège, 1994

Evaluating the Impact of Morphosyntactic Ambiguity in Grammatical Error Detection

Arantza Díaz de Ilarraza, Koldo Gojenola and Maite Oronoz
Department of Computer Languages and Systems
University of the Basque Country
{jipdisaa, koldo.gojenola, maite.oronoz}@ehu.es

Abstract

We present a study of the impact of morphological and syntactic ambiguity in the process of grammatical error detection. We will present three different systems that have been devised with the objective of detecting grammatical errors in Basque and will examine the influence of ambiguity in their results. We infer that the ambiguity rate in the input to an error detection tool can have a considerable impact on the quality of the system.

Keywords

Grammatical error detection, morphosyntactic ambiguity

1 Introduction

The relationship between ambiguity and error detection has been mentioned in very few occasions [3, 13]. Similarly to most NLP areas, the development of tools for grammatical error detection and correction finds ambiguity as a main obstacle for the design of efficient and accurate systems. Typically the errors accumulated through the linguistic analysis make difficult the process of detecting grammatical errors. Birn [3] states the following relation between ambiguity, linguistic analysis and grammar error detection.

> "The relationship between disambiguation and grammar error detection is intricate. On the one hand, ... disambiguation is a prerequisite for any effort at precise error detection. On the other hand, a grammar error may disturb the disambiguation, ... and this in turn may disturb the error detection"

In this paper we will study this statement over three systems designed for the detection of errors ranging from a restricted and limited context (errors in date expressions and complex postpositions) to the more general case of agreement errors between verb and sentence elements. We will concentrate on morphological and syntactic ambiguity:

- Morphological ambiguity: each word-form can receive multiple morphological analyses, e.g. noun/verb is a typical example of categorial ambiguity. For agglutinative languages there are additional sources of ambiguity (number, case, ...). This poses a problem for grammatical error detection/correction.

Level	Linguistic features	Method
M1	POS	CG + HMM
M2	POS + SubPOS	CG + HMM
M3	POS + SubPOS + Case	CG + HMM
M4	All in MORFEUS	CG

Table 1: *Disambiguation levels in* EUSTAGGER.

- Syntactic ambiguity: this is typically added on top of morphological ambiguity. For example, it is important to exactly know whether an NP is the subject or the object of a verb in order to detect agreement errors.

The remainder of this paper is organized as follows. Section 2 comments on the general morphosyntactic analyzer for Basque, and its parameterization to investigate the impact of ambiguity in error detection. Section 3 will present the experiments with different degrees of ambiguity in three settings. Section 4 compares our work with related systems, ending with the main conclusions.

2 Linguistic resources and parameterization of ambiguity

For the analysis of the input texts, we will use the Basque shallow syntactic analyzer [1]. Instead of using a general purpose analyzer, an alternative approach to error analysis could be the development of specially tailored resources for error processing, but as the creation of tools (morphological analyzer, tagger,...) is a very expensive task, we decided to use the one within our reach, and perform the necessary adaptations to deal with ill-formed sentences.

Let us focus in the parts related to ambiguity:

- *Morphosyntactic disambiguation* (linguistic and stochastic disambiguation in figure 1). After morphosyntactic analysis (MORFEUS), the tagger/lemmatiser EUSTAGGER obtains the lemma and category of each form and also performs disambiguation using the part of speech (POS), fine grained part of speech (SubPOS) and case. Disambiguation is performed by linguistic rules using Constraint Grammar (CG) [16] and stochastic rules (HMMs) [9]. Table 1 shows the parameterizable disambiguation levels in EUSTAGGER.

International Conference RANLP 2009 - Borovets, Bulgaria, pages 155–160

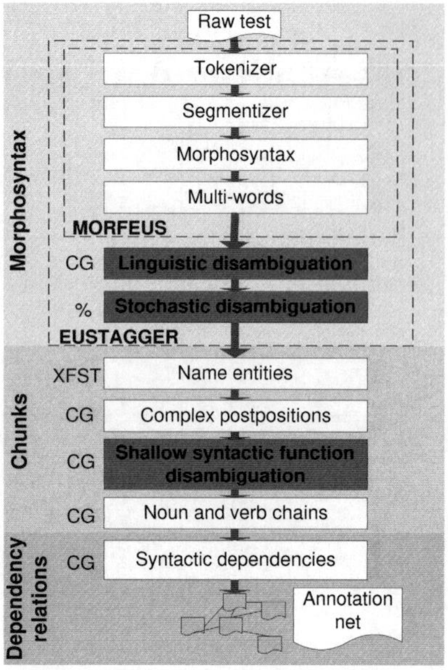

Fig. 1: *The syntactic analyzer for Basque.*

- *Shallow syntactic function disambiguation.* This is carried out in two levels:
  - S1: functions related to noun chunks (@<CM, ...) and functions of verbal chunks (@+FMAINVERB, ...) are disambiguated[1].
  - S2: functions included in S1 and main syntactic functions (@SUBJ, @OBJ...) are disambiguated.

For local error detection only morphosyntactic disambiguation will be used. In the case of agreement errors, however, both morphosyntactic and syntactic function treatment are necessary. For that reason, the experiments will use combinations of morphosyntactic and shallow syntactic function disambiguation. For example the combination M1-S2 indicates the morphosyntactic level M1, and the syntactic disambiguation level S2.

3 Estimation of the impact of ambiguity in Error Detection

We have divided grammatical errors into two groups depending on the context they occur. On the one hand, we will treat "local syntactic errors" that appear in windows of five-six consecutive words following the linear order of a sentence, that is, they usually occur within phrases or chunks. Several tools based on finite-state automata or transducers, such as Constraint Grammar, The Xerox Finite State Tool [17] or Foma [14] can be used to detect these types of errors. On the other hand, there is a group of grammatical errors that needs more sophisticated techniques. For example, in the detection of agreement errors, the elements to be analyzed (verb, subject, object and indirect object) may appear far from each other in the sentence. In the particular case of Basque, they could appear in many different positions due to its free constituent order of nominal elements with respect to the verb. We call these types of errors "global syntactic errors". We will use *Saroi* [6], a tool that we have developed to allow the definition of declarative rules for the detection of errors in dependency-trees. Although, in local syntactic errors correction has also been implemented, the results presented in this paper concern error detection in all cases.

With regard to the corpus used, we use not only general error corpora, but also "correct" corpora. The latter will allow us to test the systems negatively, that is, we will test systems' behavior in respect to false alarms. We think that this approach is interesting for a good evaluation of automatic error detection.

3.1 Local Syntactic Errors: Date Expressions and Complex Postpositions

Errors in date expressions and complex postpositions can be deemed as representative of local syntactic errors. Despite their similarity because their context for detection is limited to a few consecutive words, they also have important differences:

- *Date expressions.* These structures are hardly ambiguous. For example, the following succession of elements is almost always a date:

  `[ place name, ]`[2] `year month day`

  An example of this structure is, *"1995eko maiatzaren 15"* (15th of May, 1995). It is incorrectly written because in Basque the day number after a month in genitive case must take a case mark. In erroneous date constructions, it is usual to find 2 or 3 errors in the same structure.

- *Complex postpositions.* Postpositions in Basque play a role similar to that of prepositions in languages like English or Spanish, so that, postposition suffixes are attached to the last element of the noun phrase. We have treated those postpositions that are formed by a suffix followed by a lemma (main element) that can also be inflected:

etxearen			*gainetik*		
etxe	+	*-aren*	*gain*	+	*-etik*
(house)		(of the)	(top)		(from the)
from	the	top	of	the	house

Frequently the incorrect uses of some complex postpositions can have the same form as correct uses of adverbs or names. This makes postpositions morphosyntactically and semantically very ambiguous. Usually, erroneous constructions contain an unique error.

[1] @<CM: modifier of the noun carrying case. @+FMAINVERB: finite main verb.

[2] [ ] symbols indicate that the place name is optional.

3.1.1 Date expressions

We have performed the detection and correction of grammatical errors in date expressions [8] using finite-state transducers (FSTs). Finite-state constraints, encoded in the form of automata and transducers by means of the Xerox Finite State Tool (XFST), are applied to the morphosyntactic analysis of dates. The system is composed of two groups of FSTs, one for error detection and the other one for the generation of correct dates. The system deals with the nine most frequent error types occurring in dates in Basque.

The system was evaluated in a "test list" (items where month-names appear) of 658 sentences (411 for **Dev**elopment and 247 for **Test**), including correct dates, incorrect dates, and also structures similar to dates. Those sentences were extracted from a corpus composed of i) 267 essays written by students and ii) texts from newspapers (presumably correct), more than 500,000 words altogether. Only detection was evaluated, as the generation of correct date expressions guarantees the correction of all the errors in the expression even if not all of them were detected.

In order to evaluate the impact of morphosyntactic ambiguity, we have analyzed the corpora considering different levels of disambiguation (see table 1). Table 2 shows the results. Without disambiguation (WD), or using M1, M2 and M4 disambiguation levels, values of 95.9% recall[3] and 97.8% precision[4] are reached in the development corpus. The system gives 92.1% recall and 89.7% precision over the test corpus (247 test items) in WD, M1 and M2. However, the detection goes down when using the major number of features for disambiguation (M3 includes POS, SubPOS and case) obtaining 76.3% and 87.7% precision and recall in the test corpus. The reason for this reduction is the removal of the analyses needed for error detection, and in consequence, the decrease in the number of detected errors (75 from 93 in the development corpus and 29 from 35 in the test one). There are no changes in the false alarm rate.

3.1.2 Complex Postpositions

We designed and evaluated a set of rules, based on the Constraint Grammar (CG) formalism to detect errors in complex postpositions, constructions that are semantically and syntactically ambiguous [7]. For the description of the incorrect structures, apart from morphosyntactic and syntactic features, the rules were extended with several classes of semantic restrictions (animate nouns, names representing places, ...). For error correction we applied a morphosyntactic generator that uses information extracted from the incorrect structure and from correction schemas.

Being a local error, for the evaluation of this structure we used again "test lists", but in this occasion we made a distinction between those extracted from an error corpus (994,658 word-forms), and those obtained from a "correct" corpus composed of newspapers (8,207,919 word-forms).

[3] recall = correctly detected errors/all errors

[4] precision = correctly detected errors/(correctly detected errors + false alarms)

The first experiment was carried out again, without disambiguating the analyzed texts. Table 3 shows the evaluation results. In the error corpus we obtained a recall of 81.6% and a precision of 96% (development) and 65% recall and 67% precision (test). The corpus composed of newspapers is lexically richer than the error corpus, and in consequence, the semantic variability of some complex postpositions was higher. That causes an increment of the false alarm rate, leaving the precision in values ranging from 40% to 42%.

	Newspapers Corp.		Error Corp.	
	Dev	**Test**	**Dev**	**Test**
Sentences	26679	17786	3884	2590
Errors	-	-	60	29
Undetected	-	-	11	10
Detected	30	24	49	19
False alarms	45	33	2	9
Recall	-	-	81.6%	65%
Precision	40%	42%	96%	67%

Table 3: *Complex Postpositions. Evaluation.*

As the goal of the present work is to analyze the impact of the ambiguity in grammar error detection and not the error detection task itself, we decided to use the biggest corpus for this experiment, in this case the **Dev** corpus. Table 4 shows the evaluation results. Although much variability in the results could be observed, still the option that makes a deeper morphosyntactic disambiguation gives the worse results. The precision falls from 96% in the WD option, to 84.9% in M3 due to the appearance of more false alarms. This may be caused because a deeper disambiguation can remove the correct interpretation of a word-form, which can then be flagged as incorrect.

	Error Corpus. Development				
	Detect	Undetect	FA	Recall	Precision
WD	49	11	2	81.6%	96.0%
M1	43	17	4	71.6%	91.48%
M2	43	17	4	71.6%	91.48%
M3	45	15	8	75.0%	**84.9%**
M4	42	18	3	**70.0%**	93.3%
Sentences	3884				
Errors	60				

Table 4: *Impact of ambiguity in postpositions.*

3.2 Global Syntactic Errors: Agreement

Agreement errors in Basque are very frequent. Finite verbs agree with the subject, object or indirect object of the sentence. These elements can appear in any order in the sentence, and each of them must agree with the verb in case, number and person. This is a source of many syntactic errors, considerably higher than in languages with a more reduced kind of agreement, as English or Spanish.

3.2.1 *A tool for inspecting dependency trees*

For the detection of agreement errors we applied *Saroi*, a system that is used to apply query-rules

	Development					Test				
	Detect	Undetect	FA	Recall	Precision	Detect	Undetect	FA	Recall	Precision
WD	93	4	2	**95.9%**	**97.8%**	35	3	4	**92.1%**	**89.7%**
M1	93	4	2	**95.9%**	**97.8%**	35	3	4	**92.1%**	**89.7%**
M2	93	4	2	**95.9%**	**97.8%**	35	3	4	**92.1%**	**89.7%**
M3	75	4	2	77.3%	97.4%	29	3	4	76.3%	87.7%
M4	93	4	2	**95.9%**	**97.8%**	34	3	4	89.5%	89.5%
Sentences	411					247				
Errors	97					38				

Table 2: *Impact of ambiguity in date error detection.*

to dependency-trees. *Saroi* has as input a group of analysis-trees and a group of rules, and obtains as output the dependency-trees that fulfill the conditions described in the rules. Its main objective is the analysis of linguistic phenomena in corpora. Figure 2 shows an example of a rule that detects the error in the dependency-tree of figure 3. In the sentence the subject *zentral nuklearrak* (nuclear power station), in absolutive case, and the auxiliary verb, *dute*, which needs the subject to be in ergative case, do not agree. Specifically the first rule asks that the current word (which should be the main verb) has a subject, and this subject has a modifier (which contains the grammatical case). The verb has an auxiliary verb as dependent (linked by the auxmod dependency arc), which is transitive. If these two conditions hold, then the auxiliary verb and the subject should agree in case. If they do not, then an agreement error occurs.

```
AGREEMENT_SUBJ_CASE_N_NK
(
Detect (
      @!ncsubj!ncmod∼ &
      @!auxmod.type == 'transitive' &
      @!ncsubj!ncmod.case != @!auxmod.nork.case
      )
)
```

Fig. 2: *Example of a rule.*

Saroi uses as input the result of the partial syntactic analyzer (see section 2), in which the relations between the elements of the sentence are ambiguously represented. *Saroi* constructs all the set of non ambiguous trees starting from an initially ambiguous tree (see figure 4). The error-detection rules are applied to the full set of dependency-trees. Having in mind the errors accumulated in the analysis chain, we choose a conservative approach: we decide that an agreement error occurs in a sentence when an error detection rule matches all the analysis-trees.

3.2.2 Experiments

Due to morphosyntactic and syntactic ambiguity, a number of trees ranging from 1 to more than 100 is generated for each sentence. In addition, several difficulties must be taken into account:

- NP ellipsis is common in Basque. This makes it difficult to know if a sentence is correct or not, as there may be several ellided elements.

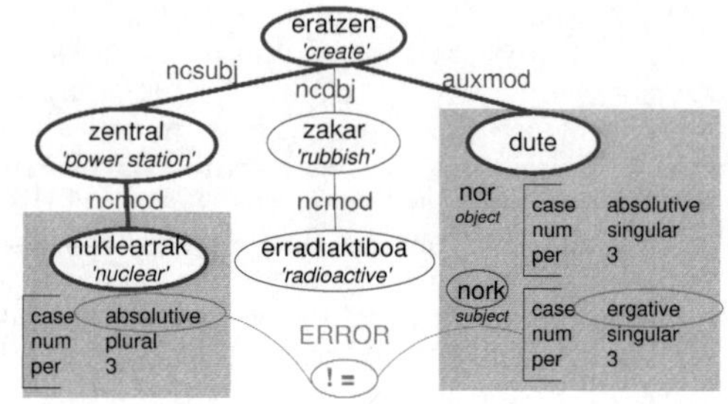

Fig. 3: *Dependency-tree for the sentence* *Zentral nuklearrak zakar erradiaktiboa eratzen dute *(*Nuclear power station create radioactive rubbish).*

- The syntactic analyzer obtains partial analyses and, therefore, not all the elements of the sentence appear in the dependency-trees due to lack of coverage, increasing false alarms.

We decided that in agreement error detection the best option for disambiguation should be chosen before starting the evaluation because to test the rules with all the possible disambiguation options is too time consuming. Considering all the disambiguation combinations, the best criteria should be the ones that:

- Detects the higher number of errors in ungrammatical sentences.
- Gives the lower number of false alarms in grammatical sentences.
- Generates the lower number of analysis trees for each sentence (efficiency).

Our strategy to obtain the best disambiguation option was to chose first the morphosyntactic disambiguation level, and then we selected the best option for syntactic disambiguation.

In order to choose the best morphosyntactic disambiguation level we selected a set of 10 ungrammatical sentences and their respective corrections, which were analyzed with the eight disambiguation combinations (see table 5). The combinations generating the lower number of trees, with aceptable detection and false alarm rates were those making the deepest morphosyntactic disambiguation (M3-S1 and M3-S2).

Next, we aimed at selecting the best syntactic function disambiguation level. We soon realized that the grammar that assigns the dependency-relations to grammatical texts needed of relaxation when applied

	Disambiguation combinations							
	M1-S1	M2-S1	**M3-S1**	M4-S1	M1-S2	M2-S2	**M3-S2**	M4-S2
Number of trees	67,7	67,7	**27,8**	46,7	22,11	22,11	**11,6**	10,33
Errors in ungrammatical	5	5	**6**	6	5	5	**6**	6
False alarms in grammatical	0	0	**1**	1	0	0	**1**	0

Table 5: *Looking for the best morphosyntactic disambiguation-combination.*

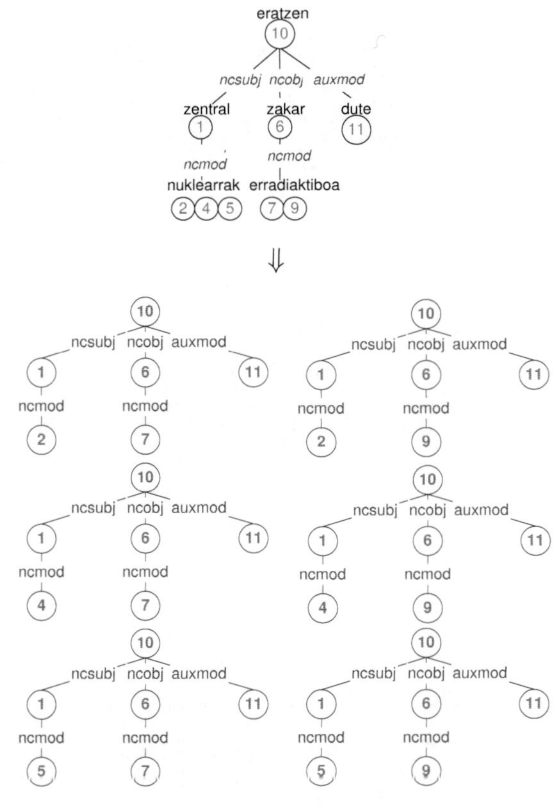

Fig. 4: *Ambiguous dependency tree and the corresponding non-ambiguous trees.*

to ill-formed texts. For example, in the incorrect sentence "*nik ez nago konforme" (*I do not agree*), the word "nik" (*I*) was not tagged as *subject* because it carries the ergative case, and the auxiliary verb "nago" asks for a subject in absolutive case. We experimented relaxing all the conditions referred to the type of auxiliary verb in the rules assigning *subject*, *object* and *indirect object* relations. In a second experiment we used a corpus of 75 sentences containing an agreement error and 75 of their corrections. The sentences were analyzed with the following combinations: M3-S1-Relaxed, M3-S1-NotRelaxed, M3-S2-Relaxed and M3-S2-NotRelaxed. Table 6 shows that the best results were obtained with the M3-S2-Relaxed option. In this experiment we reach interesting conclusions related to error detection:

- In 76.9 % of the cases (20 out of 26), the error was not detected because dependency-relations were incorrectly assigned.
- Sometimes the error was detected due to an incorrect analysis. A false detection occurs.

Opposite to what happened in local error detection, in this case the combination with the best results was the one that disambiguates most.

The work carried out in agreement error detection shows us that when the dependency-relations are incorrectly tagged, error detection is very difficult. The improvement of the syntactic analyzer will bring as a result a better error detection.

4 Related work

To choose the more appropiate approach to face up the problem of grammatical error detection is not a trivial decision. In this section we review some error detection approaches, and at the same time we try to justify our choice of using knowledge-based techniques, as opposite to statistic-based ones.

In our opinion, for error types related to the omission, replacement or addition of elements, empirical approaches are suitable. For example, in [19] and [5] machine learning techniques are used to detect errors involving prepositions in non-native English speakers. Although both English prepositions and Basque postpositions have in some part relation with semantic features, postpositions are, in our opinion, qualitatively more complex, as they are distributed across two words, and they also show different kinds of syntactic agreement, together with a high number of variants. A deeply studied area using machine learning techniques is that of the "context-sensitive spelling correction" [12, 4]. Izumi *et al.* [15] use empirical techniques to detect omission- and replacement-type grammatical and lexical errors in Japanese learners of English. Bigert and Knutsson [2] prove that precision in error detection is significantly improved when unsupervised methods are combined with linguistic information.

The error types we are working with are in all cases related to agreement. Linguistic features of several elements belonging to phrases or sentences must be compared in order to be able to detect the potential errors. This is one of the reasons why we decided to use a knowledge-based approach. Similar methods have been used for grammatical error detection using approaches based on context free grammars (CFG) or finite state techniques. In the first case, for analyzing ungrammatical sentences by means of CFGs, the "relaxation" of some constraints in the grammar has been necessary [18, 11], or error grammars have been developed [10]. When finite state techniques are used, error patterns encoded in rules are applied to the analyzed texts. We follow the second approach as rules encoded using CG, XFST or the query-rules of *Saroi* are applied to the linguistic analysis of the texts.

Disambiguation combinations				
	Relaxed		NotRelaxed	
	M3-S1	M3-S2	M3-S1	M3-S2
Errors in ungrammatical (EE)	42	**40**	36	34
False alarms in grammatical (FA)	23	**16**	18	15
Real detection (EE - FA)	19 (25.33%)	**24 (32%)**	18 (24%)	19 (25.33%)

Table 6: *Looking for the best syntactic function disambiguation-combination.*

5 Conclusions and future work

In this work we have presented the impact of morphosyntactic and syntactic ambiguity across three different types of error detection systems. Two of the systems detect and correct local syntactic errors, and the last one detects global syntactic errors. The results of the experiments show that the influence of morphosyntactic ambiguity in grammatical error detection is undeniable. We can assert that it is not always true that "it is obvious that disambiguation is a prerequisite for any effort at precise error detection". In local syntactic error detection the best results have been obtained when the analyzed texts are not disambiguated (in the case of dates the same results are achieved if some types of disambiguation are performed). The reason is that before the disambiguation process starts, all the set of interpretations for each word is within our reach, both "correct" and "incorrect" interpretations. When disambiguation is performed, sometimes the interpretations we are interested in, are removed. We must bear in mind that disambiguation rules are generally written having grammaticality in mind. In the case of global syntactic error detection, nevertheless, the best results are obtained when the deepest disambiguation is used at morphosyntactic level, and also at syntactic level. In our opinion, this phenomenon is due to the explosion in the number of generated trees when "all" the possible ambiguity is considered. We think that each kind of error type asks for a specific study of the influence of ambiguity, specially when using knowledge-based techniques.

In all the presented systems one of the main goals is to process real texts with high precision error detection, minimizing false alarms, which are the main bottleneck in current grammar checking systems.

Acknowledgments

This research is supported by the Basque Government (IT-397-07).

References

[1] I. Aduriz, M. Aranzabe, J. M. Arriola, A. Díaz de Ilarraza, K. Gojenola, M. Oronoz, and L. Uria. A cascaded syntactic analyser for Basque. In A. Gelbukh, editor, *Computational Linguistics and Intelligent Text Processing: 5th International Conference CICLing2004, Seoul, Korea, February 15-21*, volume 2945 of *Lecture Notes in Computer Science*, pages 124–134. Springer-Verlag GmbH, 2004.

[2] J. Bigert and O. Knutsson. Robust error detection: A hybrid approach combining unsupervised error detection and linguistic knowledge. In *Romand 2002 (Robust Methods in Analysis of Natural language Data)*, Frascati, Italy, 2002.

[3] J. Birn. Detecting grammar errors with Lingsoft's Swedish grammar-checker. In *Proceedings from the 12th Nordiske datalingvistikkdager*, Department of Linguistics, Norwegian University of Science and Technology (NTNU), 2000.

[4] A. J. Carlson, J. Rosen, and D. Roth. Scaling up context-sensitive text correction. In *Proceedings of the Thirteenth Innovative Applications of Artificial Intelligence Conference (IAAI-01)*, pages 45–50, Menlo Park CA, 2001.

[5] M. Chodorow, J. Tetreault, and N.-R. Han. Detection of Gramatical Errors Involving Prepositions. In *4th ACL-SIGSEM workshop on Prepositions*, Prague, 2007.

[6] A. Díaz de Ilarraza, K. Gojenola, and M. Oronoz. Design and development of a system for the detection of agreement errors in Basque. In A. Gelbukh, editor, *Computational Linguistics and Intelligent Text Processing: 6th International Conference CICLing2005, Mexico City, Mexico, February 13-19*, volume 3406 of *Lecture Notes in Computer Science*, pages 793–803. Springer-Verlag GmbH, 2005.

[7] A. Díaz de Ilarraza, K. Gojenola, and M. Oronoz. Detecting Erroneus Uses of Complex Postpositions in an Agglutinative Language. In *Proceedings of the 22nd International Conference on Computational Linguistics (COLING 2008)*, Manchester, 2008.

[8] A. Díaz de Ilarraza, K. Gojenola, M. Oronoz, M. Otaegi, and I. Alegria. Syntactic error detection and correction in date expressions using finite"-state transducers. In *Proceedings of Finite"-State Methods and Natural Language Processing (FSMNLP07)*, Postdam, Germany, 2007.

[9] N. Ezeiza, I. Aduriz, I. Alegria, J. Arriola, and R. Urizar. Combining stochastic and rule-based methods for disambiguation in agglutinative languages. In *COLING 1998*, Montreal, 1998.

[10] J. Foster and C. Vogel. Good reasons for noting bad grammar: Constructing a corpus of ungrammatical language. In *Pre-Proceedings of the International Conference on Linguistic Evidence: Empirical, Theoretical and Computational Perspectives*, Tübingen, Germany, 2004.

[11] K. Gojenola and K. Sarasola. Aplicación de la relajación gradual de restricciones para la detección y corrección de errores sintácticos. In *Actas del X congreso de la Sociedad Española para el Procesamiento del Lenguaje Natural, (SEPLN)*, volume 4, Córdoba, Spain, 1994.

[12] A. R. Golding and D. Roth. A Winnow-Based Approach to Context-Sensitive Spelling Correction. *Machine Learning*, 34(1-3):107–130, 1999.

[13] S. Hashemi. Detecting Grammar Errors in Children's Writing: A Finite State Approach. In *Proceedings of the 13th Nordic Conference on Computational Linguistics (NoDaLiDa'01)*, Uppsala, Sweden, 2000.

[14] M. Hulden. Foma: a Finite-State Compiler and Library. In *Demo in the proceedings of EACL*, 2009.

[15] E. Izumi, K. Uchimoto, T. Saiga, T. Supnithi, and H. Isahara. Automatic error detection in the Japanese learners' English spoken data. In *ACL '03: Proceedings of the 41st Annual Meeting on Association for Computational Linguistics*, pages 145–148, Morristown, NJ, USA, 2003.

[16] F. Karlsson, A. Voutilainen, J. Heikkila, and A. Anttila. *Constraint Grammar: Language-independent System for Parsing Unrestricted Text.* Prentice-Hall, Berlin, 1995.

[17] L. Karttunen, T. Gaál, and A. Kempe. Xerox finite state tool. Technical report, Xerox Research Centre Europe, 1997.

[18] R. Teixeira Martins, R. Hasegawa, M. D. G. Volpe Nunes, G. Montilha, and J. Osvaldo Novais De Oliveira. Linguistic issues in the development of ReGra: A grammar checker for Brazilian Portuguese. *Natural Language Engineering*, 4(4):287–307, 1998.

[19] J. Tetreault and M. Chodorow. The ups and downs of preposition error detection in esl writing. In *Proceedings of Coling,*, Manchester, 2008.

Fast Boosting-based Part-of-Speech Tagging and Text Chunking with Efficient Rule Representation for Sequential Labeling

Tomoya Iwakura
Fujitsu Laboratories Ltd.
1-1, Kamikodanaka 4-chome, Nakahara-ku, Kawasaki 211-8588, Japan
iwakura.tomoya@jp.fujitsu.com

Abstract

This paper proposes two techniques for fast sequential labeling such as part-of-speech (POS) tagging and text chunking. The first technique is a boosting-based algorithm that learns rules represented by combination of features. To avoid time-consuming evaluation of combination, we divide features into not used ones and used ones for learning combination. The other is a rule representation. Usual POS taggers and text chunkers decide the tag of each word by using the features generated from the word and its surrounding words. Thus similar rules, for example, that consist of the same set of words but only differ in locations from current words, are generated. We use a rule representation that enables us to merge such rules. We evaluate our methods with POS tagging and text chunking. The experimental results show that our methods show faster processing speed than taggers and chunkers without our methods while maintaining accuracy.

1 Introduction

Several machine learning algorithms such as Support Vector Machines (SVMs) and boosting-based learning algorithms have been applied to Natural Language Processing (NLP) problems successfully. The cases of boosting include text categorization [11], POS tagging [5] and text chunking [7, 5], and so on. Furthermore, parsers based on boosting-based learners have shown fast processing speed [7, 5]. However, to process large data such as WEB data and e-mails, processing speed of base technologies such as POS tagging and text chunking will be important.

This paper proposes two techniques for improving processing speed of POS tagging and text chunking. The first technique is a boosting-based algorithm that learns rules. Instead of specifying combination of features manually, we specify features that are not used for the combination of features as atomic. Our boosting algorithm learns rules that consist of features or a feature from non-atomic features, and rules consisting of a feature from atomic features.

The other is a rule representation for sequential labeling such as POS tagging and text chunking. Usual POS taggers and text chunkers decide the tag of each word by using features generated from the current word and its surrounding words. Thus each word and its attributes, such as character-types, are evaluated several times in different relative locations from current word. We propose a representation that enables us to merge similar rules that consist of the same set of words and attributes that only differ in positions from current word.

The experimental results with English POS tagging and text chunking show the taggers and chunkers based on our methods show faster processing speed than without our methods while maintaining competitive accuracy.

2 Boosting-based Learner

2.1 Preliminaries

Let $\mathcal{X}$ be the set of examples and $\mathcal{Y}$ be a set of labels $\{-1,+1\}$. Let $\mathcal{F}=\{f_1,f_2,...,f_M\}$ be M types of features represented by strings.

Let S be a set of training samples $\{(\mathbf{x}_1,y_1),...,(\mathbf{x}_m,y_m)\}$, where each example $\mathbf{x}_i \in \mathcal{X}$ consists of features in $\mathcal{F}$, which we call a feature-set, and $y_i \in \mathcal{Y}$ is a class label. The goal is to induce following mapping from S:

$$F:\mathcal{X}\rightarrow\mathcal{Y}.$$

Let $|\mathbf{x}_i|$ $(0<|\mathbf{x}_i|\leq M)$ be the number of features included in a feature-set $\mathbf{x}_i$, which we call the size of $\mathbf{x_i}$, and $x_{i,j}\in\mathcal{F}$ $(1\leq j\leq|\mathbf{x}_i|)$ be a feature included in $\mathbf{x}_i$. We call a feature-set of size k as a k-feature-set. We call $\mathbf{x}_i$ is a subset of $\mathbf{x}_j$, if a feature-set $\mathbf{x}_j$ contains all the features in a feature-set $\mathbf{x}_i$. We denote subsets of feature-sets as

$$\mathbf{x_i}\subseteq\mathbf{x_j}.$$

Then we define weak hypothesis based on the idea of the real-valued predictions and abstaining [11]. Let $\mathbf{f}$ be a feature-set, called a rule, c be a real number, called a confidence value, and $\mathbf{x}$ be an input feature-set, then a weak-hypothesis for feature-sets is defined as

$$h_{\langle\mathbf{f},c\rangle}(\mathbf{x})=\begin{cases}c & \mathbf{f}\subseteq\mathbf{x}\\ 0 & otherwise\end{cases}.$$

2.2 Boosting-based Rule Learning

We use a boosting-based algorithm that has shown fast training speed by treating a weak learner that learns several rules at each iteration [5]. The learner learns a final hypothesis F consisting of R types of rules defined as

$$F(\mathbf{x})=sign(\textstyle\sum_{r=1}^{R}h_{\langle\mathbf{f}_r,c_r\rangle}(\mathbf{x})).$$

We use a learning algorithm that generates several rules from a given training samples $S=\{(\mathbf{x}_i,y_i)\}_{i=1}^{m}$ and weights over samples $\{w_{r,1},...,w_{r,m}\}$ as weak learner. $w_{r,i}$ is the weight of sample number i after selecting $r-1$ types of rules, where $0<w_{r,i}$, $1\leq i\leq m$ and $1\leq r\leq R$.

Given such input, the weak learner selects ν types of rules with $gain$:

$$gain(\mathbf{f})\stackrel{\text{def}}{=}|\sqrt{W_{r,+1}(\mathbf{f})}-\sqrt{W_{r,-1}(\mathbf{f})}|,$$

where $\mathbf{f}$ is a feature-set, and $W_{r,y}(\mathbf{f})$ is

$$W_{r,y}(\mathbf{f})=\textstyle\sum_{i=1}^{m}w_{r,i}[[\mathbf{f}\subseteq\mathbf{x_i}\wedge y_i=y]],$$

where $[[\pi]]$ is 1 if a proposition π holds and 0 otherwise.

The weak learner selects a feature-set having the highest $gain$ as the r-th rule, and the weak learner selects ν types of feature-sets having $gain$ in top ν as $\{\mathbf{f}_r,...,\mathbf{f}_{r+\nu-1}\}$ at each iteration.

Then the boosting-based learner calculates the confidence value of each rule in the selected ν rules and updates the weight of each sample. The confidence value c_r for the first rule $\mathbf{f}_r$ in the selected ν rules is defined as

International Conference RANLP 2009 - Borovets, Bulgaria, pages 161–165

```
## F_k : A set of k-feature-sets
## \mathcal{R}_o : ν optimal rules (feature-sets)
## R_{k,ω} : ω k-feature-sets for generating candidates
## selectNBest(\mathcal{R}, n, S, W_r): Select n best rules in \mathcal{R}
##   with gain on {w_{i,r}}_{i=1}^m and training samples S
## \mathcal{FN}, \mathcal{FA} : non-atomic, atomic features
procedure weak-learner(F_k, S, W_r)
 ## ν best feature-sets as rules
 \mathcal{R}_o = selectNBest( \mathcal{R}_o ∪ F_k, ν, S, W_r);
 if (ζ ≤ k) return \mathcal{R}_o; ## Size constraint
 ## ω best feature-sets in F_k for generating candidates
 R_{k,ω} = selectNBest(F_k, ω, S, W_r);
 τ = min_{f ∈ \mathcal{R}_o} gain(f); ## The gain of ν-th optimal rule
 Foreach ( f_k ∈ R_{k,ω})
  ## Pruning candidates with upper bound of gain
  if ( u(f_k) < τ) continue;
  Foreach (f ∈ \mathcal{FN}) ## Generate candidates
   F_{k+1} = (F_{k+1} ∪ gen(f_k, f));
  end Foreach
 end Foreach
 return weak-learner(F_{k+1}, S, W_r);
```

Fig. 1: *Find rules with given weights.*

$$c_r = \frac{1}{2}\log(\frac{W_{r,+1}(\mathbf{f}_r)+\varepsilon}{W_{r,-1}(\mathbf{f}_r)+\varepsilon}),$$

where ε is a value to avoid to happen that $W_{r,+1}(\mathbf{f})$ or $W_{r,-1}(\mathbf{f})$ is very small or even zero [10]. We set ε to 1. After the calculation of c_r for $\mathbf{f}_r$, the learner updates the weight of each sample with

$$w_{r+1,i} \quad = \quad w_{r,i}exp(-y_i h_{\langle \mathbf{f}_r, c_r \rangle}(\mathbf{x}_i)). \qquad (1)$$

Then the learner adds ($\mathbf{f_r}$, c_r) to F as the r-th rule and its confidence value. When we calculate the confidence value c_{r+1} for $\mathbf{f}_{r+1}$, we use $\{w_{r+1,1}, ..., w_{r+1,m}\}$ as the weights of samples. After processing all the selected rules, the learner starts the next iteration. The learner continues training until obtaining R rules.

2.3 Learning Rules

We extend a weak learner that learns several rules from a small portion of candidate rules called a bucket used in [5]. Figure 1 describes an overview of the weak learner.

At each iteration, one of the $|B|$ types of buckets is given as an initial 1-feature-sets F_1 to the weak learner. We use *W-dist* that is a method to distributes features to $|B|$-buckets. To distribute features to buckets, *W-dist* calculates the weight of each feature that is defined as $W_r(f) = \sum_{i=1}^m w_{r,i}[[\{f\} \subseteq \mathbf{x}_i]]$ $(f \in \mathcal{F})$. Then *W-dist* sorts features based on the weight of each feature, and insert each feature to one of the buckets.

The weak learner finds ν best feature-sets as rules from feature-sets that include one of the features in F_1. The weak learner generates candidate k-feature-sets $(1 < k)$ from ω best (k-1)-feature-sets in F_{k-1} with $gain$.

We define two types of features, $\mathcal{FA}$ and $\mathcal{FN}$ (i.e $\mathcal{F} = \mathcal{FA} \cup \mathcal{FN}$). $\mathcal{FA}$ and $\mathcal{FN}$ are a set of atomic features and a set of non-atomic features. When we generate candidate rules that consist of more than a feature, we only use non-atomic features in $\mathcal{FN}$.

For example, if we use features $\mathcal{FA} = \{A, B, C\}$ and $\mathcal{FN} = \{a, b, c\}$, we examine followings as candidates; $\{A\}$,$\{B\}$,$\{C\}$,$\{a\}$,$\{b\}$, $\{c\}$, $\{a, b\}$, $\{b, c\}$ and $\{a, b, c\}$.

The gen is a function to generate combination of features. We denote $\mathbf{f}' = \mathbf{f} + f$ as the generation of $k+1$-feature-set $\mathbf{f}'$ that consists of a feature f and a k-feature-set $\mathbf{f}$. Let $ID(f)$ be the integer corresponding to f, called id, and ϕ be 0-feature-set. Then the gen is defined as follows.

$$gen(\mathbf{f}, f) = \begin{cases} \phi & if\ (\ \mathbf{f} \subseteq \mathcal{FA}\ ) \\ \mathbf{f} + f & if\ ID(f) > \max_{f' \in \mathbf{f}} ID(f') \\ \phi & otherwise \end{cases}.$$

```
## S = {(x_i, y_i)}_{i=1}^m : x_i ⊆ \mathcal{X}, y_i ∈ {±1}
## W_r = {w_{r,i}}_{i=1}^m : Weights of samples after learning
## r types of rules.
## |B| : The size of bucket B = {B[0], ..., B[|B| − 1]}
## b, r : The current bucket and rule number
## distFT: distribute features to buckets
procedure AdaBoost.SDFAN()
B = distFT(S, |B|); ## Distributing features into B
## Initialize values and weights:
 r = 1; b = 0; c_0 = \frac{1}{2} log(\frac{W_{+1}}{W_{-1}});
For i = 1,...,m: w_{1,i} = exp(c_0);
While (r ≤ R) ## Learning R types of rules
 ##Select ν rules and increment bucket id b
 \mathcal{R} = weak-learner(B[b], S, W_r); b++;
 Foreach (f ∈ \mathcal{R}) ##Update weights with each rule
  c = \frac{1}{2} log(\frac{W_{r,+1}(f)+1}{W_{r,-1}(f)+1});
  For i=1,..,m w_{r+1,i} = w_{r,i} exp(−y_i h_{⟨f,c⟩}(x_i));
  f_r = f; c_r = c; r++;
 end Foreach
 if (b == |B|) ## Redistribution of features
  B = distFT(S, |B|); b=0;
 end if
end While
return F(x) = sign(c_0 + \sum_{r=1}^R h_{⟨f_r, c_r⟩}(x))
```

Fig. 2: *An overview of AdaBoost.SDFAN.*

The gen excludes the generation of candidates that include an atomic feature. We assign smaller integer to more infrequent features as id. If there are features having the same frequency, we assign id to each feature with lexicographic order of features as in [4].

We also use the following pruning techniques.

- **Size constraint** (ζ): We examine candidates whose size is no greater than a threshold ζ.
- **Upper bound of gain**: The upper bound is defined as

$$u(\mathbf{f}) \stackrel{\mathrm{def}}{=} max(\sqrt{W_{r,+1}(\mathbf{f})}, \sqrt{W_{r,-1}(\mathbf{f})}).$$

For any feature-set $\mathbf{f}' \subseteq \mathcal{F}$, which contains $\mathbf{f}$ (i.e. $\mathbf{f} \subseteq \mathbf{f}'$), the $gain(\mathbf{f}')$ is bounded under $u(\mathbf{f})$, since $0 \leq W_{r,y}(\mathbf{f}') \leq W_{r,y}(\mathbf{f})$ for $y \in \{\pm 1\}$. Thus if $u(\mathbf{f})$ is less than τ, the $gain$ of the current optimal rule, candidates that contain $\mathbf{f}$ are safely pruned.

Figure 2 describes an overview of our algorithm, which we call AdaBoost for a weak learner learning *S*everal rules from *D*istributed *F*eatures consist of *A*tomic and *N*on-atomic (*AdaBoost.SDFAN*, for short). [1]

3 Efficient Rule Representation

3.1 A Problem of Conventional Methods

When identifying the POS tags of words and chunks of words in usual parsers, we firstly generate features from current word and its surrounding words.

Let "I am happy ." be a sequence of words. If we identify a tag of "am" with 3-word window, we use "I", "am" and "happy" as features. To distinguish words that appear different locations, we usually express words with relative locations from current word like "I:-1", "am:0" and "happy:1", where the -1, 0 and 1 after ":" are location-markers for relative locations. When "happy" is a current word, we have to express "am" as "am:-1". Thus similar rules that differ in relative locations are generated.

3.2 Efficient Rule Representation

We propose a rule representation, called *Compressed Sequential Labeling Rule Representation* (*CSLR-rep*, for

[1] To reflect imbalance class distribution, we use the default rule defined as $\frac{1}{2}\log(\frac{W_{+1}}{W_{-1}})$, where $W_y = \sum_{i=1}^m [[y_i = y]]$ for $y \in \{\pm 1\}$.

```
## f: a rule generated by AdaBoost.SDFAN
## sc : the score of f
## cl : the class of f
## s(f): the feature-stem of a feature f
## p(f): the location-marker of a feature f
## fn: the conversion result of f
## RC[fn]: scores for fn
procedure ruleConv( f, sc, cl)
  bp = min_{f∈f} p(f) ## select the base position
  Foreach f ∈ f ## generate new rule
   lm = p(f) − bp ## new location-marker of f
   ## append new representation of f
   fn = fn + "s(f):lm"
  endForeach
  RC[fn] = RC[fn] ∪ (−bp, cl, sc)
```

Fig. 3: *Generating CSLR-rep based rules.*

short), to merge similar rules. To use *CSLR-rep*, we convert weak-hypotheses (*WH*s, for short) generated by AdaBoost.SDFAN to *CSLR-rep*. A *CSLR-rep*-based *WH* is represented as

$$\langle \mathbf{rule}, \{(p_1, cl_1, c_1), ..., (p_q, cl_q, c_q)\}\rangle.$$

The $\mathbf{rule}$ is a rule generated by merging rules learned by AdaBoost.SDFAN. p_p, called scoring-position, denotes the position of a word to assign a score c_p of a class cl_p ($1 \leq p \leq q$) from current word.

We describe an example. Let $\langle\{I{:}{-2}, am{:}{-1}\}, JJ, c_0\rangle$, $\langle\{I{:}-1, am{:}0\}, VBP, c_1\rangle$ and $\langle\{I{:}0, am{:}1\}, PRP, c_2\rangle$ be *WH*s generated by AdaBoost.SDFAN, and JJ, VBP and PRP be class tags. These *WH*s are converted to the following *CSLR-rep*-based rule; $\langle\{I{:}0, am{:}1\}, \{(2, JJ, c_0), (1, VBP, c_1), (0, PRP, c_2)\}\rangle$,

When the converted *WH* in the example is applied to a word sequence "I am happy .", we can assign scores to all the three words by just checking $\{I{:}0, am{:}1\}$. The scores for "JJ", "VBP" and "PRP" are assigned to "happy", "am" and "I", respectively.

When we use the three original *WH*s in the example, we have to check three rules to assign scores to the words.

Figure 3 shows an overview for the rule conversion. We assume each feature is divided into a location-marker and a feature-stem. A location-marker is the relative location from a current word. A feature-stem is a word or one of its attributes such as character-types without a location-marker.

We use the relative location of a feature appeared in left-most word in each rule as base-position (*bp*, for short). Then we convert each feature to a new feature that consists of its feature-stem and new location-marker. The new location-marker means a relative location from the *bp*. We add the value of (*bp* $\times$ -1) as the scoring-position of the current score.

3.3 Rule Application

We describe an overview of the application of rules represented by *CSLR-rep*. We consider two types of features, **static-features** and **dynamic-features**, in this application. Static-features are generated from input word sequences. Dynamic-features are dynamically generated from the tag of each word assigned with the highest score. We define W as a word window size that means using a current word and its surrounding words appearing $\frac{W-1}{2}$ left and $\frac{W-1}{2}$ right of the current word.

Figure 4 shows an overview of the application. Let $\{\mathbf{wd}_1, .., \mathbf{wd}_N\}$ be an input that consists of N ($1 \leq N$) words. Each word $\mathbf{wd}_i$ ($1 \leq i \leq N$) has $|\mathbf{wd}_i|$ types of attributes. We denote j-th attribute of $\mathbf{wd}_i$ as $wd_{i,j}$. $\mathcal{RC}$ is a set of rules represented by *CSLR-rep* and $\mathcal{RC}[\mathbf{rc}]$ is the set of $\langle$ scoring-position, class, score $\rangle$ of $\mathbf{rc}$.

The application has two stages for static-features and dynamic-features. Our algorithm firstly assigns scores with rules consisting of only Static-features to each word in the direction of beginning of sentence (BOS) to end of sentence (EOS) direction. $\mathbf{Rs}[i]$ keeps the status of rule applications for i-th word. If the algorithm finds a subset of rules while applying rules from i-th word, the algorithm adds the subset of rules to $\mathbf{Rs}[i]$. [2] We define subsets of rules as follows:

Definition 1 *Subsets of rules*
If there exists $\mathbf{rule}$ *in* $\langle\mathbf{rule}, scores\rangle \in \mathcal{RC}$ *that satisfies* $\mathbf{rc} \subseteq \mathbf{rule} \wedge \mathbf{rc} \neq \mathbf{rule}$, *we call* $\mathbf{rc}$ *is a subset of rules of* $\mathcal{RC}$ *and denote it as*

$$\mathbf{rc} \subset \mathcal{RC}$$

Then we apply rules that include dynamic-features. All the subsets of rules are kept in $\mathbf{Rs}$ after examining all the Static-features, we can assign scores to words by just checking dynamic-feature of each word with $\mathbf{Rs}$. When checking rules that include the dynamic-feature of i-th word we check subsets of rules of words in ($i - \frac{W-1}{2} - \Delta$) to (i + $max(\frac{W-1}{2}, \Delta)$ - 1). We use the tags of words with in Δ in the direction of EOS.

We describe an example. Let $\mathcal{RC}$ ={ {I:0, am:1}, {I:0, VBP:1}, {I:0, VBP:1, JJ:2} } be a set of rules. When applying the rules to "I am happy ." with $(W, \Delta) = (3, 2)$, we check "I:0" first. "I:0" is inserted to $\mathbf{Rs}[1]$ because of {I:0} $\subset \mathcal{RC}$. Then we check "am:1" with "{I:0}" in $\mathbf{Rs}[1]$, and {I:0, am:1} is found. Finally we check "happy:2" with $\mathbf{Rs}[1]$. We check the other words like this. After checking all the words from BOS to EOS direction, we start to check rules that include dynamic-features from EOS to BOS direction. If the dynamic-features of "am" and "happy" are VBP and JJ, we check VBP and JJ with $\mathbf{Rs}$. For example, VBP is treated as "VBP:1" from the position of "I" and "VBP:0" from the position of "am". When we check "VBP:1" with "{I:0}" in $\mathbf{Rs}[1]$, {I:0, VBP:1} is found and inserted to $\mathbf{Rs}[1]$. Then we check "JJ:2" with "I:0" and {I:0, VBP:1} in $\mathbf{Rs}[1]$. Then we check these dynamic-features with $\mathbf{Rs}[2]$.

Unfortunately, the *CSLR-rep* has some drawbacks. One of the drawbacks is the increase of dynamic-features. When we convert rules that consist of more than a feature to *CSLR-rep*, the number of types of dynamic-features increases. Since original rule representation only handles dynamic-features within Δ, the total number of types of dynamic-features is up to "$\Delta \times CL$", where CL is the number of classes in each task. However, the total number of dynamic-features in *CSLR-rep* is up to " ($\frac{W-1}{2}$ + Δ + $max(\frac{W-1}{2}, \Delta)$ -1) $\times$ CL " because we express each feature with the relative location from the base-position of each rule.

4 POS tagging and Text Chunking

4.1 English POS Tagging

We used the Penn Wall Street Journal treebank [8]. We split the treebank into training (sections 0-18), development (sections 19-21) and test (sections 22-24) as in [5]. We used the following features:

[2] We use a TRIE structure called double array for representing rules [1]. To keep the statuses of rule applications, we store the last position in a TRIE where each subset of rules reached.

$\mathcal{RC}[\mathbf{rc}]$: pairs of score-positions and scores of $\mathbf{rc}$
$\mathbf{Rs}[i]$: subset of rules of i-th word
Initial value for each word is 0-feature-set
procedure **ruleApplication**($\{\mathbf{wd}_1, .., \mathbf{wd}_N\}, \mathcal{FN}$)
For Static-feature
For $i' = 1; i' \leq N; i'$++ # beginning position
 For $i = i'; i < i + W; i$++ # combination position
  For $j = 1; j \leq |\mathbf{wd}_i|; j$++# attributes
   Foreach $\mathbf{rc} \in \mathbf{Rs}[i']$
    $lm = i - i'$ ## current location-marker
    $\mathbf{rc}' = \mathbf{rc}$ + "$wd_{i,j}$:lm"
    # If $\mathcal{RC}[\mathbf{rc}']$ is applied,
    # assign the scores with base position i'
    assignScores($\mathcal{RC}[\mathbf{rc}'], i'$)
    If $\mathbf{rc}' \subset \mathcal{RC}$ $\mathbf{Rs}[i'] = \mathbf{Rs}[i'] \cup \mathbf{rc}'$
   endForeach
 # If no subset of rules for i', go to $i' + 1$-th word
 If $\mathbf{Rs}[i'] = \{\phi\}$ **break**
 endFor
endFor
For Dynamic-feature : EOS to BOS direction
For $i' = N; 1 \leq i'; i'--$ # beginning position
 # Checking rules including Dynamic-feature
 $db = i' - \frac{W-1}{2} - \Delta; de = i' + max(\frac{W-1}{2}, \Delta);$
  For $i = db; i < de; i$++
  Foreach $\mathbf{rc} \in \mathbf{Rs}[i]$
   $lm = j - i'$ ## current location-marker
   $\mathbf{rc}' = \mathbf{rc}$ + "$dft_{i':lm}$" # dft_j is the tag of i'-th word
   assignScores($\mathcal{RC}[\mathbf{rc}'], i$)
   If $\mathbf{rc}' \subset \mathcal{RC}$ $\mathbf{Rs}[i] = \mathbf{Rs}[i] \cup \mathbf{rc}'$
  endForeach
 endFor
endFor

Fig. 4: *Application of CSLR-rep based rules.*

· words, words that are turned into all capitalized, in a W-word window size, tags assigned to Δ words on the right.
· whether the current word has a hyphen, a number, a capital letter, the current word is all capital, all small
· prefixes and suffixes of current word (up to 4)
· candidate-tags of words in a W-word window
We collect candidate POS tags of each word, called candidate feature, from the automatically tagged corpus provided for the shared task of English Named Entity recognition in CoNLL 2003 as in [5]. [3] [4] We express these candidates with one of the following ranges decided by their frequency fq: $10 \leq fq < 100$, $100 \leq fq < 1000$ and $1000 \leq fq$.

If 'work' is annotated as NN 2000 times, we express it like "1000≤NN". If 'work' is current word, we add 1000≤NN as a candidate POS tag feature of the current word. If 'work' appears the next of the current word, we add 1000≤NN as a candidate POS tag of the next word.

4.2 Text Chunking

We used the data prepared for CoNLL-2000 shared tasks. [5] This task aims to identify 10 types of chunks, such as, NP, VP and PP, and so on. The data consists of subsets of Penn Wall Street Journal treebank: training (sections 15-18) and test (section 20). We prepared the development set from section 21 of the treebank as in [5]. [6]

Each base phrase consists of one word or more. To identify word chunks, we use **IOE2** representation. The chunks are represented by the following tags: E-X is used for end word of a chunk of class X. I-X is used for non-end word in an X chunk. O is used for word outside of any chunk.

[3] http://www.cnts.ua.ac.be/conll2003/ner/
[4] We collected POS tags for each word that are annotated to the word more than 9 times in the corpus as candidates.
[5] http://lcg-www.uia.ac.be/conll2000/chunking/
[6] We used http://ilk.uvt.nl/~sabine/chunklink/chunklink_2-2-2000_for_conll.pl for creating development data.

Table 1: *Training data for experiments. POS and ETC indicate POS tagging and text chunking. ♯ of S, ♯ of cl and M indicate the number samples, the number of class in each data set and the distinct number of feature types for each pair of (W, Δ).*

			M (W, Δ)		
data	♯ of S	♯ of cl	$(3, 1)$	$(5, 2)$	$(7, 3)$
POS	912,344	45	283,979	440,725	593,065
ETC	211,727	22	56,917	93,333	128,651

Table 2: *Accuracy on Test Data.*

POS tagging

		-Atomic		+Atomic	
(W, Δ)/ ζ	1	2	3	2	3
(3,1)	96.81	97.09	97.05	97.00	97.04
(5,2)	96.96	97.30	97.30	97.25	97.28
(7,3)	96.99	**97.36**	97.30	97.31	**97.34**

text chunking

		-Atomic		+Atomic	
(W, Δ)/ ζ	1	2	3	2	3
(3,1)	92.40	93.87	93.69	93.91	93.82
(5,2)	92.87	94.31	94.14	**94.34**	94.31
(7,3)	93.09	**94.32**	94.11	94.12	94.11

For instance, "[He] (NP) [reckons] (VP) [the current account deficit] (NP)..." is represented by IOE2 as follows; "He/E-NP reckons/E-VP the/I-NP current/I-NP account/I-NP deficit/E-NP".

We used the following features:
· words and POS tags in a W-word window.
· tags assigned to Δ words on the right.
· candidate-tags of words in a W-word window.
We collected the followings as candidate-tags for chunking from the same corpus used in POS tagging.
• Candidate-tags expressed with frequency information as in POS tagging
• The ranking of each candidate decided by frequencies in the automatically tagged data
• Candidate tags of each word
If we collect "work" annotated as I-NP 2000 times and as E-VP 100 times, we generate the following candidate-tags for "work"; 1000≤I-NP, 100≤E-VP<1000, rank:I-NP=1 rank:E-NP=2, candidate=I-NP and candidate=E-VP. [7]

5 Experiments

We tested R=200,000, $|B|$=1,000, ν = 10, ω=10, ζ={1,2,3} and (W, Δ)={(3,1), (5,2), (7,3)}. Table 1 shows that the number of training samples, classes, features.

We examine two types of training, "-Atomic " and " +Atomic ", in this experiment. "-Atomic " indicates training with all the features as non-atomic. " +Atomic " indicates training by using atomic features. We specify prefixes, suffixes and candidate-tags as atomic for POS tagging, and candidate-tags as atomic for text chunking.

To extend AdaBoost.SDFAN to handle multi-class problems, we used the one-vs-the-rest method. To identify proper tag sequences, we use Viterbi search. [8]

5.1 Tagging and Chunking Accuracy

Table 2 shows accuracy obtained with each rules on POS tagging and text chunking. We calculate label accuracy for

[7] We converted the chunk representation in the corpus to IOE2 and we collected chunk tags of each word appearing more than 9 times.
[8] We map the confidence value of each classifier into the range of 0 to 1 with sigmoid function defined as $s(X) = 1/(1+exp(-\beta X))$, where $X = F(\mathbf{x})$ is a output of a classifier. We used β=5 in this experiment. We select a tag sequence which maximizes the sum of those log values by Viterbi search.

Table 3: *Tagging and Chunking Speed. Each number is average processed words per second. We examine three times measurements for each tagger or chunker. Each time is obtained with all rules.*

POS tagging

$(W,\Delta)/\zeta$	-Atomic 1	-Atomic 2	-Atomic 3	+ Atomic 2	+ Atomic 3
without *CSLR-rep*					
(3,1)	9477	4023	2505	5450	5096
(5,2)	8118	2564	1445	3915	3389
(7,3)	6615	1842	1007	3033	2464
with *CSLR-rep*					
(3,1)	19467	4258	2013	10969	9644
(5,2)	18261	2807	1102	8212	5934
(7,3)	15658	2195	754	7474	4939

text chunking

$(W,\Delta)/\zeta$	-Atomic 1	-Atomic 2	-Atomic 3	+Atomic 2	+Atomic 3
without *CSLR-rep*					
(3,1)	14510	3995	1036	13975	12221
(5,2)	11266	1681	401	9571	7018
(7,3)	9434	961	230	6849	4595
with *CSLR-rep*					
(3,1)	27705	4282	863	19496	16169
(5,2)	25471	2477	352	13692	8475
(7,3)	23338	1758	206	10058	5701

POS tagging as accuracy. As for text chunking, we calculate F-measure ($F_{\beta=1}$) given by $2rp/(r+p)$ as accuracy, where r and p are recall and precision. Each accuracy on a test data is calculated with the number of rules that show the best accuracy on development data.

We obtain almost the same accuracy even if we use part of features as atomic.

5.2 Tagging and Chunking Speed

Table 3 shows tagging and chunking speed. We measure the number of words processed by per second.[9] We obtain faster processing speed by using *CSLR-rep*-based rules traind with $\zeta = \{1, 2\}$ and - Atomic. These show that *CSLR-rep* contributes to improved processing time. When we use rules trained with $\zeta = 1$, we can get more improvement than using rules trained with $\zeta = 2$.

However, the performance obtained with *CSLR-rep*-based rules trained with ($\zeta = 3, -Atomic$) is slower than with the original rules. We guess this is caused due to the following two reasons. Our *CSLR-rep* reduces the number of times of rule evaluation up to $1/W$. Thus *CSLR-rep* reduces processing time linearly. However, the number of combination of features exponentially increases. The other reason is that the number of times to generate dynamic-features is increased as described in the end of section 3.3.

We obtain much improvement by using atomic features with *CSLR-rep*. For example, processing speed obtained with the text chunker using rules ($\zeta = 3, W = 7$, +Atomic) is about 28 times faster than the speed obtained with the chunker using rules ($\zeta = 3, W = 7$, -Atomic).

6 Related Work

We list previous best results on English POS tagging and Text chunking in Table 4. The tagger and chunker based on AdaBoost.SDFAN show competitive F-measure with previous best results.

[9] We used a machine with 3.6GHz DualCore Intel Xeon and 10 GB memory.

Table 4: *Comparison with previous best results.*

POS tagging		Text Chunking	
Guided learning [12]	97.33	LaSo [2]	94.4
Boosting [5]	97.32	Boosting [5]	94.30
CRF [13]	97.40	CRF [13]	95.15
This paper	97.34	**This paper**	94.34

As for fast classification methods, techniques for converting or pruning models or rules generated by machine learning algorithms are proposed. Model conversion techniques for SVMs with polynomial kernel that converts kernel-based classifier into a simple liner classifier are proposed in [3, 6]. For AdaBoost, a pruning method for hypotheses is proposed in [9].

Our method uses a rule conversion technique for sequential labeling problems. Although *CSLR-rep* can only be used in tasks that use each word as different features time and again, such as POS tagging and text, we obtain faster processing speed without loss in accuracy.

7 Conclusion and Future Work

We have proposed techniques for fast boosting-based POS tagging and text chunking. To reduce time-consuming rule evaluation, our method controls the generation of combination of features by specifying part of features that are not used for combination. We have also proposed a rule representation that enables us to merge similar rules. Experimental results have showed our techniques improve classification speed while maintaining accuracy.

References

[1] J. Aoe. An efficient digital search algorithm by using a double-array structure. In *IEEE Transactions on Software Engineering*, volume 15(9), 1989.

[2] H. Daumé III and D. Marcu. Learning as search optimization: approximate large margin methods for structured prediction. In *Proc. of ICML 2005*, pages 169–176, 2005.

[3] H. Isozaki and H. Kazawa. Efficient Support Vector classifiers for named entity recognition. In *Proc. of COLING 2002*, pages 390–396, 2002.

[4] T. Iwakura and S. Okamoto. Fast training methods of boosting algorithms for text analysis. In *Proc. of RANLP 2007*, pages 274–279, 2007.

[5] T. Iwakura and S. Okamoto. A fast boosting-based learner for feature-rich tagging and chunking. In *Proc. of CoNLL 2008*, pages 17–24, 2008.

[6] T. Kudo and Y. Matsumoto. Fast methods for kernel-based text analysis. In *Proc. of ACL-03*, pages 24–31, 2003.

[7] T. Kudo, J. Suzuki, and H. Isozaki. Boosting-based parse reranking with subtree features. In *Proc. of ACL 2005*, pages 189–196, 2005.

[8] M. P. Marcus, B. Santorini, and M. A. Marcinkiewicz. Building a large annotated corpus of english: The Penn Treebank. pages 313–330, 1994.

[9] D. D. Margineantu and T. G. Dietterich. Pruning adaptive boosting. In *Proc. of ICML 1997*, pages 211–218, 1997.

[10] R. E. Schapire and Y. Singer. Improved boosting algorithms using confidence-rated predictions. *Machine Learning*, 37(3):297–336, 1999.

[11] R. E. Schapire and Y. Singer. Boostexter: A boosting-based system for text categorization. *Machine Learning*, 39(2/3):135–168, 2000.

[12] L. Shen, G. Satta, and A. Joshi. Guided learning for bidirectional sequence classification. In *Proc. of ACL 2007*, pages 760–767, 2007.

[13] J. Suzuki and H. Isozaki. Semi-supervised sequential labeling and segmentation using giga-word scale unlabeled data. In *Proc. of ACL-08: HLT*, pages 665–673, June 2008.

Cross-document Event Extraction and Tracking: Task, Evaluation, Techniques and Challenges

Heng Ji* **Ralph Grishman†** **Zheng Chen*** **Prashant Gupta‡**

*Computer Science Department, Queens College and The Graduate Center, The City University of New York

†Computer Science Department, New York University

‡Computer Science Department, Indian Institute of Information Technology Allahabad

hengji@cs.qc.cuny.edu

Abstract

This paper proposes a new task of cross-document event extraction and tracking and its evaluation metrics. We identify important person entities which are frequently involved in events as 'centroid entities'. Then we link the events involving the same centroid entity along a time line. We also present a system performing this task and our current approaches to address the main research challenges. We demonstrate that global inference from background knowledge and cross-document event aggregation are crucial to enhance the performance. This new task defines several extensions to the traditional single-document Information Extraction paradigm beyond 'slot filling'.

Keywords

Information Extraction, Cross-document Extraction, Event Extraction

1. Introduction

Consider a user monitoring or browsing a multi-source news feed, with assistance from an Information Extraction (IE) system. Various events are evolving, updated, repeated and corrected in different documents; later information may override earlier more tentative or incomplete facts. In this environment, traditional single-document IE would be of little value; a user would be confronted by thousands of *unconnected* events with tens of thousands of arguments. Add to this the fact that the extracted results contain *unranked, redundant* and *erroneous* facts and some crucial facts are *missing*, and it's not clear whether these IE results are really beneficial. How can we take proper advantage of the power of extraction to aid news analysis? In this paper we define a new cross-document IE task beyond 'slot filling' to generate more *coherent, salient, complete* and *concise* facts.

A high-coherence text has fewer conceptual gaps and thus requires fewer inferences and less prior knowledge, rendering the text easier to understand [1]. In our task, coherence is the extent to which the relationships between the events in the documents can be made explicit. We aim to provide a more coherent presentation by linking events based on shared arguments. In the news from a certain period some entities are more central than others; we propose to identify these *centroid entities,* and then link the events involving the same centroid entity on a time line. In this way we provide coherent event chains so that users can more efficiently review and analyze events, such as tracking a person's movement activities and trends. This will offer a richer set of views than is possible with document clustering for summarization or with topic tracking.

To sum up, the specific goals of this paper are to:

- Formulate a tractable but challenging task of cross-document IE, producing a product useful for browsing, analysis, and search;
- Propose a set of metrics for this task;
- Present a first cut at a system for performing this task;
- Lay out the potential research challenges and suggest some directions for improving this system's performance.

2. Traditional Single-document IE and Its Limitations

We shall start by illustrating, through the ACE [1] event extraction task, the limitations of traditional single-document IE.

2.1 Terminology and Task

ACE defines the following terminology:

entity: an object or a set of objects in one of the semantic categories of interest, e.g. persons, locations, organizations.

mention: a reference to an entity (typically, a noun phrase)

relation: one of a specified set of relationships between a pair of entities.

event: a specific occurrence involving participants, including 8 types of events, with 33 subtypes; for the purpose of this paper, we will treat these simply as 33 distinct event types.

event mention: a phrase or sentence within which an event is described.

event trigger: the main word which most clearly expresses an event occurrence.

event argument: an entity involved in an event with some specific role.

event time: an exact date normalized from time expressions and a role to indicate that an event occurs before/after/within the date.

[1] http://www.nist.gov/speech/tests/ace/

International Conference RANLP 2009 - Borovets, Bulgaria, pages 166–172

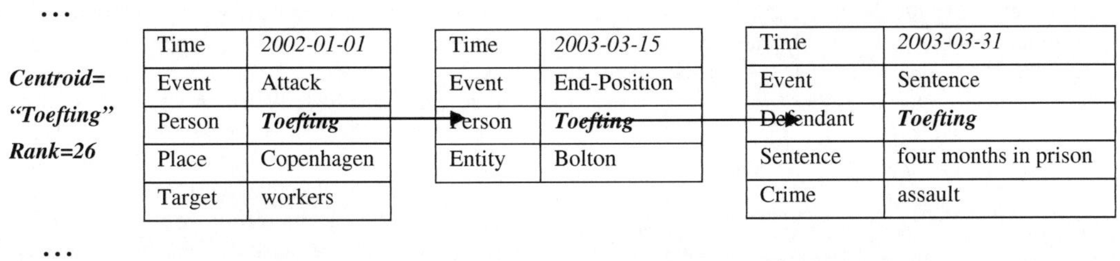

Figure 1. Example of Ranked Cross-document Temporal Event Chains

For example, for the following text:

Barry Diller on Wednesday quit as chief of Vivendi Universal Entertainment, the entertainment unit of French giant Vivendi Universal.

A single-document ACE IE system should detect the following information:

entity: person: {Barry Diller, chief}; ...
mention: person: "Barry Diller"; ...
relation: part-whole: "the entertainment unit" is part of "French giant"
event mention: Personnel_End Position event: "Barry Diller on Wednesday quit as chief of Vivendi Universal Entertainment."
event trigger: quit ; **event time**: Wednesday (2003-03-05).
event argument: position: chief**; person: "Barry Diller"**

2.2 Evaluation Metrics

As for other ACE tasks, the ACE 2005 official evaluation scorer can produce an overall score called "ACE value" for event extraction. However, most of the ACE event extraction literature (e.g. [3]; [4]) used a simpler argument-based F-measure to evaluate ACE event extraction, and we will adapt this measure to our task.

2.3 Limitations

In the ACE single-document event extraction task, each event mention is extracted from a single sentence. The results are reasonably useful for hundreds of documents. However, when we apply the same system to process much larger corpora, the net result is a very large collection of events which are:

(1) Unconnected. Related events (for example, "Tony Blair's foreign trips) appear unconnected and unordered.

(2) Unranked. Event mentions are presented in the order in which they appear in the corpus and considered equally important. It will be beneficial to rank the myriad events by some salience criteria. Centroid-based multi-document text summarization (e.g. [5]; [6]) detects the 'centroid' words that are statistically important to a cluster of documents, and then ranks sentences by incorporating centroid word confidence values. We will adopt the same strategy to rank event arguments.

(3) Redundant. More critically, many events are frequently repeated in different documents. Cross-document event aggregation is essential, in order to enable the users to access novel information more rapidly.

(4) Erroneous and Incomplete. Like many other NLP applications, ACE event extraction systems faced a 'performance ceiling', -- they barely exceeded 50% F-score on argument labeling. Some extraction errors came from limitations on the use of facts already extracted from other documents because of the single-document extraction paradigm.

3. A New Cross-document IE Task

As one initial attempt to address the limitations as described above, we shall propose a cross-document IE task. Since this task is quite new to the IE community, there is no baseline system covering all the aspects for comprehensive comparison. Therefore it is valuable to develop new task standards (section 3.1) and scoring metrics (section 3.2). We shall elaborate the motivations for these changes over the traditional IE task.

3.1 Terminology and Task Definition

We extend the ACE terminology from single document to cross-document setting, and define the following new terminology:

centroid entities: N person entities most frequently appearing as arguments of events.
temporal event chain: a list of temporally-ordered events involving the same centroid entity.

Our cross-document IE task is defined as follows:

Input: A test set of documents
Ouput: Identify a set of centroid entities, and then for each centroid entity, link and order the events centered around it on a time line. For example, Figure 1 presents a temporal event chain involving "Toefting".

3.2 Evaluation Metrics

We introduce the following new measures to gauge the effectiveness of a cross-document IE system.

(1) Centroid Entity Detection

To measure how well a system performs in *selecting the correct centroid entities* in a set of documents, we compute the Precision, Recall and F-measure of the top N centroid entities identified by the system as a function of N (the value of N can be considered as reflecting the 'compression ratio' in a summarization task):

- *A centroid entity is correctly detected* if its substring matches a reference centroid.

In the reference the centroids are the top N entities ranked by the number of events in which that entity appears as an argument.

For those correctly identified centroid entities, we will use a standard ranking metric, normalized Kendall tau distance [7], to evaluate how a system performs in ranking:

• Normalized Kendall tau distance (Centroid Entities) = the fraction of correct system centroid entity pairs out of salience order.

• Centroid Entity Ranking Accuracy = 1- Normalized Kendall tau distance (Centroid Entities)

(2) Browsing Cost: Incorporate Novelty/Diversity into F-Measure

It's important to measure how well a system performs at *presenting the events involving the centroid entities accurately*. The easiest solution is to borrow the argument based F-Measure in the traditional IE task. However, as we pointed out in section 2.3(3), many events are reported redundantly across multiple documents, we should incorporate novelty and diversity into the metric and assign penalties to the redundant event arguments. We define an evaluation metric *Browsing Cost which is* similar to the Search Length i metric [8] for this purpose:

- *An argument is correctly extracted* in an event chain if its event type, string (the full or partial name) and role match any of the reference argument mentions.
- *Two arguments in an event chain are redundant* if their event types, event time, string (the full or partial name) and roles overlap.
- *Browsing Cost (i)* = the number of incorrect or redundant event arguments that a user must examine before finding i correct event arguments.

If an event chain contains more redundant information, then the browsing cost is larger. We examine the centroid entities in rank order and, for each argument, the events in temporal order, inspecting the arguments of each event.

(3) Temporal Correlation: Measure Coherence

Since the traditional IE task doesn't evaluate event ordering, we shall use the correlation metric to evaluate how well a system performs at *presenting the events in proper temporal order for each event chain*. Assume the event chain *ec* includes a set of correct arguments *argset*, then the *temporal correlation* is measured by:

- *Temporal Correlation (ec)* = the correlation of the temporal order of *argset* in the system output and the answer key.

The overall system performance is measured by the average value of the temporal correlation scores of all the event chains. In assessing temporal correlation, we should also take into account the number of argument pairs over which temporal order is measured:

- *Argument recall* = number of unique and correct arguments in response / number of unique arguments in key

The general idea follows the event ordering metric in TempEval [9], but we evaluate over event arguments instead of triggers because in our task the representation of a node in the chain is extended from an event trigger to a structured aggregated event including fine-grained information such as event types, arguments and their roles. Also similar to TempEval we focus more on the temporal order of events instead of the exact date associated with each individual event. This is different from other time identification and normalization tasks such as TERN[2]. We believe for a cross-document IE task, the exact date normalization results are less crucial. In some cases the system can insert the events into the correct positions in the chains even by only detecting rough date periods (e.g. "a few weeks ago"). Our temporal correlation metric is able to assign appropriate credit to these cases.

4. A Cross-document IE System

We have developed a system performing this new cross-document IE task.

4.1 System Overview

Figure 2 depicts the overall architecture of our system.

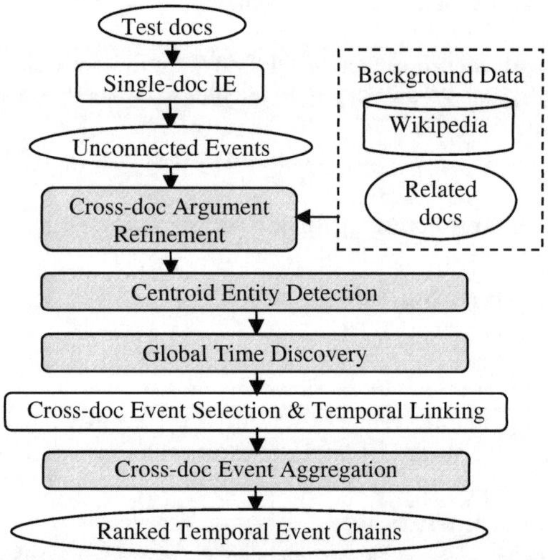

Figure 2. Cross-document IE System Overview

4.2 Baseline Single-document IE System

We first apply a state-of-the-art English ACE single-document IE system [10] which can extract events from individual documents. This IE system includes entity extraction, time expression extraction and normalization, relation extraction and event extraction. The event extraction component combines pattern matching with a set of Maximum Entropy (MaxEnt) classifiers for trigger labeling, argument identification and argument classification. Each of these classifiers produces local confidence values [3].

4.3 What's New

The following sections will describe the various challenges in this new task and our current techniques to address them, including:

[2] http://fofoca.mitre.org/tern.html

- More Salient: Detecting centroid entities using global confidence (section 5);
- More Accurate and Complete: Correcting and enriching arguments from the background data (section 6);
- More Concise: Conducting cross-document event aggregation to remove redundancy (section 7).

Except for the cross-document argument refinement techniques in section 6.1 which is based on prior work, all other components are newly developed in this paper.

5. Centroid Entity Detection

After we harvest a large inventory of events from single-document IE, we label those person entities involved frequently in events with high confidence as centroid entities. We first construct the candidates through a simple form of cross-document coreference (section 5.1) and then rank these candidates (section 5.2).

5.1 Cross-document Name Coreference

We merge two person name mentions <*$mention_i$, $mention_j$*> into one candidate centroid if they satisfy either of the following two conditions:

- identified as coreferential by single-document coreference resolution; or
- in different documents, there is a $name_i$ referring to $mention_i$ and a $name_j$ referring to $mention_j$ (if several names, taking the maximal name in each document), and $name_i$ and $name_i$ are equal or one is a substring of the other.

Using this approach we can avoid linking "Rod Stewart" and "Martha Stewart" into the same entity. In the future we intend to exploit more advanced cross-document person name disambiguation techniques (e.g. [11], [12]) to resolve ambiguities.

5.2 Global Entity Ranking

Because the candidate entities are extracted automatically, and so may be erroneous, we want to promote those arguments which are both central to the collection (*high frequency*) and more likely to be accurate (*high confidence*). We exploit global confidence metrics to reach both of these goals. The intuition is that if an entity is involved in events frequently as well as with high extraction confidence, it is more salient.

Our basic underlying hypothesis is that the salience of an entity e_i should be calculated by taking into consideration both its confidence and the confidence of other entities $\{e_j\}$ connected to it, which is inspired by PageRank [13]. Therefore for each entity e_i, we construct a set of related entities as follows:

$\{n_j \mid n_j$ *is a name*, n_j and e_i are coreferential or linked by a relation; and n_j is involved in an event mention$\}$

Then we compute the salience of e_i based on local confidence *lc* by the baseline single-document event extraction, and select the top-ranked entities as centroid entities:

$$salience(e_i) = \sum_j \sum_k lc(n_j, event_k)$$

6. Cross-document Event Refinement

Any extraction errors from the baseline system, especially on name and time arguments, will be compounded in our new cross-document IE task because they are vital to centroid detection and temporal ordering. We shall exploit knowledge derived from the background data (related documents and Wikipedia) to improve performance.

6.1 Cross-document Argument Refinement

We apply the cross-document inference techniques as described in [3] to improve name argument labeling performance. We detect clusters of similar documents and aggregate similar events across documents, and then for each cluster (a "super-document") we propagate highly consistent and frequent arguments to override other, lower confidence, extraction results, by favoring interpretation consistency across sentences and related documents.

6.2 Global Time Discovery

About 50% of the event mentions produced by single-document IE don't include explicit time arguments. However, many documents come from a topically-related news stream, so we can recover some event time arguments by gleaning knowledge from other documents.

(1) Time Search from Related Documents and Wikipedia

We analyze the entire background data and store the extracted events into an offline knowledge base:

Event type, {argument entity$_i$, role$_i$ | i =1 to n}, Event time, global confidence

Then if any event mention in the test collection is missing its time argument, we can search for this event type and arguments in the knowledge base, seeking the time argument with the highest global confidence. In the following we give two examples for discovering time from related documents and Wikipedia respectively.

In the following example, the single-document IE system is not able to identify a time argument for the *"interview"* event in the test sentence. The related documents, however, do include the time "Wednesday" (which is resolved to 2003-04-09), so we can recover the event time in the test sentence.

[***Test Sentence***]
<entity>Al-Douri</entity> *said in the* ***<entity>AP </entity> interview*** *he would love to return to teaching but for now he plans to remain at the United Nations.*
[***Sentence from Related Documents***]
In an ***interview*** *with* ***<entity>The Associated Press </entity> <time>Wednesday<time>*** *night,* ***<entity> Al-Douri</entity>*** *said he will continue to work at the United Nations and had no intention of defecting.*

For some biographical facts for famous persons, hardly any time arguments can be found from the news articles. However, we can infer them from the knowledge base extracted from Wikipedia. For example, we can find the time argument for the *start-position* event involving *"Diller"* in the following test sentence as "1966":

Relation	$Event_i$ Arguments	$Event_j$ Arguments	Centroid	Event Type	Event Time
Coreference	Entity[Ariel Sharon] Place [Jerusalem]	Entity[Sharon] Place[Jerusalem]	Powell	Contact-Meet	2003-06-20
Subset	Entity[Bush]	Entity[Bush] Place[Camp David]	Blair	Contact-Meet	2003-03-27
Subsumption	Destination[Mideast]	Destination[Egypt]	Bush	Movement-Transport	2003-06-02
Complement	Sentence[nine-year jail] Crime[corruption]	Adjudicator[court] Place[Malaysia] Sentence[nine-year prison]	Anwar Ibrahim	Justice-Sentence	2003-04-18

Table 1. Cross-document Event Aggregation Examples

[***Test Sentence***]
<person>Diller</person> started *his entertainment career at* ***<entity>ABC</entity>****, where he is credited with creating the ``movie of the week" concept.*
[***Sentence from Wikipedia***]
<person>Diller</person> ***was*** *hired* ***by*** *<entity> ABC</entity>* ***in*** *<time>1966</time>* ***and was soon placed in charge of negotiating broadcast rights to feature films.***

(2) Statistical Implicit Time Prediction

Furthermore, we exploited a time argument prediction approach as described in [14]. We manually labeled 40 ACE05 newswire texts and trained a MaxEnt classifier to determine whether a time argument from an event mention EM_i can be propagated to the other event mention EM_j. The features used include the event types of EM_i and EM_j, whether they are located in the same sentence, if so the number of time expressions in the sentence; whether they share coreferential arguments, if so the roles of the arguments. This predictor is able to propagate time arguments between two events which indicate some precursor/consequence, subevent or causal relation (e.g. from a "Conflict-Attack" event to a "Life-Die/Life-Injure" event).

7. Cross-document Event Aggregation

The degree of similarity among events contained in a group of topically-related documents is much higher than the degree of similarity within an article, as each article is apt to describe the main point as well as necessary shared background. Therefore we also take into account other events that have already been generated to maximize *diversity* among the event nodes in a chain and *completeness* for each event node. In order to reach these goals, a simple event coreference solution is not enough. We also aggregate other relation types between two events: Subset, Subsumption and Complement as shown in Table 1.

Besides using cross-document name coreference to measure the similarity between a pair of arguments, we adopted some results from ACE relation extraction, e.g. using "PART-WHOLE" relations between arguments to determine whether one event subsumes the other. Earlier work on event coreference (e.g. [15]) in the MUC program was limited to several scenarios such as terrorist attacks and management succession. In our task we are targeting wider and more fine-grained event types.

8. Experimental Results

In this section we will describe our answer-key event chain annotation and then present experimental results.

8.1 Data and Answer-key Annotation

We used 106 newswire texts from ACE 2005 training corpora as our test set. Then we extracted the top 40 ranked person names as centroid entities, and manually created temporal event chains by two steps:
(1) Aggregated reference event mentions;
(2) Filled in the implicit event time arguments from the background data.

The annotations of (1) and (2) were done by two annotators independently and adjudicated for the final answer-key. In total it took one annotator about 8 hours and the other 10 hours. The inter-annotator agreement is around 90% for step (1) and 82% for step (2). We used 278,108 texts from English TDT-5 corpus and 148 million sentences from Wikipedia as the source as our background data. In these event chains there are 140 events with 368 arguments (257 are unique). The top ranked centroid entities are "Bush", "Ibrahim", "Putin", "Al-douri", "Blair", etc.

8.2 Centroid Entity Detection

First we use the arguments generated directly from single-document IE to detect 40 centroid entities, obtaining an F-measure of 55%. When we apply the cross-document name argument refinement techniques before argument ranking, the F-measure is enhanced to 67.5%, and we can cover all key centroid entities by using the top 76 system output arguments.

The ranking accuracy of the 40 correct system centroid entities is 72.95%. For comparison we computed two baselines: (1) random ranking: with accuracy about 42%; (2) ranked by the position where the first mentions of the centroid entities appear as event arguments in the test corpus, with accuracy 47.31%. We can see that our cross-document IE method achieved much higher accuracy than both baselines.

8.3 Browsing Cost

For all the system generated event chains which center around the 40 correct centroid entities, we present the browsing cost results in Figure 3.

Figure 3 indicates that for the event chains generated entirely from single-document IE, a user needs to browse 117 incorrect/redundant arguments before seeing 71 correct arguments. By adding cross-document event aggregation, the browsing effort is slightly reduced to seeing 103 incorrect/redundant arguments. The most notable result is that after applying cross-document name argument correction, the number of correct arguments is increased to 79 while the number of incorrect/redundant arguments is significantly reduced to 54. Global time discovery provided further gains: 85 correct arguments after seeing 51 incorrect/redundant ones. The final system resulted in a 60.7% user browsing effort reduction compared to the baseline before seeing 71 correct arguments; and extracted an additional 19.7% unique correct arguments.

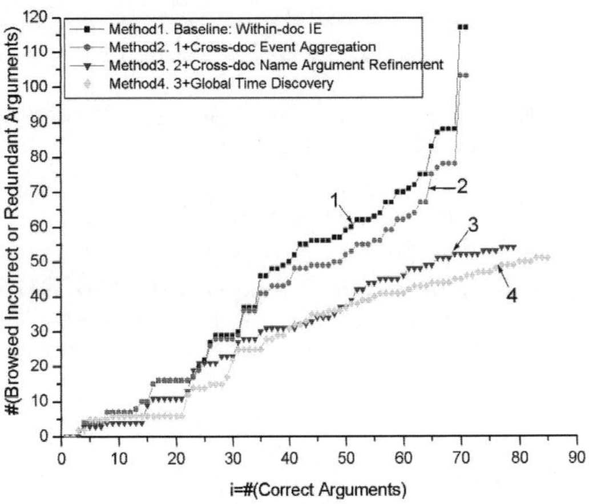

Figure 3. Argument Browsing Cost

8.4 Temporal Correlation

Table 2 shows the argument temporal ordering correlation score for each step. The 4 methods are listed in the legend for Figure 3. The difference among these methods is partly reflected by the number of scored argument pairs, as shown in the argument recall scores. As a first (crude) approximation, events can be ordered according to the time that they are reported. We treat this as our baseline.

Method	Temporal Correlation	Argument Recall
Baseline	3.71%	27.63%
Method1	44.02%	27.63%
Method2	46.15%	27.63%
Method3	55.73%	30.74%
Method4	70.09%	33.07%

Table 2. Temporal Correlation

As we can see, for news stories text order by itself is a poor predictor of chronological order (only 3.71% correlation with the true order). We can generally conclude that our cross-document IE-driven methods can produce significantly better temporal order than the baseline, and thus more coherent extraction results.

9. Related Work

To the best of our knowledge, no research group has combined ranking and linking for cross-document IE. Hence in this section, we present related work in other areas for ranking and linking separately.

Text summarization progressed from single-document to multi-document processing by centroid based sentence linking and ranking (e.g. [5], [6]). Accurate ranking techniques such as PageRank [13] have greatly enhanced information retrieval.

Recently there has been heightened interest in discovering temporal event chains, especially, the shared task evaluation TempEval [9] involved identifying temporal relations in TimeBank [17]. For example, [18] applied supervised learning to classify temporal and causal relations simultaneously for predicates in TimeBank. [19] extracted narrative event chains based on common protagonists. Our work is also similar to the task of topic detection and tracking [20] under the condition that each 'node' for linking is an event extracted by IE instead of a story.

Several recent studies have stressed the benefits of going beyond traditional single-document extraction and taking advantage of information redundancy. In particular, [3, 16, 21, 22, 23, 24, 25] have emphasized this potential in their work. As we present in section 6, the central idea of cross-document argument refinement can be applied to discover knowledge from background data, and thus significantly improve local decisions.

In this paper we import these ideas into IE while taking into account some major differences. Following the original idea of centering [2] and the approach of centering events involving protagonists [19], we present a similar idea of detecting 'centroid' arguments. We operate cross-document instead of single-document, which requires us to resolve more conflicts and ambiguities. In addition, we study the temporal event linking task on top of IE results. In this way we extend the representation of each node in the chains from an event trigger to a structured aggregated event including fine-grained information such as event types, arguments and their roles. Compared to [5, 6], we also extend the definition of "centroid" from a word to an entity; and target at linking extracted facts instead of sentences. On the other hand, we cannot simply transfer the traditional relevance or salience based ranking approaches in IR and multi-document summarization because of the incorrect facts extracted from IE. Therefore we incorporate quality into the ranking metric. Furthermore by incorporating global evidence we correct the original extracted facts and discover implicit time arguments.

10. Conclusion and Future Work

We have defined a new task of cross-document event extraction, ranking and tracking. These new modes can lay the groundwork for an improved browsing, analysis, and search process, and can potentially speed up text comprehension and knowledge distillation.

Then we presented and evaluated a system for performing this task. We investigated various challenging aspects of this new task and showed how to address them by exploiting techniques such as cross-document argument refinement, global time discovery and cross-document event aggregation. Experiments have shown that the performance of cross-document event chain extraction is significantly enhanced over the traditional single-document IE framework.

In this paper we presented event chains involving person entities, but this approach can be naturally extended to other entity types, such as tracking company start/end/acquire/merge activities. In addition we plan to automatically adjust cross-document event aggregation operations according to different compression ratios provided by the users. We are also interested in identifying more event types and their lexical realizations using paraphrase discovery techniques.

Acknowledgements

This material is based upon work supported by the Defense Advanced Research Projects Agency under Contract No. HR0011-06-C-0023, and the National Science Foundation under Grant IIS-00325657, Google Research, CUNY Research Enhancement Program and GRTI Program. Any opinions, findings and conclusions expressed in this material are those of the authors and do not necessarily reflect the views of the U. S. Government.

References

[1] Danielle S McNamara. 2001. Reading both High-coherence and Low-coherence Texts: Effects of Text Sequence and Prior Knowledge. *Canadian Journal of Experimental Psychology.*

[2] Barbara Grosz, Aravind Joshi, and Scott Weinstein. 1995. Centering: A Framework for Modelling the Local Coherence of Discourse. *Computational Linguistics, 2(21).*

[3] Heng Ji and Ralph Grishman. 2008. Refining Event Extraction Through Unsupervised Cross-document Inference. *Proc. ACL-HLT 2008.*

[4] Zheng Chen and Heng Ji. 2009. Language Specific Issue and Feature Exploration in Chinese Event Extraction. *Proc. HLT-NAACL 2009.*

[5] Regina Barzilay, Noemie Elhadad and Kathleen R. Mckeown. 2002. Inferring strategies for sentence ordering in multi-document news summarization. *Journal of Artificial Intelligence Research*, v.17, pp. 35-55, 2002.

[6] Dragomir R. Radev, Hongyan Jing, Malgorzata Stys and Daniel Tam. 2004. Centroid-based Summarization of Multiple Documents. *Information Processing and Management.* 40 (2004) pp. 919-938.

[7] Maurice Kendall. 1938. A New Measure of Rank Correlation. Biometrica, 30, 81-89.

[8] W. S. Cooper. 1968. Expected search length: A Single Measure of Retrieval Effectiveness based on the Weak Ordering Action of retrieval systems. *Journal of American Society of Information Science*, 19(1), 30-41.

[9] Marc. Verhagen, Robert Gaizauskas, Frank Schilder, Mark Hepple, Graham Katz and James Pustejovsky. 2007. SemEval-2007 Task 15: TempEval Temporal Relation Identification. *Proc. ACL 2007 workshop on SemEval*, 2007.

[10] Ralph Grishman, David Westbrook and Adam Meyers. 2005. NYU's English ACE 2005 System Description. *Proc. ACE 2005 Evaluation Workshop.*

[11] K. Balog, L. Azzopardi, M. de Rijke. 2008. Personal Name Resolution of Web People Search. *Proc. WWW2008 Workshop: NLP Challenges in the Information Explosion Era (NLPIX 2008).*

[12] Alex Baron and Marjorie Freedman. 2008. Who is Who and What is What: Experiments in Cross-Document Co-Reference. *Proc. EMNLP 2008.*

[13] Lawrence Page, Sergey Brin, Rajeev Motwani and Terry Winograd. 1998. The PageRank Citation Ranking: Bringing Order to the Web. *Proc. the 7th International World Wide Web Conference.*

[14] Prashant Gupta and Heng Ji. 2009. Predicting Unknown Time Arguments based on Cross-event propagation. *Proc. ACL-IJCNLP 2009.*

[15] Amit Bagga and Breck Baldwin. 1999. Cross-document Event Coreference: Annotations, Experiments, and Observations. Proc. ACL1999 Workshop on Coreference and Its Applications.

[16] Gideon Mann. 2007. Multi-document Relationship Fusion via Constraints on Probabilistic Databases. *Proc. HLT/NAACL 2007.*

[17] J. Pustejovsky, P.Hanks, R. Sauri, A. See, R. Gaizauskas, A. Setzer, D. Radev, B.Sundheim, D. Day, L. Ferro and M. Lazo. 2003. The Timebank Corpus. *Corpus Linguistics.* pp. 647-656.

[18]Steven Bethard and James H. Martin. 2008.Learning semantic links from a corpus of parallel temporal and causal relations. *Proc. ACL-HLT 2008.*

[19] Nathanael Chambers and Dan Jurafsky. 2008. Unsupervised Learning of Narrative Event Chains. *Proc. ACL-HLT 2008.*

[20] James Allan. 2002. Topic Detection and Tracking: Event-based Information Organization. Springer.

[21] Doug Downey, Oren Etzioni, and Stephen Soderland. 2005. A Probabilistic Model of Redundancy in Information Extraction. *Proc. IJCAI 2005.*

[22] Jenny Rose Finkel, Trond Grenager and Christopher Manning. 2005. Incorporating Non-local Information into Information Extraction Systems by Gibbs Sampling. *Proc. ACL 2005.*

[23] Roman Yangarber. 2006. Verification of Facts across Document Boundaries. Proc. International Workshop on Intelligent Information Access.

[24] Siddharth Patwardhan and Ellen Riloff. 2007. Effective Information Extraction with Semantic Affinity Patterns and Relevant Regions. *Proc. EMNLP-CONLL 2007.*

[25] Siddharth Patwardhan and Ellen Riloff. 2009. A Unified Model of Phrasal and Sentential Evidence for Information Extraction. 2009. *Proc. EMNLP 2009.*

Co-Parsing with Competitive Models

Lidia Khmylko
Natural Language Systems Group
University of Hamburg, Germany
khmylko@informatik.uni-hamburg.de

Kilian A. Foth
smartSpeed GmbH & Co. KG
Hamburg, Germany
kilian.foth@smartspeed.com

Wolfgang Menzel
Natural Language Systems Group
University of Hamburg, Germany
menzel@informatik.uni-hamburg.de

Abstract

We present an asymmetric approach to a runtime combination of two parsers where one component serves as a predictor to the other one. Predictions are integrated by means of weighted constraints and therefore are subject to preferential decisions. Previously, the same architecture has been successfully used with predictors providing partial or inferior information about the parsing problem. It has now been applied to a situation where the predictor produces exactly the same type of information at a fully competitive quality level. Results show that the combined system outperforms its individual components, even though their performance in isolation is already fairly high.

Keywords

Dependency Parsing, Hybrid Parsing

1 Introduction

Machine learning techniques for automatically acquiring processing models from a data collection and traditional methods of eliciting linguistic knowledge from human experts are usually considered as two alternative roadmaps towards natural language processing solutions. Since the resulting components exhibit quite different performance characteristics with respect to coverage, robustness and output quality, they might be able to provide some kind of complementary information, which could even lead to a notable degree of synergy between them when combined within a single system solution.

For the task of dependency parsing the high potential for such a synergy has indeed been demonstrated already.

A popular approach for combining alternative decision procedures is voting [18]. It makes use of a symmetric architecture, where a meta component chooses from among the available candidate hypotheses by means of a (weighted) voting scheme. Such an approach not only requires the target structures of all components to be of the same kind, but in case of complex structures like parse trees also requires sophisticated decision procedures which are able to select the optimal hypotheses with respect to additional global constraints (e.g. the tree property). Since this optimization problem has to be solved by the individual parser anyhow, an asymmetric architecture suggests itself as an alternative.

In asymmetric architectures, a master component, i.e. a full fledged parser, is solely in charge of deciding on the target structure, whilst the others (so called helper or predictor components) provide additional evidence which is integrated into the global decision by suitable means. Such a scheme has been extensively investigated for the Weighted Constraint Dependency Grammar, WCDG [3]. External evidence from the predictor components is integrated by means of constraints, which check for compatibility between a local structure and a prediction, and penalize this hypothesis in case of a conflict. So far, however, all the additional information sources which have been considered in this research differed considerably from the master component: They either focused on particular aspects of the parsing problem (e.g. POS tagging, chunking, PP attachment), or used a simplified scheme for structural annotation (e.g. projective instead of non-projective trees).

This paper takes one step further by investigating the same architecture under the additional condition that (1) the helper component provides the very same kind of target structure as the master, and (2) the quality levels are considered in isolation.

As a helper component MSTParser [9], a state-of-the-art dependency parser for non-projective structures based on a discriminative learning paradigm, is considered. The accuracy of MSTParser differs insignificatly from that of WCDG with all the previously used helper components active.

Section two introduces WCDG with a special emphasis on the soft integration of external evidence while section three describes MSTParser which is used as a new predictor component. Since parsing results for these systems have been reported in quite different experimental settings we first evaluate them under comparable conditions and provide the results of using MSTParser as a guiding predictor for WCDG in section four and discuss whether the expected synergies have really materialized. Section five concentrates on a comparative error analysis.

International Conference RANLP 2009 - Borovets, Bulgaria, pages 173–179

2 WCDG

The formalism of a Constraint Dependency Grammar was first introduced by H. Maruyama [8] and suggests modeling natural language with the help of constraints. I. Schröder [17] has extended the approach to Weighted Constraint Dependency Grammar, WCDG, where weights are used to further disambiguate between competing structural alternatives. A WCDG models natural language as labeled dependency trees and is entirely declarative. It has no derivation rules — instead, constraints license well-formed tree structures. The reference implementation of WCDG for the German language used for the experiments described below contains about 1,000 manually compiled constraints.[1]

The values of weights of the WCDG constraints have to be determined by the grammar writer experimentally. They lie in the interval from zero to one, a lower value of the weight reflects its greater importance. Constraints having zero weights are referred to as hard and are used for prohibitive rules. Constraints with a weight greater than zero, also called defeasible, may express universal principles or vague preferences for language phenomena. Empirically, the absolute values of defeasible constraints usually do not matter greatly as long as the relative importance of the rules remains preserved.

If a set of dependency edges in a parse found by the system violates any of the constraints, it is registered as a *constraint violation* between the structure and the rules of the language. The *score* of an analysis is the product of all the weights for constraint violations occurring in the structure. Therefore, it becomes possible to differentiate between the quality of different parse results: the analysis with a higher score is considered preferable. Under these conditions, an analysis having only a few grave conflicts may be preferred by the system against another one with a great number of smaller constraint violations. However, an analysis which violates any of the hard constraints always receives the lowest possible score.

The parsing problem is being treated in the WCDG system as a Constraint Satisfaction Problem. While a complete search is intractable for such a problem, *transformation-based solution methods* provide a reliable heuristic alternative. Starting with an initial guess about the optimal tree, changes of labels, subordinations, or lexical variants are applied, with constraint violations used as a control mechanism guiding the transformation process [5].

A transformation-based search cannot guarantee to find the best solution to the constraint satisfaction problem. Compared to the resource requirements of a complete search, however, it is not only more efficient, but can also be interrupted at any time. Even if interrupted, it will always return an analysis, together with a list of constraint violations it was not able to remove. The algorithm terminates on its own if no violated constraints with a weight above a predefined threshold remain. Alternatively, a timeout condition can be imposed.

The same kind of constraints that describe grammar rules, can also be used as an interface to external predictor components. Thus, the formalism turned out to be flexible enough to incorporate other sources of knowledge into the decision process on the optimal structural interpretation. Previously, five additional statistical components have been successfully integrated into WCDG: POS tagger, chunker, supertagger, PP attacher and a shift-reduce oracle parser [4]. This study has shown that the accuracy also improves if multiple components interact and consistent predictions no longer can be guaranteed. Even though the predictor components have an accuracy that is mostly — with the exception of the tagger — below that of the parser itself, WCDG not only avoids error propagation successfully, it also improves consistently by slight, but noticeable margins.

3 MSTParser

MSTParser [9] is a state-of-the-art language independent data-driven parser. It processes the input in two separate stages. In the first, the dependency structure is determined, labeling is applied to it successively in the second. The reasons of its efficiency lie in the successful combination of discriminative learning with graph-based solution methods for the parsing problem.

In this edge-factored graph-based model, each edge of the dependency graph is assigned a real-valued score that expresses the likelihood of creating a dependency edge between two words. The score of the graph is defined as the sum of its edge scores.

If a scoring function for edges is known, the parsing problem becomes equivalent to finding the highest scoring directed spanning tree in the complete graph over the given sentence, and the correct parse can be obtained by searching the space of valid dependency graphs for a tree with a maximum score.

This formalism allows to find efficient solutions for both projective and non-projective trees. When only features over single edges are taken into account, the complexity falls to unprecedented $O(n^2)$ [12].

Not only a single edge, but also adjacent edges may be included into the scoring function. As a result, intractability problems arise for the non-projective algorithm, but an efficient approximate algorithm based on exhaustive search is provided for this case [10]. This algorithm was also used for our experiments.[2]

The parsing model of MSTParser has the advantage that it can be trained globally and eventually be applied with an exact inference algorithm. On the other hand, the parser has only limited access to the history of parsing decisions. To avoid complexity problems, the scores (and the feature representations) are restricted to a single edge or adjacent edges. Outsourcing labeling into a separate stage comes at the price of not being able to combine knowledge about the label and the structure it is attached to. Such combined evidence, however, might be helpful for some disambiguation problems.

[1] Freely available from `http://nats-www.informatik.uni-hamburg.de/view/CDG/DownloadPage`

[2] MSTParser is freely available from `http://sourceforge.net/projects/mstparser`

4 Guiding WCDG by Predictions of MSTParser

MSTParser predictions are integrated into the decision procedure of WCDG by means of two additional constraints, which monitor each dependency hypothesis for being in accord with the prediction and penalize it if a mismatch has been found. One of the constraints checks the attachment point being the same, while the other takes care of the dependency label.

To properly adjust the weights of these constraints, it has to be determined how valuable the information of the predictor is relative to the information already present in the system. This gradation is needed to establish a balance between the influence of the grammar and the predictor. According to the scoring principles of WCDG, a low weight strongly deprecates all deviations from the prediction, thus forcing the system to follow them almost without exception. Higher weights, on the other hand, enable the grammar to override a prediction. This, however, also means that predictions have less guiding effect of the transformation process. Typically for WCDG, the best suitable weights have to be tuned on development data.

To determine the best constraint weights the WCDG grammar is extended with three additional constraints similar to those used for the shift-reduce predictor in the previous experiments [3]:

```
#pragma predict MST 'mst.pl -v 3 -' cat

{X!SYN} : 'MST:regent' : stat : W :
      predict(X@id, MST, gov) = X^to;

{X|SYN} : 'MST:null' : stat : W :
      predict(X@id, MST, gov) = 0;

{X:SYN} : 'MST:label' : stat : W :
      predict(X@id, MST, lab) = X.label;
```

The first two constraints advise WCDG on the structural information, whereby the second deals with the elements modifying the root and the first with all the others; the third fetches the edge label predicted. W, $0 \leq W \leq 1$, stands for the constraint weight chosen for the experiment.

As a result of these experiments, the optimum weight for the attachment predictions has been adjusted to 0.75. Compared to a weight of 0.9 for the shift-reduce parser, this is a rather strong influence, which also reflects the differences in the reliability of these two information sources. With a weight of 0.9, the integration of the label predictions is considerably weaker, which is consistent with their lower degree of accuracy.

Evaluation

The most common general measures for the quality of dependency trees are *structural accuracy* that points out the percentage of words correctly attached to their regent, and *labeled accuracy* which is the ratio of the correctly attached words which also have the correct label. Still, it is difficult to directly compare the results reported for different parsers, as the evaluation results are influenced by the data used during the experiment, the domain of the data, and different annotation guidelines. Moreover, the particular kind of POS information might be relevant, which either can be obtained from the manual annotations or be provided by a real tagger. Even such a condition as the treatment of punctuation has not yet become a standard. Following the evaluation procedure in the CoNLL-X shared task [2], we will not include punctuation into the performance measures, as was done in previous WCDG experiments [4]. The source of POS tagging information will need to be specified in each individual case.

All the evaluations were performed on a thousand sentences (18,602 – 19,601) from the NEGRA treebank, the same data set that was previously used in the performance evaluations of WCDG, e.g. in [3]. The NEGRA treebank is a collection of newspaper articles; in the original, it stores phrase structure annotations. These have been automatically translated into dependency trees and then manually corrected to bring them in accord with the annotation guidelines of WCDG. The major difference consists in a different treatment of non-projectivity, where WCDG only allows non-projectivity in the attachment of verbal arguments, relative clauses and coordinations, i.e., the cases where it helps to decrease ambiguity. Furthermore, corrections were applied when the annotations of NEGRA itself turned out to be inconsistent (usually in connection with co-ordinated or elliptical structures, adverbs and subclauses).

Unfortunately, these manually corrected data were only available for a small part (3,000 sentences) of the NEGRA corpus, which is not sufficient for training MSTParser on WCDG-conforming tree structures. Previous evaluations of the MSTParser have used much larger training sets. E.g., during the CoNLL-X shared task 39,216 sentences from the TIGER Treebank [1] were used.

Therefore, we used 20,000 sentences from the online archive of `www.heise.de` as an alternative training set. They have been manually annotated according to the WCDG guidelines (called `heiseticker` in the following). The texts in this corpus are all from roughly the same domain as NEGRA, and although very many technical terms and proper nouns are used, the sentences have only a slightly longer mean length compared to the NEGRA corpus.

Using POS tags from the gold annotations, MSTParser achieves 90.5% structural and 87.5% labeled accuracy on the aforementioned NEGRA test set (Table 1). Even a model trained on the inconsistent NEGRA data excluding the test set reaches state-of-the-art 90.5 and 87.3% for structural and labeled accuracy respectively, despite the obvious mismatch between training and test data. This performance is almost the same as the 90.4%/87.3% reported on the TIGER data during the CoNLL-X 2006 shared task. Another MSTParser experiment has been conducted with a real POS tagger [6]. Generally, in ambiguous cases, it can predict several POS tags per word sorted by the predicted POS category probabilities in descending order. But only the first of these predictions was used for the experiments with MSTParser as, contrary to WCDG, it does not provide an interface to use POS tag variants by default. As is to be expected, if a real POS tagger is used, the accuracy is

Experiment	structural	labeled
MSTParser-h	90.5	87.5
MSTParser-N	90.5	87.3
MSTParser(CoNLL-X)	90.4	87.3
WCDG + MST	92.9	91.3
WCDG + MST + 5P	93.3	92.0

Table 1: *Structural/labeled accuracy results with POS tagging from the gold standard. WCDG — no statistical enhancements used. MSTParser-h — MSTParser trained on the* `heiseticker`. *MSTParser-N — MSTParser trained on NEGRA. 5P — with all five statistical predictors of WCDG.*

reduced quite expectedly by approximately one percent to 89.5%/86.0% (Table 2 (B)). All the results obtained with a real POS tagger are summarized in Table 2. For comparison, under the same evaluation conditions, the performance of WCDG with different predictors is summarized in Table 2 (A).

	Experiment	structural	labeled
(A)	**WCDG**	**88.0**	**86.0**
	CP	88.6	86.5
	PP	89.4	87.3
	ST	90.8	89.2
	SR	90.0	88.4
	PP+SR	90.2	88.6
	ST+SR	91.0	89.4
	ST+PP	90.8	89.2
	5P	**91.3**	**90.0**
(B)	**MSTParser**	**89.5**	**86.0**
(C)	**WCDG + MST**	**92.0**	**90.5**
	PP	92.0	90.6
	CP	92.1	90.6
	SR	92.2	90.6
	ST	92.4	90.9
	CP+SR	92.3	90.7
	CP+ST	92.6	91.0
	ST+SR	92.9	91.4
	PP+CP+ST	92.6	91.1
	PP+ST+SR	92.8	91.3
	CP+ST+SR	92.9	91.4
	5P	**92.9**	**91.4**

Table 2: *Structural/labeled accuracy results with a real POS tagger. (A) WCDG experiments with different statistical enhancements (B) MSTParser experiment with a real POS tagger. (C) Combined experiments of WCDG and MSTParser with other statistical enhancements of WCDG. CP — chunker, ST — supertagger, PP — prepositional attacher, SR — shift-reduce oracle parser, 5P — POS + CP + PP + ST + SR.*

The combined experiments in which MSTParser was used as a predictor for WCDG have achieved higher accuracy than each of the combined components in isolation: the structural accuracy rises to 92.0% while the labeled accuracy also gets over the 90%-boundary (WCDG + MST experiment in Table 2 (C)) .

Finally, the MSTParser predictor was evaluated in combination with the other predictors available for WCDG. The results of the experiments are shown in Table 2 (C). Every combination of MSTParser with other predictors (first four experiments) improves the accuracy. The increase is highest (0.4%) for the combination with the supertagger. This confirms earlier experiments with WCDG, in which the supertagger also contributed the largest gains.

The experimental results again confirm that WCDG is a reliable platform for information integration. Although the use of multiple predictors does not lead to an accumulation of the individual improvements, the performance of predictor combinations is always higher that using them separately. A maximum performance of 92.9%/91.4% is reached with all the six available predictors active. For comparison, the same experiment with POS tags from the gold standard has achieved even better results of 93.3%/92.0% (Table 1).

Unfortunately, the PP attacher brings accuracy reductions when it is working parallel to the shift-reduce predictor (experiment PP + CP + SR in Table 2 (C)). This effect has already been observed in the experiments that combined the two alone (experiment PP + SR in Table 2 (A)). When MST was combined with the PP attacher (experiment PP in Table 2 (C)), the increase of the performance was also below a tenth of a percent. The possible reasons why the use of an additional information source does not improve the performance in this case may be the disadvantages of the PP attacher compared to a full parser.

5 Error Analysis

A very useful property of WCDG is that it not only can be used as a parser, but also as a diagnostic tool for dependency structures. Applied to a given dependency tree, any constraint violation reported by the constraint solver indicates an inconsistency between the structure and the WCDG constraint grammar.

Among the most frequent hard constraint violations found in the MSTParser results are double subjects, double objects and direct objects in passive, projectivity violations, conjunctions without a clause as well as subordinate clause without conjunction.

These findings are in line with the analysis of [11]. For example, the errors in distinguishing noun complements of the verb may be due to the fact that MSTParser is more precise for longer dependency arcs and has no access to the parsing history.

In absolute figures, MSTParser commits 1509 attachment errors of which 902 are corrected by WCDG. On the other hand, WCDG adds another 542 errors of its own, so that the final result still contains 1149 errors.

For most labels, accuracy of the predictor combination is higher than in each of the parsers alone. A particularly large gain has been observed for coordinated elements (KON and CJ), subordinate (NEB)

	(1)		(2)		(3)	
Label	*p*	*r*	*p*	*r*	*p*	*r*
DET	98.4	99.3	98.7	99.5	99.3	99.5
PN	97.4	97.4	98.0	98.0	98.0	98.7
PP	67.6	98.1	78.3	97.4	80.1	98.5
ADV	76.6	94.7	79.4	95.4	82.2	97.2
SUBJ	94.0	90.9	91.3	86.4	95.8	94.0
ATTR	95.2	95.8	97.7	98.2	98.3	98.4
S	89.2	90.1	89.3	90.5	90.5	91.0
AUX	95.9	94.2	98.6	97.8	98.7	97.6
OBJA	87.9	83.9	83.8	72.5	92.5	88.7
APP	85.1	88.5	88.9	90.9	90.9	94.0
KON	78.9	88.1	78.9	88.3	86.0	89.2
CJ	85.6	86.5	90.9	91.4	93.0	93.5
GMOD	90.7	90.7	89.0	85.3	96.3	95.8
KONJ	88.6	91.9	91.9	95.7	95.1	95.7
PRED	90.3	75.0	85.4	60.4	91.7	76.4
NEB	68.9	82.8	73.0	66.4	79.5	90.2
REL	64.8	77.9	59.0	77.0	68.9	86.9

Table 3: *Per label structural precision (*p, %*) and label recal (*r, %*) in comparison for the experiments with the real POS tagger (1) WCDG, (2) MSTParser, (3) WCDG combined with MSTParser*

and relative (REL) clauses, indirect accusative objects (OBJA), genitive modifiers (GMOD) and apposition (APP), (Table 3). Here, the measures of structural precision, the ratio of the number of correct attachment of a given label to the number of all the predictions for that label made by the parser, and label recall, the ratio between the number of correct labeling decisions and desired labeling are used.

In this respect, the increase in the structural precision of the PP attachment seems worth mentioning. MSTParser attaches 79.3% of PPs correctly on the used test set. Although MSTParser does not use any special PP-attachment resolution mechanisms, it is comparable with the result of WCDG combined with the PP attacher that achieves 78.7% structural precision for PP edges.

If MSTParser is trained on NEGRA excluding the test set — the rest of NEGRA lacking consistence mentioned above — it performs even better, attaching 80.4% of PP-s correctly. Thus, MSTParser as a statistical parser trained on a full corpus becomes a strong competitor for a PP attacher that has been trained on restricted four-tuples input.

As for the errors in the MSTParser output that are most often corrected in the hybrid experiment, this happens for both the structural precision and label recall of most verb complements, such as direct and indirect objects, or clausal objects as well as for subordinate and relative clauses for such subordinate clauses.

It even comes to one case in which the synergy took place in spite of the incorrect predictions. Although MSTParser has predicted possessive modifiers more seldom than WCDG alone (the label recall of MSTParser for possessive modification was over 5% below that of WCDG) its structural precision and label recall in the combined experiment are by around 6% greater than WCDG result.

Cases in which WCDG performs worse with the predictor than its predictor alone can hardly be found. Still, one may observe many cases in which the predictor has a negative influence on the performance of WCDG, such as for different kinds of objects (indirect objects, object clauses and infinitive objects) and parenthetic matrix clauses. For all, the result of MSTParser was below that of the baseline WCDG with only the POS tagger active. Same can be said about the labeled accuracy for split verb prefixes and nominal time expressions. This worsening effect can be attributed to the lower values of the WCDG constraints for the corresponding labels and edges than for the MSTParser predictor. Thus, the search could not find a decision scoring better than that when the MSTParser prediction has been followed.

Around 15% of the sentences in the test set are not projective. The accuracy of MSTParser on the projective sentences of the test set is higher than that on the non-projective sentences by more than 3 percent (Table 4), although these values cannot be compared directly as the mean length of non-projective sentences is longer (25.0 vs. 15.3 words).

Experiment	Non-proj.	Proj.
MSTParser (POS)	88.2	91.7
WCDG (POS)	87.2	90.2
WCDG (POS + SR)	88.7	92.2
WCDG (POS + MST)	91.3	93.6

Table 4: *Structural accuracy, (%), for different parsing runs for non-projective vs. projective sentences.*

MSTParser generally tends to find many more non-projective edges than the data has, while the precision remains restricted. The number of non-projective edges was determined by counting how often an edge crosses some other edge. Thus, if a non-projective edge crossed three other edges the number of non-projective edges equals three. For MSTParser experiments with a real POS tagger (MSTParser POS-experiment in Table 5), the non-projective edge recall, the ratio of the non-projective edges found in the experiment to the corresponding value in the gold standard, is at 23% and non-projective edge precision, the ratio of the correctly found non-projective edges to all non-projective edges found, is also only 36% (second column in Table 5).

Precision and recall of non-projective sentences is a less rigid measure. If at least one edge-crossing is correctly identified in a non-projective sentence, it is added to the correctly identified non-projective sentences, even if the identified edge-crossing is not the one annotated in the gold standard and the ratios are calculated respectively (right column of Table 5). Under these relaxed conditions, MSTParser correctly identifies slightly less than a half of the non-projective sentences and over a third of non-projective edges.

Experiment	Edges r	Edges p	Sentences r	Sentences p
MSTParser (POS)	23	36	35	44
WCDG (POS)	37	53	51	63
WCDG (POS + SR)	41	47	57	55
WCDG (POS + MST)	48	53	61	61

Table 5: *Recall* (r, %) *and precision* (p, %) *of the non-projective edges and sentences for different parsing runs.*

In fact, WCDG under the same conditions (WCDG POS-experiment in Table 5) has a non-projective sentence precision of 63% and a non-projective edge precision of 53%. Still, WCDG misses a considerable amount of non-projectivities. More importantly, as the present shift-reduce predictor has not been designed for non-projective parsing, its inclusion reduces the non-projective sentence and edge precision of WCDG — to 55% and 47% respectively — WCDG (POS+SR) in Table 5.

The expected benefits for the non-projective sentences have not yet been observed to the full extent. The precision of the combined system to find non-projective sentences and edges remained limited by the performance that WCDG was able to achieve alone (WCDG (POS+MST) in Table 5). While MSTParser in many cases predicts non-projectivity correctly WCDG is seldom capable of accepting this external evidence. On the contrary, WCDG often accepts an incorrect projective solution of the predictor instead of relying on its own cues. In its interaction with external predictors WCDG should typically decide about the alternatives.

6 Related Work

So far, approaches to hybrid parsing have been mainly based on the idea of a post-hoc selection which can be carried out for either complete parses, or individual constituents and dependency edges, respectively. The selection component itself can be based on heuristics, like a majority vote. Alternatively, a second-level classifier is trained to decide which component to trust under which conditions and therefore the approach is often referred to as classifier stacking.

In a series of experiments, J. C. Henderson and E. Brill [7] combined three constituency-based parsers by a selection mechanism for either complete parsing results (parser switching) or individual constituents (parse hybridization), using both a heuristic decision rule as well as a naïve Bayesian classifier in each case. Among the heuristics considered were majority votes for constituents and a similarity-based measure for complete trees. Tests on Penn Treebank data showed a clear improvement of the combined results over the best individual parser. Constituent selection outperformed the complete parse selection scheme, and Bayesian selection was slightly superior.

Instead of coupling different data-driven parsers which all provide comparable analyses for complete sentences, C. G. Rupp etal. [15] combined differently elaborated structural descriptions (namely chunks and phrase structure trees) obtained by data-driven components with the output of a HPSG-parser. Driven by the requirements of the particular application (speech-to-speech translation), the focus was not only on parse selection, but also on combining incomplete results. However, no quantitative evaluation of the results has been published.

D. Zeman and Z. Žabokrtský [18] applied the selection idea to dependency structures and extended it by using more context features. They combined seven different parsers for Czech, among them also a system based on a manually compiled rule set. Some of the individual parsers had a fairly poor performance, but even a simple voting scheme on single edges contributed a significant improvement while the best results have been obtained for a combination that did not include the worst components. Alternatively the authors experimented with a trained selection component which not only had access to the alternative local parsing results, but also to their structural context. Neither a memory-based approach nor a model based on decision trees did result in further gains.

In two separate experiments, K. Sagae and A. Lavie [16] combined a number of dependency and constituent parsers, respectively. They created a new weighted search space from the results of the individual component parsers using different weighting schemes for the candidates. They then reparsed this search space and found a consistent improvement for the dependency structures, but not for the constituent-based ones.

While all these approaches attempt to integrate the available evidence at parse time, J. Nivre and R. McDonald [14] pursued an alternative architecture, where integration is achieved already at training time. They combined the two state-of-the-art data-driven dependency parsers, MaltParser [13] and MSTParser [10], by integrating the features of each of the classifiers into the parsing model of the other one at training time. Since the two parsers are based on quite different model types (namely a history-based vs. a structure-based one), they exhibit a remarkable complementary behavior [11]. Accordingly, significant mutual benefits have been observed. Note, however, that one of the major benefits of MaltParser, its incremental left-to-right processing, is sacrificed under such a combination scheme.

7 Conclusion

Integrating MSTParser as a full predictor with WCDG is beneficial for both of them. Since these systems take their decisions based on completely different sources of knowledge, combining both helps avoid many mistakes each of them commits in isolation. Altogether, with a real POS tagger, an accuracy level of 92.9%/91.3% has been reached (the last row in Table 2 (C)), which is higher than what any of the parsers achieved alone. With POS tagging from the gold standard, the accuracy has been at 93.3%/92.0% (the last row in Table 1). To the knowledge of the authors, these accuracy values are also better than any previous parsing results on the NEGRA test set.

WCDG can profit from the combination not only with ancillary predictors for specific parsing subtasks, but also with another full parser. This result was achieved even though the second parser is very similar to WCDG with respect to both the richness and the accuracy of its target structures. The probable reason lies in the considerable difference in the error profiles of both systems as regards specific linguistic phenomena. WCDG was also used as a diagnostic tool for the errors of MSTParser.

Possibly, a higher degree of synergy could be achieved if a stronger coupling of the components is established by also using the scores of MSTParser as additional information for WCDG, reflecting the intuitive notion of preference or plausibility of the predictions. This could be done for the optimal parse tree alone as well as for the complete hypothesis space. Alternatively, the output of MSTParser can be used as a initial state for the transformation procedure of WCDG. Vice versa, MSTParser could be enriched with additional features based on the output of WCDG, similar to the feature-based integration of data-driven parsers evaluated by J. Nivre and R. McDonald [14].

At the moment, the integration constraints treats all attachment and label predictions as being uniformly reliable. To individualize them with respect to their type or origin could not only make the system sensitive to qualitative differences between predictions (for instance, with respect to different labels). It would also allow the parser to accommodate multiple oracle predictors and to carefully distinguish between typical configurations in which one prediction should be preferred over an alternative one. MaltParser [13] is certainly a good candidate for carrying out such experiments.

References

[1] S. Brants, S. Dipper, S. Hansen, W. Lezius, and G. Smith. The TIGER treebank. In *Proceedings of the Workshop on Treebanks and Linguistic Theories*, Sozopol, 2002.

[2] S. Buchholz and E. Marsi. CoNLL-X shared task on multilingual dependency parsing. In *Proc. CoNLL*, pages 149 – 164, 2006.

[3] K. A. Foth. *Hybrid Methods of Natural Language Analysis.* Doctoral thesis, Hamburg University, 2006.

[4] K. A. Foth and W. Menzel. Hybrid parsing: using probabilistic models as predictors for a symbolic parser. In *Proc. 21st Int. Conference on Computational Linguistics and ACL-44*, pages 321–328, 2006.

[5] K. A. Foth, W. Menzel, and I. Schröder. A Transformation-based Parsing Technique with Anytime Properties. In *4th Int. Workshop on Parsing Technologies, IWPT-2000*, pages 89 – 100, 2000.

[6] J. Hagenström and K. A. Foth. Tagging for robust parsers. In *Proc. 2nd. Int. Workshop, Robust Methods in Analysis of Natural Language Data, ROMAND-2002*, 2002.

[7] J. C. Henderson and E. Brill. Exploiting diversity in natural language processing: Combining parsers. In *Proc. 4th Conference on Empirical Methods in Natural Language Processing*, pages 187–194, 1999.

[8] H. Maruyama. Structural disambiguation with constraint propagation. In *Proc. 28th Annual Meeting of the ACL (ACL-90)*, pages 31–38, 1990.

[9] R. McDonald. *Discriminative Learning and Spanning Tree Algorithms for Dependency Parsing.* PhD dissertation, University of Pennsylvania, 2006.

[10] R. McDonald, K. Lerman, and F. Pereira. Multilingual dependency analysis with a two-stage discriminative parser. In *Proc. CoNLL*, pages 216 – 220, 2006.

[11] R. McDonald and J. Nivre. Characterizing the errors of data-driven dependency parsing models. In *Proc. EMNLP-CoNLL*, pages 122 – 131, 2007.

[12] R. McDonald, F. Pereira, K. Ribarov, and J. Hajič. Non-projective dependency parsing using spanning tree algorithms. In *Proc. HLT/EMNLP*, pages 523 – 530, 2005.

[13] J. Nivre, J. Hall, J. Nilsson, G. Eryiğit, and S. Marinov. Labelled pseudo-projective dependency parsing with support vector machines. In *Proc. CoNLL-2006*, pages 221–225, 2006.

[14] J. Nivre and R. McDonald. Integrating graph-based and transition-based dependency parsers. In *Proc. ACL-08: HLT*, pages 950–958, 2008.

[15] C. G. Rupp, J. Spilker, M. Klarner, and K. L. Worm. Combining analyses from various parsers. In W. Wahlster, editor, *Verbmobil: Foundations of Speech-to-Speech Translation*, pages 311–320. Springer-Verlag, Berlin etc., 2000.

[16] K. Sagae and A. Lavie. Parser combinations by reparsing. In *Proc. HLT/NAACL*, pages 129–132, 2006.

[17] I. Schröder. *Natural Language Parsing with Graded Constraints.* PhD thesis, Dept. of Computer Science, University of Hamburg, Germany, 2002.

[18] D. Zeman and Z. Žabokrtský. Improving parsing accuracy by combining diverse dependency parsers. In *Proc. 9th International Workshop on Parsing Technologies (IWPT-2005)*, pages 171–178, Vancouver, B.C., 2005.

Robust Compositional Polarity Classification

Manfred Klenner & Stefanos Petrakis & Angela Fahrni
Computational Linguistics
Zurich University, Switzerland
{klenner,petrakis}@cl.uzh.ch
angela.fahrni@swissonline.ch

Abstract

We describe a pattern-based system for polarity classification from texts. Our system is currently restricted to the positive, negative or neutral polarity of phrases and sentences. It analyses the input texts with the aid of a polarity lexicon that specifies the prior polarity of words. A chunker is used to determine phrases that are the basis for a compositional treatment of phrase-level polarity assignment. In our current experiments we focus on sentences that are targeted towards persons, be it the writer (I, my, me, ..), the social group including the writer (we, our, ..) or the reader (you, your, ..). We evaluate our system on a manually annotated set of sentences taken from texts from a panel group called 'I battle depression'. We present the results of comparing our system's performance over this gold standard against a baseline system.

Keywords

sentiment analysis, polarity composition

1 Introduction

Polarity classification aims at identifying the positive and negative polarities of text, at various levels, including document, sentence, phrase and word level.

Such a task can be guided by the principle of compositionality[5], which states that:

> "The meaning of a complex expression is determined by its structure and the meanings of its constituents."

Based on this principle, the polarity of a portion of text can be composed from the polarities of its constituents in a systematic way[11]. An example of such compositionality appears in the following sentence,

> "He is a good liar"

which is classified as negative[1], since a positive adjective and a negative noun yield a negative noun phrase. In principle, such an incremental compositional interpretation might proceed up the sentence level — negating, confirming and intensifying already computed phrase polarities. In the sentence:

> "He is a quite good liar."

the positive polarity of the adjective is confirmed and intensified ('quite'), whereas in the sentence

> "He is not an extremely good liar."

the positive polarity of the adjective remains but is decreased. This happens because the adverb 'extremely' is shifted by the "not" negator and does not function as an intensifier anymore. Negation is the most common form of so-called polarity shifters. Another example is 'without' - 'without hope' is negative, but 'without fear' is positive.

In the simplest case, word polarities are provided by a polarity lexicon. Commonly used lexicons are the subjectivity lexicon from [15], the semi-automatically derived SentiWordNet [6] or lexicons generated from the General Inquirer lexicon [12].

Ambiguity turns out to be a problem: 'a cheap therapy' might be regarded as positive if 'cheap' means 'low price' but negative if it means 'low quality'. However, we have identified only few cases of ambiguity in our experiments. In principle, we identify ambiguity of this type as a challenging problem, although we don't cope with it in our current setup.

Another problem is 'out of the blue' non-neutral polarity. That is, combinations of two or more neutral words might yield a non-neutral polarity. For instance, the phrase 'long waiting time (to see the doctor)' is negative, although all parts are neutral. No prior polarity lexicon can cope with these cases. We have proposed a corpus-based approach to solve these cases in [7].

Finally, figurative language such as irony and sarcasm might as well occur in such texts. Consider the following example:

> "I also am being charged 100 for missing a doctor's appt. What a way to make me feel better"

The intended meaning of the second sentence clearly is not positive, although the literal interpretation suggests this.

We introduce a system for polarity classification based on the prior lexicon from [15] and the output of the TreeTagger chunker [14].

It is shown that our cascaded, pattern-based compositional polarity determination yields good empirical performance on texts from a self-help group called 'I battle depression'. The evaluation of our system involved constructing a gold standard used for testing a baseline system's performance against our own.

[1] With an overtone of admiration

International Conference RANLP 2009 - Borovets, Bulgaria, pages 180–184

2 Resources and tools

We have searched for texts where people are expressing strong emotions. A website called "the experience project"[2] has proved interesting for our purposes. On that website, groups can be found to rather diverse topics such as 'I quit smoking', 'I love cats (music, books, lyrics)', 'I want to loose weight' etc. For our experiments, we have taken 2290 texts from a panel group called 'I battle depression'"[3].

Here, people explicitly describe their emotional states, their feelings, their experiences, their hopes and fears and even give each other advice how to overcome mental problems such as for instance social anxiety.

In a first step, we wanted to analyse the polarity of phrases and sentences from these texts. In order to achieve this, a polarity lexicon was necessary. We have experimented with the subjectivity lexicon from [15].

The subjectivity lexicon [15] is a resource compiled from various other resources - including the general inquirer (GI). This was done mainly manually, but in part also automatically. The lexicon comprises about 8,000 polarity tagged words (adjectives, verbs, nouns, adverbs), where each word either is positive, negative or objective. A non-objective word also might be weak or strong subjective (we have not used this information).

3 The composition of polarity

The predominant approach in the area of sentiment detection can be characterised as 'machine learning on top of a bag of word representation of the input data'. There are very few notable exceptions, namely [11] and lately, [3] (see section related work).

The bag of words approach ignores the fact that sentiment interpretation is compositional. To a certain extent, a machine learning algorithm is able to approximate composition, e.g. the effect of negation ('I don't like ..'). However, sentiment composition is a phenomenon that can be fixed with a relatively small set of simple rules with very few exceptions. So there is no need to learn these regularities.

ADJ	NOUN	→	NP	Example
NEG	POS	→	NEG	disappointed hope
NEG	NEG	→	NEG	a horrible liar
POS	POS	→	POS	a good friend
POS	NEG	→	NEG	a perfect misery
POS	NEU	→	POS	a perfect meal
NEG	NEU	→	NEG	a horrible meal

Fig. 1: *NP composition*

Fig. 1 gives the regularities for NP level composition, where an adjective is combined with a noun. The sentiment orientation of the words comes from a pre-compiled polarity lexicon. So for example, the positive adjective 'perfect' combined with the negative noun 'misery' yields a negative noun phrase.

[2] Their slogan is: "Share your experiences anonymously. Meet new friends who understand you".

[3] http://www.experienceproject.com/group_stories.php?g=109

Adverbs act as intensifiers, that is, they leave the orientation, but alter the strength. So a 'very good friend' is more than just a 'good friend' etc.

NP	Prep	NP	→	PP	
POS	to	NEG	→	POS	solution to my problem
POS	for	POS	→	POS	hope for relief
NEG	of	NEG	→	NEG	pain of disappointment
NEG	of	POS	→	NEG	lost of hope

Fig. 2: *NP-PP composition*

Fig. 2 shows some regularities holding for NP-PP composition. With NP-PP composition, the effect also depends on the preposition.

Verbs might as well bear a polarity orientation. The Verb 'love' is positive, 'hate' is negative. 'To enjoy', 'to like', but also 'to detest', 'to dislike' etc. are all verbs with a clear polarity. The question is, how the combination with their direct objects must be interpreted in terms of compositionality. Is the verbal phrase from the sentence 'He loves nasty films' positive or negative, given that 'nasty films' is negative. Accordingly, is 'He hates good books' positive or negative?

If the mental state of the subject is in question, then the verb overwrites the NP polarity, i.e. the VP with love is positive independent from the polarity of the direct object (accordingly for 'hate'). If however, the character (in the sense of morality) of the subject is in question, then the VP with love is negative. To love negative things is negative[4].

Some verbs like 'fail', 'stop' etc., are polarity shifters. A polarity shifter inverts the polarity of the embedded phrase. 'Fail to make someone angry' then is positive: a negative embedded phrase is inverted.

Other polarity shifters are adverbs such as hardly ('this is hardly true') and negation ('I don't like action films').

We have implemented our sentiment composition as a cascade of transducers operating on the prior polarities of the subjectivity lexicon, the output of the TreeTagger chunker [14] and manually written pattern-matching rules.

4 Cascaded sentiment composition

We propose an engineering approach to sentiment composition, a system combining both domain-specific and domain-independent knowledge. Our system operates based on the assumption that since sentiment composition takes place in a rather canonical and straightforward way and therefore its reqularities can be captured by a limited number of rules. This set of rules is what we mentioned as domain-independent knowledge as it takes effect across different domains. The other basic module of this system is the polarity lexicon, and that is - at least in part - domain-specific.

[4] How to evaluate the following sentence from the group 'I Quit Smoking': I like smoking?

It can be modified or completely replaced to suit specific domains. An immediate advantage of such an approach compared to other dominant approaches in the field, namely machine learning, is that we do not need neither a training corpus nor a training phase to bootstrap our system. For our system to operate in a new domain we need only adapt the polarity lexicon. We discuss problems with the determination of the polarity of words in section 6.

Our system receives as input text that has been syntactically chunked. In our current setup we have used the tree-tagger chunker [14] which is currently available for three languages (English, French, German), but other chunkers should also work well with our system.

The chunked text that is inputted to our system is a flat structure, which is evaluated via a cascade of transducers. Simpler rules are taking effect first, and their output is then consumed by more complex ones, moving from word level to sentence level sentiment composition. The rules are written in our own pattern-matching language, devised to facilitate the engineering process. A sample of a basic set of rules is the following:

```
vc_to=_,_POS;nc=_ ->POS
vc_to=_,_NEG;nc=_ ->NEG
?vc_*=_:SHI,*=vb:POS;POS ->NEG
?vc_*=_:SHI,*=vb:POS;NEG ->POS
```

Rule 1 and 2 operate in a similar fashion. A verb chunk (vc) that contains a "to" item and a positive (POS) or a negative (NEG) one, is adjoined with a noun chunk (nc) to compose a positive constituent, e.g. 'to enjoy the sun', or a negative one, e.g. 'to envy the success'. Rules 3 and 4 are also alike, they bring together a shifted (SHI) verb chunk that contains a positive verb (vb:POS) followed by a POS or NEG item to produce a NEG constituent, e.g. 'not succeed to love', or a POS constituent 'not earn the contempt', respectively.

Given for instance the sentence 'I did not achieve to cheer him', we get the chunked text that is shown in Fig. 3.

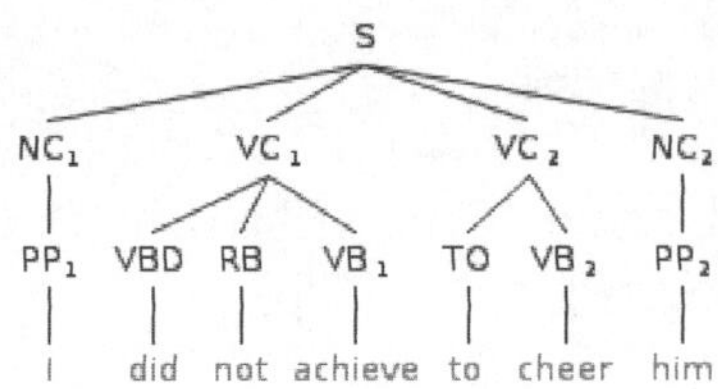

Fig. 3: *Example 1*

The rules mentioned above would then be applied in the following cascade[5] :

to cheer$^+$ him	$\rightarrow$	POS_1
I did not* achieve$^+$ POS_1	$\rightarrow$	NEG_2

[5] Indices indicate succession, $\rightarrow$ means 'rewrite' and the polarity of lexical items is indicated by the superscript where '+' means positive, '-' means negative and '*' indicates a polarity shifter

The result is a negative polarity at the sentence level. Another example would be the sentence 'She did not manage to hurt his feelings', seen in Fig. 4.

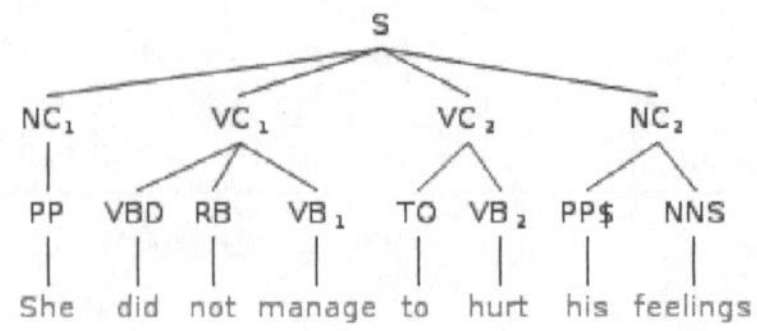

Fig. 4: *Example 2*

resulting in a positive polarity at the sentence level, evaluated in the following way:

to hurt$^-$ his feelings	$\rightarrow$	NEG_1
She did not* manage$^+$ NEG_1	$\rightarrow$	POS_2

Another part of our system is polarity strength. Each word has a polarity strength that ranges from 0 to 1. A word with positive polarity and strength 1 is strongly positive, and a negative word with strength 1 is strongly negative. Intensifiers have no polarity but a strength value. Polarity strength adds up while rules are applied, except for intensifiers which are multiplied with word or phrase strength.

For example, 'good friend' yields a positive NP polarity, the polarity strength is the sum of the polarities of 'good' and 'friend' (currently 1 respectively). Intensifiers duplicate the polarity without altering it. So 'a very good friend' has a polarity strength of 4. Shifters such as 'not' invert the polarity without altering the strength. In order to determine sentence-level polarity(e.g. in sentences with more than one target) all phrase-level polarities are added up and the polarity class with the highest strength is chosen (e.g. a sentence has positive polarity, if the sum of positive strength is higher than the sum of negative strength).

5 Empirical evaluation

We have previously[9][10] evaluated our system using customer reviews data as described in [4] and texts from the depression group of the experience project[1]. In those evaluations we have used the same set of composition rules and the same lexicon, the only difference being the selection of targets. In the customer reviews data evaluation, the targets were already identified in the gold standard, while in the depression group texts we set as targets the first person singular, second person singular and first person plural personal pronouns (we call these targets I-targets).

Our system produced promising results during both of these evaluations. We present here yet another type of evaluation for our system in an effort to test it exhaustively. In this evaluation we produce a gold standard from the depression group texts. Then we setup a baseline system and we compare the performance of our system with it. An additional difference from the previous evaluations, is that we focus on sentence rather on phrase level polarity of the depression group texts.

5.1 Gold standard

We set about building a gold standard, annotated by two different annotators. We work with texts from the depression group of the experience project. From these texts we chose those sentences that contain an I-target. We have a set of 346 sentences, where each sentence is labelled as positive, negative or neutral.

The interannotator agreement was measured first as a simple percentage, which gave us a 68%. We also calculated two more measures of agreement, following [2]. The expected interannotator agreement was 46.5% and finally the chance corrected interannotator agreement was 41.15%. Finally, the set of sentences that both annotators agreed on was selected to be used as our gold standard. That gave us a set of 222 sentences that we used in our evaluation.

5.2 Systems specifications

Our system, PolArt, uses as a prior lexicon the subjectivity lexicon from [15]. We enchanced the lexicon by adding 'not' as well as a few other polarity shifters. We have also added polarity strengths, but we did it uniformly (strength of 1). Only selected words are given a fine-grained polarity strength - in order to carry out some experiments. The set of rules, 70 in total remains the same as the one we used in prior evaluations.

The baseline procedure determines the majority class for each sentence, by examining each word inside the sentence. To examine each word and retrieve a polarity value for it, the baseline system is also using the subjectivity lexicon. The majority class is determined by counting positive and negative words inside the sentence. The most frequent polarity is assigned to the whole sentence. Note, that although the baseline system is not meant to work in a compositional-way, we make an exception for the shake of reliability of the results. This exception covers the special case of a shifter like "not" which inverts the polarity (e.g. 'not guilty' is positive).

5.3 Results

We ran both systems with our gold standard as input. The baseline system correctly classified 64 out of the 222 sentences, which translates into an accuracy of 28.82%. PolArt correctly classified 114 sentences, scoring a 51.35% accuracy which is a rather mediocre score. The interannotator agreement metrics for our gold standard indicate that even for human experts, sentiment classification is a demanding task, neither trivial nor unanimous.

During the evaluation phase, we also asked the annotators to state which of the two systems came closer to their classification of each sentence. We think of this metric as a proximity score[6]. From the 222 sentences of the gold standard, the baseline system got 36.48% on proximity while PolArt got a 63.51%.

In Fig 5, the scores for precision, recall and F-measure are given for negative (NEG), positive (POS) and neutral (NEU) classification of sentences, for each of the two systems.

[6] This score is more meaningful for these sentences where both of the systems disagreed with the gold standard

[Baseline/Polart]	Recall	Precision	F-measure
NEG	0.20/0.59	0.79/0.74	0.33/0.66
POS	0.48/0.4	0.15/0.19	0.23/0.25
NEU	0.56/0.13	0.16/0.11	0.25/0.12

Fig. 5: *Recall, precision and F-Measure scores for the baseline system and the PolArt*

PolArt performed rather well when it came to negative classifications and moderately well in the case of positive classifications. In neutral classifications it performed poorly, as did the baseline system.

The explanation for this is that neutral polarity, in both the baseline system and PolArt, occurs as a mutual neutralization of accumulated POS and NEG values. This treatment of neutrality is brittle as it is based on a weak concept. It also stands quite separate from the human perception of neutral polarity, as this was made obvious by the annotated gold standard. The following examples present sentences that the annotators classified as neutral, giving a good idea of their view of where neutral polarity lies:

> I 'm not sure if he is a deep enough human being to understand
>
> That 's not her real name , but it will suffice
>
> I may have been melancholy or depressed , but I had no real physical symptoms
>
> I read somewhere that age will increase the hormonal mood problems

In these examples both annotators agreed on the neutral polarity of the sentences, while both of the systems disagreed with the annotators, classifying the sentences either as negative or positive.

In order to improve our system's performance, it is crucial to find another way to define and handle neutrality.

6 Open problems with polarity determination

There are remaining problems with polarity determination to be dealt with in subsequent work:

- composition principles are debatable (or application dependent): 'a perfect$^+$ spy$^-$' - positive or negative?
- composition principles are not deterministic: if 'a perfect$^+$ spy$^-$' is positive why then is 'a perfect$^+$ hassle$^-$' in any case negative?
- words without a prior polarity combine to a non-neutral phrase polarity: 'a cold answer' is negative although both words are neutral
- implicit attitudes and figurative language (irony, even slang): 'I was happy that my stepfather disappeared'. The negative attitude towards the stepfather is only implicitly given.

- disambiguation might be necessary before polarity determination 'a cheap therapy' might be regarded as positive if 'cheap' means 'low price' but negative if it means 'low quality'.

7 Related work

Only a limited number of approaches in the field of sentiment analysis copes with the problem of sentiment composition.

The first, fully compositional account to sentence-level sentiment interpretation on the basis of a manually written grammar is presented in [11]. Since based on a normative grammar, their approach is brittle, while our pattern-matching approach operates well in the presence of noise.

More recently, [3] have introduced a machine learning approach to sentiment composition, but they also have experimented with a pattern-matching approach. Their empirical results are based on the MPQA corpus [15]. In the near future, we shall also experiment with the MPQA corpus to enable a direct comparison.

8 Conclusion and future work

We presented in this paper an engineering approach to dealing with polarity classification. The goal was to perform this task outside of the machine learning paradigm. What we managed to prove is that employing a set of compositional rules and a polarity lexicon can be a feasible solution.

What usually dictates the use of machine learning techniques is domain independence. In the case of sentiment composition, pattern matching rules can operate in a domain independent way. We work with a set of 70 such rules that operate in cascades of rewrite operations. A polarity lexicon is necessary and - although at least partially domain dependent - a moderate sized one like the one we use in our system is not a costly resource.

We worked with texts from a panel group called "I battle depression". We prepared a gold standard, as well as a baseline system to measure our system's performance. The results were encouraging, although there exist various tough points to overcome. Among these is the conceptual and practical treatment of neutral polarity.

The texts we worked with were in English. We have tested our system with German [8] as well as with French[13] texts and have made a demo version[7] available. We are also experimenting with the use of a dependency parser instead of a chunker, since word order in languages such as French and German is less restricted.

All in all, a pattern-based approach to sentiment analysis seems to be a choice of reason. The polarity lexicon - being the most volatile of our resources and the most dependent on domain specific knowledge - is, however, a good candidate for machine learning.

[7] Visit http://www.cl.uzh.ch/kitt/polart/ for a demo version of our system for English, German and French

Acknowledgments

This work is funded by the Swiss National Science Foundation (grant 100015_122546/1).

References

[1] Experience project, 2009. http://www.experienceproject.com.

[2] R. Artstein and M. Poesio. Inter-coder agreement for computational linguistics. *Comput. Linguist.*, 34(4):555–596, 2008.

[3] Y. Choi and C. Cardie. Learning with compositional semantics as structural inference for subsentential sentiment analysis. In *Proc. of EMNLP*, 2008.

[4] X. Ding and B. Liu. The utility of linguistic rules in opinion mining. In *SIGIR*, 2007.

[5] D. R. Dowty, R. E. Wall, and S. Peters. *Introduction to Montague Semantics*. Reidel, Dordrecht, 1981.

[6] A. Esuli and F. Sebastiani. SentiWordNet: A publicly available lexical resource for opinion mining. In *Proc. of LREC-06*, Genova, IT, 2006.

[7] A. Fahrni and M. Klenner. Old Wine or Warm Beer: Target-Specific Sentiment Analysis of Adjectives. In *Proc.of the Symposium on Affective Language in Human and Machine, AISB 2008 Convention, 1st-2nd April 2008. University of Aberdeen, Aberdeen, Scotland*, pages 60 – 63, 2008.

[8] M. Klenner. Süsse Beklommenheit und schmerzvolle Ekstase. Automatische Sentimentanalyse in den Werken von Eduard von Keyserling. In *Tagungsband der GSCL- Tagung, Gesellschaft für Sprachtechnologie und Computerlinguistik (GSCL)(erscheint)*, Potsdam, 30.9. - 2.10 2009.

[9] M. Klenner, A. Fahrni, and S. Petrakis. An Experimental Tool for Polarity Classification of Human Affect from Panel Group Texts. In *Acii 2009, Ansterdam, The Netherlands*, 2009.

[10] M. Klenner, A. Fahrni, and S. Petrakis. PolArt: A Robust Tool for Sentiment Analysis. In *NODALIDA 2009, Odense, Dänemark, 14-16.5.*, 2009.

[11] K. Moilanen and S. Pulman. Sentiment composition. In *Proc. of RANLP-2007*, pages 378–382, Borovets, Bulgaria, September 27-29 2007.

[12] M. S. P. Stone, D. Dumphy and D. M. Ogilvie. *The General Inquirer: a computer approach to content analysis.* MIT Press, Cambridge, MA, 1966.

[13] S. Petrakis, M. Klenner, E. Ailloud, and A. Fahrni. Composition multilingue de sentiments. In *TALN (Traitement Automatique des Langues Naturelles) (Demo paper)*, Senlis, France, 2009.

[14] H. Schmid. Probabilistic part-of-speech tagging using decision trees. In *Proc. of Intern. Conf. on New Methods in Language Processing*, 1994.

[15] J. W. T. Wilson and P.Hoffmann. Recognizing contextual polarity in phrase-level sentiment analysis. In *Proc. of HLT/EMNLP 2005*, Vancouver, CA, 2005.

Feature Subset Selection in Conditional Random Fields for Named Entity Recognition

Roman Klinger and Christoph M. Friedrich
Department of Bioinformatics
Fraunhofer Institute for Algorithms and Scientific Computing (SCAI)
53754 Sankt Augustin, Germany
{roman.klinger,christoph.friedrich}@scai.fraunhofer.de

Abstract

In the application of Conditional Random Fields (CRF), a huge number of features is typically taken into account. These models can deal with inter-dependent and correlated data with an enormous complexity. The application of feature subset selection is important to improve performance, speed and explainability.

We present and compare filtering methods using information gain or χ^2 as well as an iterative approach for pruning features with low weights.

The evaluation shows that with only 3 % of the original number of features a 60 % inference speed-up is possible. The F_1 measure decreases only slightly.

1 Introduction

Feature selection is well established for many machine learning methods, for instance for feed-forward neural networks [2] or decision trees [17]. The main advantages are an improvement of prediction performance, faster training and prediction as well as a better understanding of the models [4]. Methods can be distinguished between filters not using the learning algorithm and wrappers using the learning algorithm as a black box [8]. An overview of approaches for classification tasks is given by Liu and Motoda [11], more specifically for text classification by Yang and Pederson [25].

Such feature selection methods are not well established for Conditional Random Fields [9], a Maximum Entropy-based method [1] for structured data. We propose methods coping with the demanding task of handling sequential data represented by a huge number of features. Reported numbers are for instance 1,686,456 for a gene name tagger [5]. Due to this high complexity, training and inference times can explode. These high numbers of features are generated by automated methods, i. e., for every token in the training set, features are generated. Then, all other tokens are tested for these features. This method is typically applied to determine the identity of words as well as for prefixes or suffixes of different length or for learning schemata of regular expression-like patterns [20].

Only a few approaches dealing with feature handling for CRFs are published. The work by McCallum [12] demonstrates a method for iteratively constructing feature conjunctions that would increase conditional log-likelihood if added to the model. An analysis of different penalty terms for regularization is shown by Peng and McCallum [15]. Goodman [3] presented a related analysis of exponential priors for Maximum Entropy models. The very recent work of Vail et al. [23, 22] shows feature selection in Conditional Random Fields by L_1-norm regularization in the robotics domain, a work which is related to the selection in Maximum Entropy models proposed by Koh et al. [7].

These methods incorporate the training procedure in the selection process. In contrast, we present different filter methods for feature selection to limit the complexity before starting the training. It is demonstrated how the sequential structure of text can be respected by filtering approaches originally developed for classification problems (especially in Section 3.1.2 and 3.1.3). These filter methods are compared to an iterative approach.

The paper is organized as follows. A short description of Conditional Random Fields is given in Section 2. We introduce different approaches for feature selection in Section 3, namely the adaption of classification methods to filter features and an iterative approach to remove features with low weights. In Section 4, an evaluation of the feature selection methods is given. The results show a reduction of complexity leading to improved speed and better explainability.

2 Conditional Random Fields and Sequential Data

Conditional Random Fields [9, 13] are a family of probabilistic, undirected graphical models for computing the probability $P_{\vec{\lambda}}(\vec{y}|\vec{x})$ of a possible label sequence $\vec{y} = (y_0, \ldots, y_n)$ given the input sequence $\vec{x} = (x_0, \ldots, x_n)$. In the context of Named Entity Recognition, this observation sequence $\vec{x}$ corresponds to the tokenized text. The label sequence is encoded in a label alphabet $\mathcal{L} = \{$*I-<entity>*, *O*, *B-<entity>*$\}$ where $y_i = O$ means that x_i is outside an entity, $y_i =$ *B-<entity>* means that x_i is the beginning and $y_i =$ *I-<entity>* means that x_i is inside an entity.

In general, a CRF is given by

$$P(\vec{y}|\vec{x}) = \frac{1}{Z(\vec{x})} \prod_{j=1}^{n} \Psi_j(\vec{x}, \vec{y}) \qquad (1)$$

International Conference RANLP 2009 - Borovets, Bulgaria, pages 185–191

with normalization $Z(\vec{x}) = \sum_{\vec{y} \in \mathcal{Y}} \prod_{j=1}^{n} \Psi_j(\vec{x}, \vec{y})$, where Ψ_j are the different factors and $\mathcal{Y}$ is the set of all possible label sequences. These factor functions combine different features f_i of the considered part of the text and label sequence and usually correspond to maximal cliques on the independence graph.

For simplicity, we focus on the linear-chain CRF as a special case of the general CRF. The factors are given in the form

$$\Psi_j(\vec{x}, \vec{y}) = \exp\left(\sum_{i=1}^{m} \lambda_i f_i\Big(y_{j-1}, y_j, \vec{x}, j\Big)\right). \quad (2)$$

Each feature $f_i(\cdot)$ is weighted by $\lambda_i \in \mathbb{R}$. These weights are the parameters to be learned in the model and later used in the iterative approach for feature subset selection (in Section 3.2). An example formulation of features $f_i(\cdot)$ is

$$f_i\Big(y_{j-1}, y_j, \vec{x}, j\Big) = \begin{cases} 1, \text{if } y_{j-1} = s_i' \text{ and } y_j = s_i'' \text{ and } \varphi_k(x_j) \\ 0, \text{otherwise,} \end{cases} \quad (3)$$

where $s_i', s_i'' \in \mathcal{L}$.

There are two kinds of features. First, the ones representing the token sequence as a feature vector sequence[1] (these features are referred to as $\varphi_k \in \mathfrak{F}$). An example is that $\varphi_k(x_j)$ holds if and only if x_j is a capital word. Second, the feature functions representing $\varphi_k(x_j)$ with label transitions, to be referred to as $f_i \in \mathcal{F}$.

Optimization of the parameters λ_i is often performed with the limited-memory Broyden-Fletcher-Goldfarb-Shanno algorithm (L-BFGS, Nocedal, [14]) on the convex function $L(\mathcal{T})$ with the training data $\mathcal{T}$, including a penalty term:

$$L(\mathcal{T}) = \log P_{\vec{\lambda}}(\vec{y}|\vec{x})) - \sum_{i=1}^{m} \frac{\lambda_i^2}{2\sigma^2}. \quad (4)$$

3 Feature Selection Methods for CRFs

An exhaustive search to find the optimal feature subset is not possible due to the large number of features and comparatively long training times. Hence, a wrapper approach considering the CRF as a black box is impractical. We compare different approaches for feature subset selection of sequential data in CRFs, i. e., filtering methods (in Section 3.1) and an iterative method (in Section 3.2).

3.1 Filter

To apply filter methods for classification tasks, the sequence data have to be represented as classification instances. For a pair of sequences $(\vec{y}, \vec{x})$ this is done with respect to the incorporated factors in the CRF. For every factor $\Psi_j(\vec{y}, \vec{x})$, an instance is built. The labels are all dependencies on $\vec{y}$, the features have the values at the corresponding position for $\vec{x}$.

For the factors in a linear-chain CRF as shown in Equation 2, the instance $\mathcal{I}_j = (\mathfrak{L}_j, \vec{\varphi}_j)$ at position j $(0 < j \leq n)$ has the label $\mathfrak{L}_j = (y_{j-1}, y_j)$ from a set of all possible transitions[2] $\mathfrak{L}_j \in \mathcal{L}^2$. The feature values are $\varphi_k(x_j)$. Instances are built for all positions in all training examples from $\mathcal{T}$.

The features are ranked by measures presented below. The best p_{filter} features (where p_{filter} is a parameter specifying the percentage of kept features) are selected to represent the text data.

In the following, the number of generated instances is denoted with h, the number of instances with feature $\varphi(x_j)$ with value 1 with h_j^1 and with value 0 with h_j^0. The number of instances with label $\mathfrak{L}_\ell$ is $h(\ell)$, with feature values 1 or 0 of those with $h_j^1(\ell)$ and $h_j^0(\ell)$ respectively.

3.1.1 Simple Information Gain

Our first approach for measuring the quality of a feature is the use of information gain of a feature $IG(\varphi(x_j))$ to differentiate between all possible labels $\mathfrak{L}_\ell$. It is defined as

$$IG(\varphi(x_j)) = I\left(\frac{h_j^1}{h}, \frac{h_j^0}{h}\right) - R(\varphi(x_j)) \quad (5)$$

where $I(\cdot)$ is the information content

$$I(p_1, p_2) = -p_1 \log_2 p_1 - p_2 \log_2 p_2 \quad (6)$$

with probabilities p_1 and p_2. $R(\varphi(x_j))$ is the remainder of bits of information after testing feature $\varphi(x_j)$:

$$R(\varphi(x_j)) = \sum_{\ell=1}^{|\mathcal{L}^2|}\left(\frac{h(\ell)}{h} I\left(\frac{h_j^1(\ell)}{h(\ell)}, \frac{h_j^0(\ell)}{h(\ell)}\right)\right). \quad (7)$$

For comparing the features it is sufficient to compute $R(\cdot)$ because $I(\cdot)$ is constant for one feature [18]. Determining this measure for m features with $|\mathcal{L}|$ different labels lasts $\mathcal{O}(m|\mathcal{L}^2|)$.

Ranking the features with this approach cannot lead to differences between transitions in the CRF. Therefore, it is referred to as *Simple IG*.

3.1.2 Information Gain One-Against-All

The limitation of *Simple IG* is the disregard of differences between transitions in CRF. To cope with that, we assign a list of the best p_{filter} features to every transition $\mathfrak{L}_\ell$. In general, every clique in the graph has its own evaluation of features $\varphi(\cdot)$.

The remainder, the measure for the quality of a feature in Equation 7, changes slightly to

$$R_{OAA}(\varphi(x_j), \mathfrak{L}_\ell) = \left(\frac{h(\ell)}{h} I\left(\frac{h_j^1(\ell)}{h(\ell)}, \frac{h_j^0(\ell)}{h(\ell)}\right)\right) + \left(\frac{\bar{h}(\ell)}{h} I\left(\frac{\bar{h}_j^1(\ell)}{\bar{h}(\ell)}, \frac{\bar{h}_j^0(\ell)}{\bar{h}(\ell)}\right)\right) \quad (8)$$

[1] For simplicity, we only consider boolean features.

[2] For the linear-chain CRF of order 1. In general, $\mathfrak{L}_j \in \mathcal{L}^{c+1}$ with order c holds.

	$\varphi(x_j)=1$	$\varphi(x_j)=0$	$\sum$
$\mathfrak{L}_\ell$	$h_j^1(\ell)$	$h_j^0(\ell)$	$h(\ell)$
$\mathfrak{L}_{\neq\ell}$	$\bar{h}_j^1(\ell)$	$\bar{h}_j^0(\ell)$	$\bar{h}(\ell)$
$\sum$	h_j^1	h_j^0	h

Table 1: The 2×2 contingency table.

where

$$\bar{h}(\ell) = \sum_{l \in \{1,\ldots,|\mathcal{L}|^2\} \setminus \ell} h(l)\,,$$

and $\bar{h}_j^1(l)$ and $\bar{h}_j^0(l)$ analogous. This approach is applied to rank the features $\varphi(x_j)$ for every transition $\mathfrak{L}_\ell$ separately. It is referred to as *Information Gain One-Against-All (IG-OAA)*. The runtime is $\mathcal{O}(m|\mathcal{L}|)$ and therefore less than *Simple IG*.

3.1.3 χ^2-Statistics

Another well-known and often incorporated ranking method are χ^2*-statistics* [16]. The 2×2 contingency table is defined for each feature $\varphi(x_j)$ and each transition $\mathfrak{L}_\ell$ compared to all other transitions (cf. Table 1). The χ^2-statistic is then computed by

$$\chi^2(\varphi(x_j), \mathfrak{L}_j) = \frac{\left(h_j^1(\ell) \cdot \bar{h}_j^0(\ell) - h_j^0(\ell) \cdot \bar{h}_j^1(\ell)\right)^2 \cdot h}{h(\ell) \cdot \bar{h}(\ell) \cdot h_j^0 \cdot h_j^1} \tag{9}$$

Similar to *IG OAA*, this is performed to rank the features $\varphi(x_j)$ for every transition $\mathfrak{L}_\ell$ separately. Therefore, the runtime is also $\mathcal{O}(m|\mathcal{L}|)$. We refer to this method as χ^2 *OAA*.

3.1.4 Random

The most simple method is a *random* ranking and selection of features. This is used as a baseline to evaluate the other measures presented in the previous sections.

3.2 Iterative Feature Pruning

Training a CRF is commonly performed by the iterative algorithm L-BFGS to assign weights λ_i to all feature functions $f_i \in \mathcal{F}$ such that $\mathcal{L}(T)$ is maximized (compare to Equation 4). Typically, many weights are close to 0. The idea of Iterative Feature Pruning (IFP) is that feature functions with low absolute weight value have a low impact on the output sequence.

Based on this assumption, the algorithm (see pseudo code in Figure 1) starts with a fully optimized CRF using all features representing the training data (Line 2). The next step is the removal of features with lowest absolute value (3). The parameter $p = 1 - \frac{|S|}{|\mathcal{F}|}$ specifies the percentage of features to be removed in each iteration (13–15). S is the set of remaining features after one iteration of IFP.

In each step, a retraining with L-BFGS is performed to allow an adaption of the model by adjusting the weights for the remaining features (16). After that, the pruning is repeated (17) until no features are left (11).

```
1: function IFP(crf,trainData, valData, p)
2:     crf = BFGS(crf, trainData, valData)
3:     log = PRUNING-STEP(crf, trainData, valData, p)
4:     crf = SELECTFEATURESET(log)
5:     crf = BFGS(crf, trainData+valData,null)
6: end function
7: function PRUNING-STEP(crf, trainData, valData, p)
8:     log ← EVALUATE(trainData, valData, crf)
9:     F = GETFEATURESET(crf)
10:    if F = ∅ then
11:        return log
12:    end if
13:    S = features with lowest weights such that
           p = 1 − |S|/|F|
14:    F = F\S
15:    SETFEATURESET(crf,F)
16:    crf = BFGS(crf, trainingData)
17:    return PRUNING-STEP(crf, trainData, valData)
18: end function
```

Figure 1: Iterative Feature Pruning Algorithm (starting with method IFP($\cdot$) in Line 1)

During this process, at each iteration of pruning, the current performance of the model is evaluated and stored (8). This information can be used to select the final feature set (Line 4, an heuristic is shown in Section 4.3) and to train a full model with the identified feature subset (Line 5).

To illustrate the process of IFP, it is shown exemplarily by means of extreme examples for one data set[3] in Figure 2. On the horizontal axis, all L-BFGS training iterations are shown consecutively with the intermediate pruning steps. The blue dotted line shows the decrease of the number of features, the red solid line the F_1 measure for the training data, the green dashed line the F_1 measure for one validation data set. Removing 40 % of the features in each step ($p = 0.4$) clearly depicts the process of removing and retraining of the model. Experiments[4] have shown that in general lower numbers of features can be achieved with comparable F_1 measures if smaller values of p are used. The drawback is the higher number of iterations needed. We focus on $p = 0.1$ which leads to good results as shown in Section 4.

4 Results

In this section, the methods proposed in Section 3 are evaluated on the data sets and configurations of the CRFs described in Section 4.1. The hypotheses to be analyzed are:

Selecting a reasonable subset of features:

A1 Improves explainability of the CRF model,

A2 Improves training time and tagging time which is beneficial for developing as well as applying the model,

A3 Improves performance in F_1 measure or does not decrease it dramatically.

Additionally, we assume that one method is superior to all others:

B One method outperforms the others.

[3]CoNLL data set introduced in Section 4.1

[4]Results not shown here due to page limitation.

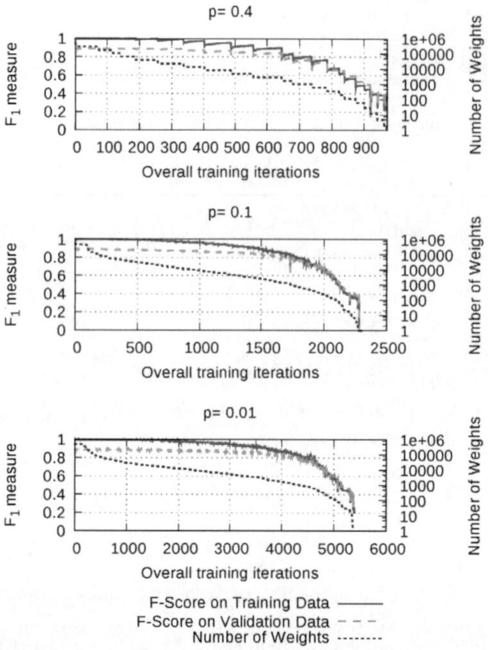

Figure 2: Iterative Feature Pruning for CRF trained on CoNLL data with different percentages of features pruned in each iteration.

The evaluations in the following form the basis for the discussion of these hypotheses in Section 4.4.

4.1 Data Sets used for Evaluation

The results and evaluations are shown on the basis of two data sets with slightly different configurations of the CRF. Quantities of entities are given in Table 2.

The BioCreative 2 Gene Mention Task data (BC2) contains entities of the class *Gene/Protein* with the specialty of acceptance of several boundaries for entities [24]. We incorporate the configuration of the CRF as described in a participating system using only the shortest possible annotation as exact true positive per entity [6, 21].

Name	Training Set		
	B-	I-	O
BC2	18165	15017	382983
CoNLL	29466	13180	213499
	Test Set		
	B-	I-	O
BC2	6290	4801	128915
CoNLL	5654	2458	38554

Table 2: Numbers of labels in data sets, the different entity classes are added in CoNLL.

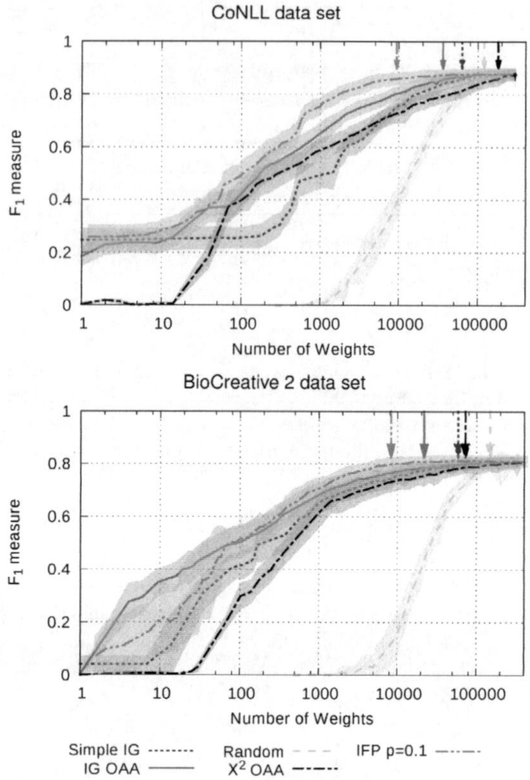

Figure 3: Comparison of the average F_1 measure using 10-fold cross-validation. Used features are determined with methods described in Section 3. The transparent band shows the standard deviation. The arrows show a possible selection of the model features ($g = 2 \cdot 10^{-6}$, $\Delta = 0.02$, cf. Section 4.3).

The CoNLL data [19] is an annotation of the Reuters corpus [10] containing the classes *person*, *organization*, *locations* and *misc*. We use an order-one CRF with offset conjunction combining features of one preceding and succeeding token for each position in the text sequence. The feature set is fairly standard with Word-As-Class, prefix and suffix generation of length two, three and four as well as regular expressions detecting capital letters, numbers, dashes and dots separately and as parts of tokens. The combination of the provided sets "train" and "testa" is used for training and "testb" for testing.

For evaluating the inference time on a larger set, a uniform sample from the Medline[5] database of 10,000 entries is used additionally. Each one comprises titles, author names, and abstracts. The number of tokens is 958869 for BC2 and 960744 for CoNLL (additionally to BC2 tokenization, splitting on all dots is performed for CoNLL data).

4.2 Cross-Validation on the Training Sets

As a basis for parameter selection (presented in Section 4.3) and to evaluate the impact of feature selection, 10-fold cross

[5] http://www.nlm.nih.gov/databases/databases_medline.html

validation is performed on the training sets (Section 4.1). The results are shown in Figure 3. The curves depict the average F_1 measure[6] of the 10 partitions. The different numbers of features are detected with different parameters specified for the respective selection method. The transparent band around the line depicts the standard deviation for the according number of features.[7] The significance of the difference of the methods is tested regarding the area under the curves in Figure 3 via Welch's t-test with a significance level of $\alpha = 0.05$.

Comparing the results on the two data sets, the methods lead to similar results whereas the differences are clearer on CoNLL data. All approaches outperform the random selection significantly. The approach of χ^2 *OAA* is worse than the conceptionally similar *IG OAA* and the more naive *Simple IG* on BC2 data.

IG OAA outperforms all other filtering approaches. Assuming the goal to reach the highest possible F_1 measure, *IFP* leads to better results than *IG OAA* on both data sets. Only if an extremely small number of features remains (fewer than about 50), *IG OAA* leads to better results. The superiority of *IFP* to χ^2 *OAA* is significant ($p = 0.02$) on the CoNLL data set.

4.3 Results on independent test sets

We need to find the parameter assignment to determine the feature subset in the final model. For the filter approaches, the parameter is p_{filter}. For *IFP*, the meaningful number of features at which the pruning is stopped has to be detected. Based on the smoothed[8] values of F_1 measure in 10-fold cross-validation (see Figure 3), we define two measures to automatically detect these parameters: The maximally accepted loss in F_1 measure is denoted with Δ, the threshold for the gradient is g. The detection of the feature subset is performed via backward selection starting with high numbers of features. The first position on the curve for which the gradient is smaller than g or the F_1 measure is smaller than Δ is selected. The values $g = 2 \cdot 10^{-6}$ and $\Delta = 0.02$ lead to the positions denoted by arrows in Figure 3. The results for these values are evaluated in the following. The advantage of backward selection to forward selection is that it may capture interacting features more easily [8].

A model is built on the full training set applying *IFP* or filtering with the detected parameters. In Figure 4 the results on independent test sets mentioned in Section 4.1 are depicted. The smallest numbers of features are achieved by *IFP* followed by *IG OAA*.

The F_1 measures decrease up to the accepted $\Delta = 0.02$ on BC2 data and to a lower amount for the CoNLL data. The best trade-off between F_1 measure and the number of features (depicted in third bar chart) is always achieved by *IFP* followed by *IG OAA*.

A smaller number of features should induce a faster model in training and inference. The time of evaluating $P_{\vec{\lambda}}(\vec{y}|\vec{x})$ (compare to Equation 1) on all training examples is shown in the fourth bar charts. This computation is crucial for training durations as it has to be performed many times. These numbers correspond roughly to the number of features, the durations are smaller than for the original model. The ratio is not linear due to the necessary forward-backward algorithm calls (whose runtime is quadratic in the number of possible labels) and dynamic memory allocation times.

These numbers naturally lead to dramatically reduced training times. Training the full CoNLL model lasts 5788 seconds, $2397s$ for BC2 respectively. With the feature set detected by *IFP*, these numbers reduce to $2156s$ and $670s$. This improvement is not helpful in practice, as the *IFP* procedure incorporates training the model. However, filtering via *IG OAA* improves overall training time as it is computationally inexpensive. It leads to $5230s$ and $1002s$ for training a model.[9]

Reducing the number of features also leads to a faster inference[10]: The fifth bar charts show durations for tagging 10000 sampled abstracts from Medline. Best results are achieved by *IFP* (CoNLL: $10.52s$ instead of $17.56s$, BC2: $2.42s$ instead of $4.56s$), followed by the filtering methods which do not differ remarkably (*IG OAA*: CoNLL: $14s$, BC2: $2.65s$).

Summarizing, a reduced training iteration time of $76\,\%$ of original time evaluating $P_{\vec{\lambda}}(\vec{y}|\vec{x})$ with a loss of only $1.7\,\%$ F_1 (absolute value) on the BC2 data is possible with *IFP*. The tagging time is reduced to $53\,\%$. On the CoNLL data, a loss of only $0.57\,\%$ in F_1 occurs with savings of even $54\,\%$ of original computing time. Tagging time is reduced to $60\,\%$.

4.4 Discussion

Comparing the methods, the results are similar for the data sets: In 10-fold cross-validation, the random method is dominated by all other methods. *Simple IG* or χ^2 *OAA* are second worst, depending on the data set. *IFP* is the best method, closely followed by *IG OAA*.

The *Simple IG* lacks the representation of different transitions in the features which is especially important for the CoNLL data with 4 entity classes of interest. No dictionaries with members of these classes have been used in the presented setting, so all classes are memorized with automatically generated features, hence, a large number of different features is needed for the different transitions in the CRF.

The method χ^2 *OAA* always leads to worse results compared to *IG OAA* on the 10-fold cross-validation although it is a systematically similar approach. The reason is presumably the unbalancedness of the labels in the generated classification instances[11] which is taken into account in the

[6] $F_\beta = \frac{(1+\beta^2)\cdot \mathit{precision}\cdot \mathit{recall}}{\beta^2\cdot \mathit{precision}+\mathit{recall}}$, where $\beta = 1$

[7] In iterative feature pruning, different numbers of features can occur at the same iteration of pruning. In that case, the closest detected number of features is used to compute average and standard deviation.

[8] Smoothing via computation of median in a running window.

[9] The relation to the numbers of features and the iteration durations is not linear as the needed numbers of training iterations differs.

[10] Measuring only the computation, not the time to read the data from hard disk and to extract the features.

[11] Transitions of intermediate terms (like (*O*,*O*)) are for instance much more frequent than those of beginnings of entities (like (*B*,*B*)).

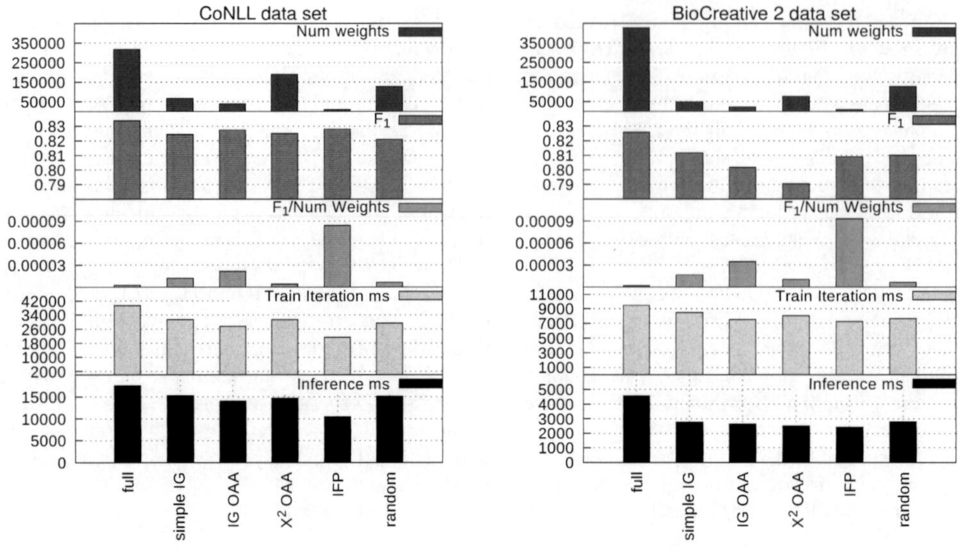

Figure 4: Results on independent test sets (Note the different scales for some of the histograms.)

information remainder (Equation 7 and 8) but not in χ^2 (Equation 9).

IFP leads to better results than *IG OAA* for high F_1 measures. The reason is the limitation of *IG OAA* to use the same number of features (but not the same set) for each transition (specified by p_{filter}). This does not hold for *IFP* as it only relies on the model structure itself. The drawback is the higher computational cost due to the incorporated L-BFGS optimization.

The *random* method does not lead to good results, but it should be noted, that even this approach can remove 30 %–40 % without a dramatic decrease in F_1 measure. The reason are unessential redundancies in the full feature set.

Mainly all these results are reflected on the independent test sets. *IFP* or *IG OAA* has the best trade-off between F_1 measure and the number of features. Good inference speed-ups can be achieved with both methods, corresponding to the low numbers of features. However, *IFP* cannot be used to speed up training as it incorporates the training procedure itself. Hence, *IG OAA* is proposed for this instance. For reducing tagging time as well as for understanding the model, *IFP* should be used as it leads to the smallest numbers of features.

In Table 3, the percentages and numbers of remaining features accepting maximally 0.01 loss in F_1 measure are depicted. Much more features can be ignored in the BC2 than in the CoNLL setting. This can be an indicator for the need for better generalizing features: as the classes have to be memorized by automatically generated features, less features can be eliminated. In BC2, features with better generalization characteristics are implemented.

We conclude the results with an investigation of the hypotheses:

A1 The explainability of models applying feature selection is improved by the lower complexity. The need for many automatically generated features can be an indicator for a possible improvement by implementation of features with better generalization properties. Detected relevant features representing words or important pre- and suffixes help understand the different entity classes of interest. The fact that noisy features are removed allows for an investigation of the remaining features which can be assumed as meaningful[12]

A2 Training and tagging time are decreased by the lower complexity of the CRF. To improve training time, the use of a filtering approach like *IG OAA* is proposed as these methods are computationally inexpensive. To improve tagging time, *IFP* should be used as it leads to the lowest numbers of features.

A3 A small decrease in F_1 measure has to be accepted for the benefit of a model with a considerable lower number of features.

B The recommendation for a method depends on the application: For improving training time, a filtering method should be used, preferably *IG OAA* as it shows best results. For improving tagging time, the computationally more expensive *IFP* can be applied.

	Number of Features		
Data Set	Original	Remaining	%
CoNLL	269506	17377	6.45
BC 2	492611	11096	2.25

Table 3: Minimal numbers of original features needed to lose maximally 0.01 of F_1 measure applying IFP.

[12]Lists of all features of the models are available online to demonstrate the explainability comprehensively. `http://www.scai.fraunhofer.de/ranlp-crf-fs.html`

5 Conclusion and Future Work

A huge number of features is typically used to represent input text in CRFs. We presented different approaches for feature subset selection, novel adaptations of filtering to the sequential structure of text as well as an iterative method. The methods have been evaluated on two domains, showing a decrease of computing time and complexity of the model. The F_1 measure varies slightly.

Summarizing, *IG OAA* is the best filter approach, a lower number of features can only be achieved with Iterative Feature Pruning (*IFP*) with a similar F_1 measure. *IFP* relies only on the CRF structure itself, so it is able to deal with different numbers of features per transition in contrast to the One-Against-All methods. Its main disadvantage is its higher computing cost due to the incorporated training process. It is notable that *IFP* and *IG OAA* are methods taking the sequential structure of the text into account, *IFP* via using the model itself, *IG OAA* via different feature sets for different transitions. The method *Simple IG*, which does not select features with respect to transitions, leads to worse results.

Building a new Named Entity Recognizer often includes annotation of a corpus. It has to be investigated, how the need for features changes during the process of enriching the training set with examples (e. g. via active learning).

Another point is that the proposed methods allow for more complex feature generations (e.g. with more context information). It has to be studied if new features, which could not be implemented before due to an exhaustive memory consumption or run-time demand, could improve the state-of-the-art results.

6 Acknowledgments

We thank especially Günter Rudolph, Katrin Tomanek, Juliane Fluck, Corinna Kolářik and Martin Hofmann-Apitius for fruitful discussions. Many thanks to the reviewers for comprehensive comments. This work has been partially funded by the Max-Planck-Society–Fraunhofer-Society Machine Learning Collaboration (`http://lip.fml.tuebingen.mpg.de/`).

References

[1] A. L. Berger, S. D. Pietra, and V. J. D. Pietra. A Maximum Entropy Approach to Natural Language Processing. *Computational Linguistics*, 22(1):39–71, 1996.

[2] C. M. Bishop. *Neural Networks for Pattern Recognition*. Clarendon Press, 1995.

[3] J. Goodman. Exponential Priors for Maximum Entropy Models. In *Proceedings of the Human Language Technology Conference of the North American Chapter of the Association for Computational Linguistics (HLT-NAACL)*, pages 305–312, 2004.

[4] I. Guyon and A. Elisseeff. An Introduction to Variable and Feature Selection. *Journal of Machine Learning Research*, 3:1157–1182, 2003.

[5] C.-N. Hsu, Y.-M. Chang, C.-J. Kuo, Y.-S. Lin, H.-S. Huang, and I.-F. Chung. Integrating high dimensional bi-directional parsing models for gene mention tagging. *Bioinformatics*, 24(13):i286–i294, Jul 2008.

[6] R. Klinger, C. M. Friedrich, J. Fluck, and M. Hofmann-Apitius. Named Entity Recognition with Combinations of Conditional Random Fields. In *Proc. of the Second BioCreative Challenge Evaluation Workshop*, pages 89–91, 2007.

[7] K. Koh, S.-J. Kim, and S. Boyd. An Interior-Point Method for Large-Scale l_1-Regularized Logistic Regression. *Journal of Machine Learning Research*, 8:1519–1555, 2007.

[8] R. Kohavi and G. H. John. Wrappers for Feature Subset Selection. *Artifical Intelligence – Special Issue on relevance*, 97(1-2):273–324, 1997.

[9] J. D. Lafferty, A. McCallum, and F. C. N. Pereira. Conditional Random Fields: Probabilistic Models for Segmenting and Labeling Sequence Data. In *Proc. of the Eighteenth International Conference on Machine Learning (ICML 2001)*, pages 282–289. Morgan Kaufmann Publishers, 2001.

[10] D. D. Lewis, Y. Yang, T. Rose, and F. Li. A New Benchmark Collection for Text Categorization Research. *Journal of Machine Learning Research*, 5:361–397, 2004.

[11] H. Liu and H. Motoda. *Computational Methods of Feature Selection*. Data Mining and Knowledge Discovery Series. Chapman & Hall/CRC, 2008.

[12] A. McCallum. Efficiently Inducing Features of Conditional Random Fields. In *Proc. of the 19th Conference in Uncertainty in Articifical Intelligence (UAI-2003)*, pages 403–410, 2003.

[13] R. McDonald and F. Pereira. Identifying Gene and Protein Mentions in Text Using Conditional Random Fields. *BMC Bioinformatics*, 6 Suppl 1:S6, 2005.

[14] J. Nocedal. Updating Quasi-Newton Matrices with Limited Storage. *Mathematics of Computation*, 35(151):773–782, July 1980.

[15] F. Peng and A. McCallum. Accurate Information Extraction from Research Papers using Conditional Random Fields. In *Proc. of Human Language Technology Conference and North American Chapter of the Association for Computational Linguistics (HLT-NAACL)*, pages 329–336, 2004.

[16] R. L. Plackett. Karl Pearson and the Chi-Squared Test. *International Statistical Review*, 51(1):59–72, 1983.

[17] J. R. Quinlan. Induction of Decision Trees. *Machine Learning*, 1:81–106, 1986.

[18] S. Russell and P. Norvig. *Artificial Intelligence – A Modern Approach*. Prentice Hall, 2003.

[19] E. F. T. K. Sang and F. De Meulder. Introduction to the CoNLL-2003 Shared Task: Language-Independent Named Entity Recognition. In W. Daelemans and M. Osborne, editors, *Proc. of CoNLL-2003*, pages 142–147. Edmonton, Canada, 2003.

[20] B. Settles. ABNER: an open source tool for automatically tagging genes, proteins and other entity names in text. *Bioinformatics*, 21(14):3191–3192, 2005.

[21] L. Smith, L. K. Tanabe, R. J. nee Ando, C.-J. Kuo, I.-F. Chung, C.-N. Hsu, Y.-S. Lin, R. Klinger, C. M. Friedrich, K. Ganchev, M. Torii, H. Liu, B. Haddow, C. A. Struble, R. J. Povinelli, A. Vlachos, W. A. Baumgartner, L. Hunter, B. Carpenter, R. T.-H. Tsai, H.-J. Dai, F. Liu, Y. Chen, C. Sun, S. Katrenko, P. Adriaans, C. Blaschke, R. Torres, M. Neves, P. Nakov, A. Divoli, M. Maa-Lpez, J. Mata, and W. J. Wilbur. Overview of BioCreative II gene mention recognition. *Genome Biol*, 9 Suppl 2:S2, 2008.

[22] D. L. Vail. *Conditional Random Fields for Activity Recognition*. PhD thesis, Computer Science Department, Carnegie Mellon University, Pittsburgh, USA, 2008.

[23] D. L. Vail, J. D. Lafferty, and M. M. Veloso. Feature Selection in Conditional Random Fields for Activity Recognition. In *Proc. of the IEEE/RSJ International Conference on Intelligent Robots and Systems (IROS)*, pages 3379–3384, 2007.

[24] J. Wilbur, L. Smith, and L. Tanabe. BioCreative 2. Gene Mention Task. In *Proc. of the Second BioCreative Challenge Evaluation Workshop*, pages 7–9, 2007.

[25] Y. Yang and J. O. Pederson. A Comparative Study on Feature Selection in Text Categorization. In *Proceedings of the International Conference on Machine Learning*, 1997.

User's Choice of Precision and Recall in Named Entity Recognition

Roman Klinger and Christoph M. Friedrich
Fraunhofer Institute for Algorithms and Scientific Computing (SCAI)
Department of Bioinformatics
Schloss Birlinghoven
53754 Sankt Augustin, Germany
{roman.klinger,christoph.friedrich}@scai.fraunhofer.de

Abstract

Conditional Random Fields are commonly trained to maximize likelihood. The corresponding F_β measure, the weighted harmonic mean of precision and recall, which is established for evaluation in information retrieval and text mining, is not necessarily the optimal result for the user's choice of β.

Some approaches have been published to optimize multivariate measures like F_β to overcome this inconsistency. The limitation is that constraints like the value of β have to be known at training time.

This publication proposes a method of multi-objective optimization of both precision and recall based on a preceding likelihood training. The output is an estimation of pareto-optimal solutions from which the user can select the best for the actual application. Evaluated on two publicly available data sets in the field of named entity recognition, nearly all F_β values are superior to those resulting from log-likelihood training.

Keywords

Named Entity Recognition, Conditional Random Fields, Multi-Objective Optimization, NSGA-II, F_β measure, Recall, Precision

1 Introduction

In information retrieval, the F_β measure, the weighted harmonic mean between recall and precision, is established as evaluation measure. The corresponding β value to be chosen is application-depend. Methods for selecting β at training time exist for Support Vector Machines [18], Logistic Regression as well as Conditional Random Fields (CRF) [11] all of which are classically optimized by means of accuracy-related measures [7, 8, 20]. A similar goal is known from the AmilCare system [4] with the main focus on user involvement.

At inference time, a parameter to select between higher precision or recall can be introduced by changing the decision threshold for an adequate decision function $d(\cdot) \in \mathbb{R}$. In sequential segmentation tasks like named entity recognition (NER), precision can be increased with this approach without retraining. Increasing recall is possible with the allowance of overlaps as demonstrated for gene and protein names [3]. This requires the computation of reliable confidences, which increasing runtime is a drawback especially during inference [5, 20].

In contrast to optimizing one special value or selecting the set of output entities in prediction phase, we propose to use an evolutionary optimization scheme to optimize recall and precision in a multi-objective way to yield different model configurations, which can be selected by an end-user depending on the respective task with higher recall or higher precision without retraining. Thereby, the non-intentional choice of precision and recall by optimization of accuracy (which is performed by maximizing the log-likelihood of the model given the training data in the case of CRFs) is avoided.

The main contribution of this paper is therefore the presentation of multi-objective optimization for Conditional Random Fields (MOCRF). The feasibility of evolutionary optimization in such models is demonstrated. The resulting possibility to choose a β for F_β evaluation is meaningful for information retrieval tasks often demanding for a high recall or information extraction with the need for a high precision.

2 Methods

2.1 Conditional Random Fields and Text Segmentation

Conditional Random Fields (CRF) [11, 13] are a family of probabilistic, undirected graphical models for computing the probability $P_{\vec{\lambda}}(\vec{y}|\vec{x})$ of a possible label sequence $\vec{y} = (y_0, \ldots, y_n)$ given the input sequence $\vec{x} = (x_0, \ldots, x_n)$. In the context of named entity recognition, this observation sequence $\vec{x}$ corresponds to the tokenized text. The label sequence is encoded in a label alphabet $\mathcal{L} = \{I\text{-}\langle entity\rangle, O, B\text{-}\langle entity\rangle\}$ where $y_i = O$ means that x_i is outside an entity, $y_i = B\text{-}\langle entity\rangle$ means that x_i is the beginning and $y_i = I\text{-}\langle entity\rangle$ means that x_i is inside an entity. Using this IOB alphabet, named entity recognition is modelled as text segmentation task. An example for an input sequence and possible output sequences is shown in Table 1 taken from data of [21].

International Conference RANLP 2009 - Borovets, Bulgaria, pages 192–196

$\vec{x} = ($	or	chicken	beta-actin	(	cBA	)	gene	were	injected	$)^T$
$\vec{y^*} = ($	O	B	I	O	B	O	O	O	O	$)^T$
$\vec{y'} = ($	O	B	I	O	O	O	O	O	O	$)^T$
$\vec{y''} = ($	O	B	I	B	I	I	I	O	O	$)^T$

Table 1: Named Entity Recognition example input sequence with possible output sequences. For better perceptibility, segments have been underlined additionally. The correct sequence is $\vec{y^*}$, $\vec{y'}$ and $\vec{y'}$ are possible predictions. (annotations from [21])

		Correct	
		C_1	$\neg C_1$
Predict	C_1	TP	FP
	$\neg C_1$	FN	TN

Table 2: Contingency table for two classes C_1 and not C_1 ($\neg C_1$) used to compute different evaluation measures.

Assuming $\vec{y^*}$ to be the correct segmentation and $\vec{y''}$ to be the predicted sequence, the result is 1 TP (true positive), 1 FN (false negative) and 1 FP (false positive). Only predicting the first segment and not the second one leads to a better result with 1 TP and 1 FN (as $\vec{y'}$ in Table 1). This is a reason why it is easier to get a high precision than a high recall (compare with measures in Section 2.2). Given a predicted sequence and confidence scores, it is therefore easy to increase precision by removing unconfident entities. But it can easily be seen that adding entities to a result is not straight-forward, as searching for candidates is necessary.

A linear-chain CRF is given by $P_{\vec{\lambda}}(\vec{y}|\vec{x}) = \exp(\sum_{j=1}^{n}\sum_{i=1}^{m}\lambda_i f_i(y_{j-1}, y_j, \vec{x}, j))/Z(\vec{x})$ with $Z(\vec{x}) = \sum_{\vec{y} \in \mathcal{Y}} \exp\left(\sum_{j=1}^{n}\sum_{i=1}^{m}\lambda_i f_i\left(y_{j-1}, y_j, \vec{x}, j\right)\right)$ as normalization, where $\mathcal{Y}$ is the set of all possible label sequences. Each feature $f_i(\cdot)$ is weighted by $\lambda_i \in \mathbb{R}$. These weights are the parameters to be learned in the model. Optimization of the parameters λ_i is typically performed with the limited-memory Broyden-Fletcher-Goldfarb-Shanno algorithm (L-BFGS [16]) on the logarithmic likelihood, the convex function $L(\mathcal{T})$ with the training data $\mathcal{T}$, including a penalty term: $L(\mathcal{T}) = \log P_{\vec{\lambda}}(\vec{y}|\vec{x})) - \sum_{i=1}^{m}(\lambda_i^2/2\sigma^2)$.

2.2 Evaluation Measures

All measures used in this work are based on the contingency table shown in Table 2 [22]. The entries in the table denote frequencies of instances being true positives (TP), false positives (FP), true negatives (TN), or false negatives (FN). These values are functions of a model configuration $\vec{\lambda}$ and some data $\mathcal{D} \ni (\vec{x}, \vec{y})$ consisting of text sequences $\vec{x}$ and given label sequences $\vec{y}$. Optimizing a CRF with respect to $L(\mathcal{T})$ corresponds to maximization of accuracy which is defined as

$$\text{acc}(\vec{\lambda}, \mathcal{D}) = \frac{TP + TN}{TP + FP + TN + FN}. \quad (1)$$

Closely related is the precision

$$\text{prec}(\vec{\lambda}, \mathcal{D}) = \frac{TP}{TP + FP} \quad (2)$$

which is combined with recall

$$\text{rec}(\vec{\lambda}, \mathcal{D}) = \frac{TP}{TP + FN} \quad (3)$$

to form the F_β measure

$$F_\beta(\vec{\lambda}, \mathcal{D}) = \frac{(1+\beta^2) \cdot \text{prec}(\vec{\lambda}, \mathcal{D}) \cdot \text{rec}(\vec{\lambda}, \mathcal{D})}{\beta^2 \cdot \text{prec}(\vec{\lambda}, \mathcal{D}) + \text{rec}(\vec{\lambda}, \mathcal{D})} \quad (4)$$

The discrepancy between optimizing accuracy and evaluating F_β measures is based on the fact that the first is not differentiating between false positives and false negatives nor between true positives and true negatives while the latter does by incorporating recall and precision.[1]

2.3 Non-dominated Sorting Genetic Algorithm II (NSGA-II)

The NSGA-II is an evolutionary optimization scheme for multi-objective optimization presented here briefly. For details, we refer to the original work [6].

As usual in evolutionary computation [1], main aspects are recombination, mutation and selection of a population of individuals representing solutions of a problem. Each has one or more assigned objective values. For multi-objective optimization the population is maintained to consist of diverse solutions. The result of the process is a population of non-dominated individuals near the real pareto-optimal front. Domination means that a solution has at least one better and no worse objective value than another solution.

In each iteration of the optimization procedure, sorting of the individuals is necessary with respect to the non-domination. The result is a partition of the population into domination fronts, i.e., each individual I has an assigned rank $\text{r}(I) \in \mathbb{N}$.

As mentioned, the population needs to be divers and cover the pareto-front with a good spread. This is achieved by assigning a *crowding distance* $c(I) \in \mathbb{R}^+$ to each individual. This measure represents the average distance to the individuals with most similar objective values in the same front.

[1] A state-of-the-art approach to overcome this is the minimum classification error (MCE) framework [20].

These two values are used to define the comparator $\prec$ and sort the individuals of a population:

$$I_1 \prec I_2 \text{ if } \begin{cases} & (r(I_1) < r(I_2)) \\ \text{or} & (r(I_1) = r(I_2) \text{ and } c(I_1) > c(I_2)) \,. \end{cases} \quad (5)$$

This operator is used to select the individuals to form the succeeding population; in the original work, a tournament selection [15] is proposed.

The general workflow is as follows: First, the initial parent and offspring population is generated. In the evaluation step, the individuals are sorted with respect to $\prec$. By selection of the q first individuals, the succeeding population is created. If the stop criterion (e.g. based on iteration number or values of objective functions) is not satisfied, this population is used in the next iteration to generate offspring by recombination and mutation and so on. The final set of solutions is defined by the last population.

2.4 Multi-Objective Optimization of CRFs (MOCRF)

To apply NSGA-II to optimize precision and recall we need to define initialization, recombination and mutation operators manipulating the parameters $\vec{\lambda} = \{\lambda_1, \ldots, \lambda_m\}$ of a CRF. Each individual in the following is represented by such a vector, therefore we refer to them as $\vec{\lambda}_k$ $(1 \leq k \leq q)$.

For initializing, a maximization of log-likelihood of an individual $\vec{\lambda}_1$ via L-BFGS is performed until convergence of the training algorithm. The initial population $P = \{\vec{\lambda}_1, \ldots, \vec{\lambda}_q\}$ consists of this individual and $n-1$ copies of the resulting parameters. The individuals $\vec{\lambda}_2, \ldots, \vec{\lambda}_q$ are modified with the mutation operator $\text{mut}(\vec{\lambda})$: We add a normally distributed random value to each parameter:

$$\text{mut}(\lambda_k) = \lambda_k + \mathcal{N}(0, \sigma) \,, \quad (6)$$

with $\mathcal{N}(\mu, \sigma)$ as a normally distributed random number with expectation value μ and standard deviation $\sigma \in \mathbb{R}$.

The recombination operator creates offspring from two parents (chosen by tournament selection). Two crossover variants are incorporated, in each application of recombination one is selected randomly: Intermediate recombination $\text{im}(\vec{\lambda}_1, \vec{\lambda}_2)$ or one-point crossover $\text{co}(\vec{\lambda}_1, \vec{\lambda}_2)$ [1] ($\lambda_{i,j}$ denotes component j of individual $\vec{\lambda}_i$; $r \in [1, n] \subset \mathbb{N}$ a uniformly distributed random variable):

$$\text{im}(\vec{\lambda}_1, \vec{\lambda}_2) = \Big((\lambda_{1,1} + \lambda_{2,1})/2, \ldots, (\lambda_{1,n} + \lambda_{2,n})/2\Big)^T \,, \quad (7)$$

$$\text{co}(\vec{\lambda}_1, \vec{\lambda}_2) = \Big(\lambda_{1,1}, \ldots, \lambda_{1,r}, \lambda_{2,r+1}, \ldots, \lambda_{2,n}\Big)^T \,. \quad (8)$$

The objective functions are $\text{prec}(\vec{\lambda}, \mathcal{D})$ and $\text{rec}(\vec{\lambda}, \mathcal{D})$.

The implementation used in this work is based on [14]. It should be noted, that computing the objective functions can easily be done in parallel to decrease duration of the optimization process.

3 Experiments

In this section, the results for the proposed optimization approach are evaluated on two data sets from the field of named entity recognition. Parameter settings via cross-validation or bootstrapping are not a topic of this paper due to page limitations.

The standard deviation σ (step size) used for mutating the individuals representing solutions is set to $\sigma = 0.01$. Greater step sizes would lead to a better exploration but a worse approximation of the real pareto-front. All experiments are performed with a population size of $q = 100$ and 100 iterations of the multi-objective optimization.

3.1 Data Sets

The results and evaluations are shown on the basis of two data sets with slightly different configurations of the CRF.

The BioCreative 2 Gene Mention Task data (BC2) contains entities of the class *Gene/Protein* with the specialty of acceptance of several boundaries for entities [21]. We incorporate the configuration of the CRF as described in a participating system using only the shortest possible annotation as exact true positive per entity [10, 19].

The ConLL data [17] is an annotation of the Reuters corpus [12] containing the classes *person*, *organization*, *locations* and *misc*. We use an order-one CRF with offset conjunction combining features of one preceding and succeeding token for each position in the text sequence. The feature set is fairly standard with Word-As-Class, prefix and suffix generation of length two, three and four as well as several regular expressions detecting capital letters, numbers, dashes and dots separately and as parts of tokens. The combination of the provided sets "train" and "testa" is used for training and "testb" for testing.

In both settings, a feature selection based on information gain is performed (namely *IG-OAA* [9]). For CoNLL, we use 38095 features and 22993 for BC2.

3.2 Results

Figure 1 depicts the final population for both data sets. The estimated pareto-fronts for the training and test sets are shown, each individual forming one position in the plot on each front is connected with a line. The boxes show the results of the initial individual trained to maximize log-likelihood. The blue, green and red line show the individual with highest F_2, F_1 and $F_{0.5}$ measure respectively.

The pareto-front on the training set is the one determined by MOCRF. The results shown as pareto-front on the test set are the results of the same individuals connected by a line. The absence of crossings to a

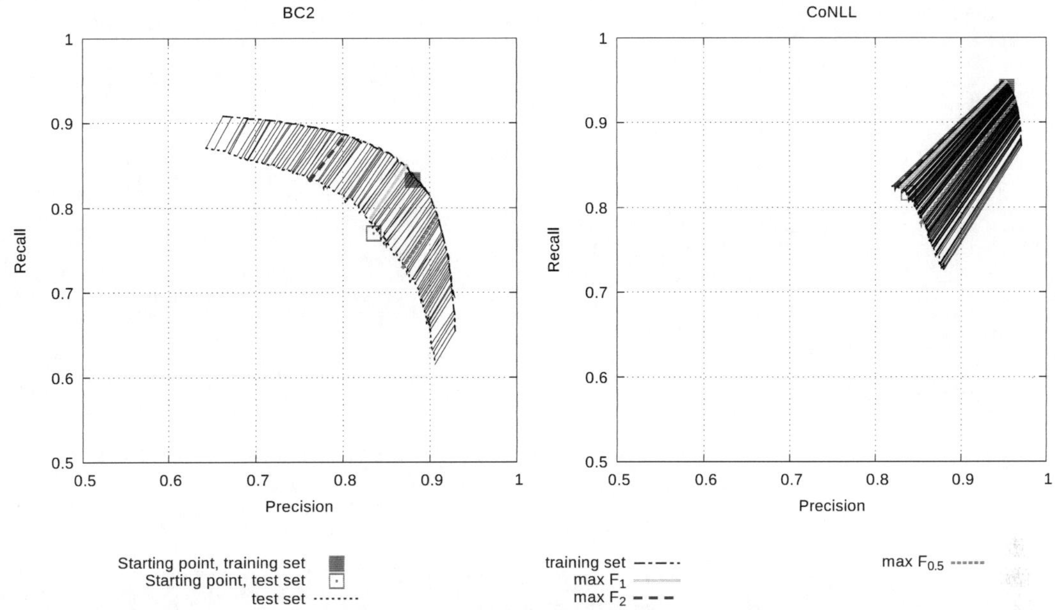

Figure 1: Results of the final population for $\sigma = 0.01$ without smoothing. Best F_1, $F_{0.5}$ and F_2 values are shown in bold colored lines, selected on the training set with the according values on the test set.

	L-BFGS					MOCRF				
Data Set	$F_{0.25}$	$F_{0.5}$	F_1	F_2	F_4	$F_{0.25}$	$F_{0.5}$	F_1	F_2	F_4
BC2	0.83	0.82	0.80	0.78	0.78	0.88	0.84	0.81	0.82	0.85
CoNLL	0.84	0.83	0.83	0.82	0.82	0.87	0.84	0.83	0.83	0.83

Table 3: Results for classic L-BFGS training in comparison to MOCRF. Given are the best available F_β measures for $\beta = \{0.25, 0.5, 1, 2, 4\}$, as well as the result for L-BFGS for different data sets. All results are equal or better than for L-BFGS training which does not optimize with respect to a special β value. These results are shown graphically in Figure 2.

large extent shows that the generalization from the results on the training set to the results on the test set is feasible.

It is noticeable, that the fronts seem to be differently well explored in BC2 and CoNLL data. On BC2 data, precision as well as recall can be increased at the expense of the other measure: The starting point is an F_1 measure of 0.86 with a precision of 0.88 and a recall of 0.83 on training data, highest possible precision is 0.93 (difference 0.05), highest possible recall is 0.90 (difference to start: 0.07). On ConLL data, the starting point is an F_1 measure of 0.94 with a precision of 0.95 and a recall of 0.94 on training data, highest possible precision is 0.97 (difference 0.02), highest possible recall is 0.95 (difference to start: 0.01). This difference between the data sets is founded by the structure of the problem and the different dependencies of the objective functions on the data sets. In both cases, a spread set of solutions is made available by the proposed method.

Assuming a user asking for a model characterized by an F_β measure with fixed β, the provided system multi-objectively trained exhibits better performance than the one trained to maximize log-likelihood. This is shown in Table 3 and Figure 2. On BC2 data, the results are better for all β values, for CoNLL data the results are the same for F_1, but superior for all other values.

On both data sets, the precision is higher than the recall for the model trained on log-likelihood. Therefore, F_β is monotonically decreasing for that method. For MOCRF, higher values of precision than for recall are achieved. On BC2 data, this even leads to a minimum of F_β for $\beta = 1$ as the same precision and recall are more difficult to achieve than other weightings. On CoNLL data, the exploration of recall is not as successful as on BC2 data.

4 Conclusions and Future Work

This paper presents the application of multi-objective optimization via NSGA-II to maximize precision and recall in Conditional Random Fields for named entity

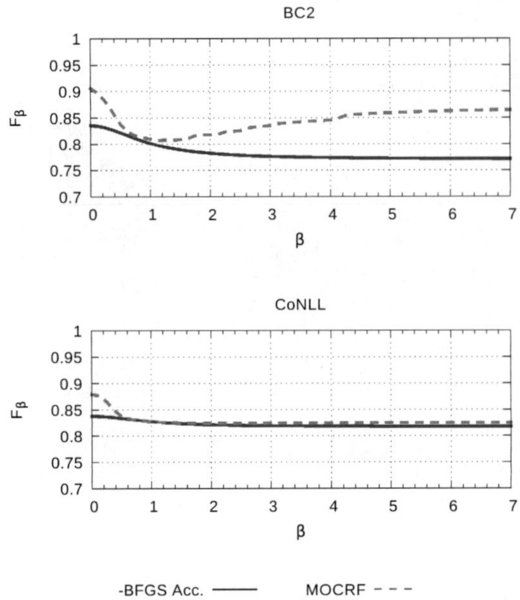

Figure 2: Results in F_β for different β on the result obtained via L-BFGS training w.r.t. log-likelihood and MOCRF.

recognition. It is shown on both data sets that F_β measures for nearly all β could be increased in comparison to classical maximization of log-likelihood via L-BFGS. This enables an end-user to choose a model with higher recall or precision without retraining or time-consuming computation of confidence measures. Possible applications include information retrieval with the need for a high recall to find most of the possible results, e.g. documents from a database as well as information extraction, where a high precision can help to detect correct relations between named entities.

Main future work is to evaluate other multi-objective optimization heuristics to improve the result in terms of a higher spread of solutions and possibly a better approximation of the real pareto-front. An integration of the initial training into the multi-objective optimization is also desirable.

References

[1] T. Bäck, D. Fogel, and Z. Michaelewicz, editors. *Handbook of Evolutionary Computation*. Institute of Physics Publishing and Oxforf University Press, Bristol. UK, 1997.

[2] A. L. Berger, S. D. Pietra, and V. J. D. Pietra. A Maximum Entropy Approach to Natural Language Processing. *Computational Linguistics*, 22(1):39–71, 1996.

[3] B. Carpenter. LingPipe for 99.99 In *Proceedings of the 2nd BioCreative workshop*, Madrid, Spain, 2007.

[4] F. Ciravegna and D. Petrelli. User involvement in customizing adaptive Information Extraction: position paper. In *Proceedings of the IJCAI-2001 Workshop on Adaptive Text Extraction and Mining*, Seattle, US, August 2001.

[5] A. Culotta and A. McCallum. Confidence Estimation for Information Extraction. In *Proceedings of HLT-NAACL*, pages 109–112, 2004.

[6] K. Deb, A. Pratap, S. Agarwal, and T. Meyarivan. A Fast and Elitist Multiobjective Genetic Algorithm: NSGA-II. *IEEE Transactions on Evolutionary Computation*, 6(2):182–197, 2002.

[7] M. Jansche. Maximum Expected F-Measure Training of Logistic Regression Models. In *Proceedings of HLT/EMNLP*, Vancouver, October 2005.

[8] T. Joachims. A Support Vector Method for Multivariate Performance Measures. In *Proceedings of the International Conference on Machine Learning (ICML)*, pages 377–384, Bonn, 2005.

[9] R. Klinger and C. M. Friedrich. Feature Subset Selection in Conditional Random Fields for Named Entity Recognition. In *Proceedings of Recent Advances in Natural Language Processing (RANLP)*, Borovets, Bulgaria, 2009.

[10] R. Klinger, C. M. Friedrich, J. Fluck, and M. Hofmann-Apitius. Named Entity Recognition with Combinations of Conditional Random Fields. In *Proc. of the Second BioCreative Challenge Evaluation Workshop*, pages 89–91, 2007.

[11] J. D. Lafferty, A. McCallum, and F. C. N. Pereira. Conditional Random Fields: Probabilistic Models for Segmenting and Labeling Sequence Data. In *Proc. of the Eighteenth International Conference on Machine Learning (ICML 2001)*, pages 282–289. Morgan Kaufmann Publishers, 2001.

[12] D. D. Lewis, Y. Yang, T. Rose, and F. Li. A New Benchmark Collection for Text Categorization Research. *Journal of Machine Learning Research*, 5:361–397, 2004.

[13] R. McDonald and F. Pereira. Identifying Gene and Protein Mentions in Text Using Conditional Random Fields. *BMC Bioinformatics*, 6 Suppl 1:S6, 2005.

[14] J. Melcher. Java Non-Dominated Sorting Genetic Algorithm II (JNSGA II) – Implementation. Software, 2007. `http://sourceforge.net/projects/jnsga2`.

[15] B. L. Miller and D. E. Goldberg. Genetic algorithms, tournament selection, and the effects of noise. *Complex Systems*, 9:193–212, 1995.

[16] J. Nocedal. Updating Quasi-Newton Matrices with Limited Storage. *Mathematics of Computation*, 35(151):773–782, July 1980.

[17] E. F. T. K. Sang and F. De Meulder. Introduction to the CoNLL-2003 Shared Task: Language-Independent Named Entity Recognition. In W. Daelemans and M. Osborne, editors, *Proc. of CoNLL-2003*, pages 142–147. Edmonton, Canada, 2003.

[18] B. Schölkopf and A. J. Smola. *Learning with Kernels*. The MIT Press, 2002.

[19] L. Smith, L. K. Tanabe, R. J. nee Ando, C.-J. Kuo, I.-F. Chung, C.-N. Hsu, Y.-S. Lin, R. Klinger, C. M. Friedrich, K. Ganchev, M. Torii, H. Liu, B. Haddow, C. A. Struble, R. J. Povinelli, A. Vlachos, W. A. Baumgartner, L. Hunter, B. Carpenter, R. T.-H. Tsai, H.-J. Dai, F. Liu, Y. Chen, C. Sun, S. Katrenko, P. Adriaans, C. Blaschke, R. Torres, M. Neves, P. Nakov, A. Divoli, M. Maa-Lpez, J. Mata, and W. J. Wilbur. Overview of BioCreative II gene mention recognition. *Genome Biol*, 9 Suppl 2:S2, 2008.

[20] J. Suzuki, E. McDermott, and H. Isozaki. Training Conditional Random Fields with Multivariate Evaluation Measures. In *Proceedings of the 21st International Conference on Computational Linguistics and 44th Annual Meeting of the ACL*, pages 217–224. Association for Computational Linguistics, July 2006.

[21] J. Wilbur, L. Smith, and L. Tanabe. BioCreative 2. Gene Mention Task. In *Proc. of the Second BioCreative Challenge Evaluation Workshop*, pages 7–9, 2007.

[22] C. J. van Rijsbergen. *Information Retrieval*. Butterworth, 1979.

Semi-Supervised Learning for Word Sense Disambiguation: Quality vs. Quantity

Sandra Kübler
Indiana University
skuebler@indiana.edu

Desislava Zhekova
University of Bremen
zhekova@uni-bremen.de

Abstract

In this paper, we discuss the importance of the quality against the quantity of automatically extracted examples for word sense disambiguation (WSD). We first show that we can build a competitive WSD system with a memory-based classifier and a feature set reduced to easily and efficiently computable features. We then show that adding automatically annotated examples improves the performance of this system when the examples are carefully selected based on their quality.

Keywords

word sense disambiguation, memory-based learning, semi-supervised learning

1 Introduction

Word sense disambiguation (WSD) [7] is concerned with lexical ambiguity: It is the task of automatically assigning the correct meaning to occurrences of polysemous words in their context. Thus, word sense disambiguation is a necessary component for many applications in Computational Linguistics, such as machine translation, information retrieval, information extraction, or question answering. However, most of the WSD approaches reported so far rely on supervised learning techniques, relying on the data sets provided by the SensEval[1] and SemEval[2] competitions. This makes them susceptible for well known problems in supervised machine learning such as data sparseness or lacking domain independence.

In the present paper, we will investigate a semi-supervised approach to WSD. Semi-supervised learning starts with a supervised learner trained on available data. In a second step, data are added from automatically annotated sources. Semi-supervised approaches, especially when they do not optimize for individual words, often result in no or minimal improvements. Gonzalo and Verdejo [5] show that the good results for individual words cannot compare to supervised results. This either means that the quality of the data is not good enough to be used for the given purpose, or that the approach in employing the data is not optimal. If the former is true, future approaches to semi-supervised learning must concentrate on distinguishing reliably from unreliably annotated examples.

Our hypothesis is that the automatically annotated examples that are added to the training material are not of high enough quality to improve the results. In order to investigate the problem, we start with the SensEval-3 English lexical sample task data set[3] and then add examples extracted from a selection of lexicons and corpora. The results show that only reliably annotated examples should be considered and that they can be included in approaches different from the ones previously proposed (e.g. by Mihalcea [12]). We will show that a careful selection of automatically annotated examples gives a modest improvement over the supervised results, as compared to a significant drop in accuracy when all examples are added.

2 Related work

There is a considerable amount of work published on word sense disambiguation for English. We will concentrate here on some systems that took part in the SensEval-3 task and that we will use to place our system as well as on semi-supervised approaches.

Yarowsky [21] suggested an unsupervised self-training approach to WSD. This approach can also be used in a semi-supervised manner if the initial data is manually annotated, which results in an increase in accuracy from 90.5% for the unsupervised approach to 95.5%. A very successful approach to automatic acquisition of sense-tagged corpora is Mihalcea's [12] co-training and self-training approach. This approach is based on the creation of several (co-training) or a single (self-training) word-experts on labeled data and their further usage for labeling unannotated data. In the case that the optimal selection of parameters is chosen for each word independently, the approach for both co- and self-training strategies achieve an error reduction of 25.5%. Moreover, in order to improve the co-training method, a combination of co-training with majority voting was used. The improved co-training algorithm with a global parameter selection scheme resulted in a considerable error reduction of 9.8% as compared to the basic classifier.

Gonzalo and Verdejo [5] discuss multiple encouraging results with regard to the automatic acquisition of sense-tagged corpora. One such result is the observation that under certain circumstances, the quality of the automatically extracted data equals the quality of

[1] http://www.senseval.org

[2] http://nlp.cs.swarthmore.edu/semeval/

[3] http://www.senseval.org/senseval3/data.html

International Conference RANLP 2009 - Borovets, Bulgaria, pages 197–202

the manually prepared one. Another interesting remark is the fact that employing web data reaches better results than unsupervised approaches but the final system performance is still far lower than the performance of fully supervised systems.

The development of fully supervised WSD systems, however, has been given considerably more attention than the automatic acquisition of sense-tagged corpora. This is proven by approaches as the ones presented by Mihalcea et al. in the overview of the SensEval-3 English lexical sample competition [13] - naïve Bayes systems (e.g. htsa3 [6]), systems based on kernel methods (e.g. IRTS-Kernels [19]; nusels [8]), based on the Lesk algorithm [9] (e.g. wsdiit [18]), maximum entropy models (e.g. Cymfony [15]) and many others (e.g. Prob0 [17] and clr04-ls [10]). Those systems constitute the set of best performing systems from the SensEval-3 evaluation exercise.

3 The system for WSD

In order to examine evidence for our hypothesis that only automatically annotated examples of high quality can be used successfully, we designed a memory-based learning system, which we used to train multiple word-experts/classifiers, first on the SensEval training data, and in a second step with the automatically acquired data. The remainder of the section is structured as follows: In section 3.1, we will describe the supervised baseline system, section 3.2 describes the feature and parameter optimization, section 3.3 the data sets that were collected, and section 3.4 the preprocessing steps for the new data sets.

3.1 The supervised baseline system

The supervised system uses memory-based learning, in the implementation of the Tilburg Memory-Based Learner (TiMBL) [2]. Memory-based learning is a member of the k-nearest neighbor (k-NN) [14] paradigm. This approach bases the classification of a new instance on the k most similar instances found in the training data. It has been shown to be successful for a range of problems in NLP [1]. Daelemans et al. [1] argue that MBL has a suitable bias for such problems because it allows learning from atypical and low-frequency events, thus enabling a principled approach to the treatment of exceptions and sub-regularities in language. Another advantage of MBL lies in the fact that it can work with features with a large number of different values. This allows the usage of complete words as feature values. As a consequence, however, MBL is also sensitive to large numbers of features that are only relevant for the classification of specific instances but not for all instances. For this reason, the best results using memory-based learning are reached by a rather small data set, as shown by Dinu and Kübler [3] for Romanian.

The classifier is trained on the SensEval-3 English lexical sample task data set, which contains 57 ambiguous words along with examples of their use. We trained and optimized separate classifiers for individual words. The features we employed are based on the feature set by Dinu and Kübler [3]. , they are listed in Table 1. As shown in section 4.1, these features also give competitive results for English when compared to systems participating in SensEval-3.

Feature	Description
CT_{-3}	TP -3 from TW
CT_{-2}	TP -2 from TW
CT_{-1}	TP -1 from TW
CT_0	TW
CT_1	TP 1 from TW
CT_2	TP 2 from TW
CT_3	TP 3 from TW
CP_{-3}	POS of TP -3 from TW
CP_{-2}	POS of TP -2 from TW
CP_{-1}	POS of TP -1 from TW
CP_0	POS of target word
CP_1	POS of TP 1 from TW
CP_2	POS of TP 2 from TW
CP_3	POS of TP 3 from TW
NA	first noun after TW
NB	first noun before TW
VA	first verb after TW
VB	first verb before TW
PA	first preposition after TW
PB	first preposition before TW

Table 1: *Featured used for the word-experts (TP x is the token at position x and TW is the target word)*

3.2 System Optimization

Since memory-based learning is sensitive to irrelevant features (cf. e.g. [11]), it is important to optimize features for each word-expert. Following Mihalcea [11] and Dinu and Kübler [3], we used forward and backward feature selection. This resulted in a considerable reduction in the number of features actually used for individual words as well as in a considerable improvement in accuracy (see section 4.1 for details).

We also performed a non-exhaustive optimization of system parameters. The most straightforward parameters that can be optimized for a k-NN approach are the distance metric and the values for k representing the k nearest neighbors used for classifying a new instance.

We selected the overlap metric as the distance metric and tested the following values for the number of nearest neighbors, or rather the number of nearest distances in the TiMBL system: $k = 1$, $k = 3$, $k = 5$. The parameters are optimized for each word-expert individually, and only the results for the best setting are described in the results. Since the individual optimization of parameters for word-experts results in a high number of training runs, we did not explore other parameter settings, but rather used the setting found optimal for Romanian by Dinu and Kübler [3].

3.3 Data collection

For the investigation whether adding automatically annotated examples to the training set can increase coverage and consequently accuracy, we extracted examples from several dictionaries and corpora. Table 2

```
activate   [Show phonetics]
verb [T]
1 to cause something to start:
    The alarm is activated by the lightest pressure.

2 SPECIALIZED to make a chemical reaction happen more quickly, especially by heating
```

Fig. 1: *The entry for the word "activate" from the Cambridge Learner's Dictionary*

```
ascertain the size of the overdose. Evacuation of the stomach, gastric lavage, and
administration of activated charcoal. Delay in evacuating the stomach may result in
delayed absorption, leading to relapse during
```

Fig. 2: *An example for the word "activate" extracted from the BNC*

lists all dictionaries and corpora plus the number of examples extracted from these sources.While the dictionaries do contain word sense information, the sense inventories are generally different from the one used in the SensEval-3 English data set and thus cannot be used directly. For this reason, we only extracted examples without keeping track with which sense an example was associated. Figure 1 shows the entry for the word `activate` from the Cambridge Learner's Dictionary (minus the formatting). From this entry, only the example sentence for sense 1 is extracted.

Sources	No. ex.
Dictionaries	
Dictionary.com Unabridged (v 1.1)[4]	114
Cambridge Advanced Learner's Dictionary[5]	405
American Heritage Dictionary of the English Language[6]	194
The Longman Dictionary of Contemporary English Online[7]	709
WordNet 3.0[8]	300
Corpora	
British National Corpus (BNC)	15 472
ukWaC	158 072

Table 2: *The dictionaries and corpora used for the extraction of additional examples*

Additionally, we used two different corpora: the British National Corpus (BNC) and the ukWaC. The BNC contains approximately 100 million words. It was designed to be representative of current British English, both spoken and written. The second source is the ukWaC corpus [4]. The corpus was automatically constructed and consists of more than 2 billion tokens. For the examples extracted from the corpora, no sense information was available. We extracted a context of maximally 100 words. In most cases, the actual text was shorter, restricted by the corpus interface. Figure 2 shows an example from the BNC for the word `activate`.

Annotation	Source	Train	Tests
Manual	Senseval-3	7 860	3 944
Automatic	Dictionaries	1 722	
	BNC	15 472	
	ukWaC	158 072	
Total		183 126	3 944

Table 3: *The collection of examples in our system*

Table 3 gives an overview of the data sources used in the experiments, the set amounts to approximately 183 000 instances for training. For testing, we used the original test set from the SensEval-3 competition to make our results comparable to previous work.

3.4 Data preprocessing

For the additional examples, we had to preprocess the text to change the representation so that it was comparable to the SensEval examples. For preprocessing, punctuation was stripped off, words were tokenized, and meta characters were deleted. Additionally, we used a POS tagger to assign morpho-syntactic annotation to the words. For this purpose, we used the POS tagger by Tsuruoka and Tsujii [20], which is accurate and very efficient, a definite concern with regard to the text size of the newly acquired examples.

In a next step, the examples from the dictionaries and corpora had to be annotated for senses. For this purpose we used the generalized framework for WSD - `WordNet::SenseRelate::TargetWord`[9] developed by Pedersen, Patwardhan, and Banerjee [16]. `WordNet::SenseRelate::TargetWord` uses a modification of the Lesk algorithm [9] that also includes glosses of related words from WordNet. The best sense for a word is then selected based on its semantic relatedness to these words from the context and from WordNet. Based on a manual evaluation of a small data set, we chose the local module for determining relatedness.

The reason for not using self-training, as Mihalcea [12] did, was that we wanted to avoid a bias towards

[4] `http://dictionary.reference.com`
[5] `http://dictionary.cambridge.org`
[6] `http://education.yahoo.com/reference/dictionary`
[7] `http://www.ldoceonline.com`
[8] `http://wordnetweb.princeton.edu/perl/webwn`
[9] `http://www.d.umn.edu/ tpederse/senserelate.html`

majority senses in the training data. We intend the additional examples to complement the available training set from SensEval-3. This means, we are interested in adding examples for minority senses where at all possible. If we used our main machine learning approach, to which we will add these examples in the end, it would show a tendency to annotate the new examples with majority senses. For this reason, we chose a method that is based on semantic similarity measures.

System/Team	Coarse	Fine
nusels/Nat.U.Singapore	78.8	72.4
htsa3/U.Bucharest	79.3	72.9
IRST-Kernels/ITC-IRST	**79.5**	72.6
our system	79.3	**75.1**

Table 5: *Comparison with the three best supervised systems in the Senseval-3 lexical sample task [13]*

4 Experiments

We investigate the question whether automatically annotated examples can help a supervised system. Our hypothesis is that such additional examples can be beneficial if we can select high quality examples from the large pool with high confidence. For this reason, we present five sets of experiments: 1) The supervised experiment in which only the designated SensEval-3 training set is used. 2) A lower bound experiment in which we use the complete set of automatically annotated examples as the training set. This will show that the sheer size of the automatically annotated examples is not sufficient for gaining competitive results. 3) The first semi-supervised approach, in which all automatically examples are added to the training set. 4) The second semi-supervised experiment, in which the set of automatically annotated examples is sampled based on the sense distribution of the SensEval-3 training set. 5) The third semi-supervised experiment, the set of automatically annotated examples is sampled based on quality.

The results of the system were evaluated by the SensEval-3 scoring software *scorer2*[10]. The scorer calculates precision and recall, for both fine-grained and coarse-grained evaluations. However, since our classifier assigns senses to all instances, we will present only accuracy, which is equivalent to precision and recall.

Experiment		Coarse	Fine
	MFS [13]	64.5	55.2
1)	supervised	79.3	75.1
2)	unsupervised	56.2	47.5
3)	semi-supervised: all	64.5	57.8
4)	semi-supervised: ratio	77.5	72.7
5)	semi-supervised: quality	79.4	75.0

Table 4: *The results of the experiments*

4.1 The Supervised WSD System

The results of the system (using the features presented in section 3.1) when trained only on the SensEval-3 training set are shown in row 1 in Table 4.

A comparison to the best participating systems in the third SensEval evaluation exercise, shown in Table 5, confirms that our system is highly competitive. Note that our results are based on a much more restricted feature set than the ones used by all the other system. For example, we do not use any context features apart from the closest nouns, verbs, and prepositions. Instead, the features are all easily and efficiently computable. It is noteworthy that our system with the restricted feature set reaches a fine-grained accuracy that is significantly higher than that of all participating systems. These results give us a good basis for using our system in further experiments with data that has been automatically gathered and annotated.

4.2 Training on automatically annotated examples

The experiment described here uses all examples collected from the dictionaries and from the corpora. As described in Section 3.4, they were automatically annotated by `WordNet::SenseRelate::TargetWord`. The whole set of examples was then used as training data for the memory-based classifier, using the same feature set as for the baseline system. The results of this experiment are shown in row 2 of Table 4.

The results show that the accuracy based on this training set is considerably lower than that for the supervised approach with the same feature set. As expected, a larger size of training data, without quality control, is not sufficient for reaching good results in WSD.

4.3 Semi-supervised WSD with all automatically annotated examples

In this experiment, we used the SensEval-3 training set and added all the automatically annotated examples. The results of this experiment are shown in row 3 of Table 4. The surprising result here is that adding more examples does not improve accuracy. On the contrary, the results are approximately 15 percent points lower than the baseline results in the coarse evaluation and approximately 17 percent points for the fine-grained evaluation. These results corroborate earlier findings that adding more examples is not always beneficial.

4.4 Semi-supervised WSD with filtering based on ratio

One reason for the disappointing results in the previous section might be that the sense distribution of the newly added examples does not correspond to the distribution in the SensEval-3 data. For this reason, we conducted one experiment in which we filtered the automatically annotated data so that the sense distribution in the SensEval-3 training set is maintained. We

[10] `http://www.cse.unt.edu/~rada/senseval/senseval3/scoring/scoring.tar.gz`

are aware that the sense distribution in the training set does not necessarily correspond to the distribution in the test set. But since in a real-world setting, there is no possibility of determining the sense distribution in the test set short of manually annotating it, we use the distribution in the training set as the best estimate available to us.

In the present experiment, filtering is defined as excluding all examples that violate the distribution of senses in the SensEval-3 training set. To clarify the procedure, we will use a simple example. Let us consider one of the words in the training set - the verb `suspend`. Let us suppose that in the original manually annotated training set, this word appears with 3 senses and the following distribution: 19, 12, and 48. We record this distribution and filter our automatically prepared examples in such a way that the senses for the word have the same proportional distribution. If we assume that we have 39, 60, and 100 additional examples for the three senses, then the maximal ratio for sense 1 is 2, which restricts us to adding 38, 24, and 96 examples.

The results of adding the ratio filtered examples to the original training set are shown in row 4 of Table 4. Filtering the training set in order to preserve the distribution of senses as it is in the SensEval-3 lexical sample task training set improves results considerably when we compare this experiment to the one using all automatically annotated examples: Accuracy improves by 13 percent points in the coarse evaluation and by 15 percent points in the fine-grained evaluation. This comparison shows that the new examples have a radically different sense distribution than the SensEval data. It also shows that obtaining a similar sense distribution to the one in the test data is of utmost importance. However, the results are still below the results for supervised learning, which shows that the sense distribution is not the only factor that needs to be taken into account when adding new examples.

4.5 Semi-supervised WSD with filtering based on quality

Since filtering based on ratio only partially helps closing the gap between the supervised system and the one with all examples, we maintain our hypothesis that the quality of the added examples must be high in order for them to be useful in classifying the test data. To test this hypothesis, we carried out a final experiment, in which we filtered the new examples based on their quality.

Filtering based on quality works as follows: First, we have the supervised baseline system classify each of the instances from our automatically annotated example set. We determine the quality of this example by its distance to the nearest neighbors in the original SensEval training set. The distance is provided by TiMBL. Second, based on the distances, we extract only those instances that differ only minimally (distance < 2) from the manually annotated training set. We then add the resulting collection of examples (consisting of 141 instances) to the SensEval training set. The experiment achieves the results shown in row 5 of Table 4.

The results for this experiment show a slight improvement in the coarse evaluation over the supervised baseline. However, we have to keep in mind here that we only added a minimal number of examples (141). This means that the number of examples added for an individual word never exceeds 6 instances so that the overall changes in accuracy are only minimal. The reason for this is that we concentrated on using only the examples of the highest quality. In order to show the differences that adding these few examples makes, we show the result for those words for which new examples were added in Table 6.

The results show that for seven words, the results improve for both types of evaluation. In three cases, only the coarse evaluation improves, and in two cases, the fine-grained evaluation. The highest improvement is reached for the word `add`, for which adding 2 examples results in an improvement of both scores from 84.8% to 87.5%. Apart from the improvements, however, we also have a decrease in performance for seven words.

5 Conclusion and future work

We described the design and performance of a memory-based word sense disambiguation system with a very limited feature set, which makes use of automatic feature selection and minimal parameter optimization. We showed that the system performs competitively to other state-of-art systems, and we used it further for the evaluation of automatically acquired data for word sense disambiguation.

We also investigated the extension of the supervised training set by extracting additional examples from online lexicons and corpora, which are then annotated automatically with a WSD system based on semantic distance. Adding these examples, however, results in a dramatic drop in performance. Filtering the additional examples to maintain the original distribution of senses improves results, but they still do not reach the quality of supervised training only. However, filtering the additional examples for quality does increase overall performance slightly. This corroborates our hypothesis that additional examples can only be used successfully if they are of high quality. Since this method still results in a decrease in performance for several words, we are planning to refine the definition of how to determine the quality of examples in the future.

References

[1] W. Daelemans, A. van den Bosch, and J. Zavrel. Forgetting exceptions is harmful in language learning. *Machine Learning*, 34:11–43, 1999. Special Issue on Natural Language Learning.

[2] W. Daelemans, J. Zavrel, K. van der Sloot, and A. van den Bosch. TiMBL: Tilburg memory based learner – version 6.1 – reference guide. Technical Report ILK 07-07, Induction of Linguistic Knowledge, Tilburg University, 2007.

[3] G. Dinu and S. Kübler. Sometimes less is more: Romanian word sense disambiguation revisited. In *Proceedings of the International Conference on Recent Advances in Natural Language Processing, RANLP 2007*, Borovets, Bulgaria, 2007.

[4] A. Ferraresi, E. Zanchetta, M. Baroni, and S. Bernardini. Introducing and evaluating ukWaC, a very large web-derived corpus of English. In *Proceedings of the 6th Language Resources and*

Word	Baseline no. ex.	Filtered no. ex.	Baseline coarse	Baseline fine	Filtered coarse	Filtered fine
activate	228	234	83.8	83.8	84.2	84.2
add	263	265	84.8	84.8	87.5	87.5
appear	265	271	76.7	76.7	76.7	76.7
arm	266	272	90.2	90.2	90.2	90.2
ask	261	262	64.1	64.1	63.4	63.4
atmosphere	161	165	71.0	71.0	69.8	69.8
audience	200	203	97.0	79.5	99.0	79.5
bank	262	267	88.6	80.7	87.9	79.9
decide	122	128	85.5	85.5	82.3	82.3
degree	256	261	86.7	77.0	89.8	78.9
difference	226	230	66.2	60.1	70.2	58.8
eat	181	187	90.8	90.8	92.0	92.0
encounter	130	136	96.9	72.3	96.9	70.8
expect	156	162	87.2	87.2	86.5	86.5
express	110	111	89.1	80.0	89.1	80.0
interest	185	191	75.3	73.7	71.0	71.0
note	132	138	79.1	79.1	79.1	79.1
organization	112	118	87.5	81.2	89.3	80.4
party	230	234	72.8	71.6	72.8	72.0
plan	166	171	88.7	88.7	88.1	86.9
produce	186	192	68.1	67.0	69.1	69.1
provide	136	142	98.6	95.7	100.0	97.1
remain	139	145	92.9	92.9	94.3	94.3
shelter	196	202	72.4	72.4	68.4	68.4
sort	190	196	87.0	75.5	87.0	75.5
talk	146	151	79.5	79.5	79.5	79.5
watch	100	102	92.2	80.4	92.2	82.4

Table 6: *System results for individual words under the supervised and the semi-supervised condition with quality-based filtering*

Evaluation Conference (LREC 2008), Marrakech, Morocco, May 2008.

[5] J. Gonzalo and F. Verdejo. Automatic Acquisition of Lexical Information and Examples. In E. Agirre and P. Edmonds, editors, *Word Sense Disambiguation*, pages 253–274. Springer, 2007.

[6] C. Grozea. Finding optimal parameter settings for hight performance word sense disambiguation. In *SENSEVAL-3: Third International Workshop on the Evaluation of Systems for the Semantic Analysis of Text*, pages 125–128, Barcelona, Spain, July 2004.

[7] N. Ide and J. Véronis. Word sense disambiguation: the state of the art. *Computational Linguistics*, 24(1):1–40, 1998.

[8] Y. K. Lee, H. T. Ng, and T. K. Chia. Supervised word sense disambiguation with Support Vector Machines and multiple knowledge sources. In *SENSEVAL-3: Third International Workshop on the Evaluation of Systems for the Semantic Analysis of Text*, Barcelona, Spain, July 2004.

[9] M. Lesk. Automated sense disambiguation using machine-readable dictionaries: How to tell a pine cone from an ice cream cone. In *Proceedings of the 1986 SIGDOC Conference*, Toronto, Canada, 1986.

[10] K. C. Litkowski. SENSEVAL-3 task automatic labeling of semantic roles. In *SENSEVAL-3: Third International Workshop on the Evaluation of Systems for the Semantic Analysis of Text*, pages 9–12, Barcelona, Spain, 2004.

[11] R. Mihalcea. Instance based learning with automatic feature selection applied to word sense disambiguation. In *Proceedings of the 19th International Conference on Computational Linguistics, COLING'02*, Taipeh, Taiwan, 2002.

[12] R. Mihalcea. Co-training and self-training for word sense disambiguation. In *Proceedings of the Conference on Natural Language Learning (CoNLL 2004)*, Boston, MA, 2004.

[13] R. Mihalcea, T. Chklovski, and A. Kilgarriff. The SENSEVAL-3 English lexical sample task. In *SENSEVAL-3: Third International Workshop on the Evaluation of Systems for the Semantic Analysis of Text*, pages 25–28, Barcelona, Spain, 2004.

[14] H. T. Ng and H. B. Lee. Integrating multiple knowledge sources to disambiguate word sense: An examplar-based approach. In *Proceedings of the 34th Annual Meeting of the Association for Computational Linguistics (ACL-96)*, pages 40–47, Santa Cruz, CA, 1996.

[15] C. Niu, W. Li, R. K. Srihari, H. Li, and L. Crist. Context clustering for word sense disambiguation based on modeling pairwise context similarities. In *SENSEVAL-3: Third International Workshop on the Evaluation of Systems for the Semantic Analysis of Text*, pages 187–190, Barcelona, Spain, July 2004.

[16] S. Patwardhan, S. Banerjee, and T. Pedersen. SenseRelate::TargetWord - a generalized framework for word sense disambiguation. In *Proceedings of the 20th National Conference on Artificial Intelligence*, pages 1692–1693, Pittsburgh, Pennsylvania, USA, 2005.

[17] J. Preiss. Probabilistic WSD in SENSEVAL-3. In *SENSEVAL-3: Third International Workshop on the Evaluation of Systems for the Semantic Analysis of Text*, pages 213–216, Barcelona, Spain, 2004.

[18] G. Ramakrishnan, B. Prithviraj, and P. Bhattacharyya. A gloss-centered algorithm for disambiguation. In *SENSEVAL-3: Third International Workshop on the Evaluation of Systems for the Semantic Analysis of Text*, pages 217–221, Barcelona, Spain, 2004.

[19] C. Strapparava, A. Gliozzo, and C. Giuliano. Pattern abstraction and term similarity for word sense disambiguation: IRST at senseval-3. In *SENSEVAL-3: Third International Workshop on the Evaluation of Systems for the Semantic Analysis of Text*, Barcelona, Spain, 2004.

[20] Y. Tsuruoka and J. Tsujii. Bidirectional inference with the easiest-first strategy for tagging sequence data. In *Proceedings of HLT/EMNLP*, pages 467–474, Vancouver, Canada, 2005.

[21] D. Yarowsky. Unsupervised word sense disambiguation rivaling supervised methods. In *Proceedings of the 33rd Annual Meeting of the Association for Computational Linguistics*, pages 189–196, Cambridge, MA, 1995.

Treelex Meets Adjectival Tables

Anna Kupść
Université de Bordeaux / CLLE-ERSS, Signes, IPIPAN

Abstract

The paper presents Treelex, a valence lexicon of French adjectives automatically extracted from a treebank. The corpus contains morphological and syntactic annotations but no subcategorisation information is present for adjectives. Due to rich corpus annotations, our extraction method is guided by linguistic knowledge. The obtained lexicon (about 2000 adjectives and 40 frames) has been evaluated against hand-crafted adjectival tables described in [13] and achieved 0.46 F-measure.

Keywords

adjectives, valence, treebank, syntactic lexicon, lexicon-grammar tables, French

1 Introduction

The importance of subcategorisation information is unquestionable with respect to performance of various NLP applications [4, 15, 5, 9]. So far, creating valence lexicons has been mostly devoted to obtaining such resources for verbs whereas valence lexicons for other predicates, e.g., nouns, adjectives or adverbs, are scarce. For French, the only available resources for adjectives (lexicon-grammar tables in [8] and [13]) exist only on paper and have not been adapted yet to automatic processing. In this paper, we present a method for obtaining an electronic valence lexicon of French adjectives which can be used in various NLP applications.

The adopted technique consists in automatically extracting the lexicon from a treebank. We exploit a journalistic corpus, richly annotated with both morphological and syntactic information (constituents and functions), cf. [1]. The corpus is relatively small as it contains about 1 million words. The treebank has been automatically pre-tagged and then manually verified by human experts following annotation guidelines in [2]. We rely on linguistic knowledge and corpus annotations in order to obtain subcategorisation patterns for adjectives.

Syntactic annotations in the corpus provide information about major constituents (including adjectival phrases) but grammatical functions are indicated only for phrases related to verbs. Therefore, no distinction between argumental and non-argumental dependents of adjectives is made in the treebank. Specifying valence (i.e., arguments) of adjectives is more difficult than for verbs. First, in most cases, the syntactic realization of adjective's arguments is optional. For instance, [12] mentions just a few adjectives, such as *enclin* 'inclined', *exempt* 'exempted' or *désireux* 'desirous', among those for which a complement is obligatory. This makes the strongest 'obligatoriness' criterion, often used to identify complements of verbs, practically inapplicable to adjectives. Also results of other linguistic tests, e.g., topicalisation or pronominalisation, are in general less reliable than for verbs, cf. [13]. Second, syntactic realization of adjective's arguments is more variable than with verbs: several equivalent syntactic realizations of one semantic argument are possible. For example, *affable* 'affable' may appear with two semantically equivalent PP complements: *affable envers/avec les clients* 'affable towards/with customers'. Such variability makes the specification of required components even more challenging. Finally, adjectives may appear in many syntactic constructions, e.g., comparative or impersonal phrases. Hence, arguments specific to individual adjectives should be distinguished from elements regularly appearing in a particular construction.

Despite the difficulties in defining complements of adjectives, the subject of an adjective can be quite easily identified. In the paper, we focus on specifying these two types of arguments: both the subject and complements are incorporated into valence frames of adjectives.

2 Method

As mentioned above, we exploit corpus annotations and use linguistic knowledge in order to obtain subcategorisation information for adjectives. In particular, we refer to constituent types (to identify APs and their components) as well as to functions associated with direct dependents of verbs, especially with respect to predicative adjectives.

2.1 Arguments of Adjectives

In French, complements of adjectives can be mainly realised by three syntactic categories: prepositional phrases, subordinate clauses or infinitive clauses, tagged in the corpus, respectively, as PP, Ssub and VPinf.

(1) sûr [PP de son retour] / [Ssub qu'il
sure of his return that-he
reviendra] / [VPinf de revenir]
will-be-back to be-back
'sure of his return/ that he'll be back / to be back'

International Conference RANLP 2009 - Borovets, Bulgaria, pages 203–207

Nominal phrases (NP), on the other hand, can serve only as the subject of an adjective.[1] We adopt the notion of the subject also for attributive adjectives: the modified noun is a semantic argument of the adjective and can be considered its semantic subject. Therefore, we consider that the subject is present in both predicative (2) and attributive (3) uses of an adjective:

(2) predicative use:

[NP La maison] est **grande**.
the house is big

'The house is big.'

(3) attributive use:

Je vois une **grande** [N maison].
I see a big house

'I see a big house.'

2.2 Linguistic Cues in the Treebank

Corpus annotations indicate adjectival phrases (AP) but they do not specify arguments of adjectives: functional annotations are absent within APs. Moreover, an argument of an adjective can be outside of an AP, for example the subject of a predicative adjective (2). Therefore, we use linguistic knowledge, applied to corpus annotations, in order to identify predicate-argument structure of adjectives. In particular, we aim at providing a 'normalized' valence, i.e., to separate constituents which occur with individual adjectives from components of productive constructions (elements which can appear with almost any adjective).

If no complement and no subject have been identified for an adjective in the corpus, we assume that its valence contains only the NP subject.

2.2.1 Arguments

In the corpus, predicative adjectives are arguments of a verb and they are assigned a grammatical function: a subject complement (ATS) or an object complement (ATO), i.e., a predicate referring either to the sentential subject (2) or to the direct object (4).

(4) [NP Jacques] trouve [AP inevitable] [Ssub
SUJ Jacques finds ATO unavoidable OBJ
qu'elle chante].
that-she sings

'Jacques finds unavoidable that she sings.'

In such cases, the subject of the adjective can be easily identified as it is indicated by the grammatical function of another argument of the verb: SUJ for ATS, and OBJ for ATO adjectives. As (4) shows, the subject of an adjective does not have to be nominal.

Adjectives can also appear in impersonal constructions with an accompanying Ssub or VPinf, (5). The status of the propositional components in (5) is different from those in (6), as indicated also by corpus annotations. The crucial difference is that Ssub or VPinf in (5) can be preposed to become the sentential subject, whereas this is not possible in (6).

(5) Il est [AP agréable] [Ssub qu'il fasse
it is ATS nice OBJ that-it makes
beau] / [VPinf de sortir].
beautiful OBJ to go out

'It's nice that the weather is good / to go out.'

(6) Paul est [AP heureux [Ssub qu'il fasse
Paul is ATS happy that-it makes
beau] / [VPinf de sortir]].
beautiful to go out

'Paul is happy that the weather is good / to go out.'

In (6), corpus annotations indicate that Ssub or VPinf is embedded within AP, unlike in (5). We consider the propositional constituents in (5) the extraposed subject of the adjective, i.e., in impersonal constructions (the subject is *il* or *ce*), OBJ is the subject of ATS adjective. On the other hand, if no construction-specific elements are present (sec. 2.2.2), the subordinate component in (6) is treated as a complement of the adjective.

French clitics are always attached to a verb but they can replace dependents of other predicates as well. Although clitics often pronominalise arguments, they may refer to adjuncts, for instance to locative phrases. In the corpus, clitics are direct dependents of a verb and they are assigned a function. In copular predicative constructions, as the copula itself does not have a clitic, the clitic can only indicate a dependent of the predicative adjective. The clitic function specifies whether it is a complement or an adjunct.

2.2.2 Non-arguments

Constituents which regularly appear in syntactic constructions are not related to a specific adjective and do not belong to its valence list. We filter out such components (PP, VPinf or Ssub) based on linguistic cues.

In comparative constructions, an adjective is often accompanied by a PP or Ssub, annotated in the corpus as an internal component of AP. If the adjective appears with a comparative adverb, *plus* 'more', *moins* 'less', *autant* 'as much as', etc., the embedded constituent is not considered part of the adjective frame (in contrast to (6) where there is no adverb).

(7)–(8) illustrate another type of productive constructions where the embedded constituent of AP is not an argument of the adjective. Again, the presence of an intensifier adverb, such as *si* 'so', *trop* 'too', *tellement* 'so much', etc., is decisive for the status of Ssub or VPinf constituent within AP. Only if no such adverb is present, the constituent can be considered an argument of the adjective.

(7) Paul est [AP si heureux [Ssub qu'il saute
Paul is ATS so happy that-he jumps
de joie]].
of joy

'Paul is so happy that he jumps out of joy.'

[1] [13] mentions two apparent exceptions: *bleu roi* 'royal blue' and *rouge cerise* 'cherry red'. Such adjectives, however, can be considered multi-word units, cf. [8].

(8) Cette histoire est [AP trop belle [VPinf
this story is ATS too beautiful
pour être vraie]].
for be true
'This story is too good to be true.'

2.2.3 Lexicon of Prepositions

Apart from comparative phrases, PPs do not appear in adjectival constructions. Therefore, no other linguistic observations can help us specify the status of PPs in APs. In particular, there is no general rule which would permit to distinguish a PP complement of an adjective from a PP attached to an adjective in complex NP restructured constructions, [11]. Instead, we use PrepLex [7], a lexicon of argumental and non-argumental prepositions, i.e., prepositions which can or cannot introduce an argument. We adopt it to filter out PPs which cannot be complements of an adjective. We added to the list of non-argumental prepositions a few complex ones found in the treebank which are not present in PrepLex.

3 Extracted Frames

The described method results in a lexicon of 2153 adjectives[2] and 40 frames. The vast majority of adjectives (1849) appear only with a basic frame, i.e., with the nominal subject, whereas the remaining 304 adjectives were found with a different frame. Tab.1 presents 23 extracted frames which appeared more than once along with their frequency counts and the number of corresponding adjective entries.

Before proceeding to a quantitative evaluation (sec. 4), we provide a brief impressionisitic analysis of the obtained results. As far as Ssub and VPinf arguments are concerned, their identification should be quite reliable since elimination of these non-argumental phrases is targeted by the adjectival constructions. However, a few issues still remain. First, our list of intensifier adverbs is not exhaustive and 2 adjectives were mistakenly assigned a VPinf[pour] complement. Second, certain impersonal constructions have not been recognized. At the beginning of the sentence, a predicative adjective is often followed by its extraposed VPinf subject, as in a regular impersonal construction (5), but neither the impersonal pronoun nor the copula are present. In such cases, as no construction-specific adverb is present either, the embedded VPinf is misinterpreted as a complement. Even more problematic is recognition of PP-complements since it is based on purely lexical rather than contextual information. Most prepositions listed in PrepLex are ambiguous, i.e., whether they introduce a complement or not depends on the context. Another issue related to PP-arguments is a verification of their semantic content. Although adjectives can admit several different PP-realisations of a single semantic argument, the corresponding prepositions should be semantically equivalent. At present, we have no means of verifying this requirement other than manually. Finally, a few singleton frames (i.e., of frequency 1, not listed in Tab. 1) resulted from occasional annotation problems, mostly related to incorrectly assigned syntactic structure.

[2] Numerals, quantifiers and interrogative adjectival pronouns have been excluded.

FRAME	freq.	#adjs
SUJ:NP (basic)	15485	2087
SUJ:NP|P-OBJ:PP[à]	278	81
SUJ:NP|P-OBJ:PP[de]	204	94
SUJ:NP|P-OBJ:VPinf[de]	83	44
SUJ:VPinf[de]	66	29
SUJ:NP|P-OBJ:VPinf[à]	53	16
SUJ:NP|P-OBJ:PP[pour]	35	29
SUJ:NP|P-OBJ:PP[en]	30	23
SUJ:NP|P-OBJ:VPinf[pour]	24	6
SUJ:NP|P-OBJ:PP[dans]	22	14
SUJ:SsubI[que]	18	11
SUJ:NP|OBJ:Ssub[que]	18	4
SUJ:NP|P-OBJ:PP[par]	13	12
SUJ:NP|OBJ:SsubI[que]	12	3
SUJ:NP|P-OBJ:PP[sur]	11	11
SUJ:NP|P-OBJ:PP[avec]	9	6
SUJ:NP|P-OBJ:PP[loc]	8	8
SUJ:NP|P-OBJ:PP[entre]	5	3
SUJ:SsubS[que]	6	5
SUJ:NP|P-OBJ:PP[chez]	4	3
SUJ:NP|P-OBJ:PP[depuis]	3	3
SUJ:VPinf[de]|P-OBJ:PP[à]	3	3
SUJ:NP|P-OBJ:PP[après]	2	2

Table 1: *Extracted frames with their frequency and the number of adjectival entries in which they appear. Abbreviations: functions: SUJ – subject, P-OBJ – PP or VPinf object, OBJ – object without an introducing element, categories: NP – noun phrase, PP – prepositional phrase, Ssub – a subordinate clause, either in subjunctive (SsubS) or indicative (SsubI) mode, VPinf – an infinitive clause.*

4 Comparison with Adjective Tables

In order to get a more objective evaluation of Treelex, we compared it with adjectives listed in lexicon-grammar tables in [13], the only available syntactic lexicon of French adjectives we are aware of. This reference resource is not ideal for our purpose. First, the tables exist only on paper so they cannot be directly used. Second, they contain constructions rather than 'normalized' frames we aim at producing here. Finally, tables do not describe adjectives that appear only with the NP subject, which leaves the status of missing adjectives unclear. Despite these inconveniencies, we decided to use the tables for our preliminary evaluation.

From 419 adjectives in [13], 266 are also present in our lexicon and we used them for evaluation. This list contains 177 adjectives found only with a basic frame in the corpus and there are 127 adjectives occurring with different frames in text. Out of all 40 frames discovered in Treelex (sec. 3), 30 are present in the evalua-

Baseline Results	
Precision	0.69
Recall	0.19
F-measure	0.30

Results for evaTreelex	
Precision	0.74
Recall	0.33
F-measure	0.46

Table 2: *The baseline results and the overall evaluation obtained for Treelex frames*

tion sublexicon (evaTreelex). We manually translated the corresponding entries in Picabia into our format, which produced 75 frames, and then compared each evaTreelex entry with frames obtained for the adjective in Picabia (evaPicabia). If a Treelex frame was equivalent to the corresponding construction present in the evaPicabia entry, the format difference was not taken into account and the frame was marked as appearing in both lexicons.

To set a baseline for our evaluation, we assumed that all adjectives have only a basic frame. We adopted standard evaluation metrics: Precision (P), Recall (R) and F-measure (F), following their definitions in [10]:

(9) $P = \frac{\text{evaTreelex} \cap \text{evaPicabia}}{\text{evaTreelex}}$

(How many entries in evaTreelex are correct?)

(10) $R = \frac{\text{evaTreelex} \cap \text{evaPicabia}}{\text{evaPicabia}}$

(How many evaPicabia entries found in evaTreelex?)

(11) $F = \frac{2PR}{P+R}$ (harmonic mean)

The results obtained for all frames in evaTreelex and the baseline figures are given in Tab. 2. The overall results do not seem very impressive: [14] obtain F-measure of 0.719 for English adjectives. However, our evaluation sample is much bigger (266 vs. 30 test adjectives used for English) and so is the number of frames in the reference lexicon (75 vs. 30). On the other hand, our extraction precision is quite high (0.75) whereas the low recall (0.33) is probably due to the corpus size and the choice of the reference resource. Note that 177 out of 266 evaluated adjectives were not found with a complement in the corpus (being listed in Picabia's tables, they should have a non-subject argument). Since the adjectival tables do not come from a corpus investigation, another explanation of the low recall is a possible rarity of adjective-frame uses (constructions) presented in Picabia. For example, many contructions containing a Ssub introduced by a complex complementizer *de ce que* 'of that' or *à ce que* 'to that' were not found in the corpus.

It is clear nevertheless that Treelex does much better than the baseline, especially in identifying non-basic frames. The difference in precision is smaller due to the fact that many of evaTreelex entries only have the frame used as the baseline.

20 out of 30 frames present in evaTreelex are found also in Picabia's tables. Evaluation of each individual frame present in the common part is shown in Tab. 3. The numbers confirm the observation made for the overall performance: the precision of each frame is higher than its recall. Again, this discrepancy is directly related to the amount of data available. There is no clear correlation between extraction accuracy for propositional (Ssub and VPinf) and prepositional (PP) arguments as could have been expected from the adopted technique. Note however that, in addition to the problems mentioned in sec. 3, the frame frequencies are counted with respect to adjective entries (rather than to their frequency in text). Hence, the numbers in Tab. 3 are quite low and not fully reliable.

5 Related Work

As mentioned in sec. 4, a method for automatically extracting various syntactic lexica for English, including adjectives, has been proposed in [14]. This approach is also corpus-based but it uses a set of pre-defined frame patterns to classify adjectives in the corpus rather than discovers frames themselves. Although the authors use a reference standard for evaluation, it has been extracted from a corpus and, for adjectives, it has been specifically created for this purpose. This allows them to provide an evaluation with respect to the same-origin resource rather than use a completely independent lexicon as a reference standard.

In a recent study, [3] provides 15 classes of French adjectives based on their combinatorial properties, i.e., roughly corresponding to valence frames we presented here. His classes, however, are more general than our frames. For example, most prepositions in PP complements are not explicitly indicated, nor is the type of a propositional argument (VPinf or Ssub). More importantly, his work does not aim at creating a lexicon and he uses only a few adjectives to illustrate specific classes.

6 Conclusion

The lexicon presented in the paper has been automatically extracted from a treebank, providing a resource of over 2000 adjective entries and discovering 40 frames. The quality of the lexicon has been evaluated with respect to adjectival tables listed in [13]. Although the quantitative results do not achieve the state-of-the-art performance yet, they are well above the baseline we set, which clearly indicates that adjective valence cannot be ignored in the text.

In order to obtain a better coverage and improve the quality, the lexicon should be extended. We plan to complement it by adopting statistical techniques on a much larger corpus, e.g., [6]. This will also allow us to validate the remaining Treelex frames and verify performance for individual adjectives.

The lexicon is freely available from the site: `http://erssab.u-bordeaux3.fr/spip.php?article150`.

Frame	Freq.	P	R	F
SUJ:NP	183	0.77	0.94	0.85
SUJ:NP|P-OBJ:PP[à]	40	0.89	0.66	0.75
SUJ:NP|P-OBJ:PP[de]	36	0.80	0.42	0.55
SUJ:NP|P-OBJ:VPinf[à]	11	1.00	0.15	0.26
SUJ:NP|P-OBJ:VPinf[de]	10	0.77	0.30	0.43
SUJ:VPinf[de]	8	0.62	0.80	0.69
SUJ:SsubI[que]	7	1.00	1.00	1.00
SUJ:NP|P-OBJ:PP[pour]	5	0.50	0.36	0.42
SUJ:VPinf[de]|P-OBJ:PP[à]	3	1.00	1.00	1.00
SUJ:NP|P-OBJ:PP[en]	3	0.25	0.23	0.24
SUJ:NP|P-OBJ:PP[loc]	2	1.00	0.67	0.80
SUJ:NP|P-OBJ:PP[avec]	2	0.50	0.25	0.33
SUJ:NP|OBJ:SsubI[que]	2	1.00	1.00	1.00
SUJ:NP|P-OBJ:PP[de]|P-OBJ:PP[à]	1	1.00	0.25	0.40
SUJ:Ssub[que]	1	1.00	0.04	0.07
SUJ:NP|P-OBJ:PP[sur]	1	0.33	0.50	0.40
SUJ:SsubS[que]	1	1.00	1.00	1.00
SUJ:VPinf[de]|P-OBJ:PP[pour]	1	1.00	0.33	0.50
SUJ:NP|P-OBJ:PP[dans]	1	0.25	0.50	0.33
SUJ:NP|P-OBJ:VPinf[pour]	3	0.00	0.00	NONE

Table 3: *Evaluation measures for 20 frames present both in Treelex and in Picabia's tables*

References

[1] A. Abeillé, L. Clément, and F. Toussenel. Building a treebank for French. In *Treebanks*. Kluwer, 2003.

[2] A. Abeillé, F. Toussenel, and M. Chéradame. Corpus le Monde. annotations en constituants. guide pour les correcteurs. LLF, UFRL, Paris7, 2004.

[3] N. Barrier. *Une méta-grammaire des adjectifs du français. Une appalication aux TAG.* PhD thesis, Université Paris 7, 2009.

[4] J. Carroll and A. Fang. The automatique acquisition of verb subcategorisations and their impact on the performance of an HPSG parser. In *Proceedings of the 1st International Conference on Natural Language Processing*, Sanya City, China, 2004.

[5] L. Danlos. *La génération automatique de textes.* Masson, 1985.

[6] C. Fabre and D. Bourigault. Exploiter des corpus annotés syntaxiquement pour observer le continuum entre arguments et circonstants. *Journal of French Language Studies*, 18(1):87–102, 2008.

[7] K. Fort and B. Guillaume. Preplex: a lexicon of French prepositions for parsing. In *ACL SIGSEM07*, 2007.

[8] M. Gross. *Méthodes en syntaxe.* Hermann, 1975.

[9] C. Han, J. Yoon, N. Kim, and M. Palmer. A Feature-Based Lexicalized Tree Adjoining Grammar for Korean. Technical report, IRCS, 2000.

[10] F. I., F. G., and G. C. Evaluating synlex. In *Proceedings of TALN 2007*, Toulouse, 2007.

[11] M. Meydan. La restructuration du GN sujet dans les phrases adjectivales à substantif approprié. *Langages*, (133):59–80, 1999.

[12] M. Noailly. *L'adjectif en français.* Ophrys, 1999.

[13] L. Picabia. *Les construction adjectivales en français.* Droz, Genève-Paris, 1978.

[14] J. Preiss, T. Briscoe, and A. Korhonen. A system for large-scale acquisition of verbal, nominal and adjectival subcategorization frames from corpora. In *ACL 2007*, 2007.

[15] M. Surdeanu, S. Harabagiu, J. Williams, and P. Aarseth. Using predicate-argument structures for information extraction, 2003.

Integrating WordNet and FrameNet using a knowledge-based Word Sense Disambiguation algorithm

Egoitz Laparra and German Rigau
IXA group. University of the Basque Country, Donostia
{*egoitz.laparra,german.rigau*}@*ehu.com*

Abstract

This paper presents a novel automatic approach to partially integrate FrameNet and WordNet. In that way we expect to extend FrameNet coverage, to enrich WordNet with frame semantic information and possibly to extend FrameNet to languages other than English. The method uses a knowledge-based Word Sense Disambiguation algorithm for linking FrameNet lexical units to WordNet synsets. Specifically, we exploit a graph-based Word Sense Disambiguation algorithm that uses a large-scale knowledge-base derived from WordNet. We have developed and tested four additional versions of this algorithm showing a substantial improvement over previous results.

1 Introduction

Predicate models such as FrameNet [6], VerbNet [16] or PropBank [23] are core resources in most advanced NLP tasks, such as Question Answering, Textual Entailment or Information Extraction. Most of the systems with Natural Language Understanding capabilities require a large and precise amount of semantic knowledge at the predicate-argument level. This type of knowledge allows to identify the underlying typical participants of a particular event independently of its realization in the text. Thus, using these models, different linguistic phenomena expressing the same event, such as active/passive transformations, verb alternations and nominalizations can be harmonized into a common semantic representation. In fact, lately, several systems have been developed for shallow semantic parsing and semantic role labeling using these resources [11], [26], [14].

However, building large and rich enough predicate models for broad–coverage semantic processing takes a great deal of expensive manual effort involving large research groups during long periods of development. Thus, the coverage of currently available predicate-argument resources is still unsatisfactory. For example, [7] or [25] indicate the limited coverage of FrameNet as one of the main problems of this resource. In fact, FrameNet1.3 covers around 10,000 lexical-units while for instance, WordNet3.0 contains more than 150,000 words. Furthermore, the same effort should be invested for each different language [27]. Following the line of previous works [26], [7], [15], [24], [8], [29], we empirically study a novel approach to partially integrate FrameNet [6] and WordNet [12]. The method relies on the use of a knowledge-based Word Sense Disambiguation (WSD) algorithm that uses a large-scale graph of concepts derived from WordNet [12] and eXtented WordNet [19]. The WSD algorithm is applied to semantically coherent groupings of words belonging to the same frame. In that way we expect to extend the coverage of FrameNet (by including from WordNet closely related concepts), to enrich WordNet with frame semantic information (by porting frame information to WordNet) and possibly to extend FrameNet to languages other than English (by exploiting local wordnets aligned to the English WordNet).

WordNet[1] [12] (hereinafter WN) is by far the most widely-used knowledge base. In fact, WN is being used world-wide for anchoring different types of semantic knowledge including wordnets for languages other than English [4], domain knowledge [17] or ontologies like SUMO [22] or the EuroWordNet Top Concept Ontology [3]. It contains manually coded information about English nouns, verbs, adjectives and adverbs and is organized around the notion of a *synset*. A synset is a set of words with the same part-of-speech that can be interchanged in a certain context. For example, <*student, pupil, educatee*> form a synset because they can be used to refer to the same concept. A synset is often further described by a gloss, in this case: "a learner who is enrolled in an educational institution" and by explicit semantic relations to other synsets. Each synset represents a concept which is related to other concepts by means of a large number of semantic relationships, including hypernymy/hyponymy, meronymy/holonymy, antonymy, entailment, etc.

FrameNet[2] [6] is a very rich semantic resource that contains descriptions and corpus annotations of English words following the paradigm of Frame Semantics [13]. In frame semantics, a Frame corresponds to a scenario that involves the interaction of a set of typical participants, playing a particular role in the scenario. FrameNet groups words (lexical units, LUs hereinafter) into coherent semantic classes or frames, and each frame is further characterized by a list of participants (lexical elements, LEs, hereinafter). Different senses for a word are represented in FrameNet by assigning different frames.

Currently, FrameNet represents more than 10,000 LUs and 825 frames. More than 6,100 of these LUs also provide linguistically annotated corpus examples. However, only 722 frames have associated a LU. From those, only 9,360 LUs[3] where recognized by WN (out of 92%) corresponding to only 708 frames.

LUs of a frame can be nouns, verbs, adjectives and adverbs representing a coherent and closely related set of meanings that can be viewed as a small semantic field. For example, the frame EDUCATION_TEACHING contains LUs referring to the teaching activity and their par-

[1] `http://wordnet.princeton.edu/`
[2] `http://framenet.icsi.berkeley.edu/`
[3] Word-frame pairs

International Conference RANLP 2009 - Borovets, Bulgaria, pages 208–213

ticipants. It is evoked by LUs like *student.n*, *teacher.n*, *learn.v*, *instruct.v*, *study.v*, etc. The frame also defines core semantic roles (or FEs) such as STUDENT, SUBJECT or TEACHER that are semantic participants of the frame and their corresponding LUs (see example below).

[Bernard Lansky]$_{STUDENT}$ *studied* [the piano]$_{SUBJECT}$ [with Peter Wallfisch]$_{TEACHER}$.

Table 1 presents the result of the our WSD process on some LUs of the Frame EDUCATION_TEACHING. We also include the polysemy degree of each word (#senses) and the definition (Gloss) of the sense (Synset) selected by the algorithm.

The contribution of this new resource is threefold[4]. First, we extend the coverage of FrameNet. For instance, the frame EDUCATION_TEACHING only considers *instruct.v* and *instruction.n*, but not *instructor.n* which is a synonym in WN of the LU *teacher.n*. Second, we can extend the coverage of semantic relations in WN. For instance, in WN there is no a semantic relation connecting <*student, pupil, educatee*> and < *teacher, instructor*> directly. Third, we can also automatically extend FrameNet to languages other than English by exploiting local wordnets aligned to the English WN. For instance, the Spanish synset aligned to <*student, pupil, educatee*> is <*alumno, estudiante*> and the Italian one is <*allievo, alunno, studente*>. Furthermore, we can also transport to the disambiguated LUs the knowledge currently available from other semantic resources associated to WN such as SUMO [22], WN Domains [17], etc. For instance, now the LU corresponding to *student.n* can also have associated the SUMO label *SocialRole* and its corresponding logical axioms, and the WN Domains *school* and *university*.

The paper is organized as follows. After this short introduction, in section 2 we present the graph-based Word Sense Disambiguation algorithm and the four additional versions studied in this work. The evaluation framework and the results obtained by the different algorithms are presented and analyzed in section 3, and finally, in section 4, we draw some final conclusions and outline future work.

2 SSI algorithms

Structural Semantic Interconnections (SSI) is a knowledge-based iterative approach to Word Sense Disambiguation [21]. The original SSI algorithm is very simple and consists of an initialization step and a set of iterative steps.

Given W, an ordered list of words to be disambiguated, the SSI algorithm performs as follows. During the initialization step, all monosemous words are included into the set I of already interpreted words, and the polysemous words are included in P (all of them pending to be disambiguated). At each step, the set I is used to disambiguate one word of P, selecting the word sense which is closer to the set I of already disambiguated words. Once a sense is disambiguated, the word sense is removed from P and included into I. The algorithm finishes when no more pending words remain in P.

In order to measure the proximity of one synset (of the word to be disambiguated at each step) to a set of synsets

[4] Available at `http://adimen.si.ehu.es/WordFrameNet`

Algorithm 1 SSI-Dijkstra algorithm

Function SSI-Dijkstra (T: list of terms)
$(I, P) := InitialInterpretation(T)$
for *each* $\{p \in P\}$ **do**
  $s := BestSense(p, I, \emptyset)$
  $I := I \cup \{s\}$
end for
Function InitialInterpretation (T: list of terms)
$(I, P) := SelectMonosemous(T)$
Function SelectMonosemous (T: list of terms)
$I := \emptyset$
for *each* $\{t \in T\}$ **do**
  if t *is monosemous* **then**
    $I := I \cup \{the\ unique\ sense\ of\ t\}$
  else
    $P := P \cup \{t\}$
  end if
end for
Function BestSense (t: term, I: list of senses, P: list of terms)
$BestSense := \emptyset$
$MinDistance := 0$
for *each* $\{sense\ s\ \in t\}$ **do**
  $d := MinDistanceS(s, I)$
  if $MinDistance = 0$ *or* $d < MinDistance$ **then**
    $BestSense := s$
    $MinDistance := d$
  end if
end for
Function MinDistance (s: sense, I: list of senses)
$d := 0$
for *each* $\{sense\ s' \in I\}$ **do**
  $d := d + DijkstraShortestPath(s, s')$
end for

(those word senses already interpreted in I), the original SSI uses an in-house knowledge base derived semi-automatically which integrates a variety of online resources [20]. This very rich knowledge-base is used to calculate graph distances between synsets. In order to avoid the exponential explosion of possibilities, not all paths are considered. They used a context-free grammar of relations trained on SemCor to filter-out inappropriate paths and to provide weights to the appropriate paths.

Instead, we used a version of the SSI algorithm called SSI-Dijkstra [9] (see algorithm 1. SSI-Dijkstra uses the Dijkstra algorithm to obtain the shortest path distance between a node and some other nodes of the whole graph. The Dijkstra algorithm is a greedy algorithm that computes the shortest path distance between one node an the rest of nodes of a graph. BoostGraph[5] library can be used to compute very efficiently the shortest distance between any two given nodes on very large graphs. As [9], we also use already available knowledge resources to build a very large connected graph with 99,635 nodes (synsets) and 636,077 edges (the set of direct relations between synsets gathered from WN[6][12] and eXtended WN[7] [19]. For building this graph we used WN version 1.6 and the semantic relations appearing between synsets and disambiguated glosses of WN 1.7. To map the relations appearing in eXtended WN to WN version 1.6 we used the automatic WN Mappings[8] [10]. On that graph, SSI-Dijkstra computes several times

[5] http://www.boost.org/doc/libs/1_35_0/libs/graph/doc/index.html
[6] http://wordnet.princeton.edu
[7] http://xwn.hlt.utdallas.edu
[8] http://www.lsi.upc.es/ nlp/tools/mapping.html

Lexical Unit	synset	#senses	Gloss
education.n	00567704-n	2	"activities that impart knowledge"
teacher.n	07632177-n	2	"a person whose occupation is teaching"
instruct.v	00562446-v	3	"impart skills or knowledge"
study.v	00410381-v	6	"be a student; follow a course of study; be enrolled at an institute of learning"
student.n	07617015-n	2	"a learner who is enrolled in an educational institution"
pupil.n	07617015-n	3	"a learner who is enrolled in an educational institution"

Table 1: *Partial result of the WSD process of the LUs of the frame EDUCATION_TEACHING*

the Dijkstra algorithm.

SSI-Dijkstra has very interesting properties. For instance, as the Dijkstra algorithm always provides the minimum distance between two synsets, the SSI-Dijkstra algorithm always provides an answer being the minimum distance close or far. In contrast, the original SSI algorithm not always provides a path distance because it depends on a predefined grammar of semantic relations. In fact, the SSI-Dijkstra algorithm compares the distances between the synsets of a word and all the synsets already interpreted in I. At each step, the SSI-Dijkstra algorithm selects the synset which is closer to I (the set of already interpreted words).

Previously, the SSI-Dijkstra algorithm have been used for constructing KnowNets [9]. KnowNets are very large knowledge bases, which have been acquired by semantically disambiguating the Topic Signatures obtained from the web [1]. Basically, the method uses SSI-Dijkstra to assign the most appropriate senses to large sets of ordered topic words (for instance, *underclassman*, *overachiever*, *seminarian*, *college*, etc.) associated to a particular synset (for instance, *pupil#n#1*).

Initially, the list I of interpreted words should include the senses of the monosemous words in W, or a fixed set of word senses. Note that when disambiguating a Topic Signature associated to a particular synset, the list I always includes since the beginning of the process at least the sense of the Topic Signature (in our example *pupil#n#1*) and the rest of monosemous words of W. However, many frames only group polysemous LUs. In fact, a total of 190 frames (out of 26%) only have polysemous LUs. Thus, SSI-Dijkstra provides no results when there are no monosemous terms in W. In this case, before applying SSI, the set of the LUs corresponding to a frame (the words included in W) have been ordered by polysemy degree. That is, the less polysemous words in W are processed first.

Obviously, if no monosemous words are found, we can adapt the SSI algorithm to make an initial guess based on the most probable sense of the less ambiguous word of W. For this reason we implemented two different versions of the basic SSI-Dijkstra algorithm: **SSI-Dijkstra-FirstSenses-I** (hereinafter FSI) and **SSI-Dijkstra-AllSenses-I** (hereinafter ASI). Thus, these two versions perform as SSI-Dijkstra when W contains monosemous terms, but differently when W contains only polysemous words. In fact, FSI and ASI always provide an interpretation of W.

While FSI includes in I the sense having minimal cumulated distance to the first senses of the rest of words in W, ASI includes in I the sense having minimal cumulated distance to the all the senses of the rest of words in W. The rationale behind the FSI algorithm is that the most frequent sense for a word, according to the WN sense ranking is very competitive in WSD tasks, and it is extremely hard to improve upon even slightly [18]. Thus, this algorithm expects that the first sense in WN will be correct for most of the words in W. Regarding ASI, this algorithm expects that the words in W (corresponding to a very close semantic field) will establish many close path connections between different synsets of the same word (because of the fine-grained sense distinction of WN).

At each step, both the original SSI and also the SSI-Dijkstra algorithms only consider the set I of already interpreted words to disambiguate the next word of P. That is, the remaining words of P are not used in the disambiguation process. In fact, the words in P are still not disambiguated and can introduce noise in the process. However, the knowledge remaining in P can also help the process. In order to test the contribution of the remaining words in P in the disambiguation process, we also developed two more versions of the basic SSI-Dijkstra algorithm. **SSI-Dijkstra-FirstSenses-P** (hereinafter FSP) and **SSI-Dijkstra-AllSenses-P** (hereinafter ASP). When a word is being disambiguated, these two versions consider the set I of already interpreted words of W and also the rest of words remaining in P. That is, at each step, the algorithm selects the word sense which is closer to the set I of already disambiguated words and the remaining words of P all together. While FSP selects the sense having minimal cumulated distance to I and the first senses of the words in P, ASP selects the sense having minimal cumulated distance to I and all the senses of the words in P.

3 Experiments

We have evaluated the performance of the different versions of the SSI algorithm using the same data set used by [28] and [29]. This data set consists of a total of 372 LUs corresponding to 372 different frames from FrameNet1.3 (one LU per frame). Each LUs have been manually annotated with the corresponding WN 1.6 synset. This Gold Standard includes 9 frames (5 verbs and 4 nouns) with only one LU (the one that has been sense annotated). Obviously, for these cases, our approach will produce no results since no context words can be used to help the disambiguation process[9]. Table 2 presents the main characteristics of the datasets we used in this work. In this table, *FN* stands for FrameNet[10], *GS* for the Gold-Standard, *mono* for those Gold-Standard frames having at least one monosemous LU and *poly* for those Gold-Standard frames having only polysemous LUs. The table shows for each dataset, the number of frames and the average distribution per frame of

[9] In fact, FrameNet has 33 frames with only one LU, and 63 with only two.

[10] We removed frames with no LUs assigned or not present in WN

	FN	GS	mono	poly	10
#Frames	708	372	299	73	195
Nouns	5.87	7.90	9.35	1.95	13.58
Verbs	5.77	6.49	7.32	3.09	9.70
Adjectives	2.49	3.24	3.86	0.71	5.36
Other	0.11	0.14	0.14	0.09	0.24
Not in WN	1.07	1.30	1.51	0.42	2.13
Monosemous	4.40	5.79	7.20	0.00	9.87
Polysemous	8.77	10.68	11.96	5.42	16.88
#senses	3.64	3.45	3.28	5.64	3.63
Total	14.24	17.77	20.67	5.84	28.88

Table 2: *Number of frames and average distribution of words per frame of the different datasets*

each POS, the words not represented in WN, the number of monosemous and polysemous words, the polysemy degree and the total words. The number of words per frame in this Gold Standard seems to be higher than the average in FrameNet. This data set also has 73 frames having only polysemous LUs (20% of the total). That is, these frames do not have monosemous LUs. Possibly, because its small size (5.84 words on average).

Table 3 presents detailed results per Part-of-Speech (POS) of the performance of the different SSI algorithms in terms of Precision (P), Recall (R) and F1 measure (harmonic mean of recall and precision). In bold appear the best results for precision, recall and F1 measures. As baseline, we also include the performance measured on this data set of the most frequent sense according to the WN sense ranking. Remember that this baseline is very competitive in WSD tasks, and it is extremely hard to beat. However, all the different versions of the SSI-Dijkstra algorithm outperform the baseline. Only SSI-Dijkstra obtains lower recall for verbs because of its lower coverage. In fact, SSI-Dijkstra only provide answers for those frames having monosemous LUs, the SSI-Dijkstra variants provide answers for frames having at least two LUs (monosemous or polysemous) while the baseline always provides an answer.

As expected, the SSI algorithms present different performances according to the different POS. Also as expected, verbs seem to be more difficult than nouns and adjectives as reflected by both the results of the baseline and the SSI-Dijkstra algorithms. For nouns and adjectives, the best results are achieved by both FSI and ASI variants. Remember that these versions perform as SSI-Dijkstra on frames having monosemous LUs but performing an initial guess on frames having only polysemous LUs. While FSI makes an initial guess including in I the sense of the less polysemous word having minimal cumulated distance to the *first senses* of the rest of words in W, ASI makes an initial guess including in I the sense of the less polysemous word having minimal cumulated distance to *all* the senses of the rest of words in W. In fact, FSI and ASI behave differently than SSI-Dijsktra in the 73 frames having only polysemous LUs in the data set. Interestingly, the best results for verbs are achieved by FSP, not only on terms of F1 but also on precision. Remember that FSP always uses I and the first senses of the rest of words in P as context for the disambiguation. It seems that for verbs it is useful to consider not only the disambiguated words but also the most frequent senses of the rest of words being disambiguated. However, for nouns and adjectives the best precision is achieved by the original SSI-Dijkstra. This fact suggests the importance of having monosemous or correctly disambiguated words in I at the beginning of the incremental disambiguation process, at least for nouns and adjectives.

To our knowledge, on the same dataset, the best results so far are the ones presented by [29]. They presented a novel machine learning approach reporting a Precision of 0.76, a Recall of 0.61 and an F measure of 0.68[11]. Note that these results are below the most-frequent sense according to the WN sense ranking (F1=0.69) and all versions of SSI-Dijkstra (F1 from 0.69 to 0.74).

In order to measure the contribution of the different SSI-Dijkstra versions on those frames having at least one monosemous LU, Table 4 presents detailed results per POS of its performance in terms of Precision (P), Recall (R) and F1 measure (F). Again, in bold appear the best results, and as a baseline, we again include the results measured on this data set of the most frequent sense according to the WN sense ranking. Obviously, FSI and ASI variants are not included since for frames having monosemous LUs both approaches obtain the same result as of the SSI-Dijkstra algorithm. Interestingly, when having monosemous LUs, all SSI algorithms obtain substantial improvements over the baseline, which is very high. Also interesting is that SSI-Dijkstra obtains the best results for nouns and adjectives while FSP obtains the best results for verbs.

In order to measure the contribution of the different SSI-Dijkstra versions on those 73 frames having only polysemous LUs, Table 5 presents detailed results per POS of its performance in terms of Precision (P), Recall (R) and F1 measure (F). Again, in bold appear the best results, and as a baseline, we again include the results measured on this data set of the most frequent sense according to the WN sense ranking. Obviously, the original SSI-Dijkstra is not included. For these subset of frames, the algorithms behave similarly as for the whole data set. In fact, as before, verbs seem to be more difficult than nouns and adjectives. However, according to the baseline, without monosemous LUs the task seems to be much more difficult. This is specially acute for nouns and verbs where the the first sense heuristic obtains accuracies of 58% and 48% respectively. The algorithms also present different performances according to the different POS. Again, the the best results are achieved by both FSI and ASI variants on nouns and adjectives, and FSP on verbs. However, in this data set only ASI slightly outperforms the baseline in precision and F1. Since these versions do not provide answers for frames having only one LU, the recall is below precision.

Although the set of frames having only polysemous LUs seems to be much more difficult than the set of frames having monosemous LUs, the results shown in tables 4 and 5 also suggest room for improving the SSI algorithms. In fact, not only for frames having no monosemous LUs, but also in general. For instance, for disambiguating verbs. These results suggest that possibly, a new version of the SSI-Dijkstra algorithm processing nouns and adjectives as FSI (or ASI) and verbs as FSP would clearly outperform the current versions. We expect for this new algorithm improved results also for nouns, verbs and adjectives, since the whole incremental disambiguation process will benefit from a better disambiguation of I. Possibly, during the incremental and iterative disambiguation process, a better disambiguation of verbs will improve the disambiguation

[11] In fact, both evaluations are slightly different since they perform 10-fold cross validation on the available data, while we provide results for the whole dataset.

	nouns			verbs			adjectives			all		
	P	**R**	**F**	**P**	**R**	**F**	**P**	**R**	**F**	**P**	**R**	**F**
wn-mfs	0.75	0.75	0.75	0.64	0.64	0.64	0.80	0.80	0.80	0.69	0.69	0.69
SSI-dijktra	**0.84**	0.65	0.73	0.70	0.56	0.62	**0.90**	0.82	0.86	**0.78**	0.63	0.69
FSI	0.80	**0.77**	**0.79**	0.66	0.65	0.65	0.89	**0.89**	**0.89**	0.74	**0.73**	0.73
ASI	0,80	**0,77**	**0,79**	0,67	0,65	0,66	0,89	**0,89**	**0,89**	0,75	**0,73**	**0,74**
FSP	0.75	0.73	0.74	**0.71**	**0.69**	**0.70**	0.79	0.79	0.79	0.73	0.72	0.72
ASP	0.72	0.69	0.70	0.68	0.66	0.67	0.75	0.75	0.75	0.70	0.69	0.69

Table 3: *Results of the different SSI algorithms*

	nouns			verbs			adjectives			all		
	P	**R**	**F**	**P**	**R**	**F**	**P**	**R**	**F**	**P**	**R**	**F**
wn-mfs	0.78	0.78	0,78	0,67	0,67	0,67	0,80	0,80	0,80	0,73	0,73	0,73
SSI-dijktra	**0,84**	**0,84**	**0,84**	0,70	0,70	0,70	**0,90**	**0,90**	**0,90**	**0,78**	**0,78**	**0,78**
FSP	0,80	0,78	0,79	**0,73**	**0,73**	**0,73**	0,80	0,80	0,80	0,76	0,76	0,76
ASP	0,78	0,78	0,78	0,71	0,71	0,71	0,76	0,76	0,76	0,74	0,74	0,74

Table 4: *Evaluation of frames with at least one monosemous word*

of nouns, and a better disambiguation of nouns will also improve the disambiguation of verbs and adjectives.

However, still remains unclear if the problem of frames having no monosemous LUs is because the lack of correctly disambiguated words in I, the small number of LUs per frame or its high polysemy degree. We expect to clarify this issue in future experiments and analysis.

Although the experimental setting is different, [8] also present a direct evaluation of their integration of WN and FrameNet for the LU induction task [5]. They apply a combination of knowledge and distributional based methods to carry out the mapping process. In order to aliviate their data sparseness problem, they reduced the whole dataset in two ways. First, they neglected LUs occurring less than 50 times in the British National Corpus. Second, they excluded frames having less than 10 LUs. This leaves them with 220 frames, involving 4,380 LUs. They focused the study of the quality of their automatic mapping on four frames (i.e. KILLING, PEOPLE_BY_AGE, STATEMENT and CLOTHING) with 306 LUs. On this dataset, they report a precision of 0.80, a recall of 0.79 and an F measure of 0.80. Unfortunately, they do not report detailed performances per POS nor baselines. Trying to be more representative of the whole resource, the dataset used in our study covers a large set of frames but only one LU per frame has been annotated. Obviously, the results of these four frames will not allow to make appropriate conclusions.

In order to establish a fair comparison with our evaluation framework, Table 6 also presents detailed results per POS of the performance of the SSI versions in terms of Precision (P), Recall (R) and F1 measure (F) on the 195 frames having at least 10 LUs[12]. Again, in bold appear the best results, and as a baseline, we again include the results measured on this reduced data set of the most frequent sense according to the WN sense ranking. Note that the average result for this baseline is the same as the one reported for the whole dataset although it presents a different behaviour depending on the POS. Regarding SSI algorithms, they behave similarly as with the whole dataset (better precision for SSI-Dijkstra, better performance for FSI and ASI on nouns and adjectives and FSP for verbs, and better performance overall for FSI and ASI). Surprisingly, the different SSI algorithms only obtain for nouns better performances than with the whole dataset. Slightly worst results are obtained for verbs and adjectives. Possibly, the cause of this phenomena would be the different POS distribution per frame on this particular dataset. However, overall, the results improve with respect the complete Gold-Standard.

Although both approaches are not directly comparable due to the different evaluation dataset, our results seem to be very close to those reported by [8]. In fact, their dataset excluded low frequent LUs and was centered only on the LUs of four frames. Moreover, we applied a unique knowledge based approach. Furthermore, we expect even better results with the improved version of the SSI-Dijkstra using FSI for nouns and adjectives, and FSP for verbs.

4 Conclusions and future work

In this work, we have presented a novel approach to integrate FrameNet and WordNet. The method uses a knowledge based Word Sense Disambiguation (WSD) algorithm called SSI-Dijkstra for assigning the appropriate synset of WordNet to the semantically related Lexical Units of a given frame from FrameNet. This algorithm relies on the use of a large knowledge base derived from WordNet and eXtended WordNet. Since the original SSI-Dijkstra requires a set of monosemous or already interpreted words, we have devised, developed and empirically tested four different versions of this algorithm to deal with sets having only polysemous words. The resulting new algorithms obtain improved results over state-of-the-art.

As a result of this empirical study, we are currently developping a new version of the SSI-Dijkstra using FSI for nouns and adjectives, and FSP for verbs. We also plan to further extend the empirical evaluation with other available graph based algorithms that have been proved to be competitive in WSD such as UKB[13] [2].

Finally, using the same automatic approach, we also plan to disambiguate the Lexical Elements of a given frame.

[12] We did not remove unfrequent LUs

[13] `http://ixa2.si.ehu.es/ukb/`

	nouns			verbs			adjectives			all		
	P	R	F	P	R	F	P	R	F	P	R	F
wn-mfs	0.58	**0.58**	0.58	0.48	0.48	0.48	**0.80**	**0.80**	**0.80**	0.54	**0.54**	0.54
FSI	**0,64**	0,55	**0,59**	0,50	0,44	0,47	**0,80**	**0,80**	**0,80**	0,58	0,51	0,54
ASI	**0,64**	0,55	**0,59**	0,53	0,46	0,49	**0,80**	**0,80**	**0,80**	**0,59**	0,52	**0,55**
FSP	0,56	0,48	0,52	**0,59**	**0,51**	**0,55**	0,60	0,60	0,60	0,58	0,51	0,54
ASP	0,48	0,41	0,44	0,53	0,46	0,49	0,60	0,60	0,60	0,52	0,45	0,48

Table 5: *Results of the different SSI algorithms on frames having only polysemous LUs*

	nouns			verbs			adjectives			all		
	P	R	F	P	R	F	P	R	F	P	R	F
wn-mfs	0.76	0.76	0.76	0.61	0.61	0.61	0.76	0.76	0.76	0.69	0.69	0.69
SSI-dijktra	**0,86**	0,78	0,82	0,66	0,63	0,64	**0,88**	0,85	0,87	**0,77**	0,72	0,75
FSI	0,85	**0,85**	**0,85**	0,64	0,64	0,64	**0,88**	**0,88**	**0,88**	0,76	**0,76**	**0,76**
ASI	0,85	**0,85**	**0,85**	0,64	0,64	0,64	**0,88**	**0,88**	**0,88**	0,76	**0,76**	**0,76**
FSP	0,81	0,81	0,81	**0,67**	**0,67**	**0,67**	0,74	0,74	0,74	0,73	0,73	0,73
ASP	0,76	0,76	0,76	0,63	0,63	0,63	0,71	0,71	0,71	0,69	0,69	0,69

Table 6: *Results of the different SSI algorithms on frames having at least 10 LUs*

Thus, the resulting resource will also integrate the core semantic roles of FrameNet. For example, for the frame EDUCATION_TEACHING we will associate the appropriate WordNet synsets to the Lexical Elements STUDENT, SUBJECT or TEACHER.

References

[1] E. Agirre and O. L. de la Calle. Publicly available topic signatures for all wordnet nominal senses. In *Proceedings of LREC*, Lisbon, Portugal, 2004.

[2] E. Agirre and A. Soroa. Personalizing pagerank for word sense disambiguation. In *Proceedings of the 12th conference of the European chapter of the Association for Computational Linguistics (EACL-2009)*, Athens, Greece, April 2009. Eurpean Association for Computational Linguistics.

[3] J. Álvez, J. Atserias, J. Carrera, S. Climent, A. Oliver, and G. Rigau. Consistent annotation of eurowordnet with the top concept ontology. In *Proceedings of Fourth International WordNet Conference (GWC'08)*, 2008.

[4] J. Atserias, L. Villarejo, G. Rigau, E. Agirre, J. Carroll, B. Magnini, and P. Vossen. The meaning multilingual central repository. In *Proceedings of GWC*, Brno, Czech Republic, 2004.

[5] C. Baker, M. Ellsworth, and K. Erk. Semeval-2007 task 19: Frame semantic structure extraction. In *Proceedings of the Fourth International Workshop on Semantic Evaluations (SemEval-2007)*, pages 99–104, Prague, Czech Republic, June 2007. Association for Computational Linguistics.

[6] C. Baker, C. Fillmore, and J. Lowe. The berkeley framenet project. In *COLING/ACL'98*, Montreal, Canada, 1997.

[7] A. Burchardt, K. Erk, and A. Frank. A WordNet Detour to FrameNet. In *Proceedings of the GLDV 2005 GermaNet II Workshop*, pages 408–421, Bonn, Germany, 2005.

[8] D. D. Cao, D. Croce, M. Pennacchiotti, and R. Basili. Combining word sense and usage for modeling frame semantics. In *Proceedings of The Symposium on Semantics in Systems for Text Processing (STEP 2008)*, Venice, Italy, 2008.

[9] M. Cuadros and G. Rigau. Knownet: Building a large net of knowledge from the web. In *22nd International Conference on Computational Linguistics (COLING'08)*, Manchester, UK, 2008.

[10] J. Daudé, L. Padró, and G. Rigau. Validation and Tuning of Wordnet Mapping Techniques. In *Proceedings of RANLP*, Borovets, Bulgaria, 2003.

[11] K. Erk and S. Pado. A powerful and versatile xml format for representing role-semantic annotation. In *Proceedings of LREC-2004*, Lisbon, 2004.

[12] C. Fellbaum, editor. *WordNet. An Electronic Lexical Database*. The MIT Press, 1998.

[13] C. J. Fillmore. Frame semantics and the nature of language. In *Annals of the New York Academy of Sciences: Conference on the Origin and Development of Language and Speech*, volume 280, pages 20–32, New York, 1976.

[14] A.-M. Giuglea and A. Moschitti. Semantic role labeling via framenet, verbnet and propbank. In *ACL-44: Proceedings of the 21st International Conference on Computational Linguistics and the 44th annual meeting of the Association for Computational Linguistics*, pages 929–936, Morristown, NJ, USA, 2006. Association for Computational Linguistics.

[15] R. Johansson and P. Nugues. Using WordNet to extend FrameNet coverage. In *Proceedings of the Workshop on Building Frame-semantic Resources for Scandinavian and Baltic Languages, at NODALIDA*, Tartu, Estonia, May 24 2007.

[16] K. Kipper. *VerbNet: A broad-coverage, comprehensive verb lexicon*. PhD thesis, University of Pennsylvania, 2005.

[17] B. Magnini and G. Cavaglià. Integrating subject field codes into wordnet. In *Proceedings of LREC*, Athens. Greece, 2000.

[18] D. McCarthy, R. Koeling, J. Weeds, and J. Carroll. Finding predominant senses in untagged text. In *Proceedings of ACL*, pages 280–297, 2004.

[19] R. Mihalcea and D. Moldovan. extended wordnet: Progress report. In *Proceedings of NAACL Workshop on WordNet and Other Lexical Resources*, Pittsburgh, PA, 2001.

[20] R. Navigli. Semi-automatic extension of large-scale linguistic knowledge bases. In *Proc. of 18th FLAIRS International Conference (FLAIRS)*, Clearwater Beach, Florida, 2005.

[21] R. Navigli and P. Velardi. Structural semantic interconnections: a knowledge-based approach to word sense disambiguation. *IEEE Transactions on Pattern Analysis and Machine Intelligence (PAMI)*, 27(7):1063–1074, 2005.

[22] I. Niles and A. Pease. Towards a standard upper ontology. In *Proceedings of the 2nd International Conference on Formal Ontology in Information Systems (FOIS-2001)*, pages 17–19. Chris Welty and Barry Smith, eds, 2001.

[23] M. Palmer, D. Gildea, and P. Kingsbury. The proposition bank: An annotated corpus of semantic roles. *Computational Linguistics*, 31(1):71–106, March 2005.

[24] M. Pennacchiotti, D. D. Cao, R. Basili, D. Croce, and M. Roth. Automatic induction of FrameNet lexical units. In *Proceedings of Empirical Methods in Natural Language Processing (EMNLP)*, Honolulu, Hawaii, USA, 2008.

[25] D. Shen and M. Lapata. Using semantic roles to improve question answering. In *Proceedings of the 2007 Joint Conference on Empirical Methods in Natural Language Processing and Computational Natural Language Learning (EMNLP-CoNLL)*, pages 12–21, 2007.

[26] L. Shi and R. Mihalcea. Putting pieces together: Combining framenet, verbnet and wordnet for robust semantic parsing. In *Proceedings of CICLing*, Mexico, 2005.

[27] C. Subirats and M. R. Petruck. Surprise: Spanish framenet! In *Proceedings of the International Congress of Linguists*, Praga, 2003.

[28] S. Tonelli and E. Pianta. A novel approach to mapping framenet lexical units to wordnet synsets. In *Proceedings of IWCS-8*, Tilburg, The Netherlands, 2009.

[29] S. Tonelli and D. Pighin. New features for framenet - wordnet mapping. In *Proceedings of the Thirteenth Conference on Computational Natural Language Learning (CoNLL'09)*, Boulder, CO, USA, 2009.

Sampling-based multilingual alignment

Adrien Lardilleux Yves Lepage
GREYC, University of Caen Basse-Normandie, France
Firstname.Lastname@info.unicaen.fr

Abstract

We present a sub-sentential alignment method that extracts high quality multi-word alignments from sentence-aligned multilingual parallel corpora. Unlike other methods, it exploits low frequency terms, which makes it highly scalable. As it relies on alingual concepts, it can process any number of languages at once. Experiments have shown that it is competitive with state-of-the-art methods.

Keywords

Sub-sentential alignment, low frequency term, hapax, sampling.

1 Motivation

Sub-sentential alignment from parallel corpora covers a variety of applications, such as the constitution of lexical resources or machine translation.

The widely used IBM models [2] and their extensions, implemented in the open source tool Giza++ [14], constitute the standard. Many alternatives or improvements have been proposed in the past years. Most of them are based on statistics, *e.g.* [6, 12, 13, 17], other ones are non-statistical methods, *e.g.* [1, 5]. All of them mainly address the issue of *quality* of alignments, *i.e.*, getting as close to human judgment as possible, or making machine translation as efficient as possible. Yet quality is only one aspect of alignment. Other issues still deserve to be explored:

- Some applications require alignments in more than two languages. This is particularly true for multilingual lexicography. As sub-sentential alignment was introduced as a *bilingual* problem since its early stages, obtaining truly multilingual alignments (in at least three languages) always required pair-by-pair processing of languages [16]. But the quality of alignments is hindered when relying on "pivot" languages.

- Traditional statistical methods may not scale up, nor even scale *down* [1]. Despite the growing availability of resources for numerous languages, some will probably never reach a coverage that could make them usable in real applications. On the other hand, huge amounts of input, while known to produce better results, quickly turn out to be a plague in processing time.

- These models are generally complex. This makes them difficult to integrate in actual applications, unless some free tool is available.

We propose a different approach to sub-sentential alignment that solely relies on *low frequency terms*. While often neglected, they actually provide an elegant solution to the above-mentioned issues.

This paper is organized as follows. Section 2 gives an overview of the concepts of the proposed multilingual alignment technique. Section 3 describes the technique in more details. Section 4 addresses the issue of multilingual alignment scoring. Section 5 compares the method with state-of-the-art tools.

2 Rationale

2.1 From high to low frequencies

Intuitively, one naturally trusts high frequency words, because of their statistical significance. As a result, low frequency words are often neglected and discarded, *e.g.* by removing all words which frequency is below a given threshold.

A practical answer has been long known: increase the amount of input data. Doing so naturally increases all word frequencies, turning low frequency words into high frequency ones. However, new words are always introduced meanwhile, that bear low frequencies. This is a vicious circle!

If one could safely align low frequency terms instead of focusing on high frequency ones, one would not need to indefinitely increase the amount of input data. Instead, *removing* input data would do the job, by turning high frequency words into low frequency ones. This would inherently lead to less processing, less resources required, and simpler mechanisms.

2.2 *Hapax legomena*

Amongst low frequency terms, *hapax legomena* (hapaxes for short), *i.e.*, words that appear only once in a corpus, are certainly those that show the greatest potential. While usually discarded, we have shown that they can be safely aligned [10]. Indeed, given a sentence-aligned parallel corpus in multiple languages, *sequences of hapaxes* contained in a particular sentence in all languages can be safely assumed to be lexical equivalences. Note that any number of languages can be processed simultaneously with this principle.

It is worth reminding that hapaxes typically represent 50% of the total vocabulary of a text [10]. As they are massively present, they can serve as the basis for the design of a sub-sentential alignment method.

Another advantage of hapaxes is that they are *unambiguous* in their corpus. Because they occur only once, they only have one possible meaning within this

International Conference RANLP 2009 - Borovets, Bulgaria, pages 214–218

corpus. In other words, high frequency words can be naturally disambiguated — temporarily — by the simple means of removing data.

2.3 Bringing together low and high frequencies

Starting from the previous remarks, one could design a sub-sentential alignment method that consists in removing input data until some term to be aligned become a corpus hapax. By filtering input sentences so that this term be the only hapax in a particular sentence, hapaxes of the corresponding sentences in other languages would be expected to be its translations.

While some experiments have shown that this principle already delivers promising results, it simply lacks the ability to align very high frequency terms like periods, which appear in almost all sentences of a corpus. The only way to make a period become a hapax is to cut the corpus down to one sentence only. However, all words on this sentence would become hapaxes as well, which prevents them from being aligned separately.

This problem can easily be tackled by noticing that alignments of hapaxes are just a particular case of what we shall refer to as "perfect alignments," *i.e.*, sequences of words that strictly appear in the same sentences. An example is shown in Fig. 1. Most of these alignments are alignments of hapaxes [10], but they also include high frequency terms. Again, this is not restricted to language pairs: any number of languages can be processed simultaneously.

3 The method

We now describe the process by which alignments can be extracted from parallel corpora in multiple languages simultaneously. A free implementation is available at:

`http://users.info.unicaen.fr/~alardill/anymalign/`

3.1 Introducing *alingual* corpora

As stated previously, one of the main advantage of the method is that it can align any number of languages simultaneously. Fig. 1 shows examples in three languages. More languages could be added with absolutely no change. More surprising, the principle still holds with a *monolingual* corpus. Indeed, the simple process of searching words that strictly appear on the same lines (assuming one sentence per line) can be applied to a single language. What we obtain then is just some particular case of collocations. Doing so in multiple languages simultaneously is thus tantamount to extract "multilingual collocations."

Therefore, the whole alignment process can heavily be simplified by assimilating a multilingual input corpus to a monolingual one. This is done by discriminating all surface forms according to the language they come from: words with identical surface forms from different languages are considered to be different. Boundaries between languages are removed, and recovered after the alignment process, based on the origin of words.

Such a corpus is a view over multiple languages, and does not involve any language-dependent concept. We thus refer to it as an *alingual* corpus. It is the entry point of all subsequent processing. An example of alingual corpus is shown in Fig. 2.

3.2 Sampling input data

The core of the method consists in removing data from the input to decrease word counts. This process makes new "perfect alignments" appear, most of them being hapaxes. More precisely, numerous subcorpora are forged from which alignments are extracted.

We set on a sampling-based approach. In addition to be straightforward, this approach appears to be the most accurate because the natural distribution of words in the alingual corpus is left untouched. Because of its randomness, the complete coverage of input data cannot be ensured. This issue is easily tackled by extracting alignments from numerous random subcorpora of various sizes. Handling a large number of subcorpora is no problem since processing a subcorpus is fast. In addition, since all subcorpora are independent, parallel processing is possible.

Biasing the sampling

We note x the number of subcorpora of size k to be processed. We define it as follows: it must ensure that the probability that none of the sentences from a subcorpus of length k is ever chosen is below a certain threshold t, an indicator of the coverage of the input corpus. The lower t is, the better the coverage.

With n the size of the (alingual) input corpus ($1 \leq k \leq n$):

- the probability that a particular sentence is chosen is k/n;
- the probability that this sentence is not chosen is $1 - k/n$;
- the probability that none of the k sentences is chosen is $(1 - k/n)^k$;
- the probability that none of these k sentences is ever chosen is $(1 - k/n)^{kx}$.

Hence, the number of random subcorpora of size k to forge by sampling is defined by $(1 - k/n)^{kx} \leq t$, which yields:

$$x \geq \frac{\log t}{k \log (1 - k/n)}$$

Processing at least x random subcorpora of size k will thus ensure a proper coverage of the input corpus.

However, rather than setting in advance some particular degree of coverage (hence imposing a fixed number of subcorpora to process), we deduce from the above result a probability distribution to randomly draw the sizes of the subcorpora to process:

$$\mathrm{p}(k) = \frac{-1}{k \log (1 - k/n)} \qquad \text{(to be normalized)}$$

The numerator ($\log t$) was substituted for -1 because t is a constant: $t \leq 1 \Rightarrow \log t \leq 0$. This distribution highly favors small subcorpora. Experiments have shown that they provide more accurate and more numerous alignments than large subcorpora, in addition to be much faster to process [11].

Input corpus:

	English		French		German
1	One coffee , please .	↔	Un café , s'il vous plaît .	↔	Einen Kaffee , bitte .
2	This coffee is not bad .	↔	Ce café est correct .	↔	Dieser Kaffee ist nicht schlecht .
3	One strong tea .	↔	Un thé fort .	↔	Einen starken Tee .

⇓

"Perfect alignments:"

The words:					appear on lines:
One	↔	Un	↔	Einen	1 3
coffee	↔	café	↔	Kaffee	1 2
, please	↔	, s'il vous plaît	↔	, bitte	1
.	↔	.	↔	.	1 2 3
This is not bad	↔	Ce est correct	↔	Dieser ist nicht schlecht	2
strong tea	↔	thé fort	↔	starken Tee	3

Fig. 1: *Extracting "perfect alignments" from a toy parallel corpus in English, French, and German. Each line in the input corpus is a triple of aligned sentences. Sequences of words that strictly appear on the same lines are expected to be translations of each other.*

1	One$_1$ coffee$_1$,$_1$ please$_1$.$_1$ Un$_2$ café$_2$,$_2$ s'il$_2$ vous$_2$ plaît$_2$.$_2$ Einen$_3$ Kaffee$_3$,$_3$ bitte$_3$.$_3$
2	This$_1$ coffee$_1$ is$_1$ not$_1$ bad$_1$.$_1$ Ce$_2$ café$_2$ est$_2$ correct$_2$.$_2$ Dieser$_3$ Kaffee$_3$ ist$_3$ nicht$_3$ schlecht$_3$.$_3$
3	One$_1$ strong$_1$ tea$_1$.$_1$ Un$_2$ thé$_2$ fort$_2$.$_2$ Einen$_3$ starken$_3$ Tee$_3$.$_3$

Fig. 2: *Assimilating a multilingual corpus to a monolingual one (same corpus as the one presented in Fig. 1, but words have been discriminated with subscripts: 1 for English, 2 for French, and 3 for German).*

3.3 Extracting alignments

To extract "perfect alignments" from all subcorpora obtained by sampling, the same process as depicted in Fig. 1 is applied, except that it runs on alingual sentences (see Fig. 2). In addition, since we can safely assume that "perfect alignments" yield good translations, the remaining parts of the sentences they appear on are likely to be translations of each other as well [3].

In other words, each "perfect alignment" yields up to two multilingual alignments per line:

1. the sequence of words that consists of the "perfect alignment" itself, preserving word order from the sentence;
2. the complementary of this sequence on the line (*i.e.*, its context), ordered as well.

Fig. 3 illustrates the process. Any alignment may be obtained a plurality of times, from different subcorpora and different lines. The result is a list of alignments along with the number of times they have been obtained.

In the general case, the method outputs non-contiguous sequences of words. They can subsequently be filtered according to specific criteria, like word contiguity, number of languages covered, or the number of words in a given language.

4 Scoring alignments

We propose two ways to score multilingual alignments by generalizing two well-known bilingual scoring techniques to the case of multilingual contexts.

4.1 Translation probabilities

Translation probabilities reflect the probability that some monolingual sequence of words of a multilingual alignment translates into the sequences of words in the remaining languages. We use the principle proposed in [9] to compute phrase translation probabilities, except that we generalize it to multilingual contexts: since there is no "source" and "target" languages in our multilingual alignments, each language becomes the "source" in turn, and *all* remaining languages together become a single "target" one.

In other words, assuming an input corpus in L languages, a score is computed for each language i ($1 \leq i \leq L$). It is the probability that the sequence of words s_i generates the rest of the alignment. It is computed by dividing the count of the current multilingual alignment, $C(s_1, \ldots, s_L)$, by the sum of the counts of all alignments in which s_i appears, $C(s_i)$:

$$P(s_1, \ldots, s_{i-1}, s_{i+1}, \ldots, s_L | s_i) = \frac{C(s_1, \ldots, s_L)}{C(s_i)}$$

Table 1 gives an example of actual data in three languages: each alignment is assigned three scores.

In the case of bilingual alignment, these scores directly correspond to the traditional pair $P(source|target)$ and $P(target|source)$. If the input data is monolingual, the score is always $C(s_1)/C(s_1) = 1$.

4.2 Lexical weights

Lexical weights were proposed in [9] to validate the quality of alignments. Given a bilingual alignment to score, it consists in checking how well each source word translates into the target words it links to. When a source word links to multiple target words, the average of their translation probabilities is used. A source-to-target lexical weight is then the product of all scores. The same holds from target to source, and the result is a pair of lexical weights between 0 and 1. We adapt this technique with three major changes.

First, since there is no source and target languages in multilingual alignments, we use the same principle as previously: each language becomes the source in turn, and the rest of the alignment is assimilated to the target. We end up with as many lexical weights per alignment as there are input languages.

Input corpus: see Fig. 2

⇓

Extract "perfect alignments" and their contexts:

The words:	appear on lines:	from which we extract:
One$_1$ Un$_2$ Einen$_3$	1	One$_1$ Un$_2$ Einen$_3$ coffee$_1$,$_1$ please$_1$.$_1$ café$_2$,$_2$ s'il$_2$ vous$_2$ plaît$_2$.$_2$ Kaffee$_3$,$_3$ bitte$_3$.$_3$
	3	One$_1$ Un$_2$ Einen$_3$ strong$_1$ tea$_1$.$_1$ thé$_2$ fort$_2$.$_2$ starken$_3$ Tee$_3$.$_3$
coffee$_1$ café$_2$ Kaffee$_3$	1	coffee$_1$ café$_2$ Kaffee$_3$ One$_1$ _ ,$_1$ please$_1$.$_1$ Un$_2$ _ ,$_2$ s'il$_2$ vous$_2$ plaît$_2$.$_2$ Einen$_3$ _ ,$_3$ bitte$_3$.$_3$
	2	coffee$_1$ café$_2$ Kaffee$_3$ This$_1$ _ is$_1$ not$_1$ bad$_1$.$_1$ Ce$_2$ _ est$_2$ correct$_2$.$_2$ Dieser$_3$ _ ist$_3$ nicht$_3$ schlecht$_3$.$_3$
⋮	⋮	⋮

⇓

Collect alignments, count them, and restore boundaries between languages:

English		French		German	Count
One	↔	Un	↔	Einen	2
coffee , please .	↔	café , s'il vous plaît .	↔	Kaffee , bitte .	1
strong tea .	↔	thé fort .	↔	starken Tee .	1
coffee	↔	café	↔	Kaffee$_3$	2
One _ , please .	↔	Un _ , s'il vous plaît .	↔	Einen _ , bitte .	1
This _ is not bad .	↔	Ce _ est correct .	↔	Dieser _ ist nicht schlecht .	1
		⋮			⋮

Fig. 3: *Extracting multilingual alignments from an alingual corpus. Underscores (_) mark discontinuities within one language.*

English (e)		French (f)		German (g)	Count	Translation probabilities $P(f,g\|e)$	$P(e,g\|f)$	$P(e,f\|g)$	Lexical weights $W(f,g\|e)$	$W(e,g\|f)$	$W(e,f\|g)$
loud applause	↔	vifs applaudissements	↔	lebhafter beifall	122	0.730	0.760	0.826	0.936	0.995	0.990
loud applause	↔	vifs applaudissements	↔	starker beifall	24	0.144	0.143	0.820	0.936	0.995	0.895
loud applause	↔	vifs applaudissements	↔	(lebhafter beifall)	12	0.072	0.092	0.667	0.936	0.995	0.060
loud applause	↔	applaudissements prolongés	↔	lebhafter beifall	8	0.048	0.167	0.048	0.916	0.995	0.990
loud applause	↔		↔	beifall	1	0.006	0.000	0.006	0.836	1.000	0.991

Table 1: *Alignments of the English word sequence "loud applause" obtained from a sample of the Europarl corpus [7], along with their associated scores.*

Second, as we start without any word-to-word alignment, we estimate a simple lexical translation probability distribution D based on relative word frequencies from the input corpus:

$$D(w_j|w_i) = \frac{C(w_i, w_j)}{C(w_i)}$$

where w_i is a word in language i and w_j is a word in language j $(i \neq j)$.

Lastly, the sampling-based approach does not *link* words, as would statistical models do. For example, in the first alignment of Table 1, one would expect English "loud" to link to French "vifs," and "applause" to "applaudissements." Our method does not permit this; instead, the complete phrase "loud applause" is considered to be a translation of the phrase "vifs applaudissements" as a whole. Therefore, where [9] computed the *average* of relative word frequencies for those words that link together, we actually compute the *maximum* of relative word frequencies for *all* possible links, *i.e.*, from all "source" words to all "target" words.

Formally, within an alignment, we look for the best possible translation of a word w_i from sequence s_i (in language i) amongst all words in other languages, according to distribution D, and retain this probability. The lexical weight for language i is the product of all probabilities retained, after determining the best translation for each word in s_i:

$$W(s_1, \ldots, s_{i-1}, s_{i+1}, \ldots, s_L|s_i) = \prod_{w_i \in s_i} \max_{w_j \in \bigcup_{i \neq j} s_j} D(w_j|w_i)$$

5 Evaluation

We evaluate the method by comparing the output of the Moses statistical machine translation decoder [8] using its default phrase tables (refined alignments from Giza++ [14]), against those produced by our method. We present results on two tasks: the IWSLT07 Japanese to English classical task [4], and a Spanish to French task using the Europarl corpus [7].

For each task, a standard Giza++ training is run using the default set of options, and processing time is

System	BLEU score	Entries in phrase table	Input corpus coverage
Giza++ ($t = 404s$)	0.45	141,338	69%
Our system ($t/2$)	0.42	241,810	89%
+ lexical weights	0.44		
Our system (t)	0.42	324,213	89%
+ lexical weights	0.45		
Our system ($t \times 2$)	0.42	**420,391**	**90%**
+ lexical weights	**0.46**		

Table 2: *Evaluation results on the IWSLT07 Japanese to English machine translation task. The input corpus consists in roughly 40,000 aligned sentences (average sentence length: 10 words).*

System	BLEU score	Entries in phrase table	Input corpus coverage
Giza++ ($t = 27,791s$)	**0.32**	**9,614,327**	67%
Our system ($t/2$)	0.29	1,393,278	85%
+ lexical weights	0.30		
Our system (t)	0.30	1,953,576	85%
+ lexical weights	0.31		
Our system ($t \times 2$)	0.30	2,690,782	**86%**
+ lexical weights	0.31		

Table 3: *Evaluation results on a Spanish to French machine translation task. The input corpus consists in roughly 200,000 aligned sentences (average sentence length: 31 words).*

measured. This time serves as a reference for our system, which can be stopped at any time. Three runs are performed: the first one is stopped after half of the reference time has elapsed, the second takes the same amount of time as the reference time, and the last one takes twice as long. All phrase tables have the five same features (two translation probabilities, two lexical weights, and length penalty). We systematically measure the contribution of lexical weights by removing them from the phrase tables and performing an additional run with the decoder.

Results are presented in Tables 2 and 3. We use BLEU [15] to measure translation quality. As for the Japanese to English task, the best results are obtained by running our system twice as long as the standard Giza++ training. Lexical weights give a significant performance boost. This is certainly due to the fact that our phrase tables contain noise (hence their size), that lexical weights help reduce. For example, on the third line of Table 1, the last score is very low because of the presence of brackets in the alignment.

This performance hint is not as visible on the Spanish to French task, because our phrase tables are much smaller than Moses' default. We still could come very close to Giza++'s quality.

Note that in a sample-based approach, quality is not a matter of time; coverage is: the method consists in continuously outputting "perfect alignments" and their contexts from various samples of the input corpus. The time, subcorpus, and sentence they have been extracted from do not matter: all alignments are on an equal footing from the quality point of view. The randomness of this process requires numerous subcorpora to be forged to ensure a proper coverage. However, Tables 2 and 3 show that the coverage of our phrase tables is always much higher than that obtained with Giza++, even within less time ($t/2$) or when the phrase table is smaller.

6 Conclusion

We described a complete alignment method, which allows multiple languages to be aligned simultaneously from parallel corpora. It solely relies on the use of low frequency terms. It makes it highly flexible regarding the amount of input data. The sample-based approach allows the user to interrupt the alignment process at any time and still produce high quality translation tables. Experiments show that it can match the accuracy of Giza++, while exhibiting a much higher coverage of input data, and being by far simpler.

References

[1] T. Andriamanankasina, K. Araki, and K. Tochinai. Sub-sentential alignment method by analogy. In *Proceedings of PACLIC 13*, pages 277–284, Taiwan, 1999.

[2] P. Brown, S. D. Pietra, V. D. Pietra, and R. Mercer. The mathematics of statistical machine translation: Parameter estimation. *Computational Linguistics*, 19(2):263–311, 1993.

[3] I. Cicekli. Similarities and differences. In *Proceedings of SCI2000*, pages 331–337, Orlando, FL, USA, 2000.

[4] C. S. Fordyce. Overview of the IWSLT 2007 evaluation campaign. In *Proceedings of IWSLT 2007*, pages 1–12, Trento, Italy, 2007.

[5] E. Giguet and P.-S. Luquet. Multilingual lexical database generation from parallel texts in 20 european languages with endogenous resources. In *Proceedings of COLING/ACL 2006*, pages 271–278, Sydney, Australia, 2006.

[6] D. Gildea. Loosely tree-based alignment for machine translation. In *Proceedings of ACL 2003*, pages 80–87, Sapporo, Japan, 2003.

[7] P. Koehn. Europarl: A parallel corpus for statistical machine translation. In *Proceedings of MT Summit X*, Phuket, Thailand, 2005.

[8] P. Koehn, H. Hoang, A. Birch, C. Callison-Burch, M. Federico, N. Bertoldi, B. Cowan, W. Shen, C. Moran, R. Zens, C. Dyer, O. Bojar, A. Constantin, and E. Herbst. Moses: Open source toolkit for statistical machine translation. In *Proceedings of ACL 2007*, Prague, Czech Republic, 2007.

[9] P. Koehn, F. J. Och, and D. Marcu. Statistical phrase-based translation. In *Proceedings of HLT-NAACL 2003*, volume 1, pages 48–54, Edmonton, Canada, 2003.

[10] A. Lardilleux and Y. Lepage. The contribution of the notion of hapax legomena to word alignment. In *Proceedings of LTC'07*, pages 458–462, Poznań, Polland, 2007.

[11] A. Lardilleux and Y. Lepage. A truly multilingual, high coverage, accurate, yet simple, sub-sentential alignment method. In *Proceedings of AMTA 2008*, pages 125–132, Waikiki, Hawai'i, USA, 2008.

[12] I. D. Melamed. Models of translational equivalence among words. *Computational Linguistics*, 26(2):221–249, 2000.

[13] R. Moore. Association-based bilingual word alignment. In *Proceedings of the ACL Workshop on Building and Using Parallel Texts*, pages 1–8, Ann Arbor, Michigan, USA, 2005.

[14] F. Och and H. Ney. A systematic comparison of various statistical alignment models. *Computational Linguistics*, 29:19–51, 2003.

[15] K. Papineni, S. Roukos, T. Ward, and W.-J. Zhu. Bleu: a method for automatic evaluation of machine translation. In *Proceedings of ACL 2002*, pages 311–318, Philadelphia, Pennsylvania, USA, 2002.

[16] M. Simard. Text-translation alignment: Three languages are better than two. In *Proceedings of EMNLP/VLC*, College Park, Maryland, USA, 1999.

[17] Y. Zhang and S. Vogel. An efficient phrase-to-phrase alignment model for arbitrarily long phrase and large corpora. In *Proceedings of EAMT-05*, Budapest, Hungary, 2005.

Using Semantic Networks to Identify Temporal Expressions from Semantic Roles

Hector Llorens, Borja Navarro, Estela Saquete
Natural Language Processing Research Group
University of Alicante, Spain
{*hllorens,borja,stela*}@*dlsi.ua.es*

Abstract

Nowadays, the temporal aspects of natural language are receiving a great research interest. TimeML has been adopted as a standard for temporal information annotation by a large number of researchers. Available TimeML resources are very limited in size and in diversity of languages. This paper analyzes a combination of semantic roles and semantic networks information for improving this situation. An automatic approach using semantic networks to convert temporal semantic roles into TimeML TIMEX3 elements is presented. This approach has been quantitatively evaluated for English and Spanish. The results point out that the presented approach can help in a semi-automatic creation of TimeML resources for the evaluated languages and could be also valid for other European languages.

Keywords

TimeML, TimeBank, TE identification, Semantic Roles

1 Introduction

In recent years, the research interest on automatic treatment of temporal information of natural language (NL) text has experienced an important growth [8]. One of the main reasons for that are the benefits that temporal information brings to Question answering (QA), summarization and many other natural language processing (NLP) areas [17]. Specialized workshops and conferences [12, 15], and evaluation forums [20, 21] reflect the importance of this field. Furthermore, the development of language independent systems has become an important issue among NLP community. This has been reflected in many conferences such as CLEF[1], as well as in works specific to Temporal Expression (TE) recognition field [24, 10]. In this paper, we present an approach to temporal expression identification from a multilingual point of view.

There are different ways to represent temporal information in NL. One of them is TimeML [13], which has been recently adopted as *de facto* standard annotation scheme by a large number of researchers [17].

A different way to represent time is defined in Semantic role labeling (SRL). SRL consists of determining basic event structures in a sentence, detecting semantic relations among entities and events. The temporal information of the events is represented by the temporal semantic role. SRL field has achieved important results in the last years [5].

Currently, the major problem of TimeML lies on the lack of resources, specially the lack of corpora for languages other than English. Specifically, this work is focused on the benefits that available semantic networks and semantic roles corpora can introduce to TE identification. To achieve the proposed objective, we present an automatic system that identifies TimeML TEs from semantic roles using semantic networks as validation method. Furthermore, this system is designed to handle the task multilingually, provided that there are semantic networks and semantic roles resources available for the target language. To measure the performance and the possibilities of the presented proposal, an evaluation for English and Spanish is carried out, as well as an in-depth analysis of the results.

The paper is structured as follows: Section 2 focuses on the background of temporal information processing and SRL fields and Section 3 provides detailed information about our proposal to obtain TimeML TEs from semantic roles and semantic networks. Section 4 includes the evaluation and error analysis and, finally, conclusions and further work lines are presented.

2 Background

The importance of temporal aspects of NL is not a new issue in artificial intelligence (AI) [1]. Several efforts have been done in order to define standard ways to represent temporal information in NL. Since temporal information extraction was included in Message Understanding Conference context, there have been three important annotation schemes for temporal information: STAG [18], TIDES [4] and TimeML [13]. TimeML is a rich specification language for events and TEs in NL that combines and extends features of both preceding schemes. It was designed to address time stamping, ordering and reasoning about TEs and events of NL. Fig. 1 illustrates an example annotation. In the example, "*came*" (EVENT) represents an event which is linked to the temporal expression "*Monday*" (TIMEX3) through a temporal link (TLINK), in which the temporal signal "*on*" (SIGNAL) is involved.

An English corpus illustrating TimeML annotation, TimeBank [14], was created together with the first version of this annotation scheme. The last version of the corpus, TimeBank 1.2, is considered a gold standard and has been published by Linguistic Data Consor-

[1] European Cross-Language Evaluation Forum

International Conference RANLP 2009 - Borovets, Bulgaria, pages 219–224

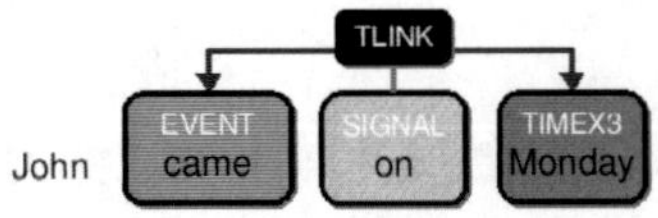

Fig. 1: *TimeML example*

tium. An in-depth analysis of TimeBank corpus can be found in [2]. Unfortunately, there are not TimeML corpora available for other languages like Spanish.

There have been different works on developing systems for automatically tagging NL text following TIMEX3 specifications. On the one hand, the work of Boguraev and Ando [2] presents an evaluation on automatic TimeML annotation over TimeBank using machine learning techniques. The results for TIMEX3 recognition using 5-fold cross validation were 89.6% and 81.7% $F_{\beta=1}$ for relaxed and strict span. On the other hand, TTK [22] accomplishes this task using the GUTime module. TTK has not been evaluated for TIMEX3. However, it was benchmarked on training data from TERN 2004 [20] at 85% and 78% $F_{\beta=1}$ for TIMEX2 relaxed and strict span respectively.

As introduced in previous section, another way of representing temporal information in NL texts, is through semantic roles. They represent temporality from a different perspective. Essentially, Semantic role labeling consists of determining basic event structures in a sentence, detecting semantic relations among entities and events. The temporal semantic role (TSR) represents "*when*" an event takes place. Fig. 2 illustrates how semantic roles represent temporal information through the temporal semantic role.

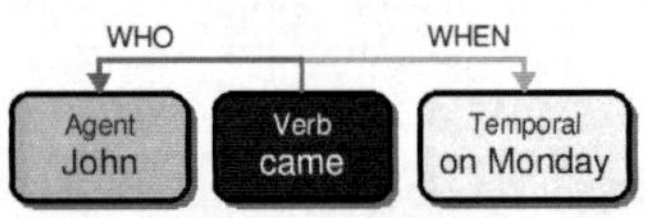

Fig. 2: *Semantic roles example*

Only one reference about using semantic roles for temporal information processing has been found in literature [6]. That work used them as complementary information to identify temporal relations.

Semantic networks have been used in many NLP fields for different purposes. WordNet [3] and EuroWordNet [23] represent the most used semantic networks for English and European languages respectively. Specifically, in temporal expression identification task, semantic networks have been used in the following works: Negri et al. [11] used WordNet to create a list of temporal named entities such as Bastille Day, Hanukkah, etc., by collecting all hyponyms tree of "*calendar_day*" synset. Also, in [16], semantic networks where used to expand a list of temporal triggers by adding all the synonyms. These works show that the information contained in semantic networks can be useful for temporal information extraction task.

3 Proposal

In order to study the benefits that semantic networks and semantic roles can introduce to temporal expressions identification task, this section presents an automatic system that identifies TimeML TEs using such resources. Two versions are described, firstly, TIPSem, which uses morphosyntactic information to transform temporal semantic role (TSR) into TIMEX3 element, and secondly, TIPSem+WN, which uses semantic networks to validate TIMEX3 elements identified by TIPSem system.

3.1 TIPSem

Temporal role is not defined exactly as a TIMEX3. A TSR represents a complete semantic predicate with a temporal function. However, the full extent of a TIMEX3 tag must correspond to one of the following categories: noun phrase ("*yesterday*" NP), adjective phrase ("*3-day*" ADJP) or adverbial phrase ("*3 days ago*" ADVP). As shown in example 1, both representations are not equivalent.

(1) She was born [in 1999 TSR]
She was born in <TIMEX3>1999</TIMEX3>

TIPSem (Temporal Information Processing based on Semantic roles) implements the following set of transformation rules from TSR to TIMEX3 solving the main differences between them.

1. **Removing TSR overlapping**: Due to the fact that each verb has its own roles, it is possible to find overlapped TSRs. In such cases, TIPSem system keeps only the TSR representing the minimum syntactic unit (NP, ADJP or ADVP).

2. **Removing subordination of TSR**: If a TSR corresponds to a subordination clause it does not correspond to a TIMEX3. The system detects and removes it using the syntactic tree.

3. **Splitting TSR**: A TSR composed of more than one NP can contain a set of related TIMEX3, linked by a temporal preposition or a coordination conjunction. There are two exceptions for this rule. Times "*[ten minutes to four]*", where the "*to*" preposition is denoting an specification relation, and the preposition "*of*" ("*the end of 1999*"), which is usually part of the expression. Our system looks for prepositions or coordination conjunctions in every TSR containing more than one NP. If they are found and do not represent an exception, the TSR is split in n TIMEX3 corresponding to each NP.

4. **TSR syntactic reduction**: As described above, a TSR generally differs from a TIMEX3 on its boundaries. If a TSR has any element out of the minimum syntactic unit (NP, ADJP or ADVP), this element is not included as part of the TIMEX3. The most common cases are the ones in which the TSR consists of a prepositional phrase

(PP). This PP normally contains some preposition (before, at, etc.) or a combination adverb-preposition (later in, ahead of, etc.) followed by an NP which represents the TIMEX3 element.

5. **Tagging resulting TSR as TIMEX3**: Finally, after the application of all the previous rules, resulting TSR are directly tagged as TIMEX3.

Furthermore, due to the fact that SRL relies on verbs, nominal sentences can not be labeled. These sentences are commonly found in titles, brackets, notes, etc. Hence, as a post-processing step, a TE tagger capable of identifying basic explicit TEs (only times and dates) is executed for these sentences.

3.2 TIPSem+WN

There are cases in which TSR does not contain a TIMEX3. These cases represent one of the main problems of the TIPSem approach. Example 2 illustrates the problem showing a sentence annotated with the TSR, the correct TIMEX3 annotation and the incorrect TIMEX3 annotation obtained by TIPSem.

(2) **TSR**: She ate [before the meeting TSR]
Correct TIMEX3: She ate before the meeting
Incorrect TIMEX3 (TIPSem):
She ate before <TIMEX3>the meeting</TIMEX3>

As shown in the example 2, "*the meeting*" is incorrectly tagged as TIMEX3 by TIPSem approach. In this case the temporal information provided by the TSR corresponds to a TimeML EVENT instead. The difficulty arises on how to differentiate this kind of events from real TEs. The following example illustrates the reasons why this is not an easy issue.

(3) (S(NP (PRP She))(VP (VBD ate)
(PP (IN before)(NP (DT the) (NN night)))))

(S(NP (PRP She))(VP (VBD ate)
(PP (IN before)(NP (DT the) (NN meeting)))))

In example 3, "*before the night*" and "*before the meeting*" are represented by a TSR at semantic roles level, and are identical at morphosyntactic level. However, "*the night*" corresponds to a TIMEX3, but not "*the meeting*". In this manner, it is not trivial to distinguish between them using only morphosyntactic and semantic roles information.

One possible solution would be to manually encode a list of temporal triggers. This solution is costly and language dependent. For that reason, we propose an automatic multilingual solution to problem using the multilingual temporal information encoded in different languages semantic networks such as WordNet [3], EuroWordNet [23]. A list of different languages "*WordNets*" can be found at Global WordNet site[2].

For each word sense (synset), semantic networks bring, among other things, the complete hypernyms hierarchy. Our hypothesis is that all words related to time should have a general time concept among their hypernyms. Example 4 shows two words related to a general time concept.

(4) hour (hypernyms hierarchy)
=> **time_unit** => measure => abstraction => entity

Monday (hypernyms hierarchy)
=> day_of_the_week => calendar_day => **time_period**
=> measure => abstraction => entity

The unique exception we include in this hypothesis are purely numeric dates and times such as "*1999, 12-12-2001 and 18:25*".

Taking this hypothesis into consideration, we define a TE validation algorithm based on semantic networks. It is defined as follows:

- A TSR is validated to be a TIMEX3 if at least one of its words has a hypernym that matches a general temporal concept or a numeric date/time.
- To handle polysemous words, the word part-of-speech (PoS) is used to query the semantic networks. If the word has different senses with the same PoS, if at least one of them is related to a time concept the system validates it, because if the word is contained by a temporal role, this is probably the correct sense.
- The algorithm also searches for multiword expressions to handle compound temporal concepts like "*Corpus Christi*" and "*Saint Joseph*".

The described algorithm has been implemented for English and Spanish. WordNet has been used for English, taking as general time concepts: *time_period*, *time_unit* and *time*. EuroWordNet has been used for Spanish, taking as general time concepts the same as in English: *periodo*, *unidad_de_tiempo* and *tiempo*[3]. Fig. 3 illustrates the TIPSem+WN system architecture.

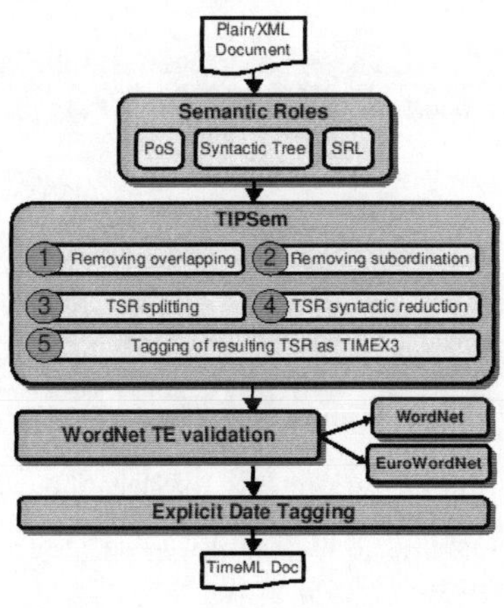

Fig. 3: *TIPSem+WN Architecture*

[2] http://www.globalwordnet.org/

[3] time_period, time_unit and time

4 Evaluation

The objective of the evaluation is to provide a quantitative study on how well does TIPSem and TIPSem+WN approaches perform in TIMEX3 identification task and which are the effects of the usage of semantic networks. It covers English and Spanish, and also includes a Baseline implementation, that tags every TSR as TIMEX3, to measure how accurate are temporal roles by their own on representing TIMEX3.

4.1 Evaluation Environment

4.1.1 Corpora

The presented approaches have been evaluated using TimeBank 1.2 corpus [14] for English, and a manually annotated sample of AnCora [19, 9] for Spanish.

- **English (TimeBank)**: TimeBank 1.2 consists of 183 news articles tagged following the TimeML 1.2.1 specification. For this evaluation, this corpus has been automatically annotated using the SRL tool developed by University of Illinois CCG group [7], which uses PropBank role set. This tool obtained a 77.44% $F_{\beta=1}$ in TSR (AM-TMP PropBank role) labeling in CoNLL 2005.

- **Spanish (AnCora TimeML Sample)**: Due to the lack of TimeML corpus for Spanish, we have developed a Spanish TimeML TIMEX3 corpus sample annotating manually 30 docs of AnCora. AnCora is the largest corpus annotated at different linguistic levels in Spanish and Catalan. It consists of 500K words in each language, mainly taken from newspaper texts. The corpus is annotated and manually reviewed at: morphological level, syntactic level, and semantic level.

Both corpora statistics are shown in Table 1. In the table, the *in TEXT* value indicates the TIMEX3 tags found in corpus text (between *TEXT* tags), ignoring explicit dates in documents headers.

Corpus	docs	words	TIMEX3 (in TEXT)
TimeBank	183	61.8K	1414 (1228)
AnCora Sample	30	7.3K	155 (125)

Table 1: *Corpora statistics*

4.1.2 Criteria

The presented approaches have been tested in TE identification within the previously described corpora and the results have been compared to the original TIMEX3 annotation. The explicit dates of document headers have been ignored to make a more reliable test. We applied the criteria used in TERN-2004. The measures, inherited from it, are:

- **ACT**: TIMEX3 tags returned by the system.
- Correct (**corr**): Correct instances
- Incorrect (**inco**): Wrongly bounded instances
- Missing (**miss**): Not detected instances
- Spurious (**spur**): False positives
- Precision (**prec**): corr/ACT
- Recall (**rec**): corr/POS
- $\mathbf{F}_{\beta=1}$: (2*prec*rec)/(prec+rec)

An adaptation to TIMEX3 of the TERN-2004 scorer[4] has been used to calculate these measures.

4.2 Results

Tables 2 and 3 show the obtained results for English and tables 4 and 5 the ones obtained for Spanish. For each system, span relaxed ***R*** and span strict ***S*** results are indicated. *S* refers to strict match of both boundaries of a TIMEX3 expression (exact extent) while *R* results consider as correct every tag including a TIMEX3 even if it is wrongly bounded.

System		ACT	corr	inco	miss	spur
Baseline	R	1410	764	0	464	646
	S	1410	368	396	464	646
TIPSem	R	1245	908	0	320	337
	S	1245	817	91	320	337
TIPSem+WN	R	1020	905	0	323	115
	S	1020	815	90	323	115

Table 2: *TIMEX3 results for English (1)*

System		prec %	rec %	$F_{\beta=1}$ %
Baseline	R	54.2	62.2	**57.9**
	S	26.1	30.0	**27.9**
TIPSem	R	72.9	73.9	**73.4**
	S	65.6	66.5	**66.1**
TIPSem+WN	R	88.7	73.7	**80.5**
	S	79.9	66.4	**72.5**

Table 3: *TIMEX3 results for English (2)*

For English, the Baseline obtains a 57.9% $F_{\beta=1}$ for R, but it falls to 27.9% for S. Nevertheless, TIPSem achieves a 66.1% $F_{\beta=1}$ for S, and TIPSem+WN outperforms the previous two obtaining a 72.5%.

System		ACT	corr	inco	miss	spur
Baseline	R	147	93	0	32	54
	S	147	44	49	32	54
TIPSem	R	144	108	0	17	36
	S	144	102	6	17	36
TIPSem+WN	R	114	107	0	18	7
	S	114	101	6	18	7

Table 4: *TIMEX3 results for Spanish (1)*

For Spanish, the Baseline obtains a 68.4% $F_{\beta=1}$ for R, but it falls to 32.4% for S. However, TIPSem achieves a 75.8% $F_{\beta=1}$ for S, and TIPSem+WN surpasses them obtaining an 84.5%.

Although both corpora consist of news articles and have a similar TE distribution, English and Spanish results are not strictly comparable due to the difference in size of the corpora. Thus, prior to analyzing the results obtained for different languages, we studied the comparability of the results. The English corpus is approximately 10 times greater in size than the Spanish corpus. For that reason, we created a TimeBank

[4] http://fofoca.mitre.org/tern.html#scorer

System		prec %	rec %	$F_{\beta=1}$ %
Baseline	R	63.3	74.4	**68.4**
	S	29.9	35.2	**32.4**
TIPSem	R	75.0	86.4	**80.3**
	S	70.8	81.6	**75.8**
TIPSem+WN	R	93.9	85.6	**89.5**
	S	88.6	80.8	**84.5**

Table 5: *TIMEX3 results for Spanish (2)*

normalized corpus dividing TimeBank corpus into 10 parts whose average statics are closer to the Spanish (18 docs, 6.1 K words, 140 TIMEX3 and 122 TIMEX3 in TEXT). The approaches have been evaluated over each part and the results have been averaged. The normalized corpus and the complete TimeBank corpus show same quality results with an average difference of 0.47% $F_{\beta=1}$. Therefore, the results can be compared taking into account these numbers. Fig. 4, illustrates the strict span $F_{\beta=1}$ results for the three presented approaches in both evaluated languages.

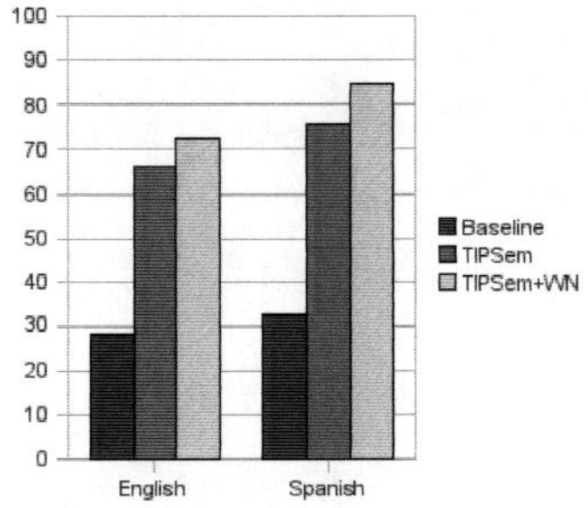

Fig. 4: *Strict span $F_{\beta=1}$ results comparison*

As shown in the Fig. 4, the results for both languages follow the same pattern and offer similar quality. The Spanish evaluation achieved better results than the English evaluation. This may be because contrary to English, Spanish SRL has been done manually in AnCora corpus.

Results show that, taking TSR as TIMEX3 without any post processing (Baseline), they are reasonably good in the span relaxed identification case, but not in the strict case. However, TIPSem approach obtains much higher results. It indicates that the transformation rules of TIPSem approach have resolved several differences between TSR and TIMEX3.

Focusing on the benefits that the usage of semantic networks introduced to TIPSem approach, we can observe that $F_{\beta=1}$ results have been increased in both languages. The improvement in strict span $F_{\beta=1}$ is a 9.68% for English and a 11.48% for Spanish. This fact indicates that the method defined in this paper accomplishes the objectives for which it was created. TIPSem+WN improves the TIPSem precision via reducing spurious errors produced by the problem described in section 3.2. Moreover, TIPSem+WM does not sacrifice the recall (-0.1% English S, -0.8% Spanish S), see next section (4.3) for details.

There are no strictly comparable results in the literature. Currently, there are no published results for TIMEX3 identification in Spanish. The closest evaluation is the one done by Boguraev and Ando [2] for English using TimeBank, which is described in section 2. Our approach obtains similar quality results specially in the case of Spanish which has been done over a corpus manually labeled with semantic roles.

4.3 Error analysis

The aim of this section is to show in which aspects is TIPSem+WN failing and analyze the error reduction introduced by semantic networks method.

- **Spurious** (8% EN / 6% ES): False positives have been reduced drastically by the application of the method based on semantic networks defined in this paper, which confirms that the proposed hypothesis is valid for this task. Specifically, it decreases TIPSem spurious errors from 27% to 8% for English and from 25% to 6% for Spanish.

  The few errors that remain spurious, apart from SRL errors, are indefinite TEs[5] (see example 5). The problem is that, although they are indeed TEs, they do not correspond to TIMEX3 elements following the TimeML specifications.

  (5) **EN**: in just a moment
  ES: en ese momento[6]

- **Missing** (27% EN / 14% ES): This problem appears because semantic roles not always cover all possibilities of TE in NL.

  - The major problem appear in nominal sentences, parenthesis, titles and, in general, all kinds of NL text where verbs are not present. Due to the fact that semantic roles are mainly related to verbs, and semantic networks method is only applied to TSR, TIPSem+WN is not applicable in these sentences (see example 6).

    (6) **EN**: The 1999 results
    ES: Tres años en Francia[7]

  - Also, cases in which a TE has no temporal function in the sentence (i.e., *Agent* role) but it is a TIMEX3 (see example 7). Semantic networks have not been applied to roles other than TSR, because the ambiguity would introduce noise, for example, in proper nouns like "*Doris Day*".

    (7) **EN**: [He A0][spent V][6 days A3]
    ES: [Estas semanas A0][fueron V][nefastas A1][8]

  - Very few correct TEs obtained by TIPSem have been missed by TIPSem+WN approach, which indicates that the used semantic networks are enough complete in temporal information relations to satisfy this task needs. Example 8 shows the unique cases.

[5] TEs with an indefinite temporal value (a moment, a while,...)
[6] at that time
[7] Three years in France
[8] These weeks were terrible

(8) **EN1**: nineteen seventy-nine
EN2: as soon as possible
EN3: second (adjective)
ES: el primer cuatrimestre[9]

– Minor problems are caused by SRL errors.

- **Incorrect** (6% EN / 5% ES): Span errors are mostly produced by SRL errors. For example, in "*[10 p.m]. [Wednesday]*" the error is produced because the last period of "*10 p.m.*" has been interpreted as a sentence separation mark.

5 Conclusions

This paper studied the application of semantic networks to the identification of temporal expressions from semantic roles following TimeML specifications. For this purpose, two approaches have been defined (1) TIPSem, which does not use semantic networks, and (2) TIPSem+WN using them. They both, together with a Baseline, have been evaluated in TIMEX3 identification for English and Spanish.

The TIPSem+WN approach obtained a 80.5% and 89.5% $F_{\beta=1}$ for English and Spanish respectively. This means a significant improvement over the Baseline, and an important improvement over TIPSem approach (S $F_{\beta=1}$: +9.68% English and +11.48% Spanish).

The results and errors analysis have confirmed that semantic networks usage produces a reduction of spurious values, but not an increment of missing ones. In this manner, the precision has been increased and the recall maintained, producing a final $F_{\beta=1}$ increase.

The results for both languages follow the same pattern and offer similar quality, facing equivalent error percentages and types. Hence, we can confirm that the approach is valid for English and Spanish. Due to the fact the presented approach is based on semantic roles and multilingual semantic networks information, it could be valid also for other European languages that share several features at this level.

The results lead us to propose potential applications as further work. On the one hand, taking into account that same quality results have been obtained for English and Spanish using the same approach, this study will be extended to other languages to confirm if the analyzed hypothesis could be considered multilingual. On the other hand, due to the lack of TimeML corpora, it will be analyzed if the presented study could be exploited as part of a semi-automatic process of building TimeML corpora for other languages.

Acknowledgments. This paper has been supported by the Spanish Government, project TIN-2006-15265-C06-01, where Llorens is funded (BES-2007-16256).

References

[1] J. F. Allen. Maintaining knowledge about temporal intervals. *Communications of ACM*, 26(11):832–843, 1983.

[2] B. Boguraev and R. K. Ando. Effective Use of TimeBank for TimeML Analysis. In F. Schilder, G. Katz, and J. Pustejovsky, editors, *Annotating, Extracting and Reasoning about Time and Events, International Seminar*, volume 4795 of *LNAI, LNCS*, pages 41–58. Springer, 2007.

[3] C. Fellbaum. *WordNet: An Electronic Lexical Database*. The MIT Press, May 1998.

[4] L. Ferro, L. Gerber, I. Mani, B. Sundheim, and G. Wilson. TIDES 2005 Standard for the Annotation of Temporal Expressions. Technical report, MITRE, 2005.

[5] D. Gildea and D. Jurafsky. Automatic labeling of semantic roles. *Computational Linguistics*, 28(3):245–288, 2002.

[6] C. Hagège and X. Tannier. XRCE-T: XIP temporal module for TempEval campaign. In *TempEval (SemEval)*, pages 492–495, Prague, Czech Republic, 2007. ACL.

[7] P. Koomen, V. Punyakanok, D. Roth, and W.-t. Yih. Generalized inference with multiple semantic role labeling systems (shared task paper). In *CoNLL-2004*, pages 181–184, 2005.

[8] I. Mani, J. Pustejovsky, and R. J. Gaizauskas, editors. *The Language of Time: A Reader*. Oxford University Press, 2005.

[9] M. A. Martí, M. Taulé, L. Márquez, and M. Bertran. Anotación semiautomática con papeles temáticos de los corpus CESS-ECE. In *Sociedad Española para el Procesamiento del Lenguaje Natural*, volume 38, 2007.

[10] T. Moia. Telling apart temporal locating adverbials and time-denoting expressions. In *Proceedings of the workshop on Temporal and Spatial information processing*, pages 1–8, NJ, USA, 2001. ACL.

[11] M. Negri and L. Marseglia. Recognition and Normalization of Time Expressions: ITC-irst at TERN 2004. Technical report, Information Society Technologies, 2004.

[12] J. Pustejovsky. TERQAS: Time and Event Recognition for Question Answering Systems. In *ARDA Workshop*, 2002.

[13] J. Pustejovsky, J. M. Castaño, R. Ingria, R. Saurí, R. J. Gaizauskas, A. Setzer, and G. Katz. TimeML: Robust Specification of Event and Temporal Expressions in Text. In *IWCS-5, 5th Int. Workshop on Computational Semantics*, 2003.

[14] J. Pustejovsky, P. Hanks, R. Saurí, A. See, R. J. Gaizauskas, A. Setzer, D. R. Radev, B. Sundheim, D. Day, L. Ferro, and M. Lazo. The TIMEBANK Corpus. In *Corpus Linguistics*, pages 647–656, 2003.

[15] J. Pustejovsky, I. Mani, Belanger, B. Boguraev, Knippen, Litman, Rumshisky, See, Symonen, and Guilder. ARDA summer workshop on graphical annotation toolkit for TimeML. Technical report, MITRE, 2003.

[16] E. Saquete, P. Martínez-Barco, and R. Muñoz. Automatic Multilinguality for Time Expression Resolution. In *MICAI*, volume 2972 of *LNCS*, pages 458–467, 2004.

[17] F. Schilder, G. Katz, and J. Pustejovsky. *Annotating, Extracting and Reasoning About Time and Events*, volume 4795 of *LNCS*. Springer, 2007.

[18] A. Setzer and R. Gaizauskas. Annotating Events and Temporal Information in Newswire Texts. In *LREC 2000*, pages 1287–1294, Athens, 2000.

[19] M. Taulé, M. A. Martí, and M. Recasens. AnCora: Multilevel Annotated Corpora for Catalan and Spanish. In ELRA, editor, *LREC*, Marrakech, Morocco, 2008.

[20] TERN-2004. Time Expression Recognition and Normalization Evaluation Workshop (http://fofoca.mitre.org/), 2004.

[21] M. Verhagen, R. J. Gaizauskas, M. Hepple, F. Schilder, G. Katz, and J. Pustejovsky. Semeval-2007 task 15: Tempeval temporal relation identification. In *Proceedings of the 4th International Workshop on Semantic Evaluations*, pages 75–80, Prague, 2007. ACL.

[22] M. Verhagen, I. Mani, R. Saurí, R. Knippen, S. B. Jang, J. Littman, A. Rumshisky, J. Phillips, and J. Pustejovsky. Automating temporal annotation with TARSQI. In *ACL*, pages 81–84, NJ, USA, 2005. ACL.

[23] P. Vossen, editor. *EuroWordNet: a multilingual database with lexical semantic networks*. Kluwer Academic Publishers, MA, USA, 1998.

[24] G. Wilson, I. Mani, B. Sundheim, and L. Ferro. A multilingual approach to annotating and extracting temporal information. In *Proceedings of the workshop on Temporal and Spatial information processing*, pages 1–7, NJ, USA, 2001. ACL.

[9] the first four-month period

The Design of an Experiment in Anaphora Resolution for Referring Expressions Generation

Diego Jesus de Lucena
University of São Paulo (USP/EACH)
Av. Arlindo Bettio, 1000
São Paulo, Brazil
diego.si@usp.br

Ivandré Paraboni
University of São Paulo (USP/EACH)
Av. Arlindo Bettio, 1000
São Paulo, Brazil
ivandre@usp.br

Abstract

We present a pilot experiment to measure the effects of redundancy in the resolution of definite descriptions as performed by a small number of human readers. Although originally intended to provide evidence of how much redundancy should ideally be included in generated anaphoric descriptions, preliminary findings reveal a number of little explored issues that are relevant to both referring expressions generation and interpretation.

Keywords
Referring expressions generation, Anaphora resolution.

1. Introduction

Human speakers routinely make use of redundant information when referring to world or discourse objects via definite descriptions, and they often do so even when the sole purpose of referring is the identification of the target object. By contrast, Natural Language Generation (NLG) systems usually implement referring expressions generation (REG) algorithms that are far less prepared to include redundant information in their output.

One possible reason for this difference between real language use and NLG output is the fact that generating redundancy without a proper reason comes with a price, namely, false logic implicatures in the sense defined by H. P. Grice [1]. For instance, in a context containing only one object of type 'door', a redundant (from the point of view of identification) reference to the colour attribute of the referent as in "please open the *red* door" may cause the hearer to consider whether there is any special reason for mentioning such 'unnecessary' information at all.

To avoid this sort of mishap, most REG algorithms to date (including one of the most influential works in the field, the Incremental algorithm in [2]) attempt to avoid the inclusion of any information not strictly necessary for the identification of the intended referent. Referring expressions produced in this way are suitably brief, but they may look unnaturally so. In extreme cases, certain instances of short descriptions may actually make the identification of the intended referent a daunting task. One such example is the case of *deictic* references in structurally-complex (e.g., spatial) domains. Deictic referents may be unidentifiable unless a certain amount of redundant information is added [3]. For example, a distinguishing description such as "the girl in white shoes" is not of much help if, say, the referred person is part of a large crowd. Redundancy in this case (e.g., "the girl in white shoes, *next to the elevator*") may facilitate the resolution of these expression (here understood as the task of interpreting the referring expression and identifying the intend referent.)

The implication of this for REG algorithms is that redundancy should be somehow taken into account at least when generating instances of *space deixis*, and this is precisely the kind of insight needed to design NLG systems that describe objects in physical contexts. For other kinds of application, however, this may be only a minor issue. This is the case, for example, of systems that generate textual reports or documents making intensive use of *anaphoric* referring expressions. In these cases, it is far less clear whether the same principle of 'redundancy as a means to help resolution' is applicable, and if not, what role redundancy should play at all.

In this work we investigate the effects of redundant information in anaphora resolution to gather evidence on how to generate more human-like anaphoric descriptions. More specifically, we designed a small pilot experiment to measure reader's search behaviour under a number of controlled situations of anaphora resolution. Preliminary findings suggest that some of the existing evidence on deixis may not hold for anaphora, and reveal a number of little explored issues that are relevant not only to REG, but to research on language interpretation as well.

2. Background

Probably the best-known REG algorithm to date is the Incremental algorithm in [2]. The input to the algorithm is a context set C containing a number of objects – a target object and its distractors – with their corresponding semantic properties (represented as attribute-value pairs as in 'colour-blue'), and the intended referent r to be described by means of a definite description. The goal of the algorithm is to compute a list of properties L such that L denotes the intended referent r and no other distractor in C. Redundancy in this case is merely a by-product of a more general strategy to cope with the computational complexity of the task: once an attribute is selected for inclusion in L, it can never be removed (and, crucially, not even if a subsequent addition makes this attribute redundant), which gives the name 'incremental to the approach.

In previous work [3] we describe an experiment to measure the effort involved in the resolution of deictic descriptions in spatial domains, whose results suggest that under certain circumstances the inclusion of logical redundancy may be necessary if the hearer is to identify

International Conference RANLP 2009 - Borovets, Bulgaria, pages 225–229

the intending referents at all. The findings in [3] however do not cover anaphora, and it is unclear whether they are still applicable to these cases. For a start, unlike space deictic expressions, anaphors do not normally convey location information to help find the antecedent term[1], e.g., in a context with only one object of the type 'cup', the redundancy in "the cup *on the table*" may facilitate search for the intended referent in a deictic situation, but less clearly so in an anaphoric context.

Secondly, anaphora resolution involves not only searching for the antecedent term in the text (as when searching for domain objects in space deixis) but also interpreting multiple candidate descriptions (including those of the competing discourse objects, or distractors, and the real antecedent term.) Descriptions of distractor objects may vary greatly in the number of attributes that they share with the referring expression, which may somehow have an impact on the overall resolution effort. For instance, given the antecedent term "the large white cat" and the anaphor "the white cat", the reader may come across distractors such as "the small cat", "the large black cat" and so on, each of them representing a particular obstacle to resolution.

Finally, the work in [3] does not distinguish between *discriminatory* and *non-discriminatory* redundancy, that is, it is not clear how redundant information impacts resolution when it may help ruling out distractors (e.g., the use of a redundant attribute 'white' in a context in which all distractors are black) or not (e.g., the same, in a context in which some of the distractors are also white.)

3. Experiment Design

We are interested in collecting evidence of how redundancy may affect anaphora resolution (i.e., the task of interpreting the referring expression and then identifying the antecedent term in the previous text), so that in the future this information could be taken into account in the development of more human-like REG algorithms. To this end, we designed an experiment in which subjects were instructed to identify anaphoric antecedents of descriptions conveying various degrees of redundancy in a number of documents in electronic format, while their navigation steps and resolution times were recorded with millisecond precision.

Subjects. 38 native speakers of Brazilian Portuguese.

Procedure. All subjects were shown 13 documents in electronic format in random order. Each document conveyed a short text in a randomly selected domain (e.g., cars, pets, books etc.) Each text was shown one paragraph at a time. Subjects were told to read each paragraph and scroll down to reveal the next one. Upon reaching the end of the text, an instruction of the kind 'Click on the expression that refers to a X in the text' was displayed, in which X was an unambiguous anaphoric expression. Although subjects most likely did not read the entire text, but simply skimmed through it to find each instruction at the end, the experiment setting forced them to browse the text in linear order from the beginning, and did not allow them to skip to the instructions. This was done to provide a general idea of the text topic and size.

After interpreting the given instruction and hitting a 'start' button at the end of each document, the subject was free to backtrack and locate the referred antecedent term in the previous text. Because the text was shown one paragraph at a time, the subject was forced to use the navigation (up / down) arrows to find the required information, which ensured incremental interpretation.

Each text conveyed a number of clickable elements representing the actual antecedent *a* and alternative candidates. To prevent subjects from trying to find the answer simply by looking for special formatting (e.g., hyperlinks), clickable elements were visible only when the mouse pointer was passed over them. Clicking on a wrong answer or going beyond the antecedent position would produce an error message and a new text to be randomly selected, that is, the experiment could only be finalized once the 13 correct answers were found[2].

After each correct answer the subject was directed to the next text, until the end of the experiment. The instruction conveying the referring expression was permanently shown at the bottom of the screen to remind the subjects of their task. All navigation steps and times were recorded during the entire resolution procedure, that is, from the moment that the 'start' button was hit until the correct answer was selected.

Redundancy. We would like to test whether adding logically redundant attributes (either discriminatory or not) to a referring expression may affect resolution times. Redundancy in this case is viewed as a combination of two factors: the number of redundant attributes conveyed by the referring expression and their discriminatory power. Starting from a basic expression conveying the referent type and a single discriminatory attribute (e.g., 'the black cat'), we will consider the addition of four degrees of redundancy: minimal descriptions or zero redundancy (0), one discriminatory attribute (+1), one non-discriminatory attribute (-1) and two attributes (2), in this case being one attribute discriminatory and the other not. Other attribute combinations were not considered for practical reasons[3].

Referential Context. Besides looking into situations of reference with various degrees of redundancy, we will also vary the degree of complexity of the context by making use of *distractors*, that is, discourse objects of the

[1] Unless we were to consider the special case of *textual anaphora* as "the first word in the above paragraph" [4].

[2] This allowed us also to filter out subjects that produced an overly large number of mistakes, and who may not have taken the experiment seriously.

[3] The degree of redundancy expressed by two simultaneous attributes seemed less relevant to our present investigation, and perhaps less common in language use as well.

same type as the antecedent a, and which are placed between the anaphoric expression and a, so that the reader is forced to take them into account during resolution. Contextual complexity will be modelled as the number of distractors found before the antecedent a, which may vary from zero to two (recall that the reader searches backwards from the referring expression.)

Of course another relevant factor in contextual complexity would be the degree of contrast of the distractor compared to a, that is, the number of attributes that the distractor shares with a. In our experiment setting this means that we should take into account two kinds of distractor: a less contrastive kind that we call *c1*, which differs from a by one attribute, and a more contrastive variety called *c2*, which differs from a by two attributes. For instance, a possible *c1* distractor for the referent of "large black cat" would be "large white cat", and a *c2* distractor would be "small white cat".

The issue of how many attributes are shared between distractor and antecedent terms may be an interesting one, but in order to avoid testing every referring expression in 6 different contexts (3 context sizes * 2 distractor types) we presently do not take distractor types into account, that is, we eliminate this possible effect by using a uniform distribution for individual *c1* and *c2* distractors, and also for the presentational order of (*c1*,*c2*) pairs. In practice this means that (depending on the random text selection used in each experiment) different subjects may come across more objects of type *c1* or *c2*. As we discuss later, this has no impact on our hypothesis testing regarding *c1* and *c2* objects since we will limit this investigation to the cases in which both appear simultaneously.

The four degrees of redundancy (0, +1, -1 and 2) and the three degrees of contextual complexity (0, 1 or 2 obstacles) give rise to 4 * 3 = 12 situations of reference to be examined, each of them corresponding to a statement in the experiment.

Table 1 – Research statements

#	Redundancy	Distractors
01	0	0
02	0	1
03	0	2
04	+1	0
05	+1	1
06	+1	2
07	-1	0
08	-1	1
09	-1	2
10	2	0
11	2	1
12	2	2

Research questions. Results in [3] suggest that adding redundant attributes to *deictic* descriptions in spatial domains (e.g., buildings divided into rooms etc.) may facilitate resolution. However, given that anaphora resolution involves interpreting multiple candidate descriptions and matching them to the anaphor term to decide which one is co-referential, our central hypothesis is that the effect of redundancy may in this case be *precisely the opposite*, that is: longer descriptions demand more time for the identification of discourse objects (i.e., the antecedent term and distractors.) But this is not to say that one should expect an increase in the overall resolution time when redundancy is included: unlike space deictic descriptions that use redundant information to *locate* the intended referent (e.g., "the cup *on the table*" in a context in which there is only one such cup), anaphora resolution is not generally facilitated in this way, and it is unlikely that finding an antecedent in the text will take any longer if we write e.g., "the cup on the table" instead of simply "the cup". For that reason, instead of looking into overall resolution times we will examine the identification times of individual discourse components, namely, the antecedent term a and *c1* and *c2* distractor objects.

We will use the notation *time(r, x)* to represent the average identification time spent in contexts conveying 0..2 distractors while examining the object x (which can be the antecedent a or a distractor *c1* or *c2*) given a description of redundancy degree r. All times are measured from the moment in which x is displayed on screen until the moment that a navigation action is performed (e.g., moving up or down in the text, or selecting x) in which presumably the antecedent or distractor has been identified as such. The relationship between redundancy and identification will be tested by comparing identification times of a given short description (0 degree of redundancy) and a long one (+1, -1 or 2 degrees of redundancy.) Additionally, we will also compare short (+1 and -1 descriptions) with long (2) descriptions when relevant.

In our pilot experiment we consider the following four research questions (*h1*-*h4*):

h1: The use of longer descriptions increases the identification time of anaphoric antecedents.

$$time(0, a) < time(r, a), r \neq 0.$$

This hypothesis will be tested by comparing the time spent examining the antecedent of short descriptions (statements 01..03) and those conveying +1, -1 or 2 degrees of redundancy (statements 04..12) Additionally, we will compare descriptions conveying one degree of redundancy (r=+1 and -1) with those conveying two degrees (r=2). In all cases we expect longer descriptions to demand longer identification time.

h2: The use of longer descriptions increases the identification time of less contrastive distractors.

$$time(0, c1) < time(r, c1), r \neq 0.$$

This hypothesis will be tested by comparing the time spent examining *c1* distractors (and hence deciding that *c1* was not the correct antecedent term) in contexts involving both *c1* and *c2*. More specifically, we will compare the time spent on *c1* given a short description (statement 03) with the time spent given descriptions of +1, -1 or 2 degrees of redundancy (statements 06, 09 and

12.) In all cases we expect longer descriptions to demand longer identification time[4].

h3: The use of longer descriptions increases the identification time of more contrastive distractors.

$$time(0, c2) < time(r, c2), r \neq 0.$$

This hypothesis is analogous to *h2*. We will compare the time spent on *c2* given a short description (statement 03) with the *c2* time given descriptions of +1, -1 or 2 degrees of redundancy (statements 06, 09 and 12) In all cases we expect longer descriptions to require longer identification time.

h4: Identifying more contrastive distractors (c2) is faster than identifying less contrastive ones (c1).

$$time(r, c2) < time(r, c1), r \neq 0.$$

This hypothesis states that *c1* distractors always require longer identification time than *c2* regardless of the degree of redundancy of the referring expression. This will be tested by comparing the time spent on *c2* and *c1* in all situations in which both occur (statements 03,06,09 and 12.) In all cases we expect more contrastive distractors to require shorter identification time.

We had originally made additional predictions about the possible relationship between degrees of redundancy and misidentification (e.g., selecting *c1* or *c2* instead of the antecedent term.) However, misidentification turned out to be almost inexistent in our data due to our strict implementation that forces the subjects to carefully select each antecedent to obtain the required 13 correct answers to reach the end of the experiment. Thus, this analysis was not possible in our experiment setting.

Materials. 146 purpose-made documents in electronic format, conveying one statement each. Two documents were only intended to familiarize the subject with the experiment setting, and had no other research purpose. The reminder 144 research documents represent our 12 possible document configurations in 12 different domains (pets, vehicles etc.) This level of variation was deemed necessary to avoid domain and other linguistic effects[5], and also to prevent the subjects from relying on memory. It should however be made clear that each subject had only to find the correct answer in 12 different (and randomly selected) research documents, being each one in a different domain and presented in random order (besides the practice documents at the beginning.)

All documents kept the same sentence structure and number of words between the referring expression and the antecedent term. The language used was kept as simple as possible, and making use of highly visual, concrete discourse objects. Besides the basic entity type, referring expressions conveyed three kinds of attribute: colour, location and size. In all statements, colour and location were discriminatory attributes that could be made redundant or not depending on the contents of the description in which they appeared, whereas size was always non-discriminatory and thus always redundant.

4. Preliminary Results

38 Information Systems students completed the experiment. Table 2 shows the average identification time for the antecedent *a* and distractors of type *c1* and *c2* in situations involving 0, 1, -1 and 2 degrees of redundancy (denoted as *r0*, *r1*, *r-1* and *r2*.)

Table 2 – Average identification times (seconds)

object	r0	r1	r--1	r2
a	2.72	3.58	2.93	3.67
c1	1.81	2.00	2.16	3.03
c2	2.01	1.84	2.04	1.79

Informally speaking, it is immediate to observe that for the three kinds of objects (antecedent *a*, *c1* and *c2*) the data show a tendency (either of increase or decrease) from *r0* to *r2* that is interrupted only by the *r-1* cases. In fact, if we disregard the *r-1* column in Table 1 above we notice that the identification times of both antecedent and *c1* always *increase* according to the degree of redundancy, and, analogously the identification times of *c2* always *decrease*. In addition to that, the above identification times show that the difference from *r0* to *r2* is fairly large, but less so between *r0* and *r1* or *r-1*. This seems to suggest that our experiment setting was not entirely adequate to measure the subtle effect of adding one single attribute to a non-redundant description, or to distinguish between discriminatory (*r1*) and non-discriminatory (*r-1*) redundancy. Accordingly, our results below were mainly significant when comparing the difference between *r0* and *r2*, and for that reason we will refer to them simply as short/long descriptions.

The results for hypotheses *h1-h3* (those comparing identification times for *a*, *c1* and *c2* in short and long descriptions) using Wilcoxon signed-rank test are significant as stated in the following Table 3-5. In *h3* the observed effect was in the opposite direction.

Table 3 – h1: antecedent identification

Test	N	T	%	p
r0 < r1	24	47.50	71.05	0.0034
r0 < r2	21	42.00	60.53	0.0106
r–1 < r2	22	59.00	71.05	0.0284

[4] Contexts involving one distractor only (statements 02,05,08 and 11) convey *either c1* or *c2*, which does not allow us to draw a balanced comparison between them.

[5] For example, a reader more familiar with (or more interested in) a particular subject may pay more attention to that text, and this may impact resolution.

Table 4 – h2: c1 identification

Test	N	T	%	p
r0 < r–1	19	49.00	55.26	0.0642
r0 < r2	24	87.50	63.16	0.0742
r1 < r2	23	77.50	65.79	0.0658

Table 5 – h3: c2 identification

Test	N	T	%	p
r0 > r2	20	60.50	63.16	0.0966

Results for hypothesis *h4* (the comparison between *c1* and *c2* identification times) are significant as in Table 6 below, that is, only for the longest descriptions.

Table 6 – h4: c2 < c1 test

Redundancy	N	T	%	p
r2	20	35.00	76.32	0.0090

5. Discussion

When the shortest (*r0*) and the longest (*r2*) descriptions are compared, all tests showed significant change in resolution times of the antecedent, *c1* and *c2* distractors. On the other hand, as suggested in the previous section, our experiment setting was unable to detect significant differences between *r0* and *r1* / *r-1* descriptions in most tests. The exceptions were two significant effects in antecedent identification (those between *r0* and *r1*, and between *r-1* and *r2*) and one effect in *c1* identification (between *r0* and *r-1*.)

Despite these limitations, these results seem to suggest that redundancy does increases identification times of antecedent terms and *c1* (i.e., less contrastive) objects, which can be explained by the fact that reading longer descriptions simply takes longer. The effect is particularly significant for antecedent identification (*h1*), but also observable for *c1* (hypothesis *h2*.)

On the other hand, results for *c2* (i.e., more contrastive) objects were remarkably opposite to the predictions in *h3*: redundancy in this case actually *decreases* identification times, that is, making resolution easier. This is further confirmed by the findings for *h4*, in which the identification of *c1* objects took much longer that the identification of *c2* (recall that these were measured under exactly the same situations of reference.)

A possible explanation for this difference is the cognitive load involved in the identification of various competing descriptions (of *a*, *c1* or *c2*). Given a referring expression *i* and a candidate referent *j*, the reader is supposed to interpret both *i* and *j* and decide whether they match. Even though redundancy does increase reading times, matching *i* and *j* may still require relatively little cognitive effort when both *i* and *j* share a large number of properties (or words) if compared to matching a more dissimilar description pair. In other words, we hypothesize that for a closely-related pair of descriptions (i.e., an anaphor and a *c1* object, or an anaphor and the actual antecedent term) the readers may benefit from some form of shallow processing to quickly decide, for example, that the reference "the small black cat" is not the same as (*c1*) "the small white cat", but that it does co-refer with an antecedent term "the black cat".

By contrast, when facing a more complex match between "the small black cat" and a candidate conveying two unexpected attributes (*c2*) as in "the large white cat", it may be necessary to resort to a somewhat deeper analysis, which would explain why *c2* reading times are longer. Although we presently do not seek to validate this claim, this intuition seems to be consistent with the behaviour reported in informal interviews with some of the experiment subjects. We believe that more research will be required to clarify this issue.

Finally, with respect to the comparison between deixis and anaphora resolution, our preliminary results for anaphora are quite dissimilar from those reported in [4] for space deixis. Although this was to a large extent to be expected (as hypothesised in *h1-h3*), the present outcome seems to suggest a far more complex picture that once again will require further investigation.

6. Final Remarks

Despite the small scale of our pilot experiment, preliminary results suggest a number of interesting issues to be taken into account in the design of REG algorithms. Chief among them, we found that redundancy may in fact *increase* anaphora resolution times. While this is not to say that redundancy should be simply avoided (e.g., redundancy may reduce misidentification or improve comprehension), this insight is quite contrary to existing knowledge on the generation of deictic descriptions.

In addition to that, redundancy seems to have different effects depending on the kinds of redundant attribute used (i.e., discriminatory or not) and affects more or less contrastive distractors in different ways. All in all, there is no straight answer as to whether to generate redundant descriptions or not, but rather that a number of context details need to be taken into account.

The experiment provided us with a large and complex data set that we have only started to analyse. As future work we intend to make additional inferences from these results and redesign a number of aspects of the experiment setting including a larger number of subjects.

7. Acknowledgements

This work has been supported by CNPq and FAPESP.

8. References

[1] Grice, H. P. "Logic and Conversation". In P. Cole and J. L. Morgan (eds.) *Syntax and Semantics*, Vol. iii: Speech Acts. New York, Academic Press, pages 4-158, 1975.

[2] Dale, R. and E. Reiter. "Computational interpretations of the Gricean maxims in the generation of referring expressions". Cognitive Science 19(2), 1995.

[3] Paraboni, I., K. van Deemter and J. Masthoff "Generating Referring Expressions: Making Referents Easy to Identify". Computational Linguistics 33(2), 229-254.

[4] Lyons, John. *Semantics*. Cambridge Univ. Press, 1977.

A Model for the Cross-Modal Influence of Visual Context upon Language Processing

Patrick McCrae
CINACS Graduate Research Group
Department of Informatics
Hamburg University
Vogt-Kölln-Straße 30, 22527 Hamburg, Germany
patrick.mccrae@informatik.uni-hamburg.de

Abstract

In this paper, we present a novel, cognitively motivated framework for modelling the cross-modal influence of visual scene context upon language processing. We illustrate how semantic relations in a knowledge representation of visual scene context can effect syntactic attachment modulations in a weighted-constraint dependency parser. In line with a central tenet of conceptual semantics, visual scene context and linguistic processing are hypothesised to interact via an intermediate, cross-modally integrated level of semantic representation. Cross-modal interaction in our model is restricted by conceptual compatibility between the concepts activated linguistically and contextually.

We apply our framework to syntactically ambiguous sentences of German and parse them in the presence of biasing visual scene contexts. The observed modulations in syntactic attachment support our two modelling hypotheses: 1) The influence of visual context upon syntactic processing is mediated by semantics. 2) The compatibility of concepts from different modalities is a suitable criterion to restrict the scope of cross-modal interaction.

Keywords

Cross-Modal Interaction, Parsing, Syntax-Semantics Interface, Context Integration, Information Fusion.

1 Introduction

The vision-language interface has become considerably more accessible to scientific enquiry with the advent of eye tracking technology. [3] showed a semantic interaction between vision and language for single-word processing with co-present visual stimuli as early as 1974. About two decades later, [13] investigated subjects' eye movements for syntactically ambiguous sentences with a particular focus on the aspect of incrementality in linguistic processing. Yet another decade later, [1] investigated whether the eye movement patterns observed as a result of the interaction between vision and language were contingent upon the visual stimulus being co-present with the linguistic stimulus. In this paper we present a successful implementation of a framework for the integration of visual context information into the process of syntactic parsing. Starting from the review of central empirical investigations of the vision-language interface, we begin with the identification of elementary requirements for the design of a cognitively motivated framework for the cross-modal integration between vision and language. Adopting a weighted-constraint model of language processing, we outline how in our framework the interpretation of visual context constitutes an additional constraint on the cross-modally integrated semantic representation which is built up based on linguistic and contextual input.

In the following section, we provide a brief overview over selected key findings from milestone experiments at the vision-language interface to motivate the requirements for our framework. In Section 3, we outline how the components of our framework interact with each other and which procedures we employ to achieve cross-modal interaction. In Section 4, we provide experimental results from the integration of visual context into parsing for a particular class of syntactically ambiguous sentences. In Section 5, we summarise our central points and draw conclusions.

2 Milestone Investigations into the Vision-Language Interface

Cooper demonstrated that spoken word semantics influenced subjects' fixation patterns on co-present visual stimuli [3]. More specifically, Cooper was able to show that, from a selection of nine co-present visual stimuli, subjects preferably fixated those that were either direct depictions of referents denoted by the words heard or depictions of items semantically related to the words' referents. Cooper interpreted these eye movement patterns as a reflection of the on-line activation of word semantics from speech.[1]

In another milestone investigation into the vision-language interface, [13] recorded subjects' eye movements when presented with a visual scene depiction and syntactically ambiguous sentences. With their focus on eye movements in incremental sentence processing, Tanenhaus et al. concluded that *"people seek to establish reference (...) during the earliest moments of linguistic processing"*. The eye movement patterns observed support their hypothesis

[1] Moreover, Cooper had the foresight that this novel methodology constituted an experimental paradigm whose *"linguistic sensitivity (...) together with its associated small latencies suggests its use as a practical new research tool for the real-time investigation of perceptual and cognitive processes"*. His methodology subsequently became known as the *visual-world paradigm*.

International Conference RANLP 2009 - Borovets, Bulgaria, pages 230–235

that referentially relevant non-linguistic information *immediately* affects linguistic processing. Tanenhaus et al. further showed that eye movements and linguistic processing are tightly time-locked, which they interpret as an indication for a close and continual interaction between visual and linguistic processing.[2]
While both [3] and [13] observed anticipatory eye movements, neither of them investigated the cognitive mechanisms that drive those eye movements or ventured a hypothesis on the structure of the mental representations feeding those mechanisms. In our view, the control of the anticipatory eye movements must originate from a suitably detailed mental representation of the visual field. This mental representation must be accessible at the point in time at which the corresponding linguistic stimulus occurs. [1] examined the question of underlying mental representation by employing the *blank-screen paradigm*, a variation of the visual-world paradigm in which the visual stimulus is removed shortly before the onset of the linguistic stimulus. Given sufficiently small inter-stimulus intervals, eye movements are very similar to those obtained in the visual-world condition can be observed, even in the absence of a visual stimulus at the time of interaction. [1] concluded that the eye movements are not the result of a direct online interaction between language and the visual scene but rather result from the interaction between language and a mental representation of the visual scene.[3]

Today, there is substantial and significant empirical evidence for an online interaction between visual and linguistic processing. [1] provides solid support for the hypothesis that the cross-modal interaction between vision and language occurs at representational level. This interpretation is also in line with Jackendoff's Conceptual Structure Hypothesis [6]. Based on a wide range of linguistic and cognitive evidence, Jackendoff argues that "*there is a layer of mental representation, Conceptual Structure, at which linguistic, sensory, and motor information are mutually compatible*". While Jackendoff provides a series of subsequent refinements to this hypothesis and the model underlying it, e.g. [7], the central message remains the same, namely that cross-modal integration occurs in Conceptual Structure, a semantic level of mental representation that brings together concepts, concept instances, semantic relations, linguistic representations and is accessible to reasoning. It was our intention to include this cognitive architecture centring around an integrating level of semantic representation into our model. We hence derive the following high-level modelling requirements from these initial considerations:

R1. Visual and linguistic processing must interact continuously.

R2. The interaction between vision and language must be semantic in nature.

R3. The interaction between vision and language requires the presence of a mental representation of the visual scene rather than the physical presence of the visual scene itself.

R4. Cross-modal interaction must occur at a single representational level that encodes concepts, concept instances and semantic relations such that different modalities – be they sensory or representational in nature – are compatible with each other.

R5. The level of integrated representation must be accessible to reasoning to permit to draw elementary inferences and conclusions.

[2] This finding is of particular relevance in the context of the discussion to what degree the linguistic processor acts as an encapsulated unit. The degree of interactivity of the linguistic parser clearly has a bearing on the mechanisms by which and the point in time when it can engage in interaction with information provided by other sensory or representational modalities.

[3] While beyond the scope of this paper, it should be mentioned for completeness' sake that there is some scientific debate regarding the contents and degree of detail of this mental representation as well as its actual location in memory.

3 Framework Implementation

3.1 The Syntax-Semantics Interface and Cross-Modal Integration

Our framework implements the architecture for cross-modal integration as proposed by [9]. Core component of the architecture in [9] is WCDG, a weighted constraint dependency parser for German which provides a generic interface to incorporate additional, possibly non-linguistic, information into the parsing process [10, 5]. Constraint-based systems have the succinct advantage that in principle any modelled property of the target structure – be it linguistic or non-linguistic – can be constrained by the mere addition of appropriate further constraints. For cross-modal interaction, we use integration constraints that stipulate to what degree the cross-modally integrated semantic representation comply with the representation of visual context. A predictor component provides the contextual information to the parser.
Discussing the application of their architecture to PP-attachment, [8] proposes to achieve cross-modal integration in the parser by imposing additional context constraints upon dependencies about which the parser itself has no or only insufficient information. The additional penalty scores are provided by a predictor and are calculated based on queries to a representation of visual context through a reasoning engine. Our framework implements this approach.
Since the parser is constraint-based, a predictor influences dependency assignments by providing graded dependency vetoes. These vetoes are evaluated in the integration constraints and may further constrain the set of acceptable solutions. In our model, the predictor assigns graded penalties to semantic dependencies. These prediction scores are based on context information accessible to the predictor but unavailable to the parser.
When adopted into the cross-modally integrated semantic representation, the score on a semantic dependency affects the overall score of the syntax-semantics analysis. In our implementation, context-based prediction scores are calculated for all semantic dependencies after accessing the knowledge representation of visual context. We use the FaCT++ reasoner to do so [4]. The context representation contains instances of ontological concepts linked by thematic relations. Following [6], we assume that this kind of representation results from visual understanding.
During parsing, the parser builds up layers of syntactic and semantic representation that interface with each other. The syntax-semantics interface in our model contains correspondence rules that interlock the syntactic and semantic

levels of analysis and require consistency between them.[4] For context integration, the parser's semantic levels of representation are constrained to be consistent with the syntactic representation and the thematic relations asserted in visual context. The integration constraints stipulate just how rigidly the consistence of thematic relations be enforced between modalities. The interaction between the different levels of representation in the parser is shown schematically in Figure 1. The overall solution score comprises all levels of representation and is optimised for a minimisation of constraint violation severity.

Syntactic Representation ⇆ Semantic Representation
↑
Visual Scene Context

Fig. 1: *Representational interactions during the influence of visual context upon syntactic parsing in our model.*

3.2 Scoring Thematic Relations based on Visual Context

Having outlined the overall interaction of the various components in the framework we now take a closer look at the actual scoring process inside the predictor. The precondition for a thematic relation in visual context to be able to affect a thematic dependency assignment in the semantic representation is that the word in the linguistic modality map onto one or more concept instances in visual context. Only if this mapping is successful can the thematic relations in visual context provide relevant information for the dependency assignment to a given dependant-regent word pair. Consequently, the first step in cross-modal interaction must be the mapping of linguistic entities onto sets of concept instances in visual context. This process is referred to as *cross-modal matching* [2].
With WCDG, cross-modal matching is subject to a technical limitation that, at present, cannot be overcome: the predictor is invoked *prior to* the commencement of the parsing process, i.e. at a stage at which no syntactic information is available yet. As a result, the predictor can only provide dependency scores for word pairs – and not for syntactically more complex units such as phrases or clauses. To map an individual word in the input sentence to a set of concept instances in the representation of visual context, the predictor passes through the following steps (cf. Figure 2):

1. WCDG maps every surface string to a corresponding set of uniquely identified lexical entries. Each lexical entry is characterised by a unique set of lexical features. The surface string 'fragen' *ask*, e.g., can map to the infinitive lexical entry with POS tag `VVFIN` or to the finite verb form with POS tag `VVINF`.[5]

2. The predictor normalises each lexical entry to a form which, in the majority of cases, coincides with the lexical base form in the lexicon. For nouns, the normalisation typically is the nominative singular form, for verbs it is the infinitive.

3. Every normalisation activates a set of concepts in an ontology embedded in our model of Conceptual Structure. Specifically, every word activates those concepts that are lexicalised by the word's normalisation. By permitting the activation of an entire set of concepts through a single word in the linguistic input, our model robustly handles lexical ambiguity and homophony.

4. At the same time, each individual in the representation of visual context instantiates a concept from the ontology.

5. With a reasoner, the predictor determines the set of concepts instantiated in visual context that are compatible with the set of concepts activated by each word in the linguistic input.

6. A thematic relation asserted in visual context becomes relevant in cross-modal integration if the concept instances it connects instantiate concepts that have been matched to words in the input sentence.

In our framwork, dectecting a cross-modally relevant thematic relation in visual context has three effects upon the semantic level of representation in the parser:

a. The detected thematic dependency is integrated for the corresponding dependant-regent word pair. The dependency's score now contributes to the total score of the integrated representation.

b. The assignment of any other thematic dependency between the same dependant-regent word pair is penalised.

c. The assignment of any other thematic dependency originating from the same dependant or pointing to the same regent is penalised. These penalties may subsequently be overwritten if analysis of another thematic relation in visual context provides concrete positive evidence for such an additional thematic relation.

Note that b. results from the uniqueness of a thematic role assignment within any situation frame. Consequence c. reflects the assumption that the interaction between vision and language occurs in a closed-world. We hence assume that the cross-modal interaction occurs on the basis of the information available to the system at the time of interaction. Clearly, this information may be incomplete. In cases in which this information is subsequently revised, – e.g. because an additional scene participant has been detected in the visual scene – a new cross-modal interaction between vision and language based on the revised visual context representation must result.

4 Applying the Framework

To demonstrate the effectiveness of the framework, we have applied it to different classes of syntactic ambiguity phenomena in German: Genitive-Dative ambiguity of feminine nouns, subject-object ambiguities and PP attachment.

[4] Note that – since all constraints are weighted – the parser may also find solutions in which conflicts between syntactic and semantic representations occur. The parser will, however, always favour those solutions in which the overall severity of constraint violations is minimised.

[5] WCDG employs the Stuttgart-Tübingen POS tag set (STTS) [12] which is standard for German.

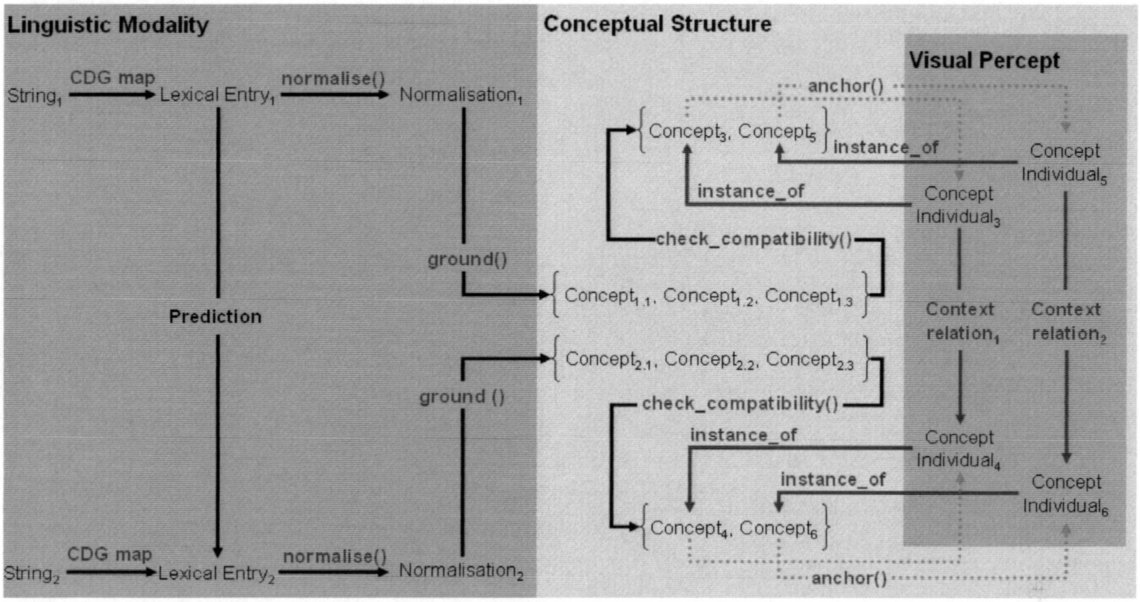

Fig. 2: *Mapping procedure in cross-modal integration.*

The latter class of ambiguity phenomena has already been envisioned as a possible application of the framework by [8].

While a detailed discussion of the application of the framework to these classes of syntactic ambiguities is beyond the scope of this paper, we now discuss how the framework processes one globally ambigous sentence that is representative of the class of German Genitive-Dative ambiguities in feminine nouns as studied by [14]. To improve comparability of the sentences, we have normalised the different introductory main clauses to 'Er weiß, dass ... ' *He knows that ...* for all sentences. Consider (1) with the structural ambiguity highlighted.

(1) Er weiß, dass die Ärztin ***der Patientin*** den Leidenden präsentierte.

He knows that ...

a. Binary Situation (Genitive reading)
... the female patient's female doctor presented the male sufferer.

b. Ternary Situation (Dative reading)
... the female doctor presented the male sufferer to the female patient.

The parser's default analysis of (1) in the absence of contextual information is the Dative reading which corresponds to the syntactic structure shown in Figure 4. We can, however, modulate the semantic representation – and via the syntax-semantics interface also the syntactic analysis – by integrating a visual context that corresponds to the Genitive reading in (1) b.

The question arises how detailed such a context representation needs to be in order to be cognitively plausible and have the desired effect upon the integrated semantic representation in the parser. How, for instance, would one be able to differentiate based on the visual modality alone whether the observed scene was a 'präsentieren' *to present* or a 'zeigen' *to show* situation? In [11] Spivey argues for a level of representational detail which balances the economy of information storage against the need for access to cognitively salient information. Spivey concludes that while the mental representation of visual context need not necessarily be complete it must provide anchor points for access to information not stored in the representation via the process of active vision.

To preempt a discussion on the level of representational granularity provided by the visual modality, we have reduced the level of detail provided by the visual modality to the situation arity – i.e. the number of situation participants –, the participants' ontological category as well as their thematic role in the situation. Our model hence does not impose any restriction on how specific the ontological categorisation of participants or the situation verb needs to be. A typical context model is visualised in figure 3.

The concept instances we include need to be general enough to be attainable based on visually perceptible features. In Figure 3 we have identified the central situation verb as an instance of a generic binary situation concept and thus have intentionally underspecified the specific nature of the observed action. This visual context can be interpreted as 'I can see who is doing something to whom – even if I cannot discern exactly what it is that they are doing'.

While our framework permits to define instantiations of specific situation concepts such as 'präsentieren' *present* or 'Ärztin' *female doctor*, we think that it is cognitively questionable whether such detailed and strongly lexicalised information is really provided by the visual modality. Since our model does not rely on the one-to-one mapping of word in the linguistic modality to a concept instance in visual context we can safely model visual context with

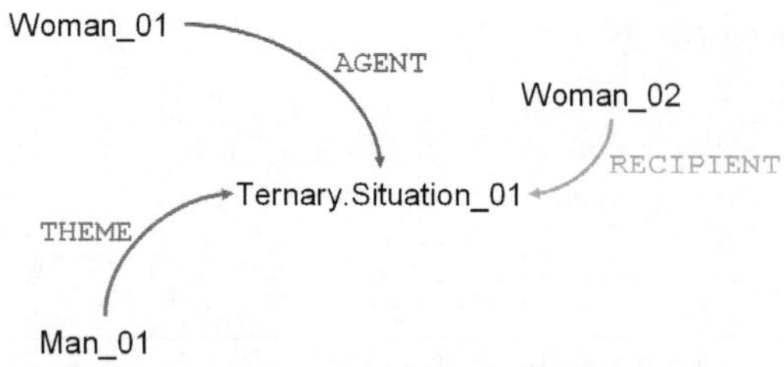

Fig. 3: *Representation of visual context for the ternary situation (Dative reading) of sentence (1).*

instances of less specific concepts. Less specific concepts are superclasses of the more specific concepts in the ontology and therefore exhibit equally or a less restrictive concept compatibility. Our results from larger evaluations show that even such rather general context information is sufficient to impart the correct situation arity to the parser's semantic representation.
The result of integrating the binary visual context into the parsing of (1) is the syntactic dependency structure in Figure 4. Integration of a visual context corresponding to the Genitive reading (1) a. has indeed succeeded in overriding the parser's default ternary situation analysis which previously was obtained in the absence of a visual context.

5 Conclusions

In this paper we have described the implementation of a framework for the cross-modal influence of visual context upon linguistic processing in a weighted constraint dependency parser. Our framework utilises semantic relations between concept instances in combination with structural constraints to achieve cross-modal interaction between visual context and syntactic analysis. In our implementation, semantic information from a parser-external knowledge representation of visual context is aligned with the semantic representation in the parser. Syntactic analysis is modulated via the syntax-semantics interface.
We have outlined that in the parser correspondence rule constraints demand the alignment between the syntactic and semantic levels of analysis and another class of constraints – the integration constraints – demand alignment of the thematic dependencies on the semantic levels with the thematic relations asserted in visual context. We found that concept instantiations related by thematic relations provide a suitable first approximation for the representation of visual context. Our account concludes with the discussion of an application of our framework to a sentence representative of an entire class of syntactic ambiguities in German. The example shows how the integration of visual context in our model permits to modulate syntactic attachment decisions.

Acknowledgements

This work has been generously funded by the German Research Foundation (DFG) as part of the CINACS project "Multimodal Representations in Communication". We would also like to express our sincere thanks to the five anonymous reviewers for their detailed and constructive feedback on an earlier version of this paper.

References

[1] G. T. M. Altmann. Language-mediated eye movements in the absence of a visual world. *Cognition*, 93:B79–B87, 2004.

[2] E. W. Bushnell. *The development of intersensory perception: comparative perspectives*, chapter A Dual-Processing Approach to Cross-Modal Matching: Implications for Development, pages 19–38. Lawrence Erlbaum Associates, 1994.

[3] R. M. Cooper. The control of eye fixation by the meaning of spoken language. a new methodology for the real-time investigation of speech perception, memory, and language processing. *Cognitive Psychology*, 6:813–839, 1974.

[4] FaCT-PlusPlus Download Page. `http://code.google.com/p/factplusplus/`, 2009. Link verified: 20 April 2009.

[5] K. A. Foth. *Hybrid Methods of Natural Language Analysis*. PhD thesis, Department of Informatics, Hamburg University, Germany, 2007.

[6] R. S. Jackendoff. *Semantics and Cognition*. Cambridge, MA: MIT Press, 1983.

[7] R. S. Jackendoff. *Patterns in the Mind*. New York: Basic Books, 1994.

[8] P. McCrae. Integrating cross-modal context for PP attachment disambiguation. In *Proceedings of the 3rd International Conference on Natural Computation, Haikou (ICNC 2007)*, volume 3, pages 292–296, Los Alamitos, CA, 2007. IEEE.

[9] P. McCrae and W. Menzel. Towards a system architecture for integrating cross-modal context in syntactic disambiguation. In B. Sharp and M. Zock, editors, *Proceedings of the 4th International Workshop on Natural Language Processing and Cognitive Science, Madeira (NLPCS 2007)*, pages 228–237. INSTICC Press, 2007.

[10] I. Schröder. *Natural Language Parsing with Graded Constraints*. PhD thesis, Department of Informatics, Hamburg University, Germany, 2002.

[11] M. J. Spivey, D. C. Richardson, and S. A. Fitneva. *The Interface of Vision, Language, and Action*, chapter Thinking outside the brain: Spatial indices to linguistic and visual information, pages 161–189. Number 5. New York: Psychology Press, 2004.

[12] STTS Tag Set. `http://www.sfs.nphil.uni-tuebingen.de/Elwis/stts.html`, 2009. Link verified: 24 July 2009.

[13] M. K. Tanenhaus, M. J. Spivey-Knowlton, K. M. Eberhard, and J. C. Sedivy. Integration of visual and linguistic information in spoken language comprehension. *SCIENCE*, 268:1632–1634, 1995.

[14] A. van Kampen. *Syntaktische und semantische Verarbeitungsprozesse bei der Analyse strukturell mehrdeutiger Verbfinalsätze im Deutschen: Eine empirische Untersuchung*. PhD thesis, Freie Universität Berlin, 2001.

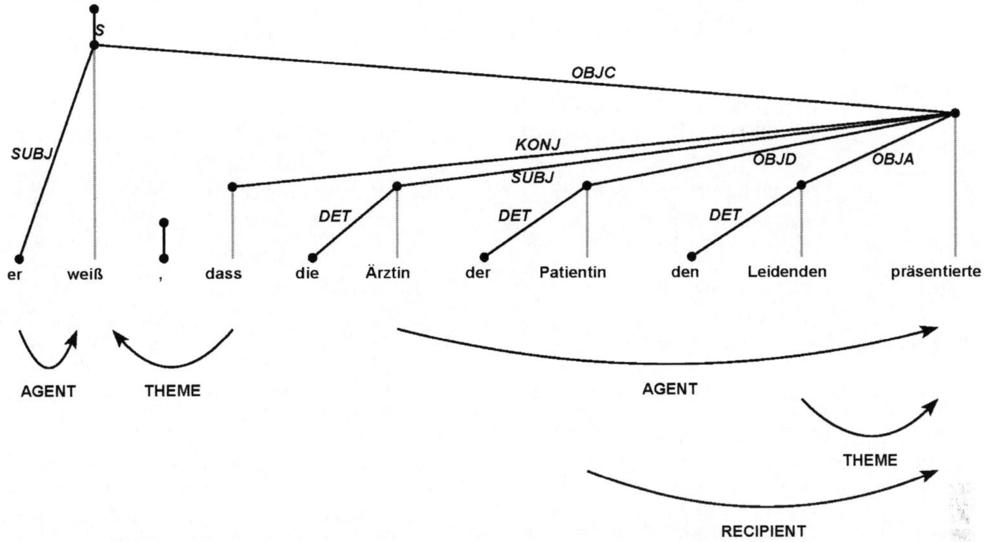

Fig. 4: *The parser's default analysis in the absence of visual context (Dative reading).*

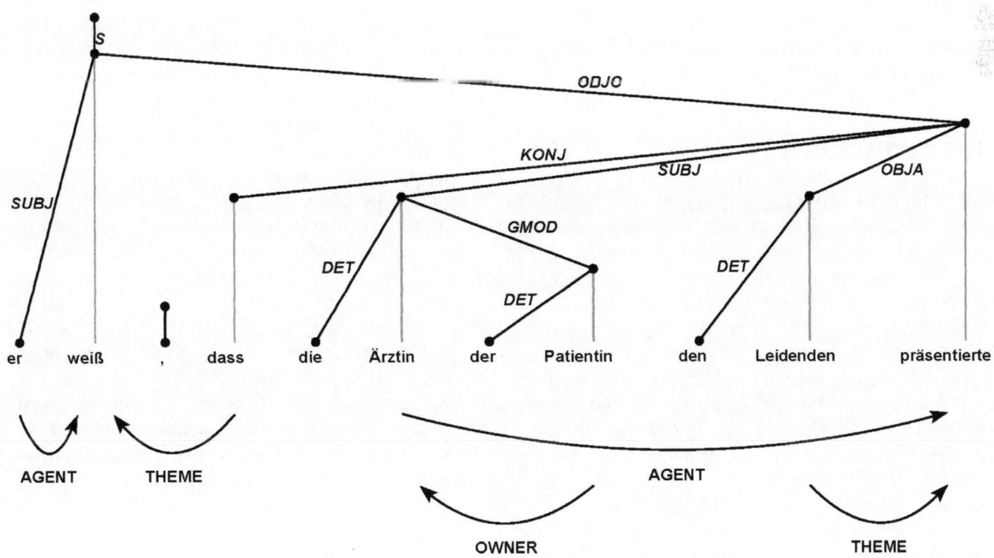

Fig. 5: *The parser's cross-modally integrated analysis with a binary visual context (Genitive reading).*

Bimodal Corpora Terminology Extraction: Another Brick in the Wall

Claudiu Mihăilă*
University of Wolverhampton
Wulfruna Street
Wolverhampton WV1 1LY
claudiu.mihaila@info.uaic.ro

Dalila Mekhaldi
University of Wolverhampton
Wulfruna Street
Wolverhampton WV1 1LY
dalila.mekhaldi@wlv.ac.uk

Abstract

This paper presents a new study on automatic terminology extraction in the context of bimodal corpora that were generated from lectures and meetings. More specifically, the study aims to observe to which extent written text (discussed documents) and spoken text (dialogue transcript) share keywords. Using a hybrid terminology extraction approach, experiments have been performed on a collection of bimodal English corpora, including one scientific conference presentations corpus and two decision-making meetings corpora respectively. The evaluation results highlight a difference between keywords extracted from written text and from spoken text. Moreover, the obtained results emphasise the importance of considering text obtained from different modalities in order to generate rich and consistent keyword lists for bimodal corpora.

Keywords

bimodal corpus, keyword extraction, keyword similarity, spoken document, written document.

1 Introduction

Corpora, which are defined as large bodies of linguistic evidence composed of attested language use [9], are increasingly used in natural language processing field(NLP), such as in machine translation, automatic summarisation, etc. However, the diversity of NLP tasks that are based on corpora is proportional to the variousness of types of the latter. Therefore many corpora types have been distinguished [9], mainly monolingual corpora, parallel corpora and comparable corpora. Whilst most of the existing studies are based on these corpora types, bimodal corpora, which are originally built in the context of multimodal and multimedia applications, have recently appeared as a new corpora type that needs to be studied. Bimodal corpora are defined as pairs of texts either used or generated during multimedia events (e.g. meetings or lectures), each of them obtained through a different modality (e.g. text of written documents, speech transcript, text extracted from video recording frames).

*The author is also affiliated to the Faculty of Computer Science, "Al.I. Cuza" University of Iaşi, Romania

From another side, terminology extraction (TE) consists in the identification and retrieval of the important lexical units, i.e. keywords, from a corpus. One of the challenges in TE is the definition of a keyword, which greatly depends on the context of the application. Other challenges are morphological and lexical variation of keywords, the consideration of single-word and multi-word keywords, etc. Once these challenges are addressed, the extracted keywords are particularly useful for conceptualising a knowledge domain or for supporting the creation of domain ontologies, due to their high specificity and low ambiguity. The accuracy in the identification of keywords may influence NLP tasks like analysis, understanding, generation, translation, automatic summarisation [12], and multiple-choice test item generation [5] of textual documents.

Terminology extraction from bimodal corpora, which is studied in this paper, represents the basis of many NLP and NLP-related fields of study. The task of multimodal document alignment framework, defined in [10], is based on the semantic similarity between spoken and written documents, which might benefit from their commonly extracted keywords. Moreover, bimodal terminology extraction might be useful for the disambiguation of words in the spoken corpora when they contain noise. Another use case of bimodal terminology extraction is the disambiguation of words between written and spoken corpora, e.g. the meaning of an abbreviation in a written document may be fully understood when its corresponding explicit phrase is used in speech, and vice-versa. Additionally, the bimodal terminology extraction could be exploited for the creation of digital libraries and multimedia archives, as well as management tasks related to their resources, including indexing, topic segmentation, automatic summarisation, etc.

This paper is structured as follows: section 2 highlights some of the recent works in terminology extraction field. In section 3, our system and the corpora on which this work was performed are described. Finally, the results of the evaluation are presented and discussed in section 4.

2 Existing studies

Research methods in TE are usually classified as linguistic, statistical or hybrid. Linguistic and statistical methods can be further subdivided into term-based (intrinsic) and context-based (extrinsic) [4].

International Conference RANLP 2009 - Borovets, Bulgaria, pages 236–240

Linguistic approaches use the linguistic information associated to words at different levels to identify the keywords. Part-of-speech sequences [7] or morphological features [1], as well as boundary markers [3], are used in the recognition of terms.

Statistical approaches are based on statistical features such as word frequency, inverse document frequency, mutual information, etc. Statistical frameworks have been explored in the context of mutual bilingual terminology extraction from textual documents, showing that probabilistic models are a viable approach for incorporating alignment scores in automatic terminology [6].

3 Bimodal Corpora TE

Our work is based on three bimodal English corpora in different domains obtained from the recordings of one scientific conference and two decision-making meetings respectively. Each corpus is composed of multiple pairs of spoken text (speech transcripts) and written text. The spoken text corresponds to the manual transcription of the dialogue recording (with a total number of 59 805 words), whilst the written text is manually extracted from the printed documents that were discussed or presented (articles, slideshows, posters, etc.), with a total of 42 427 words. Our assumption is that, during meetings and lectures, speakers use roughly the same keywords that appear in the written documents.

Our bimodal terminology extraction system is based on a hybrid approach, combining both linguistic and statistical features. Thus, the main component of the system is statistical, enriched with shallow linguistic information. The system developed for this task comprises two main parts: corpus parsing and a keyword extraction module.

The written and spoken text files are first preprocessed using Machinese, a publicly available lemmatiser and POS-tagger[1]. The extracted linguistic features will be used by our system for the identification of candidate keywords, in the form of a morphological filter which only permits phrases having certain morphological structures to be considered by the user (noun, adjective, verb, etc.). However, in the current study the morphological category was not restricted and all types of candidates were considered. Moreover, an additional filter based on a stopword list is used to restrict the selection of semantically insignificant words.

The extraction module offers to the user a fully parametrised interface: it is possible to change easily the corpus, the files to analyse, the stopword list, the morphological categories to which the keywords belong, the methods used for scoring the keywords candidates and the number of extracted keywords. In addition to the TF method (term frequency), three other statistical scoring methods (TF·IDF, TF·IDF$_L$, and TF·IDF$_A$) are computed according to the formulae [8]:

$$TF \cdot IDF(t) = \frac{tf(t)}{df(t)} \qquad (1)$$

[1] http://www.connexor.eu/technology/machinese/

$$TF \cdot IDF_L(t) = tf(t) \log\left(\frac{N}{df(t)}\right) \qquad (2)$$

$$TF \cdot IDF_A(t) = 0.5 + \frac{0.5tf(t)}{max(tf(t))} \log\left(\frac{N}{df(t)}\right) \qquad (3)$$

where N is the total number of documents in the corpus, $tf(t)$ is the term frequency in the current file, and $df(t)$ is the frequency of the term t in the corpus.

These metrics were chosen as starting point for this preliminary study due to their extensive use and simplicity. However, more complex formulae will be used in the future, which might generate better results.

4 Evaluation

The evaluation approach consists of three steps. First, a common keyword golden standard was manually created by a domain expert for each pair of spoken and written texts in each corpus. In addition to the main author, an expert has been involved in the task of creating the golden corpus. Second, an automatic extraction of keywords from each written and spoken text was performed and then generated keyword lists are evaluated against the golden standard. Finally, the obtained spoken and written keyword lists for each pair were compared in order to measure their overlap.

The four scoring methods (TF, TF·IDF, TF·IDF$_A$, and TF·IDF$_L$) were experimented in order to extract keywords from the test data. However, the TF·IDF$_L$metric has generated the best results, and thus was used for further evaluation. This is mainly due to the fact that this method normalises the score by using only the logarithm. On the other hand, TF·IDFand TF·IDF$_A$divide the term frequency by the document frequency or by the maximum term frequency in the texts of the corpus, which helps increase the score for the candidates which appear only in the current text. Since written texts in evaluated corpora have different contents one from the other, many keyword candidates obtain the maximum score. However, in this study we have limited the number of selected keywords to 10 per text (the same number of keywords has been extracted for the golden standard).

For each spoken/written text pair, a pair of spoken/written keyword lists is created by the system. Based on the manually extracted list of keywords (golden standard), the precision, recall, and F-measure are computed for the respective keyword lists. A match is counted if a term from the list returned by the system is present in the golden standard in the exact variation form. However, problems may occur in the case of orthographic variations (*oxidization* vs. *oxidisation*) or syntactic variations (*lung cancer* vs. *cancer of the lung*).

In order to measure the overlap between the extracted written and spoken keyword lists, the Jaccard similarity coefficient, in equation 4, has been used.

$$J = \frac{|K_w \cap K_s|}{|K_w \cup K_s|} \qquad (4)$$

where K_w and K_s represent the written and, respectively, spoken keyword lists.

However, Jaccard coefficient does not show the rate of the actual keywords in the overlap between spoken/written keywords. Thus, an additional similarity coefficient was implemented, which is based on Jaccard index and considers the golden standard. This new coefficient, called KSim, is defined in equation 5.

$$KSim = \frac{|K_w \cap K_s \cap K_g|}{|K_w \cup K_s|} \quad (5)$$

where K_w, K_s, and K_g represent the written, spoken and golden corpus keyword sets respectively. This similarity coefficient gives the percentage of actual common keywords between the written and spoken texts.

In the following paragraphs, the results of the evaluation obtained for the three corpora are presented and analysed.

4.1 Scientific conference corpus

The first evaluated corpus corresponds to the material of a scientific conference in the domain of physics of particles, CHEP'04. More specifically, the corpus contains eight pairs of scientific papers (i.e. written text) with a total of 34 047 words, and their corresponding transcribed presentations (i.e. spoken text) with a total of 38 206 words. The duration of this corpus is 237 minutes. Each pair of written/spoken texts was cleaned from the data that might be noisy for our evaluation. Thus, the references section was removed from the written text due to the lack of relevant information (e.g. names of authors and editors, publishers, years), as well as non-textual information comprised in the documents (e.g. images, equations, charts). In the spoken text, the question-answering section was removed due to the non-clarity of the speech.

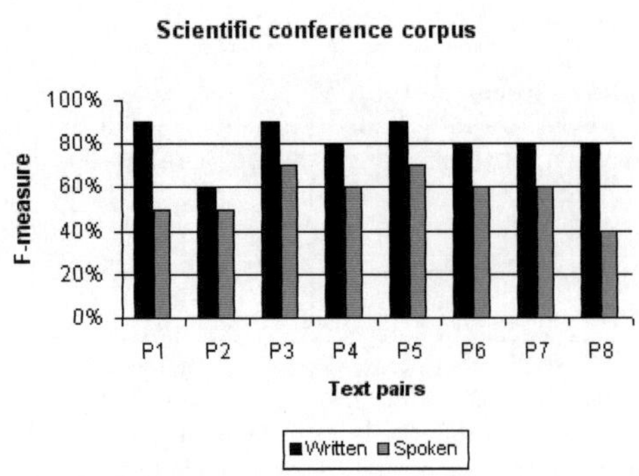

Fig. 1: *F-measures for written and spoken keywords using* TF·IDF$_L$

The obtained values of the F-measure for this corpus are presented in Fig. 1. As shown, there is a divergence between the F values of the written and spoken keywords for each pair, with an average F value of 81.25% for the written texts, and 57.5% for spoken texts.

One possible reason that leads to a lower average score for the spoken texts is that they are more spontaneous and less formal than written texts. An additional reason is that synonym words and phrases are more likely to be used in speech, replacing the actual keywords in the written texts. Furthermore, additional factors such as the misunderstanding, spelling errors, or lack of expertise of the human transcriber in the domain have affected the quality of the transcription, and thus the accuracy of retrieved keywords. After a human annotator performed a manual correction to remove inaccuracies, the score for the spoken text increases considerably from 57.5% up to 62%.

After computing the individual scores for each spoken and written text, a comparison of the two lists of extracted keywords is performed in order to measure their similarity. Fig. 2 shows the results of the overlap using Jaccard and KSim coefficients.

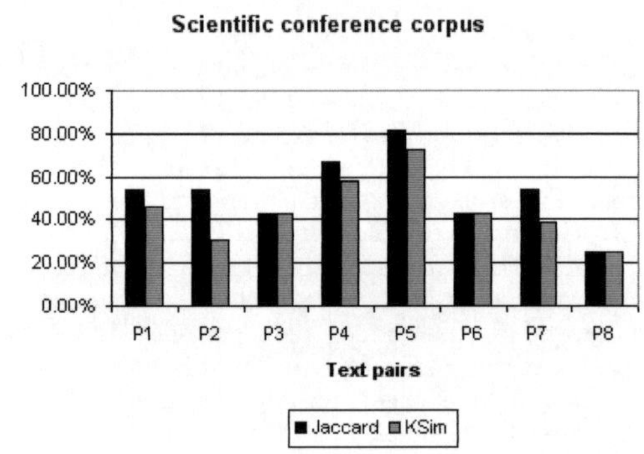

Fig. 2: *Comparison between written and spoken keywords using Jaccard and KSim coefficients*

As seen in the figure, Jaccard index has a relatively high value with an average of 52.59% (+ 5% if the effects caused by speech noise are ignored), showing that the two automatically extracted sets of keywords are quite similar [2]. The obtained average using KSim coefficient is 44.64% (which increases to 49.85% if the speech noise effect is ignored).

Amongst the eight pairs of texts, three have the same value for Jaccard and KSim coefficients, which means that the intersection for those three pairs contains only actual keywords. The average percentage of actual keywords inside the intersection between spoken and written texts, which is obtained by dividing the KSim value by Jaccard value, is 84.88% (86.25% if speech noise is ignored).

4.2 Movies corpus

The second corpus corresponds to a movie-club, a decision-making meeting about the movie to display, which lasts 48 minutes. This meeting has been recorded at the IDIAP Smart Meeting Room [11]. The generated corpus from this meeting is composed of one spoken text (12 563 words) and eight written documents including three articles, two slideshows and three posters (3 576 words). In order to have more than one spoken/written text pair, the eight written documents were categorised into three main sets according to their topics. Similarly, the spoken text has been divided into three topics. Subsequently, our movie corpus was decomposed into three written/spoken text pairs, M1, M2 and M3.

The scores of the F-measure of extracted keywords for the movie corpus pairs in this corpus are shown in Fig. 3, where the average F value is 26.66% (+6.66% if ignoring speech noise) for both written and spoken texts, which is less than the scores achieved in the previous corpus.

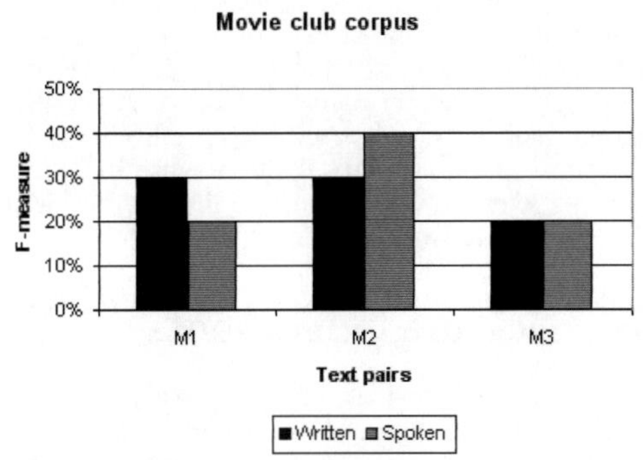

Fig. 3: *F-measures for written and spoken keywords using* TF·IDF$_L$

Fig. 4 shows the results of the comparison of written and spoken keywords, where the average is 18% using Jaccard coefficient and 8% using KSim coefficient. Thus, the percentage of actual keywords in the intersection is 44.5%. Even with the manual correction, the scores for these two similarities remained unchanged, due to the fact that the correction did not add any common keywords for written and spoken texts.

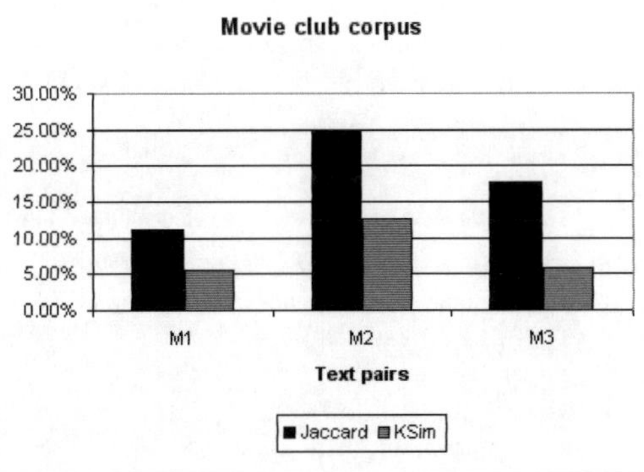

Fig. 4: *Comparison between written and spoken keywords using Jaccard and KSim coefficients*

The main reason for these low scores, either for individual keywords extraction or for keyword lists overlap for written/spoken text, is due to the nature of this corpus and the meeting scenario adopted by speakers. The speech is more spontaneous and informal compared to the previous academic corpus, and speakers interact more and rely less on the written documents.

4.3 Furniture corpus

The last corpus used in our evaluation is obtained from a furniture proposal meeting which aims at determining the type of furniture to buy. This meeting has been registered by ISSCO Research Group [13] and has a duration of 37 minutes. The corpus generated from this meeting is composed of one spoken text (9 036 words) and six written documents, three articles and three slideshows (4 804 words). Similarly to the previous corpus, this corpus was decomposed into three pairs, according to the topics of the written documents (F1, F2 and F3).

The F-measure values for this corpus (presented in Fig. 5) generated lower scores when compared to the scientific conference corpus, with an average of 43.33% (+ 6.66% when correcting noise effects) for written texts and 26.66% (+ 3.33% if correcting speech noise) for spoken texts.

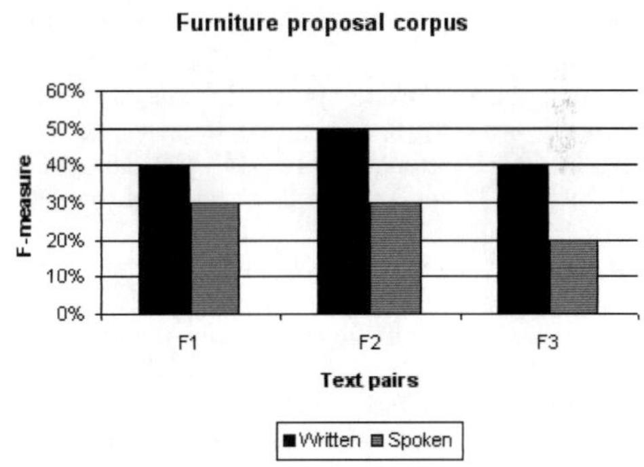

Fig. 5: *F-measures for written and spoken keywords using* TF·IDF$_L$

From written texts perspective, the content of discussed documents is less formal than the academic content in the scientific corpus, containing more informal vocabulary such as pronouns and phrasal verbs. From spoken texts perspective, some possible causes of the low scores are due to the spontaneity of speech and high interaction between speakers.

When comparing both spoken and written keywords (Fig. 6), the similarity obtained is 30.56% (+ 3.17% without speech noise effect) using Jaccard coefficient, and 19.72% (+ 2.8% without speech noise effect) using KSim coefficient, with a percentage of actual keywords in the intersection of 64.54% (+ 2.4% without speech noise effect). These lower results compared to the scientific conference are due to the fact that half of the written documents in this corpus were not discussed by speakers.

4.4 Discussion

The evaluation performed on the various bimodal corpora has highlighted several important aspects about the relationship between the nature of the corpora and the used language style (academic, spontaneous, etc.) from one side, and the accuracy of their terminology extraction from the other side. As seen in the evaluation section, the written texts provide more rele-

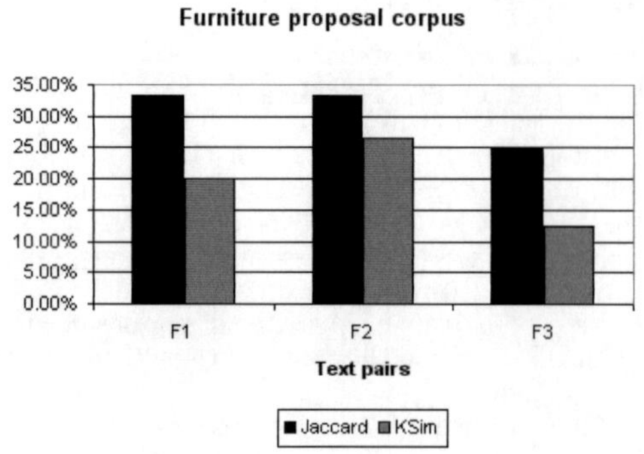

Fig. 6: *Comparison between written and spoken keywords using Jaccard and KSim coefficients*

vant keywords, when compared to spoken text. This is caused by the nature of spoken language which is more informal and rich with a variety of features such as colloquialisms, synonyms, phrasal verbs, variation in syntax and orthography (e.g. in the scientific conference corpus *GRID3* is sometimes referred to as *GRID*), in addition to other speech features such as repairs and word fragments, external noise, etc. Other factors that affected the accuracy of keywords extracting are the expertise of the transcriber in the domain. For instance, in the scientific conference corpus phrases like (*C++*, *C ++*, *Cplusplus*, and *C plus plus*) or (*daq*, *das*, and *data acquisition*) refer to the same concept respectively, but were transcribed differently.

From another side and by computing the symmetric difference for written/spoken pairs, it was revealed that there are cases where the spoken text provides additional keywords that are not present in the written text, and vice-versa. This emphasises the importance of using text extracted from different modalities for bimodal corpora terminology extraction.

5 Conclusions and future work

In this paper, we present a study about the extraction of keywords from bimodal corpora, generated from multimedia events mainly meetings and lectures, and composed of speech transcripts and the written texts of documents being discussed. The extracted written/spoken keyword lists for the respective corpora were evaluated against a manual golden standard. Later on, the overlap of each written/spoken keyword pair was measured by comparing the lists one to the other using specific similarity measures.

According to the obtained results, the system has generated more accurate keywords for written text compared to spoken text, mainly due to the nature of the latter and its ill-formed structure. This leads to the conclusion that written texts are more conducive to obtaining relevant keywords when compared to dialogue transcripts. Nevertheless, in some cases the latter has provided additional keywords that were not identified in the written text.

The extracted bimodal keywords might be used in the multimodal document alignment framework [10] defined in the context of lectures and meetings, in order to prune discovered thematic links between written documents and speech transcript of meetings. These bimodal keywords might be also useful for other tasks such as meeting indexing, searching and retrieval, etc.

As future work, other methods for terminology extraction will be used, which consider other features such as deeper linguistic information and other statistical features. From another side, the speech in the studied bimodal corpora was manually transcribed in order to avoid the negative effects of automatic speech recognition systems on this preliminary study (mainly due to the noise and error rate). However, in the future, automatically transcribed speech should be considered. Finally, focus will be put on bilingual bimodal corpora so as to verify if documents in different languages and obtained through different modalities can be aligned at keyword level.

6 Acknowledgements

We would like to express our gratitude to Alexandra Dobrinescu for her expertise and valuable comments provided during the golden standard compilation.

References

[1] S. Ananiadou. A methodology for automatic term recognition. In *Proceedings of the 15th International Conference on Computational Linguistics (COLING94)*, pages 1034–1038, Kyoto, Japan, 1994.

[2] M. R. Anderberg. *Cluster Analysis for Applications.* Academic Press, London, 1973.

[3] D. Bourigault. *LEXTER, un Logiciel d'EXtraction de TERminologie. Application à l'acquisition des connaissances à partir de textes.* PhD thesis, École des Hautes Études en Sciences Sociales, 1994.

[4] D. Bourigault, C. Jacquemin, and M.-C. L'Homme. *Recent Advances in Computational Terminology.* John Benjamins, Amsterdam, 2001.

[5] L. A. Ha. *Advances In Automatic Terminology Processing: Methodology And Application In Focus.* PhD thesis, University of Wolverhampton, 2007.

[6] L. A. Ha, R. Mitkov, and G. Corpas. Mutual terminology extraction using a statistical framework. In *Proceedings of the 24th edition of the conference of the Spanish Society for Natural Language Processing (SEPLN 2008)*, Madrid, Spain, September 2008.

[7] J. S. Justeson and S. L. Katz. Technical terminology: some linguistic properties and an algorithm for identification in text. *Natural Language Engineering*, 3(2):259–289, 1996.

[8] C. D. Manning and H. Schütze. *Foundations Of Statistical Natural Language Processing.* MIT Press, Cambridge, Massachusetts, 1999.

[9] T. McEnery. *Corpus-based Language Studies: an Advanced Resource Book.* Routledge, London, 2005.

[10] D. Mekhaldi. *A Study on Multimodal Document Alignment: Bridging the Gap between Textual Documents and Spoken Language.* PhD thesis, University of Fribourg, 2006.

[11] D. Moore. The IDIAP smart meeting room. Technical report, IDIAP-Com, 2002.

[12] C. Orăsan, V. Pekar, and L. Hasler. A comparison of summarisation methods based on term specificity estimation. In *Proceedings of Fourth International Conference on Language Resources and Evaluation (LREC-04)*, pages 1037–1041, Lisbon, Portugal, 2004.

[13] A. Popescu-Belis and D. Lalanne. Detection and resolution of references to meeting documents. In S. Renals and S. Bengio, editors, *Proceedings of MLMI'06, Machine Learning for Multimodal Interaction'06*, pages 64–75, Berlin, 2006. Springer-Verlag.

Exploiting Latent Semantic Relations in Highly Linked Hypertext for Information Retrieval in Wikis

Tristan Miller*
InQuira UK Ltd
50–52 Paul Street
London EC2A 4LB, United Kingdom
tmiller@inquira.com

Bertin Klein*
7P Consulting GmbH
Balcke-Dürr-Allee
40882 Ratingen, Germany
bertin.klein@7p-group.com

Elisabeth Wolf*
Ubiquitous Knowledge Processing Lab
Technische Universität Darmstadt, Germany
wolf@tk.informatik.tu-darmstadt.de

Abstract

Good hypertext writing style mandates that link texts clearly indicate the nature of the link target. While this guideline is routinely ignored in HTML, the lightweight markup languages used by wikis encourage or even force hypertext authors to use semantically appropriate link texts. This property of wiki hypertext makes it an ideal candidate for processing with latent semantic analysis, a factor analysis technique for finding latent transitive relations among natural-language documents. In this study, we design, implement, and test an LSA-based information retrieval system for wikis. Instead of a full-text index, our system indexes only link texts and document titles. Nevertheless, its precision exceeds that of a popular full-text search engine, and is comparable to that of PageRank-based systems such as Google.

Keywords

latent semantic analysis, LSA, latent semantic indexing, LSI, information retrieval, search engines, Wikipedia, wikis, hypertext, hyperlinks, large corpora

1 Introduction

1.1 Hypertext information retrieval

Traditional information retrieval systems are based on a flat, vector-space document model designed for searching plain-text corpora. Such systems are deficient when it comes to hypertext, however, as they fail to account for the topological structure of the corpus. This led to the development of the first hypertext document scoring algorithms, PageRank [22, 7, 5] and HITS [18], which score documents on the basis of the source and number of incoming and outgoing links. These scores are computed as a fixed point of a linear equation; later scoring studies [11, 6] investigated statistical or hybrid approaches.

In real-world IR applications, such as Google, the document scoring algorithm is combined with traditional vector-space IR techniques, plus metadata such as the document titles and link texts. The use of this metadata is predicated on the assumption that it is semantically related to the document under consideration. That is, the document title should reflect the document content, and likewise the text of links should accurately describe the target document—practices which are mandated by authoritative hypertext style guides [24, 10, 9, 4].

However, these guidelines are routinely ignored in HTML Web pages, for two reasons. First, few HTML authoring tools remind, encourage, or compel the writer to adhere to them. For example, in a random sample of documents from a Web corpus [15], we found that 6% of document titles were either missing, empty, a copy of the filename, or some default string such as "Untitled Document"; a further 2 to 3% were so vague as to be meaningless when read out of context. Of 2545 hyperlinks examined, 256 (10%) had no link text; 340 (13%) had link text corresponding to the URL or e-mail address of the target document; and dozens more were meaningless, referred only to navigation mechanics (e.g., "Click here"), or identified targets in a manner more suited to printed literature than to online hypertext (e.g., "Page 1").

The second reason for poor hypertext style is willful abuse of Internet search engines; authors can deliberately mislabel their documents and links in an attempt to influence page rankings for political purposes or commercial gain ("Google bombing" or "spamdexing", respectively) [2, 16]. Such manipulation is made possible by the prevailing access control structure of the Web, whereby anyone is free to post documents to be indexed, but the poster has exclusive control over their contents. This has resulted in an arms race of sorts between spamdexers and search engine developers, the former seeking new methods of artificially inflating their page ranks and the latter modifying their search algorithms to nullify those methods.

*The research described in this paper was carried out while the authors were at the Knowledge Management Research Group of the German Research Center for Artificial Intelligence (DFKI GmbH) in Kaiserslautern, Germany.

1.2 Wikis

In recent years, the Internet has witnessed a surge in the popularity of wikis, web applications for collaborative hypertext authoring [23]. Wikis have a number of important differences from regular HTML websites. Most significantly for the purposes of this study, wiki hypertext tends to be on-topic and have comparatively good hypertext style. This is a consequence of the following features:

Forced document validation. All wiki documents reside on a central Web server and as such must be retrieved and submitted through a Web browser. The wiki software provides a standardized editing interface, composed of HTML forms, which all users must use to submit new documents or changes to existing ones. The program which processes the form input resides on the server and can reject or fix invalid input, as well as automatically add important metadata such as the author's name and timestamp. For example, the wiki editing form will prompt the author for the document title, and if the author neglects to fill it in and submits the document anyway, the server will reject it and prompt him to correct it. By contrast, the file transfer protocol used to publish regular web pages does not enforce the semantic or syntactic validity of uploaded documents.

Lightweight markup language. Wikis accept documents not in HTML but in a lightweight markup language known as wikimarkup or wikitext [26]; the server then converts the wikitext to HTML for readers. Wikitext syntax varies from implementation to implementation, but nearly all dialects encourage or require link text to correspond to the target document title. Even where the wikitext dialect permits a disparity, the wiki software can tag the link with metadata[1] indicating the target document's true title.

Open access control structure. Wikis are designed for collaborative writing, where membership in the collaborative group can be restricted to a few named individuals or open to the general public. In the former case, abuse (in the form of spam, vandalism, or other off-topic posts) is practically nonexistent and easily rectified by blocking the perpetrator. Abuse is also low-risk in the latter case, provided the wiki is well-maintained. Popular open-access wikis such as Wikipedia are frequently policed by contributors, and any large-scale attempts at vandalism or spamdexing are immediately noticed and thwarted [25].

We posit that since wikis tend to be topically cohesive and employ stylistically correct hypertext, they do not benefit from typical Internet search engines' attempts to compensate for low-quality corpora. Any attempts to identify and suppress spamdexing, for example, can only result in false positives. Even search engines that assume their corpus documents are authoritative might not make the same assumption for the semantic correspondence between links and document titles. We therefore propose that wikis may benefit from special-purpose search engines optimized for their particular features. In particular, we believe that the semantic coherence of documents enforced by link text–document title correspondence makes wikis an excellent candidate for processing with latent semantic analysis [13, 20], a factor analysis technique which is able to discover latent semantic relations between terms and documents.

[1] For example, by using the `title` attribute of the `a` element in HTML.

2 Algorithm

In this section we describe document indexing and search algorithms which exploit both the explicit semantic relations found in wikis and the implicit semantic relations discovered by LSA.

2.1 Document indexing

The input to the document indexing phase is a collection of wiki articles; each article is assumed to contain a unique title, plus wikitext which may contain any number of internal hyperlinks to other wiki articles. We assume that the text of a hyperlink (the *link text*) is identical to the target article's title; for wikitext dialects where this is not necessarily the case, we substitute the target article title for the link text. Each document title or link text is considered to be a single token, even if it contains multiple words.

The next and crucial step in indexing documents is to discard all text except for the title and link texts. This drastically reduces the size of the corpus—typically by 99% or more. Throwing out all this text is justified on the grounds that it is only the link texts that encapsulate the strongest semantic relations among documents, so by comparison all other information is simply noise to LSA. This is similar to the use of a stop word list to remove function words of negligible semantic content (e.g., *and*, *the*, *of*), but on a much larger scale. The net effect is essentially lossy compression of the document corpus, and allows large corpora to be indexed and searched in a tiny fraction of the storage space and time that would normally be required.

The term–document co-occurrence matrix corresponding to this reduced corpus is then tabulated, preprocessed with any desired information-theoretic transformations (e.g., tf–idf), and then dimensionality-reduced with singular value decomposition.

Figure 1 shows a sample wiki article in various forms: (a) the source code, written in a fictitious wikitext dialect where `==...==` marks the article title and `[[...]]` indicates a hyperlink; (b) how the article might be rendered in a web browser; and (c) the document vector for the article as it would appear before SVD.

2.2 Search

A search query Q consists of one or more possibly weighted terms, represented internally as a document vector. Thus the most basic query algorithm would

```
==Abraham Lincoln==
Abraham Lincoln (* 12. Februar [[1809]]
bei [[Hodgenville]], Hardin County,
[[Kentucky]]; &dagger; [ermordet] 15.
April [[1865]] in [[Washington (D.C.)]])
war 16. [[Präsident der USA]]
([[1860]]&ndash;[[1865]]).
```

(a) Wikitext source

Abraham Lincoln
Abraham Lincoln (* 12. Februar 1809 bei Hodgenville, Hardin County, Kentucky; † [ermordet] 15. April 1865 in Washington (D.C.)) war 16. Präsident der USA (1860–1865).

(b) Presentation in browser

Term	Frequency
1809	1
1860	1
1865	2
Abraham␣Lincoln	1
Hodgenville	1
Kentucky	1
Präsident␣der␣USA	1
Washington␣(D.C.)	1

(c) Document vector

Fig. 1: *A sample wiki document*

be to perform pairwise vector comparisons[2] of Q with each document vector in the matrix, and return the best matches.

In the special case where Q consists of a single term which is also found in our corpus, we can use any of three additional algorithms which exploit the fact that each link text (term) in our corpus corresponds to a single document title. In the first algorithm, *Document–Document*, we find the corpus document with title Q, perform pairwise vector comparisons of its vector with each other document vector in the matrix, and return the best matches. In the second algorithm, *Link–Link*, we find the corpus term vector corresponding to Q and compare it pairwise with each other term vector in the matrix. The best-matching terms returned are link texts, but since each link text is also an article title, we return the documents with these titles. The last approach, *Link–Document*, is a hybrid of the first two, where the corpus term vector corresponding to Q is compared with each document vector.

[2] In practice, any vector comparison function [17, 21] could be used, but in this study we use the cosine metric, which returns a similarity measure in the range $[-1, 1]$.

	corpus		
	original	C_T	C_L
documents	775 696	10 419	10 419
words	195 374 109	113 019 521	658 447
links	8 196 071	N/A	658 447
kilobytes	1 891 382	775 500	6 564

Table 1: *Corpus statistics*

3 Evaluation

To test our system, we set up a user-focused experiment wherein human judges rated the relevance of search results obtained from various queries using various search engines, some of which are variations on our LSA technique and some of which are popular third-party systems.

For our document corpus, we used a subset of the German-language version of Wikipedia [1] as of 29 October 2005. The complete German Wikipedia is too large to work with efficiently for testing purposes (over 1.9 GB), so we pared it down by removing all non-articles (e.g., help and discussion pages), all leaf articles (i.e., those without any outgoing links), and all "orphan" articles of indegree < 100 (i.e., those with fewer than 100 incoming links). We refer to this corpus as C_T, as it contains the full text of the articles. From this corpus we derived a link text–only corpus C_L by removing all text outside of hyperlinks (except for the document title), plus all hyperlinks which do not target a document in the corpus. Table 1 gives some statistics on the size of our corpora.

We then selected at random three article titles which appeared in both Wikipedia's list of featured articles of 2005 and our corpora: *Abraham Lincoln*, *Dampflokomotive* (steam locomotive), and *Todesstrafe* (death penalty). Each article title formed a search query Q which was passed to seven search engine configurations:

LSA Document–Document (LSA DD). We use LSA to compare the document with title Q to all documents in C_L, and return the top four matching document titles.

LSA Link–Link (LSA LL). We use LSA to compare the term Q to all terms (i.e, link texts) in C_L, and return the top four matching link texts.

LSA Link–Document (LSA LD). We use LSA to compare the term Q to all documents in C_L, and return the top four matching document titles.

InQuery Term–Document (IQ TD). We use the InQuery search engine [3, 8] to index C_T, submit Q as a query, and return the top four matching document titles.

InQuery Link–Document (IQ LD). We use the InQuery search engine to index C_L, submit Q as a query, and return the top four matching document titles.

Google Term–Document (Google TD). We submit Q as a query to Google with the `site:de.wikipedia.org` directive to limit the search to German Wikipedia. Since our corpus is a subset of Wikipedia, we select the top four matching document titles which are also in our corpus.

Random outgoing links. This naïve algorithm, intended as a baseline, finds the document with title Q in C_L and returns four randomly selected outgoing hyperlink texts.

We could have obtained up to 28 unique results per topic, but since various search engines returned the same documents, we ended up with 14, 18, and 20 results for the respective topics.

We recruited 25 human judges who self-identified as fluent in German. The judges were asked to imagine that they were research assistants for three authors writing comprehensive reports on Abraham Lincoln, the steam locomotive, and the death penalty, respectively. We told them that they were to begin their research by finding relevant encyclopedia articles from Wikipedia. For each topic, we presented the judges with the combined search results for that topic. The judges were to read or skim through each Wikipedia article presented and rate them for relevance to the topic on a four-point scale from not at all relevant (1) to very relevant (4).

Implementation details

The data processing and experiments were carried out on a Sun Solaris machine using various GNU utilities, the Telcordia "Infoscale" LSA suite [12], InQuery, and a web browser for Google access.

The LSA indexing step was run with logarithmic local weighting and entropy global weighting. Since the degree of dimensionality reduction must be determined empirically, we made preliminary tests with various values and eventually settled on 1000 factors.

The three LSA-based query algorithms were implemented in a simple Bash shell script which took as input a query term, matched that term to a term or document vector from the corpus, and called the Telcordia `syn` program to perform pairwise comparisons with all the other term or document vectors. Processing each query took about three seconds of real time.

4 Results

Interjudge agreement (Pearson r) was generally very high. Mean agreements for the judges' relevance ratings for the three topics were $r = 0.747$, 0.715, and 0.767. Figure 2 is a box-and-whisker plot showing interjudge agreement for all three topics combined; the boxes delimit the first and third quartiles, the whiskers extend to the minimum and maximum, and the lines dividing the boxes show the median scores. There were no obvious outliers; we can therefore conclude that all judges basically agreed on what constituted a relevant document and that our aggregate ratings are meaningful.

We next performed a two-factor repeated-measures analysis of variance (ANOVA) to determine how the

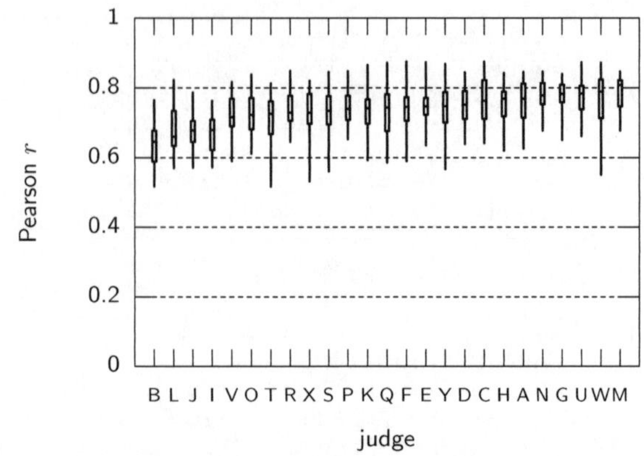

Fig. 2: *Interjudge agreement*

rank	search engine	mean relevance
1	Google TD	3.247
1	LSA LD	3.117
3	LSA LL	2.953
4	IQ TD	2.523
4	IQ LD	2.463
4	LSA DD	2.413
7	Random	1.540

Table 2: *Search engine rankings*

choice of search engine and query affected the ratings. The two-way interaction between the search engine and query was significant at the 0.05 confidence level ($p < 0.0001$), as was the query alone ($p < 0.0001$). However, this was not entirely unexpected given the small number of queries we used in the study. Given our uniformly high interjudge agreement across queries, though, we felt justified in continuing on to perform a single-factor ANOVA across search engines. In this ANOVA, variation between groups was, of course, also statistically significant ($p < 0.0001$) so we proceeded to perform 21 pairwise t-test means comparisons. All comparisons were significant except for those between Google TD and LSA LD ($p = 0.0848$), IQ TD and IQ LD ($p = 0.3147$), IQ TD and LSA DD ($p = 0.1337$), and IQ LD and LSA DD ($p = 0.6234$). On this basis we can partition search algorithm performance into three discrete ranks, as shown in Table 2.

Figure 3 plots the combined rating scores for each of the seven search engines tested. The graph type is the same as for Figure 2, except that the dividing lines show the mean instead of the median.

As expected, the random link search algorithm performed the poorest, with a mean relevance score of 1.540. The top-ranking position is tied between Google and our LSA Link–Document algorithm. The next rank is occupied by LSA Link–Link. No statistically significant difference was observed among the InQuery Term–Document, InQuery Link–Document, and LSA Document–Document algorithms, which occupy the following rank.

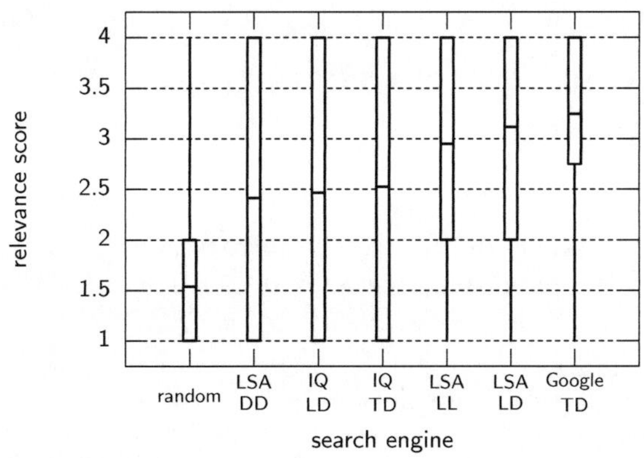

Fig. 3: *Search engine performance*

5 Conclusion

In this paper we have proposed a document indexing algorithm and family of LSA-based search algorithms which are designed to take advantage of the semantic properties of well-styled hyperlinked texts such as wikis. Performance was measured by having human judges rate the relevance of the top four search results returned by the system. When given single-term queries, our highest-performing search algorithm performs as well as the proprietary PageRank-based Google search engine, and significantly better than the non–hypertext-aware InQuery search engine. The performance with respect to Google is especially promising, given that our system operates on less than 1% of the original corpus text, whereas Google uses not only the entire corpus text but also metadata internal and external to the corpus.

Acknowledgments

The research described in this paper was supported in part by a grant (№ 01 ISC 13C) from the German Federal Ministry of Education and Research.

References

[1] *Wikipedia, die freie Enzyklopädie.* Accessed 2009-04-09 from `http://de.wikipedia.org/`.

[2] *Proceedings of the First International Workshop on Adversarial Information Retrieval on the Web, 14th International World Wide Web Conference*, 2005.

[3] J. Allan, J. P. Callan, W. B. Croft, L. Ballesteros, D. Byrd, R. C. Swan, and J. Xu. INQUERY does battle with TREC-6. In *Proceedings of the 6th Text REtrieval Conference (TREC-6)*, pages 169–206, 1997.

[4] T. Berners-Lee. *Style Guide for Online Hypertext*, chapter Make your (hyper)text readable. W3C, 1998.

[5] M. Bianchini, M. Gori, and F. Scarselli. Inside PageRank. *ACM Transactions on Internet Technology*, 5(1):92–128, 2005.

[6] A. Borodin, G. O. Roberts, J. S. Rosenthal, and P. Tsaparas. Finding authorities and hubs from link structures on the world wide web. In *WWW '01: Proceedings of the 10th international conference on World Wide Web*, pages 415–429, New York, NY, USA, 2001. ACM Press.

[7] S. Brin and L. Page. The anatomy of a large-scale hypertextual Web search engine. In *WWW7: Proceedings of the Seventh International Conference on World Wide Web 7*, pages 107–117, Amsterdam, 1998. Elsevier Science Publishers B. V.

[8] J. Broglio, J. P. Callan, W. B. Croft, and D. W. Nachbar. Document retrieval and routing using the INQUERY system. In D. Harman, editor, *Proceedings of the 3rd Text REtrieval Conference (TREC-3)*, NIST Special Publication 500-225, pages 22–29, 1994.

[9] W. Chisholm, G. Vanderheiden, and I. Jacobs, editors. *Web Content Accessibility Guidelines 1.0*, chapter 6.13: Provide clear navigation mechanisms. W3C Recommendation. W3C, May 1999.

[10] W. Chisholm, G. Vanderheiden, and I. Jacobs, editors. *HTML Techniques for Web Content Accessibility Guidelines 1.0*, chapter 6.1: Link text. W3C Note. W3C, Nov. 2000.

[11] D. Cohn and H. Chang. Learning to probabilistically identify authoritative documents. In *ICML '00: Proceedings of the Seventeenth International Conference on Machine Learning*, pages 167–174, San Francisco, CA, USA, 2000. Morgan Kaufmann Publishers Inc.

[12] S. Deerwester. *A Brief Infoscale Tools Tutorial.* University of Chicago, second edition, 16 May 1990.

[13] S. Deerwester, S. T. Dumais, G. W. Furnas, T. K. Landauer, and R. Harshman. Indexing by latent semantic analysis. *Journal of the American Society For Information Science*, 41:391–407, 1990.

[14] G. W. Furnas, T. K. Landauer, L. M. Gomez, and S. T. Dumais. Statistical semantics: Analysis of the potential performance of key-word information systems. *Bell System Technical Journal*, 62(6):1753–1806, 1983.

[15] Google Corp. Google programming contest, February 2002. Corpus and software. `http://www.google.com/programming-contest/`.

[16] S. Johnson. The art of Googlebombing. *Discover*, 25(7):22–23, July 2004.

[17] W. P. Jones and G. W. Furnas. Pictures of relevance: A geometric analysis of similarity measures. *Journal of the American Society for Information Science*, 38(6):420–442, 1987.

[18] J. M. Kleinberg. Authoritative sources in a hyperlinked environment. In *SODA '98: Proceedings of the Ninth Annual ACM-SIAM Symposium on Discrete algorithms*, pages 668–677, Philadelphia, 1998. Society for Industrial and Applied Mathematics.

[19] A. Kontostathis and W. M. Pottenger. A mathematical view of latent semantic indexing: Tracing term co-occurrences. Technical Report LU-CSE-02-006, Computer Science and Engineering Department, Lehigh University, 2002.

[20] T. K. Landauer, P. W. Foltz, and D. Laham. An introduction to latent semantic analysis. *Discourse Processes*, 25(2&3):259–284, 1998.

[21] M. McGill, M. Koll, and T. Noreault. An evaluation of factors affecting document ranking by information retrieval systems. Technical report, School of Information Studies, Syracuse University, Syracuse, NY, October 1979.

[22] L. Page, S. Brin, R. Motwani, and T. Winograd. The PageRank citation ranking: Bringing order to the Web. Technical report, Stanford Digital Library Technologies Project, 1998.

[23] L. Sanger et al. Wiki. In *Wikipedia, the Free Encyclopedia.* Retrieved 2009-04-09 from `http://en.wikipedia.org/wiki/Wiki`.

[24] A. Swartz. Don't use "click here" as link text. In W3C QA Team, editor, *Quality Tips for Webmasters.* W3C, Sept. 2001.

[25] F. B. Viégas, M. Wattenberg, and K. Dave. Studying cooperation and conflict between authors with *history flow* visualizations. In *CHI '04: Proceedings of the SIGCHI Conference on Human Factors in Computing Systems*, pages 575–582, New York, 2004. ACM Press.

[26] Wiki Markup Standard Working Group et al. WikiMarkupStandard. In *Meatball Wiki.* Retrieved 2009-04-01 from `http://www.usemod.com/cgi-bin/mb.pl?WikiMarkupStandard`.

Large vocabulary continuous speech recognition for Bulgarian

Petar Mitankin
Institute for Parallel Processing
Bulgarian Academy of Sciences
petar@lml.bas.bg

Stoyan Mihov
Institute for Parallel Processing
Bulgarian Academy of Sciences
stoyan@lml.bas.bg

Tinko Tinchev
Faculty of Mathematics and Informatics
Sofia University
tinko@fmi.uni-sofia.bg

Abstract

The paper presents the results of a project completed by the authors for realizing a continuous speech recognition system for Bulgarian. The state-of-the-art speech recognition technology used in the system is discussed. Special attention is given to the problems with some specifics of the Bulgarian language namely the large vocabulary (450000 wordforms). Some implementation details of the language module are given. At the end the paper provides evaluation of the accuracy of recognition.

Keywords

Speech recognition, language model

1 Introduction

Speech is a preferable medium for enabling comfortable and effective human-computer interface. This explains the wide interest in speech technology. There are a number of implementations of computer speech synthesis systems, which deliver intelligible and naturally sounding voices. For Bulgarian the SpeechLab system [1] is widely used by the visually impaired people.

Speech recognition is a considerably more difficult problem especially in the case of continuous speech and large vocabulary. There exist sophisticated implementations for English and some other major European and Asian languages. There are no reports for a large vocabulary continuous speech recognition (LVCSR) systems for Bulgarian. This paper will present the result of a project for realizing a LVCSR system for Bulgarian, which has been executed by the authors.

After some background information given in the next section we will describe the basic modules of our system. Section 3 and Section 4 will provide technical details of the Bulgarian acoustic and language models correspondingly. The recognition process is discussed in Section 5. In Section 6 we present the implementation details of the language model and Section 7 shows our accuracy evaluation. The conclusion presents some general discussions and further development directions.

2 Background

The problem of speech recognition can be considered as the task to find the set of possible word sequences which sound close to the observed speech signal and are admissible according to a given language model. The recognition of isolated words is significantly simpler. This task can be solved using various techniques with modest computational efforts. The computational complexity might be linear in regards of number of words in the vocabulary and no language model is required. A LVCSR system has to recognize a sequence of words from a large vocabulary without information of the word boundaries. A naive method would require an exponential number of word permutations to be considered.

The state-of-the-art approach to this problem is the Hidden Markov Model (HMM) framework. An HMM represent a statistical process, where the elements of a sequence of observed variables are regarded as emissions of the state variables in a Markov chain. The observed variables in our case represent the characteristics of a short slice (frame) of the speech signal. The states in the Markov chain represent the phases of the phonemes, which we assume to be pronounced.

3 Acoustic model

Our implementation of the acoustic model consists of two parts. The first part is the digital signal processing (DSP) module, which extracts a vector of features for each frame of the speech signal. The second part consists of the phoneme models.

The audio input is sampled at 16 KHz. First an emphasis filter is applied for emphasizing the higher frequencies. Afterwards, the signal is sliced into frames using a 30 ms Hamming window in 10 ms steps rolling. The next step is extracting the most characteristic, in respect to the human perception, features of the signal. For that purpose we extract the Mel-frequency

International Conference RANLP 2009 - Borovets, Bulgaria, pages 246–250

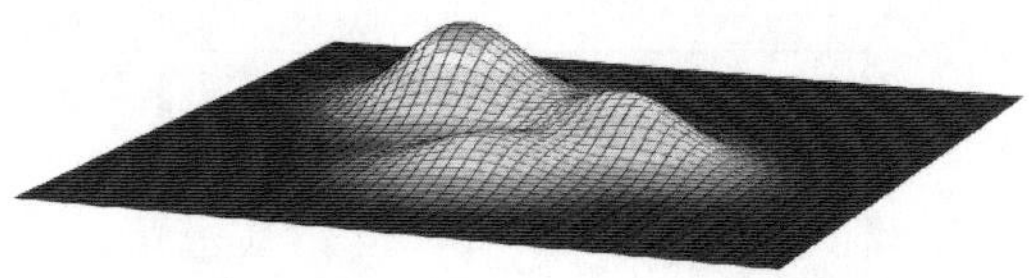

Fig. 1: *A two-dimensional Gaussian mixture with three components.*

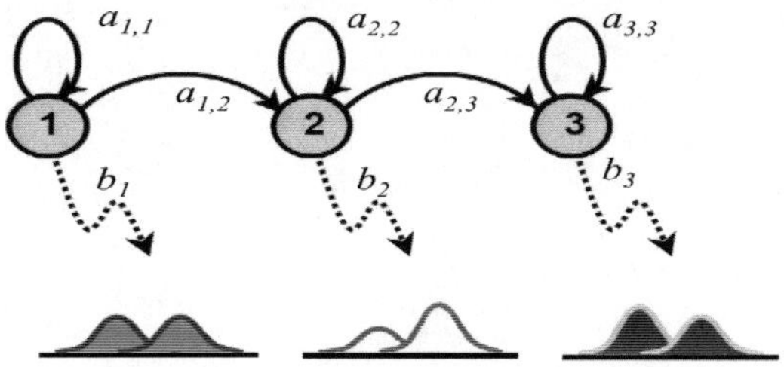

Fig. 2: *A continuous 3-state left-to-right first-order HMM.*

cepstrum coefficients. The idea behind is to compensate for some specifics of the human ear like logarithmic energy and frequency perception, and to be able to separate the source of the signal from the articulation configuration (the filter). More details on the articulation model and the DSP part might be found in [7, 5]. The characteristic feature vector we obtain from each frame consists of the first and second derivative of the frame energy, the 16 cepstrum coefficients and their first and second derivatives – 50 parameters in total.

We use Bayesian classifiers for classifying the frames based on the extracted feature vectors. The Bayesian classifiers are implemented as Gaussian mixtures.

$$f(x; c_k, \mu_k, \Sigma_k) = \sum_{k=1}^{K} c_k \frac{1}{\sqrt{(2\pi)^n |\Sigma|}} e^{-\frac{1}{2}(x-\mu)^t \Sigma (x-\mu)};$$

$$c_k \geq 0; \sum_{k=1}^{K} c_k = 1$$

Clearly each Gaussian mixture is a n-dimensional continuous probability distribution (see Figure 1). The Gaussian mixture is used to define the probability for every feature vector to belong to a given class. In our implementation we have 50 dimensions and we use mixtures with up to 16 components.

Our phoneme models are based on continuous 3-state left-to-right HMM (Figure 2). More formally a continuous 3-state left-to-right first-order HMM is a tuple consisting of a sequence of states $\langle 1, 2, 3 \rangle$, transition probabilities $\langle a_{0,1}, a_{1,1}, a_{1,2}, a_{2,2}, a_{2,3}, a_{3,3} \rangle; a_{0,1} = 1; a_{1,1} + a_{1,2} = 1; a_{2,2} + a_{2,3} = 1; a_{3,3} = 1$ and emissions $\langle b_1, b_2, b_3 \rangle$, such that every emission b_i is a n-dimensional Gaussian mixture. In that case if a sequence of T feature vectors $O_1, O_2, \ldots, O_T \in \mathbb{R}^n$ is given, then the probability this sequence to be observed along the sequence of hidden states $s_1, s_2, \ldots, s_T \in \{1, 2, 3\}$ is:

$$P(O_1, O_2, \ldots, O_T | s_1, s_2, \ldots, s_T) = \prod_{i=1}^{T} a_{i-1,i} b_i(O_i)$$

The probability the sequence $O_1, O_2, \ldots, O_T \in \mathbb{R}^n$ to be observed by the HMM model is the sum of the probabilities this sequence to be observed along all the sequences of hidden states:

$$P(O_1, O_2, \ldots, O_T) = \sum_{s_1, s_2, \ldots, s_T} P(O_1, O_2, \ldots, O_T | s_1, s_2, \ldots, s_T)$$

A	мерак	l	лек, лампа	g	град
a	мазе, кедър	m	мама	d	дар
e	тел, перо	n	нар	v	жар
i	бик, пирон	p	пек	z	зар
O	конче	r	ръка	k	кана
o	борба, кичур	s	син	4	чар
U	Тунис	t	тих	6	шах
Y	катър	f	фар	j	край, Кольо
b	баба	h	хол	0	чорбаджия
w	Варна	c	цар	9	годзила

Table 1: *Phonemes*

The acoustic model consists of 30 continuous 3-state left-to-right HMMs – one for each phoneme. The training of the HMMs is performed using a variant of the Baum-Welch algorithm [10, 5].

Our phonetic system uses different phonemes for the stressed and unstressed vowels "а", "о", "у" and "ъ". The unstressed vowels "а" and "ъ" are merged into one phoneme. The same applies to the unstressed "о" and "у". The palatalized consonants are considered as a pair of the corresponding not palatalized consonant followed by the semivowel "й". Table 1 presents the 30 phonemes used in our system.

4 Recognition model

The Recognition model has to provide a mapping between an audio signal represented as a sequence of feature vectors and the sequence of the pronounced words. This mapping is ambiguous because of the ambiguous positions of the word boundaries and the homophony phenomenon. For example there is no difference in the pronunciation of the Bulgarian phrases *Петко рита* and *Пет корита*. Because of that the Recognition model has to provide an evaluation (probability) of the correspondence of the audio signal and a sequence of words in regards to the following criteria:

1. Acoustic similarity between the signal and the pronunciation of the words;
2. The syntactic correctness of the word sequence;
3. The semantic correctness of the word sequence in respect to the context.

The speech recognition task is then reduced to finding the most probable sequence of words for a given signal

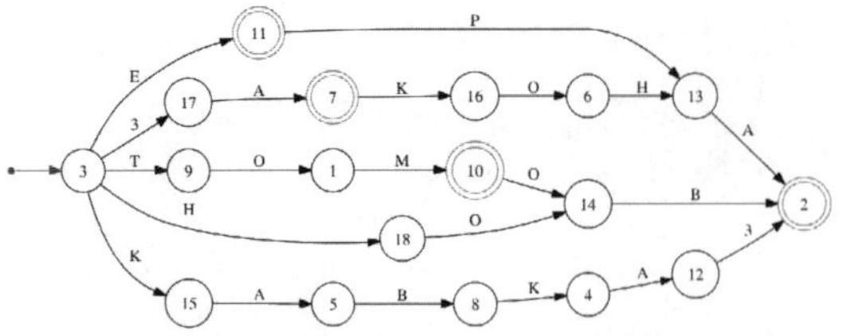

Fig. 3: *Dictionary if the wordforms* Е, ЕРА, ЗА, ЗАКОНА, КАВКАЗ, НОВ, ТОМ, ТОМОВ *represented as a deterministic finite-state automaton.*

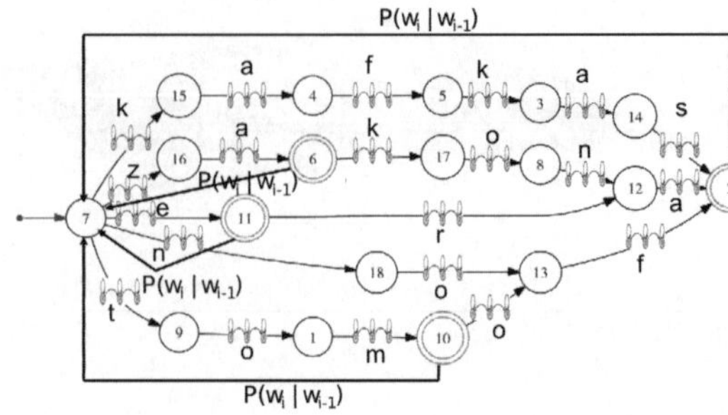

Fig. 4: *The Recognition model.*

in respect to the Recognition model.

The Recognition model is built in several steps. First a deterministic finite-state automaton D recognizing all the wordforms from the vocabulary is constructed using the methods presented e.g. in [2]. On Figure 3 the minimal deterministic finite-state automaton for 8 wordforms is shown. On the next step the vocabulary of phonetized wordforms is built. For this task we have used the phonetization rules for Bulgarian developed in the framework of the SpeechLab project [1]. The ruleset is represented as a composition of replace rules. For example the rule for de-voicing a sequence of consonants ending with an unvoiced consonant is (refer to [6]):

```
(w→f)|(z→s)|(g→k).../
_ (voiced|unvoiced)*.unvoiced.(vowel|sonor)
```

All the phonetization rules are represented as regular relations, which are composed into one relation R using the techniques presented in [6, 4]. The finite-state automaton representing the phonetized vocabulary $R(D)$ is derived by the mapping of D through R using the following regular operations: $R(D) = range(id(D) \circ R)$.

In the next steps the phonemes in the network $R(D)$ are substituted with the corresponding acoustic models – the 3-state left-to-right HMMs discussed in the previous section. In this way we derive a huge HMM which models the acoustic probability a sequence of feature vectors to be mapped against a given word.

Finally the Recognition model has to incorporate a language model which evaluates the possible sequences of words. The most common language model for a task of this scope is based on bigram probability estimates, relating the likelihood of co-occurrence for two consecutive words in a sequence.

The final recognition network is constructed from the phonetized vocabulary HMM by creating bigram-weighted transitions from the end of each word (the final states) to the beginning of every other word (the starting state). The bigram-weights are calculated dynamically as explained in section 6. The Recognition model is illustrated on Figure 4.

5 Recognition process

As discussed above, the recognition process is reduced to finding the most probable sequence of states in the Recognition model in regards to the feature vectors derived from the audio signal. The general scheme of the recognition process is given on Figure 5.

The computational complexity of the naive approach, which considers all possible sequences of hidden states would be $O(M^T)$, where M is the number of states in the language model HMM and T is the length of the sequence of feature vectors. The Viterby algorithm [10] might be used for reducing the complexity to $O(M^2T)$. In the case of LVCSR M is in the order of millions and T is in the order of a thousand. Therefore a full Viterby search can hardly be performed in real time. To reduce the computations a common approach is to employ beam search. In the Viterby algorithm at each step only a limited number – the best scoring paths are regarded. I.e. the dynamic programming traversal of the network is a partial breadth-first traversal, where the lower scoring paths are discarded. Only the N-best continuation "active" states are considered. In our evaluation we have experimented with the following values for N: 1000, 1500, 2000, 2500 and 3000.

The number of word sequences, which are derived using a full Viterby search is in the order of $10^{60} - 10^{70}$. The beam search approach reduces the number of word sequences for a given utterance to about 10^{10}. The result of the traversal is stored into a weighted acyclic word lattice. An example of the word lattice for the utterance "петкорита" is shown on Figure 6. The weights correspond to the acoustic and word bigram probabilities, summed with particular weights. The acoustic probability is calculated from the acoustic models of the phonemes in the sequence and the bigram probabilities are derived from the bigram language model. On a second step the acoustic and bigram probabilities are re-scored using other weights. The system returns the best sequences in the word lattice in respect to the new weights. More details of this approach are presented in [8, 5].

Our system implements the Microsoft Speech API version 5.1. In this way the Bulgarian speech recognition is accessible under the Microsoft Windows operating system from all applications utilizing the Speech API like Microsoft Office. The memory used by the system is below 120 MB. The speed of the processing is under 0.9 times the real time on a modest computer in case of 2000 active states. This means that the user can use the system without the need to awaiting the processing.

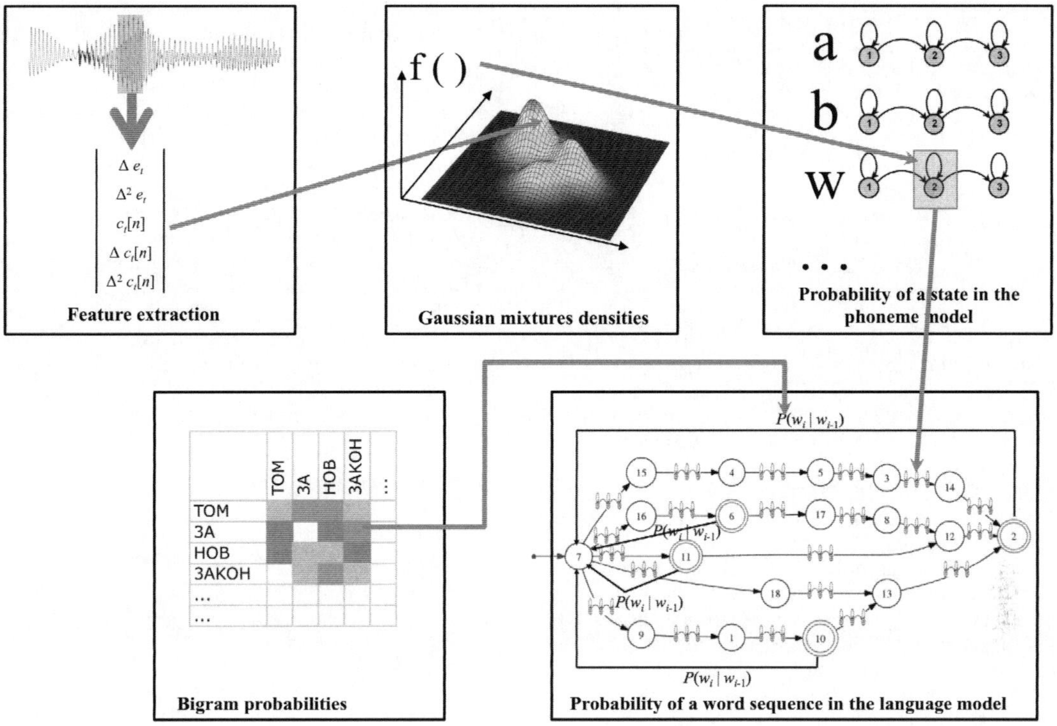

Fig. 5: *General scheme of the speech recognition process.*

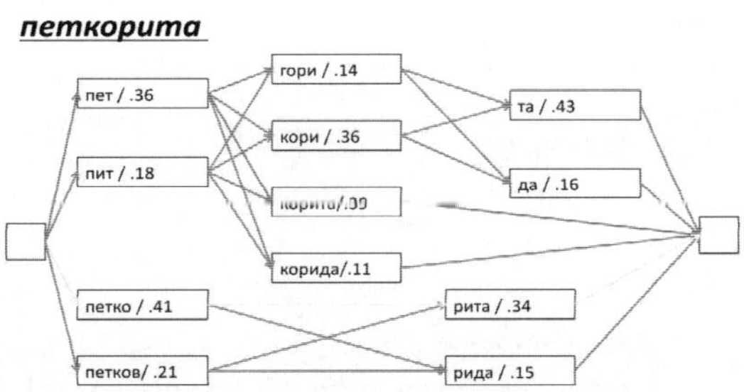

Fig. 6: *Word lattice.*

6 Implementation details of the Language model

Consider the sequence of n words $v_1, v_2, \ldots, v_n$. Its probability is approximated as $P(v_1) \cdot \prod_{i=1}^{n-1} P(v_{i+1} \mid v_i)$. A bigram language model can be considered as a data structure used for solving the following problem: given a bigram (pair of words) $w_1 w_2$, find $P(w_2 \mid w_1)$.

We use a corpus of legal texts to evaluate a bigram language model. The corpus consists of $200 \cdot 10^6$ words. 90% of the sentences in the corpus are used for the computation of the bigrams, while the other 10% are used for the calculation and minimization of the cross-entropy. The number of the words (monograms) in our dictionary is 442, 501. In our implementation we use a bigram cut-off threshold: we take into account only the bigrams with at least two occurrences in the corpus. The number of these bigrams is 4, 108, 409. To smooth the monogram and bigram probabilities, we apply the absolute discounting algorithm, [9], in backing-off variant.

In [3] Jan Daciuk and Gertjan van Noord present a technique for very compact representation of language models. However their method requires binary search in sorted arrays. Since the time complexity is crucial for a good speech recognition system, we choose an approach that requires constant time for a bigram probability evaluation. The constant is small and does not depend on the number of the monograms and bigrams.

Every word is represented as a 32-bit integer. Its value is the position of the word in the lexicographical order of all words. Every byte of this 32-bit integer is considered as a separate symbol. Thus every word has exactly four symbols and every bigram is a string of eight symbols. The number of all symbols is 256. We keep all such eight-symbol strings in a perfect hash. The perfect hash is represented as a minimal acyclic deterministic finite state automaton $A = \langle \Sigma, Q, i, \delta, \sigma, f \rangle$ over alphabet Σ, where $|\Sigma| = 256$, Q is the set of states, $|Q| = 631, 501$, $\delta : Q \times \Sigma \to Q$ is a partial transition function, the number of the transitions is 4, 264, 244, i is the initial state and f is the only one final state. Every transition of A is associated with a nonnegative whole number by the

Active states	1000	1500	2000	2500	3000
Juridical texts					
1-LER	93.72%	95.32%	96.05%	96.16%	96.51%
1-WER	81.46%	84.85%	87.10%	87.41%	88.08%
Speed (x RT)	0.32	0.55	0.82	1.21	1.67
Memory (MB)	100.73	108.3	111.54	116.0	137.21
Common texts					
1-LER	94.13%	94.83%	95.30%	95.50%	95.64%
1-WER	80.41%	82.37%	83.53%	84.07%	84.42%
Speed (x RT)	0.3	0.52	0.77	1.13	1.55
Memory (MB)	103.94	110.59	119.17	120.6	139.31

Table 2: *Evaluation table.*

function $\sigma : Q \times \Sigma \rightarrow \mathbb{N}$. A has the property that if the bigram $b = b_1 b_2 \ldots b_8$ is accepted by A, then $\sum_{k=1}^{8} \sigma(\delta^*(i, b_1 b_2 \ldots b_{k-1}), b_k)$ is the position of the bigram b in the lexicographical order of all $4,108,409$ bigrams. Here δ^* is the extended transition function. The function δ induces a sparse transition matrix and we use Tarjan's table, [11], to represent this matrix. The table has $4,895,828$ entries. Every entry represents a transition. The size of one entry is 12 bytes: 4 bytes encode a symbol, 4 - a value of σ and 4 - a destination state. We have achieved 87,1% utilization of the Tarjan's table leaving 12,9% empty entries. Using this table, given a state s and a symbol $a \in \Sigma$, we can compute in constant time $\delta(s, a)$ and $\sigma(s, a)$. We have another table Pr of $4,108,409$ four-byte floating-point numbers. In Pr we keep the $-log$ probabilities of the bigrams. Let us explain how our language model solves the following problem: given a bigram $b = b_1 b_2 \ldots b_8$, find $P(b)$. We start a traversal of A with b. If b is accepted by A then $P(b) = Pr[\sigma^*(i, b)]$, where σ^* is the extended version of σ. If the traversal fails after b_4 then we use the smoothing formulae and the monogram model to compute $P(b)$. If the traversal fails before b_4 then $P(b) = P(b_5 b_6 b_7 b_8)$ and we use the monogram model to compute it. The representation of the monogram model is trivial: it is a table of $442,501$ four-byte floating-point numbers - one number for every word.

The size of the whole language model is 82,3 MB. The computation of a bigram probability $P(w_2 \mid w_1)$ requires constant time.

7 Evaluation

We performed our experiments on a notebook with a Mobile AMD Sempron 3400+ processor and 2 GB RAM. The acoustic model was trained by adapting a speaker independent model with one hour of speaker's speech data. The vocabulary consists of about 450000 wordforms.

The test set consists of 63 utterances from juridical texts and 1276 utterances from common texts. We have evaluated the letter accuracy defined as $1 -$ letter error rate (1-LER) and the word accuracy defined as $1 -$ word error rate (1-WER). The speed indications are in respect to the real time. Table 2 summarizes the evaluation results.

A manual review of the recognition results revealed some specific classes of mistakes. As expected the complex clitics grammar in Bulgarian resulted in many cases of wrong word boundary segmentation e.g.:

да ли ↔ *дали*, *би ли* ↔ *били*, *за кон и* ↔ *закони*.

The full form of the definite article inflection in masculine nouns was another major source of recognition errors. Since the "т" in the full form article inflections "ът", "ят" is often pronounced without an explosion the system confused it often with the wordform with the non-full form of the definite article e.g.:
конят ↔ *коня*, *мъжът* ↔ *мъжа*.

The single most frequent source of errors are the proposition "в" and "с". Their unvoiced phonetizations are the phonemes "f" and "s", which are very easily confused with any noise like speaker's aspiration especially at the utterance start. Since those are between the most frequent words in Bulgarian this resulted some times in the wrong insertion of an additional proposition in front of the utterance, especially in case of more noisy environment.

8 Conclusion

This paper presented the result of the project for building a LVCSR system for Bulgarian. Sophisticated techniques were applied to cope with the very large Bulgarian vocabulary. The evaluation results showed less than 4% letter error rate and 13% word error rate on speech recognition of juridical texts using real time processing speed on a modest notebook computer. The system has been packaged as a software product implementing the Microsoft Speech API 5.1.

An informal user feasibility test has been conducted in a company specialized in providing law information services. This test proved that although a user adaptation period is required, the system is already in a state permitting daily use for text dictation.

References

[1] M. Andreeva, I. Marinov, and S. Mihov. Speechlab 2.0 – a high-quality text-to-speech system for bulgarian. In *Proceedings of the RANLP 2005*, pages 52 – 58, Borovets, 2005.

[2] J. Daciuk, S. Mihov, B. Watson, and R. Watson. Incremental construction of minimal acyclic finite state automata. *Computational Linguistics*, 26(1), 2000.

[3] J. Daciuk and G. van Noord. Finite automata for compact representation of tuple dictionaries. *Theor. Comput. Sci.*, 313(1):45–56, 2004.

[4] H. Ganchev, S. Mihov, and K. U. Schulz. One-letter automata: How to reduce k tapes to one. In F. Hamm and S. Kepser, editors, *Logics for Linguistic Structures*, number 201 in Trends in Linguistics, pages 35–56. Mouton de Gruyter, Hillsdale, New Jersey, 2008.

[5] X. Huang, A. Acero, and H.-W. Hon. *Spoken Language Processing*. Prentice-Hall, 2001.

[6] R. M. Kaplan and M. T. Kay. Regular models of phonological rule systems. *Computational Linguistics*, 20(3):331–378, 1994.

[7] S. E. Levinson. *Mathematical models for speech technology*. Wiley, 2005.

[8] R. Mosur. *Efficient Algorithms for Speech Recognition*. PhD thesis, Carnegie Mellon University, 1996.

[9] Ney, Hermann, U. Essen, and R. Kneser. On structuring probabilistic dependences in stochastic language modeling. *Computer Speech and Language*, 8:1–38, June 1994.

[10] L. Rabiner. A tutorial on hidden markov models and selected applications in speech recognition. *Proc. IEEE*, 77, 1989.

[11] R. E. Tarjan and A. C. Yao. Sorting a sparse table. *Communications of the ACM*, 22(11):606–611, November 1979.

Diacritization for Real-World Arabic Texts

Emad Mohamed
Indiana University
emohamed@indiana.edu

Sandra Kübler
Indiana University
skuebler@indiana.edu

Abstract

For Arabic, diacritizing written text is important for many NLP tasks. In the work presented here, we investigate the quality of a diacritization approach, with a high success rate for treebank data but with a more limited success on real-world data. One of the problems we encountered is the non-standard use of the hamza diacritic, which leads to a decrease in diacritization accuracy. If an automatic hamza restoration module precedes diacritization, the results improve from a word error rate of 9.20% to 7.38% in treebank data, and from 7.96% to 5.93% on selected real-world texts. This shows clearly that hamza restoration is a necessary step for improving diacritization quality for Arabic real-world texts.

Keywords

Arabic diacritization, memory-based learning

1 Introduction

The problem of diacritization, or vocalization, is essential to many tasks in Arabic NLP. Arabic is generally written without the short vowels, which means that one written form can have several pronunciations, each pronunciation carrying its own meaning(s). The word form 'mskn' is an example for a highly ambiguous word. Its possible pronunciations include 'maskan' (home), 'musakkin' (analgesic), 'masakn' (they-*fem.* have held), or 'musikn' (they-*fem.* have been held). The importance of diacritization becomes clear when we look at how Google Translate renders 'A$tryt Almskn mn AlSydlyp' (I bought a pain killer from the pharmacy): as 'I bought the home from the pharmacy'. This error would not occur if the input to the translation system were diacritized in a first step before the actual translation process. However, diacritization is far from trivial: the example above shows that the diacritized forms of a single undiacritized word differ in their parts of speech (POS) as well as in their meaning. This shows that to a certain degree, diacritization performs implicit POS tagging and word sense disambiguation. It also shows very clearly that word forms cannot be diacritized in isolation; the task is heavily dependent on the context of the word.

The goal of the work reported here is the creation of a diacritization system that works reliably on real-world data taken from websites. The first step towards this problem is a system that reaches a high accuracy in an *in-vitro* evaluation, i.e. on data from the same treebank on which it was trained. After we obtain a reliable system for the treebank data, we will test it to determine how well it works in an *in-vivo* evaluation, i.e. on real-world data. More importantly, in the second step, we will investigate how the system needs to be modified in order to produce reliable diacritizations in the in-vivo situation.

In the first step, we concentrate on investigating how important different types of context are for diacritization. We follow Zitouni et al. [16] in defining diacritization as a classification problem in which we decide for each character in the undiacritized word whether it is followed by a short vowel. Additionally, the classification task includes the shadda and sokoon (lack of a vowel). The shadda is consonant gemination and is usually found in combination with another vowel, thus resulting in 3 classes, *~a, ~i, ~u*. The shadda plays an important role in the interpretation of Arabic words because it is used, inter alia, to discriminate between the base form of a verb and its causative form: *kataba* (to write), *kat~aba* (to make write). At present, we ignore case endings, mood endings, and nunation (syntactic indefiniteness marker for a noun or adjective). In this setting, we also ignore the hamza, the glottal stop.

Most experiments are performed on treebank data, which is preprocessed and standardized to a very high degree. When such a model is used for naturally occurring data, such as newspaper texts published on the world-wide web, the results are considerably lower than the results published by Zitouni et al. [16], for example.

For the second set of experiments, our intention is to investigate how such a treebank trained diacritization system performs on real-world data. For this experiment, we use the diacritization approach that proved optimal on the treebank data (from the Penn Arabic Treebank (ATB) [1]) and use it to diacritize articles from the Agence France Press (AFP) Arabic website. Although, data from AFP were included in the training set, so that there are no cross-genre problems, our first results were disappointing. Examination of the data shows that one major difference between our training data from the ATB and the real-world test data is that the latter collapses the different forms of 'hamza', the glottal stop, into the long vowel alef, a common, but non-standard, practice. In the real-world texts, however, practices vary considerably in terms of whether the hamza is used carefully or carelessly, or even whether it is used at all. Some texts, like those of the AFP news agency do not use hamzas at all. In other texts, such as the Egyptian Al-Ahram [1], they are used correctly. From these findings, we conclude that a hamza restoration program is

[1] www.ahram.org.eg

International Conference RANLP 2009 - Borovets, Bulgaria, pages 251–257

necessary for the treatment of such texts.

In further experiments, we examine the different options of hamza restoration or normalization in search of the optimal settings of diacritization. For this purpose, we conduct two kinds of experiments: 1) in-vitro experiments, in which we test the different settings in a controlled setting on data from the Arabic Treebank, and 2) in-vivo experiments, in which we use the best settings from step 1) for diacritizing real-world data.

2 Related work

The first approaches to the diacritization of Arabic define the problem word-based, i.e. the task is to determine for each word the complete diacritized form. Gal [10] uses a bigram Hidden Markov Model for diacritizing the Qur'an and achieves a word error rate (WER) of 14%. His error analysis shows that the errors result mostly from unknown words. Kirchhoff et al. [12] design a diacritization module for use in a speech recognition system. Their system uses a unigram model extended by a heuristic for unknown words, which retrieves the most similar unlexicalized word and then applies edit distance operations to turn it into the unknown word. They reach a WER (for diacritization) of 16.5% on conversational Arabic. Nelken and Shieber [14] tackle the problem with weighted finite-state transducers. For known words, morphological units are used for retrieving the diacritization while unknown words are diacritized based on the sequence of characters. They reach a WER of 12.8%. Zitouni et al. [16] use a maximum entropy model in combination with a character based classification. Their features are based on single characters of the focus word, morphological segments, and POS tags. They reach a WER of 17.9%. Habash and Rambow [11] perform a full diacritization including case endings and nunation. They use the Buckwalter analyzer [3] to obtain all possible morphological analyses, including all diacritics. Then they train individual classifiers to disambiguate between these analyses. Residual ambiguity is resolved via an n-gram language model. Habash and Rambow reach a WER of 14.9% on the test set of Zitouni et al. [16]. Shaalan et al. [15] compare a lexicon-based approach with an approach using word bigram statistics and a Support Vector Machine (SVM) classifier. The SVM approach uses features from automatic segmentation, POS tagging, and chunk parsing. Shaalan et al. show that the best results for diacritization are reached by combining all three approaches. Unfortunately, they use the Ummah section of the treebank for training and testing, which can be shown to give better results than the An Nahar News section that Zitouni et al. and Habash and Rambow use (see Section 3.3). To our knowledge, Shaalan et al. are the first to include case endings as features in the task. however, a comparison of the SVM approach with and without case endings shows that their inclusion results in a considerable decrease in performace: The WER increases from 16.26% to 69.94%.

A comparison of the different approaches shows that the definition of diacritization as inserting vowels between characters results in the best WER. However, these studies leave the lexical context of words for the most part unexplored. In the present study, we will investigate this area of research. The studies also concentrate on treebank data, which means that it is unclear how well they work on real-world data.

We are not aware of any automatic approaches to hamza restoration. For example, Diab et al. [9] do not consider the hamza in their diacritization since "most Arabic encodings do not count the hamza a diacritic, but rather a part of the letter". The relaxed attitude towards the hamza in the Arabic orthography is part of what Buckwalter [4] calls "suboptimal orthography".

3 The baseline system

3.1 Data

For the baseline system, we use the Penn Arabic Treebank (ATB) [1] as the data source. The treebank is encoded in Buckwalter transliteration [3] and is available in a diacritized and an undiacritized version. Based on the treebank, we performed three different experiments: 1) In order to test the limits of the approach, we decided to use a large and varied data set, with 10-fold cross-validation (CV). 2) To ensure that our results can be compared with the results of Zitouni et al. [16], we perform a second experiment on their data set. 3) Based on the results from the first experiment, we selected one fold of this experiment as test set and the other 9 folds as training set for the third experiment. This data set will also be used in the experiments concerning the hamza restoration. In order to keep consistency with the real-world test set from the internet in this second series of experiments, we chose the set including AFP data. An earlier version of the first two experiments described here was published in [13].

For the first experiment, we extract 170 000 words from the AFP section (part 1 version 2.0) and approximately 160 000 words from the Ummah section (part 2 version 2.0), in a 10-fold CV setting. This experiment is intended to determine the optimal parameter settings for the machine learner and the optimal context used for diacritization. For the second experiment, which serves as comparison to Zitouni et al., the data are taken from part 3, version 1.0. This data set contains news items from the An Nahar News text, it is split into a training set of approximately 288 000 words and a devtest set of approximately 52 000 words. For the third experiment, we chose a subset of the first experiment, part 1, version 2.0, in order to use data that originates from the same source, AFP, as the real-world test files. In this setting, the 90% from the beginning of the data set serve as training data and the tail 10% are used for testing.

As mentioned previously, we define diacritization as a classification problem: For each character in the focus word, the learner needs to decide whether the character is followed by a short vowel and what the short vowel is. We will call this character the focus character. The task also involves the restoration of the shadda (gemination).

The features used for determining the short vowel following the focus character consist of the focus character itself (c), its local context in terms of neighboring

w_{-5}	w_{-4}	w_{-3}	w_{-2}	w_{-1}	c_{-5}	c_{-4}	c_{-3}	c_{-2}	c_{-1}	c	c_1	c_2	c_3	c_4	c_5	w_1	w_2	w_3	w_4	w_5	v
kl	$y"	tgyr	fy	HyAp	_	_	_	_	_	A	l	m	t	$	r	styfn	knt	EndmA	Evrt	Ely	_
kl	$y"	tgyr	fy	HyAp	_	_	_	_	A	l	m	t	$	r	d	styfn	knt	EndmA	Evrt	Ely	_
kl	$y"	tgyr	fy	HyAp	_	_	_	A	l	m	t	$	r	d	_	styfn	knt	EndmA	Evrt	Ely	u
kl	$y"	tgyr	fy	HyAp	_	_	A	l	m	t	$	r	d	_	_	styfn	knt	EndmA	Evrt	Ely	a
kl	$y"	tgyr	fy	HyAp	_	A	l	m	t	$	r	d	_	_	_	styfn	knt	EndmA	Evrt	Ely	a
kl	$y"	tgyr	fy	HyAp	A	l	m	t	$	r	d	_	_	_	_	styfn	knt	EndmA	Evrt	Ely	~i

Fig. 1: *The word 'Almt$rd' represented with one instance per word; the class represents the vowel to be inserted after the character.*

characters within the focus word, and a more global context of neighboring words. For the local context, 5 characters to the left ($c_{-5} \dots c_{-1}$) and 5 characters to the right ($c_1 \dots c_5$) are used; for the lexical context, 5 words to the left ($w_{-5} \dots w_{-1}$), and 5 words to the right ($w_1 \dots w_5$). The last value in the vector (v) provides the correct classification, i.e. the short vowel to be inserted after c, or - in cases where no vowel is inserted in that position. The instances for the Arabic word 'Almt$rd', for example, are shown in Figure 1. The last instance contains an example of the shadda, represented by the tilde sign.

3.2 Methods

For classification, we use a memory-based learner, TiMBL [7]. Memory-based learning is a lazy-learning paradigm, which assumes that learning does not consist of abstraction of the training instances into rules or probabilities. Instead, the learner uses the training instances directly. As a consequence, training consists in storing the instances in an instance base, and classification finds the k nearest neighbors in the instance base and chooses their most frequent class as the class for the new instance. Memory-based learning has been proven to have a suitable bias for many NLP problems [5, 6]. One of the reasons for this success is that natural language exhibits a high percentage of subregularities or irregularities, which cannot be distinguished from noise. Eager learning paradigms smooth over all these cases while memory-based learning still has access to the original instance. Thus, if a new instance is similar enough to one of these irregular instances, it can be correctly classified as such.

Memory-based learning was chosen for two reasons: First, this approach weights features based on information gain or gain ratio [7], thus giving some indication of the most and the least important features. Additionally, it is a paradigm that is capable of handling symbolic features with a high number of different feature values. This allows us to use complete context words as features.

Parameter settings for TiMBL need to be determined first. The best results are obtained for all experiments with the IB1 algorithm with similarity computed as weighted overlap, i.e. with a standard city block metric as distance measure. Relevance weights are computed with gain ratio, and the number of k nearest neighbors (or in TiMBL's case, nearest distances) is set to 1. The latter setting is noteworthy in that it signals that only the closest training examples provide reliable information for classifying a character. Normally, higher values of k are beneficial since they provide a certain smoothing factor. A more detailed investigation of different options in feature settings, as well as optimal training set sizes can be found in [13].

For the experiments to determine the effect of context on diacritization accuracy, we use 10-fold cross validation (CV). For the experiments with the data set from Zitouni et al. and for the AFP set, we use a designated test set. For the 10-fold CV experiments, we do not build the folds randomly but rather sequentially, thus ensuring that a single fold contains consecutive articles. This may result in folds which cover different topics from the other folds. We are convinced that this approach is closer to real-world situations since we cannot be sure that the training data will be from the same time period and thus cover the same topics. However, we make sure that all instances of a word are put in the same fold.

For evaluation, we calculate the error rate based on characters (CER) and based on words (WER). A decision of the classifier is considered correct if both the vowel to be inserted and the shadda (if present) are correct. Since previous work has been evaluated on all words in the texts, including punctuation and other non-diacritized words such as numbers, we will present these results to allow a comparison to previous work. However, we believe that words that are never diacritized (such as numbers or punctuation signs) should not be considered in the evaluation. For this reason, we also provide results where such words were present in the classification, but were excluded in the evaluation.

3.3 Baseline results for treebank data

Before we start with the evaluation proper, we need to establish the level of difficulty of the task. One measure for difficulty is the average number diacritizations per word. A closer look at the large data set used for the fist experiment shows that a word on average has only 1.67 diacritizations. This figure is considerably lower than the average in normal texts. Debili et al. [8] found that on average, each undiacritized word type has 2.9 diacritized versions, and there is an average of 11.6 diacritized versions per word token in a text. We assume that the difference is a consequence of the different text genres.

The results of our experiments with regard to different contexts on the large data set are shown in the first part of Table 1. The first experiment uses only a character context of 5 characters to each side of the focus character but ignores the context words, i.e. the features from c_{-5} to c_5 in Figure 1 are used. The next experiment uses the lexical context to the left of the

	With punct.		W/o punct.	
	CER	WER	CER	WER
Character context	2.22	6.64	6.20	14.40
Left word context	2.26	7.06	2.33	7.57
Word context	2.35	6.86	2.64	9.91
Zitouni data set	5.70	17.50	5.70	20.49
Zitouni et al.	5.5	18.0	n/a	n/a
AFP data set	2.53	7.39	2.83	13.65

Table 1: *The results of the diacritization experiments on different parts of the ATB*

focus word in addition to the character context but ignores the context words on the right, i.e. the features from w_{-5} to c_5 are used. Finally, the last experiment uses all features shown in Figure 1, i.e. it uses the character context as well as the lexical features to the left and to the right of the focus word. The results show that in the evaluation including punctuation and words that are never diacritized, both the CER and the WER are slightly worse when context is added. However, in the evaluation where punctuation and non-diacritized words are excluded, we find a considerable improvement when words from the left context are added. Adding the right context, in contrast, has a negative effect on both error rates. From these results, we conclude that the left context is more important (which is also corroborated by the weights assigned to the word features). And we assume that the inclusion of words from the right context lead to data sparseness problems. For this reason, all the remaining experiments are carried out with the character context plus 5 words on the left of the focus word.

The experiment on the data set by Zitouni et al. shows that there is considerable variability in the data sets of the Penn Arabic Treebank. Here, the error rates are more than twice as high as on the first, larger data set. A comparison of our approach on this data set shows that the results are comparable to those by Zitouni et al., which are listed in the row below ours. This is notable since our system does not have access to any linguistic preprocessing. The system by Zitouni et al., in contrast, has access to morphological segments and POS tags.

The third experiment is performed on a data set that is a subset of the first set, namely the AFP section from part 1, version 2.0. Here, the error rates are slightly worse than for the first set. This is the data set that will be used for the experiments in the following section.

4 Beyond treebank data

In this section, we will investigate the question how the system presented in the previous section needs to be modified in order to be usable for real-world texts, which is not as clean as the treebank data. A first informal evaluation of some real-world texts shows a surprisingly high number of errors in diacritization. A closer look at these errors shows that many of them involved a non-standard use of the hamza. For this reason, we decided to carry out a series of experiments to determine a usable strategy to improve the results.

As mentioned before for all experiments reported in this section, we use the Arabic Treebank part 1, version 2.0, where the 90% from the beginning serve as training data and the tail 10% are used for testing. This section is based on AFP news, the same genre as the real-world texts we use for evaluation. This ensures that the effects we will see in the results are due to our modifications and not due to out-of-domain phenomena. All the experiments are conducted with the optimal parameter and feature settings as determined in the first experiment described in Section 3.

We conduct four experiments to test the effect of hamza presence or absence on diacritization as detailed below:

1. **Pure treebank**: In order to determine the upper bound, we train and test the diacritization system on the treebank in its original form.

2. **Normalized treebank**: For this experiment, we normalized all hamzas both in the training and the test set. To this end, we replaced all hamzas with the alef (A in Buckwalter transliteration [2]). The intuition behind this experiment is to test a simple normalization of non-standard uses of the hamza, which might solve the problems with non-conventional diacritization. If this experiment reaches the same results as the upper bound from experiment 1, hamzas are not important for diacritization.

3. **Hamza-free test set**: Here, we train on the original training set (with all hamzas) and test on the test set with all hamzas removed. This experiment is intended to show whether the variation in hamzas between the training and test sets has any bearing on diacritization. If there are no differences, then we can reach good results on real-world texts by simply removing all hamzas.

4. **Hamza-free training set**: This experiment is the exact opposite of experiment 3. Here, we train on the training set without hamzas and test on the original test set (containing all hamzas).

4.1 Results

The results of the experiments presented above are shown in Table 2. For the upper bound experiment, in which the original treebank data are used for both training and testing, the memory-based diacritization system reached an overall CER of 2.53% and a WER of 7.39% when punctuation is included in the evaluation and a CER of 2.83 and WER of 13.65 when punctuation is excluded. A word is considered ill-diacritized if any of its vowels is wrong. These results are in the range of other published results although they are slightly worse than the best results of the first experiment described in Section 3. The reason for this can be found in the choice of the training set, which is here restricted to one part of the treebank. Additionally, in the present experiments, we do not use 10-fold CV but a single fold for testing.

When we remove all hamzas from the training and test set (normalized treebank), the diacritization system reaches a CER of 3.08% and a WER of 9.20%

	With punct.		W/o punct.	
	CER	WER	CER	WER
Pure treebank (AFP set)	2.53	7.39	2.83	13.65
Normalized treebank	3.08	9.20	3.43	17.02
Hamza-free test set	6.51	18.11	7.26	33.48
Hamza-free training set	3.53	10.48	3.94	19.38
Hamza-restored	2.54	7.38	2.83	13.66

Table 2: *The results of the in-vitro experiments with the AFP part of the ATB*

including punctuation. When punctuation is not included in evaluation, the WER increases by approximately 3.5 percent points. These results show that removing the hamzas from both the training and testing sets decreases the accuracy of diacritization at both the character and word level so that we have to conclude that the hamza is important for diacritization and should not be normalized. The normalization option may also be dis-preferred for lingustic reasons as it collapses different characters into one, and these characters may at times distiniguish minimal pairs. For example, the words vAr and v>r (in Buckwalter transliteration) mean "to revolt" and "revenge" respectively. The difference is not merely allophonic. Similar meaning-distinguishing hamzas include the pairs: fAr (fugitive) and f>r (mouse), <rm (a city name) and Arm (throw, imperative), mAl (money) and m|l (destination).

The experiments in which either the training set or the test set contained hamzas show the worst results: For the hamza-free training set, the WER reached 10.48% including punctuation and 19.38% when punctuation is excluded. For the experiment with the hamza-free test set, both the CER (6.51% with punctuation and 7.26% without punctuation) and the WER (18.11% with punctuation and a staggering 33.48% without punctuation) are the highest for all experiments. This shows that the standard approach for diacritizing real-world data, i.e. training on the ATB treebank and testing on texts that may not contain hamzas is the worst possible setting.

5 Creating a hamza restoration module

The experiments described above lead to the conclusion that we need a hamza module that can take the raw text and restore the hamzas if necessary, before the text is passed to the diacritization system. However, such an approach is only feasible if the hamza restoration module reaches a high accuracy. Otherwise, incorrectly placed hamzas may even further harm diacritization results.

In order to test the usefulness of hamza restoration, we designed a hamza restoration module using the same training and testing sets as the AFP experiment in Section 3. The module uses TiMBL with the following settings, which proved to be optimal in a non-exhaustive search: IB1, with similarity computed as weighted overlap, relevance weights computed with gain ratio, and the number of k nearest neighbors set to ???. Similar to diacritization, hamza restoration is treated as a classification problem, in which the classifier assigns one of the four classes A, |, <, > (alef and the 3 hamza forms) to each potential hamza location, whether it occurs word-initially, word-medially, or word-finally. In order to remove non-standard diacritization, the module removes all hamza forms first, including the alef, and then re-assigns a hamza form or an alef to each location. We use the focus hamza location and a context of the previous and following 5 characters as features. The hamza restoration accuracy we obtain using this module is 98.09%.

Given a hamza restoration module with sufficient accuracy, we need to test the effect of hamza restoration on diacritization. For this experiment, we use the normalized treebank version from Section 4 (with all hamzas replaced by alephs). This version is passed to the hamza restoration module, and subsequently to the diacritization system, now with the original training set, and the hamza-restored file as the test set. We obtain considerably improved results: a CER of 2.54% and a WER of 7.38% including punctuation and a CER of 2.83% and a WER of 13.66% without punctuation (cf. experiment *hamza-restored* in Table 2). This means, our results are nearly identical to the results when both training and test data contain perfect hamza information, at least on treebank data.

In the next section, we describe the in-vivo experiments, using our hamza restoration module for diacritizing text obtained from the AFP website. This experiment will show whether the method presented here can also improve results for real-world texts.

6 Diacritizing real-world texts

The test corpus we selected for this experiment consists of four news stories from the AFP Arabic website published on December 2, 2008. The resulting test set consists of 1 332 words. None of these texts have any hamza represented in the texts.

We conduct two experiments on these four files: The first one uses the texts in the original form as taken from the website as input for the diacritization system. The second experiment passes the texts through the hamza restoration module before sending them to the diacritization system. We use the same parameter settings and features as for the the experiments in Section 4.

The resulting diacritized versions were given to two independent raters for evaluation. Both raters are native speakers of Arabic and graduate students; one of them teaches undergraduate Arabic courses. Each rater was familiarized with the task and was given

Text	No. of words	No hamza restoration		With hamza restoration	
		No. incorrect words	WER	No. incorrect words	WER
1	272	20	7.35	11	4.04
2	556	51	9.17	37	6.65
3	252	19	7.54	20	7.94
4	252	16	6.35	11	4.37
Total	1332	106	7.96	79	5.93

Table 3: *Diacritization of real-world texts with and without hamza restoration*

instructions to correct all wrongly diacritized words. Then the two texts were compared, and the first author, a native speaker of Arabic, served as arbitrator.

It is worth noting that rater A found 3 errors that require a very deep knowledge at the discourse level. The news item talks about prisoners. The number of the prisoners is declared to be two towards the end of the story. This requires some change in the diacritization of the word "prisoners" to reflect the dual. Even an expert Arabicist would not find the correct diacritization for these three consecutive words (1 noun and 2 adjectives) without reading the whole story first. This indicates that diacritization is sometimes challenging even for native speakers. These three errors are not included in the calculation.

The results of the experiments on real-world texts are shown in Table 3. The comparison of the results with and without hamza restoration before diacritization show that using hamza restoration reduces the word error rate by 2 percent points. This corresponds to an error reduction of 25.5%.

The results for diacritization with hamza restoration are clearly better than the results for the same approach on the treebank data (experiment hamza-restored in Table 2). We assume that the high results are due to the selection of a small number of short news stories in order not to overtax the human raters. These texts are in general easier to diacritize than the treebank texts.

7 Conclusion and Future Work

We presented a system for diacritization trained on the Penn Arabic Treebank. After parameter and feature optimization, the system reaches competitive error rates as compared to systems such as the one by Zitouni et al. [16] although it does not use any linguistic preprocessing. In a next step, we investigated how well such a treebank trained system performs on texts that differ in whether the hamza is present or not. The results show that inconsistencies between training and test set in this respect lead to a higher number of errors in diacritization. In a last experiment, we tested our approach on real-world data taken from the AFP website, with parallel improvements for the version with the integrated hamza restoration module. The experiments here show clearly that hamza restoration is a necessary step for improving diacritization quality for Arabic real-world texts. Treebanks tend to be more perfect than naturally occurring texts in terms of adherence to spelling conventions, especially with regard to diacritization. This makes them suboptimal for training modules that are intended for real-world texts.

For the future, we are planning to investigate a post-processing module for hamza restoration, which checks whether the suggested hamza belongs to the confusion set allowed in a certain context. We are also planning to integrate linguistic information such as segmentation and POS tagging into the diacritization module. Additionally, we are planning to investigate how diacritization affects POS tagging. We assume that reliable POS tags will improve diacritization while at the same time, reliable diacritics will improve POS tagging, thus leading to a circular optimization problem.

References

[1] A. Bies and M. Maamouri. Penn Arabic Treebank guidelines. Technical report, LDC, University of Pennsylvania, 2003.

[2] T. Buckwalter. Arabic morphological analyzer version 1.0. Linguistic Data Consortium, 2002.

[3] T. Buckwalter. Arabic morphological analyzer version 2.0. Linguistic Data Consortium, 2004.

[4] T. Buckwalter. Issues in Arabic morphological analysis. In A. Soudi, A. van den Bosch, and G. Neumann, editors, *Arabic Computational Morphology: Knowledge-Based and Empirical Methods*. Springer Verlag, 2007.

[5] W. Daelemans and A. van den Bosch. *Memory Based Language Processing*. Cambridge University Press, 2005.

[6] W. Daelemans, A. van den Bosch, and J. Zavrel. Forgetting exceptions is harmful in language learning. *Machine Learning*, 34:11–43, 1999. Special Issue on Natural Language Learning.

[7] W. Daelemans, J. Zavrel, K. van der Sloot, and A. van den Bosch. TiMBL: Tilburg memory based learner – version 6.1 – reference guide. Technical Report ILK 07-07, Induction of Linguistic Knowledge, Computational Linguistics, Tilburg University, 2007.

[8] F. Debili, H. Achour, and E. Souissi. De l'etiquetage grammatical a la voyellation automatique de l'arabe. Technical report, Correspondances de l'Institut de Recherche sur le Maghreb Contemporain, 2002.

[9] M. Diab, M. Ghoneim, and N. Habash. Arabic diacritization in the context of statistical machine translation. In *Proceedings of the Machine Translation Summit (MT-Summit)*, Copenhagen, Denmark, 2007.

[10] Y. Gal. An HMM approach to vowel restoration in Arabic and Hebrew. In *Proceedings of the ACL-02 Workshop on Computational Approaches to Semitic Languages*, Philadelphia, PA, 2002.

[11] N. Habash and O. Rambow. Arabic diacritization through full morphological tagging. In *Proceedings of the North American Chapter of the Association for Computational Linguistics (NAACL)*, Rochester, NY, 2007.

[12] K. Kirchhoff, J. Bilmes, J. Henderson, R. Schwartz, M. Noamany, P. Schone, G. Ji, S. Das, M. Egan, F. He, D. Vergyri, D. Liu, and N. Duta. Novel speech recognition models for Arabic - final report of the JHU summer workshop. Technical report, Johns Hopkins University, 2002.

[13] S. Kübler and E. Mohamed. Memory-based vocalization of Arabic. In *Proceedings of the LREC Workshop on HLT and NLP within the Arabic World*, Marrakech, Morocco, 2008.

[14] R. Nelken and S. Shieber. Arabic diacritization using weighed finite-state transducers. In *Proceedings of the ACL Workshop on Computational Approaches to Semitic Language*, Ann Arbor, MI, 2005.

[15] K. Shaalan, H. Abo Bakr, and I. Ziedan. A hybrid approach for building Arabic diacritizer. In *Proceedings of the EACL Workshop on Computational Approaches to Semitic Languages*, Athens, Greece, 2009.

[16] I. Zitouni, J. Sorensen, and R. Sarikaya. Maximum entropy based restoration of Arabic diacritics. In *Proceedings of the 21st International Conference on Computational Linguistics and 44th Annual Meeting of the Association for Computational Linguistics, COLING-ACL-2006*, Sydney, Australia, 2006.

Multi-entity Sentiment Scoring

Karo Moilanen and Stephen Pulman
Oxford University Computing Laboratory
{ *Karo.Moilanen* | *Stephen.Pulman* }@*comlab.ox.ac.uk*

Abstract

We present a compositional framework for modelling entity-level sentiment (sub)contexts, and demonstrate how holistic multi-entity polarity scoring emerges as a by-product of compositional sentiment parsing. A data set of five annotators' multi-entity judgements is presented, and a human ceiling is established for the challenging new task. The accuracy of an initial implementation, which includes both supervised learning and heuristic distance-based scoring methods, is 5.6∼6.8 points below the human ceiling amongst sentences and 8.1∼8.7 points amongst phrases.

Keywords

Entity-level sentiment analysis, sentiment scoring, sentiment parsing, sentiment annotation, compositional semantics

1 Introduction

The ability to detect author sentiment towards various entities in text is a fundamental goal in sentiment analysis, and holds great promise for many applications. Entities, which can comprise anything from mentions of people or organisations to concrete or even abstract objects, condition what a text is ultimately about. Besides the intrinsic value of entity scoring, the success of document- and sentence-level analysis is also decided by how accurately entities in them can be modelled. Deep entity analysis unfortunately presents the most difficult challenges, be they linguistic or computational. One of the most recent developments in the area - *compositional semantics* - has shown potential for sentence- and expression-level analysis in both logic-oriented [11],[9] and machine learning-oriented [3] paradigms. Our goal in this paper is to further that avenue by extending it to entity-level sentiment analysis.

Entity-level approaches have so far involved relatively shallow methods which usually presuppose some pre-given topic or entity of relevance to be classified or scored (§5.3). Other proposals have attempted specific semantic sentiment roles such as evident sentiment HOLDERs, SOURCEs, TARGETs, or EXPERIENCERs (§5.2). What characterises these approaches is that only a few specific entities in text are analysed while all others are left unanalysed. While shallow approaches can capture some amount of explicitly expressed sentiment, they ignore all layers of implicit sentiment pertaining to a multitude of other entities. We believe that access to these rich layers is required for deeper logical sentiment reasoning in the future.

We take a different view on the problem and investigate the possibility of a holistic *multi*-entity analysis in that we make no categorical distinctions between individual entity mentions, topics, or sentiment roles of any kind. We instead refer to all base nouns simply as **entity markers** which may (or may not) serve the above metafunctions, and aim at classifying *all* such markers in sentences using a single, unified approach. For the sentence in Ex. 1, we envisage a classifier that classifies all of the bracketed entities as positive$^{(+)}$, neutral$^{(N)}$, or negative$^{(-)}$ (NB. / = 'or'):

(1) *"Here's the* `[thing]`$^{(N)/(+)}$*: Other* `[studies]`$^{(N)/(+)}$ *have found that* `[clergy]`$^{(+)}$, *and not* `[psychologists]`$^{(-)/(+)}$ *or other mental* `[health]`$^{(+)}$ `[experts]`$^{(+)/(-)}$, *are the most common* `[source]`$^{(+)/(N)}$ *of* `[help]`$^{(+)}$ *sought in* `[times]`$^{(N)/(-)}$ *of psychological* `[distress]`$^{(-)}$*."*

Note that, in this kind of deep analysis, not only can the polarity of an entity differ from the global, sentential reading but it may also depend heavily on one's subjective point of view: for example, the entity `[experts]` is logically either positive or negative, arguably. Simple keyword spotting, window-based techniques, and even statistical features have limited power in multi-entity analysis because of the inherently overlapping and interdependent nature of entities. We argue in this paper that the analytical strategy towards this problem needs to be grammatical in nature.

Going beyond existing shallow single-entity approaches to deep multi-entity scoring requires the 'conventional' definitional scope of sentiment to be extended to include not only 1) explicit subjective expressions of sentiment, opinions, and emotions, but also 2) implicit subjective expressions and connotations describing some positive (desirable, favourable), negative (undesirable, unfavourable), or neutral (objective) state of affairs in the world. Our classification task is accordingly much wider than most past work in the area. We now illustrate how existing compositional approaches can be extended for multi-entity scoring purposes.

2 Sentiment Parsing

We adopted the compositional sentiment model described in [11] as a basis for our scoring framework. In *idem.*, polarity classification is broken down into binary combinatory steps whereby two syntactic input (`IN`) constituents are combined at a time, and a three-valued polarity logic controlled by a sentiment grammar calculates a polarity for the resultant composite constituent. The process starts with word-level lexical

International Conference RANLP 2009 - Borovets, Bulgaria, pages 258–263

Table 1: *Sample Constituent Rankings*

Mod:AdjP	≫	Head:N	*[funny blunders]*$^{(+)}$
Mod:Nom	≪	Head:N	*[error reduction]*$^{(+)}$
Mod:AdvP	≫	Head:Adj	*[badly decorated]*$^{(-)}$
Head:Adj	≫	Comp:PP	*[sick of fame]*$^{(-)}$
Head:N	≪	Comp:VP	*[market gone sour]*$^{(-)}$
Head:Pred	≫	Comp:DirObj	*[end the hostility]*$^{(+)}$
Head:Pred	≪	Adjunct:Adv	*[smiled painfully]*$^{(-)}$
...			

seeds, proceeds recursively via intermediate syntactic levels, and terminates at the top sentence level.

2.1 Compositional Processes. The model in *idem.* operates with positive (POS), negative (NEG), and neutral (NTR) polarities, and reversive (¬) and equative (=) polarity shifting values. Non-neutral sentiment propagation is modelled by allowing non-neutral (POS, NEG) constituents to override NTR ones (e.g. *"[funny$^{(+)}$things$^{(N)}$]$^{(+)}$"*). The model supports polarity-reversing compositions (cf. [14]) in which reversive (¬) constituents reverse non-neutral ones (e.g. *"[no$^{[¬]}$talent$^{(+)}$]$^{(-)}$"*; *"[tax$^{(-)}$decreases$^{[¬]}$]$^{(+)}$"*), and the resolution of non-neutral polarity conflicts (e.g. *"[bad$^{(-)}$luck$^{(+)}$]$^{(-)}$"*; *"[cancer$^{(-)}$cure$^{(+)}$]$^{(+)}$"*).

2.2 Sentiment Grammar. Since the polarity of a composite constituent can differ from the two IN polarities, the IN constituents can not be equally salient. The model assigns relative weights to the two IN constituents to dictate whose sentiment dominates: the stronger of the two (superordinate (SPR)) dominates the weaker one (subordinate (SUB)) (i.e. SPR ≫ SUB). The weights are not stored in any individual IN constituents but are latent in specific syntactic constructions such as [Mod:Adj Head:N] (i.e. adjectival premodification of head nouns) or [Head:V Comp:NP] (i.e. direct object complements of verbs). Crucially then, a constituent may be superordinate in one syntactic environment but subordinate somewhere else: consider *"helpline$^{(+)}$"* in *"[abuse helpline]$^{(+)}$"* vs. *"[useless helpline]$^{(-)}$"*, for example. The effects of different syntactic environments on IN constituent rankings are specified in a hand-written sentiment grammar which is described in more detail in [11]. Table 1 illustrates some sample grammatical rankings.

2.3 Pre-processing. Raw text is first processed with a dependency parser[1]. A flat parse tree is then generated in which each constituent head is linked to zero or more pre- and/or post-head dependents. Each leaf node is assigned a prior sentiment polarity and reversal value. These are obtained from an extensive word-class-specific, general-purpose main sentiment lexicon of 57103 sentiment words (22402 ADJ, 6487 ADV, 19004 N, 9210 V), and from an auxiliary list of 312343 known NTR words. Our main lexicon, which was compiled manually based on WordNet 2.1 synsets and glosses, contains 21341 POS, 7036 NTR, and 28726 NEG entries; 1700 (3%) have (¬) reversal features.

2.4 Parsing. Sentiment analysis starts with the main lexical head verb of the root clause (or the head noun of a main clausal NP), and first descends recursively down to its lowermost atomic leaf constituents. Through a recursive bottom-up traversal of the dependency tree, each constituent's internal polarity is resolved before it is combined with its parent constituent. When parsing a constituent, the parser follows a fixed order in combining the constituent head (H_i) first with j post-head ($R_{i+1\,:\,i+j}$) dependents and then with k pre-head ($L_{i-k\,:\,i-1}$) dependents (schematised in Fig. 1). Each combinatory step operates on the head and only one of its dependents, and consults the sentiment grammar (§2.2) to determine which element is SPR and assigns the resultant compositional polarity to the head-dependent pair.

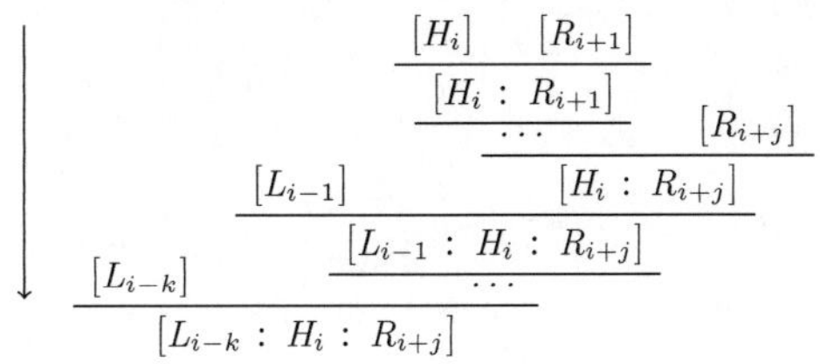

Fig. 1: *Head-dependents combination schema*

3 Entity Scoring

Since each constituent - a head with k pre- j post-head dependents - stands for a unique (sub)part of the sentence (i.e. $[L_{i-k} : H_i : R_{i+j}]$), a constituent and its internal polarity constitutes a **sentiment (sub)context** in the sentence. Each constituent consequently shapes the polarities of the entity marker(s) inside it. Leaf-node (sub)contexts holding but a single entity marker can be seen as intrinsically **lexical** for they represent atomic pieces of information without alluding to any higher context(s). In contrast, (sub)contexts in which entity markers fall under the influence of other words are extrinsically **contextual**. Importantly then, the very possibility of expressing opinions and sentiments about an entity means that a sentence can exhibit many contextual polarities for it. These can and often do differ from the atomic lexical polarity of the entity and the polarity of the sentence. In the headline *"[EU opposes* [credit] *crunch rescue package]$^{(-)}$"*, the entity [credit] is shaped by six (sub)contexts (Ex. 2):

(2)	1: [		[credit]	]$^{(+)}$
	2: [		[credit] *crunch*	]$^{(-)}$
	3: [		[credit] *crunch rescue*	]$^{(+)}$
	4: [		[credit] *crunch rescue package*	]$^{(+)}$
	5: [	*opposes*	[credit] *crunch rescue package*	]$^{(-)}$
	6: [	*EU opposes*	[credit] *crunch rescue package*	]$^{(-)}$

We aim at including in our analysis not only the two extremes (1: atomic lexical, 6: global sentential) but all intermediate levels of sentiment as well. Seen as a stack of (sub)contexts, the occurrences of an entity across all (sub)contexts along the atomic-global continuum give rise to three gradient polarity distribution scores (#POS, #NTR, #NEG). Entity-level sentiment scoring thus involves measuring how many times each entity was found in POS, NTR, and NEG (sub)contexts. The scoring process is incremental in that each time the parser has calculated a compositional polarity for a constituent (i.e. a (sub)context), we locate all entity markers inside the (sub)context, and, for each found entity marker, use the polarity distribution within the

[1] Connexor Machinese Syntax (www.connexor.com)

(sub)context to increment the entity's polarity counts, accordingly.

The main challenge is how (sub)contexts' polarity distributions are actually measured. We experimented with two possible scoring methods. Our scoring framework is however not restricted to any particular scoring method(s) per se as other scorers can be plugged in.

3.1 Distance Scoring. The most basic method for measuring the polarity distribution of a (sub)context is a bidirectional polarity search around an entity marker word. For polarity $p \in \{\texttt{POS}, \texttt{NTR}, \texttt{NEG}\}$, in a (sub)context with n neighbouring words with p around an entity marker word at word ID w_m, the following distance scoring function is used within each (sub)context:

$$dist(p) = \sum_{i=1}^{n} \frac{1}{worddist(w_m, w_i^p)} \cdot \frac{\Theta}{clausedist(w_m, w_i^p)}$$

In addition to the raw distance between the entity marker and a neighbouring word (*worddist*), the distance between their respective (full) clause IDs is also considered (*clausedist*). The Θ coefficient, which was set experimentally at 1.75, boosts neighbouring words that are in the same (full) clause as the entity marker. Because only some higher-level (sub)contexts contain subregions with contrasting polarities (e.g. multiple clauses), distance scoring often suggests similar polarity distributions for all entities in a given (sub)context.

3.2 Syntactic Scoring. Distance scoring takes no notice of syntactic or lexical evidence around entity markers. Such blanket coverage risks being too broad. For more complex scoring, we used supervised learning with Support Vector Machines[2]. We apply the feature template in Table 2 to ±3 words around each entity marker (within a (sub)context). The `PRIOR_POLARITY` and `POLARITY_REVERSAL` features refer to a word's raw prior lexical polarity and polarity reversal values while `GLOBAL_POLARITY` indicates the current (sub)context's internal polarity (as suggested by the parser). The `DEPENDENCY_TYPE`, `GRAMMATICAL_RELATION`, `SYNTACTIC_ROLE`, and `WORD_CLASS` features reflect the tags assigned to each word by the dependency parser. `POLARITY_WSD_TYPE` indicates whether a word is tagged in the lexicon as capable of bearing more than one polarity (e.g. *"lean$^{(N)(+)(-)}$"*, *"chicken$^{(N)(-)}$"*, *"bliss$^{(+)}$"*). `UNIGRAM` features are also included. In total, 19502 binary features (§4.1) were used to train a polynomial kernel.

Based on the observed variability in human annotations in the training data (§4.1), we trained five separate models (one per annotator), and run them as a committee. In each (sub)context, each entity marker word is submitted to the committee and the number of classifiers returning polarity $p \in \{\texttt{POS}, \texttt{NTR}, \texttt{NEG}\}$ as a class label is used to increment the entity's corresponding polarity counts:

$$svmvote(p) = \#\text{ of SVMs classifying entity as } p$$

SVMs' predicted class labels are required to fulfill one post-classification polarity axiom: if a (sub)context does not contain any words with `POS` or `NEG` prior polarities (i.e. it is fully `NTR`), non-neutral predictions are discarded and asserted as `NTR` instead.

[2] Johnson, M. (2008). SVM.NET 1.4. (`www.matthewajohnson.org/software/svm.html`). Based on Chang, C. & Lin, C. (2001). LIBSVM. (`www.csie.ntu.edu.tw/~cjlin/libsvm/`).

Table 2: *SVM entity feature template*

PRIOR_POLARITY	GLOBAL_POLARITY	UNIGRAM
POLARITY_REVERSAL	POLARITY_WSD_TYPE	
DEPENDENCY_TYPE	SYNTACTIC_ROLE	
GRAMMATICAL_RELATION	WORD_CLASS	

3.3 Weights. The sentiment parsing process scores entities incrementally by measuring the polarity distribution of one (sub)context at a time and updating the entities in it. The cumulative polarity distributions $D_1 \ldots D_n$ of an entity across all of its hosting (sub)contexts $z_1 \ldots z_n$ ultimately determine the entity's final sentiment scores. However, simple cumulative sums do not suffice. In particular, individual (sub)contexts' scores need to be weighted because not all of them are equally salient: atomic (sub)contexts are evidently not very important, for example.

We experimented with three empirically discovered coefficients to control the weight of each (sub)context. g estimates the information gain of a (sub)context over its predecessor by boosting longer (sub)contexts. β measures the length of a (sub)context in the sentence: longer (sub)contexts are again boosted. Abrupt polarity changes between (sub)contexts are boosted by v: for example, a `NEG` (sub)context followed by a `POS` one may indicate a shift in perspective or negation. For each entity, the cumulative score for polarity $p \in \{\texttt{POS}, \texttt{NTR}, \texttt{NEG}\}$ in a sentence with n (sub)contexts ($z_1 \ldots z_n$) is obtained as follows:

$$scr(p) = \sum_{i=1}^{n} \frac{g\beta v D_i}{len(z_i)}$$

D_i = $dist(p)$ or $svmvote(p)$ score from (sub)context z_i
g = $length(z_i)$ - $length(z_{i-1})$
β = $length(z_i)$ / $length(sentence)$
v = 1.75 if polarity of z_i is not polarity of z_{i-1}, else 1

3.4 Sample Analysis. Consider Ex. 3:

(3) *"**Finch** said the **decision** to withdraw the **application** was a 'dispiriting **decision which** will harm **London's reputation** as a **city which** is well governed, and **which** hitherto has had a welcoming **attitude** to major overseas **investors**'."*

Since the sentence depicts a state of affairs that is negative/undesirable/unfavourable, all entities in it could be classified uniformly as `NEG`. However, the sentential negativity *does not entail* that *"[a city which is well governed]$^{(+)}$"* and *"[a welcoming attitude to major overseas investors]$^{(+)}$"* are `NEG` as such: instead, it merely makes an allusion to their involvement in a `NEG` context. The same holds for *"[London's reputation]$^{(N)(+)}$"*. We therefore expect the algorithm to assign different degrees of negativity (and positivity and neutrality) to the entities. Ex. 4 visualises the parser's entity scores. The polarity scores of the entity `[London]` (29% `POS`, 18% `NTR`, 53% `NEG`), which are illustrated in Table 3, reflect the statement in that (i) `[London]` is `NTR` in itself, (ii) it has a positively-evaluated reputation, and (iii) it is affected by a `NEG` event. The other entities, from the most `NEG` `[decision]` to the most `NTR` `[Finch]`, are tenable, too. Note that the scores represent each entity's involvement in three polarity contexts and may not as such indicate sentiment/polarity strength although small margins amongst the three values signal mixed (sub)contexts while large(r) margins can be equated with pure(r) polarities. We observed that interpreting these kinds of multi-entity scores is similar to interpreting automatically generated summaries in that, due to subjective scaling and class in- and exclusion preferences, the scores often afford *many* possible interpretations: whether the `NEG` score for `[application]` should be .82, `SOMEWHAT_NEG`, or some other arbitrary value, for example, is secondary to the fact that the parser ranked the entity sensibly as `NEG` $\gg$ `NTR` $\gg$ `POS`.

(4)

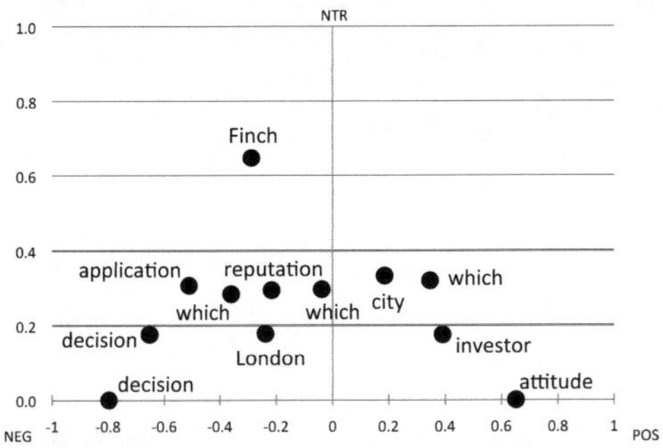

4 Evaluation

4.1 Gold Standard. Most existing gold standards used in past sentiment research such as MPQA[3] [20] or FBS[4] [4] come with incomplete entity annotations as only some entities (e.g. sentiment roles or product features) are usually included per text region. In contrast, we wish to evaluate *all* entity markers in a given text region. To achieve that, a new multi-entity data set was compiled from a cross-genre pool of 24 documents' dependency parses. Five annotators (three paid linguistics students, one of the authors, one volunteer) annotated 7904 entity markers as `POS`, `NTR`, or `NEG` (cf. Ex. 1). Cases displaying mixed sentiment or those infected with inescapable ambiguity were marked as ambiguous. In order to preclude misaligned annotations between annotators (cf. [20]: 34-42; [7]: 6), we made a decision to confine ourselves to base nouns only (cf. Ex. 1).

The data set contains two subsections. The first (`GS_PHR`) contains 4765 entities from 1500 syntactic constituent phrases of differing lengths (from six documents) while the second (`GS_SNTC`) encompasses 3139 entities from 500 full sentences (from 18 documents). Both subsets were further split into 4/5 training and 1/5 testing sections, yielding for training 2490 entities (`GS_SNTC`) vs. 3877 entities (`GS_PHR`) (§3.2). 649 and 888 entities are given for testing, respectively. For syntactic scoring, the SVM classifier committee consisted of five separate models, each trained on 6367 entities (with 19502 features) from one annotator's combined `GS_SNTC` and `GS_PHR` training sections (§3.2).

4.2 Human Ceiling. In order to estimate human performance in the new task, we compared each annotator against all others, and obtained five average accuracy and Kappa scores (Table 4). It is apparent that the task is highly subjective because the figures are only modest in a three-way condition (accuracy 62%; k .43~.45) (see §4.4). However, the task is considerably less vague in a two-way non-neutral condition (86~89% accuracy; k .70~.78).

4.3 Error Classification. The inter-annotator agreement levels point towards increased ambiguity with `NTR` polarity due to differing personal degrees of sensitivity towards neutrality/objectivity. Not all classification errors are then equal for classifying a `POS` case as `NTR` is more tolerable than classifying it as `NEG`, for example. We found it useful to characterise three distinct error classes or disagreements between human H and algorithm A. `FATAL` errors $(H^{(\alpha)}A^{(\neg\alpha)}\ \alpha\in\{+\ -\})$ are those where the non-neutral polarity is completely wrong: such errors affect the performance of the parser adversely. `GREEDY` errors $(H^{(N)}A^{(\alpha)}\ \alpha\in\{+\ -\})$ are those where the algorithm wrongly made a decision to jump one way or the other, displaying oversensitivity towards non-neutral polarities. `LAZY` errors $(H^{(\alpha)}A^{(N)}\ \alpha\in\{+\ -\})$ indicate that the algorithm chose to sit on the fence and displayed oversensitivity towards `NTR` polarity.

4.4 Test Conditions. The highest-scoring polarity (1st rank) amongst each entity's three polarity counts is compared against the gold standard. All ambiguous cases were excluded, as were a few tie scores amongst short phrases. We compare the DIST and SVM scorers against a fully-COMPOSitional baseline that simply uses the internal polarity of a (sub)context to score its entities. A hybrid DIST+SVM method is also evaluated. All experiments were conducted under a (i) three-way `ALL_POL` (`POS:NTR:NEG`), and a (ii) two-way `NON_NTR` (`POS:NEG`, with `FATAL` errors only) classification condition. The proportions of finding a match in the algorithm's 1st, 2nd, and 3rd polarity ranks are included. The algorithm's average figures against five annotators are given in Table 5.

4.5 Results. In absolute terms, the results are modest. But in comparison with the low human ceiling, the algorithm's best scores are only 5.6~8.7 points behind (`ALL_POL`). Both scorers outperformed the fully `COMPOS`itional baseline - a realisation implying that entity-level sentiment is weakly compositional although, interestingly, non-compositional scoring can be approached compositionally. Shorter constituents with less contextual evidence (`GS_PHR`) were, as expected, more challenging than longer, holistic constituents (`GS_SNTC`). Most notable is the performance of the heuristic DIST method which generally equalled or outperformed the SVM committee. The hybrid combination (DIST+SVM) resulted in a small boost. The two complementary scoring methods appear to neutralise each other's errors as DIST displays oversensitivity towards `POS` and `NEG` labels (cf. more `GREEDY` errors) while SVM suggests `NTR` in many cases (cf. mostly `LAZY` errors). The correct label was in the parser's 1st and 2nd ranks in 79~85% of the cases (`ALL_POL`) which confirms that the parser generally points at the right direction. Matching past observations in the area, the average gap between three-way `ALL_POL` and two-way `NON_NTR` classification accuracy is noticeable at 20~25 points.

4.6 Future Work. Further research is needed to address cases of 'sentiment overflow' where an entity's scores are incorrectly shaped by (sub)contexts beyond its natural sentiment zone boundaries. Although en-

[3] `http://www.cs.pitt.edu/mpqa/`

[4] `http://www.cs.uic.edu/~liub/`

Table 3: *Sample analysis of (sub)contexts containing the entity "London" (with POS:NTR:NEG scores)*

SUBCONTEXT	TYPE	ENTITY MARKER
*[**London's**]$^{(N)}$*	Lexical	[London] 0:100:0
*[**London's** reputation]$^{(+)}$*	Contextual	[London] 5:95:0
*[which will harm **London's** reputation as a city which is well governed, and which hitherto has had a welcoming attitude to major overseas investors']$^{(-)}$*	Contextual	[London] 27:30:43
*[a 'dispiriting decision which will harm **London's** ... investors']$^{(-)}$*	Contextual	[London] 28:24:48
*[the decision to withdraw the application was ... **London's** ... investors']$^{(-)}$*	Contextual	[London] 29:20:51
*[Finch said the decision to withdraw the application was a 'dispiriting decision which will harm **London's** reputation as a city which is well governed, and which hitherto has had a welcoming attitude to major overseas investors']$^{(-)}$*	Contextual, global	[London] 29:18:53

Table 4: *Human accuracy and inter-annotator agreement scores on the gold standard*

	GS_SNTC (3139)				GS_PHR (4765)			
	k ALL_POL	*k* NON_NTR	Acc ALL_POL	Acc NON_NTR	*k* ALL_POL	*k* NON_NTR	Acc ALL_POL	Acc NON_NTR
Human-1	.50	**.82**	66.82	**90.99**	**.49**	**.74**	66.83	**87.90**
Human-2	.48	.77	65.03	88.67	**.49**	.71	**66.87**	86.43
Human-3	.34	.79	52.79	89.60	.33	.72	55.09	86.73
Human-4	**.51**	.80	**66.90**	89.70	.47	.66	64.46	82.88
Human-5	.40	.72	58.80	86.21	.36	.69	54.89	85.14
Avg	.45	.78	62.07	89.03	.43	.70	61.63	85.81

tity markers (and any sentiment roles therein) are linked through a variety of complex means [16][18][6], taking discourse structure, Named Entities, semantic roles, and reported speech into account would be beneficial. Entity markers can be chained through anaphora/co-reference resolution which can lead to significant boosts [6]. The values for the weighting coefficients (§3.3) and the exploratory learning features for syntactic scoring (§3.2) can be optimised, and other scorers may be employed.

5 Related Work

5.1 Compositional Analysis. A few systems that exploit the compositional properties of sentiment in differing degrees have been proposed. The system closest to our framework is [9] who describe a tool for phrase- and sentence-level classification. A sentiment composition model is described which uses a cascade of transducers relying on lexical sentiment seeds, a phrasal chunker, and hand-written pattern-matching rules. Instead of making use of compositional rules (cf. §2.2), [3] incorporated compositional semantics into structured inference-based learning with lexical, negator, and voting features. [12] describe a hybrid system for detecting sentiment expressions about a topic that combines a rule-based sentiment extractor with a learning-based topic classifier. For the former, phrasal chunking and shallow parsing patterns are used to combine elements in specific syntactic cases. However, no explicit details about compositional processes are given. [17] uses scored prior polarities from sentiment lexica and knowledge bases with dependency parsing to generate verb-centric ACTOR-ACTION-OBJECT frames (each with optional internal modifiers), and calculate contextual polarities at different structural levels using hand-written polarity combination rules. A shallow compositional affect sensing approach with lexical, phrasal, and sentential linking and ranking patterns is proposed in [13].

5.2 Entities. In classifying raw entity mentions without deep sentiment semantics, the primary focus has been on relatively shallow techniques restricted to specific topical mentions, or product names, features, and attributes. Goalwise, the approach closest to our multi-entity framework is [6] who classify entities (topics) expressed in IR search queries. Matched query entities are expanded through co-reference and meronymy analysis of concrete entities' parts and features to generate a set of topical entity mentions. These are paired with topically relevant sentiment expressions targeting them, and aggregate scores for the query entities are calculated using a sentiment propagation graph. For each sentiment expression, candidate target mentions are ranked with proximity-based, heuristic, and supervised learning-based scorers.

The product feature mining and summarisation system described in [5] classifies feature mentions based on neighbouring adjectives and sentential polarity frequencies. [4] propose a more complex approach targeting products' parts and attributes with a holistic lexicon- and distance-based method that exploits local and global clause-, sentence-, and review-level evidence and patterns in disambiguating ambiguous words, irregular/idiomatic constructions, and polarity conflicts. A relaxation labelling technique was used in [15] to classify product feature mentions by sequential analyses of words, features, and sentences with syntactic dependency, lexical, and collocational constraints. [10] extract opinions with fixed opinion frames which capture for a given entity an attribute and a sentiment expression with its HOLDER.

5.3 Sentiment Roles. The inventory of possible semantic roles *specific* to sentiment is unclear. Past proposals have targeted some of the most obvious roles encompassing opinion HOLDERs, SOURCEs, TARGETs, or EXPERIENCERs. [1] model the information filtering structures of opinions and facts with a supervised approach to identify the hierarchical structure of perspective and speech expressions using syntactic dominance features, and to recursively determine local and global parent-child relations amongst such ex-

Table 5: *Multi-entity scoring results*

		ALL_POL		NON_NTR		Ranks (ALL_POL)				Errors (ALL_POL)		
Data set	Scoring	Acc	k	Acc	k	1	2	3	1+2	FATAL	GREEDY	LAZY
GS_SNTC	HUMAN	62.07	.45	89.03	.78					17.99	41.01	41.01
	COMPOS	52.20	.28	71.71	.45					38.66	38.13	**23.20**
	DIST	**56.44**	**.35**	79.32	.59	**56.44**	28.04	15.52	**84.48**	28.32	35.69	35.99
	SVM	50.04	.28	79.49	.58	50.04	30.64	19.31	80.69	**14.60**	**14.11**	71.28
	DIST+SVM	54.12	.33	**82.21**	**.64**	54.12	30.31	15.56	84.44	16.03	19.56	64.42
GS_PHR	HUMAN	61.63	.43	85.81	.70					18.38	40.81	40.81
	COMPOS	48.70	.24	65.56	.34					32.28	44.48	**23.23**
	DIST	51.42	**.27**	68.73	.40	51.42	27.51	21.07	78.93	27.41	39.68	32.91
	SVM	52.74	.25	**77.70**	**.52**	52.74	24.73	22.53	77.47	**12.42**	**20.70**	66.88
	DIST+SVM	**52.92**	**.27**	73.60	.48	**52.92**	26.08	21.00	**79.00**	18.52	28.71	52.77

pressions. However, only SOURCEs were targeted. A global Integer Linear Programming-driven constraint-based inference approach was used in [2] for joint extraction of sentiment expressions, SOURCEs, and their link relations using sequence tagging and relation classifiers with lexical, positional, and syntactic frame features. [7] extract HOLDERs and TOPICs using opinion verbs and adjectives, and FrameNet-driven semantic frame role labelling. In detecting HOLDERs, Maximum Entropy modelling with syntactic dependency features between sentiment expressions and candidate entities was used in [8]. [16], who highlight the insufficiency of automatic semantic role labelling in resolving SOURCEs and TARGETs, discuss the complexity involved in the task ranging from attribution, multiple SOURCEs and TARGETs, semantic scope, referents, discourse structure, inference, and TARGET relations, amongst others. The interrelation between sentiment roles and discourse structures is discussed further in [18] who propose transitive opinion frames for linking TOPICs. The role of co-reference resolution is discussed in [19] alongside a TOPIC annotation scheme that links opinions based on topical co-reference (cf. [6]).

6 Conclusion

This paper presents a principled, structural framework for modelling entity-level sentiment (sub)contexts, and in doing that, it sheds light on the role of (non-)compositional semantics in entity-level sentiment analysis. We demonstrated how compositional sentiment parsing lends itself naturally to multi-entity sentiment scoring with minimal modification. Initial results obtained from two scoring methods suggest that, despite the inherent complexity and subjectivity of the task, compositional sentiment parsing can generate sensible analyses that emulate human multi-entity sentiment judgements effectively.

References

[1] E. Breck and C. Cardie. Playing the telephone game: determining the hierarchical structure of perspective and speech expressions. In *Proceedings of COLING 2004*, pages 120–126, Geneva, Aug. 2004.

[2] Y. Choi, E. Breck, and C. Cardie. Joint extraction of entities and relations for opinion recognition. In *Proceedings of EMNLP 2006*, pages 431–439, Sydney, Jul. 2006.

[3] Y. Choi and C. Cardie. Learning with compositional semantics as structural inference for subsentential sentiment analysis. In *Proceedings of EMNLP 2008*, pages 793–801, Honolulu, Oct. 2008.

[4] X. Ding, B. Liu, and P. S. Yu. A holistic lexicon-based approach to opinion mining. In *Proceedings of the 1st ACM Intl. Conference on Web Search and Data Mining (WSDM 2008)*, pages 231–240, Palo Alto, Feb. 2008.

[5] M. Hu and B. Liu. Mining and summarizing customer reviews. In *Proceedings of the ACM SIGKDD Intl. Conference on Knowledge Discovery & Data Mining (KDD 2004)*, pages 168–177, Seattle, Aug. 2004.

[6] J. S. Kessler and N. Nicolov. Targeting sentiment expressions through supervised ranking of linguistic configurations. In *Proceedings of the 3rd Intl. Conference on Weblogs and Social Media (ICWSM 2009)*, San Jose, May 2009.

[7] S.-M. Kim and E. Hovy. Extracting opinions, opinion holders, and topics expressed in online news media text. In *Proceedings of the COLING/ACL 2006 Workshop on Sentiment and Subjectivity in Text*, pages 1–8, Sydney, Jul. 2006.

[8] S.-M. Kim and E. Hovy. Identifying and analyzing judgment opinions. In *Proceedings of HLT/NAACL-2006*, pages 200–207, New York, Jun. 2006.

[9] M. Klenner, S. Petrakis, and A. Fahrni. A tool for polarity classification of human affect from panel group texts. In *Proceedings of the Intl. Conference on Affective Computing and Intelligent Interaction (ACII 2009)*, Amsterdam, Sep. 2009.

[10] N. Kobayashi, K. Inui, and Y. Matsumoto. Extracting aspect-evaluation and aspect-of relations in opinion mining. In *Proceedings of EMNLP/CoNLL 2007*, pages 1065–1074, Prague, Jun. 2007.

[11] K. Moilanen and S. Pulman. Sentiment composition. In *Proceedings of RANLP 2007*, pages 378–382, Borovets, Sep. 2007.

[12] K. Nigam and M. Hurst. Towards a robust metric of opinion. In Y. Qu, J. Shanahan, and J. Wiebe, editors, *Computing Attitude and Affect in Text: Theory and Applications*, pages 265–280. Springer, 2006.

[13] A. Osherenko. Towards semantic affect sensing in sentences. In *Proceedings of the AISB 2008 Symposium on Affective Language in Human and Machine*, pages 41–44, Aberdeen, Apr. 2008.

[14] L. Polanyi and A. Zaenen. Contextual valence shifters. In Y. Qu, J. Shanahan, and J. Wiebe, editors, *Computing Attitude and Affect in Text: Theory and Applications*, pages 1–10. Springer, 2006.

[15] A.-M. Popescu and O. Etzioni. Extracting product features and opinions from reviews. In *Proceedings of HLT/EMNLP 2005*, pages 339–346, Vancouver, Oct. 2005.

[16] J. Ruppenhofer, S. Somasundaran, and J. Wiebe. Finding the sources and targets of subjective expressions. In *Proceedings of LREC 2008*, Marrakech, May 2008.

[17] M. A. M. Shaikh. *An Analytical Approach for Affect Sensing from Text.* PhD thesis, University of Tokyo, 2008.

[18] S. Somasundaran, J. Wiebe, and J. Ruppenhofer. Discourse level opinion interpretation. In *Proceedings of COLING 2008*, pages 801–808, Manchester, Aug. 2008.

[19] V. Stoyanov and C. Cardie. Annotating topics of opinion. In *Proceedings of LREC 2008*, Marrakech, May 2008.

[20] J. Wiebe, T. Wilson, and C. Cardie. Annotating expressions of opinions and emotions in language. *Language Resources and Evaluation*, 39(2-3):165–210, May 2005.

A morphological and syntactic wide-coverage lexicon for Spanish: The *Leffe*

Miguel A. Molinero
Grupo LYS
Univ. of A Coruña
A Coruña, Spain
mmolinero@udc.es

Benoît Sagot
Project ALPAGE
INRIA
Paris, France
benoit.sagot@inria.fr

Lionel Nicolas
Équipe RL
Laboratoire I3S
Sophia Antipolis, France
lnicolas@i3s.unice.fr

Abstract

In this paper, we introduce the *Léxico de Formas Flexionadas del Español* (*Leffe*), a wide-coverage morphological and syntactic Spanish lexicon based on the Alexina lexical framework. We explain how the *Leffe* has been created by merging together several heterogeneous lexicons and how the Alexina lexical framework has been applied to Spanish. We also introduce a semi-automatic technique based on a tagger to detect the lexicon's deficiencies. A preliminary evaluation shows the potential of the *Leffe* and the relevance of both creation and extension processes.

1 Introduction

High-level Natural Language Processing (NLP) tools require reliable linguistic resources, such as lexicons and grammars. Nowadays, such relevant resources exist for English, but are often absent or incomplete for other languages, even major ones. For example, some lexical resources exist for Spanish, but none of them combines satisfactorily the following properties:

- coverage: all words, including rare ones, in all categories should be included;
- quality: manually and automatically developed resources contain various errors;
- richness: applications such as (deep) parsing require at least morphological and syntactic information, including subcategorization frames.

The *Leffe*[1] is a wide-coverage morphological and syntactic lexicon based on the Alexina framework [13, 15, 1]. This lexicon follows the linguistic criteria applied on the French lexicon *Lefff*[2] taking advantage of the linguistic proximity between Spanish and French as Romance languages.

The main contributions of this piece of research are the following:

- we present a morphological and syntactic wide coverage lexicon for Spanish;
- we describe an enhanced available lexical framework,
- we expose a simple semi-automatic PoS tagger-based approach to detect numerous missing entries in a lexicon (including homonyms).

The work described here is one of the starting points of the recently created Victoria project. This project aims at developing techniques and tools for an efficient acquisition and correction of the linguistic resources necessary to symbolic syntactic parsers. The first phase of the project focuses on Spanish, Galician[3] and French.

This paper is organized as follows: we present first a brief description of Spanish language in Section 2. In Section 3 we describe the lexical framework used to formalize the linguistic information. Then, we briefly describe how some available resources were used to develop the *Leffe*. In Section 5 we present a semi-automatic technique to correct and extend the lexicon. Finally in Section 6 we show preliminary evaluations of the lexicon and present our conclusions in Section 7.

2 The Spanish language in brief

Spanish is a Romance Language, just like Italian, French, Portuguese, and many others. Despite being spoken as a mother tongue by more than 400 million people, this language is little formalized within the framework of NLP when compared with English.

Spanish is an inflected language, with a two-gender system, about fifty conjugated forms per verb, but limited inflections for nouns, adjectives, and determiners. It is morphologically characterized with the Latin alphabet plus the letter *ñ* and the digraphs *ch*, *ll* and *rr*. Apart from this, the acute accents are commonly used and they enable homophones to be distinguished: e.g., *te* ('you', object pronoun) and *té* ('tea').

Regarding syntax and grammar, it is right-branching, uses prepositions, and usually, though not always, places adjectives after nouns. Its syntax is generally Subject Verb Object, though variations are valid and very common. The subject is usually omitted but appears in an implicit fashion. Contrary to English, but similarly to other Romance languages, it is verb-framed, i.e., many Spanish verbs directly encode motion path, and may leave out the manner of motion or express it in a complement of manner: e.g., *entrar* (go in), *salir* (go out), *subir* (go up). It also use a noticeable range of pronominal verbs.

[1] *Léxico de formas flexionadas del español* - Lexicon of Spanish inflected forms
[2] *Lexique des formes fléchies du français* - Lexicon of French inflected forms
[3] A co-official language in north-west Spain.

International Conference RANLP 2009 - Borovets, Bulgaria, pages 264–269

A corner stone of this work relies on the fact that Spanish is similar to other Romance Languages in many ways. Indeed, a network of correspondances can easily be established between their features.

This led us to consider the benefits of reusing resources describing related languages when building the *Leffe*. Such approach presents many advantages :

- a more flexible and complete formalism could be found to develop the *Leffe*,
- establishing interlingual links between resources written with a common formalism results easier,
- the data contained in resources describing other related languages can be more easily acquired.

According to these statements, we identified the *Lefff*, an enhanced morphological and syntactic wide-coverage French lexicon based on the Alexina format (See section 3), as the best candidate.

3 The Alexina framework

A detailed lexical description of all words (or as many as possible) belonging to a language is needed in order to perform high-level NLP tasks such as deep parsing. This information is usually compiled into a lexicon, which could be defined as a list of lexical forms associated with morphological and syntactic information. Alexina is a framework that represents lexical information in a complete, efficient and readable way [11, 1], and is compatible with the LMF[4] [2] standard. The flexibility and completeness of the Alexina format allow a straightforward integration with deep grammatical formalisms (LFG, LTAG) which require detailed syntactic data for all forms, and allow to model lexical information for diverse languages. It is indeed the lexical framework of the *Lefff*, a large-coverage morphological and syntactic lexicon for French, but also that of other lexical resources for languages such as Polish, Slovak, and soon English.

The Alexina model is based on a two-level representation, detailed below, that separates the description of a lexicon from its use:

- The intensional lexicon factorizes the lexical information by associating each lemma with a morphological class and deep syntactic information; it is used for lexical resource development
- The extensional lexicon, which is generated automatically by *compiling* the intensional lexicon, associates each inflected form with a detailed structure that represents all its morphological and syntactic information; it is directly used by NLP tools such as parsers.

The first task achieved by the compilation process, which turns an intensional lexicon (an `.ilex` file) into an extensional lexicon (a `.lex` file), is to inflect lemmas according to their morphological class. Morphological classes are defined in a formalized morphological description described in [11, 12]. In case a lemma inflects in a very specific way, and/or if a lemma has additional inflected forms apart from those generated by its morphological class, these forms are "manually" listed in an additional file (the corresponding `.mf` file).

As sketched above, the compilation process also maps deep syntactic information into surface syntactic information. Deep syntactic information (deep subcategorization frames and other syntactic information) is common to all redistributions, whereas each redistribution corresponds to different surface syntactic information, and therefore to different extensional entries.

3.1 The Intensional format

Each entry in the intensional lexicon is usually defined by a lemma and a POS. Nevertheless, it is possible to find several entries with same lemma and POS but differing in the morphological and syntactic information. This allows to split one lemma into different semantic meanings which implies different syntactic constructions.

An intensional entry details the following information:

- a *morphological class*, which defines the patterns that build all inflected forms of the lemma [12];
- a *category* (or part-of-speech, often written POS), that is taken from the chosen tagset — *Leffe* uses the Multext (Parole) tagset; categories can be divided in two types: open (productive) categories (adjectives, adverbs, verbs, nouns) and closed (grammatical) categories;
- a (deep-syntax) *subcategorization frame*, that explicits how the lemma might be used in valid syntactic constructions: it lists the canonical syntactic functions of the lemma's possible arguments,[5] and the possible realizations of each of these functions;[6,7]
- additional syntactic information (control, raising, attributes...);
- possible *(re)distributions*, that define how the deep-syntax subcategorization frame is to be transformed so as to build extensional surface-syntax subcategorization frames (usual (re)distributions are *%actif, %passif, %se_moyen*).[8]

For example, here is the intensional (slightly simplified[9] for clarity reasons) entry in the *Leffe* for the Spanish lemma

[4] Lexical Markup Framework, the ISO/TC37 standard for NLP lexicons.

[5] The *Leffe* uses the following syntactic functions: *Suj* for subjects, *Obj* for direct objects that can be cliticized into an accusative clitic pronoun, *Objà* for indirect objects introduced by the preposition *a*, *Loc* and *Dloc* for locative and delocative arguments, *Att* for (subject, object or *a*-object) attributes, and *Obl* (and *Obl2*) for other (non-cliticizable) arguments. More detailed defining criteria for their French counterparts in the *Lefff* can be found in [14].

[6] Possible realizations are threefold:
– clitic pronouns: *cln* (nominative clitic), *cla* (accusative clitic), *cld* (dative clitic), *serefl* (reflexive *se*);
– direct phrases: *sn* (noun phrase), *sa* (adjectival phrase), *sinf* (infinitive clause), *scompl* (completive clause), *qcompl* (interrogative clause);
– prepositional phrases: a direct phrase introduced by a preposition (e.g., *a-sn*)

[7] Note that realizations have the same (French) names as their French counterparts in the *Lefff*. This should change in the next version of the *Leffe*.

[8] As for realizations, redistributions have the same (French) names as their French counterparts in the *Lefff*. This should also change in the next version of the *Leffe*.

[9] In particular, additional syntactic features such as control information are not shown.

diagnosticar$_1$, i.e., *diagnosticar* in the sense of the English *to diagnose*.

```
diagnosticar1
        V4
        Lemma;v;
        <arg0:Suj:cln|scompl|sinf|sn,
        arg1:Obj:(cla|scompl|sn)>;
        %actif,%passif
```

It describes a transitive entry with the following informations:

- its morphological class is `V4`, the class of the first-conjugation verbs (ending *-ar*) whose stem changes for present subjunctive(*c* changes to *que*);
- its semantic predicate can be represented by the `Lemma` as is, i.e., *diagnosticar*;
- its category is *verb* (`v`);
- it has two arguments canonically realized by the syntactic functions `Suj` (subject) and `Obj` (direct object). Each syntactic function is associated with a list of possible realizations. ;
- it allows for two different redistributions: active (`%actif`) and passive (`%passif`).

3.2 The Extensional format

The compilation process builds one extensional entry for each inflected form and each compatible redistribution, by applying formalized definitions of these redistributions. For example, the only inflected forms of *diagnosticar* that are compatible with the passive redistribution are the past participle forms. The (simplified) extensional passive entry for *diagnosticados* (*diagnosed*) is the following (`MP00SM` is the morphological tag for past participle masculine plural forms):

```
diagnosticados     v
[pred='diagnosticar1<arg1:Suj:cln|scompl|sn,
arg0:Obl2:(por-sn)>',@passive,@pers,@MP00PM];
%passif
```

As can be seen the original direct object (Obj) has been transformed into the passive Subject and an optional Agent (Obl2) realized by a noun phrase preceded by a preposition (*por-sn*) was added.

4 Reusing other lexical resources

In order to create a first version of the Le*ff*e, the first step was of course to reuse available Spanish lexical resources.

Reusing available linguistic resources is a handy way to start developing new ones. However, it requires to interpret all input resources even though their lexical models are partially incompatible, convert them into a common model and format, and finally merge the converted lexicons. None of these three steps is trivial.

Indeed, available resources might describe a given language from different points of view and/or using different linguistic criteria. This can be used to acquire information covering different aspects of a language. When considering whether a resource was worth using or not for this task, we payed more attention to quality or richness than coverage. After all, combining several resources shall lead to a good coverage that will generally be wider than the largest of them. Thus, we ensured as more important the reliability of the information put into the new resource. The application of the technique described in section 5 allowed us later to regain more coverage.

As stated in the introduction, several resources are available for Spanish, but none of them fulfilled our requirements:

- wide coverage, good precision and satisfying richness,
- complete separation between lexical and grammatical information, i.e., independence from the grammatical formalism it is going to be used with,
- clear and compact format easily readable by humans,
- free availability in terms of access, modification and distribution;
- easily linkable with resources in other languages.

Nevertheless, in order to create a first version of the Le*ff*e, we reused the following resources:

Multext is an international project [6] which aims, among other things, at developing standards and specifications for the encoding and processing of linguistic corpora.

The USC lexicon is a large morphological Spanish lexicon [16], created for PoS tagging tasks in the research group *Gramática del Español* of the University of Santiago de Compostela (Spain).

ADESSE is a database of Spanish verbs developed at the University of Vigo (Spain) [3] with syntactic and some semantic information. It is a high quality work which includes subcategorization frames for more than 4,000 verbs. However, it is restricted to verbs and does not include morphological information;

The Spanish Resource Grammar (SRG) is an open-source multi-purpose large-coverage and precise grammar for Spanish [7] grounded in the theoretical framework of Head-driven Phrase Structure Grammar (HPSG). It includes a lexicon describing syntactic information for Spanish in a well organized hierarchy of syntactic classes. However, it is not easily readable, and specific to the HPSG formalism.

In order to merge these resources, we followed a process described in details in [9]. We briefly remind it here.

As mentioned in Section 2, Multext and USC lexicons only include morphological information, whereas the SRG Lexicon and ADESSE include syntactic information. Therefore, we proceeded in the following way:

1. we built a morphological baseline lexicon by converting the Multext lexicon into the Alexina format and added some Alexina-specific entries (prefixes, suffixes, named entities, punctuation signs);
2. we converted the USC Lexicon into the Alexina format and merged it with the baseline lexicon extracted from Multext, so as to obtain the morphological base of the Le*ff*e;
3. we converted the syntactic information from ADESSE and the SRG lexicon into the Alexina format;

4. we merged the morphological *Leffe* from step 2 and both verbal syntactic lexicons built during step 3; the result was the *Leffe* beta.

The final result is a morphological and syntactic lexicon with an important coverage in terms of morphological information but a more restricted one in terms of syntactic information. Indeed, for morphological entries[10] for which no syntactic information could be found, we added default syntactic features corresponding to the most common ones among entries with the same PoS. For example, all verbal lemmas that were not covered by ADESSE or SRG received the following subcategorization frame: `<Suj:sn|cln,Obj:(sn|cla)>` (transitive verb with optional direct object). However, the application of semi-automatic techniques to extend and correct a lexicon, as described in [10], should help us fixing this aspect.

5 Tagger-based identification of missing entries

The next step after obtaining a first version of the *Leffe* was to continue upgrading it by adding missing entries. Usually, this task is manually performed and thus, is a time-costly process. We now present a simple but effective semi-automatic technique which greatly eases the process by identifying possible missing entries.

We distinguish two types of missing entries:

1. totally non referenced forms,
2. missing homonyms of forms referenced in the lexicon, i.e., forms non associated to a different Part-of-Speech (PoS).

In order to detect missing entries, a PoS tagger [5, 8] might be used to discover new PoS tags thanks to its ability to guess PoS tags for unknown words. The tagger we use is trained with a Spanish training corpus of approx. 500,000 words extracted from the Ancora[11] corpora and *Leffe* as an external lexicon.

According to the kind of missing entries we are trying to identify, the tagger is used in two different ways.

When looking for non referenced forms, we simply rely on the tagger's ability to guess tags for unknown words.

When looking for missing homonyms, we allow the tagger to assign new tags to known forms that are different from those included in its lexicon by forcing it to consider known forms as unknown. Indeed, the default strategy for most taggers when facing a form included in their internal lexicon is to consider as candidate tags only the ones associated there. Thus, when facing a missing homonym of a form, the tagger will never consider as a potential candidate the correct missing tag. In order to obtain such behavior, we simply bypass the internal lexicon. Thus, the tagger guesses new tags basing itself on the morphology of the form and its local context.

Obviously, such a process introduces ambiguity on purpose. In order to keep it beyond limits, we only force one form in a sentence at a time to be considered as unknown. Thus, to guess PoS tags for all words in the sentence, the sentence is entirely tagged several times.

[10] The condition to add an entry to the *Leffe* was to acquire at least its morphological information.

[11] http://clic.ub.edu/ancora/index.php, July 2009.

Since forms belonging to closed categories[12] are generally well described (and their homonyms correctly included too), only forms belonging to open categories[13] are forced as unknown.

Of course, taggers make mistakes, particularly when dealing with unknown (forced or not) forms. A well-known situation for a tagger is to consider an unknown proper noun as a common noun. However, the scope of the process span an entire corpora and not only one sentence. Thus, considering a large amount of text allows us to compute a statistical ranking of the suspected missing forms which balance the false positives produced by tagging errors. This ranking takes into account the precision rate $prec_t$ for a tag t, as evaluated relatively to the training corpus, and n_{wt} and the number of occurrences of the form w tagged as t. More precisely, we assign to each couple form w and tag t a *score* $S_{\mathrm{sc}}(w,t)$ defined as follows:

$$S_{\mathrm{sc}}(w,t) = prec_t \cdot \log(n_{w/t}) \qquad (1)$$

Thanks to this *ranking*, we are able to generate an ordered list of candidate pairs *(form,PoS)* which minimizes the appearance of false positives. As we will see in section 6, this list was good enough to be manually reviewed in a short amount of time.

6 Preliminary Evaluation

In order to evaluate the quality of *Leffe*, currently in beta version, we performed the following tests: on the one hand, we compared *Leffe* with other known Spanish lexicons in terms of coverage; on the other hand, we measured the improvement achieved on the baseline lexicon after adding the information extracted from all other sources.

Regarding coverage, the *Leffe* contains more than 165,000 unique *(lemma,PoS)* pairs, which correspond to approx. 1,590,000 extensional entries that associate a form with both morphological and syntactic information (approx. 680,000 unique *(form,PoS)* pairs). We computed the following properties for the other lexicons:

- SRG: 76,000 unique *(lemma,PoS)* pairs[14] (53.9% fewer than *Leffe*), some of them associated with syntactic information;
- Multext: 510,710 unique *(form,PoS)* pairs[15] (24.9% fewer than *Leffe*), and no syntactic information is provided;
- Spanish gilcUB-M Dictionary: 70,000 lemmas[15](57.6% fewer than *Leffe*), and no syntactic information is provided;
- USC Lexicon: 490,000 unique *(form,PoS)* pairs (27.95% fewer than *Leffe*), and no syntactic information is provided.

We also tested the morphological coverage of our lexicon in the context of a real application: a morphological

[12] Such as prepositions, pronouns and determiners.

[13] Adverbs, common nouns, proper nouns, verbs, adjectives.

[14] As provided by Freeling (`http://garraf.epsevg.upc.es/freeling/`) in a version from April 2008.

[15] According to ELRA webpage `http://catalog.elra.info`, April 2009.

pre-processor [4] developed by the COLE[16] and LYS[17] groups. We first performed a test with our baseline lexicon and another one with the L*effe*.

The corpus of raw text we used as input for these tests was obtained from Wikipedia Sources[18]. It includes more than 4,322,000 words after clearing Wikipedia references and foreign expressions. The evaluation took into account how many words were not tagged by the pre-processor and thus remained unknown. It is worth noting that unknown words are the main cause of PoS-tagging errors. Such problems can be tackled by relying on (very) large coverage lexicons.

As can be observed in Table 1, the process has noticeable benefits. The L*effe* has beaten other large lexicons in the morphological preprocessing task. Even if the difference is slight, this demonstrates the advantage of merging existing resources to create an enhanced one.

In order to measure the syntactic coverage of the lexicons at all stages of the merging process, we used the notion of *expanded intensional entry* [9] which is just a defactorized Alexina subcategorization frame. Thus, each *expanded intensional entry* describes one fully-specified syntactic behaviour.

The expanded intensional lexicon acquired from SRG contains 42,689 unique entries, i.e., fully-specified subcategorization frames, while the one obtained from the ADESSE contains 39,040 entries. After merging these lexicons, the number of such unique entries jumps to 66,028. Finally, the L*effe*, which associates default syntactic information with all verbs not covered by the result of this merging, contains 91,507 unique expanded entries. After factorization, the L*effe* contains 16,311 verbal entries.

Once the first version of L*effe* was built, we used the technique described in section 5 to upgrade its coverage. We used a corpus built from a subset of the Spanish part of the Europarl[19] containing approx. 6 million words. The only restriction applied to this corpus was to avoid the inclusion of sentences containing foreign words, since they would lead to false positives.

A ranking of suspected missing pairs *(form, tag)* was obtained. The quality of this list was not exceptional since it included many false positives, but, thanks to this list, we did include in the L*effe* at a very small cost (it was manually done by one person in two days) nothing less than 1,800 lemmas. We must note that the original coverage of the L*effe* was very high and thus it is reasonable to think that the proportion of false positive would have been reduced when dealing with lexicons with a smaller coverage.

Table 2 shows the number of lemmas added to the L*effe* classified by categories. The great majority were proper nouns, since they were very incomplete in L*effe* up to this point. The approx. 1,800 intensional entries added to the L*effe* correspond to more than 3,700 inflected forms in the extensional lexicon. For example, we added the verbs it abstraer (to abstract) and *documentar* (to document), the adjective francoespañol (Franco-Spanish), the common noun *biocarburante* (biofuel), the adverb *precipitadamente* (hastily) and the proper noun *Niza* (Nice).

Apart from the correct entries, the list allowed us to detect some systematic deficiencies, such as diminutives/augmentatives and adverbs ending in *-mente*. In a near future, they will be automatically generated after updating the morphological rules used to obtain the extensional lexicon from the intensional one (see sect.3).

[16] http://www.grupocole.org, April 2009

[17] http://www.grupolys.org, April 2009

[18] http://download.wikimedia.org, January 2009

[19] A parallel corpus from the European Parliament proceedings

7 Conclusion

In this work we have presented a morphological and syntactic wide-coverage lexicon for Spanish built by taking advantage of existing lexical resources in Spanish and French. Nowadays, for many languages, several scattered linguistic resources exist, but usually none of them is satisfying in terms of coverage, richness or precision. Nevertheless, the amount of work invested in their development should not be ignored. In fact, we believe reusing already formalized knowledge is a handy and productive way to build and/or upgrade other linguistic resources and it will be the usual strategy in the near future.

We also described a tagger-based approach to detect missing entries in a lexicon. Even when applied to a quite exhaustive lexicon, such as L*effe*, this simple approach has allowed us to add more than 3,700 lexical forms in a very short amount of time.[20]

The resulting lexicon, the L*effe*, is currently in beta version and will soon be distributed under a LGPL-LR license[21]. Although it is still far from perfect, we have shown that the L*effe* has already overtaken other well-known Spanish lexicons in terms of morphological and syntactic coverage.

In the near future, we plan to further evaluate the L*effe* by comparing the coverage and precision of different deep parsers that rely on the same grammar but using different morphological and syntactic lexicons such as the L*effe*.

Acknowledgements

This work was supported in part by the Ministerio de Educación y Ciencia of Spain and FEDER (HUM2007-66607-C04-02), the Xunta de Galicia (INCITE08PXIB302179PR, INCITE08E1R104022ES, PGIDIT07SIN005206PR) and the "Galician Network for Language Processing and Information Retrieval" (2006-2009).
We would like also to thank the group *Gramática del Español* from USC, and especially to Guillermo Rojo, M. Paula Santalla and Susana Sotelo, for granting us access to their lexicon.

References

[1] L. Danlos and B. Sagot. Constructions pronominales dans dicovalence et le lexique-grammaire – intégration dans le L*efff*. In *Proceedings of the 27th Lexicon-Grammar Conference*, L'Aquila, Italy, 2008.

[20] The use of a tagger with a lower error rate, in particular on words unknown to the tagger's training corpus, should allow to scale up the efficiency of this approach. Such a tagger is under development in the team of one of the authors.

[21] As explained in this paper, the construction of the L*effe* involved the Spanish morphological lexicon developed within the Multext project, which is freely available for research. The L*effe* beta is the result of the research work described here. It merges lexical information coming from various resources, most of them with a coverage that is larger than the Spanish Multext lexicon. For this reason, we consider it appropriate to publish the L*effe* beta under the LGPL-LR.

	TOTAL UNKNOWN WORDS	UNIQUE UNKNOWN WORDS
USC Lexicon	70,026	25,888
Baseline	86,521	27,234
Leffe	69,756	24,703

Table 1: *Results obtained by applying the morphological preprocessor with different lexicons.*

	LEMMAS (INTENSIONAL)	INFLECTED FORMS (EXTENSIONAL)
Adjectives	88	298
Adverbs	54	54
Verbs	26	1,693
Common nouns	117	231
Proper nouns	1,518	1,518
Total	1,803	3,740

Table 2: *Lemmas acquired using the tagger-based technique.*

[2] G. Francopoulo, M. George, N. Calzolari, M. Monachini, N. Bel, mandy Pet, and C. Soria. Lexical Markup Framework (LMF). In *Proceedings of LREC'06*, Genoa, Italy, 2006.

[3] J. M. García-Miguel and F. J. Albertuz. Verbs, semantic classes and semantic roles in the ADESSE project. In *Proceedings of the Interdisciplinary Workshop on the Identification and Representation of Verb Features and Verb Classes*, Saarbrücken, Germany, 2005.

[4] J. Graña, F. M. Barcala, and J. Vilares. Formal methods of tokenization for part-of-speech tagging. *Computational Linguistics and Intelligent Text Processing, Lecture Notes in Computer Science*, 2002.

[5] J. Graña. *Técnicas de Análisis Sintáctico Robusto para la Etiquetación del Lenguaje Natural (robust syntactic analysis methods for natural language tagging)*. Doctoral thesis, Universidad de La Coruña, Spain, 2000.

[6] N. Ide and J. Véronis. Multext: Multilingual text tools and corpora. In *Proceedings of COLING'94*, Kyoto, Japan, 1994.

[7] M. Marimon, N. Seghezzi, and N. Bel. An open-source lexicon for Spanish. In *Sociedad Española para el Procesamiento del Lenguaje Natural, n. 39*, 2007.

[8] M. A. Molinero, F. M. Barcala, J. Otero, and J. Graña. Practical application of one-pass viterbi algorithm in tokenization and pos tagging. *Recent Advances in Natural Language Processing (RANLP). Proceedings, pp. 35-40*, 2007.

[9] M. A. Molinero, B. Sagot, and L. Nicolas. Building a morphological and syntactic lexicon by merging various linguistic resources. In *Proceedings of NODALIDA'09*, Odense, Denmark, 2009.

[10] L. Nicolas, B. Sagot, M. A. Molinero, J. Farré, and É. Villemonte de La Clergerie. Computer aided correction and extension of a syntactic wide-coverage lexicon. In *Proceedings of COLING'08*, Manchester, United Kingdom, 2008.

[11] B. Sagot. Automatic acquisition of a Slovak lexicon from a raw corpus. In *Lecture Notes in Artificial Intelligence 3658 (© Springer-Verlag), Proceedings of TSD'05*, pages 156–163, Karlovy Vary, Czech Republic, 2005.

[12] B. Sagot. Building a morphosyntactic lexicon and a pre-syntactic processing chain for Polish. In *Proceedings of the 3rd Language & Technology Conference (LTC'05)*, pages 423–427, Poznań, Poland, 2007.

[13] B. Sagot, L. Clément, E. Villemonte de La Clergerie, and P. Boullier. The *Lefff* 2 syntactic lexicon for French: architecture, acquisition, use. In *Proceedings of LREC'06*, 2006.

[14] B. Sagot and L. Danlos. Améliorer un lexique syntaxique à l'aide des tables du lexique-grammaire – Constructions impersonnelles. *Cahiers du Cental*, 2007.

[15] B. Sagot and L. Danlos. Méthodologie lexicographique de constitution d'un lexique syntaxique de référence pour le français. In *Proceedings of the workshop "Lexicographie et informatique : bilan et perspectives"*, Nancy, France, 2008.

[16] C. Álvarez, P. Alvariño, A. Gil, T. Romero, M. P. Santalla, and S. Sotelo. Avalon, una gramática formal basada en corpus. In *Procesamiento del Lenguaje Natural (Actas del XIV Congreso de la SEPLN)*, pages 132–139, Alicante, Spain, 1998.

How Limited is the Limit?

Prakash Mondal
International Institute of Information Technology, Gachibowli
Hyderabad 500032
prakash.mondal@research.iiit.ac.in

Abstract

In this paper an exploratory map of what intelligent natural language processing systems can achieve will be drawn up, given the advances that have been made in recent years as revealed in the latest developments in practical applications of natural language technology in areas as diverse as natural language generation, natural language understanding, machine translation, dialog system etc. Here a mathematical exploration of the issue in question will lay out the constraints on what they can achieve in their goal of automatizing language processing that humans do. It will be shown that these constraints together constitute a fundamental limit which these systems seem to fail to cross.

Keywords

Intelligent natural language processing systems; constraints; mathematical exploration; language processing.

1. Introduction

In recent years we have encountered a massive change in our conception of what natural language processing systems have achieved [1]. We have also gained a broader understanding of conceptual and empirical challenges that we face today in designing and implementing better systems that can be robust without incurring heavy computational costs [2]. With all this we are perhaps moving more towards the goal of automatization of human language processing in machines. But in spite of what has been gained in terms of theoretical and conceptual understanding of the problems, challenges, prospects in building natural language processing systems, there still seems to be an enormous gap between the level of performance these systems have come up to and how human language processing occurs [3] [4]. Is there any fundamental reason why the gap cannot be bridged? If there is any reason, why cannot we overcome it? And what is it about us that makes us do effortlessly all that these systems are designed to do, but are still far behind fully being capable of doing? It would be argued that a fundamental answer to all these questions perhaps exists. And the fundamental answer underlies a fundamental nature of human language processing mechanism.

2. What has been achieved

In recent years we have seen a spurt in the growth of computational models and practical systems in natural language processing. In the domain of natural language generation systems we have seen massive developments in phrase-based and feature-based systems of natural language generation [5], [6]. In the case of natural language understanding we have gone through ELIZA, PARRY, SIR etc. and we have viewed a range of rule-based and statistical natural language understanding systems for tutoring, medical advising etc. [7], [8] [9]. At the same time developments in parsing technology have moved on from rule-based models to data-driven statistical models and now future progress is moving toward hybrid models [10]. In addition, parallel progress has been made in machine translation systems and spoken dialog systems as well [11], [12], [13]. However, even if a lot has been achieved so far, a whole lot more is still to be achieved, which is upon the future generation high-computing technology [14].

3. What next?

3.1 The seemingly unbridgeable gap

Against this background, it seems that there is something missing. And such concerns are also recently found in a few recent works [15], [16], [17]. The missing link underpins the disparity between the level of performance of these systems as enumerated above and the seemingly effortless capabilities of human language processing. Can we really hope to scout out this missing link? Can there be a possible role of some hidden constraints, variables which operate in cognitive processing of human language, but are missing in inert machines? Even if the answers to these questions may not be easy to be spelled out, here it will be proposed that there is some deeply hidden fundamental law or law-like contingency that reflects the missing link. Before that a general architecture of cognitive processing of language will be drawn up to show that such a model of general cognitive processing is viable for placing linguistic processing in its ecological niche which has perhaps been ignored by the community [4].

3.2 Cognitive topography of human language processing

It is now necessary to present a model of the cognitive substrate of language processing by fitting the functional system of language into an architecture incorporating other cognitive domains so that how this architecture of language interacts with other cognitive domains can be linked to neural processing at the lower level. The broader picture in Figure 1 below is symmetric with certain constraints on mutual interaction of the cognitive domains/systems such that not all information passes from one domain/system to

International Conference RANLP 2009 - Borovets, Bulgaria, pages 270–274

another. Such constraints- computational, algorithmic and implementational in Marr's [18] sense- are specified by our genome.

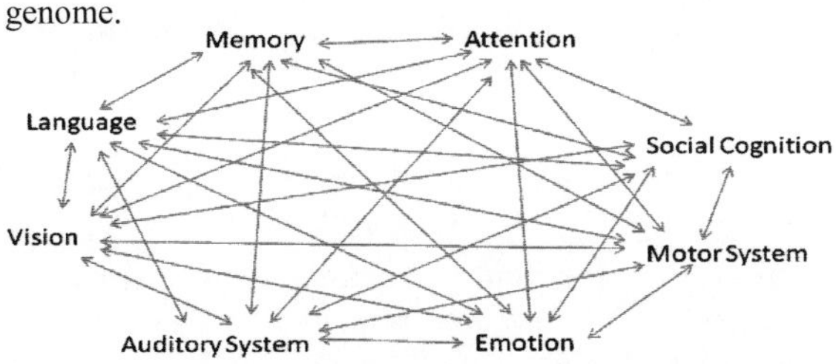

"Figure 1. Interconnection of Language to other Cognitive Domains/Systems."

Here the architecture is much more general in having a broader interconnected network of connections spanning through a plexus of cognitive domains. Such a network resembles Hopfield network more [19]. And research in a number of fields like biology, dynamical systems theory, behavioral genetics is moving more toward such interconnected models because of overlapping and shared neural mechanisms between many of them. [20], [21].

4. The hidden fundamental

4.1 Two fundamental variables

4.1.1 Meaning

It has generally been realized by philosophers, linguists, computer scientists, and perhaps neuroscientists what meaning in language is not, rather than what meaning in language is. However, despite the progress made in understanding meaning in language we are no nearer to having a complete grasp of what it is [22], [23]. And because of this the problem persists in fields which heavily rely on linguistic meaning, such as the field of natural language processing or AI.

Here the notion of meaning in language as we know it will be taken in a natural and general sense, even if no attempt will be made to define it given that there exists a serious danger in defining what meaning is. Roughly it can be said that meaning in language is what we understand in given circumstances from a linguistic structure- whether lexical or phrasal or sentential or discoursal. And it can correspond to a concept as is customary in *conceptual semantics* [24] or to a formal specification in *formal semantics* [25], or to a neurally connected network of activation patterns [26]. So meaning is here being treated as a fundamental variable in language in that language is impossible without this entity. Meaning is inherent in language as a system or language processing. It is so fundamental that it is perhaps least vulnerable in language disorders [27], [28].

4.1.2 Structure

Now the focus can be thrown on the other fundamental variable of language. The concept of structure has also a long history of varying implications. Right from the start linguistic structure has had a privileged place in the history of linguistic studies. Structural linguistics was entirely based on the conception of linguistic structure. Then with the advent of Generative grammar more stress has been given on syntactic structure as it is thought to be the computational systems with semantics and phonology as interpretive systems [29]. Here (linguistic) structure will be used in a general sense as it was done for meaning. It will be used to mean lexical structure, or phrasal structure or sentential or discoursal structure and phonological structure. The form of each type of structure is what has been characterized in the literature in terms of hierarchical organization [22].

Structure in language is also fundamental in terms of the scaffolding it provides to language. It is uncontroversial that natural language in any modality- auditory or visual (sign language) – must have structures which are constituted by phonological, lexical and syntactic structures. The exact representation of these kinds of structures may vary from one theoretical framework to another, but the fact that they form the skeletal architecture of language is fairly established.

4.2 The fundamental principle

Here the entire system of language has been reduced to two fundamental variables of language, namely, structure and meaning both of which can be either stable or variable; even if it is true that language interfaces with other cognitive domains/systems, which falls out of the architecture in Figure 1. above. However, soon this notion of language will be interwoven with the cognitive architecture shown above. Before that let us proceed to the fundamental principle that meaning and structure in language give rise to. Meaning and structure in language show a fundamental duality, in that what language is is manifested at varying levels either as meaning or as structure. For example, in the well-known case of tip-of-the-tongue phenomenon, what exists in mind is meaning, not the structure. Similar things happen in cases where we feel that a meaning is so intricate that it cannot be expressed in linguistic structure. Or for example in the case of patients with Broca's aphasia what is missing in them is structure at some level, but not meaning. The reverse is also found in a range of cases, though it is relatively rarer. Consider the case of *semantic satiation* where the structure of a word or phrase is repeated to the extent that it is bleached of its meaning [19]. Or for example, take the case of reading a poem which has linguistic structures in it, but often readers do not understand the meaning, even if they can decode the structures. In addition, in language itself we find specific words or phrases that have no meaning despite having structure; for example, light verbs like 'keep', the word 'of' in English are of such a nature.

Structure-meaning duality is actually at the heart of language and is perhaps more pervasive than has been realized. In particular, it can be emphasized that this duality does not in itself diminish the complexity of language as we know it, rather it adds to it. It is because in the absence of structure it is meaning that fills up the vacuum and perhaps vice versa. We understand it more deeply when we see a complementarity between the two in our everyday affairs. Pre-linguistic children understand the meaning, but are not capable of producing structure [19]. We so often fail to understand the convoluted structures in language, though we sense the meaning. In fact, in our normal day-to-day life we transform meaning into structure and structure into meaning. And this can be simply expressed in the following manner-

$$f(\mathrm{M}) = \mathrm{S} \quad \ldots (1)$$

and

$$f(\mathrm{S}) = \mathrm{M} \quad \ldots (2)$$

By treating them equivalent we get

$$f(\mathrm{M}) = f(\mathrm{S}) \quad \ldots (3)$$

But if we become more refined, the duality can be represented in the following way-

$$\mathrm{M} = \mathrm{S} \cdot k \quad \ldots (4)$$

Here M denotes meaning as has been characterized above; S denotes structure and k is a constant specifying the constraints that operate on structure. What this ultimately amounts to is that meaning is actually equivalent to structure and vice versa. On the face of it, it may seem to be counterintuitive, since there is a general feeling that sometimes more meaning comes out of a given structure, so meaning cannot be equivalent to structure. But let us stop for a moment to understand what we mean by it. What is being claimed is that at a given instant, a given structure must be equivalent to meaning or vice versa, hence for example no one can compute two meanings from a single pattern of structure within a temporal window of, say, 100-200 milliseconds, which falls within the neural threshold for action potentials [30]. In the same way, no human being can compute two structures from a single meaning within the same temporal window. But it is of course possible to have

$$\mathrm{M} > \mathrm{S} \quad \ldots (5)$$

or

$$\mathrm{S} > \mathrm{M} \quad \ldots (6)$$

In that case we must have the following scenario as can be represented here as

$$\mathrm{C(t)} = \sum_{i=1}^{n} A(\mathrm{t}_1 \ldots \mathrm{t}_n).\ \delta^{(h)} \quad \ldots (7)$$

where C(t) refers to total conceptual emergence, A is a mapping from S to M or vice versa with different instants from $t_1 \ldots t_n$ and $\delta^{(h)}$ is the distribution of them in a linear (or real or complex) space Ś.

Now this total conceptual emergence C(t) defined over the mapping A can be related to processing function $P^{(d)}$ relativized to a cognitive domain d. First we have as $P^{(d)}$

$$P^{(d)} = \sum_{i=1}^{N} P_i \int \mathrm{d}_{\mathrm{p}1,\ldots}\, \mathrm{d}_{\mathrm{pN}}\, \delta(_{\mathrm{p}1 \ldots \mathrm{pN}}).\ \Delta\psi \quad \ldots (8)$$

Here $_{\mathrm{p}1} \ldots {}_{\mathrm{pN}}$ are differential probability functions coming out of the interaction dynamics of language with other cognitive domains (Fig. 1); $\Delta\psi$ is a temporal continuum distribution. Relating C(t) to $P^{(d)}$, we get

$$\frac{\partial\, \mathrm{C(t)}}{\partial t} = \frac{P^{(d)} \rho_i (\mathrm{C(t)})}{P^{(d)} \rho_j (\mathrm{C(t)})} \quad \ldots (9)$$

What this boils down to is that C(t) if at time t, C(t) exists with the processing function P(d) with the probability density ρj, then it is true at any other time as well when there exists a current form of probability function ρi.

4.3 Layers of recursive emergence

It should now be clarified at this moment that the equation (1) derives from A which is an emergent reality that is embedded in another emergent reality at a higher level characterized by $P^{(d)}$. So it appears that here we have got a case of recursive emergence with one being nested inside a larger one. However, it may be noted that reading meaning-structure equivalence into language is itself an emergent reality which is nested inside another layer of emergent level representing $P^{(d)}$. And this $P^{(d)}$ is a non-algorithmic process as being mediated by dynamical non-linearity [19], [21], [30]. Interestingly, being an emergent level of fundamentality, this duality can never be broken down into either meaning or structure separately. In other words, if one tries to treat meaning representations or specifications in a way thinking that they are actually representing meaning which, to them, is a phenomenologically different entity altogether even if it stands for the structure in question, they are misled into a wrong direction. The reason is quite simple. Let us suppose that in a given scenario a meaning M' stands for or is symbolized by a structure S'; and assume that M'≠ S'. In a certain case let us say that S' is non-existent, but M' is not, since M' exists. In that scenario (for example, tip-of-the-tongue situation) quite often we get another S'' that is a sort of surrogate of S' when the speaker tries to substitute another structure for the one missing. What if we get another surrogate S''' for S'' itself? It will of course lead us into an infinite regress, which does not of course happen in normal situations. The point to be made is that if meaning had not been equivalent to structure, this would have never happened. Meaning is not tied to any specific structure, rather we can say meaning is structure or vice versa.

4.4 Meaning-structure equivalence and multiple grammars

Where does meaning-structure equivalence come from? Thus the concept of meaning-structure as specified above can be more generally linked to the concept of multiple grammars. Recently the concept of multiple grammars has been proposed to account for the existence of a range of hypotheses about grammar in language acquisition, the existence of overlapping but diverging grammars in language change [31] etc. And this can be generalized to the extent that it may well be said that at any stage in language processing a number of grammars operate in a hyperspace of potentiality from where the best one(s) that help(s) interpret the structure or convert the meaning into structure are chosen or utilized. Here the word 'grammar' is being used in a more general sense. It is of such nature that it may be used in interpreting structure(s) or for converting meaning into structure; so in this sense it is not just syntax that constitutes grammar, it may include semantic/pragmatic, morphological, phonological rules as well. In fact, meaning or structure is an actualization or realization of a selection form a wave of probability density of multiple grammars. It can be represented as

$$\sum_{i=1}^{n} h\,(P_1(G_1), \ldots, P_n(G_n)).\ P_1(G_1).\,, \ \ldots\,,\ .\ P_n(G_n) \qquad \ldots (10)$$

At any time there exist grammars $G_1, \ldots, G_n$ with the probabilities $P_1, \ldots, P_n$,where m is an arbitrary number and $n \leq m$, $n \geq 2$. But it must be the case that $m \geq 2$, since $n \geq 2$. This picture becomes much clearer in cases of ambiguity in natural language. Even in cases where there does not apparently exist any ambiguity; a selection must occur from that potential probability waving through the hyperspace. What is realized as structure or meaning at any time from that potential probability is an actualization at an emergent level. It may well be the case that this emergent actualization is unique in most instances [32].

5. Natural language processing, machine intelligence and meaning-structure equivalence

Below are some reasons for why machines cannot manifest any signs of meaning-structure equivalence.

First, natural language processing or even AI in general is still mostly based on linear, logical, rule-governed, algorithmic, and perhaps deterministic view of language processing, whereas the meaning-structure equivalence is a an emergent property of natural intelligence belonging to humans. We still find algorithms in natural language processing that are of such nature and that is why in the absence of meaning, machines cannot provide for structure in substitution of the missing meaning [33].

Second, it is indeed true that language computations are bound below by NP-hardness and are NP complete as has been mathematically proved by Ristad [34]. Where does this complexity come from? It can be said that this is the essence of natural language which reflects emergent non-linearity of meaning-structure equivalence.

Third, computational modeling of meaning-structure equivalence fails for the following reason. Let us suppose that there is a mapping function W from meaning-structure equivalence $M\text{-}S^E$ to an algorithm K. Then we get $W(M\text{-}S^E) \rightarrow K$. Now if one has to computationally model this mapping, that mapping has to be embedded in another mapping function, say, Q which maps the above mapping to another potential algorithm for the purpose of modeling nested layers of emergence. Given that the goal of natural language processing is to build a robust system without incurring greater computational costs, such a computational modeling as depicted above will certainly involve greater computational costs.

6. What is the limit?

So what is the limit then? The limit lies in what the duality of meaning and structure shows machines to be confined to. It seems that in this way computation of natural language is bound from below by the constraints posed by meaning-structure equivalence in humans. We can put it here in the following fashion

$$\varphi \leq W(M\text{-}S^E) \qquad \ldots (11)$$

Here the functional mapping $W(M\text{-}S^E)$ is bound below by the threshold limit φ which is not crossed by computers. This is what makes the problem of computational tractability. Indeed, it leads to a different view of constraints as operating on natural language processing. They allow us to refine our understanding of what it means to process language not just in a robust way which is a perfect epiphenomenon of this duality, but also in a broader view. The duality is like a self-referential loop as one gets the same thing in dealing with either.

7. Conclusion

This is a preliminary sketch of what it is that is behind the limitations today's natural language processing systems are facing. The paper has proposed that there is a natural reason behind all that. And it is this very fundamental of meaning-structure equivalence that is so elusive that it escapes computational tractability. There is of course no logical reason why the future cannot forge a different picture of natural language processing. Perhaps the future lies in a hybrid model of neural fuzzy systems combined with evolutionary computation subsumed under a dynamical non-linear approach. This has the potential of handing over to the research community the necessary self-organizing dynamics in language processing that we urgently require. But whether that will really place us in a position to claim that we have succeeded in building natural or seemingly natural intelligence into machines will depend on our emerging views about language processing, human intelligence and perhaps cognition in general.

References

[1] Robert Dale, H. L. Somers and Hermann Moisl.(Eds.), Handbook of Natural Language Processing. Marcel Dekker, New York, 2000.

[2] Shalom Lappin. A Sequenced Model of Anaphora and Ellipsis Resolution. In António Branco, Tony McEnery and Ruslan Mitkov (Eds.), Anaphora Processing: Linguistic, Cognitive and Computational Modeling. John Benjamins, Amsterdam, 2005.

[3] J. A. Feldman. Computational Cognitive Linguistics. In Proceedings of 20th International Conference on Computational Linguistics. Association for Computational Linguistics, Morristown, New Jersey, 2004.

[4] Roger K. Moore. Towards a Unified Theory of Spoken Language Processing. In Proceedings of 4th IEEE International Conference on Cognitive Informatics, Irvine, USA, 2005.

[5] Eduard Hove. Language Generation. In Ronald Cole, Joseph Mariani, Hans Uszkoreit, Givanni Battista Virile, Annie Zaenen, and Antonio Zampoli. (Eds.), Survey of the State of the Art in Human Language Technology. Cambridge University Press, New York, 1998.

[6] C. L. Paris, W. R. Swartout, and W. C. Mann. (Eds.). Natural Language Generation in Artificial Intelligence and Computational Linguistics. Kluwer Academic, Boston, 1990.

[7] James Allen. Natural Language Understanding. CA: Benjamin/Cummings, Redwood City, 1994.

[8] Nicholas L. Cassimatis, Arthi Murugesan and Magdalena D. Bugajska A Cognitive Substrate for Natural Language Understanding. In Proceedings of the First Conference on Artificial General Intelligence, University of Memphis, 2008.

[9] Mark G. Core and Johanna D. Moore. Robustness versus Fidelity in Natural Language Understanding. In Proceedings of the Human Language Technology-North American Chapter of the Association for Computational Linguistics, Boston, USA, 2004.

[10] A. Murugesan, and N.L. Cassimatis. A Model of Syntactic Parsing Based on Domain-General Cognitive Mechanisms. In Proceedings of the 28th Annual Conference of the Cognitive Science Society, Canada, Vancouver, 2006.

[11] S. Nirenburg, H. L Somers and York Wilks. (Eds.), Readings in Machine Translation. MIT Press, Cambridge, Mass., 2003.

[12] Yorick Wilks: Machine Translation: Its Scope and Limits. Springer, New York, 2009.

[13] Egidio Giachin. Spoken Language Dialogue. In Ronald Cole, Joseph Mariani, Hans Uszkoreit, Givanni Battista Virile, Annie Zaenen, and Antonio Zampoli. (Eds.), Survey of the State of the Art in Human Language Technology. Cambridge University Press, New York, 1998.

[14] Jeremy Pekham. (Ed.). Recent Developments and Applications of Natural Language Processing. Kogan Page, London, 1989.

[15] S. Nireburg and Victor Raskin. Ontological Semantics. MIT Press, Cambridge, Mass., 2004.

[16] N.L. Cassimatis Cognitive Science and Artificial Intelligence Have the Same Problem. In Proceedings of the 2006 AAAI Spring Symposium on Between a Rock and a Hard Place: Cognitive Science Principles Meet AI-Hard Problems, 2000.

[17] Martin Kay. A Life of Language. Computational Linguistics 31(4): 425-438, 2005.

[18] David Marr. Vision: A Computational Investigation into the Human Representation and Processing of Visual Information. W. H. Freeman, San Francisco, 1982.

[19] Michael Spivey. The Continuity of Mind. Oxford University Press, New York, 2007.

[20] Klaus Mainzer. Thinking in Complexity: The Computational Dynamics of Matter, Mind and Mankind. Springer, New York, 1994.

[21] Myrna Estep. Self-Organizing Natural Intelligence: Issues of Knowing, Meaning and Complexity. Springer, Dordrecht, 2006.

[22] Ray Jackendoff. Foundations of Language. Oxford University Press, Oxford, 2002.

[23] P. Reccah. What is an Empirical Theory of Linguistic Meaning a Theory of? In Z. Frajzyngier, A. Hodges, and D. S. Rood. (Eds.), Linguistic Diversity and Language Theories. John Benjamins, Amsterdam, 2007.

[24] Ray Jackendoff. Semantic Structures. MIT Press, Cambridge, Mass., 1990.

[25] G. Chierchia and S. McConnell-Ginet. Meaning and Grammar: An Introduction to Semantics. MIT Press, Cambridge, Mass., 2000.

[26] A. M. Collins and M. R. Quillian. Retrieval Time from Semantic Memory. Journal of Verbal Learning and Verbal Memory. 8, 240-247, 1969.

[27] P. Fletcher and J. F. Miller. (Eds.), Developmental Theory and Language Disorders. John Benjamins, Amsterdam, 2005.

[28] Ewa Dąbrowska. Language, Mind and Brain. Edinburgh University Press, Edinburgh, 2004.

[29] Noam Chomsky. The Minimalist Program. MIT Press Cambridge, Mass., 1995.

[30] Eugene M. Izhikevich. Dynamical Systems in Neuroscience: The Geometry of Excitability and Bursting. MIT Press, Cambridge, Mass., 2007.

[31] Charles Yang. Knowledge and Learning in Natural Language. Oxford University Press, New York, 2002.

[32] Evelyne Andreewsky. Complexity of the Basic Unit of Language: Some Parallels in Physics and Biology. In M. Mugur-Schachetr, and Alwyn van der Merwe. (Eds.), Quantum Mechanics, Mathematics, Cognition and Action. Springer, Amsterdam, 2002.

[33] C. Havasi, R. Speer and J. Alonso. ConceptNet3: A Flexible Multilingual Semantic Network for Common Sense Knowledge. In Proceedings of the Recent Advances in Natural Language Processing, Borovets, Bulgaria, 2007.

[34] Eric Sven Ristad. The Language Complexity Game. MIT Press, Cambridge, Mass., 1993.

Dependency Parsing and Semantic Role Labeling as a Single Task

Roser Morante, Vincent Van Asch
CLiPS - Computational Linguistics
University of Antwerp
Prinsstraat 13
B-2000 Antwerpen, Belgium
Roser.Morante, Vincent.VanAsch@ua.ac.be

Antal van den Bosch
Tilburg Centre for Creative Computing
Tilburg University
P.O. Box 90153
NL-5000 LE Tilburg, The Netherlands
Antal.vdnBosch@uvt.nl

Abstract

We present a comparison between two systems for establishing syntactic and semantic dependencies: one that performs dependency parsing and semantic role labeling as a single task, and another that performs the two tasks in isolation. The systems are based on local memory-based classifiers predicting syntactic and semantic dependency relations between pairs of words. In a second global phase, the systems perform a deterministic ranking procedure in which the output of the local classifiers is combined per sentence into a dependency graph and semantic role labeling assignments for all predicates. The comparison shows that in the learning phase a joint approach produces better-scoring classifiers, while after the ranking phase the isolated approach produces the most accurate syntactic dependencies, while the joint approach yields the most accurate semantic role assignments.

Keywords

Joint learning, dependency parsing, semantic role labeling

1 Introduction

In their currently popular definitions, dependency parsing and semantic role labeling are partly overlapping tasks. In their standard definitions they map to differently structured output spaces: dependency graphs span over sentences, while semantic role assignments center around individual predicates. Yet, the spaces overlap; in a dependency graph verbal predicates will tend to have dependency relations with the same modifiers that have a semantic role as argument of that predicate. In general, even though the labels are different, syntactic dependencies between two words often co-occur with the existence of certain semantic roles. Although they do not signify the same, the "subject" dependency relation, for example, often co-occurs with the "A0" label that denotes the agent role in the PropBank annotation scheme [14]. Overlaps such as these naturally suggest the possibility of jointly learning the two labeling tasks as if they were one.

In this paper we present a system that performs dependency parsing and semantic role labeling jointly, which we submitted to the CoNLL Shared Task 2009 [8]. The task combines the identification and labeling of syntactic dependencies and semantic roles for seven languages. Details about the task setting and the data sets used can be found in the web page of the task[1]. Additionally, we present a comparison of the joint system with another version of the system (*"isolated" system*) that processes semantic and syntactic dependencies separately. In this way, we are able to evaluate whether and where the joint learning approach is more efficient and successful than the isolated approach. As far as we know, this is the first time that such a comparison is performed.

In the joint system, the two labeling tasks are learned jointly by merging the syntactic and semantic dependencies, which implies that the number of labels increases, and the average number of examples per label decreases. This does not rule out the application of a machine learning classifier to the joint task, but the classifier should not be too sensitive to a fragmented class space with many labels. This is the main reason our system relies on local memory-based classifiers: they are largely insensitive in terms of training and processing efficiency to the number of class labels [4].

Memory-based algorithms have been previously applied to processing semantic and syntactic dependencies separately. As for semantic role labeling, [10] describes a memory-based semantic role labeling system for Spanish based on gold standard dependency syntax; [11] report on a semantic role labeling system for English based on syntactic dependencies produced by the MaltParser system of Nivre *et al.* [13]. As for dependency parsing, MaltParser uses memory-based learning as one of its optional local classifiers. Canisius *et al.* [2] present another type of memory-based dependency parser, extended later in [3] to a constraint satisfaction-based dependency parser. The latter parser combines local memory-based classification with a global optimization method based on soft weighted constraint-satisfaction inference, where the local classifiers estimate syntactic relations between pairs of words, the direction of the relation from children to parents, and the relations that parents have with children. Our current joint system adopts a similar strategy, but uses ranking rather than weighted constraint satisfaction inference.

[1] `http://ufal.mff.cuni.cz/conll2009-st/`

We briefly discuss the issue of joint learning of two tasks in Section 2. The two versions of the system are described in Section 3, Section 4 presents and discusses the results, and in Section 5 we put forward some conclusions and future research.

2 Joint learning

When two tasks share the same feature space, there is the natural option to merge them and consider the merge as a single task. For example, Sejnowski and Rosenberg [15] train a back-propagation multi-layered perceptron network on the joint task of mapping a letter in its context within an English word onto a joint label representing its phonemic mapping and a marker indicating stress on that phoneme. Van den Bosch [16] demonstrates that the joint learning of these two tasks indeed produces superior generalization performance as compared to learning the letter-phoneme task and the stress marker assignment task separately. Buchholz [1] transposes this idea to shallow parsing, and shows that POS tagging and base phrase chunking could be learnd as a single task without any significant performance loss. Wang *et al.* [17] jointly learn Chinese word segmentation, named entity recognition, and part-of-speech tagging, outperforming a pipeline architecture baseline. Recently, Finkel and Manning show that joint learning of parsing and named entity recognition produce mildly improved performance for both tasks [6].

The merging of two tasks will typically lead to an increase in the number of class labels, and generally a more complex class space. In the worst case, the number of classes in the new class space is the product of the number of classes in the original tasks. In practice, if two combined tasks are to some extent related, the increase will tend to be limited, as class labels from the original tasks will tend to correlate. For instance, the POS tag for "determiner" will typically co-occur with the chunk marker for "beginning of noun phrase", and less so, or not at all with other chunk markers. Yet, even a mild increase of the number of classes leads to a further separation of the class space, and thus to less training examples per class label.

Joint learning can therefore only lead to positive results if the data sparsity effect of the separation of the class space is counter-balanced by an unharmed, or even improved learnability. The latter is the primary reason for doing joint learning in the first place: certain parts of either of the combined tasks may be learned with more ease and with better success when it is co-learned with a part of another tasks. Learning this new separate part of the class space may in theory be easier than learning that particular part of the the larger unseparated class space of either of the composing tasks.

Here, in the joint system, we treat the syntactic and semantic tasks as one and the same task. For example, given a pair of words A and B, where B would be a verbal predicate, we train a local classifier to assign the label "SBJ:A0", signifying that A is the modifier in a subject dependency relation with its head B, as well as that A is the argument with the A0 role of predicate B. Thus, we merge the class labels of the two tasks into single labels, and present the classifiers with examples with these labels. Further on the system, as we describe in the next section, we do make use of the compositionality of the labels, as in the end we have to produce syntactic dependency graphs and semantic role assignments separately.

Apart from our system, three more joint systems participated in the CoNLL Shared Task 2009. The system described by [9] extends the Eisner parser to accomodate semantic dependencies. The system of [5] decomposes the joint learning task in four subtasks: semantic dependency identification and labeling, and syntactic dependency identification and labeling. A pipeline approach is set up in order to use the output of one task as input of another, and features not available at a certain step are incorporated iteratively. The system described by [7] is based on an incremental parsing model with synchronous syntactic and semantic derivations and a joint probability model for both types of dependency structures.

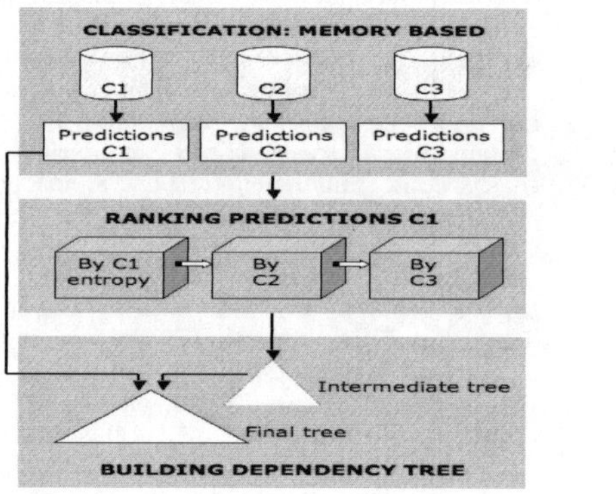

Fig. 1: Architecture of the joint system for dependency parsing and semantic role labeling

3 System description

In this section we describe the joint system, and compare it to the isolated version of the system. The joint system operates in three phases (see Figure 1): a classification phase in which three memory-based classifiers predict different aspects of joint syntactic and semantic labeling; a ranking phase in which the output of the classifiers is combined per sentence; and a phase in which the syntactic and semantic dependency graphs are built.

As a first step, before generating the instances of the joint classifiers, we merge the semantic and syntactic dependencies into single labels. Table 1 lists the merged versions of the dependencies in an example sentence. The "Merged"' column contains for each token its one or more merged dependencies, separated by blank spaces; each dependency is expressed in labels with the following format: < *headID* >::< *dependencylabel* >:< *semanticrolelabel* >. If a syntactic or semantic label is absent, it is encoded by an underscore, "_".

N	Token	Synt.	Sem.	Merged
1	Housing	2:NMOD	2:A1	2::NMOD:A1
2	starts	3:SBJ	2:A2 4:A1 6:A1 13:A0	2::_:A2 3::SBJ:_ 4::_:A1 6::_:A1 13::_:A0
3	are	0:ROOT	_	0::ROOT:_
4	expected	3:VC	_	3::VC:_
5	to	4:OPRD	4:C-A1	4::OPRD:C-A1
6	quicken	5:IM	_	5::IM:_
7	a	8:NMOD	_	8::NMOD:_
8	bit	6:OBJ	6:A2	6::OBJ:A2
9	from	6:ADV	6:A3	6::ADV:A3
10	August	13:NMOD	13:AM-TMP	13::NMOD:AM-TMP
11	's	10:SUFFIX	_	10::SUFFIX:_
12	annual	13:NMOD	13:AM-TMP	13::NMOD:AM-TMP
13	pace	9:PMOD	_	9::PMOD:_
14	of	13:NMOD	13:A2	13::NMOD:A2
15	1,350,000	16:NMOD	_	16::NMOD:_
16	units	14:PMOD	_	14::PMOD:_
17	.	3:P	_	3::P:_

Table 1: *Example sentence with isolated and merged dependency labels*

3.1 Phase 1: Classification

In the classification phase, three classifiers predict different local aspects of the global output structure. All three operate at the word level. Two classifiers consider pairs of words, and predict the identity or the presence, respectively, of a joint semantic and syntactic dependency between them. The third classifier focus on single words only, and predicts the relations one word has with other words, without making reference to these other words. The hyperparameters of the classifiers were optimized on English, by training on the full training set and testing on the development set; these optimized settings were then used for the other six languages as well. The hyperparameters and features used per classifier can be found in [12].

Classifier 1: Pairwise semantic and syntactic dependencies. Classifier 1 predicts the merged semantic and syntactic dependencies that hold between two tokens. Instances represent combinations of pairs of tokens within a sentence. Each token is combined with all other tokens in the sentence. The class predicted is a joint $< dependencyrelation >:< semanticrole >$ label, or NONE if no relation is present between the tokens. The amount of occurring classes for all seven languages is shown in Table 2.

	Cat	Chi	Cze	Eng	Ger	Jap	Spa
C1	111	309	395	551	152	103	124
C2	111	1209	1221	1957	300	505	124

Table 2: *Number of classes per language predicted by Classifiers 1 (C1) and 2 (C2)*

The three most frequent merged class labels in the case of English carry a syntactic dependency only: NMOD:_ (16.2% of all joint dependency labels), P:_ (10.1%), and PMOD:_ (8.7%). The syntactic dependency components of these three labels also co-occur with semantic roles in other joint labels, such as NMOD:A1, which is the sixth-most frequent joint label (3.9%). The fourth most frequent class is a semantic-role-only label: _:A0 (5.5%). The fifth most frequent class is the most frequent example of a joint syntactic and semantic dependency: OBJ:A1 (4.5% of all joint dependency labels). The joint label SBJ:A0 ranks number 12 in the frequency list, covering 2.5% of all labels. At the other end of the frequency list, many joint labels occur only rarely; for English, 287 classes of the 551 occur only once.

Classifier 2: Per-token relations. Classifier 2 predicts the labels of the dependency relations of a token with its syntactic and/or semantic head(s). Instances represent single tokens. For example, the instance that represents token 2 in Table 1 would have as class: _:A2-SBJ:_-_:A1-_:A1-_:A0. The amount of classes per language is shown in Table 2 under "C2". The number of classes exceeds 1,000 for Chinese, Czech, and English. These numbers are higher than those for Classifier 1, as single tokens can have several semantic heads, along with always one syntactic head.

Classifier 3: Pairwise detection of a relation. Classifier 3 is a binary variant of Classifier 1 that predicts whether two tokens have a dependency relation. Instance representation follows the same scheme as with Classifier 1.

3.1.1 Results

The results of the Classifiers in terms of micro-averaged F-scores (with $\beta = 1$) over all class labels are presented in Table 3. The performance of Classifiers 1 and 3 is mostly above 90%, which is promising, leaving a clear margin of error nonetheless. The micro-averaged F-scores for Classifier 2 are lower, especially for Chinese, Czech, and English. There appears to be a correlation with the high number of Classifier 2 class labels (more than one thousand) for these three languages in particular, as witnessed by Table 2. The data sparsity induced by this high fragmentation of the class space may be hampering performance of Classifier 2 for these three languages.

Lang.	C1	C2	C3
Cat	94.77	86.30	97.96
Chi	92.97	70.11	95.47
Cze	91.49	67.87	93.88
Eng	94.17	76.16	95.37
Ger	92.76	83.23	93.77
Jap	91.55	81.22	96.75
Spa	94.76	84.40	96.39

Table 3: *Micro-averaged F-scores of the joint system per classifier (C) and per language on the test corpora*

The isolated version of the system consists of six classifiers: each of the three classifiers described above, applied separately to syntax and semantics. These classifiers learn the content of the columns "Synt." and "Sem." in Table 1 in isolation, instead of learning it jointly.

English	C1		C2		C3	
Dependencies	ISO	JOINT	ISO	JOINT	ISO	JOINT
Synt	94.65	95.19	87.32	_	95.88	_
Sem	96.29	97.87	80.42	_	95.43	_
Synt/Sem	92.24	94.17	_	76.16	94.42	95.37

Table 4: *Comparison of Micro-averaged F-scores per classifier (C) on English test data in the joint and the isolated systems*

Table 4 compares the results per classifier for the joint ("JOINT") and the isolated ("ISO") systems. For Classifier 1 we compute the results for syntax, semantics and for the combination. To compute the combined results of the isolated system we recombine the results of the syntax and semantics classifiers. For Classifier 2 we can only compare the results of the combined syntactic and semantic labels in the joint system with the results that we obtain separately for syntax and semantics in the isolated system. For Classifier 3 it is not possible to compute the results of syntax and semantics separately for the joint system, as its binary labels do not distinguish between syntax and semantics.

Results of Classifiers 1 and 3 indicate that learning the tasks jointly produces a moderately better performance. The results of the main classifier, C1, show that syntactic and semantic dependencies are better learned within the joint setting. This might be explained by the fact that merged class labels are more fine-grained, and that certain merged labels can be predicted better separately than when lumped together in the original coarser-grained syntactic or semantic labels. By analysing the scores per class, we find that the scores per syntactic class improve for classes that split into several classes in the joint setting and are frequent. For example, the syntactic class NMOD, which splits into 13 classes and is very frequent, scores 5 points higher in the joint system, whereas the class MNR, which splits into 8 classes and is not frequent, scores 4 points lower. We observe the same trend in the scores per semantic class. For example, class A1, which is the most frequent and splits into 20 combined classes, scores 18 point higher in the joint setting.

3.2 Phase 2: Ranking

The classifier at the root of generating the desired output (dependency graphs and semantic role assignments) is Classifier 1, which predicts the semantic and syntactic dependencies that hold between two tokens. However, the classifier predicts incorrect dependencies to a certain degree, and does not produce a graph in wich all tokens have at least a syntactic head. The evaluation of the overall joint syntactic and semantic labeled accuracy based on the output of Classifier 1 produces a baseline score of 51.3% labeled macro F-score. The ranking phase intends to improve over this performance. This is done in two steps: (i) reranking alternative predictions of Classifier 1 in order to construct an intermediate dependency tree, and (ii) adding extra semantic dependencies to the tree that do not align with syntactic dependencies.

3.2.1 Ranking predictions of Classifier 1

In order to disambiguate between all possible dependencies predicted by Classifier 1 between tokens, the system applies re-ranking rules. It analyses the dependency relations that have been predicted for a token with its potential parents in the sentence, and ranks them. For example, for a sentence with 10 tokens, the system would make 10 predictions per token. The predictions are first ranked by entropy of the class distribution for that prediction, then using the output of Classifier 2, and next using the output of Classifier 3.

Ranking by entropy. In order to compute entropy we use the (inverse-linear) distance-weighted class label distributions among the nearest neighbors that Classifier 1 is able to find. For example, the prediction for an instance may be: { NONE (2.74), NMOD:_ (0.48) }. The system ranks the prediction with the lowest entropy in position 1, while the prediction with the highest entropy is ranked in the last position. The rationale behind this is that the lower the entropy, the more confident the classifier is about the predicted dependency. Table 5 lists the first six heads for the predicate word 'starts' ranked by entropy (cf. Table 1).

Head	Predicted label	Distribution	Entropy
Housing	NONE	{ NONE (8.51) }	0.0
expected	_:A1	{ _:A1 (5.64) }	0.0
to	NONE	{ NONE (4.74) }	0.0
quicken	_:A0	{ _:A0 (4.13), _:A1 (0.18), _:A2 (0.31) }	0.56
are	NONE	{ NONE (2.56), SBJ:_ (0.52) }	0.65
starts	_:A0	{ _:A0 (7.90), _:A1 (0.61), _:A2 (1.50) }	0.93

Table 5: *Output of Classifier 1 for the first six heads of 'starts', ranked by entropy*

Ranking by Classifier 2. The next ranking step is performed by using the predictions of Classifier 2, i.e. the estimated labels of the dependency relations of a token with its syntactic and/or semantic head(s). The system re-ranks the predictions that are not in the set of possible dependencies predicted by Classifier 2 to the bottom of the ranked list. Because this is done after ranking by entropy, the instances with the lowest entropy are still at the top of the list. Table 6 displays the re-ranked six heads of 'starts', given that Classifier 2 has predicted that possible relations to heads are SBJ:A1 and _:A1, and given that only 'expected' is associated with one of these two relations.

Head	Predicted label	Distribution	Entropy
expected	_:A1	{ _:A1 (5.64) }	0.0
Housing	NONE	{ NONE (8.51) }	0.0
to	NONE	{ NONE (4.74) }	0.0
quicken	_:A0	{ _:A0 (4.13), _:A1 (0.18), _:A2 (0.31) }	0.56
are	NONE	{ NONE (2.56), SBJ:_ (0.52) }	0.65
starts	_:A0	{ _:A0 (7.90), _:A1 (0.61), _:A2 (1.50) }	0.93

Table 6: *Output of Classifier 1 for the first six heads of 'starts', ranked by entropy and Classifier 2*

Ranking by Classifier 3. The final ranking step makes use of Classifier 3, which predicts the existence of a relation between two tokens. The dependency relations predicted by Classifier 1 that are not confirmed by Classifier 3 are moved to the end of the ranked list. Table 7 lists the resulting ranked list.

Head	Predicted label	Distribution	Entropy
expected	_:A1	{ _:A1 (5.64) }	0.0
quicken	_:A0	{ _:A0 (4.13), _:A1 (0.18), _:A2 (0.31) }	0.56
starts	_:A0	{ _:A0 (7.90), _:A1 (0.61), _:A2 (1.50) }	0.93
Housing	NONE	{ NONE (8.51) }	0.0
to	NONE	{ NONE (4.74) }	0.0
are	NONE	{ NONE (2.56), SBJ:_ (0.52) }	0.65

Table 7: *Output of Classifier 1 for the first six heads of 'starts' ranked by entropy, Classifier 2, and Classifier 3*

After ranking the predictions of Classifier 1, the system selects as syntactic head for every token the prediction with the best ranking that has a syntactic dependency value different from "_". This is motivated by the fact that every token has one and only one syntactic head. The tree that results from this step (*intermediate* tree) can have more than one root, or no root at all. To make sure that every sentence has one and only one root, we apply some extra rules.

The error reduction rate at each step of the ranking process is shown in Table 8.

Ranking	Labeled Macro F1	Error Reduction
No ranking	53.40	-
C1 Entropy	68.66	32.74
By C2	71.48	8.99
By C3	75.88	15.42

Table 8: *Effect of the ranking steps in the final results of the joint system on the test data of English*

The product of this step is a tree in which every token is uniquely linked to a syntactic head. Because syntactic and semantic dependencies have been linked, the tree contains also semantic dependencies. However, the tree is missing the semantic dependencies predicted by Classifier 1 that do not have a syntactic dependency part. The final step, described in Subsection 3.3 adds these relations to the dependency tree. We first describe how ranking in the isolated system is implemented.

3.2.2 Ranking in the isolated system

In the isolated system the same ranking process is applied to the syntactic dependency task in order to build a syntactic graph, where every node has only one syntactic head. The ranking algorithm takes as input the output of the classifiers that learn syntactic dependencies in isolation.Table 9 shows the error reduction rates of syntactic dependencies for English at every step of the ranking process, comparing the joint system and the isolated system. The results show that the effect of the ranking process outperforms the scores of the joint system slightly, despite the fact that the individual classifiers produced better scores in the joint setting.

	Joint		Isolated	
Ranking	LAS	ER	LAS	ER
No ranking	51.08	-	51.02	-
C1 Entropy	70.84	40.39	71.93	42.69
By C2	74.22	11.29	74.71	9.90
By C3	80.35	23.77	81.08	25.18

Table 9: *Comparison of the ranking effects in the isolated and joint systems for syntactic dependencies on the test data of English (LAS "Labeled Attachment Score", ER "Error Reduction")*

It is not possible to make the same comparison for semantic dependencies in isolation, as the ranking aims to select one syntactic head. In the semantic dependency graph, a token can have more than one head.

3.3 Phase 3: Adding extra semantic dependencies

In order to find the tokens that have only a semantic relation with a predicate, the system analyses for each predicate the list of predictions made by Classifier 1, selecting the predictions in which the syntactic part of the label is "_" and the semantic part of the label is not "_". On the test data for English, applying this rule produces another 9.57% error reduction on labeled macro F1: from 75.88% to 78.19%.

In the isolated system semantic dependencies are processed differently. Classifiers 1, 2 and 3 learn the semantic dependencies in isolation. Then, the predictions of Classifier 1 are ranked by entropy. All AM arguments (e.g. AM-TMP) are kept because a predicate can have more than one, but the redundant basic arguments (such as A0, A1, etc.) are filtered out because each predicate can have only one of them. If there is more than one, we keep the one that occupies the highest position in the ranking. Additionally, some relations are filtered out by using Classifiers 2 and 3. The results obtained for semantics in the isolated and in the joint system are not directly comparable, because we cannot process them in the exact same way.

3.4 Predicate sense disambiguation

In the setting of the CoNLL Shared Task, processing the semantic dependencies of a predicate involves also disambiguating the sense of the predicate. This is performed in the joint and the isolated systems by a classifier for each language that predicts the sense of the predicate. An exception is made for Japanese, as with that language the lemma is taken as the sense. We use the IGTREE algorithm. Instances represent predicates; the features used are the word, lemma and POS of the predicate, and the lemma and POS of two tokens before and after the predicate. The results per language are presented in Table 10. We observe relatively high scores for Chinese and English.

Lang.	Cat	Chi	Cze	Eng	Ger	Spa
F1	82.40	94.85	87.84	93.64	73.57	81.13

Table 10: *Micro-averaged F-score for the predicate sense disambiguation*

4 Overall results

For each language, a full system is developed by training the three classifiers on the training set and testing on the development set. The final results are obtained by processing the test set provided by the CoNLL 2009 Shared Task. Table 11 lists the syntactic and semantic dependency prediction evaluated separately. The labeled attachment score (LA) indicates low scores for Chinese and Czech, and relative success for English and Japanese. In terms of semantic role labeling scores, precision is higher than recall for all languages, and markedly lower scores are obtained with German and Japanese.

The comparison of the final results of the joint and the isolated system presented in Table 12 indicates a moderately better performance of the isolated system

	Syntax	Semantics		
Lang.	LAS	F1	Precision	Recall
Cat	77.33	70.14	72.49	67.94
Chi	67.92	67.63	69.48	65.86
Cze	60.03	77.28	80.73	74.11
Eng	80.35	75.97	79.04	73.13
Ger	73.88	61.01	65.15	57.36
Jap	86.17	68.82	77.66	61.80
Spa	73.07	68.48	69.62	67.38

Table 11: *Labeled attachment score (LAS) for syntactic dependencies and F scores of semantic dependencies per language in the joint system*

for syntactic dependencies, and a drop in performance of the isolated system for semantic dependencies. In particular, the isolated system produces considerably lower recall rates. This cannot be caused by the performance of the classifiers, since their results in the isolated setting are less than 2 points lower. Therefore, the ranking process customized to semantic dependencies is suboptimal.

	Syntax	Semantics		
System	LAS	F1	Precision	Recall
Joint	80.35	75.97	79.04	73.13
Isolated	81.08	63.89	72.00	57.42

Table 12: *Comparison of labeled attachment score (LAS) of syntactic dependencies and F scores of semantic dependencies in the joint and the isolated systems for English*

5 Conclusions

In this paper we presented two systems, one that performs dependency parsing and semantic role labeling, based on local classifiers that learn the semantic and syntactic information jointly, and a second that performs the tasks based on local classifiers that learn the semantic and syntactic information in isolation. The isolated system was designed with the purpose of extracting conclusions about the effect of joint learning. By comparing the systems using English data, we found that in the joint learning setting the classifiers achieve slightly better scores.

The analysis of the results per class of the main classifier in the joint and the isolated setting shows that classes that are frequent and split into several merged classes in the joint setting have the highest increase of scores in the joint setting compared to the isolated setting. This suggests that separation of the class into finer-grained intersections of semantic and syntactic labels space facilitates the learning process, provided that there are enough examples for these finer-grained joint labels.

As for the joint system, the comparatively low scores on most languages (compared to other competing systems in the CoNLL 2009 shared task) can be likely improved (1) by making use of the available morphosyntactic features, which we did not use in the present system; (2) by optimising the classifiers per language; and (3) by further improving the ranking algorithm. We also observe a relatively low recall on the semantic task as compared to the overall scores, indicating that syntactic dependencies are identified with a better precision-recall balance than the semantic roles. More detailed tuning of our downsampling strategy may be used to improve the balance for the semantic task.

Acknowledgments

This study was made possible through financial support from the University of Antwerp (GOA project BIOGRAPH), and from the Netherlands Organisation for Scientific Research.

References

[1] S. Buchholz. *Memory-Based Grammatical Relation Finding*. PhD thesis, Tilburg University, 2002.

[2] S. Canisius, T. Bogers, A. van den Bosch, J. Geertzen, and E. T. K. Sang. Dependency parsing by inference over high-recall dependency predictions. In *Proc. of CoNLL-X*, pages 3–8, New York City, NY, 2006.

[3] S. Canisius and E. Tjong Kim Sang. A constraint satisfaction approach to dependency parsing. In *Proc. of the CoNLL Shared Task Session of EMNLP-CoNLL 2007*, pages 1124–1128, 2007.

[4] W. Daelemans and A. van den Bosch. *Memory-based language processing*. Cambridge University Press, Cambridge, UK, 2005.

[5] Q. Dai, E. Chen, and L. Shi. An iterative approach for joint dependency parsing and semantic role labeling. In *Proc. of the CoNLL 2009: Shared Task*, pages 19–24, Boulder, CO, 2009.

[6] J. R. Finkel and C. D. Manning. Joint parsing and named entity recognition. In *Proc. of Human Language Technologies: The 2009 Annual Conference of the NAACL*, pages 326–334, Boulder, Colorado, June 2009. ACL.

[7] A. Gesmundo, J. Henderson, P. Merlo, and I. Titov. A latent variable model of synchronous syntactic-semantic parsing for multiple languages. In *Proc. of the CoNLL 2009: Shared Task*, pages 37–42, Boulder, CO, 2009.

[8] J. Hajič, M. Ciaramita, R. Johansson, D. Kawahara, M. A. Martí, L. Màrquez, A. Meyers, J. Nivre, S. Padó, J. Štěpánek, P. Straňák, M. Surdeanu, N. Xue, and Y. Zhang. The CoNLL-2009 shared task: Syntactic and semantic dependencies in multiple languages. In *Proc. of CoNLL-2009: Shared Task*, Boulder, Colorado, USA, 2009.

[9] X. LLuís, S. Bott, and L. Márquez. A second-order joint eisner model for syntactic and semantic dependency parsing. In *Proc. of the CoNLL 2009: Shared Task*, pages 79–86, Boulder, CO, 2009.

[10] R. Morante. Semantic role labeling tools trained on the Cast3LB-CoNLL-SemRol corpus. In *Proc. of the LREC 2008*, Marrakech, Morocco, 2008.

[11] R. Morante, W. Daelemans, and V. Van Asch. A combined memory-based semantic role labeler of english. In *Proc. of the CoNLL 2008*, pages 208–212, Manchester, UK, 2008.

[12] R. Morante, V. Van Asch, and A. van den Bosch. Joint memory-based learning of syntactic and semantic dependencies in multiple languages. In *Proc. of the CoNLL 2009: Shared Task*, pages 25–30, Boulder, CO, 2009.

[13] J. Nivre. *Inductive Dependency Parsing*. Springer, 2006.

[14] M. Palmer, D. Gildea, and P. Kingsbury. The proposition bank: An annotated corpus of semantic roles. *Computational Linguistics*, 31(1):71–105, 2005.

[15] T. Sejnowski and C. Rosenberg. Parallel networks that learn to pronounce English text. *Complex Systems*, 1:145–168, 1987.

[16] A. Van den Bosch. *Learning to pronounce written words: A study in inductive language learning*. PhD thesis, Universiteit Maastricht, 1997.

[17] X. Wang, J. Nie, D. Luo, and X. Wu. A Joint Segmenting and Labeling Approach for Chinese Lexical Analysis. In *Proc. of the European conference on Machine Learning and Knowledge Discovery*, pages 538–549, Berlin, 2008. Springer Verlag.

Structured Output Learning with Polynomial Kernel

Hajime Morita
Department of Computational Intelligence and Systems Science, Tokyo Institute of Technology
morita@lr.pi.titech.ac.jp

Hiroya Takamura
Precision and Intelligence Laboratory, Tokyo Institute of Technology
takamura@pi.titech.ac.jp

Manabu Okumura
Precision and Intelligence Laboratory, Tokyo Institute of Technology
oku@pi.titech.ac.jp

Abstract

We propose a new method which enables the training of a kernelized structured output model. The structured output learning can flexibly represent a problem, and thus is gaining popularity in natural language processing. Meanwhile the polynomial kernel method is effective in many natural language processing tasks, since it takes into account the combination of features. However, it is computationally difficult to simultaneously use both the structured output learning and the kernel method. Our method avoids this difficulty by transforming the kernel function, and enables the kernelized structured output learning. We theoretically discuss the computational complexity of the proposed method and also empirically show its high efficiency and effectiveness through experiments in the task of identifying agreement and disagreement relations between utterances in meetings. Identifying agreement and disagreement relations consists of two mutually-correlated problems: identification of the utterance which each utterance is intended for, and classification of each utterance into approval, disapproval or others. We simultaneously use both of the structured output learning and the kernel method in order to take into account this correlation of the two problems.

Keywords

Structured Output Learning, Machine Learning, Passive-Aggressive Algorithm, Kernel, Meeting Records, Dialog Act, Adjacency-Pairs.

1 Introduction

Structured output learning is a method that learns a model in order to predict the structured label of an instance. Typically, the structure is complex, and the set of possible labels is very large. Examples of structured labels are graphs, trees and sequences. Recently, for the algorithms of structured output learning, Support Vector Machine (Thochantaridis, 04) and Passive Aggressive Algorithm (Crammer, 06) were expanded. Structured output learning plays an important role in natural language processing (NLP), including parsing and sequential role labeling.

In NLP, the polynomial kernel has proven effective because it can take into account the interaction between features. For example, for complicated tasks like dependency structure analysis, we need to consider a combination of features (Kudo, 00). The use of a kernel is necessary for non-linear classification, as well as for improvement of performance. However, structured output learning is hardly ever used with a kernel, mainly because evaluation of all possible labels by kernels would be necessary, and is computationally prohibitive. We construct a kernelized classifier that identifies agreement/disagreement relations between utterances in dialogue. Identifying agreement and disagreement relations consists of two mutually-correlated problems: identification of the utterance which each utterance is intended for, and classification of each utterance into approval, disapproval or others. This problem can be seen as the problem of finding edges between pairs of nodes, where the number of nodes is fixed, and it is equivalent to restricting the possible structure output in the output of structured output learning. We can apply our method to the problems that can be seen as identification of a graph with a fixed number of nodes.

Furthermore, when using structured output learning for complex NLP tasks, predicting a structure might include a number of different problems. In order to simultaneously learn a number of different problems as elements of a structured label, we define cost functions in consideration of the case where the proportion of classes differs among the problems.

In this paper, we propose a method that transforms the kernel to reduce the computational complexity of learning with restricted structured output and kernels, and propose cost functions to take into account the different class proportions among the problems, in order to apply structured output learning to a larger area of application. We evaluate our method on the task of identifying agreement and disagreement relations in the MRDA corpus (Shriberg, 04). On the large set of labels, experiments show that our method is exponentially faster than the conventional methods.

2 Related work

In structured output learning, we need to find the best label from an exponentially large set of labels in order to predict the label. Therefore, the complexity of predicting the label determines whether the problem can be solved in practical time or not. Specialized algorithms for each problem to improve efficiency are thus used for predicting a label. For example, if the label is a sequence, the Viterbi algorithm might be useful (Sittichai, 08), and if the label is a parse tree, parsing algorithms like CKY can be used to search for the best label (McDonald, 05). In general, these problems are learned by linear models.

When training a kernel-based model, the increasing number of support vectors has a bad influence on the complexity. For this reason, Orabona (2008) proposed a method that approximates a new vector through the existing support vectors in order to reduce the overall number of obtained support vectors. Similarly, the complexity of

International Conference RANLP 2009 - Borovets, Bulgaria, pages 281–286

classification increases according to the increase of the set of support vectors in the Support Vector Machine (SVM). Keerthi (2006) proposed a method to approximate the size of the support vector set.

Another approach to overcome the increase of the support vectors is a technique that expands the kernel so that it avoids dealing with the support vectors (Moh, 08). This method expands a polynomial kernel in order to treat the induced feature space as the feature vector in linear models. However, this is infeasible for a large feature set.

3 Passive Aggressive Algorithm

Passive Aggressive Algorithm (Crammer, 06) is a family of perceptron-like online max margin algorithms. It has linear complexity in the number of examples. Therefore, this algorithm is faster than batch-algorithms such as SVM, and requires less memory. Crammer proposed an expansion to structured output learning, and a derivation algorithm for learning with a kernel. At each step, this algorithm conservatively updates the model so that it can correctly classify the misclassified instance $\mathbf{x}$. For details, refer to (Crammer, 06).

Algorithm 1 shows the expansion to structured output learning with kernel. Each instance $\mathbf{x}^{(i)}$ is paired with a correct label $\mathbf{y}^{(i)}$. We call the pair $(\mathbf{x}, \mathbf{y})$ added to the model $\mathcal{W}$ a *support vector*, such as in SVM, and τ is the weight of the support vector. So the model $\mathcal{W}$ is a set of tuples:(τ , $\mathbf{x}$, $\mathbf{y}$). Each pair of an instance and a label corresponds to a feature vector that is given by $\Phi(\mathbf{x}^{(i)}, \mathbf{y})$. The prediction problem is reduced to finding the best label $\hat{\mathbf{y}}$ from the possible labels $\mathcal{Y}$:

$$\bar{\mathbf{y}} = \underset{\mathbf{y} \in \mathcal{Y}}{\operatorname{argmax}} \sum_{\{\tau^{(t)}, \mathbf{x}^{(t)}, \mathbf{y}^{(t)}\} \in \mathcal{W}} \tau^{(t)} K(\Phi(\mathbf{x}^{(t)}, \mathbf{y}^{(t)}), \Phi(\mathbf{x}^{(i)}, \mathbf{y}))$$

To assign a different cost for each misclassified instance during the learning, a cost function $\rho(\mathbf{y}, \mathbf{y}')$ is introduced, associated with every pair of correct label $\mathbf{y}$ and predicted label $\hat{\mathbf{y}}$. We assume that $\rho(\mathbf{y}, \mathbf{y}') = 0$ if $\mathbf{y}' = \mathbf{y}$ and that $\rho(\mathbf{y}, \mathbf{y}') \geq 0$ whenever $\mathbf{y} \neq \mathbf{y}'$. At each update step, the algorithm updates the model so that the following constraint is going to be satisfied,

$$\mathcal{W}_{\text{updated}} = \mathcal{W} \cup (\tau, \mathbf{x}^{(i)}, \mathbf{y}^{(i)}) \cup (-\tau, \mathbf{x}^{(i)}, \bar{\mathbf{y}}).$$

At step 4, the algorithm maximizes the following expression by finding the label that violates this constraint to the highest extent,

$$\bar{\mathbf{y}} = \underset{\mathbf{y} \in \mathcal{Y}}{\operatorname{argmax}} \sum_{\{\tau^{(t)}, \mathbf{x}^{(t)}, \mathbf{y}^{(t)}\} \in \mathcal{W}} \tau^{(t)} K(\Phi(\mathbf{x}^{(t)}, \mathbf{y}^{(t)}), \Phi(\mathbf{x}^{(i)}, \mathbf{y})) + \sqrt{\rho(\mathbf{y}^{(i)}, \mathbf{y})}. \quad (1)$$

At steps 5 and 6, unless there is a sufficient margin between the example with the correct label and the other examples, we calculate the weight τ. τ is a real number that ensures necessary margin between the example with the correct label and the example with the resultant label $\bar{\mathbf{y}}$. Step 7 updates the model by τ and $\bar{\mathbf{y}}$ as follows:

$$\mathcal{W}_{\text{updated}} = \mathcal{W} \cup (\tau, \mathbf{x}^{(i)}, \mathbf{y}^{(i)}) \cup (-\tau, \mathbf{x}^{(i)}, \bar{\mathbf{y}}).$$

There are two problems with simultaneous use of structured output and polynomial kernel. One is clear from formula (1). Following the increase in the number of support

Algorithm 1 Passive Aggressive Algorithm

Input: $S = ((\mathbf{x}^{(1)}, \mathbf{y}^{(1)}), ..., (\mathbf{x}^{(N)}, \mathbf{y}^{(N)})), C$
1: initialize model
2: **for** $iteration = 1, 2, \ldots$ **do**
3:   **for** $i = 1, ..., N$ **do**
4:     get most violated label $\bar{\mathbf{y}}$
5:     **if** $(\bar{\mathbf{y}} \neq \mathbf{y}^{(i)})$ **then**
6:       calculate τ from $\rho(\mathbf{y}^{(i)}, \bar{\mathbf{y}})$
7:       update model
8:     **end if**
9:   **end for**
10: **end for**
11: return model

vectors, the computational complexity increases compared to a linear model. Since a maximization (1) is carried out at each iteration, the computational complexity increases not only during classification, but also during learning.

We should also notice that the number of support vectors tends to be large in online learning. In addition, since structured output learning has as many examples as the number of pairs of an instance and a label, the number of support vectors tends to be even larger.

The second problem is that since the algorithm classifies the instances in the kernel space, we cannot evaluate the intermediate scores corresponding to the elements of label structures and their features. Therefore, most of the available conventional decoding algorithms such as Viterbi cannot be used. Moreover, since step 4 requires the maximization of the sum of more than one polynomial kernel function, it is difficult to solve this problem efficiently.

4 Formal definition

In this section, we give a formal definition of the problem of applying the polynomial kernel to structured output prediction.

- label $\mathbf{y}$

  In this paper, we assume that the label is a binary vector of length m. Most of the data structures, such as graphs or sequences, can be represented by binary vectors.

- instance $\mathbf{x}$

  $\mathbf{x}$ denotes the vector representing an instance.

- Φ function

  In algorithm 1, the Φ function generates a feature vector from a label and an instance. $\oplus$ denotes an operator that concatenates two vectors, m denotes the label length, and y_i denotes a label element. We define the Φ function as follows,

  $$\Phi(\mathbf{y}, \mathbf{x}) = (y_1\mathbf{x}) \oplus (y_2\mathbf{x}) \oplus \cdots \oplus (y_m\mathbf{x}).$$

  For example, for a given pair $\mathbf{y} = (1, 0, 1, 0), \mathbf{x} = (1, 2, 3, 4)$, we obtain $\Phi(\mathbf{y}, \mathbf{x}) = (1, 2, 3, 4,\ 0, 0, 0, 0,\ 1, 2, 3, 4,\ 0, 0, 0, 0)$. By combining each of the label elements with the vectors that represent the instances, this Φ function generates a range of features in a vector corresponding to each label element. That is, the weights of each feature can be determined for each label element. We can decide whether the feature is a positive evidence or a negative evidence for each label element.

- cost function

  We define three cost functions for the labels, each one of which is represented as a binary vector. Section 6 explains the cost functions in detail.

5 Transformation of the polynomial kernel

As a kernelized learner, we often use a polynomial kernel in NLP in order to treat the combination of features such as words and dependencies. Let m be the label length, and $K(\mathbf{v}, \mathbf{v}')$ be a p degree polynomial kernel. We transform this kernel to reduce the computational complexity. The transformation is composed of integrating the Φ function and polynomial kernel, and decomposing the integrated kernel.

5.1 Integrating the Φ function and the kernel

Let us first consider reducing the computational complexity per kernel function evaluation. For calculating the kernel, we must regenerate the feature vector from $\mathbf{x}$ and $\mathbf{y}$, or cache the kernel values. However it is impractical to hold all the $N2^m$ feature vectors. In addition, we must deal with all feature vectors at each iteration. The access to feature vectors does not have locality of reference. Therefore caching support vectors is not efficient. For this reason, we calculate the kernel value directly, by integrating the polynomial kernel and the Φ function.

Let us calculate the kernel between the vectors generated by the Φ function in due order. For simplicity, the constant term in the polynomial kernel is dropped out, without loss of generality. The p degree polynomial kernel can be expanded as follows:

$$\begin{aligned} & K(\Phi(\mathbf{y}, \mathbf{x}), \Phi(\mathbf{y}', \mathbf{x}')) \\ = \; & ((y_1 \cdot \mathbf{x} \oplus y_2 \cdot \mathbf{x} \oplus \ldots \oplus y_m \cdot \mathbf{x}) \cdot \\ & (y'_1 \cdot \mathbf{x}' \oplus y'_2 \cdot \mathbf{x}' \oplus \ldots \oplus y'_m \cdot \mathbf{x}'))^p. \end{aligned}$$

Since in the kernel space an inner product can be obtained by the range of features corresponding to each label element, the above formula can be tranformed as follows:

$$K(\Phi(\mathbf{y}, \mathbf{x}), \Phi(\mathbf{y}', \mathbf{x}')) = \{(y_1 \cdot y'_1)(\mathbf{x} \cdot \mathbf{x}') + \ldots + (y_m \cdot y'_m)(\mathbf{x} \cdot \mathbf{x}')\}^p,$$

and we can extract the products of the dot-product of instance vectors $(\mathbf{x} \cdot \mathbf{x}')$, $K(\Phi(\mathbf{y}, \mathbf{x}), \Phi(\mathbf{y}', \mathbf{x}')) = ((\mathbf{y} \cdot \mathbf{y}')(\mathbf{x} \cdot \mathbf{x}'))^p$. Thus, a kernel can be represented by a dot-product of labels $(\mathbf{y} \cdot \mathbf{y}')$ and a dot-product of instance vectors $(\mathbf{x} \cdot \mathbf{x}')$. It turns out that we can evaluate the polynomial kernel without the Φ function. Here, let the kernel integrated with Φ function be denoted by K_{ex} as follows:

$$K_{ex}(\mathbf{y}, \mathbf{x}, \mathbf{y}', \mathbf{x}') = ((\mathbf{y} \cdot \mathbf{y}')(\mathbf{x} \cdot \mathbf{x}'))^p. \quad (2)$$

Refer to Figure 1 for intuitive explanation. Through the kernel integrated with Φ, we can evaluate a kernel by only the dot-product between the instance vectors, regardless of the label length.

If we do not integrate Φ with the kernel, evaluation of the kernel costs (label length) $\times$ (feature size) computational time and memory. By contrast, evaluation costs only

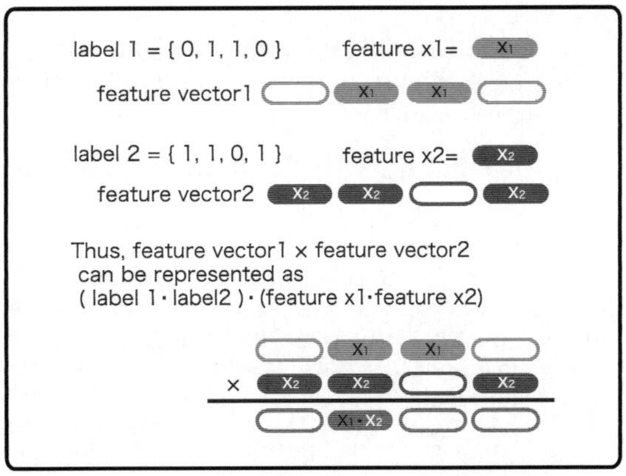

Fig. 1: *Integrating Φ function and kernel*

(label length) + (feature size) for both in our calculation. Since we have to only cache the kernel between the instances, cache efficiency increases significantly.

5.2 Decomposing the kernel

In order to reduce the number of calls to the kernel function as much as possible, we expand the integrated kernel further, limiting ourselves to the case of second degree polynomial kernels for the sake of simplicity.

In the Passive Aggressive Algorithm with a kernel, the number of suppor vectors increases during the iterations, and becomes an arbitrarily large set. For this problem, Moh (2008) proposed a method that expands a second degree polynomial kernel to an induced feature space, and treated it as a linear model to avoid treating support vectors for memory complexity. However, since Moh's method must treat a large space that is of a square of the size of a feature set, this has the opposite effect that the computational space is increasing. Thus, this method cannot treat a large number of features. If we expand the kernel in a feature space, it cannot benefit from the kernel trick and it must treat a large feature space as in Moh(2008). We expand the kernel not only in the feature space, but also in the label space. Therefore, we can expand the kernel efficiently, if label length < feature size.

K_{ex} can be decomposed and represented as a combination of y_i that belongs to $\mathbf{y}$, where the constant term in a polynomial kernel is dropped out without loss of generality,

$$K_{ex}(\mathbf{y}, \mathbf{x}, \mathbf{y}', \mathbf{x}') = ((\mathbf{y} \cdot \mathbf{y}')(\mathbf{x} \cdot \mathbf{x}'))^2 = (\mathbf{y})^2 \left((\mathbf{y}')^2 (\mathbf{x} \cdot \mathbf{x}')^2\right).$$

Here, we consider the calculation of the kernel score $S(\mathbf{y}, \mathbf{x})$ between an example $(\mathbf{y}, \mathbf{x})$ and the support vectors $\{\tau^{(t)}, \mathbf{y}^{(t)}, \mathbf{x}^{(t)}\}$. We decompose $\mathbf{y}$ and $\mathbf{y}^{(t)}$ to each y_i and $y_i^{(t)}$, and expand the square. So let γ_{ij} denote $\sum_{\{t | (\tau^{(t)}, \mathbf{y}^{(t)}, \mathbf{x}^{(t)}) \in \mathcal{W}\}} \tau^{(t)} y_i^{(t)} y_j^{(t)} (\mathbf{x} \cdot \mathbf{x}^{(t)})^2$, because γ_{ij} is constant in terms of $\mathbf{y}$. We then obtain the score of the example:

$$\begin{aligned} S(\mathbf{y}, \mathbf{x}) &= \sum_{(\tau^{(t)}, \mathbf{y}^{(t)}, \mathbf{x}^{(t)}) \in \mathcal{W}} \tau^{(t)} K_{ex}(\mathbf{y}, \mathbf{x}, \mathbf{y}^{(t)}, \mathbf{x}^{(t)}) \\ &= \sum_{\{i,j | i \neq j,\ i,j < m\}} y_i y_j \gamma_{ij} + \sum_{\{i | i \leq m\}} y_i^2 \gamma_{ii}. \end{aligned}$$

As shown above, support vectors can box in the parameters $\gamma \in \mathcal{R}^{m^2}$. For the same instance vector $\mathbf{x}$ and the same model, we can calculate the score using γ for each $\mathbf{y}$ without calls to the kernel. We call the expanded kernel a "transformed kernel".

5.3 Predicting with polynomial kernelization

At step 4 of Algorithm 1, we solve the maximization problem. We exploit the expansion so that we obtain the label which violates the constraints to the highest extent.

Algorithm 2 predicts $\bar{\mathbf{y}}$ using the transformed kernel. $\mathbf{1}$ denotes the label, each element of which is 1. $\mathbf{e}_i$ denotes a label that is the vector with a 1 in the i-th element and 0 elsewhere. And $\tau^{(k)}$ denotes the weight on the k-th support vector. $\mathbf{sv}_{ki} = \Phi(\mathbf{e}_i, \mathbf{SV}_k)$ denotes the feature vector generated by Φ from the k-th support vector and $\mathbf{e}_i$. We henceforth define $y^{(0)}$ as always equal to 1, so that we calculate γ with a constant term, and the label whose length is m implicitly includes the constant term $y^{(0)}$.

Algorithm 2 for finding $\bar{\mathbf{y}}$.

Input: $\mathbf{x} = \Phi(\mathbf{1}, \mathbf{x}), \tau, \mathcal{W} = \{\mathbf{sv}_1, ..., \mathbf{sv}_n\}$
Input: $\mathtt{true\_y}$ //correct label(in training only)

for all $\{(i,j)|0 < i \leq j \leq m\}$ **do**

$$\gamma_{ij} = \sum_{\mathbf{sv}_k \in \mathcal{W}} \tau^{(t)} \beta_{ij} K(\mathbf{sv}_{ki}, \mathbf{x}) K(\mathbf{sv}_{kj}, \mathbf{x})$$

$$\beta_{ij} = \begin{cases} 1 & if(i = j) \\ 2 & otherwise \end{cases}$$

end for
for $0 \leq i \leq m$ **do**

$$\gamma_{0i} = \gamma_{i0} = \sum_{\mathbf{sv}_k \in \mathcal{W}} \tau^{(t)} K(\mathbf{sv}_{ki}, \mathbf{x})$$

// processing constant terms.
end for
$\bar{\mathbf{y}} = \underset{\mathbf{y} \in \{0,1\}^m}{\text{argmax}}\, S(\mathbf{y}, \mathbf{x})$ //when classifying
$\bar{\mathbf{y}} = \underset{\mathbf{y} \in \{0,1\}^m}{\text{argmax}}\, S(\mathbf{y}, \mathbf{x}) + \rho(\mathbf{true\_y}, \mathbf{y})$ //when training
return $(\bar{\mathbf{y}})$

Calculating γ requires calling the kernel function $n(m+1)^2$ times, but the evaluation of each label requires only the calculation of the polynomial expression whose coefficient is γ. Thus, even the evaluation of all possible labels has only to call the kernel $n(m+1)^2$ times.

Additionally, the Passive Aggressive Algorithm trains the model incrementally, and the weight of the support vector added to the model does not change. In this way, if we hold γ for all instances, γ can be updated according to the support vectors newly added to the model. Thus, complexity can be reduced even further.

5.4 Discussion

Here, we discuss the computational complexity of the learning. Let N be the number of examples, and let h be the number of support vectors included in the model at a given point. Let H be the number of the final support vectors, I be the number of iterations needed to obtain H support vectors, and m be the label length.

We assume that the misclassification rate of training data is constant while training the model. We then need to perform classification calculation $\lambda = \frac{NI}{H}$ times in order to obtain one support vector. In the following, we will see the number of calls to the kernel required to obtain all the support vectors for each case of without transformation and with transformation.

- Without kernel transformation

  Since evaluation of each example requires $h2^m$ calls to the kernel function, obtaining one support vector requires $h2^m\lambda$ calls. Thus, the number of calls to the kernel to obtain H support vectors is, $\sum_{h=1}^{H} h\lambda 2^m = NI(H+1)2^{m-1}$. In practice, misclassifications decrease in number with training and one support vector requires more classification examples. Hence complexity can become larger.

- When transforming the kernel

  Since evaluation of the examples requires only the calculation of the kernel of the new support vectors, it needs $\frac{H(m+1)^2}{I}$ calls to the kernel function on average. Therefore, the number of calls to the kernel to get H support vectors is, $H\frac{H(m+1)^2}{I}\lambda = NH(m+1)^2$.

In the cases where the label length is long or training needs many iterations, the computational complexity benefits from the transformation of the kernel.

6 Cost function

In structured output learning, for a given pair of labels, a cost is calculated by a cost function. Hereby, we can introduce a "near error" and a "distant error", and impose a little penalty to near error and a large penalty to distant error. We define three cost functions. Each cost function defines what is "near" and "distant". s is a scale parameter in the following.

- 0/1 cost

  $$\rho_{0/1}(\mathbf{y}, \mathbf{y}') = \begin{cases} 0 & if\ \mathbf{y} = \mathbf{y}' \\ s & otherwise \end{cases}$$

  It returns s if the labels differ, and 0 otherwise. It is the most basic cost function that can be defined for general labels.

- average cost

  $$\rho_{average}(\mathbf{y}, \mathbf{y}') = \frac{1}{m}\sum_{i=1}^{m} \begin{cases} 0 & if\ y^{(i)} = y'^{(i)} \\ s & otherwise \end{cases}$$

  It returns $s \times$ (the number of different elements in the label) divided by the label length. It means that errors in several label elements induce a larger penalty.

- Asymmetric cost

  $$\rho_{asm}(\mathbf{y}, \mathbf{y}') = \frac{1}{m}\sum_{i=1}^{m} \begin{cases} 0 & y^{(i)} = y'^{(i)} \\ s \cdot j_i & y^{(i)} = 1, y^{(i)} \neq y'^{(i)} \\ s & otherwise \end{cases}$$

  This cost function returns $s \cdot j_i$ if a positive element is incorrectly classified as a negative element. If there is a bias between positive and negative label elements, the model will learn disproportionally by rote, because of which it gains a rather oversized margin, and the rest cannot gain sufficient margin. In order to remedy the bias and gain decent margins, an asymmetric cost function gives a different cost when the positive or negative elements are mistaken. It changes the width of the margin that must be

Table 1: *Dialogue example*

A	wait, is this a computer science conference ?
A	or is it a
B	um, well, it's more . . .
B	it's both right.
B	it's it's sort of t- cognitive neural psycho linguistic
B	but all for the sake of doing computer science
B	so it's sort of cognitive psycho neural plausibly motivated architectures of natural language processing
B	so it seems pretty interdisciplinary

reserved. We assign different parameters j_i to each label, so that this function can absorb the positive and negative bias that is different for each element.

7 Experiments

We examine the task of identifying agreement and disagreement between utterances to verify the efficiency and the effectiveness of our method. Identifying agreement and disagreement between utterances is to predict whether each utterance shows agreement or disagreement, and inter-utterances have a link.

7.1 Data

We used the MRDA corpus that has been used by related works (Galley, 2004). This corpus contains dictated text and audio data collected from 75 multi-party meetings in ICSI. The meetings, one hour duration each, have been held on a weekly basis by 6.5 researchers on average. For all utterances in this corpus, annotators labeled that the Dialog Acts, speakers, Adjacency-Pairs, etc.

Each Dialog Act is a category of utterances defined according to their intent. There are 44 Dialog Acts. Among them, we regard 4 tags, Acknowledge-answer("bk"), Accept("aa"), Accept-part("aap"), Maybe("am"), as agreement. We regard other 2 tags, Reject("ar"), Reject-part("arp") as disagreement. Adjacency-Pairs are another kind of tags. We regard an utterance pair is linked if they are annotated with the Adjacency-Pairs tag. We show the dialogue example in Table 1.

7.2 Experimental settings

In this experiment, we aim to predict the agreement and disagreement relations between the utterances, segmented into groups of 3 continuous utterances: first, second, and third utterances. There are 3 possible links. For each link, there are 3 possible values: agreement, disagreement, others. Therefore, the label length m is 9. In this paper, we train and classify shifting the segments by 1 utterance. That is, the second utterance from an example is the first utterance on the next example. We also used as features the preceeding and succeeding 3 utterances, 7 utterance in all, to classify on our method. The features that denote the content of utterances are the word length, uni-grams, bi-grams, tri-grams, head 2 words, and tail 2 words. The features that denote relations between utterances are whether the speaker is the same or not, and the time interval. We cannot evaluate this problem precisely by accuracy, since the classes are biased in size. Thus, we used F-value in order to evaluate. We used 12499 examples to train, and 9200 examples for testing. We do not determine an iteration limit in the Passive Aggressive Algorithm; instead, we used the model of the point of convergence. The second degree polynomial kernel was used, and the constant term is set to 1.

7.3 Execution time

We also measure the execution time. When the kernel is not integrated, the execution time tends to be prohibitively long. So we experimented with a small training dataset in that case.

Additionally, we used fixed parameters, because parameters influence the execution time. The number of iterations is 15. We used the average cost. We set the scale factor of the cost function s to 10. We used the second degree polynomial kernel in the evaluations of both the transformed and non-transformed kernels.

8 Results

8.1 Effect of the cost function

We show the result of our examination of the performance of the cost function in Table 2. We first compare the result with the zero-one cost with the result with the average cost. When the zero-one cost is used, the utterance position changes the result significantly, but classifying each position utterance is the same problem.

On the other hand, when the average cost is used, the utterance position does not change results much. Since the zero-one cost judges only the overall correctness of the predicted relations, it learns to reserve margin against both near errors and distant errors. As a result, it reserves oversized margin against mistakes of the label elements during learning. But, when the average cost is used, the mistakes of label elements change the score; So it learns to reserve an appropriate margin against elements of each label.

Furthermore, when the asymmetric cost is used, the method performs well for all label elements. This is because this asymmetric cost absorbs the proportion of positive contents and negative contents, by implementing differential penalty for the mistakes. We show the effect of the parameters of asymmetric cost in the next section.

Table 2: *Performance of the cost function*

Cost function	0/1	Average	Asymmetric (j=3)
Agreement (utterance 1)	0.337	0.394	0.490
Agreement (utterance 2)	0.170	0.343	0.462
Agreement (utterance 3)	0.097	0.237	0.414
Disagreement (utterance 1)	0.016	0.000	0.134
Disagreement (utterance 2)	0.000	0.032	0.032
Disagreement (utterance 3)	0.000	0.000	0.076
Link(utterance 1-2)	0.030	0.074	0.305
Link(utterance 2-3)	0.021	0.088	0.366
Link(utterance 1-3)	0.012	0.083	0.277

8.2 Effect of the parameters j

We show the results with different values of parameters $\mathbf{j} \in \{j_i\}^m$ in Table 3. We can change the penalty that is given when the positive content is incorrectly classified, by changing $\mathbf{j}$. We observe an improvement in the classification of agreements or links, and particularly in the classification of disagreements where these are few positive examples. Increasing $\mathbf{j}$ does not improve the performance unlimitedly. The optimal values for $\mathbf{j}$ can be determined from the proportion of the positive and negative examples, and we must fit $\mathbf{j}$ to the corresponding problem.

Table 3: *Influence of* **j**

j	0.5	1	10	50	100
Agreement (1)	0.290	0.382	**0.526**	0.500	0.479
Agreement (2)	0.226	0.327	**0.510**	0.497	0.460
Agreement (3)	0.160	0.216	**0.514**	0.507	0.464
Disagreement (1)	0.000	0.000	0.245	**0.320**	0.287
Disagreement (2)	0.000	0.000	0.201	**0.306**	0.277
Disagreement (3)	0.000	0.000	0.258	**0.320**	0.316
Link (1-2)	0.173	0.088	0.472	**0.508**	0.445
Link (2-3)	0.038	0.142	**0.529**	0.518	0.456
Link (1-3)	0.027	0.069	0.431	**0.450**	0.413

Table 4: *Comparison with linear model*

Model	Kernelized	Linear
Agreement	**0.512**	0.501
Disagreement	**0.316**	0.263
Link(utterance 2-3)	**0.550**	0.494
Link(utterance 1-3)	**0.454**	0.418

8.3 Effect of the kernel

Based on the results above, we optimized the weight **j** for agreement/disagreement and link, and compared with the linear model. The weight parameters are as follows: $j_{yea} = 3$, $j_{nay} = 10$, $j_{link_{1-2,2-3}} = 6$, $j_{link_{1-3}} = 5$. We set the scale factor of the cost function s to 5. In linear model: $j_{yea} = 3$, $j_{nay} = 100$, $j_{link_{1-2,2-3}} = 6$, $j_{link_{1-3}} = 5$. We set the scale factor of linear model s_{linear} to 4. We chose the parameters for test data. Thus, the results are the upper limit that we can obtain by tuning the parameters.

We show the results with this settings in Table 4. The linear model cannot deal with corresponding words among the utterances because it cannot treat a combination of features, and slows down the performance, especially when classifying links. In classification of agreements/disagreements, the polynomial kernel improves the performance, too.

8.4 Computational complexity

We measured the execution times and compared them in Table 5. For both cases of using transformation or not, the execution time is proportional to (example size) $\times$ (support vector size).

Without overheads, the difference of these execution times is close to the theoretical complexity difference when the kernel is called $2^m = 512$ times and the complexity for each kernel is $m = 9$ times higher, coming together as in total 4608 times.

Table 5: *Execution time*

Number of training examples	50	100	150
Support vectors	118	183	294
Using non-transformed kernel	15523s	56227s	139590s
Using transformed kernel	3. 19s	8.14s	28.65s
Ratio	$\times$4866	$\times$6907	$\times$4872

9 Conclusion

In this paper, we proposed the cost functions to take into account the different class proportions between the problems, and a method that transforms the kernel to reduce the computational complexity of learning with structured output and kernels. This algorithm is based on one of the online max margin algorithm, Passive Aggressive Algorithm, so it learns fast and uses a small amount of memory. We evaluated our method on the task of identifying agreement and disagreement relations, and we empirically and theoretically showed the computational complexity of the proposed method, and also the efficiency of using a polynomial kernel for structured output learning.

References

[1] Koby Crammer, Ofer Dekel, Joseph Keshet, Shai Shalev-Shwartz, Yoram Singer, Online Passive-Aggressive Algorithms. *Journal of Machine Learning Research*, Vol. 7, pp. 551–585, 2006.

[2] Michel Galley, Kathleen McKeown, Julia Hirschberg, Elizabeth Shriberg, Identifying agreement and disagreement in conversational speech: Use of bayesian networks to model pragmatic dependencies. In *Proceedings of the 42nd Annual Meeting on Association for Computational Linguistics*, pp. 669–676, 2004.

[3] Taku Kudo, Yuji Matsumoto, Japanese dependency structure analysis based on support vector machines. In *Proceedings of the 2000 Joint SIGDAT Conference on Empirical Methods in Natural Language Processing and Very Large Corpora*, pp. 18–25, 2000.

[4] Elizabeth Shriberg, Raj Dhillon, Sonali Bhagat, Jeremy Ang, and Hannah Carvey, The ICSI meeting recorder dialog act (MRDA) corpus. In *Proceedings of the 5th SIGdial Workshop on Discourse and Dialogue*, pp. 97–100, 2004.

[5] Ioannis Tsochantaridis, Thomas Hofmann, Thorsten Joachims, Yasemin Altun, Support Vector Learning for Interdependent and Structured Output Spaces. In *Proceedings of the 21st International Conference on Machine Learning*, pp. 823–830, 2004.

[6] Yasemin Altun, Ioannis Tsochantaridis, Thomas Hofmann, Hidden Markov Support Vector Machines. In *Proceedings of the 20th International Conference on Machine Learning*, pp. 3–10, 2003.

[7] Yvonne Moh,Thorsten, Joachim Buhmann, Kernel Expansion for Online Preference Tracking. In *proceedings of The International Society for Music Information Retrieval*, pp. 167–172, 2008.

[8] Ioannis Tsochantaridis, Thomas Hofmann, Thorsten Joachims, Yasemin Altun, Support Vector Learning for independent and Structured Output Spaces. In *Proceedings of the 21st International Conference on Machine Learning* , p. 104 , 2004.

[9] Francesco Orabonal, Joseph Keshet, Barbara Caputo, The projectron: a bounded kernel-based Perceptron. In *Proceedings of the 25th International Conference on Machine Learning*, pp. 720–727 , 2008.

[10] Jiampojamarn Sittichai, Cherry Colin, Kondrak Grzegorz, Joint Processing and Discriminative Training for Letter-to-Phoneme Conversion. In Proceedings of 2008 Annual Meeting on Association for Compurational Linguistics and Human Language Technology Conference, pp. 905–913, 2008.

[11] S. Sathiya Keerthi, Olivier Chapelle, Dennis DeCoste, Building Support Vector Machines with Reduced Classifier Complexity. *The Journal of Machine Learning Research*, Volume 7, pp. 1493–1515, 2006.

[12] Ryan McDonald, Koby Crammer, Fernando Pereira, Online Large-Margin Training of Dependency Parsers. In *Proceedings of the 43rd Annual Meeting on Association for Computational Linguistics*, pp. 91–98 , 2005.

Unsupervised Word Sense Induction from Multiple Semantic Spaces with Locality Sensitive Hashing

Claire Mouton - CEA LIST - Exalead
CEA LIST - Claire.Mouton@cea.fr
Exalead - 10 place de la Madeleine - 75008 Paris
Claire.Mouton@exalead.com

Guillaume Pitel - Epiphyte
10 rue de Vouillé - 75015 Paris
Guillaume.Pitel@epiphyte.eu

Gaël de Chalendar - CEA LIST
18, route du Panorama
BP6, FONTENAY AUX ROSES
F-92265 France
Gael.de-Chalendar@cea.fr

Anne Vilnat - LIMSI/CNRS
bât. 508 - Université Paris XI
BP 133 - 91403 Orsay Cedex France
Anne.Vilnat@limsi.fr

Abstract

Word Sense Disambiguation is the task dedicated to the problem of finding out the sense of a word in context, from all of its many possible senses. Solving this problem requires to know the set of possible senses for a given word, which can be acquired from human knowledge, or from automatic discovery, called Word Sense Induction. In this article, we adapt two existing meta-methods of Word Sense Induction for the automatic construction of a disambiguation lexicon. Our adaptation is based on multiple semantic spaces (also called Word Space Models) produced from a syntactic analysis of a very large number of web pages. These adaptations and the results presented in this article differ from the original methods in that they use a combination of several high dimensional spaces instead of one single representation. Each of these competing semantic spaces takes part in a clustering phase in which they vote on sense induction.

Keywords

semantic space, word space model, dimensionality reduction, locality sensitive hashing, word sense induction, words clustering, multi-represented data

1 Introduction

A single word may potentially convey many different senses but despite this potential for ambiguity, misinterpretations occur relatively rarely in actual human linguistic interactions, including written texts. As a consequence, it is possible to draw the hypothesis that a wordsense should be inferable from the context it appears in (letting aside the question of the context size). Word Sense Disambiguation is the task dedicated to this problem of finding out the sense of a word in context. For a more detailed study, [1] and [12] have covered an exhausting overview of the task. However, solving this problem requires first to know the set of possible senses for a given word. The mere possibility of doing this exhaustively is a much debated issue, because even among humans, it is very difficult to agree on a set of senses for any given word. However if we consider it possible to obtain a list of the senses, even if it is incomplete, then it can be acquired from human knowledge (as one can find in any good dictionary), or from automatic discovery, a task which is generally called Word Sense Induction.

This task (and consequently Word Sense Disambiguation itself) is often tackled using methods that are able to group similar words together, in order to perform a clustering over the neighbors of the target, and thus to discover one 'sense' for each cluster found. This approach puts a large part of the burden into the similarity measure. While some methods use graph-based measures (thus making use of manually crafted structured resources), many unsupervised approaches are based on the Word Space Model paradigm, sometimes also called Semantic Vector Space paradigm. This paradigm relies on the hypothesis that a word-sense depends on the contexts it appears in [8]. For instance, all words that designate a *mammal* will tend to occur with verbs like *eat*, *run* or *breathe*. Because of this, if we represent each word by a normalized vector of the cooccurrence counts of this word with every other words in a given corpus, two words that share a lot of semantic features will tend to have a small angular distance.

Semantic spaces are interesting because they are built completely automatically from a corpus. They do not require error prone and costly manual work and can be quickly updated to reflect the emergence of new words in a constantly evolving domain . Semantic spaces can be built using various context types such as documents, paragraphs or occuring words, or again lemmas appearing near the source word (cooccurents). In [16], dimensions of Vector Space Model represent the terms occurrence frequencies in each document where each column represent a document. In [11], dimensions correspond to the most frequent terms of the vocabulary and the values are the number of cooccurrences, in fixed-size windows, between the line term and the column term (or possibly the mutual information). In [13] and [7], each dimension corresponds to a context obtained through a given syntactic

International Conference RANLP 2009 - Borovets, Bulgaria, pages 287–291

relation and the value is their cooccurrence frequency.

With these semantic spaces where each word is represented by a vector from which is derived a measure of similarity with other words, similar words can be grouped together Senses of polysemic words can be induced from various term selections. In [10], clusters are built in one step from the full vocabulary, each word may appear in several clusters. These clusters represent synonym classes and senses of words belonging to several clusters are thus discriminated. [17] approach consists in clustering all the occurence contexts in a corpus of each word for which senses are being learned. Finally, some systems like [4], [20] or [6] cluster cooccurrents of the words they want to distinguish the senses and [14] cluster the nearest neighbors in the semantic space.

Our work largely follows [14] as we also group nearest neighbors but differs from it as we dispose of a panel of different semantic spaces (built on different syntactic relations) with different specificities that we combine, instead of using a unique semantic space.

Section 2 of this paper details the conception of the semantic spaces we use. We present in Section 3 the method of dimensionality reduction we use. Section 4 describes the clustering methods developed to take into account differences between spaces. Finally, Section 5 gives perspectives on the results and some directions towards future works.

2 Description of the semantic space

Semantic spaces we use for word sense induction are issued from the work of [7] . The semantic spaces are built using the results of a large scale syntactic analysis. When we extracted them for our work, the French corpus on which this semantic space is built was made of two millions urls of French language pages on which a syntactic analysis (including lemmatization) was processed using LIMA, the CEA LIST natural language processing system [2].

This parser is a dependency analyser. Thus it extracts binary relations between tokens, like subject_verb, object_verb, noun_complement, etc. These relations are oriented: for example in the phrase *'advance in NLP'*, *NLP* appears in the context of *advance* for the noun_complement relation but *advance* appears in the context of *NLP* for the noun_complement reverse relation.

The dictionary used to build the matrices (i.e. the semantic space) is made of the 68,000 most frequent words of the French language. To each binary relation is associated a distinct matrix that registers the cooccurrence frequencies of these 68,000 words through the given relation. In order to be able to take into account the information given by all words, even the rare ones, we work with mutual information matrices computed from the frequencies matrices. Mutual information is computed according to the following formula, where P_i is the probability of occurrence of the term described by line i in any context of the given relation, P_j is the probability of occurence of the context defined by column j, and $P_{i,j}$ is the probability of cooccurrence of the term i with the context j in the given relation.

$$MI = log(\frac{P_{i,j}}{P_i * P_j}) \quad (1)$$

The same process is applied on reverse relations and on cooccurrences in fixed-size windows (5, 10, 20). Finally, we obtain 71 sparse square matrices of 68,000 dimensions. We will see later that these matrices contain different and complementary kind of information.

3 Approximative KNN

Given the size of these matrices, it is highly desirable to perform a dimensionality reduction before using them for nearest neighbor search and clustering. A linear Principal Component Analysis method such as Latent Semantic Analysis [9] would have been an alternative if not for the original dimensionality of our data and the quadratic ($O(n^3)$) complexity of the underlying Singular Vector Decomposition. On the other hand, Random Indexing [19] while more scalable, was not a real option because of its reported low quality. We chose to use Locality Sensitive Hashing which is supposed to be more scalable than LSA and whose quality was still to be tested on complex tasks. [3] has defined a family of LSH functions for which the hashed signatures keep their angular similarity for any input vectors pair. [15] has shown that this hashing is particularly well adapted to set up a fast nearest neighbors search method.

3.1 Dimension reduction: Locality sensitive hashing

The goal of a hashing is to obtain a footprint smaller than the original signature. Here, we want a function h giving a smaller footprint and respecting the property that if two vectors v_1 and v_2 from the initial space are similar, then the two hashed vectors $h(v_1)$ and $h(v_2)$ are also similar.The hashing functions family proposed by [3] allows to approximate the cosinus measure whose efficiency has already been shown for proximities of the elements in word spaces. We outline the method below.

We draw randomly according to a Gaussian distribution d unit vectors $\overrightarrow{r}$. This drawing provides an equidistributed breakdown on the unitary hypersphere.

Let a family of functions be defined by:

$$h_{\overrightarrow{r}}(\overrightarrow{u}) = \begin{cases} 0 \; if \; \overrightarrow{r}.\overrightarrow{u} \geq 0 \\ 1 \; if \; \overrightarrow{r}.\overrightarrow{u} < 0 \end{cases} \quad (2)$$

Let two vectors $\overrightarrow{u}$ and $\overrightarrow{v}$, the probability to draw a random vector defining a hyper plane that separates them is:

$$Pr[h_{\overrightarrow{r}}(\overrightarrow{u}) \neq h_{\overrightarrow{r}}(\overrightarrow{v})] = \theta(\overrightarrow{u}, \overrightarrow{v})/\pi \quad (3)$$

On a number of randomly drawn vectors this probability can be measured. Indeed, the probability that a randomly drawn hyperplane has separated the original two vectors u and v is the probability that the hyperplane has given a different bit for the two hash results for u and v. The formula 4 gives this probability:

$$Pr[h_{\overrightarrow{r}}(\overrightarrow{u}) \neq h_{\overrightarrow{r}}(\overrightarrow{v})] = hamming\_distance(\overrightarrow{u}, \overrightarrow{v})/d \quad (4)$$

By combining 3 and 4 the following approximation is obtained:

$$\theta(\overrightarrow{u}, \overrightarrow{v}) \approx hamming\_distance(\overrightarrow{u}, \overrightarrow{v})/d * \pi \quad (5)$$

3.2 Fast approximate nearest neighbors search

A fast approximate nearest neighbor search in a space with a Hamming distance was proposed by [3] and picked up by [15]. The method consists in pulling random p permutations of d elements. For each permutation, (a) the signatures are permuted bit by bit, (b) all the elements are sorted following lexicographic order, and (c) the B elements closest to the n source elements which cosine approximation is lower than a given threshold are kept.

We build the list of nearest neighbours words we want to cluster, using the main trends of that algorithm.

3.3 Results

We have been able to compute the list of k nearest neighbors of polysemous words for each of the syntactic spaces and we see for example in table 1 the results with $k = 10$ for the word *vol*[1] in various spaces.

We notice that the nearest neighbors obtained for the word *vol* are quite different depending on which space is used. Some spaces gather nearest neighbors oriented towards a precise meaning, while others return mixed meanings. uses can be separated into: *media type*, *computers aspect* and *content and uses*, the distinction between spaces remains unclear except for the *apposition* relation. We observed that these distinctions largely depend on the polysemous word processed: the discriminating spaces, when they exist, are not always the same. Therefore we can assume that each space contains different information which is worth being taken into account.

Our goal is to build sets of nearest neighbors representing different uses. Since automatic induction exploits the contexts of words occurrences in a corpus, various usages of even monosemous words can appear and be discriminated in the same way as different senses of polysemous words would. We thus prefer the term *use* to the term *sense*. Depending on the words, spaces discriminate quite heterogeneously their various *uses*. We propose in the next section a clustering method taking into account the specificity of each space while allowing the inter-space consolidation.

4 Word sense induction by multi-represented words clustering

In our approach, we want to cluster the nearest neighbors of a word into several clusters so that each of them represents a sense. We wish to be able to distinguish different clusters as in the manually built example of

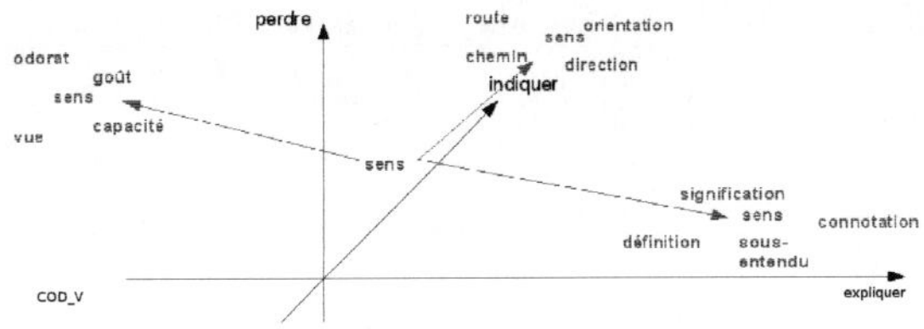

Fig. 1: *Senses discrimination in the object_verb base*

Figure 1. This figure shows a 3-dimensional projection where object_verb contexts should allow the discrimination of three meanings of the word *sens*: the *sens* as the ability to perceive, the *sens* giving an orientation indication, and the *sens* giving a semantic indication.

Traditional clustering methods are used on a single vector space, as illustrated in the ideal example above. But we have seen previously that the various spaces emphasized different closenesses. It can be seen for example in table 1) that the object_verb relation highlights the semantic proximity on *flying* meaning of the word *vol* while the *apposition* space does not highlight it at all, but stresses the proximities of *theft* meaning. We thus assume that the spaces peculiarities will help to better distinguish clusters of meaning if each of them is separately taken into account rather than considering a global space built by concatenation of all the matrices. To do this, we are guided by Shared Nearest Neighbors clustering algorithms adapted and used by [5] and [6] and by the Hyperlex algorithm developed by [20]. We propose two "clustering by vote" methods.

For each of the parts of speech for which we want to produce senses, *i.e.* *noun, verb, adjective*, we retain the relevant spaces . For instance when dealing with a verb, we do not consider the complement_noun space involving only nouns and we use the reverse object_verb space and not the object_verb one. We also consider only spaces involving relations between plain words (noun, verb, adverb, adjective). For example, we leave out the relationship between a determiner and its noun.

After experimentation, we choose to cluster the words that appear at least twice in the 30 nearest neighbors of the selected spaces. Let E be this set. The following sections present the two methods.

4.1 Method based on the shared nearest neighbors algorithm

This method processed in three steps. First, a number of seeds (not fixed in advance) is extracted. The remaining elements are then assigned to these clusters. Finally clusters whose seeds are too close are joined and elements belonging to clusters considered as too small are reassigned.

The algorithm we propose is based on the [5] SNN algorithm seed selection method for which there is no need to choose *a priori* the number of seeds. However, experiments give us better results with a direct neighbors graph than with the shared nearest neighbors graph. We then keep the first one. One possible explanation for this surprising result compared

[1] which means *fly* or *steal*

vol	complement_noun	vol, avion, voyage, retour, course, achat, opération, première, journée, premier
	object_verb	vol, voyage, retour, création, attaque, changement, mise, mariage, acte, fin
	apposition	vol, meurtre, racket, fraude, chantage, assassinat, homicide, rapine, violence, crime
	apposition.reverse	vol, meurtre, viol, prostitution, rapine, adultère, proxénétisme, idolâtrie, agression, luxure

Table 1: *10 nearest neighbors of words vol*

to the results presented in [5] is that we use a small part of the original space elements. There is therefore too few data to use this second level of information. We also retain the idea of defining the seeds using the *strong links*. The name Shared Nearest Neighbors being no longer relevant, we now refer to this algorithm as MultiNN.

In each space (object_verb, subject_verb, ...):

1. we build the nearest neighbors graph in which each element of E has a corresponding node and every distance between two of the elements is represented by an edge weighted by their approximate cosine distance.
2. we define a strong link threshold (eg. 0.2 of the maximum distance in the space) and discard edges whose values are below this threshold;
3. for each node in the graph (elements of E) we compute the sum of its remaining links.
4. if this sum is larger than a certain threshold (eg. 0.3 of the maximum in the space), we say that this is a *local seed* for this space.

For each element of E, we know the number of spaces in which it is a *local seed*. If this number is bigger than a threshold (eg 0.8 of the number of collaborating spaces), then this element is said to be a *global seed*.

We build clusters around each global seed in this way:

- In each space, we remove the elements of E which have been called *global seed*.
- In each space and for each element of E, we store a vote for its nearest global seed (highest approximate cosine).
- We sum the votes on all spaces and assign each element to its most popular seed (possibly several ones in case of equality).
- In each space, if two seeds have a total value exceeding a certain threshold, the space votes for the merging of the two clusters involved.
- If a sufficient number of spaces votes for this merging, the two clusters are merged into one.
- The elements of the clusters considered too small compared to the number of elements to be clustered are reassigned one by one to large clusters.

4.2 Method based on the HyperLex algorithm

We adapt a second method to our multi-representation of words. This is the Hyperlex algorithm presented by [20]. It was originally applied to a list of co-occurrences but in our case we apply it to a list of nearest neighbors.

The the first part of the original algorithm proceeds as follows.

Let E be the set of words to cluster.

- Take the most frequent element (hub) in E. If the number of its connected nodes whose weight is below a certain threshold φ is greater than a given number k, this hub becomes the seed of a component.
- Remove this hub and if it has been determined to be a seed, remove also its connected nodes from E.
- Repeat until E is empty.

In the scope of our multiple representations, we define the distance from any element of E to the source as the average distance over the spaces and use the decreasing distances as the order in which to test whether a node is a seed. We assume that a word close to the source will be a good sense representation. We do not need to test the high frequency term in first place because our graph is a nearest neighbours graph in which a high frequency of a term does not infer more outgoing edges. Instead of being discarded, items related to a seed are candidates to become elements of the seed component. The different spaces vote to validate this attribution. In this first study we do not implement the second part of the algorithm (spanning tree calculation) as we assume that the process of voting will filter out the words which are not part of a component and let them be attached to a forthcoming seed.

4.3 Results

The results were evaluated manually in this first step by comparing our results with those obtained by the original algorithms for a predefined list of words. For instance, table 2 presents the results of the four methods (the two original and our two modified versions) for the word *barrage*.

The comparison of our clusters with those of the original algorithms is difficult because we did not try to group the same type of terms (cooccurrents vs. syntactic nearest neighbors). We can notice that the distinguished senses are not always the same. We find firstly in 3.1, 4.1 and 4.4, the usage of *barrage* as *hydraulic dam* which was discriminated for its use as an *industrial system* and in 3.2 and 4.2 as a *building on a river*. The senses 3.3 and 4.3 of *barrage* correspond to the meanings *roadblock, police barrage or factory strike* that we cannot well distinguish. The dictionary *Petit Larousse* used during the ROMANSEVAL campaign [18] does not itself distinguish them and simply considers them as *obstacles*. This is the same physical object, but the usage is different. Finally, we could not find the sportive meaning of *play-off match*, whose use is present in very few locutions such as *match de barrage*. The fact that hardly no nearest neighbour can express this meaning and the sparseness of its occurrences can both explain the difficulty we have to extract it. Nevertheless, for the word *vol*, our algorithm correctly extracted the *theft offence* and *flight* meanings, which was not the case for the HyperLex algorithm.

As Word Sense Induction systems group different initial terms and learn on different corpus bearing potentially different semantic content, an automatic evaluation of our

Source word	barrage
HyperLex [20]	1.1 : eau, construction, ouvrage, rivière, projet, retenue, crue
	1.2 : routier, véhicule, camion, membre, conducteur, policier, groupement
	1.3 : frontière, Algérie, militaire, efficacité, armée, Suisse, poste
	1.4 : match, vainqueur, victoire, rencontre, qualification, tir, football
SNN [6]	2.1 : manifestant, forces_de_l'ordre, préfecture, agriculteur, protester, incendier, calme, pierre
	2.2 : conducteur, routier, véhicule, poids_lourd, camion, permis, trafic, bloquer, voiture, autoroute
	2.3 : fleuve, lac, rivière, bassin, mètre_cube, crue, amont, pollution, affluent, saumon, poisson
	2.4 : blessé, casque_bleu, soldat, milicien, tir, milice, convoi, évacuer, croate, milicien, combattant
MultiHyperLex	3.1 : infrastructure, défense, établissement, installation, aménagement
	3.2 : rivière, digue, pont, canal, lac
	3.3 : train, station, usine, bâtiment, route, véhicule
MultiNN	4.1 : bâtiment, usine, véhicule, aménagement, bassin, chantier, infrastructure
	4.2 : pont, barrière, digue, écluse
	4.3 : route, rivière, train, défense
	4.4 : station, canal, centrale, établissement, infrastructure, installation

Table 2: *Comparison of clusters built for the word* barrage

results by comparing the resulting clusters with those produced by other methods (whatever the mapping method used) can prove to be inaccurate. A more reliable evaluation would be to perform a more applicative task based on those clusters (like Word Sense Disambiguation or Information Retrieval) and to evaluate the results of the latter. An automatic evaluation of this kind is still to be performed in order to judge which of the two proposed approaches give the better results and to assess the cluster discrimination quality.

5 Discussion and future work

Although we do not have to choose the number of clusters to obtain, allowing a different number of meanings for each word, fixing the values of the parameters involved in the two algorithms remains a real problem in the sense that we currently have no way to learn the optimal parameters. We are thus forced to choose them by experimentation.

An advantage of these methods can be put forward: in addition to distinguishing clusters of meaning, we assume that the use of nearest neighbors as a set of elements to cluster (not using cooccurrents) will allow the use of those clustered neighbors as learning data for a classifier performing word sense disambiguation. This hypothesis will be tested soon.

Furthermore, the finalization of this work requires to quickly carry out various studies. To highlight the contributions of the method presented here, we want to build clusters from the same set of closest neighbors, using various spaces configuration: first the window cooccurrences space only, second each of the syntactic spaces alone, and third the concatenation of all matrices, which should differ highly from our combination.

Finally, we plan to automatically build clusters of those sense-clusters to define WordNet-like *synsets*. We will use them to disambiguate and index a collection of documents and study the contribution of this disambiguation to information retrieval.

References

[1] E. Agirre and P. Edmonds, editors. *Word Sense Disambiguation: Algorithms and Applications (Text, Speech and Language Technology)*. Springer-Verlag New York, Inc., Secaucus, NJ, USA, 2006.

[2] R. Besançon and G. de Chalendar. L'analyseur syntaxique de lima dans la campagne d'valuation easy. In M. Jardino, editor, *Actes de TALN 2005 (Traitement automatique des langues naturelles)*, Dourdan, June 2005. ATALA, LIMSI.

[3] M. Charikar. Similarity estimation techniques from rounding algorithms. In *Proceedings of the 34th Annual ACM Symposium on Theory of Computing*, 2002.

[4] B. Dorow and D. Widdows. Discovering corpus-specific word senses. In *EACL 2003*, 2003.

[5] L. Ertz, M. Steinbach, and V. Kumar. Finding topics in collections of documents: A shared nearest neighbor approach. In *Text Mine 01, Workshop of the 1st SIAM International Conference on Data Mining*, 2001.

[6] O. Ferret. Discovering word senses from a network of lexical cooccurrences. In *COLING '04: Proceedings of the 20th international conference on Computational Linguistics*, page 1326, Morristown, NJ, USA, 2004. Association for Computational Linguistics.

[7] G. Grefenstette. Conquering language : Using nlp on a massive scale to build high dimensional language models from the web. In *Proc. of the 8th CICLing Conference*, pages 35–49, Mexico, 2007.

[8] Z. Harris. Distributional structure. In J. J. Katz, editor, *The Philosophy of Linguistics*, pages 26–47. Oxford University Press, New York, 1985.

[9] T. K. Landauer and S. Dumais. A solution to plato's problem: The latent semantic analysis theory of the acquisition, induction, and representation of knowledge. *Psychological Review*, 104(2):211–240, 1997.

[10] D. Lin. Automatic retrieval and clustering of similar words. In *Proceedings of COLING-ACL98*, pages 768–774, 1998.

[11] K. Lund and C. Burgess. Producing high-dimensional semantic spaces from lexical co-occurrence. *Behavior Research Methods, Instruments, and Computers*, 28:203–208, 1996.

[12] R. Navigli. Word sense disambiguation: A survey. *ACM Comput. Surv.*, 41(2):1–69, 2009.

[13] S. Padó and M. Lapata. Dependency-based construction of semantic space models. *Comput. Linguist.*, 33(2):161–199, 2007.

[14] P. Pantel and D. Lin. Discovering word senses from text. In *Proc. of ACM SIGKDD Conference on Knowledge Discovery and Data Mining 2002*, Edmonton, Canada, 2002.

[15] D. Ravichandran, P. Pantel, and E. Hovy. Randomized algorithms and nlp: Using locality sensitive hash functions for high speed noun clustering. In *Proceedings of ACL*, Ann Arbour(MI), 2005.

[16] G. Salton, A. Wong, and C. S. Yang. A vector space model for automatic indexing. 18(11):613–620, 1975.

[17] H. Schütze. Automatic word sense discrimination. *Computational Linguistics*, 24(1):97–123, 1998.

[18] F. Segond. Framework and results for french. *Computers and the Humanities, Special Issue on SENSEVAL*, 34(1-2), 2000.

[19] L. Sellberg and A. Jönsson. Using random indexing to improve singular value decomposition for latent semantic analysis. In *Proceedings of the 6th Conference on Language Resources and Evaluation*, Marrakech, Morocco, 2008.

[20] J. Véronis. Hyperlex: lexical cartography for information retrieval. *Computer Speech and Language*, 18:223–252, 2004.

Unsupervised Extraction of False Friends from Parallel Bi-Texts Using the Web as a Corpus

Svetlin Nakov and Preslav Nakov*
Department of Mathematics and Informatics
Sofia University "St Kliment Ohridski"
5, James Bourchier Blvd.,1164 Sofia, Bulgaria
{*svetlin.nakov, preslav.nakov*}@*fmi.uni-sofia.bg*

Elena Paskaleva
Linguistic Modeling Department
Institute for Parallel Processing
Bulgarian Academy of Sciences
25A, Acad. G. Bonchev St., 1113 Sofia, Bulgaria
hellen@lml.bas.bg

Abstract

False friends are pairs of words in two languages that are perceived as similar, but have different meanings, e.g., *Gift* in German means *poison* in English. In this paper, we present several unsupervised algorithms for acquiring such pairs from a sentence-aligned bi-text. First, we try different ways of exploiting simple statistics about monolingual word occurrences and cross-lingual word co-occurrences in the bi-text. Second, using methods from statistical machine translation, we induce word alignments in an unsupervised way, from which we estimate lexical translation probabilities, which we use to measure cross-lingual semantic similarity. Third, we experiment with a semantic similarity measure that uses the Web as a corpus to extract local contexts from text snippets returned by a search engine, and a bilingual glossary of known word translation pairs, used as "bridges". Finally, all measures are combined and applied to the task of identifying likely false friends. The evaluation for Russian and Bulgarian shows a significant improvement over previously-proposed algorithms.

Keywords

Cognates, false friends, cross-lingual semantic similarity, Web as a corpus, statistical machine translation.

1 Introduction

Words in two languages that are orthographically and/or phonetically similar are often perceived as mutual translations, which could be wrong in some contexts. Such words are known as *cognates*[1] when they are mutual translations in all contexts, *partial cognates* when they are mutual translations in some contexts but not in other, and *false friends* when they are not mutual translations in any context.

For example, the Bulgarian *слънце* (*slynce*) and the Russian *солнце* (*solnce*) are cognates, both meaning *sun*. However, the Bulgarian *син* (*sin*) and the Russian *сын* (*syn*) are only partial cognates: while they can both mean *son* in some contexts, the Bulgarian word can also mean *blue* in other. Finally, the Bulgarian *бистрота* (*bistrota*) and the Russian *быстрота* (*bystrota*) are false friends meaning *clearness* and *quickness*, respectively.

False friends are important not only for foreign language learning, but also for various natural language processing (NLP) tasks such as statistical machine translation, word alignment, automated translation quality control, etc.

In this paper, we propose an unsupervised approach to the task of extracting pairs of false friends from a sentence-aligned corpus (a bi-text). While we experiment with Bulgarian and Russian, our general method is language-independent.

The remainder of the paper is organized as follows: Section 2 provides an overview of the related work, Section 3 present our method, Section 4 lists the resources we are using, Sections 5 and 6 describe the experiments and discuss the evaluation results, Section 7 concludes and suggests directions for future work.

*Also: Department of Computer Science, National University of Singapore, 13 Computing Drive, Singapore 117417, nakov@comp.nus.edu.sg

[1] We should note that linguists define *cognates* as words derived from a common root regardless of whether they differ in meaning or not. For example, the *Electronic Glossary of Linguistic Terms* gives the following definition [3]:

> Two words (or other structures) in related languages are cognate if they come from the same original word (or other structure). Generally cognates will have similar, though often not identical, phonological and semantic structures (sounds and meanings). For instance, Latin *tu*, Spanish *tú*, Greek *sú*, German *du*, and English *thou* are all cognates; all mean 'second person singular', but they differ in form and in whether they mean specifically 'familiar' (non-honorific).

Following previous researchers in *computational* linguistics [2, 24, 25], we will adopt a simplified definition which ignores origin, defining cognates as words in different languages that are mutual translations and have a similar orthography.

International Conference RANLP 2009 - Borovets, Bulgaria, pages 292–298

2 Related work

Previous work on extracting false friends from text can be divided into the following categories: (1) methods for measuring orthographic and phonetic similarity, (2) methods for identifying cognates and false friends from parallel bi-texts, and (3) semantic methods for distinguishing between cognates and false friends.

Most of the research in the last decade has focused on orthographic methods for cognate identification that do not try to distinguish between cognates from false friends. While traditional orthographic similarity measures like *longest common subsequence ratio* and *minimum edit distance* have evolved over the years towards machine learning approaches for identifying cross-lingual orthographic transformation patterns [2, 26]), recent research has shown interest in using semantic evidence as well [26, 27].

However, little research was conducted on extracting false friends from parallel bi-texts. Very few authors proposed such algorithms [31], while most research focused on word to word alignment [39] and extracting bilingual lexicons with applications to identifying cognates [9].

2.1 Orthographic/phonetic similarity

In this subsection, we describe some relevant methods based on orthographic and phonetic similarity.

2.1.1 Orthographic similarity

The first methods proposed for identifying cognates were based on measuring orthographic similarity. For languages sharing the same alphabet, classical approaches include *minimum edit distance* [22], *longest common subsequence ratio* [25], and variants of the Dice coefficient measuring overlap at the level of character bigrams [5].

The Levenshtein distance or *minimum edit distance* (MED) is defined as the minimum number of INSERT, REPLACE, and DELETE operations at the character level needed to transform one string into another [22]. For example, the MED between the Bulgarian word *първият* ('*the first*') and the Russian word *первый* ('*first*') is 4: there are three REPLACE operations, namely, *ъ* → *е*, *и* → *ы*, and *я* → *й*, and one DELETE operation (to remove *т*). To be used as a similarity measure, it is typically normalized by dividing it by the length of the longer word; this normalized measure is known as the *minimum edit distance ratio* (MEDR):

$$\text{MEDR}(\textit{първият}, \textit{первый}) = 1 - 4/7 \approx 0.43$$

The *longest common subsequence ratio* (LCSR) [25] is another classic normalized orthographic similarity measure. It is calculated as the ratio of the length of the longest common subsequence of the two words and the length of the longer word. For example, LCS(*първият*, *первый*) = *пръ*, and thus we have:

$$\text{LCSR}(\textit{първият}, \textit{первый}) = 3/7 \approx 0.43$$

Other approaches to measuring orthographic similarity between two words have been proposed by [1] who calculate the Dice coefficient for character bigrams. Their idea is further extended by [5], who used a weighting version of the Dice coefficient, and by [19], who proposed a generalized n-gram measure.

2.1.2 Phonetic similarity

The phonetic similarity measures the degree to which two words sound alike. Unlike orthographic similarity, it operates with sounds rather than letter sequences.

Although a number of specialized algorithms for measuring phonetic similarity have been proposed [11, 17], it can be also measured using orthographic similarity methods after the words have been phonetically transcribed. This approach also works for languages that use different alphabets.

2.1.3 Using transformation rules

Recently, some researchers have proposed to apply transformation rules that reflect typical cross-lingual transformation patterns observed for the target pair of languages before measuring orthographic similarity. This is a good idea when the languages do not use exactly the same alphabet or the same spelling systems. Of course, such substitutions do not have to be limited to single letters and could be defined for letter sequence such as syllables, endings, and prefixes. For example, [16] use manually constructed transformation rules between German and English for expanding a list of cognates: e.g., replacing the German letters *k* and *z* by the English *c*, and changing the ending German *-tät* to the English *-ty*.

Other researchers have tried to learn automatically cross-lingual transformation rules that reflect regular phonetic changes between two languages. For example, [27] do that using MED and positive examples provided as a list of known cognates. Unlike them, [2] use both positive and negative examples to learn weights on substring pairings in order to better identify related substring transformations. Starting with MED, they first obtain an alignment at the letter level. They then extract corresponding substrings that are consistent with that alignment, which in turn are used with a support vector machine (SVM) classifier to distinguish between cognates and false friends.

2.2 Using parallel bi-texts

There is little research on extracting false friends from text corpora directly. Most methods first extract candidate cognates and false friends using some measure of orthographic or phonetic similarity, and then try to distinguish between cognates and false friends in a second step [26].

Fung [9] extracted semantically similar cross-lingual word pairs from parallel and comparable corpora using binary co-occurrence vectors – one for each side of the bi-text.

Brew and McKelvie [5] used sentence alignment to extract cognates and false friends from a bi-text using co-occurrence statistics in the aligned sentences.

Nakov and Pacovski [31] extracted false friends from a paragraph-aligned Bulgarian-Macedonian[2] bi-text, assuming that false friends are unlikely to co-occur in paragraphs that are translations of each other, while cognates tend to do so. Several formulas formalizing this assumption have been proposed and evaluated.

2.3 Semantic approaches

2.3.1 Corpus-based approaches

There has been a lot of research during the last decade on measuring semantic similarity with applications to finding cognates and false friends. Most of the proposed approaches are based on the *distributional hypothesis*, which states that words occurring in similar contexts tend to be semantically similar [12]. This hypothesis is typically operationalized using the vector-space model [38], where vectors are built using words from the local context of the target word as coordinates and their frequencies as values for these coordinates. For example, Nakov & al. [33] defined the local context as a window of a certain size around the target word, while other researchers have limited the context to words in a particular syntactic relationship with the target word, e.g., direct object of a verb [7, 23, 28]. These vectors are typically compared using the cosine of the angle between them as in [33], but other similarity measures such as the Dice coefficient have been used as well [28].

Kondrak [18] proposed an algorithm for measuring semantic similarity using WordNet [8]. He used the following eight semantic similarity levels as binary features: gloss identity, keyword identity, gloss synonymy, keyword synonymy, gloss hypernymy, keyword hypernymy, gloss meronymy, and keyword meronymy. These features were combined with a measure of phonetic similarity and used in a naive Bayes classifier to distinguish between cognates and non-cognates.

Mitkov & al. [26] proposed several methods for measuring the semantic similarity between orthographically similar pairs of words, which were used to distinguish between cognates and false friends. Their first method uses comparable corpora in the two target languages and relies on distributional similarity: given a cross-lingual pair of words to compare, a set of the most similar words to each of the two targets is collected from the respective monolingual corpus. The semantic similarity is calculated as the Dice coefficient between these two sets, using a bilingual glossary to check whether two words can be translations of each other. The method is further extended to use taxonomic data from EuroWordNet [40] when available. The second method extracts co-occurrence statistics for each of the two words of interest from a respective monolingual corpus using a dependency parser. In particular, verbs are used as distributional features when comparing nouns. Semantic sets are thus created, and the similarity between them is measured using the Dice coefficient and a bilingual glossary.

[2] There is a heated linguistic and political debate about whether Macedonian represents a separate language or is a regional literary form of Bulgarian. Since no clear criteria exist for distinguishing a dialect from a language, linguists remain divided on that issue. Politically, Macedonian remains unrecognized as a language by Bulgaria and Greece.

2.3.2 Web-based approaches

The idea of using the Web as a corpus is getting increasingly popular and has been applied to various problems. See [15] for an overview. See also [20, 21] for some interesting applications, and [14, 29] for a discussion on some issues.

Many researchers have used the Web to identify cognates and false friends. Some used Web search engines as a proxy for n-gram frequency, i.e., to estimate how many times a word or a phrase is met on the Web [13], whereas others directly retrieved contexts from the returned text snippets [33]. There have been also some combined approaches, e.g., that of Bollegala & al. [4], who further learned lexico-syntactic templates for semantically related and unrelated words using WordNet, which were used for extracting information from the text snippets returned by the search engine.

3 Method

We propose a method for extracting false friends from a bi-text that combines statistical and semantic evidence in a two-step process: (1) we extract cross-lingual pairs of orthographically similar words, and (2) we identify which of them are false friends.

For the sake of definiteness, below we will assume that our objective is to extract pairs of false friend between Bulgarian and Russian.

3.1 Finding candidates

We look for cross-lingual pairs of words that are perceived as similar and thus could be cognates or false friends. First, we extract from the bi-text[3] all cross-lingual Bulgarian-Russian word pairs (w_{bg}, w_{ru}). We then measure the orthographic similarity between w_{bg} and w_{ru}, and we accept the pair as a candidate only if that similarity is above a pre-specified threshold. In the process, we ignore part of speech, gender, number, definiteness, and case, which are expressed as inflections in both Bulgarian and Russian.

We measure the orthographic similarity using the *modified minimum edit distance ratio* (MMEDR) algorithm [30]. First, some Bulgarian-specific letter sequences are replaced by Russian-specific ones. Then, a weighted minimum edit distance that is specific to Bulgarian and Russian is calculated between the resulting strings. Finally, that distance is normalized by dividing it by the length of the longer word and the result is subtracted from 1 so that it can become a similarity measure.

Let us consider for example the Bulgarian word *първият* (*'the first'*) and the Russian one *первый* (*'first'*). First, they will be normalized to *първи* and *перви*, respectively. Then, a single vowel-to-vowel REPLACE operation will be performed with the cost of 0.5. Finally, the result will be normalized and subtracted from one:[4]

[3] We extract pairs from the whole bi-text ignoring sentence alignment, i.e., the words in a pair do not have to come from corresponding sentences.

[4] Compare this result to MEDR and LCSR, which severely underestimate the similarity: they are both 0.43 for *първият* and *первый*.

$$\text{MMEDR}(\textit{пъвеият}, \textit{первый}) = 1 - 0.5/7 \approx 0.93$$

Although MMEDR is an orthographic approach, it reflects phonetics to some extent since it uses transformation rules and edit distance weights that are motivated by regular phonetic changes between Bulgarian and Russian as reflected in the spelling systems of the two languages. See [30] for more details.

While the MMEDR algorithm could be improved to learn transformation rules automatically, e.g., following [2, 26, 27], this is out of the scope of the present work. Our main focus below will be on distinguishing between cognates and false friends, which is a much more challenging task.

3.2 Identifying false friends

Once we have collected a list of orthographically and/or phonetically similar cross-lingual word pairs, we need to decide which of them are false friends, i.e., distinguish between false friends and cognates.[5] We use several approaches for this purpose.

3.2.1 Sentence-level co-occurrences

First, we use a statistical approach, based on statistics about word occurrences and co-occurrences in a bi-text. The idea is that cognates tend to co-occur in corresponding sentences while false friends do not. Following [31], we make use of the following statistics:

- $\#(w_{bg})$ – the number of Bulgarian sentences in the bi-text containing the word w_{bg};
- $\#(w_{ru})$ – the number of Russian sentences in the bi-text containing the word w_{ru};
- $\#(w_{bg}, w_{ru})$ – the number of corresponding sentence pairs in the bi-text containing the word w_{bg} on the Bulgarian side and the word w_{ru} on the Russian side.

Nakov & Pacovski [31] tried various combinations of these statistics; in their experiments, the best-performing formula was the following one:

$$F_6(w_{bg}, w_{ru}) = \frac{\#(w_{bg}, w_{ru}) + 1}{\max\left(\frac{\#(w_{bg})+1}{\#(w_{ru})+1}, \frac{\#(w_{ru})+1}{\#(w_{bg})+1}\right)}$$

Now, note that we have the following inequalities:

$$\#(w_{bg}) \geq \#(w_{bg}, w_{ru})$$
$$\#(w_{ru}) \geq \#(w_{bg}, w_{ru})$$

Thus, having a high number of co-occurrences $\#(w_{bg}, w_{ru})$ should increase the probability that the words w_{bg} and w_{ru} are cognates. At the same time, a big difference between $\#(w_{bg})$ and $\#(w_{ru})$ should increase the likelihood of them being false friends. Based on these observations, we propose the following extra formulas (E_1 and E_2):

$$E_1(w_{bg}, w_{ru}) = \frac{(\#(w_{bg}, w_{ru}) + 1)^2}{(\#(w_{bg}) + 1)(\#(w_{ru}) + 1)}$$

$$E_2(w_{bg}, w_{ru}) = \frac{(\#(w_{bg}, w_{ru}) + 1)^2}{P \times Q}$$

where

$$P = \#(w_{bg}) - \#(w_{bg}, w_{ru}) + 1$$
$$Q = \#(w_{ru}) - \#(w_{bg}, w_{ru}) + 1$$

Finally, unlike [31], we perform lemmatization before calculating the above statistics – Bulgarian and Russian are highly inflectional languages, and words are expected to have several inflected forms in the bi-text.

3.2.2 Word alignments

Our next information source are lexical probabilities for cross-lingual word pairs: they should be high for cognates and low for false friends. Such probabilities can be easily estimated from word alignments, which in turn can be obtained using techniques from statistical machine translation.

We start by tokenizing and lowercasing both sides of the training bi-text. We then build separate directed word alignments for Bulgarian→Russian and Russian→Bulgarian using IBM model 4 [6], and we combine them using the *intersect+grow heuristic* described in [34]. Using the resulting undirected alignment, we estimate lexical translation probabilities $\Pr(w_{bg}|w_{ru})$ and $\Pr(w_{ru}|w_{bg})$ for all Bulgarian-Russian word pairs that co-occur in aligned sentences in the bi-text. Finally, we define a cross-lingual semantic similarity measure as follows:

$$lex(w_{bg}, w_{ru}) = \frac{\Pr(w_{bg}|w_{ru}) + \Pr(w_{ru}|w_{bg})}{2}$$

Note that the above definition has an important drawback: it is zero for all words that do not co-occur in corresponding sentences in the bi-text. Thus, we will never use $lex(w_{bg}, w_{ru})$ alone but only in combination with other measures.

3.2.3 Web similarity

Next, we use an algorithm described in [33], which, given a Russian word w_{ru} and a Bulgarian word w_{bg} to be compared, measures the semantic similarity between them using the Web as a corpus and a glossary G of known Russian-Bulgarian translation pairs, used as "bridges". The basic idea is that if two words are translations, then the words in their respective local contexts should be translations as well. The idea is formalized using the Web as a corpus, a glossary of known word translations serving as cross-linguistic "bridges", and the vector space model. We measure the semantic similarity between a Bulgarian and a Russian word, w_{bg} and w_{ru}, by construct corresponding contextual semantic vectors V_{bg} and V_{ru}, translating V_{ru} into Bulgarian, and comparing it to V_{bg}.

[5] Since our ultimate objective is to extract pairs of false friends, we do not need to distinguish between true and partial cognates; we will thus use the term *cognates* to refer to both.

The process of building V_{bg}, starts with a query to Google limited to Bulgarian pages for the target word w_{bg}. We collect the resulting text snippets (up to 1,000), and we remove all stop words – prepositions, pronouns, conjunctions, interjections and some adverbs. We then identify the occurrences of w_{bg}, and we extract the words from its local context – three words on either side. We filter out the words that do not appear on the Bulgarian side of G. We do this for all text snippets. Finally, for each retained word, we calculate the number of times it has been extracted, thus producing a frequency vector V_{bg}. We repeat the procedure for w_{ru} to obtain a Russian frequency vector V_{ru}, which is then "translated" into Bulgarian by replacing each Russian word with its translation(s) in G, retaining the co-occurrence frequencies. In case there are multiple Bulgarian translations for some Russian word, we distribute the corresponding frequency equally among them, and in case of multiple Russian words with the same Bulgarian translation, we sum up the corresponding frequencies. As a result, we end up with a Bulgarian vector $V_{ru \to bg}$ for the Russian word w_{ru}. Finally, we calculate the semantic similarity between w_{bg} and w_{ru} as the cosine of the angle between their corresponding Bulgarian vectors, V_{bg} and $V_{ru \to bg}$, as follows:

$$sim(w_{bg}, w_{ru}) = \frac{V_{bg}.V_{ru \to bg}}{|V_{bg}| \times |V_{ru \to bg}|}$$

3.2.4 Combined approach

While all three approaches described above – sentence-level co-occurrences, word alignments, and Web similarity – are useful for distinguishing between cognates and false friends, each of them has some weaknesses.

Using sentence-level co-occurrences and word alignments is a good idea when the statistics for the target words are reliable, but both work poorly for infrequent words. Unfortunately, most words (and thus most word pairs) will be rare for any (bi-)text, according to the Zipf law [41],

Data sparsity is less of an issue for the Web similarity approach, which uses statistics derived from the largest existing corpus – the Web. Still, while being quite reliable for unrelated words, it sometimes assigns very low scores to highly-related word pairs. The problem stems from it relying on a commercial search engine like Google, which only returns up to 1,000 results per query and rates too high sites about news, e-commerce, and blogs, which introduces a bias on the local contexts of the target words. Moreover, some geographical and cultural notions have different contexts on the Web for Bulgarian and Russian, despite being very related otherwise, e.g., person names and goods used in e-commerce (due to different popular brands in different countries).

A natural way to overcome these issues is to combine all three approaches, e.g., by taking the average of the similarity each of them predicts. As we will see below, this is indeed quite a valuable strategy.

4 Resources

For the purpose of our experiments, we used the following resources: a bi-text, lemmatization dictionaries, a bilingual glossary, and the Web as a corpus.

4.1 Bi-text

We used the first seven chapters of the Russian novel *Lord of the World* by Alexander Belyaev and its Bulgarian translation consisting of 759 parallel sentences. The text has been sentence aligned automatically using the alignment tool *MARK ALISTeR* [36], which is based on the Gale-Church algorithm [10].

4.2 Morphological dictionaries

We used two large monolingual morphological dictionaries for Bulgarian and Russian created at the Linguistic Modeling Department of the Institute for Parallel Processing in the Bulgarian Academy of Sciences [35]. The Bulgarian dictionary contains about 1M wordforms and 70K lemmata, and the Russian one contains about 1.5M wordforms and 100K lemmata.

4.3 Bilingual glossary

We built a bilingual glossary by adapting an online Russian-Bulgarian dictionary. First, we removed all multi-word expressions. Then we combined each Russian word with each of its Bulgarian translations – due to polysemy/homonymy some words had multiple translations. We thus obtained a glossary of 59,583 pairs of words that are translations of each other.

4.4 Web as a corpus

In our experiments, we performed searches in Google for 557 Bulgarian and for 550 Russian wordforms, and we collected as many as possible (up to 1,000) page titles and text snippets from the search results.

5 Experiments and evaluation

We performed several experiments in order to evaluate the above-described approaches – both individually and in various combinations.[6]

First, we extracted cross-lingual pairs of orthographically similar words using the MMEDR algorithm with a threshold of 0.90. This yielded 612 pairs, each of which was judged by a linguist[7] as being a pair of false friends, partial cognates, or true cognates. There were 35 false friends (5.72%), 67 partial cognates (10.95%), and 510 true cognates (83.33%).

Then, we applied different algorithms to distinguish which of the 612 pairs are false friends and which are cognates (partial or true). Each algorithm assigned a similarity score to each pair and then the pairs were sorted by that score in descending order. Ideally, the false friends, having a very low similarity, should appear at the top of the list, followed by the cognates.

[6] Some of the experiments have been published in [32].
[7] The linguist judged the examples as cognates or false friends by consulting Bulgarian-Russian bilingual dictionaries.

Following [2] and [33], the resulting lists were evaluated using *11-pt average precision*, which is well-known in information retrieval [37]; it averages the precision at 11 points corresponding to recall of 0%, 10%, 20%, ..., 100%, respectively.

We performed the following experiments:

- BASELINE – word pairs in alphabetical order: it behaves nearly like a random function and is used as a baseline;
- COOC – the sentence-level co-occurrence algorithm of [31] with their formula F_6;
- COOC+L – the algorithm COOC with lemmatization;
- COOC+E1 – the algorithm COOC with the formula E_1;
- COOC+E1+L – the algorithm COOC with the formula E_1 and lemmatization;
- COOC+E2 – the algorithm COOC with the formula E_2;
- COOC+E2+L – the algorithm COOC with the formula E_2 and lemmatization;
- WEB+L – the Web-based semantic similarity with lemmatization;
- WEB+COOC+L – averaging the values of WEB+L and COOC+L;
- WEB+E1+L – averaging the values of WEB+L and E1+L;
- WEB+E2+L – averaging the values of WEB+L and E2+L;
- WEB+SMT+L – the algorithm WEB+L combined with the statistical machine translation similarity measure by averaging the values of WEB+L and the estimated lexical translation probability;
- COOC+SMT+L – the algorithm COOC+L combined with the machine translation similarity by averaging the similarity scores;
- E1+SMT+L – the algorithm E1+L combined with the machine translation similarity by averaging the similarity scores;
- E2+SMT+L – the algorithm E2+L combined with the machine translation similarity by averaging the similarity scores;
- WEB+COOC+SMT+L – averaging WEB+L, COOC+L, and the machine translation similarity;
- WEB+E1+SMT+L – averaging WEB+L, E1+L, and the machine translation similarity;
- WEB+E2+SMT+L – averaging WEB+L, E2+L and the machine translation similarity.

The results are shown in Table 1. We also tried several ways of weighting the statistical and semantic components in some of the above algorithms, but this had little impact on the results.

Algorithm	**11-pt average precision**
BASELINE	4.17%
E2	38.60%
E1	39.50%
COOC	43.81%
COOC+L	53.20%
COOC+SMT+L	56.22%
WEB+COOC+L	61.28%
WEB+COOC+SMT+L	61.67%
WEB+L	63.68%
E1+L	63.98%
E1+SMT+L	65.36%
E2+L	66.82%
WEB+SMT+L	69.88%
E2+SMT+L	70.62%
WEB+E2+L	76.15%
WEB+E1+SMT+L	76.35%
WEB+E1+L	77.50%
WEB+E2+SMT+L	78.24%

Table 1: *Performance of the different methods sorted by 11-pt average precision (in %).*

6 Discussion

Table 1 shows that most algorithms perform well above the baseline, with the exception of E_1 and E_2 when used in isolation. However, when combined with lemmatization, both E_1 and E_2 perform much better than the original formula F_6 (the COOC algorithm) of [31]: Bulgarian and Russian are highly inflectional languages and thus applying lemmatization is a must. Not surprisingly, the best results are obtained for the combined approaches.

Overall, we observe significant improvements over the original algorithm of [31], but the results are still not perfect.

7 Conclusions and future work

We have presented and compared several algorithms for acquiring pairs of false friends from a sentence-aligned bi-text based on sentence-level co-occurrence statistics, word alignments, the Web as a corpus, lemmatization, and various combinations thereof. The experimental results show a significant improvement over [31].

There are many ways in which the results could be improved even further. First, we would like to try other formulas for measuring the semantic similarity using word-level occurrences and co-occurrences in a bi-text. It would be also interesting to try the contextual mapping vectors approach of [9]. We could try using additional bi-texts to estimate more reliable word alignments, and thus, obtain better lexical probabilities. Using non-parallel corpora as in [26] is another promising direction for future work. The Web-based semantic similarity calculations could be improved using syntactic relations between the words as in [4]. Finally we would like to try the algorithm for other language pairs and to compare our results directly with those of other researchers – on the same datasets.

Acknowledgments

The presented research is supported by the project FP7-REGPOT-2007-1 SISTER.

References

[1] G. W. Adamson and J. Boreham. The use of an association measure based on character structure to identify semantically related pairs of words and document titles. *Information Storage and Retrieval*, 10(7-8):253–260, 1974.

[2] S. Bergsma and G. Kondrak. Alignment-based discriminative string similarity. In *Proceedings of the Annual Meeting of the Association for Computational Linguistics (ACL'07)*, pages 656–663, Prague, Czech Republic, 2007.

[3] A. Bickford and D. Tuggy. Electronic glossary of linguistic terms. http://www.sil.org/mexico/ling/glosario/E005ai-Glossary.htm, 2002.

[4] D. Bollegala, Y. Matsuo, and M. Ishizuka. Measuring semantic similarity between words using web search engines. In *Proceedings of the 16th international conference on World Wide Web (WWW'07)*, pages 757–766, New York, NY, USA, 2007. ACM.

[5] C. Brew and D. McKelvie. Word-pair extraction for lexicography. In *Proceedings of the 2nd Int. Conference on New Methods in Language Processing*, pages 44–55, 1996.

[6] P. Brown, V. D. Pietra, S. D. Pietra, and R. Mercer. The mathematics of statistical machine translation: parameter estimation. *Computational Linguistics*, 19(2):263–311, 1993.

[7] J. R. Curran and M. Moens. Improvements in automatic thesaurus extraction. In *Proceedings of the ACL-02 workshop on Unsupervised lexical acquisition*, pages 59–66, 2002.

[8] C. Fellbaum, editor. *WordNet: An Electronic Lexical Database*. MIT Press, 1998.

[9] P. Fung. A statistical view on bilingual lexicon extraction: From parallel corpora to non-parallel corpora. In *Proceedings of the 3rd Conference of the Association for Machine Translation in the Americas (AMTA'98)*, pages 1–16, 1998.

[10] W. A. Gale and K. W. Church. A program for aligning sentences in bilingual corpora. *Computational Linguistics*, 19(1):75–102, 1993.

[11] J. B. M. Guy. An algorithm for identifying cognates in bilingual wordlists and its applicability to machine translation. *Journal of Quantitative Linguistics*, 1(1):35–42, 1994.

[12] Z. S. Harris. Distributional Structure. *Word*, 10:146–162, 1954.

[13] D. Z. Inkpen. Near-synonym choice in an intelligent thesaurus. In *Proceedings of the Human Language Technology Conference of the North American Chapter of the Association of Computational Linguistics (HLT-NAACL'07)*, pages 356–363, Rochester, New York, USA, 2007.

[14] F. Keller and M. Lapata. Using the Web to obtain frequencies for unseen bigrams. *Computational Linguistics*, 29:459–484, 2003.

[15] A. Kilgariff and G. Grefenstette. Introduction to the special issue on the web as corpus. *Computational Linguistics*, 29(3):333–347, 2003.

[16] P. Koehn and K. Knight. Learning a translation lexicon from monolingual corpora. In *Proceedings of ACL workshop on Unsupervised Lexical Acquisition*, pages 9–16, 2002.

[17] G. Kondrak. Identifying complex sound correspondences in bilingual wordlists. In *In Proceedings the 4th International Conference on Computational Linguistics and Intelligent Text Processing (COLING'03)*, pages 432–443, 2003.

[18] G. Kondrak. Combining evidence in cognate identification. In *Advances in Artificial Intelligence, 17th Conference of the Canadian Society for Computational Studies of Intelligence, Canadian AI 2004*, volume 3060 of *Lecture Notes in Computer Science*, pages 44–59, London, Ontario, Canada, 2004. Springer.

[19] G. Kondrak and B. J. Dorr. Automatic identification of confusable drug names. *Artificial Intelligence in Medicine*, 36(1):29–42, 2006.

[20] M. Lapata and F. Keller. The web as a baseline: Evaluating the performance of unsupervised web-based models for a range of NLP tasks. In *Proceedings of the Human Language Technology Conference of the North American Chapter of the Association of Computational Linguistics (HLT-NAACL'04)*, 2004.

[21] M. Lapata and F. Keller. Web-based models for natural language processing. *ACM Trans. Speech Lang. Process.*, 2(1):3, 2005.

[22] V. Levenshtein. Binary codes capable of correcting deletions, insertions, and reversals. *Doklady Akademii Nauk SSSR*, 163(4):845–848, 1965.

[23] D. Lin. Automatic retrieval and clustering of similar words. In *Proceedings of the 17th international conference on Computational linguistics*, pages 768–774, 1998.

[24] G. Mann and D. Yarowsky. Multipath translation lexicon induction via bridge languages. In *Proceedings of the Annual Meeting of the North American Association for Computational Linguistics (NAACL'01)*, pages 1–8, Pittsburgh, PA, USA, 2001.

[25] D. Melamed. Bitext maps and alignment via pattern recognition. *Computational Linguistics*, 25(1):107–130, 1999.

[26] R. Mitkov, V. Pekar, D. Blagoev, and A. Mulloni. Methods for extracting and classifying pairs of cognates and false friends. *Machine Translation*, 21(1):29–53, 2007.

[27] A. Mulloni and V. Pekar. Automatic detection of orthographic cues for cognate recognition. In *Proceedings of the conference on Language Resources and Evaluation (LREC-06)*, pages 2387–2390, 2006.

[28] A. Mulloni, V. Pekar, and R. M. D. Blagoev. Semantic evidence for automatic identification of cognates. In *Proceedings of the RANLP'2007 workshop: Acquisition and management of multilingual lexicons.*, pages 49–54, Borovets, Bulgaria, 2007.

[29] P. Nakov and M. Hearst. A study of using search engine page hits as a proxy for n-gram frequencies. In *Proceedings of Recent Advances in Natural Language Processing (RANLP'2005)*, pages 347–353, Borovets, Bulgaria, September 2005.

[30] P. Nakov, S. Nakov, and E. Paskaleva. Improved word alignments using the Web as a corpus. In *Proceedigs of Recent Advances in Natural Language Processing (RANLP'07)*, pages 400–405, Borovets, Bulgaria, 2007.

[31] P. Nakov and V. Pacovski. *Readings in Multilinguality, Selected Papers from Young Researchers in BIS-21++*, chapter Acquiring False Friends from Parallel Corpora: Application to South Slavonic Languages, pages 87–94. Incoma Ltd, Shumen, Bulgaria, 2006.

[32] S. Nakov. Automatic identification of false friends in parallel corpora: Statistical and semantic approach. *Serdica Journal of Computing*, 3(2):133–158, 2009.

[33] S. Nakov, P. Nakov, and E. Paskaleva. Cognate or false friend? Ask the Web! In *Proceedings of the RANLP'2007 workshop: Acquisition and management of multilingual lexicons.*, pages 55–62, Borovets, Bulgaria, 2007.

[34] F. J. Och and H. Ney. A systematic comparison of various statistical alignment models. *Computational Linguistics*, 29(1):19–51, 2003.

[35] E. Paskaleva. Compilation and validation of morphological resources. In *Workshop on Balkan Language Resources and Tools (Balkan Conference on Informatics)*, pages 68–74, 2003.

[36] E. Paskaleva and S. Mihov. Second language acquisition from aligned corpora. In *Proceedings of International Conference "Language Technology and Language Teaching"*, pages 43–52, 1998.

[37] G. Salton and M. J. McGill. *Introduction to Modern Information Retrieval*. McGraw-Hill, Inc., New York, NY, USA, 1986.

[38] G. Salton, A. Wong, and C. S. Yang. A vector space model for automatic indexing. *Commun. ACM*, 18(11):613–620, 1975.

[39] J. Tiedemann. Word to word alignment strategies. In *Proceedings of the 20th international conference on Computational Linguistics (COLING'04)*, page 212, 2004.

[40] P. Vossen, editor. *EuroWordNet: a multilingual database with lexical semantic networks*. Kluwer Academic Publishers, Norwell, MA, USA, 1998.

[41] G. Zipf. The psycho-biology of language. Houghton Mifflin, Boston, MA, 1935.

Evaluating term extraction

Adeline Nazarenko
Laboratoire d'Informatique de Paris-Nord
CNRS UMR 7030 - Univ. Paris 13
99, avenue J.B. Clément
F-93430 Villetaneuse
nazarenko@lipn.univ-paris13.fr

Haïfa Zargayouna
Laboratoire d'Informatique de Paris-Nord
CNRS UMR 7030 - Univ. Paris 13
99, avenue J.B. Clément
F-93430 Villetaneuse
haifa@lipn.univ-paris13.fr

Abstract

In contrast with other NLP tasks, only few and limited evaluation challenges have been carried out for terminology acquisition. It is nevertheless important to assess the progress made, the quality and limitations of terminological tools. This paper argues that it is possible to define evaluation protocols for tasks as complex as computational terminology. We focus on the core task of term extraction for which we propose evaluation metrics. We take into account the specificity of computational terminology, the complexity of its outputs, the application, the user's role and the absence of well-established gold standard.

Keywords

Term extraction, evaluation, terminological distance.

1 Introduction

Stemming from traditional terminology and natural language processing (NLP), computational terminology aims at building automatically or semi-automatically terminological resources from acquisition corpora. The growing needs in information management and localization make it more and more necessary to assist and automate terminological tasks.

A lot of terminological tools have been developed since the early research works of the 90s and many content management companies now rely on them [20]. However, despite the progress made, it remains difficult to get a clear idea of the maturity of computational terminology and to compare the proposed approaches. Unlike many other NLP fields, only few effort has been made to set up an evaluation protocol adapted to the specificity of terminological tasks.

We nevertheless argue that an evaluation is possible in computational terminology and that defining a clear and consensual evaluation protocol would benefit to the whole field. This paper focuses on technical aspects of evaluation putting aside the ergonomic and software aspects. We propose a comparative and application-independent evaluation protocol for monolingual term extraction as a first step towards more global and application-oriented evaluations.

Sections 2 and 3 review the first experiments that have been carried out for evaluating terminological tools and the difficulties that such evaluations raise. Sections 4 and 5 present our proposal: a protocol for evaluating term extractors and the specific metrics on which it relies. Section 6 describes experiments for meta-evaluating the proposed metrics.

2 State of the art

Various experiments have been made to evaluate terminological tools. Some were technologically oriented and took the form of evaluation challenges while others put focus on the application context.

2.1 Evaluation challenges

Traditionally, evaluation challenges aim at evaluating a set of systems on a specific task and for a common data set. The systems are compared to each other or wrt. a common data set. This enables the ranking of the systems for the specified task. The first evaluation challenges proposed interesting protocols.

The NTCIR[1] initiative was launched in 1999 and aimed at evaluating information retrieval and term recognition in Japanese [15]. The term recognition task (*TEMREC*) was decomposed into three subtasks: term extraction, key-word extraction and key-word roles analysis. The systems were evaluated on the basis of a standard set of terms. Unfortunately, this task was not very popular and it was eliminated in posterior NTCIR initiatives. [9] explains that TEMREC suffered from the limited number of participants and the absence of previous evaluation initiative for computational terminology.

CoRReCT proposed interesting data set and protocol [7]. The goal was to evaluate term recognition in corpora, a task that is close to controlled indexing. Participating systems took a corpus and a terminology as inputs and indexed the corpus with the terms of the input terminology and their variant forms. The incremental annotation of the corpus is an originality of CoRRecT.

CESART is the most complete challenge [14]. Three different tasks were planned (term extraction, controlled indexing and relation extraction) but only the first one gave rise to a real evaluation, due to the reduced number of participants. CESART nevertheless proposed an interesting protocol for term extraction. A gold standard list of terms and a corresponding acquisition corpus were chosen for a specific domain.

[1] http://research.nii.ac.jp/ntcir/

International Conference RANLP 2009 - Borovets, Bulgaria, pages 299–304

The systems were given the acquisition corpus as input. They extracted terms from the acquisition corpus and the resulting lists of terms were compared with the gold standard, using traditional precision and recall metrics. The originality of CESART was to consider term relevance on a 5-value scale rather than as a Boolean value. An adjudication phase allowed to add some missing relevant terms to the gold standard. Despite the small number of term extractors that participated in CESART, the challenge highlighted the heterogeneity of their results, especially regarding the length of the output lists of terms[2]. This reflects the diversity of the their methods and the differences in their underlying conceptions of what a terminology should be.

2.2 Application-based Evaluation

Smaller experiments have been carried out to evaluate the impact of terminological tools on parsing sublanguages [3], indexing and retrieving documents [6, 16, 19], building back-of-the-book indexes [1] or automatically translating specialised documents [12].

These experiments proposed original approaches to evaluate computation terminology without any terminological gold standard. The impact of terminologies is measured through the own application quality criteria.

Even if they reported very positive results, none of the mentioned experiences gave a global idea of the impact of terminological tools on an application. Coming to such a conclusion would require, for each application, to integrate various term extractors in various application systems, to really assess the impact of the first ones on the second ones and to compare various extracting methods independently on how they are integrated.

This is the reason why we consider that application oriented evaluations are more complex to set up than technological ones, which are addressed in this paper.

3 Evaluation Difficulties

Despite these first evaluation experiences, no comprehensive and global framework has yet been proposed for computational terminology as there exist for many other NLP fields. Beside economic factors, it seems that evaluating terminology acquisition raises some specific intrinsic difficulties.

Heterogeneity of terminology acquisition tools Computational terminology quickly developed in the 1990s and diversified into many subtasks at the end of the decade [4, 8, 5].

The first works focused on term extraction and a large variety of tools have been developed. Some of them rely on a morphological and syntactic analysis to identify the textual units that can be considered as terms. Others are based on statistics and word cooccurrences. Statistical extractors generally produce ranked lists of terms while linguistic ones output unordered ones. Depending on the extractor, focus is put on term well-formedness or on analysis robustness and result coverage. The results produced by these tools are therefore difficult to compare, which makes evaluation more complex.

Following term extraction, many additional terminological functionalities have been proposed. Terminology acquisition now covers a large variety of tools and this diversification also hinders evaluation. We argue that, for evaluation purposes, computational terminology must be split into several, clearly identified, independent and elementary tasks. We focus on the first one in this paper: term extraction.

Complexity of terminological resources The diversity of terminological tools reflects in the resulting terminological resources. Terms are often multi-word units that follow various variation rules in corpora. Terms can also be related to each others by morphological (*schedule/schedules*), synonymy (*plan/schedule*) or hyponymy (*time schedule/schedule*) relations. The quality of the resulting terminology cannot be measured with a single metric, as it is the case with word error rate in speech recognition, for instance. This also leads to decompose term acquisition into several tasks to be evaluated independently.

Gradual relevance The quality of extracted lists of terms would be easy to measure if terms were either relevant or irrelevant because one could rely on the well-known evaluation metrics such as recall and precision. Unfortunately, the underlying hypothesis that relevance is a binary value does not hold for term extraction: a term candidate can be different from a standard term but nevertheless close to it and interesting. In biology, it was reported that extractors often propose incomplete terms, such as *core rna*, which are nevertheless kept in a modified form (*core rna polymerase*) by terminologists [2]. CESART strategy to avoid this binary relevance constraint consisted in defining four levels of precision.

Gold standard variability A major difficulty comes from the fact that, even for a same domain and corpus, different terminologists will produce different terminologies, which reflects their different points of view, different terminological traditions and different choices regarding the granularity of the description. There is usually not a single gold standard but a large set of "acceptable solutions". To palliate the variability of the gold standards, we propose to tune the output of the terminology chosen as standard. This is an original way to free evaluation from the imperfection and relativity of the gold standard. It plays the same role as adjudication but it can be used on a larger scale and it is less costly.

Application role The application for which the terminology is designed also determines what must be evaluated. Although the role of application is important, we do not propose an application-oriented evaluation here. We focus on technological evaluation, which we consider as a first generic step towards more global evaluations.

Interaction Since terminology acquisition is seldom seen as a fully automatic process, terminological tools are generally assisting tools that integrate

[2] The extractors were evaluated on the basis of their first 10,000 terms but some systems outputted 20 times more.

the terminologist role in the resource building process. This also makes evaluation complex because it is difficult to distinguish what comes from the acquisition tools and what results from the terminologist's work. It is nevertheless interesting to compare the output of the system with its amended version. It gives and interesting feed-back for interactive tools.

4 Protocol

Despite those difficulties, we argue that it is possible to design a generic protocol to evaluate term extraction.

4.1 Comparative Protocol

We identified three scenarios for evaluating terminological tools and term extraction in particular. They all rely on comparison. The first scenario compares the output of a term acquisition tool with an independent gold standard. The second takes interaction into account and measures the effort required to turn the draft terminology into an acceptable one. This effort corresponds to the minimal number of elementary operations (term deletion, addition or modification) that allows to transform the draft terminology into the final one. The third scenario evaluates the terminology indirectly through an application (*e.g.* machine translation) using the application own quality criteria.

The comparative protocol that we propose can be used in the two first scenarios: the output of a system (O) is compared with a gold standard (R) that is either an external resource or the validated output[3].

4.2 Choice of the gold standard

Even if, as mentionned above, *gold standard* is variable. There are several ways to build it. One may reuse an existing terminology as in CESART but this terminology may be only partially related to the acquisition corpus. A costly solution consists in asking one or several terminologists to build that standard terminology out of the acquisition corpus. A third solution consists in having the terminologists validating the results of the systems. In that case, the gold standard is the fusion of the validated outputs of the systems, as in CoRReCT. This last solution is not exhaustive but it is less costly than the second one.

The metrics proposed in the following for term extraction are compatible with any of these gold standard building methods.

4.3 Sub-tasks Decomposition

As mentioned above, term extraction is not the only terminological task. Other tasks such as variation calculus, relation extraction, term normalisation must be considered as well, even if they are left apart here. As far as evaluation is concerned, those tasks must be considered as independently as possible. This is especially important for term extraction and variation calculus, which consists in clustering terms that are variant forms of each others. The term lists output by the systems must be considered as unstructured lists even if the systems propose some variation relations among the terms. Those systems have to be evaluated twice (for the term extraction in the first place and for the variation in a second phase) but the quality of one task must not affect the evaluation of the other.

[3] In that case, there is no need for a standard terminology but recall cannot be measured or only partially because validation consists in deleting rather than adding terms.

5 Metrics

As mentioned above, traditional metrics of precision and recall are not appropriate for term extraction evaluation. One problem is that term relevance is a gradual rather than a binary notion and that one cannot expect all extractors or terminologists to deliver ranked list of terms. This led us to stem relevance on a terminological distance. A second problem is that no terminological standard can be considered as a stable and unique gold standard. We propose to overcome that difficulty by tuning the system output to the granularity of the chosen gold standard in order to avoid arbitrarily favouring one system against another.

It is important however to have simple and well-known metrics [13], so we adapt traditional metrics of precision and recall rather than defining new ones[4].

The proposed metrics are implemented in a tool, called TermoMeter. It takes two unstructured term lists as input (the output O of a term extractor and the gold standard R without any hypothesis on the type, length and granularity of that gold standard) and it computes the terminological precision and recall (resp. TP and TR) of O wrt. R. For a perfect system ($O = R$), TermoMeter gives $TP = TR = 1$. A system that extracts in addition terms that are close to the gold standard is not penalised or only a little bit. TermoMeter gives $TP = TR = 0$ for systems that give only irrelevant terms ($S \cap R = \emptyset$).

Let us consider the cases where $R = \{$*data base*$\}$ and we have the following output lists: $O_1 = \{$*data base, data bases*$\}$, $O_2 = \{$*data bases*$\}$ et $O_3 = \{$*data base, table of content*$\}$. We expect O_1 and O_2 to be of similar quality: O_1 gives the term of R along with a second redundant but relevant one; O_2 gives a single term that is close but not exactly that one of R. O_3 has a lower quality since the extra term, which is to too far from the term of R, is considered as noise.

5.1 Term Distance

Several methods have been proposed to measure word distance. They rely on character string comparison, on Levenshtein distance and the minimal number of editing operations required to transform one word into another [17], or on morphological and linguistic transformation rules. However, since terms are generally multi-word units having their own variation rules, two independent levels must be considered in term distance: the word level (*base* vs *bases*) and the phrase level (*file system* vs *disk file system*). [18] proposed to

[4] Recall that:

$$precision = \frac{|O \cap R|}{|O|} \qquad recall = \frac{|O \cap R|}{|R|}$$

where $|O|$ is the number of elements retrieved by the system, $|O \cap R|$ is the number of relevant elements retrieved by the system, and $|R|$ is the number of elements in the gold standard.

exploit Levenshtein distance to compute distances on these two levels in an homogeneous way but our approach differs from this work because we avoid relying on external linguistic knowledge. This allows to keep computation simple, which is important if one considers the number of distances that must be computed in real evaluation conditions. To keep distance unbiased, it is also important to avoid using for evaluation the linguistic knowledge (such as term variation rules or POS-tagging) that may be used by extractors.

We define a first distance on character strings (d_s. It is a normalised Levenshtein distance, where the sum of the costs of the elementary editing operations (character insertion, deletion, substitution) required to transform a string into another is divided by the length of the longer string. The normalisation allows to compare the distances of various string pairs. If all the elementary operations have an equal cost of 1, TermoMeter gives the following distances :

$$d_s(base, bases) = 1/5 = 0.2$$
$$d_s(base, basement) = 4/8 = 0.5$$
$$d_s(base, relational) = 9/10 = 0.9$$

Of course, that distance does not always match with linguistic intuition but it must be evaluated globally through the evaluation of a list of terms (see Sec. 6) and not on individual pairs of words.

The distance on complex terms is based on the same principle, except that editing operations apply on words instead of characters. The distance between two complex terms (d_c) is the sum of the elementary operations (word insertion, deletion or substitution) required to transform a term into another. To search for the best word alignment that minimizes the global cost, TermoMeter relies on Hungarian algorithm [11]. The cost of an insertion or deletion is 1 while the cost of a substitution is equal to the normalised Levenshtein distance (d_s) of the corresponding words. This gives the following distances, for instance:

$$d_c(\textit{data base, data bases}) = 0.1$$
$$d_c(\textit{relational data base, data base}) = 0.33$$
$$d_c(\textit{relational data base, web site}) = 0.88$$

This measure allows to take into account word permutations that are frequent in term variation as for *expression of gene* and *gene expression*. Its drawback is that it relies on a necessarily arbitrary word segmentation method.

Finally the term distance (d_t) is defined as the mean of the distances on strings and on complex terms :

$$d_t(t_1, t_2) = (d_s(t_1, t_2) + d_c(t_1, t_2))/2$$

d_t is a normalised distance ranging between 0 and 1. The following examples show that the d_c factor allows for permutation but that the d_s factor both attenuates that effect and limits the impact of segmentation choices:

$d_t(\textit{precise gene localization, precise localization of gene}) = (10/25 + 1/4)/2 = 0,34$
$d_t(\textit{porte folio, portefolios}) = (1/11 + 3/11)/2 = 0,4$

This term distance is robust, quick to compute and easy to interpret. It does not require any external knowledge and is language independent. It takes a gradual relevance into account without considering the eventual variants that systems may propose and that must be evaluated on a separate task.

5.2 Gradual relevance

The terminological precision and recall metrics take that gradual relevance into account. The global relevance of a term list with respect to a gold standard is defined as the function $Pert(O, R)$ that verifies

$$|O \cap R| \leq Pert(O, R) \leq min(|0|, |R|)$$

and reflects the global distance between O and R. It is based on the term distances $d_t(e_o, e_r)$ between the terms of the output O and that of the gold standard R. The relevance of a term e_o of O is based on its distance to the closest term e_r of R:

$$pert_R(e_s) = \begin{cases} 1 - min_{e_r \in R}(d_t(e_o, e_r)) \\ \text{ if } min_{e_r \in R}(d_t(e_o, e_r)) < \tau \\ 0 \text{ otherwise} \end{cases}$$

where τ is a threshold such that if the distance between two terms is superior to τ, they are considered as totally different.

5.3 Output tuning

Since any terminology is a relative gold standard, it would be artificial to compare directly the output of the systems with it. It might favour the systems that would have made "by chance" the same granularity choice. The evaluation scores and system ranking might be too dependent on the gold standard. To avoid this problem, the output is transformed to find its maximal correspondence with the gold standard, which means that the output is tuned to the terminological type and granularity of the gold standard.

Since several output terms may correspond to the same standard term, they are considered all together. The precision and recall measures are not computed directly on O but on a partition of O that is defined relatively to R. This partition $\mathcal{P}$(O) is such that any part p of $\mathcal{P}$(O) either contains a set of terms of O that are close to the same term of R and with a distance inferior to the threshold τ, or contains a single term that matches with no term of R:

$$p = \begin{cases} \{e_1, e_2, ..., e_n\} \\ \text{ if } (\exists e_r \in R)((\forall i \in [1, n])(\forall e'_r \in R) \\ (d_t(e_i, e'_r) \geq d_t(e_i, e_r))(d_t(e_i, e_r) \leq \tau)) \\ \{e\} \text{ if } (\nexists e_r \in R)(d_t(e, e_r) \leq \tau)\} \end{cases}$$

$$\text{where } e \in O \text{ and } \forall i \in [1, n])(e_i \in O)$$

The relevance of a part p of $\mathcal{P}(\mathcal{O})$ wrt. R is defined as follows[5].

$$Pert_R(p) = max_{e \in p}(pert_R(e))$$

Terminological precision (TP) and recall (TR) are defined as follows:

$$TP = \frac{Pert(O, R)}{|\mathcal{P}(\mathcal{O})|} = \frac{\sum_{p \in \mathcal{P}(\mathcal{O})} Pert_R(p)}{|\mathcal{P}(\mathcal{O})|}$$

[5] Note that the relevance is null if p contains only one term of O with a distance superior to τ to any term of R.

$$TR = \frac{Pert(O,R)}{|R|} = \frac{\sum_{p \in \mathcal{P}(O)} Pert_R(p)}{|R|}$$

As expected, TermoMeter gives $TP = TR = 1$ for a perfect system, TP and TR tend towards 0 for systems that extract mainly irrelevant terms and TR decreases when the size of the gold standard increases wrt. that of the output.

6 Meta-evaluation of metrics

As it has been done for machine translation [10], it is important to meta-evaluate the proposed metrics before starting to use them in real evaluation conditions, either challenges or benchmark comparisons.

To achieve this meta-evaluation at low cost, existing independent data have been exploited. Two series of tests have been made on terminological results provided by MIG laboratory of INRA. These data sets are used to test the robustness of TermoMeter and its adequacy to initial specifications.

6.1 Terminological *vs.* usual metrics

The first experiment is based on the following data: (i) an English corpus specialised in Genomics and composed of 405,000 words, (ii) the outputs of three term extractors in which only frequent candidate terms (more than 20 occurrences) have been kept to alleviate the terminologist's work. The outputs of the systems S_1, S_2 and S_3 respectively contain 194, 307 and 456 candidate terms and (iii) a gold standard (GS) of 514 terms, which has been built by asking a terminologist to validate the outputs of the three extractors[6].

Table 1 presents the evaluation of these systems wrt. the gold standard. As expected, the terminological measures (TP and TR) follow the same curves as the classical ones (P and R), but they are higher, which proves that the terminological measures take into account the gold standard approximation. A difference of 10 points in F-measure (F) is significant.

	P	R	F	TP	TR	F
GS	1.0	1.0	1.0	1.0	1.0	1.0
S_1	0.71	0.42	0.52	0.95	0.48	0.63
S_2	0.77	0.68	0.72	0.94	0.70	0.80
S_3	0.76	0.28	0.40	0.95	0.34	0.50

Table 1: *Results of the output of three term extractors, τ = 0.4 for terminological measures (TP, TR)*

The output partitioning leads to cluster mostly morphological (singular/plurial) or typographic (lower/upper cases) variants. The analysis of the incomplete terms (8.5% of the extracted terms as reported by the terminologist) shows that most of them are considered as close to the corresponding complete terms that the terminologist has added to the gold standard. For instance, *acid residue* is considered as close to *amino acid residues* with a distance of 0.35. In fact, four terms are clustered in the same output part associated to *amino acid residues*: acid residue (distance=0.35), amino acid residue (distance=0.05), acid residues (distance=0.29), amino acid residues (distance=0.0).

6.2 Large scale experiment

The second experiment exploited the following data: (i) an English patent corpus in the agrobiotech domain, (ii) the raw output of an extractor (4,200 candidate terms extracted from the corpus) without any ranking or filtering. It contains almost and (iii) a gold standard of 1,988 terms resulting from the validation of the extractor output by two terminologists[7].

This experiment allows to analyse globally the behaviour of TermoMeter and its metrics on a large scale sample: comparing the output to the gold standard led to compute around $8 * 10^6$ term distances, which required only few minutes on a standard PC.

The results are presented on Figure 1[8]. It shows the correlation between τ (the threshold above which a candidate term is not clustered with others) and terminological precision (Fig. 1 a.). When $\tau = 0$, there is no clustering at all ($TP = precision$) but TP increases with τ. The threshold value has a direct impact on the size of the output partition (Fig. 1 b.): the higher the threshold is, the more numerous are the terms that are clustered and match with the gold standard. When τ has its maximal value, all the candidate terms match with the gold standard and the terminological precision cannot get higher. The shapes of the curve show that it should be possible to determine the threshold value automatically (between 0.4 and 0.5 in the present case).

The relative quality of the system output and the lists validated by a single terminologist have also been measured. Three output lists of terms have been considered: the raw system output (O_r) and the outputs validated by the two terminologists independently (V_1 and V_2). They all have been compared with the gold standard (V_{12}) that resulted from the join validation of the two same terminologists. Table 2 shows that the expected quality ranking of the three outputs is verified:

$$TP(S_b) < TP(V_1) < TP(V_{12})$$
$$TP(S_b) < TP(V_2) < TP(V_{12})$$

and that the first terminologist judgement is closer to the gold standard than that of the second one.

	S_b	V_1	V_2	V_{12}
TP	0.55	0.91	0.97	1.0

Table 2: *Terminological precision, τ = 0.4*

7 Conclusion

After 15 years of research in computational terminology it is important to assess the maturity of terminological tools. Evaluating term extraction is a first step in that direction.

[6] The terminologist was allowed to supplement the incomplete terms.

[7] Inter-annotator variations (11% of the candidate terms) have been solved through discussion.

[8] Only precision measures are presented. The gold standard cannot be used to measure recall since terminologists validated or deleted terms without adding any new one.

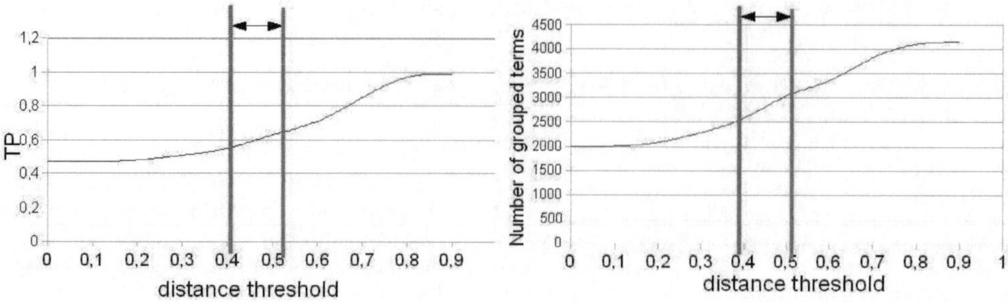

Fig. 1: *Curves of terminological precision (TP) (a) and the number of candidate terms matching with the gold standard (b) wrt. the threshold values.*

The fact that terminological tools are often assisting tools for terminologists and application dependent, the relativity of any standard terminology, the complexity of terminological resources make the evaluation difficult in computational terminology. However, this paper proposes an evaluation protocol and the associated metrics that take into account terminological specificity and nevertheless enable to set up comparative evaluations in a simple way. The proposed terminological measures differ from traditional precision and recall in two ways: they take into account the gradual relevance of terms and the relativity of the gold standard.

The first meta-evaluation experiments have shown that the TermoMeter tool globally behaves as expected on large scale term lists and that it gives a more precise evaluation of terminological extractors than traditional measures.

Further work will consist in setting up evaluation experiments for term extraction and to define adequate protocols for other terminological tasks such as term variation calculus and term relation extraction.

Acknowledgments. The authors would like to thank Olivier Hamon (ELDA-LIPN) and Jonathan van Puymbrouck (LIPN) for fruitful discussions and Sophie Aubin (MIG) for helpful material used in meta-evaluation. This work was partly realized as part of the Quaero Programme, funded by OSEO, French State agency for innovation.

References

[1] T. Ait El Mekki and A. Nazarenko. An application-oriented terminology evaluation: the case dof back-of-the-book indexes. In R. C. *et al.*, editor, *Proceedings of the Workshop "Terminology Design: Quality Criteria and Evaluation Methods" (LREC-TerEval)*, pages 18–21, Genova, Italy, May 2006.

[2] S. Aubin. Comparaison de termes extraits par acabit, nomino, syntex de fréquence supérieures ou égales à 20. Livrable 3.2, Projet ExtraPloDocs, INRA-MIG, 2003.

[3] S. Aubin, A. Nazarenko, and C. Nédellec. Adapting a general parser to a sublanguage. In *Proceedings of the International Conference on Recent Advances in Natural Language Processing (RANLP'05)*, pages 89–93, Borovets, Bulgaria, 2005.

[4] M. Cabré Castellv, R. Estopà, and J. Vivaldi Palatresi. Automatic term detection: A review of current systems. In D. Bourigault, C. Jacquemin, and M.-C. L'Homme, editors, *Recent Advances in Computational Terminology*. John Benjamins, Amsterdam, 2001.

[5] B. Daille, K. Kageura, H. Nakagawa, and L.-F. Chien, editors. *Terminology. Special issue on Recent Trends in Computational Terminology*, volume 10. John Benjamins, 2004.

[6] B. Daille, J. Royauté, and X. Polenco. Evaluation d'une plateforme d'indexation des termes complexes. *Traitement Automatique des Langues*, 41(2):396–422, 2000.

[7] C. Enguehard. Correct : Démarche coopérative pour l'évaluation de systèmes de reconnaissance de termes. In *Actes de la 10ème conférence annuelle sur le Traitement Automatique des Langues (TALN 2003)*, pages 339–345, Nancy, 2003.

[8] C. Jacquemin and D. Bourigault. Term extraction and automatic indexing. In R. Mitkov, editor, *Handbook of Computational Linguistics*, chapter 19, pages 599–615. Oxford University press, Oxford, GB, 2003.

[9] K. Kageura, T. Fukushima, N. Kando, M. Okumura, S. Sekine, K. Kuriyama, K. Takeuchi, M. Yoshioka, T. Koyama, and H. Isahara. Ir/ie/summarisation evaluation projects in japan. In *LREC2000 Workshop on Using Evaluation within HLT Programs*, pages 19–22, 2000.

[10] P. Koehn, N. Bertoldi, O. Bojar, C. Callison-Burch, A. Constantin, B. Cowan, C. Dyer, M. Federico, E. Herbst, H. Hoang, C. Moran, W. Shen, and R. Zens. Factored translation models. In J. H. University, editor, *CLSP Summer Workshop Final Report WS-2006*, 2006.

[11] B. H. W. Kuhn. The hungarian method for the assignment problem. *Naval Research Logistics Quarterly*, 2:83–97, 1955.

[12] P. Langlais and M. Carl. General-purpose statistical translation engine and domain specific texts: Would it work? *Terminology*, 10(1):131–152, 2004.

[13] A. F. Martin, J. S. Garofolo, J. C. Fiscus, A. N. Le, D. S. Palett, and M. A. P. ang Gregory A. Sanders. Nist language technology evaluation cookbook. In *Proceedings of Fourth International Conference on Language Resources and Evaluation (LREC 2004)*, 2004.

[14] W. Mustafa el Hadi, I. Timimi, M. Dabbadie, K. Choukri, O. Hamon, and Y. Chiao. Terminological resources acquisition tools: Toward a user-oriented evaluation model. In *Proceedings of the Language Resources and Evaluation Conference (LREC'06)*, pages 945–948, Genova, Italy, May 2006.

[15] National Center for Science Information Systems, editor. *Proceedings of the First NTCIR Workshop on Research in Japanese Text Retrieval and Term Recognition*, 1999.

[16] A. Névéol, K. Zeng, and O. Bodenreider. Besides precision & recall: Exploring alternative approaches to evaluating an automatic indexing tool for medline. In *Proceedings of the AMIA Annual Symposium*, pages 589–593, 2006.

[17] P. M. Sant. Levenshtein distance. in *Dictionary of Algorithms and Data Structures* [online], Paul E. Black, ed., U.S. National Institute of Standards and Technology, 2 April 2009 2004. (accessed 2 April 2009) Available from: http://www.itl.nist.gov/div897/sqg/dads/HTML/rootedtree.html.

[18] A. Tartier. *Analyse automatique de l'évolution terminologique : variations et distances.* PhD thesis, Université de Nantes, 2004.

[19] N. Wacholder and P. Song. Toward a task-based gold standard for evaluation of np chunks and technical terms. In *Proceedings of HTL-NAACL.*

[20] D. Zielinski and Y. R. Safar. t-survey 2005: An online survey on terminology extraction an terminology management. In *Proceedings of Translating and the Computer.*

Question Answering over Structured Data: an Entailment-Based Approach to Question Analysis

Matteo Negri and Milen Kouylekov
FBK-irst - Fondazione Bruno Kessler
Via Sommarive 18, 38100 Povo (TN), Italy
negri,kouylekov@fbk.eu

Abstract

This paper addresses question analysis in the framework of Question Answering over structured data. The problem is set as a relation extraction task, where all the relations of interest in a given domain have to be extracted from natural language questions. The proposed approach applies the notion of Textual Entailment to compare the input questions with a repository of relational textual patterns. The underlying assumption is that a question expresses a certain relation if a pattern for that relation is entailed by the question. We report on a number of experiments, testing different simple distance-based entailment algorithms over a dataset of 1487 English questions covering the domain of cultural events in a town, and 75 relations that are relevant in this domain. The positive results obtained demonstrate the feasibility of the overall approach, and its effectiveness in the proposed QA scenario.

Keywords

Restricted-Domain Question Answering, Textual Entailment, Relation Extraction.

1 Introduction

Question analysis is the Question Answering (QA) subtask that consists in analysing a natural language question in order to identify all the relevant information needed to extract the correct answer from a given data source. Depending on the QA application, relevant information may include the identification of: *i)* the Expected Answer Type (*i.e.* the semantic category of the sought-after answer), *ii)* the word sense of the question terms, *iii)* the most important keywords, *iv)* named entities, and *v)* relations between entities. In the framework of QA over structured data, extracting from an input question all the relevant relations in a given domain becomes crucial, as it allows to fully capture the context in which the request has to be interpreted and, in turn, to determine the constraints on the database query. For instance, given the question *"What movie can I see today at cinema Astra?"*, an effective database query will select a concept of type MOVIE, with specific relations with a DATE (*e.g.* HASDATE(MOVIE:?, DATE:"today")) and a CINEMA (*e.g.* HASMOVIESITE(MOVIE:?, SITE:"Astra")). Successful answer retrieval depends on capturing *all and only* the relations expressed in the question: unrecognized relations will determine underspecified queries (often leading to redundant answers), while spuriously recognized relations will determine overspecified queries (leading to answer extraction failures).

While in open-domain QA any type of relation is potentially relevant, making their automatic identification unfeasible in an exhaustive manner, QA over structured data in a restricted domain presents a reasonable setting to address the task. In this paper we investigate the applicability of Textual Entailment (TE) as a possible solution to the problem. TE has been recently proposed as a comprehensive framework for applied semantics [4], where the mapping between linguistic objects is carried out by means of semantic inferences at the textual level. In the TE framework, a text (T) is said to entail the hypothesis (H) if the meaning of H can be derived from the meaning of T. According to such framework, we aim at discovering entailment relations between an input question Q (the *text* in the TE terminology) and a set of relational patterns (the *hypotheses*) that represent possible lexicalizations of the relations of interest in a given domain. The assumption is that, if an entailment relation holds between Q and a pattern p associated to a relation R_i, then R_i is among the relations expressed in Q.

In contrast with traditional approaches to QA over structured data, the proposed solution allows for a more flexible mapping between linguistic expressions (*e.g.* lexical items, syntactic structures) and data objects (*e.g.* concepts and relations in a knowledge base). This is because much of the machinery implied in such mapping, such as the construction of a logical form [1], [11], is not required in the TE framework, where inferences are performed at the textual level.

A TE-based approach to QA over structured data has been recently proposed in [9], which describes a system for the Italian language based on Linear Distance, a word-level TE Recognition (RTE) algorithm. Even though the preliminary results reported by the authors are encouraging, several aspects of the methodology have not been investigated, leaving room for more comprehensive evaluations. This paper represents a significant step forward, as it extensively addresses the following open issues: *i)* how do different RTE algorithms perform in the task of recognizing relevant relations in a dataset of domain-specific questions? *ii)* what is the impact on performance obtained by varying the number of available patterns associated to each relation?, *iii)* what is the impact of the TE-

International Conference RANLP 2009 - Borovets, Bulgaria, pages 305–311

based approach to Relation Extraction (RE) on the overall performance of a QA system?, and *iv)* what is the relationship between the general TE Recognition task, as it is formulated within the Pascal-RTE Challenge [5], and the specific application scenario here proposed? By answering these questions, the main contribution of this work consists in providing exhaustive experiments to demonstrate that QA over structured data can be cast as an RTE-related problem.

The paper is organized as follows. Section 2 defines the TE-based RE task. Sections 3 and 4 describe our approach to RTE, and our experimental setting. Section 5 discusses evaluation results. Section 6 overviews related works, and Section 7 concludes the paper drawing final remarks.

2 Task Definition

We define the TE-based RE task as a classification problem, where a question Q annotated with entities has to be assigned to all the relations $R_1,...,R_n$ it expresses, selected from a predefined set R. For instance, given the question *"What can I see [DATE: today] at cinema [SITE: Astra]?"*, the following relations represent the expected output of the system:
R1: HASMOVIESITE(MOVIE:?, SITE:"Astra")
R2: HASDATE(MOVIE:?, DATE:"today")

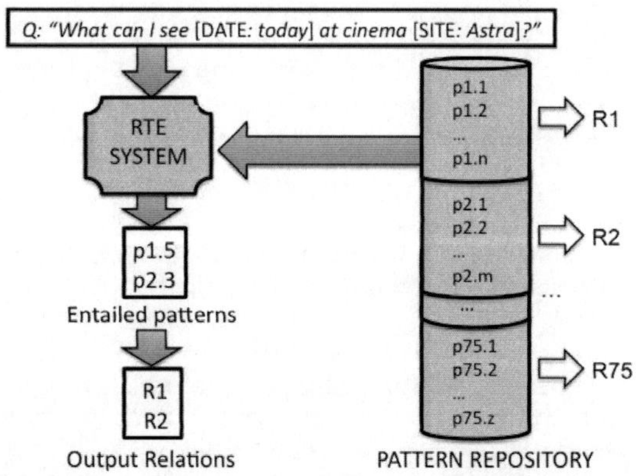

Fig. 1: *TE-based Relation Extraction process.*

As shown in Figure 1, the classification is carried out by means of an RTE system, which compares the question Q against a set of textual patterns stored in a *Pattern Repository (P)*. P contains n sets of relational patterns, each set representing possible lexicalizations of one relation R_i in R. Given the question Q, the RTE system attempts to verify, for each relation R_i, if an entailment relation holds between Q and at least one of R_i's patterns. If so, the relation is added to the output of the system. In case no relation is found, this is interpreted as evidence that the question is out of domain. Considering the example reported in Figure 1, since the input question entails patterns for the relations R1 and R2, the two relations are returned as output by the system. This task formulation is consistent with the one adopted in the Pascal-RTE initiative for the creation of TE pairs, as it is reported in [5].

2.1 Minimal Relational Patterns (MRPs)

Relational patterns represent an important aspect in our formulation of the task. In general, we say that a relational pattern p expresses a relation $R(arg1, arg2)$ in a certain language L if speakers of L agree that the meaning of p expresses the relation R between $arg1$ and $arg2$, given their knowledge about the entities. For instance, all the examples in Table 1 represent relational patterns for the relation HASMOVIESITE(MOVIE, SITE).

In order to be profitably used in the proposed entailment framework, valid patterns should have the additional property of representing only *one* relation. Patterns representing multiple relations, in fact, would be entailed only by questions containing all those relations, thus resulting limited in their usage. For instance, only patterns (1)-(3) in Table 1 will be entailed by the question *"What can I see at cinema [SITE: Astra]?"*. Since (4) also contains the relation HASDATE(MOVIE, DATE), it will be entailed only by questions that lexicalize both relations.

Single-relation patterns, or *Minimal Relational Patterns* (MRPs), can be formally defined in terms of TE. Given two sets of relational patterns $P1$ and $P2$ for the relations $R1$ and $R2$, a pattern p_k belonging to $P1$ is a MRP for $R1$ if condition (1) holds.

$$\forall p_i \in P2, p_k \mapsto p_i = \emptyset \quad (1)$$

In other words, a pattern p is minimal for a relation R if none of the patterns for the other relations can be derived from p (*i.e.* is entailed by p). According to such definition, patterns (1)-(3) are MRPs for the relation HASMOVIESITE(MOVIE, SITE), while (4) is not, since it also entails patterns for the relation HASDATE(MOVIE, DATE).

3 Distance Based RTE

Edit distance approaches to RTE, such as the one proposed in [8], assume that the distance between T and H is a characteristic that separates the positive pairs, for which entailment holds, from the negative pairs, for which entailment does not hold. Such distance is computed as the cost of the editing operations (*i.e.* insertion, deletion and substitution) which are required to transform T into H. Each edit operation on two text fragments A and B (denoted as $A \rightarrow B$) has an associated cost (denoted as $\gamma(A \rightarrow B)$). The entailment score for a T-H pair is calculated on the minimal set of edit operations that transform T into H. An entailment relation is assigned to a T-H pair only if the overall cost of the transformation is below a certain threshold empirically estimated over training data. The entailment score function is defined in the following way:

$$score_{entailment}(T, H) = 1 - \frac{\gamma(T, H)}{\gamma_{nomap}(T, H)}$$

where $\gamma(T, H)$ is the function that calculates the edit distance between T and H, and $\gamma_{nomap}(T, H)$ is the *no mapping* distance equivalent to the cost of inserting

(1)	<ARG2:MOVIE:X> *is shown at cinema* <ARG1:CINEMA:Y>
(2)	*What* <ARG2:*movie*> *is on at* <ARG1:CINEMA:Y>*?*
(3)	*Is there any* <ARG2:*movie*> *that I can see at* <ARG1:CINEMA:Y>*?*
(4)	*Can I see* <ARG2:MOVIE:X> *at cinema* <ARG1:CINEMA:Y> *on* <ARG?:DATE:Z>*?*

Table 1: *Examples of relational patterns.*

the entire text of H, and deleting the entire text of T. The entailment score function has a range from 0 (when T is identical to H), to 1 (when T is completely different from H).

3.1 Algorithms

In this paper we experiment with the following two simple distance-based algorithms.

Linear Distance (LD) As for Linear Distance, *Levenshtein Distance* has been applied to RTE [8], by converting both the text T and the hypothesis H into sequences of words. Accordingly, edit operations have been defined as follows:

- **Insertion** ($\Lambda \rightarrow A$): insert a word A from H into T.
- **Deletion** ($A \rightarrow \Lambda$): delete a word A from T.
- **Substitution** ($A \rightarrow B$): substitute a word A from T with a word B from H.

Tree Edit Distance (TED) As regards Tree Edit Distance, [8] reports on an implementation for RTE based on [13], where the dependency trees of both T and H are considered. Edit operations are defined in the following way:

- **Insertion** ($\Lambda \rightarrow A$): insert a node A from the dependency tree of H into the dependency tree of T. When a node is inserted it is attached to the dependency relation of the source label.
- **Deletion** ($A \rightarrow \Lambda$): delete a node A from the dependency tree of T. When A is deleted all its children are attached to the parent of A. It is not required to explicitly delete the children of A, as they are going to be either deleted or substituted in a following step.
- **Substitution** ($A \rightarrow B$): change the label of a node A in the source tree into a label of a node B of the target tree. In case of substitution the relation attached to the substituted node is changed with the relation of the new node.

3.2 Cost Schemes for Edit Operations

The core of the edit distance approach is the mechanism for the definition of the cost of edit operations. This mechanism is defined separately from the distance algorithm and should reflect the knowledge of the user about the processed data. The principle behind it is to capture certain phenomena that facilitate the algorithm to assign small distances to positive T-H pairs, and large distances to negative pairs. Different semantic representations of the text allow different ways of defining the cost of edit operations. In the following paragraphs we describe the cost schemes we have used.

Default Cost Scheme (DEF)

$$\gamma(\Lambda \rightarrow A) = length(T)$$
$$\gamma(A \rightarrow \Lambda) = length(H)$$
$$\gamma(A \rightarrow B) = \begin{cases} 0 & A = B \\ \gamma_{i+d}(A \rightarrow B) & otherwise \end{cases}$$

In this scheme the cost of the insertion of a text fragment from H in T is equal to the length (*i.e.* the number of words) of T, and the deletion of a text fragment from T is equal to the length of H. The substitution cost is set to the sum of the insertion and the deletion of the text fragments, if they are not equal. This means that the algorithm would prefer to delete and insert text fragments rather than substituting them, in case they are not equal[1]. Setting the insertion and deletion costs respectively to the length of T and H is motivated by the fact that a shorter text T should not be preferred over a longer one T' while computing their overall mapping costs with the hypothesis H. Setting the costs to fixed values would in fact penalize longer texts (due to the larger amount of deletions needed) even though they are very similar to H.

When creating a cost scheme we can take advantage of other features of the processed text fragments. In the following two cost schemes we consider the depth and the width of the dependency trees representing the T-H pairs.

Depth-based Scheme (DS)

$$\gamma(\Lambda \rightarrow A) = depth(Tree_H) - depth(A)$$
$$\gamma(A \rightarrow \Lambda) = depth(Tree_T) - depth(A)$$

In this scheme the cost of the insertion of a node from the dependency tree of H in T, and of the deletion of a node from the dependency tree of T are inversely proportional to the depth (distance from the root) of the nodes in the dependency trees of T and H. The rationale behind this cost scheme is that words that are important to the meaning of the sentence, like verbs, subjects and objects, are usually in the top of the dependency tree and thus they should have higher costs of insertion and deletion.

[1] This is the default substitution setting for all the following schemes and will be omitted in their representation.

Width-based Scheme (WS)

$$\gamma(\Lambda \rightarrow A) = children(A)$$
$$\gamma(A \rightarrow \Lambda) = children(A)$$

In this scheme the cost of inserting and deleting a node is proportional to the number of children of the node in the dependency trees of T and H. The rationale is that the words that connect the phrases of the sentence are meaning preserving, and should have higher costs of insertion and deletion.

4 Experimental Setting

The main elements of our experimental setting are: *i)* the question corpus, and *ii)* the Pattern Repository.

4.1 Question Corpus

We experiment with a corpus of 1487 English questions extracted from the QALL-ME benchmark[2] [3], a multilingual corpus of annotated spoken requests in the domain of cultural events in a town (*e.g.* cinema, theatre, exhibitions, etc.). The available questions are manual transcriptions of *1223 read* and *264 spontaneous* telephone requests, annotated with different types of information. As far as relation annotation is concerned, questions are marked as containing one or more relations chosen from a set of 75 binary relations defined in the QALL-ME ontology[3]. As an example, the annotation of the question *Q2536: "What is the name of the director of 007 Casino Royale, which is shown today at cinema Modena?"* contains three relations, namely:

HasDate(Movie,Date)
HasMovieSite(Movie,Site)
HasDirector(Movie,Director).

The annotated questions contain 2 relations on average (min 1, max 6). A Kappa value of 0.94 (*almost perfect agreement*) was measured for the agreement between two annotators over part of the dataset (150 questions), showing the reliability of the annotation.

The annotated questions are used to create the *training* and *test* sets for our experiments. For this purpose, the question corpus was randomly split in two sets, respectively containing 999 and 488 questions. Such separation was carried out guaranteeing that, for each relation R, the questions marked with R are distributed in the two sets in proportion 2/3-1/3. The larger set of 999 questions is used for the acquisition of MRPs and, together with the resulting Pattern Repository, is used to train our RTE system (*i.e.* to empirically estimate an entailment threshold for each relation, considering positive and negative examples). The smaller set of 488 questions (which remained "unseen" in the MRP acquisition phase) is used as test set for the experiments described in Section 5.

[2] The QALL-ME benchmark has been developed within the EU funded QALL-ME project (http://qallme.fbk.eu).

[3] The QALL-ME ontology contains 107 properties (relations), and 122 classes (concepts). Our 75 relations, selected from the 107 properties, involve 27 concepts.

4.2 Pattern Repository

According to the definition in Section 2.1, for each relation R we manually[4] extracted a set of MRPs from the training questions annotated with R. Given Q, the set of all the questions annotated with R, we adopt the following pattern creation guidelines:

1. A valid MRP describes only one relation.
2. A valid MRP has to be entailed by all the questions in Q.

For instance, given the following training examples for the relation HasDirector(Movie,Director):

Q493: *"What is the title of the last action movie directed by Martin Campbell?"*
Q2056: *"Is Gabriele Muccino's movie La Ricerca Della Felicitá on tomorrow?"*
Q2893: *"What is the name of the director of dreamgirls today at Nuovo Roma cinema?"*

the extracted MRPs are:

p1: movie directed by [Person]
p2: [Person]'s movie
p3: director of [Movie]

Adopting the aforementioned criteria, we populated our Pattern Repository with a total of 449 patterns, with at least 1 MRP per relation (6 on average).

5 Experiments and Discussion

5.1 Comparison of Different Algorithms

The objective of our first experiment was to determine the impact on RE performance of different configurations of the RTE system. As a baseline we used the *Longest Common Subsequence* (**LCS**), a similarity measure often used by RTE systems [2]. Given a text $T =< t_1, ..., t_n >$, and a hypothesis $H =< h_1, ..., h_n >$, the LCS is defined as the longest possible sequence $W =< w_1, ..., w_n >$ with words in W also being words in T and H in the same order.

For a meaningful comparison, we considered the following combinations of distance algorithms and cost schemes described in Section 3:

- Linear Distance + Default Scheme (**LD+DEF**) - to compare this word-level algorithm with those based on syntactic structures matching;
- Tree Edit Distance + Dynamic Scheme (**TED+DEF**) - to evaluate the contribution of considering dependency tree representations of the T-H pairs (obtained using Minipar[5]);
- Tree Edit Distance + Depth Scheme (**TED+DS**);
- Tree Edit Distance + Width Scheme (**TED+WS**).

[4] Even though automatic pattern acquisition (from local corpora or from the Web) is an active research area, this aspect falls beyond the scope of this paper, and is left for future work.

[5] http://www.cs.ualberta.ca/~lindek/minipar.htm

	LCS	LD+DEF	TED+DEF	TED+DS	TED+WS	ALL	ALL+PS
Precision	0.557	0.724	0.687	0.693	0.802	0.832	0.860
Recall	0.233	0.521	0.470	0.468	0.501	0.592	0.633
F1	0.318	0.606	0.559	0.559	0.617	0.692	**0.729**

Table 2: *Performance of different configurations of the RTE system on the test set.*

The distances resulting from the previous configurations are also used as features to train a classifier with a Random Forest Learning algorithm[6], obtaining the last experimented configuration:

- **ALL** - to evaluate the potential of a combination of all distances.

Each configuration was trained on the training set (999 questions), and then run on the test set (488 questions). Table 2 reports the results achieved on the test set. Precision/Recall/F1 scores indicate the system's ability to recognize the relations expressed in the test questions. Considering these results, we can draw the following conclusions:

1. All the configurations of the system significantly outperform the baseline (LCS), showing that distance-based algorithms are more suitable to capture entailment relations than simple word matching techniques.

2. As far as the single distance-based algorithms are concerned, TED taken in isolation slightly improves over LD only in one case (TED+WS). In general, we observe that TED alone achieves lower recall than LD. This can be explained by the parser difficulties in processing questions, and handling some syntactic structures like conjunctions, appositions, and relative clauses. TED+WS performs better than the other TED configurations as it handles compound nouns and PP phrases more effectively (*i.e.* it assigns lower costs of deletion to words that connect the main verb with its complements). Consider, for instance, the following T-H pair:

Q7: *"Where can I see the movie* [Movie:*Shrek*] *?"*
p: *where can i see [*MOVIE*]*

In this case, to make the complete mapping between T and H, the edit distance algorithm has to delete from T the word *"movie"*, which is part of a compound noun phrase. Using TED+WS, the contribution of such edit operation to the overall entailment score of the T-H pair will be lower than in the other TED-based configurations.

3. In spite of a lower recall, TED+WS achieves higher precision than LD. This validates the hypothesis that, when T and H have similar structures, words with a higher number of children (*i.e.* those connecting the phrases of the sentence) are meaning preserving, and should have higher costs of insertion and deletion.

4. The best result, achieved by the combined configuration (ALL), demonstrates that the different combinations of distance algorithms and cost schemes cover different entailment phenomena, and together they improve over the baseline up to +117% (from 0.318 to 0.692 F1).

[6] Implemented in Weka: http://www.cs.waikato.ac.nz/ml/weka/

5. The combined configuration (ALL) achieves good results especially in terms of Precision. This is particularly important in view of the overall QA application, for which high precision is a requirement. The possibility of answering a question Q, in fact, depends on system's ability to avoid overspecified queries due to false positives in the RE phase (*i.e.* recognized relations that are not present in Q).

5.2 Pattern Selection

Another important aspect in our approach is the relation between the number of patterns available in the Pattern Repository, and the performance of the system under different configurations. On the one side, we could expect that the more the patterns, the less the workload of the RTE system. Under this hypothesis, larger amounts of patterns will increase the possibility of discovering entailment relations. On the other side, dealing with many patterns could affect system's performance, as they might reduce the distance between positive and negative examples for a given relation in the training phase. This happens, for instance, when one of the variants for a relation $R1$ has many words in common with a pattern for another relation $R2$. To investigate this aspect, a pattern selection process has been carried out to select, for each relation R, the subset of the available MRPs (from the *power set* P(S) of the patterns for R) with highest precision on the training set. The pattern selection process has been carried out for each system configuration, and evaluated on the test data.

The last column of Table 2 (**ALL+PS**) reports the highest result, achieved by the combined configuration. This result demonstrates the positive impact of the pattern selection process, with an F1 improvement of +5.34% (from 0.692 to 0.729). The performance increase in the combined configuration is due to improved F1 results under *all* the configurations (the F1 improvements for the single configurations, not reported in Table 2, range from +0.16% for TED+WS, to +6% for LD+DEF). The minimal increase achieved by TED+WS shows that, in general, such configuration makes a better use of the available patterns. Such conclusion is supported by Table 3, which reports the number of patterns discarded under each configuration. As can be seen, the pattern selection algorithm eliminates significantly more patterns for the LD-based configuration than for the TED-based ones. The discovered correlation between *i)* the variations in the number of patterns available, *ii)* the system's performance variations, and *iii)* the type of TE recognition algorithm used, shows that larger amounts of patterns can be profitably used only with more sophisticated (*i.e.* semantically oriented) algorithms.

LD+DEF	TED+DEF	TED+DS	TED+WS
74	48	48	46

Table 3: *Discarded MRPs in each system configuration.*

5.3 Extrinsic Evaluation: Impact on QA

The third experiment aims at estimating the impact of our TE-based approach to question analysis on the overall performance of a QA system. For this purpose, each relation R in the Pattern Repository (P) can be associated to an SQL query to the database. The idea is that the system will first try to establish an entailment relation between an input question and each of the MRPs in P. Then, the SQL queries associated to the relations for which entailed patterns have been found will be joined in a single query. Our assumption is that effective database queries depend on recognizing all and only the relevant domain relations expressed in a question. As shown in the example below (referring to a question Q expressing the relations $R1$, $R2$, and $R3$), four types of queries can be obtained depending on the output of the RE phase:

- Type 1 - $[R1, R2, R3]$. Optimal case: the question analysis component correctly recognized all and only the relations expressed in Q. The conjunction of the SQL query portions associated to the three relations will correctly constraint the query, allowing for exact answer retrieval.
- Type 2 - $[R1, R2]$. Underspecified query: the missing constraint (*i.e.* the SQL query associated to $R3$) will lead to answers in which the sought-after information might come with non-relevant information[7].
- Type 3 - $[R1, R2, R3, R4]$. Overspecified query: the conjunction of a spurious SQL query portion (associated to $R4$) will lead to an answer extraction failure.
- Type 4 - $[R1, R2, R4]$. Mixed situation, leading to an answer extraction failure.

Table 4 reports the distribution of the four query types over the 488 test questions, obtained by the best configuration of the system (ALL), with and without pattern selection. Such distribution reflects the high precision of our TE-based question analysis component, especially when pattern selection is applied. In this case, around 36.5% of the test questions (178 out of 488) fall in the optimal case and, more important, around 83% of the questions (408) fall in the first two types (which at least lead to answers containing the sought-after information). As far as pattern selection is concerned, it's worth noting how its contribution comes both in terms of more Type 1 queries, and in terms of less Type 4 queries.

[7] This, however, is a quite strong assumption. In some cases, in fact, missing relations do not affect the output of the system (*e.g.* given *"Who is the director of Casino Royale, today at Astra?"*, missing HASDATE(MOVIE,DATE), or HASMOVIESITE(MOVIE,SITE), will not affect answer retrieval.)

	Type 1	Type 2	Type 3	Type 4
ALL	164	232	20	72
ALL+PS	178	230	29	51

Table 4: *Query types distribution over 488 test questions.*

5.4 Evaluation over the RTE-3 Dataset

Our final experiment aims at better understanding the relationship between the general RTE task, as it is formulated within the Pascal-RTE Challenge, and the TE-based RE task here proposed. To compare the complexity of the two tasks the best configuration of our RTE system (ALL) has been trained and evaluated also on the RTE-3 dataset [6][8]. The resulting *63%* Accuracy roughly corresponds to the average performance of the systems participating in the challenge. Even though the two datasets are not comparable, the positive results achieved in both the evaluations demonstrate that systems designed for the general RTE task are perfectly suitable to address the problems posed by our application-oriented scenario.

6 Related Work

This section overviews related works, focusing on the differences between our approach and other TE-based approaches to QA and RE.

Question Answering. Several recent works document the use of TE as a mechanism for approximating the types of inference needed for QA. However, the QA subtasks addressed up to date (answer validation and ranking) differ completely from the problem discussed in the present work (question analysis). For instance, both in the Pascal-RTE Challenge, and in the CLEF-AVE task [10], the QA problem is modeled considering a question Q turned into an affirmative sentence as the hypothesis, and a text passage containing a candidate answer A as the text (*i.e.* systems have to decide whether A supports, or *entails*, Q). The same perspective is also adopted in [7], where TE is applied to filter and rank candidate answers returned by a QA system. While the application of TE for extracting relations in a given question is not documented in the QA field, similarities with our approach can be found in the RE area.

Relation Extraction. The most similar approach based on TE is described in [12], which reports experiments on a dataset of protein interactions. In spite of the similarities (*i.e.* the use of entailing templates for RE, and a syntax-based entailment checking), this approach differs from ours in several aspects. First, while [12] deals with a single relation, we consider a large number of possible target relations (*i.e.* 75), assuming that more than one relation can appear in a given question at the same time. Second, while [12]

[8] The Pascal-RTE3 dataset consists of 800 T-H pairs (the development set, which was used for training), and 800 T-H pairs (the test set, which was used for test).

deals with only one type of entities (*i.e.* proteins), in our multiple-relations scenario up to 27 entity types can participate in different relations. Finally, in [12] both the entities involved in the relation are given *a priori*, and the system has to decide whether, given two entities, they are involved in the relation or not. This assumption is not valid in our scenario, since it is not guaranteed that both the entities involved in a relation will appear in a given question.

7 Conclusions and Future Work

This paper addressed question analysis in the framework of QA over structured data, focusing on the task of extracting relations from a natural language question. We approached the problem by applying the notion of Textual Entailment to compare the input question with a repository of patterns representing different lexicalizations of the relevant relations in a given domain. The reported experiments demonstrate: *i)* the feasibility of the approach, *ii)* the correlation between the number of available patterns and the performance of different RTE algorithms, *iii)* the positive impact of our approach on the overall performance of a QA system, and *iv)* the suitability of systems designed for the general RTE task for the proposed application-oriented scenario.

Showing that even basic (general-purpose) RTE algorithms are suitable to address the task, our results motivate further research, with improved algorithms, along the same direction. Future work will thus concentrate on improving QA performance with more semantically oriented RTE algorithms. For example, enhanced cost schemes should apply *entailment rules* considering different features of the terms involved in the transformations, such as their *semantic similarity* (*e.g.* lower substitution costs for synonyms), and their *weight* (*e.g.* the insertion cost of a term t will be proportional to the number of relations whose patterns contain t). A complementary research direction is the automatic acquisition of relational patterns from the available dataset of questions. This will enhance the scalability of our approach (*i.e.* the possibility to enlarge the set of relevant domain relations), and its portability across domains.

References

[1] I. Androutsopoulos, G. Ritchie, and P. Thanisch. Natural Language Interfaces to Databases – An Introduction. *Journal of Natural Language Engineering*, 1(1), 1995.

[2] W. Bosma and C. Callison-Burch. Paraphrase Substitution for Recognizing Textual Entailment. In *Revised Selected Papers of CLEF 2006*, 2006.

[3] E. Cabrio, B. Coppola, R. Gretter, M. Kouylekov, B. Magnini, and M. Negri. Question Answering Based Annotation for a Corpus of Spoken Requests. In *Proceedings of the Workshop on Semantic Representation of Spoken Language SRSL07*, Salamanca, Spain, 2007.

[4] I. Dagan and O. Glickman. Generic Applied Modeling of Language Variability. In *Proceedings of the PASCAL Workshop on Learning Methods for Text Understanding and Mining*, Grenoble, France, 2004.

[5] I. Dagan, O. Glickman, and B. Magnini. The PASCAL Recognising Textual Entailment Challenge. In *Machine Learning Challenges (MLCW 2005)*, volume 3944 of *LNAI*. Springer-Verlag, 2006.

[6] D. Giampiccolo, B. Magnini, I. Dagan, and B. Dolan. The Third PASCAL Recognizing Textual Entailment Challenge. In *Proceedings of the ACL 2007 PASCAL Workshop on Textual Entailment and Paraphrasing*, Prague, Czech Republic, 2007.

[7] S. Harabagiu and A. Hickl. Methods for Using Textual Entailment in Open-Domain Question Answering. In *Proceedings of COLING/ACL 2006*, Sydney, Australia, 2006.

[8] M. Kouylekov and B. Magnini. Combining Lexical Resources with Tree Edit Distance for Recognizing Textual Entailment. In *Machine Learning Challenges (MLCW 2005)*, volume 3944 of *LNAI*. Springer-Verlag, 2006.

[9] M. Negri, M. Kouylekov, and B. Magnini. Detecting Expected Answer Relations through Textual Entailment. In *Proceedings of CICLing 2008*, Haifa, Israel, 2008.

[10] A. Penas, A. Rodrigo, V. Sama, and F. Verdejo. Overview of the Answer Validation Exercise 2006. In *Evaluation of Multilingual and Multi-modal Information Retrieval*, volume 4730 of *LNCS*. Springer-Verlag, 2006.

[11] A. Popescu, O. Etzioni, and H. Kautz. Towards a Theory of Natural Language Interfaces to Databases. In *Proceedings of the Conference on Intelligent User Interfaces*, Miami, Florida, 2003.

[12] L. Romano, M. Kouylekov, I. Szpektor, I. Dagan, and A. Lavelli. Investigating a Generic Paraphrase-based Approach for Relation Extraction. In *Proceedings of the 11th EACL Conference*, Trento, Italy, 2006.

[13] K. Zhang and D. Shasha. Fast Algorithm for the Unit Cost Editing Distance Between Trees. *Journal of Algorithms*, 11, December 1990.

A Semi-supervised Approach for Generating a Table-of-Contents

Viet Cuong Nguyen, Le Minh Nguyen, and Akira Shimazu
School of Information Science
Japan Advanced Institute of Science and Technology
1-1 Asahidai, Nomi, Ishikawa 923-1211, Japan
{cuongnv,nguyenml,shimazu}@jaist.ac.jp

Abstract

This paper presents a semi-supervised model for generating a table-of-contents as an indicative summarization. We mainly focus on using word cluster-based information derived from a large amount of unannotated data by an unsupervised algorithm. We integrate word cluster-based features into a discriminative structured learning model, and show that our approach not only increases the quality of the resulting table-of-contents, but also reduces the number of iterations in the training process. In the experiments, our model shows better results than the baseline model in generating a table-of-contents, about 6.5% improvement in terms of averaged ROUGE-L score.

Keywords

text generation, text summarization, semi-supervised learning

1 Introduction

In our research, to help people quickly having an overview of a topic or an event, we automatically collect articles from online newspapers related to that topic or event, and summarize them. We should be able to make a summarized document from those articles by extracting important sentences. However, there is a lot of articles with many useful information which makes the document too long as well as does not contain the deep comments of the authors of those articles about the topic or event. Our aim is to make a concise summary in the form of table-of-contents, automatically.

A table-of-contents is a hierarchical structure of titles and locations of segments in a very long text such as books or a set of texts such as multiple documents which describe the same topic [2]. It is a type of indicative summarization that is especially suited for locating and accessing information. With a table-of-contents as a navigation tool, a reader can quickly get not only an overview of the content of a very long text or multiple documents via the titles of segments, but also the location of needed information via the locations of segments.

The task of automatically generating a table-of-contents involves two subtasks: (1) separating every article into a hierarchical structure of segments (a tree of segments) and merge them to make a unique tree of segments [6, 11, 12, 15] and (2) generating a title for each segment in that tree to make a table-of-contents [1, 2]. In this paper, we focus on subtask two with the assumption that the tree of segments are easily got from existing methods such as *C99* [6] or *TextTiling* [11] with a text structuring method [5].

The subtask two is previously mentioned in [1, 2]. In [1], for each segment, they used the most important noun phrase based on its frequency to make the title of that segment. This method made the title too short and having very low quality. In [2], they made a better table-of-contents with a supervised learning method which accounts for a number of features at word level and word sequence level. However, in their experiments, a large amount of titles in the result table-of-contents were not related to the content of the corresponding segments. The lack of semantic information might be a reason. Moreover, their model required a large number of iterations in the training process.

In this paper, we propose a model that tries to integrate semantic information into the learning model which is based on [2]. With the support of semantic information, the new model could make the meaningful titles with strong relation to the content of the corresponding segments. Another motivation of our approach is to reduce the number of iterations in the training process [13, 16].

Our learning model is a two-stage semi-supervised learning model [16]. The semantic information used in our model is derived from word clusters which are, in turn, built from a large unannotated data by an unsupervised learning algorithm, the Brown algorithm [3]. After that, we use those word cluster-based information in a supervised learning model. The key of our approach is the way of integrating the word clustering information into the learning model. We encode word cluster-based information as features in a discriminative learning model. The learning algorithm used in this research is based on the Perceptron learning algorithm because of its simplicity, powerful and high speed. Especially, it is appropriate for structured learning tasks.

Our experiments show that, by incorporating word clustering information and using the same corpus, our model not only produces a better table-of-contents than baseline model, but also reduces the number of iterations in the training process. Our model even generated titles which is the same with original titles in the test data.

The remainder of this paper is structured as follows: Section 2 presents our approach on using a

International Conference RANLP 2009 - Borovets, Bulgaria, pages 312–317

structured learning model for generating a table-of-contents. Section 3 describes word clustering and the reason of using the word clustering information to support a supervised learning model. Section 4 designs features for the learning model and the way of incorporating word clustering information in our model. Section 5 presents our experimental results with discussion about the results. Section 6 gives some conclusions and future works.

2 The learning model

In this section, we mainly focus on the subtask of generating a table-of-contents from a tree of segments. In this task, automatically generating a table-of-contents can be seen as a structured learning task, in which the trained model produces a tree of titles $\mathcal{T}$ as the output from a tree of segments $\mathcal{S}$ as the input. $\mathcal{T}$ contains $\mathcal{T}_i$ that is the title of a segment $\mathcal{S}_i$ in $\mathcal{S}$.

We formulate this task as a two-steps structured learning. First, our algorithm learns a model for generating a title $\mathcal{T}_i$ from a segment $\mathcal{S}_i$. Second, our algorithm learns another model for generating a tree of titles $\mathcal{T}$ from a tree of segments $\mathcal{S}$.

A trivial algorithm for the second model is that we construct $\mathcal{T}$ from all $\mathcal{T}_i$ generated by the first model, separately. However, due to our experiments, this trivial algorithm produces a $\mathcal{T}$ with many duplicating titles at the same level in its hierarchical structure and this makes reader have confused. Therefore, we must use another learning algorithm to construct $\mathcal{T}$ from $\mathcal{T}_i$ which makes $\mathcal{T}$ more coherent, for example, without duplicating titles. In the Section 5, we will show the experimental results of the both algorithms.

To keep the learning process as simple as possible and to make the model easier in incorporating new features, we use an instance of the discriminative structured learning algorithm with the *LaSO* technique [10]. Due to this technique, the process of learning for generating a table of contents is as follow:

- First, for each text segment $\mathcal{S}_i$ in the tree of segments, our model learns to generate a list of candidate titles which are ranked by the scores which are the products of the weight vector of the model and the feature vectors of the $\mathcal{S}_i$ and the candidate titles.

- Second, our model learns to generate a table-of-contents from the candidate titles of segments which are produced by the above step. The scores are also computed by using another weight vector.

In this paper, the model used for the first learning step is called the local model and the second one is called the global model. The details of learning algorithm and decoding algorithm of the above two models are described in next sections.

2.1 The local model

In the learning step of the local model, a vine-growth strategy [10] is used to learn a model for generating a title for a text segment. The learning process simulates the process of building a title $\mathcal{T}_i$ incrementally from words inside a segment $\mathcal{S}_i$ as in Algorithm 1. To reduce the size of searching space, it maintains a beam $\mathcal{B}$ which contains partial titles. This strategy has been successfully applied in other tasks such as parsing [7], chunking [10], and machine translation [9].

Algorithm 1 Training algorithm for the local model

Input:
- $\mathcal{D} = \{(s,t)\}$ is a set of *(segment, title)*
- N is the number of iterations
- k is the beam size

Output:
- w_l is the weight vector of the local model

1: **for** $i = 1 \rightarrow N$ **do**
2:   **foreach** $(s,t) \in \mathcal{D}$ **do**
3:     **for** $j = 1 \rightarrow |t|$ **do**
4:       $\mathcal{B} = \text{GetTop}(\text{PartialGen}(s,\mathcal{B}),\text{k})$
5:       **if** $t[1..j] \notin \mathcal{B}$ **then**
6:         $w_l = w_l + f(s, t[1..j]) - \sum_{z \in \mathcal{B}} f(s,z)$
7:         $\mathcal{B} = \{t[1..j]\}$
8:       **end if**
9:     **end for**
10:   **end for**
11: **end for**
12: $w_l = w_l/(N * |\mathcal{D}|)$

In Algorithm 1, $\mathcal{D}$ contains a list of *(segment, title)* pairs (s,t) which is provided as the training data of the learning process. N is the number of iterations of the perceptron algorithm. At the line 4, $\mathcal{B}$ is a beam of partial titles. By using *PartialGen*, $\mathcal{B}$ is grown by appending every word in s into every title in $\mathcal{B}$ to make a list of titles of length j. After that, by using *GetTop*, $\mathcal{B}$ is pruned to contain top k ranked titles based on the scores $w_l \cdot f(s,z)$, $\forall z \in \mathcal{B}$. w_l is a weight vector of the perceptron model and the f is a function which produces a feature vector of a segment s and a partial title $t[1..j]$ which is a prefix of the title t with length of j words.

In the decoding step of the local model, Algorithm 2 will produce a list of candidate titles by incrementally generating titles from the words in the text segment. It uses a same strategy, beam search, in Algorithm 1 to reduce the size of searching space.

In Algorithm 2, s is the sequence of words w_i in the text segment, l is length of desired title of that segment. $\mathcal{B}$ is a beam containing partial titles which is similar to $\mathcal{B}$ in Algorithm 1. $\mathcal{Q}$ is a sorted list of the titles made by appending every word s_i into every title z_i of $\mathcal{B}$. The output of this algorithm is a list of k candidate titles that are the input of the global model.

2.2 The global model

In the learning step of the global model, the input is a tree of candidate titles, in which each node contains a list of k candidate titles, and the output is a tree of titles, in which each node contains a title. The input and the output of this model are hierarchical structure (a tree) which are different from the local model, a flat structure of words (a title).

Algorithm 2 Generating a list of candidate titles for a text segment

Input:
- s is the sequence of words in the text segment
- l is the length of desired title
- k is the beam size

Output:
- A list of k candidate titles.

$\mathcal{B}$ = a set that contains an empty string
for $i = 1$ to l **do**
  foreach $w_i \in s$ **do**
    $\mathcal{Q} = \{\}$
    foreach $z_i \in \mathcal{B}$ **do**
      $\mathcal{Q} = \mathcal{Q} + \{(z_i + w_i, w_l * f(s, z_i))\}$
    end for
    $\mathcal{B} = \{$top k partial titles of $\mathcal{Q}\}$
  end for
end for

In this model, we can still use a learning algorithm which is similar to the one used in the local model by traversing the tree of titles in pre-order. With this technique, we can also incrementally build the tree of titles.

In the training process, at each node of the tree in the traversing process, our algorithm create a beam $\mathcal{B}$ containing a list of partial trees ranked by the scores which are similarly computed as in the local model. Because the global model use those candidate titles returned by the local model, therefore, at some nodes, the true title may not be among the candidate titles. In this cases, our algorithm chooses the best title in those candidate titles which is closest to the title of the corresponding segment in the training data by using ROUGE-1 score[1]. The output of this learning step is a weight vector w_g.

In the decoding step, we use the same strategy as in the local model. We incrementally generate the tree of titles by traversing the tree in pre-order with beam search strategy. However, the output of this step is a tree of titles which is called a table-of-contents.

3 Word Clustering

In this research, we use word clustering information to make the learning model take into account semantic information, in terms of the word similarity. With this information, we can choose better words which are semantically related for generating titles of segments in the table-of-contents. For example, normally, "tree" is no more similar to "graph" than "plant". However, by using word clusters derived from a large amount of text in computer science, "graph" and "tree" may have semantic relations. This approach is successful on other natural language processing tasks such as name-entity recognition [16] and dependency parsing [13].

To get the word clusters, we use the Brown algorithm described in [3]. This is a bottom-up agglomerative clustering algorithm which is used to produce

[1] ROUGE-1 computes the number of overlapping words of two word sequences.

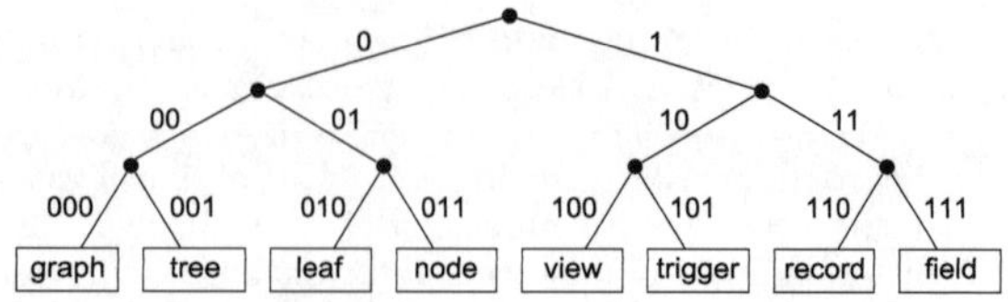

Fig. 1: *An example of a Brown word cluster tree. Each word at the leaf is encoded by a binary string with respect to the path from the root, where 0 indicates a left branch and 1 indicates a right branch*

a hierarchical cluster of words. The input of this algorithm is a large sequence of words and the output is a binary tree, in which leaves of the tree are words. Every word in this tree is uniquely identified by a path from a root. This path is encoded by a binary string, where 0 indicates a left branch and 1 indicates a right branch. For example, in Figure 1, "tree" is encoded by "001", "node" is encoded by "011" and so on.

In the word cluster tree, by selecting an inner node of the tree, we have a set of leaves of the corresponding subtree. Therefore, we have a set of words semantically related which forms a word cluster. This cluster is also identified by a path from the root to the chosen inner node. For example, in Figure 1, we might select three clusters {graph, tree} encoded by "00", {leaf, node} encoded by "01" and {view, trigger, record, field} encoded by "1".

4 Feature Design

The features are divided into two sets. The first set is used for the local model. It contains the features that capture selection constrains at word level and contextual constrains at word sequence level. The selection features in the model captures word information of a text segment, which are:

- The position of the word;
- The TF*IDF value of the word;
- The part-of-speech tag of the word;
- Whether the parent segment contains that word and its position;
- Whether the sibling segments contain that word and its position;
- The word cluster information of the word.

To use the word cluster-based information, we encoded each word cluster in a unique code with respect to the binary string described in previous section. A word cluster-based feature is an indicative function which has a value 1 if the current word is in the corresponding cluster and a value 0 otherwise. It is an interesting point of our approach.

The contextual features record bi-gram and tri-gram language model scores, both for words and POS tags. To eliminate generic phrases from the generated titles, such as "*the following section*", it also captures

111011011101	microcomputer
111011011101	peripheral
111011011101	minicomputer
111011011101	magnetic
111011011101	PC
111011011101	computer
....	
01101010	Dijkstra
01101010	Clanton
01101010	Rooney
01101010	Nakagama
01101010	Shannon
....	
011001011010	Japan
011001011010	Colombia
011001011010	Austria
011001011010	Russia
011001011010	Brazil
....	

Fig. 2: *Examples of word clusters derived from BLLIP corpus*

the collocational properties of noun phrases in the title.

In the global model, to avoid duplicating titles of the segments in the same section and to make them more coherent, we use some types of features that describe interaction between different titles. The first type is for title redundancy that includes title duplication and title similarity. The second type is for capturing parallel construction of titles of segments in the same section. For example, in the section describing sorting algorithms, we may see some titles of subsections with the same prefix such as "*Bubble sort algorithm*" and "*Quick sort algorithm*". The last type of features is to take into account the process of selecting the best title in the list of candidate titles at every node of the table-of-contents. It helps to choose a better title in the list of ranked titles produced by the local model.

5 Experiments

5.1 Data

In our experiments, we used two dataset. The first dataset is a large sequence of words used for Brown algorithm to derive word clusters. The second dataset is a table-of-contents readily in a books used for learning model.

To build word clusters, we used the BLLIP corpus [4], which contains a collection of three-year Wall Street Journal (WSJ) from the ACL/DCI corpus with approximately 30 million words. All the text is cleaned, separated into sentences and joined into a large text file. The Brown algorithm ran on that cleaned text to produce 1000 clusters. Figure 2 shows some result word clusters with their code (binary string) and some words in those clusters. In these word clusters, the words related to PC hardware are grouped into a cluster, the countries' name are grouped into a cluster and so on.

We used the content and the table-of-contents of the textbook "*Introduction to Algorithm*" [8] as the corpus for the learning model which is the same as [2]. However, we used Charniak's tool[2] to get part-of-speech information for words in the book.

We considered the table-of-contents of the above book as a collection of smaller table-of-contents. In this book, parts are at level 1, chapters are at level 2, sections are at level 3 and so on. Level 1 is removed to make a set of trees of titles which have root at level 2 of the original tree. With this technique, we had 39 trees and 540 titles to used as training and testing data. The average depth of trees is 4.

We randomly choose 80% of these trees for training and the rest for testing. In our experiments, we choose ten different randomizations and get the average score to make the experiments fairly.

5.2 Evaluation

In our experiments, we used ROUGE scores[3] with the default settings as the measure of performance. It contains ROUGE-1, ROUGE-L and ROUGE-W used to compute similarity score between candidate title and original title [14].

- ROUGE-1 is based on 1-gram overlapping between two titles.
- ROUGE-L is based on longest common subsequence of two titles.
- ROUGE-W is based on weighted longest common subsequence of two titles.

We did two type of experiments. In the first type, the models generated table-of-contents without hierarchical constrains described in Section 2. And in the second type, the models used hierarchical constrains to generate table of contents.

In both two type of experiments, we did three experiments. In the first experiment, the baseline model was trained and tested with the best configuration which is published on the web [2]. The local model was trained in 50 iterations and the global model was trained in 200 iterations. This experiment is denoted by BS. The beam size used in the local model and the global model were 50 and 250, respectively.

In the second experiment, we ran our model on the same configuration with the baseline model. This experiment is denoted by EX1.

We ran our model in a series of experiments with different configurations. The best result was reported in the third experiment. In this experiment, the local model was trained in 10 iterations and the global model was trained in 40 iterations. The size of beams used in the local model and the global model were the same to the baseline model. This experiment is denoted by EX2.

Every experiment was done with 10 randomizations. The experimental results were averaged based on three ROUGE scores: ROUGE-1, ROUGE-L and ROUGE-W.

[2] http://www.cs.brown.edu/~ec/#software
[3] http://berouge.com

Original:	Baseline:	Our model:
hash tables	many dictionaries	dictionary operations
direct address tables	direct address dictionary	direct address table
hash tables	computer address	hash function
collision resolution by chaining	chaining a same slot	chaining all the elements
analysis of hashing with chaining	creating an same chaining hash	hash table with load factor
open addressing	address hash	address hash
linear probing	hash probing	hash function
quadratic probing	quadratic hash	quadratic probing
double hashing	double hash	double hashing

Fig. 3: *Fragments of the table-of-contents generated by our model and the baseline model*

	ROUGE-1	ROUGE-L	ROUGE-W
BS	0.235	0.215	0.169
EX1	0.236	0.216	0.169
	+0.001	+0.001	0.000
EX2	**0.292**	**0.281**	**0.222**
	+0.057	**+0.066**	**+0.053**

Table 1: *In these experiments, the features that captures hierarchical constrains were not used*

	ROUGE-1	ROUGE-L	ROUGE-W
BS	0.246	0.226	0.178
EX1	0.252	0.231	0.182
	+0.006	+0.005	+0.004
EX2	**0.301**	**0.290**	**0.229**
	+0.055	**+0.064**	**+0.076**

Table 2: *In these experiments, we used the features that help to avoid duplicate titles and make titles more coherent*

The results of the first type of experiments are shown on Table 1. Table 2 contains the results of the second type of experiments.

In Figure 3, we show a subtree of table-of-contents of the original table-of-contents and the table-of-contents generated by the baseline model to compare with the table-of-contents generated by our model. In EX2, the averaged number of exact match titles is 13.

5.3 Discussion

Our experiments show that word clustering information is useful in generating a table-of-contents task. It could be also useful in the title generation task in general. By using this information as features in a discriminative learning model, we can not only improve the quality of generated table-of-contents and reduce the number of iterations in training process.

In terms of quality, by using word clustering information, it reduces the sparsity of data, thereby, it makes our model to be better at setting the parameter values. Moreover, word cluster-based features help the model choose the words that are semantically related even those words did not occur in the training data. In our experiments, our model gets higher results than the baseline model, about 6.5%. A fragment of the generated table-of-contents in Figure 3 is an example of the better quality of our model. For example, "*dictionary operations*" is close to "*hash tables*" than "*many dictionaries*". It also has some generated titles that match with the original titles.

In terms of speed, with additional semantic information derived from word clustering, the model converges faster, therefore, the number of iterations are reduced in the training process, about 5 times in our experiments.

The word cluster in our experiments was derived from the BLLIP corpus that is a general corpus (multi-domains). Therefore, its could be used without re-generate word clusters. However, the training data, which is a book about algorithm, should be replaced by suitable data. For example, we can use Reuters corpus, which contains articles and their titles, to generate a table-of-contents for a set of news articles.

In this research, the Brown word clustering algorithm uses only correlation of words at the sentence level. However, to generate a title for a document, we need the correlation of words at the document level. This problem could be solved by using topic information by using topic modeling. This should be an extension of this research.

6 Conclusion

We presented a two-stage semi-supervised learning approach for generating a table-of-contents automatically. The main contribution is to use semantic information derived from word clusters in a discriminative learning model to generate titles which have strong relations to the corresponding segments. It helps our model not only makes a better table-of-contents but also reduces the number of iterations in training process. This method could be successfully applied in other NLP tasks which requires semantic information of the text, such as summarization, machine translation and so on.

References

[1] R. Angheluta, R. D. Busser, and M.-F. Moens. The use of topic segmentation for automatic summarization. In *In Workshop on Text Summarization in Conjunction with the ACL 2002 and including the DARPA/NIST sponsored DUC 2002*

Meeting on Text Summarization, pages 11–12, Philadelphia, Pennsylvania, USA, 2002.

[2] S. R. K. Branavan, P. Deshpande, and R. Barzilay. Generating a table-of-contents. In *Proceedings of the 45th Annual Meeting of the Association of Computational Linguistics*, pages 544–551, Prague, Czech Republic, 2007.

[3] P. F. Brown, P. V. Desouza, R. L. Mercer, and J. C. Lai. Class-based n-gram models of natural language. *Computational Linguistics*, 18(4):467–479, 1992.

[4] E. Charniak, D. Blaheta, N. Ge, K. Hall, J. Hale, and M. Johnson. *BLLIP 1987-89 WSJ Corpus Release 1*. Linguistic Data Consortium, 2000.

[5] E. Chen, B. Snyder, and R. Barzilay. Incremental text structuring with online hierarchical ranking. In *Proceedings of the 2007 Joint Conference on Empirical Methods in Natural Language Processing and Computational Natural Language Learning*, pages 83–91, Prague, Czech, 2007.

[6] F. Y. Y. Choi. Advances in domain independent linear text segmentation. In *Proceedings of NAACL '00*, pages 26–33, Seattle, USA, 2000.

[7] M. Collins and B. Roark. Incremental parsing with the perceptron algorithm. In *Proceedings of the 42nd Meeting of the Association for Computational Linguistics (ACL'04), Main Volume*, pages 111–118, Barcelona, Spain, 2004.

[8] T. H. Cormen, C. E. Leiserson, R. L. Rivest, and C. Stein. *Introduction to Algorithms*. The MIT Press, Cambridge, Massachusetts, second edition, 2001.

[9] B. Cowan, I. Kučerová, and M. Collins. A discriminative model for tree-to-tree translation. In *Proceedings of the 2006 Conference on Empirical Methods in Natural Language Processing*, pages 232–241, Sydney, Australia, 2006.

[10] H. Daumé III and D. Marcu. Learning as search optimization: Approximate large margin methods for structured prediction. In *International Conference on Machine Learning (ICML)*, Bonn, Germany, 2005.

[11] M. A. Hearst. Texttiling: Segmenting text into multi-paragraph subtopic passages. *Computational Linguistics*, 23(1):33–64, 1997.

[12] X. Ji and H. Zha. Domain-independent text segmentation using anisotropic diffusion and dynamic programming. In *SIGIR '03: Proceedings of the 26th annual international ACM SIGIR conference on Research and development in information retrieval*, pages 322–329, Toronto, Canada, 2003.

[13] T. Koo, X. Carreras, and M. Collins. Simple semi-supervised dependency parsing. In *Proceedings of ACL-08: HLT*, pages 595–603, Columbus, Ohio, USA, 2008.

[14] C.-Y. Lin. Rouge: A package for automatic evaluation of summaries. In *Proceedings of the Workshop on Text Summarization Branches Out (WAS 2004)*, pages 25–26, Barcelona, Spain, 2004.

[15] I. Malioutov and R. Barzilay. Minimum cut model for spoken lecture segmentation. In *Proceedings of the 21st International Conference on Computational Linguistics and 44th Annual Meeting of the Association for Computational Linguistics*, pages 25–32, Sydney, Australia, 2006.

[16] S. Miller, J. Guinness, and A. Zamanian. Name tagging with word clusters and discriminative training. In *HLT-NAACL 2004: Main Proceedings*, pages 337–342, Boston, Massachusetts, USA, 2004.

Towards efficient production of linguistic resources: the *Victoria* Project

Lionel Nicolas⋆, Miguel A. Molinero◇, Benoît Sagot⊕,
Elena Sánchez Trigo•, Éric de La Clergerie⊕, Miguel Alonso Pardo◇,
Jacques Farré⋆, Joan Miquel Vergés•.

⋆ Équipe RL, Laboratoire I3S, UNSA+CNRS, France	{lnicolas,jf}@i3s.unice.fr
◇ Grupo LYS, Univ. de A Coruña, España	mmolinero@udc.es
⊕ Projet ALPAGE, INRIA Rocquencourt + Paris 7, France	{benoit.sagot, Eric.De_La_Clergerie}@inria.fr
• Grupo Cole, Univ. de Vigo, España	{etrigo,jmv}@uvigo.es, alonso@udc.es

Abstract

In order to produce efficient Natural Language Processing (NLP) tools, reliable linguistic resources are a preliminary requirement. When available for a given language, the resources are generally far below the expectations in terms of quality, coverage or usability. This paper presents a project whose ambition is to enhance the production capacities of linguistic resources through the creation and intensive use of interconnected acquisition and correction tools, inter-lingual transfer processes and a collaborative online development framework.

1 Introduction

The efficiency and linguistic relevance of most NLP tools depends directly or indirectly on the quality and coverage of the resources they rely on. For major languages such as Spanish and French, many well known and widely used resources are still in a precarious state of development. For languages with a smaller speech community, such as Galician[1], they are generally non-existent.

Such an absence is a direct consequence of the cost induced by their development: their complexity and/or size makes their manual improvement a labor-intensive, complex and error prone task requiring massive expert work.

Such an important effort could obviously be balanced by sharing it among several people or groups interested in those resources. Nevertheless, long-term collaboration can be problematic for license, management, distance, time or financial reasons. Thus, linguistic resources are generally developed in a somewhat isolated way.

Owing to these issues, building linguistic resources takes years of constant effort which often fails to achieve visible or useful results. Therefore, quick and efficient acquisition and correction of linguistic resources is an unsolved problem of considerable interest to the NLP community.

In order to face it, the *Victoria* project aims at:

- First and foremost, developing a chain of tools automatizing the acquisition and correction processes in order to reduce labor work and enhance the quality, homogeneity, connectivity and coverage of the linguistic resources produced.
- Exploring inter-lingual transfer processes of linguistic knowledge in order to build or upgrade resources for a given language taking advantage of similar resources formalizing other linguistically related languages.
- Allowing people to combine their efforts through a shared web development framework.

These three objectives are dedicated to the more general goal of producing and providing freely available high-quality linguistic resources.

In its current state of development, the project focuses on the resources necessary to build symbolic syntactic parsers[2] for French, Spanish and Galician. As a long term goal, the project will extend to other kinds of resource and other Romance languages.

The main contributions of this paper are the following:

1. It exposes a strategy with several guidelines that may be reused for other projects with similar objectives.
2. It reports the viability of transferring some formalized linguistic knowledge between two related languages.
3. It presents theoretical and generic techniques to sequentially and incrementally detect and correct shortcomings in linguistic resources.
4. It lists the tools, techniques and resources that have already been produced.

This paper is organized as follows. In section 2, we shortly introduce the project itself and briefly recall the past and existing projects with common points to ours. In section 3 and section 4, we explain our strategy for enhancing the production capacities. We then detail in section 5 what has been achieved and what is still ongoing. Finally, in section 6, we detail our future orientations and developments and conclude in section 7.

2 Overview

This project brings together researchers from the computer science field and researchers from the human translation field of four different French and Spanish teams. The

[1] A co-official language spoken in the north-west of Spain.

[2] Morphological rules, morpho-syntactic lexicons and lexicalised grammar.

International Conference RANLP 2009 - Borovets, Bulgaria, pages 318–323

COLE team (Grupo COLE) from the Univ. of Vigo, the LYS team (Grupo Lys) from the Univ. of A Coruña, the Alpage project (Projet Alpage) from the Univ. of Paris 7 and the INRIA Institute of Rocquencourt and the RL team (Équipe RL) from the I3S laboratory of the Univ. of Nice Sophia Antipolis and the CNRS Institute.

The project officially started in November 2008 thanks to the financiation of the Galician Goverment (INCITE08PXIB302179PR, INCITE08E1R104022ES).

2.1 Related projects

There have been various projects aiming at building lexical resources for a large spectrum of languages. The most famous are probably the MULTEXT project[3] and its follow-up MULTEXT-East.[4] Other projects focused on specification, standardization and/or development of lexical resources, such as GENELEX , EAGLES and PAROLE.

As for the syntactic level, the DELPHIN project[5] based on the LKB framework as well as the AGFL project[6] have permitted the creation of various formalized grammars. Some other existing projects, such as LinGO Grammar Matrix[7], explore the possibility of sharing formalized linguistic knowledge among several resources in different languages.

The ongoing CLARIN[8] and FLARENET[9] initiatives aim at managing and bringing under a common framework many existing resources.

Obviously, describing each project is a complex task that would fall beyond the scope of this paper. We shall just highlight that, in most cases, resources have been built with little (or no) computer aid. So far, we are not aware of any large-scale project regarding automatic acquisition of linguistic information from plain corpora. This causes a common situation where the resources are developed until a (more or less) advanced state of development where it becomes difficult to find errors/deficiencies manually. Then, they usually get stuck and do not evolve much.

Furthermore, manual development is one of the main reasons for the poor (free) availability of the resources. Indeed, manual development greatly increases the cost of development, which sometimes prevents resources from being freely distributed.

2.2 Guidelines of the project

By studying the weaknesses and strengths of related projects, we established several guidelines to achieve our objectives. Those guidelines, detailed in section 3 and 4, can be resumed as follows:

- In order to allow collaborative work, easily accessible online consultation and edition interfaces should be available for every kind of resource produced.
- So as to maximize feedback, the resources shall always be under non-restrictive public open-source distribution license in order to avoid restricting their availability.
- In order not to limit the scope of the project to a particular set of languages or tools, the formalisms used to describe the resources shall be as general as possible.
- Existing available resources should always be considered when upgrading a particular resource, including those describing another language.
- Tools automatizing the processes of detection and correction of linguistic resources are an absolute necessity when aiming toward for the construction of high quality linguistic resources.
- The tools developed shall use as input plain text which is daily produced for most languages.

3 Enhancing collaborative work, availability and usability

To our knowledge, there are three reasons that may limit collaborative work.

First, it is unusual to find resources with dedicated consultation or edition interfaces. Manual edition is often error-prone since humans can make typing errors or introduce incoherent data. Thus, collaborative work is generally restricted to a smaller number of skilled persons.

Second, collaborative work can be limited if it cannot be achieved from anywhere.

Third, collaborative work can be technically restrained by some operating systems or platforms.

In order to prevent edition errors and allow users to focus on the data themselves without worrying about the underlying formalism, we are willing to develop a dedicated query and management interface for every resource and technique output. In order to overcome distance troubles, every dedicated interface shall be accessible online. So as to avoid technical problems that could restrain access, all interfaces shall be developed with stable Web technologies handled by most web browsers without additional installations.

In order to maximize feedback and federate people with linguistic skills around the common beneficial goal of providing high-quality resources for everybody, all formalized linguistic knowledge should be available to anybody willing to consult, use or collaborate in its development. The availability of the produced techniques, formalisms and resources by the *Victoria* project in terms of access, modification and distribution is guaranteed by a non-restrictive public open-source distribution. Such an objective is fulfilled thanks to non-restrictive public licenses like LGPL-LR[10] and CeCILL-C.[11]

In order to maximize the usability[12] of the resources produced, the choice of the most suitable formalisms has been made according to the following principles:

- Since the combined use of resources is usually a requirement when designing advanced NLP tools, all the formalisms designed and used should be general and extensible enough to permit combined uses.

[3] http://aune.lpl.univ-aix.fr/projects/MULTEXT/
[4] http://nl.ijs.si/ME/
[5] http://wiki.delph-in.net/moin/LkbTop
[6] http://www.agfl.cs.ru.nl/
[7] http://www.delph-in.net/matrix/
[8] http://www.clarin.eu
[9] http://www.flarenet.eu/

[10] Lesser General Public License for Linguistic Resources
[11] LGPL-compatible, http://www.cecill.info/.
[12] By usability, we mean the capacity of the resource to be integrated in NLP tools or applied to a particular language

- Foreseeing the exhaustive list of those uses is simply impossible. Therefore, it is essential for the formalisms to be compared to various kind of languages and practical tools in order to adapt and extend them.

- The formalisms need to be regularly maintained so as to guarantee their extension to uncovered phenomena.

In order to develop our morphological and lexical resources, we chose to use the Alexina framework [7, 8, 2]. This framework, which is compatible with the LMF standard [3] represents morphological and syntactic information in a complete, efficient and readable fashion. The Alexina model is based on a two-level representation distinguishing the description of a lexicon from its use. The intensional level, used for an efficient description, factorizes the lexical information by associating each lemma with a morphological class and deep syntactic information (a deep subcategorization frame, a list of possible restructurations, and other syntactic features such as information on control, attributes, mood of sentencial complements, etc.). The extensional level, used in practice by tools, is generated automatically by *compiling* the intensional lexicon thanks to the morphological rules. It associates each inflected form with a detailed structure that represents all its morphological and syntactic information: morphological tag, surface subcategorization frame corresponding to one particular redistribution, and other syntactic features. Alexina has already been used to develop morpho-syntactic wide-coverage lexicons for French, Spanish, Slovak and Polish and has been combined with syntactic parsers based on commonly used grammatical formalisms (TAG and LFG).

Regarding grammatical knowledge, our resources rely on a meta-grammar formalism [1] which represents the syntactic rules of a language in a hierarchical structure of classes. The classes on top of the hierarchy define general concepts as Part-of-Speech (noun, verb, etc.) and their possible attributes. Classes are then refined while descending towards the bottom of the hierarchy, adding constraints, allowed/forbidden constructions, etc. This meta-grammar formalism is theoretically compilable in most commonly used grammar formalisms. In practice, we compile our grammars into a hybrid TAG/TIG parser. Such a generic formalism is extremely useful since it permits an easy adaptation of an existing grammar to a linguistically related language. For example, Romance languages, which include major languages (Spanish, French, Italian, Portuguese, etc.) and many others with smaller speech communities (Galician, Catalan, Occitan, Sardinian, etc.), are very similar in terms of syntactic behaviors. Hence, many definitions, constraints and rules can be reused when building a new grammar for another related language. It is worth noting that the outputs produced by our parser are dependency trees.

4 Enhancing extension/correction

4.1 Using existing resources

Existing resources are generally valuable sources of data when building new resources or extending others. Ignoring the great efforts invested in order to build existing resources does not seem reasonable or productive. Such an approach depends on the resource and the kind of data one is trying to adapt. Nevertheless, various practical experiments (see sect. 5.3.2 and [2]), have shown that existing resource usually share common points. Adapting a large part of the available existing resources is often a reasonable objective.

4.1.1 Interlingual transfer processes

Since related languages share large parts of their linguistic knowledge, we do not restrict the scope of this approach to a single language and consider the existing resources describing other related languages. Such an approach is especially beneficial when working on languages with smaller speech communities and limited digital resources. It also facilitates the establishment of interlingual links required for multilingual tasks. Informally, we could say that the proximity between linguistically related languages can be used to "transfer" formalized knowledge from one resource to another.

In order to achieve such a task, one should consider separately the formalisms and the formalized knowledge.

Extending/adapting the formalisms used to describe a given language to a related one is generally fast. This statement has been verified in practice when building new resources for Spanish from French ones (see sect. 5.3)

Transferring linguistic knowledge depends on the kind of knowledge we are dealing with.

Transferring morphological knowledge seems improbable. Applying the morphological rules of a language to a related one seems risky; we have not considered it so far.

Regarding lexical knowledge, the following idea seems promising: whoever has learned two common-rooted languages must have realized that many "direct" translations are effective, i.e., it seems possible to apply a basic morphological alignment to translate some words. This concept, similar to cognates, is known as very delicate. Nevertheless, when studied more closely, this statement seems to apply mainly to less frequent words since they are generally the ones that have evolved the least from the root language (Latin in our case). For example, an infrequent word ending with *-tion* in French can often be translated by a word ending with *-ción* in Spanish.

As regards grammatical knowledge, grammars are abstract and static enough to not evolve much. Consequently, a grammar designed for French could be used as a starting point to build a grammar for a related language such as Spanish (see sect. 5.3). In addition, since many grammar rules are shared by both grammars, establishing interlingual syntactic links between constructions results easier. Such an approach is already effective for French and Spanish (see sect. 5.3). The results should even be further enhanced when considering Spanish with other Iberian languages such as Galician.

4.2 Using correction and extension processes

We now describe a generic approach which has been abstracted from practical research results described essentially in [9] and [5].

In order to efficiently produce new formalized knowledge, a source of data is needed to detect and acquire the missing knowledge. Since this source should be available in sufficient quantity for any language, we have discarded annotated data[13] which is only available in limited quantities for a small number of languages, and opted for plain digital text which is daily produced for most languages.

In order to extend and correct a resource from plain text, we apply the following two-step generic approach:

- identify as accurately as possible which part of the text is not covered by a resource,
- generate corrections for the detected shortcomings and rank them in order to prepare an easier manual validation.

We now present generic approaches to achieve these two steps. Practical implementations have already proved to be effective in practice (see sect. 5.2).

4.2.1 Identifying shortcomings in a resource

Identifying possible shortcomings in a studied resource can be achieved by studying unexpected/incorrect behaviors of some tools relying on the resource. To do so, one needs first to establish what can be considered as unexpected (incorrect) behavior. Once identified, one must ensure they are not due to some incorrect data given as input or some other resource the tool relies on.

The first situation can easily be avoided by giving as input corpora considered as linguistically correct (error-free), i.e., the corpora one wants the resources to cover. We use law texts and some selected journalistic productions and discard corpora we consider as having a poor quality, like those composed of emails.

The second situation, i.e., when the tool relies on various resources, can be solved through a global study of the unexpected behaviors. Indeed, natural languages are ambiguous and thus, difficult to formalize. Nevertheless, this ambiguity has the advantage of being randomly distributed on the different aspects of a language. Depending on the state of development of the resources, it can be truly rare for two resources to be incorrect at the same time for a given element, i.e., many unexpected behaviors can be induced by only one resource at a time. In a restricted scope, it is difficult and hazardous to identify a culprit for a given unexpected behavior. However, such an aspect can be balanced by a global study of the behaviors when processing a massive set of text. Indeed, if among the elements of a given resource, some are always found when unexpected behaviors occur, then such an element can be (statistically) suspected to be incorrectly described in the resource.

For example, in [9], the authors are looking for shortcomings in a lexicon. The tool they observe is a syntactic parser and parse failures are considered as unexpected behaviors of the parser. Each parse failure can be due to deficiencies of the grammar and/or of the lexicon the parser relies on. Determining for a given parse failure which resource is the true culprit can be utterly complex. In order to detect incorrect lexical entries, the authors use a fixed point algorithm which emphasizes the lexical forms that occur more than expected in non parsable sentences.

When doing so, one must keep in mind that:

1. enough plain text should be provided as input in order to ensure the validity of the statistics,
2. the statistical models might make assumptions keeping the computations within certain limits and produce irrelevant suspicions. In order to balance this aspect, we generally designed our techniques in a *semi-automatic* fashion implying a human post-validation.

4.2.2 Generating relevant corrections

As explained earlier, it may be rare for two resources A and B jointly used to be incorrect at the same time and thus be both responsible for a given unexpected behavior. Hence, if we believe resource A to be responsible for an unexpected behavior, we can often rely on resource B to generate relevant corrections. Of course, the kind of corrections depends on the data the resources interact on, i.e., not every pair of resources are suitable for this purpose.

For example, a grammar that interacts with the syntactic part of a lexicon can be used to generate corrections for it while morphological rules clearly cannot. In [5], the authors use a grammar to guess corrections for a lexicon.

Another highly convenient feature is the following: if resource B cannot be used any longer to provide relevant corrections for resource A, we can consider the left-over unexpected behaviors as mostly representing shortcomings of resource B since it does not cover them. We thus obtain an incremental and sequential way to obtain for both resources corpora representing mostly their shortcomings. Thus, correcting resource A thanks to resource B generate useful data to correct resource B. Once resource B corrected, it is possible to correct resource A. And so on.

For example, in [5], the improvement of a lexicon thanks to a grammar is limited by the quality of the grammar used. Nevertheless, the authors expose that the non-parsable part of the corpus used to guess lexical correction has become globally representative of shortcomings of the grammar. This corpus can then be used to update the grammar. Once the grammar is updated, the corpus can be used again to correct the lexicon. And so on.

5 Results

5.1 Online development framework

The recently created (incomplete) online development framework[14] aims at allowing collaborative work. In order to fulfill such a goal, it is essential to offer dedicated interfaces to consult, manage and download the resources. So far we have concentrated our efforts on developing a dedicated interface for morpho-syntactic wide-coverage lexicons which, among the three kinds of resources developed, is clearly the one requiring most collaborative work.

The current version of this interface allows us to search for entries with logical equations, consult and edit the data related to the matched entries, and trace the changes.

5.2 Techniques

According to the ideas explained in section 4.2, we established a conceptual map of a sequential chain of tools (see figure 1) which aims at helping to upgrade from plain text, in a semi automatic fashion, all the basic components of a symbolic syntactic parser, namely, morphological rules, morpho-syntactic lexicons and lexicalised grammars.

[13] we actually consider it as an existing resource, see sect 4.1

[14] soon available at `http://www.victoria-project.org`

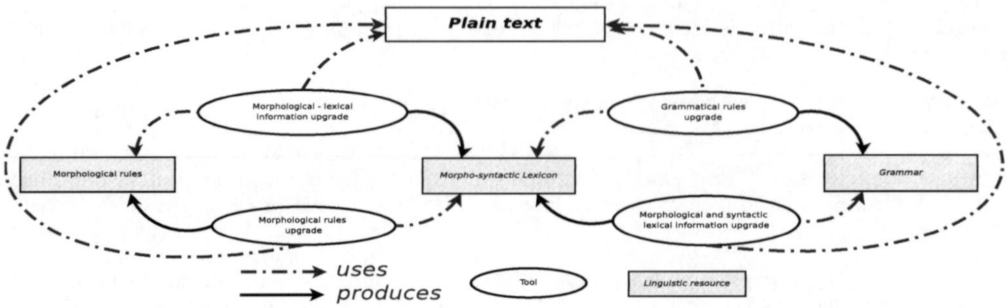

Fig. 1: *conceptual map of the semi-automatic upgrade of linguistic resources*

5.2.1 Morphological lexical information improvement

To achieve this task, we apply the technique described in [6] where the observed tool is a lexicon access system, the unexpected behaviors are the absence of some lexical forms, and the resources A and B are morphological rules and the morphological data of a morpho-syntactic lexicon.

The morphological rules are used to predict hypothetical lemmas for all forms of a corpus missing in the lexicon. A statistical fixed-point algorithm is used to rank the hypothetical lemmas according to the number of inflected forms found in the corpus. The manual validation of the best ranked lemmas improves the coverage of the lexicon and increases the quality of subsequent executions.

5.2.2 Syntactic lexical information improvement

To achieve this task, we apply the technique described in [5] where the tool observed is a syntactic parser, the unexpected behaviors are parsing failures, and the resources A and B are a morpho-syntactic lexicon and a grammar.

In order to correct and extend a lexicon, the authors firstly detect lexical forms suspected to be responsible for some parse failures thanks to two techniques.

A statistical computation which emphasizes "suspicious" lexical forms present more frequently than the rest in non-parsable sentence [10]. Lexical forms are even more "suspicious" if present in non-parsable along with forms "cleared" by their presence in parsable ones [9].

A tagger-based approach which highlights absent entries by relying on the tagger's ability to guess a tag for unknown words and forcing the tagger to use it on forms that are in fact known. If the tag answered represents data absent in the lexicon, the form is suspected.

Once the suspicious forms have been identified, the authors rely on the grammar to generate lexical corrections for the identified forms. To achieve this task, they study the expectations of a grammar for the identified forms in non-parsable sentences, i.e., they observe what lexical information would have not led to conflicts with the grammar rules and would have permitted syntactic parses. Such a goal is fulfilled by underspecifying the lexical restrictions of the suspected form in order to allow the parse to explore originally non explored grammar rules. They later extract from the parse outputs the information assigned to the suspected form and translate it back to the lexicon's format.

5.2.3 Morphological rules acquisition from a lexicon

As explained earlier in section 3, the Alexina framework employed to describe our lexicons requires morphological rules to be functional. In order to create lexicons for both Spanish and Galician (see sect. 5.3.2) and according to our statement to always consider using existing resources to build or upgrade new ones, we used the following idea to extract morphological rules from existing available morphological lexicons. For each lemma, we extract the longest prefix that is common to all its inflected forms, which is considered as the stem, and build an ordered list of *(suffix,tag)* pairs.[15] If at least 3 lemmas lead to the same list of *(suffix,tag)* pairs, this list is turned into the definition of a morphological class, and all corresponding lemmas are associated with this class. Moreover, the stems of all these lemmas are analyzed, so as to build the most specific (reasonable) regular pattern that matches them all. The result is not only a set of morphological classes but also a list of lemmas classified under such a set of classes.

5.3 Linguistic resources

High-quality linguistic resources are the final goal of the *Victoria* project. Apart from the fact that they constitute the practical results which support our theories, we are using them to complete syntactic parsers.

5.3.1 Morphological rules

According to the technique described earlier in section 5.2.3, we used two existing morphological lexicons for Spanish and Galician in order to extract morphological descriptions from a set of *(form,lemma,tag)* triples. Morphological classes are associated to PoS, but several classes are always required to cover all the inflection cases for one PoS. Finally, we obtained a set of 237 morphological classes for Spanish (approx. 7,250 inflection cases) and 154 for Galician (approx. 4,160 inflection cases).

5.3.2 Morphological and syntactic lexicons

Two wide coverage lexicons for Spanish and Galician have already been produced following the Alexina format. Both

[15] At this point, the process discards all entries that do not have their lemma as one of their inflected forms.

lexicons are currently being upgraded using the techniques described in section 5.2 and will be available under LGPL-LR licenses soon.

The Spanish lexicon L*effe* [16] has overtaken other well known Spanish lexicons in terms of coverage despite being in beta version. It has been obtained by merging several existing Spanish linguistic resources [4]. Nowadays, the L*effe* beta contains more than 165,000 unique *(lemma,PoS)* pairs, corresponding to approx. 1,590,000 inflected entries that associate a form with morpho-syntactic information (approx. 680,000 unique *(form,PoS)* pairs).

The L*effga*[17] has been created after the Galician lexicon developed in the CORGA[18] project. The L*effga* is still in alpha version (April 2009), and less developed than the L*effe*. It contains more than 52,000 unique *(lemma,PoS)* pairs (approx. 515,000 unique *(form,PoS)* pairs). The complete lexicon includes more than 742,000 inflected entries with little syntactic information to this point.

5.3.3 Grammars

The Spanish meta-grammar (SPMG) takes as its starting point a French meta-grammar (FRMG) [11]. Nowadays, it contains 244 classes organized in a hierarchical structure. We can confirm the ease of building such a grammar for Spanish using a French one. In fact, there are few major syntactic differences between those languages. Simply by fixing these differences it is possible to achieve a coverage somewhat similar to the original French grammar. We only needed to achieve slight modifications in a dozen classes to obtain this grammar. We evaluated its coverage by extracting more than 4,000 sentences with 25 words or less from the Europarl-Spanish[19] corpus. In such a corpus we completed non-robust parses for 53% of the sentences using a parser based on L*effe* and SPMG. It is worth noting that many parsing errors might be caused by the lexicon, since the number of completed parses depends both of the quality of the grammar and the lexicon.

6 Future work

Online tools Before considering other kind of resource, the interface dedicated to the lexicon shall be finalised.

In order to obtain plain text given as input to our techniques, we are developing a tool using the RSS system to trace journalistic production on websites, extract it (if we are allowed to) and index it in the TEI format[20].

Techniques The extension and correction techniques regarding lexical knowledge are already effective. We shall thus concentrate on developing techniques for extending morphological rules and grammars. Since we are able to produce corpora representing mostly shortcomings of both kinds of resource, we shall follow the methodology described in section 4.2. We also plan to investigate an idea explained in [5], where an entropy classifier is trained to recognize non-grammatically covered sentences. The statistical model might be an interesting starting point to guess non covered syntactic structures.

We will also work on the theory about infrequent words in order to transfer lexical information between French and Spanish. Infrequent words being the major part of a lexicon, such transfer process would be extremely useful.

Resources Thanks to the techniques explained in 5.2, we shall further extend and correct the L*effe* and we hope to convert it into a lexical resource comparable in terms of quality and coverage with what currently exists for English.

We will extend the morphological information of the L*effga* and adapt, in the same way we adapted the French one to Spanish, the Spanish meta-grammar to Galician. Once a beta meta-grammar is achieved, we will be able to extend syntactic lexical information in the L*effga*.

7 Conclusion

In order to allow efficient production of linguistic resources, the *Victoria* project is dealing with wide coverage resources, useful techniques and a collaborative development framework, i.e., objectives that can be considered, one by one, as challenging.

Even if modest when compared to its ambitious objectives, the practical achievements obtained in only a few months demonstrates its validity and coherence and indicates that it is following a productive path.

The combination of transfer processes with efficient formalisms and extension and correction techniques is already allowing us to produce resources with noticeable qualities in a very short amount of time when manual construction would not have permitted anything similar.

References

[1] M.-H. Candito. *Organisation modulaire et paramétrable de grammaires électroniques lexicalisées*. PhD thesis, Univ. of Paris 7, 1999.

[2] L. Danlos and B. Sagot. Constructions pronominales dans dicovalence et le lexique-grammaire. In *Proceedings of the 27th Lexicon-Grammar Conference*, L'Aquila, Italy, 2008.

[3] G. Francopoulo, M. George, N. Calzolari, M. Monachini, N. Bel, mandy Pet, and C. Soria. Lexical markup framework (LMF). In *Proceedings of LREC'06*, Genoa, Italy, 2006.

[4] M. A. Molinero, B. Sagot, and L. Nicolas. Building a morphological and syntactic lexicon by merging various linguistic ressources. In *Proceedings of NODALIDA 2009*, Odense, Danemark.

[5] L. Nicolas, B. Sagot, M. A. Molinero, J. Farré, and É. Villemonte de La Clergerie. Computer aided correction and extension of a syntactic wide-coverage lexicon. In *Proceedings of COLING'08*, Manchester, United Kingdom, 2008.

[6] B. Sagot. Automatic acquisition of a Slovak lexicon from a raw corpus. In *Lecture Notes in Artificial Intelligence 3658 (© Springer-Verlag), Proceedings of TSD'05*, pages 156–163, Karlovy Vary, Czech Republic, 2005.

[7] B. Sagot, L. Clément, É. Villemonte de La Clergerie, and P. Boullier. The Lefff 2 syntactic lexicon for French: architecture, acquisition, use. In *Proceedings of LREC'06*, Genoa, Italy, 2006.

[8] B. Sagot and L. Danlos. Méthodologie lexicographique de constitution d'un lexique syntaxique de référence pour le français. In *Proceedings of the workshop "Lexicographie et informatique : bilan et perspectives"*, Nancy, France, 2008.

[9] B. Sagot and É. Villemonte de La Clergerie. Error mining in parsing results. In *Proceedings of ACL/COLING'06*, pages 329–336, Sydney, Australia, 2006.

[10] G. van Noord. Error mining for wide-coverage grammar engineering. In *Proceedings of ACL 2004*, Barcelona, Spain.

[11] E. Villemonte de La Clergerie. From metagrammars to factorized TAG/TIG parsers. In *Proceedings of IWPT'05*, pages 190–191, Vancouver, Canada, 2005.

[16] *Léxico de formas flexionadas del español / Lexicon of Spanish inflected forms*
[17] *Léxico de formas flexionadas do galego / Lexicon of Galician inflected forms*
[18] http://corpus.cirp.es/corga/
[19] http://www.statmt.org/europarl/
[20] http://www.tei-c.org

A Classification-driven Approach to Document Planning

Rafael L. de Oliveira, Eder M. de Novais, Roberto P. A. de Araujo, Ivandré Paraboni
University of São Paulo (USP)
School of Arts, Sciences and Humanities (EACH)
Av. Arlindo Bettio, 1000 - São Paulo, Brazil
{ rafaellage, eder.novais, roberto.araujo, ivandre } @usp.br

Abstract

Document Planning - the task of deciding which content messages should be realised in a target document based on raw data provided by an underlying application, and how these messages should be structured - is arguably one of the most crucial tasks in Natural Language Generation (NLG). In this work we present a machine learning approach to Document Planning that is entirely trainable from annotated corpora, and which paves the way to our long-term goal of developing a text generator system based on a series of classifiers for a simple NLG application in the education domain.

Keywords

Document Planning; Content Selection.

1. Introduction

Natural Language Generation (NLG) systems are used whenever simple, 'canned' text is not sufficient, and greater (i.e., closer to human performance) linguistic variation is required. The traditional NLG architecture is often depicted in simplified form as a 3-stages pipelined process (Document Planning, Sentence Planning and Surface Realisation, cf. [1]), a division that is at least partially motivated by the sheer complexity of the task. Starting from a high-level communicative goal of describing a given domain concept, the system builds up a plan to represent the input data up to the point in which fully-specified text in natural language is produced. The Document Planning module is responsible for deciding what information to communicate (this being the task of *Content Determination*) and then how this information should be structured for presentation (this being the task of *Document Structuring*.) For a more comprehensive discussion of the role of Document Planning and its subtasks in the NLG architecture we report to [3].

Document Planning is arguably one of the most crucial components of an NLG system [1]: if a generated document presents the required information in a reasonably coherent structure, then the system may be considered successful even if the text shows surface flaws or limited linguistic variation. On the other hand, if the required information is missing from the text, or if the text is poorly structured, then the overall results are most likely unsatisfactory regardless of how well the individual sentences were realised.

When speaking of Data-to-Text generation[1], Document Planning is often preceded by a *Data Interpretation* stage [2] that processes raw data application in the first place. In what follows, we discuss the early stages of a simple Data-to-Text NLG application addressing some aspects of both issues, namely, which chunks of information – or messages - should be included in the generated text from the raw data provided by an underlying application, and how such messages should be structured within a standard RST framework [4]. We will argue that at least in simple NLG applications, some of these issues may be tackled using trainable and (at least partially) domain-independent methods. The focus of this paper is one such method, in which we apply standard machine learning techniques to both Content Determination and Document Structuring, and which can be viewed as a first step towards the development of a trainable text-generating application based on a series of classifiers.

2. Application and Training Data

We envisage a simple NLG application in which grades obtained by University students in a given course are described as short reports generated automatically from raw data (i.e., the numeric grades themselves) available from their academic records. Thus, the input to our system will be a student's record, and the output is a report conveying a series of statements such as "You fared well in the regular exams and your grades on this subject were above the average of your class" etc. Such reports can be useful to both students keen to learn how their professors interpret their efforts, and to the professors themselves who may have an at-a-glance view of the student's progress.

A substantial part of our work consisted of preparing training data. We started by collecting 241 records of students' academic performance data in five courses taught by a single professor (who can be viewed as the domain expert) in an academic term. Each record consists of a set of 25 values representing various aspects of a student's academic performance: figures about attendance records, examination grades at various stages throughout the course, and the average grades obtained by the entire class in the same examinations. Additional attributes describe how the available grades should be interpreted in that particular course or term (e.g., whether a given practical exercise was compulsory etc.) From these data we intend to generate textual descriptions of both what each student achieved individually, and how their performance compares to their peers'.

[1] For a large-scale application of this kind, see [5].

International Conference RANLP 2009 - Borovets, Bulgaria, pages 324–329

For each one of the 241 data records, the domain expert has also authored a short (about 5-sentences long, and to some extent normalised) sample report conveying a series of statements about the overall progress of the student. The reports are entirely purpose-made, i.e., written so as to provide training data for a machine-learned NLG application. Similar methodology has been employed in an NLG system (also in the education domain) described in [6], and it contrasts the use of naturally-occurring texts as a model for the application.

Unlike common practice in many domain-independent NLP tasks, we have collected aligned data-text instances produced by a *single author*. In the present case this was necessary because we are interested in establishing the mappings from raw data (e.g., students' grades) to semantics (i.e., the interpretation of the data according to the professor in charge), and which may vary wildly across domain experts[2]. The fact that we are dealing with a domain- and author-dependent problem should not be viewed as unappealing to the wide research community, though: as our approach is intended to be trainable from a collection of text-data alignments, our work remains in principle adaptable to a particular author or domain, as we will discuss later.

As suggested in [7], the collected reports were manually segmented and annotated with information about the meanings or content messages that they intend to convey[3]. In doing so, we faced the question of how these messages should be defined: on the one hand, content messages could be sufficiently detailed so as to represent the meaning of atomic text units (e.g., single words.) On the other hand, meanings could span over entire sentences or even paragraphs. As pointed out in [1], the level of granularity of content messages should presumably be determined by the expected linguistic variation of the output text. In our case, given the regularity of our target documents, each text was simply segmented in meaningful units from which the corresponding messages were readily identified. The resulting list of messages and the segmentation scheme were then refined for completeness, and infrequent instances were eliminated (which of course reduced the possible linguistic variation of the output.) As a result, the possible contents of each document could be modelled as a 14-messages vector represented in flat semantics as attribute-value pairs, and each text segment in the document was annotated with one such message.

Put together, data and corresponding reports make a complete training data set for corpus-based NLG that we have called the *SINotas* corpus. The corpus consists of a structured collection of the above 241 data-text alignments annotated in XML format, including basic sentence segmentation (provided at the message level only, as discussed above), part-of-speech information and partial discourse structure represented as manually annotated RST relations [4].

The *SINotas* corpus is a valuable NLG resource in its own right, and a ready-to-use testbed for NLG research in Portuguese and related languages. However, as we have abstracted away from the application raw data by modelling the underlying semantics as content messages, *SINotas* does not convey the kind of low-level representation available from, e.g., the SUMTIME-METEO corpus described in [8], which aligns text directly with domain data[4].

3. Document Planning as Classification

We will use the *SINotas* data-text aligned corpus described in the previous section to develop a number of modules of a simple corpus-based NLG system as a series of classifiers, using off-the-shelf learning algorithms. Serialised classifiers have been applied to other NLG tasks, e.g., surface realisation as in [9,10][5].

Regarding related work in the field, we notice that the early stages of Document Planning (and particularly, Content Determination issues) seem to be somewhat misrepresented in the NLG literature, a gap that might be explained by the domain-dependent nature of the task (i.e., the dealing with raw application data.) Content Determination has been performed using statistical techniques in [11], followed by a machine learning approach to select relevant information. The same general principal is applied in [12] in the domain of American football matches, and taking contextual dependencies into account in a so-called 'collective' content selection approach. An extension of this work has been recently presented in [13] for the domain of cricket game with a novel alignment technique. In all these cases, the main focus is the automatic data-text alignment (which in our case was performed manually via corpus annotation) and they do not address our second subtask, Document Structuring.

3.1 Content Determination

Content Determination can be viewed as the task of computing content messages (e.g., in the form of predicate-argument structures) from the input data provided by the underlying application. In our work this is implemented as a 2-steps process: first, we compute all possible messages derivable from the application data (a task that can be viewed as a simplified form of *data interpretation* as in [2]) and then we select the subset of

[2] Had we mixed data produced by various authors in a single training set, it would not be possible to establish meaningful data-text mappings. For example, a grade 5.0 may be rated as 'good' by a particular professor, but simply as 'poor' by a less benign one.

[3] For an example of automatic alignment technique applicable to this task see [12].

[4] In other words, *SINotas* does not contain personal data (e.g., student's grades) but simply text and semantic features derived from them for research purposes.

[5] For instance, the system *Amalgam* described in [10] uses a series of 18 decision-trees to implement various tasks ranging from lexical choice to punctuation.

messages that should actually be realised in a particular document (which we will call *content selection.*) We will discuss each step in turn.

Data interpretation is performed as follows: given the 25 input values produced by the application, we intend to produce the set of 14 messages representing the semantic contents of the target document (some of which possibly conveying '*null*' values that stand for missing or irrelevant information.) This procedure was implemented by means of a classifier in which the 25 input values are learning features to each of the 14 output classes (annotated as messages in the *SINotas* corpus.)

For example, given a low grade in the examinations we would expect the corresponding *provas_aval* class to be assigned a negative value such as "*insufficient*". Using the application data and the *SINotas* corpus, 241 * 14 = 3374 training instances of data interpretation were used to classify each of the 14 output messages as below[6]:

```
[val1,val2...val25, message1]
...
[val1,val2...val25, message14]
```

The second Content Determination task – content selection - consists of deciding which of the generated messages should end up realised as surface text. This is necessary because not all available information appears in the output, that is, different value combinations may result in different reports altogether, and some values that are highly prominent in one context may be even discarded in other situations in which different information should be spelled out. For example, good overall results may make a single low grade not worth mentioning at all. Similarly, a student that has decided not to sit the final exams does not need to be told that his/her grades were 'below average' etc.

Given as an input the original 14-messages vector, we would like to filter out irrelevant content based on what is actually shown (or not shown) in the sample output texts as seen in the corpus. To this end, we defined a set of 14 learning features comprising the previously generated messages and 14 binary classes representing whether each of them were actually realised as text (true) or simply omitted (false). Once again, 241 training instances of content selection were extracted from the corpus to classify each of the 14 '*realise*' binary classes) making 3374 instances as below:

```
[msg1, msg2...msg14, realise_msg1]
...
[msg1, msg2...msg14, realise_msg14]
```

Each classification task was performed individually, that is, we did not use the reminder (13) binary classes as learning features to each class. This may in principle seem counter-intuitive, as the textual realisation of one message could hinge on whether others are realised or not, but such dependencies were not observed in our data. By contrasts, see for instance the collective selection approach in [12].

[6] In practice, however, none of the classification tasks required the use of all 25 learning features, as we discuss in section 5.

3.2 Document Structuring

We are interested in two particular aspects of Document Structuring (and which to some extent cover aspects of Microplanning in the standard pipeline NLG architecture in [1] as well): the task of organising the content messages computed in the previous Content Determination stage into sentences, and then organising these sentences in a global rhetorical structure. Both tasks consist of computing RST relations between content messages, in the first case within sentences (which we will call *within-sentence structuring*) and in the second case between sentences (called *between-sentences structuring.*) In our classification-driven approach this will be performed in a bottom-up fashion, that is, content messages are first aggregated into sentences conveying intra-sentential rhetorical relations, and then the inter-sentential relations are established.

Within-sentence structuring is performed as follows. Given a list of (filtered) content messages produced in the previous Content Determination stage, we would like to have them distributed across a number of individual sentences. To this end, we defined training instances of within-sentence structuring as relations between message pairs in the form (m_1, m_2, *relation*) in which m_1 and m_2 are messages represented as attribute-value pairs, and *relation* is a rhetorical relation (which in our data could be either *concession, joint* or *contrast*). For each positive instance of within-sentences structuring (m_i,m_j), we have also defined counter-examples (conveying the '*none*' value of the *relation* class) covering every other possible message combination. Thus, our goal was to use messages as learning features for classifying *relation* as one of its possible RST values, or as the special *none* case. 12,247 such training instances of within-sentence structuring were extracted from the *SINotas* corpus, being 394 two-message sentences (in which messages are linked by a RST relation) and the reminder 11,853 instances being one-message (*none*) sentences as follows:

```
[attr1,val1, attr2, val2, relation]
```

Between-sentences structuring follows a similar approach. Our goal in this case is to learn possible rhetorical relations between the sentences produced in the previous stage (which in our data could be either *contrast, elaboration* or *none.*) Thus, every related sentence pair in the corpus produced a positive training instance in the form (m_1, m_2, *relation*) in which m_1 and m_2 are messages from one sentence each, and which are found in the nucleus and satellite (or vice-versa) of a inter-sentential rhetorical relation.

For each positive instance of between-sentences structuring (m_i,m_j), we have also defined 12 negative instances (conveying the '*none*' value of the *relation* class) covering every other possible message combination (m_i,m_k)such that $j \neq i$ and $j \neq k$. In this way, 3432 training instances were extracted from the corpus, being 176 cases of *contrast*, 88 cases of *elaboration* and 3168 counter-examples (*none*). The structure of the training instances is the same used for within-sentence structuring, though considering inter-sentential RST relations:

```
[attr1,val1, attr2, val2, relation]
```

4. Implementation

The message generator was implemented as a module that produces a 14-message vector from the given set of input values (e.g., students' grades etc.) Similarly, the message selector was implemented as a subsequent module that reduces this vector to those (possible fewer) messages that should actually be passed on to the next stage. Both modules were integrated (or rather, pipelined) as a Content Determination component corresponding to the first stage in our NLG application under development.

Following the same approach, within-sentence and between-sentence structuring were pipelined in a Document Structuring module. In this case however it was necessary an additional procedure for submitting all possible message pair combinations to each classifier in order to decide which message pairs should make sentences and which sentences should be linked by rhetorical relations.

A complete example of our classification-driven Document Planning works as follows. First, Content Determination: given a student's record showing (among other information) a 6.6 grade in the final exams, data interpretation produces a fixed 14-message vector conveying all relevant facts about the input, including the message *mf_aval=bom* (which stands for a 'good' grade in the final exams.) Next, content selection takes this vector as an input, eliminates all unnecessary messages and outputs the (sub)set of those that should actually appear in the text.

The second stage is Document Structuring: within-sentence structuring could determine that the generated message should be aggregated in a single sentence with, say, a message *mf_turma=abaixo* (which says that the grade falls below the overall class results) using a *concession* rhetorical relation. Finally, between-sentences structuring could link the generated sentence to a second one using a *contrast* rhetorical relation. In this example, the single piece of information about the final exams (had we implemented the entire system, of course) could eventually be realised as "Your grades in the final exams were good but below average", and then linked to another sentence as "On the other hand, your substitutive examination grades were pretty good".

5. Results

To each of our four Document Planning subtasks – data interpretation, content selection, within-sentence and between-sentences structuring - we have applied J48 Weka [14] decision-tree induction using 10-fold cross-validation and its default parameter values.

With respect to data interpretation, we notice that each message actually depends only on a small set of features. This does not come as a surprise as our 25 learning features cover a wide range of phenomena in the application semantics, e.g., from weekly attendance to average grades. Thus, all decision-trees were revised to determine which learning features were actually needed for each classification, and pruned accordingly. As a result, the 14 classification tasks were performed using on average only 2.2 learning features each.

Four messages types (*sub_aval*, *sub_turma*, *corel_nota_falta* and *aband_rec*) could not be classified automatically due to the heavy imbalance in their value distributions and/or data sparseness. These cases will be implemented separately following a knowledge-engineered approach. Table 1 below shows the results for the reminder (i.e., machine-learned) classes only as compared to a baseline approach that simply selects the most frequent value for each class.

Table 1. Data interpretation results

	Decision-tree induction			Baseline
Class	Prec.	Recall	F-measure	Correctness
provas_aval	0.970	0.968	0.982	0.349
provas_turma	0.989	0.989	0.989	0.415
progresso	0.756	0.754	0.752	0.270
eps_aval	0.710	0.635	0.659	0.502
dev_ep1	0.963	0.963	0.963	0.859
freq_aval	0.918	0.948	0.945	0.780
mf_aval	0.956	0.958	0.977	0.336
mf_turma	0.988	0.984	0.986	0.560
rec_aval	0.928	0.931	0.925	0.830
rec_turma	0.652	0.716	0.680	0.846

A number of observations are due. First, the frequency-based baseline would only approach decision-tree induction when data are extremely sparse (e.g., the class *rec_turma* in which 85% of values are '*null*'.) On the other hand, when these problems do not occur (e.g., the values of the class *mf_aval* are evenly distributed in the corpus) results of the machine-learned approach are far superior to the baseline.

Second, we notice that accuracy rates for some classes are extremely high, which is mainly the case of classes of well-defined semantics (for example, University policies determine that a 5.0 grade should be considered average, and this kind of knowledge was taken into account by the domain expert when writing the reports.) However, this is not the case when we consider more subjective classes such as, e.g., *progresso*, which describes the student's performance curve throughout the term (e.g., rising, falling, U-shaped etc.), or sparse data such as in *rec_turma* (modelling recuperation exams attended by very few of the students.)

In addition to that, we notice that the results hide some extreme situations in all classes. For example, the data do not provide sufficient evidence to classify instances conveying *rec_turma=media* (i.e., an average result in the recuperation exams) which occurred only twice in the training data. In practice, this means that we should expect the system to rate an 'average' grade as something else in 2 out of 241 cases (0.83%), a relatively minor error rate that we expect to accommodate in the subsequent (and also classification-driven) stages of the generation process. In either case, we believe that the overall positive results in message classification should be interpreted as more indicative of the simplicity of the underlying semantics (allowing the authoring of highly consistent reports as seen in the corpus) and less of the performance of the annotation task or computational approach undertaken.

With respect to the second task - content selection – we notice that some of the message realisations turned out to be trivially derivable from the input messages. This was the case of five messages conveying highly prominent information (*mf_turma*, *corel_nota_falta*, *provas_turma*, *dev_ep1* and *abandon_rec*) that is always included in the output text unless they contained a '*null*' value. For all these cases, no learning approach was actually required. Below we show the results for the reminder (machine-learned) classes and the correctness rates of a possible baseline algorithm that simply includes all non-null messages in the output text.

Table 2. Content selection results

	Decision-tree induction			Baseline
Class	Prec.	Recall	F-measure	Correctness
provas_aval	0.995	0.981	0.987	0.784
sub_aval	0.995	0.944	0.968	1.000
sub_turma	0.875	0.991	0.924	0.938
progresso	0.989	0.963	0.975	0.983
eps_aval	0.894	0.916	0.904	0.784
freq_aval	0.884	0.884	0.884	0.817
mf_aval	0.821	0.923	0.849	0.784
rec_aval	0.963	0.992	0.977	0.988
rec_turma	0.993	0.937	0.963	0.946

Although content selection turned out to be a straightforward procedure – the simple baseline algorithm achieves superior results in 4 out of 9 classes - we notice that by applying the generated models to the 241 input message vectors in the *SINotas* corpus we have actually obtained output sets of average 5.1 messages each[7], that is, the next module to be implemented – document structuring – will have to deal with an average of 5 messages in each text, and not 14, a considerable reduction in the task complexity that we expect to become evident in the next stages of development of our generation system.

Results for the third task - within-sentence structuring – are as follows.

Table 3. Within-sentence structuring results

	Decision-tree induction		
Class	Precision	Recall	F-measure
concession	0.980	0.916	0.947
joint	0.847	0.756	0.799
contrast	0	0	0
null	0.993	0.997	0.995

The high correctness rates in this case are due to the regularity of the sentence structures in the corpus, most of which either comparing two opposite values (e.g., a low and a high grade in a *concession* relation) or simply stating them as two otherwise independent facts (linked by a *joint* relation.) The corpus contained only eight instances of intra-sentential *contrast* relations. These cases could not be classified automatically, and will be left out from our output documents. Given the high F-measure rates above, we do not explicitly provide a baseline algorithm. By comparison to this case we notice that the simple choice for, e.g., the most frequent meaningful class (*concession*) would have achieved 70.8% correctness rate, but only if we could disregard the negative instances, that is, if the system somehow 'knew' in advance that the two messages should be linked by a RST relation in the first place.

Finally, results for the fourth task - between-sentences structuring - are as follows.

Table 4. Between-sentences structuring results

	Decision-tree induction		
Class	Precision	Recall	F-measure
contrast	0.933	0.875	0.903
elaboration	0.882	0.852	0.867
null	0.990	0.995	0.992

Once again, we observe high correctness rates due to the uniform rhetorical structure of our corpus. By means of comparison, a possible baseline strategy that chooses always the '*null*' class would achieve up to 92.3% correctness (although obviously not performing any useful document structuring.)

6. Final Remarks

We have presented a corpus-based approach to NLG Document Planning addressing the initial stages of Content Determination (here including both aspects of data interpretation and content selection) and Document Structuring (which we called within- and between-sentences structuring.) Although still domain-dependent - in the sense that it requires annotated training data – results in both cases were highly satisfactory, suggesting that the general methodology is in principle applicable to the development of simple NLG systems of this kind. Moreover, as automatic (or semi-automatic) methods for data-text alignment become more widespread (e.g., [12]), the current knowledge acquisition bottleneck is likely to become more treatable.

We are currently working on the late stages of Macroplanning / Microplanning, that is, generating abstract sentence specifications for a future surface

[7] This relatively low average number of output messages is greatly influenced by several records of students that did not sit any of the expected exams, producing single-sentence reports of the kind "Unfortunately you do not seem to have followed the course regularly".

realisation module, which should ultimately lead to a simple NLG system made of a series of classifiers.

7. Acknowledgements

The authors acknowledge support by CNPq, FAPESP and the University of São Paulo (USP).

8. References

[1] Reiter, E. and R. Dale "Building Applied Natural Language Generation Systems". Cambridge University Press, 2000.

[2] Reiter, E. "An Architecture for Data-to-Text Systems". In Proceedings of ENLG-2007, pages 97-104, 2007.

[3] Mellish, C. et. al. "A Reference Architecture for Natural Language Generation Systems". Natural Language Engineering 12 (1) pages 1–34, 2006.

[4] Mann, W. C. and S. A. Thompson "Rhetorical Structure Theory: A Theory of Text Organisation". L. Polanyi (ed.) The Structure of Discourse. Ablex, Norwood, 1987.

[5] Portet, F., E. Reiter, A. Gatt, J. Hunter, S. Sripada, Y. Freer, C. Sykes "Automatic Generation of Textual Summaries from Neonatal Intensive Care Data". Artificial Intelligence 173, pages 789-816, 2009.

[6] Williams, S. and Ehud Reiter "Deriving content selection rules from a corpus of non-naturally occurring documents for a novel NLG application". Corpus Linguistics workshop on Using Corpora for Natural Language Generation, 2005.

[7] Geldof, S. "Corpus analysis for NLG". In: Reiter, E., Horacek, H. and van Deemter, K. (Eds.) 9th European Workshop on NLG, pages 31-38, 2003.

[8] Sripada, S., E. Reiter, J. Hunter, and J. Yu "Exploiting a parallel text-data corpus". Corpus Linguistics 2003, pages 734–743, 2003.

[9] Marciniak, T. and M. Strube "Using an Annotated Corpus As a Knowledge Source For Language Generation". Corpus Linguistics'05 Workshop Using Corpora for NLG (UNNLG-2005), pages 19-24, 2005.

[10] Smets, Martine, Michael Gamon, Simon Corston-Oliver and Eric Ringger "French Amalgam: A machine-learned sentence realization system". TALN-2003, Batz-sur-Mer, 2003.

[11] Duboue, Pablo A. and Kathleen R. McKeown. "Statistical Acquisition of Content Selection Rules for Natural Language Generation". EMNLP '03, pages 121–128, 2003.

[12] Barzilay, Regina and Mirella Lapata. "Collective Content Selection for Concept-To-Text Generation". In HLT'05, pages 331–338, 2003.

[13] Kelly, Colin, Ann Copestake and Nikiforos Karamanis "Investigating Content Selection for Language Generation using Machine Learning". 12th European Workshop on Natural Language Generation, Athens, Greece, 2009.

[14] Witten, I. H. and E. Frank. "Data Mining: Practical machine learning tools and techniques". 2nd edition, Morgan Kaufmann, San Francisco, 2005.

Interactive machine translation based on partial statistical phrase-based alignments

Daniel Ortiz-Martínez
Dpto. de Sist. Inf. y Comp.
Univ. Politécnica de Valencia
46071 Valencia, Spain
dortiz@dsic.upv.es

Ismael García-Varea
Dpto. de Sist. Inf.
Univ. de Castilla-La Mancha
02071 Albacete, Spain
ivarea@info-ab.uclm.es

Francisco Casacuberta
Dpto. de Sist. Inf. y Comp.
Univ. Politécnica de Valencia
46071 Valencia, Spain
fcn@dsic.upv.es

Abstract

State-of-the-art Machine Translation (MT) systems are still far from being perfect. An alternative is the so-called Interactive Machine Translation (IMT) framework. In this framework, the knowledge of a human translator is combined with a MT system. We present a new technique for IMT which is based on the generation of partial alignments at phrase-level. The proposed technique partially aligns the source sentence with the user prefix and then translates the unaligned portion of the source sentence. The generation of such partial alignments is driven by statistical phrase-based models. Our technique relies on the application of smoothing techniques over the phrase models to appropriately assign probabilities to unseen events. We report experiments investigating the impact of the different smoothing techniques in the accuracy of our system. In addition, we compare the results obtained by our system with those obtained by other well-known IMT systems.

Keywords

Statistical machine translation, interactive machine translation, phrase-based translation, phrase-based alignments, smoothing.

1 Introduction

Information technology advances in modern society have led to the need of more efficient methods of translation. It is worth mentioning that current MT systems are not able to produce ready-to-use texts. Indeed, MT systems usually require human post-editing in order to achieve high-quality translations.

One way of taking advantage of MT systems is to combine them with the knowledge of a human translator, constituting the Interactive Machine Translation (IMT) paradigm. This IMT paradigm can be considered a special type of the so-called Computer-Assisted Translation (CAT) paradigm.

An important contribution to IMT technology was carried out within the TransType (TT) project [11, 7, 5]. This project entailed a focus shift in which interaction directly aimed at the production of the target text, rather than at the disambiguation of the source text, as in former interactive systems. The idea proposed in that work was to embed data driven MT techniques within the interactive translation environment.

Following these TT ideas, [1] proposed a new approach to IMT. In this approach, fully-fledged statistical MT (SMT) systems are used to produce full target sentence hypotheses, or portions thereof, which can be partially or completely accepted and amended by a human translator. Each partial correct text segment is then used by the SMT system as additional information to achieve further, hopefully improved suggestions. Figure 1 illustrates a typical IMT session.

In this paper, we also focus on the IMT approach to CAT. Specifically, we propose a new IMT engine based on the generation of partial alignments at phrase-level. The proposed technique partially aligns the source sentence with the user prefix and then translates the unaligned portion of the source sentence. The partial alignments are generated using the statistical knowledge provided by a phrase-based model. As it will be shown, the techniques proposed here require the application of smoothing techniques over the phrase-based models to correctly assign probabilities to unseen events.

2 Statistical interactive MT

IMT can be seen as an evolution of the SMT framework. The fundamental equation of the statistical approach to MT is:

$$\hat{\mathbf{e}} = \underset{\mathbf{e}}{\operatorname{argmax}} \{Pr(\mathbf{f} \mid \mathbf{e}) \cdot Pr(\mathbf{e})\} \quad (1)$$

where $Pr(\mathbf{f} \mid \mathbf{e})$ is approached by a *translation model* that tries to represent the correlation between source and target sentence and $Pr(\mathbf{e})$ is approached by *language model* representing the well-formedness of the candidate translation $\mathbf{e}$.

Current MT systems are based on the use of phrase-based models [19, 10] as translation models. The basic idea of Phrase-based Translation (PBT) is to segment the source sentence into phrases, then to translate each source phrase into a target phrase, and finally to reorder the translated target phrases in order to compose the target sentence. If we summarize all the decisions made during the phrase-based translation process by means of the hidden variable $\tilde{a}_1^K$, we arrive to the following expression:

$$Pr(\mathbf{f}|\mathbf{e}) = \sum_{K,\tilde{a}_1^K} Pr(\tilde{f}_1^K, \tilde{a}_1^K \mid \tilde{e}_1^K) \quad (2)$$

International Conference RANLP 2009 - Borovets, Bulgaria, pages 330–336

source	Para ver la lista de recursos
interaction-0	To view the resources list
interaction-1	To view [a] list of resources
interaction-2	To view a list[i]ng resources
interaction-3	To view a listing [o]f resources
acceptance	To view a listing of resources

Fig. 1: *IMT session to translate a Spanish sentence into English. In interaction-0, the system suggests a translation. In interaction-1, the user moves the mouse to accept the first eight characters "To view " and presses the key [a], then the system suggests completing the sentence with " a list of resources". Interactions 2 and 3 are similar. In the final interaction, the user completely accepts the present suggestion.*

where each $\tilde{a}_k \in \{1 \dots K\}$ denotes the index of the target phrase $\tilde{e}$ that is aligned with the k-th source phrase $\tilde{f}_k$, assuming a segmentation of length K.

According to Eq. (2), and following a maximum approximation, the problem stated in Eq. (1) can be reframed as:

$$\hat{\mathbf{e}} \approx \arg\max_{\mathbf{e},\mathbf{a}} \{p(\mathbf{e}) \cdot p(\mathbf{f}, \mathbf{a} \mid \mathbf{e})\} \quad (3)$$

State-of-the-art statistical machine translation systems model $p(\mathbf{f}, \mathbf{a}|\mathbf{e})$ following a loglinear approach [14], that is:

$$p(\mathbf{f}, \mathbf{a}|\mathbf{e}) \propto \exp\left[\sum_i \lambda_i f_i(\mathbf{f}, \mathbf{e}, \mathbf{a})\right] \quad (4)$$

In the IMT scenario we have to find an extension $\mathbf{e}_s$ for a given prefix $\mathbf{e}_p$. For this purpose we reformulate Eq. (3) as follows:

$$\hat{\mathbf{e}}_s \approx \arg\max_{\mathbf{e}_s,\mathbf{a}} \{p(\mathbf{e}_s \mid \mathbf{e}_p) \cdot p(\mathbf{f}, \mathbf{a} \mid \mathbf{e}_p, \mathbf{e}_s)\} \quad (5)$$

where the term $p(\mathbf{e}_p)$ has been dropped since it does not depend on $\mathbf{e}_s$ and $\mathbf{a}$.

Thus, the search is restricted to those sentences $\mathbf{e}$ which contain $\mathbf{e}_p$ as prefix. It is also worth mentioning that the similarities between Eq. (5) and Eq. (3) (note that $\mathbf{e}_p\mathbf{e}_s \equiv \mathbf{e}$) allow us to use the same models if the search procedures are adequately modified [2, 1].

3 Related work

Several IMT systems have been proposed in the literature. For example, in [7] a maximum entropy version of IBM 2 model is used as word-based translation model. In [15] the Alignment Template approach to IMT is proposed. In that work a pre-computed word translation graph is used in order to achieve fast response times. This approach is compared with the use of a direct translation modeling [2]. In [4] an IMT approach based on stochastic finite-state transducers is presented. In that work, also word translation graphs are used to resolve real-time constraints. In [18] a phrase-based approach is presented.

Recently, in [1] the IMT approach to CAT is proposed, establishing the state-of-the-art in this discipline. In this work the last three approaches mentioned above are compared.

In the following sections, we present a new IMT technique which is based on the generation of partial alignments at phrase-level. The proposed technique partially aligns the source sentence with the user prefix and then translates the unaligned portion of the source sentence. The generation of such partial alignments is driven by statistical phrase-based models. Our technique relies on the application of smoothing techniques over the phrase models to appropriately assign probabilities to unseen events.

The IMT system we propose is similar to those presented in [2] and [18]. The so-called *interactive* generation strategy presented in [2] does not use word graphs as well as our proposal. The key difference between their system and the system we propose is that they use error-correcting techniques instead of smoothing techniques to assign probabilities to unseen events. Specifically, the error correcting costs are introduced as an additional weight in their log-linear model. We think that our approach is better motivated from a theoretical point of view, as it has been deeply studied and demonstrated in the field of language modelling. In addition, our system needs much less time per iteration (hundredths of seconds vs. seconds, as will be shown in section 7) than the system presented in [2].

The work presented in [18] is based on filtering the phrase table to obtain translations that are compatible with the user prefix. Since this approach seems too restrictive (phrase models always present coverage problems in complex tasks, as is discussed in section 4), we guess that also any sort of smoothing is taken into account, but as far as we know the exact technique that is used is not explained. Because of this, we think that the work presented in [18] can benefit from the study on smoothing techniques presented here.

4 Phrase-based alignments

The problem of finding the best alignment at phrase level has been studied in [16, 8, 13]. The concept of phrase-based alignment can be formalized as follows:

Let $\mathbf{f} \equiv f_1, f_2, \dots, f_J$ be a source sentence and $\mathbf{e} \equiv e_1, e_2, \dots, e_I$ the corresponding target sentence in a bilingual corpus. A phrase-alignment between $\mathbf{f}$ and $\mathbf{e}$ is defined as a set $\mathcal{S}$ of ordered pairs included in $\mathcal{P}(\mathbf{f}) \times \mathcal{P}(\mathbf{e})$, where $\mathcal{P}(\mathbf{f})$ and $\mathcal{P}(\mathbf{e})$ are the set of all subsets of consecutive sequences of words, of $\mathbf{f}$ and $\mathbf{e}$, respectively. In addition, the ordered pairs contained in $\mathcal{S}$ have to include all the words of both the source and target sentences.

A phrase-based alignment of length K ($\tilde{A}_K$) of a sentence pair $(\mathbf{f}, \mathbf{e})$ is defined as a triple $\tilde{A}_K \equiv$

$(\tilde{f}_1^K, \tilde{e}_1^K, \tilde{a}_1^K)$, where $\tilde{a}_1^K$ is a specific one-to-one mapping between the K segments/phrases of both sentences ($1 \leq K \leq \min(J, I)$).

Then, given a pair of sentences $(\mathbf{f}, \mathbf{e})$ and a phrase alignment model, we have to obtain the best phrase-alignment $\tilde{A}_K$ (or Viterbi phrase-alignment $V(\tilde{A}_K)$) between them. Assuming a phrase-alignment of length K, $V(\tilde{A}_K)$ can be computed as:

$$V(\tilde{A}_K) = \arg\max_{\tilde{A}_K} \{p(\tilde{f}_1^K, \tilde{a}_1^K | \tilde{e}_1^K)\} \quad (6)$$

where, following the assumptions of [19], $Pr(\tilde{f}_1^K, \tilde{a}_1^K | \tilde{e}_1^K)$ can be efficiently computed as:

$$p(\tilde{f}_1^K, \tilde{a}_1^K | \tilde{e}_1^K) = \prod_{k=1}^{K} p(\tilde{f}_k | \tilde{e}_{\tilde{a}_k}) \quad (7)$$

The model parameters ($\{p(\tilde{f}|\tilde{e})\}$) are typically estimated via relative frequencies as $p(\tilde{f}|\tilde{e}) = N(\tilde{f}, \tilde{e})/N(\tilde{e})$, where $N(\tilde{f}|\tilde{e})$ is the number of times that $\tilde{f}$ has been seen as a translation of $\tilde{e}$ within the training corpus.

On the basis of Eq. (7), a very straightforward technique can be proposed for finding the best phrase-alignment of a sentence pair $(\mathbf{f}, \mathbf{e})$. This can be conceived as a sort of *constrained* translation. In this way, the search process only requires the use of a regular SMT system which filters its phrase-table in order to obtain those translations of $\mathbf{f}$ that are compatible with $\mathbf{e}$.

As noted in [16], this technique has no practical interest when applied on regular tasks. Specifically, the technique is not applicable when the alignments cannot be generated due to coverage problems of the phrase-based model (i.e. one or more phrase pairs required to compose a given alignment have not been seen during the training process). Coverage problems are very frequent in complex translation tasks as will be shown in section 7. In order to solve this problem, an alternative technique is proposed. The alternative technique is able to consider every source phrase of $\mathbf{f}$ as a possible translation of every target phrase of $\mathbf{e}$. For this purpose, it uses a general mechanism for assigning probabilities to phrase pairs based on the application of smoothing techniques over the phrase-table. In addition, the search algorithm that is used no longer filters its phrase-table to generate the sentence $\mathbf{e}$, but instead it can efficiently explore the set of possible alignments between $\mathbf{f}$ and $\mathbf{e}$ (see [16] for more details).

4.1 A log-linear approach to phrase-to-phrase alignments

The score for a given alignment can be calculated according Eq (7). This scoring function does not allow control of basic aspects of the phrase alignment, such as the lengths of the source and target phrases, and the reorderings of phrase alignments. This problem can be alleviated following the approach stated in Eq. (4), thus introducing different feature functions as scoring components in a log-linear fashion.

We use the same set of feature functions proposed in [16]:

- $f_1(\mathbf{f}, \mathbf{e}, \mathbf{a}) = \log(\prod_{k=1}^{K} p(\tilde{e}_{\tilde{a}_k} | \tilde{f}_k))$: direct phrase model log-probability
- $f_2(\mathbf{f}, \mathbf{e}, \mathbf{a}) = \log(\prod_{k=1}^{K} p(\tilde{f}_k | \tilde{e}_{\tilde{a}_k}))$: inverse phrase model log-probability
- $f_3(\mathbf{f}, \mathbf{e}, \mathbf{a}) = \log(\prod_{k=1}^{K} p(|\tilde{e}_k|))$: target phrase length model. This component can be modeled by means of a uniform distribution (penalizes the length of the segmentation) or a geometric distribution (penalizes the length of the target phrases)
- $f_4(\mathbf{f}, \mathbf{e}, \mathbf{a}) = \log(\prod_{k=1}^{K} p(\tilde{a}_k | \tilde{a}_{k-1}))$: distortion model. This component is typically modeled by means of a geometric distribution (penalizes the reorderings)
- $f_5(\mathbf{f}, \mathbf{e}, \mathbf{a}) = \log(\prod_{k=1}^{K} p(|\tilde{f}_k| \mid |\tilde{e}_{\tilde{a}_k}|))$: source phrase length model given the length of the target phrase. This component can be modeled by means of different distributions: uniform (does not take into account the relationship between the length of source and target phrase), Poisson or geometric

The corresponding weights $\lambda_i, i \in \{1, 2, \ldots, 5\}$ can be computed by means of MERT training.

5 Smoothing

As was mentioned in section 4, the application of smoothing techniques is crucial in the generation of phrase-alignments. Most of the well-known language model smoothing techniques (see for example [12]) can be imported to the SMT field and specifically to the PBT framework, as it is shown in [6]. However, PBT and the generation of phrase-alignments differ in a key aspect. While in PBT the probabilities of unseen events are not important (since the decoder only proposes phrase translations contained in the model, see [6]), in the generation of phrase alignments, assigning probabilities to unseen events is one of the most important problems that has to be solved (see [16]).

In the rest of this section, we describe the smoothing techniques that has been used in our work.

5.1 Statistical estimators

Training data can be exploited in different ways to estimate statistical models. Regarding the phrase-based models, the standard estimation technique is based on the relative frequencies of the phrase pairs. Taking this standard estimation technique as a starting point, a number of alternative estimation techniques can be derived.

We have implemented the following estimation techniques for phrase-based models: Maximum-likelihood (ML), Good-Turing (GT), Absolute-discount (AD), Kneser-Ney smoothing (KN), and Simple discount (SD). The SD estimation technique works in a similar way to AD estimation but it subtracts a fixed probability mass instead of a fixed count.

A good way to tackle the problem of unseen events is the use of probability distributions that decompose phrases into words. In our work we have used the

IBM 1 model as defined in [3] to assign probabilities to phrase pairs instead of sentence pairs (this distribution will be referred to as LEX).

5.2 Combining estimators

The statistical estimators described above can be combined in the hope of producing better models. We have chosen three different techniques for combining estimators: Linear interpolation, Backing-off, and Log-linear interpolation. Specifically, we have implemented combinations of two estimators, a phrase-based model estimator (ML, GT, AD, KN or SD estimator) and the LEX estimator.

The key difference between interpolation and backing off is that the latter only uses information from the smoothing distribution (the LEX distribution) for low frequency or unseen events. Since for phrase alignment generation, better prediction of unseen events has a great impact, backing-off seems a specially suitable approach.

Finally, the main difference between linear and log-linear combination is that the former moderates extreme probability values and preserves intermediate values, whereas the latter preserves extreme values and makes intermediate values more extreme. When assigning probabilities to unseen events, the phrase-based model statistical estimators will produce very low or zero probabilities that will be moderated by linear combination (using the LEX distribution), and preserved by log-linear combination. Because of this, we expect linear combination to work better than log-linear combination.

6 IMT based on partial phrase-based alignments

In this section we propose a new IMT technique based on the generation of *partial phrase-alignments* between the source sentence $\mathbf{f}$ and the user prefix $\mathbf{e}_p$. The concept of partial phrase-alignment is similar to the concept of complete phrase alignment described in section 4. Specifically, we define a partial alignment between $\mathbf{f}$ and $\mathbf{e}_p$ as the set $\mathcal{S}'$ of ordered pairs that contains all the words of $\mathbf{e}_p$ and only a subset of the words of $\mathbf{f}$.

The generation of the suffix in IMT can be seen as a two-stage process. First we partially align the prefix $\mathbf{e}_p$ with a part of $\mathbf{f}$, and second, we translate the unaligned portion of $\mathbf{f}$ (if any) giving the suffix $\mathbf{e}_s$. For this purpose, we propose the use of a *stack-decoding* algorithm [9]. The stack-decoding algorithm attempts to iteratively *expand* partial solutions, called hypotheses, until a complete translation is found. The expanded hypotheses are stored into a stack data structure which allows the efficient exploration of the search space.

The expansion process consists of appending target phrases as translation of previously uncovered source phrases of a given hypothesis. Let us suppose that we are translating the sentence $\mathbf{f} \equiv$ "Para ver la lista de recursos", and that the user has validated the prefix $\mathbf{e}_p \equiv$ "To view a" (interaction 1 of the IMT session given in Figure 1). Figure 2 shows an example of the results obtained by the expansion algorithm that we propose for two hypotheses h_1 and h_2.

Hypothesis h_1 has covered the source phrase "Para ver la" (covered phrases are noted with underlined words in Figure 2), appending the target phrase "To view a". Since for h_1, the user prefix $\mathbf{e}_p$ has already been generated, the expansion process works in the same way as the one executed in a regular translator. Let us suppose that we are covering the source phrase $\tilde{f} \equiv$"lista de recursos" given by the source positions $u = \{4,5,6\}$. We generate the new hypotheses h_3 and h_4 by appending target phrases $\tilde{e}$ from the set $\mathcal{T}_{\tilde{f}}$ of translations for $\tilde{f}$ contained in the phrase table.

Regarding the hypothesis h_2, it has covered the source phrase "Para" appending the target phrase "To". In this case, the prefix $\mathbf{e}_p$ has not been completely generated. Let $\mathbf{e}_r \equiv$ "view a" be the remaining words that are to be appended to h_2 to complete the user prefix. In this case, we have to take into account whether we are covering the last source phrase positions or not. For example, let us suppose that we cover the phrase positions $u = \{2,3,4,5,6\}$ ($\tilde{f} \equiv$ "ver la lista de recursos"). Since those are the last positions to be covered, we have to ensure that the whole prefix $\mathbf{e}_p$ is generated. For this purpose, we append $\mathbf{e}_r$ to h_2, resulting in the hypothesis h_5. In addition, we can append phrases $\tilde{e}$ contained in the set $\mathcal{T}_{\tilde{f}}$ having $\mathbf{e}_r$ as sub-prefix (if any). This allows the generation of hypotheses like h_6 that takes advantage of the information contained in the phrase table.

In contrast, if we are not covering the last phrase positions of h_2, we can also append strings from the set $\mathcal{S}_{\mathbf{e}_r}$ of sub-prefixes of $\mathbf{e}_r$ to the newly generated hypotheses, allowing the translation system to complete the whole prefix $\mathbf{e}_p$ in subsequent expansion processes. For example, let us suppose that we cover the phrase positions $u = \{2\}$ ($\tilde{f} \equiv$ "ver"). In this case we can append the phrase "view" which is a subprefix of $\mathbf{e}_r$, resulting in the hypothesis h_7. In addition, we can also append $\mathbf{e}_r$ itself, resulting in the hypothesis h_8. Finally, appending phrases from $\mathcal{T}_{\tilde{f}}$ having $\mathbf{e}_r$ as subprefix (if any) can also be considered, although this situation has not been depicted in Figure 2.

Algorithm 1 shows the expansion algorithm that we propose for its application in IMT. The algorithm is a formalization of the ideas depicted in Figure 2.

The time cost of the IMT expansion algorithm can be reduced by the introduction of pruning techniques. Such pruning techniques include hypotheses recombination, stack length limitation and restrictions on the maximum number of target phrases that can be linked to an unaligned source phrase during the expansion process. Specifically, in those cases where $\mathbf{e}_p$ has not already been generated, only a subset of the strings contained in the set $\mathcal{S}_{\mathbf{e}_r}$ are considered as candidates for the expansion process. One possible criterion to choose the substrings is based on the length of the phrase $\tilde{f}$ to be translated determined by u. Only those substrings with lengths similar to the length of $\tilde{f}$ are considered. In addition, the set of expanded hypotheses that is returned by the algorithm can be sorted by score, keeping only the best ones.

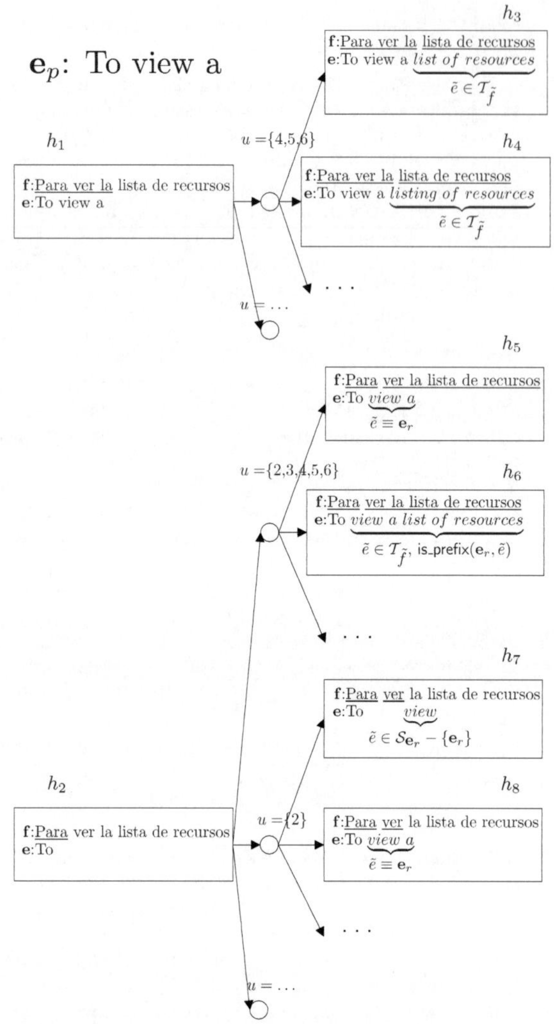

Fig. 2: *Example of the expansion of two hypotheses h_1 and h_2 given $\mathbf{f} \equiv$ "Para ver la lista de recursos" and the user prefix $\mathbf{e}_p \equiv$ "To view a"*

```
input    : e_p (user validated prefix), hyp (hypothesis to
           be expanded)
output   : hyp_vector (Vector of expanded hypotheses)
auxiliar: U_hyp (set of uncovered phrase positions of
           hyp), S_{e_r} (set of sub-prefixes of e_r), T_f̃ (set
           of translations for f̃ in phrase table)
begin
  forall u ∈ U_hyp do
    f̃ =get_source_phrase(hyp,u);
    if hyp does not contain e_p then
      e_r =get_remaining_prefix (hyp,e_p);
      if u is the last phrase to be covered then
        forall ẽ ∈ S_{e_r} − {e_r} do
          add(hyp_vector,append(hyp,u,ẽ))
      add(hyp_vector,append(hyp,u,e_r));
      forall ẽ ∈ T_f̃ do
        if is_prefix(e_r,ẽ) and e_r ≠ ẽ then
          add(hyp_vector,append(hyp,u,ẽ))
    else
      forall ẽ ∈ T_f̃ do
        add(hyp_vector,append(hyp,u,ẽ))
end
```

Algorithm 1: Pseudocode for the IMT hypothesis expansion algorithm

7 Experimental results

In this section we describe the experiments we carried out to test the IMT techniques that we have presented in previous sections.

7.1 Experimental setup

The experiments were performed using the XEROX XRCE corpus [17], which consist of translation of Xerox printer manual involving three different pairs of languages: French-English, Spanish-English, and German-English. The main features of these corpora are shown in Table 1. Partitions into training, development, and test were performed by randomly selecting (without replacement) a specific number of development and test sentences and leaving the remaining ones for training. In order to get a first impression of the complexity of these corpora, the BLEU score and the number of sentences with coverage problems of the test partition (for both translation directions) are also reported. As can be seen, there is a great number of sentences that present coverage problems for the different corpora.

It is worth noting that the manuals were not the same in each pair of languages, therefore the figures for the different English counterparts are shown.

IMT experiments were carried out for both directions of the three different corpora.

7.2 Assessment criteria

The evaluation of the techniques presented in this papers were carried out using the *Key-stroke and mouse-action ratio* (KSMR) measure [1], which is calculated as the number of keystrokes plus the number of *mouse movements* plus one more count per sentence (aimed at simulating the user action needed to accept the final translation), divided by the total number of reference characters.

In the experiments we carried out only one reference translation was considered.

7.3 IMT results

In Table 2 the IMT results using different phrase-to-phrase alignment smoothing techniques are presented, for three different language pairs and translation directions, Geometric distributions were selected to implement both the f_3 and f_5 feature functions. The first row of the table shows the baseline, which consists of the results obtained using a maximum likelihood estimation (ML) without smoothing. The rows labelled with (GT, AD, KN, and SD) show the results for the phrase-based model estimators presented

		Spa	**Eng**	**Fre**	**Eng**	**Ger**	**Eng**
Train	Sent. pairs	55761		52844		49376	
	Running words	657172	571960	573170	542762	440682	506877
	Vocabulary	29565	25627	27399	24958	37338	24899
Dev	Sent. pairs	1012		994		964	
	Running words	13808	12111	9801	9480	8283	9162
	Perplexity (3-grams)	34.0	46.2	74.1	96.2	124.3	68.4
Test	Sent. pairs	1125		984		996	
	Running words	9358	7634	9805	9572	9823	10792
	Running characters	57536	45770	62885	54757	70963	61327
	Perplexity (3-grams)	59.6	107.0	135.4	192.6	169.2	92.8
	BLEU score	58.7	51.1	26.7	24.9	24.8	16.4
	Sents. with coverage problems	617	633	615	653	724	722

Table 1: XEROX *corpus statistics for three differente language pairs*

in section 5.1. The rest of the rows corresponds to different estimation techniques combined with linear interpolation (LI), backing-off (BO), and log-linear interpolation (LL). As was expected (see section 5.2) linear interpolation and backing-off obtains better results than log-linear interpolation.

The baseline system obtained by far the worst results. In contrast, all those experiments that included the LEX distribution outperformed the others due to improved assignment of probabilities to unseen events.

Smooth.	**Spa-Eng**	**Fre-Eng**	**Ger-Eng**
ML	36.7/32.5	59.4/53.2	63.6/57.2
GT	28.6/29.4	51.9/49.4	57.7/53.0
AD	30.3/28.1	50.4/46.7	58.4/52.5
KN	30.3/28.1	50.4/46.7	58.4/52.4
SD	28.5/29.4	51.6/49.2	57.1/52.5
ML+LEX$_{\mathrm{LI}}$	21.2/21.3	39.9/39.2	43.9/42.4
GT+LEX$_{\mathrm{LI}}$	21.1/21.3	39.9/39.2	44.2/42.2
AD+LEX$_{\mathrm{LI}}$	21.4/22.2	40.2/40.5	45.1/42.2
KN+LEX$_{\mathrm{LI}}$	21.5/22.2	40.1/40.5	45.0/42.2
SD+LEX$_{\mathrm{LI}}$	21.2/21.2	39.9/39.0	44.0/41.8
GT+LEX$_{\mathrm{BO}}$	21.1/21.0	39.8/39.0	45.3/42.3
SD+LEX$_{\mathrm{BO}}$	21.2/21.0	39.8/39.2	45.1/42.3
ML+LEX$_{\mathrm{LL}}$	37.5/35.5	59.5/53.7	64.3/58.0
GT+LEX$_{\mathrm{LL}}$	24.0/25.8	43.2/43.3	50.9/46.9
AD+LEX$_{\mathrm{LL}}$	30.8/29.2	51.3/46.9	59.7/52.1
KN+LEX$_{\mathrm{LL}}$	30.9/29.1	51.4/46.9	59.7/52.0
SD+LEX$_{\mathrm{LL}}$	23.6/27.7	43.2/42.7	50.7/45.9

Table 2: *KSMR results for the three* XEROX *corpora (for both direct and inverse translation directions separated by the symbol "/") for different smoothing techniques. Geometric distributions were selected to implement the f_3 and f_5 feature functions*

In order to study the effect of the different probability distributions used for the feature functions f_3 (target phrase length model) and f_5 (source phrase length model) an exhaustive experimentation was carried for all smoothing techniques, and their respective combinations with the Lexical distribution. Table 3 reports the KSMR results for all possible combinations of the probability distributions used for f_3 (Uniform (U) and Geometric (G)) and for f_5 (Uniform (U), Geometric (G), and Poisson (P)). As can be seen in this table slight KSMR differences are obtained. In Table 3 only the results obtained for the best smoothing technique (Good-Turing) are reported. The best results were obtained when U+G distribution were used for the GT smoothing estimation, and G+G for the BO combination. As was mentioned in section 4.1, the use of a uniform distribution for f_3 penalizes the length of the segmentation and the use of a geometric distribution penalized the length of the source phrases. Correspondingly, the use of a geometric distribution for f_5 makes it possible to establish a relationship between the length of source and target phrases (the use of a Poisson distribution also worked well).

Smooth.	f_3, f_5	**Spa-Eng**	**Fre-Eng**	**Ger-Eng**
GT	U,U	30.1/29.0	53.8/50.7	58.0/53.9
	U,P	29.5/28.6	52.9/49.7	57.6/53.4
	U,G	28.7/28.0	51.7/48.7	57.3/52.7
	G,U	30.5/29.7	54.6/51.5	58.5/54.4
	G,P	29.7/29.4	53.3/50.5	58.2/53.7
	G,G	28.6/29.4	51.9/49.4	57.7/53.0
GT+ LEX$_{\mathrm{BO}}$	U,U	21.8/21.6	40.4/39.1	44.8/42.2
	U,P	21.5/21.4	40.2/39.0	44.3/42.0
	U,G	21.3/21.4	40.1/38.8	44.0/41.8
	G,U	21.6/21.5	40.3/39.1	44.6/42.1
	G,P	21.4/21.3	40.0/39.0	44.2/41.9
	G,G	21.1/21.0	39.8/39.0	45.3/42.3

Table 3: *KSMR results for the three* XEROX *corpora (for both direct and inverse translation directions separated by the symbol "/") for all possible combinations of the probability distributions for the f_3 and f_5 feature functions when using two different smoothing techniques*

In Table 4 the IMT results for the three considered corpora (for both translation directions) are shown. MERT training for the development corpus was performed to adjust the weights of the log-linear model. In this case, only the Good-Turing (GT) and Simple Discount (SD) results are reported, showing that both techniques yielded similar results. The last column of Table 4 shows the average time in seconds per iteration needed to complete a new translation given a user validated prefix. Clearly, these times allow the system to work on a real time scenario.

Finally, in Table 5 a comparison of the best results obtained in this work (Partial Statistical Phrase-based Alignments (PSPBA)) with state-of-the-art IMT systems is reported (95% confidence intervals are shown). We compared our system with those presented in [1]: the alignment templates (AT), the stochastic finite-state transducer (SFST), and the phrase-based (PB)

Corpus	Smooth.	KSMR	secs./iter.
Spa–Eng	GT+LEX$_{BO}$	19.6	0.086
	SD+LEX$_{BO}$	19.6	0.090
Eng–Spa	GT+LEX$_{BO}$	17.5	0.093
	SD+LEX$_{BO}$	17.6	0.094
Fre–Eng	GT+LEX$_{BO}$	36.9	0.204
	SD+LEX$_{BO}$	37.0	0.205
Eng–Fre	GT+LEX$_{BO}$	34.4	0.148
	SD+LEX$_{BO}$	34.4	0.147
Ger–Eng	GT+LEX$_{BO}$	39.5	0.170
	SD+LEX$_{BO}$	39.5	0.184
Eng–Ger	GT+LEX$_{BO}$	39.1	0.152
	SD+LEX$_{BO}$	39.2	0.154

Table 4: *KSMR results for the three* XEROX *corpora, using geometric distributions for f_3 and f_5 feature functions. MERT training was performed. The average time (in secs.) per iteration is also reported*

Corpus	AT	PB	SFST	PSPBA
Spa–Eng	24.0±1.3	18.1±1.2	26.9±1.3	19.6±1.1
Eng–Spa	23.2±1.3	16.7±1.2	21.8±1.4	17.6±1.1
Fre–Eng	40.5±1.4	37.2±1.3	45.5±1.3	37.0±1.4
Eng–Fre	40.4±1.4	35.8±1.3	43.8±1.6	34.4±1.2
Ger–Eng	45.9±1.2	36.7±1.2	46.6±1.4	39.5±1.1
Eng–Ger	44.7±1.2	40.1±1.2	45.7±1.4	39.2±1.1

Table 5: *KSMR results comparison of our system and three different state-of-the art IMT systems. 95% confidence intervals are shown*

approaches to IMT. As can be seen, our system obtains similar results and in some cases clearly outperforms the results obtained by these IMT systems. Specifically, our results were better than those obtained by the SFST and the AT systems. In contrast, the KSMR results with respect to the PB approach were similar.

8 Conclusions

We have presented a new technique for IMT which is based on the generation of partial alignments at phrase-level. The generation of such partial alignments is driven by statistical phrase-based models and relies on the application of smoothing techniques to assign probabilities to unseen events.

The experiments we carried out show the great impact of the smoothing techniques in the accuracy of our system. The combination of a phrase-based model estimator with a lexical distribution yielded the best results. Three different combination techniques were tested: backing-off, linear interpolation and log-linear interpolation. As we expected, backing-off and linear interpolation worked better than log-linear

Finally, we have compared the results obtained by our system with those obtained by state-of-the-art IMT systems. Our system obtained similar results and in some cases clearly outperformed the results obtained by the state-of-the-art systems.

Acknowledgments

Authors wish to thank Antonio Lagarda and Luis Rodríguez for their corpus preprocessing software. This work has been partially supported by the Spanish research programme Consolider Ingenio 2010: MIPRCV (CSD2007-00018) and the EC (FEDER), the Spanish MEC under grant TIN2006-15694-CO2-01 and the Spanish JCCM under grant PBI08-0210-7127.

References

[1] S. Barrachina, O. Bender, F. Casacuberta, J. Civera, E. Cubel, S. Khadivi, A. L. H. Ney, J. Tomás, and E. Vidal. Statistical approaches to computer-assisted translation. *Computational Linguistics*, page In press, 2008. doi: 10.1162/coli.2008.07-055-R2-06-29.

[2] O. Bender, S. Hasan, D. Vilar, R. Zens, and H. Ney. Comparison of generation strategies for interactive machine translation. In *Conference of the European Association for Machine Translation*, pages 33–40, Budapest, Hungary, May 2005.

[3] P. F. Brown, S. A. Della Pietra, V. J. Della Pietra, and R. L. Mercer. The mathematics of statistical machine translation: Parameter estimation. *Computational Linguistics*, 19(2):263–311, 1993.

[4] J. Civera, J. M. Vilar, E. Cubel, A. L. Lagarda, S. Barrachina, E. Vidal, F. Casacuberta, D. Picó, and J. González. From machine translation to computer assisted translation using finite-state models. In *Proc. of EMNLP*, Barcelona, 2004.

[5] G. Foster. *Text Prediction for Translators*. PhD thesis, Université de Montréal, 2002.

[6] G. Foster, R. Kuhn, and H. Johnson. Phrasetable smoothing for statistical machine translation. In *Proc. of the EMNLP*, pages 53–61, Sydney, Australia, July 2006. ACL.

[7] G. Foster, P. Langlais, and G. Lapalme. User-friendly text prediction for translators. In *Proc. of EMNLP'02*, pages 148–155, 2002.

[8] I. García-Varea, D. Ortiz, F. Nevado, P. A. Gómez, and F. Casacuberta. Automatic segmentation of bilingual corpora: A comparison of different techniques. In *Proc. of the 2nd IbPRIA*, volume 3523 of *LNCS*, pages 614–621. Estoril (Portugal), June 2005.

[9] F. Jelinek. A fast sequential decoding algorithm using a stack. *IBM Journal of Research and Development*, 13:675–685, 1969.

[10] P. Koehn, F. J. Och, and D. Marcu. Statistical phrase-based translation. In *Proc. of the Human Language Technology and North American Association for Computational Linguistics Conference (HLT/NAACL)*, pages 48–54, Edmonton, Canada, May 2003.

[11] P. Langlais, G. Lapalme, and M. Loranger. Transtype: Development-evaluation cycles to boost translator's productivity. *Machine Translation*, 15(4):77–98, 2002.

[12] C. D. Manning and H. Schütze. *Foundations of Statistical Natural Language Processing*. MIT Press, Cambridge, Massachusetts 02142, 2001.

[13] D. Marcu and W. Wong. A phrase-based, joint probability model for statistical machine translation. In *emnlp*, pages 1408–1414, Philadelphia, USA, July 2002.

[14] F. J. Och and H. Ney. Discriminative Training and Maximum Entropy Models for Statistical Machine Translation. In *Proc. of the 40th ACL*, pages 295–302, Philadelphia, PA, July 2002.

[15] F. J. Och, R. Zens, and H. Ney. Efficient search for interactive statistical machine translation. In *EACL '03: Tenth Conf. of the Europ. Chapter of the Association for Computational Linguistics*, pages 387–393, Budapest, Hungary, Apr. 2003.

[16] D. Ortiz-Martínez, I. García-Varea, and F. Casacuberta. Phrase-level alignment generation using a smoothed loglinear phrase-based statistical alignment model. In *Proc. of EAMT'08*, Hamburg, Germany, September 2008.

[17] SchlumbergerSema S.A., I. T. de Informática, R. W. T. H. A. L. für Informatik VI, R. A. en Linguistique Informatique Laboratory University of Montreal, C. Soluciones, S. Gamma, and X. R. C. Europe. TT2. TransType2 - computer assisted translation. Project technical annex., 2001.

[18] J. Tomás and F. Casacuberta. Statistical phrase-based models for interactive computer-assisted translation. In *Proceedings of the Coling/ACL2006*, pages 835–841, Sydney, Australia, 17th-21th July 2006. http://acl.ldc.upenn.edu/P/P06/P06-2107.pdf.

[19] R. Zens, F. J. Och, and H. Ney. Phrase-based statistical machine translation. In *Advances in artificial intelligence. 25. Annual German Conference on AI*, volume 2479 of *LNCS*, pages 18–32. Springer Verlag, Sept. 2002.

Topic Modeling of Research Fields: An Interdisciplinary Perspective

Michael Paul and Roxana Girju
University of Illinois at Urbana-Champaign
{mjpaul2,girju}@illinois.edu

Abstract

This paper addresses the problem of scientific research analysis. We use the topic model Latent Dirichlet Allocation [2] and a novel classifier to classify research papers based on topic and language. Moreover, we show various insightful statistics and correlations within and across three research fields: Linguistics, Computational Linguistics, and Education. In particular, we show how topics change over time within each field, what relations and influences exist between topics within and across fields, as well as what trends can be established for some of the world's natural languages. Finally, we talk about trend prediction and topic suggestion as future extensions of this research.

Keywords

topic models; scientific research analysis; statistical approaches

1 Introduction

No one can predict (at least not in detail) the stringent issues that science and society will consider in the next decades. However, if we look at some top-priority issues of today - such as health, economy, homeland security, stem-cell research, science teaching - and pressing research questions, such as how to enhance child development and learning and even how to make sense of the huge amount of information with which we deal daily, we can say that future topics will be so complex as to require insights from multiple disciplines.

Interdisciplinary research will thus facilitate the integration of information, data, techniques, tools, perspectives, concepts, and/or theories from two or more disciplines or sources of specialized knowledge to advance fundamental understanding or to solve problems whose solutions are beyond the scope of a single discipline or field of research.

We believe that like other disciplines, Computational Linguistics (CL) will drastically benefit from an interdisciplinary perspective. This research is part of a larger project whose goal is to design a system which will help foster interdisciplinary research in order to make breakthrough predictions for future directions. The system is also intended to promote interdisciplinary collaborations by providing novel topic suggestions to professionals who would like to engage in research discussions with other parties, but who are not familiar with those areas.

This paper presents details about the current version of our system which *researches* a set of three fields: Linguistics, Computational Linguistics, and Education (we include here Educational psychology). Based on various topic models which classify research papers into topic and language categories, the system displays a series of statistics, correlations, and graphics which show the dynamics of topics and local and global trends based on the proceedings of the major conferences and journals in the three fields over many years. In particular, we show how topics change over time within each field, what relations exist between topics, what temporal correlations and topic influences can be determined across fields, as well as what trends can be established for some of the world's natural languages. Finally, we mention some future extensions of this research including suggestions for novel topics by combining research ideas across fields as well as predicting future trends from this combination.

2 Previous Work

Most of the work on the analysis of scientific research deals with citations [11]. This includes the examination of the frequency, patterns and graphs of citations in articles and books. Citation analysis uses citations in scholarly works to establish a graph with links between works and researchers. The web has had a major impact on this type of research leading to the creation of databases such as *Scopus* (www.scopus.com) and *Google Scholar* (scholar.google.com) which allow the analysis of citation patterns of academic papers.

Citation analysis, however is limited in that the citation graphs created are sparse and they do not span related fields. For example, the citation analysis literature [9] shows that 90% of papers published in academic journals are never cited. Moreover 50% of papers are never read by anyone else but their authors, referees, and journal editors.

Another approach to the analysis of scientific research relies on topic models which uncover structures used to explore text collections. In particular, they divide documents according to their topics and use the hidden structure to determine similarity between documents. Popular unsupervised topic models such as Latent Dirichlet Allocation (LDA) [2] and hierarchical models [7] have been successfully applied to various publications such as *The American Political Science Review* and *Science*. In Computational Linguistics, the only work of which we are aware is that of Hall et al. 2008 [4] who study the history of ideas using LDA and topic entropy.

In this paper we extend over the work of Hall et al. 2008 [4] by adding two related fields (Linguistics and Education) and by employing various novel topic models for scientific research analysis.

3 Approach

In this section we present the data used in this research and the topic models employed. We categorize both by topics

International Conference RANLP 2009 - Borovets, Bulgaria, pages 337–342

Field	Venue	Number of documents	Year range
LING	Language	1031	78-08
LING	Linguistics, Journal of	152	97-08
LING	Linguistic Inquiry	338	98-08
LING	Ling. & Philosophy	652	77-08
CL	ACL	1826	79-08
CL	EACL	517	83-06
CL	NAACL	543	01-07
CL	Applied NLP	262	83-00
CL	COLING	1549	63-
EDU	Education, Journal of	491	75-06
EDU	Educational Psych.	1116	90-08

Table 1: *This table presents the number of documents per field and publication venue. CL stands for Computational Linguistics, LING - Linguistics, EDU - Education.*

and by language.

3.1 The Data

Our corpus consists of approximately 4,700 papers (1965-2008) from the ACL Anthology [1], 2,300 papers from Linguistics journals (1977-2008), and 1,700 papers from Education journals (1975-2008). The exact distribution is shown in Table 1. To best represent each field, we chose top journals (Linguistics and Education) and conferences (CL) that have broad topic coverage of their respective fields. The papers were obtained from library and publisher websites. Only titles and abstracts were freely (and electronically) available for papers in the Linguistics and Education journals.

3.2 Modeling the Research Fields

3.2.1 Modeling Linguistics

Some, albeit only a small fraction, of the Linguistics papers were already categorized (with overlap) in their original publications. Specifically, *Language*, *Journal of Linguistics*, and *Linguistic Inquiry* provided 320 labels for 190 of these papers. Moreover, we manually labeled an additional 147 papers with 185 labels to increase coverage and to create more training data for underrepresented categories. We labeled these papers with categories from the original set as well as new topics that were missing, such as *typology, pragmatics*, and *metaphor*. In the end, there were 86 distinct categorization topics. Of the remaining 2,149 unlabeled papers, we had abstracts for 281, and only titles for the rest. The small training set and document lengths make this a difficult classification problem. To begin, we constructed a basic Naïve Bayes classifier that assigns each document D a probability of belonging to each category c_j, defined as

$$P(c_j|D) = P(c_j) \prod_{f_i \in F_D} (P(f_i|c_j)) \tag{1}$$

where F_D is the feature set of document D. The feature space consists of both words from the text, titles and abstracts of documents as well as the bigrams from these strings. Bigrams are useful here – for example, the word "languages" is not so informative, but the phrases "languages in" and "languages of" indicate discussion of languages in a certain region or family, and thus should tilt toward the *language documentation* and *typology* categories.

Since some categories are significantly under-labeled, instead of defining $P(c_j)$ as the observed probability, we assume that the categories have a uniform distribution. The probability of a feature given a class is estimated using Laplace smoothing [10]:

$$P(f_i|c_j) = \frac{n_i + 1}{n + |F|} \tag{2}$$

where n_i is the number of examples labeled c_j that have f_i as an active feature, n is the number of unique active features among all examples labeled c_j, and F is the feature set.

We want to allow a paper to be placed into multiple categories, or none, if it does not match any category. For such an any-of classification task, one would typically create a binary classifier for each class and determine membership in each class individually [8]. We do not do this here because papers were labeled with some but not all of the categories they might belong to, so we cannot assume that the absence of a label implies that a document can be used as a negative example for membership to a class.

Instead, we label a paper with some subset of categories in which $P(c_j|D)$ is significantly greater than the others. To do this, we first perform z-score normalization on the probabilities [5]. The z-score of a value p is defined as $\frac{p-\bar{P}}{\sigma}$, where $\bar{P}$ is the average over each p_j and σ is the standard deviation.

We then say that a paper D belongs to all categories such that the z-score of $P(c_j|D)$ is above some threshold. This means that the probability assigned to the category is greater than the average by some distance relative to the standard deviation of the probability values.

In an attempt to strengthen the training data, we took a semi-supervised approach and added to the training set documents that were labeled with a probability above a constant confidence threshold. This process was iteratively repeated until no new examples were added to the training set.

For an estimate of this classifier's performance, we performed 10-fold cross validation. Table 2 shows however that its initial performance was not good enough to make accurate observations.

We improved over this approach employing a model proposed by Zelik & Hirsh 2000 [12]. The idea is to use an unlabeled corpus of background knowledge to match unlabeled examples with labeled examples. Thus, if a labeled document A is similar to some document W in the background corpus and an unlabeled document B is similar to the same document W, then perhaps B should have the same label as A. This method is particularly useful when the training set is very small and when the strings to classify are short.

To create our background corpus, we grabbed the Wikipedia articles categorized under *Linguistics*, truncating the documents down to the main content part and removing the HTML tags. Each article is represented as a vector of the tf-idf measures of the words in its text, with log term frequencies and $\text{IDF}(t) = log(\frac{|d|}{|d_t|})$.

The same tf-idf representation is used for our labeled and unlabeled research papers. The cosine measure is used to calculate the similarity $sim(D_i, W_j)$ between a paper and a Wikipedia article. Let $v_{D,c}$ be the score assigned to a document D for a category c based on this matching through Wikipedia. We define this as

$$v_{D,c} = \sum_{A_i \in W_D} \sum_{L_j \in X_{Ai}} I(c \in L_j) sim(L_j, A_i)^2 sim(A_i, D) \quad (3)$$

where W_D is the set of Wikipedia articles that are similar to D above a threshold cosine score λ_c, X_{Ai} is the set of labeled papers with similarity scores to an article A_i greater than λ_c, and I is the indicator function. λ_c is defined as some constant k standard deviations above the mean similarity measurement between a category c and each article. This assigns a larger v to the categories with the highest similarity to the Wikipedia articles which are highly similar to D (the paper we are attempting to label).

We can now classify a document by augmenting the original Naïve Bayes probability $P(c|D)$ with this new v score as follows.

During testing, we noticed that $P(c|D)$ was a more accurate weight than $v_{D,c}$ (or vice versa) for certain categories. For example, Naïve Bayes alone could correctly label a paper as *historical linguistics* in the presence of a word such as "history", but matching through Wikipedia would usually point the classifier to an irrelevant class.

To compensate for this problem, we introduce a bias factor α, defined as the mean value of $P(c|D)$ or $v_{D,c}$ for each document D in the training set that is labeled as c, where both $P(c|D)$ and $v_{D,c}$ have been normalized to the same range. We calculate α values during a run of the cross-validation test, then rerun the classifier with these values.

Finally, to label a document, we assign each document a weight toward a class c, defined as

$$w_{D,c} = log(1+(frac_{NB,c}P(c|D)))+log(1+(frac_{W,c}v_{D,c})) \quad (4)$$

where $frac_{Z,c} = \frac{\alpha_{Z,c}}{\alpha_{NB,c}+\alpha_{W,c}}$.

$frac$ distributes the weights between the methods (Naïve Bayes or Wikipedia matching) according to how they usually perform on the class c.

$w_{D,c}$ increases with the size of class c, so we adjust the confidence threshold according to this. Then, a paper D is labeled as the category c if the z-score of $w_{D,c}$ is above the variable threshold δ_c, which is defined as the prior probability $P(c)$ normalized to fit the range $[\delta_L, \delta_U]$ for some constant lower/upper threshold bounds.

This classification performance is listed in Table 2 (Combined NB + Wikipedia). This performance is actually slightly worse than the semi-supervised Naïve Bayes classifier. However, it was able to correctly classify papers that Naïve Bayes could not.

We then took an additional step of semi-supervision and extracted the top results (with a score above some threshold) of our combined Naïve Bayes with Wikipedia classifier and added them to the training set. We re-ran our original semi-supervised Naïve Bayes classifier with this new training set to get our final results (last row in Table 2).

3.2.2 Modeling Computational Linguistics

Most of the papers in the ACL Anthology are not categorized, so unsupervised methods were needed to label them.

Model	P	R	F
Supervised NB	0.59	0.68	0.63
Semi-supervised NB	0.89	0.68	0.77
Combined NB + Wikipedia	0.85	0.67	0.75
Semi-super. w/ new labels	0.91	0.78	0.84

Table 2: *Classification performance for the Linguistics data. NB stands for Naïve Bayes.*

We chose to use the generative model Latent Dirichlet Allocation [2], which represents documents as random mixtures over latent topics, where each topic is characterized by a multinomial distribution of words.

After removing a standard list of stop words, we ran LDA to induce 100 topics on the text of the papers and saved 72 topics that were relevant. A sample of these topics is shown in Table 3.

3.2.3 Modeling Education

We used a similar process for the field of Education. We ran LDA on the Education papers using the words from the titles and abstracts, as the full text was not available. We used these data to induce 30 topics and chose 18 that were relevant. Two of these 18 topics were specifically relevant to language – *reading/language comprehension* and *reading/language instruction*. We repeated the LDA process on this subset of language-related papers and grouped them into 8 additional topics. Samples of these topics are shown in Table 3.

3.3 Categorizing by Language

In addition to labeling papers by topic, we noted which languages were discussed in papers. Thus, we simply labeled a paper with the languages that appear in its text above a certain frequency threshold. Intuitively, this should work except for a few cases and with a few languages. English, for example, is not always explicitly mentioned in papers that focus on English, and Greek returns false positives in Education because of Greek culture studies. Otherwise, empirically this works quite well – if a language is mentioned at least a few times in a paper, then we would like this paper to be labeled as such.

4 Data Analysis

In the following subsections we present insightful observations on the data classification and discuss potential trends.

4.1 Changes Over Time

To measure a topic's prominence over time, we look at the fraction of papers within that topic dated in a given year out of all papers from that year. We perform least squares linear regression on the temporal data points for each topic to see if and by how much a topic has a general upward/downward trend.

Within Computational Linguistics, our findings are similar to those presented by Hall et al. 2008 [4]. Thus, *text classification* has the largest upward trend. *Natural language interfaces* and *speech act interpretation* are

Topic	Keywords
	Linguistics
Pragmatics	pragmatics attitudes meaning semantics pragmatic inference communication
Prosody	accent intonation initial prosodic prosody contour fall stress phonological
Psycholinguistics	mental psychological language processing psychology representations triggers
Quantifiers	quantifier quantification quantifiers existential scope generalized polyadic
Semantics	semantic semantics meaning lexical content pragmatics meanings conceptual
	Computational Linguistics
Morphology	morphological word morphology lexical level forms form lexicon stem words
MT Evaluation	evaluation score human scores sentence automatic quality reference metrics
Multimodal NLP	multimodal speech gesture user language input figure spoken based systems
Named Entities	entity names named entities ne information person location muc extraction
Optimality Theory	constraints constraint dominance theory language phonological structure stress
	Education
Race/Ethnicity Issues	american students african teachers ethnic minority stereotypes Educational
Reading Instruction	reading children phonological instruction awareness grade spelling skills
Reading Comprehension	reading language comprehension english children vocabulary word readers
Self Concept/Efficacy	self concept efficacy academic model relations skill domain ability
Teaching Effectiveness	learning multimedia students evaluations teaching effectiveness factor

Table 3: *Slice of topics and their top keywords in Linguistics, Computational Linguistics, and Education.*

among the strongest-declining topics. In general, *formal semantics* and similar theoretical topics have taken a nose-dive since the 1980s, while *statistical/probabilistic methods* have strongly increased. Within the area of *semantics*, there are some topics on the rise, such as *word sense disambiguation*, *semantic role labeling*, and *event/temporal semantics*.

In Linguistics, no topic showed a strong rise in prominence, at least not among topics that were large enough to give accurate trends over time. For the most part, topics fluctuate year-to-year, but do not have an overall trend. There were, however some topics with a noticeable decline. Thus, an interesting observation is that while in Computational Linguistics *formal semantics* took a significant plunge, it has declined less dramatically in the field of Linguistics while still remaining relatively prominent (see Table 1). The statistics indicate that *language documentation, historical linguistics*, and *pragmatics* show the most marked decline in Linguistics. *Discourse* shows a sudden decline in the late 1990s – to compare, *discourse segmentation* has a steady rise in CL, but *discourse Centering Theory* has a steady decline. Interestingly, the prevalence of computational Linguistics papers in the linguistics journals peaked in the late-80s and early-90s and has since declined. Moreover, *language acquisition* has declined in the Linguistics field in the past decade, whereas it has risen in the Education field in the same time period.

Morphology, prosody, and *quantifiers* have a steady decline in CL, whereas they stayed fairly consistent (but small) in Linguistics.

In Education, there is a markedly strong rise in prominence of topics about *language and reading*. *Student performance* is another topic with a strong increase, while *epistemology* has slightly declined. These are shown in Figure 2.

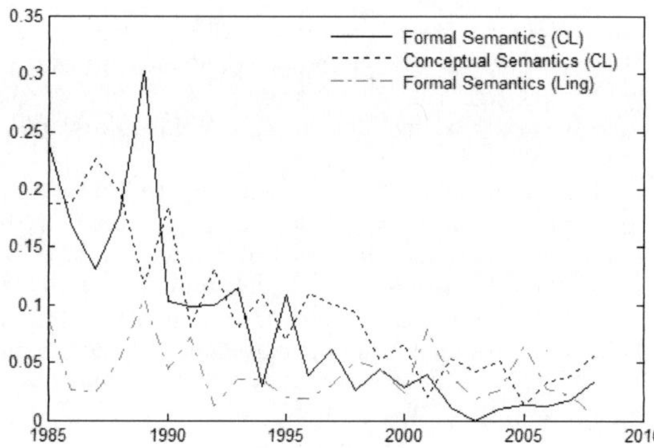

Fig. 1: Semantics *in Computational Linguistics and Linguistics over time.*

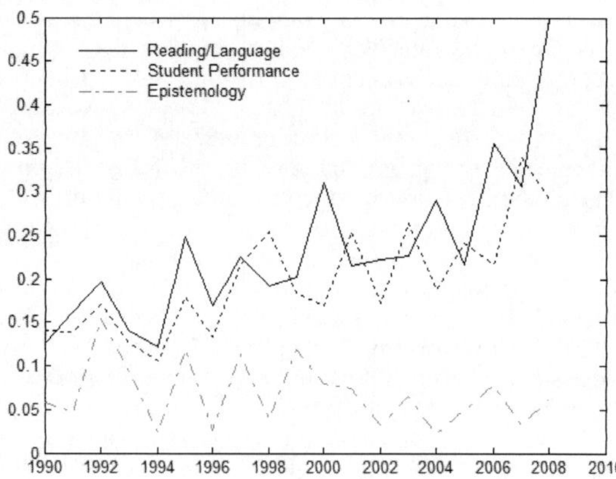

Fig. 2: *Most prominent upward/downward trends in Education.*

4.2 Relations Between Topics

We can see how different research areas are related by allowing papers to be assigned to multiple topics. For example, within computational Linguistics we found that the *dialogue systems* topic overlaps with *natural language interfaces* and *speech recognition* - some percentage of papers labeled as *dialogue systems* have also been labeled with these topics.

Of course, we also want to see how topics relate across

fields. Since we only modeled topics within each distinct field, we must determine which topics of different fields are similar. Thus, we create a topic meta-document for each topic by concatenating the words of every document within the class. We can then represent each topic as a vector of words from these documents (again weighted by their tf-idf value) and compute the similarity of these topic vectors by their cosine.

Figure 3 highlights the interdisciplinary nature of these fields. The links in the diagram show a sample of the highest-scoring similarity matches, where line thickness indicates increasing similarity value.

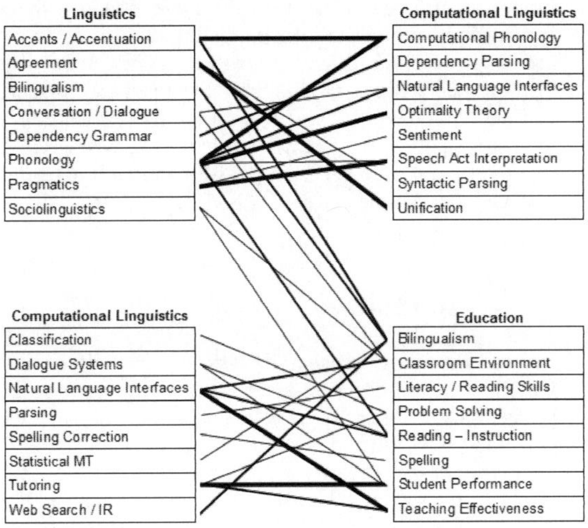

Fig. 3: *Similarity of topics across fields.*

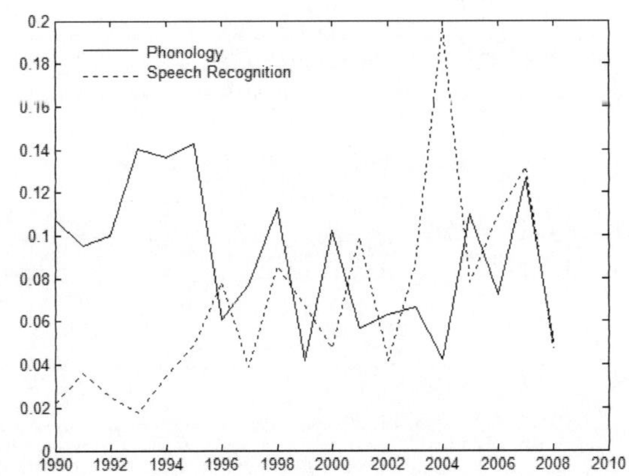

Fig. 4: *Similarity of topics across the speech and phonology fields.*

4.3 Language Trends

The most prominent languages (after English) within computational Linguistics are Japanese, German, French, Chinese, and Spanish. Within each language, we can look at the distribution of topics – although they were not strikingly different for the most part, there were some differences. The most prominent topic for Chinese, for example, is *word segmentation*, which did not receive the same attention in the other languages.

The Education field differs slightly in that its most prominent languages are Chinese, Spanish, German, and Korean in this order. Chinese and German have a pretty general topic distribution, while Spanish- and Korean-related papers are predominately about *bilingualism* and *language learning*. Japanese, German, Spanish, and French were found as the most prominent within Linguistics.

In Computational Linguistics, English and Japanese have remained consistently prominent throughout the years. Chinese and Arabic show strong increases, while Russian and Italian have a slight downward trend. French, German, and Spanish all rose through the late 80s and 90s and have since slightly declined.

Chinese and Spanish are on the rise in Education and Linguistics seems to be taking an increasing interest in Japanese.

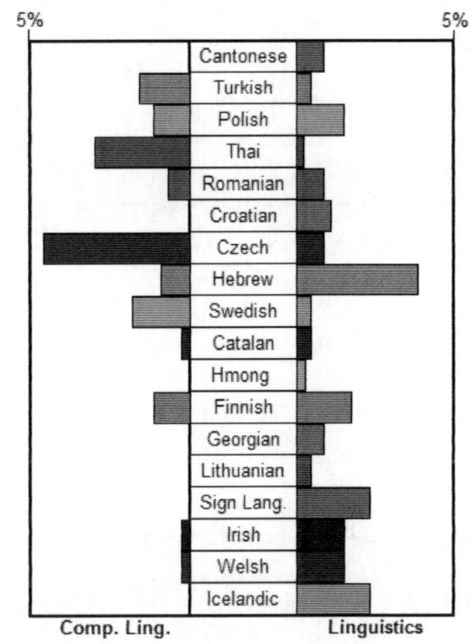

Fig. 5: *Comparison of less-spoken languages in Computational Linguistics and Linguistics.*

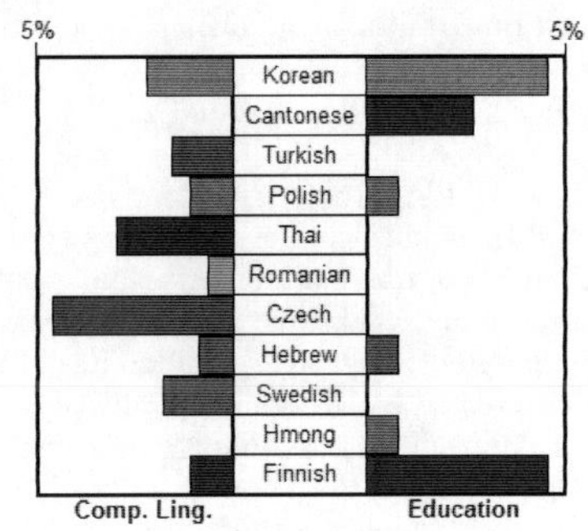

Fig. 6: *Comparison of less-spoken languages in Computational Linguistics and Education.*

It is also important to look at less-spoken but still prominent languages (Figures 5 and 6). There are some differences in the languages being discussed in Computational Linguistics compared to Linguistics and Education. For example, Czech, Thai, and Swedish are prominent in CL, Hebrew, Icelandic, sign languages, Irish, Welsh in Linguistics, and Korean, Finnish and Cantonese in Education[1].

We also compared specific topics over time across languages. For example, all Arabic papers in CL were in the *morphology* topic. The other top languages were mostly the same: *statistical MT* and *parsing* at the top.

5 Discussion

The statistics and observations presented in this paper have an important significance for the research community at large. Besides the potential of identifying novel topics, this information is useful for assessing which areas are important and which areas might currently be overlooked. Moreover, we showed that such a system can indicate interesting correlations among related fields, correlations which can be put to work in various ways. For example, these data can be very useful to computational linguists who can get ideas of novel topics or theoretical models from Linguistics, build sophisticated systems and apply them to Education. Another possibility is to use large-scale empirical Computational Linguistics models to help identify and develop new theories in Linguistics.

Most importantly this kind of research will hopefully foster collaboration among related fields. Moreover, tools such as the one presented here will be beneficial to young researchers who start their graduate studies looking for research topics within their field, but also in an interdisciplinary context.

In the next subsections we provide some detailed suggestions.

5.1 Suggestions for Research Directions

Although languages such as Arabic, Russian, and Korean have been studied in Computational Linguistics, they seem to be somewhat under-represented in the field relative to their importance in the world and other fields. Spanish is one such example – in spite of being one of the most-spoken world's languages and in spite of its rising importance in Education research, it continues to be underrepresented in Computational Linguistics. Cantonese, Hmong, Finnish, and Hebrew are significantly more prominent in Linguistics and Education than in CL.

Another general area that seems under-represented in Computational Linguistics is that of *dialects* and *dialectology*. While this has certainly been covered in Computational Linguistics, its prominence is small compared to that in Linguistics, and studies have mostly focused on a small subset of languages. Inconsistencies in natural language processing created by different dialects of a language is a known problem in the community [3], so this should be studied further.

Language evolution is a topic of interest in Linguistics, but very little has been done to study it using computational methods, at least among the papers in our collection. We did find a few papers on computational phylogeny in the Linguistics and Computational Linguistics corpora, but this appears to be a topic that could use more research.

[1] It seems that the Education field has focused mostly on languages spoken in the western education systems.

5.2 Trend Prediction and Topic Suggestion

We can go even further with the analysis of such correlations among related fields. For example, we have already shown in Section 4.3 that some fields seem to influence others on some particular topics, such as *phonology, speech recognition*, and *dialog systems*. Such possible influences indicate that we can go a step further towards trend prediction. Moreover, another goal for our research is to be able to suggest novel and interesting topics. For example, a closer look at our data collection, statistics, and trends indicates a potential research topic: *automatic note-taking* (i.e., how to build a system which takes notes automatically say, in an academic environment). To our knowledge the topic is novel in Computational Linguistics and has direct implications in Linguistics and Education. While in Linguistics it has not been studied[2], the topic has been well researched in Education (in particular from a learning and knowledge retention perspective). However, in oder to make trend prediction and topic suggestion possible, a much deeper analysis is needed on much larger text collections. This is left for future research.

6 Conclusions

In this paper we presented various novel topic models which classify research papers based on topic and language. Moreover, we gave various insightful statistics and correlations within and across three research fields: Linguistics, Computational Linguistics, and Education. In particular, we showed a number of trends in each field along with relations between topics, temporal correlations and topic influences across fields, as well as language trends.

References

[1] S. Bird. Association for Computational Linguistics Anthology. In *http://www.aclweb.org/anthology-index/*, 2008.

[2] D. Blei, A. Ng, and M. Jordan. Latent dirichlet allocation. *Journal of Machine Learning Research*, 3:993–1022, 2003.

[3] N. Habash. Arabic Natural Language Processing for Machine Translation. In ACL, editor, *Tutorial at the 8th Conference of the Association for Machine Translation in the Americas (AMTA)*. MIT Press, 2008.

[4] D. Hall, D. Jurafsky, and C. Manning. Studying the history of ideas using topic models. In *Empirical Natural Language Processing Conference*, 2008.

[5] J. Han and M. Kamber. *Data Mining: Concepts and Techniques*. 2nd Edition. Morgan Kaufmann, San Francisco, 2006.

[6] R. Janda. Note-taking english as a simplified register. *Discourse Processes*, 8:437–454, 1985.

[7] W. Li and A. McCallum. Dag-structured mixture models of topic correlations. In *International Conference on Machine Learning*, 2006.

[8] C. Manning, P. Raghavan, and H. Schutze. *Introduction to Information Retrieval*. Cambridge University Press, 2008.

[9] L. Meho. The Rise and Rise of citation analysis. *Physics World*, to appear.

[10] T. Mitchell. *Machine Learning*. McGraw Hill, New York, 1997.

[11] R. Rubin. *Foundations of Library and Information Science*. 2nd ed. New York: Neal-Schuman, 2004.

[12] S. Zelikovitz and H. Hirsh. Improving short text classification using unlabeled background knowledge to assess document similarity. In *The 17th International Conference on Machine Learning (ICML)*, 2000.

[2] Actually, note-taking has been studied in Linguistics by Richard Janda [6], but the paper was published in a different journal.

An Interaction Grammar of interrogative and relative clauses in French

Guy Perrier
LORIA - université Nancy 2
BP 239
54506 Vandœuvre-lès-Nancy cedex - France
guy.perrier@loria.fr

Abstract

We present a fairly complete grammar of interrogative and relative clauses in French, written in the formalism of Interaction Grammars. Interaction Grammars combine two key ideas: a grammar is viewed as a constraint system which is expressed through the notion of tree description, and the resource sensitivity of natural languages is used as a syntactic composition principle by means of a system of polarities.

Keywords

Syntax, grammatical formalism, tree description, polarity, interrogative clause , relative clause, interaction grammar

1 Introduction

This article is a contribution to the construction of formal grammars from linguistic knowledge. This task is motivated by both applicative and scientific considerations. From an applicative point of view, it is essential for NLP systems requiring a fine and complete syntactic analysis of natural languages. From a scientific point of view, formalization can be very helpful for linguists, who aim at capturing the complexity of a natural languages with relevant generalizations. In this task, one of the most difficult challenges is to get the largest possible coverage of these formal grammars.

Regarding this challenge, relative and interrogative clauses in French are a good test because they illustrate the complexity of natural languages in a very obvious manner. They give rise to interference between several phenomena, which are present in both types of clauses and justify a common study. In the following, a clause which is a relative clause or an interrogative clause is called a *wh-clause*. In this paper, we have highlighted four phenomena occurring with wh-clauses:

- *Wh-extraction*: a particular constituent is extracted from its canonical position in the wh-clause to be put in front of it: if the clause is interrogative, it contains the requested information and if the clause is relative, it contains a reference to the antecedent of the relative clause; in both cases, they are represented with grammatical words, which we call *wh-words*. The difficulty lies in the fact that extraction can occur through a chain of a possibly indeterminate number of embedded clauses. This gives rise to an unbounded dependency which is subject to special constraints, called *island constraints*.
- *Pied-piping*: in some cases, wh-words drag a complex phrase along with them in the extraction movement. Another unbounded dependency may be generated from the fact the wh-word can be embedded less or more deeply in the extracted phrase.
- *Subject inversion*: contrary to canonical constructions of clauses where the subject precedes the verb, wh-clauses allow subject inversion under some conditions. These conditions depend on various factors.
- *Interrogative and declarative marking*: in French, relative clauses and interrogative clauses often use the same wh-words but they differ in the fact that the first ones are marked declaratively, whereas the second ones are marked interrogatively. If we consider only written texts, there are four main ways of marking clauses interrogatively or declaratively: the punctuation, the position of subject clitics with respect to the verb, the construction of clauses as objects of verbs expecting questions, and special terms like *est-ce que*.

If we aim at capturing all these phenomena most fairly, we need a rich formalism but which is at the same time simple enough to keep the formal representations readable. We have chosen the formalism of Interaction Grammar (IG) [8], for two main reasons:

- The basic objects of the formalism are pieces of underspecified syntactic trees, which can combine very freely by superposition. Such a flexibility is used at the same time in the construction of modular grammars and then in the process of syntactic composition. In our application, underspecification will be used to represent unbounded dependencies related to wh-extraction and pied-piping.
- The resource sensitivity of natural languages is used as a principle of syntactic composition under the form of a system of polarities. In this way, syntactic composition consists in superposing pieces of syntactic trees under the control of polarities with the goal of saturating them. The

International Conference RANLP 2009 - Borovets, Bulgaria, pages 343–348

use of polarities for managing the interrogative and declarative marking of clauses is an elegant illustration of this principle.

In section 2, we give an informal presentation of IG with the help of an example. Then, we show how to build an IG of wh-clauses focusing on four phenomena: wh-extraction (section 3.1), pied-piping (section 3.2), subject inversion (section 3.3), interrogative and declarative marking (section 3.4). We end with an evaluation of the grammar.

2 Presentation of Interaction Grammars

2.1 Tree descriptions and polarities

The basic objects of IG [8] are *tree descriptions*, which can be viewed as partially specified syntactic trees. Their nodes represent syntactic constituents and they are labelled with feature structures representing the morpho-syntactic properties of constituents. The nodes are structured by two kinds of relations: dominance and precedence. Both can be underspecified.

Tree descriptions combine by superposition under the constraints of polarities expressing their saturation state. Polarities are attached to features, so that features are triples (name, polarity, value), which are called *polarized features*. Tree descriptions labelled with polarized feature structures are called *polarized tree descriptions (PTD)*.

The superposition of two PTDs is realized by merging some of their nodes. When two nodes merge, their feature structures are composed according to an operation, which reduces to classical unification if we forget polarities.

There are 5 polarities: neutral ($=$), positive ($\rightarrow$), negative ($\leftarrow$), virtual ($\sim$), saturated ($\leftrightarrow$). Polarities are composed according to an operation, denoted $\oplus$, defined by the following table .

$\oplus$	$=$	$\rightarrow$	$\leftarrow$	$\sim$	$\leftrightarrow$
$=$	$=$				
$\rightarrow$			$\leftrightarrow$	$\rightarrow$	
$\leftarrow$		$\leftrightarrow$		$\leftarrow$	
$\sim$		$\rightarrow$	$\leftarrow$	$\sim$	$\leftrightarrow$
$\leftrightarrow$				$\leftrightarrow$	

In this table, an empty entry means that the corresponding polarities fail to be composed. The neutral polarity applies to features that behave as non consumable resources, agreement features for instance. Other polarities interact together with the aim of being saturated. Thus, according to the table, there are two kinds of interactions:

- *Linear interactions*: a linear interaction occurs between exactly one positive feature $f \rightarrow v_1$ and one negative feature $f \leftarrow v_2$ to combine in a saturated feature $f \leftrightarrow v_1 \wedge v_2$[1]; in this way, both features become saturated. Then, they can only combine with virtual features; they cannot combine any more with another positive, negative or saturated feature. This mainly expresses interaction between predicates and arguments, in which one predicate requires exactly one argument for each function.
- *Non linear interactions*: a non linear interaction occurs between one saturated feature $f \leftrightarrow v$ and n (n being possibly equal to 0) virtual features $f \sim v_1, \ldots, f \sim v_n$ to saturate these virtual features into a feature $f \leftrightarrow v \wedge v_1 \cdots \wedge v_n$. This interaction can be viewed as an absorption of any number of virtual polarities by a saturated polarity. It mainly models two types of interactions: context requirements and applications of modifiers to constituents.[2]

The system of polarities presented here is not the only possible one. It is important to understand that the polarity system is a parameter of any IG. For instance, the system used in the initial presentation of IG [8] differs from the present system on one point: neutral features have the property of absorbing virtual features.

2.2 Syntactic composition and parsing

In IG, a *syntactic composition process* is defined as a sequence of PTD superpositions controlled by interactions between polarities. One superposition is composed of elementary operations of *node merging*. When two nodes merge, their feature structures are composed, which can give rise to some interactions between their polarized features.

A particular IG is defined by a finite set of PTDs, the *elementary PTDs (EPTDs)* of the grammar. In practice, the actual IGs are totally lexicalized: each EPTD has a special node that is linked to a word of the language; this node is unique and it is called the *anchor* of the EPTD.

All *valid syntactic trees* generated from the grammar are the *saturated trees* resulting from a syntactic composition process of a finite set of EPTDs. A saturated tree is a PTD that is a completely specified tree in which all polarities are neutral or saturated The language generated by the grammar is the set of the *yields* of the valid syntactic trees, that is the sequences of words attached to the leaves of the trees.

To parse a sentence with a particular IG, we first have to select an EPTD for each word of the sentence: the anchor of the PTD must be linked with the corresponding word. Then, we have to perform the syntactic composition of the selected EPTDs to find a valid syntactic tree, the yield of which is the parsed sentence.

The parsing problem for IG in its whole generality is NP-hard, which can be shown with an encoding of

[1] Feature values v_1 and v_2 are disjunctions of atoms and $v_1 \wedge v_2$ represents their conjunction.

[2] If we look at the polarity composition table carefully, we remark that a virtual feature can also be absorbed by a positive or a negative feature but these features must then combine with a dual feature to become saturated. Apart from the order, this leads to the same result as a linear interaction followed by a non linear interaction. From this consideration, it is logical to extend the notion of non linear interaction to any interaction between a virtual feature and a positive or negative feature.

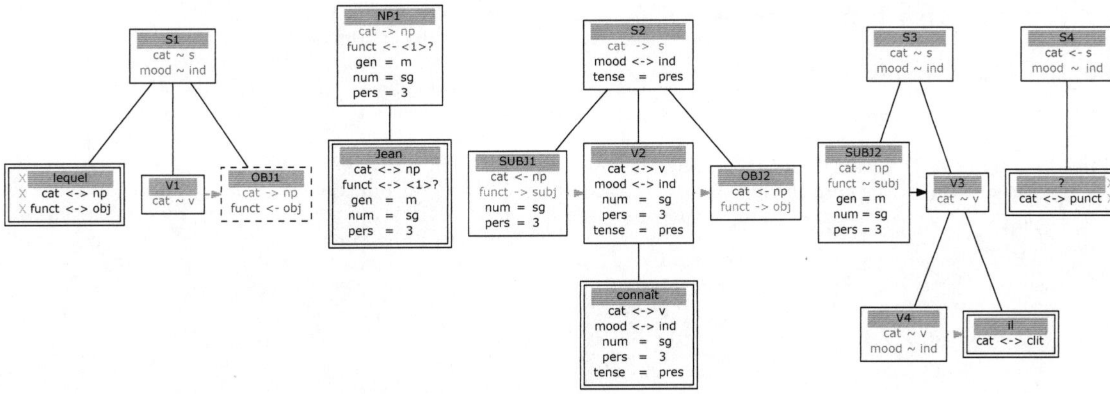

Fig. 1: *EPTDs selected from an IG for sentence 1*

the Intuitionistic Implicative fragment of linear logic. Nevertheless, grammars aiming at modelling real natural languages allow the use of original methods for parsing, which are based on polarities and make parsing tractable. This is not the concern of this article and the reader can refer to [3, 4, 2] for an in-depth study of parsing with IG.

2.3 An example

Consider the following sentence to parse with an IG:

(1) *Lequel* *Jean* *connaît-il* *?*
which one Jean does he know ?
'Which one does Jean know ?'

Figure 1 represents a possible selection from the grammar for the words of sentence 1. The EPTD associated with *connaît* represents a syntactic construction where the transitive verb is used in the active voice. Node S_2 represents the clause with *connaît* as its head. It is composed of three constituents: the verbal kernel, the subject and the object of the verb, which are respectively represented by nodes V_2, $SUBJ_1$ and OBJ_2. The basic constituent of the verbal kernel is the bare verb, the anchor of the EPTD, represented with a double frame. In $SUBJ_1$, the negative feature *cat* $\leftarrow$ *np* and the positive feature $funct \rightarrow subj$ mean that *connaît* expects a noun phrase to provide it with the subject function. Underspecified strict precedence between the three nodes is represented with dashed arrows.

The EPTD associated with *il* represents its construction as a subject clitic pronoun, put just after the verb as a duplication of the actual subject to make the clause interrogative. Node V_4 represents the bare verb, which is concatenated with *il* to constitute the cliticized verb V_3. The *cat* features of nodes V_3 and V_4 are virtual to express that *il* acts as a modifier of an actual verb: nodes V_3 and V_4 have to merge with actual verbs. Nodes S_3 and $SUBJ_2$ represent a required context: a finite clause with a third person singular male subject. This is expressed with virtual features.

The EPTD associated with *lequel* represents its construction as an object interrogative pronoun. The interrogative clause is represented by the node S_1. The pronoun *lequel* is put in front of the clause to represent an extracted object[3] and the canonical position of the object is occupied by a trace, the node $OBJ1$ which is represented with a dashed box to express that the trace has an empty phonological form.

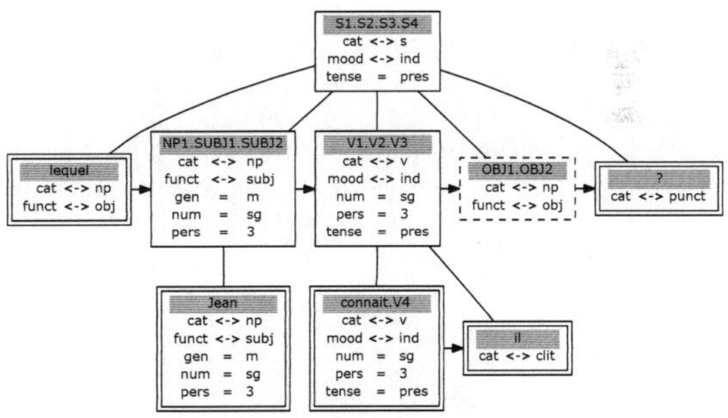

Fig. 2: *Parse tree of sentence 1*

The EPTD associated with *Jean* contains two *funct* features with an undetermined value, which is expressed with a question mark. It means that the noun phrase can receive any syntactic function in the sentence. The index $<1>$ that is put before the value indicates that the *funct* features of nodes *NP1* and *Jean* share the same value.

Punctuation signs are considered as ordinary words and they are also associated with EPTDs. So, the question mark is associated with an EPTD, the root of which represents the interrogative sentence.

The parsing succeeds because the syntactic composition of the EPTDs from figure 1 ends with the valid syntactic tree given by figure 2. On the figure, the head of the box representing each node contains the names of the nodes from the initial EPTDs that were merged into this node. The parsing of the sentence is composed of 9 mergings, including themselves 5 linear interactions and 12 non linear interactions. Among the 12 non linear interactions, only one realizes the action of a modifier; the others realize context requirements.

[3] The crosses on the left of the box representing *lequel* mark that the node is the leftmost daughter of node *S1*.

3 Modelling interrogative and relative clauses in French

3.1 Wh-extraction

Wh-extraction is a common property to relative and interrogative clauses in French: wh-words appear at the beginning of the clause and they play the role of a constituent that is lacking in the clause. The empty position in the clause is usually marked with a trace.

(2) ***Où*** *Pierre pense-t-il que Marie*
where Pierre does he believe that Marie
veut aller □ *?*
wants to go ?
'Where does Pierre believe that Marie wants to go ?'

In sentence 2, the trace is indicated with a □ symbol. The wh-word is bold. Contrary to sentence 1, in sentence 2, the trace is located in a clause which is not the interrogative clause introduced by the wh-word but an embedded object clause. The clause *aller* □ is an infinitive clause, which is included in the finite clause *que Marie veut aller* □ , which is itself included in the interrogative clause *où Pierre pense-t-il que Marie veut aller* □. The number of embedded clauses between the trace and the wh-word is undetermined, hence an unbounded dependency between the wh-word and the verb that has the trace as its complement.

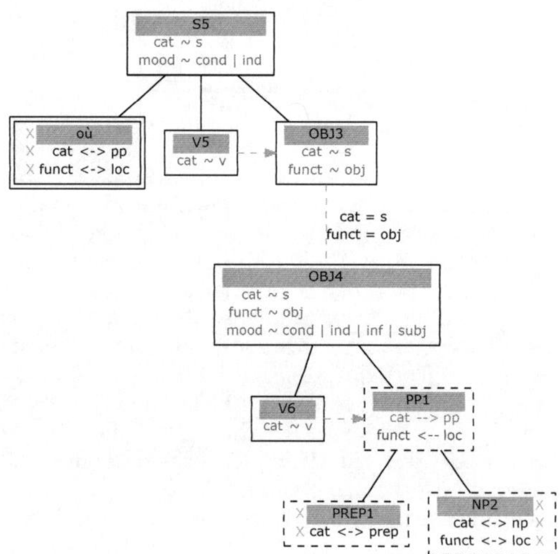

Fig. 3: *EPTD for the interrogative pronoun* où

IG uses an underspecified dominance relation to model this unbounded dependency. Figure 3 shows the EPTD used in sentence 2 to represent the interrogative pronoun *où*. Node *OBJ3* represents the object clause that is immediately included in the main clause, *que Marie veut aller* □ in our example. Node *OBJ4* represents the last embedded object clause, which has the trace as an immediate constituent, the infinitive clause *aller* □ in our example. There is an underspecified dominance relation from *OBJ3* to *OBJ4* , in order to express that there is an undetermined number of object clauses inserted between them. Dominance relations must be understood in a large sense: *OBJ3* may merge with *OBJ4*.

The underspecified dominance relation is represented in figure 3 with a dashed vertical line. The line is labelled with two neutral features *cat* = *s* and *funct* = *obj*, which mean that all nodes dominated by *OBJ3* and dominating *OBJ4* in a large sense, must be equipped with both features. The features labelling dominance relations interact with the feature structures of the concerned nodes by unification. This mechanism models the fact that all constituents included in the main interrogative clause and containing the trace are object clauses, which is a way of implementing island constraints. Lexical Functional Grammar (LFG) [5] uses a similar form of constraint on underspecified dominance: *functional uncertainty*.

In figure 3, the trace is represented by the subtree rooted at node *PP1*. This node is labelled with a positive feature *cat* → *pp* and a negative feature *funct* ← *loc*. It means that it provides a prepositional phrase which expects to receive a locative function. Both polarized features will be saturated by the verb *aller*.

3.2 Pied-piping

Pied-piping represents the ability of wh-words to drag complex phrases along with them when brought to the front of interrogative or relative clauses. Here is an example of pied-piping in which the extracted phrase is put between square brackets.

(3) *[Dans la maison du père de* ***qui****]*
in the house of father of whom
Pierre pense-t-il que Marie veut aller
Pierre does he believe that Marie wants to go
□ *?*
?
'in the house of whom father does Pierre believe that Marie wants to go ?'

In sentence 3, the wh-word is embedded more or less deeply in the extracted phrase, via a chain of noun complements introduced by the preposition *de*. Besides extraction, such a construction is a second source of unbounded dependency and IG also uses an underspecified dominance relation to model it.

Figure 4 gives an example of EPTD associated with the interrogative pronoun *qui* used with pied-piping. The only change with respect to figure 3 lies in the subtree rooted at node *PP2* representing the complex extracted phrase. In sentence 3, *PP2* represents *dans la maison du père de qui*. Anchor *qui* is embedded in a chain of noun complements introduced by the preposition *de*. Nodes *PP4* and *PP5* represent the extremities of the chain and the underspecified dominance relation between them means that the number of elements of the chain is undetermined. In particular, it can be null when *PP5* is identified with *PP4*. The features labelling the dominance relation express a constraint on the nodes constituting the chain. These nodes must be only nouns, noun phrases or prepositional phrases with either no syntactic function or complements introduced by the preposition *de*.

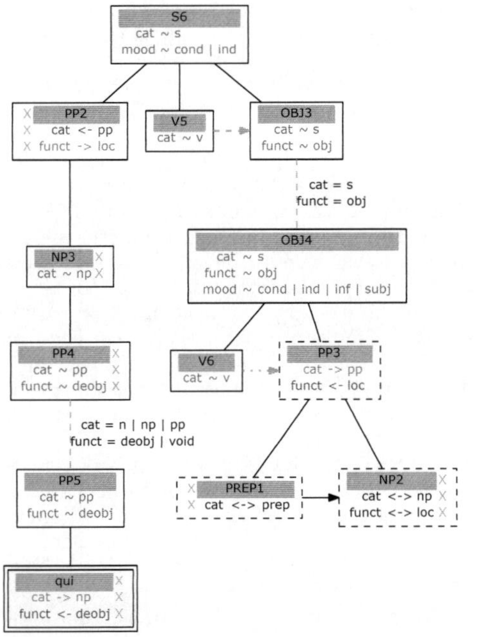

Fig. 4: *EPTD for the interrogative pronoun* qui

3.3 Subject inversion

Subject inversion is allowed in interrogative and relative clauses under some conditions. For the relative clauses, inversion is usually possible, but there is a case in which it is strictly forbidden: when there is a possible confusion between the inverted subject and an object of the verb. For the interrogative clauses, besides the presence of an object for the verb, some interrogative words prevent subject inversion while others force it. In the first class, there is *pourquoi* (*why*) and in the second case, there is *que* (*what*). Others like *où* (*where*) are unconcerned with the subject-verb order.

(4) *Que fait Marie ?*
what is doing Marie ?
'What is Marie doing?'

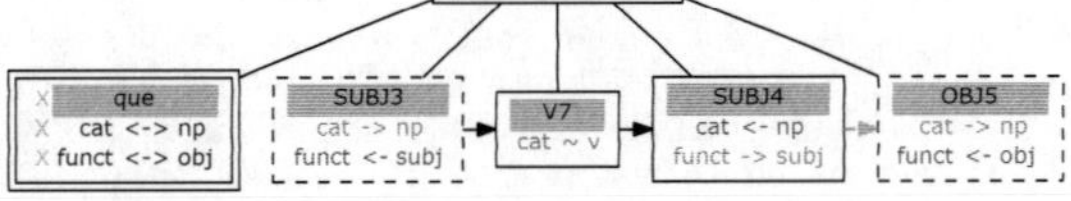

Fig. 5: *EPTD for the interrogative pronoun* que

Figure 5 shows how subject inversion in sentence 4 is modeled in an EPTD associated with the interrogative pronoun *que*. Node *SUBJ3* represents the trace of the subject at the initial position just before the verbal kernel represented by node *V7*. Node *SUBJ4* represents an expected noun phrase just after the verbal kernel, to which the EPTD gives the *subject* function. The interest of this way of representing subject inversion is that the same EPTD for a transitive verb is used in the canonical construction and the inverted construction of the subject-verb order. The doubling of the number of EPTDs for transitive verbs in the grammar is avoided this way.

3.4 Declarative and interrogative marking

Nodes representing clauses are equipped with a *typ* feature, which can take three values, *decl*, *inter* or *inj*, according to the type of the clause: declarative, interrogative or injunctive. The feature is polarized and since grammars are lexicalized, there is a subtle interaction between words to saturate them.

The interaction is especially complex for interrogative clauses. In direct interrogations, sentence 2 for instance, the question mark brings a negative feature *typ* ← *inter* and in indirect interrogations, the same feature is brought by the main verb which expects a question.

In direct interrogations, like sentence 2, if there is a subject clitic put just after the main verb, this clitic brings the positive feature *typ* → *inter*. Otherwise, the positive feature is brought by the wh-word.

The declarative marking of relative clauses is simpler: the relative pronoun brings the feature *typ* ↔ *decl* to the relative clause.

This way of marking interrogative and declarative clauses is not the only possible with IG. Its system of polarities is rich and flexible enough to provide other solutions.

4 Organization of the grammar

In previous sections, we focused on four main aspects of the grammar of the interrogative and relative clauses in French but the whole grammar is more complex and its implementation is a real challenge.

For this, we used the XMG tool [7]. XMG provides a high level language dedicated to grammar description. A grammar is designed as a set of classes, each class defining a set of PTDs. The initial classes are composed into complex classes by means of two operations: *conjunction* and *disjunction*. Classes are ranked by family. Figure 6 shows the architecture of our IG of interrogative and relative clauses in French. We call it IG_{Wh}. Ovals represent families and an arrow from an oval to another one means that some classes from the first family are used in the definition of classes of

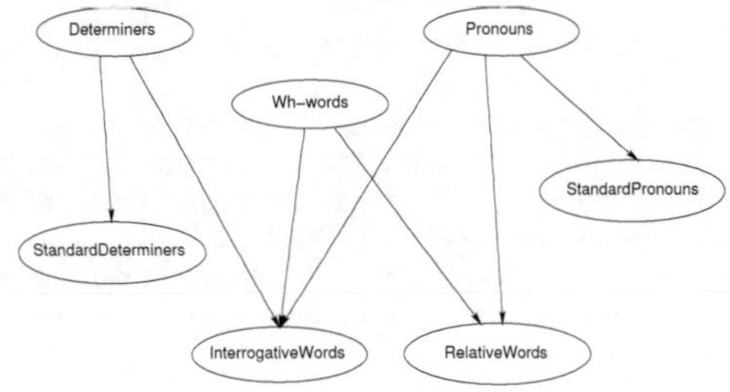

Fig. 6: *Organization of the grammar*

Some classes are distinguished as *terminal classes* and they are compiled by XMG into a set of EPTD constituting an IG usable for automated parsing. IG_{Wh} is composed of 40 classes. Among them, 16 terminal classes are distributed in 4 relative classes and 12 interrogative classes. These terminal classes are compiled into 77 EPTDs anchored with relative pronouns and 295 EPTDs anchored with interrogative pronouns and determiners.

5 Evaluation and comparison with other works

The evaluation of IG_{Wh} has two aspects:

- its precision measures the extent to which all parse trees generated from IG_{Wh} reflect valid constructions in French;
- its recall measures the extent to which all constructions with interrogative or relative clauses in French are captured by IG_{Wh}.

The use of treebanks on large real corpora with a classical F-measure is not well suited to such an evaluation: even if they are very large, their grammatical coverage of relative and interrogative clauses is too limited and they only include positive sentences, when ungrammatical sentences are necessary to spot overgeneration. Finally, the construction of such treebanks is very costly and for French, they are too limited both in number and size.

The least costly way of evaluating IG_{Wh} is to use it for parsing a test suite of grammatical and ungrammatical sentences illustrating most rules of the French grammar related to interrogative and relative clauses. Unfortunately, there exists no test suite satisfying this specification. The TSNLP [9] contains no relative clause and only direct interrogative sentences covering the grammar of these sentences very partially. The EUROTRA test suite [6] contains relative clauses but its coverage is limited and it does not contain any ungrammatical sentence.

We have built our own test suite, consisting in a hundred grammatical sentences and a hundred ungrammatical sentences. These sentences cover most syntactic phenomena related to relative and interrogative clauses. Of course, these sentences need a complete grammar to be parsed but, as we focus on relative and interrogative clauses, we take care to choose only simple rules with regard to other phenomena. For the parsing, we used LEOPAR[4], which is a parser devoted to IG. The hundred grammatical sentences were parsed successfully, all parse trees were verified manually and the hundred ungrammatical sentences were rejected by the parser.

Another way of evaluating our grammar is to compare it with other existing grammars of interrogative and relative clauses in French. Unfortunately, there are very few works about this question. Anne Abeillé [1] has developed a grammar of French in the formalism of Tree Adjoining Grammar (TAG). This grammar covers relative and interrogative clauses. Like our grammar, it is lexicalized, but the main difference is that all syntactic constructions related to wh-clauses are attached to the head verb of these clauses. From a computational point of view, this is an important drawback because it inflates the number of elementary trees associated with verbs, which makes the selection of relevant trees more difficult. Even if it fits on with the locality principle[5], such a feature is determined by the rigidity of the operation of syntactic composition, adjunction, which does not allow for flexibility about the way of attaching syntactic information to words. Nevertheless, the attachment of the syntactic constructions related to wh-clauses to verbs presents one advantage over the attachment to wh-words: the absence of a direct objet just after the head verb of the wh-clause can be made explicit in the elementary tree attached to this verb, so that subject inversion is completely controlled. Wh-extraction, interrogative and declarative marking are expressed with the TAG machinery: the mechanism of adjunction combined with an important system of control features. Another illustration of the limited expressivity of adjunction is the inability to represent the extraction of noun complements. Finally, a point remains unclear: the modelling of unbounded dependencies generated by pied-piping.

Other formalisms, such as HPSG [10] and LFG [5] propose solutions for relative and interrogative clauses and other languages than French but in this article, we have stressed the combination of four aspects, which is very specific to French, and an exhaustive comparison would be lengthy for this article.

References

[1] A. Abeillé. *Une grammaire électronique du français*. CNRS Editions, Paris, 2002.

[2] G. Bonfante, B. Guillaume, and M. Morey. Dependency constraints for lexical disambiguation. In *11th International Conference on Parsing Technology, IWPT'09*, Paris, France, 2009.

[3] G. Bonfante, B. Guillaume, and G. Perrier. Analyse syntaxique électrostatique. *Traitement Automatique des Langues (TAL)*, 44(3):93–120, 2003.

[4] G. Bonfante, B. Guillaume, and G. Perrier. Polarization and abstraction of grammatical formalisms as methods for lexical disambiguation. In *CoLing'2004*, pages 303–309, Genève, Switzerland, 2004.

[5] J. Bresnan. *Lexical-Functional Syntax*. Blackwell Publishers, Oxford, 2001.

[6] B. Daille, L. Danlos, and O. Laurens. L'analyse du français dans le projet EUROTRA. *Traitement Automatique des Informations*, 32(2):89–106, 1992.

[7] D. Duchier, J. Le Roux, and Y. Parmentier. XMG : Un compilateur de méta-grammaires extensible. In *TALN 2005, Dourdan, France*, 2005.

[8] B. Guillaume and G. Perrier. Interaction Grammars. *Research on Language and Computation*, 2009. To appear. A preliminary report is available at http://www.loria.fr/ ∼ perrier/langcomp2009.pdf.

[9] S. Lehmann, S. Oepen, S. Regnier-Prost, K. Netter, V. Lux, J. Klein, K. Falkedal, F. Fouvry, D. Estival, E. Dauphin, H. Compagnion, J. Baur, L. Balkan, and D. Arnold. TSNLP — Test Suites for Natural Language Processing. In *Proceedings of COLING 1996,Kopenhagen*, 1996.

[10] I. A. Sag, T. Wasow, and E. M. Bender. *Syntactic Theory: a Formal Introduction*. Center for the Study of Language and INF, 2003.

[4] `http://www.loria.fr/equipes/calligramme/leopar`

[5] A predicate and its arguments must be present in the same elementary tree.

Comparing Statistical Similarity Measures for Stylistic Multivariate Analysis

Marius Popescu
University of Bucharest
Department of Computer Science
Academiei 14, Bucharest, Romania
mpopescu@phobos.cs.unibuc.ro

Liviu P. Dinu
University of Bucharest
Department of Computer Science
Academiei 14, Bucharest, Romania
ldinu@funinf.cs.unibuc.ro

Abstract

The goal of this paper is to compare a set of distance/similarity measures, some motivated statistically, others motivated stylistically, regarding their ability to reflect stylistic similarity between texts. To assess the ability of these distance/similarity functions to capture stylistic similarity between texts, we have tested them in the two most frequently employed multivariate statistical analysis settings: cluster analysis and (kernel) principal components analysis.

Keywords

Stylistic Multivariate Analysis, Statistical Similarity Measures, Cluster Analysis, Kernel Principal Components Analysis

1 Introduction

Computational stylistics investigates texts from the standpoint of individual style (author identification) or functional style (genres, registers). Because in all computational stylistic studies/approaches, a process of comparison of two or more texts is involved, in a way or another, there was always a need for a distance/similarity function to measure similarity (or dissimilarity) of texts from the stylistic point of view.

Usually, the distance/similarity measures are implicitly or explicitly used by multivariate statistical analysis techniques typically applied in computational stylistic approaches. In [5], these approaches are characterized as: "[The]...technique essentially picks the N most common words in the corpus under investigation and computes the occurrence rate of these N words in each text or text-unit, thus converting each text into an N-dimensional array of numbers. Multivariate statistical techniques are then applied to the data to look for patterns. The two techniques most frequently employed are principal components analysis and cluster analysis."

The goal of this paper is to compare a set of distance/similarity measures, some motivated statistically, others motivated stylistically, regarding their ability to reflect stylistic similarity between texts.

As style markers we have used the function word frequencies. Function words are generally considered good indicators of style because their use is very unlikely to be under the conscious control of the author and because of their psychological and cognitive role [3]. Also function words prove to be very effective in many author attribution studies.

The distance/similarity between two texts will be measured as distance/similarity between the function words frequencies corresponding to the respective texts. For this study we selected some similarity/distance measures. We started with the most natural distance/similarity measures: euclidean distance and (taking into account the statistical nature of data) Pearson's correlation coefficient. Since function words frequencies can also be viewed as ordinal variables, we also considered for comparison some specific similarity measures: Spearman's rank-order coefficient, Spearman's footrule, Goodman and Kruskal's gamma, Kendall's tau. Finally, we have added a stylistically motivated similarity measure: Burrows's delta, that has interesting statistic interpretations.

To assess the ability of these distance/similarity functions to capture stylistic similarity between texts, we have tested them in the two most frequently employed multivariate statistical analysis settings: cluster analysis and principal components analysis.

Clustering is a very good test bed for a distance/similarity measure behavior. We plugged the distance/similarity measures selected for comparison into a standard hierarchical clustering algorithm and applied it to a collection of 21 nineteenth century English books [6]. The family trees thus obtained revealed a lot about the distance/similarity measures behavior.

If clustering explicitly uses a distance/similarity function as its base, principal components analysis implicitly uses the euclidean distance. Kernel principal components analysis [8] allows the replacement of the implicitly used euclidean distance with other similarity measures, *the kernels*. Not all the distance/similarity measures selected for comparison can be transformed into kernels because a kernel has to be a positive definite function. For those similarity measures that can be transformed into kernels (Spearman's rank-order coefficient, Kendall's tau) we have compared the results of kernel principal components analysis (using the respective kernels) with the result of standard principal components analysis (that implicitly uses the euclidean distance).

The main finding of our comparison is that the similarity measures that treat function words frequencies as ordinal variables performed better than the others distance/similarity measures. Treating function words

International Conference RANLP 2009 - Borovets, Bulgaria, pages 349–354

frequencies as ordinal variables means that in the calculation of distance/similarity function the ranks of function words according to their frequencies in text will be used rather than the actual values of these frequencies. Usage of the ranking of function words in the calculation of the distance/similarity measure instead of the actual values of the frequencies may seem as a loss of information, but we consider that the process of ranking makes the distance/similarity measure more robust acting as a filter, eliminating the *noise* contained in the values of the frequencies. The fact that a specific function word has the rank 2 (is the second most frequent word) in one text and has the rank 4 (is the fourth most frequent word) in another text can be more relevant than the fact that the respective word appears 34% times in the first text and only 29% times in the second.

Also, the experiments shown that Burrows's Delta achieved good results. Burrows's Delta is a stylistically motivated distance function especially designed as a measure for authorship attribution and used until now only in classification experiments. As far as we know this is the first time when Burrows's Delta is used in a clustering setting.

In the next section we present the distance/similarity measures involved in the comparison study. Section 3 briefly describes the multivariate statistical analysis techniques used: cluster analysis and (kernel) principal component analysis. In section 4 are presented the experiments and the results obtained, and the last section contains discussion and suggestions for future work.

2 Similarity Measures

If we treat texts as random variables whose values are the frequencies of different words in the respective texts, then various statistical correlation measures can be used as similarity measures between that texts. For two texts X and Y and a fixed set of words $\{w_1, w_2, \ldots, w_n\}$ let us denote by x_1 the relative frequency of w_1 in X, by y_1 the relative frequency of w_1 in Y and so on by x_n the relative frequency of w_n in X, by y_n the relative frequency of w_n in Y.

2.1 Pearson's Correlation Coefficient

The Pearson's correlation coefficient [9] is:

$$r = \frac{\sum_{i=1}^{n} \left(\frac{x_i - \overline{x}}{s_x}\right)\left(\frac{y_i - \overline{y}}{s_y}\right)}{n-1}$$

where $\overline{x}$ is the mean of X, $\overline{y}$ the mean of Y and s_x is the standard deviation of X, s_y the standard deviation of Y.

The correlation coefficient measures the tendency of two variables to change in value together (i.e., to either increase or decrease). r is related with the Euclidean distance, the $\sqrt{2(1-r)}$ being the Euclidean distance between the standardized versions of X and Y.

2.2 Correlation Statistics for Ordinal Data

The random variables X, Y representing texts can also be treated as ordinal data, in which data is ordered but cannot be assumed to have equal distance between values. In this case the values of X (and Y respectively) will be the ranks of words $\{w_1, w_2, \ldots, w_n\}$ according to their frequencies in text X rather than of the actual values of these frequencies. The most common correlation statistic for ordinal data is *Spearman's rank-order coefficient* [9]:

$$r_{sc} = 1 - \frac{6}{n(n^2-1)} \sum_{i=1}^{n} (x_i - y_i)^2$$

To be noted that, this time, x_i, y_i are ranks and actually, the Spearman's rank-order coefficient is the Pearson's correlation coefficient applied to ranks.

The Spearman's footrule [9] is the l_1-version of Spearman's rank-order coefficient:

$$r_{sf} = 1 - \frac{3}{n^2-1} \sum_{i=1}^{n} |x_i - y_i|$$

Another set of correlation statistics for ordinal data are based on the number of concordant and discordant pairs among two variables. The number of concordant pairs among two variables X and Y is $P = |\{(i,j) : 1 \leq i < j \leq n,\ (x_i - x_j)(y_i - y_j) > 0\}|$. Similarly, the number of discordant pairs is $Q = |\{(i,j) : 1 \leq i < j \leq n,\ (x_i - x_j)(y_i - y_j) < 0\}|$.

Goodman and Kruskal's gamma [9] is defined as:

$$\gamma = \frac{P-Q}{P+Q}$$

Kendall developed several slightly different types of ordinal correlation as alternatives to gamma. *Kendall's tau-a* [9] is based on the number of concordant versus discordant pairs, divided by a measure based on the total number of pairs (n = the sample size):

$$\tau_a = \frac{P-Q}{\frac{n(n-1)}{2}}$$

Kendall's tau-b [9] is a similar measure of association based on concordant and discordant pairs, adjusted for the number of ties in ranks.It is calculated as $(P-Q)$ divided by the geometric mean of the number of pairs not tied on X (X_0) and the number of pairs not tied on Y (Y_0):

$$\tau_b = \frac{P-Q}{\sqrt{(P+Q+X_0)(P+Q+Y_0)}}$$

All the above three correlation statistics are very related, if n is fixed and X and Y have no ties, then P, X_0 and Y_0 are completely determined by n and Q.

2.3 Burrows's Delta

In his 2001 Busa Award lecture, John F. Burrows proposed a new measure for authorship attribution which he termed 'Delta', defined as: "the mean of the absolute differences between the z-scores for a set of word-variables in a given text-group and the z-scores for the same set of word-variables in a target text." [2]

Let $\mathcal{C} = \{X, Y, \ldots\}$ be a fixed set of texts, *a corpus*, and $\{w_1, w_2, \ldots, w_n\}$ a fixed set of words. Let σ_i be the standard deviation of the relative frequency of w_i in the corpus $\mathcal{C}$. For each $X, Y \in \mathcal{C}$, Delta is defined as [1]:

$$\Delta(X,Y) = \frac{1}{n}\sum_{i=1}^{n}\left|\frac{x_i - y_i}{\sigma_i}\right|$$

As it is defined, $\Delta(X, Y)$ depends not only on X and Y, but also on the entire data set (corpus) from which X and Y are drawn. This will not be a problem for clustering, because the family tree obtained from a cluster analysis depends anyway on the entire data set (adding a new text to a data set can change the family tree completely).

3 Multivariate Analysis Techniques

3.1 Clustering Analysis

An agglomerative hierarchical clustering algorithm [4] arranges a set of objects in a family tree (dendogram) according to their similarity, similarity which in its turn is given by a distance function defined on the set of objects. The algorithm initially assigns each object to its own cluster and then repeatedly merges pairs of clusters until the whole tree is formed. At each step the pair of nearest clusters is selected for merging. Various agglomerative hierarchical clustering algorithms differ in the way in which they measure the distance between clusters. Note that although a distance function between objects exists, the distance measure between clusters (set of objects) remains to be defined. In our experiments we used the *complete linkage* distance between clusters, the maximum of the distances between all pairs of objects drawn from the two clusters (one object from the first cluster, the other from the second).

3.2 (Kernel) Principal Components Analysis

Principal components analysis (PCA) [4] is a method of dimensionality reduction. The motivation for performing PCA is often the assumption that directions of high variance will contain more information than directions of low variance. The PCA aims to transform the observed variables (function word frequencies, in our case) to a new set of variables which are uncorrelated and arranged in decreasing order of importance. These new variables, or components, are linear combinations of the original variables, the first few components accounting for most of the variation in the original data. Typically the data are plotted in the space of the first two components.

PCA works in the euclidean space and so implicitly use euclidean distance and standard inner product. Kernel principal components analysis [8] allows the replacement of the implicitly used euclidean distance with other similarity measures, *the kernels.*

Group	Author	Book
American Novelists	Hawthorne	Dr. Grimshawe's Secret
		House of Seven Gables
	Melville	Redburn
		Moby Dick
	Cooper	The Last of the Mohicans
		The Spy
		Water Witch
American Essayists	Thoreau	Walden
		A Week on Concord
	Emerson	Conduct Of Life
		English Traits
British Playwrights	Shaw	Pygmalion
		Misalliance
		Getting Married
	Wilde	An Ideal Husband
		Woman of No Importance
Bronte Sisters	Anne	Agnes Grey
		Tenant Of Wildfell Hall
	Charlotte	The Professor
		Jane Eyre
	Emily	Wuthering Heights

Table 1: *The list of books used in the experiments*

Kernel-based algorithms work by embedding the data into a feature space (a Hilbert space). The embedding is performed implicitly, that is by specifying the inner product between each pair of points rather than by giving their coordinates explicitly. The kernel function captures the intuitive notion of similarity between objects in a specific domain and can be any function defined on the respective domain that is symmetric and positive definite. Because of the positive definite restriction not all distance/similarity measures described in section 2 can be transformed into a kernel, but some can. For example, from the Spearman's rank-order coefficient the following kernel can be obtained: $k(X, Y) = e^{-\frac{r_{sc}(X,Y)}{2}}$ Also, P, the number of concordant pairs among two variables X and Y (see section 2.2) can be proved to be a kernel, but the prove of that is beyond the scope of this paper. For details of how a method like PCA ca be transformed into a kernel method and which distance/similarity functions can be a kernel see [8].

4 Experiments

For our experiments we used a collection of 21 nineteenth century English books written by 10 different authors and spanning a variety of genres (Table 1). The books were used by Koppel et al. [6] in their authorship verification experiments.

To perform the experiments, a set of words must be fixed. The most frequent function words may be selected or other criteria may be used for selection. In all our experiments we used the set of function words identified by Mosteller and Wallace [7] as good candidates for author-attribution studies.

In a first set of experiments we used the agglomerative hierarchical clustering algorithm coupled with the various distance similarity functions employed in the comparison to cluster the works the Table 1.

The resulted dendograms for euclidean distance and Pearson's correlation coefficient are very similar, which is no surprise taking into account the close relation between the two measures (see section 2.1). We present only the dendogram for Pearson's correlation coefficient in Figure 1. The problem of this family tree (and also of the family tree corresponding to euclidean distance) is that the works of Melville are not grouped together: one being clustered with the novels of Cooper (Moby Dick) and the other with the novels of Hawthorne. Also, apart from authorship relation, the dendogram reflects no other stylistic relation between the works (like grouping the works according to genre or nationality of the authors: American / English).

The dendogram for Spearman's footrule (not shown because of lack of space) is a good one, accurately reflecting the stylistic relations between books. The books were grouped in three big clusters (the first three branches of the tree) corresponding to the three genre: dramas (lower branch), essays (middle branch) and novels (upper branch). Inside each branch the works were first clustered according to their author. The only exceptions are the two essays of Emerson which instead of being first clustered together and after that merged in the cluster of essays, were added one by one to this cluster.

Spearman's rank-order coefficient, Goodman and Kruskal's gamma and Kendall's tau produced the same dendogram (modulo the scale). Figure 2 shows the dendogram for Spearman's rank-order coefficient. The dendogram is perfect: all works are clustered according to theirs author. More over, the first two branches correspond to the nationality of the authors: British writers on lower branch, American writers on upper branch. Further more, inside each of these two branches, the works are clustered according to genre: drama and novels in the case of British writers, novels and essays in the case of American writers.

The family tree obtained when Burrows's Delta was used resembles the dendogram produced by Spearman's rank-order coefficient (Figure 2), but this time, in the case of American writers, the works are no longer grouped according to genre.

A second set of experiments aim to compare the standard principal components analysis (that implicitly uses the euclidean distance) with kernel principal components analysis, based on kernels derived from distance/similarity measures selected for this study. The works in the Table 1 are plotted in the space of the first two principal components, to see if the stylistic similarity is reflected in the spatial configuration.

The plot obtained using standard principal components analysis is shown in Figure 3. Generally, the works of the same author are plotted close together, but again (as in the case of the euclidean distance and Pearson's correlation coefficient clustering) the works of Melville ($\times$) are an exception. One is placed close to works of Emerson ($\Box$) and the other alone in a different region. Also, the works of Emerson ($\Box$) and the works of Cooper ($+$) are not clearly separated. An interesting fact is that the American writers and the British writers are separated in the plane by a vertical line ($x = 0$).

For comparison, in Figure 4 we present the plot obtained using kernel principal components analysis with the kernel derived from Spearman's rank-order coefficient[1] (see section 3.2). The works of the same author are plotted close together and different authors are clearly separated. Even more interesting than in the case of standard components analysis, a vertical line, $x = 0$, separates the British writers (left) from the American writers (right), and a horizontal line, $y = 0$ separates different genres: drama (above) from novels (below) in the case of British writers, essays (above) from novels (bellow) in the case of American writers.

[1] Because of space limitation we have presented the kernel principal components analysis only in the case of the best performing kernel, the kernel derived from Spearman's rank-order coefficient.

5 Discussion

In this paper we have compared a set of distance/similarity measures, some motivated statistically, others motivated stylistically, regarding theirs ability to reflect stylistic similarity between texts. To assess the ability of these distance/similarity functions to capture stylistic similarity between texts, we tested them in the two most frequently employed multivariate statistical analysis settings: cluster analysis and (kernel) principal components analysis.

The experiments have shown that the similarity measures that treat function words frequencies as ordinal variables (Spearman's rank-order coefficient, Spearman's footrule, Goodman and Kruskal's gamma, Kendall's tau) performed better than the distance/similarity measures that use the actual values of function words frequencies (Euclidean distance, Pearson's correlation coefficient).

Also we have shown how Burrows's Delta, a distance function especially designed as a measure for authorship attribution, can be used in clustering analysis with good results.

In future work it would be useful to test these distance/similarity measures on other data sets. Also, it would be interesting to further investigate the ability of some of the similarity measures (Spearman's rank-order coefficient, Goodman and Kruskal's gamma, Kendall's tau) to distinguish between the different nationality of English language writers; for example, by adding to the data set works of Australian writers from the same period.

References

[1] S. Argamon. Interpreting burrows's delta: Geometric and probabilistic foundations. *Literary and Linguistic Computing*, 23(2):131–147, 2008.

[2] J. Burrows. 'delta': a measure of stylistic difference and a guide to likely authorship. *Literary and Linguistic Computing*, 17(3):267–287, 2002.

[3] C. K. Chung and J. W. Pennebaker. The psychological function of function words. In K. Fiedler, editor, *Social communication: Frontiers of social psychology*, pages 343–359. Psychology Press, New York, 2007.

[4] R. O. Duda, P. E. Hart, and D. G. Stork. *Pattern Classification (2nd ed.)*. Wiley-Interscience Publication, 2001.

[5] D. I. Holmes, L. J. Gordon, and C. Wilson. A widow and her soldier: Stylometry and the american civil war. *Literary and Linguistic Computing*, 16(4):403–420, 2001.

[6] M. Koppel, J. Schler, and E. Bonchek-Dokow. Measuring differentiability: Unmasking pseudonymous authors. *Journal of Machine Learning Research*, 8:1261–1276, 2007.

[7] F. Mosteller and D. L. Wallace. *Inference and Disputed Authorship: The Federalist.* CSLI Publications, Stanford, 2007.

[8] J. S. Taylor and N. Cristianini. *Kernel Methods for Pattern Analysis.* Cambridge University Press, New York, NY, USA, 2004.

[9] G. Upton and I. Cook. *A Dictionary of Statistics.* Oxford University Press, Oxford, 2008.

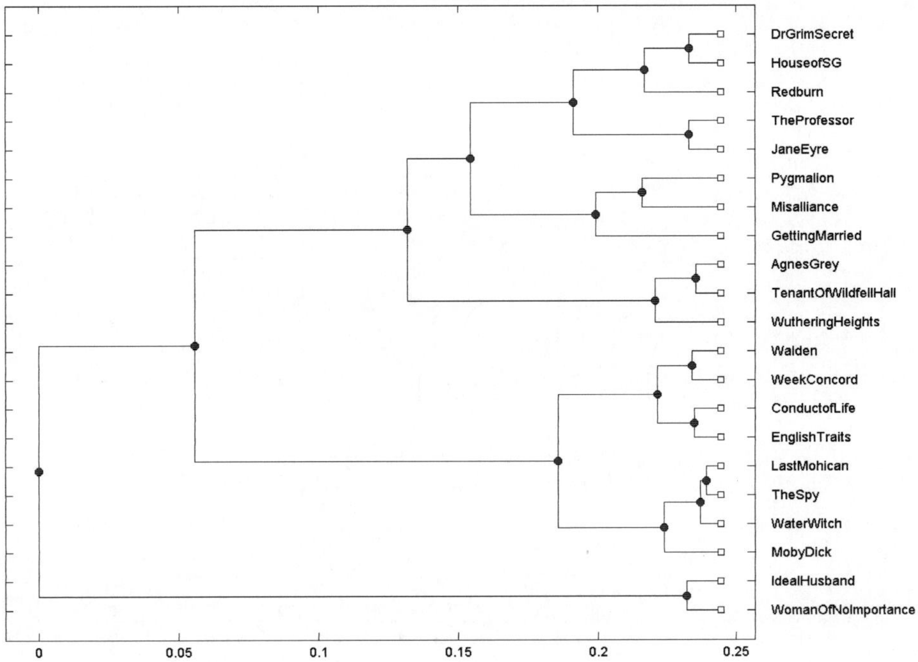

Fig. 1: *Dendogram of 21 nineteenth century English books (Pearson's correlation coefficient)*

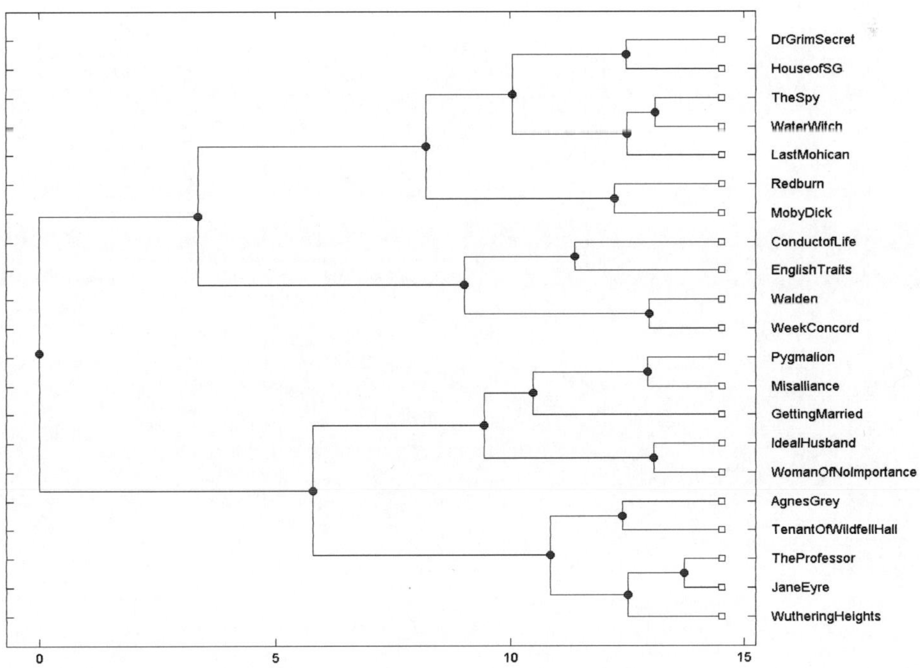

Fig. 2: *Dendogram of 21 nineteenth century English books (Spearman's rank-order coefficient)*

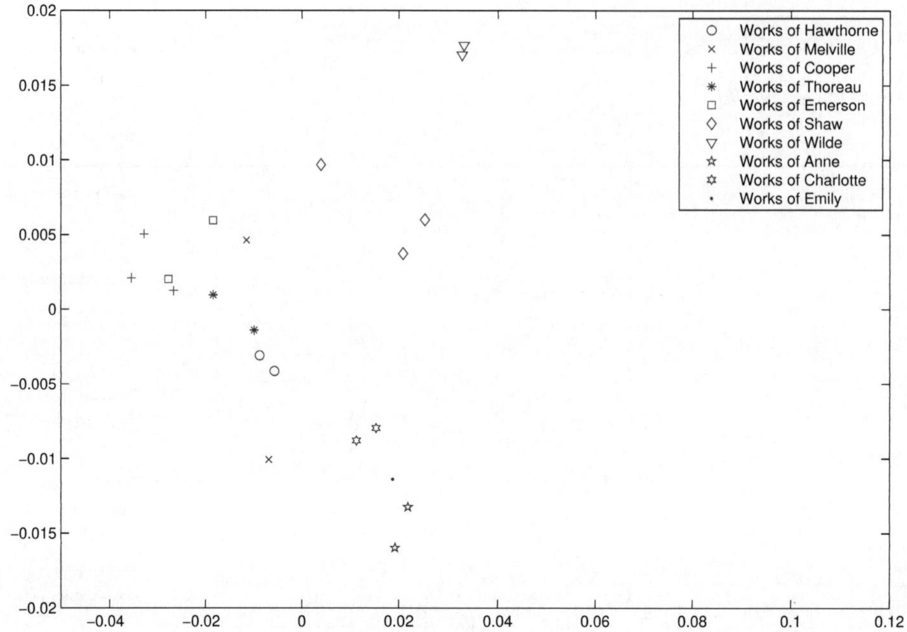

Fig. 3: *Standard principal components plot of 21 nineteenth century English books*

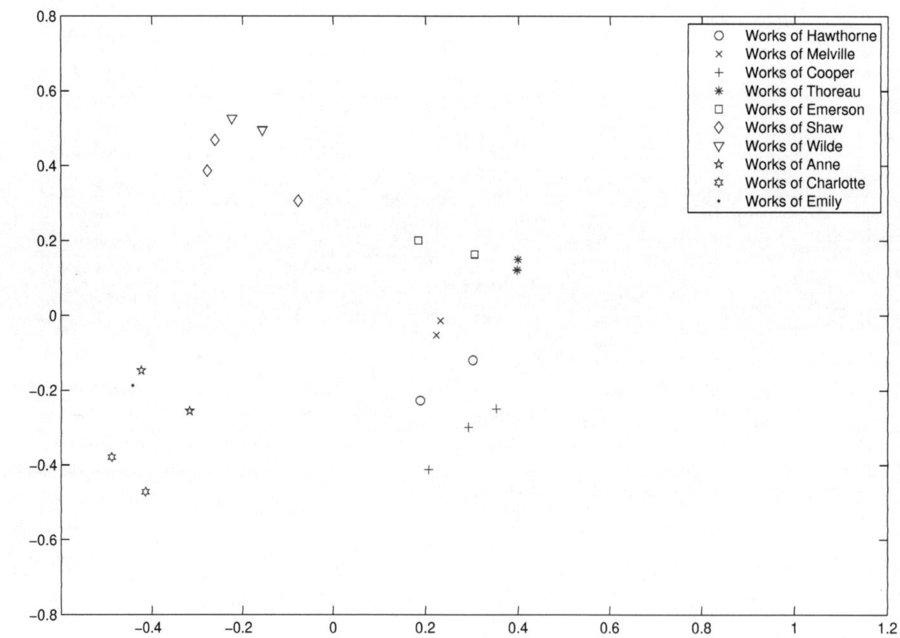

Fig. 4: *Kernel principal components plot of 21 nineteenth century English books (Spearman's rank-order coefficient kernel)*

From Bag of Languages to Family Trees From Noisy Corpus

Taraka Rama and Anil Kumar Singh
Language Technologies Research Centre, IIIT, Hyderabad, India
taraka@students, anil@research@students.iiit.ac.in

Abstract

In this paper, we use corpus-based measures for constructing phylogenetic trees and try to address some questions about the validity of doing this and applicability to *linguistic areas* as against language families. We experiment with four corpus based distance measures for constructing phylogenetic trees. Three of these measures were earlier tried for estimating language distances. We use a fourth measure based on phonetic and orthographic feature n-grams. We compare the trees obtained using these measures and present our observations.

Keywords

Language distances, similarity measures, phylogenetic trees

1 Introduction

Establishing relationships among languages which have been in contact for a long time has been a topic of interest in historical linguistics [6]. However, this topic has been much less explored in the computational linguistics community. Most of the previous work is focused on reconstruction of phylogenetic trees for a particular language family using handcrafted word lists [12, 3, 2, 14] or using synthetic data [4].

In this paper we pose the following questions. What happens when we try to construct phylogenetic trees using inter-language distances in the context of a *linguistic area*[1]? Can the phylogenetic trees be used for evaluating the robustness of the inter-language distance measures and the meaningfulness of the distances? To our knowledge these questions have not been addressed previously. As Singh and Surana [18] showed, corpus based measures can be successfully used for comparative study of languages. Can these distances, estimated from a noisy corpus[2], meaningfully be used to construct phylogenetic trees? Can the information represented by the tree give meaningful interpretations about the languages involved? In this paper, we try to answer these questions. By using meaningful measures for estimating the distance between languages, we try to establish that the answers to these questions are affirmative. Overall, the contributions of the paper are the following a) use a new measure for estimating language distance b) present results of the experiments on constructing phylogenetic trees from corpus based word lists rather than handcrafted ones c) validate the hypothesis that India is a linguistic area [10].

The paper is organized as follows. Related work is discussed in Section 2. A brief discussion of various inter-language measures is given in Section 3. The experimental setup and the analysis of the results have been given in Section 4 and Section 5, respectively. We present a summary of our experiments, analysis of the results and future directions of the work in Section 6.

2 Related Work

In recent years, the methods developed in computational biology [13, 15, 11, 19] have been successfully adapted in computational linguistics for constructing the phylogeny[3]. All these methods are character based or distance based methods. The major disadvantage of these approaches is that they require handcrafted lists. Moreover, the methods inspired from glottochronology take a boolean matrix as input, which denotes the change in the state of the 'characters' (the 'characters' can be lexical, morphological or phonological) to infer the phylogenetic trees.

Ellison and Kirby [9] discuss establishing a probability distribution for every language through intralexical comparison using confusion probabilities. They use normalized edit distance to calculate the probabilities. Then the distance between every language pair is estimated as a distance between the probability distributions formed for individual languages. The distances (between languages) are estimated using KL-divergence and Rao's distance. The same measures are also used to find the level of cognacy between the words. The experiments are conducted on Dyen's [8] classical Indo-European dataset. The estimated distances are used for constructing a phylogenetic tree of the Indo-European languages.

Bouchard-Cote et al. [5], in a novel attempt, combine the advantages of classical comparative method and the corpus-based probabilistic models. The word forms are represented by phoneme sequences which un-

[1] The term *linguistic area* or *Sprachbund* [10] refers to a group of languages that have become similar in some way as a result of proximity and *language contact*, even if they belong to different families. The best known example is the Indian (or South Asian) linguistic area.

[2] By noisy corpus we mean a corpus that includes wrongly spelled words and spelling variations.

[3] Phylogeny is the (study of) evolutionary development and history of a species or higher taxonomic grouping of organisms. The term is now also used for other things such as tribes and languages. Phylogenetic trees represent this evolutionary development.

International Conference RANLP 2009 - Borovets, Bulgaria, pages 355–359

dergo stochastic edits along the branches of a phylogenetic tree. The robustness of the model is proved when it selects the linguistically attested phylogeny. The stochastic models successfully model the language change by using synchronic languages to reconstruct the word forms in Vulgar Latin and Classical Latin. Although it reconstructs the ancient word forms of the Romance Languages, a major disadvantage of this model is that some amount of data of the ancient word forms is required to train the model, which may not be available in many cases.

In another novel attempt, Singh and Surana [18] used corpus based simple measures to show that corpus can be used for comparative study of languages. They used both character n-gram distances and Surface Similarity [16] to identify the potential cognates[4], which in turn are being used to estimate the inter-language distance. Both diachronic and synchronic experiments are performed and the results very well attest to the linguistic facts. They also argued that there is a common orthographic as well as phonetic space for languages with a long history of contact which can be exploited for developing inter-language (rather than intra-language) measures, in contrast to the position taken by Ellison and Kirby [9]. Having followed this line of argument, we explain some corpus measures which we adopted from their work and also use a new measure which we call phonetic (and orthographic) feature n-gram based distance.

3 Inter-Language Measures

Such measures can be broadly divided into three categories. Character n-gram measures, cognate based measures and feature n-gram measures. The following sections describe each measure in more detail. One important point that can be mentioned here is that all the languages we experimented on use Brahmi origin scripts, which have almost one-to-one correspondence between letters and phonemes. Moreover, these scripts are similar in a lot of ways, especially the fact that the alphabets used by them can be seen as subsets of the same abstract alphabet, although the letters may have different shapes so that to a lay person the scripts seem very different. In fact, there is a 'super encoding' or 'meta encoding' called ISCII that can be used to represent this common alphabet. The letters of this common alphbet can be approximately treated like phonemes for computational purposes. For languages which do not use such scripts, we will first have to convert the text into a phonetic notation to be able to use the methods described below, except perhaps the first one.

3.1 Symmetric Cross Entropy (SCE)

The first measure is purely a letter n-gram based measure similar to the one used by Singh [17] for language and encoding identification. Note that since letters in Brahmi origin scripts can almost be treated like phonemes, we could call this method a phoneme n-gram based measure. To calculate the distance, letter 5-gram models are prepared from the corpora of the languages to be compared. Then the n-grams of all sizes (unigrams, bigrams, etc.) are combined and sorted according to their probability in descending order. Only the top N n-grams are retained and the rest are pruned. This is based on the results obtained by Cavnar [7] and validated by Singh, which show that the top N (300 according to Cavnar) n-grams have a high correlation with the identity of the language. At this stage there are two probability distributions which can be compared by a measure of distributional similarity. The measure used here is symmetric cross entropy:

$$d_{sce} = \sum_{g_l = g_m} (p(g_l)\ log\ q(g_m) + q(g_m)\ log\ p(g_l)) \quad (1)$$

where p and q are the probability distributions for the two languages and g_l and g_m are n-grams in languages l and m, respectively. The probabilities of bigrams and larger n-grams are relative frequencies over a single distribution consisting of n-grams of all sizes up to 5 (the 'order' of the n-gram model), not conditional probabilities, as in standard n-gram models for calculating sequence probabilities.

The disadvantage of this measure is that it does not use any linguistic (e.g., phonetic) information, but the advantage is that it can easily measure the similarity of distributions of n-grams. Such measures have proved to be very effective in automatically identifying languages of text, with accuracies nearing 100% for fairly small amounts of training and test data [1, 17].

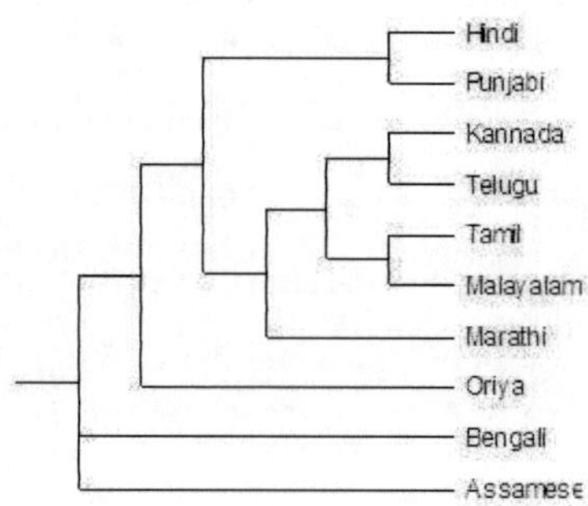

Fig. 1: *Phylogenetic tree using SCE*

3.2 Measures based on Cognate Identification

The other two measures are based on potential cognates, i.e., words of similar form. Both of them use an algorithm for identification of potential cognates. Many such algorithms have been proposed. For identifying cognates, Singh and Surana [18] used the Computational Phonetic Model of Scripts or CPMS [16]. This model takes into account the characteristics of Brahmi origin scripts and calculates Surface Similarity.

[4] Potential cognates are words of different languages which are similar in form and therefore are likely to be cognates. They might include some 'false friends', i.e., words which are not etymologically inherited. It is worthwhile to experiment (using statistical techniques) on potential cognates, even without removing the 'false friends' because a large percentage of them are actually cognates in the linguistic sense.

It consists of a model of alphabet that represents the common alphabet for Brahmi origin scripts, a model of phonology that maps the letters (which are, for the most part, phonemes) to phonetic and orthographic features, a Stepped Distance Function (SDF) that calculates the phonetic and orthographic similarity of two letters and a dynamic programming (DP) algorithm that calculates the Surface Similarity of two words or strings. The CPMS was adapted by Singh and Surana for identifying the potential cognates.

In general, the distance between two strings can be defined as:

$$c_{lm} = f_p(w_l, w_m) \tag{2}$$

where f_p is the function (implemented as a DP alignment algorithm) which calculates Surface Similarity using the CPMS based cost between the word w_l of language l and the word w_m of language m.

Those word pairs are identified as cognates which have the least cost.

3.2.1 Cognate Coverage Distance (CCD)

The second measure used is a corpus based estimate of the coverage of cognates across two languages. Cognate coverage is defined ideally as the number of words (from the vocabularies of the two languages) which are of the same origin, but which is approximately estimated by identifying words of similar form (potential cognates). The decision about whether two words are cognates or not is made on the basis of Surface Similarity of the two words as described in the previous section. Non-parallel corpora of the two languages are used for identifying the cognates.

The normalized distance between two languages is defined as:

$$t'_{lm} = 1 - \frac{t_{lm}}{max(t)} \tag{3}$$

where t_{lm} and t_{ml} are the number of (potential) cognates found when comparing from language l to m and from language m to l, respectively.

Since the CPMS based measure of Surface Similarity is asymmetric, the average number of unidirectional cognates is calculated:

$$d^{ccd} = \frac{t'_{lm} + t'_{ml}}{2} \tag{4}$$

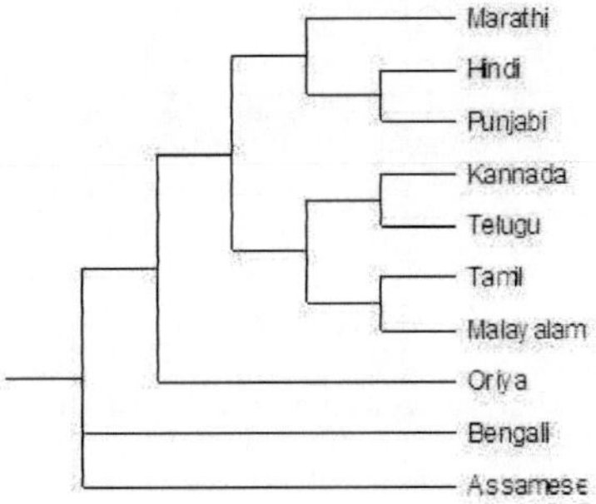

Fig. 2: *Phylogenetic tree using CCD*

3.2.2 Phonetic Distance of Cognates (PDC)

Simply finding the coverage of cognates may indicate the distance between two languages, but a measure based solely on this information does not take into account the variation between the cognates themselves. To include this variation into the estimate of distance, Singh and Surana [18] used another measure based on the sum of the CPMS based cost of n cognates found between two languages:

$$C^{pdc}_{lm} = \sum_{i=0}^{n} c_{lm} \tag{5}$$

where n is the minimum of t_{lm} for all the language pairs compared.

The normalized distance can be defined as:

$$C'_{lm} = \frac{C^{pdc}_{lm}}{max(C^{pdc})} \tag{6}$$

A symmetric version of this cost is then calculated:

$$d_{pdc} = \frac{C'_{lm} + C'_{ml}}{2} \tag{7}$$

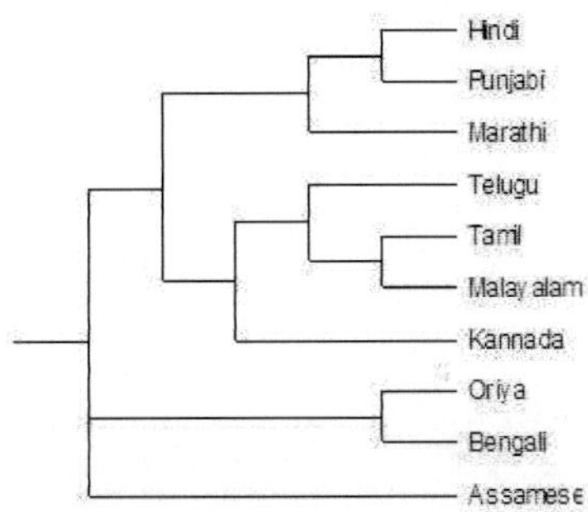

Fig. 3: *Phylogenetic tree using PDC*

3.3 Feature N-Grams (FNG)

The idea in using this measure is that the way phonemes occur together matters less than the way the phonetic features occur together because phonemes themselves are defined in terms of the features. Therefore, it makes more sense to a have measure directly in terms of phonetic features. But since we are experimenting directly with corpus data (without any phonetic transcription) using the CPMS [16], we also include some orthographic features as given in the CPMS implementation. The letter to feature mapping that we use comes from the CPMS. Basically, each word is converted into a set of sequences of feature-value pairs such that any feature can follow any feature, which means that the number of sequences for a word of length l_w is less than or equal to $(N_f \times N_v)^{l_w}$, where N_f is the number of possible features and N_v is the number of possible values. We create sequences of feature-value pairs for all the words and from this 'corpus' of feature-value pair sequences we build the feature n-gram model.

The formula for calculating distributional similarity based on these phonetic and orthographic features is the same (SCE) as given in equation 1, except that the distribution in this case is made up of features rather than letters. Note that since we do not assume the features to be independent, any feature can follow any other feature in a feature n-gram. All the permutations are computed before the feature n-gram model is pruned to keep only the top N feature n-grams. The order of the n-gram model is kept as 3, i.e., trigrams.

The feature n-grams are computed as follows. For a given word, each letter is first converted into a vector consisting of the feature-value pairs which are mapped to it by the CPMS. Then, from the sequence of vectors of features, all possible sequences of features up to the length 3 (the order of the n-gram model) are computed. All these sequences of features (feature n-grams) are added to the n-gram model. Finally the model is pruned as mentioned above. We expected this measure to work better because it works at a higher level of abstraction and is more linguistically valid.

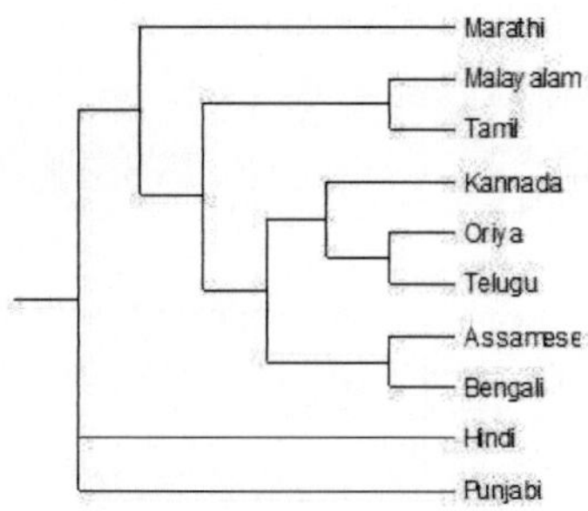

Fig. 4: *Phylogenetic tree using feature n-grams*

4 Experimental Setup

Although the languages we selected belong to two different language families, there are a lot of similarities among them which allow us to choose them for our experiments [10]. The corpora used for our experiments are all part of the CIIL multilingual corpus. The experiments were conducted using word lists prepared from the raw corpus for every language. No morph analyzer or stemmer has been applied to the words. Initially the word types with their frequencies are extracted from the corpus. Then the word types are sorted based on their corresponding frequency. Only the top N_w of these word types are retained. This is done with the aim of including as much of the core vocabulary as possible for comparing the languages[5]. For using cognate based measures for estimation of language distance, cognates are extracted from the word lists between these languages. For feature n-gram measures, the feature n-gram models are prepared as explained in Section 3.

[5] For our experiments we fixed N_w at 50,000. This number is different from N, the number of top n-grams that are retained after pruning the n-gram model.

We calculate the distance between every pair of languages available. We compare the results between all the four measures discussed above by constructing trees using these measures. The trees are constructed using the NEIGHBOR program in the PHYLIP package[6]. The NEIGHBOR programs provides two distance-based tree construction algorithms: Neighbour Joining and UPGMA. For our experiments we used Neighbour Joining as it does not assume a constant rate of evolution and it produces unrooted trees unlike UPGMA which assumes constant rate of evolution (the length of the leaves from the root of the tree is same across all the leaves) and produces rooted trees. We do not do any outgrouping as outgrouping makes sense only when all the languages belong to a single family.

	BN	HI	KN	ML	MR	OR	PA	TA	TE
AS	0.02	0.39	0.71	0.86	0.61	0.20	0.61	0.93	0.73
	0.12	0.25	0.39	0.61	0.45	0.11	0.58	0.95	0.46
	0.05	0.30	0.51	0.50	0.43	0.18	0.42	0.70	0.64
	0.02	0.06	0.07	0.12	0.09	0.05	0.09	0.13	0.05
BN		0.32	0.68	0.86	0.57	0.07	0.56	0.96	0.70
		0.29	0.42	0.64	0.42	0.05	0.56	0.90	0.50
		0.29	0.47	0.45	0.43	0.14	0.42	0.74	0.43
		0.06	0.07	0.13	0.08	0.04	0.09	0.11	0.02
HI			0.61	0.81	0.42	0.40	0.20	0.93	0.61
			0.17	0.56	0.16	0.27	0.16	0.87	0.38
			0.43	0.46	0.16	0.33	0.20	0.74	0.34
			0.09	0.09	0.06	0.08	0.03	0.15	0.13
KN				0.77	0.68	0.75	0.73	0.88	0.53
				0.45	0.17	0.31	0.50	0.82	0.25
				0.18	0.38	0.52	0.58	0.42	0.09
				0.10	0.09	0.02	0.08	0.10	0.03
ML					0.89	0.88	0.88	0.62	0.72
					0.65	0.59	0.77	0.56	0.31
					0.42	0.53	0.55	0.07	0.19
					0.13	0.13	0.11	0.07	0.15
MR						0.64	0.52	0.95	0.68
						0.40	0.37	0.94	0.46
						0.34	0.39	0.60	0.30
						0.08	0.06	0.13	0.09
OR							0.63	0.98	0.74
							0.45	0.89	0.44
							0.65	0.83	0.64
							0.07	0.10	0.00
PA								0.90	0.71
								0.90	0.59
								0.92	0.48
								0.14	0.07
TA									0.85
									0.81
									0.39
									0.08
AS: Assamese, **BN:** Bengali, **HI:** Hindi, **KN:** Kannada **ML:** Malayalam, **MR:** Marathi, **OR:** Oriya, **PA:** Punjabi, **TA:** Tamil, **TE:** Telugu									

Table 1: *Inter-language comparison among ten major South Asian languages using four corpus based measures. The values have been normalized and scaled to be somewhat comparable. Each cell contains four values: by CCD, PDC, SCE and FNG.*

[6] `http://evolution.genetics.washington.edu/phylip/phylip.html`

5 Analysis of Results

Table 1 shows the results obtained for the four distance measures. Figures 1 to 4 show the trees obtained using all the above measures. There are three subgroupings of the languages which are clearly visible in all the trees. Namely, Northern Indo-Aryan (Hindi and Punjabi), Eastern Indo-Aryan (Assamese, Bengali and Oriya) and Dravidian languages (Tamil, Kannada, Malayalam and Telugu). There are clearly some similarities in the trees which are generated by all the methods. All the methods group Hindi and Punjabi, Tamil and Malayalam together. CCD gives the normalized measure of the number of cognates between every language pair. In the case of CCD tree, although Bengali and Assamese are grouped together, Oriya is placed incorrectly, which is correctly placed in the case of feature n-grams.

Oriya is incorrectly grouped with Bengali in the case of PDC tree. The reason can be because of the huge number of shared words which cause a lower phonetic distance between the languages. Kannada and Telugu are not grouped together in the case of PDC. Marathi is either classified with Northern Indo-Aryan languages or with Dravidian languages. It is grouped with Indo-Aryan languages in the case of cognate distance measures and grouped with Dravidian languages in the other cases. The reason for grouping it with Dravidian languages is the influence of Dravidian languages due to long history of contact.

The distance of a terminal node from its parent gives very important information[7]. For example, Tamil is always at a greater distance from its parent node, although grouped with Malayalam, compared to other languages. Especially in the case of feature n-grams and SCE, the distance is very evident. The reason for this is the lower number of 'characters' (elements from which n-grams are made) when compared to other languages in the case of SCE. In the case of feature n-grams, the lack of phonemic distinction in writing between voiced and unvoiced sounds for Tamil decreases the number of shared feature n-grams. Moreover, the number of borrowings from Indo-Aryan Languages are comparatively less in the case of Tamil.

6 Conclusion and Future Work

In this paper we discussed the possibility of using corpus based measures for constructing phylogenetic trees. Four corpus based measures were used for the construction of phylogenetic trees. Out of these measures, the second, the third and the fourth measure are linguistically well grounded measure. We considered the differences between each tree and tried to explain the reasons for the anomalies in the tree structure. We have shown that by using noisy corpus and simple but linguistically well founded measures, we can very nearly achieve the desired family tree. These measures can be very useful for languages which do not have linguistically hand-crafted lists. The experiments also demonstrate that the technique can be applicable even to *linguistic areas*, not just language families.

[7] The trees in the figures are not scaled, but the distances are given in the table.

Acknowledgment

We would like to acknowledge the valuable suggestions made by Sudheer Kolachina from LTRC, IIIT, Hyderabad. We are also thankful to the reviewers for their constructive comments which we tried to take into account as far as possible.

References

[1] G. Adams and P. Resnik. A Language Identification Application Built on the Java Client/Server Platform. *From Research to Commercial Applications: Making NLP Work in Practice*, pages 43–47, 1997.

[2] Q. Atkinson and R. Gray. How old is the Indo-European language family? Progress or more moths to the flame. *Phylogenetic Methods and the Prehistory of Languages (Forster P, Renfrew C, eds)*, pages 91–109, 2006.

[3] Q. Atkinson, G. Nicholls, D. Welch, and R. Gray. From words to dates: water into wine, mathemagic or phylogenetic inference? *Transactions of the Philological Society*, 103(2):193–219, 2005.

[4] F. Barbançon, T. Warnow, S. Evans, D. Ringe, and L. Nakhleh. An experimental study comparing linguistic phylogenetic reconstruction methods. Technical report, Technical Report 732, Department of Statistics, University of California, Berkeley, 2007.

[5] A. Bouchard-Cote, P. Liang, T. Griffiths, and D. Klein. A probabilistic approach to language change. NIPS, 2000.

[6] L. Campbell. *Historical linguistics: an introduction.* MIT Press, 2004.

[7] W. Cavnar and J. Trenkle. N-gram-based text categorization. *Ann Arbor MI*, 48113:4001, 1994.

[8] I. Dyen, J. Kruskal, and P. Black. An Indoeuropean classification: a lexicostatistical experiment. Amer Philosophical Society, 1992.

[9] T. Ellison and S. Kirby. Measuring language divergence by intra-lexical comparison. In *Proceedings of the 44th annual meeting of the ACL*, pages 273–280. Association for Computational Linguistics Morristown, NJ, USA, 2006.

[10] M. Emeneau. India as a Lingustic Area. *Language*, pages 3–16, 1956.

[11] J. Felsenstein. Inferring Phylogenies. Sunderland, MA. *Sinauer Press. Chapters*, 1(7):11, 2003.

[12] R. Gray and Q. Atkinson. Language-tree divergence times support the Anatolian theory of Indo-European origin. *Earth Planet. Sci*, 23:41–63, 1995.

[13] J. Huelsenbeck, F. Ronquist, R. Nielsen, and J. Bollback. Bayesian inference of phylogeny and its impact on evolutionary biology. *Science*, 294(5550):2310–2314, 2001.

[14] L. Nakhleh, D. Ringe, and T. Warnow. Perfect phylogenetic networks: A new methodology for reconstructing the evolutionary history of natural languages. *Language*, 81(2):382–420, 2005.

[15] N. Saitou. The neighbor-joining method: a new method for reconstructing phylogenetic trees, 1987.

[16] A. K. Singh. A computational phonetic model for indian language scripts. In *Proceedings of the Constraints on Spelling Changes: Fifth International Workshop on Writing Systems*, Nijmegen, The Netherlands, 2006.

[17] A. K. Singh. Study of some distance measures for language and encoding identification. In *Proceeding of ACL 2006 Workshop on Linguistic Distances*, Sydney, Australia, 2006.

[18] A. K. Singh and H. Surana. Can corpus based measures be used for comparative study of languages. In *Proceedings of the ACL Workshop Computing and Historical Phonology*, Prague, Czech Republic, 2007.

[19] D. Swofford, G. Olsen, P. Waddell, and D. Hillis. Phylogenetic inference. *Molecular systematics*, 2:407–514, 1996.

Language-Independent Sentiment Analysis Using Subjectivity and Positional Information

Veselin Raychev and Preslav Nakov*
Department of Mathematics and Informatics
Sofia University "St Kliment Ohridski"
5, James Bourchier Blvd.,1164 Sofia, Bulgaria
{*veselin.raychev, preslav.nakov*}@*fmi.uni-sofia.bg*

Abstract

We describe a novel language-independent approach to the task of determining the polarity, positive or negative, of the author's opinion on a specific topic in natural language text. In particular, weights are assigned to attributes, individual words or word bi-grams, based on their position and on their likelihood of being subjective. The subjectivity of each attribute is estimated in a two-step process, where first the probability of being subjective is calculated for each sentence containing the attribute, and then these probabilities are used to alter the attribute's weights for polarity classification. The evaluation results on a standard dataset of movie reviews shows 89.85% classification accuracy, which rivals the best previously published results for this dataset for systems that use no additional linguistic information nor external resources.

Keywords

Sentiment analysis, subjectivity identification, polarity classification, text categorization.

1 Introduction

Recently, there has been growing research interest in determining the polarity, positive or negative, of the author's opinion on a specific topic in natural language texts. Such analysis has various potential applications ranging from components for web sites to business and government intelligence [6]. Previous research on document sentiment classification has shown that machine learning based classifiers perform much better compared to rule-based systems [7]. However, the task remains challenging since opinions are typically expressed in a specific manner, using many rare words and language expressions. As previous research has shown [8], even words with a single occurrence on training can turn out to be good predictors on testing. As a result, the classification accuracy for sentiment analysis using machine learning approaches tends to be much lower compared to that for other text classification tasks like topic identification.

*Also: Department of Computer Science, National University of Singapore, 13 Computing Drive, Singapore 117417, nakov@comp.nus.edu.sg

2 Related work

Pang & al. [7] pioneered the field of sentiment analysis. They worked on a *sentiment polarity classification* task, choosing between a positive and negative label using Naïve Bayes and support vector machines (SVM), where each text document was represented as a bag-of-words with weights for word presence. They further tried to use negation, word positions and part-of-speech (POS) information without much success, and found that many techniques that typically help for topic classification negatively affected the accuracy for sentiment polarity. The experiments were carried out on a set of 2,000 movie reviews mined from the web, 1,000 positive and 1,000 negative, without explicit information about polarity, i.e., without ranks, scores, or number of stars. The dataset was made publicly available[1] and has since become the de-facto standard for training and evaluation in most of the subsequent research.

In the case of movie reviews, sentiment polarity classification has been found to be hard not only because of many informative words being rare, but also due to large portions of the movie reviews consisting of non-subjective sentences that just narrate the movie plot without actually contributing much sentiment information. In an attempt to get rid of such sentences, Pang and Lee [5] proposed a pre-processing filter that removes all non-subjective sentences while retaining the subjective ones to be used for sentiment polarity classification. In order to train that filter, they created a special dataset consisting of 5,000 subjective and 5,000 non-subjective sentences mined from the *Internet Movie DataBase*[2] (IMDB). This gave rise to a new task, *subjectivity classification*, as an intermediate step for polarity classification. In their experiments, Pang and Lee used a Naïve Bayes classifier, which yielded 92% accuracy for the subjectivity filter. Using the filter to help choose subjective sentences for polarity classification yielded 86.4% accuracy, which represents about 3% absolute improvement for the sentiment polarity classification with a Naïve Bayes classifier; there were no improvements when using an SVM classifier.

Matsumoto & al. [4] experimented with an SVM classifier and a more recent version of the polarity dataset. Using several innovative features based on linguistic analysis, including unigrams, bigrams and all pairs of

[1] http://www.cs.cornell.edu/people/pabo/movie-review-data
[2] http://www.imdb.com

International Conference RANLP 2009 - Borovets, Bulgaria, pages 360–364

words within the same sentence, they achieved over 88.1% accuracy when only language-independent features were used, and 92% when additional English-specific linguistic information was introduced.

There have been some attempts to use language models (LM) for polarity classification, but the resulting accuracy was low. Hu & al. [2] tried using language models (LM) for polarity classification with several different kinds of smoothing, but found that a model based on unigrams, i.e., without sequence information, performed better. One possible explanation could be found in the observation that, for the task of sentiment polarity classification, the Naïve Bayes classifier works better when the feature weights are binary (i.e., when only term presence/absence is taken into account, but repetitions are ignored) rather than frequency-based, while language models calculate the probability to generate a document taking term repetitions into account.

Below we propose a novel approach that assigns weights to individual attributes, words or word bigrams, based on their position in the text and on their likelihood of being subjective. Using the Naïve Bayes classifier, we achieve 89.85% accuracy, which is an improvement over the best previously published language-independent results that use no additional linguistic information sources such as parsers, POS taggers, stemmers, etc.

3 Method

In this section, we first describe the multinomial Naïve Bayes classifier and the way we are changing it. We then explain how we use the subjectivity dataset to improve the results further.

3.1 Naïve Bayes

We use the Naïve Bayes multinomial classifier, which makes the naïve assumption that the occurrences of the attributes (in our case: words and word bigrams) in a document are conditionally independent given the document class (in our case: 'positive' or 'negative'). It further assumes that the occurrences of the attributes are position- and context-independent, and that the document length is class-independent. Each document is represented as a vector of attribute counts x and its class-conditional probability is given by a multinomial distribution over the set of attributes:

$$\Pr(x|c) = \Pr(l_x)\frac{l_x!}{\prod_d x_d!}\prod_d \Pr(d|c)^{x_d} \quad (1)$$

where l_x denotes the length of document x, c is a candidate class, d ranges over the set of all attributes occurring in document x, and x_d is the occurrence frequency of attribute d in document x.

Using the Bayes rule, we can express the posterior probability for class c given document x as follows:

$$\Pr(c|x) = \frac{\Pr(c)\prod_d \Pr(d|c)^{x_d}}{\sum_{c'}\Pr(c')\prod_d \Pr(d|c')^{x_d}} \quad (2)$$

Then, the most likely class $\hat{c}$ for a document x is selected as follows:

$$\hat{c} = \arg\max_c \Pr(c|x) \quad (3)$$

After removing the denominator, which is independent of c, and after taking a logarithm, we obtain the following formula for the classification decision:

$$\hat{c} = \arg\max_c [\log \Pr(c) + \sum_d x_d \log \Pr(d|c)] \quad (4)$$

Let N_{cd} be the sum of the values x_d of all attributes d that occur in training documents x that belong to class c:

$$N_{cd} = \sum_{x:class(x)=c} x_d \quad (5)$$

Then the conditional probabilities $\Pr(d|c)$ can be estimated as follows:

$$\Pr(d|c) = \frac{N_{cd}}{\sum_{d'} N_{cd'}} \quad (6)$$

In order to avoid zero-valued estimates of attribute values, the above probability should be smoothed [3]. In our experiments, we use Laplace smoothing, which estimates $\Pr(d|c)$ as follows:

$$\Pr(d|c) = \frac{N_{cd} + s}{\sum_{d'}(N_{cd'} + s)} \quad (7)$$

We set the smoothing parameter s to 1, which is a commonly used default value.

3.2 Positional Information

The above-described multinomial Naïve Bayes model does not take into account the position of occurrence of the attributes. for topic categorization tasks, the occurrence frequency x_d of attribute d in document x is typically used as a feature weight, in the multinomial Naïve Bayes model and for sentiment polarity classification, binary attributes for word presence have been reported to yield better classification accuracy [7]. Still, in both cases, no positional information is being used.

In the above description, each occurrence of attribute d in document x would contribute a count of 1 to the frequency x_d regardless of the position it occurs at. However, position seems to be playing an important role since opinions in movie reviews tend to be expressed around the end of the document. In order to account for this observation, we introduce a new schema, where instead of 1, an occurrence of attribute d in document x contributes a different value to the frequency x_d depending on its position in x: an attribute starting at position 0 counts as some constant a, $a \geq 0$, and one starting at the last word in the document counts as $b = a + q$, $q > 0$. Attributes occurring in between get position-dependent fractional counts that are obtained using a simple linear interpolation, namely $a + q \times \frac{p}{|x|-1}$, where p is the position of occurrence of the attribute and $|x|$ is the length of document x in words.

Consider, for example, the following sample document (tokenized and lowercased):

```
i have to admit that i was a little
skeptical as to how much I could really
get out of another " anti-slavery " movie .
fortunately , i turned out to be wrong .
```

The attribute for the word *have* occurs at position 1 and thus will get a fractional count of $a + q \times \frac{1}{34}$; this will be also the value of its x_d. Similarly, the attribute for the bigram *be wrong* occurs at position 32, and thus its x_d will be $a + q \times \frac{32}{34}$. Finally, the attribute for the word *to* occurs three times, at positions 2, 11, and 31, which count as $a + q \times \frac{2}{34}$, $a + q \times \frac{11}{34}$, and $a + q \times \frac{31}{34}$, respectively; the corresponding weight x_d should be the sum of the three fractional counts. However, since we are interested in sentiment polarity classification, where binary attributes for word presence work better, we will only take into account the last occurrence of the attribute and thus we will set the value of x_d to be the fractional count for that last occurrence.

Let us now see how using such fractional counts impacts the classifier. First, let a be 0. According to eq. (6), the conditional probability $\Pr(d|c)$ will be independent of the value of the parameter q; however, as eq. (7) shows, this will not be the case if smoothing is being used. Let $a \neq 0$: then the fractional counts are in the interval $[a;a+q]$, which can be seen as a scaled version of the interval $[1;1+q']$, where $q' = q/a$. Now, let us further take into account the fact that in the movie reviews dataset there is an equal number of positive and the negative reviews. Then, we can rewrite eq. (4) as follows:

$$\hat{c} = \arg\max_{c} \sum_{d} x_d \log \Pr(d|c) \tag{8}$$

From the last equation, we can see that, if we multiply the values of all attributes by the constant a, $a \neq 0$, the classification decision will remain the same (provided that we use no smoothing).

Thus, it is enough to consider two groups of classifiers, `0+q` and `1+q`. For `0+q`, the classifiers are equivalent for all values of q (except for smoothing), which means that it is enough to test with $q = 1$. Note that changing q would be equivalent to updating the smoothing parameter s for Laplace smoothing.

For comparison purposes, we also apply a simpler scheme where we remove all attributes that appear at the first k positions in the document, assuming they contribute no sentiment information. This is similar to the approach adopted by Pang and Lee [5], where some of the objective sentences were filtered out.

3.3 Subjectivity

Pang and Lee [5] used a subjectivity filter to eliminate the non-subjective sentences in a target movie review, so that they could apply their polarity classifier on a smaller set of higher-quality sentences. Although 92% accurate, their filter is not perfect, which could result in some useful features being lost. In contrast, our weighting scheme can benefit from the potential subjectivity of the last sentences while still giving some smaller weight to the words in the earlier sentences.

In order to further benefit from the position-dependent weights, we propose to move the subjective sentences to the end of the document. We thus train a Naïve Bayes classifier on the subjectivity dataset, and we use its posteriors to estimate the likelihood of each sentence being subjective; we then use this likelihood to sort the sentences in decreasing order.

A potential drawback of this approach is that, if all sentences turned out to be subjective, it would be unable to take this into account. This could be addressed by combining the approach with non-subjective sentence filtering: if we only sort sentences according to subjectivity, `0+q` methods should perform well, while when we also use filtering, `1+q` methods should be better since the first subjective sentences would get a high positive weight rather than one close to 0.

4 Experiments and evaluation

In our experiments, we used the above-described sentiment polarity dataset. Unfortunately, it is not divided into proper training and testing subsets, and thus we were forced to use a 10-fold cross-validation in order to be directly comparable to previous publications.

However, there are some complications since we further want to be able to optimize some parameters such as the value of q. Normally, this requires having three separate datasets: (1) training, (2) development, and (3) testing. In order to obtain a development dataset, for each iteration of the 10-fold cross-validation, we further perform an internal 5-fold cross-validation which divides the training dataset into a train-train and a train-dev datasets: the former is used for training the classifier, while the latter is used for tuning the additional parameters. After having chosen the values for the parameters, we can train on the full training dataset.

4.1 Using unigrams only

Unigrams, or just words, are the most widely used attributes in sentiment analysis, and we show that the approaches proposed in sections 3.2 and 3.3 do yield improvements in accuracy when used with unigrams.

Our baseline accuracy on the sentiment polarity dataset was 83.33% for the multinomial Naïve Bayes classifier with Laplace smoothing.

Figure 1 shows that removing attributes performs worse than updating their weights. Fully removing the first few words in the documents yields a decrease when done for the first 10% of the words. However, there are some benefits of having less noise, e.g., when removing all words after the first 10% up until 50%.

The figure further shows that using `1+q` has little effect, i.e., useless attributes are not penalized enough. For `0+q`, the best result is achieved for $q = 0.5$, which yields 85.55% accuracy with a corresponding 95% Wilson confidence interval [1] of [83.94%, 87.02%]; it is a statistically significant improvement over the baseline. However, the value of $q = 0.5$ was chosen aposteriori, and we need further verification to choose a value for

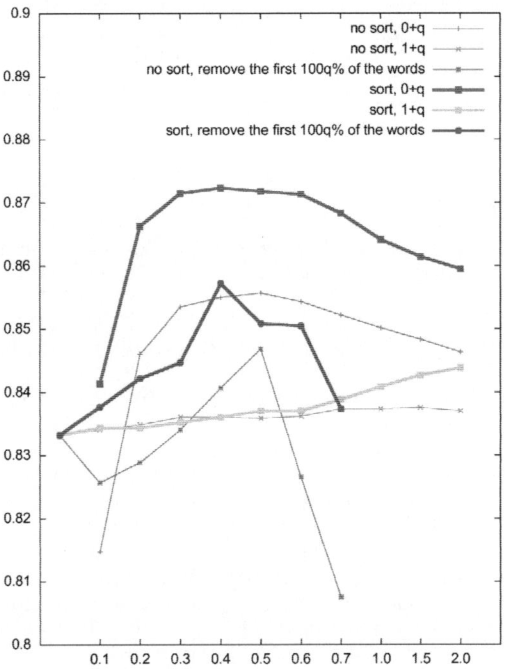

Fig. 1: *Accuracy with unigrams only: using filtering and sorting sentences by subjectivity. The horizontal axis shows the value of the parameter q.*

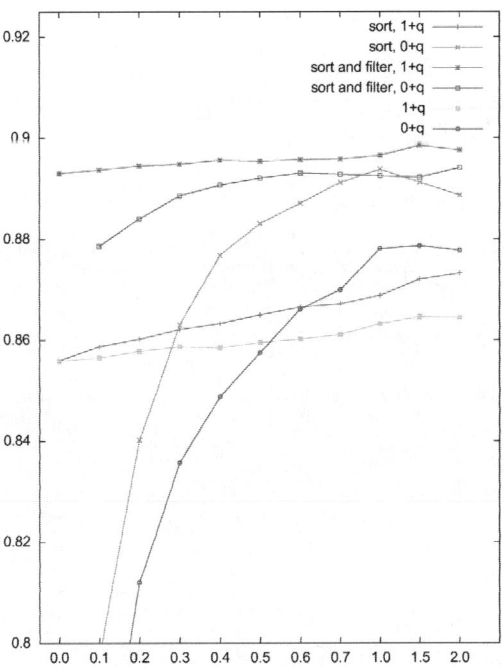

Fig. 2: *Accuracy with unigrams and bigrams: using filtering and sorting sentences by subjectivity. The horizontal axis shows the value of the parameter q.*

q based on the training dataset only. Using the above-described nested cross-validation, we achieved 86.42% accuracy, which shows that the reported accuracy was not due to the aposteriori selection.

We also experimented using the subjectivity dataset to improve the accuracy of the classifier even further. When we used filtering of the objective sentences as a baseline, we achieved 86.31% accuracy, which is very close to what previous publications have reported [5].

All methods proposed in this paper for weighting attributes yield improvements in accuracy when the sentences are sorted according to subjectivity compared to when no sorting is used. The `0+q` method with subjectivity sorting achieves 87.23% accuracy for $q = 0.4$. Again, we need to prove that this value of q does not yield a randomly good score just because of the choice being made aposteriori. Choosing a value based on the training dataset only, using the nested 5-fold cross-validation, yielded 87.62% accuracy, which means that it is very likely that the method performs at least as good as the reported accuracy.

4.2 Using unigrams and bigrams

A natural extension of the above methods is to add more features. Previous research has shown that using different sets and methods to add bigrams may improve or damage the accuracy of the classifier [4, 7]. We show that adding bigrams improves the accuracy when using the movie reviews dataset v2.0 with the full set of 1,000 positive and 1,000 negative documents. Using unigrams and bigrams with the Naïve Bayes multinomial classifier yields 85.59% accuracy, which is significantly better than the accuracy of 83.33% for unigrams only. Similarly, when using the subjectivity dataset to filter objective sentences first, unigram features yield 86.31% accuracy while using unigrams and bigrams together yields 89.30% accuracy.

With position-dependent attribute weights, we have three experimental conditions with respect to the subjectivity dataset: (1) not using it, (2) using it to sort sentences by subjectivity, and (3) using it to filter the objective sentences and then sort the remaining sentences by subjectivity.

The results are presented on Figure 2. Not using the dataset yields the maximum accuracy of 87.81% for the `0+q` method for $q = 1$. The corresponding 95% Wilson confidence interval is [86.30%, 89.17%]. This is a statistically significant improvement compared to the baseline, which does not use the subjectivity dataset: 85.59% accuracy.

Using the subjectivity dataset allows for higher accuracy to be achieved by the `0+q` method. Sorting the sentences by subjectivity yields 89.38% accuracy for $q = 1$. However, this is not a statistically significant improvement compared to the baseline that filters objective sentences. Thus, the method does not perform that well with unigrams and bigrams in combination with the subjectivity dataset. The highest accuracy achieved by our methods is 89.85%; it is not statistically better than our baseline, but still shows the potential of the method.

Method	Accuracy	Reference	Subj.?
Naïve Bayes, unigrams	83.33	[5]	−
Unigrams, 0+q, $q = 0.5$	85.55	this work	−
Naïve Bayes, unigrams and bigrams	85.59	this work	−
Naïve Bayes, unigrams, subjectivity filter	86.40	[5]	+
Unigrams, 0+q, $q = 0.4$, subjectivity sort	87.25	this work	+
Unigrams and bigrams, 0+q, $q = 1$	87.81	this work	−
SVM, unigrams and bigrams	88.10	[4]	−
Naïve Bayes, unigrams and bigrams, subjectivity filter	89.30	this work	+
Unigrams and bigrams, 0+q, $q = 1.5$, subjectivity sort and subjectivity filter	**89.85**	this work	+

Table 1: *Comparing our results to those in previous publications using the sentiment polarity dataset: accuracy is shown in %. The last column indicates whether the subjectivity dataset was used.*

5 Discussion

The polarity classification task of movie reviews has attracted a lot of research interest and many classifiers have been applied to it so far. As a result, support vector machines have been found to be among the most accurate; however, as Pang and Lee [5] have shown, although the SVM classifier perform very well on the polarity classification task, removing subjective sentences fails to improve their accuracy. Matsomoto & al. [4] experimented with several methods to add different features and reported that an SVM classifier with unigrams and bigrams yields 88.1% accuracy. Our best approach achieves 89.85% accuracy using multinomial Naïve Bayes; the corresponding 95% Wilson confidence interval is [88.45%, 91.10%], which makes it significantly better than the result for SVM. Note, however, that we are using the subjectivity dataset in addition to the sentiment polarity one.

Language modeling represents another common approach to document classification. Its popularity could be explained by its simplicity and by the existence of several easy-to-use state-of-the-art implementations. However, for polarity classification, language modeling approaches generally perform poorly: the best accuracy we could find is that of Hu & al. [2], who achieved a maximum accuracy of only 84.13%.

Table 1 shows a summarized comparison of the results from our experiments with those reported in previous publications using the sentiment polarity dataset. The table also indicates which results have been obtained using the subjectivity dataset as an additional dataset.

Acknowledgments

The presented research is supported by the project FP7-REGPOT-2007-1 SISTER.

6 Conclusion and future work

We have described a novel approach to the task of determining the polarity, positive or negative, of the author's opinion on a specific topic in natural language text. The approach uses language-independent features only and makes no use of linguistic analysis. The evaluation results on a standard dataset of movie reviews have shown classification accuracy that rivals the best previously published results for this dataset for systems that use no additional linguistic information nor external resources.

There are many ways in which the presented approach could be extended. First, we would like to try combining our attribute weighting scheme with more complex features such as subtrees of dependency trees, as proposed by Matsumoto & al. [4]; note that this would make the resulting approach dependent on a particular dependency parser, thus yielding its language-independence questionable. Another possible research direction would be using an additional classifier such that, given a list of the document sentences sorted by the likelihood of being subjective in increasing order, it can find the position after which all sentences are actually subjective; they will be then given higher weights. We would also like to experiment with other position-dependent weighting functions, e.g., non-linear. Using other classifiers is another interesting direction; in particular, we are interested in finding a way to improve SVM using the subjectivity dataset. Finally, we plan to apply our approach to other domains and languages, thus assessing the extent of validity of its underlying assumption.

References

[1] A. Agresti and B. Coull. Approximate is better than 'exact' for interval estimation of binomial proportions. *The American Statistician*, (52):119–126, 1998.

[2] Y. Hu, R. Lu, X. Li, Y. Chen, and J. Duan. A language modeling approach to sentiment analysis. In *ICCS '07: Proceedings of the 7th international conference on Computational Science, Part II*, pages 1186–1193, 2007.

[3] A. Juan and H. Ney. Reversing and smoothing the multinomial naive Bayes text classifer. In *In Proceedings of the 2nd Int. Workshop on Pattern Recognition in Information Systems (PRIS 2002*, pages 200–212, 2002.

[4] S. Matsumoto, H. Takamura, and M. Okumura. Sentiment classification using word sub-sequences and dependency sub-trees. In *Proceedings of PAKDD'05, the 9th Pacific-Asia Conference on Advances in Knowledge Discovery and Data Mining*, pages 301–311, 2005.

[5] B. Pang and L. Lee. A sentimental education: Sentiment analysis using subjectivity summarization based on minimum cuts. In *Proceedings of the 42nd Meeting of the Association for Computational Linguistics (ACL'04), Main Volume*, pages 271–278, 2004.

[6] B. Pang and L. Lee. Opinion mining and sentiment analysis. *Foundations and Trends in Information Retrieval*, 2(1-2):1–135, 2008.

[7] B. Pang, L. Lee, and S. Vaithyanathan. Thumbs up? Sentiment classification using machine learning techniques. In *Proceedings of the 2002 Conference on Empirical Methods in Natural Language Processing*, pages 79–86, 2002.

[8] J. Wiebe, T. Wilson, R. Bruce, M. Bell, and M. Martin. Learning subjective language. *Computational Linguistics*, 30(3):277–308, 2004.

All Words Unsupervised Semantic Category Labeling for Hindi

Siva Reddy, Abhilash Inumella, Rajeev Sangal, Soma Paul
Language Technologies Research Center
International Institute of Information Technology,
Gachibowli, Hyderabad, India - 500032
{*gvsreddy, abhilashi*}*@students.iiit.ac.in*, {*sangal, soma*}*@iiit.ac.in*

Abstract

In the task of semantic category labeling, given a text, every word in it has to be assigned a semantic category. Our language of interest is Hindi. We use the ontological categories defined in Hindi Wordnet as semantic category inventories. In this paper we present two unsupervised approaches namely Flat Semantic Category Labeler (FSCL) and Hierarchical Semantic Category Labeler (HSCL). The former method treats semantic categories as a flat list, whereas the latter one exploits the hierarchy among the semantic categories in a top down manner. Further our methods use simple probabilistic models, using which the category labeling becomes a simple table look up with little extra computation and thus opening the possibility of it's use in real-time interactive systems.

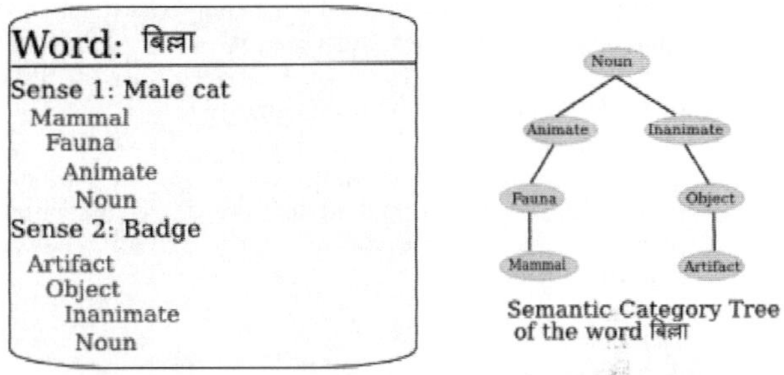

Fig. 1: Hindi wordnet entry of the word *billA*. The word has two senses meaning male cat and badge. Ontological category mappings of the two senses are shown on the left side of the figure. On the right, the semantic category tree(SCT) of the word is shown.

Keywords

word sense disambiguation, Semantic category labeling, unsupervised

1 Introduction

Given a word, its admissible semantic categories and its context, the task of semantic category labeling is to assign the most appropriate semantic category to the word. Our language of interest is Hindi.[1] An example is shown in *Table 1*. We use Hindi Wordnet Ontological categories [5] as semantic category inventories rather than Wordnet synsets. We justify the reason behind this later.

1.1 Ontological Categories

Hindi Wordnet's Ontology is a hierarchical organization of concepts. A separate ontological hierarchy exists for each syntactic category (noun, verb, adjective adverb). Number of nodes (categories) in noun, verb, adjective and adverb hierarchy are 101, 31, 25 and 11 respectively. The maximum depth of the hierarchy is 5. Each synset of the wordnet is mapped to some place in the hierarchy. Figure 1 depicts an example showing the mapping from the synsets of the word *billA* to ontological categories.

1.2 Ontological Categories versus Synsets ?

During manual annotation of few hindi sentences, we found that the inter annotator agreements were more when we used ontological categories compared to synsets. This is because various synsets (fine grained) are mappped to the same ontological category (coarse grained). A similar behavior was observed for English in earlier works. In the English Lexical Sample Task [7, 11] of Senseval-2, the inter annotator agreement of verbs rose to 82% using the grouped senses (coarse) from 73% using Wordnet 1.7 ungrouped senses. Ramakrishnan et al. [4] states that, sense disambiguation systems should not commit to a particular sense, but rather, to a set of senses which are not necessarily orthogonal or mutually exclusive. With coarse grained senses, this problem does not arise much. Fine grained senses might be useful for human users but are not necessary for many computer applications (chapter 3 of Agirre et al. [1]). So we use ontological categories of wordnet as semantic category inventories. For a detailed discussion on fine grained vs coarse grained senses, refer to chapter 4 of [1].

1.3 Semantic Category labeling is interesting

Recently, in the work on Hindi dependency parser by Bharati et al.[3], the use of semantic features has been exploited. They used just two features namely, human-nonhuman and animate-inanimate to boost the accuracy of dependency parser. For some labels, the increase is 5-10%. This is an encouraging result which shows the effect of using minimal semantic features on parsing accuracy. Other tasks that can benefit from using our system are Machine translatio, building dictionaries from parallel corpora, named entity recognition, information extraction

[1] Hindi is the official language of India. Urdu is a close cousin to Hindi. Hindi and Urdu are spoken by approximately 500 million people in the world.

1.	*kuwwe/Dog*	ko	*xeKawe/seeing*	hI	**billA/cat**	*pedZa/tree*	para/on	caDZa/climbed gayA
	Mammal		*NaturalEvent*		*Mammal*	*NaturalObject*		*VerbOfAction*
2.	*saBA/Meeting*	meM/in	*Aye/came*	saBI/all	*svayaMsevaka/volunteers*	**billA/badge**	lagAye/wear hue We	
	Event		*VerbOfAction*		*Group*	*Artifact*	*VerbOfState*	

Table 1: Examples showing the task of semantic category labeling.

etc. This motivates us to present, all words unsupervised semantic category labeling using raw or pos tagged text.

The methodology presented here has the capability of performing both unsupervised and supervised (using sense annotated corpora) sense disambiguation. For reasons of clarity and space, we focus in this paper only on the description of unsupervised approach.

Our paper is organized as follows. In section 2 we present the related work. In section 3 we give the definitions. Our developed methods are presented in section 4. Section 5 covers the evaluation aspects. Section 6 has concluding remarks.

2 Related work

Earlier work on Hindi WSD has been done by Sinha et al. [10] using wordnet synsets. They used Lesk like algorithm [8] where the target word's synset which has maximum overlap of its gloss, its hypernymy gloss and its hyponymy gloss with the words in the context of target word is chosen as the sense of the word. Lesk alogrithm cannot be used here since the definition of our semantic (ontological) categories is very general and does not have sufficient gloss to cover all its occurrences. To our knowledge, ours is the first attempt to work on Hindi semantic category labeling using ontological categories.

Patwardhan et al. [12] WSD systems disambiguates a target word by using WordNet-based measures of semantic relatedness to find the sense of the word that is semantically most strongly related to the senses of the words in the context of the target word. Sinha and Mihalcea [13] present Graph based unsupervised word sense disambiguation. Their work combines the word semantic similarity measures and graph centrality measures for sense disambiguation.

Semantic relatedness measures between ontological categories of hindi wordnet have yet to be studied and expored. In this scenario, we present approaches which do not need such semantic relatedness measures.

Yarowsky [14] unsupervised WSD uses Bayesian theoretical framework where words that are indicative to each category are identified and weighed and these words are used in selection of a category. We use a probabilistic model slightly similar to the one used by Yarowsky.

3 Definitions

We first introduce the task formally and define some terms which are used in further discussion. The task of semantic category labeling can be formally defined as follows. Given a sequence of words $W = \{w_1, w_2, \ldots, w_n\}$ with each word w_i having semantic categories $SC_{w_i} = \{c_{w_i}{}^1, c_{w_i}{}^2, \ldots, c_{w_i}{}^{N_{w_i}}\}$, we have to assign a category to each word w_i from the set of it's semantic categories SC_{w_i}.

Definition 3.1. *First order collocational features* of a word *w* are the set of features describing the context of the word *w*. A feature *f* is a tuple which can be defined by one of the following templates (*sw*) or (*sw*, posOf(*sw*)) or (*sw*, posof(*sw*), posOf(*w*)) etc. where *sw* is the surrounding word of *w*, posOf(*w*) is the pos tag of *w*. Consider the following sentences.

- I ate an orange.
- Monkey is eating a banana.
- She eats an apple everyday.

If we define a feature of a word as (*sw*) within a distance of 2 words, then the first order collocational features of *eat, orange, banana* and *apple* are {*I, orange, monkey, banana, she, apple*}, {*eat*}, {*eat*}, and {*eat, everyday*} respectively.

Definition 3.2. *Second order collocates*: A word *x* is said to be second order collocate of *y* with respect to feature *f*, iff the feature *f* is a first order collocational feature of *x* and *y*. In the above example, {*orange, banana, apple*} are second order collocates w.r.t feature *eat* because *eat* is a first order collocational feature of all the three words *orange, banana and apple*

Definition 3.3. *Semantic Category Tree (SCT)*: As already said, hindi wordnet has an ontological hierarchy and each sense of a word is mapped to some place in this hierarchy. The SCT of a word is a sub tree of this hierarchy which is shared with all the senses of this word. For example the SCT of word *billA* is shown in figure 1. If the pos tag of the word is known beforehand, only the subtree corresponding to this pos-tag is considered as SCT.

4 Our Approach

Our approach is inspired from the work Lin [9]. He uses syntactic dependency as local context to do word sense disambiguation. His work is based on the intuition that

> Two different words are likely to have similar meanings if they occur in identical local contexts.

Our assumption similar to Lin [9] is

> Two different words are likely to have similar semantic category if they have identical first order collocational features i.e. if they are second order collocates to each other.

In this section, we present the methods Flat Semantic Category Labeler (FSCL) and Hierarchical Semantic Category Labeler (HSCL). FSCL treats semantic categories as a flat list whereas HSCL exploits the hierarchy among the categories. Both these methods take the following steps.

- **Training Phase**
  - **Step 1:** Collect second order collocates w.r.t all the features present in the training corpus.
  - **Step 2:** Build training models from second order collocation sets. Aim of this step is to calculate the likelihood of a category cat given a feature.
- **Disambiguation Phase**
  - **Step 3:** Using the above training models for Semantic Category labeling.

Detailed discussion of each step is given below.

Step 1: First order collocational features F of all the words present in the training corpus are collected using feature templates. We tried out different feature templates and the best are presented here.

1. (sw_k)
2. (sw_k , posOf(sw_k) , posOf(sw_0))

where sw_k (sw_{-k}) denote the kth surrounding word to the right (left) of word of interest sw_0. k can be only in the range of ($-m$, m) where $2 * m + 1$ is the size of window. posOf(sw) is the part of speech tag of sw.

For every feature f_j in F, **S**econd **O**rder **C**ollocate sets w.r.t f_j, SOC_{f_j}, are calculated i.e. all the words which have feature f_j as first order collocational feature are collected.

In the following sections, we discuss two different methods that differ in the way *steps 2,3* are performed.

4.1 Flat Semantic Category labeler (FSCL)

Based on our assumption that second order collocates w.r.t a feature f_j, SOC_{f_j}, are likely to have same semantic category, we calculate the expectation of the occurrence of each semantic category with feature f_j. Only the leaf semantic categories of the all the words in the second order collocate set SOC_{f_j} are considered. Hierarchial information of the semantic categories is not used.

Step 2: Aim of this step is to calculate the expectation of occurrence of category cat with feature f_j. To calculate this, we use the following equations.

$$Pr(cat|f_j) = \frac{Count(cat, SOC_{f_j})}{\sum_{cat} Count(cat, SOC_{f_j})}$$
$$AE(cat|f_j) = \frac{Pr(cat|f_j)}{Pr(f_j)} \quad (1)$$

where $Pr(cat|f_j)$ denotes the probability of the occurence of category cat with feature f_j. $Count(cat, SOC_{f_j})$ denotes the number of words in SOC_{f_j} which have category cat as their leaf semantic category. $AE(cat/f_j)$ is the above expectation measure which gives the expectation of occurrence of cat with feature f_j. Some of the most frequent features consisting of function words, occur with almost all the categories. This measure penalizes such words and rewards the salient features of a category. A similar AE measure can be found in Kavalec et al. [6]. In his work, the measure *above expectation* (AE) is employed for non taxonomic relation extraction.

Step 3: This is the disambiguation phase where an utterance of a word w_i with leaf semantic categories SC_{w_i}= $\{c_1, c_2, \ldots\}$ is assigned a category according to the following equation.

$$\underset{c_k \in SC_{w_i}}{\text{argMax}} \sum_{j=1}^{F} AE(c_k|f_j)$$

where $f_1, f_2, \ldots, f_F$ are the first order collocational features of w_i. $AE(c_k|f_j)$ is the expectation of the occurrence of c_k with feature f_j which is calculated in the previous step (training phase). The expected occurrence of each admissible leaf category of w_i is calculated w.r.t all its first order collocational features and the category with highest score is chosen. We used summation over all features because AE is an expectation measure and not a probability measure.

4.2 Hierarchical Semantic Category labeler (HSCL)

This method uses the hierarchical information of the semantic category tree (FSCL uses only leaf categories). In the training phase, given a feature, the expectation of each category at each level of the semantic category tree are calculated. The disambiguation algorithm runs in a top down fashion and takes a decision at each level based on the available expectation scores at that level. The details are as follows.

Step 2: Given a feature f_j, the aim of this step is to calculate the expectation of each category at each level of the semantic category tree (SCT). Let c_h^i denote i^{th} category at the level h of SCT. This phase is summarized below.

- Aggregate the semantic category trees of all of the words in the set SOC_{f_j}: The semantic category trees of the second order collocates w.r.t feature f_j are obtained. They are aggregated in this step to form the aggregate tree AGT_{f_j}. To perform the aggregation we take the union of semantic category trees of all the words in SOC_{f_i}. Union of two trees is a simple operation by doing which, the nodes common to both the trees get their scores summed up and the for others it remains the same. Initially each tree node carries a score of .

  $$node.score = \frac{1}{|node.siblings| + 1}$$

  Aggregation of trees:

  $$AGT_{f_j} = \{ \bigcup_{w \in SOC_{f_j}} SCT(w)\}$$

- Normalize the scores of each node in the tree AGT_{f_j} to calculate $Pr(c_h^i|f_j)$: The nodes in of the tree AGT_{f_j} carry the summed up scores as a result of aggregation operation performed in previous step. These scores are normalized according the following equation.

  $$Pr(c_h^i|f_j) \simeq \frac{n_h^i.score}{|SOC_{f_j}|}$$
  $$AE(c_h^i|f_j) = \frac{Pr(c_h^i|f_j)}{Pr(f_j)} \quad (2)$$

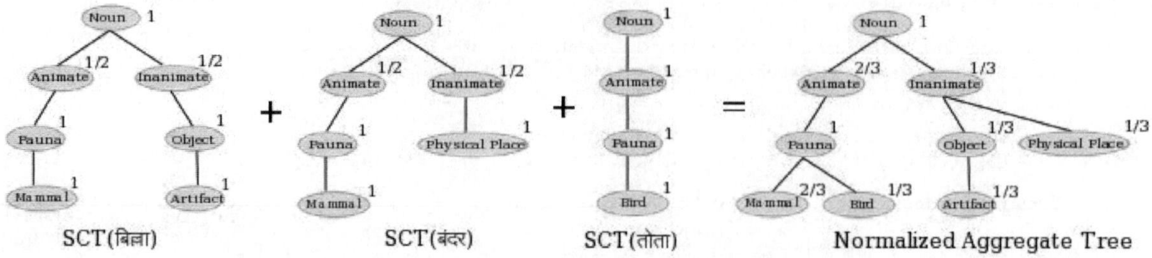

Fig. 2: Aggregation and Normalization of Semantic Category trees

where n_h^i is the node in AGT_{f_j} corresponding to the category c_h^i. $AE(c_h^i|f_j)$ is the above expectation measure which gives the expectation of the occurrence of c_h^i when the feature f_j. Note: $Pr(c_h^i|f_j)$ is not the exact probability. This measure gives more preference to the words in SOC_{f_j} which are less ambiguous.

The example shown in the figure 2 clarifies the aggregation and normalization steps used in this algorithm. The feature used in this example is *(caDZa/climb)*. The set $SOC_{\text{(caDZa/climb)}}$ consists of words *billA/Cat, baMxara/Monkey, wowA/Parrot*. The semantic category trees of these words are shown on the left with their initial scores. The right most tree is formed after the normalization of the aggregated tree $AGT_{\text{(caDZa/climb)}}$.

In this paragraph, we discuss an alternative scoring mechanism. The same example in figure 2 is used to explain this mechanism. The probabilities in this are calculated as follows. Take initial $node.score$ to be 1 for each tree. Aggregate all of them to form an aggregate tree. In the example figure, scores on nodes $Noun$, $Animate$, $Inanimate$ of the aggregate tree will be 3, 3, 2 respectively. Normalization is performed using the following equation

$$Pr(c_h^i|f_j) = \frac{n_h^i.score}{\sum_k n_h^k.score}$$

Scores on nodes $Noun$, $Animate$, $Inanimate$ of the aggregate tree after the normalization are $3/3$, $3/5$, $2/5$ respectively. The ratio of the probability of $Animate$ and $Inanimate$ is $(3/5)/(2/5) = 3/2$. Using the former scoring mechanism it is $(2/3)/(1/3) = 2$. The former mechanism accumulates a higher confidence for the category $Animate$ compared to $Inanimate$ because it gives more preference to words with one sense (here wowA/parrot) and the latter model gives equal preference to all the words. To put it in other words, our scoring mechanism gives preference to semantic category of the words with single sense assuming that this semantic category is more likely to occur with the given feature.

Step 3: To disambiguate an occurrence a word w_i with it's collocational features f_j a top down walk is performed on the semantic category tree of w_i. The set of categories at level h (denoted by $SCT^h(w_i)$) are disambiguated first before moving to disambiguate at level $h+1$. Once a category is decided at level h, then the algorithm considers only the children of this category in level $h+1$. This results in reducing the semantic category search space of disambiguation algorithm. For more details, refer to the algorithm below.

Algorithm 1 HSCL Disambiguation phase

Input: w_i and it's collocational features f_j
Output: A semantic category path.
cur=TOP
for each level $h \in \{0, 1, \ldots\}$ **do**
  $pList = \{c | c \in SCT^h(w_i) \& parent(c) == cur\}$
  //pruning the list of categories at level h
  $cur = \underset{cat \in pList}{\text{argMax}} \sum_{j=1}^{F} AE(cat|f_j)$
  append cur to output
end for

Advantages of HSCL:

- HSCL disambiguates level by level. Number of categories to be disambiguated in the top level are less compared to the number of leaves of the semantic category tree. This reduces the search space while disambiguation and hence it becomes simpler.
- No need of semantic similarity/relatedness measures.
- The nodes at top levels are shared by large number of words. This makes the learning effective for these nodes and hence the method takes better decisions at top levels.
- This can handle unseen category instances because the disambiguation proceeds in top down manner.
- This method can stop at a level which has high confidence score.

5 Evaluation

We trained our methods on a 1.2 million word corpus. We used a separate corpus for evaluating the proposed algorithms. The testing data comprises of 7200 manual annotated sentences which cover 133 semantic categories.

It is desirable to have high precision and low recall systems in certain scenarios. To achieve this, a word is committed to a category only if the confidence score is greater than the set threshold value. The threshold value is chosen to be the k times the average of the set S consisting of all category scores over all the features.

$$\theta = k * averageoftheSet(S)$$

where $\forall cat \forall j Pr(cat|f_j) \in S$. Set S is collected during Training phase. As k is increased, precision increases (with decrease in recall)

5.1 FSCL accuracies

The **baseline** system assigns the semantic category of first sense of the word. The evaluation results of FSCL for **nouns** is shown in table 2.

Model	P	R
Baseline	85.6	85.6
FSCL trained on raw text	75.6	75.6
FSCL with k=2 trained on raw text	84.7	53.9
FSCL with k=3 trained on raw text	87.8	50.0
FSCL with k=2 trained on pos tagged text	83.2	63.4

Table 2: Accuracies of FSCL and Baseline for **nouns** (P: precision and R:recall)

As discussed in *Section 4*, feature (sw_k) and (sw_j, $pos(sw_j)$, $pos(sw_0)$) are used as features for training on raw and pos-tagged text repectively. Window size of 20 is used in all the models.

As k value is increased, FSCL method performs better than the baseline. We believe that the reason for low recall is because of the size of training corpus. For English, huge corpora above 100 million words are available. But for Hindi, such huge corpora does not exist. Once if our models are built using such huge corpora, recall can also be increased since the number of salient words for each category increases.

We see that the precision of the model trained on pos-tagged text is less compared to others because of the low accuracy of the hindi pos-tagger which is about 78%. Training corpus is pos tagged using [2].

5.2 Level wise accuracies of HSCL

	Baseline		HSCL ($k = 5$)	
Level	P	R	P	R
1	96.9	96.9	99.4	94.0
2	91.5	91.5	96.4	63.8
3	89.8	89.8	95.4	52.0
4	87.7	87.7	94.4	46.4
5	76.8	76.8	83.1	64.4

Table 3: Level wise accuracies of HSCL for **nouns**

For each level, the **baseline** system assigns the semantic category of the first sense of the word corresponding to that level.

The results obtained using HSCL method with $k = 5$ are shown in the table 3. Window size of 20 is taken. Raw text is used for training. We see that HSCL outperforms the baseline (first sense) in terms of precision. The recall values of HSCL are low compared to baseline.

Comparing HSCL with FSCL, precision values of HSCL are very high and the recall values of HSCL are comparable with FSCL. This shows us that high precision values can be achieved with HSCL compared to FSCL for the same recall values.

6 Conclusion

In this paper we have introduced the problem of semantic category labeling and also presented two unsupervised methods for performing this task. These methods do not use semantic similarity measures. To label an utterance of size n, an efficient implementation of our disambiguation procedure takes a time $O(n * s)$, where s is the maximum number of senses of a word in this utterance. Besides presenting the evaluations of our algorithms, we also presented a simple parameter tuning procedure to obtain a precision recall tradeoff.

In the near future, we are integrating our system with Hindi dependency parser and study the effect of semantic features on parsing accuracies. Also, we are interested to apply the methods discussed here to English language using the synset hierarchy of English Wordnet.

References

[1] E. Agirre and P. Edmonds. *Word Sense Disambiguation: Algorithms and Applications (Text, Speech and Language Technology).* Springer-Verlag New York, Inc., Secaucus, NJ, USA, 2006.

[2] Avinesh.PVS and K. Gali. Part-of-speech tagging and chunking using conditional random fields and transformation based learning. In *IJCAI-07 Workshop on "Shallow Parsing in South Asian Languages"*, 2007.

[3] A. Bharati, S. Husain, B. Ambati, S. Jain, D. M. Sharma, and R. Sangal. Two semantic features make all the difference in parsing accuracy. In *International Conference on Natural Language Processing (ICON-08), CDAC, Pune, India*, 2008.

[4] A. D. P. B. Ganesh Ramakrishnan, B. P. Prithviraj and S. Chakrabarti. Soft word sense disambiguation. In *The Second Global Wordnet Conference, Masaryk University Brno, Czech Republic*, pages 33–64, 2004.

[5] S. Jha, D. Narayan, P. Pande, and P. Bhattacharyya. A wordnet for hindi. In *International Workshop on Lexical Resources in Natural Language Processing, Hyderabad, India, January*, 2001.

[6] M. Kavalec, E. Maedche, and V. Svtek. Discovery of lexical entries for non–taxonomic. In *In: Proceedings of SOFSEM 2004: Theory and Practice of Computer Science, LNCS 2932*, pages 249–256, 2004.

[7] A. Kilgarriff. English lexical sample task description. In *In Proceedings of the SENSEVAL -2 workshop, ACL Workshop.*, 2001.

[8] M. Lesk. Automatic sense disambiguation using machine readable dictionaries: how to tell a pine cone from an ice cream cone. In *SIGDOC '86: Proceedings of the 5th annual international conference on Systems documentation*, pages 24–26, New York, NY, USA, 1986. ACM.

[9] D. Lin. Using syntactic dependency as local context to resolve word sense ambiguity. In *In Proceedings of ACL/EACL-97*, pages 64–71, 1997.

[10] P. P. L. K. Manish Sinha, Mahesh Kumar and P. Bhattacharyya. Hindi word sense disambiguation. In *In: International Symposium on Machine Translation, Natural Language Processing and Translation Support Systems, Delhi, India, November, 2004.*, 2004.

[11] S. C. L. D. Martha Palmer, Christiane Fellbaum and H. T. Dang. English tasks: All-words and verb lexical sample. In *In Proceedings of the SENSEVAL -2 workshop, ACL Workshop.*, 2001.

[12] S. Patwardhan, S. Banerjee, and T. Pedersen. Using measures of semantic relatedness for word sense disambiguation. In *Proceedings of the Fourth International Conference on Intelligent Text Processing and Computational Linguistics*, pages 241–257, Mexico City, Mexico, February 2003.

[13] R. Sinha and R. Mihalcea. Unsupervised graph-basedword sense disambiguation using measures of word semantic similarity. In *ICSC '07: Proceedings of the International Conference on Semantic Computing*, pages 363–369, Washington, DC, USA, 2007. IEEE Computer Society.

[14] D. Yarowsky. Word-sense disambiguation using statistical models of roget's categories trained on large corpora. In *In Proceedings of COLING-92*, pages 454–460, 1992.

Sentiment Analysis of Figurative Language using a Word Sense Disambiguation Approach

Vassiliki Rentoumi*† *vrentoumi@iit.demokritos.gr*

George Giannakopoulos*† *ggianna@iit.demokritos.gr*

Vangelis Karkaletsis* *vangelis@iit.demokritos.gr* George A. Vouros† *georgev@aegean.gr*

Abstract

In this paper we propose a methodology for sentiment analysis of figurative language which applies Word Sense Disambiguation and, through an n-gram graph based method, assigns polarity to word senses. Polarity assigned to senses, combined with contextual valence shifters, is exploited for further assigning polarity to sentences, using Hidden Markov Models. Evaluation results using the corpus of the Affective Text task of SemEval'07, are presented together with a comparison with other state-of-the-art methods, showing that the proposed method provides promising results, and positive evidence supporting our conjecture: figurative language conveys sentiment.

1 Introduction

Metaphors and expansions are very common phenomena in everyday language. Exploring such cases, we aim at revealing new semantic aspects of figurative language. Detection of sentiments and implicit polarity, is within our focus. We thus propose a methodology for sentiment analysis that can be valuable in detecting new semantic aspects of language. Recent studies have shown that subjectivity is a language property which is directly related to word senses [14]. We believe that subjectivity and thus, senses related to meanings that convey subjectivity, are valuable indicators of sentiment. In order to prove this, we are led to the exploration of non-literal senses. Work presented in [11] provides evidence that non-literal senses, such as metaphors and expanded senses, tend to indicate subjectivity, triggering polarity. In order to capture the polarity that figurative language conveys [12], it is necessary to resolve ambiguities and detect the cases where words have non-literal meaning. Detecting this property for words, we can further assign polarity to the enclosing context, as it is shown in [12]. Towards this goal, other elements in discourse such as valence shifters [9] affect evaluative terms such as figurative expressions and modify the polarity of the whole context. In this paper we introduce a methodology for polarity detection that applies word sense disambiguation (WSD), exploits the assessed word senses and assigns polarity to the enclosing sentences, exploiting other contextual features as well.

In Section 2 we briefly present related work while in Section 3 we present the theoretical background of this work, together with evidence for the conjectures made. Section 4 presents a detailed description of the overall methodology and of the specific methods used. Section 5 details the evaluation of the specific techniques used as well as the overall evaluation of the system. Section 6 concludes this article with a brief presentation of future research.

*National Centre for Scientific Research "Demokritos", Inst. of Informatics and Telecommunications, Greece

†University of the Aegean, Dpt. of Information and Communication System Enginneering, Greece

2 Related Work

Sentiment analysis aims to determine the exact polarity of a subjective expression. Specifically in [3] there is an effort using semi-supervised machine learning methods to determine orientation of subjective terms by exploiting information given in glosses provided by WordNet. In particular this approach is based on the assumption that terms with similar orientation tend to have similar glosses. Therefore, by means of glosses classification authors aim to classify the terms described by these glosses. Moreover in [16] the authors try to achieve a classification of phrases and sentences into positive/negative, by exploiting their context. In our approach we exploit the context where figurative expressions appear and perform disambiguation to reveal their senses which are considered as indicators of sentiment.

There are contextual elements in discourse that could modify the valence of words bearing opinion, thus affecting the overall polarity of a sentence. These contextual valence shifters are studied in [9].

Words, as shown in [14] can be assigned a subjective (with polarity) sense or an objective (neutral) sense. In this paper we support that we need to relate word senses with polarity, rather than the words themselves. It has also been shown through an empirical evaluation in [11], that especially metaphorical and expanded senses are strongly polar. Recent approaches follow this trend by developing sense tagged lists [4].

The methodology we propose aims to perform sentiment analysis on figurative language, detecting the writer's attitude. The suggested approach shows: (a) the necessity of WSD for assigning polarity to figurative expressions, (b) that figurative expressions combined with valence shifters drive the polarity of the sentence in which they appear, (c) that it seems

International Conference RANLP 2009 - Borovets, Bulgaria, pages 370–375

promising even for the cases where the language is not figurative.

3 Theoretical Background and Corpus Study

We claim that metaphors and expansions drive the polarity of the whole sentence, as they constitute intense subjective expressions. The author, as shown in the following examples, transmits his opinion: (a)"Ice storm **cripples** central U.S", (b)"Woman **fights** to keep drunken driver in jail". In (a) the author uses "cripple" to express implicitly his frustration about the physical disaster. The same is happening in (b) with the expanded sense of "fight", where the writer expresses indirectly a positive attitude towards this woman.

We consider figurative language as the language which digresses from literal meanings. We conjecture that expanded senses and metaphors, being part of figurative language, can be used as expressive subjective elements since they display sentiment implicitly [12], [15]. To provide evidence for this, we used the corpus of the Affective Text task of Sem Eval ´07[1] comprising 1000 newspaper headlines as it contains strongly personal and figurative language. We extracted headlines containing metaphorical and expanded expressions, using criteria inspired by Lakoff [6]. Lakoff's theory follows the principle of "from more concrete to more abstract meaning". For this reason, we mostly considered as metaphorical those headlines whose word senses do not coincide with the default reading. The "default reading" of a word is the first sense that comes to mind in the absence of contextual clues, and it usually coincides with the literal one: the more concrete connotation of a word. In contrast, headlines containing figurative language invoke a deduction to a more abstract reading.

We manually extracted from the corpus 277 headlines in total[2]; 190 containing expanded senses (95 positive and 95 negative) and 87 containing metaphors (39 positive and 48 negative). These are annotated, as described in [13], according to a valence scale in which 0 represents a neutral opinion, -100 a negative opinion, and 100 a positive opinion. The average polarity assigned to headlines containing expansions and metaphors is above 40 which provides evidence that figurative language conveys significant polarity.

We consider that in the headlines, there can be contextual indicators, referred to as "valence shifters", that can strengthen, weaken or even reverse the polarity evoked by metaphors and expansions. We first examine valence shifters that reverse the polarity of a sentence. Let us consider the following examples: (a)"Blazing Angels" for PS3 **fail** to **soar**, (b)"**Stop/halt/end**, violent nepal strikes". In example (a) we observe, as is also claimed in [9], that "fail" has a negative connotation. On the other hand "to soar" in this context, has a positive connotation. The evaluative term such as "to soar", under the scope of "fail" will be neutralized, "fail" preserves its negative orientation and propagates it to the whole sentence. Moreover, in example (b) additional valence shifters are presented which are used as expanded senses, and they act as polarity reversers. These are the verbs "halt", "end" and "stop".

In the following examples we meet two more categories of valence modifiers: the diminishers and the intensifiers: (c)"Tsunami **fears ease** after quake", (d) "New Orleans violence **sparks** tourism **fears**". In example (c) "ease" functions as a valence diminisher for "fears", as it means " to calm down". The polarity of the whole sentence becomes less negative. In example (d), "spark" is used with its expanded sense denoting "to trigger a reaction", thus strengthening the evaluative term it modifies.

There are words that always act as valence shifters, while certain polysemous words, act as valence shifters when they are used under a specific sense (i.e. as expanded senses or metaphors). We manually compiled a list of 40 valence shifters derived from our corpus. It contains common valence shifters (e.g. negations) and words used as such on a per context basis. In the near future we intend to exploit a WSD approach in order to detect the specific word senses of non literal expressions that act as valence shifters.

4 The Proposed Method For Sentiment Analysis

Our methodology involves three steps:(a) disambiguation of word senses (WSD). (b) assignment of polarity to word senses, based on the results derived from the WSD step. (c) polarity detection on a sentence level, by exploiting polarities of word senses and contextual cues such as valence shifters. The specific methods that implement these steps are presented in more detail in the subsequent sections.

4.1 First Step: Word Sense Disambiguation (WSD)

For WSD we chose an algorithm[3], [8] that assigns to every word in a sentence the sense that is most closely related to the WordNet[4] senses of its neighbouring words, revealing the meaning of that word. We used a context window of 8 words, as the mean length of each headline consists of 8-10 words. This WSD algorithm performs disambiguation for every word of each headline of our corpus, taking as input a headline and a relatedness measure [8]. Given such a measure, it computes similarity score for word sense pairs, created using every sense of a target word and every sense of its neighbouring words. The score of a sense of a target word is the sum of the maximum individual scores of that sense with the senses of the neighbouring words. The algorithm then assigns the sense with the highest score to the target word. The algorithm supports several WordNet based similarity measures, and among

[1] `http://www.cse.unt.edu/~rada/affectivetext/`

[2] The SemEval 07 corpus subset, annotated with metaphors and expansions can be downloaded from: `http://www.iit.demokritos.gr/~vrentoumi/corpus.zip`

[3] `http://www.d.umn.edu/~tpederse/senserelate.html`

[4] `http://wordnet.princeton.edu`

these, Gloss Vector (GV) performs best for non literal verbs and nouns [11]. GV creates a co-occurence matrix of words. Each cell in this matrix indicates the number of times the words represented by the row and the column occur together in a WordNet gloss. Every word existing within a WordNet gloss is represented in a multi-dimensional space by treating its corresponding row as a vector. A context vector is created for each word in the gloss, using its corresponding row in the co-occurence matrix. Then the gloss of each word sense is represented by a GV that is the average of all these context vectors. In order to measure similarity between two word senses, the cosine similarity of their corresponding gloss vectors is calculated. The input to the algorithm is the corpus enriched with Part-of-Speech (POS) tags performed by the Stanford POS tagger [5].

4.2 Second Step: Sense Level Polarity Assignment

This step detects polarity of the senses computed during the first step. To do this, WordNet senses associated with words in the corpus are mapped to models of positive or negative polarity. These models are learned by exploiting corresponding examples from the General Inquirer (GI). GI [6] is a lexical resource containing 1915 words labeled "positive" and 2291 labeled "negative". Results from preliminary experiments (Section 5) show that GI provides correct information concerning polarity of non literal senses. On the other hand, SentiWordNet [4] is a resource for opinion mining assigning every synset in WordNet three scores, which represent the probability for a sense of a word to be used in a positive, negative or objective manner. Our method assumed binary classification of polarity while SentiWordNet performs ternary polarity classification. In the training procedure for SentiWordNet's construction a seed list consisting of positive and negative synsets was compiled and was expanded iteratively through WordNet lexical relations. Our method uses GI's positive and negative terms together with their definitions, instead. Moreover, after experimental evaluation with various WordNet features in order to detect sense level polarity for non literal senses, we decided that the best representative combination in judging the polarity for non literal senses is the combination which consists of synsets and GlossExamples (GES) of non literal senses. On the other hand SentiWordNet uses synsets and the whole gloss of every WordNet sense, in order to judge sense level polarity.

To compute the models of positive and negative polarity and produce mappings of senses to these models, we adopt a graph based method based on character n-grams [5], which takes into account contextual (neighbourhood) and sub-word information.

A (character) n-gram S^n contained in a text T can be any substring of length n of the original text. The *n-gram graph* is a graph $G = \{V^G, E^G, L, W\}$, where V^G is the set of vertices, E^G is the set of edges, L is a function assigning a label to each vertex and edge, and W is a function assigning a weight to every edge.

[5] http://nlp.stanford.edu/software/tagger.shtml

[6] http://www.wjh.harvard.edu/~inquirer/

n-grams label the vertices $v^G \in V^G$ of the graph. The (directed) edges are labeled by the concatenation of the labels of the vertices they connect in the direction of the connection. The edges $e^G \in E^G$ connecting the n-grams indicate proximity of these n-grams in the text within a given window D_{win} of the original text [5]. The edges are weighted by measuring the number of co-occurrences of the vertices' n-grams within the window D_{win}. Subsequent paragraphs explain how the models of polarity are generated from the General Inquirer and how mappings of WordNet senses to these models are calculated by exploiting n-gram graph representations.

4.2.1 Constructing models using n-gram Graphs

To compute models of polarity using n-gram graphs, we have used two sets of positive and negative examples of words and definitions provided by the General Inquirer (GI). To represent a text set using n-gram graphs, we have implemented an *update/merge* operator between n-gram graphs of the same rank. Specifically, given two graphs, G_1 and G_2, each representing a subset of the set of texts, we create a single graph that represents the merging of the two text subsets: $\text{update}(G_1, G_2) \equiv G^u = (E^u, V^u, L, W^u)$, such that $E^u = E_1^G \cup E_2^G$, where E_1^G, E_2^G are the edge sets of G_1, G_2 correspondingly.

The weights of the resulting graph's edges are calculated as follows: $W^i(e) = W^1(e) + (W^2(e) - W^1(e)) \times l$. The factor $l \in [0, 1]$ is called the learning factor: the higher the value of learning factor, the higher the impact of the second graph to the first graph. The model construction process for each class (e.g. of the positive/negative polarity class) comprises the initialization of a graph with the first document of a class, and the subsequent update of this initial graph with the graphs of the other documents in the class using the union operator. As we need the model of a class to hold the average weights of all the individual graphs contributing to this model, functioning as a representative graph for the class documents, the i-th graph that updates the class graph (model) uses a learning factor of $l = \frac{i-1}{i}, i > 1$.

When the model for each class is created, we can determine the class of a test document by computing the similarity of the test document n-gram graph to the models of the classes: the class whose model is the most similar to the test document graph, is the class of the document. More specifically, for every sense x of the test set, the set of its synonyms (synsets) and Gloss Example Sentences (GES) extracted from WordNet, are being used for the construction of the corresponding n-gram graph X for this sense.

4.2.2 Graph Similarity

To represent a character sequence or text we use a set of n-gram graphs, for various n-gram ranks (i.e. lengths), instead of a single n-gram graph.

To compare two graph sets $\mathbb{G}_1, \mathbb{G}_2$ (one representing a sense and the other the model of a polarity class) we first use the *Value Similarity (VS)* for every n-gram rank [5], indicating how many of the edges contained in graph G^i of rank n are also contained in graph G^j also of rank n, considering also the weights of the matching edges. In this measure each matching edge e having weight w_e^i in graph G^i contributes $\frac{\mathrm{VR}(e)}{\max(|G^i|,|G^j|)}$ to the sum, while not matching edges do not contribute i.e. if an edge $e \notin G^i$ then $w_e^i = 0$. The *ValueRatio (VR)* scaling factor is defined as $\mathrm{VR}(e) = \frac{\min(w_e^i, w_e^j)}{\max(w_e^i, w_e^j)}$. Thus, the full equation for *VS* is:

$$\mathrm{VS}(G^i, G^j) = \frac{\sum_{e \in G^i} \frac{\min(w_e^i, w_e^j)}{\max(w_e^i, w_e^j)}}{\max(|G^i|, |G^j|)} \quad (1)$$

VS is a measure converging to 1 for graphs that share their edges and have identical edge weights.

The overall similarity VS^O of the sets $\mathbb{G}_1, \mathbb{G}_2$ is computed as the weighted sum of the VS over all ranks:

$$\mathrm{VS}^O(\mathbb{G}_1, \mathbb{G}_2) = \frac{\sum_{r \in [L_{\min}, L_{\mathrm{MAX}}]} r \times \mathrm{VS}^r}{\sum_{r \in [L_{\min}, L_{\mathrm{MAX}}]} r} \quad (2)$$

where VS^r is the VS measure for extracted graphs of rank r in $\mathbb{G}$, and $L_{\min}$, L_{MAX} are arbitrary chosen minimum and maximum n-gram ranks. For our task we used $L_{\min}$= 3 and L_{MAX}= 5.

4.3 Third Step: Sentence Level Polarity Detection

For the sentence level polarity detection we train two HMMs [10] - one for the positive, and one for the negative cases. The reason behind the choice of HMMs was that they take under consideration transitions among observations which constitute sequences. In our case the POS of a word combined with the word's polarity constitutes an observation. This information is provided by the POS tagging, and the graph based polarity assignment method upon metaphorical and expanded senses of the input sentences. The transitions among these observations yield the polarity of the sentential sequences. Structured models have been exploited for polarity detection showing promising results [2]. To exploit valence shifters, these are manually annotated in the corpus: they are assigned a predefined value depending on whether they revert, strengthen or weaken the polarity, in order to be integrated in the HMM.

This choice of features is based on the assumption that polarity of sentences is implied by patterns of parts of speech appearance, by the polarity assigned to specific senses in the specific context, and by the presence of valence shifters types in a sentence. We need to emphasize that the sequences are constructed using only non literal senses and valence shifters (if present), as we believe that these sequences enclose and determine the polarity of the sentences in which they participate. Having trained two HMM's, one for positive and one for negative cases, we determine the polarity of each headline sentence by means of the maximum likelihood of the judged observations given by each HMM. In order to evaluate this method of classifying headlines containing metaphors and expanded senses into positive and negative, we have used a 10-fold cross validation method for each of the two subsets.

5 Experimental Results

We evaluated the performance of the whole system (Table 4), but also the distinct steps comprising our method in order to verify our initial hypotheses, (a) WSD helps in polarity detection of non literal sentences and (b) the polarity of figurative language expressions drives the overall polarity of the sentences where these are present.

To evaluate the WSD method selected, we manually annotated the metaphorical and expanded cases with their corresponding senses in WordNet, indicated by their synsets and glosses. Two annotators were instructed to assign the most appropriate senses derived from WordNet according to the semantics of each headline's context and a third one refereed any disagreement In order to evaluate the polarity assignment to senses, we manually aligned the senses of metaphors and expansions indicated by the WSD step, with the corresponding senses existing in GI, in order to assign to them the polarity provided by the latter.

In assigning polarities to senses, three annotators participated. Two of them mapped senses to GI, and the third refereed any disagreement. The annotators aligned metaphorical and expanded senses from WordNet, considering synsets and GES, with the corresponding senses from GI and took into account the polarity orientation (pos/neg) assigned to these senses. As synsets and GES denote the contextual use of the given sense, they can also reveal its polarity orientation in a given context. For each corpus subset (metaphors and expansions) there were two sets of senses, one extracted manually and one using automatic WSD. The annotators performed the alignment of all four of these sense sets with GI, which was exploited in the experimental evaluation. The results for the four polarity alignment tasks concern disagreement upon polarity alignment between annotators. In particular for metaphors, annotators disagreed in 10 senses for manual and 13 senses for automatic disambiguation, out of a total of 128 senses. Moreover for expansions annotators disagreed in 20 senses for manual and 24 senses for automatic disambiguation, out of a total of 243 senses. In preliminary research we performed an extra alignment with GI in order to detect if the figurative senses investigated are polar. Results show us that according to GI, the majority of metaphors (positive: 38.28%, negative: 35.15%) and expansions (positive: 31.27% negative: 37.8%) are polar. This verifies our initial hypothesis concerning the polarity of metaphors and expansions.

5.1 Evaluation of WSD in Polarity Detection

We first defined a baseline WSD method. In this method all senses were assigned the first sense given by WordNet. Since WordNet ranks the senses depending on their frequency, the first sense indicates the most common sense. We then compared the performance of the baseline method against a method without WSD for the polarity detection process and we observed that the former performs better than the latter. In Table 1 results are presented, in terms of recall and precision (prec), concerning polarity classification of headlines containing metaphors (Met) and expansions (Exp), with WSD (GVbasedWSD/baselineWSD) and without the use of WSD (nonWSD). The results presented in Table 1 are based on automatic WSD and Sense level polarity assignment. It is deduced that even crude WSD, like the baseline method, could help the polarity classification of non literal sentences. Table 1 shows that polarity detection using the GV based WSD method performs much better than the one without WSD (nonWSD), for both categories of headlines. We further performed t-tests [7], to verify if the performance boost when GV based WSD is exploited is statistically significant over that when WSD is absent. Indeed, the method exploiting GV based WSD is better - within the 1% statistical error threshold (p-value 0.01).

Table 1 shows that polarity classification using GV based WSD outperforms the one using baseline WSD for both subsets of headlines. For metaphors, the GV based WSD method is better than the one using baseline WSD, within the 1% statistical error threshold (p-value 0.01). On the other hand, for expanded senses we cannot support within 5% statistical error that GV based WSD performs better than baseline (p-value 0.20). The above results verify our initial hypothesis that WSD is valuable in the polarity classification of headlines containing non literal senses.

In order to evaluate the GV based WSD method, we first compared the output of the GV based WSD step with that of the manually performed WSD. This comparison is performed for both metaphorical and expanded cases. We detected that in the WSD process for metaphorical senses, GV based WSD had a 49.3% success and for expanded senses 45%. The mediocre performance of GV based WSD is attributed to the fact that disambiguation of metaphors and expansions is itself a difficult task. Additionally, the restricted context of a headline makes the process even more difficult. In order to find out to which extent the errors introduced in the disambiguation step can affect the performance of the whole system, we compare two versions of our system. These versions are differentiated by the automation of different components of the system.

In Table 2, we see the performance of both versions in terms of recall and precision for polarity classification of headlines containing metaphors and expansions. The first version is based on manual WSD and manual sense level polarity assignment (manual/manual(a)), and the second is based on automatic WSD and manual polarity assignment upon the senses that the automatic WSD method indicated (auto/manual(b)). Both versions use HMM models for headlines classification. We can also deduce from these results, that errors introduced during automatic WSD do not affect the system significantly. This is attributed to the fact that the prototypical core sense of a word remains, even if the word can be semantically expanded, acquiring elements from relative semantic fields. This core sense can bear a very subtle polarity orientation, which becomes stronger and eventually gets activated as the word sense digresses (as in the cases of expansions and metaphors) from the core one. There also exists the rare case when the polarity of a word is reversed because of a semantic change. The above lead to the deduction that WSD helps indeed to improve sentiment analysis, even though the "exact" sense is not always correct.

	GVbasedWSD		nonWSD		baselineWSD	
	recall	prec	recall	prec	recall	prec
Met	72.6	76.5	46.75	48.5	54.20	57.00
Exp	67.9	68.0	48.1	48.0	63.12	63.00

Table 1: *Polarity classification results of headlines containing metaphors (Met) and expansions (Exp) with or without the use of WSD*

WSD	manual		auto		manual	
Sense Pol	manual(a)		manual(b)		n-gram graphs	
	recall	prec	recall	prec	recall	prec
Met	78.5	81.5	71.00	74.5	62.57	66.00
Exp	79.1	79.5	75.36	75.5	62.53	62.95

Table 2: *Evaluation of GV based WSD (auto) and n-gram graphs steps, Sense Pol: sense level polarity, manual(a): manual polarity assignment on the manually disambiguated senses, manual(b): manual polarity assignment on the automatically disambiguated senses*

5.2 Evaluation of n-gram graphs for sense level polarity assignment

In order to evaluate the n-gram graph method used for sense level polarity assignment, we first compare the output of n-gram graphs, with that of the manual procedure. The n-gram graphs scored 60.15% success for metaphorical senses, and 67.07% for expanded senses.

We present in Table 2 the performance of the system, with n-gram graphs (manual/n-gram graphs) and with manual sense level polarity assignment (manual/manual(a)). The significant drop of the performance when n-gram graphs are used, led to the assumption that sense level polarity assignment errors affect our system's performance because they change the input of the decisive HMM component.

5.3 Metaphors and Expansions: Enough for sentence level polarity detection

We also performed experiments to verify that figurative language expressions represent the polarity of the sentences in which they appear. For that we performed two more experiments - all steps of which are performed automatically - one for metaphors and one for expansions, where we trained HMMs with input

headlines with met				headlines with exp			
met		all words		exp		all words	
rec	prec	rec	prec	rec	prec	rec	prec
72.6	76.5	55.9	57.45	67.89	68.0	59.4	59.8

Table 3: *Evaluation of the system for polarity classification of headlines containing metaphors and expansions (headlines with met/headlines with exp) using only non literal expressions (metaphors(met) and expansions(exp)) vs using all words*

Our System						CLaC		CLaC - NB	
head. met.		head. exp.		1000 headlines		1000 headlines			
rec	prec	rec	prec	rec	prec	rec	prec	rec	prec
72.6	76.5	67.9	68.0	55.60	55.65	9.20	61.42	66.38	31.18

Table 4: *Evaluation of the performance of the system*

sequences containing all the words of each headline instead of only the non literal expressions. In Table 3 the system's performance for polarity classification, in terms of recall and precision, is presented, for each subset. Results are shown for the cases when all words of the sentence are used and for the cases where only the non literal expressions are used. The experiments with only the non literal expressions have much better results. This verifies our initial hypothesis that the polarity of figurative language expressions can represent the polarity of the sentence in which they appear.

5.4 System Evaluation, Comparison with state-of-the-art systems

Table 4 presents results for our system as well as two state-of-the-art systems CLaC and CLaC-NB [1], in terms of recall and precision, compared to the Gold Standard polarity annotation. For our system we present in Table 4 three sets of results, for headlines containing metaphors (head. met), expanded senses (head. exp) and for the whole corpus (1000 headlines). The last set of results is presented in order to have a comparison with the two other systems under a common data set. As mentioned in the beginning of this paper, our system aims to fill the gap for polarity detection in sentences containing figurative language. The results for the individual cases (exp. and met.) show that the system performs well under these circumstances. This leads to the result that the specific combination of GV based WSD, n-gram graphs and HMMs works well for these two subsets. As results in Tables 4 and 2 show, the performance of the overall method, compared to configurations where some of the steps are performed manually, is very promising.

When our system is applied to the overall corpus (Table 4), although the peak values are lower than the two other systems, they are high enough to spark further research. We can see that although precision in the CLaC system is quite high, it suffers a low recall value. The authors attribute this to the fact that the system was based on an unsupervised knowledge-based approach in which they aimed to achieve results of higher quality, thus missing a lot of sentiment bearing headlines [1]. On the contrary CLaC-NB has a high recall and relatively low precision. This system is based on supervised machine learning and the authors attributed this behaviour to the lack of significant corpus to train the statistical classifier. The strength of our system is that we achieved relatively high values in both recall and precision.

6 Conclusions and Future Work

This paper presents a new methodology for polarity classification of non literal sentences. We showed through experimental evaluation that WSD is valuable in polarity classification of sentences containing figurative expressions. Moreover, we showed that polarity orientation hidden in figurative expressions prevails in sentences where such expressions are present and combined with contextual valence shifters, can lead us to assessing the overall polarity for the sentence. So far evaluation results of our methodology, seem comparable with the state-of-the art methodologies tested upon the same data set. Testing our methodology in a more extended corpus is our next step.

Acknowledgments.
We would like to thank Giota Antonakaki, Ilias Zavitsanos, Anastasios Skarlatidis, Kostas Stamatakis and Jim Tsarouhas for their invaluable help.

References

[1] A. Andreevskaia and S. Bergler. Clac and clac-nb: Knowledge-based and corpus-based approaches to sentiment tagging. *Proceedings of the Fourth International Workshop on Semantic Evaluations (SemEval-2007)*, pages 119–120, 2007.

[2] Y. Choi, E. Breck, and C. Cardie. Joint extraction of entities and relations for opinion recognition. In *Proc. EMNLP*, 2006.

[3] A. Esuli and F. Sebastiani. Determining the semantic orientation of terms through gloss analysis. *Proc. CIKM-2005*, 2005.

[4] A. Esuli and F. Sebastiani. Sentiwordnet: A publicly available lexical resource for opinion mining. *Proceedings of LREC*, pages 417–422, 2006.

[5] G. Giannakopoulos, V. Karkaletsis, G. Vouros, and P. Stamatopoulos. Summarization system evaluation revisited: N-gram graphs. *ACM Transactions on Speech and Language Processing (TSLP)*, 5(3), 2008.

[6] G. Lakoff and M. Johnson. Metaphors we live by. *Cultural Metaphors: Readings, Research Translations, and Commentary*, 2001.

[7] M. O'Mahony. *Sensory evaluation of food: Statistical methods and procedures*. CRC Press, 1986.

[8] T. Pedersen, S. Banerjee, and S. Patwardhan. Maximizing semantic relatedness to perform word sense disambiguation. *Supercomputing institute research report umsi*, 25, 2005.

[9] L. Polanyi and A. Zaenen. Contextual valence shifters. *Computing Attitude and Affect in Text: Theory and Applications*, pages 1–9, 2004.

[10] L. Rabiner. A tutorial on hidden Markov models and selected applications inspeech recognition. *Proceedings of the IEEE*, 77(2):257–286, 1989.

[11] V. Rentoumi, V. Karkaletsis, G. Vouros, and A. Mozer. Sentiment analysis exploring metaphorical and idiomatic senses: A word sense disambiguation approach. *Proccedings of International Workshop on Computational Aspects of Affectual and Emotional Interaction (CAFFEi 2008)*, 2008.

[12] E. Riloff and J. Wiebe. Learning extraction patterns for subjective expressions. *Proceedings of the Conference on Empirical Methods in Natural Language Processing (EMNLP-2003)*, pages 105–112, 2003.

[13] C. Strapparava and R. Mihalcea. SemEval-2007 Task 14: Affective Text. In *Proceedings of the thInternational Workshop on Semantic Evaluations (SemEval 2007), Prague, Czeck Republic*, pages 70–74, 2007.

[14] J. Wiebe and R. Mihalcea. Word sense and subjectivity. *Proceedings of the 21st International Conference on Computational Linguistics and the 44th annual meeting of the ACL*, pages 1065–1072, 2006.

[15] J. Wiebe, T. Wilson, and C. Cardie. Annotating expressions of opinions and emotions in language. *Language Resources and Evaluation*, 39(2):165–210, 2005.

[16] T. Wilson, J. Wiebe, and P. Hoffmann. Recognizing contextual polarity in phrase-level sentiment analysis. *Proceedings of HLT/EMNLP 2005*, 2005.

Global Evaluation of Random Indexing through Swedish Word Clustering Compared to the People's Dictionary of Synonyms

Magnus Rosell
KTH CSC
Stockholm, Sweden
rosell@csc.kth.se

Martin Hassel
DSV, KTH - Stockholm University
Kista, Sweden
xmartin@dsv.su.se

Viggo Kann
KTH CSC
Stockholm, Sweden
viggo@nada.kth.se

Abstract

Evaluation of word space models is usually local in the sense that it only considers words that are deemed very similar by the model. We propose a global evaluation scheme based on clustering of the words. A clustering of high quality in an external evaluation against a semantic resource, such as a dictionary of synonyms, indicates a word space model of high quality.

We use Random Indexing to create several different models and compare them by clustering evaluation against the People's Dictionary of Synonyms, a list of Swedish synonyms that are graded by the public. Most notably we get better results for models based on syntagmatic information (words that appear together) than for models based on paradigmatic information (words that appear in similar contexts). This is quite contrary to previous results that have been presented for local evaluation.

Clusterings to ten clusters result in a recall of 83% for a syntagmatic model, compared to 34% for a comparable paradigmatic model, and 10% for a random partition.

Keywords

Random Indexing, Word Space Model, Word Clustering, Evaluation, Dictionary of Synonyms

1 Introduction

Word space models (see among others [1, 16, 11, 6, 15]) map words to vectors in a multidimensional space by extracting statistics about the context they appear in from a large sample of text. Words that thus become represented by similar vectors (as measured by a similarity measure such as the cosine measure) are considered related. What this (meaning) relation could be referred to in ordinary (human) semantics is not obvious. It may capture something like synonymy, but may as well regard for instance antonyms, and a hyponym and its hyperonym as highly related.

Relations between words based on their contexts can be divided into two categories [15]: Two words have a relation that is

syntagmatic if they appear together.
paradigmatic if they appear in similar contexts.

Word space models can be constructed in attempts to capture either of these two relations. In this work we use Random Indexing (see Section 2) to construct several different word space models.

Word space models have been evaluated using several different schemes [15]. They are all *local* in that they only consider a small part of the words in the model. We introduce a new *global* evaluation scheme that takes all words in the model into consideration, using word clustering and a list of synonyms.

The paper is organized as follows. Sections 2 and 3 describe Random Indexing and word clustering. We discuss evaluation of word space models in general and present our proposed global evaluation scheme in Section 4. In Section 5 we describe and discuss our experiments: the text set we have used (Section 5.1) and evaluation against a list of Swedish synonyms, called the People's Dictionary of Synonyms (Section 5.2). Finally, Section 6 contains some conclusions.

2 Random Indexing

Random Indexing (RI) [6, 13] is an efficient and scalable implementation of the word space model idea. It can be used for attempts at capturing both syntagmatic and paradigmatic relations, and has been shown to perform on par with other implementations. In the paradigmatic version RI assigns a sparse *random vector* to each word, usually with a dimension of a few thousands, say n. The random vectors only contain $2t$ ($t \ll n$) randomly chosen non-zero elements, half of which are assigned one (1), and half minus one (-1).

The random vectors are used to construct *context vectors* for all words. The method runs through the texts word by word focusing on a center word. A portion of the surrounding words are considered being in a *sliding window*. We have used symmetric windows with ω words on both sides of the center word included. As the sliding window moves through the text the random vectors of the surrounding words are added to the context vector of the the current center word. The addition may be either constant or weighted depending on the distance, d, between the center word and the particular surrounding word. We have used constant weighting and the commonly used exponential dampening: 2^{1-d}. The resulting word vectors will be similar for words that appear in similar contexts. We measure the similarity/relatedness between two words by the cosine similarity of their corresponding context

International Conference RANLP 2009 - Borovets, Bulgaria, pages 376–380

vectors (the dot product of the normalized vectors)[1].

In the syntagmatic version of RI random vectors are assigned to each text. If a word appears in a text the random vector of the text is added to the context vector of the word[2]. We define the similarity between two words as in the paradigmatic version. It now measures to what extent the words appear in the same texts.

Although, being reasonable approximations of syntagmatic and paradigmatic relations the two RI versions are closely related, as noted in [15]. Consider the constant weighting function for the paradigmatic version. If we increase ω until it covers whole texts each word in the text is updated with the sum of all the random vectors in the text (except the one associated with itself, a very small part of the sum for large enough texts). This sum serves as a "random vector" (albeit not sparse) for the text, which means that we have a method that is similar to the syntagmatic version[3]. These dense "random vectors" become similar if the texts share a lot of words. In such cases the paradigmatic model is prevented from being fully transformed into a syntagmatic one. However, if the syntagmatic model performs better than a corresponding paradigmatic one, we conjecture that the latter will gain from having its sliding window increased.

3 Word Clustering

We use the K-Means clustering algorithm (see for instance [12]) to cluster the words based on the word space models. K-Means improves on k centroids (component-wise average vectors), that represent k clusters, by iteratively assigning words to the cluster with the most similar centroid. We have set 20 iterations as maximum, as the quality of clustering usually improves most at the beginning of the process.

We use the dot product for similarity between the normalized word vectors and the centroids, i.e. the average cosine similarity between the word and all words in a cluster. In each iteration all words are compared to all centroids, meaning that when a word is assigned to a cluster all other words are taken into consideration. This is an appealing property of the algorithm in its own right. It also makes it suitable for the evaluation scheme we present in the next section.

4 Evaluation

Word space models have been evaluated using several different resources and evaluation metrics [15]. In [14] evaluation methods are divided into two categories: *indirect* schemes evaluate a word space model through an application and are therefore not concerned with the model per se, while *direct* schemes compare a model to some lexical resource, to judge its ability to model the information it contains.

The existing evaluation schemes are *local* – they only consider a small part of the words in the model. The most common direct evaluation scheme is to use a synonym test: for each question the model is considered successful if the similarity of the test word to the correct alternative is higher than to the other. Here, only the words in the synonym test are regarded. How they relate to the other words is not taken into consideration. In fact, it is only the words within the same question that are considered at the same time.

4.1 Global Evaluation

The *global* evaluation scheme we propose takes the relation between all words of the model into account. We cluster all words represented in a model; all words are assigned to one of several clusters by means of the similarity measure. In the assignment of each word all other words are considered via the clusters they appear in. This is true for most clustering algorithms, and in particular for the K-Means algorithm, see Section 3.

> *The global evaluation scheme considers a word space model to be of high quality if it leads to clusterings of high quality. This quality reflects how all the words relate to each other.*

When the clustering evaluation is performed using a lexical resource (such as a list of synonyms), we have a global and direct word space model evaluation. There are many measures of clustering quality that could be used to compare the models. The next section discusses word clustering evaluation, in particular the evaluation measures appropriate for our experiments.

In [8] it is argued that the most interesting information of a word space model is found in the local structure, rather than in the global. This should not be confused with our global evaluation. It is the local relations (similarities between words) that drives the clustering; it takes *all* local relations into consideration. Further, when the evaluation is made against a lexical resource, it concerns the local structure (there are few synonyms to each word compared to the number of words in the model).

4.2 Word Clustering Evaluation

Clustering evaluation can be internal or external. We are interested in how the underlying word space model relation compares to what words humans consider related; i.e. we want to compare the clustering result to a resource through external evaluation. Depending on the resource this could be achieved in several ways.

In the following experiments (Section 5) we compare the results to a synonym dictionary that consists of pairs of synonyms (Section 5.2). There are several measures (see for instance [12] and [4]), that compare a clustering to a known categorization based on pairs of words. Each pair can be either in the same or in two different clusters, and in the same category or not. This gives us the four counts presented in the left part of Table 1: *tp* is for true positives, the number of pairs of words that appear in the same cluster *and* in the same category, fp, fn, and *tn* are for false positives,

[1] The method corresponds to a projection of the words represented in a space defined by the ordinary word-word-co-occurrence-matrix to a random subspace. When the original data matrix is sparse and the projection is constructed well the distortions in the similarities are small [9].

[2] This results in a random matrix projection of the common term-by-document matrix used in search engines.

[3] For the paradigmatic RI version with a weighting function that decreases with the distance d this relatedness is not as strong, but could perhaps be of some significance.

Cluster	Category		In/not in
	Same	Different	dictionary
Same	tp	fp	tp
Different	fn	tn	fn

Table 1: *Number of Pairs in the Same and Different Clusters, and in a Categorization or a Dictionary*

false negatives, and true negatives. Using these several measures can be constructed, the most straightforward perhaps precision (p) and recall (r): $p = \frac{tp}{tp+fp}$, $r = \frac{tp}{tp+fn}$. These measures depend on that we know a full categorization, which is not the case in our experiments; pairs that are not in the synonym dictionary may still be synonymous or have some other relation. We do not know what these relations might be, so we can not use the pairs not in the dictionary.

The only counts we can define using a dictionary of synonyms are the ones in the right part of Table 1. Hence, the only measure we can define is recall, r. It denotes the part of the synonym pairs that appear in the same cluster. It is important to note that a high recall does not necessarily imply that most of the words in a cluster are related, only that the synonym pairs are not split between clusters.

To put the evaluation in perspective we present the results for random partitions as well as the results for the clustering algorithm applied on the different models. In a random partition with k parts (clusters), for each word in a pair the probability for the other word of being in the same cluster is $1/k$. Thus the recall for the entire random partition is $1/k$. The clustering result, of course, has to outperform the random partition to be considered any good at all.

4.3 Local Evaluation via Clustering

If we cluster just the words that also appear in the resource we compare the clustering to, we make a *local* evaluation, which is much more similar to previously used schemes. It does, however, consider the relations between all the words in the resource. This is usually not the case for other local schemes, as described for the synonym test previously.

5 Experiments

We have clustered the words based on several different RI models, that we constructed using a freely available tool-kit called JavaSDM[4]. In all models we have used eight non-zero elements in the random vectors ($t = 4$). We use the following notation to abbreviate differences between the models, see Section 2: "n-winω", or "n-text". winω means a sliding window with ω words before and after the center word, text means that we have used texts as contexts, and n is the dimension of the vectors. We have used the exponential dampening weighting function for the n-winω-methods. We indicate constant weighting thus: "n-winω-const".

[4] http://www.nada.kth.se/~xmartin/java/JavaSDM/

As K-Means is not deterministic we cluster the words ten times for each representation and calculate averages and standard deviations. We can only compare results for the same number of clusters. For two results to be considered different they, as a rule of thumb, must not overlap with the standard deviations.

5.1 Text Set

The RI:s have been trained on a text set consisting of all texts from the Swedish Parole corpus [3], 20 million words, the Stockholm-Umeå Corpus [2], 1 million words, and the KTH News Corpus [5], 18 million words. In all they contain 114 691 files/texts. We tokenized and lemmatized all texts using GTA, the Granska Text Analyzer [10], removed stop words (function words and extremely frequent words) and all words that appeared less than four times.

5.2 People's Dictionary of Synonyms

For the evaluation we have used the People's Dictionary of Synonyms [7], a dictionary produced by the public. In 2005 a list of possible synonyms was created by translating all Swedish words in a Swedish-English dictionary to English and then back again using an English-Swedish dictionary. The generated pairs contained lots of non-synonyms. The worst pairs were automatically removed using Random Indexing.

Every user of the popular dictionary Lexin online was given a randomly chosen pair from the list, and asked to judge it. An example (translated from Swedish): *"Are 'spread' and 'lengthen' synonyms?* Answer using a scale from 0 to 5 where 0 means *I don't agree* and 5 means *I do fully agree*, or answer *I do not know*." Users of the dictionary could also propose pairs of synonyms, which subsequently were presented to other users for judgment.

All responses were analyzed and screened for spam. The good pairs were compiled into the dictionary. Millions of contributions have resulted in a constantly growing dictionary of more than 75 000 Swedish pairs of synonyms. Since it is constructed in a giant cooperative project, the dictionary is a free downloadable language resource[5].

An interesting feature of the People's Dictionary of Synonyms is that the synonymity of each pair is graded. It is the mean grading by the users who have judged the pair. The available list contains 18 053 pairs that have a grading of 3.0 to 5.0 in increments of 0.1. Through the rest of the paper we refer to this part of the dictionary as *Synlex*. (See Table 4 and our complementing paper[6].)

5.3 Results

The results in Table 2 follow the global evaluation scheme of Section 4.1, while Table 3 uses the local scheme presented in Section 4.3. Where the standard deviation is 0.00 for the random partitions[7] we have

[5] http://lexin.nada.kth.se/synlex

[6] http://www.csc.kth.se/ rosell/publications/papers/rosellkannhassel09complement.pdf

[7] This is the case for large enough sets of words.

k	Representation dim-context(-const)	Recall (stdv) K-Means	Random
100	**1800-text**	0.56 (0.10)	0.01
100	1800-win4	0.15 (0.01)	0.01
5	500-text	0.48 (0.12)	0.20
5	**1000-text**	0.77 (0.07)	0.20
5	**1800-text**	0.83 (0.01)	0.20
10	**500-text**	0.77 (0.05)	0.10
10	**1000-text**	0.80 (0.05)	0.10
10	**1800-text**	0.83 (0.02)	0.10
5	500-win4	0.41 (0.02)	0.20
5	1000-win4	0.42 (0.02)	0.20
5	1800-win4	0.44 (0.03)	0.20
10	500-win4	0.32 (0.01)	0.10
10	1000-win4	0.31 (0.01)	0.10
10	1800-win4	0.34 (0.02)	0.10
5	500-win30	0.44 (0.03)	0.20
5	1000-win30	0.43 (0.03)	0.20
5	1800-win30	0.45 (0.03)	0.20
10	500-win30	0.34 (0.03)	0.10
10	1000-win30	0.34 (0.01)	0.10
10	1800-win30	0.33 (0.01)	0.10
5	500-win250	0.42 (0.02)	0.20
5	1000-win250	0.41 (0.03)	0.20
5	1800-win250	0.44 (0.02)	0.20
10	500-win250	0.33 (0.01)	0.10
10	1000-win250	0.34 (0.02)	0.10
10	1800-win250	0.33 (0.01)	0.10
5	500-win30-const	0.45 (0.03)	0.20
5	1000-win30-const	0.43 (0.02)	0.20
5	1800-win30-const	0.44 (0.03)	0.20
10	500-win30-const	0.34 (0.02)	0.10
10	1000-win30-const	0.34 (0.02)	0.10
10	1800-win30-const	0.34 (0.01)	0.10
5	**500-win250-const**	0.72 (0.07)	0.20
5	1000-win250-const	0.66 (0.04)	0.20
5	1800-win250-const	0.76 (0.09)	0.20
10	500-win250-const	0.58 (0.03)	0.10
10	1000-win250-const	0.56 (0.03)	0.10
10	1800-win250-const	0.60 (0.01)	0.10
5	**500-win1000-const**	0.67 (0.04)	0.20
5	1000-win1000-const	0.68 (0.05)	0.20
5	1800-win1000-const	0.69 (0.06)	0.20
10	500-win1000-const	0.58 (0.02)	0.10
10	1000-win1000-const	0.60 (0.03)	0.10
10	1800-win1000-const	0.60 (0.03)	0.10

Table 2: Global Evaluation. *The Effect of Different Contexts. Recall for Word Clustering of All Words, RI in Table 4. (k – the number of clusters) The table is divided into four sections by horizontal double lines. The top one contains results for clusterings to 100 clusters. The second one contains the results for the syntagmatic models, and the two following the results for the paradigmatic models with two different weightings: those with the exponential damping and those with constant (-const). The best representation for each number of clusters is presented in bold face letters (for ties: both). The standard deviation for the random "clustering" is 0.00 in all cases.*

not reported it. The best representation for each number of clusters is presented in bold face letters. For ties, i.e. results with overlapping standard deviations, we present them both with bold face letters.

We present the number of words and pairs in Synlex

k	Representation dim-context	Recall (stdv) K-Means	Random
5	500-text	0.22 (0.01)	0.20
5	1000-text	0.30 (0.03)	0.20
5	**1800-text**	0.45 (0.06)	0.20
10	500-text	0.11 (0.00)	0.10
10	1000-text	0.19 (0.04)	0.10
10	**1800-text**	0.31 (0.08)	0.10
5	**500-win4**	0.39 (0.00)	0.20
5	**1000-win4**	0.40 (0.01)	0.20
5	**1800-win4**	0.40 (0.00)	0.20
10	**500-win4**	0.27 (0.01)	0.10
10	**1000-win4**	0.27 (0.02)	0.10
10	**1800-win4**	0.28 (0.01)	0.10

Table 3: Local Evaluation. *Recall for Word Clustering of Words Only in Synlex, Synlex*RI in Table 4. (k – the number of clusters) The best representation for each number of clusters is presented in bold face letters (for ties: both). The standard deviation for the random "clustering" is 0.00 in all cases.*

and the RI:s in Table 4. See also our complementing paper[6]. The pairs in Synlex that are not in the RI are mostly multi-word tokens, words in non lemma form, and slang words that the public has wanted to include.

5.4 Discussion

Our major finding is that the syntagmatic RI versions perform much better than the paradigmatic versions in our global evaluation. This is apparent in Table 2, which contains the results for the syntagmatic versions ("n-text") and several paradigmatic versions. This result differ to local direct evaluations that have been performed against synonym resources, where paradigmatic versions have been more successful [15].

This, present, result may seem counterintuitive, as synonyms have a paradigmatic relation. A plausible explanation is that for the syntagmatic versions the cluster centroids actually capture something very similar to paradigmatic relations. Consider a clustering of the words represented in the the term-by-document matrix that the syntagmatic RI model is an approximation of (see Section 3). Synonyms usually appear with a set of shared words. These words will be likely to be assigned to the same cluster as they often appear together. As the synonyms also appear with them chances are that they also will end up in that cluster. The centroid associates synonyms via the words they both appear together with – a paradigmatic relation extracted from a syntagmatic representation.

The paradigmatic RI models are approximations of the word-word-cooccurence matrix (see Section 3) that contains the overall distribution of the close context of each word. It is a direct attempt at capturing the paradigmatic relations between words. However, the clustering can not find associations between words that appear further apart within specific documents. It is only for really large windows and the constant weighting scheme ("-const") a paradigmatic version can compete. This is in line with the argument in Section 2 that a paradigmatic version with large windows and constant weighting scheme is closely related to the syn-

	Pairs	Words (n)	Possible Pairs $(n(n-1)/2)$
Synlex	18 053	15 296	$1.67 \cdot 10^8$
RI	$9.43 \cdot 10^9$	137 364	$9.43 \cdot 10^9$
Synlex*RI	14 051	11 173	$6.24 \cdot 10^7$

Table 4: *Pairs and Words in Synlex and RI.* Synlex*RI *means pairs that appear in both Synlex and RI.*

tagmatic version. The paradigmatic version with constant weighting scheme improves with increasing window size ($2 \cdot \omega$), but seems to be saturated at $\omega = 250$, since results do not improve for $\omega = 1000$. A window size of 500 covers most texts in their entire. That the paradigmatic versions with exponential weighting (not "-const") does not improve with increasing window size is not surprising; the impact of words far away from the center word is limited.

The syntagmatic versions perform better with increasing dimensionality (n). This suggests that they might benefit more from even larger dimensionality. The paradigmatic versions are not effected.

The results for the local evaluation (see Section 4.3) in Table 3 gives a different view. The syntagmatic models perform much worse than in the global evaluation, while the paradigmatic models perform similarly. Here, the paradigmatic models outperform the syntagmatic models, for low dimensionalities. In fact, the syntagmatic model performs as a random partition for $n = 500$. However, as in the global evaluation the syntagmatic version performs better with increasing dimensionality. For $n = 1800$ it performs comparable to the syntagmatic version.

The syntagmatic model exploits the information in all of the words it contains and performs much better when it is allowed to use them (global vs. local evaluation). Then it outperforms the paradigmatic models. The results for the paradigmatic models are unaffected by whether they are allowed to consider all other words. Both versions obviously have their merits. We observe that the best performing of the evaluated models is 1800-text, the syntagmatic model with a dimension of $n = 1800$. It performs superior to all paradigmatic models in the global evaluation and comparable in the local evaluation. In the global evaluation, for ten clusters, it achieves 83% recall, compared to 34% for the paradigmatic models with exponential dampening, and 10% for the random partitions.

None of the models is able to separate the different Synlex gradings. We have confirmed this in two ways (see our complementing paper[6]): by plotting the distributions of gradings and model similarities, and by evaluating using only the synonym pairs of high grade (results were similar to Table 2). The models do, however, give higher similarity to synonyms in the dictionary than to other word pairs.

6 Conclusions

We have presented and used a new *global* evaluation scheme for word space models. While local evaluation only considers a portion of the words in the model, global evaluation takes them all into consideration.

We constructed word space models (realized using Random Indexing) on Swedish texts and used a list of synonyms called the The People's Dictionary of Synonyms for evaluation. In our global evaluation scheme models that attempt to capture syntagmatic relations between words performed better than models that attempt to capture paradigmatic relations. This result is contrary to previous results using local evaluation against synonym resources.

This work addresses the theoretic matter of how to evaluate word space models. Though we hope that the use of a combination of both local and global evaluation will promote the investigation of the nature of word space models and the word (meaning/similarity) relation they define, we conclude the paper with a more tangible question. The syntagmatic models perform very well when they are allowed to take all words into consideration. How can this be exploited in applications?

References

[1] S. C. Deerwester, S. T. Dumais, T. K. Landauer, G. W. Furnas, and R. A. Harshman. Indexing by latent semantic analysis. *J. of the Society for Inform. Science*, 41(6):391–407, 1990.

[2] E. Ejerhed, G. Källgren, O. Wennstedt, and M. Åström. *SUC - The Stockholm-Umeå Corpus*, version 1.0 (suc 1.0). CD-ROM. The Dept of Linguistics, University of Stockholm and the Dept of Linguistics, University of Umeå. ISBN 91-7191-348-3, 1992.

[3] M. Gellerstam, Y. Cederholm, and T. Rasmark. The bank of Swedish. In *Proc. of Second Int. Conf. on Lang. Resources and Evaluation. LREC-2000*, Athens, Greece, 2000.

[4] M. Halkidi, Y. Batistakis, and M. Vazirgiannis. On clustering validation techniques. *J. of Intelligent Information Systems*, 17(2-3):107–145, 2001.

[5] M. Hassel. Automatic construction of a Swedish news corpus. In *Proc. 13th Nordic Conf. on Comp. Ling. – NODALIDA '01*, 2001.

[6] P. Kanerva, J. Kristofersson, and A. Holst. Random indexing of text samples for latent semantic analysis. In *Proc. of the 22nd annual conference of the cognitive science society*, 2000.

[7] V. Kann and M. Rosell. Free construction of a free Swedish dictionary of synonyms. In *Proc. 15th Nordic Conf. on Comp. Ling. – NODALIDA '05*, 2005.

[8] J. Karlgren, A. Holst, and M. Sahlgren. Filaments of meaning in word space. *Advances in Information Retrieval*, 2008.

[9] S. Kaski. Dimensionality reduction by random mapping: Fast similarity computation for clustering. In *Proc. of IJCNN'98, Int. Joint Conf. on Neural Networks*, volume 1. IEEE Service Center, Piscataway, NJ, 1998.

[10] O. Knutsson, J. Bigert, and V. Kann. A robust shallow parser for Swedish. In *Proc. 14th Nordic Conf. on Comp. Ling. – NODALIDA '03*, 2003.

[11] T. K. Landauer and S. T. Dumais. A solution to Plato's problem: The latent semantic analysis theory of the acquisition, induction, and representation of knowledge. *Psychological Review*, 104:211–240, 1997.

[12] C. D. Manning, P. Raghavan, and H. Schütze. *Introduction to Information Retrieval*. Cambridge University Press, 2008.

[13] M. Sahlgren. An introduction to random indexing. In *Methods and Applications of Semantic Indexing Workshop at the 7th Int. Conf. on Terminology and Knowledge Engineering, TKE 2005*, 2005.

[14] M. Sahlgren. Towards pertinent evaluation methodologies for word-space models. In *In Proc. of the 5th Int. Conf. on Lang. Resources and Evaluation*, Genoa, Italy, 2006.

[15] M. Sahlgren. *The Word-Space Model: using distributional analysis to represent syntagmatic and paradigmatic relations between words in high-dimensional vector spaces*. PhD thesis, Stockholm University, 2006.

[16] H. Schütze. Word space. In S. Hanson, J. Cowan, and C. Giles, editors, *Advances in Neural Information Processing Systems 5*. Morgan Kaufmann Publishers, 1993.

Identifying Semantic Relations in Context: Near-misses and Overlaps

Alla Rozovskaya and Roxana Girju
University of Illinois at Urbana-Champaign
{rozovska,girju}@illinois.edu

Abstract

This paper addresses the problem of semantic relation identification for a set of relations difficult to differentiate: *near-misses* and *overlaps*. Based on empirical observations on a fairly large dataset of such examples we provide an analysis and a taxonomy of such cases. Using this taxonomy we create various contingency sets of relations. These semantic categories are automatically identified by training and testing three state-of-the-art semantic classifiers employing various feature sets. The results show that in order to identify such near-misses and overlaps accurately, a semantic relation identification system needs to go beyond the ontological information of the two nouns and rely heavily on contextual and pragmatic knowledge.

Keywords

lexical semantics; semantic relations; machine learning

1 Introduction

Although semantic relations have been studied for a long time both in linguistics and natural language processing, they received special attention recently due to research done in various knowledge-rich tasks such as question answering [3, 17], information retrieval [11], and textual entailment [24].

The identification of semantic relations between nominals is the task of recognizing the relationship between two nouns in context. For example, the noun pair (cycling, happiness) encodes a Cause-Effect relation in the sentence *He derives great joy and happiness from cycling*. This task requires several local and global decisions needed for relation identification. This involves the meaning of the two noun entities along with the meaning of other words in context.

The problem, while simple to state is hard to solve. The reason is that the meaning encoded by the two nouns is not always expliciteły stated in context. Despite the encouraging results obtained by the participating systems at the SemEval-2007 - Task 4: *Classification of Semantic Relations between Nominals* [9], the problem needs further analysis. For example, the set of semantic relations considered for this problem needs to be better understood. Thus, a more thorough analysis of semantic relations needs to be done before building systems capable of recognizing them automatically in context. Particular attention should be given to those semantic relations that are difficult to differentiate (near-misses) and those relations that coexist in some particular contexts (overlaps). Consider for example the following sentences:

(1) a. I got home and big $\langle e1 \rangle$branches$\langle /e1 \rangle$ had fallen off the $\langle e2 \rangle$tree$\langle /e2 \rangle$ into the driveway.

b. He fell off the $\langle e1 \rangle$tree$\langle /e1 \rangle$ and hit every $\langle e1 \rangle$branch$\langle /e1 \rangle$ on the way down.

(2) Whisk together the mustard, vinegar and two $\langle e1 \rangle$teaspoons$\langle /e1 \rangle$ of the remaining $\langle e2 \rangle$lemon juice$\langle /e2 \rangle$.

(1)a and (1)b are near-misses since the same noun-noun concept pair *branch - tree* encodes Origin-Entity in (1)a and Part-Whole in (1)b (the branches are still part of the tree). In example (2) the noun-noun concept pair *teaspoon - lemon_juice* encodes Part-Whole (in particular Portion-Mass, a subtype of Part-Whole relations), but also Measure and Content-Container, so these three relations coexist in the context of the same sentence.

These semantic relations are difficult to differentiate, and thus pose a challenging problem to the learning models. Some of these relations can coexist only in some contexts, and this overlap is not genuine but is influenced by contextual and pragmatic factors. Consider, for example, Part-Whole, Content-Container, and Measure. These relations coexist for some special classes of nouns (e.g., *glass, cup* can mean either container or quantity) which have a dual semantic nature and thus, performing what is called a metonymic shift. For example, a simple analysis of the hits returned by Google for the noun phrase *glass of wine* showed that its interpretation is highly contextual: ".. I enjoyed/broke a glass of wine", etc. Here, the verb selects either the *wine* or the *glass* as point of focus. In case the focus is *wine*, the meaning is Measure, and since liquid substances come in containers then it also implies Content-Container. However, when the focus is on *glass*, the Content-Container interpretation does not necessarily imply Measure (the glass might not be full). This is just an example of many other clusters of such relations which need to be further analyzed.

Although there have been recent attempts in this direction (the consideration of near-misses as negative examples for each semantic relation at SemEval 2007 - Task 4), to our knowledge there is no systematic study of clusters of closely related and overlapping semantic relations.

In this paper we provide an analysis of a set of five most frequently occurring semantic relations which are near-misses (Part-Whole, Origin-Entity, Purpose) and overlaps (Part-Whole, Measure, Content- Container). Moreover, we compare the performance of three state-of-the-art relation identification systems which employ different feature sets: (1) an improved implementation of a supervised model, SemScat2 [2], (2) the SNoW machine learning architecture [23], and (3) a competitive 1007 SemEval-Task 4 system [1]. The systems were trained and tested on a corpus of 1,000 examples.

The results show that in order to identify such near-misses and overlaps accurately, a semantic relation iden-

International Conference RANLP 2009 - Borovets, Bulgaria, pages 381–387

tification system needs to go beyond the ontological information of the two nouns and rely heavily on contextual and pragmatic knowledge.

The paper is organized as follows. In the next section we present previous work, followed by an analysis of semantic relations. In particular, we provide a classification of clusters of near-miss and overlapping relations based on empirical observations. In Section 4 we present the models employed. Finally, we present various experiments and discuss the results.

2 Previous Work

Most of the attempts in the area of noun - noun semantic interpretation have tackled the problem either out of context (mostly in linguistics: [26], [15]) or in different limited syntactic contexts (linguistics and computational linguistics), such as noun–noun compounds and other noun phrases (e.g., "N preposition N", "N, such as N"), and "N verb N". More recently, in the datasets provided as part of the SemEval-2007, Task 4, the nouns could occur anywhere in the sentence. Moreover, in what concerns the set of semantic relations used, state of the art systems follow roughly two main directions: interpretation based on semantic similarity with previous seen examples [22], [16], [20], and semantic disambiguation relative to an underlying predicate or semantically-unambiguous paraphrase [13], [12].

Most methods employ rich ontologies, such as WordNet or look for local paraphrases (such as "N prep. N" or "N verb N") and disregard the sentence context in which the nouns occur, partly due to the lack of annotated contextual data on which they are trained and tested, and partly due to the claim that axioms and ontological distinctions are more important than the information derived from the context in which the nouns occur. We also support this claim, based on the results of our recent experiments [2] which show that some relations such as Part-Whole, Origin-Entity, and Content-Container are better fitted for an ontological approach than others. However, even these relations are difficult to identify from a pool of examples containing near misses. For example, at SemEval 2007, Origin-Entity was identified as one of the most difficult relation. 99% and 73% of the 11 B-type systems (WordNet-based) identified the relation as one of the three, and respectively two most difficult relations to classify.

In this paper we show that for near miss and overlapping contextual semantic and pragmatic data, semantic interpretation systems need to explore both the linguistic context of the sentence and the context of use (pragmatics).

3 Semantic Relations: Analysis of Near-misses and Overlaps

There are to date several sets of semantic relations that have been widely used in the computational linguistics community. In 1995 Lauer [14] proposed a set of 8 prepositions as semantic classification categories: {*of, for, with, in, on, at, about, from*}. Others [20] have used more specific relations organized into a two-level hierarchy, splitting 5 relations in the top level (Causal, Participant, Spatial, Temporal, Quality) into 30 more specific. Moldovan & Girju [18] presented a list of 35 semantic relations which overlaps considerably with that of Nastase & Szpakowicz [20].

In 2007, the SemEval-Task 4 organizers introduced a collection of 7 semantic relations which were chosen from the most frequently used ones in the literature: Cause-Effect, Instrument-Agency, Product-Producer, Origin-Entity, Theme-Tool, Part-Whole, and Content-Container.

Thus, these semantic relations need to be studied in more detail in order to build accurate relation classifiers.

A closer look at the inter-annotator agreements reported in the computational linguistics literature on various relations and the annotation comments from the freely available SemEval-Task 4 dataset [9] shows that some relations cluster together either as near-misses or overlaps. For example, Girju et al. [5] report a Kappa inter-annotator agreement of about 0.83 on Part-Whole[1], while Panachiotti & Pantel [21] list an agreement of about 0.73 on two non overlapping relations, Part-Whole and Cause-Effect. For larger sets of semantic relations the inter-annotator agreement is much lower. For example, Girju et al. [7] report a Kappa agreement of about 0.6 on a set of 35 relations and SemEval organizers report an average agreement of about 70.3% on the 7 SemEval relations (a much higher agreement was obtained after discussions). Moreover, the SemEval annotators' comments and suggestions made and listed as part of the released datasets, along with our own observations on various data collections show that annotation disagreements are mainly attributed to the fact that various semantic relations can occur in very similar contexts or can even coexist/overlap in the context of the same sentence. These relations form what we call a `contingency set`.

For this research, we focused on the SemEval-Task 4 datasets and the publicly available cluvi-europarl text collection[2] [4]. The cluvi-europarl collection is presented in the SemEval Task 4 format and is based on a set of 22 semantic relations overlapping with that of one used at SemEval 2007. The collection contains 2,031 (1,023 europarl and 1,008 cluvi) instances. The Kappa values were obtained on europarl (N N: 0.61; N P N: 0.67) and cluvi (N N: 0.56; N P N: 0.68).

In the next subsections we present the data used in this research, an evaluation of the frequently occurring set of such semantic relations, and propose a classification of contingency relations.

3.1 SemEval Task 4: Classification of Semantic Relations between Nominals

The SemEval 2007 task on semantic relations between nominals is to identify the underlying semantic relation between two nouns in the context of a clause. Since there is no concensus on the number and abstraction level of semantic relations, the SemEval effort focused on seven frequently occurring semantic relations listed by many researchers in their lists of relations [20, 6, 8]: Cause–Effect, Instrument–Agency, Product–Producer, Origin–Entity, Theme–Tool, Part–Whole, and Content–Container. The dataset provided consists of a definition file and 140

[1] Girju et al. [5] trained the annotators providing explicit annotation schemas based on a well defined classification of 6 subtypes of Part-Whole relations [25].

[2] This collection is freely available at: *http://apfel.ai.uiuc.edu/resources.html*.

training and about 70 test sentences for each of the seven relations considered. The definition file for each relation includes a detailed definition, restrictions and conventions, and prototypical positive and near–miss negative examples. For example, the Part–Whole relation is defined as follows [9]:

Definition Part–Whole(X, Y) is true for a sentence S that mentions entities X and Y iff:

(a) X and Y appear close in the syntactic structure of S (we do not assign the relation to entities from separate clauses in a composite sentence);

(b) according to common sense, the situation described in S entails that X is the part of Y.

(c) X and Y follow the constraints proposed by Winston et al. 1987 [25] in a classification into six specialized types of the Part-Whole relation, of which we consider five [..]

Winston et al. 1987 [25] performed psycholinguistic experiments to identify Part–Whole instances based on the way in which the parts contribute to the structure of the wholes. Here detailed restrictions are listed for X and Y for five subtypes of Part–Whole relations: Component–Integral (e.g., *wheel–car*), Member–Collection (e.g., *soldier–army*), Portion–Mass (e.g., *slice–pie*), Stuff–Object (e.g., *silk–dress*), and Place–Area (e.g., *oasis–desert*).

For each relation, the instances were selected by applying wild–card search patterns on Google. The patterns were built manually, using the approach of Hearst 1992 [10] and Nakov & Hearst 2006 [19]. Examples of queries which potentially select Part–Whole instances are "* is part of *", "* has *", "* contains *".

Each SemEval-Task4 organizer was responsible for a particular semantic relation for which they collected a corpus of instances. Each instance in this corpus was then annotated by two other organizers. In each training and test example sentence, the nouns were identified and manually labeled with their corresponding WordNet 3.0 senses (given as sense keys). The average inter-annotator agreement on relations (true/false) after the independent annotation step was 70.3%, and the average agreement on WordNet sense labels was 71.9%. In the process of arriving at a consensus between annotators, the definition of each relation was revised to cover explicitly cases where there had been disagreement.

Table 1 shows all seven relations considered along with the positive/negative instance distribution and examples.

Moreover, each example was accompanied by the heuristic pattern (query) the relation organizer used to extract the sentence from the web and the position of the arguments in the relation. Positive and negative instances of the Part–Whole relation are listed in the examples (3) and (4) below. Part–Whole relations are semantically similar to other relations such as Origin–Entity, and Content–Container, and thus difficult to differentiate automatically. Instances encoding these relations are called near–miss examples, as shown in (4).

(3) 026 "He caught her <e_1>arm</e_1> just above the <e_2>wrist</e_2>."
WordNet(e_1) = "arm%1:08:00::", WordNet(e_2) = "wrist%1:08:00::", Part-Whole(e_2, e_1) = "true", Query = "* just above the *"
Comment: Component–Integral object

(4) "Not sure what brand of model it came from but the <e_1>wings</e_1> are from a <e_2>trashed plane</e_2> my buddy had."
Comment: Origin–Entity

The example in (4) is interpreted by inferring that the wings have been taken from a plane of which they used to be part. This goes way beyond sentential context into very complex inferences about our knowledge about the world.

The task is defined as a binary classification problem. Thus, given a pair of nouns and their sentential context, a semantic interpretation system decides whether the nouns are linked by the target semantic relation. Based on the information employed, systems can be classified in four types of classes:

(A) systems that use neither the given WordNet synsets nor the queries,
(B) systems that use only WordNet senses,
(C) systems that use only the queries, and
(D) systems that use both WordNet senses and queries.
Detailed information about the SemEval-Task4 data and procedure can be found in [9].

3.2 The Data

We have identified some initial contingency sets of relations from the annotations, comments, definitions, and constraints provided as part of the SemEval datasets. Then we looked in cluvi and europarl datasets for examples involving these contingency sets. The most frequently occurring contingency sets we identified are {Part-Whole, Origin-Entity}, {Part-Whole, Purpose}, {Origin-Entity, Purpose}, {Part-Whole, Measure}, {Part-Whole, Content-Container}. It is interesting to note that most of these contingency sets involve Part-Whole.

As a next step, we relabeled the Part-Whole relations in the mentioned datasets with their five subtypes according to the context of the sentence. This was a relatively easy task since the five Part-Whole subtypes are well defined and many of the Part-Whole relations in SemEval and cluvi-europarl collections were already identified with these subtypes in the "Comment" sections.

For the other relations in the identified contingency sets, we selected only those examples in which the noun-noun pair was one of the five subtypes of Part-Whole. For example, Origin-Entity relations can hold between Component-Integral nouns (e.g., *apple - seed*: "The seeds were removed from the apple") as well as between Entity-Location nouns (e.g., *China - cup*: "I got the cup from China"). The rational was to focus only on semantic relations that are near misses.

Thus we built an initial corpus of 1,109 examples. The distribution is shown in Table 2.

In order to provide a fairly balanced corpus of examples for the set of semantic relations considered, we followed the procedure used by the SemEval annotators and searched the web using various relevant queries. Since we found only a few examples for Place-Area, Phase-Activity, and Indeterminate (the relation was not clear from the context) we did not include them in the final corpus.

Two annotators familiar with the task provided the semantic relations and the noun sense keys in context following the format used at SemEval 2007. This was somewhat a trivial task since all of the examples from SemEval

Relation	Training data		Test data		Example
	positive	total size	positive	total size	
Cause-Effect	52.14%	140	51.25%	80	laugh (cause) wrinkles (effect)
Instrument-Agency	50.71%	140	48.71%	78	laser (instrument) printer (agency)
Product-Producer	60.71%	140	66.67%	93	honey (product) bee (producer)
Origin-Entity	38.57%	140	44.44%	81	message (entity) from outer-space (origin)
Theme-Tool	41.43%	140	40.84%	71	news (theme) conference (tool)
Part-Whole	46.43%	140	36.11%	72	the door (part) of the car (whole)
Content-Container	46.43%	140	51.35%	74	apples (content) in the basket (container)

Table 1: *Data set statistics on each of the seven SemEval relations considered along with he positive/negative instance distribution and examples.*

Relations	Number of examples			Total
	SemEval	cluvi, europarl	web	
Component-Integral	25	140	3	168
Portion-Mass	3	2	167	172
Member-Collection	32	112	26	170
Stuff-Object	6	8	86	100
Place-Area	0	6	4	10
Phase-Activity	0	3	5	8
Origin-Entity	44	6	31	81
Measure	6	22	126	154
Purpose	0	26	95	121
Content-Container	70	18	32	120
Indeterminate	0	0	5	5
Total	1,109			

Table 2: *Semantic relation counts in all the text collections considered.*

and cluvi-europarl collections had the nouns already annotated with corresponding sense keys. The annotators, however, paid special attention to the semantic relation annotation. They provided new labels if they did not agree with the initial annotation (in case of SemEval and cluvi and europarl datasets) or if they thought multiple relations are possible. After this, a third judge analyzed the conflicting cases (total and partial disagreements) and identified 290 partial disagreements (overlaps among the labels proposed by the annotators per example) by collapsing the sets proposed by the annotators. The resulting sets were {Portion-Mass, Member-Collection, Measure}, {Portion-Mass, Measure, Content-Container}, {Portion-Mass, Member-Collection, Measure, Content-Container}, and {Measure, Content-Container}. The data was thus relabeled to reflect these overlaps. The content of the resulting corpus (1,000 examples) is presented in Table 3 along with examples. Since Portion-Mass and Member-Collection both involve homeomerous parts, we collapsed them in one class called P-Whp – P-W with homeomerous parts (e.g., the whole comprises other parts similar with the part in question). These subtypes of Part-Whole are involved in similar overlaps.

3.3 Data Analysis

Based on the literature and our own observations with the corpus created and presented in the previous subsection and with other text collections, we identified two classes of contingency sets: near-misses and overlaps. We present next a detailed account of each type.

Overlaps

So far we have identified the following types of overlaps:

(A) Genuine, when two or more relations coexist in the same context,

(B) Indeterminate, when two or more relations are possible due to insufficient context information, and

(C) Ill-defined or too general, when two or more relations coexist since some of them are either ill-defined or too general. These include those which overlap with other relations in just one or few of their subtypes. Thus, they need to be revised and further refined.

Overlaps type (A) and (B) are valid overlaps, while overlaps of type (C) are not. These are exemplified in sentences (5) - (7) below. The genuine overlaps we have identified so far are directional. For instance, in (5) Place-Area entails Location (and not the other way around since there are other types of Location which are not Place-Area) and in (6) Measure entails Content-Container. However, the entailment in (6) is of pragmatic nature. This example suggests the idea of amount/measure and Content-Container coexists with Measure, but it is pragmatically inferred from it – since liquids, and especially coffee are usually served in cups. Thus, while the overlap in (5) always holds, the overlaps in (6) and (7) are most of the time resolved by the linguistic context (syntax, semantics) and the context of use (pragmatics).

(5) "Darfur is a $\langle e1\rangle$region$\langle /e1\rangle$ in western $\langle e2\rangle$Sudan$\langle /e2\rangle$, Africa.", Relation(e1,e2) = {Place-Area; Location}

(6) "Making a delicious $\langle e1\rangle$cup$\langle /e1\rangle$ of $\langle e2\rangle$coffee$\langle /e2\rangle$ is not a magical experience or a hit-and-miss stroke of luck." Relation(e2,e1) = {Measure; Content-Container}

(7) "I set on fire the $\langle e1\rangle$branches$\langle /e1\rangle$ of the $\langle e2\rangle$tree$\langle /e2\rangle$, Relation(e2,e1) = {Origin-Entity, Component-Integral}.

The interpretation of the noun pair in example (7) is indeterminate since there is not enough context, so both relations are possible. Sure, we can extend the context to include the entire paragraph or the document it came from. However, even in such situations the interpretation may remain indeterminate. Consider for example the instance *the girl's shoes* which can mean the shoes the girl made, dreams of, buys, wears, etc.

An example of relation which creates a type (C) overlap is Part-Whole. As mentioned in the previous section, this relation belongs to the following contingency set: {Origin-Entity, Purpose, Measure, Content-Container}. However, it does not interact in the same way with each of the relations in the set. For instance, it forms a near-miss set with Origin-Entity and Purpose and overlaps with Measure and Content-Container. The specialization of this relation into its 5 subtypes gives the following contingency relations: Near misses – {Component-Integral, Origin-

No.	Set of semantic categories	Number of instances	Examples
1	Component-Integral	168	"When the first transplant took place at St. Paul's in 1986, the vast majority of *patients* received a new *kidney* from a deceased donor."
2	$Part - Whole_{hp}$	36	"The *catalogue* contained *books* published in 1998 warning of the upcoming millennium bug and other similarly germane works, but neither of Brock's bestsellers."
3	Stuff-Object	100	"Typically, an unglazed *clay pot* is submerged for 15 to 30 minutes to absorb water."
4	Origin-Entity	81	"I got home and big *branches* had fallen off the *tree* into the drive way."
5	Measure	104	"Ensure that you don't lose a *drop* of *juice* by nestling your shellfish in salt."
6	Purpose	121	"023 "All he had on underneath was a phoney *shirt collar*, but no shirt or anything."
7	Content-Container	120	"Among the contents of the *vessel* were a set of carpenter's *tools*, several large storage jars, ceramic utensils..
8	$Part - Whole_{hp}$/ Measure	156	"The contents of the boxes included phone cards, disposable cameras and razors, travel-size toiletries, snack food, and *lots* of *candy*."
9	$Part - Whole_{hp}$/ Measure/ Content-Container	75	"I would have ripe olives and about a *cup* of that leftover *tea*."
10	Measure/ Content-Container	69	"Is enjoying a *glass* of red *wine* with dinner each evening beneficial to your health?"

Table 3: *The set of 10 semantic relation categories considered along with examples.*

Entity, Purpose}, and overlaps – {Portion-Mass, Member-Collection, Measure}, {Portion-Mass, Measure, Content-Container}, {Portion-Mass, Member-Collection, Measure, Content-Container}, and {Measure, Content-Container}. Similarly, other semantic relations may be decomposed into finer grain types, so more specific relation taxonomies may be built.

Near-misses
Near misses are sets of mutually exclusive relations in the context of the same sentence. As shown above, in the empirical investigations of this research we identified the following set of near misses: {Component-Integral, Origin-Entity, Purpose}. For instance, although the pair *branch - tree* (as shown in the examples below) can encode Component-Integral, Origin-Entity and Purpose, only one relation is possible in a given context:

(8) "He grabbed the $\langle e1\rangle$branches$\langle /e1\rangle$ of the $\langle e2\rangle$tree$\langle /e2\rangle$ to get closer to the nest up high." Relation(e1,e2) = {Component-Integral}

(9) "He took the $\langle e1\rangle$branches$\langle /e1\rangle$ he cut from the old $\langle e2\rangle$tree$\langle /e2\rangle$ and burned them." Relation(e2,e1) = {Origin-Entity}

(10) "'These plastic $\langle e1\rangle$branches$\langle /e1\rangle$ are for the green $\langle e2\rangle$tree$\langle /e2\rangle$', said he while showing me how to assemble them." Relation(e2,e1) = {Purpose}.

Table 4 shows the contingency relations identified in this research, types of encountered overlaps, plus constraints observed on the data. Due to an insufficient number of examples, we have not performed any experiments with the {Content-Container, Stuff-Object} contingency set.

4 Models

In order to test the validity of the new set of contingency classes we trained and tested three state-of-the-art classifiers on the 1,000 sentence corpus: (1) our implementation of a supervised semantic interpretation model, Semantic Scattering2 [2], (2) the SNoW machine learning architecture [23], and (3) a competitive SemEval type-B system [1].

Semantic Scattering is a supervised model which uses only semantic information about the two nouns. It consists of a set of iterative procedures of specializations of the training examples on the WordNet IS-A hierarchy. Thus, after a set of necessary specialization iterations the method produces specialized examples from which the model learns a discrimination function.

We implemented the model and improved it. In our implementation we obtain similar performance, but with a much smaller number of training examples[2].

SNoW is a learning architecture that learns a sparse network of linear functions and can deal very well with a large number of features. SNoW has been used successfully in a number of NLP tasks. The features that we used include word-level and part-of-speech information of context words, as well as grammatical categories (subject, object) of the two nouns. All features were implemented as boolean features.

Our SemEval system is a type-B system which participated competitively in the evaluations of SemEval - Task 4 [1]. It makes use of the WordNetIS-A hierarchy to get semantic information about the two nouns, but it also employs various shallow contextual features.

The classification task is defined as a multi-class classification problem on different classification sets.

Contingency relations	Type of overlap	Constraints
{Part-Whole_hp, Content-Container, Measure}	P-Whp $\models$ M	1) Whole must exist before the parts; the part has to be homeomerous with other parts of the whole; it entails the idea of separation of the part from the whole.
	P-Whp $\models$ M $\models_p$ C-C	2) the semantic head noun is a container (this condition is in addition to those at 1) above)
	M $\models_p$ C-C	3) the head noun is a container (this condition is in addition to all of the above), but it is not P-W (the existence of the whole is not a condition for the existence of the parts)
	M	4) the head noun is not a container and the existence of the whole is not presupposed
	P-Wnp	5) when the parts are not homeomerous
{Component-Integral, Purpose, Origin-Entity}	$(C-I \cap PRP \cap O-E = \emptyset)$	6) mutually exclusive; C-I and O-E: encoded by specific instances; parts have a function in regard to the whole and can be (potentially) separated; PRP: encoded by generic instances
{Content-Container, Stuff-Object}	$(C-C \cap S-O = \emptyset)$	7) mutually exclusive; the whole and can be separated for C-C and it cannot for S-O.

Table 4: *Sets of contingency relations along with types of overlap and constraints.*

5 Experimental results

Using the three classifiers described in the previous section, we performed two sets of experiments on the annotated corpus. In the experiment set I each classifier was trained and tested with a 10-fold cross validation one-vs-all approach for each relation (as positive examples those annotated with the relation and as negative the remaining examples in the corpus). Table 5 shows that the best overall results are obtained by the SemEval system, while the worst results are obtained by SemScat2. These results can be partially explained by the fact that the SemEval and SNoW systems relied on contextual information, while SemScat relied only the WordNet information of the two nouns.

System	P [%]	R [%]	F [%]
SemScat	60	52	55
SNoW	64	63	63
SemEval	72	60	65

Table 5: *The overall performance of the three systems using a 10-fold cross validation one-vs-all approach.*

In the second round of experiments we trained and tested the classifiers using a 10-fold cross validation, one-vs-contingency_set approach. Each classifier was trained per relation as in the previous experiments, but this time as negative examples we considered only those belonging to the corresponding contingency set. Thus, we split the 1,000 example corpus into three datasets corresponding to the following contingency sets: {Component-Integral, Origin-Entity, Purpose}, {Content-Container, Measure/Content-Container, P-Whp/Measure/Content-Container}, and {P-Whp/Measure, Measure, P-Whp}.

Tables 6, 7 and 8 show the results which vary per system and differ from those presented in Table 5. Particular attention should be given to SemScat which obtained the lowest results overall. It differentiates poorly between PW_{hp}/M/C-C and M/C-C, since most of the noun - noun pair examples had the same e1-e2 order (i.e., the container followed by the content as in *a cup of soup* – Measure/Content-Container vs. *a cup of that soup* – Measure/Portion-Mass/Content-Container). SemScat performed much better on the last contingency set, in particular to identify PW_{hp}/M. This is explained by the fact that many of these examples are of the type *lots/bunch/couple of cats/flowers*. These are called *vague measure partitives* since they refer to both the amount (Measure) and the parts of the whole (Member-Collection).

This shows one more time that for relations which are very difficult to differentiate, the ontological information about the two nouns is not very helpful.

Better results are obtained by SNoW and the SNoW and Semeval systems due to their contextual features. In particular, these systems classified well the near miss examples in Table 6 due to various lexical and syntactic features such as verbs and the prepositions "from" and "for". The SemEval system however did not perform well for PW_{hp}/M/C-C and M/C-C since it disregards stop words, including determiners and definite articles which are very important here (in many PW_{hp}/M/C-C examples, the whole is preceeded by a definite article/determiner; e.g.: *a cup of that soup*).

We also performed a quick error analysis. In particular we looked at some of the examples which were misclassified by the Semeval system. Many of the examples required a combination of world knowledge about other words in context as well as pragmatic information. Instances (11) and (12) below indicate such cases. The systems labeled the instance as P-Whp/Measure/Content-Container due to lexical cues such as the verb *pour* and the determiners *that* and *this*. However, the correct interpretation is Measure/Content-Container since *tea* and *wine* here refer to a kind of tea, respectively wine (generic noun) and not to a particular one (specific noun). Example (12) is actually more problematic since it involves pragmatic knowledge.

(11) "I'd also pour you a $\langle e1 \rangle$cup$\langle /e1 \rangle$ of that apricot $\langle e2 \rangle$tea$\langle /e2 \rangle$ you like so you could sit and visit with me next week."

(12) The waiter stood politely near the table while Mary decided to order: "I'd like to try a ⟨e1⟩glass⟨/e1⟩ of this ⟨e2⟩wine⟨/e2⟩", said she pointing at the menu.

No. rel	Relation	SemScat	SNoW	SemEval system
1	C-I	61.2	87	86.3
4	O-E	57.3	77	78.0
6	PRP	59.1	87	88.7

Table 6: *The performance of the SemEval system on the semantic classification categories representing near-misses: Component-Integral (C-I), Origin-Entity (O-E), and Purpose (PRP).*

No. rel	Relation	SemScat	SNoW	SemEval system
7	C-C	63.7	84	85.3
9	PW_{hp}/M/C-C	54.4	83	75.6
10	M/C-C	56.8	72	71.1

Table 7: *The performance of the SemEval system the semantic classification categories representing overlaps: Content-Container (C-C), Part-Whole/Measure/Content-Container (PW_{hp}/M/C-C), and Measure/Content-Container (M/C-C).*

No. rel	Relation	SemScat	SNoW	SemEval system
2	PW_{hp}	64.0	50	74.3
5	M	66.2	84	78.7
8	PW_{hp}/M	70.0	80	85.1

Table 8: *The performance of the SemEval system the semantic classification categories representing overlaps: Part-Whole (PW_{hp}), Measure (M), Part-Whole/Measure (PW_{hp}/M).*

6 Discussion and Conclusions

This paper addresses the problem of semantic relation identification for a set of relations difficult to differentiate: *near-misses* and *overlaps*. Based on empirical observations on a fairly large dataset of such examples we provided an analysis and a taxonomy of such cases. Using this taxonomy we created various contingency sets of relations. These semantic categories were identified by training and testing three state-of-the-art semantic classifiers employing various feature sets. The results showed that relation identification systems need to rely on both the information provided by the linguistic context and the context of use (pragmatics).

The taxonomy of near-miss and overlapping relations presented here is by no means exhaustive and we intend to extend it in future research. Moreover, we would like to explore ways to learn the contingency sets automatically.

References

[1] B. Beamer, S. Bhat, B. Chee, A. Fister, A. Rozovskaya, and R. Girju. UIUC: A Knowledge-rich Approach to Identifying Semantic Relations between Nominals. In *SemEval-2007*, 2007.

[2] B. Beamer, A. Rozovskaya, and R. Girju. Automatic Semantic Relation Extraction with Multiple Boundary Generation. In *The National Conference on Artificial Intelligence (AAAI)*, 2008.

[3] R. Girju. Automatic Detection of Causal Relations for Question Answering. In *Association for Computational Linguistics (ACL 2003), Workshop on "Multilingual Summarization and Question Answering - Machine Learning and Beyond"*. 2003.

[4] R. Girju. Improving the interpretation of noun phrases with cross-linguistic information. In *Proceedings of ACL*, 2007.

[5] R. Girju, A. Badulescu, and D. Moldovan. Automatic discovery of part-whole relations. *Computational Linguistics*, 32(1), 2006.

[6] R. Girju, A. Giuglea, M. Olteanu, O. Fortu, O. Bolohan, and D. Moldovan. Support vector machines applied to the classification of semantic relations in nominalized noun phrases. In *In Proceedings of the HLT/NAACL Workshop on Computational Lexical Semantics.*, Boston, MA., 2004.

[7] R. Girju, D. Moldovan, M. Tatu, and D. Antohe. On the semantics of noun compounds. *Computer Speech and Language*, 19(4):479–496, 2005.

[8] R. Girju, D. Moldovan, M. Tatu, and D. Antohe. On the Semantics of Noun Compounds. *Computer Speech and Language - Special Issue on Multiword Expressions*, 2005.

[9] R. Girju, P. Nakov, V. Nastase, S. Szpakowicz, P. Turney, and D. Yuret. Semeval-2007 task 04: Classification of semantic relations between nominals. In *SemEval-2007*, 2007.

[10] M. Hearst. Acquisition of Hyponyms from Large Text Corpora. In *Proceedings of the 14th International Conference on Computational Linguistics (COLING-92)*, pages 539–545, Nantes, France, 1992.

[11] C. S. G. Khoo, S. H. Myaeng, and R. N. Oddy. Using cause-effect relations in text to improve information retrieval precision. *Information Processing & Management*, 37(1):119–145, 2001.

[12] S. N. Kim and T. Baldwin. Interpreting semantic relations in noun compounds via verb semant ics. In *International Computational Linguistics Coference (COLING)*, 2006.

[13] M. Lapata. The disambiguation of nominalisations. *Computational Linguistics*, 28(3):357–388, 2002.

[14] M. Lauer. Corpus statistics meet the noun compound: Some empirical results. In *In the Proceedings of the Association for Computational Linguistics*, pages 47–54, Cambridge, Mass, 1995.

[15] J. Levi. *The Syntax and Semantics of Complex Nominals.* Academic Press, New York, 1978.

[16] D. Moldovan, A. Badulescu, M. Tatu, D. Antohe, and R. Girju. Models for the semantic classification of noun phrases. In *Proceedings of the HLT/NAACL Workshop on Computational Lexical Semantics*, Boston, MA., 2004.

[17] D. Moldovan, C. Clark, S. Harabagiu, and D. Hodges. A semantically and contextually enriched logic prover for question answering. *Journal of Applied Logic*, 5:49–69, 2005.

[18] D. Moldovan and R. Girju. Knowledge discovery from text. In *The Tutorial Proceedings of the 41st Annual Meeting of the Association for Computational Linguistics*, Sapporo, Japan, 2003.

[19] P. Nakov and M. Hearst. Using verbs to characterise noun-noun relations. In *Proceedings of the 12th International Conference on Artificial In telligence: Methodology, Systems and Applications*, 2006.

[20] V. Nastase and S. Szpakowicz. Augmenting wordnet's structure using ldoce. In *CICLing-2003*, 2003.

[21] M. Pennacchiotti and P. Pantel. Ontologizing semantic relations. In *COLING/ACL-06*, 2006.

[22] B. Rosario and M. Hearst. Classifying the semantic relations in noun compounds. In *Proceedings of the 2001 Conference on Empirical Methods in Natural Language Processing*, 2001.

[23] D. Roth. The SNoW learning architecture. Technical Report UIUCDCS-R-99-2101, UIUC Computer Science Department, May 1999.

[24] M. Tatu and D. I. Moldovan. A Logic-Based Semantic Approach to Recognizing Textual Entailment. In *Proceedings of the Association for Computational Linguistics - Poster session*, 2006.

[25] M. Winston, R. Chaffin, and D. Hermann. A taxonomy of part-whole relations. *Cognitive science*, 11(4):417–444, 1987.

[26] K. Zimmer. Some general observations about nominal compounds. *Stanford Working Papers on Linguistic Universals*, 5:C1-C21, 1971.

Statistical Confidence Measures for Probabilistic Parsing

Ricardo Sánchez-Sáez, Joan-Andreu Sánchez and José-Miguel Benedí
Instituto Tecnológico de Informática
Universidad Politécnica de Valencia
Camí de Vera s/n, Valencia 46022 (Spain)
{rsanchez, jandreu, jbenedi}@dsic.upv.es

Abstract

We introduce a formal framework that allows the calculation of new purely statistical confidence measures for parsing, which are estimated from posterior probability of constituents. These measures allow us to mark each constituent of a parse tree as correct or incorrect. Experimental assessment using the Penn Treebank shows favorable results for the classical confidence evaluation metrics: the CER and the ROC curve. We also present preliminar experiments on application of confidence measures to improve parse trees by automatic constituent relabeling.

1 Introduction

Many parsing methods exist in the literature, including those based on Probabilistic Context-Free Grammars (PCFGs). Great effort has been undertaken to improve performance of these parsers. First, lexicalization of grammars with elaborate smoothing accomplished very promising results [4, 5]. Then, manual tree annotation and nonterminal spliting greatly shortened the gap between unlexicalized models and their better performing lexicalized counterparts [10, 12]. Later, automatic tree annotation systems, using a nonterminal split-and-merge approach and a hierarchy of progressively refined grammars, provided superior results over the best lexicalized approaches [14, 16, 17]. Last but not least, the most impressive results were achieved by reranking systems, as shown in the semi-supervised method of [15], or the forest reranking approach of [9] which uses packed parse forests (compact structures that contain many possible tree derivations).

Given the difficulty and importance of parsing in all of its applications [13], there exists an increasing necessity to detect erroneous syntactic structures therein. This need is even more present in parse trees that are obtained using current high performing systems, especially if error-free trees are desired. In such a case, the few remaining erroneous parts need to be quickly detected and manually corrected (possibly using interactive methods). Assessing the correctness of the different parts of the parsing is needed for the construction of efficient computer-assisted interactive predictive parsing systems, which will be useful in the creation of new gold standard treebanks [6]. This paper is a step forward in introducing Confidence Measures into the parsing world.

Confidence measures are a powerful formalism that have been used to detect individual erroneous words in Automatic Speech Recognition (ASR) and Statistical Machine Translation (SMT) output sentences [19, 18]. Once these errors are detected and marked, they can be more easily corrected, either by automatic or manual methods.

In parsing, confidence measures detect erroneous constituents. Some confidence measures for parsing in the form of combinations of characteristics calculated from n-best lists were proposed in [2]. In our work, we present an alternative more akin to word graph-based methods in ASR and SMT.

Other works have proposed to improve parsing results by defining parsing algorithms that try to maximize alternative objective functions. In [8], Goodman derived an algorithm that maximized the labeled recall evaluation criterion (rather than maximizing the whole tree probability as the classical CYK-Viterbi does) which presents some similarities with the confidence measure framework presented here.

Goodman's algorithm presented the problem of producing trees that were not grammatical, and as such, unsuitable for downstream processing. However, many applications can benefit from maximizing the number of correct constituents, regardless of the grammaticality of the tree, for example, machine translation systems.

The *max-rule* parser, which is a variation of Goodman's algorithm that solves the ungrammaticality issue, has been used in very recent top performing parsing systems [14, 17]. In [17], the authors also proposed different objective functions for parsing with posterior probabilities.

The performance of our proposal is assessed by classical metrics, the Confidence Error Rate (CER) and the Receiver Operating Characteristic (ROC) curve, which are widely used for confidence measure evaluation [19, 18]. Additionally, we introduce experimentation exemplifying the use of confidence measures for automatic constituent relabeling for the improvement of F_1 and POS tag accuracy results.

2 Statistical confidence measures

In ASR and SMT, confidence measures refer to the probability of single words being correct in an output sentence, and they are mostly calculated from the posterior probability of each word.

One way to estimate the posterior probability is to use n-best lists. In this case, the probability of a word being correct is determined by how many times the word appears in a similar position over all the n-best sentences.

More recently, the posterior probability is obtained using a forward-backward expression over word graphs [19, 18]. Word graphs can be seen as a condensing of the information contained in an n-best list. In the ideal case of a non-pruned word graph, it represents all the possible out-

International Conference RANLP 2009 - Borovets, Bulgaria, pages 388–392

put sentences for a given input. In practice, word graphs are usually pruned, so they contain only information about the most probable outputs. This approach presents greater flexibility than n-best lists since word graphs are not limited by a predefined number of n outputs, but rather take form depending on the concentration of probability mass.

2.1 Edge posterior probability

A tree t is composed of substructures that are usually referred to as constituents or edges. Given a tree t associated to a string $x_{1|x|}$, a constituent c_{ij}^A is defined by a nonterminal symbol (or syntactic tag) A that spans the substring x_{ij}.

In this paper, we establish a framework for probabilistic calculation of confidence measures for edges c_{ij}^A, which uses edge posterior probability. This is similar to the calculation of posterior probability over word graphs and its use as a confidence measure presented in SMT [18].

Let G be a probabilistic Context-Free Grammar, and let $\boldsymbol{x} = x_1 \ldots x_{|x|}$ an input sentence. The parser analyzes the input sentence $\boldsymbol{x} = x_1 \ldots x_{|x|}$ and then produces the most probable parse tree $\hat{t} = \arg\max_{t \in \mathcal{T}} p_G(t|\boldsymbol{x})$, where $p_G(t|\boldsymbol{x})$ is the probability of the tree, and $\mathcal{T}$ is the set of all possible parse trees for $\boldsymbol{x}$.

The posterior probability of a constituent can be considered as a measure of the degree to which the constituent is believed to be correct. The posterior probability of a constituent given the string $\boldsymbol{x}$ is

$$p_G(c_{ij}^A|\boldsymbol{x}) = \frac{p_G(c_{ij}^A, \boldsymbol{x})}{p_G(\boldsymbol{x})} = \frac{\sum_{t' \in \mathcal{T}:\, c_{ij}^A \in t'} p_G(t'|\boldsymbol{x})}{p_G(\boldsymbol{x})}, \quad (1)$$

that is, the normalized probability of the constituent c_{ij}^A being placed on the tree in the exact position that spans the $x_i \ldots x_j$ substring. The upper part is the sum of probabilities of all possible parse trees for $\boldsymbol{x}$ containing the nonterminal A with the same exact start and end points i and j.

Eq. (1) can be efficiently computed with the inside ($\beta_A(i,\, j) = p_G(A \Rightarrow^* x_i \ldots x_j)$) and outside ($\alpha_A(i,\, j) = p_G(S \Rightarrow^* x_1 \ldots x_{i-1}\, A\, x_{j+1} \ldots x_{|\boldsymbol{x}|})$) probabilities introduced in [1] (see Fig. 1):

$$p_G(c_{ij}^A|\boldsymbol{x}) = \frac{\beta_A(i,\, j)\, \alpha_A(i,\, j)}{\beta_S(1,\, |\boldsymbol{x}|)}\,. \quad (2)$$

The posterior probability can now directly be used as a measure of the confidence in each individual edge

$$\mathcal{C}(c_{ij}^A) = p_G(c_{ij}^A|\boldsymbol{x})\,. \quad (3)$$

Eq. (2) is the same expression that is maximized in [8] for the labeled recall parsing algorithm, which can indeed be seen as a confidence measure-based parsing algorithm.

Fig. 2 shows a synthetic example in order to clarify the confidence measure concept. This figure shows the only four possible parse trees for the string *abc*. Let all productions in the grammar of the example carry the same probability, and suppose that the parser returns *(a)* tree. Then the following confidence measure values are obtained for the edges in the *(a)* tree: $\mathcal{C}(c_{13}^S) = 1$, $\mathcal{C}(c_{12}^Z) = 2/4$, $\mathcal{C}(c_{11}^A) = 1$, $\mathcal{C}(c_{22}^B) = 1$ and $\mathcal{C}(c_{33}^D) = 1/4$. If the correct parse tree is *(e)*, which is unobtainable by the example grammar, then setting a confidence threshold would allow us to know that the c_{33}^D edge is incorrect in the *(a)* tree.

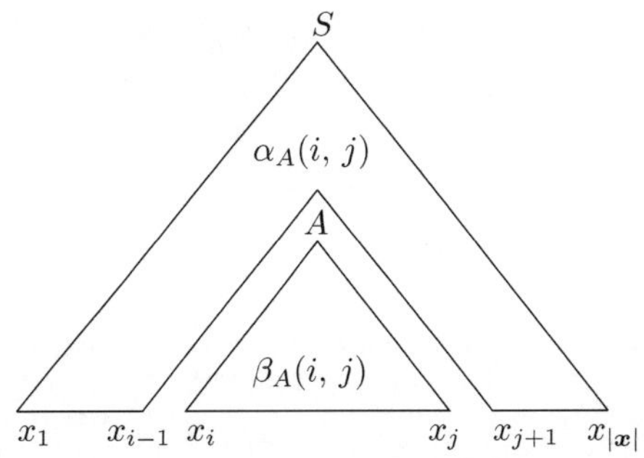

Fig. 1: The product of the the inside probability $\beta_A(i,\, j) = p_G(A \Rightarrow^* x_i \ldots x_j)$ and the outside probability $\alpha_A(i,\, j) = p_G(S \Rightarrow^* x_1 \ldots x_{i-1}\, A\, x_{j+1} \ldots x_{|\boldsymbol{x}|})$, comprises the upper part of expression (2)

3 Experiments

In the experiments presented in this section, we show how confidence measures can help parsing through the detection of erroneous constituents. We introduce evaluation metrics that assess the performance of confidence measures in section 3.1, we define the experimental framework on section 3.2, and we present empirical results on section 3.3. Additionally, we introduce experimentation showing how confidence measures can be used for tree improvement by automatic constituent relabeling in section 3.4.

3.1 Evaluation metrics

Performance of a confidence measure refers to its ability to detect erroneous constituents. We report results on two classical metrics: the Confidence Error Rate (CER) and the Receiver Operating Characteristic (ROC) curve with its corresponding integrated area (IROC) [19, 18]. The results for these metrics are presented for both syntactic constituents and POS tag together as well as separately. At this point, the F-measure cannot be used to evaluate the performance of confidence scores because there is only one set of parse trees with confidence scores attached. Two sets of parse trees are necessary for F-measure comparison, so it is not reported until section 3.4.

Given a tree with a number of constituents n (some correct and some incorrect) and a confidence score attached to each one, each constituent is marked as either correct or incorrect depending on whether its confidence exceeds the confidence threshold τ, which is obtained beforehand using a development set.

The $CER(\tau) = \frac{n_{fr}(\tau)+n_{fa}(\tau)}{n}$ is the total number of incorrect marks divided by the total number of constituents (false rejection $n_{fr}(\tau)$ is the number of constituents that are correctly obtained by the parser but that are deemed incorrect by the confidence measure; false acceptance $n_{fa}(\tau)$ is the number of erroneus constituents marked correct due to their high confidence value).

In the ideal case of perfect confidence measures, incorrect and correct constituents are discriminated without mistakes and the CER is zero. The baseline CER is the one obtained assuming that all syntactic edges are correct (the only possible assumption when confidence measures are not available), it is the number of erroneous constituents

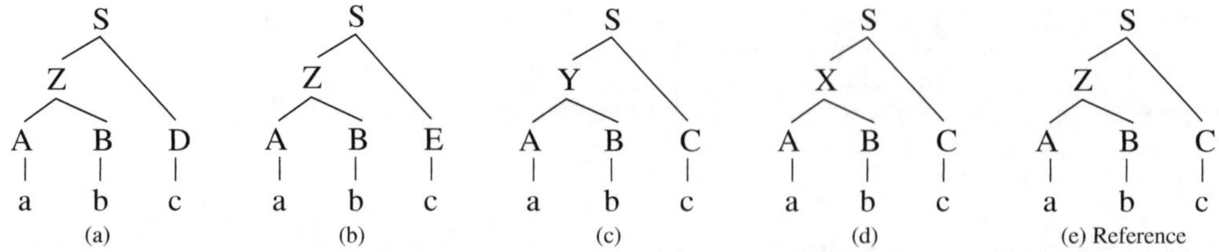

Fig. 2: Synthetic example of a confidence measure calculation. Assume that all productions in the grammar have the same probability. The grammar can only generate the *(a), (b), (c)* and *(d)* parse trees for the abc input string. The reference parse tree is unobtainable. Confidence measures for the edges in the (a) tree are $\mathcal{C}(c_{13}^{S}) = 1$, $\mathcal{C}(c_{12}^{Z}) = 2/4$, $\mathcal{C}(c_{11}^{A}) = 1$, $\mathcal{C}(c_{22}^{B}) = 1$ and $\mathcal{C}(c_{33}^{D}) = 1/4$

divided by the total.

Another measure that determines the goodness of confidence measures globally over all possible thresholds is the ROC curve, which is the plot of the correct rejection rate against the correct acceptance rate for all possible values of $\tau \in [0,1]$. The worst case ROC is a diagonal line, and the further it lies from the diagonal towards 1.0 on both axes, the better the ROC is. A ROC curve provides a qualitative analysis of the adequacy of the confidence measure. Its corresponding IROC (integrated area under a ROC curve taking values in the interval $[0,1]$) accounts for the corresponding quantitative metric.

Once incorrect constituents are detected, actions to correct them can be carried out. In Section 3.4, we present some experimentation that does this by automatic relabeling incorrect constituents.

3.2 Experimental framework

Standard train and test splits were defined over the Penn Tree bank. Sections 2 to 21 were used to obtain a vanilla Penn Treebank Grammar; the test set was the whole section 23; and the development set was comprised of the first 346 sentences of section 24.

Since CYK works with grammars in the Chomsky Normal Form (CNF), we obtained several binarized versions of the train grammar. We used the CNF transformation method from the open source NLTK[1] to obtain several right-factored binary grammars of different sizes. This method implements the vertical (v value) and horizontal (h value) markovizations [12].

We modified the CYK to perform the confidence measure calculation at parsing time, using equation (1) as described in section 2.

For out-of-vocabulary words, when an input word could not be derived by any of the preterminals in the treebank grammar, a very small probability for that word was uniformly added to all of the preterminals.

An unbinarization process was performed over the obtained parse trees in order to compare them to the reference trees. Newly introduced nonterminals were removed, and their children became attached to their original parents.

The constituents in each proposed solution tree were then automatically compared to the ones in the gold-standard corpus. Each constituent was marked as correct or incorrect depending on whether or not the corresponding constituent existed in the reference tree.

[1] http://nltk.sourceforge.net/

With the edges labeled as either correct or incorrect, the baseline CER and the confidence measure CER were calculated for the test set. Since the CER depends on the selected threshold, the separate development set was used to obtain the best threshold. ROC curves with their IROC values for the test set were also calculated.

3.3 CER and ROC results

We calculated metric results for the presented confidence measure using the three different markovizations of the train grammar shown in Table 1. Increasing the v markovization parameter produces better performing PCFGs, but also increases the number of nonterminals. When parsed with these grammars, the 346 sentences in the development set produced about 16k elements (7k syntactic constituents and 9k POS tags), and the 2416 sentences in the test set produced about 101k ones (44k syntactic constituents and 57k POS tags).

PCFG	Size
h=0,v=1	561
h=0,v=2	2,034
h=0,v=3	5,058

Table 1: Grammar size after each markovization (number of nonterminals).

Performance of the confidence measure is reflected in the classical confidence evaluation metrics discussed in section 3.1: improvement of the best CER over the baseline CER; the ROC curve, and its corresponding IROC. The results for the test set are presented in Table 2.

The confidence measures are able to discriminate an high number of incorrect constituents, as show by the clear improvements over the baseline CER for all markovizations of the PCFG, both for syntactic constituents and for POS tags.

Even for the PCFG with the best baseline CER (*h=0,v=3*), the confidence measures allowed us to detect that 2.4% of the edges could be erroneously labeled (4.9% of syntactic constituents, and 1% of POS tags), this is a relative reduction of 14.6% (15.9% for syntactic constituents, and 20% for POS tags). The ROC curves for the mentioned PCFG are presented in Fig. 3. This figure shows that the confidence measures discriminate better over POS tags than over syntactic constituents, which is consistent with the baselines and relative CER gains for each category of constituents.

PCFG	F1 Basel.	F1 Relabel.	F1 Δ	POS tag accuracy Basel.	POS tag accuracy Relabel.	POS tag accuracy Δ
h=0,v=1	67.87	68.01	.14±.08	96.11	96.35	.24±.11
h=0,v=2	71.09	71.20	.11±.07	96.30	96.54	.24±.09
h=0,v=3	71.17	71.31	.14±.07	96.23	96.51	.28±.10

Table 3: F_1 and POS tag accuracy for the test set: baseline scores, relabeling scores, and increments. Accuracy values are bootstrap estimates with $B = 10^4$; the improvement interval is a 95% confidence interval based on the standard error estimate [3].

PCFG	TAGS	Basel. CER	Confidence M. CER	Confidence M. RelR	Confidence M. IROC
h=0	all	17.8	12.3	30.9%	0.81
v=1	syn	34.3	22.8	33.5%	0.65
	pos	5.2	4.2	19.2%	0.86
h=0	all	16.4	13.2	19.5%	0.77
v=2	syn	31.1	24.6	20.9%	0.57
	pos	5.0	4.4	12.0%	0.86
h=0	all	16.4	14.0	14.6%	0.75
v=3	syn	30.9	26.0	15.9%	0.50
	pos	4.9	4.5	8.1%	0.86

Table 2: Metric results for the test set: baseline CER, confidence CER (with the best development threshold), CER relative reduction, and IROC for each PCFG.

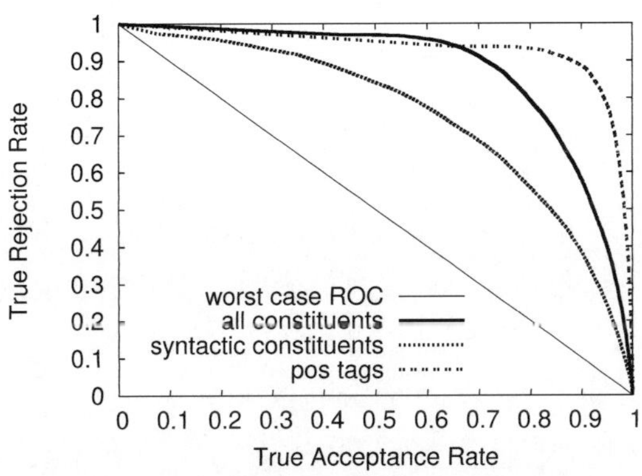

Fig. 3: ROC curves for markovization *h=0,v=3*.

Our results can be compared to the ones presented in [2], in which confidence measures were calculated from n-best lists obtained by the Charniak parser. Comparing the CERs presented here to the ones shown in the cited work, we observe that our relative reductions are consistently higher. Note that, in our work, we carried out unlexicalized parsing; therefore, our baseline CERs are slightly worse than the ones reported in the cited paper.

3.4 Confidence measures for automatic constituent relabeling

Finally, we employed confidence measures in an experiment that consisted of improving trees by constituent relabeling.

After obtaining the best parse tree, the confidence value of each available nonterminal was calculated for each element (both syntactic constituent and POS tags) position and span. The nonterminal that yielded the maximum confidence value was introduced as the new label of the constituent. As we mentioned above, this process does not guarantee the grammaticality of the resulting trees.

The results are shown in Table 3. We obtained small but statistically significant (95% confidence intervals as in [3]) improvements, not only in POS tag accuracy but also in LP/LR F_1.

In syntactic tags, the advantage obtained by our system is marginal. This is possibly due to the more severe structural errors present in the start and end points of the bracketings. A better approach would be to completely discard groups of incorrect constituents and calculate completely new ones.

Although the results presented in this section are far from the current state of the art, the improvements presented here both exemplify one of the possible uses of confidence measures and support the good confidence measure metric results presented in section 3.3. These experiments discover a new path that is worth exploring in order to achieve further parsing improvements.

4 Conclusions

A new formal framework for calculating a purely statistical confidence measure (based on inside-outside estimated posterior probability of constituents) for probabilistic parsing has been introduced.

Experiments were performed on the Penn Treebank: CERs showed that the proposed confidence measure is able to discriminate a high number of correct constituents from incorrect ones. This is confirmed by similarly good IROC values. The relabeling experiment also resulted in consistent improvements in F_1 and POS tag accuracy.

Future work involves using confidence measures for improving state-of-the-art parsing and reranking systems as well as building efficient computer-aided predictive interactive parsing systems.

Acknowledgements

Work supported by the EC (FEDER) and the Spanish MEC under the MIPRCV "Consolider Ingenio 2010" research programme (CSD2007-00018), the iTransDoc research project (TIN2006-15694-CO2-01), and the FPU fellowship AP2006-01363.

References

[1] Baker, J. 1979. *Trainable grammars for speech recognition*. In Speech Communications, MASA'79, 31-35.

[2] Benedí, José-Miguel, Joan-Andreu Sánchez and Alberto Sanchís. 2007. *Confidence measures for stochastic parsing*. In RANLP '07, 58-63,.

[3] Bisani, Maximilian and Hermann Ney. 2004. *Bootstrap estimates for confidence intervals in asr performance evaluation*. In ICASSP '04, I:409-412.

[4] Charniak, Eugene. 2000. *A maximum-entropy-inspired parser*. In NAACL '00, 132-139.

[5] Collins, Michael. 2003. *Head-driven statistical models for natural language parsing*. In Computational Linguistics, 29(4):589-637.

[6] De la Clergerie, Éric, Olivier Hamon, Djamel Mostefa, Christelle Ayache, Patrick Paroubek and Anne Vilnat. 2008. *PASSAGE: from French Parser Evaluation to Large Sized Treebank*. In LREC'08.

[7] Earley, Jay. 1970. *An efficient context-free parsing algorithm*. In Communications of the ACM'70, 8(6):451-455.

[8] Goodman, Joshua. 1996. *Parsing algorithms and metrics*. In ACL '96, 177-183.

[9] Huang, Liang. 2008. *Forest reranking: discriminative parsing with non-local features*. In ACL '08.

[10] Johnson, Mark. 1998. *PCFG models of linguistic tree representation*. In Computational Linguistics '98, 24:613-632.

[11] Klein, Dan and Chistopher D. Manning. 2001. *Parsing with treebank grammars: Empirical bounds, theoretical models, and the structure of the Penn treebank*. In ACL '01, 338-345.

[12] Klein, Dan and Chistopher D. Manning. 2003. *Accurate Unlexicalized Parsing*. In ACL '03, 423-430.

[13] Lease, Matthew, Eugene Charniak, Mark Johnson and David McClosky. 2006. *A look at parsing and its applications*. In National Conference on Artificial Intelligence '96, vol. 21-II, 1642-1645.

[14] Matsuzaki, Takuya, Yasuke Miyao and Jun'ichi Tsujii. 2005. *Probabilistic CFG with latent annotations*. In ACL '05, 75-82.

[15] McClosky, David, Eugene Charniak and Mark Johnson. 2006. *Effective self-training for parsing*. In HLT-NAACL '06.

[16] Petrov, Slav, Leon Barrett, Romain Thibaux and Dan Klein. 2006. *Learning accurate, compact and interpretable tree annotation*. In ACL '06, 433-440.

[17] Petrov, Slav and Dan Klein. 2007. *Improved inference for unlexicalized parsing*. In NAACL-HLT '07.

[18] Ueffing, Nicola and Hermann Ney. 2007. *Word-level confidence estimation for machine translation*. In Computational Linguistics 33(1), 9-40.

[19] Wessel, Frank, Ralf Schlüter, Klaus Macherey and Hermann Ney. 2001. *Confidence measures for large vocabulary continuous speech recognition*. In IEEE Tran. on Speech and Audio Processing, 3(9):288-298.

Exploring the Vector Space Model for Finding Verb Synonyms in Portuguese

Luís Sarmento[1], Paula Carvalho[2] and Eugénio Oliveira[1]
[1]Faculdade de Engenharia da Universidade do Porto - DEI - LIACC
Rua Dr. Roberto Frias, s/n, 4200-465 Porto, Portugal
[2]Faculdade de Ciências da Universidade de Lisboa - DI - XLDB
Campo Grande, 1749-016 Lisboa, Portugal
las@fe.up.pt, *pcc@xldb.di.fc.ul.pt* and *eco@fe.up.pt*

Abstract

We explore the performance of the Vector Space Model (VSM) in finding verb synonyms in Portuguese by analyzing the impact of three operating parameters: (i) the weighting function, (ii) the context window used for automatically extracting features, and (iii) the minimum number of vector features. We rely on distributional statistics taken from a large n-gram database to build feature vectors, using minimal linguistic pre-processing. Automatic evaluation of synonym candidates using gold-standard information from the OpenOffice and Wiktionary thesaurus shows that low frequency features carry most information regarding verb similarity, and that a [0, +2] window carries more information than a [-2, 0] window. We show that satisfactory precision levels require vectors with 50 or more non-nil components. Manual evaluation over a set of *declarative verbs* and *psychological verbs* show that VSM-based approaches achieve good precision in finding verb synonyms for Portuguese, even when using minimal linguistic knowledge. This lead us to proposing a performance baseline for this task.

Keywords

Vector Space Model, Semantics, Relation Extraction, Statistical Methods, Language Resources, Evaluation

1 Introduction

Large-coverage and fine-grained linguistic resources are crucial for the majority of the applications in natural language processing, but they are still scarce and, in most cases, they do not satisfy every particular information need. Manual creation of linguistic resources is time-consuming and requires linguistic expertise. Therefore, there is a rising interest in developing automatic or semi-automatic methods and techniques for building language resources with minimal human intervention. However, automatic methods usually involve a large set of parameters, whose impact on final results is difficult to assess, and thus to optimize. In this paper, we address the task of automatically creating a lexicon of verb synonyms for Portuguese using the Vector Space Model (VSM), and we explore the impact of three of its core parameters: (i) the *context* used for extracting vector features, (ii) the function used for weighting features, and (iii) the *cut-off threshold* for removing vectors with insufficient feature information. We rely on n-gram information collected from a large dump of the Portuguese web, in order to obtain distributional statistics for verb lemmas. For performing parameter exploration, we evaluate results automatically using gold-standard information extracted from the OpenOffice thesaurus and from Wiktionary. Fine-grained evaluation was achieved by manually assessing the synonym candidates obtained for a sample of two syntactic-semantic classes of verbs: *psychological verbs* and *declarative verbs*. We chose these two specific verb classes for two reasons. First, they exhibit different syntactic and semantic behavior, and thus present different challenges for the task of synonymy finding. Psychological verbs do not have a prototypical syntactic structure and they usually convey a plurality of meanings, which can only be disambiguated in context. In contrast, declarative verbs are less ambiguous and the syntactic structure where they occur is better defined. Second, these two verb classes are crucial in several information extraction task, such as for example quotation extraction from news or opinion mining, so it is particularly interesting to evaluate the performance over them for practical reasons.

To the best of our knowledge, this study is pioneer for Portuguese. Since our approach relies only on minimal linguistic processing, the results presented can be considered a *baseline* for other methods that try to perform the same task, using additional linguistic information.

2 Related Work

Curran [5] follows an experimental methodology for testing several parameters of the VSM in the process of automatically computing a language thesaurus – the context for extracting features, functions for weighting those features, functions for computing vector similarity, cut-off thresholds for input data and algorithms for computing pairwise vector similarity. The author performs large scale experimentation on the parameter space and evaluates results automatically by computing precision at several ranks, inverse ranks (InvR) and direct comparison with a gold standard built by aggregating 5 thesauri: the *Roget's Thesaurus*, the *New Roget's Thesaurus*, the *Moby Thesaurus*, the *New Oxford Thesaurus of English* and the *Macquire Encyclopedic Thesaurus*. WordNet was also used to automatically check if results on synonymy are contaminated with antonyms, hyponyms or meronyms. Detailed error analysis was performed for a sample of 300 words. Results show that when the number of features associated to vector drops below 1000, or for words with frequencies below 5000, performance decays significantly. Additionally, direct comparison and InvR measures tend to increase for words with multiple senses with larger number of senses while the precision measures are fairly stable. Results also demonstrate that it is more difficult to find synonyms for words related with certain Wordnet classes such as *entities* and *abstractions*.

Sahlgren [11] builds vector spaces for capturing either *paradigmatic* or *syntagmatic* relations, and tests how such spaces can then be used for different tasks – thesaurus generation, synonym finding, antonym detection and POS guessing. The author evaluates the impact of several VSM parameters such as (i) the context (paradigmatic vs. syntagmatic), size of the context window (narrow vs. wide and small vs. large), the weighting of the windows (constant vs. aggressive decay) feature weighting functions (raw frequency vs. binary vs. tf-idf vs. logarithmic). For the specific task of finding synonyms the author concludes that spaces built using paradigmatic contexts clearly outperform those built using syntagmatic contexts. Additionally, vectors built by extracting word features from *narrow windows* (with two or three context words around the headword) lead to better performance. Interestingly, wide windows lead to better results for the task of finding *antonyms*.

In im Walde [9], a set of experiments on clustering German verbs (by synonymy) is presented. Verbs are described by vectors whose features are extracted from 3 types of contexts with increasing levels of semantic information: (i) syntactical relations (from a set of 38 possible frames); (ii) syntactical relations + information about prepositional preferences, and (iii) 15 possible semantic categories of the verb arguments (mostly nouns and noun phrases) taken from GermaNet. The author concludes that the addition of more informative features – from (i) to (iii) – has a positive effect on clustering results. Also, they observe that (a) similarity metrics such as the Kullback-Liebler and its variants tended to produce better results in larger data-sets, and (b) low-frequency verbs had a negative impact in the quality of the clusters. More importantly, the authors conclude that the choice of features and the overall success of the clustering approach greatly depends on definition of *verb group* one wishes to replicate automatically.

The work by Chklovski and Pantel [2] also focus on finding semantic relations between verbs, namely *similarity*, *strength*, *antonymy*, *enablement* and *happens-before*. The procedure involves querying a search engine for co-occurrences of pairs of verbs in specific lexical-syntactic patterns that indicate that the verbs might establish one of such relations. Results were evaluated by human assessors. Lin [10] uses a broad-coverage parser to obtain grammatical relationships between pairs of words. Each word is then represented by a vector whose features are derived from the set grammatical relations it establishes with other words. Raw frequency values are weighted using a variation of the Mutual Information function. Pairs-wise similarity between nouns, verbs and adjectives/adverbs that occurred at least 100 times was computed, using several similarity metrics. Then for each word, a thesaurus entry was created using the top most similar words. Evaluation was performed using WordNet and the Roget Thesaurus.

Related work on VSM generally takes advantage of significant linguistic information, usually extracted from *annotated* corpora. In this study, we rely mostly on the information directly derived from data, in particular, on raw n-grams statistics taken from a large non-annotated collection of web documents. Apart from dictionary-based filtering and lemmatization, no additional linguistic processing (e.g. POS annotation, word-sense disambiguation) is used. Given the increasing availability of large databases of n-grams computed from non-annotated terabyte web collections (e.g. Goolge's N-gram database) and the lack of publicly available resources for Portuguese with refined semantic information, we believe that this is an interesting approach.

3 VSM Parameters

The Vector Space Model provides a convenient framework for finding semantic similarities between words, because it allows to express a strong intuition regarding semantic similarity: the *Distributional Hypothesis* [8]. There are several parameters related to the VSM, the most crucial being perhaps the choice of the appropriate *context* for extracting features capable of leading to *meaningful* vector representations of words. Usually, relevant features can be found at lexical level (by exploring the lexical surroundings of words) or at syntactical level (by exploring syntactic relations between words and constituents in a sentence, such as "subject-predicate" relation). The choice of a specific feature context has a huge impact on the information that is *transferred* to the Vector Space, thus directly affecting the notion of "similarity" that may be inferred from feature vectors (see [11]). There are also several *cutoff thresholds* used for limiting the feature vectors included in the space. These are important for cases where there might not be enough empirical evidence associated with the corresponding words. Such vectors might lead to noisy associations.

Another important parameter in the VSM is the choice of the *feature weighting function*, such as tf-idf [12], Mutual Information [3] and the Log-Likelihood Ratio [6]. Different weighting functions tend to promote (or demote) different sections of the feature spectrum, so choosing the appropriate weighting function for a specific word comparison task might have a deep impact in the final results (e.g. should "idiosyncratic" features be considered more important?). A closely related question is the choice of a *distance metric* for comparing the (weighted) vectors. Global performance of VSM approaches depends on the combination of a specific weighting function and a specific distance metric, and there is usually an optimal combination for different tasks (see [5]). However, in this work we will not explore this parameter in order to avoid dealing with additional complexity for now. Thus, in all our experiments we will keep the same metric (i.e. the cosine)

4 VSM for Verb Synonyms

As mentioned before, we wish to investigate the impact of considering a restricted set of lexical units that co-occur with a particular verb, in the specific task of synonymy detection. Concretely, we confined the context window to the *four* words around the verb, i.e. a [-2 : +2] window. Since Portuguese is an SVO language, we believe that such context contains, in the majority of the cases, relevant information about *verb-object* and *subject-verb* relations[1]. The right and the left contexts are specially important for the case of *transitive* and *intransitive verbs*, respectively. We also assume that features extracted from such contexts might be compiled independently, so that feature vectors can be created by aggregating the two sources of statistical evidence.

For obtaining verb context information we used a database of n-gram statistics compiled from a dump of the Portuguese web, totalling about 1000 million words. We scanned 3-gram information of the form (w_1, w_2, w_3, f) for cases where either w_1 or w_3 were verbs. N-gram information in this collection is *not* POS-tagged. Nevertheless, since the majority of verb forms are inflected, they can be unambiguously recognized using a simple dictionary (at least for the vast majority of possible forms). Hence, we used a dictionary to filter out ambiguous verb forms – i.e. those that could not be uniquely assigned to an unique (verb) lemma – so that only the 3-grams matching either of the two following selection patterns were chosen (v_{uf} = unambiguous verb form):

- *Pattern 1* = [$w_1 = v_{uf}$ & w_2 = * & w_3 = *]
- *Pattern 2* = [w_1 = * & w_2 = * & $w_3 = v_{uf}$]

Verb forms (at w_1 or at w_3) are lemmatized in order to obtain feature tuples of the form (verb lemma, "X w_2 w_3", frequency) and (verb lemma, "w_1 w_2 X", frequency), with *X* signalling the original position of the verb in relation to the extracted features. Feature information extracted for the various forms of the same lemma is merged so to that a single feature vector is obtained for each verb lemma. At this point, feature vectors contain raw frequency information regarding features extracted from the two words before the verb and from the two words after the verb. Features can then be weighted according to given weighting function to produce *weighted feature vectors*, which should be able to reflect more faithfully the association between verbs and features. Next, weighted feature vectors are compared so that we obtain all pairwise similarities. Synonyms for verb v_i are obtained among the other verbs, v_j, whose feature vectors $[V_j]$ are more similar to $[V_i]$. By this procedure, we are not producing *closed sets* of verb synonyms: we are building a network of similarities which enables a verb to be synonym of many other verbs, depending on the different senses it conveys.

However, we know in advance that the chosen context scope will not allow to differentiate between synonyms and antonyms. Opposite sense verbs tend to occur in the *same contexts*, since they usually select identical arguments and allow the same modifiers (e.g. "Please, open the door!" and "Please, close the door!"). Nevertheless, we decided to analyze how VSM performs in the detection of synonyms in Portuguese and assess the true impact of this limitation. Furthermore, we assume that antonyms could be identified in a subsequent *post-processing* step by using techniques such as the ones described in [2].

5 Evaluating Verb Synonyms

We used a publicly available resource as a gold-standard for automatic evaluation: the OpenOffice thesaurus for Portuguese[2]. From the OpenOffice thesaurus we collected (verb → list of synonyms) mappings for 2,783 verbs, each having 3.83 synonyms in average. However, this information refers only to about 50% of the verb lemmas one can find in standard on-line dictionaries for Portuguese (e.g. [1]). More important, there are serious *recall* problems for the mappings collected. For example, many high-frequency verbs have *only one* synonym in OpenOffice thesaurus: "ganhar" (to "win") → "poupar" ("to save");"afirmar" ("to state") → "declarar" ("to declare"); "chamar" ("to call") → "invocar" ("to invoke"), among many others. In order to minimize this problem, we extracted additional verb synonym information from the Portuguese version of the Wiktionary project[3]. We thus obtained additional (verb → list of synonyms) mappings for 2,171 verbs, each having in average 1.95 synonyms. By merging mappings extracted from both resources we obtained a larger gold-standard covering 3,423 verbs, with 4.53 synonyms per verb. This larger gold-standard still has coverage and recall problems, but we believe that it provides a good solution for the purpose of performing *parameter exploration*.

Nevertheless, we chose to perform a more thorough evaluation by manually analyzing results obtained two subclasses of verbs. We selected two groups of verbs with different syntactic and semantic properties (see Table 1). The first group includes 25 *declarative verbs*, such as "dizer" ("to say") or "mencionar" ("to mention"), and will be referred as V_{com}. The second group includes 25 *psychological verbs*, such as "gostar" ("to like") and "envergonhar" ("to shame"), and will be mentioned as V_{emo}. V_{emo} are related to the expression of a sentiment or an emotion, which can be experienced

[1] It should be stressed, however, that this context window is not sufficient for all cases, namely when there is a modifier between the verb and one of its arguments.

[2] Available from http://openthesaurus.caixamagica.pt/. The most recent version is dated from 2006-08-17.

[3] Available at http://download.wikimedia.org/ptwiktionary/

by the human noun occupying the subject or the complement position, according to the verb at stake. The level of polysemy of verbs in V_{com} is relatively low. On the other hand, verbs in V_{emo} are highly polysemous. This fact is somehow reflected by the vast list of possible antonyms, with various degrees of strength, that can be associated to verbs in V_{emo}. Sets V_{com} and V_{emo} can be placed in opposite ends of the spectrum regarding the performance that one expects to achieve in the task of synonym finding: performance for V_{com} should be higher than for V_{emo}.

	Verbs
V_{com}	acrescentar, adiantar, afirmar, alertar, anunciar, avisar, comunicar, confessar, contar, comentar, declarar, defender, destacar, dizer, esclarecer, explicar, frisar, indicar, mencionar, nomear, responder, referir, revelar, salientar, sublinhar
V_{emo}	aborrecer, adorar, agradar, amar, angustiar, assustar, atemorizar, chatear, decepcionar, detestar, emocionar, enternecer, entristecer, entusiasmar, envergonhar, fascinar, gostar, humilhar, impressionar, intimidar, irritar, lisonjear, orgulhar, preocupar, ridicularizar

Table 1: *Verb groups chosen for manual evaluation.*

Performance Metrics

Let V_{gold} be the set of verb entries in the *gold standard verb thesaurus*, and let V_{auto} be the set of verb entries for which synonyms mappings were obtained by the automatic method. Also, let $S_{gold}(v_i)$ be the set of verb synonyms defined for entry v_i in the gold standard thesaurus (i.e. the "true" synonyms), and $S_{auto}(v_i)$ be the set of synonyms inferred automatically for v_i. As a result of the automatic process, elements in $S_{auto}(v_i)$ are ranked according to the degree of synonymy they have with v_i. Thus, traditional metrics used in information retrieval can be used for evaluating the ranked sets of verb synonyms $S_{auto}(v_i)$ against those in $S_{gold}(v_i)$. Because verb mappings contained in the gold standard are far from being complete, we will not compute recall figures and we will mainly focus on evaluating *precision*.

More specifically, for each verb entry $v_i \in (V_{auto} \cap V_{gold})$, we will compute three precision figures. The first is *Precision at Rank 1*, $P_{@}(v_i, 1)$. The second is *Precision at Rank* $N_{gold}(v_i)$, $P_{@}(v_i, N_{gold}(i))$, with $N_{gold}(v_i)$ being the number of true synonyms contained in $S_{gold}(v_i)$. The third is *Average Precision*, $AP(v_i)$, which gives a global view of the precision by combining the values of the precision at various ranks:

$$AP(v_i) = \frac{\sum_{r=1}^{N_{gold}(i)} P_{@}(v_i, r) \times rl_{@}(v_i, r)}{N_{gold}(i)} \quad (1)$$

with $N_{gold}(i)$ being the number of elements in $S_{gold}(v_i)$, and $rl_{@}(v_i, r)$ a binary function indicating if the element of $S_{auto}(v_i)$ at rank r is element of $S_{gold}(v_i)$ (1) or not (0).

Global performance figures can be obtained by averaging $P_{@}(v_i, 1)$, $P_{@}(v_i, N_{gold}(v_i))$ and $AP(v_i)$ over all entries for which evaluation was possible, i.e for $v_i \in (V_{auto} \cap V_{gold})$. This allows us to compute three global precision figures: $P_{@}^{avg}(1)$, $P_{@}^{avg}(N)$ and MAP. A global *coverage* figure, $\mathcal{C}$, can be computed by dividing the number of entries evaluated by the total number of entries in the gold standard thesaurus: $\mathcal{C} = |V_{auto} \cap V_{gold}|/|V_{gold}|$. For manual evaluation, we are no longer limited by the number of "true" synonyms contained in the gold standard for a given entry, so we can compute the value of precision at several ranks up to a reasonable value (although we still can not list all possible synonyms of a verb). We chose to compute precision at ranks 1, 5, 10 and 20, which will be represented by $P_{@}^{man}(v_i, n)$, with $n \in \{1, 5, 10, 20\}$.

6 Experimental Setup

We wish to test the impact of three VSM parameters on the overall quality of the automatically generated synonymy mappings. First, for assessing the impact of different *weighting functions* (*Experiment Set 1*) we will run the complete procedure for automatically generating synonym mappings iteratively times, keeping the same context scope - a window of $[-2, +2]$ words - while using different feature weighting functions. We will try several well-documented (and frequently used) weighting functions, namely: tf-idf [12], Log-Likelihood Ratio (LL) [6], Z-Score [14], Pearson's χ^2 test [7], Student's T test [7], Mutual Information (MI) [3], Mutual Dependency (MD) [15] and ϕ^2 test [4]. We also run the complete experiment using no weighting function, i.e. using raw frequencies. For this set of experiments, we arbitrarily set the cutoff threshold on the minimum number of features to 1. Additionally, pairs with cosine similarity lower than 0.1 will be excluded (which can lead to different coverage values).

The second parameter to be explored is the context window used for extracting features. *Experiment Set 2* will consist in executing the complete synonymy finding procedure using only features extracted from a $[-2, 0]$ window (i.e. the two words preceding the verb) and from a $[0, +2]$ window (i.e. the two words following the verb). These experiment will be run using the *best performing* weighting function found in the previous experiment. The third parameter we wish to investigate is the *cutoff threshold* to be applied to raw frequency feature vectors based on the number of non-null features. In *Experiment Set 3* we will select the *best performing* weighting function found in Experiment Set 1, and repeat the complete synonym finding process with increasing cutoff thresholds. We expect to obtain increasing precision values, while coverage should slowly decrease.

Finally, for refining the figures obtained by automatic evaluation, we will manually evaluate two subsets of verbs that lie on the opposite ends of the spectrum in what performance is concerned. The main purpose is to define a possible baseline for the task of automatic synonym finding, knowing in advance that the VSM approach we used is almost purely lexical (it relies on a minimal set of linguistic features) and does not try to address issues related with antonymy and ambiguity. We will chose the best performing configuration, in terms of $P_{@}^{avg}1$ found in Experiment 3 and manually evaluate candidate synonyms found for 25 verbs V_{com} (related to *communication*) and 25 verbs V_{emo} (related the *expression of emotion*). Results for verbs in V_{emo} are expected to be substantially lower than those for V_{com}.

Feature information was obtained from our n-gram database ([13]). There are 173,607,555 distinct 3-grams available in the database. Selection Pattern 1 allowed collecting feature information for 4,972 verbs, described in a space with 2,002,571 dimensions. Selection pattern 2 allowed to collect feature information for 4,962 verbs over 2,066,282. Globally, by aggregating information from both patterns we were able to collect information for 5,025 verbs in a space with 4,068,853 dimensions. Table 2 presents an histogram regarding the number of word vectors and number of features.

# feat.	# vec.	# feat.	# vec.
< 10	541	200 - 499	777
10 - 19	220	500 - 1k	580
20 - 29	145	1k - 2k	456
30 - 39	136	2k - 5k	497
40 - 49	112	5k - 10k	306
50 - 99	353	10k - 50k	382
100 - 199	471	≥ 50k	49

Table 2: *Number of vectors per number features*

7 Results and Analysis

Global precision figures $P_{@}^{avg}1$, $P_{@}^{avg}N$ and MAP (mean average precision) for Experiment Sets 1, 2 and 3 (automatic evaluation) are presented in Tables 3, 4 and 5. Results of manually evaluating synonym identification for the 25 verbs related to *communication*, V_{com}, and the 25 verbs related the *expression of emotion* V_{emo} are presented in Table 6 (synonym candidates were obtained by setting the cutoff threshold to 200, i.e. best $P_{@}1$ found in Experiment Set 3). The most relevant, yet expected, fact regarding results from automatic evaluation is that precision values are all quite low, even for the best configurations (< 0.30). This is not surprising since the gold standard used has serious recall gaps, so it is possible that many correct top found synonyms can be evaluated, thus decreasing precision figures. In [11], even lower precision figures are reported. Also, we knew in advance that the context chosen for generating feature vectors does not allow to effectively differentiate between a verb and its possible opposite senses. Still, performance values obtained can be interpreted from a relative point of view.

Results presented in Table 3 confirm that the impact of the weighting function is very relevant. The best performing weighting function (Mutual Information) leads to a Mean Average Precision figure that outperforms the one obtained using the worst performing weighting function with comparable coverage (Log-Likelihood) by over 300%. Notably, the two best performing weighting functions are Mutual Information and Mutual Dependency, both grounded in information theoretic concepts (the two metrics are actually

Weighting	$P_{@}^{avg}1$	$P_{@}^{avg}N$	MAP	$\mathcal{C}$
MI	0.221	0.121	0.125	0.800
MD	0.164	0.083	0.083	0.800
Z	0.134	0.096	0.067	0.712
χ^2	0.087	0.075	0.030	0.392
ϕ^2	0.084	0.075	0.027	0.375
raw	0.083	0.041	0.043	0.798
tf-idf	0.076	0.038	0.039	0.800
T	0.073	0.040	0.040	0.800
LL	0.059	0.034	0.037	0.796

Table 3: *Experiment Set 1: context window = [-2, +2] and cutoff threshold = 1*

very similar). A well-known effect of these type of metrics is that they tend to asymptotically over-promote rare features. This suggests that rare features might be of crucial value in the task of finding semantically similar verbs. It is also quite surprising to see that most weighting functions score worse than performing not weighting at all (*raw*). This is so even in the case of popular weighting functions such as tf-idf. One possible reason for this is having set the cut-off threshold on the minimum number of non-nil features to 1, which resulted in considering many verb vectors with insufficient statistical information (see Table 2). Some of the weighting functions used might be particularly sensitive to this effect, and actually lead to worse results than performing no weighting at all. Another observation is that by imposing a minimum cosine similarity threshold of 0.1 the coverage obtained using the weighting functions χ^2 and ϕ^2 was approximately half of that obtained for the others. This confirms that there is a considerable interaction between the choice of the weighting function and the similarity metrics used.

Window	$P_{@}^{avg}1$	$P_{@}^{avg}N$	MAP	$\mathcal{C}$
[-2, 0]	0.136	0.078	0.079	0.779
[0, +2]	0.196	0.107	0.111	0.798
[-2, +2]	0.221	0.121	0.125	0.800

Table 4: *Experiment Set 2: weighting function = mutual information and cutoff threshold = 1*

Results from the Experiment Set 2 (Table 4) show that using feature information from *both* the left and right the verb lead to better results that using any of the two sides individually. From a relative point of view, the two words following the verb (i.e. context [0, +2]) appear to carry more information regarding verb synonymy than the two previous words (i.e. context [-2, 0]), which seems quite natural since most verbs are transitive.

As for Experiment Set 3, results shown in Table 5 confirm expectation: increasing the cutoff threshold lead to better precisions values, at the cost of reducing coverage. However, if threshold is set too high (≥ 200), values of precision do not increase anymore, while the global coverage figure falls continually. For even higher thresholds (≥ 500) precision figures actually drop, since by excluding word vectors below

cut.	$P^{avg}_{@}1$	$P^{avg}_{@}N$	MAP	$\mathcal{C}$
1	0.221	0.121	0.125	0.800
10	0.251	0.136	0.136	0.783
20	0.263	0.142	0.141	0.767
50	0.277	0.149	0.149	0.736
100	0.288	0.154	0.154	0.695
200	0.297	0.155	0.155	0.632
500	0.297	0.146	0.146	0.507
1000	0.290	0.141	0.141	0.398
2000	0.294	0.140	0.141	0.300

Table 5: *Experiment Set 3: weighting function = mutual information and context window [-2, +2]*

the threshold we are also removing correct word synonyms of verbs that were not filtered out, leading to a decrease in precision values for these more frequent verbs.

Group	$P^{man}_{@}1$	$P^{man}_{@}5$	$P^{man}_{@}10$	$P^{man}_{@}20$
V_{com}	0.88	0.71	0.56	0.44
V_{emo}	0.60	0.44	0.37	0.27

Table 6: *Manual evaluation of sets V_{com} and V_{emo}*

Results shown in Table 6 suggest that automatic evaluation underestimates performance. This is due mostly to the low *recall* of the gold-standard used. Also performance achieved for V_{com} is very high. Top ranked synonyms found for V_{com} are correct most of the times. More specifically, the values of $P^{man}_{@}1$ (0.88) and $P^{man}_{@}5$ (0.71) confirm that antonyms seem not to represent such a severe problem for the case of V_{com}. On the other hand, for verbs in V_{emo} antonyms populate the top ranked positions, and in some cases are best ranked candidate. An interesting case in V_{emo} is the verb "gostar" ("to like"), which scored 0, or close to 0 precision, at all ranks tested despite being a very frequent verb. As expected, performance figures obtained for V_{emo} are much lower than those obtained for V_{com}. Due to the simplicity of the VSM approach we followed, the figures obtained for V_{emo} can be considered baseline values for other automatic approaches aiming at finding verb synonyms for Portuguese.

8 Conclusions

We confirmed that the weighting function chosen has a crucial impact on the performance obtained when using the VSM for finding verb synonyms in Portuguese. Results achieved by combining the cosine distance with the Mutual Information weighting function suggest the low frequency features carry most of the information regarding verb similarity. We showed that information obtained from both sides of the verb is important for identifying possible synonyms, but the two following words seem to carry more information than the two preceding words. Also, we showed that it is beneficial to exclude word vectors with less than 50 non-nil features, but when the cutoff threshold is set too high both precision and coverage figures will be affected. Manual evaluation showed that the performance obtained by the VSM approach varies greatly depending of the linguistic and semantic properties of the verbs at stake. Results for verbs related with communication show that the VSM approach can potentially lead to very high performance figures. Results with the much more complex class of psychological verbs related with the expression of emotion exposed the limitations of this method in coping with antonymy. Because of the almost absence of linguistic pre-processing of our approach, such results – specially $P_{@}1 \simeq 0.60$ and $P_{@}5 \simeq 0.45$ – can be seen as *baseline* values for the task of automatically finding verb synonyms for Portuguese.

Acknowledgments

This work was partially supported by grants SFRH/BD/23590/2005 and SFRH/BPD/45416/2008 FCT-Portugal, co-financed by POSI.

References

[1] J. Almeida and U. Pinto. Jspell – um módulo para analise lexica genérica de linguagem natural. In *Actas do X Encontro da Associação Portuguesa de Linguística*, pages 1–15, Évora 1994, 1995.

[2] T. Chklovski and P. Pantel. VerbOcean: Mining the Web for Fine-Grained Semantic Verb Relations. In *In Proceedings of Conference on Empirical Methods in Natural Language Processing (EMNLP-04)*, Barcelona, Spain, 2004.

[3] K. Church and P. Hanks. Word association norms, mutual information, and lexicography. *Computational Linguistics*, 16(1):22–29, 1990.

[4] K. W. Church and W. A. Gale. Concordances for parallel text. In *Proceedings of the Seventh Annual Conference of the UW Center for the New OED and Text Research*, pages 40–62, September 1991.

[5] J. R. Curran. From distributional to semantic similarity. Technical report, PhD. Thesis, University of Edinburgh. College of Science, 2004.

[6] T. E. Dunning. Accurate methods for the statistics of surprise and coincidence. *Computational Linguistics*, 19(1):61–74, 1993.

[7] S. Evert. *The statistics of word cooccurrences : word pairs and collocations.* PhD thesis, Institut fr maschinelle Sprachverarbeitung, Universitt Stuttgart, 2005.

[8] Z. S. Harris. Distributional structure. *Word*, 10(23):146–162, 1954.

[9] S. S. im Walde. Experiments on the automatic induction of german semantic verb classes. *Computational Linguistics*, 32(2):159–194, 2006.

[10] D. Lin. Automatic Retrieval and Clustering of Similar Words. In *Proceedings of COLING-ACL 1998*, volume 2, page 768?773, Montreal, 1998.

[11] M. Sahlgren. *The Word-Space Model: Using distributional analysis to represent syntagmatic and paradigmatic relations between words in high dimensional vector spaces.* Sics dissertation series 44, Stockholm University, Sweden, 2006.

[12] G. Salton and M. J. McGill. *Introduction to Modern Information Retrieval.* McGraw-Hill, Inc., New York, NY, USA, 1986.

[13] L. Sarmento. BACO - A large database of text and cooccurrences. In *Proceedings of the 5th International Conference on Language Resources and Evaluation (LREC'2006)*, pages 1787–1790, Genoa, Italy, 22-28 May 2006.

[14] F. Smadja. Retrieving collocations from text: Xtract. *Computational Linguistics*, 19:143–177, 1993.

[15] A. Thanopoulos, N. Fakotakis, and G. Kokkinakis. Comparative evaluation of collocation extraction metrics. In *In Proceedings of the 3rd Language Resources Evaluation Conference*, pages 620–625, 2002.

A Unified Method for Extracting Simple and Multiword Verbs with Valence Information and Application for Hungarian

Bálint Sass
Research Institute for Linguistics, Hungarian Academy of Sciences, Budapest, Hungary
sass.balint@nytud.hu

Abstract

We present a method for extracting verb-centered constructions (VCCs) from corpora. In our framework, simple and multiword verbs, with or without valence are all VCCs. They are treated uniformly, from e.g. *to breathe* till e.g. *to take something into consideration.* In order to extract VCCs we represent the corpus as a sequence of clauses that contain a verb together with all its NP dependents. The method is a generalization of a former subcategorization frame extraction method. It is based on cumulative counting of frequent subframes: small frequency counts are inherited to one of the longest available subframes using random selection. The method finds out automatically the number of elements in VCCs; and it detects automatically whether a content word is integral part of the VCC (forming a multiword verb), or just the verb-dependent relation is important (forming a valence slot of the verb). Significance of our method lies in its capability to deal with multiword verbs and (their) valence simultaneously. The paper includes evaluation for Hungarian, we obtain precision values above 80% using *n*-best lists evaluation. The representation and the method is in essence language independent, it could be applied to other languages as well.

1 Introduction

Multiword expressions (MWEs) consist of several words, but semantically act as one unit, having non-compositional (idiomatic) meaning [12, 9]. Their meaning cannot be deduced, although the meaning of each part is known. Nevertheless, it is necessary to know their meanings if we want to deal with semantics in any field of natural language processing. Being a borderline case between grammar and lexicon, importance of MWES was underestimated until quite recently [12]. In fact, number of MWEs is large, one fifth of all verbs can be part of a MWE in runnig text [6].

In NLP applications MWEs are usually stored in a lexical resource together with their meaning, thus the main task (called lexical acquisition) is to build up such a lexicon. The traditional collocation-based approach of collecting/extracting MWEs is based on the fact that words in MWEs appear more frequently together than expected. The strength of association between these words can be measured using particular statistical *association measures* [3]. Most of them are worked out to handle exactly *two* words (bigrams), but this is too limiting, because there are longer MWEs, obviously, and there are cases when we do not even know the number of words in the MWEs beforehand.

Conventional classes ot MWEs [12, 9, 6], which can be located along a scale from most idiomatic to most literal meaning are shown below, with examples:

1. fully rigid expressions – *ad hoc*;
2. idioms – *kick the bucket*;
3. verb particle constructions (VPCs) – *hand in*;
4. support verb constructions (SVCs) – *take a walk*;
5. institutionalized phrases – *traffic light.*

It can be noticed that the [verb + NP/PP dependent(s)] – or *verb frame* – structure is very common among MWEs, we find MWEs of this general type in every classes mentioned above. These verb centered MWEs are called *multiword verbs (MWVs).* Since they cover substantial part of all MWEs, we will deal with this broad class aiming to have a comprehensive picture of MWEs in general.

Like common verbs, some multiword verbs also has one or more arguments (e.g. the *of*-phrase in *get rid of*). To our knowledge, these two research paths – MWEs and valence – have not crossed each other in the literature until recently. Our present aim is to develop a framework that is suitable to handle both aspects, extracting also verb-centered MWEs which are multiword and have valence at the same time.

Accordingly, our target are the *verb-centered constructions (VCCs).* They consist of a verb, zero or more additional NPs and zero or more valence slots; and the verb together with the NPs (if any) has a (to some degree) non-compositional/idiomatic meaning. If the core meaning of the construction is changing when we change the content word at the head of NP(s), the meaning is considered idiomatic.

Let us see example (1) and introduce the notion of *content* and *relational* units. Hungarian *-bA* ('into' in English) is a relational unit which relates a locative to the verb. Hungarian *-t* is also a relational unit which marks the direct object. The content unit in the object relation is *orr* ('nose' in English). If we change this content unit, the original meaning of this construction changes. So, according to the definition this example is a VCC, moreover a full-grown VCC: a multiword verb with one valence.

(1) beleüt orr-t -bA
knock·in nose-OBJ IN

International Conference RANLP 2009 - Borovets, Bulgaria, pages 399–403

≈ 'meddle with something'[1]

In this paper we introduce a VCC extraction method which fulfils the following two flexibility requirements: (1) the number of units is not restricted to a fixed number, the algorithm detects the number of units within a multiword expression processed; (2) the algorithm detects whether there are any integral content unit in the VCC – forming a multiword verb –, or just some relational units are relevant – forming some valence slots of the verb.

2 Related work

Within the MWE literature there is a significant amount of research in the field of multiword verb extraction. The target is almost always a specific type of VCCs, e.g. verb-particle constructions [2], or verb+noun idiomatic constructions [5]. There is also a MWV-collection and MWV-annotated corpus for Estonian (a language closely related to Hungarian) [6]. A paper studies valence of MWVs, but only one predefined type of valence, namely whether a MWV is transitive or not [1].

There are two important publications concerning Hungarian MWEs. In the first one ⟨verb+noun+casemark⟩ triplets were investigated [7]. These triplets also constitute a specific VCC type, namely multiword verbs without valence. The other paper presents an analysis of different aspects of extracting MWEs, and experiments with a particular extraction method based on rigidity if MWEs [9].

The basic idea of our method comes from a former verb subcategorization frame extraction method [15]. Subsequent further development or application of this method is not known from the literature. For evaluation, we use the n-best lists, as described in [4].

3 Unified representation

The representation is rather staightforward, we must represent the verb, the relational units and the content units. The solution can be imagined as a one-level-deep dependency structure: the verb becomes the head, the content units (the lemma of the heads of NPs/PPs beside the verb) become the dependents, and the relational units becomes the dependency relations in between. This is a kind of *mixed* clause model: the dependency structure is only one level deep, the dependents are phrases, they are not associated with internal dependency structure, just represented by their heads instead.

[1] We provide Hungarian examples with English glosses in this form. The first line contains the MWV, the verb is shown always first. The *-t* and *-bA* are casemarks. *orr-t* is not a real wordform but the lemma and the casemark (the content and the relational unit) separated by a dash for didactic purposes. Note: the upper case letter (e.g. in *-bA*) signs a vowel alternation point where the exact vowel is determined by Hungarian vowel harmony. The second line contains the word-by-word translation. The uppercase codes means relations, which can be SUBJ, OBJ or a preposition. The dot (·) separates two words, which has a one-word counterpart in the other language. The third line contains the overall English translation.

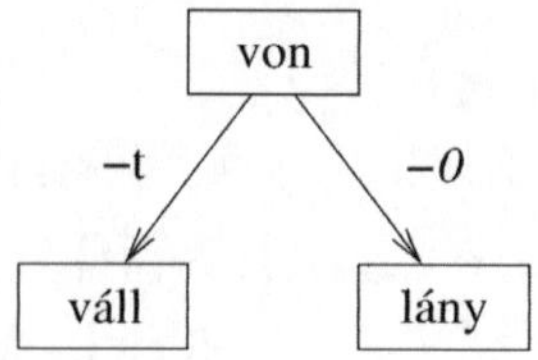

Fig. 1: *Dependency tree of sentence (2). Content unit* váll *'shoulder' is in object relation, and* lány *'girl' is in subject relation. Hungarian casemark for subject is zero suffix depicted as* -0.

Such a way, we can represent not only all kinds of VCCs but also *clause skeletons (CSs)* (i.e. the verb, the relational units and the content units in a particular clause). The dependency tree visualization of example (2) can be seen in Fig. 1.

(2) A lány váll-t von.
the girl shoulder-OBJ shrug
'The girl shrugs her shoulder.'

This model can also be seen as a flat database structure: we have labeled *positions*, which are filled or not. To be clear, these positions are not physical positions in the original clause, they have nothing to do with word order, they just record the existence of some dependent phrases and their relations to the verb. We call a position *fixed*, if there is a particular content word. Similarly, we call a position *free*, if it can be filled by several words from a broad word class. All position is fixed in clause skeletons. MWVs has fixed positions, and valences correspond to free positions (see Fig. 2). An example of a simple verb with one valence is shown in Fig. 3.

Hungarian is an agglutinative language with a relatively free word order. The surface dependencies between the verb and its NP dependents are expressed by relation markers at the end of NPs. Relation markers can be *casemarks* (e.g. *-bA* in example (1)) or *postpositions* (e.g. *mellett* 'beside'). It should be noted that using this model the VCCs need not be ordered nor continuous, so we can also represent free word order languages.

The above outlined representation seems to be language independent, in essence it only relies on the existence of predicate-argument structure. Using positions dictated by the processed language it abstracts away from actual language specific markers express-

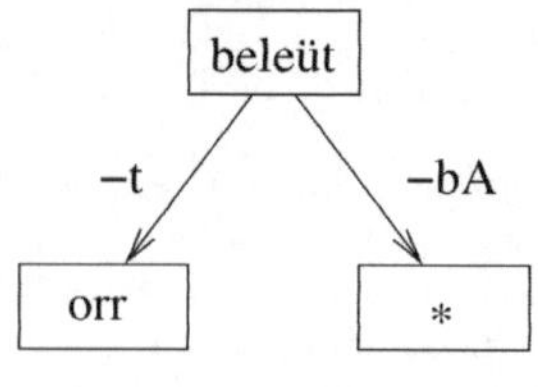

Fig. 2: *Representation of example (1), a VCC with one fixed and one free position (depicted as ∗).*

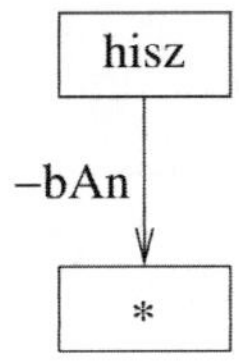

Fig. 3: *Dependency tree of the subcategorization frame* hisz -bAn *'believe IN'.*

ing the relations between the verb and its dependents: separate words (e.g. prepositions), bound morphemes (e.g. the Hungarian casemark *-bAn*), or even relational units which appear as order restrictions (e.g. the relation between the English verb and subject) included.

Input:

```
3 take consideration-INTO future-OBJ
3 take consideration-INTO information-OBJ
3 take consideration-INTO refraction-OBJ
3 take consideration-INTO rarity-OBJ
3 take consideration-INTO preference-OBJ
```

Result:

```
15 take consideration-INTO OBJ
```

Fig. 4: *An English example illustrating the method in operation. We obtain the single true VCC from a hypothetical simple input CS-list. Notation: every row consists of a frequency count, then a verb frame in unified representation (a verb followed by content unit + relation pairs).*

4 Method

According to our unified representation, verb subcategorization frames (SCFs) (i.e. verbs with some valences) constitute a subset of VCCs. We took an SCF extraction method [15], and worked out the details of extending it to our data structure, namely the unified VCC representation.

The main idea is: we should initially store not just the relational units but also the content units, and we should allow the algorithm to get rid of the content units, where they are just some words filling in a valence slot. Outline of our algorithm is the following (see text below for details):

1. We take all CSs of the corpus with frequency counts. We perform *alternating omission* of content units on all CSs (they are „fully fixed"), to have verb frames with some free positions.
2. We sort the resulting verb frame list according to *length.*
3. Starting with the longest one we discard CSs with frequency less than 5, and add their frequency to a *one-unit-shorter* frame on the list. If there are several such frames which could inherit the frequency, we choose randomly among them. Choosing at random was suggested by the original paper as the best performing possibility [15].
4. Intended VCCs are the final remaining verb frames, ranked by cumulative frequency.

Alternating omission means that (1) for every CS we add a "free" variant with all the relations kept and all the content words deleted; and (2) for CSs of length two we add two "partially free" variants (that means once we keep one lemma and delete the other, then keep the other lemma and delete the first). To make it clear, from CS of sentence (2) we could obtain these verb frames:

(3) von -0 -t

(4) von lány-0 -t

(5) von -0 váll-t

It is alternating omission (or frames in the initial list which contain fixed and free positions both) that makes possible to have not just fully-fixed MWVs but VCCs with free positions also in the resulting list of our algorithm. Regarding our example, the correct VCC is obviously (5).

The definition of length fits the intuitive length of an VCC, namely how many units belong to it (beside the verb): we count relational and content units both. In other words, we count fixed positions doubly, as they correspond to a relational unit plus a content unit together. Thus, the length of a VCC is: number of free positions + number of fixed positions · 2. (The VCCs shown in examples (1) and (5) both have length of 3; the length of the SCF on Fig. 3 is 1.) Taking this definition into account, a frame is "one-unit-shorter" if it has one less free positions *or* it has a free position instead of a fixed one.

Compared to the original method our contribution is the idea of storing all content units, the alternating omission procedure, and the suitable definition of length for VCCs.

To illustrate how the method provides true VCCs let us see the VCC in Fig. 2. It will be on the resulting list because in the corpus clauses whose main verb is *beleüt*, the *-t* position is usually filled by *orr* (so its frequency can cumulate), but the *-bA* position is much more variable (so words in this position are more easily dropped out). To make it completely clear, let us see an English example in Fig. 4. As we see, the infrequent content units are dropped out, and we obtain the desired true VCC.

5 Evaluation

To test our VCC extraction method we need a corpus equipped with a one-level-deep dependency annotation for verbs and NPs. We use the 187 million word Hungarian National Corpus, which is morphosyntactically tagged and disambiguated [14]. We lean on an automatic approximation of the dependency annotation described in [13].

In our case, because of storing all content units, size of VCC candidate list grows large, even to some mil-

Table 1: *Results. Average precision values by type and by n (of n-best list). The ± percentages point out two values corresponding to the two annotators. Most important numbers are shown in grey. Cohen's κ measuring inter-annotator agreement is shown in the last column; it corresponds to the rightmost percentage value in every row. In the 'total' line we evaluate the first 500 candidates of the whole list. Type distribution of these 500 candidates is:* `[1:01]` *– 307;* `[0:00]` *– 131;* `[2:02]` *– 33;* `[3:11]` *– 21;* `[2:10]` *– 8.*

type	$n =$ 50	100	150	200	500	Cohen's κ
[0:00]	83.0% ± 5.0%	82.0% ± 4.0%				0.53
[1:01]	94.0% ± 2.0%	92.0% ± 1.0%	92.0% ± 0.7%	91.8% ± 0.8%		0.77
object	99.0% ± 1.0%	97.0% ± 1.0%	98.0% ± 0.7%	98.0% ± 0.5%		0.75
other	79.0% ± 1.0%	79.5% ± 0.5%	78.7% ± 1.3%	79.8% ± 1.8%		0.68
[2:10]	58.0% ± 6.0%	44.0% ± 3.0%				0.64
subject	20.0% ± 6.0%	19.0% ± 6.0%				0.43
other	83.0% ± 1.0%	80.5% ± 1.5%				0.33
[2:02]	77.0% ± 7.0%	66.5% ± 8.5%				0.63
[3:11]	94.0% ± 0.0%	88.5% ± 3.5%	87.0% ± 3.0%	83.3% ± 3.3%		0.59
[4:20]	51.0% ± 7.0%	39.0% ± 5.0%				0.50
total	94.0% ± 0.0%	93.5% ± 1.5%	89.3% ± 1.3%	89.5% ± 1.5%	88.9% ± 1.3%	0.65

lion entries. Manual annotation of a list of such size is not feasible, so we cannot create P-R graphs (or calculate MAP values) [3], we can only recline upon the n-best lists method [4, 3] for evaluation. It consists of the following steps: the list of initial candidates is sorted by the extraction method; first n candidates is considered by human annotators; and *precision* = the number of true positive MWEs from the first n candidates.

Results obtained by using different evaluation methods cannot be compared directly, but we can state as a rule of thumb that values obtained from n-best lists is broadly comparable with the maximum values of P-R graphs, which are obviously larger then MAP values. We usually found n-best lists results of 50-70% in the literature. Maximum values of P-R graphs in [4] are between 55-65%. In a recent paper which compares several association measures, the best MAP value is 69% (with a baseline of 52%) [10] elsewhere a MAP value of 57% can be reached using the classic χ^2 measure [11]. Concerning the Hungarian language we mention the earlier result of 54% obtained by using n-best lists for $n = 250$ [9].

We evaluate our method using n-best lists with two annotators. We take the resulting list first as a whole (all VCC types together) to have a picture about overall performance, and then by type to map the strength and weaknesses ot the method. By *type* we mean the number of fixed and free positions a VCC has. We use the following notation for types: first comes the length (followed by a colon), then the number of fixed and free positions respectively. For example type `[2:10]` means one fixed positions (typical MWV), type of the VCC shown in Fig. 2 is `[3:11]` (typical full-grown VCC) and type of the VCC shown in Fig. 3 is `[1:01]` (typical SCF).

Applying the method to the 8000 most frequent verbs in the Hungarian National Corpus, it provides a list of 47000 possible VCCs using a cutoff-threshold of 50. We evaluated types having at most two positions. Beforehand, we filtered out candidates where the lemma was a pronoun or a named entity (trivial non-VCCs), and candidates which were erroneous because of some earlier processing step, as we wanted to evaluate only the VCC extraction step. We annotated real VCCs among the first $n = 500$; then per type among the first $n = 200$ or 100.

According to the definition of VCCs the annotation criterion was this: a candidate is a true positive VCC if and only if (1) there is no fixed positions or the verbal part (verb + occurrent fixed positions) has a (to some degree) non-compositional/idiomatic meaning; and (2) the (possibly multiword) verb truly has such a subcategorization frame which is present and this frame is complete.

Results obtained are summarized in Table 1. Compared with the results found in literature (see percentages in the text above) our results are fairly good. Inter-annotator agreement measured by Cohen's κ is also fair enough, it is mostly above 0.6, reaching 0.8 two times. We can say that our annotation criterion gives a solid foundation for annotators.

We comment the most important results (shown in grey in Table 1) in the following discussion. In type `[1:01]` we have the highest inter-annotator agreement. We get best results in the case of simple transitive verbs, with precision values coming close to 100 percent. Results of type `[1:01]` SCFs having one non-object position (see e.g. Fig. 3) are around 80 percent. Concerning to typical MWVs having one fixed position (type `[2:10]`), if the fixed position is the subject position, the expression usually have compositional meaning (typically with verb *van* 'be' acting as a copula). Conversely, if the fixed position is non-subject (see e.g. Fig. 5) we obtain far better results, but κ values are low here.

Full-grown VCCs (type `[3:11]` structures) are in the focus of this paper, these are the valence bearing multiword verbs. Number and significance of these expressions is high, and (with a moderate inter-annotator agreement) our method performs considerably well on them (see Table 1). This type does not

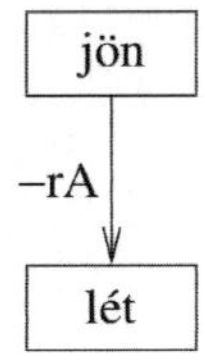

Fig. 5: *Example MWV of type [2:10]* – jön lét-rA *'come existence-INTO'.*

Table 2: *First five real VCCs of type [3:11]. 'X' means that the particular Hungarian casemark do not have an exact English counterpart.*

1.	van	szó	-rÓl
	be	word-SUBJ	ABOUT
	≈ 'something is said'		
2.	tesz	lehető-vÁ	-t
	make	possible-X	OBJ
	'make something possible'		
3.	van	szükség	-rA
	be	need-SUBJ	ONTO
	'something is wanted'		
4.	vesz	ész-rA	-t
	take	mind-ONTO	OBJ
	'became aware of something'		
5.	kerül	sor	-rA
	come	line-SUBJ	ONTO
	≈ 'something takes place'		

belong to SCFs nor to simple MWVs, as it contains free and fixed positions both. Being such a borderline case, they usually get out of field of vision, however they are as important as other MWVs having idiomatic meaning often. The main message is: handling SCFs and MWVs in a uniform general way our approach can also collect these kind of expressions. You can see first five real VCCs of type `[3:11]` in Table 2.

6 Application

The resulting list of VCCs has already been used in two projects. VCCs with fixed positions together with manual translations was integrated into the lexical resource of a Hungarian-to-English machine translation system (which is available at `http://www.webforditas.hu`). During building the Hungarian WordNet the verbal synsets was also enriched with VCCs [8].

Most frequent VCCs are also obviously important in language teaching. We are planning to create semi-automatically a "Verbal expression frequency dictionary" for Hungarian. We expect that the manual lexicographic work can be reduced using the result list of VCCs grouped by verb as a starting point.

7 Conclusion

We presented a new approach to extract all types of verb-centered constructions from corpora. Significance of our method lies in its capability of extracting structures which are in the grey area between verb subcategorization frames and multiword verbs having fixed and free positions (valences) both (see Table 2). The method matches the two requirements of flexibility stated at the beginning of this paper: it extracts VCCs with two or more units alike; it extracts VCCs with (even mixed) free and fixed positions alike. Performance of the method is good enough to automatically create reliable lexical resources of VCCs from corpora.

References

[1] T. Baldwin. The deep lexical acquisition of english verb-particle constructions. *Computer Speech and Language, Special Issue on Multiword Expressions*, 19(4):398–414, 2005.

[2] T. Baldwin and A. Villavicencio. Extracting the unextractable: A case study on verb-particles. In *Proceedings of the 6th Conference on Natural Language Learning (CoNLL-2002)*, Taipei, Taiwan, 2002.

[3] S. Evert. *The Statistics of Word Cooccurrences: Word Pairs and Collocations.* Dissertation, Institut für maschinelle Sprachverarbeitung, University of Stuttgart, 2005.

[4] S. Evert and B. Krenn. Methods for the qualitative evaluation of lexical association measures. In *Proceedings of the 39th Meeting of the Association for Computational Linguistics*, Toulouse, France, 2001.

[5] A. Fazly and S. Stevenson. Automatically constructing a lexicon of verb phrase idiomatic combinations. In *Proceedings of the 11th Conference of the EACL*, pages 337–344, Trento, Italy, 2006.

[6] H.-J. Kaalep and K. Muischnek. Multi-word verbs of Estonian: a database and a corpus. In *Proceedings of the LREC2008 workshop: Towards a Shared Task for Multiword Expressions*, pages 23–26, Marrakech, Morocco, 2008.

[7] B. Kis, B. Villada, G. Bouma, G. Ugray, T. Bíró, G. Pohl, and J. Nerbonne. A new approach to the corpus-based statistical investigation of hungarian multi-word lexemes. In *Proceedings of the 4th International Conference on Language Resources and Evaluation (LREC2004)*, volume V, pages 1677–1681, Lisbon, Portugal, 2004.

[8] J. Kuti, K. Varasdi, Á. Gyarmati, and P. Vajda. Hungarian WordNet and representation of verbal event structure. *Acta Cybernetica*, 18(2):315–328, 2007.

[9] C. Oravecz, V. Nagy, and K. Varasdi. Lexical idiosyncrasy in MWE extraction. In *Proceedings of the 3rd Corpus Linguistics conference*, Birmingham, 2005.

[10] P. Pecina. A machine learning approach to multiword expression extraction. In *Proceedings of the LREC2008 workshop: Towards a Shared Task for Multiword Expressions*, pages 54–57, Marrakech, Morocco, 2008.

[11] C. Ramisch, P. Schreiner, M. Idiart, and A. Villavicencio. An evaluation of methods for the extraction of multiword expressions. In *Proceedings of the LREC2008 workshop: Towards a Shared Task for Multiword Expressions*, pages 50–53, Marrakech, Morocco, 2008.

[12] I. Sag, T. Baldwin, F. Bond, A. Copestake, and D. Flickinger. Multiword expressions: A pain in the neck for NLP. In *Proceedings of 3rd CICLING*, pages 1–15, Mexico City, Mexico, 2002.

[13] B. Sass. The Verb Argument Browser. In *Sojka P. et al. (eds.): 11th International Conference on Text, Speech and Dialogue. LNCS, Vol. 5246.*, pages 187–192, Brno, Czech Republic, 2008.

[14] T. Váradi. The Hungarian National Corpus. In *Proceedings of the 3rd International Conference on Language Resources and Evaluation (LREC2002)*, pages 385–389, Las Palmas, Spain, 2002.

[15] D. Zeman and A. Sarkar. Learning verb subcategorization from corpora: Counting frame subsets. In *Proceedings of the 2nd International Conference on Language Resources and Evaluation (LREC2000)*, Athens, Greece, 2000.

Combining Lexical Resources for Contextual Synonym Expansion

Ravi Sinha and Rada Mihalcea
University of North Texas
ravisinha@my.unt.edu, rada@cs.unt.edu

Abstract

In this paper, we experiment with the task of contextual synonym expansion, and compare the benefits of combining multiple lexical resources using both unsupervised and supervised approaches. Overall, the results obtained through the combination of several resources exceed the current state-of-the-art when selecting the best synonym for a given target word, and place second when selecting the top ten synonyms, thus demonstrating the usefulness of the approach.

Keywords

lexical semantics, synonym expansion, lexical substitution

1 Introduction

Word meanings are central to the semantic interpretation of texts. The understanding of the meaning of words is important for a large number of natural language processing applications, including information retrieval [11, 10, 19], machine translation [4, 3], knowledge acquisition [7], text simplification, question answering [1], cross-language information retrieval [18, 5].

In this paper, we experiment with contextual synonym expansion as a way to represent word meanings in context. We combine the benefits of multiple lexical resources in order to define flexible word meanings that can be adapted to the context at hand. The task, also referred to as lexical substitution, has been officially introduced during SEMEVAL-2007 [16], where participating systems were asked to provide lists of synonyms that were appropriate for selected target words in a given context. Although it may sound simple at first, the task is remarkably difficult, as evidenced by the accuracies reported by the participating systems in SEMEVAL-2007.

In the experiments reported in this paper, we focus on the usefulness of different lexical resources – used individually or in tandem – for the purpose of contextual synonym expansion. We experiment with several resources to determine which ones provide the best synonyms for a given word in context.

2 Synonym expansion in context

Contextual synonym expansion, also known as lexical substitution [16], is the task of replacing a certain word in a given context with another, suitable word. See for example the four sentences from table 1, drawn from the development data from the SEMEVAL-2007 lexical substitution task. In the first sentence, for instance, assuming we choose *bright* as the target word, a suitable substitute could be *brilliant*, which would both maintain the meaning of the target word and at the same time fit the context.

Sentence	Target	Synonym
The sun was **bright**.	bright	brilliant
He was **bright** and independent.	bright	intelligent
His feature **film** debut won awards.	film	movie
The market is **tight** right now.	tight	pressured

Table 1: *Examples of synonym expansion in context*

We perform contextual synonym expansion in two steps: candidate synonym collection, followed by context-based synonym fitness scoring.

Candidate synonym collection refers to the task of collecting a set of potential synonym candidates for a given target word, starting with various resources. Note that this step does not account for the meaning of the target word. Rather, all the possible synonyms are selected, and further refined in the later step. For example, if we consider all the possible meanings of the word *bright*, it can be potentially replaced by *brilliant, smart, intelligent, vivid, luminous.*

The better the set of candidates, the higher the chance that one or more synonyms that are correct for the given context are found. Thus, one of the questions that we aim to answer in this paper is concerned with the role played by different lexical resources, used individually or combined, for the collection of good candidate synonyms.

Context-based synonym fitness scoring refers to picking the best candidates out of the several potential ones obtained as a result of the previous step. There are several ways in which fitness scoring can be performed, accounting for instance for the semantic similarity between the context and a candidate synonym, or for the substitutability of the synonym in the given context. Note that a factor that needs to be taken into account is the inflection of the words, which can influence the measures of fitness in context.

The better the measure of contextual fitness, the

International Conference RANLP 2009 - Borovets, Bulgaria, pages 404–410

higher the chance of identifying the correct synonyms from the input set of candidates. Hence, another question that we try to answer is the usefulness of different unsupervised and supervised methods in picking the best synonyms for a given target.

3 Lexical resources for candidate synonym selection

For the purpose of candidate synonym selection, we experiment with five different lexical resources, which are briefly described below. For all these resources, we perform several preprocessing steps, including removal of redundancies (i.e., making sure that all the candidates are unique), making sure that the target word itself is not included in the list, and also making sure that all the multiwords are normalized to a standard format (individual words separated by underscores). We also enforce that the part-of-speech of the candidates obtained from these resources coincide with the part-of-speech of the target word.

3.1 WordNet

WordNet [17] is a lexical knowledge base that combines the properties of a thesaurus with that of a semantic network. The basic entry in WordNet is a synset, which is defined as a set of synonyms. We use WordNet 3.0, which has over 150,000 unique words, over 110,000 synsets, and over 200,000 word-sense pairs. For each target word, we extract all the synonyms listed in the synsets where the word appears, regardless of its sense.

3.2 Roget's thesaurus

Roget is a thesaurus of the English language, with words and phrases grouped into hierarchical classes. A word class usually includes synonyms, as well as other words that are semantically related. We use the publicly available version of the Roget's thesaurus.[1] This version of Roget has 35,000 synonyms and over 250,000 cross-references. We query the online page for a target word, and gather all the potential synonyms that are listed in the same word set with the target word.

3.3 Encarta

Microsoft Encarta is an online encyclopedia and thesaurus resource, which provides a list of synonyms for each query word. We use Microsoft's online Encarta thesaurus[2] to extract direct synonyms for each target word, for a given part-of-speech.

3.4 TransGraph

TransGraph [5] is a very large multilingual graph, where each node is a word-language pair, and each edge denotes a shared sense between a pair of words. The graph has over 1,000,000 nodes and over 2,000,000 edges, and consists of data from several wiktionaries and bilingual dictionaries. Using this resource, and utilizing several "triangular connections" that place a constraint on the meaning of the words, we derive candidate synonyms for English words. Briefly, using the TransGraph triangular annotations, we collect the sets of all the words (regardless of language) that share a meaning with any of the meanings of the target word. From these sets, we keep only the English words, thus obtaining a list of words that have the property of being synonyms with the target word.

3.5 Lin's distributional similarity

Lin [14] proposes a method to identify distributionally similar words, which we use to derive corpus-based candidate synonyms. We use a version trained on the automatically parsed texts of the British National Corpus. From the ranked list of distributionally similar words, we select the top-ranked words in the ranking, up to a maximum of twenty if available.

To illustrate the diversity of the candidates that can be obtained from these resources, table 2 provides a snapshot of the potential candidates for the adjective *bright*. The average number of candidates selected from the different resources is 24, 19, 30, 48 and 15 from Encarta, Lin, Roget, TransGraph and WordNet respectively.

4 Methods for contextual fitness

Provided a set of candidate synonyms for a given target word, we need to select those synonyms that are most appropriate for the text at hand. We do this by using several methods to determine the fitness of the synonyms in context.

One aspect that needs to be addressed when measuring the fitness in context is the issue of morphological variations. For methods that look at substitutability in context using N-gram-based language models, we need to account for both the inflected as well as the non-inflected forms of a word. Instead, for methods that measure the similarity between a synonym and the input context, using the non-inflected form is often more beneficial. We use an online inflection dictionary[3] combined with a set of rules to derive all the inflected forms of the target word.

We describe below the three fitness algorithms used in our experiments.

4.1 Latent semantic analysis

One corpus-based measure of semantic similarity is latent semantic analysis (LSA) proposed by Landauer [13]. In LSA, term co-occurrences in a corpus are captured by means of a dimensionality reduction operated by a singular value decomposition (SVD) on the term-by-document matrix **T** representing the corpus. For the experiments reported in this paper, we run the SVD operation on the entire English Wikipedia. Using

[1] http://www.thesaurus.com
[2] http://encarta.msn.com

[3] A large automatically generated inflection database (AGID) available from http://wordlist.sourceforge.net/

Resource	Candidates
WordNet (WN)	burnished sunny shiny lustrous undimmed sunshiny brilliant
Encarta (EN)	clear optimistic smart vivid dazzling brainy lively
Roget (RG)	ablaze aglow alight argent auroral beaming blazing brilliant
TransGraph (TG)	nimble ringing fine aglow keen glad light picturesque
Lin (LN)	red yellow orange pink blue brilliant green white dark

Table 2: *Subsets of the candidates provided by different lexical resources for the adjective bright*

LSA, we can calculate the similarity between a potential candidate and the words surrounding it in context. In our experiments, we consider a context consisting of the sentence where the target word occurs.

4.2 Explicit semantic analysis

Explicit semantic analysis (ESA) [6] is a variation on the standard vector-space model in which the dimensions of the vector are directly equivalent to abstract concepts. Each article in Wikipedia represents a concept in the ESA vector. The relatedness of a term to a Wikipedia concept is defined as the tf*idf score for the term within the Wikipedia article. The relatedness between two words is then defined as the cosine of the two concept vectors in a high-dimensional space. We can also measure the relatedness between a word and a text, computed by calculating the cosine between the vector representing the word, and the vector obtained by summing up all the vectors of the words belonging to the text. As before, we consider a context consisting of the sentence containing the target word.

4.3 Google N-gram models

The Google Web 1T corpus is a collection of English N-grams, ranging from one to five N-grams, and their respective frequency counts observed on the Web [2]. The corpus was generated from approximately 1 trillion tokens of words from the Web, predominantly English. We use the N-grams to measure the substitutability of the target word with the candidate synonyms, focusing on trigrams, four-grams, and five-grams. For this method, the inflection of the words is important, as discussed above, and thus we use all the possible inflections for all the potential candidates.

For each target instance (sentence), we collect the counts for all the possible trigrams, four-grams and five-grams that have the target word replaced by the candidate synonym and its inflections, at different locations.[4] As an example, consider the trigram counts, for which we collect the counts for all the possible sequences of three contiguous words containing the target word: two words before and the target word; one word before, the target word, and one word after; the target word and two words after.

From these counts, we build several language models, as described below:

1. 3gramSum. We only consider trigrams, and we add together the counts of all the inflections of a candidate synonym. For example, if the target word is *bright* and one candidate synonym is *smart*, then we consider all of its inflections, i.e., *smart, smarter, smartest*, put them in the sequence of trigrams at different locations, collect all the counts from the Google Web 1T corpus, and then finally add them all up. This number is used as the final count to measure the substitutability of the word *smart*. After collecting such scores for all the potential candidates, we rank them according to the decreasing order of their final counts, and choose the ones with the highest counts.

2. 4gramSum. The same as 3gramSum, but considering counts collected from four-grams.

3. 5gramSum. The same as 3gramSum and 4gramSum, but considering counts collected only for five-grams.

4. 345gramSum. We consider all the trigrams, four-grams and five-grams, and add all the counts together, for the candidate synonym and for all its inflections.

5. 345gramAny. We again consider the counts associated with all the trigrams, four-grams and five-grams for the candidate synonym along with its inflections, but this time rather than adding all the counts up, we instead select and use only the maximum count.

In all the models above, the synonyms ranking highest are used as candidate replacements for the target word.

5 Experiments and evaluations

For development and testing purposes, we use the dataset provided during the SEMEVAL-2007 Lexical Substitution task. The development set consists of 300 instances (sentences) and the test set consists of 1710 instances, where each instance includes one target word to be replaced by a synonym.

We use the same evaluation metrics as used for the lexical substitution task at SEMEVAL-2007. Specifically, we measure the precision and the recall for four subtasks: *best normal*, which measures the precision and recall obtained when the first synonym provided by the system is selected; *best mode*, which is similar to *best normal*, but it gives credit only if the first synonym returned by the system matches the synonym in the gold standard data set that was most frequently selected by the annotators; *out of ten (oot) normal*, which is similar to *best normal*, but it measures the precision and recall for the top ten synonyms suggested by the system; and *out of ten (oot) mode*, which is

[4] To query Google N-grams, we use a B-tree search implementation, kindly made available by Hakan Ceylan from University of North Texas.

similar to *best mode*, but it again considers the top ten synonyms returned by the system rather than just one. For *oot*, we do not allow our system to report duplicates in the list of best ten candidates. The metrics, detailed in [16] are summarized below.

Let us assume that $\mathtt{H}$ is the set of annotators, namely $\{\mathtt{h}_1, \mathtt{h}_2, \mathtt{h}_3, ...\}$, and $\mathtt{T}$, $\{\mathtt{t}_1, \mathtt{t}_2, \mathtt{t}_3, ...\}$ is the set of test items for which the humans provide at least two responses. For each $\mathtt{t_i}$ we calculate $\mathtt{m_i}$, which is the most frequent response for that item, if available. We also collect all $\mathtt{r}_\mathtt{i}^\mathtt{j}$, which is the set of responses for the item $\mathtt{t_i}$ from the annotator $\mathtt{h_j}$.

Let the set of those items where two or more annotators have agreed upon a substitute (i.e. the items with a mode) be denoted by $\mathtt{TM}$, such that $\mathtt{TM} \subseteq \mathtt{T}$. Also, let $\mathtt{A} \subseteq \mathtt{T}$ be the set of test items for which the system provides more than one response. Let the corresponding set for the items with modes be denoted by $\mathtt{AM}$, such that $\mathtt{AM} \subseteq \mathtt{TM}$. Let $\mathtt{a_i} \in \mathtt{A}$ be the set of system's responses for the item $\mathtt{t_i}$.

Thus, for all test items $\mathtt{t_i}$, we have the set of guesses from the system, and the set of responses from the human annotators. As the next step, the multiset union of the human responses is calculated, and the frequencies of the unique items is noted. Therefore, for item $\mathtt{t_i}$, we calculate $\mathtt{R_i}$, which is $\sum \mathtt{r}_\mathtt{i}^\mathtt{j}$, and the individual unique item in $\mathtt{R_i}$, say $\mathtt{res}$, will have a frequency associated with it, namely $\mathtt{freq_{res}}$.

Given this setting, the precision (P) and recall (R) metrics we use are defined below.

Best measures:

$$\mathrm{P} = \frac{\sum_{a_i:t_i \in A} \frac{\frac{\sum_{res \in a_i} freq_{res}}{|a_i|}}{|R_i|}}{|A|}$$

$$\mathrm{R} = \frac{\sum_{a_i:t_i \in T} \frac{\frac{\sum_{res \in a_i} freq_{res}}{|a_i|}}{|R_i|}}{|T|}$$

$$\text{mode P} = \frac{\sum_{bestguess_i \in AM} 1 if\_best\_guess{=}m_i}{|AM|}$$

$$\text{mode R} = \frac{\sum_{bestguess_i \in TM} 1 if\_best\_guess{=}m_i}{|TM|}$$

Out of ten (oot) measures:

$$\mathrm{P} = \frac{\sum_{a_i:t_i \in A} \frac{\sum_{res \in a_i} freq_{res}}{|R_i|}}{|A|}$$

$$\mathrm{R} = \frac{\sum_{a_i:t_i \in T} \frac{\sum_{res \in a_i} freq_{res}}{|R_i|}}{|T|}$$

$$\text{mode P} = \frac{\sum_{a_i:t_i \in AM} 1 if\_any\_guess{\in}a_i{=}m_i}{|AM|}$$

$$\text{mode R} = \frac{\sum_{a_i:t_i \in TM} 1 if\_any\_guess{\in}a_i{=}m_i}{|TM|}$$

For each setting, we calculate and report the F-measure, defined as the harmonic mean of the precision and recall figures.

5.1 Experiment 1: Individual knowledge sources

The first set of experiments is concerned with the performance that can be obtained on the task of synonym expansion by using the individual lexical resources: Roget (RG), WordNet (WN), TransGraph (TG), Lin (LN), Encarta (EN). Table 3 shows the results obtained on the development data for the four evaluation metrics for each lexical resource when using the LSA, ESA and N-gram models.

As a general trend, Encarta and WordNet seem to provide the best performance, followed by TransGraph, Roget and Lin. Overall, the performance obtained with knowledge-based resources such as WordNet normally tend to exceed that of corpus-based resources such as Lin's distributional similarity or TransGraph.

	RG	WN	TG	LN	EN
		Best, normal			
LSA	1.55%	4.85%	2.40%	1.43%	3.80%
ESA	0.44%	3.40%	1.49%	2.42%	5.30%
3gramSum	3.04%	**9.09%**	8.63%	1.82%	7.64%
4gramSum	3.13%	8.02%	7.01%	2.95%	8.27%
5gramSum	2.97%	5.41%	4.06%	2.92%	5.07%
345gramSum	3.04%	**9.09%**	8.73%	1.82%	7.64%
345gramAny	3.04%	8.79%	7.78%	1.88%	7.44%
		Best, mode			
LSA	1.50%	4.50%	4.00%	1.99%	5.45%
ESA	0.50%	3.50%	0.50%	3.50%	6.99%
3gramSum	3.54%	13.08%	12.58%	1.99%	11.59%
4gramSum	4.68%	11.90%	9.26%	3.63%	12.45%
5gramSum	4.77%	7.94%	5.80%	4.26%	7.94%
345gramSum	3.54%	13.08%	12.58%	1.99%	11.59%
345gramAny	3.54%	**13.58%**	11.59%	1.99%	11.59%
		Oot, normal			
LSA	16.67%	21.39%	18.22%	14.93%	30.68%
ESA	15.77%	21.19%	17.47%	15.68%	26.73%
3gramSum	20.20%	21.62%	23.24%	15.90%	**32.86%**
4gramSum	15.26%	19.48%	20.98%	14.67%	30.45%
5gramSum	12.38%	17.45%	16.30%	12.59%	24.51%
345gramSum	20.50%	21.78%	23.68%	15.90%	**32.86%**
345gramAny	20.20%	21.68%	22.89%	15.80%	32.76%
		Oot, mode			
LSA	19.98%	26.48%	21.53%	16.48%	36.02%
ESA	17.49%	25.98%	23.98%	19.48%	36.02%
3gramSum	25.71%	27.21%	29.71%	18.67%	**41.84%**
4gramSum	20.12%	23.75%	27.38%	19.12%	37.25%
5gramSum	16.36%	22.77%	22.22%	17.45%	29.66%
345gramSum	26.16%	27.21%	30.71%	18.67%	**41.84%**
345gramAny	25.71%	27.21%	29.26%	18.67%	41.29%

Table 3: *F-measures for the four scoring schemes for individual lexical resources (development data)*

Based on the results obtained on development data, we select the lexical resources and contextual fitness models that perform best for each evaluation metric. We then use these optimal combinations and evaluate their performance on the test data. Table 4 shows the F-measure obtained for these combinations of resources and models on the test set. Note that, in this experiment and also in experiment 2 below, adding four-grams and five-grams to three-grams either increases the performance, albeit slightly, or keeps it the same. However, in our experiments the absolute best performances occur in cases where the four-grams and five-grams do not really contribute much and hence the score after adding them is the same as that of only using three-grams. We only depict the three-grams scores in Table 4 and in Table 6 because it shows that less computation is enough for this particular problem and the extra processing to collect the higher order N-grams is not necessarily required.

5.2 Experiment 2: Unsupervised combination of knowledge sources

In the next set of experiments, we use unsupervised combinations of lexical resources, to see if they yield

Metric	Resource	Model	F-Measure
best, normal	WN	3gramSum	10.15%
best, mode	WN	345gramAny	16.05%
oot, normal	EN	3gramSum	43.23%
oot, mode	EN	3gramSum	55.28%

Table 4: *F-measure for the four scoring schemes for individual lexical resources (test data)*

improvements over the use of individual resources. We consider the following combinations of resources:

- Encarta and WordNet. All the candidate synonyms returned by both Encarta and WordNet for a target word.
- Encarta or WordNet. The candidate synonyms that are present in either WordNet or Encarta. This combination leads to increased coverage in terms of number of potential synonyms for a target word.
- Any Two. All the candidate synonyms that are included in at least two lexical resources.
- Any Three. All the candidate synonyms that are included in at least three lexical resources.

The results obtained on development data using these unsupervised resource combinations are shown in Table 5. Overall, the combined resources tend to perform better than the individual resources.

	EN and WN	EN or WN	Any2	Any3
Best, normal				
LSA	6.36%	3.25%	3.60%	7.09%
ESA	7.45%	3.30%	4.55%	7.83%
3gramSum	**10.08**%	8.59%	6.94%	8.93%
4gramSum	8.59%	8.33%	7.82%	9.00%
5gramSum	5.24%	5.96%	5.92%	9.07%
345gramSum	**10.08**%	8.59%	6.94%	8.93%
345gramAny	10.02%	7.44%	7.14%	9.27%
Best, mode				
LSA	5.99%	5.05%	4.50%	8.99%
ESA	9.99%	3.50%	5.99%	12.49%
3gramSum	13.08%	**14.13**%	8.59%	13.08%
4gramSum	11.09%	13.44%	11.40%	13.44%
5gramSum	6.34%	10.02%	9.03%	12.20%
345gramSum	13.08%	**14.13**%	8.59%	13.08%
345gramAny	**14.13**%	12.13%	9.04%	**14.13**%
Oot, normal				
LSA	20.27%	29.83%	32.88%	30.75%
ESA	20.23%	26.53%	29.28%	30.95%
3gramSum	19.15%	36.16%	32.66%	30.42%
4gramSum	18.02%	32.65%	30.25%	28.19%
5gramSum	17.64%	23.32%	24.31%	27.60%
345gramSum	19.15%	**36.21**%	32.76%	30.42%
345gramAny	19.15%	36.06%	33.16%	30.42%
Oot, mode				
LSA	25.03%	34.02%	38.02%	42.51%
ESA	25.53%	35.52%	37.51%	44.01%
3gramSum	23.67%	**45.84**%	41.84%	43.29%
4gramSum	22.26%	40.33%	38.24%	40.78%
5gramSum	21.68%	29.11%	31.19%	39.68%
345gramSum	23.67%	**45.84**%	41.84%	43.29%
345gramAny	23.67%	45.34%	42.34%	43.29%

Table 5: *F-measures for the four scoring schemes for combined lexical resources (development data)*

Based on the development data, we select the best combinations of unsupervised resources for each of the four scoring metrics, and evaluate them on the test data. Table 6 shows the results obtained on the test set for the selected combinations of lexical resources.

Metric	Resource	Model	F-Measure
best, normal	EN and WN	3gramSum	12.81%
best, mode	AnyThree	345gramAny	19.74%
oot, normal	EN or WN	3gramSum	43.74%
oot, mode	EN or WN	3gramSum	58.38%

Table 6: *F-measures for the four scoring schemes for combined lexical resources (test data)*

5.3 Experiment 3: Supervised combination of knowledge sources

As a final set of experiments, we also evaluate a supervised approach, where we train a classifier to automatically learn which combination of resources and models is best suited for this task. In this case, we use the development data for training, and we apply the learned classifier on the test data.

We build a feature vector for each candidate synonym, and for each instance in the training and the test data. The features include the id of the candidate; a set of features reflecting whether the candidate synonym appears in any of the individual lexical resources or in any of the combined resources; and a set of features corresponding to the numerical scores assigned by each of the contextual fitness models. For this later set of features, we use real numbers for the fitness measured with LSA and ESA (corresponding to the similarity between the candidate synonym with the context), and integers for the Google N-gram models (corresponding to the N-gram counts). The classification assigned to each feature vector in the training data is either 1, if the candidate is included in the gold standard, or 0 otherwise.

One problem that we encounter in this supervised formulation is the large number of negative examples, which leads to a highly unbalanced data set. We use an undersampling technique [12], and randomly eliminate negative examples until we reach a balance of almost two negative examples for each positive example. The final training data set contains a total of 700 positive examples and 1,500 negative examples. The undersampling is applied only to the training set.

The results obtained when applying the supervised classifier on the test data are shown in Table 7. We report the results obtained with four classifiers, selected for the diversity of their learning methodology. For all these classifiers, we use the implementation available in the Weka[5] package.

To gain further insights, we also carried out an experiment to determine the role played by each feature, by using the information gain weight as assigned by Weka to each feature in the data set. Note that ablation studies are not appropriate in our case, since the features are not orthogonal (e.g., there is high redundancy between the features reflecting the individual and the combined lexical resources), and thus we cannot entirely eliminate a feature from the classifier.

[5] www.cs.waikato.ac.nz/ml/weka/

Metric	NN	LR	DL	SVM
best, normal	1.6%	9.90%	**13.60%**	3.10%
best, mode	1.5%	14.80%	**21.30%**	4.30%
oot, normal	21.8%	43.10%	**49.40%**	32.80%
oot, mode	21.6%	56.50%	**64.70%**	40.90%

Table 7: *F-measure for a supervised combination of lexical resources (test data). NN=nearest neighbor; LR=logistic regression; DL=decision lists; SVM=support vector machines*

Feature	Weight
AnyTwo	0.1862
AnyThree	0.1298
EN and WN	0.1231
EN	0.1105
EN or WN	0.0655
LSA	0.0472
WN	0.0458
4gramSum	0.0446
5gramSum	0.0258
TG	0.0245
ESA	0.0233
RG	0.0112
LN	0.011
345gramSum	0.0109
3gramSum	0.0106
345gramAny	0.0104

Table 8: *Information gain feature weight*

Table 8 shows the weight associated with each feature. Perhaps not surprisingly, the features corresponding to the combinations of lexical resources have the highest weight, which agrees with the results obtained in the previous experiment. Unlike the previous experiments however, the 4gramSum and 5gramSum have a weight higher than 3gramSum, which suggests that when used in combination, the higher order N-grams are more informative.

6 Related work

There are several systems for synonym expansion that participated in the SEMEVAL-2007 lexical substitution task [16]. Most of the systems used only one lexical resource, although two systems also experimented with two different lexical resources. Also, several systems used Web queries or Google N-gram data to obtain counts for contextual fitness. We describe below the top five performing systems.

KU [20] is the highest ranking system for the *best normal* metric. It uses a statistical language model based on the Google Web 1T five-grams dataset to calculate the probabilities of all the synonyms. In the development phase, it compares two of the resources that we use in our work, namely WordNet and Roget's Thesaurus. In the test phase, it only uses the Roget resource.

UNT [9] is the best system for both the *best mode* and the *oot mode* mode. As lexical resources, it uses WordNet and Encarta, along with back-and-forth translations collected from commercial translation engines, and N-gram-based models calculated on the Google Web 1T corpus.

System	*best, normal*	*best, mode*	*oot, normal*	*oot, mode*
		Our systems		
Unsup.indiv.	10.15%	16.05%	43.23%	55.28%
Unsup.comb.	12.81%	19.74%	43.74%	58.38%
Sup.comb.	**13.60%**	**21.30%**	*49.40%*	*64.70%*
	SEMEVAL 2007 lexical substitution systems			
KU	12.90%	20.65%	46.15%	61.30%
UNT	12.77%	20.73%	49.19%	**66.26%**
MELB	12.68%	20.41%	N/A	N/A
HIT	11.35%	18.86%	33.88%	46.91%
IRST2	6.95%	20.33%	**68.96%**	58.54%

Table 9: *Comparison between our systems and the* SEMEVAL-2007 *systems*

IRST2 [8] ranks first for the *oot normal* metric. They use synonyms from WordNet and the Oxford American Writer Thesaurus, which are then ranked using either LSA or a model based on the Google Web 1T five-grams corpus.

HIT [21] uses WordNet to extract the synonyms. For the candidate fitness scoring, they construct Google queries to collect the counts. In order to collect the queries they only look at words close to the target word in context, with the intention of keeping noise at a low level.

MELB [15], which only participated in the *best* task, also relied on WordNet and Google queries. It is similar to the other systems described above, except that for the ranking of the candidates, they also take into account the length of the query and the distance between the target word and the synonym inside the lexical resource.

Table 9 shows a comparison between the results obtained with our system and those reported by the systems participating in the SEMEVAL-2007 task. Our system outperforms all the other systems for the *best normal* and *best mode* metrics, and ranks the second for the *oot normal* and *oot mode* metrics, demonstrating the usefulness of our combined approach.

7 Conclusions

In this paper, we experimented with the task of synonym expansion, and compared the benefits of combining multiple lexical resources, by using several contextual fitness models integrated into both unsupervised and supervised approaches.

The experiments provided us with several insights into the most useful resources and models for the task of synonym expansion. First, in terms of individual resource performance, WordNet and Encarta seem to lead to the best results.

Second, in terms of performance of the contextual fitness models, methods that measure substitutability in context seem to exceed the performance of methods that measure the similarity between a candidate synonym and the input context. Moreover, for the Web N-gram substitutability models, when used individually, the trigram models seem to perform as well as higher order N-gram model, which can be perhaps explained by their increased coverage as compared to the sparser four-grams or five-grams. The increased accuracy of the four-gram and five-gram models seems instead to be more useful, and thus more heavily weighted, when used in combination inside a supervised system.

Finally, a combination of several lexical resources provides the best results, exceeding significantly the performance obtained with one lexical resource at a time. This suggests that different lexical resources have different strengths in terms of representing word synonyms, and using these resources in tandem succeeds in combining their strengths into one improved synonym representation.

Overall, the results obtained through the combination of resources exceed the current state-of-the-art when selecting the best synonym for a given target word, and place second when selecting the top ten synonyms, which demonstrates the usefulness of combining lexical resources for the task of contextual synonym expansion.

Acknowledgments

This material is based in part upon work supported by the National Science Foundation CAREER award #0747340. Any opinions, findings, and conclusions or recommendations expressed in this material are those of the authors and do not necessarily reflect the views of the National Science Foundation.

References

[1] S. Beale, B. Lavoie, M. McShane, S. Nirenburg, and T. Korelsky. Question answering using ontological semantics. In *Proceedings of the ACL Workshop on Text Meaning and Interpretation*, Barcelona, Spain, 2004.

[2] T. Brants and A. Franz. Web 1t 5-gram version 1. 2006.

[3] M. Carpuat and D. Wu. Improving statistical machine translation using word sense disambiguation. In *Proceedings of the Joint Conference on Empirical Methods in Natural Language Processing and Computational Natural Language Learning (EMNLP-CoNLL)*, Prague, Czech Republic, 2007.

[4] Y. Chan, H. Ng, and D. Chiang. Word sense disambiguation improves statistical machine translation. In *Proceedings of the Association for Computational Linguistics*, Prague, Czech Republic, 2007.

[5] O. Etzioni, K. Reiter, S. Soderland, and M. Sammer. Lexical translation with application to image search on the web. 2007.

[6] E. Gabrilovich and S. Markovitch. Computing semantic relatedness using wikipedia-based explicit semantic analysis. In *Proceedings of The Twentieth International Joint Conference for Artificial Intelligence*, pages 1606–1611, Hyderabad, India, 2007.

[7] R. Girju, A. Badulescu, and D. Moldovan. Learning semantic constraints for the automatic discovery of part-whole relations. In *Proceedings of the North American Chapter of the Association for Computational Linguistics*, pages 80–87, Edmonton, Canada, 2003.

[8] C. Giuliano, A. Gliozzo, and C. Strapparava. Fbk-irst: Lexical substitution task exploiting domain and syntagmatic coherence. In *Proceedings of the Fourth International Workshop on Semantic Evaluations (SemEval-2007)*, pages 145–148, Prague, Czech Republic, June 2007. Association for Computational Linguistics.

[9] S. Hassan, A. Csomai, C. Banea, R. Sinha, and R. Mihalcea. Unt: Subfinder: Combining knowledge sources for automatic lexical substitution. In *Proceedings of the Fourth International Workshop on Semantic Evaluations (SemEval-2007)*, pages 410–413, Prague, Czech Republic, June 2007. Association for Computational Linguistics.

[10] S. B. Kim, H. Seo, and H. Rim. Information retrieval using word senses: root sense tagging approach. In *Proceedings of the International ACM-SIGIR Conference on Research and Development in Information Retrieval*, Sheffield, UK, July 2004.

[11] R. Krovetz. Homonymy and polysemy in information retrieval. In *Proceedings of the 35th Annual Meeting of the Association for Computational Linguistics (ACL 1997)*, pages 72–79, 1997.

[12] M. Kubat and S. Matwin. Addressing the curse of imbalanced training sets: one-sided selection. In *Proceedings of the 14th International Conference on Machine Learning*, 1997.

[13] T. Landauer and S. Dumais. A solution to plato's problem: The latent semantic analysis theory of acquisition, induction, and representation of knowledge. *Psychological Review*, 104, 1997.

[14] D. Lin. An information-theoretic definition of similarity. In *Proceedings of the 15th International Conference on Machine Learning*, Madison, WI, 1998.

[15] D. Martinez, S. N. Kim, and T. Baldwin. Melb-mkb: Lexical substitution system based on relatives in context. In *Proceedings of the Fourth International Workshop on Semantic Evaluations (SemEval-2007)*, pages 237–240, Prague, Czech Republic, June 2007. Association for Computational Linguistics.

[16] D. McCarthy and R. Navigli. Semeval-2007 task 10: English lexical substitution task. In *Proceedings of the Fourth International Workshop on Semantic Evaluations (SemEval-2007)*, pages 48–53, Prague, Czech Republic, June 2007. Association for Computational Linguistics.

[17] G. Miller. Wordnet: A lexical database. *Communication of the ACM*, 38(11):39–41, 1995.

[18] C. Monz and B. Dorr. Iterative translation disambiguation for cross-language information retrieval. In *Proceedings of the 28th Annual International ACM SIGIR Conference on Research and Development in Information Retrieval*, Salvador, Brazil, 2005.

[19] C. Stokoe. Differentiating homonymy and polysemy in information retrieval. In *Proceedings of Human Language Technology Conference and Conference on Empirical Methods in Natural Language Processing*, Vancouver, British Columbia, Canada, 2005.

[20] D. Yuret. Ku: Word sense disambiguation by substitution. In *Proceedings of the Fourth International Workshop on Semantic Evaluations (SemEval-2007)*, pages 207–214, Prague, Czech Republic, June 2007. Association for Computational Linguistics.

[21] S. Zhao, L. Zhao, Y. Zhang, T. Liu, and S. Li. Hit: Web based scoring method for english lexical substitution. In *Proceedings of the Fourth International Workshop on Semantic Evaluations (SemEval-2007)*, pages 173–176, Prague, Czech Republic, June 2007. Association for Computational Linguistics.

String Distance-Based Stemming of the Highly Inflected Croatian Language

Jan Šnajder and Bojana Dalbelo Bašić
Faculty of Electrical Engineering and Computing, University of Zagreb
Unska 3, 10000 Zagreb, Croatia
{*jan.snajder, bojana.dalbelo*}@*fer.hr*

Abstract

Stemming refers to the grouping of morphologically related words into so-called *stem classes* for the purpose of improving information retrieval performance. Traditional approaches to stemming are language-specific and require a substantial amount of linguistic knowledge. A viable alternative is string distance-based stemming, in which stem classes are obtained by clustering word-forms from a corpus. In this paper, we apply string distance-based stemming to the highly inflected Croatian language using a number of string distance measures proposed in the literature. We focus on evaluating the stemming performance at both inflectional and derivational level, and investigate how this performance relates to the choice of the distance threshold value. Although our focus is on the Croatian language, we believe our results transfer well to languages of similar morphological complexity.

Keywords

Stemming, morphology, string distance,Croatian language

1 Introduction

Most information retrieval (IR) systems represent documents simply as a collection of words. The performance of such systems is negatively affected by the fact that words in texts appear in various morphological forms, either as the result of *inflection* (transformation of a word into various word-forms) or *derivation* (transformation of a word into new, but semantically related words). To reduce morphological variation, IR systems typically rely upon some sort of *morphological normalization* to conflate the various morphological forms into a single representative form. Numerous studies have shown morphological normalization to be beneficial for IR; this has been shown for English [4], as well as for other, more morphologically complex languages [13, 15].

The most common morphological normalization technique is *stemming.* Stemming refers to the removal of affixes from word-forms, yielding a stem common to all word-forms. The well-known Porter algorithm [11] is an example of such a rule-based approach to stemming. More generally, *stemming* refers to the process of grouping morphologically related word-forms into the so-called *stem classes.* Traditional rule- and dictionary-based stemming requires significant linguistic expertise and resources, which is why, for resource-poor languages, language-independent approaches are gaining popularity. Among others, string distance-based stemming, in which stem classes are derived by clustering word-forms based on their character structure, has been shown to be a viable alternative. String distance-based clustering was first proposed by Adamson and Boreham [1] for the English language, and similar approaches were later employed for Arabic [12] and Turkish [3]. More recently, Majumder et al. [9] proposed string distance measures for stemming in Bengali, as well as in Hungarian and Czech [8]. The performance of their stemming procedure has been shown to be comparable to traditional rule-based approaches.

In this paper, we investigate the applicability of string distance-based stemming to the Croatian language. The Croatian language, much like other Slavic languages, is morphologically complex, especially in the form of inflection. Previous approaches to the stemming in Croatian are rule-based [5, 7] or dictionary-based [14, 16] and are restricted to inflectional morphology. To our knowledge, the work reported here is the first application of a language-independent stemming technique to the Croatian language. The main focus of our work is a detailed evaluation of stemming performance, performed at both inflectional and derivational levels. Although our focus is on the Croatian language, we believe our results transfer well to languages of similar morphological complexity.

The rest of the paper is structured as follows. The next section describes the details of our approach: the string distance measures used, the clustering algorithm, and the evaluation methodology. Section 3 presents and discusses the experimental results. Section 4 concludes the paper and outlines future work.

2 Methodology

2.1 String distance measures

A variety of string distance measures for the clustering of morphologically related word-forms have been proposed in the literature. In [1], a Dice coefficient based on character bigrams was used as a measure of string similarity. We generalize this approach to a distance measure based on arbitrary-length n-grams:

International Conference RANLP 2009 - Borovets, Bulgaria, pages 411–415

$$Dice_n(X,Y) = 1 - \frac{2c}{x+y}, \qquad (1)$$

where x and y are the total number of n-gram tokens in words X and Y, respectively, and c is the number of n-gram tokens common to X and Y. The intuition behind this measure is that, because morphologically related words have a number of morphemes in common, they will also have a number of n-grams in common.

In [9], string distance is computed by considering character matches up to the first mismatch and penalizing all subsequent character positions. Of the four measures proposed in [9], our preliminary experiments indicated that the following two measures are most promising:

$$D_3(X,Y) = \frac{n-m+1}{m} \sum_{i=m}^{n} \frac{1}{2^{i-m}}, \qquad (2)$$

$$D_4(X,Y) = \frac{n-m+1}{n+1} \sum_{i=m}^{n} \frac{1}{2^{i-m}}, \qquad (3)$$

where m is the position of left-most character mismatch, and $n+1$ is the length of the longer of the two strings. Intuitively, measure D_4 penalizes long non-matching suffixes, whereas measure D_3 also rewards long matching prefixes.

One widely-known string distance measure is the Levenshtein distance [6], also called the *edit distance*. Edit distance between two strings is the minimal number of insertion, deletion, and substitution operations needed to transform one string into another. Of the three measures listed, edit distance is least morphologically sensitive.

2.2 Clustering

Partitioning algorithms like the k-means algorithm are widely used for clustering due to their effectiveness and simplicity. Such algorithms are not directly applicable to string distance-based clustering because they require a vector space-based measure in order to compute the cluster centroids. Thus, similar to [9] and [1], we cluster the word-forms using a hierarchical agglomerative algorithm [2]. The algorithm starts by assigning word-forms to singleton clusters and proceeds by merging at each level the two least distant clusters until a single cluster remains. From the resulting cluster tree (the *dendrogram*), clustering at specific distance levels can be obtained. The distance between two clusters is typically computed as the maximum, minimum, or average distance between elements of the two clusters, referred to as *complete-linkage*, *single-linkage*, and *average-linkage* algorithm, respectively. Complete-linkage results in small and compact clusters, single-linkage results in elongated clusters, whereas the result of average linkage is somewhere in between. In our experiments, we use average-linkage clustering. Note that, although we use a hierarchical agglomerative algorithm, we make no use of the derived hierarchical structure.

The main drawback of hierarchical agglomerative clustering is its computational inefficiency. Typical implementation makes use of an $n \times n$ distance matrix, where n is the number of elements. Thus, the space complexity of the algorithm is $\mathcal{O}(n^2)$. To construct the complete dendrogram, the distance matrix is searched for the least distant cluster pair within each of the n iterations, yielding a time complexity of $\mathcal{O}(n^3)$. Because the number of distinct word-forms in a corpus is on the order of hundreds of thousands, this problem must be addressed somehow.

Our approach is to cluster in two consecutive steps: a divisive and an agglomerative step. The idea is to use the divisive step to partition the set of word-forms into pre-clusters and then to perform agglomerative clustering on each of the pre-clusters separately. Pre-clusters must be coarse-grained so that morphologically related word-forms are assigned to the same pre-cluster, otherwise they cannot be merged in the agglomerative step. Partitioning n word-forms into pre-clusters of size m reduces the space complexity to $\mathcal{O}(m^2)$ and the time complexity to $\mathcal{O}(nm^2)$.

A straightforward approach to pre-clustering is to compute the equivalence classes of word-forms sharing a common prefix of a specified length l. We will denote this partition by $P(l)$. The size of pre-clusters is inversely proportional to l, but so is the quality of pre-clustering. If we consider longer prefixes, more morphologically related word-forms will end up being assigned to distinct pre-clusters. This problem suggests that the procedure can be further improved by taking into account the size of the obtained pre-clusters. The idea is to increase the specified prefix length and recursively partition only those clusters whose size is above the specified threshold. This procedure results in size-bounded pre-clusters of maximal quality. We will denote this partition by $M(s)$, where s is the maximum size of the pre-clusters.

2.3 Evaluation

Stemming algorithms are traditionally evaluated extrinsically, i.e., by considering their effect on the performance of IR systems. Such task-specific evaluation makes it impossible to distinguish between the case where the stemmer makes faulty conflations and the case of correct conflation not being beneficial for the task at hand. To address this, we use an intrinsic, task-independent evaluation first proposed by Paice [10]. This method evaluates a stemmer by counting the actual understemming and overstemming errors that the stemmer commits. The under- and overstemming errors are counted on a manually constructed word sample in which the words are grouped accordingly. The *understemming index UI* is computed as the proportion of pairs from the sample that are not conflated even though they belong to the same group, whereas the *overstemming index OI* is computed as the proportion of pairs that belong to different groups among those that are conflated to the same stem. The *stemming weight SW* is defined as the ratio *OI*/*UI*.

The word sample we used consisted of 10,000 distinct word-forms (nouns, verbs, and adjectives) from the Croatian newspaper "Vjesnik".[1] In order to make separate evaluation of both inflectional and derivational stemming performance possible, we grouped the

[1] `http://www.vjesnik.hr`

Table 1: *Examples of word groups from the sample*

{{arheolog}}
{{arhitekt, arhitekta}, {arhitekturi, arhitekture, arhitekturama}, {arhitektonski, arhitektonskih}}
{{arhiva, arhivima, arhivu}, {arhivske, arhivskim, arhivskoj}}
{{arija, arije, ariju}}

word-forms manually at two distinct levels. *Inflectional groups* are comprised of inflectional word-forms and have clear-cut semantic boundaries. *Derivational groups* are comprised of word-forms from morphologically and semantically related inflectional groups. More precisely, two inflectional groups are joined together if the corresponding word-forms are derivationally as well as semantically related (in the case of polysemy, it suffices if some of their senses are related). A derivational group is then obtained by a transitive closure of this pairwise relation. The semantic relations between members of such groups are less clear and are often context dependent. Our sample consists of $5,508$ inflectional and $3,833$ derivational groups. Table 1 shows an excerpt from the sample in which 17 word-forms are grouped into seven inflectional and four derivational groups.

3 Experiments and discussion

The experiments were performed on a corpus comprised of $92,465$ articles from the newspaper "Vjesnik", amounting to over 23 million word-form tokens and 560,137 word-form types.

3.1 Pre-clustering

As discussed above, the purpose of the divisive clustering step is to decrease the complexity of agglomerative clustering. Because divisive clustering results in understemming, we aim at keeping understemming errors as low as possible, while at the same time obtaining small-sized pre-clusters.

The results for both aforementioned pre-clustering partitions are depicted in Table 2. For each partition, we give the number of pre-clusters, the size of the largest pre-cluster, and the inflectional (iUI) and derivational (dUI) understemming indices. The understemming indices reflect how many errors the algorithm makes by assigning inflectionally or derivationally related word-forms to distinct pre-clusters, while the size of the largest class determines the upper bound of the algorithmic complexity. The problem of pre-clustering with a common fixed-length prefix is that, in order to obtain pre-clusters of manageable sizes, the prefix length must be at least 5. This splits apart many inflectional groups, as indicated by the high understemming values. Size-bounded partitioning, on the other hand, can be used to obtain pre-clusters of manageable sizes, while at the same time committing much less understemming errors. In particular, partition $M(500)$ seems like a reasonable trade-off between computational efficiency and stemming performance. Thus, for the divisive step, we use $M(500)$ and pre-cluster 560,137 word-forms into 10,316 pre-clusters.

Table 2: *Size and understemming indices for partitions $P(l)$ and $M(s)$*

	Pre-clusters		Understemming	
Partition	Number	Largest	iUI %	dUI %
$P(1)$	32	72108	4.21	2.49
$P(2)$	808	29716	4.79	3.76
$P(3)$	9365	10774	7.45	7.09
$P(4)$	45794	2029	16.36	20.87
$P(5)$	113532	988	28.78	38.08
$M(5000)$	1501	4932	5.62	4.70
$M(2500)$	2873	2464	6.92	6.34
$M(1000)$	5732	1000	8.17	9.29
M(500)	**10316**	**498**	**10.80**	**13.48**
$M(250)$	18108	250	15.78	21.56
$M(100)$	37155	100	29.78	43.47

3.2 Clustering

After partitioning the corpus into pre-clusters of a manageable size, we applied hierarchical agglomerative clustering on each pre-cluster separately. We used string distance measures $Dice_2$ and $Dice_3$, as defined by (1), measures D_3 and D_4, as defined by (2) and (3), respectively, and the edit distance. As a baseline, we used the partitioning method $P(l)$, which is equivalent to simply truncating a word-form to the first l characters.

The UI-OI plot on Fig. 1 shows the inflectional stemming performance of the five distance measures. As the value of the distance threshold increases, the understemming decreases and the overstemming increases. The plot reveals that all five measures perform far better than simple truncation. As expected, the edit distance performs worse than other measures. Measures D_3 and D_4 are of comparable performance and consistently outperform measures $Dice_2$ and $Dice_3$. The UI-OI plot for derivational stemming performance is shown on Fig. 2. Except for the edit distance, which performs considerably worse than the truncational baseline, the other string distance measures yield modest improvement over the baseline. Measures D_3, D_4, and $Dice_3$ perform at comparable levels, whereas measure $Dice_2$ performs slightly less well.

3.3 Optimal measure

A good string distance measure should commit as few under- and overstemming errors as possible. The trade-off between these two types of errors is similar to the trade-off between precision and recall in IR. As in IR, we define a composite measure of stemming performance, the *stemming quality*, as a harmonic mean between $1 - UI$ and $1 - OI$, as follows:

$$SQ = \frac{2(1 - UI)(1 - OI)}{2 - UI - OI}. \quad (4)$$

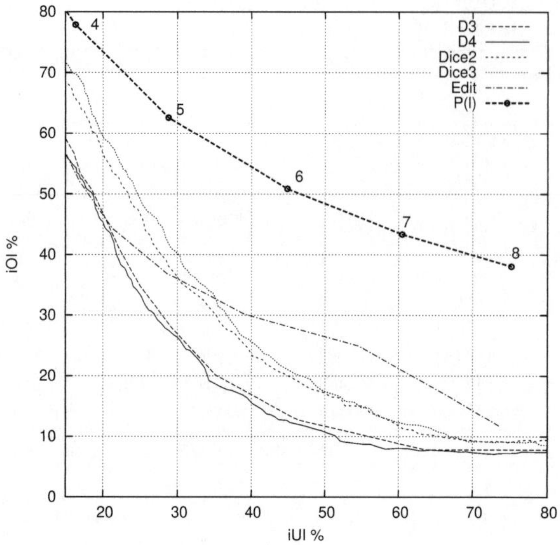

Fig. 1: *UI-OI plot for inflectional grouping*

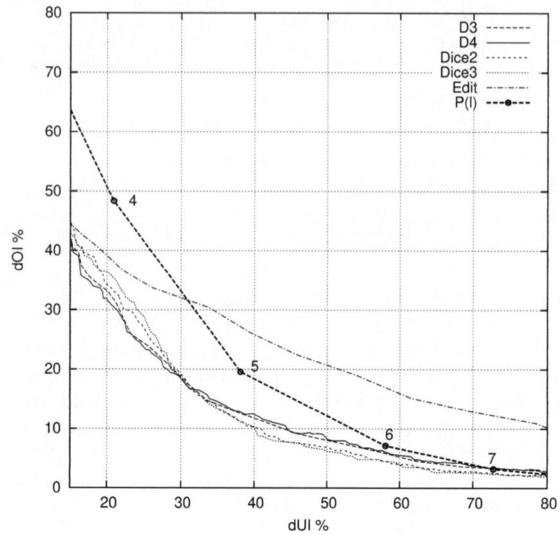

Fig. 2: *UI-OI plot for derivational grouping*

This assumes that under- and overstemming errors are equally important, though this may not be always the case. We use iSQ and dSQ to denote inflectional and derivational stemming quality, respectively; these tell us how well the string distance measure approximates the inflectional and derivational groupings.

Table 3 lists the optimal inflectional and derivational stemming quality of the five string distance measures and the corresponding threshold value t. Measure D_4 result in the best stemming quality. We can see that the stemming quality of all measures is worse on inflectional levels than on derivational levels, and that in most cases the understemming errors are more pronounced.

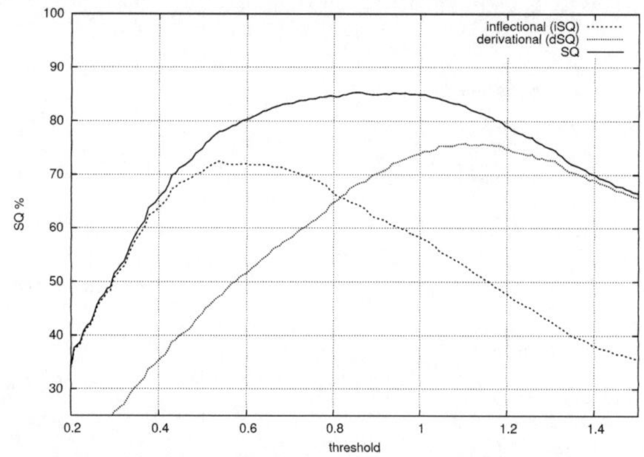

Fig. 3: *Stemming quality of measure D_4*

3.4 Optimal threshold value

The choice of the distance threshold is obviously crucial for stemming performance. A lower threshold value yields "light" and predominantly inflectional stemming, whereas a higher threshold value yields "heavy" and predominantly derivational stemming. The difficulty in choosing the optimal threshold value derives from the semantic relationships between derivationally related words being to a certain degree arbitrary. It is therefore difficult to decide how much derivational stemming is appropriate. What is certain, however, is that stemming should occur at least at the inflectional level, but should not extend beyond the derivational level. To account for this, we only have to consider inflectional understemming and derivational overstemming errors, and redefine the stemming quality SQ given by (4) in terms of indices iUI and dOI. Fig. 3 shows the so-defined stemming quality SQ of measure D_4, along with the inflectional and derivational stemming qualities iSQ and dSQ. Measure D_4 achieves optimal inflectional stemming quality for $t = 0.537$ and optimal derivational stemming quality for $t = 1.104$ (cf. Table 3). Between these two extremes, the optimal stemming quality $SQ = 85.32\%$ is reached for $t = 0.859$; this is where measure D_4 makes the least number of inflectional understemming and derivational overstemming errors, 19.38% and 9.39%, respectively.

3.5 Discussion

Among the considered measures, stemming quality is best for measure D_4; this measure seem to capture best the inflectional and derivational morphology of the Croatian language, which is mostly suffixational. Apart from this, we can make two interesting observations. Firstly, inflectional stemming quality is consistently worse than derivational stemming quality, and improvement over the simple truncational baseline is much greater for inflection than for derivation. These results are probably due to the fact that, at the level of character structure, inflectional relations are less read-

Table 3: *Optimal inflectional and derivational stemming performance of five string distance measures*

	Inflection					Derivation				
Measure	t	iUI %	iOI %	iSQ %	iSW	t	dUI %	dOI %	dSQ %	dSW
D_3	0.813	35.17	20.13	71.56	0.57	3.047	23.15	25.95	75.42	1.12
D_4	0.537	34.22	**19.23**	**72.51**	0.56	1.104	27.61	20.36	**75.84**	0.74
$Dice_2$	0.332	36.18	28.15	67.60	0.78	0.560	31.35	**16.61**	75.31	0.53
$Dice_3$	0.376	38.41	26.87	66.86	0.70	0.668	30.97	16.84	75.44	0.54
Edit	3.075	**28.59**	36.86	67.02	1.29	5.711	**22.12**	36.58	69.91	1.65

ily discernible than derivational relations. Secondly, for both inflection and derivation, understemming errors are more pronounced than overstemming errors (i.e., $SW < 1$). This difference in errors can probably be attributed to pre-clustering, which introduces additional understemming errors.

With an appropriate threshold, the stemming quality of measure D_4 can reach to over 85%. This should be contrasted with stemming quality of simple truncation, which (on the same sample) reaches to $SQ = 75.55\%$, and lexicon-based inflectional normalization [16], reaching to $SQ = 95.07\%$. This result is in favor of string distance-based stemming as a language-independent approach to stemming. A more conclusive comparison will have to be done in an extrinsic, task-specific setting.

4 Conclusion

String distance-based stemming is an alternative to the traditional language-specific stemming approaches. We have applied string distance-based stemming to the morphologically complex Croatian language, using a number of string distance measures proposed in the literature. For reasons of computational efficiency, the clustering algorithm we used combines divisive pre-clustering with agglomerative clustering.

Intrinsic evaluation of stemming performance on the given sample has shown that certain string distance measures are more adequate than others for capturing Croatian inflectional and derivational morphology. By choosing an appropriate distance threshold, stemming quality considerably outperforms the truncational baseline, and stemming errors can be kept in the range of 10–20%. While this is likely to be acceptable for many IR applications, it remains to be proven on actual IR tasks, and we leave this for future work.

Additionally, in our future work, we intend to complement the string distance-based approach with some language-specific knowledge and investigate how this refinement improves stemming quality.

Acknowledgments

The authors would like to thank the reviewers for helpful comments and suggestions on an earlier draft of this paper. This work has been supported by the Ministry of Science, Education and Sports, Republic of Croatia, under the Grant 036-1300646-1986 and the Government of Flanders under the Grant KRO/009/06 (CADIAL).

References

[1] G. Adamson and J. Boreham. The use of an association measure based on character structure to identify semantically related pairs of words and document titles. *Information Processing and Management*, 10(7/8):253–260, 1974.

[2] R. O. Duda, P. E. Hart, and D. G. Stork. *Pattern Classification*. John Wiley & Sons, New York, 2001.

[3] F. C. Ekmekcioglu, M. F. Lynch, and P. Willett. Stemming and n-gram matching for term conflation in Turkish texts. *Information Research News*, 7(1):2–6, 1996.

[4] D. A. Hull. Stemming algorithms: A case study for detailed evaluation. *Journal of the American Society of Information Science*, 47(1):70–84, 1996.

[5] D. Lauc, T. Lauc, D. Boras, and S. Ristov. Developing text retrieval system using robust morphological parsing. In V. H.-D. Damir Kalpić, editor, *Proceedings of 20th International Conference on Information Technology Interfaces (ITI'98)*, pages 61–65. SRCE, Zagreb, 1998.

[6] V. Levenshtein. Binary codes capable of correcting deletions, insertions and reversals. *Soviet Physics Doklady*, 10(8):707–710, 1966.

[7] N. Ljubešić, D. Boras, and O. Kubelka. Retrieving information in Croatian: Building a simple and efficient rule-based stemmer. In *Digital information and heritage*, pages 313–320, Zagreb, 2007. Odsjek za informacijske znanosti Filozofskog fakulteta u Zagrebu.

[8] P. Majumder, M. Mitra, and D. Pal. Hungarian and Czech stemming using YASS. In *Working Notes for the CLEF 2007 Workshop*, 2007.

[9] P. Majumder, M. Mitra, S. K. Parui, G. Kole, P. Mitra, and K. Datta. YASS: Yet another suffix stripper. *ACM Transactions on Information Systems*, 25(4):18:1–18:20, 2007.

[10] C. D. Paice. Method for evaluation of stemming algorithms based on error counting. *Journal of the American Society for Information Science*, 47(8):632–649, 1996.

[11] M. F. Porter. An algorithm for suffix stripping. *Program*, 14(3):130–137, July 1980.

[12] A. D. Roeck and W. Al-Fares. A morphologically sensitive clustering algorithm for identifying Arabic roots, 2000.

[13] J. Savoy. Light stemming approaches for the French, Portuguese, German and Hungarian languages. In *SAC '06: Proceedings of the 2006 ACM symposium on Applied computing*, pages 1031–1035, New York, NY, USA, 2006. ACM Press.

[14] M. Tadić and B. Bekavac. Inflectionally sensitive web search in Croatian using Croatian lemmatization server. In V. Lužar-Stiffler and V. H. Dobrić, editors, *Proceedings of 26th International Conference on Information Technology Interfaces (ITI'06)*, pages 481–486. SRCE, Zagreb, 2006.

[15] S. Tomlinson. Lexical and algorithmic stemming compared for 9 European languages with Hummingbird SearchServer at CLEF 2003. In *CLEF*, pages 286–300, 2003.

[16] J. Šnajder, B. Dalbelo Bašić, and M. Tadić. Automatic acquisition of inflectional lexica for morphological normalisation. *Information Processing and Management*, 44(5):1720–1731, 2008.

Classification of Emotion Words in Russian and Romanian Languages

Marina Sokolova
Children's Hospital of Eastern Ontario
401 Smyth Rd., Ottawa, Ontario, Canada
msokolova@ehealthinformation.ca

Victoria Bobicev
Technical University of Moldova
Studentilor, 7, Chisinau, Moldova
vika@rol.md

Abstract

This paper presents a machine learning study of affective words in Russian and Romanian languages. We tag the word affective meaning by one of the WordNet Affect six labels *anger, disgust, fear, joy, sadness, surprise* and group into "positive" (*joy, surprise*) and "negative" (*anger, disgust, fear, sadness*) classes. We use the word spelling, a word form, to represent words in machine learning experiments to solve the multi-class classification and binary classification problems. The results show that the word form can be a reliable source of learning the affect.

Keywords: phonosemantics, sentiment analysis, machine learning

1 Motivation

Computational Natural Language Learning have been making steady progress in various aspects of Natural Language Processing (NLP). Many tasks have been successfully solved, e.g., document topic classification obtained accuracy comparable with human evaluation. However, some problems have been a challenge for algorithmic solutions, although humans routinely solve such tasks, e.g., spotting difference between terrible accident and terrific situation.

A fundamental, essential language characteristic is the word sense which is often recognized in a rather intuitive way. Senses of words given in machine-readable dictionaries sometimes are not adequate to what people have in mind. This inadequacy was demonstrated in the field of word sense disambiguation (WSD) where the machine- readable dictionaries failed to help in text understanding [5]. At the same time, some tools have become a success. WordNet[1], a public domain lexical knowledge base, is a powerful semantic network regularly used in word sense disambiguation. Another example is Roger's Thesaurus [2] which groups words together by implicit semantic relations. Such resources map word senses to certain explanations and connections with other words.

In the current work, we use machine learning algorithms to learn relations between word meanings and their sounds. A word as a *linguistic sign* can be attributed with two essential characteristics, the sound and meaning , where meaning refers to the word reference, i.e. the concept the word describes. For example, ball and its sound directly correlate with a round, soft object which is used to throw and catch around. Relations between the word sound and meaning are far from certain. In [3], the association between the word sound and its meaning is said to be arbitrary. In contrast, Phonosemantics, the theory of sound symbolism, is based on a hypothesis that relations exist between the two characteristics [13].

The goal of this work is to build lexical resources for Russian and Romanian languages based on the WordNet-Affect domains. The resources are then used to test the hypothesis that word form is relevant to meaning, in this case – the emotions the words convey. We build two data sets, Russian and Romanian respectively, based on the WordNet Affect emotion synsets [12]. To represent the data in machine learning experiments, we use the fact that in Russian and Romanian languages the word sounds directly correspond to the word orthography. Thus, we use the word spelling, a word form, as a substitution for its sound. Specifically, we use the letter form of *transliterated* Russian words and Romanian words for machine learning classification of words' affects. The word emotions are categorized into the WordNet Affect emotion classes *anger, disgust, fear, joy, sadness, surprise.* We solve multi-class and binary classification problems. to classify the words into the six classes and into binary (*joy, surprise* vs others) classes. We apply algorithms with different learning paradigms. The obtained empirical results show that, under certain conditions, the word form can be a reliable source of learning its affect.

Our study contributes to the development of much needed tools, as in recent years, most of the Internet use growth was supported by non-native English speakers. Starting in 2000, for non-English speaking regions, the growth has surpassed 3,000 % compared with the over-all growth of 342%.[3] Consequently, the amount of text data written in languages other than English rapidly increased. This surge has prompted the demand for automated text analysis. The tool development progressed for some languages (French, German, Japanese, Chinese, Arabic), whereas some languages (Eastern European), have not yet attracted much attention from the NLP and Text Data Mining community. The presented study contributes to filling the gap.

[1] http://wordnet.princeton.edu/
[2] http://thesaurus.reference.com/
[3] http://www.internetworldstats.com/stats.htm

International Conference RANLP 2009 - Borovets, Bulgaria, pages 416–420

2 Phonosemantics

Words (rabbits) and morphemes (rabbit,-s) are commonly accepted as the meaning-bearing units which provide association between sound and meaning [7]. However, a hypothesis that smaller units, phonemes and phonetic features, can bear meaning has found supporters in Phonosemantics research [6, 8, 9]. Based on the notion of *distinctions* [15], three types of sound meaning have been suggested [8, 9]:

Onomatopoeia is the imitation of a sound like, for example, in roar or moo.

Clustering is an effect of the semantic association.

True Iconism is the visceral effect of the sound on a person.

Semantic properties of the phonetic features are unconsciously learned by a child, e.g. the smallness implicit in the /i/ sound and the wetness implicit in the /w/[4]. Once the word is assigned to its referent, i.e., concept, this intuitively apprehended semantics is masked by the referent, but it does not cease to act altogether. The effect of the sound is still influencing the word. This influence remains on the unconscious level therefore it is difficult to pick out phoneme senses.

In this work, we hypothesize that a word's form and sound have certain relations with its meaning. Consequently, the meaning of a word is in part inherited from its form. For example, slide is a smooth motion, the smoothness and slipperiness so common in /sl/ shows up in the actual referent for slide [9]. In words with a more specific reference, the component of the reference is more salient; consequently, the sound-meaning part is less salient. For example, words which denote material objects (house, train) have senses dominated by the referents. On the other hand, words which denote abstract concepts as sensations, feelings and emotions keep more sound semantics in their forms (anger, joy, agitation). Thus, words describing similar sentiments should have something similar in their sounding (vex, worry), whereas words representing opposite feelings should have much less in common (disgust, elation).

Relations between the form and meaning of English emotional words were analyzed in [10]. The authors applied K-NEAREST NEIGHBOR, a prototype-based learner, to classify affective words into multi-class and binary emotion categories. The empirical results showed that the word forms for English words expressing the same emotion are alike in certain ways. Our current study differs from [10] as follows:

1. We study Russian and Romanian emotional words. Both languages are Eastern European, belonging to *Slavic* and *Latin* families, respectively.

2. We analyze the learning abilities of different paradigms, i.e. probability-, prototype-, decision- and optimization-based algorithms.

[4] http://www.trismegistos.com/MagicalLetterPage/

Table 1: *Translation of the WordNet 05573914 n*

English	Romanian
preference	preferinta
penchant	inclinatie, slabiciune
predilection	predilectie
taste	a avea gust, a gusta, a cunoaste; a gusta; a degusta (un aliment), degustare, ...

3 Lexical Resources

WordNet Affect WordNet-Affect [5] is a lexical resource which is based on the lexical knowledge of the (English) WordNet. WordNet-Affect contains words which convey affects. A number of affective labels (*a-labels*) were manually assigned to the synonym sets (*synsets*) of nouns, adjectives, verbs, and adverbs. The words with the Emotion tag were fine-grain annotated using six labels: *joy, fear, anger, sadness, disgust, surprise* [12]. The six emotion tags were adapted from the study of human non-verbally expressed emotions [4]. We used the WordNet Affect data provided at the SemEval-2007 "Affective Text" [11].

Russian and Romanian WordNet Affects We translated the WordNet Affect synsets into Russian and Romanian. We applied a three-step approach:

Translation We manually translated every word in the six WordNet Affect emotion categories; Table 1 gives an example of a synset translation. We omitted word combinations (get happy), collocations and idioms. The other restriction was that the translations were related to the emotion of the synset. We postponed part-of-speech correspondence till the later phases. For the Romanian data set, we used the on-line dictionary Dexonline [6] to obtain all synonyms of the translated words.

Building the word sets to form the word sets for analysis, we made a list of all the translations. We edited them to delete words which meanings were not close to the emotion, e.g., for taste, only preferinta was left, all the food references were removed (Table 1). We removed duplicate translations as well. As a result, we built six sets of Russian words and six sets of Romanian words expressing the WordNet Affect emotions.

Reducing the number of the paronymous words Russian and Romanian languages are rich in derivations (schastlivyi, schastliven'kii); there were sometimes four, five – or more – words with the same root. We removed all the paronymous words. Note that Romanian and Russian languages allow letter alternation in the word root. Thus, we kept two words per root (zlo, zliti) if the number of matching letters was < 3.

[5] http://wndomains.itc.it.
[6] http://dexoline.ro

Table 2: *Data sets of affective words: English, Russian, Romanian.*

Classes	English data				Russian data			Romanian data		
	# synsets	% synsets	# words	% words	# words initial	# words	% words	# words initial	# words	% words
anger	128	21.0	318	20.7	149	105	13.0	316	151	25.0
disgust	20	3.3	72	4.7	46	31	5.0	93	43	3.9
fear	83	13.5	208	13.5	118	71	14.6	123	55	12.8
joy	228	37.2	539	35.1	253	183	36.2	510	211	37.7
sadness	29	4.7	309	20.1	217	128	25.6	241	111	16.2
surprise	124	20.3	90	5.9	54	29	5.6	91	48	4.4
Total	612	100.0	1536	100.0	837	547	100.0	1374	619	100.0

Table 3: *Distribution of the affective nouns in the Russian and Romanian data.*

Russian Data			Romanian Data		
Classes	# nouns	%	Classes	# nouns	%
anger	39	13.0	anger	51	25.0
disgust	15	5.0	disgust	8	3.9
fear	44	14.6	fear	26	12.8
joy	109	36.2	joy	77	37.7
sadness	77	25.6	sadness	33	16.2
surprise	17	5.6	surprise	9	4.4
Total	301	100.0	Total	204	100.0

Table 2 describes the WordNet-Affect synsets used in our work: **# synsets** presents the initial number of the English synsets, **% synsets** shows per cent for each class, **# words** – the unique words count for the English, **% words** – per cent of words for each emotion, **# words initial** presents the number of the Russian words before the removal of paronymous words, **# words** and **% words** list counts and per cent of the Russian words which were used in classification experiments, **# words initial, # words, % words** list the similar information for the Romanian data set. The data sets are available for research purposes. [7]

Further, the Russian and Romanian sets were *each* split into *nouns* and the other Part-of-speech. The experiments were conducted on *nouns* only; see Table 3 for details. Other part-of-speech are left for future analysis.

Previous Work Romanian WordNet was created during BalkaNet [14], a multilingual database comprising of the individual WordNets for the Balkan languages. It assigns synsets with three sentiment scores (positive, negative, objective).[8] For Russian resources, little information is available. RussNet [1] and Russian WordNet[2] are non-commercial projects. Two commercial projects are RuThes[9], an informational thesaurus, and the Russian WordNet Novosoft[10].

4 Empirical Results

We defined two *supervised* problems: (i) to classify a word as "positive" (*joy, surprise*) or "negative"(*anger, disgust, fear, sadness*) ; (ii) to classify a word with one of the six affect labels. We constructed four labelled data sets: (i) the *transliterated* Russian words (the six classes); (ii) the *transliterated* Russian words (the two classes);(iii) the Romanian words (the six classes); (iv) the Romanian words (the two classes). For each data set, we built seven representations. Five representation omit the word letter order: **Letters-All**, every letter that appeared in the word had its occurrence counted; **Vowels**, only vowels that appeared in the word were counted; **Consonants**, only consonants that appeared in the word were counted; **Letters-3**, words were represented by occurrences of the first three letters; and **Letters-4**, words were represented by occurrences of the first four letters. Two representations use the word letter order: **OrderLetters-3**, words were represented by the occurences of the first three letters and their order; and **OrderLetters- 4**, words were represented by the occurences of the first four letters and their order.

We applied the following algorithms: probability-based (NAIVE BAYES, BAYES NETS), prototype-based (K-NEAREST NEIGHBOR), decision-based (C4.5 (decision tree) and PART(decision list)), and optimization (SUPPORT VECTOR MACHINES).[11] For binary classification, we report *Accuracy*, *Precision*, *Recall* and the balanced *Fscore*. For multi-class classification, we report the *macro*-average *Precision*(P), *Recall*(R), and the balanced *Fscore*(F). To avoid the bias towards the majority class (*joy*), we report *Accuracy* obtained with the highest *Fscore*. Tables 4 and 5 list the best results of SVM, KNN, C4.5, PART. NAIVE BAYES and BAYES NETS performed considerably poorer. Both tables omit their results. SVM performed more accurately than the other learners. Only on multi-classifying the Russian words, SVM was outperformed by KNN.

The learning results differ for the two languages.The Russian words were classified more accurately when their identification was more precise: the overall best *Accuracy* corresponds to the overall best *Fscore*. The Romanian emotion words can be accurately classified without the highest precision: the overall best *Accuracy* and the overall best *Fscore* are obtained by different classifiers. The Russian words were classified the best on the first three letters, without indicating the letter order. The Romanian words were better classified if represented by vowels (the multi-class tie), the ordered first four letters (binary, the multi-class tie); the highes precision was obtained on consonants (binary) and all the letters (multi-class).

[7] http://lilu.fcim.utm.md

[8] http://sentiwordnet.isti.cnr.it/

[9] http://www.cir.ru

[10] http://research-and-development.novosoft-us.com

[11] the Weka software: http://www.cs.waikato.ac.nz/ml/weka/

Table 4: *Binary classification of the affective words, in per cent. Table reports the best Accuracy and corresponding Fscore measures for each algorithm. The overall best Accuracy and Fscore for the data are in* **bold**. *Baseline Accuracy for the Russian data – 58.7 %, for the Romanian data – 57.8 %.*

Russian Data

Feature Sets	Algorithms											
	SVM				KNN				DECISION-BASED			
	Acc	F	Pr	R	*Acc*	F	Pr	R	*Acc*	F	Pr	R
Letters-All	62.6	72.2	64.1	82.7	61.3	72.8	62.0	88.3	65.2	70.7	69.9	71.5
Vowels	62.0	71.8	63.5	82.7	63.2	72.4	64.8	82.1	60.7	69.4	63.8	76.0
Consonants	63.0	72.1	64.6	81.6	62.2	74.2	62.4	91.6	58.0	67.0	62.2	72.6
Letters-3	**71.0**	**78.9**	68.5	93.2	70.0	77.6	68.7	89.3	64.4	71.4	67.2	76.3
Letters-4	67.7	74.9	68.1	83.3	66.3	73.8	67.3	81.6	64.0	71.1	67.0	75.7
OrderLetter-3	66.6	76.7	64.9	93.9	66.6	76.7	64.9	93.9	62.3	70.6	65.1	77.1
OrderLetter-4	67.2	77.2	65.3	94.4	64.3	75.8	62.9	95.5	63.3	69.9	67.4	72.6

Romanian Data

Feature Sets	Algorithms											
	SVM				KNN				DECISION-BASED			
	Acc	F	Pr	R	*Acc*	F	Pr	R	*Acc*	F	Pr	R
Letters-All	64.7	70.0	68.9	71.2	65.7	72.2	67.9	77.1	60.8	66.7	65.6	67.8
Vowels	60.8	68.8	63.8	74.6	61.8	68.8	65.2	72.9	57.3	66.9	60.7	74.6
Consonants	64.7	**73.9**	64.6	86.4	59.8	67.7	63.2	72.9	60.3	65.8	65.5	66.1
Letters-3	59.8	69.6	61.8	79.7	58.3	68.4	60.9	78.0	57.8	65.6	62.1	69.5
Letters-4	61.3	72.7	61.4	89.0	62.8	71.4	64.2	80.5	58.3	66.9	61.9	72.9
OrderLetters-3	63.7	72.6	64.5	83.1	61.8	70.0	64.1	77.1	62.3	68.8	65.9	72.0
OrderLetters-4	**67.8**	73.0	70.6	75.4	64.2	73.3	64.5	84.7	62.8	68.6	66.9	70.3

Table 5: *Multi-class classification of the affective words, in per cent. Table reports the best Accuracy and corresponding* macro-average *Fscore measures for each algorithm. The overall best Accuracy and Fscore for the data is in* **bold**. *Baseline for the Russian data: Fscore – 8.9 %, Precision– 6.0 %; baseline for the Romanian data:Fscore– 9.7 %, Precision–6.2 %.*

Russian Data

Feature Sets	Algorithms											
	SVM				KNN				DECISION-BASED			
	Acc	F	Pr	R	*Acc*	F	Pr	R	*Acc*	F	Pr	R
Letters-All	37.4	16.6	17.2	20.4	33.4	21.5	26.4	21.5	32.1	21.0	22.5	20.9
Vowels	35.4	13.3	11.1	17.9	31.8	16.0	15.9	17.6	28.5	16.3	16.8	17.3
Consonants	38.9	15.1	12.9	19.8	36.4	15.9	22.0	19.1	27.2	16.7	18.5	17.2
Letters-3	40.0	27.1	32.6	27.4	**40.5**	**29.3**	35.5	28.3	38.9	25.8	32.8	25.4
Letters-4	38.7	16.7	18.0	20.1	35.7	19.0	18.4	20.6	37.9	19.6	21.4	21.8
OrderLetter-3	39.3	22.4	27.5	24.2	38.0	28.6	31.4	27.8	36.4	26.2	29.4	25.8
OrderLetter-4	35.4	15.8	19.6	19.0	36.4	22.6	23.5	23.4	32.8	19.7	22.7	20.7

Romanian Data

Feature Sets	Algorithms											
	SVM				KNN				DECISION-BASED			
	Acc	F	Pr	R	*Acc*	F	Pr	R	*Acc*	F	Pr	R
Letters-All	35.8	20.1	20.6	20.8	34.8	19.2	23.8	19.8	38.2	**23.8**	23.7	24.5
Vowels	**40.7**	18.8	22.7	21.0	37.3	20.9	22.0	21.6	39.2	19.9	20.4	21.3
Consonants	35.9	20.1	20.7	21.0	29.4	18.6	21.8	20.3	36.3	21.8	21.4	22.4
Letters-3	38.2	17.3	16.3	20.4	37.8	20.4	23.0	21.6	40.2	17.1	20.0	20.2
Letters-4	37.3	18.7	18.7	19.9	34.3	17.8	19.3	19.1	35.8	19.2	18.9	20.2
OrderLetters-3	36.8	19.7	19.9	20.7	36.8	19.2	19.2	20.8	36.3	19.1	18.4	20.4
OrderLetters-4	**40.7**	21.4	21.0	22.9	38.2	19.5	22.0	21.1	36.3	20.0	20.1	20.0

5 Discussion and Future Work

We have presented a study of the relations between word form and meaning for affective words. We have studied emotion words in Russian and Romanian. The obtained empirical results show the reliability of our learning approach. On the Russian and Romanian data sets, the applied algorithms performed *considerably better* than baselines. Although the difference in data sets does not allow a direct comparison, our results appear to be more accurate and precise than the results for the English affective words [10].

Based on the results of this study, we propose that there is similarity among the forms of words that express the same emotion: the word form similarity was captured by machine learning algorithms which classified words according to their emotion tags. We also sought a better word form presentation. In Russian and Romanian languages, word spelling can be considered as a word phonetic equivalent. This feature allowed us to limit the search to letter-based representations. It should be noted that letter representations provided better results for English affective words [10], although in English correspondence between the letters and phonemes is not unique, i.e. the same letter can represent different sounds depending on the neighboring letters (cat – [k],certain–[s]). Thus, we can conclude that for phonosemantic classification, letter representations may provide relevant information about the word form.

For future studies, we plan to concentrate on features which better discriminate among emotion classes. We also want to determine which sounds better correlate with the conveyed emotions. Our current hypothesis is that for every emotion there are several classes of words that share common phonological features. For example, the sound z is present in Russian words with meaning of amazement; the *transliterated* sound sh can be found in Russian words representing a kind of stupefaction (there is no absolutely precise translation of these words in English). Note that the exact translation of the English word stupefy is ostolbenet'. Hence, the *transliterated* word and its translation share the combination of sounds st. These are preliminary remarks. A thorough analysis will be able to demonstrate the existence – or the absence – of semantic relations between words with common phonetic features. Another venue would be to expand our current study to part-of-speech other than nouns. We also are interested in conducting *human evaluation.*, i.e., based on the listed word representations, query native speakers about evoked emotions.

6 Conclusions

We have constructed Russian and Romanian word sets based on the WordNet Affect domains. Although multiple efforts have been made to create lexical resources similar with English WordNet for other languages[12], lexical resources for Eastern European languages are still limited. Our study contributes to the development of the resources.

We have shown that the word forms of *transliterated* Russian words and Romanian words allow for a reliable classification of their emotions, in both multiclass and binary settings. The empirical results support our hypothesis that the word spelling is relevant to the emotion that the word conveys. The obtained results can further be used in the nested learning of sentiments in Russian and Romanian texts.

[12] http://multiwordnet.itc.it/english/home.php

Acknowledgements

This work was in part supported by the Natural Sciences and Engineering Research Council of Canada and the RANLP travel grant. We thank Elizabeth Jonker for helpful comments on the text. We thank Victoria Maxim and Natalia Burciu for assistance with building the Romanian and Russian data sets.

References

[1] I. Azarova, O. Mitrofanova, A. Sinopalnikova, M. Yavorskaya, and I. Oparin. Russnet: Building a lexical database for the russian language. In *Proceedings of the Workshop on Wordnet Structures and Standardisation and How this affect Wordnet Applications and Evaluation*, 2002.

[2] V. Balkova, A. Sukhonogov, and S. Yablonsky. Russian wordnet. In *Proceedings of the Second Global Wordnet Conference*, 2004.

[3] F. de Saussure. *Cours de linguistique générale*. Harrassowitz, Wiesbaden, 1916.

[4] P. Ekman. An argument for basic emotions. *Cognition and Emotion*, 6:169–200, 1992.

[5] N. Ide and J. Veronis. Word sense disambiguation: The state of the art. *Computational Linguistics*, 24(1):1–40, 1998.

[6] R. Jakobson and L. Waugh. *The Sound Shape of Language*. Indiana University Press, 1979.

[7] D. S. Jurafsky and J. H. Martin. *Speech and Language Processing: An Introduction to Natural Language Processing, Computational Linguistics, and Speech Recognition*. Prentice Hall, New Jersey, 2000.

[8] M. Magnus. *Gods of the Word : Archetypes in the Consonants*. Truman State University Press, 1999.

[9] M. Magnus. *What's in a Word? Studies in Phonosemantics*. PhD thesis, University of Trondheims, Norway, 2001.

[10] V. Nastase, M. Sokolova, and J. Sayyad Shirabad. Do happy words sound happy? a study of the relation between form and meaning for english words expressing emotions. In *Proceedings of the Recent Advances in Natural Language Processing (RANLP'2007)*, pages 406 – 410, 2007.

[11] C. Strapparava and R. Mihalcea. Semeval-2007 task 14: Affective text. In *Proceedings of the 2008 ACM symposium on Applied computing*, 2008.

[12] C. Strapparava, A. Valitutti, and O. Stock. The affective weight of the lexicon. In *Proceedings of the 5th International Conference on Language Resources and Evaluation*, pages 474–481, 2006.

[13] R. Tarte and M. O'Boyle. Semantic judgements of compressed monosyllables: Evidence for phonetic symbolism. *Journal of Psycholingual Research*, 11(3):183–196, 1982.

[14] D. Tufis, B. Mititelu, L. Bozianu, and C. Mihaila. Romanian wordnet: New developments and applications. In *Proceedings of the 3rd Conference of the Global WordNet Association*, pages 337–344, 2006.

[15] W. von Humboldt. *Über die Verschiedenheit des Menschlichen Sprachbauesund ihren Einflu auf die geistige Entwicklung des Menschengeschlechts*. Druckerei der Königlichen Akademie, 1836; reprinted: 1960.

Classification of Opinions with Non-affective Adverbs and Adjectives

Marina Sokolova
EHIL,
Children's Hospital of Eastern Ontario
Ottawa, Ontario, Canada
msokolova@ehealthinformation.ca

Guy Lapalme
RALI,
Université de Montréal
Montréal, Québec, Canada
lapalme@iro.umontreal.ca

Abstract

We propose domain-independent language patterns that purposefully omit the affective words for the classification of opinions. The information extracted with those patterns is then used to analyze opinions expressed in the texts. Empirical evidence shows that opinions can be discovered without the use of affective words. We ran experiments on four sets of reviews of consumer goods: books, DVD, electronics, kitchen, and house ware. Our results support the practical use of our approach and its competitiveness in comparison with other data-driven methods. This method can also be applied to analyze texts which do not explicitly disclose affects such as medical and legal documents.

1 Introduction

Opinion and sentiment analysis has recently received much attention from researchers in the Natural Language Processing (NLP) and Machine Learning (ML) communities. Most of the research addresses the primary clues of sentiments in a binary setting, e.g. positive/negative word orientation (good vs evil), subjective/objective statements (The movie was awesome vs We saw the movie yesterday), texts belonging to positive/negative opinion categories (I recommend this camera ... vs This book is awful ...). In this work, we concentrate on learning opinion from complete texts, classifying the texts as positive or negative.

In opinion learning, NLP and ML research mainly concentrates on the emotional *polarity* of texts which is expressed through the use of affective words (This is an excellent view shows positive polarity, excellent is an affective word). In this work, we, however, propose that learning opinions should allow for the use of the word categories other than affective. We present a method which uses non-affective adjectives and adverbs (future, full, perhaps), supplemented by degree pronouns and mental and modal verbs, to determine whether a text bears a positive or a negative opinion label.

The method engineers features by using the intrinsic characteristics of a language and avoids extensive and elaborate computational mechanism. Methods used to classify complete texts according to opinions and sentiments usually employ automated feature selection, e.g., [17, 15]. Although such methods can be applied to different domains, they sometimes involve complex optimization problems, e.g., NP-hard approximation problems [2].

We concentrate on expressions of stance (maybe, necessary), degree (extremely, any), time (ago, now), frequency (rare, again), size (short, high), quantity (many, few), and extent (big). We show that these indicators reliably represent texts in opinion learning. We organize the corresponding word categories – stance/degree/time/frequency adverbs, frequency/size/quantity adjectives, degree pronouns – into a semantic hierarchy. Its lowest level works with words; the middle level generalizes word categories into groups; the highest level applies to the text as a whole. The hierarchy avoids the use of emotionally-charged words. We use the hierarchy to extract lexical features from texts. Next, we use the features to represent texts in a series of machine learning experiments.

Empirical evidence obtained on four data sets shows reliability of our approach. The presented method can be applied to analyze texts which do not explicitly disclose affects, e.g., medical and legal documents. This work extends preliminary studies presented in [22]. The rest of the presentation is organized as follows: we introduce word categories used in the test representation, then the hierarchy is presented, followed by description of the information extraction procedure and empirical results; discussion of related work, results and future work conclude the paper.

2 Text representation

Studies of sentiment and subjectivity analysis mostly concentrate on the use of the affective words in expression of sentiments and opinions. Some opinion studies use topic and domain words and affect-neutral verbs [18, 21]. We propose that words which emphasize quantitative properties (high, some), time (old, yesterday) and confidence in happening (can, necessary, probably) can be used in learning opinions.

Such words constitute detailed, *specific*, description of an object or action [4, 9]. We organize them in the following word categories:

1. pronouns of degree (everybody);
2. adverbs
   (a) time (yesterday),
   (b) frequency (often, rarely),
   (c) degree (only),
   (d) stance (necessary);
3. adjectives
   (a) size/quantity/extent (large),
   (b) time (old),
   (c) relational (different);
4. comparative and superlative adjectives of the listed above categories (largest, older);
5. order words
   (a) ordinal numbers (third)
   (b) cardinal numbers (two);
6. stance verbs
   (a) modal verbs (could)
   (b) mental verbs (believe).

We use word categories 1 – 5 to build the entry level for the hierarchical text representation. To be less domain and topic-dependent, we ignore subcategories closely related to the text topics, e.g., derived (useless), topical (royal,economic), affiliative (American), foreign (ersatz) [4]. We purposefully omit evaluative/emotive adjectives (excellent, disgusting) while constructing the lexical level of hierarchy. This omission allows emphasis on the role of quantitative description in text.

3 Semantic Hierarchy

In this section, we introduce a hierarchy of text representation. Starting from the bottom, the hierarchy defines the word categories used in detailed descriptions, then groups the categories into four types of comments, and finally combines the types into direct and indirect detailed categories. The levels of the hierarchy are represented by a set of rules which capture the essential characteristics of their language indicators. The rules have the following form:

$$\textit{non-terminal} \quad \rightarrow \quad \text{alternative}_1 \mid \text{alternative}_2 \mid \ldots$$

where *non-terminal* must be replaced by one of the alternatives. Alternatives are composed of other non-terminals and `terminals` which are the pieces of the final lexical string. The lowest, lexical, level presents terminals for the word categories discussed in Section 2. The middle level organizes word categories into semantic groups. The highest, the most general, level is concerned with text pragmatics.

We determined the list of terminals by finding seed words for these word categories in [4, 6] and added their synonyms from an electronic version of Roget's Interactive Thesaurus [20]. To accommodate negative comments, we added the negation rule. There are 303 rule terminals, not counting the negation terminals. Figure 1 shows the rules for finding detailed descriptions in text; within a hierarchy level, the rules are listed in alphabetical order.

We now list some implications of the rules presented by Figure 1:

direct Details presents primary clues of quantitative evaluation and attributes of the discussed issues. Two rules of the middle level provide factual information through the word categories of the lowest level:

Estimation lists the reference attributes: physical parameters, relative and absolute time.

Quantification expresses the broadness of the discussed reference by specifying its multiplicity, frequency and extent.

indirect Details presents secondary clues of the issue evaluation. Two rules of the middle level define indirect evaluation through the word categories of the lowest level:

Comparison presents a comparative evaluation of the discussed issues, their qualities and relations among them.

Confidence reflects on the certainty about the happening of events;

4 Feature Set Construction

We hypothesize that expressed opinions can be accurately learned from non-affective adverbs and adjectives. To evaluate our hypothesis, we apply the hierarchy to find and extract features for text representation. Our core assumption is the following: the hierarchy rule terminals emphasize important characteristics of the discussed issues.

Grammatically, the rule terminals are modifiers, amplifiers and identifiers. In sentences, such words usually precede their references, especially in conversational text [4]. The extraction of words which follow the rule terminals results in the set of words most emphasized in the text. The extraction procedure is presented on Figure 2; it has only one adjustable parameter h, whose value is determined during the empirical step.

To build the set of words most emphasized in the text, we look for words with a high probability of appearance on the right side of the rule terminal. We

direct Details	$\rightarrow$	[*negation*] (*Estimation* | *Quantification*)
indirect Details	$\rightarrow$	[*negation*](*Comparison* | *Confidence*)
Comparison	$\rightarrow$	*adjComparat* | *adjRelation* | *adjSuperlat* | *numOrdinal*
Confidence	$\rightarrow$	*advStance* | *verbCognition* | *verbModal*
Estimation	$\rightarrow$	*adjPhysical* | *adjTemp* | *advTime*
Quantification	$\rightarrow$	*adjDegree* | *advDegree* | *advFrequen* | *numCardinal* | *pronDegree*
adjComparat	$\rightarrow$	`longer` | `smaller` | `older` | ...
adjDegree	$\rightarrow$	`full` | `rare` | `usual` | ...
adjPhysical	$\rightarrow$	`deep` | `long` | `small` | ...
adjRelation	$\rightarrow$	`same` | `different` | ...
adjSuperlat	$\rightarrow$	`highest` | `longest` | `oldest` | ...
adjTemp	$\rightarrow$	`belated` | `future` | `new` | ...
advDegree	$\rightarrow$	`extremely` | `only` | `roughly` | ...
advFrequen	$\rightarrow$	`often` | `rarely` | `sometimes` | ...
advStance	$\rightarrow$	`necessarily` | `perhaps` | `probably` | ...
advTime	$\rightarrow$	`ever` | `now` | `yesterday` ...
numCardinal	$\rightarrow$	`one` | `two` | ...
numOrdinal	$\rightarrow$	`first` | `second` | ...
pronDegree	$\rightarrow$	`everybody` | `few` | `some` | ...
verbCognition	$\rightarrow$	`believe` | `know` | `think`
verbModal	$\rightarrow$	`can` | `could` | `may` | `might` | ...
negation	$\rightarrow$	`not` | `no` | `can't` | `none` | ...

Fig. 1: *Rules for the identification of detailed comments in text. "|" separate alternatives, square brackets indicate optional parts and parenthesis are used for grouping. Terminals are written in this* `font`.

Step 1 build a bigram model of the data:

1. for sequences $w_{j-1}w_j, j = 1, ..., m$, calculate the probabilities of their occurrence in the data;
2. disregard the sequences with the probability of 0;

Step 2 find words appearing on the right side of the terminal:

1. for each $t_i \in T$, extract bigrams $t_i w_j$ where the pattern terminals appear on the left side;
2. build the unigram model of the extracted bigrams;
3. remove the terminal unigrams;

Step 3 find frequently modified and intensified words:

1. determine the parameter h;
2. keep w_j with $n(w_j|t_i) > h$.

Fig. 2: *The procedure for finding and extracting frequently modified and intensified words in text. The procedure uses the same notations as equations (1) and (2). The adjustable parameter h is determined empirically.*

estimate this probability $P(w_j|T)$ by computing:

$$P(w_j|T) = \sum_{t_i \in T} P(w_j|t_i), \quad (1)$$

$$P(w_j|t_i) = \frac{n(w_j|t_i)}{\sum_{j=1}^{m} n(w_j)} \quad (2)$$

where w_j is a word, T is the set of all terminals, t_i is a terminal, $w_j|t_i$ is the event where the word w_j appears after t_i in text ($t_i w_j$), m is the size of the data vocabulary, $n(x)$ is the number of occurrences of x in the data.

The idea behind the search procedure is the following: two-word sequences $t_i w_j$ - bigrams - which have terminals on their left side capture the modified and intensified words. After extracting such bigrams, we find modified and intensified words. By calculating the probability of the word occurrence after a terminal, we can find most frequently modified and intensified words. Concentrating on one-side bigrams prevents the multiple extraction of the same word.

In supervised learning experiments, each text is represented by a vector $x_1, \ldots, x_n, y$, where x_i is a number of occurrences a word w_i, a feature, appearing in the text, and y is the opinion label. As a weighting factor, we use normalization of the vector attributes with respect to the number of words in the text. It eliminates the bias introduced by the length of the text. Based on the rule terminals and the extracted words, we construct three feature sets for text representation:

I terminals of *direct Details* rules enhanced by personal pronouns; h was determined by frequencies of personal pronouns;

II terminals of all the hierarchy rules enhanced by the most frequent extracted extracted words; h was determined by frequencies of personal pronouns;

III the terminals and all the words extracted by the procedure presented in Figure 2; the cut-off threshold $h = 5$ was determined by using Katz smoothing to ensure reliability of data representation.

5 Empirical results

We ran experiments on data introduced in [5]. There are four sets of reviews of different consumer goods: books, DVD, electronics, kitchen and houseware. Each data set has 2000 labelled examples, all evenly split on 1000 positive and 1000 negative examples. Blitzer et al. deleted reviews they considered as having ambiguous opinions. A typical review contained abundance of information assigned to several fields: (**i**) product name, (**ii**) product type, (**iii**) unique id which often summarized the review contents, (**iv**) product rating, (**v**) review helpfulness rating, (**vi**) the review title, (**vii**) the date, (**viii**) the review text, etc.

For this study, we extracted the review texts; see Figure 3 for samples of the extracted reviews; in those texts we have marked the features presented by the hierarchy (Figure 1) and constructed through the procedure (Section 4) . Correspondence among information provided by different fields is left for future work. Review texts are long enough to provide meaningful communication and lexical information; Table 1 lists the descriptive statistics of the extracted data. These four sets allow us to compare our empirical results with those obtained by other methods. In order to establish how a speaker's detailed descriptions are related to her opinion, we apply *supervised learning* techniques that construct a function on a set of input and output pairs $(\vec{x}, y)$ where $\vec{x}$ represents a text and y is its opinion label (training data). This function is then used to predict opinion labels on previously unseen examples (testing data).

We want to establish a link between information extracted by patterns and the text opinion categories, e.g. positive or negative. We expect non-linear dependencies between the terminals' appearance in texts and a speaker's opinion. We applied decision-based C4.5, prototype-based K-NEAREST NEIGHBOR and kernel-based SUPPORT VECTOR MACHINE (SVM). SVM performed considerably better than other algorithms on all the four data sets. The algorithm is known for its high accuracy in text classification. SVM does not make any assumption about the data distribution and could work with non-linear dependencies, albeit on one level of learning. Further we report only the SVM's results. We use the Weka's implementation [1]. Classification measures use the following counts:

Data class	Classified as *pos*	Classified as *neg*
pos	*tp*	*fn*
neg	*fp*	*tn*

$$Accuracy = \frac{tp + tn}{tp + fn + fp + tn} \quad (3)$$

evaluates the overall performance of SVM; *tp* and *tn* provide a detailed analysis of the algorithm's performance on positive and negative classes. We use tenfold cross-validation to compute the three measures because of its generalization accuracy and the reliability of its results.

We compare text representations built on the three levels of rules presented by Figure 1. Table 2 reports learning results obtained on the three representations introduced in Section 4. As the baseline, we apply SVM on texts represented by the feature set *I*. All 62 selected words appear frequently in the data and provide substantial information about texts. These features include adverbs of degree and adverbs of frequency which were used by [3] in sentiment classification. Adding all *II* features makes a statistically significant difference in accuracy (paired t-test,

[1] http://www.cs.waikato.ac.nz/ml/weka/

Book Reviews	
Extracted review sample	Label
This thing sat on *my* shelf, half-read for *the* **longest** time. **Only** *the* notice of *the* upcoming release *this* November of Pynchon's **next** got *me* motivated **enough** to dig into *it* **again**. *It's* **not** that *it* **isn't** brilliant. **No one else** around **can** dazzle *you* with **so much** wit *and* wonder. The **first** encounter with *the* talking dog is *as* magical *as* **anything** *you*'ll **ever** read. *And* it's **not** *like* this is *the* **only** Pynchon novel that takes **some** effort to get into.	pos
I picked up *the* **first** book in this series (The Eyre Affair) based **purely** on *its* premise and was left **somewhat** underwhelmed. **Still**, *the* potential for the series seemed **so large** that *I* went ahead and *read* this **second one too** ...	neg
Kitchen and Houseware Reviews	
Extracted review sample	Label
i absolutely love *this* product. *my* neighbor has **four little** yippers *and my* shepard/chow mix was antogonized by *the* yipping on *our* side of *the* fence. *I* hung *the* device on *my* side of *the* fence *and the* noise keeps *the* neighbors dog from picking "arguments" with *my* dog. **all** barking *and* fighting has ceased. **all** *the* surrounding neighbor as *well* as *me* **can** get a *good* nights sleep **now**	pos
He **just** looks **away** from where *the* spray emits–*and* barks **again**! *It* **also** doesn't work 100 % of *the* time...and *we're* not sure why. When *we* fill *it*, *it* seems to work **fairly** *well* **right after** but *it* **either** does not have as **many** sprays as *it* is supposed to, or *it* isn't working **very long**. *It* does work *well* for *my* **other small** dog who is **not such** a persistent barker. Terriers are **just too** stubborn to care if *they're* getting sprayed, *I* guess.	neg

Fig. 3: *Samples of the extracted reviews. Terminals of rules in Figure 1 are in* **bold**; *the words found by procedure in Figure 2 are in italics; negations are ignored if they do not appear before the rule terminals. For each data set, the upper sample has a positive opinion label that labels the whole text whereas the lower sample has a negative opinion label.*

Table 1: *Customer-written reviews from Amazon.com pre-processed by J. Blitzer et al (2007). Texts (from all four data) they considered as ambiguous opinions were deleted.*

Data	# examp	# pos	# neg	Tokens	Types	Aver length
Books	2000	1000	1000	349530	39811	175
DVD	2000	1000	1000	337473	39776	169
Electronics	2000	1000	1000	222862	20664	111
Kitchen	2000	1000	1000	188137	17296	99

$P = 0.010$). When we use all the extracted words, the statistically significant difference increases (paired t-test, $P = 0.003$). For each representation, the classification results are close across the data sets. However, there is a remarkable difference between the Electronics data and the three other sets. Let's consider true classification of the positive and negative reviews. For Books, DVD, Kitchen sets, the positive reviews are always classified more correctly than the negative reviews (the only exception is a tie for Books on the II representation). The Electronics set provides the opposite results: the negative reviews are always classified more correctly then the positive ones.

It is interesting to observe that only 303 rule terminals, i.e., the *II* features, already provide an opinion accuracy of 74% – 78%. These are reliable results for opinion learning, since human agreement on whether a message provides a positive or a negative opinion about the discussed topic could be 78% for positive opinions (*tp*) and 74% for negative opinions (*tn*) [16]. On the four data sets, all extracted features provide accuracy of more than 80%. There are 1999 terminals and extracted words used. Reported *tp* and *tn* show that the extracted features provide a well-balanced classification of the classes: on all the four data sets difference between *tp* and *tn* is < 10%. This can be only achieved if the algorithm is successful in learning both positive and negative classes.

6 Related work

Opinion and sentiment analysis that focuses on whether a text is subjective, bears positive or negative opinion or expresses the strength of an opinion has received a vast amount of attention in the recent years. In this section, we discuss only research with application to *complete texts*, which sometimes are referred to

Table 2: SVM*'s classification accuracy of positive and negative opinions, in per cent. Accuracy (Acc) shows how effective is the approach in prediction of previously unseen examples, tp – prediction of positive examples, tn – prediction of negative examples. All the reported values are obtained with near-linear kernels (*exp $= 0.75, \ldots, 0.92$*) and a small error penalty for misclassification of training examples (*$C = 1.05, \ldots, 1.21$*).*

Data	Text Features								
	I			*II*			III		
	Acc	*tp*	*tn*	*Acc*	*tp*	*tn*	*Acc*	*tp*	*tn*
Books	68.70	69.00	68.40	74.75	74.70	74.80	**80.20**	81.05	79.35
DVD	70.80	73.25	68.35	73.80	76.70	70.90	**80.50**	84.10	76.80
Electronics	69.50	66.50	72.50	75.70	74.25	76.95	**82.40**	76.85	87.85
Kitchen	69.10	70.05	68.15	76.50	78.25	74.75	**85.20**	88.20	82.20

as documents. We omit research on sentiment/opinion analysis of terms, phrases, sentences and other text segments; references and discussion can be found in [7].

Some of this work relied on a list of characteristics of reviewed products. Hu and Liu extracted features based on association rule mining algorithms in conjunction with frequency to extract main product characteristics [10]. These characteristics are then used to extract adjacent adjectives which are assumed to be opinion adjectives. Later, these opinion adjectives are used to find product characteristics that are mentioned only once or few times. In contrast, we opted for a domain-independent method that does not involve the use of the domain's content words. Popescu and Etzioni (2005) extracted product characteristics from noun phases in the data and matched them with known product features. In contrast, we opted for a domain-independent method that does not involve the use of the domain's content words.

For automating recognition and the evaluation of the expressed opinion, complete texts are represented through N-grams or patterns and then classified as opinion/non-opinion, positive/negative, etc. [19]. In [5], the authors combine supervised and semi-supervised structural correspondence learning to classify the four data sets. They use fully automated feature selection based on frequency and the mutual information of words. However, the difference in evaluation technique does not allow us to directly compare the obtained results.

Syntactic and semantic features that express the intensity of terms are used to classify the text opinion intensity [23]. Benamara et al. studies the impact of combining adverbs of degree with adjectives for the purpose of opinion evaluation [3]. Our approach deals instead with opinion analysis which is broader than the analysis of sentiments. We focus on the formalization and utilization of non-emotional lexical features.

Except sentiment analysis, machine learning is used to study opinions from the point of view of predictive power [12], strength [23], and also in summarization and feature extraction studies [8]. Although Kim and Hovy (2007) generalized bi- and trigrams found in texts (e.g. NDP will win and Liberals will win became Party will win), they did it bottom-up, without providing theoretical background. We, instead, used a top-down hierarchical approach based on pragmatic and lexical rules. Wilson et al (2006) concentrated on learning subjective vs objective sentences and sentence clauses. Their initial manual clues included verbs of judgment (reprove, vilify); in the final text representation they use syntax clues. In contrast, to represent texts, we look for non-affective adverbs and adjectives.

Consumer and expert-written product reviews are intensively studied by psychology, marketing, etc. [14]. Kamakura et al. analyzed movie reviews written by 46 experts [11]. They were one of the first to do research on the information contained in unguided reviews and built a model linking the expert's history of movie evaluations and quantitative information found in reviews. However, the authors did not actually analyze the texts or language cues contained in the reviews. Their results showed that experts are not uniformly informative across movies that they scored differently. This study supports our views that specific information in product reviews relates to the speaker's opinion, although their results were obtained on expert-written reviews.

The research listed above does not consider a hierarchy of opinion disclosure. A pragmatic-lexical hierarchy of semantic verb categories was proposed in our previous work [21]. We showed that the hierarchy worked well in environment where negative opinions were expressed indirectly, without the use of negative adjectives or adverbs, e.g. debates in the US federal Senate. In contrast, in the current work, we concentrated on the use of non-affective adverbs and adjectives and degree pronouns.

7 Conclusion and future work

We have proposed a hierarchical text representation (the highest level that considers a text as a whole) and derived rules (the middle level), as well as the rules' terminal categories (the lowest level that works with words). The terminals were used to extract the emphasized information from the text. Our goal was to build domain-independent rules that do not rely on domain content words and emotional words. Further, the additionally extracted words and the rule terminals were used to represent texts in learning experiments.

In our experiments, we used four data sets which texts were gathered in different domains. We studied the relevance of detailed, specific words to the learning of positive and negative opinions. Our empirical results show that the corresponding lexical features are effective in learning opinions.

Our approach can be applied to analyze language in texts which traditionally lack emotive and affective words. Medical and legal domains provide us with such texts. It is worth note that these two domains attract more and more attention of Text Data Mining community as evidenced by many publications, for example, in the Journal of the American Medical Informatics Association [2] and the International Journal of Law and Information Technology [3]. Another venue can be a joint analysis of information contained in different fields of reviews.

In this study, we applied supervised learning algorithms that required labeled data, which is usually restricted. Our future work will be to incorporate unlabeled data and apply semi-supervised approaches, e.g., a framework of learning predictive structures [1]. A notable drawback of this framework is the need to find "good" features for data representation. We can overcome this problem by using the results of the current study. Another direction worth trying is to incorporate more pragmatic knowledge into feature construction, e.g., likelihood of the use of features in written or spoken language obtained from the British National Corpus [13].

Acknowledgements

This work was partially supported by the Natural Sciences and Engineering Research Council of Canada and the Ontario Centre of Excellence.

References

[1] R. Ando and T. Zhang. A framework for learning predictive structures from multiple tasks and unlabeled data. *Journal of Machine Learning Research*, 6:1817–1853, 2005.

[2] S. Ben-David, J. Blitzer, K. Crammer, and F. Pereira. Analysis of representataions for domain adaptation. In *Neural Information Processing Systems*, 2006.

[3] F. Benamara, C. Cesarano, A. Picariello, D. Reforgiato, and V. Subrahmanian. Sentiment analysis: Adjectives and adverbs are better than the adjectives alone. In *Proceedings of International Conference on Weblogs and Social Media (ICWSM'2007)*, 2007.

[4] D. Biber, S. Johansson, G. Leech, S. Conrad, and E. Finegan. *Longman Grammar of Spoken and Written English*. Longman, 1999.

[2] http://www.jamia.org/

[3] http://ijlit.oxfordjournals.org/

[5] J. Blitzer, M. Dredze, and F. Pereira. Biographies, bollywood, boom-boxes and blenders: Domain adaptation for sentiment classification. In *Proceedings of the 45th Annual Meeting of the Association of Computational Linguistics*, pages 440–447. Association for Computational Linguistics, 2007.

[6] D. Bolinger. *Degree Words*. Mouton De Gruyter, 1972.

[7] E. Breck, Y. Choi, and C. Cardie. Identifying expressions of opinion in context. In *Proceedings of the Twentieth International Joint Conference on Artificial Intelligence (IJCAI-2007)*, pages 2683–2688, 2007.

[8] O. Feiguina and G. Lapalme. Query-based summarization of customer reviews. In *Proceedings of the 20th Canadian Conference on Artificial Intelligence (AI'2007)*, pages 452–463, 2007.

[9] M. Hamilton. Extending an information processing model of language intensity effects. *Journal of Language and Social Psychology*, 17:109–143, 1998.

[10] M. Hu and B. Liu. Mining and summarizing customer reviews. In *Proceedings of the 10th ACM SIGKDD International Conf on Knowledge Discovery and Data Mining (KDD'04)*, pages 168–177, 2004.

[11] W. Kamakura, S. Basuroy, and P. Boatwright. Is silence golden? an inquiry into the meaning of silence in professional product evaluations. *Quantitative Marketing and Economics*, 4:119–141, 2006.

[12] S.-M. Kim and E. Hovy. Crystal: Analyzing predictive opinions on the web. In *Proceedings of the 2007 Joint Conference on Empirical Methods in Natural Language Processing and Computational Natural Language Learning (EMNLP-CoNLL)*, pages 1056–1064, 2007.

[13] G. Leech, P. Rayson, and A. Wilson. *Word Frequencies in Written and Spoken English: based on the British National Corpus*. Longman, 2001.

[14] B. Loken. Consumer psychology: Categorization, inferences, affect, and persuasion. *Annual Review of Psychology*, 57:453–485, 2006.

[15] V. Ng, S. Dasgupta, and S. M. N. Arifin. Examining the role of linguistic knowledge sources in the automatic identification and classification of reviews. In *Proceedings of the COLING/ACL 2006 Main Conference Poster Sessions*, pages 611–618. Association for Computational Linguistics, 2006.

[16] K. Nigam and M. Hurst. Towards a robust metric of opinion. In *Proceedings of the AAAI Spring Symposium on Exploring Attitude and Affect in Text*, pages 98–105. AAAI, 2004.

[17] B. Pang and L. Lee. Seeing stars: Exploiting class relationships for sentiment categorization with respect to rating scales. In *Proceedings of the 43rd Annual Meeting of the Association for Computational Linguistics (ACL'05)*, pages 115–124. Association for Computational Linguistics, 2005.

[18] A. Popescu and O. Etzioni. Extracting product features and opinions from reviews. In *Proceedings of HLTC/EMNLP 2005*, pages 339 – 346, 2005.

[19] E. Riloff, S. Patwardhan, and J. Wiebe. Feature subsumption for opinion analysis. In *Proceedings of the 2006 Conference on Empirical Methods in Natural Language Processing*, pages 440–448. Association for Computational Linguistics, 2006.

[20] roget. Roget's interactive thesaurus, 2006. http://thesaurus.reference.com/.

[21] M. Sokolova and G. Lapalme. Verbs speak loud: Verb categories in learning polarity and strength of opinions. In *Proceedings of the 21st Canadian Conference on Artificial Intelligence (AI'2008)*, pages 320–331. Springer, 2008.

[22] M. Sokolova and G. Lapalme. Learning opinions without using emotional words. In *Proceedings of the 22nd Canadian Conference on Artificial Intelligence (AI'2009)*, pages 253–256. Springer, 2009.

[23] T. Wilson, J. Wiebe, and R. Hwa. Recognizing strong and weak opinion clauses. *Computational Intelligence*, 22(2):73–99, 2006.

Amharic Part-of-Speech Tagger for Factored Language Modeling

Martha Yifiru Tachbelie and Wolfgang Menzel
Department of Informatics, University of Hamburg
Vogt-Kölln Srt. 30, D-22527 Hamburg, Germany
tachbeli, menzel@informatik.uni-hamburg.de

Abstract

This paper presents Amharic part of speech taggers developed for factored language modeling. Hidden Markov Model (HMM) and Support Vector Machine (SVM) based taggers have been trained using the TnT and SVMTool. The overall accuracy of the best performing TnT- and SVM-based taggers is 82.99% and 85.50%, respectively. Generally, with respect to accuracy SVM-based taggers perform better than TnT-based taggers although TnT-based taggers are more efficient with regard to speed and memory requirement. We have developed factored language models (with two and four parents) for which the estimation of the probability for each word depends on the previous one or two words and their POS. These language models have been used in an Amharic speech recognition task in a lattice rescoring framework and a significant improvement in word recognition accuracy has been observed.

Keywords

POS tagging, Amharic, factored language model

1 Introduction

Language models are fundamental to many natural language applications such as automatic speech recognition (ASR). The most widely used class of language models, namely statistical ones, provide an estimate of the probability of a word sequence W for a given task. However, the probability distribution depends on the available training data — large amounts of training data are required so as to ensure statistical significance.

Even if a large training corpus is available, there may be still many possible word sequences which will not be encountered at all, or which appear with a statistically insignificant frequency (data sparseness problem) [21]. In morphologically rich languages, there are even individual words that might not be encountered in the training data irrespective of its size (Out-Of-Vocabulary words problem).

The data sparseness problem in statistical language modeling is more serious for languages with a rich morphology. These languages have a high vocabulary growth rate which results in a high perplexity and a large number of out of vocabulary words [19]. Therefore, sub-words (morphemes), instead of words, have been and are being used as modeling units in language modeling so as to build more robust language models even if only insufficient training data is available.

1.1 The morphology of Amharic

Amharic is one of the morphologically rich languages. It is a major language spoken mainly in Ethiopia and belongs to the Semitic branch of the Afro-Asiatic super family. Amharic is related to Hebrew, Arabic and Syrian.

Like other Semitic languages such as Arabic, Amharic exhibits a root-pattern morphological phenomenon. A root is a set of consonants (called radicals) which has a basic 'lexical' meaning. A pattern consists of a set of vowels which are inserted (intercalated) among the consonants of a root to form a stem. The pattern is combined with a particular prefix or suffix to create a single grammatical form [4] or another stem [20]. For example, the Amharic root sbr means 'break', when we intercalate the pattern ä_ä and attach the suffix ä we get säbbärä 'he broke' which is the first form of a verb (3rd person masculine singular in past tense as in other semitic languages) [4]. In addition to this non-concatenative morphological feature, Amharic uses different affixes to create inflectional and derivational word forms.

Some adverbs can be derived from adjectives. Nouns are derived from other basic nouns, adjectives, stems, roots, and the infinitive form of a verb by affixation and intercalation. For example, from the noun lIğğ 'child' another noun lIğnät 'childhood'; from the adjective däg 'generous' the noun dägnät 'generosity'; from the stem sInIf, the noun sInIfna 'laziness'; from root qld, the noun qäld 'joke'; from infinitive verb mäsIbär 'to break' the noun mäsIbäriya 'an instrument used for breaking' can be derived. Case, number, definiteness, and gender marker affixes inflect nouns.

Adjectives are derived from nouns, stems or verbal roots by adding a prefix or a suffix. For example, it is possible to derive dIngayama 'stony' from the noun dIngay 'stone'; zIngu 'forgetful' from the stem zIng; sänäf 'lazy' from the root snf by suffixation and intercalation. Adjectives can also be formed through compounding. For instance, hodäsäfi 'tolerant, patient', is derived by compounding the noun hod 'stomach' and the adjective säfi 'wide'. Like nouns, adjectives are inflected for gender, number, and case [20].

Unlike the other word categories such as noun and adjectives, the derivation of verbs from other parts of

International Conference RANLP 2009 - Borovets, Bulgaria, pages 428–433

speech is not common. The conversion of a root to a basic verb stem requires both intercalation and affixation. For instance, from the root gdl 'kill' we obtain the perfective verb stem gäddäl- by intercalating the pattern ä_ä. From this perfective stem, it is possible to derive a passive (tägäddäl-) and a causative stem (asgäddäl-) using the prefixes tä- and as-, respectively. Other verb forms are also derived from roots in a similar fashion.

Verbs are inflected for person, gender, number, aspect, tense and mood [20]. Other elements like negative markers also inflect verbs in Amharic.

1.2 Language modeling for Amharic

Since Amharic is a morphologically rich language, it suffers from data sparseness and out of vocabulary words problems. The negative effect of Amharic morphology on language modeling has been reported by [1], who, therefore, recommended the development of sub-word based language models for Amharic.

To this end, [17, 18] have developed various morpheme-based language models for Amharic and gained a substantial reduction in the out-of-vocabulary rate. They have concluded that, in this regard, using sub-word units is preferable for the development of language models for Amharic. In their experiment, [17, 18] considered individual morphemes as units of a language model. This, however, might result in a loss of word level dependencies since the root consonants of the words may stand too far apart. Therefore, approaches that capture word level dependencies are required to model the Amharic language. [12] introduced factored language models that can capture word level dependency while using morphemes as units in language modeling. That is why we opted for developing factored language models also for Amharic.

1.3 Factored language modeling

Factored language models (FLM) have first been introduced in [13] for incorporating various morphological information in Arabic language modeling. In FLM a word is viewed as a bundle or vector of K parallel factors, that is, $w_n \equiv f_n^1, f_n^2, ..., f_n^k$. The factors of a given word can be the word itself, stem, root, pattern, morphological classes, or any other linguistic element into which a word can be decomposed. The goal of an FLM is, therefore, to produce a statistical model over these factors.

There are two important points in the development of FLM: choosing the appropriate factors which can be done based on linguistic knowledge or using a data driven technique and finding the best statistical model over these factors. Unlike normal word or morpheme-based language models, in FLM there is no obvious natural backoff order. In a trigram word based model, for instance, we backoff to a bigram if a particular trigram sequence has not been observed in our corpus by dropping the most distant neighbor, and so on. However, in FLM the factors can be temporally equivalent and it is not obvious which factor to drop first during backoff. If we consider a quadrogram FLM and if we drop one factor at a time, we can have six possible backoff paths as it is depicted in Figure 1 and we need to choose a path that results in a better model. Therefore, choosing a backoff path is an important decision one has to make in FLM. There are three possible ways of choosing a backoff path: 1) Choosing a fixed path based on linguistic or other reasonable knowledge; 2) Generalized all-child backoff where multiple backoff paths are chosen at run time; and 3) Generalized constrained-child backoff where a subset of backoff paths is chosen at run time [14]. A genetic algorithm for learning the structure of a factored language model has been developed by [7].

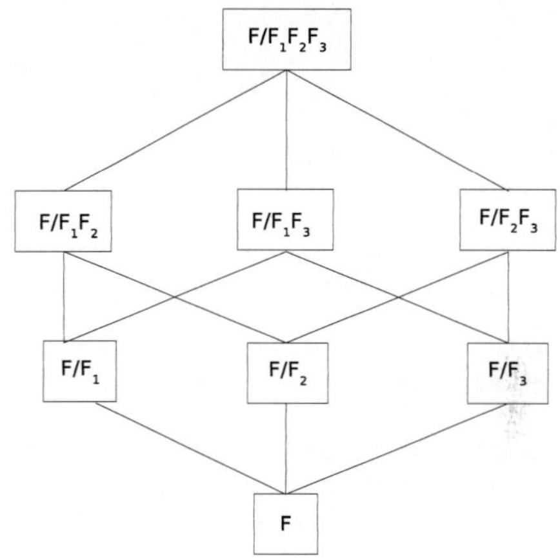

Fig. 1: *Possible backoff paths*

In addition to capturing the word level dependencies, factored language models also enable us to integrate any kind of relevant information to a language model. Part of speech (POS) or morphological class information, for instance, might improve the quality of a language model as knowing the POS of a word can tell us what words are likely to occur in its neighborhood [11]. For this purpose, however, a POS tagger is needed which is able to automatically assign POS information to the word forms in a sentence. This paper presents the development of Amharic POS taggers and the use of POS information in language modeling.

1.4 Previous works on POS tagging

[9] attempted to develop a Hidden Markov Model (HMM) based POS tagger for Amharic. He extracted a total of 23 POS tags from a page long text (300 words) which is also used for training and testing the POS tagger. The tagger does not have the capability of guessing the POS tag of unknown words, and consequently all the unknown words are assigned a UNC tag, which stands for unknown category. As the lexicon used is very small and the tagger is not able to deal with unknown words, many of the words from the test set were assigned the UNC tag.

[3] developed a POS tagger using Conditional Random Fields. Instead of using the POS tagset developed by [9], [3] developed another abstract tagset (consisting of 10 tags) by collapsing some of the categories proposed by [9]. He trained the tagger on a manually annotated text corpus of five Amharic news articles (1000 words) and obtained an accuracy of 74%.

As the data sets used to train both of the above systems are very small it is not possible to apply the taggers to large amounts of text which is needed for training a language model.

In a very recent, but independent development, a POS tagging experiment similar to the one described in this paper has been conducted by [8]. There, three tagging strategies have been compared – Hidden Markov Models (HMM), Support Vector Machines (SVM) and Maximum Entropy (ME) – using the manually annotated corpus [6] (which has also been used in our experiment) developed at the Ethiopian Language Research Center (ELRC) of the Addis Ababa University. Since the corpus contains a few errors and tagging inconsistencies, they cleaned the corpus. Cleaning includes tagging non-tagged items, correcting some tagging errors and misspellings, merging collocations tagged with a single tag, and tagging punctuations (such as '"' and '/') consistently. They have used three tagsets: the one used in [3], the original tagset developed at ELRC that consists of 30 tags and the 11 basic classes of the ELRC tagset. The average accuracies (after 10-fold cross validation) are 85.56, 88.30, 87.87 for the TnT-, SVM- and maximum entropy based taggers, respectively for the ELRC tagset. They also found that the maximum entropy tagger performs best among the three systems, when allowed to select its own folds. Their result also shows that the SVM-based tagger outperforms the other ones in classifying unknown words and in the overall accuracy for the tagset (ELRC) that is used in our experiment too.

Categories	Tags
Verbal Noun	VN
Noun with prep.	NP
Noun with conj.	NC
Noun with prep. & conj.	NPC
Any other noun	N
Pronoun with prep.	PRONP
Pronoun with conj.	PRONC
Pronoun with prep. & conj.	PRONPC
Any other pronoun	PRON
Auxiliary verb	AUX
Relative verb	VREL
Verb with prep.	VP
Verb with conj.	VC
Verb with prep. & conj.	VPC
Any other verb	V
Adjective with prep.	ADJP
Adjective with conj.	ADJC
Adjective with prep. & conj.	ADJPC
Any other adjective	ADJ
Preposition	PREP
Conjunction	CONJ
Adverbs	ADV
Cardinal number	NUMCR
Ordinal number	NUMOR
Number with prep.	NUMP
Number with conj.	NUMC
Number with prep. & conj.	NUMPC
Interjection	INT
Punctuation	PUNC
Unclassified	UNC

Table 1: *Amharic POS tagset (extracted from [6])*

2 Amharic part-of-speech taggers

2.1 The POS tagset

In our experiment, we used the POS tagset developed within "The Annotation of Amharic News Documents" project at the Ethiopian Language Research Center. The purpose of the project was to manually tag each Amharic word in its context [6]. In this project, a new POS tagset for Amharic has been derived. The tagset has 11 basic classes: nouns (N), pronouns (PRON), adjectives (ADJ), adverbs (ADV), verbs (V), prepositions (PREP), conjunction (CONJ), interjection (INT), punctuation (PUNC), numeral (NUM) and UNC which stands for unclassified and used for words which are difficult to place in any of the classes. Some of these basic classes are further subdivided and a total of 30 POS tags have been identified as shown in Table 1. Although the tagset contains a tag for nouns with preposition, with conjunction and with both preposition and conjunction, it does not have a separate tag for proper and plural nouns. Therefore, such nouns are assigned the common tag N.

2.2 The corpus

The corpus used to train and test the taggers is the one developed in the above mentioned project — "The Annotation of Amharic News Documents" [6]. It consists of 210,000 manually annotated tokens of Amharic news documents.

In this corpus, collocations have been annotated inconsistently. Sometimes a collocation assigned a single POS tag and sometimes each token in a collocation got a separate POS tag. For example, 'tmhrt bEt', which means *school*, has got a single POS tag, N, in some places and a separate POS tags for each of the tokens in some other places. Therefore, unlike [8] who merged a collocation with a single tag, effort has been exerted to annotate collocations consistently by assigning separate POS tags for the individual words in a collocation.

2.3 The software

We used two kinds of software, namely TnT and SVMTool, to train different taggers.

TnT, Trigram'n'Tags, is a Markov model based, efficient, language independent statistical part of speech tagger [5]. It has been applied on many languages including German, English, Slovene, Hungarian and Swedish successfully. [15] showed that TnT is better than maximum entropy, memory- and transformation-based taggers.

SVMTool is support vector machine based part-of-speech tagger generator [10]. As indicated by the developers, it is a simple, flexible, effective and efficient tool. It has been successfully applied to English and Spanish.

2.4 TnT-based tagger

We have developed three TnT-based taggers by taking different amounts of tokens (80%, 90% and 95%) from the corpus as training data and named the taggers as tagger1, tagger2 and tagger3, respectively. Five percent of the corpus (after taking 95% for training) has been reserved as a test set. This test set has also been used to evaluate the SVM-based taggers to make the results comparable.

Table 2 shows the accuracy of each tagger. As it is clear from the table, the maximum accuracy was found when 95% of the data (199,500 words) have been used for training. This tagger has an overall accuracy of 82.99%. The results also show that the training has not yet reached the point of saturation and the overall accuracy increases, although slightly, as the amount of training data increases. This conforms with findings for other languages that "... the larger the corpus and the higher the accuracy of the training corpus, the better the performance of the tagger" [5]. One can also observe that improvement in the overall accuracy is affected with the amount of data added. Higher improvement in accuracy has been obtained when we increase the training data by 10% than increasing by only five percent. Compared to similar experiments done for other languages and the result which has been recently reported for Amharic by [8], our taggers have worse performance. The better result obtained in [8] might be due to the use of cleaned data and a 10-fold cross-validation technique to train and evaluate the taggers. Nevertheless, we still consider the result acceptable for the given purpose.

Taggers	Accuracy in %		
	Known	Unknown	Overall
Tagger1	88.24	48.77	82.70
Tagger2	88.09	48.11	82.94
Tagger3	88.00	47.82	82.99

Table 2: *Accuracy of TnT taggers*

2.5 SVM-based tagger

We trained SVM-based tagger, SVMM0C0, using 90% of the tagged corpus. To train this model, we did not tune the cost parameter (C) that controls the trade off between allowing training errors and forcing rigid margins. We used the default value for other features like the size of the sliding window. The model has been trained in a one pass, left-to-right and right-to-left combined, greedy tagging scheme. The resulting tagger has an overall accuracy of 84.44% (on the test set used to evaluate the TnT-based taggers) as Table 3 shows.

A slight improvement of the overall accuracy and the accuracy of known words has been achieved setting the cost parameter to 0.1 (see SVMM0C01 in Table 3). The accuracy improvement for unknown words is bigger (from 73.64 to 75.30) compared to the accuracy of known words and the overall accuracy. However, when the cost parameter was increased above 0.1, the accuracy declined. We experimented with cost parameters 0.3 (SVMM0C03) and 0.5 (SVMM0C05) and in both cases no improvement in accuracy has been observed (neither for the overall accuracy nor for the accuracy of known and unknown words).

Taggers	Accuracy in %		
	Known	Unknown	Overall
SVMM0C0	86.03	73.64	84.44
SVMM0C01	86.97	75.30	85.47
SVMM0C03	86.71	73.49	85.01
SVMM0C05	86.48	71.97	84.61

Table 3: *Accuracy of SVM-based taggers*

To determine how the amount of training data affects accuracy, we trained another SVM-based tagger using 95% of the data and the cost parameter of 0.1. Only a slight improvement in the overall accuracy (85.50%) and accuracy for classifying unknown words (from 75.30% to 75.35%) has been achieved compared to the SVMM0C01 tagger which has been trained on 90% of the data. This corresponds to the findings for TnT-based taggers that improved only marginally when a small amount of data (5%) is added. For known words the accuracy declined slightly (from 86.97% to 86.95%). Although this tagger is better (in terms of the overall accuracy) than all the other ones, it performs not better than the one reported by [8] who used a 10-fold cross-validation technique and cleaned data.

Another tagger has been developed using the same data but with a different cost parameter (0.3). However, no improvement in performance has been observed. This model has an overall accuracy of 85.09% and accuracy of 86.76% and 73.40% for known and unknown tokens, respectively.

2.6 Comparison of TnT- and SVM-based taggers

The SVMM0C0 has been trained with the same data that has been used to train the TnT-based tagger, tagger2. The same test set has also been used to test the two types of taggers so that we can directly compare results and decide which algorithm to use for tagging our text for factored language modeling. As it can be seen from Table 3, the SVM-based tagger has an overall accuracy of 84.44%, which is better than the result we found for the TnT-based tagger (82.94%). This finding is in line with what has been reported by [10]. We also noticed that SVM-based taggers have a better capability of classifying unknown words (73.64%) than a TnT-based tagger (48.11%) as it has also been reported in [8].

With regard to speed and memory requirements, TnT-based taggers are more efficient than the SVM-based ones. A SVM-based tagger tags 366.7 tokens per second whereas the TnT-based tagger tags 114083 tokens per second. Moreover, the TnT-based tagger, tagger2, requires less (647.68KB) memory than the SVM-based tagger, SVMM0C0, (169.6MB). However, our concern is on the accuracy of the taggers instead of their speed and memory requirement. Thus, we preferred to use SVM-based taggers to tag our text for the experiment in factored language modeling.

Therefore, we trained a new SVM-based tagger using 100% of the tagged corpus based on the assumption that the increase in the accuracy (from 85.47 to

85.50%) observed when increasing the training data (from 90% to 95%) will continue if more training data are added. Again, the cost parameter has been set to 0.1 which yielded good performance in the previous experiments. It is this tagger that was used to tag the text for training factored language models.

3 Application of the POS information

To determine how the addition of an extra information, namely POS, improves the quality of a language model and consequently the performance of a natural language application that uses the language model, we have developed factored language models that use POS as an additional information. The language models have then been applied to an Amharic speech recognition task in a lattice rescoring framework [12]. Using factored language models in standard word-based decoders is problematic, because they do not predict words but factors.

3.1 Baseline speech recognition system

3.1.1 Speech and text corpus

The speech corpus used to develop the speech recognition system is a read speech corpus developed by [2]. It contains 20 hours of training speech collected from 100 speakers who read a total of 10850 sentences (28666 tokens). Compared to other speech corpora that contain hundreds of hours of speech data for training, for example, British National Corpus (1,500 hours of speech), it is a fairly small one and a model trained on it will suffer from lack of training data.

Although the corpus includes four different test sets (5k and 20k both for development and evaluation), for the purpose of the current investigation we have generated the lattices only for the 5k development test set, which includes 360 sentences read by 20 speakers.

The text corpus used to train the baseline backoff bigram language model consists of 77,844 sentences (868929 tokens or 108523 types).

3.1.2 Acoustic and language models

The acoustic model is a set of intra-word triphone HMM models with 3 emitting states and 12 Gaussian mixtures that resulted in a total of 33,702 physically saved Gaussian mixtures. The states of these models are tied, using decision-tree based state-clustering that reduced the number of triphone models from 5,092 logical models to 4,099 physical ones.

The baseline language model is a closed vocabulary (for 5k) backoff bigram model developed using the HTK toolkit. The absolute discounting method has been used to reserve some probabilities for unseen bigrams and the discounting factor, D, has been set to 0.5, which is the default value in the HLStats module. The perplexity of this language model on a test set that consists of 727 sentences (8337 tokens) is 91.28.

3.1.3 Performance of the baseline system

We generated lattices from the 100 best alternatives for each test sentence of the 5k development test set using the HTK tool and decoded the best path transcriptions for each sentence using the lattice processing tool of SRILM [16]. Word recognition accuracy of the baseline system was 91.67% with a language model scale of 15.0 and a word insertion penalty of 6.0.

3.2 Lattice rescoring with FLM

We substituted each word in a lattice and in the training sentences with its factored representation. A word bigram model that is equivalent to the baseline word bigram language model has been trained using the factored version of the data[1]. This language model is used as a baseline for factored representations and has a perplexity of 58.41 (see Table 4). The best path transcription decoded using this language model has a word recognition accuracy of 91.60%, which is slightly lower than the performance of the normal baseline speech recognition system (91.67%). This might be due to the smoothing technique applied in the development of the language models. Although absolute discounting with the same discounting factor has been applied to both bigram models, the unigram models have been discounted differently. While in the baseline word based language model the unigram models have not been discounted at all, in the equivalent factored model the unigrams have been discounted using Good-Turing discounting technique which is the default discounting technique in SRILM.

In addition to the baseline, we have trained models with two $(w_n|w_{n-1}pos_{n-1})$ and four parents $(w_n|w_{n-1}pos_{n-1}w_{n-2}pos_{n-2})$ for which the estimation of the probability of each word depends on the previous word/s and its/their POS. A fixed backoff strategy has been applied during backoff, dropping the most distant factor first and so on. The perplexity of the language models is indicated in Table 4.

Language models	Perplexity
Baseline word bigram (FBL)	58.41
FLM with two parents	115.89
FLM with four parents	17.03

Table 4: *Perplexity of factored language models*

The factored language models have then been used to rescore the lattices and an improvement of the word recognition accuracy was observed. As it can be seen from Table 5, the addition of the POS information makes language models more robust and consequently the word recognition accuracy improved from 91.60 to 92.92. Although normally the use of higher order ngram models also improves the word recognition accuracy, this is not the case for our factored language models.

[1] A data in which each word is considered as a bundle of features including the word itself, POS tag of the word, prefix, root, pattern and suffix.

Language models used	Word accuracy
Baseline word bigram (FBL)	91.60%
FBL + FLM with two parents	92.92%
FBL + FLM with four parents	92.75%

Table 5: *Word recognition accuracy improvement with factored language models*

4 Conclusion

This paper describes a series of POS tagging experiments aimed at providing a factored language model with an additional information source. For the POS tagger development, we used a manually tagged corpus which consist of 210,000 tokens. Two software tools, TnT and SVMTool, have been applied to train different taggers. As SVM-based taggers outperformed the probabilistic ones, we decided to use them to tag the text for our factored language modeling experiment.

We have developed factored language models (with two and four parents) which estimate the probability of each word depending on the previous one or two words and their POS. Using these language models in an Amharic speech recognition task in a lattice rescoring framework, we obtained improvement of word recognition accuracy (1.32% absolute).

Acknowledgments

We would like to thank the people who developed and made freely available the Amharic manually tagged corpus as well as TnT and SVMTool software tools. Thanks are due to the reviewers who provided constructive comments.

References

[1] S. T. Abate. *Automatic Speech Recognition for Amharic.* PhD thesis, Univ. of Hamburg, 2006.

[2] S. T. Abate, W. Menzel, and B. Tafila. An Amharic speech corpus for large vocabulary continuous speech recognition. In *Proceedings of 9th. European Confference on Speech Communication and Technology, Interspeech-2005*, 2005.

[3] S. F. Adafre. Part of speech tagging for Amharic using conditional random fields. In *Proceedings of the ACL Workshop on Computational Approaches to Semitic Languages*, pages 47–54, 2005.

[4] M. Bender, J. Bowen, R. Cooper, and C. Ferguson. *Languages in Ethiopia.* Oxford Univ. Press, London, 1976.

[5] T. Brants. TnT — a statistical part-of-speech tagger. In *Proceedings of the 6th ANLP*, 2000.

[6] G. A. Demeke and M. Getachew. Manual annotation of Amharic news items with part-of-speech tags and its challenges. *ELRC Working Papers*, II(1), 2006.

[7] K. Duh and K. Kirchhoff. Automatic learning of language model structure. In *Proceeding of International Conference on Computational Linguistics*, 2004.

[8] B. Gambäck, F. Olsson, A. A. Argaw, and L. Asker. Methods for Amharic part-of-speech tagging. In *Proceedings of the EACL Workshop on Language Technologies for African Languages - AfLaT 2009*, pages 104–111, March 2009.

[9] M. Getachew. Automatic part of speech tagging for Amharic language: An experiment using stochastic hmm. Master's thesis, Addis Ababa University, 2000.

[10] J. Giménez and L. Màrquez. Svmtool: A general pos tagger generator based on support vector machines. In *Proceedings of the 4th International Conference on Language Resources and Evaluation*, 2004.

[11] D. S. Jurafsky and J. H. Martin. *Speech and Language Processing: An Introduction to Natural Language Processing, Computational Linguistics, and Speech Recognition.* Prentice Hall, New Jersey, 2nd. ed. edition, 2008.

[12] K. Kirchhoff, J. Bilmes, S. Das, N. Duta, M. Egan, G. Ji, F. He, J. Henderson, D. Liu, M. Noamany, P. Schone, R. Schwartz, and D. Vergyri. Novel approaches to Arabic speech recognition: Report from the 2002 johns-hopkins summer workshop. In *Proceedings of International Conference on Acoustics, Speech, and Signal Processing*, volume 1, pages 1–344 – 1–347, 2003.

[13] K. Kirchhoff, J. Bilmes, J. Henderson, R. Schwartz, M. Noamany, P. Schone, G. Ji, S. Das, M. Egan, F. He, D. Vergyri, D. Liu, and N. Duta. Novel speech recognition models for arabic. Technical report, Johns-Hopkins University Summer Research Workshop, 2002.

[14] K. Kirchhoff, J. Bilmes, and kevin Duh. Factored language models - a tutorial. Technical report, Dept. of Electrical Eng., Univ. of Washington, 2008.

[15] B. Megyesi. Comparing data-driven learning algorithms for pos tagging of Swedish. In *Proceedings of the 2001 Conference on Emperical Methods in Natural Language Processing*, pages 151–158, 2001.

[16] A. Stolcke. SRILM — an extensible language modeling toolkit. In *Proceedings of International Conference on Spoken Language Processing*, volume II, pages 901–904, 2002.

[17] M. Y. Tachbelie and W. Menzel. Sub-word based language modeling for Amharic. In *Proceedings of International Conference on Recent Advances in Natural Language Processing*, pages 564–571, September 2007.

[18] M. Y. Tachbelie and W. Menzel. *Morpheme-based Language Modeling for Inflectional Language – Amharic.* John Benjamin's Publishing, Amsterdam and Philadelphia, forthcoming.

[19] D. Vergyri, K. Kirchhoff, K. Duh, and A. Stolcke. Morphology-based language modeling for Arabic speech recognition. In *Proceedings of International Conference on Spoken Language Processing*, pages 2245–2248, 2004.

[20] B. Yemam. *yäamarIña säwasäw.* EMPDE, Addis Ababa, 2nd. ed. edition, 2000 EC.

[21] S. Young, G. Evermann, M. Gales, T. Hain, D. Kershaw, X. Liu, G. Moore, J. Odell, D. Ollason, D. Povey, V. Valtchev, and P. Woodland. *The HTK Book.* Cambridge University Engineering Department, 2000.

Improving Unsegmented Statistical Dialogue Act Labelling *

Vicent Tamarit, Carlos-D. Martínez-Hinarejos and José-M. Benedí Ruíz
Instituto Tecnológico de Informática
Universidad Politécnica de Valencia
Camino de Vera s/n, 46022, Valencia, Spain
{vtamarit,cmartine,jbenedi}@iti.upv.es

Abstract

An important part of a dialogue system is the correct labelling of turns with dialogue-related meaning. This meaning is usually represented by dialogue acts, which give the system semantic information about user intentions. Each dialogue act gives the semantic of a segment of a turn, which can be formed by several segments. Probabilistic models that perform dialogue act labelling can be used on segmented or unsegmented turns. The last option is the more realistic one, but provides poorer results. An hypothesis on the number of segments can be provided in this case to improve the results. We propose some methods to estimate the probability of the number of segments based on the transcription of the turn. The new labelling model includes the estimation of the probability of the number of segments in the turn. The results show that this inclusion significantly improves the labelling accuracy.

Keywords

dialogue systems, dialogue act, statistical labelling

1 Introduction

A dialogue system is usually defined as a computer system that interacts with a human user to achieve a task using dialogue [6]. The computer system must interpret the user input, in order to obtain the meaning and the intention of the user turn. This is needed to give the appropriate answer to the user. The selection of this answer, along with other decisions that the system can take, is guided by the so-called dialogue strategy. This dialogue strategy can be rule-based [8] or data-based [17]. In the rule-based alternative, the dialogue manager selects the set of actions based on a set of production rules, usually implemented by an expert. In the data-based alternative, there are some ways to build the dialogue system. One option is using a dialogue manager whose parameters have been estimated from annotated data using supervised machine learning techniques, but this approach only take into account the strategies seen in the training data. For this reason simulated users [13] and reinforcement learning [15] are also used to obtain a more robust estimation of the dialogue manager parameters.

In either case, the dialogue strategy needs the interpretation of user turns to achieve the aim of the user. This interpretation must only take into account the essential information for the dialogue process, which is usually represented by special labels called Dialogue Acts (DA) [4]. With this approximation, each user turn can be assigned a sequence of DAs, where each DA is associated with non-overlapped sequences of words in the turn. These sequences of words are usually called segments (some authors refers to these sequences as "utterances" [14]). Each segment has an associated DA which defines its dialogue-related meaning (usually the intention, the communicative function, and the important data).

Therefore, the correct assigment of DAs to a user turn is crucial to the correct behaviour of the dialogue system. The DA tagging is a difficult task even for a human being, because similar segments can be labelled with different DAs depending on the context. Moreover, even the identification of the segments in the turn is a difficult task. To speed-up the labelling time, several models have been proposed to perform this assignment. These assignation models can be based on the annotation rules used by human labellers, but in that case it is quite difficult to code all the rules and exceptions and the model is quite rigid. In recent years, probabilistic data-based models have gained importance for this task [10, 14, 11] as they allow an easier implementation and more flexibility than rule-based models (although they require more annotated data).

The probabilistic parameters of these data-based models are estimated from appropriately labelled dialogue corpora. These dialogue corpora provide sets of dialogues that are segmented and annotated with DA labels. In the posterior use of the models, they are applied to non-annotated dialogues to obtain the most likely DA sequence for each turn. Most of the previous work on DA assignation assumed the correct segmentation of the dialogue turns. However, in a real situation, the only data that are available are the dialogue turns, and the segmentation is not available. Fortunately, these models can be easily adapted to the real situation in which segmentation is not available. In this case, the labelling accuracy is lower than that produced over correctly-segmented dialogue turns.

One possible solution for improving the results on unsegmented turns is to obtain a segmentation hypothesis of the turn before applying the DA assigna-

*Work supported by the EC (FEDER) and the Spanish MEC under grant TIN2006-15694-CO2-01 and by the Spanish research programme Consolider Ingenio 2010: MIPRCV (CSD2007-00018).

tion model, as that proposed in [1]. In that work, the authors propose a segmentation method based on some lexical and prosodic features, which is then used to make the dialogue act classification. The work presented good results but the classification task is limited to 5 classes.

The estimation of the segmentation can be also achieved in a typed dialogue, but, instead of estimating the entire segmentation, another less restricting possibility is to estimate the number of segments of a given turn. Once the estimation is made, the search for the most likely DA sequence is restricted to only having the estimated number of DA. The estimation of the number of segments can be done using the transcriptions of the turns, so it is possible to use it in typed dialogues, where only the text is available, and in spoken dialogues, because it is possible to use the output of an automatic speech recognition system as the input for the DA tagging.

In this paper, we present the formulation of a general probabilistic model of DA assignation that can be applied on the transcription of unsegmented turns. The model evolves from this general formulation to a more restricted formulation where first the probability of the number of segments is estimated, and then the most likely segmentation is obtained. Initial results show that estimating the probability of the number of segments produces significant improvements in the accuracy of the DA assignation. Following this, we present a model to estimate the number of segments given the available dialogue features (words of the turn and its length). The combination of this model with the DA assignation model shows significant improvement in accuracy with respect to the original unsegmented model.

The paper is organised as follows: In Section 2, we present the HMM-based models for labelling the turns. In Section 3, we introduce the estimation of the number of segments and describe the different approaches to the combination of features for that estimation. In Section 4, we present the experiments for testing the models as well as the results. In Section 5 we present our final conclusions and future work.

2 The HMM-based model for DA assignation

Given a word sequence $\mathcal{W}$, the main goal is to obtain the optimum DA sequence $\widehat{\mathcal{U}}$ that maximises the posterior probability $\Pr(\mathcal{U}|\mathcal{W})$.

The DA sequence $\mathcal{U}$ of the complete dialogue can be seen as $U_1^{t-1} = U_1 \cdot U_2 \cdots U_{t-1}$, which represents the DA sequence detected until the current turn t. The word sequence of the current turn is expressed as $W = W_1^l = w_1 \cdot w_2 \cdots w_l$, where l is the number of words of W. Therefore, we can reformulate the problem by introducing a new posterior probability $\Pr(U|W_1^l, U_1^{t-1})$, which represents the probability of the DA sequence U that is associated to the current user turn, given the word sequence of the user turn W_1^l and the history of the previous DA sequence U_1^{t-1}. The goal is to find the best sequence of DAs for each turn:

$$\widehat{U} = \operatorname*{argmax}_U \Pr(U|W_1^l, U_1^{t-1}) \quad (1)$$

Then, we can introduce two *hidden* variables: the number of segments r; and the segmentation of the turn, which can be described as $s = (s_0, s_1, \ldots, s_r)$. Therefore, U can be expressed as $U = u_1^r$, and W as $W_1^l = W_{s_0+1}^{s_1} W_{s_1+1}^{s_2} \ldots W_{s_{r-1}+1}^{s_r}$.

From Equation (1) we can derive two models. The usual assumption is that the segmentation s and the number of segments r are unknown and have no influence on the DA assignation. In this case, as we are under the argmax framework, we can express the probability of the DA sequence as:

$$\Pr(U|W_1^l, U_1^{t-1}) = \Pr(U|U_1^{t-1}) \Pr(W_1^l|U, U_1^{t-1}) =$$
$$\sum_{r,s_1^r} \prod_{k=1}^{r} \Pr(u_k|u_1^{k-1}, U_1^{t-1}) \Pr(W_{s_{k-1}+1}^{s_k}|u_1^k, U_1^{t-1}) \quad (2)$$

This model is simplified with three basic assumptions: the probability of the word segments depends only on the current DA; the probability of the DA depends only on the n previous DAs; and the summation is replaced by a maximisation. The resulting model is the following:

$$\Pr(U|W_1^l, U_1^{t-1}) = \max_{r,s_1^r} \prod_{k=1}^{r} \Pr(u_k|u_{k-n-1}^{k-1}) \Pr(W_{s_{k-1}+1}^{s_k}|u_k) \quad (3)$$

This model can be used when there is an available segmentation (and consequently we know the correct number of segments r) by simply eliminating the maximisation and fixing the s_k values and r to those provided by the segmentation. If there is no segmentation available, the search for the optimal DA sequence provides a segmentation that allows the maximum probability to be obtained. Consequently, we can obtain a segmentation derived from this method. This model can be considered as the baseline model.

We can develop another model from Equation (1) if we consider a different assumption: the number of segments influences the labelling. In this case, the probability of the sequence U is:

$$\Pr(U|W_1^l, U_1^{t-1}) = \sum_r \Pr(U, r|W_1^l, U_1^{t-1}) =$$
$$\sum_r \Pr(r|W_1^l, U_1^{t-1})$$
$$(\Pr(U|U_1^{t-1}, r) \Pr(W_1^l|U, U_1^{t-1}, r)) =$$
$$\sum_r \Pr(r|W_1^l, U_1^{t-1})$$
$$\prod_{k=1}^{r} \Pr(u_k|u_1^{k-1}, U_1^{t-1}, r) \Pr(W_{s_{k-1}+1}^{s_k}|u_1^k, U_1^{t-1}, r) \quad (4)$$

To simplify this expression, we do the same simplifications that we did to obtain Equation (3). Thus, the new labelling model is:

$$\Pr(U|W_1^l, U_1^{t-1}) = \sum_r \Pr(r|W_1^l, U_1^{t-1})$$

$$\max_{s_1^r} \prod_{k=1}^{r} \Pr(u_k|u_{k-n-1}^{k-1}) \Pr(W_{s_{k-1}+1}^{s_k}|u_k) \quad (5)$$

As in the previous model, we can obtain a segmentation from this Equation.

In Equations (3) and (5), $\Pr(u_k|u_{k-n-1}^{k-1})$ can be modelled as an n-gram (of degree n) and $\Pr(W_{s_{k-1}+1}^{s_k}|u_k)$ can be modelled as a HMM. The maximisation (including the segmentation and the DA decoding) can be implemented using the Viterbi algorithm. Note that, in this formula, u_{k-n-1}^{k-1} can take DAs of previous turns.

Therefore, we have derived two labelling models from Equation (1). The model described in Equation (3) does not contain any information about the number of segments of the turn nor any information about the segmentation. The model presented in Equation (5) includes the estimation of the probability of the number of segments.

To estimate the probability $\Pr(r|W_1^l, U_1^{t-1})$, the dependencies of r are substituted by a score S_c that is explained in the next section.

3 Estimation of the number of segments

In Section 2, we introduced an approach to estimate the number of segments of a turn; that is, we defined a score S_c associated with each turn, which is computed from the transcription. To estimate the number of segments, we chose the approximation $\Pr(r|W_1^l, U_1^{t-1}) = \Pr(r|S_c)$, where S_c is calculated in from the sequence of words W_1^l.

The new probability can be calculated by applying the Bayes rule:

$$\Pr(r|S_c) = \frac{p(S_c|r)p(r)}{p(S_c)} \quad (6)$$

The a priori probability $p(r)$ can be easily computed as the number of turns with r segments, N_{Tr}, divided by the total number of turns N_T:

$$p(r) = \frac{N_{Tr}}{N_T} \quad (7)$$

The conditional member $p(S_c|r)$ is estimated by a normal distribution. We calculated one distribution for each r:

$$p(S_c|r) \sim \mathcal{N}(m_r, \sigma_r) \quad (8)$$

The mean m_r and variance σ_r are computed from the scores associated with the turns with r segments.

The last element $P(S_c)$ is estimated by another gaussian distribution that is computed from all the turns:

$$p(S_c) \sim \mathcal{N}(m_{Sc}, \sigma_{Sc}) \quad (9)$$

The mean m_{Sc} and variance σ_{Sc} are computed from all the scores in the training data.

The computation of S_c is made using features that are extracted from the transcription of each turn (it is word-based). We have focused on two features to estimate the number of segments of a turn. One evident feature is the number of words of the turn. More sophisticated features can be inferred from the words (or sequences) that usually appear at the beginning or the end of segments.

First, we made a study of the features that could determine the number of segments and we evaluated the influence of some of them:

- Length of the turn. We evaluated the relation between the number of segments and the number of words in a turn.
- Final words and final n-grams. In the transcription, some words (like the interrogation mark and the period) clearly indicate the end of a segment. Combinations of the last two or three words are also useful.
- Initial words and n-grams. This is the opposite case to the final words.
- Combinations: The above features can be combined to obtain a better estimation of the number of segments.

Second, we defined some calculations for the score S_c based on the above-mentioned features.

- Based on length of the turn

  The score S_c can be calculated as the number of words in the turn:

$$S_c(W) = l \quad (10)$$

- Boundary words

  We define the score S_c of a turn W as:

$$S_c(W) = \sum_{i=1}^{l} p_f(w_i) \quad (11)$$

  where $p_f(w_i)$ is the probability of the word i being a final word in a segment. It is estimated by counting in the training corpus the number of times that the word is final divided by the total number of appearances of the word. This value is 0 for the words that never appear at the end of a segment.

  It is also possible to calculate S_c in the same way using the initial words of a segment instead of final ones.

- Boundary n-grams

  Instead of calculating the probability of a final word, we propose the estimation of the probability of the n last words of the segments. In this case, the method of estimation is the same one that we used in the above case: the number of times that the n-gram is at the end of the segment divided by the total number of appearances of the n-gram. We calculated the S_c using that estimation with:

$$S_c(W) = \sum_{i=n}^{l} p_f(W_{i-(n-1)}^{i}) \qquad (12)$$

  As we proposed in the final word estimation, the probability of initial n-grams in a segment can be computed just by counting the times an n-gram is initial.

- Composed score

  The features that we used in the estimation of the score can be combined. In this case, the score calculated for a turn is composed of various features, e.g. the score can be seen as the summation of the probability of each word to be final plus the length of the turn (by adding a number a for each word):

$$S_c(W) = \sum_{i=1}^{l} (p_f(w_i) + a) \qquad (13)$$

  Another option is to combine the final words with final n-grams, e.g., combining the final bigrams and the final words:

$$S_c(W) = \sum_{i=2}^{l} p_f(W_{i-1}^{i}) + \sum_{i=1}^{l} p_f(w_i) \qquad (14)$$

- Naive-Bayes Score

  In this case, the final probability of the number of segments is calculated by combining the probabilities for each score, i.e., if we consider:

$$\Pr(r|S_{c_1}, S_{c_2}, \cdots S_{c_n})$$

  this probability can be simplified assuming that there are no dependencies between scores (naive-Bayes assumption):

$$\Pr(r|S_{c_1}, S_{c_2}, \cdots S_{c_n}) = \Pr(r|S_{c_1}) \Pr(r|S_{c_2}) \cdots \Pr(r|S_{c_n}) \qquad (15)$$

4 Experiments and results

We present three sets of experiments that we performed using the SwitchBoard corpus [7]. The experiments were designed to show the error in the estimation of the number of segments and the accuracy of the labelling provided by the two models described in Section 2 (Equation (3) and Equation (5)).

4.1 SwitchBoard Corpus

The SwitchBoard corpus [7] is a well-known corpus of human-human conversations by telephone. The conversations are not related to a specific task, since the speakers discuss general interest topics, with no clear task to accomplish. This corpus recorded spontaneous speech, with frequent interruptions between the speakers and background noises. The transcription of the corpus takes into account all these facts and it includes special notation for the overlaps, noises and other sound effects present in the recordings.

The corpus is composed of 1,155 different conversations in which 500 different speakers participated. The number of turns in the dialogues is around 115,000, including overlaps. The vocabulary size is approximately 42,000 words.

The corpus was manually divided into segments following the criteria defined by [9], and annotated using a shallow version of the SWBD-DAMSL annotation scheme [5]. Each segment is labelled with one of the 42 different labels present in the SWBD-DAMSL annotation set. These labels represent categories such as statement, backchannel, questions, answers, etc., and different subcategories for each of these categories (e.g., statement opinion/non-opinion, yes-no/open/rethorical-questions, etc.). The manual labelling was performed by 8 different human labellers, with a Kappa value of 0.80, which reflects the difficulty of the segmentation and annotation task. This corpus is generally used in the evaluation of statistical annotation models ([14], [12], [16])

To simplify the labelling task, we-preprocessed the transcriptions of the SwitchBoard corpus to remove certain particularities. The interrupted segments were joined, thereby avoiding interruptions and ignoring overlaps between the speakers. The vocabulary was reduced by using all the words in lowercase and separating the punctuation marks from the words.

To obtain more reliable results, we performed a partition on the corpus to perform experiments with a cross-validation approach. In our case, the 1,155 different dialogues were divided into 11 partitions with 105 dialogues each one.

4.2 Estimation of the number of segments

The first set of experiments were the tests to determine the best way to estimate the number of segments of a turn. Table 1 shows the results of the different estimations of the number of segments.

These tests showed that the final bigrams provided the best estimation of the number of segments. The initial words (or bigrams) did not estimate the number of segments as well as the final ones; even the length of the turn was a better estimator. The final words and n-grams produced better results due to the presence of some words that always indicate the end of a segment (like the interrogation mark and the period). The two kinds of combination (composed and naive-vayes) did not produce any improvement in the estimation.

Estimation	Error
Length	35.8
Final Words	33.4
Final Bigrams	**27.9**
Final Trigrams	37.4
Initial Words	39.1
Initial Bigrams	39.1
Initial Trigrams	39.0
Composed length and final word score	35.6
Naive-Bayes of length and final words	34.8

Table 1: *Results of the estimation of the number of segments. The estimation column indicates the type of the score used in the estimation of r. The error column indicates the percent of the turns where the estimated number of segments is different from the real number of segments.*

4.3 Baseline

In Section 2, we presented two models for labelling. The baseline experiments used the model represented by Equation (3). We estimated the DA Error Rate (DAER) and the Turn Error Rate (TER). The DAER is the average edit distance between the reference DA sequences and the DA sequences assigned by the labelling model. The TER indicates the percent of turns that are incorrectly labelled. Table 2 shows the results using 2-grams and 3-grams for the estimation of the probability $\Pr(u_k|u_{k-n-1}^{k-1})$. It shows a comparison of the error in the labelling between the segmented and the unsegmented version. In the segmented version we knew the correct segmentation, but in the unsegmented version we did not know anything about the segmentation or the number of segments. The segmented version is a hypothetic case, because in a real system we do not know the correct segmentation.

2-gram		
Corpus	DAER/TER	C.I.
Segmented	29.9/38.3	± 0.6
Unsegmented	63.2/59.6	± 0.5

3-gram		
Corpus	DAER/TER	C.I.
Segmented	29.9/38.1	± 0.6
Unsegmented	**62.5/59.0**	± 0.4

Table 2: *DAER and TER baseline results with the model described in Equation (3). The errors are presented for both segmented and unsegmented corpus. The C.I. column indicates the 90% confidence interval of the DAER. The baseline result considered for the next experiments is shown in boldface.*

These results are boundary errors and they are similar to those provided by [12], where the authors proposed a HMM model to dialogue act labelling. The segmented turns gave us the minimum error supplied by the HMM-based model. The unsegmented turns gave us the maximum error, obtained without knowing the segmentation. We consider that the result obtained with the unsegmented version and a 3-gram is a baseline error (62.5% of DAER). This experiment is useful because it allows us to measure the difference between this model and the one with the estimation of the number of segments. We also included a 90% confidence interval for the DAER to ensure statistical significance. This confidence interval is estimated using a bootstrap estimation [3]. We used each partition as a segment for the bootstrapping and the bootstrap sample is composed by 10,000 elements.

4.4 Labelling with the estimation of the number of segments

The third set of experiments shows the labelling of the turns produced by the mathematical model presented in Equation (5), where we introduce an estimation of the probability of the number of segments. Due to the results of the estimation of r, we used the final words, final bigrams, final trigrams and length features as score estimators. We tested the labelling with 2-grams and 3-grams as estimators of the probability $\Pr(u_k|u_{k-n-1}^{k-1})$.

Table 3 shows a comparison of the errors obtained in the experiments. The error with correct r estimation was computed by labelling the unsegmented corpus, knowing the correct number of segments ($\Pr(r|S_c)$ is 1 for the correct r and 0 for the rest). The inclusion of the labelling with the correct r is only for reference, because it represents an hypothetical case. The rest of the lines refer to different estimations of the number of segments.

2-gram		
r estimation	DAER/TER	C.I.
Correct r	47.4/48.1	± 0.6
Length	54.7/54.9	± 0.5
Final Words	54.2/54.2	± 0.5
Final Bigrams	53.6/53.5	± 0.5
Final Trigrams	54.6/54.8	± 0.5

3-gram		
r estimation	DAER/TER	C.I.
Correct r	47.2/48.1	± 0.5
Length	54.6/54.8	± 0.5
Final Words	54.1/54.2	± 0.5
Final Bigrams	**53.5/53.5**	± 0.5
Final Trigrams	54.5/54.8	± 0.4

Table 3: *DAER and TER results of the labelling using the estimation of segments and different n-grams to estimate $\Pr(u_k|u_{k-n-1}^{k-1})$. Each line refers to a different estimation of the number of segments. It includes the labelling error and a 90% confidence interval for the DAER. The inclusion of the labelling with the correct r is only for reference.*

The best result was obtained with the estimation of the number of segments based on final bigrams and the probability of the dialogue act given by a 3-gram. The confidence interval for this experiment and confidence interval of the baseline show that the difference between the results given by the models are statistically significant. Thus, it can be concluded that the model

2-gram			
r estimation	Precision	Recall	F-measure
No estimation	0.44	0.32	0.37
Correct r	0.45	0.45	0.45
F. Bigrams	0.50	0.42	0.46

3-gram			
r estimation	Precision	Recall	F-measure
No estimation	0.44	0.33	0.38
Correct r	0.46	0.46	0.46
F. Bigrams	0.50	0.42	0.45

Table 4: *Precision, recall and F-measure of the labelling. It includes the results of the baseline labelling error (with no estimation), the labelling error with the correct r estimation and the labelling error using bigrams for the estimation of the number of segments.*

with the estimation of the probability of the number of segments produces a significant improvement in the labelling.

The labelling errors show that there is a relation between the estimation error of the number of segments and the labelling; however, the improvement in the estimation of segments is not translated in the same magnitude to the labelling process. This is due to the difficulty of correctly labelling some turns which were not correctly labelled in any of the experiments, even when the correct number of segments is given. As is pointed out in [14], the cause of these errors could be that some DA definitions are arbitrary and may even confuse a human labeller. To corroborate this problem, we calculated the precision, recall and F-measure of the experiments.

The precision is calculated by dividing the number of correct labelled segments by the total number of labels given by the labeller. The recall is calculated by dividing the number of correct labelled segments by the correct number of segments. The F-measure is computed as $F = 2 \cdot (\text{precision} \cdot \text{recall})/(\text{precision} + \text{recall})$.

Table 4 shows the precision, recall and F-measure of some experiments. The precision indicates the accuracy of the labeller, but the position of the labels in the labelling are not important, thus this errors are better than the corresponding DAER. The precision is similar for all the experiments, which means that the errors are produced by the labeller, even with the correct number of segments. The results also show the improvement produced by the inclusion of the probability of the number of segments in the labelling.

5 Conclusions and future work

In this work, we have shown two different models for the labelling of turns in a dialogue. Both of them are text-based methods, so they can be used in typed dialogues or in spoken dialogues with an automatic speech recogniser. One model directly labels the turns without knowing the segmentation or the number of segments in the turn, and the other model assumes the previous estimation of the probability of the number of segments. Some methods to estimate the probability of the number of segments of a turn based on the transcription are also presented.

The results show that the dialogue act labelling task can be improved by including the probability distribution of the number of segments. Even though our best result is not as good as the one obtained using the correct segmentation, it is significantly better than the error of the unsegmented model with no estimation of the number of segments. Furthermore, the estimation of the probability of the number of segments can be easily computed.

Future work is directed to obtaining a better model that estimates the number of segments. However, the estimations based on the transcription of turns does not seem to produce good enough results. In spoken dialogues, a new estimation could be to use features that are extracted directly from the audio signal, as proposed in [1], and include them into our probability model of the estimation of the number of segments. Another possibility is to repeat these experiments using a corpus of a different kind, such as a task-oriented corpus like Dihana [2]. Moreover, the experiments can be made using the output of a speech recogniser or using a modified version of the corpora with no marks such as points or commas.

References

[1] J. Ang, Y. Liu, and E. Shriberg. Automatic dialog act segmentation and classification in multiparty meetings. In *Proceedings of the International Conference of Acoustics, Speech, and Signal Processings*, volume 1, pages 1061–1064, Philadelphia, 2005.

[2] J.-M. Benedí, E. Lleida, A. Varona, M.-J. Castro, I. Galiano, R. Justo, I. López de Letona, and A. Miguel. Design and acquisition of a telephone spontaneous speech dialogue corpus in spanish: Dihana. In *Fifth International Conference on Language Resources and Evaluation (LREC)*, pages 1636–1639, May 2006.

[3] M. Bisani and H. Ney. Bootstrap estimates for confidence intervals in asr performance evaluation. *Acoustics, Speech, and Signal Processing, 2004. Proceedings. (ICASSP '04). IEEE International Conference on*, 1:I–409–12 vol.1, May 2004.

[4] H. Bunt. Context and dialogue control. *THINK Quarterly*, 3, 1994.

[5] M. G. Core and J. F.Allen. Coding dialogues with the damsl annotation scheme. In *Fall Symposium on Communicative Action in Humans and Machines*, pages 28–35. American Association for Artificial Intelligence, Nov 1997.

[6] L. Dybkjaer and W. Minker. *Recent Trends in Discourse and Dialogue*, volume 39 of *Text, Speech and Language Technology*. Springer, 2008.

[7] J. Godfrey, E. Holliman, and J. McDaniel. Switchboard: telephone speech corpus for research and development. *Acoustics, Speech, and*

Signal Processing, IEEE International Conference on, 1:517–520, 1992.

[8] A. Gorin, G. Riccardi, and J. Wright. How may i help you? *Speech Communication*, 23:113–127, 1997.

[9] D. Jurafsky, E. Shriberg, and D. Biasca. Switchboard swbd-damsl shallow- discourse-function annotation coders manual - draft 13. Technical Report 97-01, University of Colorado Institute of Cognitive Science, 1997.

[10] L. Levin, K. Ries, A. Thymé-Gobbel, and A. Levie. Tagging of speech acts and dialogue games in Spanish call home. In *Workshop: Towards Standards and Tools for Discourse Tagging*, pages 42–47, 1999.

[11] C. Martinez-Hinarejos, J. Benedí, and R. Granell. Statistical framework for a spanish spoken dialogue corpus. *Speech Communication*, 50:992–1008, 2008.

[12] C. D. Martínez-Hinarejos, R. Granell, and J. M. Benedí. Segmented and unsegmented dialogue-act annotation with statistical dialogue models. In *Proceedings of the COLING/ACL 2006 Main Conference Poster Sesions*, pages 563–570, Sydney, Australia,, 17th-21th July 2006.

[13] J. Schatzmann, B. Thomson, and S. Young. Statistical user simulation with a hidden agenda. In *Proc. SIGdial Workshop on Discourse and Dialogue*, pages 273–282, 2007.

[14] A. Stolcke, N. Coccaro, R. Bates, P. Taylor, C. van Ess-Dykema, K. Ries, E. Shriberg, D. Jurafsky, R. Martin, and M. Meteer. Dialogue act modelling for automatic tagging and recognition of conversational speech. *Computational Linguistics*, 26(3):1–34, 2000.

[15] M. A. Walker. An application of reinforcement learning to dialogue strategy selection in a spoken dialogue system for email. *Journal of Artificial Intelligence Research*, 12:387–416, 2000.

[16] N. Webb, M. Hepple, and Y. Wiks. Dialogue act classification using intra-utterance features. In *Proceedings of the AAAI Workshop on Spoken Language Understanding*, Pittsburgh, USA, 2005.

[17] S. Young. Probabilistic methods in spoken dialogue systems. *Philosophical Trans Royal Society (Series A)*, 358(1769):1389–1402, 2000.

Three issues in cross-language frame information transfer

Sara Tonelli, Emanuele Pianta
FBK-Irst
Via Sommarive 18
I-38100 Povo (Trento), Italy
{*satonelli,pianta*}@*fbk.eu*

Abstract

In this paper we address the task of transferring FrameNet annotations from an English corpus to an aligned Italian corpus. Experiments were carried out on an English-Italian bitext extracted from the Europarl corpus and on a set of selected sentences from the English FrameNet corpus that have been manually translated into Italian. Our research activity is aimed at answering the following three questions: (1) What is the best annotation transfer algorithm for the English-Italian couple? (2) What kind of parallel corpus is best suitable to the annotation transfer task? (3) How should the annotation transfer be evaluated, given the final aim of the transfer?

Keywords

Frame semantics, cross-language annotation transfer, automatic development of lexical resources.

1 Introduction

In recent years, the creation of annotated lexical resources has become crucial to the development of text processing systems, especially to train supervised learning systems and evaluate unsupervised or hand-crafted systems. The FrameNet database [8] clearly exemplifies this trend. This resource contains more than 135,000 annotated sentences pointing to more than 10,000 lexical units, with a rich repository of semantic roles (the *frame elements*) and almost 900 situation descriptions (the *frames*). FrameNet has proved to be useful in a number of NLP tasks, from textual entailment [3] to question answering [16], and the development of systems for frame recognition has become a topic of great interest for the NLP community, with a devoted task at the last SemEval workshop[1].

Given the success of the English FrameNet initiative, many researchers have focused on the development of FrameNet-like resources for other languages through manual annotation, for example [4] for German and [17] for Spanish. Manual annotation guarantees high accuracy but requires trained annotators and is expensive and time-consuming. For this reason, a second approach has been investigated, which is based on the automatic projection of frame information from English texts into a new language using bilingual parallel corpora and possibly carrying out automatic annotation of frame information on the English side. If no parallel corpora are available, manually translating an annotated English corpus and automatically transferring the annotations may represent a reliable alternative to hand-labeling a new corpus from scratch, given that translators are more easily available than linguistic annotators, particularly for complex tasks like frame annotation. In this paper we explore the possibility to develop a FrameNet database for Italian using transfer methodologies, and discuss the advantages of using a manually translated parallel corpus for the transfer task. Besides, we present and discuss two existing evaluation frameworks and propose a new evaluation approach. More specifically we try to answer the 3 following questions: (1) What is the best annotation transfer algorithm for the English-Italian couple? (2) What kind of parallel corpus is best suitable to the annotation transfer task? (3) How should the annotation transfer be evaluated, given the final aim of the transfer? We try to answer these questions in Section 3, 4, and 5.

2 The FrameNet projects

FrameNet [8] is a lexical resource for English based on corpus evidence, whose conceptual model comprises a set of prototypical situations called *frames*, the frame-evoking words or expressions called *lexical units* or *targets* and the roles or participants involved in these situations, called *frame elements*. They can be either *core*, i.e. typical of a given frame, and *non-core*, with more general meaning and several instantiations in different frames. All lexical units belonging to the same frame have similar semantics that is expressed by a set of *valence patterns*, i.e. patterns of grammatical realizations of the frame elements. We report in the table below an example frame from the FrameNet database. The WEARING frame is described with a definition, the list of frame-evoking lexical units and the core frame elements with an example sentence each:

A particular feature of the FrameNet resource is that it comprises a language-independent layer with the description of frame and frame elements (Table 1, *Def* row), and two language-dependent parts, namely the lexical unit set for every frame and the corresponding example sentences (*LUs* and *FEs* rows). For

[1] http://framenet.icsi.berkeley.edu/semeval/FSSE.html

International Conference RANLP 2009 - Borovets, Bulgaria, pages 441–448

Frame: WEARING		
Def.	The words in this frame refer to what CLOTHING a WEARER (or a specific BODY_PART of the WEARER) has on	
LUs	attired.a, bare-armed.a, bare-breasted.a, bare.v, braless.a clothed.a, coatless.a, costumed.a, decked out.a, dressed.a have got on.v, sport.v, swaddled.a, swathed.a, wear.v [...]	
FEs	BODY_PART	She was wearing a glove *on one hand.*
	CLOTHING	Lucy had *dark glasses* on.
	WEARER	She reached a group of costumed *dancers.*

Table 1: *Frame* WEARING

this reason, the FrameNet model is particularly suitable to cross-lingual induction and can be applied to languages other than English, keeping the theoretical framework as it is and populating the frames with language-specific lexical units and corpus instances. In some cases, new frame definitions may be required for the new language.

The first step towards the creation of a FrameNet database for a new language should be the annotation of frame information on a corpus of sentences in the new language. Since manual annotation is time-consuming and requires relevant financial efforts, several approaches have been proposed in the past to automatically carry out the annotation process. The most convenient alternative to manual annotation seems to be the import of English FrameNet annotation into another language exploiting a parallel corpus. [13] proposed a method to transfer frame annotation from English to German starting from parallel texts with the English side annotated with frame information. They proposed a model based on alignment at constituent level obtained through word overlap similarity. [14] tested a similar approach on a parallel English-French corpus, showing that the transfer framework can get promising results also if applied to Romance languages. [9] applied the transfer method to English-Swedish parallel texts with the English side being automatically annotated with a semantic role labeller trained on the English FrameNet database.

As for Italian, a few projects are currently aimed at developing FrameNet for Italian and at exploring new approaches to speed up manual annotation or convey fully automatic annotation. [1] have proposed a methodology to automatically transfer frame information on an English-Italian parallel corpus based on a statistical machine translation step augmented with a rule-based post-processing. [5] have trained and tested a system for automatic frame element detection using a corpus of Italian dialogs manually annotated with frame information.

3 Transfer algorithm selection

The task of frame annotation transfer is two-folded as it implies transferring the annotation of the target, which is always a lexical unit, and of frame elements, which are more complex syntactic constituents (up to full clause). Also, the annotation can be carried out at the level of strings of words or at the level of syntactic constituents, as in the work of [13] and [14]. As a consequence, the transfer algorithm can be based only on word alignment or also, when available, on syntactic structure information. [13] carried out experiments with both approaches and proved that exploiting constituent information yields substantial improvements over relying on word alignment alone. The methodology was then further optimized by [12] and applied to English-German and English-French corpora in order to transfer FE information via constituent alignment. We explored two variants of the constituent-based strategy applied to frame information transfer from English to Italian. The first variant, which was presented in [18], requires full parsing on both source and target corpus. Given an English constituent, annotated as FE, the algorithm extracts its head, aligns it with the corresponding Italian head, then looks for the maximal syntactic projection of the Italian semantic head, and transfers the English FE annotation to such constituent. In this approach, the correct alignment of the head is enough to carry out the FE transfer. However, this feature may also turn in a disadvantage, because if the semantic head is not aligned, there will be no transfer.

We present here a second version of the transfer algorithm which is more similar to [12] in that the alignment between constituents is not based on the semantic head but on the best percentage of aligned words. However, unlike [12] who considers all possible constituents in the parse tree, we take into account only constituents that are syntactically connected to the target in the Italian sentence. Note that in this approach no parsing information on the English side is required. The algorithm description is reported below:

```
Given two aligned sentences s_en and s_it
take lexunit_en ∈ s_en
if exists alignment_lexunit_en
    take aligned lexunit_it ∈ s_it
    transfer info_frame from lexunit_en to lexunit_it
    return lexunit_it+infoframe
    extract D_it from s_it
// D_it = set of syntactic dependents of lexunit_it in s_it
    for each fe_en ∈ FE_en
        Score_best = 0
        Cand_best = empty
        for each d_it ∈ D_it
            calculate Score_it
// Score_it = n. of aligned words between fe_en and d_it
            ifScore_it > Score_best
                Score_best = Score_it
                Cand_best = d_it
            end if
        end for
        return Score_best
        return Cand_best
    end for
else
    return false
```

We take the English corpus annotated with frame information C_{en} and align it at word level to the Italian corpus C_{it}, whose sentences have been previously parsed. For each sentence $s_{en} \in C_{en}$, we take the annotated lexical unit $lexunit_{en}$ and find the Italian aligned word, that we assume to be the target lexical unit $lexunit_{it}$. If no alignment is available, the transfer fails, otherwise the English frame label is assigned to the Italian $lexunit_{it}$. Then, for every English frame element fe_{en}, we take all syntactic dependents D_{it} of $lexunit_{it}$ and compute the number of aligned words between fe_{en} and $d_{it} \in D_{it}$. We consider the Italian dependent with most aligned words $Cand_{best}$ as the best candidate for annotation projection.

As an example, we report in Figure 1 the output of the first transfer algorithm applied to two parallel sentences from the *Europarl* corpus [10]. Dotted arrows connect aligned tokens.

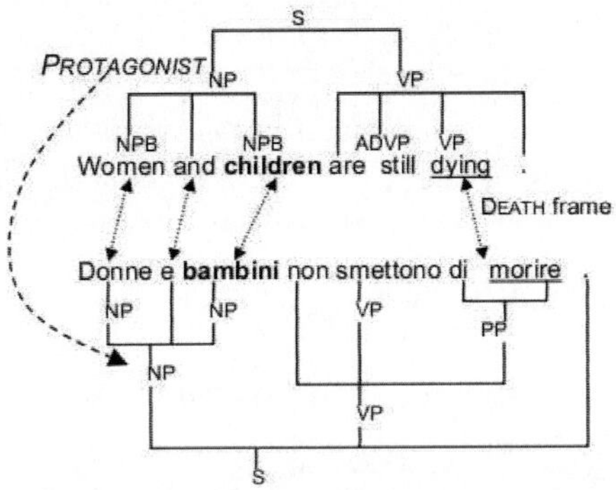

Fig. 1: *Correct transfer with Algorithm 1*

Since *"morire"* is correctly aligned with the target *"dying"*, it becomes the Italian lexical unit of the DEATH frame. As for the PROTAGONIST frame element, first *"children"* is identified as the semantic head of the constituent, then it is connected to *"bambini"*, and finally the NP node dominating *"Donne e bambini"* is selected as the best Italian constituent because it represents the highest syntactic projection of the Italian head compatible with the annotated English constituent. Algorithm 2 would not deliver any FE transfer on the same couple of sentences, as it cannot identify *"Donne e bambini"* as dependent of *"morire"*, due to the different syntactic structure of the Italian sentence. In Figure 2 we report the output of the second transfer algorithm applied to two parallel sentences from the *Europarl* corpus. Note that, unlike [12], we do not exploit any syntactic information on the English side and that the FE labels point to flat chunks, whereas in Figure 1 the sentences have been parsed on both sides.

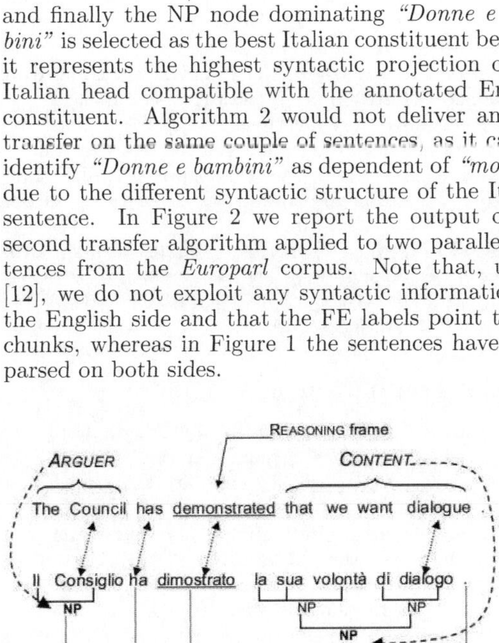

Fig. 2: *Correct transfer with Algorithm 2*

In this example, *"demonstrated"* is the target of the REASONING frame, and two frame elements are present, namely CONTENT and ARGUER. Both frame elements point to the correct constituent nodes in Italian, that are the syntactic dependents of the target *"dimostrato"*. The CONTENT frame element is correctly transferred even if only one word (*dialogue* - *dialogo*), which is not the semantic head of the constituent, has been aligned. This algorithm can cope with a different syntactic structure of the sentence in Italian, where the English secondary clause *"that we want dialogue"* is translated as *"la sua volontà di dialogo"* (i.e. *its will to dialogue*). With algorithm 1 the transfer of the CONTENT label would have failed because the semantic head of the constituent, *"want"*, has no alignment in Italian.

4 *Europarl* and *MultiBerkeley*

In order to investigate the influence of the corpus characteristics on the transfer quality, we took into account two different parallel corpora.

The first corpus was an excerpt of 987 English and Italian sentences taken from the *Europarl* multilanguage parallel corpus [10]. The English side of the corpus has been automatically annotated with part of speech and syntactic information and manually enriched with frame-semantic information as described in [13] in the context of transfer experiments between English and German. The same sentences were used also for the English-Italian transfer. The Italian sentences were parsed with Bikel's phrase-based statistical parser trained for Italian [6], which obtained the best score in the EVALITA evaluation campaign for Italian NLP tools with 70.79 f-measure. Then the English-Italian corpus was aligned at word level with KNOWA (KNowledge-intensive Word Aligner) [15]. The *coverage* of the *word alignment* process reached 65.1 coverage on the whole corpus. The Italian side of the corpus was manually annotated with frame information in order to build a gold standard to assess transfer quality. The gold standard turns out to include instances of 158 frames, mainly connected to the communication and the political scenarios, with the great majority of lexical units being verbs. This means that the variability of frames was limited, with about 6 instances for every frame. Another characteristic of the *Europarl* corpus is the presence of extremely free translations. This is due not only to the translation style, but also to the corpus structure. In fact, if we consider a set of parallel sentences from this corpus, it may include translations of the same sentence from a third language. For instance, a pair of English-Italian parallel sentences may have been translated from a French source sentence. This makes the corpus less suitable for the task of transfer annotation.

For this reason, we take into account also a second corpus called *MultiBerkeley*, which is built by manually translating in a controlled way a number of sentences from the Berkeley FrameNet corpus. The selection of sentences was guided by the desire to include in the resulting Italian corpus frames that were not already present in *Europarl*. Also, we wanted to acquire targets that are not verbs. Besides, as past experiments on annotation transfer have shown (see [2]), the automatic projection of annotation between two parallel corpora in different languages can benefit from a translation that minimizes syntactic differences from source and target language. For this reason (i) we selected 400 frames that are not represented in the *Europarl* gold standard and (ii) for each of them, we chose the target with the largest set of example sentences in the English FrameNet database. Even if the information in the FrameNet database is not statistically significant w.r.t. the frequency of the occurrence of the different targets, we assumed that a target with several attestations in the Berkeley corpus and a complete annotation should be considered significant of the frame it belongs to. Among the extracted sentences for every target, (iii) we selected the shortest one, discarding the instances where all frame elements are expressed by a personal pronoun (e.g. *"He took it"*). In the end, we obtained an English corpus composed of 400 sentences with one example per frame. The sentences are taken from the English FNet database, thus they are PoS tagged and annotated with frame information. All frame elements are also labeled with phrase type (NP, PP, VP, etc.) and grammatical function (Ext, Dep, Head, etc.). We manually translated the English corpus into Italian trying to limit "free" translations in order to enhance the correspondence between source and target texts. If possible, we preferred Italian translations minimizing divergences with English. However, priority was always given to good Italian prose. Once we created the Italian version of the corpus, the rest of the pre-processing step remained the same as for the *Europarl* corpus, with the Italian sentences being parsed with Bikel's parser and the bitext aligned at word level with KNOWA. Finally, we manually annotated all Italian sentences with frame information in order to create a second gold standard for evaluation. We call the resulting corpus *MultiBerkeley*.

We report in Table 2 some statistics about the two corpora. Note that FE parallelism is computed over the subset of sentences with frame parallelism.

	Europarl	*MBerk.*
Avg. sent. length (tokens)	23±9	10±4
Frame parallelism	0.61	0.98
FE parallelism	0.82	0.91

Table 2: *Corpus comparison*

The average sentence length in the *Europarl* corpus is more than double than that in the *MultiBerkeley* corpus due to the different selection strategy of the sentences. Different values of frame and FE parallelism depend partly on the fact that the English side had been annotated with FrameNet v. 1.1 for previous experiments [13], while we used version 1.3 for the Italian gold standard. Nonetheless, the main reason for lacking parallelism are free translations, that are particularly frequent in the *Europarl* corpus. If we apply the framework proposed by [7] to the parallel sentences with diverging frame annotation, we notice that they are mainly caused by a subset of *translation shifts* called *semantic shifts* , showing a variation of the meaning in the source and the target sentence. On the contrary, *grammatical shifts* (f.e. change of category) tend to preserve the frame label in the translated sentence. As an example, we report two pairs of sentences from *Europarl.* In (1), the change of category between *pay.v* and *pagamento.n (payment.n)* does not affect the assigned frame COMMERCE_PAY. In (2), instead, the target word *say* was translated as *sottolineare (underline)*, that led to a frame change from STATEMENT to CONVEY_IMPORTANCE[2]:

(1) I do not believe that we can solve the problem by **paying** fees. [COMMERCE_PAY]
Non credo che la soluzione consista nel **pagamento** di nuove spese. [COMMERCE_PAY]

(2) Let me **say** it again quite clearly, we have not brought up the question. [STATEMENT]
Desidero ancora una volta **sottolineare** che non abbiamo affrontato la questione. [CONVEY_IMPORTANCE]

We expect the different semantic parallelism and the different complexity of the two corpora to impact on the transfer performance.

5 Evaluation framework

In different research works about frame annotation transfer, several evaluation criteria have been applied. The common feature among them is the choice to include in the testset only sentences that present a certain degree of semantic parallelism in the parallel gold standards. We believe that this approach is not suitable for our goal. Since we aim at producing an annotated corpus with near manual annotation quality, we need to evaluate all the annotations resulting from the transfer. In the following subsections, we will illustrate two existing evaluation approaches and add our proposal for a more general and effective evaluation framework. Moreover, we will evaluate the output of our algorithms applying the presented metrics.

In order to carry out the evaluation, we divided both corpora into a development set and a testset. The former was used to tune the transfer algorithms, while the latter was employed to run the algorithms and carry out evaluation, comparing the output to the Italian gold standard. The *Europarl* corpus was split into a devset of 300 sentences and a testset of 687 sentences. The *MultiBerkeley* corpus comprised a development set of 100 sentences and a testset of 300 sentences.

5.1 Evaluation 1

In the evaluation of frame information transfer between English and German and English and French, [12] and [14] proposed to evaluate the task following three main criteria: first, they do not consider target transfer because they focus only on FE transfer. Second, they consider for evaluation only the subset of parallel sentences in the source and target gold standard having the same frame, in order to focus on the alignment and transfer quality and exclude free translations from evaluation. Third, they propose to measure performance only on frame elements using the

[2] Even if the general meaning of the first sentence might be related to the CONVEY_IMPORTANCE frame, the *say* alone is considered as a lexical unit of STATEMENT, while *clearly* should be assigned to the OBVIOUSNESS frame.

"Exact match condition", i.e. both the label and the span of the projected role have to match the gold standard annotation for the target language to count as a true positive. We first apply the same evaluation framework and compare the results obtained with algorithm 1 and 2 on *Europarl* to the results obtained by [14] for the English-French pair, given that they worked on the same subset of sentences taken from *Europarl* and used the same English gold standard. Since Italian and French are both romance languages, we assume that they should show the same degree of syntactic and semantic similarity to English. Results are reported in Table 3.

Europarl	**Precision**	**Recall**	**F1**
Algorithm 1	0.48	0.39	0.43
Algorithm 2	0.66	0.40	0.50
MultiBerkeley	Precision	Recall	F1
Algorithm 2	0.75	0.49	0.59

Table 3: *FE transfer evaluation 1 on MultiB.*

The second algorithm improves on the first for every measure. The constituent alignment strategy based on word overlap outperforms the head alignment approach, especially in precision, while recall seems to remain a weak point of both approaches. [14] report that the best full constituent-based model on the French testset, with filters for non-aligned words and arguments, achieves 63.1 as best f-measure (0.66 precision, 0.60 recall). Our best results on *Europarl* scored the same precision but a lower recall. This discrepancy may depend on different algorithm strategies (see Section 3) but also on different characteristics of the two corpora. In fact, frame instance parallelism between English and French gold standards is higher than between English and Italian, with 0.69 frame parallelism and 0.88 FE parallelism (vs. 0.61 and 0.82 on English-Italian Europarl, see Section 4). Besides, the French parser used in the pre-processing phase scores 76.3 f-measure, whereas the Bikel parser trained on Italian has 70.79 f-measure. In order to verify the impact of wrong parse trees on the algorithm performance, we applied the transfer algorithm also to the parsed Italian sentences after a manual correction of the major nodes. The corresponding evaluation on *Europarl* highlighted that for algorithm 1 the correction step enhances precision of 0.14 and recall of 0.12. With the second algorithm, the values improved respectively of 0.14 and 0.9. This proves that parsing problems are a relevant source of error.

As for *MultiBerkeley*, we could not apply algorithm 1 because it requires the source sentences to be represented as syntactic trees, whereas the English FrameNet corpus has annotation pointing to flat chunks without parsing information. Also for this second corpus, we evaluated the improvement of the algorithm on manually corrected parse trees on the Italian side. Precision scores an enhancement of 0.16, and recall of 0.11. The improvement via correction step is greater for *MultiBerkeley* than for *Europarl*. This means that in *MultiBerkeley* parsing problems are the main source of error, whereas in the *Europarl* corpus also other factors have a significant impact on the algorithm performance, for instance free translations. In general, we notice that the transfer approach performs better on a corpus like *MultiBerkeley*, where syntactic complexity is limited by the sentence length and the faithful translation of the parallel sentences enhances the performance of the aligner.

5.2 Evaluation 2

[1] presented a fully automatic transfer process based on alignment with *Moses* [11] at chunk level between English and Italian parallel sentences and a selection of the best candidate segment for semantic transfer according to some ranking and post-processing criteria. The algorithm was evaluated on the same subset of *Europarl* corpus that we used. However, they apply an evaluation framework that is different from that of [12] presented in the previous section. In fact, they consider each FE and target annotation as independent and include in the testset only those FEs having the same label both in the Italian and in the English gold standard. In order to compare this approach to ours, we decided to adopt the same evaluation measures. Accuracy is evaluated on all semantic elements of the target language (both *targets* and *frame elements* together) and only on FEs. The transfer of target annotations was considered correct if the alignment was correct, even if the frame labels were different in the two languages. As for FEs, two kinds of match were computed: Perfect Matching (the projected segments in the target language exactly match with the gold standard ones) and Partial Matching (the intersection between the target projected segments and the ones in the gold standard is not empty). Moreover, in order to measure the gap between perfect and partial matching, evaluation included also token precision, recall and f-measure computed over all transferred labels (micro-average). In Table 4 we report the evaluation of our annotation transfer with algorithm 2, which conveys better performance than algorithm 1, run on the *Europarl* corpus following the above mentioned criteria. We show the results of perfect and partial match applied to all semantic elements (targets + FEs), while the values for FEs only are reported between parenthesis.

Europarl	**PerfMatch** (FEs only)		**PartialMatch** (FEs only)
	0.77 (0.66)		0.90 (0.89)
Token	**Precision**	**Recall**	**F1**
	0.83 (0.82)	0.75 (0.78)	0.79 (0.80)

Table 4: *Evaluation 2 of Alg. 2 on Europarl*

The best model reported in [1] on the same testset scored 0.73 PerfMatch and 0.90 PartialMatch on LUs+FEs, and 0.42 and 0.78 respectively as PerfMatch and PartialMatch on FEs only. This means that both approaches reach high accuracy on target words, whereas our model performs significantly better on FEs only. In general, the two results reflect the different goals of the two approaches: [1] are interested in investigating and adopting unsupervised techniques with poor semantic and syntactic information to automatically annotate a large scale (but noisy) training set and exploit it for semantic role labelling. On the contrary, we are interested in developing annotated resources with nearly manual quality, so we consider particularly important FE transfer precision.

We report in Table 5 the evaluation of algorithm 2 on the *MultiBerkeley* corpus following the same criteria mentioned above.

MultiBerkeley	PerfMatch (FEs only)	PartialMatch (FEs only)
	0.84 (0.75)	0.92 (0.88)

Token	Precision	Recall	F1
	0.88 (0.85)	0.84 (0.86)	0.86 (0.85)

Table 5: *Evaluation 2 of Alg. 2 on M.Berkeley*

As expected, the algorithm behaves differently on the two corpora, and all values obtained on *MultiBerkeley* outperform those on *Europarl*, except for PartialMatch on FEs only (0.88 vs. 0.89). This may depend on the fact that the constituents in the *MultiBerkeley* corpus are generally quite short, so the annotation transfer tend to be either a perfect match or to fail. On the contrary, the constituents in the *Europarl* sentences tend to be more complex, thus it is likely that they have at least one aligned token with the English source FE that matches with the gold standard, but exact match is less probable.

5.3 Evaluation 3: a proposal

A common feature of the two evaluation frameworks presented in Section 5.1 and 5.2 is that they exclude from evaluation cases of missing parallelism between source and target sentences. We propose a third approach based on 3 main ideas: 1) we think that it is preferable to evaluate separately targets and frame elements, because of the different nature of the two tasks: target transfer is more influenced by word alignment quality and is generally more straightforward than FE projection. On the other hand, the latter requires a different strategy because it involves selection procedures at chunk or constituent level. While target projection is mainly based on single-word alignment, FE projection requires both role identification and boundary detection. 2) Since we are interested in the (semi) automatic creation of FrameNet for new languages, we want to evaluate the quality of the resulting corpus as a whole, so we consider all transferred annotation regardless of parallelism between the two gold standards. 3) As for the evaluation of FE transfer, we propose two different criteria for assessing the match between automatic annotation and gold standard that are looser than the exact match condition. In both cases, the automatically annotated FE matches the gold standard FE if they share at least the same semantic head. However, type 1 is more strict in that it requires that also the annotation of the corresponding targets match. Type 2, instead, considers correct all matching frame elements between automatic and manually annotated sentences regardless of whether the target has been annotated with the right frame.

We report in Table 6 the evaluation of target transfer on the two corpora. We don't distinguish between algorithm 1 and algorithm 2 on the *Europarl* corpus because the alignment step for targets is the same and relies on word alignment.

	Precision	Recall	F1
Europarl	0.71	0.50	0.59
MultiBerkeley	0.93	0.81	0.86

Table 6: *Target transfer evaluation*

Europarl	Precision	Recall	F1
Algorithm1			
Type 1	0.46	0.30	0.37
Type 2	0.64	0.41	0.49
Algorithm2			
Type 1	0.55	0.28	0.37
Type 2	0.64	0.32	0.43

Table 7: *FE transfer evaluation 3 on Europarl*

In Table 7 we report the evaluation of FE transfer on the *Europarl* corpus according to the two criteria we have proposed, using both algorithm 1 and algorithm 2. The results reflect different features of the two algorithms that had not been highlighted in the previous evaluations. In particular, algorithm 2 achieves a better performance on precision for evaluation Type 1, but the overall recall value are worse for both types. Since FE transfer in algorithm 2 depends on a correct target transfer, it is clear that missing target alignments influence in turn also the FE transfer performance. The evaluation shows that it is probably better to make the two transfer steps independent, like in algorithm1, so that one can try and align FEs even if no target has been transferred. In Table 8 we report the evaluation of FE transfer on the *MultiBerkeley* corpus according to the two criteria we have proposed and applying algorithm 2.

MultiBerkeley	Precision	Recall	F1
Type 1	0.68	0.54	0.60
Type 2	0.69	0.55	0.61

Table 8: *FE transfer evaluation 3 on MBerk.*

All results on *MultiBerkeley* generally achieve an improvement w.r.t. *Europarl*, particularly on recall. This can be explained by the nature of the corpus, that maximizes word alignment, so that less constituents are left out in the alignment step. Moreover, we noticed in the *Europarl* corpus a greater difference between type 1 and type 2 than in *MultiBerkeley*. In fact, in the former there are a lot of frames that are semantically related and share the same frame elements (for example *Cognizer* is a core FE of several frames in the corpus such as AWARENESS, CERTAINTY, COMING_TO_BELIEVE, JUDGMENT, OPINION, etc.). For this reason, the set of all matching frame elements between automatic and manually annotated sentences regardless of the frame identity (type 2) is bigger than that

considering also the corresponding target match (type 1). In *MultiBerkeley*, instead, the two sets almost coincide because the frame variability is much higher, thus it is less likely that two frame elements of different sentences are the same even if the frame is different.
Error analysis shows that transfer quality of the *Europarl* corpus is crucially affected by syntactic complexity and free translation of the target corpus, which in turn impact on alignment quality. See the example reported at (3):

(3) EN: 85% of Mexico's exports go north.
ITA: L'85 percento delle esportazioni messicane è destinato all'America del nord.
(Literal transl.: 85 percent of Mexican exports are destined to North America)

In order to determine the parallelism between the two sentences, we need to make the inference that North America is north of Mexico, which is out of the current capability of any word-alignment tool. Furthermore, *"go"* and *"essere destinato (to be destined)"* do not exactly express the same predicate and it is likely that they won't be aligned. Other problems involve both corpora and arise from different interpretations given by the annotators to the aligned sentences, which may depend also on inherent ambiguity of FrameNet definitions. For example, in the STATEMENT frame, English annotators tend to prefer to label as *Topic* the content of the communication, whereas in Italian it is mostly annotated as *Message*. Probably the difference between the two frame elements is not clear enough, especially if not applied to English. Other minor problems depend on the recognition and alignment of multiwords in Italian. In general, both algorithms fail to find the correct constituent for frame element transfer in case of complex interpolated tree nodes, where different terminals and nodes dominated by the same parent bear different FE labels.

6 Conclusions and future work

In this work, we presented two algorithms for the crosslingual projection of frame semantic information and tested it on an English-Italian parallel corpus extracted from *Europarl*. Since the comparative evaluation of the two algorithms highlighted advantages and disadvantages for each approach, we think that a combination of the two algorithms should be implemented, trying to preserve the good precision performance of algorithm 2 and to improve on recall via the head-based approach of algorithm 1. Another main concern of our investigation was to understand to what extent different types of corpora can influence the transfer process. For this reason, we tested and evaluated algorithm 2 also on the *MultiBerkeley* corpus, which was produced by manually translating a selection of English sentences from the Berkeley FrameNet database. While evaluation results on the *Europarl* subcorpus were still unsatisfactory because they did not allow for a completely automatic development of FrameNet-like resources, we noticed that *MultiBerkeley* allowed to optimize algorithm performance and minimize alignment errors. Evaluation results show that the translation effort to produce the corpus is repaid by the remarkable reduction of correction work. On the other hand, we are aware that transferring only one sentence per frame and controlling translation allows to cover only one of the possible valence patterns of the frame. For this reason, we believe that the methodology should be considered only a starting point for the creation of FrameNet-like resources for languages different from English. For example, it would be interesting to investigate procedures to automatically acquire new example sentences starting from *MultiBerkeley*, also exploiting existing lexical resources like MultiWordNet. In the future, we plan to improve the projection algorithm exploiting all annotation layers present in the FrameNet corpus. In particular, information about the grammatical function of frame elements could help improving constituent alignment and candidates selection.

References

[1] R. Basili, D. D. Cao, D. Croce, B. Coppola, and A. Moschitti. Cross-language frame semantics transfer in bilingual corpora. In *Proceedings of CICLing*. Springer-Verlag, 2009.

[2] L. Bentivogli and E. Pianta. Exploiting parallel texts in the creation of multilingual semantically annotated resources: the MultiSemCor Corpus. *Natural Language Engineering*, 11(03):247–261, 2005.

[3] A. Burchardt and A. Frank. Approximating Textual Entailment with LFG and FrameNet Frames. In *Proceedings of the 2nd PASCAL RTE Workshop*, Venice, Italy, 2006.

[4] A. Burchardt, A. Frank, S. Padó, and M. Pinkal. The SALSA corpus: a German corpus resource for lexical semantics. In *Proceedings of LREC 2006*, pages 969–974, 2006.

[5] B. Coppola, A. Moschitti, S. Tonelli, and G. Riccardi. Automatic FrameNet-Based Annotation of Conversational Speech. In *Proceedings of the 2nd IEEE Workshop on Spoken Language Technology*, Goa, India, 2008.

[6] A. Corazza, A. Lavelli, and G. Satta. Analisi Sintattica-Statistica basata su Costituenti. *Intelligenza Artificiale*, (2):38–39, 2007.

[7] L. Cyrus. Building a resource for studying translational shifts. In *Proc. of 5th LREC*, Genoa Italy, 2006.

[8] C. Fillmore, C. Johnson, and M. R. L. Petruck. Background to FrameNet. *International Journal of Lexicography*, 16:235–250, September 2003.

[9] R. Johansson and P. Nugues. A FrameNet-based Semantic Role Labeler for Swedish. In *Proc. of Coling/ACL 2006*, 2006.

[10] P. Koehn. Europarl: A Parallel Corpus for Statistical Machine Translation. In *Proceedings of MT Summit*, 2005.

[11] P. Koehn, H. Hoang, A. Birch, C. Callison-Burch, M. Federico, N. Bertoldi, B. Cowan, W. Shen, C. Moran, R. Zens, C. Dyer, O. Bojar, A. Constantin, and E. Herbst. Moses: Open source tool for statistical machine translation. In *Proceedings of ACL 2007*, Prague, CZ, 2007.

[12] S. Padó. *Cross-Lingual Annotation Projection Models for Role-Semantic Information*. PhD thesis, Universität des Saarlandes, 2007.

[13] S. Padó and M. Lapata. Cross-linguistic Projection of Role-Semantic Information. In *Proceedings of Human Language Technology Conference and EMNLP*, pages 859–866, Vancouver, Canada, 2005.

[14] S. Padó and G. Pitel. Annotation précise du français en sémantique de roles par projection cross-linguistique. In *Proceedings of TALN-07*, Toulouse, France, 2007.

[15] E. Pianta and L. Bentivogli. KNOwledge Intensive Word Alignment with KNOWA. In *Proceedings of Coling 2004*, pages 1086 – 1092, 2004.

[16] D. Shen and M. Lapata. Using Semantic Roles to Improve Question Answering. In *Proceedings of EMNLP and CONLL*, pages 12–21, Prague, CZ, 2007.

[17] C. Subirats-Rüggeberg. *FrameNet Español: un análisis cognitivo del léxico del español.* Peter Lang, Frankfurt am Main, 2009.

[18] S. Tonelli and E. Pianta. Frame Information Transfer from English to Italian. In E. L. R. Association, editor, *Proceedings of LREC 2008*, Marrakech, Morocco, 2008.

A study on Linking Wikipedia categories to Wordnet synsets using text similarity*

Antonio Toral* Óscar Ferrández† Eneko Agirre◇ Rafael Muñoz†
*Istituto di Linguistica Computazionale, Consiglio Nazionale delle Ricerche
Pisa, Italy
†Natural Language Processing and Information Systems Group
University of Alicante, Spain
◇Informatika Fakultatea, University of the Basque Country
Donostia, Basque Country

Abstract

This paper studies the application of text similarity methods to disambiguate ambiguous links between WordNet nouns and Wikipedia categories. The methods range from word overlap between glosses, random projections, WordNet-based similarity, and a full-fledged textual entailment system. Both unsupervised and supervised combinations have been tried. The gold-standard with disambiguated links is publicly available. The results range from 64.7% for the first sense heuristic, 68% for an unsupervised combination, and up to 77.74% for a supervised combination.

1 Introduction

Human languages are extremely rich and ambiguous resulting in the fact that the same information can be expressed with different words and linguistic structures. Consequently, an ambiguous text might represent several distinct meanings and a concrete meaning might be expressed by different ways. Therefore, language ambiguity and variability are considered as essential blocks to solve in order to overcome the barrier that separates the human understanding from the computer understanding.

The task of detecting semantic similarity between texts addresses properly these language phenomena and also has a lot of potential applications for Natural Language Processing [15]; examples include word sense disambiguation [16], categorisation [11], summarisation [4], etc.

In the current research, semantic similarity is applied into a methodology devoted to the automatic construction of a Named Entity Repository [18]. This method exploits the knowledge available in already existing Language Resources (LR) to support procedures of lexico-semantic acquisition from Web 2.0 collaborative semistructured resources.

Our test case for English focuses on WordNet [5] as the LR and Wikipedia as the Web 2.0 resource. The first step consists in establishing links between entries of both resources; the instantiable common nouns found in WordNet are mapped to Wikipedia categories. Obviously, these mappings are ambiguous for polysemous nouns. Another piece of research, YAGO [17], also addresses linking WordNet to Wikipedia. However, the authors do not deal with the ambiguity that arises when linking both resources (ambiguous mappings are simply manually disambiguated).

Our first attempt to resolve ambiguous mappings consisted in finding instances appearing both in a sense of the word in WordNet and in the mapped category in Wikipedia. This method offered perfect precision but suffered from low recall (39%) due to the small number of instances present in WordNet. The alternative solution we explore in this paper consists on applying semantic similarity between the LR definitions and the mapped Wikipedia abstracts.

Let us then consider our problem as a real-world testbed in which we will apply different methods for semantic similarity between contexts.

The rest of the paper is organised as follows. Next section summarises the different approaches to semantic similarity that are found in the literature. This is followed by the description of the different approaches that we have applied to perform semantic similarity. Afterwards, we present the evaluation and results. Finally, we close the paper by presenting conclusions.

2 Background

This section describes some of the most relevant works on obtaining similarities between short texts. Existing research on text similarity has focused mainly on whole documents or individual words, while short paragraphs - sentences - contexts have been mostly dismissed. Following paragraphs delve into techniques and/or approaches that were relevant for the development of this research work.

SimFinder [7] is a supervised system made up of 43 features extracted from text. It uses a log-linear regression model to determine the semantic similarity of two short text units from the evidence obtained from the different features.

[13] combines corpus-based (PMI-IR and Latent Semantic Analysis) and knowledge-based measures of

*This work has been partially funded by the EU Commission (projects ICT-2007-211423 and FP6-IST-033860) and by the Spanish Government (project TIN2006-15265-C06-01).

word similarity. The results are then combined and used to derive a similarity metric between short texts.

Semantic Text Similarity [9] combines string and semantic similarity (a modified version of the longest common subsequence and Second order Co-occurrence PMI respectively) between words and common-word order similarity.

SenseClusters [1] is a language independent and unsupervised tool that clusters short contexts. It represents contexts using first or second order feature vectors. In order to reduce dimensionality it applies Singular Value Decomposition.

Apart from the aforementioned systems, it is worth mentioning two datasets that have been used to evaluate approaches to short text similarity. The first is the Microsoft paraphrase corpus [3], extracted from news sources. It is made up of 5,801 pairs of sentences, each together with a human judgement indicating whether the two sentences can be considered paraphrases or not. The second is the Pilot Short Text Semantic Similarity Benchmark Data Set [10], which contains 30 sentence pairs from the Collins Cobuild dictionary. In this case the judgements are not binary, but on a scale (from 0.0 for minimum similarity to 4.0 for maximum similarity).

3 Methods

The current section describes the different methods that we have applied. Approaches include Textual Entailment based on lexical and semantic inferences, a graph-based algorithm based on a LR and a Random projection algorithm to term-document matrices. We present also two baseline systems to which the aforementioned ones will be confronted. Finally, we introduce three combinations of the different approaches based on voting, unsupervised and supervised schemes.

3.1 Textual Entailment

Textual Entailment has been defined as a generic framework for modeling semantic variability, which appears when a concrete meaning is described in different manners as proposed by [2]. Therefore, semantic similarity is addressed by defining the concept of Textual Entailment as a one-way meaning relation between two snippets. Moreover, a series of Workshops, called Recognising Textual Entailment (RTE[2]) challenges and the Answer Validation Exercise (AVE[3]) competitions, have been recently proposed with the objective of providing suitable frameworks to evaluate textual entailment systems .

To address the specific semantic similarity phenomenon we are dealing with in this research work (i.e. semantic similarity between WordNet glosses and Wikipedia categories), we used our in-house textual entailment system presented in [6]. This system has been previously used to support other NLP applications rather than puristic textual entailment tasks. For instance, in Question Answering [14] and automatic text summarisation [12] .

As a brief system overview, it is worth mentioning the most relevant inferences implemented aimed at solving entailment relations:

- Lexical inferences based on lexical distance measures. For instance, the Needleman-Wunsch algorithm, Smith-Waterman algorithm, a matching of consecutive subsequences, Jaro distance, Euclidean distance, IDF specificity based on word frequencies extracted from corpora, etc.

- Semantic inferences focused on semantic distances between concepts. These inferences implement several well-known WordNet-based similarity measures, verbs' similarities based on the relations encoded in VerbNet[4] and VerbOcean[5] , and reasoning about named entities correspondences between texts.

For the final application of the system to the target task of this work, we adapted it in order to manage bidirectional meaning relations. Linking WordNet glosses to Wikipedia categories is not a clear entailment phenomenon. It can occur that the gloss is implied by the category, the category is deducted by the gloss or the entailment appears in both directions. Therefore, to control these situations we opted for computing the average of the two system outputs regarding each unidirectional relation.

3.2 Personalised PageRank over WordNet

WordNet is a lexical database of English, which groups nouns, verbs, adjectives and adverbs into sets of synonyms (synsets), each expressing a distinct concept. Synsets are interlinked with conceptual-semantic and lexical relations, including hypernymy, meronymy, causality, etc.

Given a pair of texts and a graph-based representation of WordNet, our method has basically two steps: We first compute the Personalised PageRank over WordNet separately for each of the texts, producing a probability distribution over WordNet synsets. We then compare how similar these two discrete probability distributions are by encoding them as vectors and computing the cosine between the vectors.

We represent WordNet as a graph $G = (V, E)$ as follows:

- Graph nodes represent WordNet concepts (synsets) and dictionary words.

- Relations among synsets are represented by undirected edges.

- Dictionary words are linked to the synsets associated to them by directed edges.

For each text in the pair we first compute a personalised PageRank vector of graph G [8]. Basically,

[1] http://senseclusters.sourceforge.net/

[2] http://pascallin.ecs.soton.ac.uk/Challenges/RTE/

[3] http://nlp.uned.es/clef-qa/ave/

[4] http://verbs.colorado.edu/~mpalmer/projects/verbnet.html

[5] http://demo.patrickpantel.com/Content/verbocean/

personalised PageRank is computed by modifying the random jump distribution vector in the traditional PageRank equation. In our case, we concentrate all probability mass in the words present in the target text.

Regarding PageRank implementation details, we chose a damping value of 0.85 and finish the calculation after 30 iterations. We have not optimised these values for this task. We used all the relations in WordNet 3.0[6], including the disambiguated glosses[7]. This similarity method was used for word similarity [1] which report very good results on word similarity datasets.

3.3 Semantic Vectors

Semantic Vectors [19][8] is an open source (BSD license) software package that creates WORDSPACE models from plain text. Its aim is to provide an easy-to-use and efficient tool which can fit both research and production users. It uses a random projection algorithm to perform dimension reduction as this is a simpler and more efficient technique than other alternatives such as Singular Value Decomposition.

It relies on Apache Lucene[9] for tokenisation and indexing in order to create a term document matrix. Once the reference corpus has been tokenised and indexed, Semantic Vectors creates a WORDSPACE model from the resulting matrix by applying random projection.

For the current task we have gathered a corpus made up of WordNet glosses and Wikipedia abstracts. On one hand, it contains the glosses of all the synsets present in WordNet 2.1., i.e. 117,598 glosses. On the other, it contains the abstracts of all the entries present in a Wikipedia dump obtained in January 2008, i.e. 2,179,275 abstracts. The final corpus has 1,292,447 terms.

Semantic Vectors provides a class (CompareTerms) that calculates the similarity between two terms (which can be words or texts). Thus we have directly used this in our experiments.

3.4 Baselines

We provide two baselines based on sense predominance and word overlap.

3.4.1 First Sense

This baseline follows the assumption that senses in WordNet are ordered according to their usage predominance (i.e. the first sense is the most general). *First Sense* chooses always the first sense of WordNet as being the correspondent to the mapped Wikipedia category. Being Wikipedia a general resource, it is expected that the words that identify categories refer to their most common sense. E.g. it is really unexpected that the category called "Bishops" would refer to the sense "(chess) a piece that can be moved diagonally over unoccupied squares of the same color" (third and last sense of the noun "bishop" in WordNet).

3.4.2 Word overlap

This baseline calculates similarity between two texts by counting the number of overlapping words. In order to do this we have used the software package Text::Similarity[10]. This method has been applied both considering all the words that appear in the texts and discarding stop words. For the last, we have used the list of stop words of the English stemmer Snowball[11].

3.5 Combinations

Due to the fact that the methods presented belong to different paradigms, we hypothesise that their results could be complementary and therefore we consider sensible to study possible combinations of them.

The first step in this direction has been the construction of an optimal combination, which we refer to as *oracle*. Given the outputs of the different systems and the gold standard, the oracle output sense/s for each instance is/are the sense/s present in the gold standard if any system return(s) it/them. The oracle represents then an optimal upper bound, the best result that could be obtained by combining the different systems.

Once we get an insight of the improvement that could be achieved by combining the diverse systems, we come up with three combination strategies:

- Voting. For each mapping it ranks senses according to the number of times they are returned by the different systems which are combined. Finally, it outputs the first ranked sense. Voting returns more than one sense if two or more senses are ranked first with the same score.

- Unsupervised combination. Within this combination, the methods taken into account have the same relevance computing a simple average function among the outputs of the considered methods (i.e. Textual entailment, WordNet-based method, Semantic Vectors and/or Word Overlap). As a result, the value returned by the average function is associated with its corresponding *Wikipedia category-WordNet sense* pair.

- Supervised combination. The whole set of inferences carried out by the Textual Entailment system together with the scores returned by the WordNet-based, Semantic Vectors and/or Word Overlap methods are computed as features for a machine learning algorithm. Specifically, we have used the BayesNet implementation provided by Weka[12] , and we obtained the 10-fold cross validation results over our gold standard corpus.

[6] Available from http://wordnet.princeton.edu/

[7] http://wordnet.princeton.edu/glosstag

[8] http://code.google.com/p/semanticvectors

[9] http://lucene.apache.org

[10] http://text-similarity.sourceforge.net

[11] http://snowball.tartarus.org/algorithms/english/stop.txt

[12] http://www.cs.waikato.ac.nz/ml/weka/

4 Experiments and Discussion

4.1 Evaluation Framework

The evaluation data consists of a set of polysemous nouns from WordNet 2.1 which are mapped to Wikipedia categories. Additional information is provided both for nouns and categories; for the first their glosses while for the second their abstracts. The disambiguation task should then identify, for each noun, which of its senses, if any, corresponds to the mapped/s category/ies. The resulting gold standard files (corpus and key) are available for research purposes[13]. The corpus file follows the following format

```
<word id={id}>
  <sense number={num}>{sense gloss}</sense>
  [...]
  <sense number={num}>{sense gloss}</sense>
  <category id ={id}>{category abstract}</category>
  [...]
  <category id ={id}>{category abstract}</category>
</word>
```

while the key file is made up of lines with the format of Senseval-3 scorer[14]:

```
word category sense_number+
```

In order to build the corpus file we departed from a set of 254 nouns mapped to categories. 54 of them were discarded because the abstracts of the corresponding categories were empty. The final data-set contains 200 polysemous nouns mapped to 207 categories. Thus we have an evaluation set with 207 mappings.

Regarding Wikipedia abstracts, they are straightforwardly available for articles but not for categories. Therefore we developed a procedure to gather them:

```
if (category has referent_article)
  if(referent_article has abstract)
    return abstract of referent_article
if (category has article_with_same_lemma)
  if(article_with_same_lemma has abstract)
    return absract of article_with_same_lemma
if (category_body longer than N characters)
  return category_body
return empty_string
```

Besides, we have manually created a key file. It contains the correct sense/s for each mapping. In most of the cases (154, 74,4%) there is a one to one correspondence. For 37 (17,9%) mappings, more than one sense corresponds to the mapped category, this usually occurs because the WordNet senses tend to be finer-grained than the Wikipedia categories. Concerning the remaining 16 (7,7%) mappings, no sense corresponds to the mapped category. Let's take a look at an example for each of these three cases:

- One sense corresponds to one category

```
<word id="admiral">
 <sense number="1">the supreme commander of a
 fleet; ranks above a vice admiral and below
 a fleet admiral</sense>
 <sense number="2">any of several brightly
 colored butterflies</sense>
 <category id="Admirals">Admiral is the rank,
 or part of the name of the ranks, of the
 highest naval officers. It is usually
 considered a full admiral (equivalent to
 full general) and four-star rank above Vice
 Admiral and below Admiral of the Fleet/Fleet
 Admiral. </category>
</word>
```

```
admiral Admirals 1
```

- More than one sense correspond to a category

```
<word id="communist">
 <sense number="1">a member of the communist
 party</sense>
 <sense number="2">a socialist who advocates
 communism</sense>
 <category id="Communists">This category lists
 people who have, at one time or another, been
 active in communist politics through either
 identifying themselves as communists or being
 members of parties identifying themselves as
 communist. It should not be taken for granted
 that inclusion in this category implies that
 figures remained their whole life or continue
 to be communists.

 Note : communist activists should only be
 featured in this category if no existing
 subcategory (-ies) suits them better - the
 comprehensive subcategory is :Category:Communists
 by nationality . For more information on
 categories, see: Wikipedia:Categorization .
 </category>
</word>
```

```
communist Communists 1 2
```

- No sense corresponds to the category

```
<word id="chief_executive">
 <sense number="1">the person who holds the
 office of head of state of the United States
 government; "the President likes to jog every
 morning"</sense>
 <sense number="2">the office of the United
 States head of state; "a President is elected
 every four years"</sense>
 <category id="Chief_executives">Chief
 executives determine and formulate policies
 and provide the overall direction of companies
 or private and public sector organizations
 within the guidelines set up by a board of
 directors or similar governing body. They plan,
 direct, or coordinate operational activities at
 the highest level of management with the help
 of subordinate executives and staff managers.
 </category>
</word>
```

```
chief_executive Chief_executives 0
```

4.2 Result Analysis

Table 1 presents the scores obtained by the different systems and the baselines introduced in section 3. Regarding the application of the textual entailment sys-

[13] http://www.dlsi.ua.es/~atoral/#Resources
[14] http://www.senseval.org/senseval3/scoring

tem, three different experiments were carried out, each one with a specific setting:

- *TE (trained AVE'07'08 + RTE-3)*: for this experiment the system was trained with the corpora provided in the AVE competitions (edition 2007 and 2008) and RTE-3 Challenge. This configuration uses a BayesNet algorithm, and it will show the capability of the system to solve the task when specific textual entailment corpora are used as training.

- *No training phase*: in order to assess whether the training corpora are appropriate to the final decision with regards to the task tackled in this work, we also decided to make an experiment without training phase. Therefore, the highest entailment coefficient returned by the system among all sense-category pairs for each word will be tagged as the correct link. These coefficients are obtained computing the set of lexical and semantic measures integrated into the system.

- *Supervised (10-fold cross-validation)*: a BayesNet algorithm was trained with the corpus described in section 4.1, which is intended to evaluate the task. We evaluated this experiment by 10-fold cross-validation using each textual entailment inference as a feature for the machine learning algorithm. This experiment shows the system behaviour when it is trained with a specific corpus for our task.

Table 1: *System Results*

Run	Accuracy
Baseline 1st sense	64.7%
Baseline Word overlap	56.3%
Baseline Word overlap (without stop words)	62.7%
Semantic Vectors	54.1%
Personalised PageRank	61.8%
Personalised PageRank (without stop words)	64.3%
TE (trained AVE 07-08 + RTE-3)	52.8%
TE (no training)	64.7%
TE (supervised)	77.74%

The first element that comes out is the high score obtained by the 1st sense baseline (64.7%). In fact, leaving aside supervision, only one system is able to reach its score, TE without training. It is also important the role of stop words. By filtering them, substantial better results can be obtained, as it can be seen both for the Word Overlap (62.7% vs. 56.3%) and the Personalised PageRank (64.3% vs. 61.8%) systems.

Results also point out that both the AVE and RTE corpora are not appropriate to this task (52.8%). This is due to the fact that the idiosyncrasies of each corpus are somewhat different resulting in a poor training stage. Nevertheless, computing the entailment coefficient returned by the system without training (64.7%), a considerable improvement in accuracy is achieved. It proves the textual entailment inferences are suitable to support our research. Finally, as expected, the best TE result is when the dataset created for the evaluation is also processed as training and evaluated by 10-fold cross-validation (77.74%).

Table 2 presents the scores obtained by the different combinations introduced in section 3.5.

Table 2: *Combination Results*

Run	Accuracy
Oracle (PPR + SV + TE + WO)	84.5%
Voting (PPR + SV + TE + WO)	66.5%
Voting (PPR + SV + TE)	64.7%
Voting (PPR + SV + WO)	66.1%
Voting (PPR + TE + WO)	68%
Unsupervised (PPR + SV + TE + WO)	65.2%
Unsupervised (PPR + SV + TE)	64.7%
Unsupervised (PPR + SV + WO)	64.7%
Unsupervised (PPR + TE + WO)	65.7%
Supervised (PPR + SV + TE + WO)	77.24%
Supervised (PPR + SV + TE)	76.99%
Supervised (PPR + SV + WO)	75.12%
Supervised (PPR + TE + WO)	77.11%

The score achieved by the upper bound oracle (84.5%), nearly 7 points higher than the best supervised system (77.74%) seems to indicate that there is room for improving the performance by a supervised combination of the systems. However, none of the supervised combinations is able even to reach the score obtained by the supervised TE. The reason behind this is that the TE system implements some inferences which are somewhat similar to the knowledge reported by the other methods (e.g. the Smith-Waterman algorithm vs. word overlap, and WordNet Similarity measures vs. WordNet-based method). Therefore, the information gain supplied by the other methods is not enough in order to improve the TE performance.

Regarding unsupervised combinations, the best result (65.7%) is obtained by discarding Semantic Vectors, expected as out of the three systems this was the one that obtained the lowest score (54.1%). For some of these combinations the results improve the performance of the unsupervised TE configuration, but as we mentioned before, this is an slight improvement owing to the inner characteristics of the TE inferences.

Furthermore, it is worth noting though that the simple voting approach outperforms the unsupervised combination. The best result (68%) again is obtained when discarding Semantic Vectors.

5 Conclusions

This paper has presented an automatic approach to treat disambiguation when linking WordNet to Wikipedia. The proposal calculates semantic similarity between the definitions of WordNet senses and abstracts of Wikipedia categories in order to individuate which of the senses corresponds to the category. We have applied different methods based on different approaches and explored also with their combination. In order to evaluate their performance we have manually annotated a gold standard. We have also considered two baselines. The results obtained are encouraging as compared to the accuracy of the best baseline (64.7%), an unsupervised combination obtains 68% while regarding supervised schemes, a Textual Entailment system applied bidirectionally achieves 77.74%.

Regarding future work, some research lines worth exploring emerge naturally from a first analysis. First, because of the fact that some inferences from the TE system overlap with the other methods (e.g. WordNet Similarity measures of the TE system vs. WordNet-based system), we plan to explore further combinations in which such inferences of the TE will be discarded. Second, we would like to study the cases in which none of the systems is able to obtain the correct disambiguation, i.e. the 15,5% of the dataset for which the oracle fails. This will give an insight of the kind of data that none of the methods is able to disambiguate. Finally, it would be interesting to measure the statistical significance between the scores obtained by the different systems.

References

[1] E. Agirre, A. Soroa, E. Alfonseca, K. Hall, J. Kravalova, and M. Pasca. A study on similarity and relatedness using distributional and wordnet-based approaches. In *Proceedings of NAACL*, 2009.

[2] Ido Dagan and Oren Glickman. Probabilistic textual entailment: Generic appied modelling of language variability. In *Proceedings of the PASCAL Workshop on Learning Methods for Text Understanding and Mining*, Grenoble, France, 2004.

[3] William B. Dolan and Chris Brockett. Automatically constructing a corpus of sentential paraphrases. In *IWP2005*, 2005.

[4] G. Erkan and Dragomir R. Radev. Lexrank: Graph-based centrality as salience in text summarization. *Journal of Artificial Intelligence Research*, 22:457–479, 2004.

[5] Christian Fellbaum, editor. *WordNet: An Electronic Lexical Database (ISBN: 0-262-06197-X)*. MIT Press, first edition, 1998.

[6] Óscar Ferrández, Daniel Micol, Rafael Muñoz, and Manuel Palomar. A perspective-based approach for solving textual entailment recognition. In *Proceedings of the ACL-PASCAL Workshop on Textual Entailment and Paraphrasing*, pages 66–71, Prague, June 2007. ACL.

[7] Vasileios Hatzivassiloglou, Judith L. Klavans, Melissa L. Holcombe, Regina Barzilay, Min yen Kan, and Kathleen R. Mckeown. Simfinder: A flexible clustering tool for summarization. In *NAACL Workshop on Automatic Summarization*, pages 41–49, 2001.

[8] T. H. Haveliwala. Topic-sensitive pagerank. In *WWW '02: Proceedings of the 11th international conference on World Wide Web*, pages 517–526, New York, NY, USA, 2002. ACM.

[9] Aminul Islam and Diana Inkpen. Semantic text similarity using corpus-based word similarity and string similarity. *ACM Trans. Knowl. Discov. Data*, 2(2):1–25, July 2008.

[10] Yuhua Li, David McLean, Zuhair A. Bandar, James D. O'Shea, and Keeley Crockett. Sentence similarity based on semantic nets and corpus statistics. *IEEE Transactions on Knowledge and Data Engineering*, 18(8):1138–1150, 2006.

[11] Tao Liu and Jun Guo. Text similarity computing based on standard deviation. In De-Shuang Huang, Xiao-Ping Zhang, and Guang-Bin Huang, editors, *ICIC (1)*, volume 3644 of *Lecture Notes in Computer Science*, pages 456–464. Springer, 2005.

[12] Elena Lloret, Óscar Ferrández, Rafael Muñoz, and Manuel Palomar. A text summarization approach under the influence of textual entailment. In *Natural Language Processing and Cognitive Science, Proceedings of the 5th International Workshop on Natural Language Processing and Cognitive Science (NLPCS 2008)*, pages 22–31, Barcelona, Spain, 2008.

[13] Rada Mihalcea, Courtney Corley, and Carlo Strapparava. Corpus-based and knowledge-based measures of text semantic similarity. In *In AAAI06*, pages 775–780, 2006.

[14] Óscar Ferrández, Rubén Izquierdo, Sergio Ferrández, and José Luis Vicedo. Addressing ontology-based question answering with collections of user queries. *Information Processing and Management, In Press, Corrected Proof available online 31 October 2008*, 2008.

[15] Ted Pedersen. Computational approaches to measuring the similarity of short contexts : A review of applications and methods. *CoRR*, abs/0806.3787, 2008.

[16] Hinrich Schtitze. Automatic word sense discrimination. *Journal of Computational Linguistics*, 24:97–123, 1998.

[17] Fabian Suchanek, Gjergji Kasneci, and Gerhard Weikum. Yago - a large ontology from wikipedia and wordnet. *Elsevier Journal of Web Semantics*, 6(3):203–217, September 2008.

[18] Antonio Toral, Rafael Muñoz, and Monica Monachini. Named entity wordnet. In *Proceedings of the Sixth International Language Resources and Evaluation (LREC'08)*, Marrakech, Morocco, may 2008.

[19] Dominic Widdows and Kathleen Ferraro. Semantic vectors: a scalable open source package and online technology management application. In *Proceedings of the Sixth International Language Resources and Evaluation (LREC'08)*, Marrakech, Morocco, may 2008.

Ontology engineering and knowledge extraction for crosslingual retrieval

Jantine Trapman
Utrecht University
jeandix23@yahoo.com

Paola Monachesi
Utrecht University
P.Monachesi@uu.nl

Abstract

In this paper, we show that by integrating existing NLP techniques and Semantic Web tools in a novel way, we can provide a valuable contribution to the solution of the knowledge acquisition bottleneck problem. NLP techniques to create a domain ontology on the basis of an open domain corpus have been combined with Semantic Web tools. More specifically, Watson and Prompt have been employed to enhance the kick-off ontology while Cornetto, a lexical database for Dutch, has been adopted to establish a link between the concepts and their Dutch lexicalization. The lexicalized ontology constitutes the basis for the cross-language retrieval of learning objects within the LT4eL eLearning project.

Keywords

Ontology learning, eLearning, NLP, Semantic Web, cross-lingual retrieval

1 Introduction

The aim of the Language Technology for eLearning (LT4eL)[1] project is to employ Language Technology and Semantic Web resources and tools to enhance eLearning in order to develop innovative applications for education and training [8]. One important objective is to enhance the management, distribution, search and reuse of multilingual learning material [7] .

Ontologies play a relevant role in the realization of this objective. More specifically, in the LT4eL project, the ontology mediates between the user and the learning material. The relevant concepts which are attested in the learning objects constitute the backbone of the ontology. Thus, a link is created between the learning material and its conceptualization which is represented by means of the ontology allowing for the creation of individualized learning paths. However, the most important contribution of the ontology is its role as interlingua. It facilitates access to documents in various languages since it allows for cross-lingual retrieval by mediating at the conceptual level among language specific textual realizations of the concepts.

The LT4eL project has provided a prototype which has shown the feasibility of the approach that has been validated within an eLearning context. However, in order to develop a real life application, the knowledge needs to be extracted and modeled semi-automatically. Several approaches have been proposed to this end in the Natural Language Processing as well as in the Semantic Web literature, providing a valuable contribution to the solution of this problem.

Our goal is to rely on previous results and integrate, in a novel way, existing Natural Language Processing techniques such as that proposed in [2] for ontology learning from text with recent approaches emerging from the Semantic Web community. An example of which is [12], that uses dynamically selected ontologies as background knowledge to enrich existing ontologies with new concepts. Our aim is to extend (semi-automatically) the ontology developed within the LT4eL project to new domains enabling thus the cross-lingual retrieval of new learning objects. To this end, a mapping has been carried out between the ontology and various lexicalizations. In our case, the ontology has been mapped to Cornetto [14], a Dutch lexical resource. In this paper, we report our work to extend the current ontology to a new domain (i.e. music).

The structure of the paper is as follows: in the next section, we give an overview of the LT4eL project and we discuss the role that ontologies and lexicons play in supporting the learning process. In section 3, we discuss NLP techniques for ontology learning and we focus on the approach proposed by [2], which has obvious advantages in the case of our application. Section 4, shows how the ontology developed by means of NLP techniques can be enriched further by employing tools for ontology crawling, such as Watson [1] and tools for ontology merging, such as Prompt [11]. Finally, in section 5, we discuss how the ontology is mapped to an available lexical resource which has been developed for Dutch, that is Cornetto, in order to create a lexicalized ontology. The paper ends with some conclusions.

2 The LT4eL project

One of the aims of the LT4eL project is to improve the retrieval and the usability of (multilingual) learning material within a Learning Management System in order to support the learning process.

To achieve this objective, an ontology-based search functionality has been developed which is based on the following components:

- a domain ontology in the domain of the learning objects;

[1] http://www.lt4el.eu

International Conference RANLP 2009 - Borovets, Bulgaria, pages 455–459

- a lexicon for each of the languages addressed which comprises words or phrases that are mapped to concepts attested in the ontology;
- a collection of (multilingual) learning objects annotated on the basis of the ontology.

The development of the ontology which constitutes the core of the semantic search functionality is based on domain specific corpora in the area of *computing* for the various languages addressed in the project, that is Bulgarian, Czech, Dutch, English, German, Polish, Portuguese and Romanian.

Terms have been identified in the corpora and relevant concepts have been created which constitute the backbone of the domain ontology. The domain ontology has been mapped to the DOLCE upper ontology, by means of OntoWordNet [5], which is a version of WordNet mapped to DOLCE. The current ontology contains 1002 domain concepts, 169 concepts from OntoWordNet and 105 concepts from DOLCE Ultralite.

For each language represented in the project, we have developed a lexicon on the basis of the existing ontology, following [3]. The lexicons constitute the main interface between the user's query, the ontology and the semantic search functionality which is based on the ontology.

Inline annotation of the learning material is carried out on the basis of the the ontology by means of grammars implemented in the CLaRK System.[2] The regular grammars identify the relation between the domain terms in a given language and the concepts attested in the ontology. Through the annotation, a link is created between the learning material and its conceptualization which is represented by means of the ontology.

The search engine which has been developed in the LT4eL project is based on the modules previously described. In particular, when a user types a query, the search words are looked up in the lexicons of the chosen language. If lexical entries are found in the lexicon, these are related to the concepts in the ontology. The learning objects in the desired languages are retrieved on the basis of the set of found concepts. We refer to [6] and [9] for more details.

3 Ontology learning from open domain corpora

The semantic search architecture, described in the previous section, has been developed on the basis of a manually created ontology and a corpus in the *computing* domain. However, in order for the LT4eL eLearning prototype to develop into a real life application, it is necessary to create new domain ontologies and more general lexicons. It is well known that the manual creation of an ontology is a time-consuming and expensive process. Therefore, we need to create and extend domain ontologies semi-automatically on the basis of existing resources. In this paper, we explore an approach aiming at the integration of current NLP techniques and available Semantic Web tools.

[2] http://www.bultreebank.org/clark/index.html

In this section, we discuss how NLP techniques can be employed to reach this goal. Several suggestions have been made in the literature in this respect. In particular, NLP techniques can be adopted to extract terms/concepts, definitions and relations from learning material. It is thus possible to build on existing approaches which rely mainly on statistical analysis, patterns finding and shallow linguistic parsing ([10], [4] among others for an overview).

In this paper, we focus on a methodology developed by [2], in order to create a domain ontology on the basis of an open domain corpus. The main reason to adopt this approach is that it is highly compatible with the semantic search architecture assumed in the LT4eL project because the ontology extracted through this method is based on WordNet. Recall that in the LT4eL ontology, the mapping between the domain and the upper ontology occurs via OntoWordNet.

Basili et al., propose an unsupervised technique to induce domain specific knowledge from open domain corpora, on the basis of a user query. Their algorithm exploits Latent Semantic Analysis (LSA) to extract domain terminology from a large open domain corpus, as an answer to a user query. Furthermore, Conceptual Density is employed to map the inferred terms into WordNet in order to identify domain specific subregions in it. They can be considered as lexicalized kick-off ontologies for the selected domain. The main advantages of this algorythm is that it allows for the extraction of domain ontologies from WordNet on the fly without the need for domain corpora, being thus an ideal approach for our application. It can be employed to extend our ontology to new domains, more specifically we have focussed on the the *music* domain, addressed in [2].

The relevant terms are extracted through the application of LSA on the British National Corpus. The result is a terminological lexicon consisting of 181 nouns. From this lexicon a kick-off ontology has been induced which consists of 46 classes related to each other by the is-a relation. All the (numbered) leaf nodes of the ontology carry WordNet synset IDs with them. The structure of the ontology resembles WordNet but intermediate levels between two concepts are sometimes lacking. For instance, the class *quartet* is child of *quartet* > *musical_organisation* > *group*, where > denotes the is-a relation. In WordNet however, the complete subtree for this concept is *quartet* > *musical organisation / musical group* > *organisation* > *social group*> *group*.

The approach proposed in [2] has several advantages: it can be applied at run-time to an open domain corpus; in principle no specialized content is necessary. Furthermore, it is language independent and the built-in mapping to WordNet allows for easy integration in other applications related to WordNet, as in the case of the LT4eL ontology.

The result of this approach is a kick-off ontology with a taxonomic structure that constitutes the basis for further extension. In addition, a domain lexicon is produced from the terminology extraction phase. This list of extracted terms could still support a human expert in the completion of the ontology.The advantage of this list is that it contains terms that are provided with WordNet synset IDs with them. However, enhancing the kick-off ontology with these terms would still be a manual task. It is thus relevant to exploit existing resources and tools developed within the Semantic Web community to assess whether it is possible to extend this kick-off ontology in a semi-automatic way.

4 Semi-automatic ontology enrichment with new concepts

The growth of the Semantic Web has influenced also the availability of freely available ontologies. Reusing such resources can save the time and effort of manual labor. We have explored two possible strategies for the extension of our kick-off ontology described in the previous section which both exploit the use of existing resources.

One relies on *crawling semantic data* by means of Watson [1], which allows for the extraction of new concepts from relevant ontologies. Watson has been preferred to other tools such as Swoogle because of the quality of the documents retrieved and the availability of relevant plug-ins. The other approach relies on *merging* the kick-off ontology with existing resources i.e. other ontologies in the music domain by using Prompt [11].

4.1 Watson

Watson is a Semantic Web application that crawls the web to find semantic documents including existing ontologies, it is available both as web interface and as Protege plug-in. We have investigated both functionalities in the task of extending our kick-off ontology. The basic assumptions behind their use are that there are available resources on-line which contain the relevant domain information. This will greatly differ from domain to domain: several ontologies are available for *Law* and *Medicine*. However, in the *Music* domain only few resources are available, more specifically:

1. Music.owl (33 classes)
2. musicontology.rdfs (83 classes)
3. music.rdf (109 classes)
4. SUMO.owl (1524 classes)

The extension of our kick-off ontology through the Watson web interface has produced an ontology with 171 classes while the one extended with the plug-in contains about 120 classes. Expanding the kick-off ontology with the web interface version of Watson is more effective than using the plug-in since more classes are identified.

A closer analysis of the resulting ontologies reveals that the one created with the web version of Watson contains a larger number of abstract classes than the one expanded with the plug-in, even though additions in the upper layer were only made to generalize over the existing classes. It contains a set of classes that are related to the digital music industry. These classes were not found with the plug-in. This is because the plug-in only matches on classes, while the Watson web interface allows the user to include classes, properties, labels, comments, local names and/or literals. It seems thus that information types other than class names include valuable clues for retrieval. This increases the chance to come across sub areas of the domain a user might have ignored otherwise. The downside is they also cause noise i.e. irrelevant documents. It should be noticed, however, that even though the plug-in version is less efficient, it has the great advantage that one can make additions to an ontology *within* the editor environment.

More generally, on the basis of our experience with Watson, we conclude that the number of resources that contribute substantially to the enhancement of an existing ontology is rather limited. The size of the relevant resources available is still quite modest, which might be the reason why some trivial classes are not found (e.g. pianist, drummer, rhythm, chord, melody). The application allows for a relatively fast and efficient extension of the ontology (i.e. from 46 classes of the kick-off ontology to the 120-170 classes of the enhanced ontology). It should be noted that crawling of new semantic data not only enhances the kick-off ontology with new classes but it also improves its original structure.

4.2 Prompt

Watson is an appropriate tool for expanding our ontology with existing resources but it does not provide options for merging ontologies which may be quicker and more efficient than adding concepts one-by-one, as in the case of Watson. Merging could be preferable if both ontologies cover the same domain but have just a partial overlap.

In order to assess whether merging would be a better way to enhance an existing ontology, we have employed Prompt, a tool for semi-automatic ontology merging and alignment [11].

We have explored its functionalities by merging two ontologies from the music domain. More specifically, we have merged our kick-off music ontology with a domain ontology from the Music Ontology Specification Group[3]. The kick-off ontology consists of 46 classes in a purely taxonomic structure. It covers concepts related to music genre, musical groups, musicians and entertainers. The latter ontology contains 92 classes: 86 primitive and 6 defined classes. It includes three group of concepts: those covering simple editorial information, a second group covering music creation workflow and a third group of concepts related to events and time.

The overlap between both ontologies is not very large, because they are both rather small and they address different topics. The result of the merge is an ontology of 103 classes. About 20 classes originate from the kick-off ontology; most of them are leaf nodes. From the other ontology, 90% is present in the resulting ontology.

Prompt calculates linguistic matches and alignment possibilities in very short time, inherited properties and subclasses can be added to the target ontology within just one step and without risking (human)

[3] http://pingthesemanticweb.com/ontology/mo/musicontology.rdfs

mistakes, similar structures are also automatically detected, a tedious and time consuming task for any human to accomplish. Moreover, the results are automatically checked and after each execution step, mappings and matches are recalculated. It should be noticed that 74% of the operations involved in the merging process were suggested by Prompt; this is quite a high number and it shows that the algorithm works properly for the task.

To conclude: both Watson and Prompt are tools that provide valuable support to the task of enriching an ontology with new concepts. However, the one-by-one additions to the ontology which Watson supports leaves the ontology builder still with a significant amount of work. Especially when the resources include a substantial number of relevant concepts and a sound hierarchical structure, a merge between them is preferred. Merging seems more efficient but is also a more complex process. The ontology engineer is faced with the challenge to discover where multiple resources can be aligned or merged. Prompt gives significant support in the merging task. But for two ontologies to be merged they have to be available off-line. The results of our investigation is that it would be desirable to integrate the crawling and merging approach since Watson and Prompt can actually complement each other: with the former the user can find suitable candidates. Those candidates can be evaluated for the representation language and size which indicate possible mismatches on the language level and for coverage, respectively. Subsequently, Prompt can be used for merging (or aligning) the resources. We will explore this integration in future research.

5 Mapping the ontology to an existing lexical resource

The ontology we have obtained by combining NLP techniques with ontology enrichment tools developed within the Semantic Web community is an ontology representing the music domain that is partly mapped to WordNet. A shortcoming of the ontologies we have used to expand our kick-off ontology, is that they lack a mapping with WordNet. This property is one of the main motivations behind the creation method of the kick-off ontology since it enables an easy mapping to an existing lexicon.

Recall that in the LT4eLproject, in order to carry out cross-language retrieval of the learning objects, we rely not only on the ontology but also on language specific lexicons which are built on the basis of the formal definitions of the concepts of the ontology. If new domain ontologies are developed, a necessary condition is that new lexicons should also be built. In the LT4eL project, these lexicons were created manually. However, another possibilty, at least for Dutch, is to employ a lexical resource recently developed, that is Cornetto [14]. One of its features makes it especially interesting for our project: it is mapped to WordNet – a feature shared also by the kick-off ontology. Mapping the lexicon to the ontology becomes thus a straightforward process.

The Cornetto database is a lexical semantic database for Dutch which contains both combinatorial and semantic information i.e. semantic relations. It consists of three linguistic layers: Lexical Units (LU) which originate from the Referentie Bestand Nederlands (RBN), a collection of synsets from the Dutch WordNet which is aligned to the English WordNet 2.0, a formal upper ontology, that is SUMO. The main goal of the Cornetto project consisted in combining and aligning the RBN and Dutch WordNet. The core of Cornetto is therefore a table of Cornetto identifiers (CIDs). This table yields 1) the relations between LUs and synsets *within* the Cornetto database, and 2) between original word senses and the synsets from RBN and Dutch WordNet respectively: each synonym from Dutch WordNet is directly related to a lexical unit from the RBN.

Cornetto is a lexicon for an open domain from which we need to filter the relevant terms from the music domain. However, WordNet has been labeled with labels from the Dewey Decimal Classification which resulted in WordNet Domains. These domain labels are also integrated in Cornetto and filtering music related terms is thus a fairly easy task. It is reported in [13] that 985 concepts from WordNet 1.6 have been assigned the music label. The number of synsets extracted from Cornetto is actually much smaller: only 111 synsets. This is because only nouns have been extracted.

We have selected the kick-off ontology enhanced with Watson for the mapping task. Two cases can be identified: the ontology contains concepts with and without a WordNet identifier.

The former case involves a rather straightforward mapping: since the ontology includes WordNet identifiers a mapping with Cornetto amounts to the retrieval of WordNet identifiers in the database. The equivalence relations between WordNet and Dutch WordNet, captured in the database, automatically supply the mapping between the concepts from the ontology and the Dutch synsets and thus ultimately with the lexical units of the RBN. We have applied this strategy in case of equivalences and near-equivalences.

A more complex situation is due to multiple EQ_NEAR_SYNONYM relations that can exist among terms from two languages through EuroWordNet's ILI. There could be a situation in which one ontology concept maps to multiple Dutch synsets or a single Dutch synset associated with several concepts through the EQ_NEAR_SYNONYM relation. An example of the latter is the concept *Quartet_Composition* associated with synset number 06610307: *quartet:5, quartette:4*. Two Dutch synsets are near-equivalents of the English one: *kwartet:1* and *kwartet:3*. These same two Dutch synsets are also near-equivalents of the WordNet synset *quartet:2, quartette:1*, associated with the concept *Quartet_Performers* in the ontology. Hence, both synsets are mapped to two different concepts from the ontology.

After the automatic mapping, 13 of the 17 concepts with a WordNet Identifier have been assigned a mapping to 15 synsets. The fact that four concepts could not be mapped is due to the fact that not all the data was available. This leaves about 140 concepts which do not have a WordNet identifier because they originate from the enrichment of the ontology through Watson and which should be mapped to Cornetto.

The most obvious option is to carry out a syntactic mapping between the concepts and the terms from WordNet synsets in the music domain. If a concept matches any term in a WordNet synset, it will be mapped to this synset. If such a mapping has been established, a mapping to one or more Dutch synsets can be established. At the moment, there 111 Dutch synsets in the Cornetto database which are related to 126 WordNet synsets (150 English terms). So unfortunately, because the data are sparse, there are less entries and synsets in Cornetto, than there are concepts in the ontology. Preliminary investigations show that multiword phrases and ambiguity are the most common problems for optimal automatic mapping.

6 Conclusions

We have shown that the integration of exiting NLP techniques and Semantic Web tools provide a valuable contribution to the solution of the knowledge acquisition bottleneck. The integrated approach has been tested to extend the LT4eL lexicalized domain ontology to the *music* domain. In particular, on the basis of the NLP techniques proposed by [2], we have developed a kick-off ontology consisting of 46 classes related to each other by the is-a relation. In addition, all the (numbered) leaf nodes of the ontology carry WordNet synset IDs with them.

The kick-off ontology has been enhanced with new concepts by means of two Semantic Web tools. Watson, which allows for crawling of semantic data, has allowed for an extension of the kick-off ontology (46 classes) to 120 classes (plug-in version) and to 170 classes (web interface version). While Prompt has been tested for the merging of the kick-off ontology consisting of 46 classes with a new music ontology consisting of 92 classes, resulting in a new ontology of 103 classes. The version enhanced with Watson has been mapped to Cornetto by making use of the WordNet synset IDs.

The approach sketched in this paper makes possible the cross-language retrieval of learning objects, within the LT4eL project, in new domains.

References

[1] d'Aquin, M., Gridinoc, L., Sabou, M. and Angeletou, S.: (2007), Watson: Supporting next generation semantic web applications, WWW/Internet Conference 2007.

[2] Basili, R., Gliozzo, A. and Pennacchiotti, M.: (2007), Harvesting ontologies from open domain corpora: a dynamic approach, RANLP 2007, Borovets, Bulgaria.

[3] Buitelaar, P. T. Declerck, A. Frank, S. Racioppa, M. Kiesel, M. Sintek, R. Engel, M. Romanelli, D. Sonntag, B. Loos, V. Micelli, R. Porzel, P. Cimiano (2006) LingInfo: Design and Applications of a Model for the Integration of Linguistic Information in Ontologies. In: Proc. of OntoLex06, a Workshop at LREC, Genoa, Italy, May 2006.

[4] Buitelaar, P., Cimiano, P., Magnini B., (2005) Ontology from Text: Methods, Evaluation and Applications Frontiers in Artificial Intelligence and Applications Series, Vol. 123, IOS Press.

[5] Gangemi, A., Roberto Navigli, and Paola Velardi. (2003). The OntoWordNet Project: extension and axiomatisation of conceptual relations in WordNet. International Conference on Ontologies, Databases and Applications of Semantics (ODBASE 2003), Catania, Italy.

[6] Lemnitzer L., Simov K., Osenova P., Mossel E., Monachesi P. (2007) Using a domain ontology and semantic search in an eLearning environment. In: Proceedings of The Third International Joint Conferences on Computer, Information, and Systems Sciences, and Engineering. (CISSE 2007). Springer-Verlag. Berlin Heidelberg.

[7] Lemnitzer L. ,C. Vertan, A. Killing, K. Simov, D. Evans, D. Cristea and P. Monachesi. (2007). *Improving the search for learning objects with keywords and ontologies.* In: Proceedings of the ECTEL 2007 conference. Springer Verlag.

[8] Monachesi, P., L. Lemnitzer, K. Simov. Language Technology for eLearning. Proceedings of EC-TEL 2006, in Innovative Approaches for Learning and Knowledge Sharing, LNCS 0302-9743, pp. 667-672. 2006

[9] Monachesi, P., K. Simov, E. Mossel, P. Osenova, L. Lemnitzer. What ontologies can do for eLearning. Proceedings of International Conference on Interactive Mobile and Computer Aided Learning (IMCL08).

[10] Navigli, R., Velardi P. (2004) Learning Domain Ontologies from Document Warehouses and Dedicated Websites, Computational Linguistics (30-2).

[11] Noy, N. F. and Musen, M. A.: (2000), Prompt: Algorithm and tool for automated ontology merging and alignment, AAAI/IAAI, pp. 450-455.

[12] Sabou, M., dAquin, M., Motta, E. (2006) Using the Semantic Web as Background Knowledge for Ontology Mapping. International Workshop on Ontology Matching, Athens, GA.

[13] Vossen, P., Glaser, E., van Zutphen, H. and Steenwijk, R.: 2004, Validation of meaning, Wp8.1, deliverable 8.1, Irion Technologies

[14] Vossen, P., Maks, I., Segers, R., van der Vliet, H. and van Zutphen, H.: (2008), The cornetto database: Architecture and alignment issues of combining lexical units, synsets and an ontology. Proceedings of Fourth International GlobalWordNet Conference.

A method to restrict the blow-up of hypotheses of a non-disambiguated shallow machine translation system

Jernej Vičič
University of Primorska
Koper, Slovenia
jernej.vicic@upr.si

Petr Homola
Charles university
Prague, Czech republic
homola@ufal.mff.cuni.cz

Vladislav Kuboň
Charles university
Prague, Czech republic
vk@ufal.mff.cuni.cz

Abstract

The article presents two automatic methods that reduce the complexity of the ambiguous space introduced by the omission of the part of speech tagger from the architecture of a shallow machine translation system. The methods were implemented in a fully functional translation system for related languages. The language pair chosen for the experiments was Slovenian-Serbian as these languages are highly inflectional with morphologically ambiguous forms. The empirical evaluations show an improvement over the original system.

Keywords

MT, RBMT, SMT, related languages, ranking, Apertium.

1 Introduction

The article presents two automatic methods that reduce the complexity of the ambiguous space introduced by the omission of the part of speech tagger from the architecture of a shallow transfer machine translation system.
The shallow parsing machine translation architecture is suitable for the translation systems for related languages as shown in [5, 15]. Authors [12] and the authors of translation systems for related languages Apertium [5] and Česílko [11] suggest using an architecture similar to the one presented in figure 1. This architecture employs statistical part of speech (POS) tagger for disambiguation of the morphological analysis of the source language. The quality level of the tagging process of today's state-of-the-art POS taggers for highly inflectional languages like [10] and [8] is relatively low, comparing to the quality of POS taggers for the analytical languages like the English language, and also comparing to the overall quality of the translation systems for related languages.
[14] proposes a change of the basic architecture, the omission of the statistical POS tagger from the early stages of the translation process and the introduction of a ranking mechanism in the post-processing phase. The proposed architecture is presented in the figure 2. The ranking mechanism is based on the statistical trigram target language model and models the most probable sentence in the target language. The ranker selects the best translation among all available translation candidates.
The rest of the article is organized as follows: the section 2 presents the current accomplishments in the field of the machine translation for related languages, section 3 presents the basic motives that led the authors to this set of experiments. The section 4 shows the motivation that led to the experiment presented in the paper. the section 5 presents the main method and the section presents the evaluation methodology with the results. The article concludes with a discussion.

2 State of the art

The majority of the translation systems for related languages uses the shallow parsing machine translation architecture as shown in [15] and in the overview of the translation systems presented in 2.1. The figure 1 shows the architecture of the of the most known translation systems for related languages [5] and Česílko [11] and used with variations in the majority of the systems presented in 2.1.

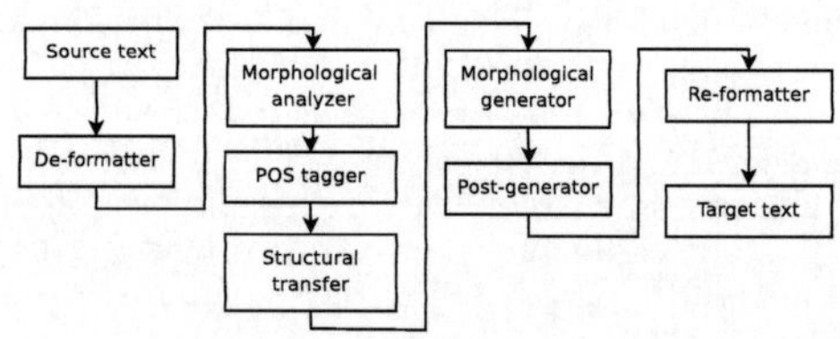

Fig. 1: *The modules of a typical shallow transfer translation system. The systems [5, 11, 17, 19] follow this design.*

2.1 Available MT systems for related languages

A few experiments in the domain of machine translation for related languages have led to the construction of more or less functional translation systems. The systems are ordered alphabetically:

- [2] for Turkic languages.
- Apertium, [5], for Romance languages.
- [7, 3, 1] for Scandinavian languages.

International Conference RANLP 2009 - Borovets, Bulgaria, pages 460–464

- Ruslan and Česílko, [9, 12], for highly inflectional Slavic languages, mostly language pairs with Czech language.
- [18] for Gaelic languages; Irish (Gaeilge) and Scottish Gaelic (G'aidhlig).
- [19] for the North Sámi to Lule Sámi language pair.
- Guat, [20], for highly inflectional Slavic languages, mostly language pairs with Slovenian language.

The experiments presented in this paper are based on technologies presented by [5] and [12].

3 Motivation

The most important motivative reasons for this research are:

- The production of a new POS tagger, especially a good quality tagger, is not a simple task. One of the easiest methods is training of a stochastic tagger based on HMM algorithm [21]. Some parts of this task can be automatized using unsupervised learning methods or supervised learning methods like [4], but it still involves the selection of a new tag set, the production of a tagged training corpus, testing of the corpus and at the end the basic learning process.
- The quality level of the tagging process of today's state-of-the-art POS taggers for highly inflectional languages like [10] and [8] is relatively low, comparing to the quality of POS taggers for the analytical languages like the English language, and also comparing to the overall quality of the translation systems for related languages.
- According to the today's most used designs for translation systems for related languages, the shallow transfer translation systems, the disambiguation module follows the source language morphological analysis at the beginning of the translation process. This design is shown on figure 1. Such design is adopted by Apertium [5] and Česílko [11]. Errors produced at the early stages of the translation process usually cause bigger problems than errors introduced at latest phases as later phases of the translation rely on the output of the preceding phases.
- Multiple translation candidates allow selection of the best candidates in the final phase when all available data for the translation has been accumulated. The most common translation errors are fluency errors of the target language and not adequacy errors. These errors commonly do not interfere with the meaning of the translation but rather on the grammatical correctness of the translation. They are mostly caused by the errors in morphological analysis or morphological syntheses.

The omission of the tagger and introduction of a ranking scheme based on target language statistical model as suggested in [13] yields better translation results as suggested in the same paper. The newly proposed architecture is shown on figure 2. This method is further described in the section 4. The introduction of multiple translation candidates generated from all possible morphological ambiguities as suggested in [13] leads to an exponential growth of the number of possible translation candidates.

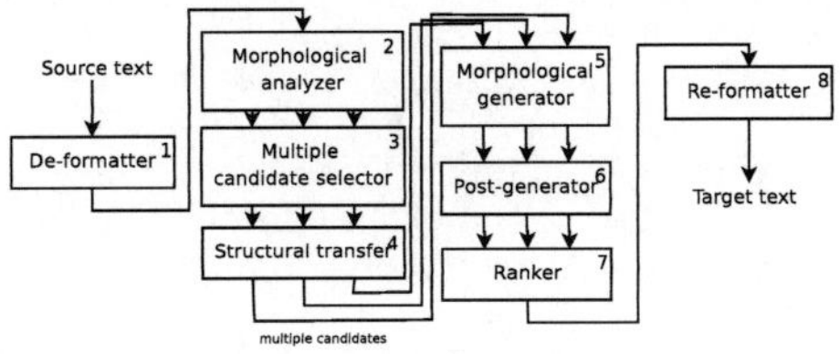

Fig. 2: *The newly proposed architecture of a shallow transfer translation system.*

The output of the morphological analysis is a set of all possible morphological tags describing each word. Every word with more than only one tag can be observed as a set of possible ambiguities. In the case of highly inflectional languages like the pair presented in this paper the number of ambiguous possibilities increases. The set of all possible translation candidates is constructed as the vector product of all ambiguous sets. The number of possible translation candidates grows exponentially with the length of the sentence, the equation 1 shows the upper limit of the number of possible translation candidates.

$$|TC| = \prod_{i=0}^{|S_{max}|} x_{max} \tag{1}$$

where TC is the set of possible translation candidates for the longest sentence S_{max} and x_{max} is the biggest number of ambiguities for a word. Although the equation 2, which shows the average number of possible translation candidates, presents much lower numbers, the complexity of the problem still remains exponential.

$$|TC| = \prod_{i=0}^{|\bar{S}|} \bar{x} \tag{2}$$

Equations 3 and 4 show empirical values for an example source sentence and typical numbers collected from a corpus test-set.

$$\begin{gathered} |\bar{S}| = 40 \\ \bar{x} = 15 \\ |TC| = \textstyle\prod_{i=0}^{40} 15 = 110,573323209e+45 \end{gathered} \tag{3}$$

$$\begin{gathered} |S| = 15 \\ x = 3 \\ |TC| = \textstyle\prod_{i=0}^{15} 3 = 14,348,907 \end{gathered} \tag{4}$$

4 Using a statistical post-processor instead of a POS tagger

A statistical language model assigns a probability to a sequence of words by means of a probability distribution. Using a language model, we assume that the training corpus used in the experiments is a good enough representation of the observed language.
The authors of the newest version of *Česílko*, the platform for MT for related languages [14], suggest a modified architecture for the translation system with the omission of the POS tagger, shown of figure 2. The experiment shown in [13] even shows a better translation performance of a similar architecture change on a different translation platform, the Apertium [5]. The experiment was conducted on a Romance language pair Portuguese - Spanish.
The exclusion of the tagger from the system has to be compensated somewhere else in the translation process since the output of the MT system is supposed to be one sentence.
An essential part of the whole MT system is the statistical post processor. The main problem with our simple MT process described in the previous sections is that both morphological analyser and transfer introduce a huge number of ambiguities into the translation. It would be very complicated (if possible at all) to resolve this kind of ambiguity by hand-written rules. That is why we have implemented a stochastic post-processor which aims to select one particular sentence that suits best the given context.

We use a simple language model based on trigrams (trained on word forms without any morphological annotation) which is intended to sort out "wrong" target sentences (these include grammatically ill-formed sentences as well as inappropriate lexical mapping). The current model has been trained on a corpus of 9 million words which have been randomly chosen from the Serbian Wikipedia[1].

Let us present an example of how this component of the system works. In the source text we had the following Slovenian segment (matrix sentence):

(5) *Kozarec* *na* *zeleni*
glass-N,M,SG,NOM on green-ADJ,F,SG,NOM
mizi ...
table-N,F,SG,NOM
"A glass on a green table ..."

The rule-based part of the system has generated four target segments: *Čaša na zelenom stolu, Čaša na zelenim stolu. Čaša na zelenim stolovima, Čaša na zelenom stolovima.*
The words *zelen* and *miza* are (fem.sg.loc and fem.du.nom). According to the language model, the ranker has (correctly) chosen the first sentence as the most probable result. There are also many homonym word forms that result in different lemmas in the target languages. For example, the word *bleda* means both "spinach beet-n.f.sg.nom" or "Beta vulgaris var cicla" and "pale-a.f.sg.nom". The ranker is supposed to sort out the contextually wrong meaning in such cases.

[1] http://sr.wikipedia.org

5 Method description

The authors of [13] suggest using a shallow parser to reduce the number of the translation candidates. The parser has to be hand-crafted. We propose a combination of two automatic methods to reduce the number of possible translation candidates:

- An automatically constructed set of local-agreement rules to discard improbable translation candidates.
- A statistical ranker of the translation candidates based on the POS tags of the source language to rank and select the remaining translation candidates from first method.

The *Guat* [20], a translation system for related languages based on *Apertium* [5], was used as the reference system and also as the sandbox for the implementation of proposed methods. Guat is automatically constructed so there is still room for improvement mainly through data correction tasks. The basic architecture of the system follows the architecture of apertium [5] and is presented in figure 1. The exponential complexity of the problem was addressed with a combination of two methods, each is presented in a separate section. The local agreement rules were used to discover and discard improbable translation candidates, the method is described in section 5.1. A statistical ranker [14] trained on the POS tags of a hand checked corpus [6] was used to select an n-best set of translation candidates, the method is presented in 5.2. The results and further discussion are presented in sections 7 and 8.

5.1 Discarding improbable translation candidates using local agreement rules

In this experiment we tried to use the agreement of morphological descriptors of adjacent words as a criterion to discard improbable translation candidates. The agreement of morphological descriptors can be modelled using rules based on regular expressions. The rules are described in section 5.1.1. The same format of rules as defined in the Apertium framework was used as it was powerful enough for the chosen task and it was already based on the same technology. The automatic induction of such rules is presented in the section 5.1.1. All the applicable rules, whose pattern regular expression describes part of the translation candidate, were applied on the translation candidate. If a rule changes part of the translation candidate, the candidate is discarded.

5.1.1 Automatic induction of local agreement rules

The automatic induction of the local agreement rules produces the same format of the rules as used by Apertium transfer module, but the method is limited to the discovery of local agreement. The requirements for the method are much simpler, just a morphologically annotated corpus of the source language.
Trigrams and bigrams with morphological descriptions

were extracted from source language part of the corpus. The corpus used as training data was [6], which was hand checked for errors in morphosyntactic tags. The source language used in our experiment was Slovenian language although the same method could be used for other languages as the method is not language specific. Each bigram and trigram was checked for agreement among tags of different words, the tags and their positions were free. If any agreements were found, a candidate for a rule was stored. The POS tags of the source bigram or trigram present the pattern part of the rule, the action part of the rule is constructed from all the morphosyntactic tags with agreement information. The rule candidates were grouped according to the pattern and action definitions, each group with a predefined number of candidates was chosen as a valid rule.

Although many improbable rules were discarded, longer sentences still yielded unmanageable number of translation candidates. Basically the growth of the problem was still exponential although the base was reduced. There is no guarantee on the upper limit of the number of translation candidates using this method. Another method was devised that coped with this problem, the ranking of translation candidates, described in section 5.2.

5.2 Ranking of the translation candidates

The empirical results in the table 2, the system named rules, show an improvement of the method that discards the improbable translation candidates using automatically induced rule, presented in section 5.1, over the original system and even over the system using all possible translation candidates. The problem of the number of possible translation candidates still rests to be resolved. The number of possible translation candidates, non-discarded by the first method, depends on the induced rules and in the worst case it is still exponential. A mechanism for ranking the remaining translation candidates and selecting a manageable subset had to be applied. A variation of the mechanism described in the section 4 was used in this experiment.

The main part of the MSD descriptors, the Category, was extracted from the source part of the training corpus [6] presenting a list of Category descriptors instead of the original words. The ranker was trained in the same way as explained in the 5.2 thus learning the most probable POS tag sequences of the source language.

Translation candidates obtained from the morphoogical analyser can be scored using this ranking scheme. A scoring scheme enables the selection of an n-best set of possible translation candidates thus reducing the problem to a fixed upper limit ensuring a limit to the worst-case translation time. The n can be an arbitrary number although lower numbers yield a translation quality penalty as shown in the ranker part of the table 2.

6 Evaluation method

The edit-distance [16] was used to count the number of edits needed to produce a correct target sentence from automatically translated sentence. The metric counts the number of deletions, insertions and substitutions that need to be performed among the observed sequences. This procedure shows how much work has to be done to produce a good translation. The metric roughly reflects the complexity of post-editing task.

The evaluation comprised of selecting 57 sentences from testing data, translating these sentences using the translation system and manually correcting the output of the system to a suitable translation. By suitable translation we mean a translation that is syntactically correct and expresses the same meaning as the source sentence. The sentences were chosen by length (shorter sentences than 15 words). This limitation enabled a fair comparison of the translation quality of all the systems, same test-set, as same systems used the full set of possible translation candidates. The complexity of each sentence was arbitrary, there was no special selection of the sentences using this criteria although shorter sentences are usually simpler in structure.

Two variants of the edit-distance [16] were calculated for each set of examples, the edit distance based on words and edit distance based on characters.

The results of this evaluation can be compared to results of the same metric used on similar systems; [14] and [20]. Language pair's properties and similarities of our system in comparison to [14] make the comparison feasible. The evaluation was conducted as a test on a low number of test translations due to the time and space limitations.

7 Results

Table 1: *The number of translation candidates for each system.*

System	All	All cand.	Used
original	57	57	57
all	44 million	44 million	34,526
rules	44 million	934,326	4,284
ranker	44 million	1,325,216	6,569
rules+ranker	44 million	437,123	4,041

Description of the table 1:

System - Name of the tested system, each system is presented in this section.

All - the number of all candidates produced from tested sentences.

All cand. - the number of all translation candidates entering the last translation phase, the ranking phase.

Used - the number of unique candidates entering the last translation phase, the ranking phase.

Description of the table 2: The figures in table 2 show the difference between 1 and the weighed edit distance, meaning higher values show better results.

System - Name of the tested system, each system is presented in this section.

Table 2: *Translation quality for each system.*

System	E. D. char.	E. D. word
original	0.848	0.778
all	0.892	0.826
rules	0.896	0.829
ranker	0.888	0.824
rules+ranker	0.896	0.829

E. D. char. - the edit distance based on characters showing the percentage of characters that were not changed.
E. D. word. - the edit distance based on words showing the percentage of words that were not changed.

Description of the systems presented on tables 1 and 2:
original - the translation system [20] based on original Apertium [5] architecture;
all - the *original* system with the omission of the statistical tagger. All possible ambiguous translation candidates were used.
rules - the *all* system with the introduction of the method based on automatically induced local agreement rules
ranker - the *all* system with the introduction of the method based on the ranking mechanism. The threshold was set at 100.000 translation candidates.
rules+ranker - the *all* system with the introduction of the method based on automatically induced local agreement rules with the ranking mechanism as a back off in case of too many translation candidates.

8 Discussion

The first experiment, the introduction of the proposed method by [14] to a new language pair, Slovenian - Serbian, showed an even bigger improvement of the proposed method as the original experiment.
The empirical evaluation showed that the introduction of the proposed methods increased the translation quality of the overall system by a statistically significant margin. The proposed methods successfully limit the number of possible translation candidates.
The empirical evaluation was conducted on a relatively small test sample due to time and resources limitations, the experiment should be evaluated on a bigger test-set. Further tests should be performed in the discovery of the best ranker threshold limit.
Some of the deterministic possibilities to restrict the blow-up of hypotheses have been explored, namely rule-based or heuristic removal of contextually inappropriate hypotheses (e.g. parser [14], tag sequences presented in this paper). Exploring different representations of the data as (multi)graph with multisets of edges and later compacting of the graph (contraction of fully/morphologically identical edges). The later approach should provide interesting results, especially for languages with high case syncretism.

References

[1] L. Ahrenberg and M. Holmqvist. Back to the future? the case for english-swedish direct machine translation. In *Proceedings of Recent Advances in Scandinavian Machine Translation*, 2005.

[2] K. Altintas and I. Cicekli. A machine translation system between a pair of closely related languages. In *Proceedings of the 17th International Symposium on Computer and Information Sciences (ISCIS 2002)*, 2002.

[3] E. Bick and L. Nygaard. Using danish as a cg interlingua: A wide-coverage norwegian-english machine translation system. In *Proceedings of NODALIDA, Tartu*, 2007.

[4] T. Brants. Tnt – a statistical part-of-speech tagger. In *Proceedings of the 6th Applied NLP Conference*. Seattle, WA, 2000.

[5] A. M. Corbi-Bellot, M. L. Forcada, S. Ortiz-Rojas, J. A. Prez-Ortiz, G. Ramirez-Sanchez, F. Sanchez-Martinez, I. Alegria, A. Mayor, and K. Sarasola. An open-source shallow-transfer machine translation engine for the romance languages of spain. In *Proceedings of the Tenth Conference of the European Association for Machine Translation*, pages 79–86, May 2005.

[6] L. Dimitrova, N. Ide, V. Petkevič, T. Erjavec, H. J. Kaalep, and D. Tufis. Multext-east: Parallel and comparable corpora and lexicons for six central and eastern european languages. In *COLING-ACL*, pages 315–319, 1998.

[7] H. Dyvik. Exploiting structural similarities in machine translation. *Computers and Humanities*, 28:225–245, 1995.

[8] T. Erjavec. Multilingual tokenisation, tagging, and lemmatisation with totale. In *Proceedings of the 9th INTEX/NOOJ Conference*, 2006.

[9] J. Hajič. An mt system between closely related languages. In *Proceedings of the third conference of the European Chapter of the Association for Computational Linguistics*, 1987.

[10] J. Hajič. Morphological tagging: data vs. dictionaries. In *Proceedings of the North American chapter of the Association for Computational Linguistics conference*, 2000.

[11] J. Hajič, P. Homola, and V. Kuboň. A simple multilingual machine translation system. In *Proceedings of the MT Summit IX*, New Orleans, 2003.

[12] J. Hajič, J. Hric, and V. Kuboň. Machine translation of very close languages. In *Proceedings of the 6th Applied Natural Language Processing Conference*, 2000.

[13] P. Homola and V. Kuboň. Improving machine translation between closely related romance languages. In *Proceedings of EAMT*, pages 72 – 77, 2008.

[14] P. Homola and V. Kuboň. A method of hybrid mt for related languages. In *Proceedings of IIS*, 2008.

[15] P. Homola, V. Kuboň, and J. Vičič. Shallow transfer between slavic languages. In *Recent Advances in Intelligent Information Systems*, page 219–232. Academic publishing house EXIT, Warsaw, 2009.

[16] V. Levenshtein. Binary codes capable of correcting deletions, insertions and reversals. *Doklady Akademii Nauk*, pages 845–848, 1965.

[17] K. P. Scannell. Machine translation for closely related language pairs. In *Proceedings of the Workshop Strategies for developing machine translation for minority languages*, 2006.

[18] K. P. Scannell. Machine translation for closely related language pairs. *unknown*, 2008.

[19] F. M. Tyers, L. Wiechetek, and T. Trosterud. Developing prototypes for machine translation between two sámi languages. In *Proceedings of EAMT*, 2009.

[20] J. Vičič. Rapid development of data for shallow transfer rbmt translation systems for highly inflective languages. In *Jezikovne tehnologije, language technologies : zbornik konference : proceedings of the conference*, pages 98–103, 2008.

[21] L. R. Welch. Hidden markov models and the baum-welch algorithm. *IEEE Information Theory Society Newsletter*, 53(4):1–14, 2003.

Sources of Performance in CRF Transfer Training: a Business Name-tagging Case Study

Marc Vilain
The MITRE Corporation
202 Burlington Rd.
Bedford, MA 01730 USA
mbv@mitre.org

Jonathan Huggins
The MITRE Corporation
202 Burlington Rd.
Bedford, MA 01730 USA
jhuggins@mitre.org

Ben Wellner
The MITRE Corporation
202 Burlington Rd.
Bedford, MA 01730 USA
wellner@mitre,org

Abstract

This paper explores methods for increasing performance of CRF models, with a particular concern for transfer learning. We consider in particular the transfer case from political news to hard-to-tag business news, and show the effectiveness of several methods, including a novel semi-supervised approach.

Keywords

Entity extraction, machine learning, business intelligence.

1. Introduction: name tagging

Named entity recognition is one of the most widely studied problems in computational language processing. It was one of the first tasks to be treated with the corpus-based method, and has remained a touchstone for benchmarking corpus-based algorithms and learning regimens. Part of the enduring interest is that name tagging continues to provide technical challenges that help drive research. In particular, while the fundamentals of training a name tagger are well understood, such barriers to practical application as robust coverage and transfer training remain active research areas.

Indeed, name-tagging systems tend to perform best when both training and test data are drawn from the same distribution of sources and sample times. However, even seemingly small divergences between training and test can lead to steep drop-offs in performance. Overcoming this lack of carry-over from training to test is thus a key precondition for practical entity recognition applications.

This paper addresses this issue in the context of training conditional random fields (CRFs) to tag named entities in business texts. We explore several orthogonal strategies for bringing a name tagger to bear on a new domain, with the aim of providing high test-time performance, robustness to out-of-training phenomena, and minimal transfer training costs. We apply these strategies to a business news corpus, and achieve substantial performance gains while only requiring modest investments in transfer training.

2. Tagging business news

The potential divergence between a name tagger's training and test performance was documented as far back as the MUC7 evaluation [15]. At issue was a shift in topic between training and test conditions: from air incidents to satellite launches. While the training and test data were otherwise comparable (same sources, same broad topic of aerospace), several system developers implicated this as a cause for poor test-time performance.

In a recent study [18], we sought to quantify this divergence in the case of business texts. Our study found a substantial training-to-test performance gap for several mature recent systems trained (or hand-configured) to process current events news. While many of the systems did well with current events, their F scores dropped by 15 to 25 points for business news and financial reports.

The present paper takes these observations as a challenge to train a business entity tagger. The business genre is primarily of interest here as a case study, though all the more interesting because it appears so challenging. The framework we have chosen towards this end is that of conditional random fields. In the few years since their introduction [10], CRF models have enjoyed a groundswell of interest, especially as a method for discriminative sequence labeling. They have been applied to conventional sequence labeling tasks like part-of-speech tagging [20] or chunking [14], and unconventional ones like anonymization [21].

For our purposes, conditional random fields provide a number of distinct advantages. A key factor is that discriminative CRF training is not confounded by conditionally dependent features. This makes it safe to include useful features that may be conditionally dependent, *e.g.* lexical and part-of-speech n-grams. This also allows for features that encode non-local dependencies and external knowledge sources: these typically capture generalizations that co-vary in useful ways with the data, and are thus not independent of other features. CRF training also scales well, even with large numbers of n-gram features.

Finally, a CRF allows for post-hoc adjustment of the prior probability of a label. By artificially decreasing the prior, one causes the CRF decoder to generate fewer instances of the label, hence increasing precision at the expense of recall [12]; this proved very useful in this work.

We used the Carafe open source CRF package.[1]

[1] Available at http://sourceforge.net/projects/carafe

International Conference RANLP 2009 - Borovets, Bulgaria, pages 465–470

Source	Token count	Description
Reuters M+A	31,000 train 33,000 dev test 47.500 eval	Mergers and acquisition
Reuters BN	22,500 train 26.500 eval	General business news
Reuters HS	15,000 eval	Hot stocks
Reuters NI	6,400 eval	New Initiatives
NYT	78,500 train	General biz.
MUC 6	153,000 train*	Political news

Table 1: data samples (* = previously annotated)

3. Outline of our experiments

The experimental conditions we investigated fall roughly into two orthogonal types of considerations: training data (on the one hand) and features (on the other). For expository purposes, we have organized these experiments into four groupings, each representing a source of performance in training a CRF-based business entity extraction system.

- Cross-training: transfer learning experiments that exploit existing MUC6 data.
- Nearly unsupervised training: supervised training based on machine-generated data.
- Non-local knowledge: various strategies based on gazetteer and found name lists.
- Validation: evaluation with other kinds of business data

We found that each of these training conditions provided an increase in performance. Most interesting, these increases were largely independent, so the performance gain achieved by combining all these methods was essentially the sum of their independent performance gains.

3.1 Experimental data

The majority of our data was drawn from the Reuters business page. These data are plentiful and easy to harvest: we used an ad-hoc Web crawler to spider several business topics, and collected news stories for select time periods in 2006 and 2007. We manually annotated a small portion of these data according to the MUC6 standard (which calls for person, organization, location, date, time, money, and percent entities). We also collected and annotated a small comparable corpus of New York Times business stories. We did not reuse the data from our earlier study primarily because the samples were small and not wholly consistent.

Table 1 shows the annotated data samples we ended up using. Our training sample consisted of all the stories from the Reuters merger and acquisition topic (M+A) on March 5, 2007. Day-to-day (dev-test) scoring was conducted with the M+A stories from February 28. A final post-development round of evaluation was run with the chronologically distant M+A stories from June 21.

The other Reuters samples (BN, HS, and NI) cover business topics distinct from M+A. We used the February 28 stories from these topics to assess the generalization of the M+A models to related but off-topic news. For our baseline-setting and first cross-training runs, we used the original MUC6 training set; the second BN and NYT samples were used as additional cross-training data. Finally, we used two entire months of M+A data (November 2006 and May 2007) for our nearly unsupervised training runs.

	M+A dev test		M+A eval test	
Train	F	Δ error	F	Δ error
MUC	75.75	—	77.44	—
MUC + M+A	89.13	-55.2%	90.86	-59.5%
M+A	87.98	—	90.40	—
M+A + MUC	89.13	-9.6%	90.86	-4.8%

Table 2: baseline and cross-training scores.

3.2 Experimental set-up

Prior to either training or testing, texts were sentence-tagged and tokenized, and then given part-of-speech tags by a revised version of the Brill tagger [1]. We included conventional-case headlines in the Reuters stories, but excluded headline-case headers from NYT and MUC6. Training was through log-likelihood learning, with LBFG-S optimization and regularization with a Gaussian prior.

We used the MUC scorer for evaluation, as it allows for comparisons to the original MUC evaluations and to our earlier study. Note that the MUC scorer gives partial credit when system responses match the answer key in extent but not type (or vice versa), yielding somewhat higher scores than the popular CoNLL scorer.

4. Cross-training

In practical applications of entity extraction, it is commonly the case that standard training sets do not align exactly with the data of interest. For business news, our earlier study showed that the widely available MUC data set does not by itself provide adequate training to capture the entity distributions and writing style of the business pages [18]. One common piece of folk wisdom for this situation suggests pairing a modest sample of task-specific data with one of the common large data sets (MUC, ACE or CoNLL). If the two data sets are reasonably consistent, we would expect the larger corpus to contain relevant training instances that provide value beyond training on the task sample alone.

In this first set of experiments, we considered this simple form of transfer learning by pairing our M+A sample with the MUC6 corpus. Table 2 summarizes our results. Training on MUC6 alone produced an uninspiring M+A dev test score of F=75.75, which is consistent with our earlier study. The combination training yielded a score of F=89.13, for a 55% reduction in the error term. The combination also outperformed training on the genre-specific M+A data alone (F=87.98), which confirms the expectation that training transfer is taking place across the genres. As the table shows, this pattern also held true for our eval test.

This approach corresponds to Daumé's all-data transfer learning case [4]. Because the transfer in our case takes place between data annotated to the exact same standard, we tend to think of it as cross-training. Though effective, this approach is less general than transfer learning efforts that seek to leverage existing data sets against data with divergent entity types, i.e., different repertoires of entities or inconsistent definitions of their common entities [16].

5. Nearly unsupervised training

Our second set of experiments aims at increasing the volume of task-specific training data (always a good thing) without requiring substantial manual annotation. Indeed, since manual annotation can be costly and time-consuming, it is important to maximize the effectiveness of annotation efforts. Tried-and-true approaches towards this end have sought to increase annotator productivity through mixed-initiative bootstrapping. Typically, a model gets built from a small initial annotated corpus, with the model then guiding subsequent annotation, either through pre-tagging [5] or by screening training cases, as in active learning [3].

Although these techniques can substantially speed up annotation, they still require an annotator to read and validate every training instance. The alternative we consider here focuses on finding large numbers of training instances with only minimal manual intervention. The basic strategy is to locate these training instances in untagged text by a high-precision (nearly) automatic method. Given a large supply of untagged texts, the instance finder need only have modest recall in order to produce a useful training corpus.

5.1 Identifying company names in Reuters

We were able to devise this kind of instance-finding scheme for company names in Reuters business news. We rely on the fact that in some 5-10% of cases, company names are marked with a stock market ticker symbol, as in:

- *Bear Stearns Cos. (BSC.N ...)*

Our instance finder identifies these ticker forms through regular expressions, and then labels the sequence of capitalized words to the left of the form as a company name. Since companies represent the most frequent entity type in business news, and are also the hardest to tag, we hoped this scheme would automatically provide us many more training instances for precisely the most critical cases.

Some subtleties preclude this method from being entirely automatic. In particular, company names regularly include prepositions, conjunctions, or punctuation, as in:

- *"Helen of Troy Ltd."*
- *"JP Morgan Chase and Co."*
- *"Wong's Kong King (Holdings) Ltd."*

The instance finder must capture these non-noun atoms in such cases, but must also exclude them in others, as in:

- *"Jeff Schuman of Keefer Bruyette Woods."*

The instance finder must also exclude non-name modifiers that happen to be capitalized at the start of a sentence:

- *"Bootmaker Timberland Cos."*

To prevent the instance finder from producing incomplete names (e.g. "Troy Ltd.") or overly long ones ("Bootmaker ..."), we included an as-needed manual review of potentially problematic contexts. The instance finder detects these contexts automatically, and after review, valid instances are cached so that they need not be queried again. Likewise predictive pre-nominals identified in the review ("bootmaker") are thereafter automatically removed from sentence-initial cases. Finally, to increase yield, the instance finder re-analyzes each story, looking for further mentions of found names. Mentions duplicating the names in their entirety or in shortened form are also labeled as companies. Except for a few easily-identified cases (e.g., "Ford" ... "Ford of Canada"), this requires no review.

This mixed-initiative strategy proved highly effective, achieving precision of P=99.9 on large samples of Reuters news, for a recall of R=38 (measured on our M+A data). In addition, caching greatly reduced the need for annotator intervention. Once the cache got going, to process an entire month of M+A news (over 1,700 stories) required 50-100 interventions over 20 minutes or less. In comparison, full manual annotation of a single weekday of M+A data required several days of effort from experienced annotators.

5.2 Partial annotation and complete sentences

A salient property of this nearly unsupervised markup is that it is partial. So while the entities reported by the instance finder are essentially always accurate, the 38% recall level still leaves another 62% of organizations unreported – to say nothing of other entity types such as persons, places, money, and the like. These unreported entities make it hard to use instance finder data directly for supervised training. The issue is that the exact same entity may appear both as a positive example (that the instance finder found) and as a negative one (that it missed). This effectively causes the training procedure to ignore both examples, thus diminishing the potential contribution of the instance finder output. While a number of researchers have made strides recently towards semi-supervised learning, where not all data are annotated (*e.g.* [11]), these approaches typically pair a fully supervised corpus with separate annotated data, and do not speak to the case of partially annotated data.

The approach we used here was to sub-select those instance finder sentences that we could guarantee to be in fact completely annotated. Ignoring numeric entities for now (dates, money, ...), a reliable gauge of complete annotation is the absence of any un-accounted-for capitalized words. We consider a capitalized word to be accounted for if either (i) it is labeled by the instance finder, or (ii) it is a closed-class word in sentence-initial position. In our trials, 8% to 9% of sentences in the corpus meet this criterion, yielding a substantial sub-corpus of fully-annotated sentences.

Train	M+A dev test		M+A eval test	
	F	Δ error	F	Δ error
M+A	87.98	—	90.40	—
+ 1 month	88.59	-5.1%	91.51	-11.6%
+ 2 months	88.28	-2.5%	91.11	-7.4%
M+A + MUC	89.13	—	90.86	—
+ 1 month	90.48	-12.5%	92.52	-18.2%
+ 2 months	90.60	-13.5%	92.49	-17.8%

Table 3: performance of nearly-unsupervised training.

The problem is that this sub-corpus is highly skewed: it necessarily contains only instances of company names, as these are the only entities identified by the instance finder. To boost the representation of other entities, we trained a CRF to identify numeric forms, and another to identify persons and places. We then artificially lowered the Viterbi decoder priors for these two models, trading off recall for precision until the decoder effectively had 100% precision. As with the entity finder, recall is only modest (30% for persons, 58% for locations). Nevertheless, these CRFs accounted for many more capitalized strings, thereby yielding many more completely annotated sentences, now up to 17% to 19% of the corpus. By extrapolation from manually annotated data, we estimate this represents around a third of the sentences that actually contain entities.

5.3 Experimental results

Table 3 reports this approach's results using our M+A training data, the MUC6 development corpus, and several months' worth of complete sentences identified by the instance finder. For the dev test, adding one month of complete sentences to the base M+A corpus yielded a modest error reduction of 5.1%, while adding a second month resulted in performance drop, with the error reduction falling to 2.5%. Results on the eval test showed a similar pattern.

We were intrigued, however, that experiments that also used the MUC6 corpus yielded much better results. The addition of one or two months of complete sentences respectively yielded dev test error reductions of 12.5%, and 13.5%, with eval test reductions topping off at 18.2%. Why such better performance with MUC6? An analysis of dev test errors for the M+A plus two months case, showed that most of the new errors were spurious organizations, all of them capitalized words. The entity distributions for these data explain what happened (Figure 4). For the complete sentences, organization names are not just the most common entity type, but form a 52% majority. While the M+A corpus starts out with only 46% of its entities as organizations, adding more complete sentences eventually causes the proportion to top 50%. The increasing skew towards organizations eventually leads the model to assign an overly strong default organization label to any potential entity, i.e., to any capitalized word.

When starting from the M+A and MUC6 data, however, this effect is moderated by the fact that the proportion

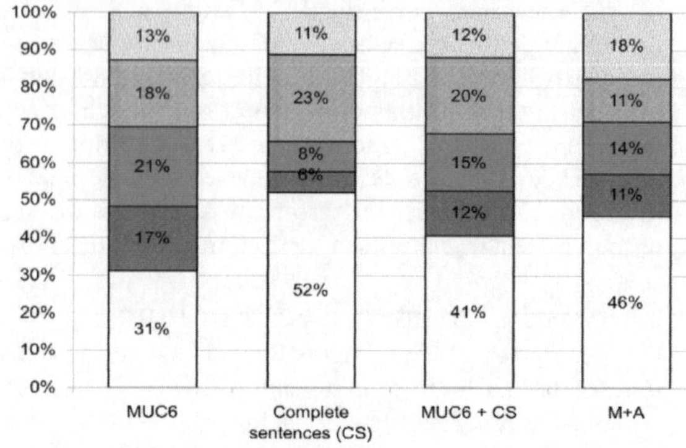

Figure 4: entity type distributions (from bottom to top: organization, person, location, money/percent, date/time)

of organizations in MUC6 is actually lower than it is in M+A. In effect the combination of MUC6 and the complete sentences yields an entity distribution that better matches that of the M+A data, hence providing greater opportunity to learn a high-performing model.

6. Non-local knowledge sources

As noted above, our post-hoc error analysis revealed cases where non-organizations were being labeled as organizations, among these person names and locations. Our third set of experiments attempted to address this problem by introducing non-local knowledge sources.

6.1 Gazetteer lists

Gazetteers of place and person names have long been used to improve the performance of name taggers [7]. We used lexical features to introduce gazetteers of given names, major geography, and numeric entity atoms (days, months, currencies). We avoided municipality lists, as they tend to also capture person names: of the 2,000 most common surnames in the US, most are also names of cities and towns.

6.2 Long-distance dependencies

One error that arose regularly in our post-hoc analysis concerned person names. The CRF generally identified full names like *"Thomas White"* but tended to mislabel surnames appearing on their own, *e.g. "White."* As Reuters avoids honorifics ("Mr.") the latter cases are hard to identify from context alone; a mechanism is thus needed to capture the implication between full names and bare surnames.

Various statistical approaches have been proposed to capture these long-distance name dependencies, *e.g.*, [2], [6], and especially [9], which presents a strategy based on the majority label for a word form. This approach proved effective for the CoNLL named entity task, so we re-implemented it here. As we detail elsewhere [19], the approach failed with our business data. Again, the prevalence of company names causes the CRF to assign the organization label to capitalized words when no countermanding

	M+A dev test		M+A eval test	
Features	**F**	**Δ error**	**F**	**Δ error**
M+A	87.98	—	90.40	—
+ gaz	89.27	-10.7%	92.07	-17.3%
+ LDD	88.74	-6.3%	91.58	-12.3%
+ gaz + LDD	90.23	-18.7%	92.82	-25.2%

Table 5: Effectiveness of non-local knowledge (NLK): gazetteers and long distance dependencies (LDD)

	M+A dev test		M+A eval test	
Train	**F**	**Δ error**	**F**	**Δ error**
M+A	87.98	—	90.40	—
M+A W/LDD	90.23	-18.7%	92.82	-25.2 %
+ 1 month	91.85	-32.2%	93.49	-32.2%
+ 2 months	91.32	-27.8%	93.06	-27.7%
M+A + MUC W/NLK	91.93	-32.9%	92.17	-18.4%
+ 1 month	93.21	-43.5%	93.95	-37.0%
+ 2 months	93.10	-42.6%	94.08	-38.3%

Table 6: Cross-training and nearly unsupervised training with non-local knowledge (NLK); Δ error is relative to M+A baseline.

evidence is available. In the case of person names, that evidence is primarily the presence of a given name, leading bare surnames to be mislabeled as organizations. Because bare surnames are more common than full names, the majority count strategy in [9] tends to perpetuate the error.

We adopted an alternative approach that captures long-distance name dependencies through evidence copying [19]. In the case of person names, if a word form α occurs in the right context of a given name, we copy this evidence to other instances of α through a non-local feature.

6.3 Experimental results

Using only our M+A development sample, we trained and evaluated CRF models with one or both of these knowledge sources active. Table 5 shows our results: while both knowledge sources were effective independently, it is particularly interesting that their combined application proved synergistic, yielding a greater performance gain than the sum of their separate yields.

Table 6 is even more telling. In this case, we activated the knowledge sources and repeated the cross-training and partially supervised training runs. The performance gains from these non-local knowledge sources were almost entirely independent of those produced by cross-training or the addition of complete sentences. Except for the final row in the table, which represents the largest training set, the non-local features contributed an additive performance boost. The configuration that performed highest on the dev test produced a compelling F score of 93.21 and an even higher F=93.95 on the eval test. Relative to training on M+A alone, this represents error reductions of 43.5% and 37% respectively.

7. Further validation runs

All of our experiments to this point were based on a single Reuters topic, mergers and acquisitions. To assess how well these M+A-trained models applied to business news in general, we annotated samples of several other business topics (previously shown in Table 1). The first two rows of Table 7 summarize performance of the M+A models on these test suites: for the most part, scores remained close to those measured on M+A data. Only the "hot stocks" topic showed degradation of more than around 1 point of F score.

Finally, to round off these cross-topic trials, we performed one more round of cross-training, adding in a sample of the BN topic along with editorially-dissimilar stories from the New York Times. The last row in Table 6 shows that cross-training was again effective at raising scores. As should be expected, performance on the BN eval test leapt higher, with a full 19% reduction in error. Interestingly, performance gains on the M+A eval test were not far behind, with a 16% reduction in error (6% for the dev test).

The most surprising gain however was with the lowest-performing HS topic, which gained over 2 points of F score, a 23% error reduction. Post-hoc analysis revealed why. The HS stories contain many references to the Dow Jones stock index (an index is not a company). In contrast. the M+A training data only had Dow Jones appearing as a company, thus leading the M+A model to mislabel HS references to the Dow as organizations. As the Times data happened to refer to the Dow as a non-name stock index, the cross-trained model removed the HS precision errors.

8. Discussion

We should begin by noting that our final F scores on blind eval data are comparable to those achieved by top-performing hand-built systems at the MUC6 and MUC7 evaluations. Further, this was achieved for business news, a genre that seems measurably harder to tag than the primarily political writing used in the MUC evaluations.

Training configuration	**M+A dev**	**M+A eval**	**BN eval**	**HS eval**	**NI eval**
M+A + MUC6 +1 month W/NLK	93.21	93.95	93.38	91.04	92.95
M+A + MUC6 +2 months W/NLK	93.10	94.08	93.12	90.56	93.06
M+A + MUC6 + BN + NYT +2 months W/NLK	93.48	95.05	94.41	92.72	93.47

Table 7: Performance on dissimilar topics

What is most interesting, however, is that this required so minimal an investment in new data annotation. While our highest scores were obtained using multiple new training sets, very respectable scores of F=93/94 (dev/test) were reached with only 31,000 words of newly annotated data, a roughly two-day annotation effort. We also did not need company lists: while these can improve recall, they are hard to keep current, and fail to capture most small businesses.

Key to our results is the roughly 40% error reduction provided by cross-training, nearly unsupervised training, and non-local knowledge. Among our core findings is that this combination of essentially orthogonal means yields an effectively additive reduction in error. This should be very encouraging to those seeking to apply entity extraction to new genres and new tasks.

It is interesting that highest performance required creative attention to both training regimens and knowledge sources. There is a methodological lesson here, as it is often tempting to focus research activities on only one or the other of these two threads.

One concern we would like to remediate in further work is the lack of direct comparison to recent efforts based on the CoNLL named entity scheme, including work on Hungarian business news [17]. The issue is complex: the CoNLL and MUC models differ not just as to scoring, but also around key annotation question.

Looking to the future, we are especially intrigued by the promise of our nearly unsupervised training strategy. While we used an instance finder that relied on the particulars of Reuters news, all that is required to apply the strategy is a high-precision instance finder with moderate recall. For the case of person names, for instance, honorifics like "Mr." act essentially like the ticker symbols we used in our company instance finder (we did not try this here because Reuters does not use honorifics). Another possibility is to generate instances through the application of gazetteers or known entity databases.

Unsupervised data have been used before as an adjunct to training for otherwise supervised entity extraction models. Approaches have included mutual bootstrapping [13] or self-training [8]. While these methods technically require no manual supervision, they tend to fail in unappealing ways once erroneous entities enter the self-generated training set. For this reason, the approach we've taken here, though requiring some manual review, may provide a valuable alternative in practice.

9. References

[1] Eric Brill. 1994. Some advances in rule-based part-of-speech tagging. Pcdgs. AAAI-94.

[2] Razvan Bunescu and Raymond J. Mooney. 2004. Collective information extraction with relational Markov networks. Pcdgs. of the 42nd ACL. Barcelona.

[3] Dagan, Ido and Sean Engelson. 1995. Committee-based sampling for training probabilistic classifiers. *Proc. ICML.*

[4] Daumé III, Hal. 2007. Frustratingly easy domain adaptation. *Proc. ACL*, Prague.

[5] Day, David, John Aberdeen, Lynette Hirschman, Robyn Kozierok, Patty Robinson, and Marc Vilain. 1997. Mixed-initiative development of language processing systems. *Proc. Applied ACL.*

[6] Jenny Rose Finkel, Trond Grenager, and Christopher Manning. 2005. Incorporating Non-local Information into Information Extraction Systems by Gibbs Sam-pling. Pcdgs. of the 43rd ACL. Ann Arbor, MI.

[7] Florian, Radu, Abe Ittycheriah, Hongyan Jing, and Tong Zhang. 2003. Named entity recognition through classifier combination. *Proc. CoNLL.*

[8] Ji, Heng and Ralph Grishman. 2006. Data selection in semi-supervised learning for name tagging. *Proc. ACL.*

[9] Krishnan, Vijay, and Christopher Manning. 2006. An effective two-stage model for exploiting non-local dependencies in named entity recognition. *Proc. ACL*, Sydney, Australia.

[10] Lafferty, John, Andrew McCallum, and Fernando Pereira. 2001. Conditional random fields: probabilistic models for segmenting and labeling sequence data. *Proc. ICML.*

[11] Mann, Gideon and Andrew McCallum. 2007. Simple, robust, scalable semi-supervised learning via expectation regularization. *Proc. ICML*, Corvalis OR.

[12] Minkov E, Wang RC, Cohen WW. 2006. NER systems that suit user's preferences: adjusting the recall-precision trade-off for entity Extraction. *Proc HLT-NAACL.*

[13] Riloff, Elen and Rosie Jones. 1999. Learning dictionaries for information extraction by multi-level bootstrapping. *Proc. AAAI.*

[14] Sha, Fei and Fernando Pereira. 2003. Shallow parsing with conditional random fields. *Proc. ACL-HLT.*

[15] Sundheim, Beth, *ed.* 1997. *Proc. of MUC-7*. Hosted at nlpir.nist.gov/related_projects/muc/proceedings/muc_7_toc.html

[16] Sutton, Chalres, and Andrew McCallum. 2005. Composition of conditional random fields for transfer learning. *Proc. HLT-EMNLP*, Vancouver, Canada.

[17] Szarvas, György, Richárd Farkas, László Felföldi, András Kocsor, & János Csirik. 2006. A highly accurate named entity corpus for Hungarian. *Proc. LREC*, Genoa.

[18] Vilain, Marc, Jennifer Su and Suzi Lubar. 2007. Entity extraction is a boring solved problem – or is it? *Proc NAACL.*

[19] Vilain, Marc, Jonathan Huggins, and Ben Wellner, 2009. Asimple feature-copying approach for long-distance dependecies. *Proc. CoNLL*, Boulder.

[20] Wellner, Ben and Marc Vilain. 2006. Leveraging machine-readable dictionaries in discriminative sequence models. *Proc. LREC*, Genoa,Italy.

[21] Wellner, Ben, Matt Huyck, Scott Mardis, John Aberdeen, Alex Morgan, Leon Peskin, Alex Yeh, Janet Hitzeman, Lynette Hirschman.2007. Rapidly retargetable approaches to de-identification. *J. Amer. Med. Informatics Assoc.* 14(5).

Extracting Synonyms from Dictionary Definitions

Tong Wang and Graeme Hirst
Department of Computer Science
University of Toronto
Toronto, ON, M5S 3G4, Canada
tong,gh@cs.toronto.edu

Abstract

We investigate the problem of extracting synonyms from dictionary definitions. Our premise for using definition texts in dictionaries is that, in contrast to free-texts, their composition usually exhibits more regularities in terms of syntax and style and thus, will provide a better controlled environment for synonym extraction. We propose three extraction methods: two rule-based ones and one using the maximum entropy model; each method is evaluated on three experiments — by solving TOEFL synonym questions, by comparing extraction results with existing thesauri, and by labeling synonyms in definition texts. Results show that simple rule-based extraction methods perform surprisingly well on solving TOEFL synonym questions; they actually out-perform the best reported lexicon-based method by a large margin, although they do not correlate as well with existing thesauri.

Keywords

Lexical semantics, synonym extraction, dictionary definition mining, maximum entropy classification

1 Introduction

1.1 Motivation

Synonymy is one of the classic lexical semantic relations based on which lexical semantic taxonomies such as WordNet (Fellbaum et al., 1998) are constructed. Despite their usefulness in various NLP studies, such taxonomies are usually considered expensive resources since they are often manually constructed. Consequently, much research effort has been devoted to automatically extracting words of certain semantic relations from various free-text corpora (e.g., Hearst 1992; Lin 1998, etc) or even building an entire taxonomy (e.g., Chodorow, Byrd, and Heidorn 1985).

Meanwhile, identifying characteristic features for synonymy is non-trivial. Many studies in this direction have started out with intuitively appealing ideas, but in practice, there are always surprises for intuition. Dependency relations used by Lin (1998) relate two nouns if, for example, they often serve as the object of the same verb. When it comes to adjectives, however, the relation established as such is no longer guaranteed to be strict synonymy, since two adjective antonyms may modify the same noun as well. As another example, when two words in one language are often translated into the same word in another language, it seems very natural to regard the two words as synonyms in the source language (Wu and Zhou, 2003), but the mapping on the lexical level between languages is far from bijective, which in turn leads to many exceptions to the hypothesis.

The difficulties in finding features for strict synonymy partly come from the syntactic and stylistic diversity in free-texts — this is the motivation behind using dictionary definitions as a resource for synonym identification. Unlike the extraction strategy used by Hearst (1992), where hyponyms would necessarily follow the phrase *such as*:

$$NP_0 \text{ such as } \{NP_1, NP_2, \ldots, (\text{and}|\text{or})\}\ NP_n$$
$$\forall i = 1, 2, \ldots, n, hyponym(NP_i, NP_0)$$

there seems to be much fewer patterns, if any, to follow for using synonyms in free-text writing.

In contrast, in the composition of dictionary definitions, there is usually much more regularity in terms of how synonyms of the word being defined should and would appear. Consequently, dictionary definition texts, as a special form of corpora, can provide a better "controlled" environment for synonym distribution and thus, it would presumably be easier to find characteristic features specific to synonymy within definition texts. Given this assumption, our goal is to find synonyms for a give word (*target word*) from the collection of all definition texts in a dictionary and subsequently evaluate the quality of the proposed synonyms.

1.2 Related Work

One of the first attempts at extracting synonyms (or semantically related words in general) from dictionary definitions is that of Reichert et al. (1969)[1], where an *inverted index* of a dictionary is built to relate a *definiendum* (the word being defined, pl. *definienda*) to its *definientia* (defining words). Despite the coarse definition of relatedness, the idea itself proved to be inspiring in formalizing the problem in graph-theoretical language, with words corresponding to nodes and edges pointing from definienda to definientia.

On the basis of this graph (usually referred to as a *dictionary graph*), many interesting variants have evolved from the original idea of inverted indexing. Taking the graph as the web, Blondel and Senellart (2002) employed an algorithm similar to PageRank (Brin et al., 1998), and similarities between words can be computed using their adjacency matrix. Alternatively, the problem can be viewed from an information theory perspective and formalized to propagate information content instead of endorsement (Ho

[1] Unfortunately, we have not been able to access the original work of Reichert et al. (1969); we resort to the description of their method by Amsler (1980) instead.

International Conference RANLP 2009 - Borovets, Bulgaria, pages 471–477

and Cédrick, 2004). Another example (Muller et al., 2006) is to simulate a random walk on the graph by building and iteratively updating a Markovian matrix, and the distance between words corresponds to the average number of steps the random walk takes from one node to the other.

Despite all these interesting variations, the original method of inverted indexing has been left unevaluated for decades, and one of the objectives of this paper is to bring the evaluation of this method into the modern paradigm of NLP. Together with this algorithm, two other extraction methods will be discussed in Section 2; evaluations of these methods are conducted in three experiments following in Section 3. Section 4 will conclude the study with prospects for future work.

2 Extraction Methods

In this section we propose three extraction methods, all of which extract synonyms from definition texts in the *Macquarie Dictionary* (Delbridge et al., 1981). The first two methods are rule-based and use original definition texts, while the third one (a maximum entropy model) is based on POS-tagged definitions[2].

2.1 Inverted Index Extraction

As mentioned above, inverted index extraction (IIE) is one of the earliest attempts at using dictionary definitions to extract synonyms or related words. Specifically, for a given target word t , the entire dictionary is scanned in search of words whose definition texts contain t, and such words are considered related to t. Since both synonymy and relatedness are symmetric, it is equivalent to say that every definiendum is related to all its definientia, or that the dictionary graph is an unweighted, undirected graph where every pair of neighbors is considered equally related.

Many problems arise with the simplicity of this notion for relatedness. For example, every word in a definition is treated equally, regardless of its POS, syntactic function, or position in the definition text. In practice, however, some definientia appear in insignificant positions (such as part of a subjunctive clause or a phrase, etc.) and thus are not as related as they are taken to be.

There are simple heuristics to deal with such false positives. Taking POS for example, one can specify the POS of a given target word and only extract words that are of the same POS. Constraints can also be applied on where a target word is allowed to appear in order to be considered a synonym of the corresponding definiendum. Apart from all these, a more pertinent issue, as it turned out in later experiments, is actually the low coverage for low-frequency target words, which do not appear often (or even not at all) in other words' definitions. In fact, this conforms with the claim made by several previous authors (e.g., Wu and Zhou 2003) that coverage is a key issue for dictionary-based methods.

2.2 Pattern-based Extraction

The intuition behind pattern-based extraction (PbE) is based on the regularity in dictionary definition text composition. In PbE, instead of relating a definiendum to every word in its definition (as in IIE), we focus more on those definientia that follow particular patterns synonyms tend to follow in definition texts. Consequently, one of the objectives of PbE is to discover such patterns.

2.2.1 Basic Algorithm

The synonym extraction and pattern finding process are related in a bootstrapping manner, as shown in Figure 1. We start with 1) a set of words containing only the target word $W_0 = \{t\}$, e.g., *split*, and 2) a small set of regular expressions P_0 capturing the most basic and intuitive patterns that synonyms usually follow in definition texts. For example, if there is only one word in the definition text, it must be a synonym of the definiendum; this corresponds to the first regex pattern in the left-most block in Figure 1, i.e., `^(\w+).$`, and the same idea applies the other two patterns as well.

Synonym extraction

Given W_0 and P_0, we now follow this procedure for synonym extraction:

1. If any word w matches any pattern $p \in P_i$, extract w as synonym of t and update the word list $W_i = W_i \cup \{w\}$.
2. If t matches any pattern $p' \in P$ in the definition text of some other word w', extract w' as synonym of t and update the word list $W_i = W_i \cup \{w'\}$.
3. Take each word $w \in W_i$ as target word and repeat 1 and 2; add all resulting synonyms to W_i and denote the new set W_{i+1}.

Pattern bootstrapping

For the moment, we assume that words in W_{i+1} appear in each other's definition in patterns other than the ones we started with in P_i.[3] We update[4] the regex set P_i by adding these new patterns, and repeat synonym extraction with W_{i+1} and P_{i+1}.

The above process will converge if our hypothesis on the regularity of definition text composition is valid, i.e., when composing definition texts, lexicographers tend not to use random patterns to include synonyms in the definition texts. In practice, it converges in all the test cases used.

Note that when combining the three steps in the synonym extraction phase, the algorithm is actually building a dictionary graph in which a definiendum is related to only those definientia following specific patterns. This is different from the dictionary graphs in IIE and its variants, which relate a definiendum to all its definientia.

2.2.2 Transitivity of Synonymy and Transitive Closure

The notion of transitivity of synonymy is implicitly adopted, especially in Step 3 in the synonym extraction

[2] We used the Stanford POS tagger for this purpose (http://nlp.stanford.edu/software/tagger.shtml).

[3] In case they do not, we can either start off with a group of known synonyms instead of one target word t, or even with another word that does lead to more appropriate situations in terms of W_{i+1}, because at this stage, we aim at bootstrapping for patterns rather than finding synonyms for any particular word.

[4] The update is currently done manually, and could be replaced by automatic recognition of the most general regular expression patterns by, for example, dynamic programming.

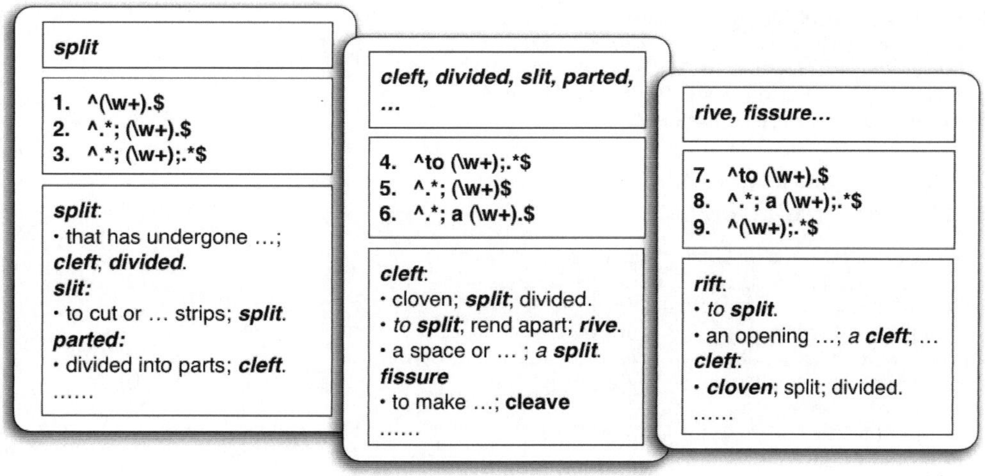

Fig. 1: *Bootstrapping between synonym extraction and pattern finding. The three rounded squares in the horizontal layout represent three iterations of bootstrapping; within each of these, the three vertically distributed squares list, from top to bottom, the extracted synonyms, newly-added regular expression patterns, and related definitions, respectively.*

phase above. In general, if a word A is synonymous to B and B to C, it is usually fair to deduce that A is a synonym of C. In the context of dictionary definitions, however, the validity of such deduction is severely compromised, because the input to the extraction process is word tokens under different senses and/or even of different POS.

Similar to IIE, there are easy remedies for confusions on POS, e.g., by specifying a POS with a target word (say, *adjective* for *split*) and looking only for definitions under the specified POS. In view of transitivity, most words following any of our patterns (e.g., *cleft*) can be safely assumed to have the same POS as that of their corresponding definienda, and starting from these words, we can follow definitions under the same POS (e.g., *cleft* as an adjective instead of a verb) for further extraction. For word senses, however, this assumption is no longer valid, since universal specification of word senses is unavailable in most dictionaries.

A more general solution to this problem is to find *transitive closure*, corresponding to circles in the dictionary graph. This idea is based on the hypothesis that definitions are circular in nature (Jurafsky and Martin, 2008). Starting from a given target word, transitivity is applied regardless of POS and word sense differences; once we encounter the target word again[5], we consider every word on this circle synonyms to the target word. As is shown in later experiments, where the extracted words are compared with existing thesauri, this approach almost triples precision at relatively low cost in recall.

2.3 Extraction using Maximum Entropy

Although PbE exhibits excellent precision in extracting synonyms (as all three experiments suggest in Section 3 below), relying solely on the limited number of patterns will again bring up the issue of coverage. This motivates more-general learning methods that would treat definition texts in a less-specific way.

As an initial attempt at machine learning approaches for processing dictionary definitions, we formulate the synonym extraction task as a classification problem: each word in a piece of definition text is a decision point, and a maximum entropy (MaxEnt) classifier is employed to decide whether or not it is a synonym of the corresponding definiendum.

The training data is based on 186,954 definition items (pairs of definiendum with corresponding definientia) in the *Macquarie Dictionary*. After POS-tagging, any word in a given definition text is labeled as a synonym of the definiendum if the word is (1) of the same POS as the definiendum, and (2) in the same WordNet synset as the definiendum. This labeled data would be partitioned and serve as both the training data for MaxEnt and the gold standard for the synonym labeling task in Section 3.3.

We choose the *opennlp.maxent* implementation of the classifier with generalized iterative scaling (GIS) capacity[6]. We use lexical features (e.g., previous, current, and next word), unigram POS features (e.g., previous, current, and next POS), and bigram POS features (e.g., previous and next POS bigrams). In addition, another group of features describes the position of each decision point by an integer counter starting from 1 to the length of a definition text. In order to capture the critical separators discussed in PbE (e.g., semicolons), a second position counter is also included, which resets to 1 whenever encountering any separators. In the definition of ***abbreviation**: reduction in length; abridgment.*, for example, the first counter assigns integers 1 to 6 to all definientia (including puncuations ";" and "."), whereas the second counter assigns 1 to 4 to definientia up to the semicolon but 1 and 2 to *abridgment* and the period.

Note that, in order to make fair comparisons with IIE and PbE, it is necessary to incorporate the dictionary graph into

[5] Or any of the words from the first round of PbE, which are usually highly synonymous to the target word

[6] Available at `http://sourceforge.net/projects/maxent/`.

MaxEnt method. Specifically, given a target word t, after extracting synonyms from its own definientia, we again go through other words' definitions in the dictionary; if t appears in the definition of another word w and is classified as a synonym, then w is taken as a synonym of t.

2.4 Interpretation of the Methods in Terms of the Dictionary Graph

So far in our discussion, the dictionary graph has been assumed to be *undirected*. For IIE, if we are to take the graph as *directed* (with edges pointing from definienda to definientia), then the in-neighbors of a target word are those related by an inverted index, and the out-neighbors are simply all its definientia. We will see how these two types of relatedness perform differently in Section 3.

In contrast, PbE and MaxEnt make fine distinctions about which part of the definitions to relate a target word to. For out-neighbors (words in the definientia of the target word), PbE and MaxEnt pick out words following specific patterns (either regular expression patterns or, implicitly, patterns learned by a classifier), as opposed to IIE which takes all definientia indiscriminately; for in-neighbors, IIE relates them all regardless of how or where the target word appears in other words' definitions, while PbE and MaxEnt, again, follow their respective patterns.

3 Evaluation

3.1 Solving TOEFL Synonym Questions

Originally introduced by Landauer and Dumais (1997), TOEFL synonym questions have gained much popularity in NLP studies as a task-driven evaluation for synonymy or semantic relatedness. The commonly used data set contains 80 questions, on which Jarmasz and Szpakowicz (2004) evaluated nine semantic similarity methods, not including a later work by Turney et al. (2003) with an accuracy of 97.5% — the highest in all reported results so far.

The popularity of this experiment partly resides in its straightforward setup and easy interpretation of results. Each question consists of one question word and four choices, one of which is a synonym to the questions word and thus, the correct answer. For a given question, we use the three extraction methods to extract synonyms for each of the five words (question word and the four choices), followed by computing the cosine similarity between the synonym set of the question word with those of the choices. The choice with the highest-scoring synonym set is proposed as the correct answer.

Ideally, due to the transitivity of synonymy, if two words are synonymous themselves, they would have a number of synonyms in common, which in turn would give a better score in the TOEFL synonym questions. Two practical issues, however, proved to be adversarial to this assumption. Firstly, finding the right answer does not necessarily depend on synonymy; relatedness, for example, is also transitive by nature. In fact, if overlapping is the only concern, one can even use sets of antonyms for finding the synonymous choice, since synonymous words share antonyms as well as synonyms. Fortunately in TOEFL synonym questions, the choices are either synonymous or unrelated to a question word, and thus, such considerations will not harm the performance on solving the questions.

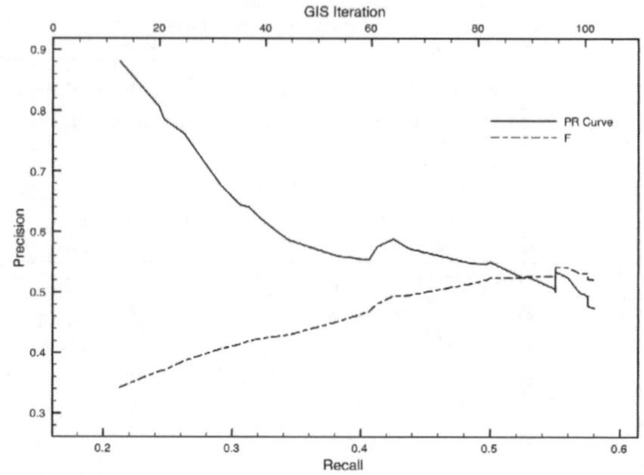

Fig. 2: *Precision-recall curve and F with respect to MaxEnt GIS training iterations (ranging from 10 to 100)*

Secondly, as mentioned earlier, if the target word is infrequent, it will have a low in-degree in the dictionary graph, and this is especially the case for TOEFL synonym questions, which tend to test the participants on a more-challenging vocabulary of relatively low-frequency words. Consequently, as it turned out in the experiment, there are often cases where the extracted set of words for the question word does not overlap with any of those of the choices. The notion of *recall* is thus borrowed to denote the percentage of questions that can be solved without such ties.

Another feature specific to the TOEFL synonym question task is lemmatization, since many of the words in these questions are inflected. As we will see shortly from the results, using these inflected words as target words for extraction gives drastically different performance from using their corresponding lemmata.

Table 1 shows the performance of various methods on the TOEFL synonym questions task. The result is reported in terms of precision, recall and F; accuracy is also included since all other published results are reported in terms of accuracy. For comparison, we separate the extraction result of IIE into in-neighbor-only, out-neighbor-only, and a combination of the two (see Section 2.4 for their differences).

The two variants of IIE with only in- or out-neighbors (IIE_{in} or IIE_{out}) perform more or less the same in terms of F, but are complementary in precision and recall. Out-neighbors are definition texts with many stop words, which are helpful in overlapping and hence the high recall (fewer ties), whereas the low frequency of the target words in TOEFL tests results in fewer in-neighbors, and thus fewer chances of overlapping and more ties.

When using the lemmatized words as target words, there is a 25% increase in recall; the best result for IIE is achieved when it is combined with lemmatization, resulting in an accuracy of 85% — better than any lexicon-based method reported in the *ACL wiki*[7]. When definition texts are combined with PbE results, precision increases by an additional 3.4 percentage points, giving the best accuracy of 88.3% on this task.

In contrast, although it is a more-sophisticated model, MaxEnt fails to perform as well; neither precision nor re-

[7] `http://aclweb.org/aclwiki/index.php?title=TOEFL_Synonym_Questions_%28State_of_the_art%29`.

Table 1: *Performance on solving TOEFL synonym questions.* IIE_{in} *and* IIE_{out} *denote variants of* IIE *with in-neighbors only and with out-neighbors only, respectively;* IIE *without subscripts corresponds to the original* IIE *method (with both in- and out-neighbors).*

	IIE_{in}	IIE_{out}	IIE_{in} + Lemma	IIE+Lemma	PbE+Lemma	PbE+DefText	MaxEnt+Lemma
Precision	**100.0**	51.3	93.8	87.2	93.6	90.6	55.0
Recall	50.0	**97.5**	75.0	**97.5**	77.5	**97.5**	54.6
F	66.7	67.2	83.4	92.1	84.8	**93.9**	54.8
Accuracy	50.0	50.0	70.4	85.0	72.5	**88.3**	30.0

call is outstanding, with an accuracy of 30% — slightly better than the simplest baseline of random guessing (25% in accuracy). In general, the number of training iterations i in the GIS algorithm has a positive correlation with the average number of words $\bar{n}$ extracted from each definition (Figure 2): $\bar{n}$ is less than one when $i = 10$, resulting in a recall as low as 15%; the best result is achieved at 80 iterations. Error analysis reveals that the words proposed by MaxEnt are far from synonymous to their corresponding definienda — partly due to the raw quality of training data as discussed in Section 3.3 below.

Performance does not improve significantly when incorporating the dictionary graph into MaxEnt (only about 1% increase in F, not reported in Table 1).

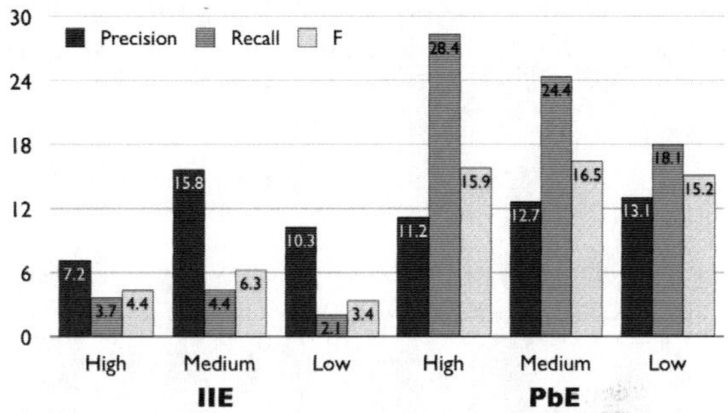

Fig. 3: *Inverted index extraction versus pattern-based extraction when compared with existing thesauri.* High, Medium, *and* Low *refer to different frequencies of target words in the* Wall Street Journal.

3.2 Comparing with Existing Thesauri

In addition to the indirect, task-driven evaluation by solving TOEFL synonym questions, we set up a second experiment in which the extracted synonyms will be directly compared with existing thesauri. The goal is to evaluate the degree of synonymy among the extracted words.

In order to compare with published results, we try to set up this experiment as close to that of Wu and Zhou (2003) as possible. The thesaurus of choice is artificially constructed, combining WordNet and *Rogets II: The New Thesaurus*[8]; target words are chosen from the *Wall Street Journal* according to different POS (nouns, adjectives, and verbs) and frequency (high, medium, and low). For each target word and each extraction method, there will be two sets of synonyms: one extracted by a given extraction method, the other from the combined thesaurus. The goal is to see how the automatically extracted set correlates with the one from the thesaurus.

With all the different POS and frequencies, the scores reported in precision, recall, and F for all three extraction methods populated a table of over 100 cells[9]. Here, we only focus on comparisons between IIE and PbE , and how their performance varies according to target word frequency (Figures 3 and 4). We also compare all three methods with published results (Figure 5).

Since POS is not of primary interest here, we average the results across the three different POS. Figure 3 shows how IIE compares with PbE across different target word frequencies. On average, PbE has slightly better precision and drastically better recall, resulting in F scores approximately 3–5 times as high as those of IIE. The performance of IIE is apparently "spiked" at medium target word frequency, conforming to our previous hypothesis that IIE would underperform when the target word frequency is too low or too high. In contrast, PbE exhibits "smoother" performance especially in precision and F score[10].

Precision of PbE increases as target word frequency decreases. We speculate that this is because the degree of polysemy of a word is approximately in proportion to its frequency; high-frequency words, being more polysemous, would have more chances of "digressing" to various branches of different senses; they also tend to appear in many different words' definitions under different senses. This is especially true when transitivity of synonymy is applied with no constraints. We will show shortly how transitive closure on the dictionary graph helps alleviate this problem.

The drop of recall in PbE with respect to frequency can be explained by different in- and out-degree of target words of different frequencies. Words of higher frequency would not only have a higher out-degree (due to their polysemy), but also a higher in-degree since they are more likely to appear in other words' definitions. In contrast, low-frequency words would have fewer senses and thus smaller numbers of definitions; if they are too infrequent to appear in other words' definitions, then these few definitions of their own would be the only source for synonyms, which would, not surprisingly, result in lower recall.

Figure 4 shows the improvement in PbE performance by finding transitive closure as mentioned in Section 2.2.2. Recall drops to about half of the original values after using transitive closure (denoted PbE_tc in the graph), but meanwhile precision is more than tripled in all frequencies. It is interesting to observe how precision responds differently to frequency change before and after using transitive closure:

[8] Available at `http://www.bartleby.com/62/`

[9] Available at `http://www.cs.toronto.edu/~tong/syn_ex/combo_thesaurus.pdf`

[10] Even recall, which seemingly drops drastically as frequency decreases, is still smoother than that of IIE if drawn at equal scale.

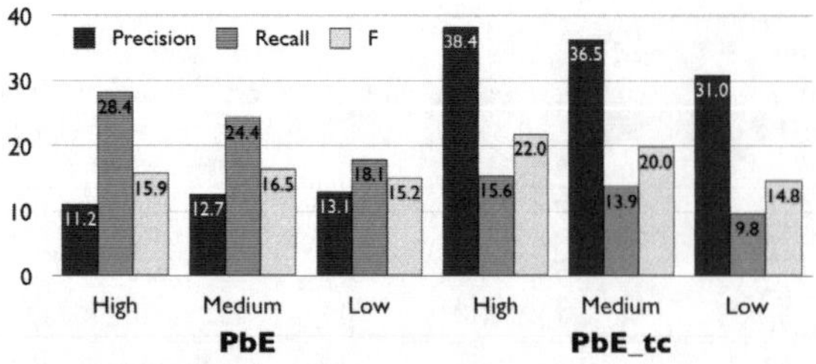

Fig. 4: *Performance before and after using transitive closure on pattern-based extraction (denoted* PbE *and* PbE_tc, *respectively).* High, Medium, *and* Low *refer to different frequencies of target words in the* Wall Street Journal.

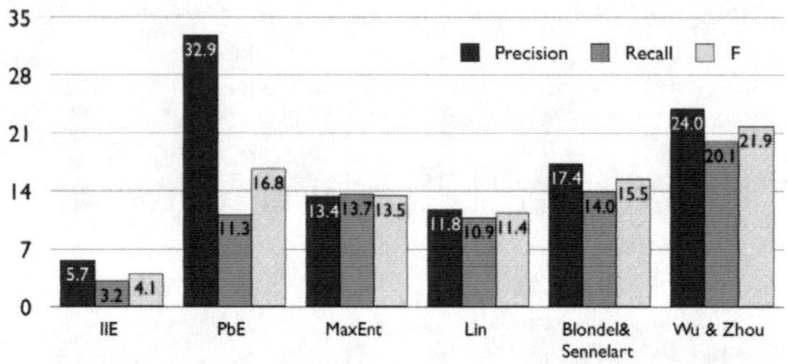

Fig. 5: *Comparing with published results on the combined thesaurus experiment*

without transitive closure, precision increases as frequency decreases, while after transitive closure is introduced, it varies in the opposite direction. This indicates that using transitive closure is most helpful for high-frequency target words. This is, again, due to their polysemy and better chances of "digression", and thus, transitive closure indeed helps to effectively eliminate false positives introduced by such digressions; low-frequency words would already have relatively better precision due to their having fewer number of senses, and transitive closure appears less helpful in this case.

Figure 5 shows how our methods compare with other published results. IIE is outperformed by all other methods by large margins. PbE has the best precision (32.9%) but falls behind that of Wu and Zhou (2003) in terms of F due to low recall. MaxEnt has better recall than both IIE and PbE, but F score is not as good as that of PbE. Results of Blondel and Senellart (2002) is included as an example of dictionary-based method for comparison, and Lin (1998) as an example of corpus-based approach[11]. Wu and Zhou (2003) combines the methods of Blondel and Senellart (2002) and Lin (1998), as well as a novel method using bilingual resources, achieving the best result among all methods being compared here.

3.3 Definition Text Labeling

Recall that the MaxEnt model labels synonyms in a piece of definition text for a given target word; in fact, PbE and IIE could also be viewed as processes of labeling synonyms in definition texts in more or less the same way. The basic

[11] Results of both Blondel and Senellart (2002) and Lin (1998) are reported by Wu and Zhou (2003).

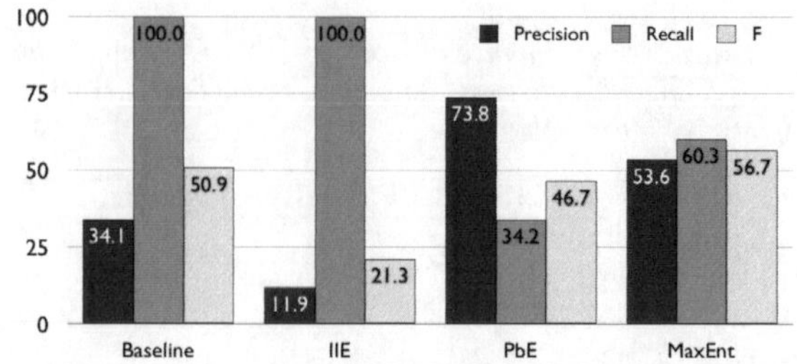

Fig. 6: *Performance on synonym labeling in definitions*

idea of this third experiment is to see how well each method performs in such a labeling task.

Note that in terms of synonym extraction, the former two experiments (Section 3.1 and 3.2) are the main approaches for evaluating the extraction quality of various methods; this section, in contrast, stresses more the nature of the training data for the MaxEnt model.

The data is prepared in the same way as described in Section 2.3; it does not necessitate any human labeling, though at the cost of the quality of synonym labels (to be discussed at the end of this section).

The labeling criteria for the three methods follow the discussion in Section 2.4: IIE takes all definientia as synonyms, while PbE takes only those following certain prespecified patterns. MaxEnt makes predictions for each defining word based on its training. We also introduce a baseline that chooses a defining word as a synonym if it shares the same POS as that of the definiendum.

The results are presented in Figure 6. The baseline and IIE both have 100% recall according to the experiment setup. IIE and PbE are both outperformed by the baseline. PbE has the highest precision and meanwhile, the lowest recall due to its dependence on specific patterns.

Due to the low quality of the training data, MaxEnt did not perform as well as expected. POS tags have many discrepancies, partly because the tagger is not trained on definition texts. On the other hand, using WordNet to create the gold standard in synonym labels also appears to be errorprone. For example, in the definition of ability (*power or capacity to do or act...*), *power* is labeled as a synonym of *ability* while *capacity* is not, since it is not in the same synset as that of *ability*. There are also cases where words in insignificant positions within the definition text happen to be in the same synset as that of the definiendum. All such cases will eventually confuse the learning process of MaxEnt.

4 Conclusions and Future Work

We proposed three methods for extracting synonyms from dictionary definition texts: by building an inverted index on the dictionary, by matching and bootstrapping regular expression patterns that synonyms tend to follow, and by developing and training a maximum entropy classifier. Their performance was evaluated in three experiments: by solving TOEFL synonym questions, by comparing against existing thesauri, and by labeling synonyms in definitions.

Our experiments show that simple extraction schemes perform surprisingly well on solving TOEFL synonym questions; IIE scores 85% in accuracy, and PbE performs even better at 88.3% — almost 10% higher than that of the best reported lexicon-based method.

Nonetheless, when compared with existing thesauri, the quality of the extracted synonyms is not as satisfactory. In addition, the results from this comparison do not correlate well with those of the TOEFL synonym question task: simple extraction schemes, such as IIE, can perform well on the TOEFL task while failing badly in the comparison experiment, whereas on the other hand, the advantage of PbE and MaxEnt is not fully reflected in the TOEFL task. This leads to the question of whether the TOEFL task, though given the name of *synonym* questions, is indeed indicative of strict synonymy.

Freitag et al. (2005) generated over 23,000 questions through an automated process to compensate for the small number of questions available in the original TOEFL synonym questions data set; although the number of questions is important, it would also be interesting to devise a set of questions that include related but not synonymous words as decoys among the choices, in hope of better evaluating the degree of strict synonymy in the extracted word sets.

As claimed earlier, the maximum entropy model is developed as an initial step towards a machine learning treatment of definition text mining; it would be interesting to employ other classifiers in the future and compare their performance.

Finally, an interesting observation on the extracted words reveals that, due to the Australian provenience of the *Macquarie Dictionary*, all extraction methods have generated some synonyms unique to Australian English or culture (such as *toilet-dunny*). This phenomenon provided evidence for the adaptability of dictionary-based methods in different domains or cultures.

Acknowledgements

This study is supported by the Natural Sciences and Engineering Research Council of Canada. Discussions with Gerald Penn helped shaping an important part of this paper, and we are sincerely grateful to all anonymous reviewers for their insightful and generous comments.

References

R.A. Amsler. *The structure of the Merriam-Webster Pocket Dictionary*. PhD thesis, The University of Texas at Austin, 1980.

V.D. Blondel and P.P. Senellart. Automatic extraction of synonyms in a dictionary. *Proc. of the SIAM Workshop on Text Mining*, 2002.

S. Brin, L. Page, R. Motwami, and T. Winograd. The PageRank citation ranking: bringing order to the web. In *Proceedings of ASIS98*, pages 161–172, 1998.

M.S. Chodorow, R.J. Byrd, and G.E. Heidorn. Extracting semantic hierarchies from a large on-line dictionary. *Proceedings of the 23rd Annual Meeting on Association for Computational Linguistics*, pages 299–304, 1985.

A. Delbridge et al. *The Macquarie Dictionary*. Macquarie Library, McMahons Point, NSW, Australia, 1981.

C. Fellbaum et al. *WordNet: An electronic lexical database*. MIT press Cambridge, MA, 1998.

D. Freitag, M. Blume, J. Byrnes, E. Chow, S. Kapadia, R. Rohwer, and Z. Wang. New experiments in distributional representations of synonymy. *Proceedings of the 9th Conference on Computational Natural Language Learning*, 2005.

M.A. Hearst. Automatic acquisition of hyponyms from large text corpora. In *Proceedings of the 14th Conference on Computational Linguistics – Volume 2*, pages 539–545. Association for Computational Linguistics Morristown, NJ, USA, 1992.

N.D. Ho and F. Cédrick. Lexical similarity based on quantity of information exchanged - synonym extraction. *Proceedings of the Research Informatics Vietnam-Francophony, Hanoi, Vietnam*, pages 193–198, 2004.

M. Jarmasz and S. Szpakowicz. Roget's Thesaurus and Semantic Similarity1. *Recent Advances in Natural Language Processing III: Selected Papers from RANLP 2003*, page 111, 2004.

D. Jurafsky and J.H. Martin. *Speech and Language Processing*. Prentice Hall, 2008.

T.K. Landauer and S.T. Dumais. A solution to Plato's problem: the latent semantic analysis theory of acquisition, induction, and representation of knowledge. *Psychological Review*, 104(2):211–240, 1997.

D. Lin. Automatic retrieval and clustering of similar words. *Proceedings of the 17th International Conference on Computational Linguistics*, pages 768 774, 1998.

P. Muller, N. Hathout, and B. Gaume. Synonym extraction using a semantic distance on a dictionary. *Proceedings of TextGraphs: The Second Workshop on Graph Based Methods for Natural Language Processing*, pages 65–72, 2006.

R. Reichert, J. Olney, and J. Paris. *Two Dictionary Transcripts and Programs for Processing Them – The Encoding Scheme, Parsent and Conix.*, volume 1. DTIC Research Report AD0691098, 1969.

P.D. Turney, M.L. Littman, J. Bigham, and V. Shnayder. Combining independent modules to solve multiple-choice synonym and analogy problems. *Proceedings of the International Conference on Recent Advances in Natural Language Processing (RANLP-03)*, pages 482–489, 2003.

H. Wu and M. Zhou. Optimizing synonym extraction using monolingual and bilingual resources. *Proceedings of the Second International Workshop on Paraphrasing*, pages 72–79, 2003.

Instance Sampling Methods for Pronoun Resolution

Holger Wunsch
University of Tübingen
wunsch@sfs.uni-tuebingen.de

Sandra Kübler
Indiana University
skuebler@indiana.edu

Rachael Cantrell
Indiana University
rcantrel@indiana.edu

Abstract

Instance sampling is a method to balance extremely skewed training sets as they occur, for example, in machine learning settings for anaphora resolution. Here, the number of negative samples (i.e. *non-anaphoric* pairs) is usually substantially larger than the number of positive samples. This causes classifiers to be biased towards negative classification, leading to suboptimal performance.

In this paper, we explore how different techniques of instance sampling influence the performance of an anaphora resolution system for German given different classifiers. All sampling methods prove to increase the F-score for all classifiers, but the most successful method is random sampling. In the best setting, the F-score improves from 0.541 to 0.608 for memory-based learning, from 0.561 to 0.611 for decision tree learning and from 0.511 to 0.584 for maximum entropy learning.

1 Introduction

Machine learning approaches to anaphora resolution are generally defined as deciding, for a pair consisting of a pronoun and a possible antecedent (*markable*), whether or not they share an anaphoric relation. In the sentence "When the car hit the tree in the dark, it lost a tire.", for example, the task is to decide whether the pronoun *it* refers to one of the noun phrases *the car*, *the tree*, *the dark*, or to any of the noun phrases in the preceding sentences in the text. This means that it is paired with each of these noun phrases individually, and the classifier decides for each case whether there is an anaphoric relationship between the two. Training data is produced in the same way. This results in a highly skewed class distribution with many more negative examples than positive ones. For example, Zhao and Ng [17] report a ratio of positive and negative examples of 1:29 for their Chinese data set. Ng and Cardie [7] report that in the MUC-6 data set, only 2% of the pairs are positive examples, all the others are negative (approximate ratio: 1:48); for MUC-7, there are 3% positive examples (approximate ratio: 1:48.5). Such an extreme skewedness of the data set tends to cause suboptimal performance in machine learning approaches. For this reason, instance sampling is often used in order to create a more balanced training set. In our case, this means restricting the number of negative examples while the positive ones remain unchanged. In the case of coreference resolution for definite noun phrases, in which case all preceding markables of a coreference chain are used for positive examples, sampling those positive examples can have a positive effect, too, as Ng and Cardie [7] show.

One often-used linguistically motivated approach to restrict the negative examples is to use only the markables between the pronoun and the actual antecedent. (cf. for example [7, 10]) Another possibility is to sample the negative examples randomly until a certain, predefined ratio is reached. To our knowledge, no systematic comparison of sampling methods has been performed. This is the aim of the work presented here. For these experiments, we used a system for pronoun resolution for German [3, 15] as the basis. The system combines a rule-based morphological pre-filter with a pronoun resolution module based on a classifier. In the original system (cf. section 5), memory-based learning was used. For this reason, we first investigated the full range of sampling methods considered here using the memory-based system. In a second round of experiments, we used the two most successful sampling methods, online sampling and random sampling, on a range of classifiers. This shows whether the success of different sampling methods is dependent on the classifier or whether there are general trends.

In the remainder of this paper, we first present the full range of sampling methods (section 3), then the data set (section 4) and the original pronoun resolution system used for the comparison (section 5). In section 6, we present and discuss the results for the following classifiers: a memory-based classifier, a decision tree classifier, and a maximum entropy classifier.

2 Pronoun resolution: Task description

The first step in pronoun resolution is a syntactic analysis, which provides the pronouns and their possible antecedents, so-called *markables*. Since we are only interested in the influence of instance sampling, we used gold standard data to identify the pronouns and the markables. The syntactic information as well as the referential information is taken from the *Tübingen Treebank of Written German, TüBa-D/Z* [11] (for more details cf. section 4).

In machine learning approaches, the task of pronoun resolution is normally defined as a classification task. Normally, this leads to the approach of pairing each anaphoric pronoun with all markables preceding it in a certain window in turn. Then for each pronoun-markable pair, the classifier decides whether there is an anaphoric relation between the two (cf. e.g. [9, 10]). We follow this approach.

International Conference RANLP 2009 - Borovets, Bulgaria, pages 478–483

German is morphologically richer than English, for which most of the work has been done, and it possesses grammatical gender. Pronouns must agree with their antecedent in gender and number. For this reason, it is effective to apply a morphological filter before using the classifier. This can lead to a considerable reduction of suitable markables, as can be seen in example (1). In this example, the relative pronoun *das* can only refer to *dem Auto (the car)* (since both are neuter), and the personal pronoun *sie* only to *die Frau (the woman)* (since both are feminine).

(1)	Die Frau	nimmt	den Ball	aus	dem	
	The woman(f)	takes	the ball(m)	from	the	
	Auto,	das	sie	gekauft	hatte.	
	car(n),	which(n)	she(f)	bought	had.	

"The woman takes the ball out of the car, which she had bought."

Morphological filtering can reduce the number of pronoun-markable pairs to about half the size of the original set. However, there are exceptions to this agreement restriction. One example can be found in the sentences *Finnland schlägt Schweden. Die Finnen haben gezeigt, daß sie spielen können.* (Finland beats Sweden. The Finns have shown that they know how to play.) where the plural personal pronoun *sie* is coreferent to *Finnland (Finland)* and to *die Finnen (the Finns)*. However, *Finnland* is singular, thus it is not compatible in number with the plural pronoun. This means that the morphological filter will exclude some of the correct pairs, thus lowering the upper limit for the machine learning approach to 95.22%.

3 Instance sampling methods

The goal of instance sampling is to reduce the number of negative examples in the training set in order to reach a more balanced ratio of positive and negative examples. Since in a highly skewed training set, the number of positive examples is low, the classifier will choose a positive answer only in a few clear cases. Thus, precision is high, but recall is low: The anaphoric relations suggested are fairly reliable, but the system finds only a subset of all relations. When we use sampling techniques, the set of positive examples remains unchanged, but we reduce the number of negative examples. We expect sampling to increase recall but also to decrease precision. We used four different sampling methods:

Local sampling is based on the intuition that anaphoric relations are closely tied to proximity: On the one hand, two entities are more likely to share an anaphoric relation if they are closer, but on the other hand, negative samples close to the pronoun are thought to be especially informative on which configurations lead to no relation, in spite of proximity. We follow Soon et al. [10] in restricting the negative examples to a linguistically defined context: Given a pair of a pronoun and a correct antecedent, we include as negative samples in the training data only those non-coreferent pairs that are located *between* the pronoun and the correct antecedent. This sampling method resulted in a sampling ratio of 1:2.1 for our data set (as compared to 1:4.29 for the whole data set).

Distance sampling tests whether a negative example is especially useful if it is very close or very far from positive examples in the search space. For this sampling method, we trained the memory-based classifier on the positive examples only, using the optimal feature settings and the feature weights from the baseline experiment without sampling. Then we classified all the negative examples from the original training set against the positive examples and looked at their distances to the closest positive example. We then selected only those negative examples that had a distance greater than 0.002[1]. The distance was chosen to reach a sampling ratio close to 1:2 (close to the ratio of the other techniques). The actual ratio with distance sampling for our data set is 1:1.82.

Incremental Learning (IB2) is a modification of the standard memory-based learning algorithm by Aha et al. [1], in which the examples are presented incrementally, and only those examples are kept for the training set that are misclassified by the current training set. While this method was originally devised for memory-based learning, it can be used for any supervised machine learning paradigm. In our case, we use a slight modification of the algorithm, in which we keep all the positive examples and add the negative ones incrementally. This is performed by a training regime in which each new example is tested against the current training set and added only when it is misclassified. Since the sampling is dependent on the individual classifier's decisions, this sampling method was carried out individually for each of the classifiers used in section 6.3, thus resulting in different sampling ratios for the individual classifiers. This method results in a comparatively low sampling ratio of 1:0.96 for memory-based learning, 1:0.83 for decision-tree learning, and 1:0.70 for maximum entropy learning.

Random Sampling is a method in which first the ratio is determined, then negative examples are randomly chosen (without replacement) until the ratio is reached. This method has been used successfully, for example, by Zhao and Ng [17] for Chinese zero pronoun resolution. Since our data was prefiltered by a morphological filter, our original ratio was considerable lower than theirs: We used sampling ratios between 1:1 and 1:4.29 (the full data set).

4 The data

Since we are only interested in the influence of instance sampling, we used gold standard data for the syntactic identification of the pronouns and the possible antecedents (*markables*). As our gold data source, we used the newspaper corpus *Tübingen Treebank of Written German (TüBa-D/Z)* [12], which is based on German newspaper articles from the newspaper *die tageszeitung (taz)*. The treebank contains 27 125 sentences in version 3. TüBa-D/Z is manually annotated syntactically as well as for referential relations. On the latter level, the treebank encodes the relations of coreference and anaphora between nominal antecedents and

[1] We also experimented with the complement, which resulted in inferior F-scores.

```
refl,OD,ON,proper,def,top,ana,diff,loc,-2,yes
refl,OD,HD,common,na,top,cata,diff,loc,-2,no
```

Fig. 1: *Feature vectors for the positive pair "sich – die AWO" and the negative pair "sich – Seniorenreisen"*

definite noun phrases and pronouns, respectively. The treebank provides full coreference chains. However, we follow standard practice in anaphora resolution and consider the closest coreferent markable as the sole antecedent of a pronoun. For pronoun resolution, the only two of the six categories in TüBa-D/Z that are relevant are *anaphoric* and *cataphoric*. A complete description of the annotation scheme for the referential annotation can be found in the annotation manual [5].

In our experiments, we only consider third person reflexive, possessive, and personal pronouns. These three types together make up 53% of all the 44 424 pronouns in the treebank; other frequent pronouns are demonstrative and relative pronouns. Out of the set of pronouns treated here, personal pronouns constitute the largest subset with 54.3%, followed by possessive pronouns with 23.4% and reflexive pronouns with 22.3%. We consider all noun phrases annotated in the treebank, including pronouns, to be markables. Each pronoun is paired with all markables in a context of three sentences previous to the pronoun. This results in 661 205 pronoun-markable pairs.

5 System description

We use a hybrid approach to pronoun resolution, combining a rule-based morphological filter with a machine learning resolution module. The system, which serves as the baseline system, was fully optimized, including an attempt to switch to a pairwise competition model. More details can be found in [16]. The modules operate sequentially on the core data set, the set of pairs of pronouns and candidate antecedents.

The morphological filter removes pronoun-markable pairs that do not agree in gender and number from further processing. In example (1), the relative pronoun *das* can only refer to the car (since both are neuter), and the personal pronoun *sie* only to the woman (since both are feminine). All other pairs are removed from the set.

The morphological filter removes 358 843 morphologically incompatible pairs, reducing the set to 46% of its original size.

The pronoun resolution module uses a trainable classifier to decide on the pairs that remain after morphological filtering. The task of pronoun resolution is reformulated as a binary classification task: a pair of a candidate antecedent and a pronoun is assigned one of the two possible classes: *anaphoric* or *not anaphoric*. For each pair in the pre-filtered list of candidates, a set of features is extracted and then bundled in a feature vector. The most informative features (determined in a non-exhaustive search) are listed in detail in Table 1. Figure 1 shows two feature vectors that correspond to two candidate pairs in the following sentence:

Feature	Description
PronType	pronoun type
PronGF	gramm. function of pronoun
NPGF	gramm. function of NP
NPType	type of NP
Definite	type of article
Embedding	embedding of NP
Direction	direction of relation
ParaGF	parallelism of gramm. function
SentDist	sentence distance
WordDist	word distance

Table 1: *Features used for the classifiers*

(2) Die AWO hat sich für Seniorenreisen
The AWO has itself for senior citizen travels
nach Mallorca von Hapaq Lloyd Provisionen
to Mallorca by Hapaq Lloyd commissions
zahlen lassen.
pay let.
"The AWO accepted commissions from Hapaq Lloyd for trips by senior citizens to Mallorca."

The reflexive pronoun *sich* is anaphoric to *die AWO*, which yields a positive pair. The pronoun is not in an anaphoric (or rather cataphoric here) relation to *Seniorenreisen*, so this gives a negative pair. The training set for the classifier will then be reduced by the different instance sampling techniques.

The original system uses the *Tilburg Memory Based Learner* (TiMBL) [2]. For the experiments reported in section 6.1, we also use TiMBL, with the IB1 algorithm, with $k = 20$ and modified value distance metric (MVDM) as the similarity metric. For the decision tree experiments, we used Weka's [14] J48 algorithm with $c = 0.25$, $m = 2$ and no subtree raising. For the maximum entropy classifier, we used Weka's Logistic algorithm with $R = 1.0E - 8$ and $M = -1$.

6 The sampling experiments

The experiments were carried out in a 10-fold cross-validation setting. As classification takes place pairwise, it is not necessary to split folds along article boundaries. Each training set contains 90% of the total number of pairs (146 153 training instances per fold). The remaining 10% are assigned to the test sets (16 239 pairs each). We evaluate the performance of the system by computing pairwise precision and recall of the classifier output against the manually annotated gold standard.[2] All experiments reported below use

[2] Since our system does not generate full coreferential chains, a pairwise evaluation metric is preferable over strategies such as the MUC-6 model-theoretic coreference scoring scheme by Vilain et al. [13].

	ratio	prec.	recall	F-score
baseline	1:4.29	**0.664**	0.457	0.541
local s.	1:2.1	0.511	0.707	0.593
distance s.	1: 2.47	0.458	**0.801**	0.583
IB2	1:0.96	0.592	0.511	0.547
random s.	1:1	0.479	0.783	0.593
	1:1.5	0.502	0.751	0.602
	1:1.75	0.521	0.720	**0.604**
	1:2	0.542	0.683	**0.604**
	1:2.25	0.552	0.662	0.602
	1:2.5	0.567	0.632	0.598
	1:3	0.598	0.570	0.584
	1:4	0.653	0.477	0.552

Table 2: *Results for training the memory-based classifier with instance sampling*

the same data split, i.e. the data for the 10-fold cross-validation was produced once and then reused for all experiments.

6.1 A comparison of all sampling methods using memory-based learning

The results of the experiments with TiMBL are shown in Table 2. For the **baseline**, we used the system as described in section 5, without any sampling. This means that the training set has a ratio of 1:4.29 of positive to negative examples. This setting results in a precision of 0.664 and a considerably lower recall of 0.457. A comparison of the baseline to the sampling experiments shows that the baseline reaches the highest precision and the lowest recall of all experiments. Thus, the experiments corroborate our assumption that instance sampling increases recall while decreasing precision.

Local sampling, i.e. reducing the negative examples to the ones found between the pronoun and its correct antecedent, increases recall by 25 percent points, but it also decreases precision by approximately 15 percent points, resulting in an increase of the F-score of 5 percent points.

Surprisingly, **distance sampling** fares considerably better, which is due to the high recall of 0.801, the highest recall of all the experiments. These results show that in order to increase recall, we need examples that are clearly different from the positive examples. However, this selection of such negative examples is also detrimental to precision: With 0.458, we get the lowest precision of all experiments.

The **incremental learning** approach IB2 presents the next surprise: The sampling ratio is the lowest of all experiments (1:0.96), which should result in high recall and low precision, but the opposite is the case: At 0.592, precision is higher than for all other sampling approaches except for random sampling with almost the complete set of negative instances (1:3) or higher. Correspondingly, recall is lower (0.511) than for most other sampling approaches, with the same exception. And while the F-score is fairly stable across the 10 folds, both precision and recall vary considerably more across the 10 folds than in all other experiments: Precision varied between 0.642 and 0.544, recall between 0.549 and 0.498.

Random sampling shows the trade-off between precision and recall dependent on the sampling rate. The more we restrict the number of negative samples, the lower precision, but the higher recall. The highest F-score is reached with a ratio between 1:2 and 1:1.75, i.e. by reducing the number of negative examples to less than half of the original set. This random combination of negative examples from all areas of the search space provides the most balanced results.

6.2 Discussion

One hypothesis to pursue would be the assumption that the only relevant factor is the sampling ratio, and there is no other significant difference between the different sampling methods. This is clearly not the case for memory-based learning. Distance sampling, for example, results in a ratio of 1:2.47 but shows results that correspond to a ratio below 1:1 in random sampling. This shows clearly that random sampling is considerably more informative than restricting the negative samples to the ones that have the longest distance from the positive examples. A comparison of local sampling and random sampling shows that the former (with a ratio of 1:2.1) results in precision and recall figures that are in the area of random sampling ratio between 1:1.5 and 1:1.75. Thus, while it is considerably more competitive than distance sampling, it reaches results that random sampling reaches with considerably fewer negative examples. The most compelling argument, however, is provided by IB2, whose results most closely resemble a random sampling ratio in the range of 1:3 and 1:4. This finding is important if efficiency is a concern. In memory-based learning, the size of the instance base is directly correlated to classification times. Thus, if efficiency is important, a smaller sampling ratio can be chosen without losing too much performance.

We can conclude that while it is linguistically reasonable to assume that the negative examples between pronoun and actual antecedent are the most informative, the best results can be reached by choosing the negative examples randomly, i.e. by including examples from all areas of the search space. One reason for this may be that both distance sampling and local sampling lead to a restricted training set, but the test set cannot be restricted in the same way since we do not know which markable is the correct antecedent or what are the closest examples. This may force the classifier to make decisions on types of pairs that it did not encounter in the training set. The results also show that random sampling with a specific ratio reaches comparable results to the other sampling methods, but with a considerably lower number of examples, such as in the comparison of the random sampling results for 1:1 with distance sampling (ratio 1:2.47).

6.3 Random sampling and IB2 sampling with different classifiers

In the previous sections, we have shown that memory-based learning profits considerably from instance sampling. The next question that arises from these results concerns the general applicability of the sampling

	ratio	memory-based			decision tree			maximum entropy		
		prec.	recall	F-score	prec.	recall	F-score	prec.	recall	F-score
baseline	1:4.29	**0.664**	0.457	0.541	**0.658**	0.489	0.561	**0.637**	0.414	0.502
IB2	1:0.96/0.65/0.7	0.592	0.511	0.547	0.476	0.789	0.594	0.380	0.737	0.501
random s.	1:1	0.479	**0.783**	0.593	0.478	**0.803**	0.600	0.443	**0.801**	0.570
	1:1.5	0.502	0.751	0.602	0.530	0.722	**0.611**	0.485	0.730	0.583
	1:1.75	0.521	0.720	**0.604**	0.551	0.680	0.608	0.514	0.667	0.581
	1:2	0.542	0.683	**0.604**	0.569	0.650	0.607	0.526	0.656	**0.584**
	1:2.25	0.552	0.662	0.602	0.584	0.627	0.604	0.548	0.614	0.579
	1:2.5	0.567	0.632	0.598	0.595	0.610	0.602	0.561	0.580	0.570
	1:3	0.598	0.570	0.584	0.618	0.559	0.587	0.594	0.513	0.550
	1:4	0.653	0.477	0.552	**0.658**	0.491	0.562	0.630	0.430	0.511

Table 3: *Results of different classifiers with instance sampling*

process: Does the success translate to other settings with other classifiers? For this reason, we repeated the experiments with two more classifiers. We chose classifiers that have been successfully used for coreference resolution: a decision tree learner [4, 7, 10], and a maximum entropy learner [6, 8]. For both classifiers, we used the Weka [14] implementations, J48 and logistic regression respectively. We were planning to include a SVM classifier in the set, but training times proved prohibitive. In order to be able to estimate the effects of instance sampling on the different classifiers, we kept the whole system and data sets constant and changed only the classifiers. This means that all classifiers are trained on exactly the same folds in the 10-fold CV and on the same feature sets. We are aware that the feature set that proved optimal for the memory-based classifier may not guarantee optimal performance for other classifiers. However, if we had optimized the feature sets for the different classifiers, we would have introduced another free variable into the experiment, and we would not have been able to distinguish differences based on sampling from differences based on the feature sets. However, we did optimize the classifiers' parameters. We are also aware that physically removing examples from the training set may not be optimal for all classifiers since some classifiers allow weighting examples so that positive examples could be assigned increased weights to balance the ratio. Again, we decided to use the same data sets since not all classifiers can use example weighting, and it is unclear whether the two methods are absolutely comparable.

For the comparative experiments, we concentrated on the best sampling method (random sampling), and the method that gave the most surprising results for memory-based learning (IB2 sampling). Note that we did not use the built-in IB2 option in the TiMBL classifier but rather used a script that would start with all positive instances as training examples and would test each negative instance separately. Negative examples were only added to the training set if they were misclassified in the test.

The results of the experiments with the different classifiers are shown in Table 3. A comparison of the **baseline** results shows very similar F-scores (0.541 for memory-based learning, 0.561 for decision tree learning, and 0.502 for maximum entropy learning). From these results, we can conclude that the selected features carry enough information for similarly successful anaphora resolution results. The fact that the first two classifiers outperform the maximum entropy learner is most likely due to the small feature set. In general, maximum entropy learning performs best in the presence of a high number of low level features while memory-based learning and decision tree learning both prefer small feature sets with more complex features.

The results for the **incremental learning** setting are surprising in that the decision tree learner reaches the third highest recall value in all the experiments presented in this section. It is only surpassed by the recall value of random sampling with the lowest ratio of 1:1. As a consequence, despite the very low precision (0.476), this method reaches a competitive F-score of 0.593. However, while the results for memory-based learning with IB2 are rather atypical with regard to the sampling ratio, the results for the combination of this sampling method with both decision tree learning and maximum entropy learning are very close to the ones for random sampling with a similar ratio (1:1). The F-score for the maximum entropy classifier does not show any improvement over the baseline for this sampling method. However, the precision and recall results are different from the baseline: precision is lower, and recall is higher.

A comparison of the **random sampling** results shows that the differences are small, again with the restriction that the maximum entropy learner has an overall performance that is 3-4 percent points lower than the other classifiers. Decision tree learning, in contrast outperforms the memory-based classifier by a small margin (F-score: 0.611 vs. 0.604), and it reaches the best results with a smaller ratio of negative examples (1:1.5 vs. 1:1.75).

An analysis of the whole table of results shows that while there are smaller differences between the classifiers, both sampling methods result in higher performance for all three classifiers. And while the results for the incremental learning approach are different for the different classifiers, the results for random sampling are very stable for the three classifiers. We can therefore cautiously conclude that using random sampling for anaphora resolution in general results in a higher F-score.

Since random sampling appears to be the most stable and the most successful sampling method, we decided to have a closer look at the curves for precision, recall, and F-score given different sampling ratios. The results for the memory-based classifier are

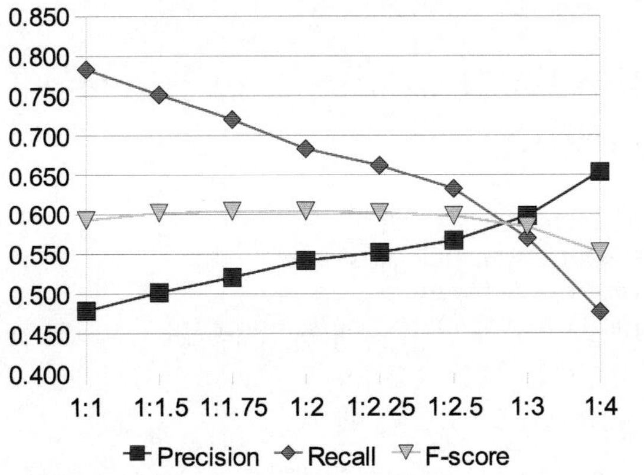

Fig. 2: *The influence of different ratios on random sampling using the memory-based classifier*

shown in Figure 2. The results for the decision tree classifier and for the maximum entropy classifier show very similar curves. The only differences are slightly lower F-scores for the maximum entropy classifier and a slight difference in ratios at which the best F-scores are reached. It is clear that across all classifiers, a low number of negative examples results in high recall, and a high number in high precision. Random sampling is therefore ideally suited for applications that may be interested in optimizing one of these measures rather than F-scores.

7 Conclusion and future work

We have shown that instance sampling is important for pronoun resolution to offset the inherent bias of the machine learner. All sampling methods (with the sole exception of maximum entropy learning with online learning) improve the F-score considerably. The highest F-score is reached for all classifiers by using random instance sampling with a ratio between 1:1.5 and 1:2. The fact that random sampling outperforms the other sampling techniques, which concentrate on different areas of the search space, clearly indicates that all examples are informative for classifications. The only function that instance sampling should perform is reducing the skewedness of the data set without fundamentally changing the distribution of the examples.

For the future, we are planning to investigate the high variance in the ten folds for IB2. Here, the sampling ratio is constant but precision and recall vary in the range of 10 and 5 percent points respectively. It is unclear why only this method should result in such a variance across the folds. One factor that does influence results is the order in which the examples are presented. But if we can resolve this issue and obtain high precision in all folds, this could be an ideal setting for classifier combination.

We also want to extend the comparison of classifiers to include feature optimization. Now that we know that all classifiers used here react favorably to random sampling given the same feature set, the next question to be answered is whether they show that same behavior with feature sets that were optimized individually.

References

[1] D. Aha, D. Kibler, and M. K. Albert. Instance-based learning algorithms. *Machine Learning*, 6:37–66, 1991.

[2] W. Daelemans, J. Zavrel, K. van der Sloot, and A. van den Bosch. TiMBL: Tilburg memory based learner – version 6.1 – reference guide. Technical Report ILK 07-07, Induction of Linguistic Knowledge, Computational Linguistics, Tilburg University, 2007.

[3] E. W. Hinrichs, K. Filippova, and H. Wunsch. A data-driven approach to pronominal anaphora resolution in German. In *Proceedings of the 5th International Conference on Recent Advances in Natural Language Processing (RANLP 2005)*, Borovets, Bulgaria, 2005.

[4] C. Müller, S. Rapp, and M. Strube. Applying co-training to reference resolution. In *Proceedings of the 40th Annual Meeting of the Association for Computational Linguistics (ACL'02)*, pages 352–359, Philadelphia, PA, 2002.

[5] K. Naumann. Manual for the annotation of in-document referential relations. Technical report, Seminar für Sprachwissenschaft, Universität Tübingen, 2006.

[6] V. Ng. Learning noun phrase anaphoricity to improve coreference resolution: Issues in representation and optimization. In *Proceedings of the 42nd Annual Meeting of the Association for Computational Linguistics (ACL'04)*, Barcelona, Spain, 2004.

[7] V. Ng and C. Cardie. Combining sample selection and error-driven pruning for machine learning of coreference rules. In *Proceedings of the Conference on Empirical Methods in Natural Language Processing (EMNLP-02)*, Philadelphia, PA, 2002.

[8] S. Ponzetto and M. Strube. Semantic role labeling for coreference resolution. In *Proceedings of the 11th Conference of the European Chapter of the Association for Computational Linguistics (EACL-2006)*, Trento, Italy, 2006.

[9] J. Preiss. Anaphora resolution with memory based learning. In *Proceedings of the 5th UK Special Interest Group for Computational Linguistics (CLUK5)*, pages 1–8, 2002.

[10] W. M. Soon, H. T. Ng, and D. C. Y. Lim. A machine learning approach to coreference resolution of noun phrases. *Computational Linguistics*, 27(4):521–544, 2001.

[11] H. Telljohann, E. Hinrichs, and S. Kübler. The TüBa-D/Z treebank: Annotating German with a context-free backbone. In *Proceedings of the Fourth International Conference on Language Resources and Evaluation (LREC 2004)*, pages 2229–2235, Lisbon, Portugal, 2004.

[12] H. Telljohann, E. W. Hinrichs, S. Kübler, and H. Zinsmeister. *Stylebook for the Tübingen Treebank of Written German (TüBa-D/Z)*. Seminar für Sprachwissenschaft, Universität Tübingen, Germany, 2006.

[13] M. Vilain, J. Burger, J. Aberdeen, D. Connolly, and L. Hirschman. A model-theoretic coreference scoring scheme. In *MUC6 '95: Proceedings of the 6th Conference on Message Understanding*, pages 45–52, Columbia, MD, 1995.

[14] I. Witten and E. Frank. *Data Mining: Practical Machine Learning Tools and Techniques*. Morgan Kaufmann, 2005.

[15] H. Wunsch. Anaphora resolution – What helps in German. In *Proceedings of the International Conference on Linguistic Evidence 2006*, pages 101–105, Tübingen, Germany, 2006.

[16] H. Wunsch. *Rule-Based and Memory-Based Pronoun Resolution for German: A Comparison and Assessment of Data Sources*. PhD thesis, Universität Tübingen, 2009.

[17] S. Zhao and H. T. Ng. Identification and resolution of Chinese zero pronouns: A machine learning approach. In *Proceedings of the 2007 Joint Conference on Empirical Methods in Natural Language Processing and Computational Natural Language Learning (EMNLP-CoNLL)*, Prague, Czech Republic, 2007.

Approximate Matching for Evaluating Keyphrase Extraction

Torsten Zesch and Iryna Gurevych
Ubiquitous Knowledge Processing Lab
Computer Science Department
Technische Universität Darmstadt, D-64289 Darmstadt, Germany
http://www.ukp.tu-darmstadt.de

Abstract

We propose a new evaluation strategy for keyphrase extraction based on approximate keyphrase matching. It corresponds well with human judgments and is better suited to assess the performance of keyphrase extraction approaches. Additionally, we propose a generalized framework for comprehensive analysis of keyphrase extraction that subsumes most existing approaches, which allows for fair testing conditions. For the first time, we compare the results of state-of-the-art unsupervised and supervised keyphrase extraction approaches on three evaluation datasets and show that the relative performance of the approaches heavily depends on the evaluation metric as well as on the properties of the evaluation dataset.

Keywords

keyphrase extraction; approximate matching

1 Introduction

Keyphrases are small sets of expressions representing a document's content. **Keyphrase extraction** is the task of automatically extracting such keyphrases from a document. The extracted phrases have to be present in the document itself, in contrast to keyphrase assignment (a multi-class text classification problem) where a fixed set of keyphrases is used which are not necessarily contained in the document. Keyphrase extraction has important applications in NLP including summarization [4, 11], clustering [9], as well as indexing and browsing [8], highlighting [22] and searching [2].

Despite the importance of the task, the evaluation of keyphrase extraction has not received much research attention in the past. In this paper, we address three core problems with the evaluation of keyphrase extraction: (i) the evaluation metric, (ii) the evaluation datasets, and (iii) the evaluation framework.

The performance of most keyphrase extraction algorithms is evaluated by comparing whether the extracted keyphrases exactly match the human assigned gold standard keyphrases. However, this is known to underestimate performance [22]. Allowing only exact matchings cannot account for variations in the extracted keyphrases that might be perfectly acceptable when presented to humans. For example, longer noun phrases like "congress party spokesman" are usually more specific and thus more informative to the reader than shorter noun phrases like "congress party". However, due to reading and writing economy, specific terms are usually not often repeated in a document [1]. Thus, longer noun phrases are unlikely to be annotated by human annotators, preventing exact matching. To compensate for these shortcomings, we propose a new approximate matching strategy that also accounts for non-exact matches and is able to give a better picture of the actual quality of a keyphrase extraction algorithm. We evaluate the validity of the new matching strategy in a human annotation study in Section 3.

The lack of standard datasets is the second problem tackled in this paper. Comparing results from different papers is difficult as no standard datasets are used, and few papers have compared their results on more than one dataset with different competing systems. Thus it cannot be judged conclusively which approaches improve results on which kind of dataset. We collected three publicly available datasets with different properties, which allows comparison of the applicability of keyphrase extraction algorithms to those datasets.

Some datasets contain annotated keyphrases that actually cannot be found in the document. This has serious implications on the comparability of results, as including them in the evaluation might significantly lower the reachable performance on the dataset. A way to solve this problem is to use a unified framework for the evaluation of keyphrase extraction. This also prevents influence from varying pre- and postprocessing. Thus, we propose a generalized framework for keyphrase extraction, which allows for fair testing conditions and a comprehensive analysis of results.

2 Related Work

In this section, we give an overview of (i) existing approaches to keyphrase extraction, (ii) the different ways to evaluate keyphrase extraction, and (iii) the datasets that have been used for evaluation.

Keyphrase Extraction Approaches Existing methods for keyphrase extraction can be categorized into supervised and unsupervised approaches.[1]

[1] Note that unsupervised approaches might use tools like NP chunkers relying on supervised approaches. However, as such

International Conference RANLP 2009 - Borovets, Bulgaria, pages 484–489

Closely related to keyphrase extraction are glossary extraction [17] and back-of-the-book indexing [3].

Unsupervised approaches usually select quite general sets of candidates (e.g. all tokens in a document), and use a subsequent ranking step to limit the selection to the most important candidates. For example, Barker and Cornacchia [1] restrict candidates to noun phrases, and rank them using heuristics based on length, term frequency, and head noun frequency. Bracewell et al. [2] also restrict candidates to noun phrases, and cluster them if they share a term. The clusters are ranked according to the noun phrase and token frequencies in the document. Finally, the centroids of the top-n ranked clusters are selected as keyphrases. Mihalcea and Tarau [15] propose a graph-based approach called *TextRank*, where the graph nodes are tokens and the edges reflect co-occurrence relations between tokens in the document. The nodes are ranked using PageRank, and longer keyphrases can be reconstructed in a post-processing step merging adjacent keywords. The method was found to yield competitive results with state-of-the-art supervised systems [15]. Wan and Xiao [24] expand TextRank by augmenting the graph with highly similar documents, which improves results compared with standard TextRank and a tf.idf baseline.

Another branch of unsupervised approaches is based on statistical analysis. Tomokiyo and Hurst [21] use pointwise KL-divergence between language models derived from the documents and a reference corpus. Paukkeri et al. [18] use a similar method based on likelihood ratios. Matsuo and Ishizuka [12] present a statistical keyphrase extraction approach that does not make use of a reference corpus, but is based on co-occurrences of terms in a single document.

Supervised approaches use a corpus of training data to learn a keyphrase extraction model that is able to classify candidates as keyphrases. A well known supervised system is *Kea* [6] that uses all n-grams of a certain length as candidates, and ranks them using the probability of being a keyphrase. *Kea* is based on a Naïve Bayes classifier using *tf.idf* and *position* as its main features. *Extractor* [22] is another supervised system that uses stems and stemmed n-grams as candidates. Its features are tuned using a genetic algorithm. *Kea* and *Extractor* are known to achieve roughly the same level of performance [23]. Hulth [10] uses a combination of lexical and syntactic features adding more linguistic knowledge which outperforms *Kea*. Medelyan and Witten [13] present the improved *Kea++* that selects candidates with reference to a controlled vocabulary from a thesaurus or Wikipedia [14]. Turney [23] augments *Kea* with a feature set based on statistical word association to ensure that the returned keyphrase set is coherent. However, this assumption might not hold if a document covers different topics. Nguyen and Kan [16] augment *Kea* with features tailored towards scientific publications such as section information and certain morphological phenomena often found in scientific papers.

tools are usually already available for most languages, we consider an approach to be unsupervised if it does not make use of any training data with annotated *keyphrases*.

Evaluation Methods The prevalent approaches for evaluating keyphrase extraction algorithms are: (i) *manual evaluation based on human judges* [1, 12, 22], (ii) *application-based evaluation* [2, 11], and (iii) *automated evaluation against human assigned keyphrases* [6, 10, 15, 16, 23].

In **manual evaluation**, human judges can easily decide whether the returned keyphrases are good representatives of a document's content or not. Thus, manual evaluation is not restricted to exact matches between gold standard keyphrases and keyphrases returned by a method. However, manual evaluation of extracted keyphrases is very costly and time-consuming. In particular, it is not suited for any kind of parameter tuning, as the output of each new system configuration involves manual re-evaluation.

An **application-based evaluation** utilizes keyphrases as part of a usually complex application, and the performance is measured in terms of the overall performance of the application. However, this entails influence of parameters besides the keyphrase extraction algorithm to be tested. For example, Bracewell et al. [2] use the information retrieval task of keyword search to determine the effectiveness of keywords at uniquely describing the document from which they were extracted. However, this method might extract keyphrase sets that are good indicators for relevant documents, but that are not acceptable when presented to humans. Litvak and Last [11] use a summary-based evaluation, where a term is used as a gold standard keyphrase if it appears in the document and in the summary.

Automated evaluation against human assigned keyphrases relies on automated matching of human annotated gold standard keyphrases with the keyphrases extracted by a certain approach. The human assigned keyphrases are either derived keyphrases assigned by authors [6, 22], or are annotated by indexers [10, 16, 24]. As this approach avoids the problems of manual evaluation (costly, time-consuming, difficult algorithm tuning), and of application-based evaluation (influence of complex applications, keyphrases unacceptable to humans), we are going to use it for evaluation in this paper.

Datasets We now describe three publicly available datasets with manually annotated gold standard keyphrases. They differ in length and domain (see Table 1), and can thus be used to assess different properties of keyphrase extraction algorithms.

The **Inspec dataset** [10] contains 2000 abstracts of journals in the Inspec database from the years 1998 to 2002. There are two sets of keyphrases assigned by professional indexers: controlled terms (restricted to the Inspec index terms, and useful for keyphrase assignment) and uncontrolled terms. Some uncontrolled terms (23.8%) are not directly found in the documents and therefore ignored in our evaluation. However, this dataset has the highest number of human assigned keyphrases per document, while the documents are rather short with an average length of $\approx$ 140 tokens. The Pearson correlation between the length of the document and the number of human assigned keyphrases is quite high ($r = 0.56$), indicating that indexers often

Name	Reference	Domain	Indexing	# Docs	∅ # Tokens	∅ # Keyphrases	r
Inspec	Hulth (2004)	Scientific	Single Indexer	2000	138.6	9.64	0.56
DUC	Wan and Xiao (2008)	News	Multiple Indexers	301	902.8	8.08	0.18
SP	Nguyen and Kan (2007)	Scientific	Multiple Indexers	134	8491.6	8.31	0.08

Table 1: *Keyphrase evaluation datasets. r is the Pearson correlation between the document length and the number of assigned keyphrases.*

exhaustively annotated keyphrases in the documents. Thus, it should be relatively easy to extract keyphrases from the documents, and we expect the performance on this dataset to be higher than on the other datasets.

The **DUC dataset** [24] consists of 308 documents from DUC2001 that were manually annotated with at most 10 keyphrases per document by two indexers. Annotation conflicts between the indexers were solved by discussion. Two documents in the DUC2001 data obtained from NIST were empty, and 5 documents had no annotated keyphrases. Thus, the final dataset used in this paper contains 301 documents.

The **SP dataset** [16] originally contains 211 scientific publications downloaded from the internet and automatically converted to plain text. Keyphrases were manually annotated by multiple indexers, but conflicts were not resolved. We removed documents for which no keyphrase annotation was available, and those with multiple conflicting annotations. The final dataset contains 134 documents.

3 Automated Evaluation

We now give an overview of the automated evaluation as introduced in the previous section. It relies on matching a set of human annotated gold standard keyphrases K_{gold} with a ranked list of keyphrases K_{ext} extracted by a certain approach. We define a matching m between a gold standard keyphrase $k_{gold} \in K_{gold}$ and an extracted keyphrase $k_{ext} \in K_{ext}$ to be a tuple $m = (k_{gold}, k_{ext})$. The matching can either be true or false, depending on whether k_{gold} and k_{ext} are equivalent according to the matching strategy. Previous works used exact matching (EXACT) that requires k_{gold} and k_{ext} to have exactly the same string representation, i.e. $\text{EXACT}(k_{gold}, k_{ext}) = \text{true} \Leftrightarrow k_{gold} = k_{ext}$.

To evaluate the overall performance of a keyphrase extraction system, we do not need to look at single matchings m, but at the full list of matchings M. Previous studies used Precision (P), Recall (R), and F-measure (F_1) at a certain fixed cutoff value, e.g. after the first 10 retrieved keyphrase matchings. However, if documents have varying numbers of keyphrases assigned (which is the case for all datasets presented in Section 2), a cutoff will distort results. For example, if we always extract 10 keyphrases, but a document only has 8 gold keyphrases assigned, then 2 extracted keyphrases will always be wrong. Thus, we propose to use the **R-precision (R-p)** measure from information retrieval [19] to evaluate keyphrase extraction systems. In information retrieval, R-p is defined as the precision when the number fo retrieved documents equals the number of relevant documents in the document collection. Hence, for keyphrase extraction we define R-p as the precision when the number of retrieved keyphrase matchings equals the number of gold standard keyphrases assigned to the document. An R-precision of 1.0 is equivalent to perfect keyphrase ranking and perfect recall.

These properties make R-p a favorable metric for keyphrase extraction, as it puts a focus on the precision on the first ranks, which is necessary for most practical systems that assign or present only a handful of keyphrases. R-p also measures whether the keyphrases on the first ranks cover the whole set of topics in the document. For example, a keyphrase extraction approach that extracts a lot of variants (e.g. "scheduling", "real-time scheduling", "embedded real-time scheduling") on the first ranks will have a lower precision than an approach that covers more topics. As an additional benefit, R-p is a single number metric allowing for more compact presentation of results and easier comparison.

We formally define R-p as the precision when $|M| = |K_{gold}|$. Precision is computed as $\frac{M_c}{M}$, where M_c is the list of correct matchings in M.

3.1 Approximate Matching Strategy

The exact matching strategy EXACT is only partially indicative of the performance of a keyphrase extraction method, as it is known to underestimate performance as perceived by human judges [22]. Additionally, it may not be a good indicator of the overall quality of the extracted set of keyphrases, as there are many cases in which exact matching fails, e.g. lexical semantic variations (*automobile sales, car sales*), overlapping phrases (*scheduling, real-time scheduling*), or morphological variants like plurals (*performance metric, performance metrics*).[2] Thus, we propose a new approximate matching strategy $\text{APPROX}(k_{gold}, k_{ext})$ that accounts for morphological variants (MORPH) and the two cases of overlapping phrases: either the extracted keyphrase includes the gold standard keyphrase (INCLUDES) or the extracted keyphrase is a part of the gold standard keyphrase (PARTOF). Exact matchings are of course still valid in addition to approximate matchings.

For overlapping phrases, we do not allow character level variations, but only token level variations, i.e. the INCLUDES category contains matchings where the extracted keyphrase contains all the tokens in the gold keyphrase plus some additional tokens. In the case of the morphological variants MORPH, we limit approximate matching to the detection of plurals. We leave the inclusion of other morphological variations and lexical semantic variants to future work.

[2] In the remainder of this paper, we present examples of matchings as (*gold keyphrase, extracted keyphrase*).

		Judges accepting matchings	
	#	4	≥ 3
INCLUDES	274	.58	.80
PARTOF	239	.31	.44
MORPH	53	.96	.96
MORPH+INCLUDES	327	.65	.83

Table 2: *Ratio of approximate keyphrase matchings acceptable to human judges (4 = all judges; ≥ 3 = at least 3 out of 4 judges).*

3.2 Approximate Matching Evaluation

For testing whether the approximate matching strategy is acceptable to humans, we randomly selected a maximum of 300 non-exact matchings from each of the three datasets (yielding a maximum of 900 randomly selected matchings). We included matchings from each of the 3 approximate matching categories (INCLUDES, PARTOF, and MORPH) using different candidate selection methods and length restrictions to account for all kinds of keyphrase variants. The total number of selected approximate matchings is 566, as some matchings were included in multiple sets of the random matchings and morphological approximate matching MORPH did not always account for 100 approximate matchings per dataset.

We had four judges annotate whether it would be acceptable to replace the gold standard keyphrase with the extracted keyphrase using the approximate matching strategy. As no context was given when judging about a matching, annotators were instructed to annotate a pair as invalid if in doubt. Thus, the annotation has a pessimistic bias and rather underestimates human agreement with the approximate matching. The results of the study are presented in Table 2.

In the MORPH category of morphological variants, agreement between judges was very high: 96% of all MORPH matchings were acceptable to all 4 judges. The only problematic case were two abbreviations (*fms*, *fmss*) and (*soa*, *soas*) where the judges could not decide about the validity without looking at the context. Agreement between all 4 judges is considerably lower for INCLUDES and PARTOF. However, given the inherent subjectivity of the task, we treat an agreement of 3 out of 4 judges as valid for accepting a match. In the INCLUDES category agreement reaches 80%, while for the PARTOF category it is only 44%.

The major source of error in the INCLUDES category was wrong pre-processing. For example, the matching (*security level*, *give security level*) was unanimously rejected by all judges, as the extracted keyphrase contains a chunking error.

A major source of error in the PARTOF category were cases when the extracted keyphrase is too general compared to the gold keyphrase, e.g. (*topic importance*, *topic*). A potential refinement of the PARTOF heuristic would be to match only extracted keyphrases whose head noun matches the head of the gold keyphrase. However, only 52% of such cases (66 out of 128) were accepted by at least 3 judges. Furthermore, in 35% of the cases (39 out of 111) a matching with a non-matching head like (*tubercolosis cases*, *tubercolosis*) was accepted by at least 3 judges. This

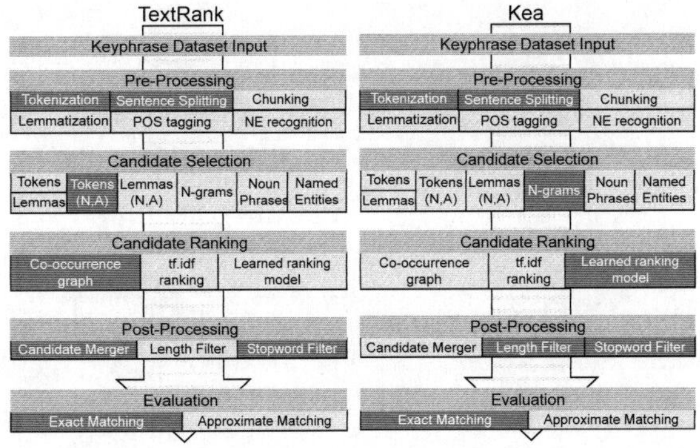

Fig. 1: *State-of-the-art keyphrase extraction systems represented in our framework.*

means, that neither is a matching head required for a keyphrase to be acceptable to human judges, nor is a matching head sufficient for an acceptable match. As we aim for an approximate matching with high precision, we decided not to use the PARTOF category due to these problems, but combined MORPH and INCLUDES to an approximate matching strategy[3] with a human agreement of 83%.

4 Extraction Framework

Most automatic keyphrase extraction methods have two stages: first they select a list of keyphrase candidates that is then ranked according to some measure of keyphrase importance. To allow for a fair comparison, the same pre- and postprocessing is necessary, as well as exactly the same evaluation strategy. We propose a generalized framework for the comprehensive analysis of keyphrase extraction as shown in Figure 1. It was designed to be as language independent as possible using either no language dependent information at all, or components that are already available for most languages (like tokenizers or chunkers). The preprocessing pipeline is based on the DKPro UIMA component repository [7].

Pre-Processing and Candidate Selection For preprocessing, we tokenize the documents, and split them into sentences. We integrated the TreeTagger for lemmatization, POS-tagging, and NP chunking [20], as well as the Stanford NER tool [5] for named entity recognition. From this pool of preprocessed data, we select as candidates *Tokens*, *Lemmas*, *N-grams*, *Noun Phrases*, and *Named Entities*. Following [15], we additionally use the restricted set of tokens *Tokens (N,A)* and lemmas *Lemmas (N,A)*.

Candidate Ranking The unsupervised graph-based methods (e.g. *TextRank*) build a co-occurence graph using the candidates. The final candidate ranking is determined by computing the centrality scores of the graph nodes using PageRank. For tf.idf ranking,

[3] It is formally defined as: $\text{APPROX}(k_{gold}, k_{ext}) = \text{EXACT} \vee \text{MORPH} \vee \text{INCLUDES}$.

	Candidates	Inspec R-p_{ex}	Inspec R-p_{ap}	DUC R-p_{ex}	DUC R-p_{ap}	SP R-p_{ex}	SP R-p_{ap}
KEA	N-grams	.16	.19	.11	.14	**.21**	**.25**
TextRank	Token N,A	**.31**	**.36**	.21	.23	.04	.10
tf.idf	Tokens	.11	.22	.05	.12	.06	.18
	Tokens (N,A)	.27	**.32**	**.12**	.15	.12	**.22**
	Lemmas	.15	.27	.06	.14	.07	.21
	Lemmas (N,A)	**.28**	**.32**	**.12**	**.16**	**.13**	**.22**
	N-grams	.10	.16	.03	.06	.06	.15
	Noun Phrases	.27	.32	**.12**	.14	.10	.21
	Named Entities	.01	.01	.11	.13	.06	.08
co-occ	Tokens	.06	.22	.00	.07	.00	.05
	Tokens (N,A)	**.31**	**.36**	.21	.23	.04	.10
	Lemmas	.07	.22	.00	.06	.00	.06
	Lemmas (N,A)	.29	.35	**.22**	**.24**	.08	.15
	N-grams	.07	.22	.03	.10	.01	.09
	Noun Phrases	.28	.34	.12	.14	**.12**	**.18**
	Named Entities	.01	.01	.09	.09	.04	.05

Table 3: *Keyphrase extraction results in terms of R-precision using exact matching (R-p_{ex}) and approximate matching (R-p_{ap}).*

the tf.idf scores are computed using token frequencies. If candidates contain more than one token, the overall tf.idf score for the candidate is the maximum tf.idf score among all the contained tokens. The supervised keyphrase extraction systems use the extraction model obtained from the training data to classify the candidates into keyphrases and rank them according to their importance in the document.

Postprocessing and Evaluation We merge candidates that are adjacent in the source document to reconstruct longer keyphrases from short candidates like *Tokens* or *Lemmas*. However, to ensure a fair comparison, we apply merging to all configurations of our keyphrase extraction framework, because also approaches with higher quality candidates like *Noun Phrases* can benefit from merging.

We use an additional post-filtering step to remove candidates or keyphrases that do not conform to length restrictions. When analyzing the length of the gold standard keyphrases in the training set, we found that - depending on the dataset - 97.7 to 99.2% of all keyphrases in the training data contain 1 to 4 tokens. Thus, we limited the length of returned keyphrases to 1 to 4 tokens.

We remove trailing stopwords from candidates, but keep stopwords that appear inside a keyphrase.[4] We also remove keyphrases that exactly match a stopword. Finally, the post-processed list of ranked keyphrases is used to compute the R-precision scores for each of the keyphrase extraction systems.

5 Experiments and Results

For our comprehensive analysis, we selected *Kea* [6] as the most widely used supervised system, and *TextRank* [15] as a state-of-the-art unsupervised system. The only external component used is the *Kea* ranking model. *TextRank* was fully modelled in our framework. We applied exactly the same pre- and post-processing to all experimental configurations.

We set aside two thirds of the documents in each dataset for training, while the rest of the data is used for evaluation.[5] We compare *Kea* and *TextRank* with all possible combinations of the candidate selection strategies and the ranking methods (tf.idf ranking as well co-occurrence graph based ranking abbreviated as "co-occ"). For comparison of the exact matching and the approximate matching strategy, we computed R-precision for exact matching (R-p_{ex}) and approximate matching (R-p_{ap}). Table 3 gives an overview of the obtained results.[6]

Theoretically, *Kea* as a supervised system is expected to yield the best performance. Tf.idf ranking based methods (that do not use any training data, but use information drawn from the whole document collection) are supposed to perform worse than supervised systems, but better than co-occurrence graph based methods like *TextRank* that only use information from a single document. However, under the controlled conditions of our keyphrase extraction framework, the unsupervised *TextRank* outperforms *Kea* by a wide margin on the Inspec and on the DUC dataset. Both datasets contain only rather small documents ($\approx$ 100–1000 tokens), making it relatively easy to select the right keyphrases.

On the SP dataset containing the longer documents, *Kea* outperforms all co-occurrence or tf.idf based system configurations by a wide margin when using exact matching. However, the approximate matching strategy reveals that the performance gap between *Kea* and the best configuration using tf.idf ranking with *Lemma (N,A)* candidates is not as large as exact matching indicates (dropping from .08 to .03).

The wide range of candidates tested within our framework allows to draw other interesting conclu-

[4] For example, we keep "United States of America" as the stopword appears inside a keyphrase, while "the weak economy" is pruned to "weak economy" as the stopword occurs at the boundary of the candidate.

[5] Note that all keyphrase extraction methods used in that paper except *Kea* did not make use of that training data. However, as we wanted to ensure a fair comparison, we tested all keyphrase extraction systems on the same evaluation data.

[6] Note that in our framework, the *TextRank* system is equivalent to using *Token (N,A)* as the candidate selection strategy and using co-occurrence graph based ranking. We duplicated this row of results as 'TextRank' for convenience.

sions: The candidate selection strategies *Tokens*, *Lemmas*, and *N-grams* generally lead to poor performance due to the overgeneration of candidates. In most cases, *Lemma (N,A)* candidates perform slightly better than *Tokens (N,A)* candidates, but the small difference does not justify the additional effort of lemmatization. The *TextRank* result on the SP dataset can almost be doubled (from .10 to .18 R-p_{ap}) by using noun phrases instead of Tokens (N,A) as candidates. This indicates that using higher quality candidates can have a positive impact on keyphrase extraction performance on longer documents.

6 Conclusions

We presented a new evaluation strategy for keyphrase extraction based on approximate keyphrase matching that accounts for the shortcomings of exact matching. In an annotation study, we showed that approximate matching (based on morphological variants and extracted keyphrases which include the gold standard keyphrases) corresponds well with human judgments. We showed that the approximate matching strategy is better suited to assess the performance of keyphrase extraction approaches.

We proposed a generalized framework for the comprehensive analysis and evaluation of keyphrase extraction systems, and compared the results of state-of-the-art unsupervised and supervised keyphrase extraction approaches on three evaluation datasets. We showed that the relative performance of the approaches heavily depends on the matching strategy as well as on the properties of the evaluation dataset especially the length of documents. We found that for small and medium sized documents ($\approx$ 100–1000 tokens), the unsupervised approach using co-occurrence graph based ranking outperforms the supervised system by a wide margin. On larger documents, the supervised system outperforms the tf.idf and co-occurrence graph based approaches, but using approximate matching reveals that the improvement over the unsupervised tf.idf ranking based approaches is small. We also find that the performance of co-occurrence graph based methods on large documents can be increased by 80% when using higher quality noun phrase candidates instead of tokens restricted to nouns and adjectives.

Acknowledgments

This work has been supported by the Volkswagen Foundation as part of the Lichtenberg-Professorship Program under grant No. I/82806, and by the German Research Foundation under grant 798/1-3. We thank Anette Hulth and Min-Yen Kan for providing evaluation datasets. We thank Melanie Hartmann, Matthieu Hermet, and Johannes Hoffart for participating in the annotation study.

References

[1] K. Barker and N. Cornacchia. Using Noun Phrase Heads to Extract Document Keyphrases. In *Canadian Conference on AI*, pages 40–52. Springer, 2000.

[2] D. B. Bracewell, F. Ren, and S. Kuriowa. Multilingual Single Document Keyword Extraction for Information Retrieval. In *Proceedings of the International Conference on Natural Language Processing and Knowledge Engineering*, pages 517–522, 2005.

[3] A. Csomai and R. Mihalcea. Investigations in Unsupervised Back-of-the-Book Indexing. In *Proceedings of the Florida Artificial Intelligence Research Society*, pages 211–216, 2007.

[4] E. D'Avanzo and B. Magnini. A Keyphrase-Based Approach to Summarization: the LAKE System at DUC-2005. In *Proceedings of DUC Workshop at HLT/EMNLP'05*, Vancouver, B.C., Canada, October 6-8 2005.

[5] J. R. Finkel, T. Grenager, and C. Manning. Incorporating Non-local Information into Information Extraction Systems by Gibbs Sampling. In *Proceedings of the 43rd Annual Meeting of the Association for Computational Linguistics (ACL'05)*, pages 363–370, 2005.

[6] E. Frank, G. W. Paynter, I. Witten, C. Gutwin, and C. G. Nevill-Manning. Domain-Specic Keyphrase Extraction. In *Proceedings of the 16th International Joint Conference on Articial Intelligence*, pages 668–673, 1999.

[7] I. Gurevych, M. Mühlhäuser, C. Müller, J. Steimle, M. Weimer, and T. Zesch. Darmstadt Knowledge Processing Repository Based on UIMA. In *Proceedings of the First Workshop on Unstructured Information Management Architecture at Biannual Conference of the GSCL*, 2007.

[8] C. Gutwin, G. Paynter, I. Witten, C. Nevill-Manning, and E. Frank. Improving Browsing in Digital Libraries with Keyphrase Indexes. *Decision Support Systems*, 27(1-2):81–104, 1999.

[9] K. M. Hammouda, D. N. Matute, and M. S. Kamel. CorePhrase: Keyphrase Extraction for Document Clustering. *Machine Learning and Data Mining in Pattern Recognition*, 2005:265–274, 2005.

[10] A. Hulth. Enhancing Linguistically Oriented Automatic Keyword Extraction. In *Proceedings of HLT/NAACL: Short Papers*, pages 17–20, 2004.

[11] M. Litvak and M. Last. Graph-Based Keyword Extraction for Single-Document Summarization. In *Proceedings of COLING*, pages 17–24, 2008.

[12] Y. Matsuo and M. Ishizuka. Keyword Extraction from a Single Document Using Word Co-occurrence Statistical Information. *International Journal on Artificial Intelligence Tools*, 13(1):157–169, 2004.

[13] O. Medelyan and I. H. Witten. Thesaurus based automatic keyphrase indexing. In *In Proceedings of the Joint Conference on Digital Libraries (JCDL) 2006*, pages 296–297, 2006.

[14] O. Medelyan, I. H. Witten, and D. Milne. Topic Indexing with Wikipedia. In *Proceeding of AAAI Workshop on Wikipedia and Artificial Intelligence*, pages 19–24, 2008.

[15] R. Mihalcea and P. Tarau. TextRank: Bringing Order into Texts. In *Proceedings of the Conference on Empirical Methods in Natural Language Processing*, pages 404–411, 2004.

[16] T. D. Nguyen and M.-Y. Kan. Keyphrase Extraction in Scientific Publications. In *Proceedings of International Conference on Asian Digital Libraries*, pages 317–326, 2007.

[17] Y. Park, R. J. Byrd, and B. K. Boguraev. Automatic Glossary Extraction: Beyond Terminology Identification. In *Proceedings of the 19th international conference on Computational linguistics*, pages 1–7, 2002.

[18] M.-S. Paukkeri, I. T. Nieminen, M. Pöllä, and T. Honkela. A Language-Independent Approach to Keyphrase Extraction and Evaluation. In *Coling 2008 Posters*, pages 83–86, 2008.

[19] G. Salton and M. J. McGill. *Introduction to Modern Information Retrieval*. McGraw-Hill, New York, 1983.

[20] H. Schmid. Probabilistic Part-of-Speech Tagging Using Decision Trees. In *International Conference on New Methods in Language Processing*, Manchester, UK, 1995.

[21] T. Tomokiyo and M. Hurst. A Language Model Approach to Keyphrase Extraction. In *Proceedings of the ACL 2003 workshop on Multiword expressions*, pages 33–40, 2003.

[22] P. D. Turney. Learning Algorithms for Keyphrase Extraction. *Information Retrieval*, 2:303–336, 2000.

[23] P. D. Turney. Coherent Keyphrase Extraction via Web Mining. In *Proceedings of the International Joint Conferences on Artificial Intelligence*, pages 434–439, 2003.

[24] X. Wan and J. Xiao. Single Document Keyphrase Extraction Using Neighborhood Knowledge. In *Proceedings of AAAI*, pages 855–860, 2008.

Too Many Mammals: Improving the Diversity of Automatically Recognized Terms

Ziqi Zhang, Lei Xia, Mark A. Greenwood and José Iria
The Department of Computer Science
The University of Sheffield, United Kingdom
{*initial.surname*}@*dcs.shef.ac.uk*

Abstract

Automatic Term Recognition systems extract domain-specific terms from text corpora. Unfortunately current systems fail to capture the whole of the domain covered by a corpus. To address this problem, we present a novel term re-ranking method that generates term lists containing terms that are not only individually salient, but also contribute to a globally diverse list that is truly representative of the corpus. We show that, even without any prior knowledge about the domain, our proposed method improves the diversity of the results produced by two popular automatic term recognition algorithms.

Keywords

Automatic Term Recognition, Diversity in Ranking, Random Walk, Semantic Similarity

1 Introduction

Automatic Term Recognition (ATR) is an important research area that deals with the recognition and extraction of technical terms from domain-specific corpora. ATR is often a processing step preceding more complex tasks, such as semantic search or ontology engineering [14, 3]. It can also be used as an end-user tool to, for instance, generate a list of terms that summarizes a text corpus provided by the user.

Whilst state-of-the-art ATR algorithms are reasonably successful in identifying the most relevant domain-specific terms from a corpus, the analysis we carried out of the output of these algorithms over several corpora led us to conclude that the ranking of terms rarely reflects the whole domain.

Having carefully studied the experimental outputs from [25], we have observed that terms from a subset of the sub-domains (of the domain covered by the corpus) tend to dominate the results, pushing other characteristic terms, which are perhaps not so globally relevant but nevertheless fundamental to get a comprehensive coverage of the domain, far down the ranking. For example, on the Wikipedia animal corpus described in Section 5, which contains 1051 random Wikipedia articles describing animals across roughly 30 scientific classes, in the top ranked 50 terms by the C-Value [10] algorithm there are the names of 13 mammals, 3 fish, 2 birds and 2 insects. Among these, 3 of the 13 mammals are species of whale, and 2 of the 3 fish are species of shark. Likewise, for the TF-IDF algorithm applied on the same corpus, in the top ranked 50 terms we obtain the names of 18 mammals, 6 birds and 4 insects. Hence terms belonging to these 3 or 4 classes dominate the results, preventing the remaining classes from being properly represented. Therefore, with current methods, taking the top-ranked terms is unlikely to produce a diverse list of terms that is fully representative of the entire domain. Unfortunately, for certain applications of ATR this is not a desirable behaviour, e.g., generating a list of terms that best summarizes a text corpus.

In this paper, we address the so-called "diversity in ranking" problem [26] in the context of ATR. Our goal is to generate term lists which contain terms that are not only individually salient, as produced by current methods, but at the same time contribute to a globally diverse list. By promoting diversity, we expect to balance the number of terms from different sub-domains appearing in the top results and provide the user with a better notion of the whole of the domain covered by the corpus. Our main contributions consist of: 1) designing and implementing a novel term re-ranking method, called TermHopper, that can be coupled with any existing ATR algorithm, 2) creating a new corpus for ATR based on Wikipedia[1], and 3) empirically showing that the proposed method provides an improved ranking of extracted terms. Furthermore, an attractive feature of the proposed approach is its domain independence, that is, it does not require any additional domain specific resources.

The remainder of this paper is structured as follows. In the following section we describe related work. Section 3 introduces our proposed ranking algorithm. Section 4 describes the application of the ranking algorithm to the ATR problem. In Section 5 we describe our experimental setup, namely the data collection and pre-processing steps, the design of the gold standard and the evaluation methodology. Sections 6 presents and discuss the results of our evaluation. We conclude with an outline of our plans for future work.

2 Related Work

[25] presented a comparison of several state-of-the-art ATR methodologies namely TF-IDF, Weirdness [1], C-Value [10], Glossex [14], and Termex [17]. TF-IDF

[1] http://www.dcs.shef.ac.uk/~ziqizhang/resources/wiki.zip

International Conference RANLP 2009 - Borovets, Bulgaria, pages 490–495

makes use of term frequencies and document frequencies in the target corpus; C-value makes use of term frequencies and the frequencies at which terms appear within longer terms. Terms which exhibit high frequency and are less often used within longer terms are given higher ranks; Weirdness compares term frequencies in both the target and a reference corpus; Glossex and Termex are similar to Weirdness in the way that they all utilise term frequencies in the target corpus versus those in a reference corpus. Glossex normalises the overall term frequencies with respect to the frequencies of the component words whilst Termex also captures domain concepts that exhibit high frequencies within a small subset of the corpus but are completely absent in the remainder of the corpus.

To the best of our knowledge, the diversity issue has been overlooked in traditional ATR methods – the closest related problem is term clustering. [2] apply the LEXTER algorithm to extract candidate terms, then applied the FASTR algorithm to cluster them. This essentially clusters terms by their canonical forms after morphological normalization and syntactic normalization. [13] run C/NC-value on 2,082 MEDLINE abstracts to extract candidate terms, then applied Nearest-Neighbour clustering to the top ranked terms. They defined contextual, functional and lexical similarity to collectively measure similarity between two terms. [20] perform similar experiments, in which they ran C/NC-value on the same corpus and then classified the extracted terms into UMLS classes. In order to do this, they extended Nenadic's method of measuring term similarity by adding another dimension called term-class similarity, which is computed by co-occurrence strength of a term to a domain-specific verb that is usually a strong indicator of a class. [6] takes document clustering and word clustering as a co-clustering task, in which the output of one task (e.g., clusters of documents) induces another (e.g., clusters of words). They viewed documents in a corpus and their words as a graph connected by edges, and treated clustering as a graph partitioning problem in which optimum clusters are produced when the crossing edges between partitions have minimum weight.

Term clustering constitutes only part of the solution to the diversity problem as we need to understand how to produce a diverse ranked list of terms given the generated clusters. Methods to improve diversity in ranking include maximum marginal relevance (MMR) [5] in the context of text summarization, mixture models [24] in the context of adaptive information filtering systems, and subtopic diversity [22] and diversity penalty [23] in the context of document retrieval. The basic underlying idea of these methods is to penalize redundancy by lowering the rank of an item if it is similar to items already ranked.

Our proposed method uses a re-ranking approach based on absorbing random walks to improve the ranking of terms that describe the domain. Contrary to methods like MMR, which partly rely on heuristics, methods based on absorbing random walks have a principled mathematical model and strong empirical performance on artificial data.

The idea of using random walks in an absorbing Markov chain to improve diversity in ranking was first introduced in [26] where it was shown to effectively improve ranking results on a text summarization task, and on a social network analysis task that identifies movie stars. Moreover, absorbing random walks have also found several other applications in the research literature. For example, [19] employ absorbing random walks in order to personalize the recommendation of items to users in a collaborative filtering task, while [18] apply them to modelling an expert finding problem. The method presented here is inspired by that of [26]. We use the same core absorbing random walks algorithm, but define a similarity metric and evaluation methodology appropriate for automatic term recognition tasks.

3 Ranking for Diversity

The ranking algorithm required to solve our problem must support the notions of centrality, diversity and prior:

1. **centrality** - a highly ranked term should be representative of a local group of terms;
2. **diversity** - the top terms should cover as many distinct groups as possible;
3. **prior** - it should be possible to incorporate an existing ranking, in our case the output from an existing ATR system, as prior knowledge.

Most ATR methods treat centrality and diversity separately and try to combine results *a posteriori*, sometimes using heuristic procedures. We, however, have chosen to adopt the GRASSHOPPER algorithm introduced in [26], which is based upon a principled mathematical model that combines centrality and diversity.

Graph-based ranking algorithms like GRASSHOPPER decide the centrality of a vertex from global information recursively drawn from the entire graph. The principle behind these models is that of voting or recommendation. When one vertex links to another one, it can be seen as casting a vote for that other vertex. The higher the number of votes that are cast for a vertex, the higher its importance. Plus, the importance of the vertex casting the vote determines how important the vote itself is. Hence, the score associated with a vertex is determined based on the votes that are cast for it, and the score of the vertices casting these votes.

In GRASSHOPPER diversity is addressed together with centrality by setting top-ranked vertices as absorbing states of a random walk over the vertices of the graph. Once the random walk reaches an absorbing state, it is absorbed and stays there. If we think about the expected number of visits to a node before absorption as its rank, we expect nodes "closer" (more similar) to the absorbing node to be less visited because the likelihood of "falling into" the nearby absorbing node is higher. This effectively places unranked vertices that are similar to absorbing nodes lower in the rank, thus encouraging diversity. In what follows we briefly describe the algorithm.

Given a graph W, represented by a $n \times n$ similarity matrix, where w_{ij} is the (non-negative) weight on the edge relating term i to term j; a probability distribution r encoding the prior ranking, obtained from a previously run ATR algorithm; and a tradeoff parameter $\alpha \in [0,1]$ (that balances domain knowledge vs. prior), the algorithm produces a (re-)ranked list of the input terms such that the top terms are not only central but also diverse.

We start by finding the top ranked term using teleporting random walks. Let $\tilde{P}$ be obtained by normalising the rows of W: $\tilde{P}_{ij} = w_{ij}/\sum_{k=1}^{n} w_{ik}$, so that $\tilde{P}_{ij}$ is the probability that the walker moves to j from i. The walk is made teleporting by interpolating each row with the available prior information[2]:

$$P = \alpha\tilde{P} + (1-\alpha)\mathbf{1} \otimes \mathbf{r},$$

where $\mathbf{1}$ is an all-1 vector, and $\mathbf{1} \otimes \mathbf{r}$ is the outer product. Due to the way it was designed (normalisation, teleportation), P is irreducible, aperiodic and ergodic, and therefore has a unique stationary distribution

$$\pi = P^\top \pi,$$

which gives the global visiting probabilities for each vertex. The states with large probabilities can be regarded as central vertices, an idea used in PageRank [4] and in many works in natural language processing such as text summarization [8] or keyword extraction [12]. The top ranked vertex is thus selected as being $a_1 = \arg\max_{i=1}^{n} \pi_i$.

The rest of the algorithm consists of an iterative procedure that takes the top ranked vertex from the previous step and sets it as being the absorbing state of the random walk at the current step. A vertex a can be turned into an absorbing state by setting $P_{aa} = 1$ and $P_{ai} = 0, \forall i \neq a$. Once the random walk reaches an absorbing state, it remains there, so we are no longer interested in the stationary distribution but rather in computing the expected number of visits to each node before absorption. The fundamental matrix

$$N = (\mathbf{I} - Q)^{-1}$$

gives the expected number of visits in the absorbing random walk [7], where Q is the submatrix of P obtained by re-arranging the terms so that those already ranked appear before unranked terms in the matrix:

$$P = \begin{bmatrix} \mathbf{I}_A & \mathbf{0} \\ R & Q \end{bmatrix}$$

The expected number of visits to vertex j is then given by the average over all possible starting states. In matrix notation:

$$\mathbf{v} = \frac{N^\top \mathbf{1}}{n - |A|}$$

where $|A|$ is the number of absorbed vertices. The vertex with the largest number of visits becomes the next term in the rank and an absorbing state for the remaining iterations: $a_{|A|+1} = \arg\max_{i=|A|+1}^{n} v_i$. The process is repeated until every vertex has been turned into an absorbing state.

4 TermHopper

Given the generic ranking algorithm introduced in the previous section, to define our TermHopper method we now need to choose a similarity matrix W. Our approach to re-ranking the output of ATR takes terms as nodes in the graph, and uses a pair wise semantic similarity function between terms to assign weights to the edges in the graph. The reasoning behind using a semantic similarity function is the belief that similar nodes in the graph, i.e., terms, will cluster together and hence the algorithm presented in the previous section will choose nodes from many different clusters rather than many nodes from the same cluster.

There have been a number of different semantic similarity functions developed in the past years. For example, distributional similarity [11] would seem like a good match for the task of re-ranking ATR output. Unfortunately, distributional similarity requires a large amount of time and data to compute and was thus deemed inappropriate for this particular application. Instead we used a WordNet [9] based similarity function for assigning edge weights.

In WordNet synonymous words are grouped into synsets. Synsets are then linked by relations such as hyponymy and hypernymy. Different WordNet based similarity functions use different parts of this structure to determine the similarity between two words. In this study we used the Lin similarity measure[3] [11].

The Lin similarity measures use corpus frequency counts to represent the informativeness of each node in WordNet, a technique developed by Resnik [16]. Nodes near the root of the hierarchy are not considered to be informative and have low values while those nearer the leaves have higher values, for example the concept *fish* would be more informative than *animal*. Numerical values representing the informativeness of each node are calculated from frequency counts of the words in that synset.

The information content (IC) for a synset, s, is calculated as $IC(s) = -\log(Pr(s))$ where $Pr(s)$ is the probability of synset s occurring in the corpus (estimated using word frequency counts). Resnik's similarity measure is provided by $sim_{Res} = IC(lcs(s_1, s_2))$, i.e. the similarity of a pair of nodes is defined to be the informativeness of their lowest common subsumer. Lin combined the same terms in a different formula:

$$sim_{Lin} = \frac{2 \times IC(lcs(s_1, s_2))}{IC(s_1) + IC(s_2)}$$

In our experiments we used information content values calculated over the BNC[4].

TermHopper can work on the output of an existing ATR system simply by taking the scores output for each term as the prior vector r introduced in the previous section.

Finally, we restrict the similarity matrix W to contain, for each term, only its k neighbour (most similar) terms. Intuitively, this has the effect of reducing the potential noise introduced by the computation of all possible pair wise similarities.

[2] We add a small teleporting constant ϵ to the prior to ensure $P_{ij} > 0, \forall i, j$

[3] We used a Java implementation of the Lin measure available at http://nlp.shef.ac.uk/result/software.html.

[4] We used the information content file distributed with the Perl WordNet::Similarity library [15]

5 Experimental Setup

In this section we describe in detail our experimental setup which is designed to validate our approach. The experiments evaluate TermHopper against the original ATR algorithms and also a random baseline. First we describe the corpus and the gold standard used, and then we present the ATR algorithms selected for comparison and the proposed random baseline. Experimental results are presented in Section 6.

5.1 Dataset Collection and Processing

The experiments presented here were conducted on the AnimalWiki corpus, a manually built corpus of Wikipedia articles about 1,051 randomly selected animals. In total, the corpus contains 1.3 million words.

The corpus was created by extracting only the main textual content from the HTML pages and ignoring any formatting or navigational elements. The corpus was then POS tagged and the linguistic filters described by [10] were applied to extract nouns and noun phrases as candidate terms. The candidate list was then filtered by removing stop words.

5.2 Algorithms

Due to space limitations, we select two popular algorithms out of the collection of ATR algorithms available in the Java Automatic Term Recognition Toolkit (JATR [5]) [25]; namely the C-Value and TF-IDF algorithms. Please refer to the related work section for an overview of these algorithms. From the output of each algorithm we select the top 500 ranked terms for reranking by TermHopper, and present the comparison between our results and the results produced by the original algorithms, over the AnimalWiki corpus.

The random baseline, which we will call RandomHopper, can be modelled using a multivariate hypergeometric distribution or, equivalently, modelling the problem as a urn sampling problem without replacement. Under this model, to determine the next term in the rank we draw one term from the urn and observe its category. We plot a curve that shows the expected number of categories observed as the number of terms drawn from the urn grows. Because there is no closed form solution to this problem, we simply simulated the urn drawing process for an appropriately large number of runs and took the average of the observations.

We also check how TermHopper behaves when using a perfect similarity function (PerfectHopper):

$$sim_{Pft}(x,y) = \begin{cases} 1, & \text{if } cat(x) = cat(y) \\ 0, & \text{otherwise} \end{cases}$$

where *cat* is a function that returns the category of a term; that is, the perfect similarity is given by consulting the categories in the gold standard.

5.3 Gold Standard Evaluation Method

We designed the gold standard for evaluation by categorising terms into different semantic categories. In order to do this, we attempted to automatically obtain the category of a term by applying a few simple heuristics over the English section of Wikipedia, using the Java Wikipedia Library [21] and the February 2007 English Wikipedia dump. If the term denotes an animal, we retrieve its corresponding Wikipedia page, and extract the scientific classification for that animal as the category for the term (Figure 1).

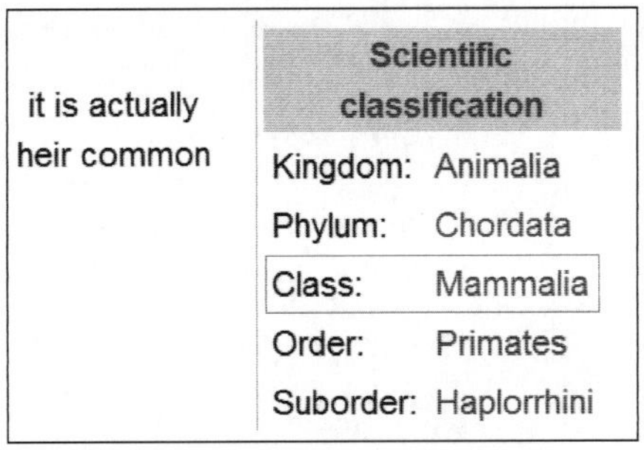

Fig. 1: *A excerpt of a Wikipedia page showing the scientific classification of an animal.*

Actinopterygii	Echinoidea
Amphibia	Gastropoda
Anthozoa	Insecta
Arachnida	Malacostraca
Aves	Mammalia
Bivalvia	Merostomata
Cephalaspidomorphi	Osteichthyes
Cephalopoda	Reptilia
Chondrichthyes	Sauropsida
Clitellata	Scyphozoa
Crustacea	Trilobita

Table 1: *Category labels derived from Wikipedia Scientific Classification "Class".*

Scientific classifications for animals in Wikipedia are subdivided into Kingdom, Phylum, Class, Order, Family, Genus, Species, etc. For the purposes of our study we have categorised terms according to Class, and we only apply the automatic labelling processes to the selected top section (500) of terms from each ATR algorithm considered. This produced 22 Wikipedia categories as listed in Table 1.

The automated process left many terms uncategorised, in particular those terms which do not denote an animal. These were manually labelled according to a further six categories, as illustrated in Table 2. *Adjective* is used to categorises terms that are used as adjectives; *Group* contains terms used for describing groups of animals; *Part* are terms used for describing body parts; *Place* and *Time* refer to terms which are generally places or time expressions; while for any other term missing a category we assign the label *Other*.

We are interested in measuring diversity in the ranking generated by the several algorithms. For that, we study how the number of observed categories grows with the number of ranked terms considered.

[5] http://www.dcs.shef.ac.uk/~ziqizhang

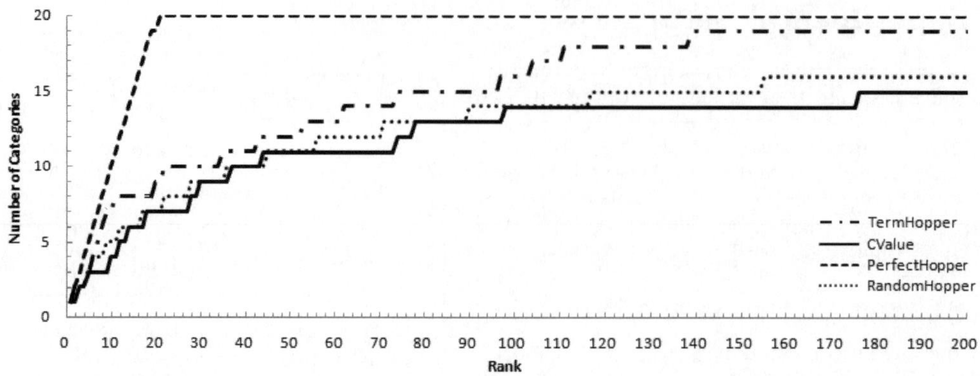

Fig. 2: *Experimental results comparing the C-Value and TermHopper algorithms, α=0.8 and k=3.*

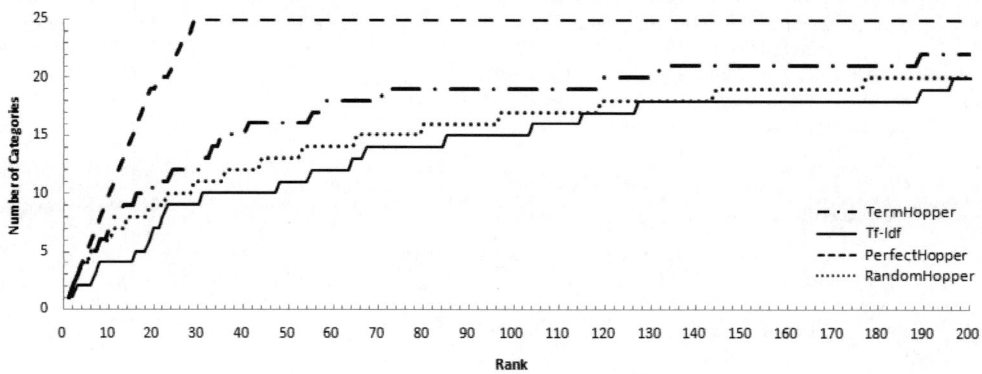

Fig. 3: *Experimental results comparing the TF-IDF and TermHopper algorithms, α=0.6 and k=10.*

Category Label	Examples
Place	river, sea, America
Time	year, month, Ice Age
Adjective	black, hybrid, male
Group	pack, colony, species
Other	range, sense, devil
Part	head, nose, mouth

Table 2: *Non-animal category labels.*

6 Results and Discussion

The performance of TermHopper in comparison to the base ATR algorithms of C-Value and TF-IDF can be seen in Figures 2 and 3 respectively. These graphs show the number of observed categories against the number of ranked terms being considered. Both graphs also show the performance of RandomHopper and PerfectHopper for comparison. In both experiments the following parameters of TermHopper were tuned using a grid method:

- the tradeoff parameter $\alpha \in [0, 1]$
- the number of (most similar) neighbours, $k \in \{3, 10, 499\}$, in the similarity matrix W

Overall, our approach consistently outperforms both the random baseline and the rankings generated by the original ATR systems. It is not surprising that the latter perform worse than the baseline, since they favour centrality only and have no notion of diversity, and thus place many (globally relevant) terms from the same category in the top ranked positions. TermHopper, on the other hand, shows more term categories sooner, both within the all-important first 10 or 20 results as well as beyond that, while at the same time ensuring, by design, that the top terms are the most central within their respective categories.

By tuning the parameters, we have observed that results improve when considering only a few (at most 10) neighbours in the similarity matrix instead of using a dense matrix with all the possible pair wise similarity values computed. This also matches our intuition that only the network of the few most similar terms should be used to semantically define a given term.

The gap between TermHopper's and PerfectHopper's curves indicates how strong the misalignment is between the adopted term similarity function and the desired gold standard classification. The proposed generic WordNet-based similarity function can be replaced with a more specific similarity function based on domain knowledge to bridge that gap. Unfortunately, doing so reduces the portability of the method. However, we believe that the results obtained are still very valuable, because they show that a considerable improvement over the baseline can be obtained even with a domain-independent, off-the-shelf similarity function.

7 Conclusions and Future Work

ATR algorithms often fail to capture the whole of the domain covered by the corpus, which for some applications may be unacceptable or undesirable. For example, a corpus summarization system aiming to provide a short summary to the user in the form of keywords needs to be able to cover all of the sub-domains in as few keywords as possible – ideally using exactly one keyword per sub-domain.

To improve diversity in ranking the automatically recognized terms, we have presented a novel term reranking method, called TermHopper. We showed that, even without encoding any knowledge about the domain, i.e., using a generic WordNet-based term similarity function, the proposed method is successful in improving the diversity of the results produced by two popular ATR algorithms on the AnimalWiki corpus. One of the advantages of the proposed method is that it can be coupled to any existing ATR system, since it runs as a post-processing step.

As future work, we plan to experiment with several similarity metrics from the literature to replace the WordNet-based similarity used here, as long as their computation cost remains low, due to the exponential cost of computing the pair wise similarity. We also plan to study the impact of deploying the new diversity-improved ATR system in our existing ontology learning tools.

Acknowledgements

This work was funded by the X-Media project (www.x-media-project.org) sponsored by the European Commission as part of the Information Society Technologies (IST) programme under EC grant number IST-FP6-026978.

References

[1] K. Ahmad, L. Gillam, and L. Tostevin. University of Surrey Participation in TREC8: Weirdness Indexing for Logical Document Extrapolation and Retrieval (WILDER). In *Proceedings of the Eighth Text REtrieval Conference (TREC-8)*, 1999.

[2] D. Bourigault. Surface Grammatical Analysis for the Extraction of Terminological Noun Phrases. In *Proceedings of the 14th International Conference on Computational Linguistics (COLING)*, 1992.

[3] C. Brewster, J. Iria, Z. Zhang, F. Ciravegna, L. Guthrie, and Y. Wilks. Dynamic Iterative Ontology Learning. In *Proceedings of the Internation Conference on Recent Advances in Natural Language Processing (RANLP 07)*, 2007.

[4] S. Brin and L. Page. The Anatomy of a Large-Scale Hypertextual Web Search Engine. In *Computer Networks and ISDN Systems*, volume 30, pages 107–117, 1998.

[5] J. Carbonell and J. Goldstein. The use of MMR, diversity-based reranking for reordering documents and producing summaries. In *Proceedings of SIGIR'98*, Australia, 1998.

[6] I. S. Dhillon. Co-clustering documents and words using bipartite spectral graph partitioning. In *Proceedings of the seventh ACM SIGKDD international conference on Knowledge discovery and data mining*, pages 269–274, San Francisco, 2001.

[7] P. Doyle and J. Snell, editors. *Random Walks and Electric Networks.* Mathematical Assoc. of America, 1984.

[8] G. Erkan and D. Radev. Lexrank: Graph-based centrality as salience in text summarization. In *Journal of Artificial Intelligence Research (JAIR)*, volume 22, pages 457–479, 2004.

[9] C. Fellbaum, editor. *WordNet: An Electronic Lexical Database and some of its Applications.* MIT Press, 1998.

[10] K. T. Frantzi and S. Ananiadou. The C-value/NC-value Domain Independent Method for Multi-Word Term Extraction. *Journal of Natural Language Processing*, 1999.

[11] D. Lin. An information-theoretic definition of similarity. In *Proceedings of the Fifteenth International Conference on Machine learning (ICML-98)*, Madison, Wisconsin, 1998.

[12] R. Mihalcea and P. Tarau. TextRank: Bringing Order into Texts. In *Proceedings of the Conference on Empirical Methods in Natural Language Processing (EMNLP 2004)*, Barcelona, Spain, 2004.

[13] G. Nenadic, I. Spasic, and S. Ananiadou. Term Clustering Using a Corpus-Based Similarity Measure. In *Proceedings of the 5th International Conference on Text, Speech and Dialogue*, pages 151–154, 2002.

[14] Y. Park, R. J. Byrd, and B. K. Boguraev. Towards Ontologies on Demand. In *Proceedings of the Workshop on Semantic Web Technologies for Searching and Retrieving Scientific Data*, 2003.

[15] T. Pedersen, S. Patwardhan, and J. Michelizzi. WordNet::Similarity - Measuring the Relatedness of Concepts. In *Proceedings of the Nineteenth National Conference on Artificial Intelligence (AAAI-04)*, San Jose, CA, 2004.

[16] P. Resnik. Using Information Content to evaluate Semantic Similarity in a Taxonomy. In *Proceedings of the 14th International Joint Conference on Artificial Intelligence (IJCAI-95)*, pages 448–453, Montreal, Canada, 1995.

[17] F. Sclano and P. Velardi. TermExtractor: A Web Application to Learn the Shared Terminology of Emergent Web Communities. In *Proceedings of the 3rd International Conference on Interoperability for Enterprise Software and Applications (I-ESA)*, 2007.

[18] P. Serdyukov, H. Rode, and D. Hiemstra. Modeling Expert Finding as an Absorbing Random Walk. In *Proceedings of the 31st Annual International ACM SIGIR conference on Research and Development in Information Retrieval*, 2008.

[19] A. P. Singh, A. Gunawardana, C. Meek, and A. C. Surendran. Recommendations using Absorbing Random Walks. In *Proceedings of NESCAI 2007*, 2007.

[20] I. Spasic, G. Nenadic, K. Manios, and S. Ananiadou. Supervised Learning of Term Similarities. In *Proceedings of the Third International Conference on Intelligent Data Engineering and Automated Learning*, 2002.

[21] T. Zesch, C. Muller, and I. Gurevych. Extracting lexical semantic knowledge from wikipedia and wiktionary. In *Proceedings of the 6th International Conference on Language Resources and Evaluation*, Marrakech, Marocco, 2008.

[22] C. X. Zhai, W. W. Cohen, and J. Lafferty. Beyond independent relevance: methods and evaluation metrics for subtopic retrieval. In *Proceedings of the 26th Annual International ACM SIGIR Conference*, pages 10–17, Toronto, Canada, 2003.

[23] B. Zhang, H. Li, Y. Liu, L. Ji, W. Xi, W. Fan, Z. Chen, and W.-Y. Ma. Improving web search results using affinity graph. In *Proceedings of the 28th Annual International ACM SIGIR Conference*, Salvador, Brazil, 2005. ACM.

[24] Y. Zhang, J. Callan, and T. Minka. Novelty and redundancy detection in adaptive filtering. In *Proc. ACM SIGIR 2002*, pages 81–88. ACM Press, 2002.

[25] Z. Zhang, J. Iria, C. Brewster, and F. Ciravegna. A Comparative Evaluation of Term Recognition Algorithms. In *Proceedings of the 6th International Conference on Language Resources and Evaluation*, Marrakech, Marocco, 2008.

[26] X. Zhu, A. B. Goldberg, J. V. Gael, and D. Andrezejewski. Improving Diversity in Ranking using Absorbing Random Walks. In *Proceedings of NAACL/HLT*, 2007.

Author Index

Association for Computational Linguistics
209 N. Eighth Street
Stroudsburg, Pennsylvania 18360

ISBN 978-1-5108-1327-4

CURRAN ASSOCIATES INC.
proceedings.com